The Wiley Blackwell
of the Psychology of
and Strengths-Based Approaches at Work

Wiley Blackwell Handbooks in Organizational Psychology

Series Editor: Jonathan Passmore

The aim of the Wiley Blackwell Handbooks in Organizational Psychology is to create a set of uniquely in-depth reviews of contemporary research, theory and practice across critical sub-domains of organizational psychology. Series titles will individually deliver the state-of-the-art in their discipline by putting the most important contemporary work at the fingertips of academics, researchers, students and practitioners. Over time, the series will grow in into a complete reference for those seeking to develop a comprehensive understanding of the field.

Published

The Wiley-Blackwell Handbook of the Psychology of Coaching and Mentoring
Edited by Jonathan Passmore, David B. Peterson, and Teresa Freire

The Wiley-Blackwell Handbook of the Psychology of Leadership, Change and Organizational Development
Edited by H. Skipton Leonard, Rachel Lewis, Arthur M. Freedman, and Jonathan Passmore

The Wiley Blackwell Handbook of Psychology of Training, Development and Performance Improvement
Edited by Kurt Kraiger, Jonathan Passmore, Sigmar Malvezzi, and Nuno Rebelo dos Santos

The Wiley Blackwell Handbook of the Psychology of Occupational Safety and Workplace Health
Edited by Sharon Clarke, Tahira Probst, Frank Guldenmund, and Jonathan Passmore

The Wiley Blackwell Handbook of the Psychology of Positivity and Strengths-Based Approaches at Work
Edited by Lindsay G. Oades, Michael F. Steger, Antonella Delle Fave, and Jonathan Passmore

Forthcoming

The Wiley Blackwell Handbook of the Psychology of Team Working and Collaborative Processes
Edited by Eduardo Salas, Ramon Rico, Neal Ashkanasy, and Jonathan Passmore

The Wiley Blackwell Handbook of the Psychology of Recruitment, Selection and Employee Retention
Edited by Harold Goldstein, Elaine D. Pulakos, Carla Semedo, and Jonathan Passmore

The Wiley Blackwell Handbook of the Psychology of the Internet at Work
Edited by Guido Hertel, Dianna L. Stone, Richard D Johnson, and Jonathan Passmore

The Wiley Blackwell Handbook of the Psychology of Positivity and Strengths-Based Approaches at Work

Edited by Lindsay G. Oades, Michael F. Steger, Antonella Delle Fave, and Jonathan Passmore

WILEY Blackwell

This edition first published 2020

Registered Office
John Wiley & Sons Ltd, The Atrium, Southern Gate, Chichester, West Sussex, PO19 8SQ, UK

Editorial Offices
350 Main Street, Malden, MA 02148-5020, USA
9600 Garsington Road, Oxford, OX4 2DQ, UK
The Atrium, Southern Gate, Chichester, West Sussex, PO19 8SQ, UK

For details of our global editorial offices, for customer services, and for information about how to apply for permission to reuse the copyright material in this book please see our website at www.wiley.com/wiley-blackwell.

Library of Congress Cataloging-in-Publication data is available

Paperback (9781119124115)

Cover image: © Ingrid H. Mair
Cover design by Wiley

Set in 9.5/11pt Galliard by SPi Global, Pondicherry, India
Printed and bound in Singapore by Markono Print Media Pte Ltd

10 9 8 7 6 5 4 3 2 1

Contents

About the Editors

Lindsay G. Oades, PhD Lindsay (MBA with Distinction, PhD) is an Associate Professor and Deputy Director (Learning & Teaching) at the *Centre for Positive Psychology*, University of Melbourne, Australia. He is also the program coordinator of the Masters in Applied Positive Psychology (MAPP). In 2013 he received an Australian Government citation for outstanding contribution to student learning. He speaks at conferences around the world, and has published more than 100 peer-reviewed journal articles and scholarly book chapters cited over 2,100 times. His research interests concern the applications of well-being in workplaces, health and education systems. In particular, he has developed intervention and organizational development programs to assist mental health services to become more recovery oriented, drawing on the empirical bases of positive psychology and well-being science. His current developing research program focuses on positive systems and well-being literacy. In 2015 he received a Vice-Chancellor's Award for excellence in research commercialiation. He is a co-editor for the multidisciplinary *International Journal of Wellbeing*; Managing Director of Life Sculpture Pty Ltd, non-executive Director of the Reach Foundation, and sits on the scientific advisory panel for the Institute of Coaching, at Harvard University's McLean Hospital. Lindsay is on the leadership team of the Wellbeing Collaborative for the Mental Health Commission of New South Wales. Lindsay enjoys traveling and cultural and outdoor adventures with his wife and two sons.

Michael F. Steger, PhD Michael is an Associate Professor of Counseling Psychology and Applied Social Psychology at Colorado State University, USA. He also is the Director for the Laboratory for the Study of Meaning and Quality of Life. His research interests concern better understanding the factors that promote human flourishing and ameliorate psychological suffering. In particular, he has focused on researching how people generate the sense that their lives are meaningful, as well as investigating the benefits of living a meaningful life. He speaks at organizations and conferences around the world, and has published more than 100 peer-reviewed journal articles and scholarly book chapters. His published works include two books, *Designing Positive Psychology* and *Purpose and Meaning in the Workplace*. He currently serves as co-Editor-in-Chief of the journal *Psychology of Well-Being*, as well as on the editorial board of several additional journals. He is the developer of the Work and Meaning Inventory, and also of the Meaning in

Life Questionnaire, which has become the most widely used measure of meaning and purpose in the world.

Antonella Delle Fave, PhD Antonella specializes in Clinical Psychology and is Professor of Psychology at the Medical School, Università degli Studi di Milano, Italy. Her research interests include the study of well-being indicators, daily experience fluctuation patterns, and the process of psychological selection across cultures and among individuals experiencing conditions of diversity and adversity. She developed intervention projects in the domains of health and education. Together with international partners she launched and implemented the project "Eudaimonic and Hedonic Happiness Investigation," aimed at identifying well-being components across cultures. She is currently conducting research and clinical studies aimed at integrating the biopsychosocial perspective of Western medicine and the Indian traditional view of health. She contributed to the development of positive psychology, as founding member and President of the International Positive Psychology Association (IPPA), the European Network of Positive Psychology (ENPP), and the Società Italiana di Psicologia Positiva (SIPP). Author of over 150 scientific articles and books, since 2010 she is Editor-in-Chief of the *Journal of Happiness Studies.*

Jonathan Passmore, D.Occ.Psych Jonathan is Professor of Psychology at the University of Evora, Portugal, and teaches at Winchester Business School and is Managing Director of Embrion, a psychology consulting company working across Europe, the Middle East, and Africa with a team of 20 trainers and psychologists. He is a chartered psychologist, holds five degrees, and has an international reputation for his work in coaching and leadership. He has published over 20 books on the themes of leadership, personal development, and change, including editing the Association for Coaching series of coaching titles. He speaks widely at conferences across the world from the United States to Europe and Asia and has published over 100 peer-reviewed journal papers and book chapters. His work has been recognized by awards from a number of professional bodies including the Association for Coaching Global Coaching Award in 2010, the British Psychology Society Research SGCP Award for his research into safety coaching in 2012, and the Association for Business Psychologists Chairman's Award for Excellence in 2015. He sits on the editorial board of several journals including *Coaching: An International Journal* and the *International Coaching Psychology Review.* Jonathan lives with his wife and two small children in the United Kingdom. In his spare time he keeps bees and likes to swim, walk, and run.

About the Contributors

Tim Anstiss, PhD, is a medical doctor focusing on behavioral medicine, well-being improvement, and staff development. A former international athlete (pole vault) and *Gladiators* contender, Tim was one of the "Slough 50" in the BBC documentary "Making Slough Happy." He has a postgraduate diploma in Occupational Medicine.

Robert Biswas-Diener, PhD, is the Managing Director at Positive Acorn as well as a prolific writer, with over 55 academic publications and several books, editor, speaker, trainer and coach. His areas of research include positive psychology interventions, strengths use and development, cross-cultural research, well-being, flourishing, and life satisfaction.

Brittany Branand is a PhD student at Claremont Graduate University, USA, and is currently a Senior Research Analyst for NORC (National Opinion Research Center) at the University of Chicago, where she evaluates innovative grant-funded interventions. Within the developmental positive psychology field, her research focuses on interpersonal relationships, including mentoring relationships, relationships in the college community, and romantic relationships in older adulthood.

Stefan P. Cantore, PhD, is Principal Teaching Fellow in Organisational Behaviour and Human Resource Management at the University of Southampton Business School, UK. Stefan has a particular interest in the role played by conversation in organization development and consulting relationships. He combines teaching with writing and organizational consultancy.

Jeanette N. Cleveland, PhD, is Professor of Industrial/Organizational Psychology at Colorado State University, USA, and elected Fellow of the Society for Industrial and Organizational Psychology and the APA. She earned her PhD from Penn State University. Her research interests include work attitudes, performance decisions, workforce diversity issues, and work–family issues.

Peter J. Clough, PhD, holds the Chair in Applied Psychology at Manchester Metropolitan University, UK. His research interests revolve around mental toughness and its relationship with performance within sport, education, and business.

Lee Crust is a Senior Lecturer in sport and exercise science at the University of Lincoln, UK, where he directs the MTOUGH research team. He is a chartered sport and exercise psychologist and has published both qualitative and quantitative research concerning mental toughness.

Mihaly Csikszentmihalyi, PhD, is the author of 14 books translated into 29 languages, and over 250 research articles. He is on the Board of the International Positive Psychology Association, an organization he co-founded in 2001.

Don E. Davis, PhD, is an Assistant Professor of Counseling Psychology at Georgia State University, USA. He earned his PhD in Counseling Psychology from Virginia Commonwealth University. His research interests focus on positive psychology, particularly virtues associated with the strengthening and repair of relationships (e.g., forgiveness, humility, or gratitude).

Cirleen DeBlaere, PhD, is an Assistant Professor of Counseling Psychology at Georgia State University, USA. She earned her PhD in Counseling Psychology from the University of Florida. Her research and clinical interests focus on the experiences of individuals with marginalized identities, particularly individuals with multiple marginalized identities.

Andrew Denovan is a Lecturer in Psychology at Manchester Metropolitan University, UK. His research interests include stress, adjustment, positive psychology, well-being, and the student experience in higher education. He is also interested in research methods.

Aylin Dulagil is a coaching and positive organizational psychologist with experience in positive psychology, employee engagement, leadership development, human resources, and organizational development. Aylin has worked as both an internal and external consultant over the last 20 years delivering organizational development initiatives to a number of Australian organizations covering a range of industries and sectors. Aylin is currently completing a PhD examining the impact of organizational climate and manager behaviors on the strengths use of individuals.

Gwenith G. Fisher, PhD, is Assistant Professor of Industrial/Organizational Psychology at Colorado State University, USA. She earned her PhD at Bowling Green State University. Her research examines individual and work factors related to worker health and well-being with a focus on aging workforce and work/non-work issues.

Suzy Green, PhD, is a Clinical and Coaching Psychologist and Founder of The Positivity Institute. Suzy lectured on Applied Positive Psychology in the Coaching Psychology Unit, University of Sydney, Australia, for 10 years and is an Honorary Vice President of the International Society for Coaching Psychology. Suzy also currently holds Honorary Academic positions at the University of Western Sydney, University of Wollongong, University of Melbourne, and Australian Catholic University, and she is an Affiliate of the Well-being Institute, University of Cambridge, UK.

Joshua N. Hook, PhD, is an Assistant Professor of Counseling Psychology at the University of North Texas, USA. He earned his PhD in Counseling Psychology from

Virginia Commonwealth University. His research interests focus on humility, forgiveness, religion/spirituality, and multicultural counseling.

Itai Ivtzan, PhD, is passionate about the combination of psychology and spirituality. He is a positive psychologist, a senior lecturer, and the program leader of MAPP (Masters in Applied Positive Psychology) at the University of East London (UEL), UK. He has published many books, journal papers, and book chapters and his main interests are spirituality, mindfulness, meaning, and self-actualization. If you wish to get additional information about his work or contact him, please visit www.AwarenessIsFreedom.com

Aaron Jarden, PhD, is a Senior Lecturer in Psychology at Auckland University of Technology, New Zealand. He is president of the New Zealand Association of Positive Psychology, co-editor of the *International Journal of Wellbeing*, lead investigator for the Sovereign New Zealand Wellbeing Index, and Senior Scientist for Work on Wellbeing.

Rebecca Jarden is a lecturer in nursing at Auckland University of Technology (AUT), New Zealand. She is a registered nurse with a background in critical care nursing, and her research and practice interests include: critical care nursing, quality in health care, student and workplace engagement and motivation, with a particular focus on well-being.

Mohita Junnarkar, PhD, completed her post-doctoral fellowship in the area of positive psychology. Her expertise deals with studying psychometric properties of various scales and validation of same for Indian population. She has to her credit national and international peer reviewed journal papers in the area of psychometric validation of positive psychology constructs.

Todd B. Kashdan, PhD, has published over 150 peer-reviewed articles and is a co-author of *The Upside of Your Dark Side*, among other books. He is Professor of Psychology and Senior Scientist at the Center for the Advancement of Well-Being at George Mason University, USA.

Sonal Khosla, MA, is a student of Positive Developmental Psychology and Evaluation at Claremont Graduate University, USA. Currently she works as a research assistant at the Quality of Life Research Center, under the supervision of Dr Jeanne Nakamura and Dr Mihaly Csikszentmihalyi.

Gaja Zager Kocjan is a psychologist and teaching assistant at the Department of Psychology, University of Ljubljana, Slovenia. Her main research interests include positive psychology and personality psychology. Currently her primary focus is on various indicators of employee well-being.

Hyjin Lee completed her BA in Psychology at the University of British Columbia, Canada, and her MA in Counselling Psychology at Ewha Womans University, South Korea. She has worked in a Human Resources consulting firm in South Korea. Her current work specializes in Assessment and Development Centers, and People Development.

Tim Lomas, PhD, is a Lecturer at the University of East London (UEL), UK, where he is the programme leader for the MSc in Applied Positive Psychology and Coaching Psychology. Tim has authored numerous books and papers in positive psychology, including a recent textbook on Applied Positive Psychology.

Shane J. Lopez, PhD, served as a Senior Scientist at Gallup and Research Director of the Clifton Strengths Institute, as well as a much-revered professor at the University of Kansas where he played a seminal role in the founding and flourishing of positive psychology. His work on the links between hope, strengths development, academic success, and overall well-being led to insights and collaboration among scholars around the world. He exemplified how giving life to one's positive characteristics could create and strengthen positive institutions. Dr. Lopez passed away in 2016, prior to the publication of his work in this volume.

Nadezhda Lyubchik works at Positive Acorn and has a number of publications on topics spanning social and positive psychology. Her areas of research include social relationships, cross-cultural research, public policy development and assessment, socio-cognitive neuroscience and positive psychology interventions.

Doug MacKie, PhD, is a business psychologist and executive coach with over 25 years' experience in the assessment and development of executive, leadership, and team capability within top companies in Australia, Asia, and the UK. He has presented at international conferences and published in leading journals on strength-based approaches to leadership development, the importance of effective evaluation, and assessing Return on Investment in coaching engagements. He is the author of a forthcoming text on strengths-based leadership coaching in organizations, based on his research in this area.

Susana C. Marques, PhD, is a researcher, full member, of the Center of Psychology at University of Porto, Portugal, and professor at the Faculty of Psychology and Education at the same university. Much of her research focuses on hope and how it can be used to help individuals, groups, and organizations flourish.

Michelle McQuaid is a best-selling author, workplace well-being teacher, and playful change activator. An Honorary Fellow at the Melbourne Graduate School of Education at the University of Melbourne, Australia, she holds a Masters of Applied Positive Psychology from the University of Pennsylvania, USA, and is currently completing her PhD. She writes for *Psychology Today*, *Huffington Post*, and *Live Happy* and her work has been featured in *Forbes*, the *Harvard Business Review*, *The Wall Street Journal*, and more.

Jeanne Nakamura, PhD, is Associate Professor, Division of Behavioral and Organizational Sciences, Claremont Graduate University, USA, where she co-directs the positive psychology concentration and the Quality of Life Research Center. She has investigated positive psychology in an adult-developmental context, including engagement and creativity, mentoring and good work, and aging well.

Christopher P. Niemiec, PhD, is a Senior Lecturer and Research Associate in Psychology and the Director of Undergraduate Studies in the Department of Clinical and Social Sciences in Psychology at the University of Rochester, USA. He also holds an honorary appointment as Visiting Associate Professor in the Faculty of Business at the University of Wollongong Sydney Business School in Australia. His program of research has extended principles from self-determination theory in social, personality, and developmental psychology, and has applied those principles to the domains of education, health, and organizational behavior.

Vanessa Placeres is an Associate Professional Counselor. She earned her Master's degree in Counseling, Marriage and Family Therapy from California State University, Fresno,

USA. She is currently working toward obtaining her Education Specialist in School Counseling. Her research interests focus on positive psychology, specifically bullying and forgiveness.

Alicia Purtell is an organization development specialist. She holds a BA from Sydney University, Australia, a Post-Graduate Certificate in Business from Macquarie Graduate School of Management, a Masters of Coaching Psychology from Sydney University. She is also currently completing a Post-Graduate Diploma in Psychology at Sydney University. Alicia has previously worked as a Senior Associate with The Positivity Institute and is currently the People and Culture Director – BCWA (Beer, Cider and Wine Australia) at Lion.

Paula Robinson, PhD, following a career as a senior executive, is now a registered, consulting psychologist, specializing in the science, application, and integration of traditional Psychology and Positive Psychology. Over the past 15 years, Paula has completed numerous research studies, academic lectures, advisory roles, keynote presentations and strategic positive change programs for government, private organizations, schools, and the wider community.

Sue Roffey, FRSA, is an educational psychologist, academic, and author. The founder of Wellbeing Australia, she is currently Associate Professor (adjunct) at Western Sydney University, Australia, and affiliated to the Well-being Institute at Cambridge, UK. Her many publications have an international readership and she works across the world as an educational consultant and speaker.

Sebastiaan Rothmann, PhD, is full professor in Industrial Psychology at the North-West University, South Africa, and Director of the Optentia Research Programme. His research interest is the assessment and development of human potential and flourishing in institutions within a multicultural context. He has published more than 160 articles and chapters in peer-reviewed journals and handbooks.

Kamlesh Singh, PhD, is actively engaged in positive psychology research, with a special focus on testing of various constructs, and development and validation of interventions for different populations. She published several book chapters and papers in national and international peer-reviewed journals. She is member of the board of directors of International Positive Psychology Association (IPPA), and founding member and secretary of National Association of Positive Psychology (NPPA) in India. For more details, please visit: http://web.iitd.ac.in/~singhk/

Gavin R. Slemp, PsyD, is a lecturer, academic, and Associate Director of Undergraduate Programs in the Centre for Positive Psychology, University of Melbourne, Australia. With a background in Organizational Psychology, his research interests are primarily in the areas of employee well-being, motivation, job crafting, and cross-cultural psychology.

Lawrence Soosai-Nathan, PhD, a Roman Catholic priest, is a psychotherapist with an eclectic approach and a holistic well-being perspective. Alongside being a trainer, he serves presently as Head of the Department of Psychology at the Anugraha Institute of Social Sciences, a rural college affiliated to Madurai Kamaraj University (Tamil Nadu, India), and is committed to the empowerment of the rural youth, especially the girls.

Gordon B. Spence, PhD, is Course Director of the Master of Business Coaching, Sydney Business School, University of Wollongong, Australia. He is a registered psychologist, lecturer, researcher, and practicing executive and workplace coach. His doctoral dissertation focused on the integration of mindfulness practice into evidence-based coaching and his current research interests include autonomous motivation, employee engagement, and workplace well-being. He is also past co-chair of the Science Advisory Council, Institute of Coaching, McLean Hospital/Harvard and author of several peer-reviewed book chapters and journal articles.

Kevin M. Walters is a graduate student in Industrial/Organizational Psychology at Colorado State University, USA, and a trainee in Occupational Health Psychology through the Mountains and Plains Education and Research Center. His research focuses on improving positive aspects of the work environment, such as health, job satisfaction, and meaningfulness of work.

Christian A. Wandeler, PhD, is an Assistant Professor in research methods and statistics, California State University, Fresno, USA. His research interests are in the development of hope and motivation, self-determination at the workplace, teacher training, and quality of vocational education and training.

Ulrich Wiesmann is the Associate Director of the Institute of Medical Psychology and the Head of the Psychotherapeutic Service at the University of Greifswald, Germany. As a psychotherapist, he specializes in the treatment of trauma disorders and has long experience as a supervisor for clinical teams. As a researcher, he is interested in the psychology of positive aging.

Paul T. P. Wong, PhD, is Professor Emeritus of Trent University, Canada, and Adjunct Professor of the Clinical PhD Program at Saybrook University, USA. He is a Fellow of the American Psychological Association (APA) and the Canadian Psychological Association (CPA), and President of the International Network on Personal Meaning (www.meaning.ca) and the Meaning-Centered Counselling Institute. Editor of the International *Journal of Existential Psychology and Psychotherapy*, he has also edited two influential volumes on *The Human Quest for Meaning*. A prolific writer, he is one of the most cited existential and positive psychologists. The originator of Meaning Therapy and International Meaning Conferences, he has been invited to speak worldwide.

Sung-Kyung Yoo, PhD, is Professor of Psychology at Ewha Womans University in South Korea. She earned her PhD at the University of Minnesota, USA, and obtained the Distinguished International Scholar award from the University of Minnesota. She is a Fulbright Visiting Scholar at Harvard University. Her research interest is career issues across developmental stages and gender in Asian culture.

Foreword

One important function of handbooks is to provide a comprehensive view of the latest information and most reliable findings related to a central topic. Almost no one reads a handbook from beginning to end, but we usually use them to identify what we know and do not yet know about certain subjects. Handbook chapters are generally considered to be the most reliable sources for advanced learning. They help us discover what's new, what's interesting, and what we have a difficult time finding elsewhere.

This handbook fulfills the highest aspirations to which handbooks aspire. It is edited by some of the best known scholars in the field of positive organizational psychology, and their choices of chapter topics and contributors are outstanding. The chapter contributors are not only luminary and internationally known for their work, but they represent the most diverse set of scholars yet to be compiled into one volume. Authors represent Africa, Asia, Australia–New Zealand, Europe, and North America. They address topics that are often neglected in the organizational psychology literature, and they highlight the application of positive organizational psychology across an impressive array of work contexts – including different sectors (e.g., education, health care, arts and crafts, agriculture, IT), different demographics (e.g., mid-career, aging), and different practices (e.g., job crafting, relationships, motivation, leadership, organizational change).

As can be expected, the fields of positive psychology and strengths-based approaches to work have met with their share of critics and detractors. These approaches to work have been accused of being biased toward the existing Western value system. They are Euro-centric and U.S.-centric and perpetuate a narrow values-bias, say the critics. Moreover, the term "positive" connotes more pizzazz than substance, and this work has garnered attention merely because the term sounds commonsense. Research findings are often invalid, overstated, and misleading, say the detractors, and misinterpreting or overclaiming results are common. Positive organizational psychology is merely a focus on "happiology," and the results perpetuate increased conformity among workers and lack of freedom.

Oades, Steger, Delle Fave, and Passmore have created a volume that provides an excellent example of counter-arguments to the critics. The perspectives are diverse. The research is rigorous and carefully crafted. The arguments are sound and well documented. And, the applications are impressive and innovative. The chapter authors are not novices or inexperienced scholars. They represent some of the best minds available. I am confident, therefore, that you will find *The Wiley Blackwell Handbook of the Psychology of Positivity and Strengths-Based Approaches at Work* to be an excellent source for the latest thinking and the most current findings about positive organizational psychology at work.

Kim Cameron
Russell William Kelley Professor of Management and Organizations
and Professor of Higher Education
University of Michigan, USA

Series Preface

Welcome to this fifth book in the Wiley Blackwell Industrial and Organizational Psychology (O/I) series. This title in the series focuses on positive psychology (PP) at work and builds on the previous four titles in the series on leadership and change, coaching and mentoring, training and development, and health and safety.

Over recent years we have seen a growth in positive psychology, which itself is rooted in humanistic approaches from the 1950s and 1960s. However the past decade or more of research in this field has provided quantitative evidence of the well-being and performance benefits of adopting positive approaches. While organizational psychology has traditionally focused on what works, as opposed to what does not work, PP offers opportunities for psychologists at work to further enhance and support their clients, helping to make work more fulfilling and more enjoyable while attaining higher levels of performance.

We believe this series differs in four ways from other titles in the field.

Firstly, the focus of the title is aimed at the academic researcher and student, as opposed to the practitioner, although scholar practitioners may also find this an interesting read. The aim of this book is to offer a comprehensive coverage of the main topics of inquiry within the domain and in each of these to offer a comprehensive critical literature review of the main topic areas. Each chapter is thus an attempt to gather together the key papers, book chapters, and ideas and to present these for the serious researcher, student, and academic as a starting point for research in the key topics of I/O psychology in a focused (10,000-word) chapter. The book thus aims to operate as a starting point for any in-depth inquiry into the field.

Secondly, while many books take a UK/European or a US/North American approach with contributors drawn predominantly from one continent or the other, in this series we have made strenuous efforts to create an international feel. For each title in the series we have drawn contributors from across the globe, and encouraged them to take an international, as opposed to national or regional, focus. Such an approach creates challenges. Challenges in terms of language and spelling, but also in the way ideas and concepts are applied in each country or region. We have encouraged our contributors to highlight such differences. We encourage you as the reader to reflect on these to better understand how and why these differences have emerged and what implications they have for your research and our deeper understanding of the psychological constructs that underpin these ideas.

Thirdly, the chapters avoid offering a single perspective, based on the ideas of a single contributor. Instead we have invited leading writers in the field to critically review the literature in their areas of expertise. The chapters thus offer a unique insight into the literature in each of these areas, with leading scholars sharing their interpretation of the literature in their area.

Finally, as series editor I have invited contributors and editors to contribute their royalties to a charity. Given the international feel of the title, we selected an international charity – The Railway Children – a charity that supports run-away and abandoned children across the world. This means approximately 10 percent of the cover price has been donated to charity and in this way we collectively are making a small contribution to making the world a slightly better place.

With any publication of this kind there are errors; as editors we apologize in advance for these.

Jonathan Passmore
Series Editor, I/O Psychology

Supported Charity

Railway Children

Railway Children supports children alone and at risk on the streets of India, East Africa, and the UK. Children migrate to the streets for many reasons, but once there they experience physical and sexual abuse, exploitation, drugs, and even death. We focus on early intervention, getting to the street kids before the street gets to them, and where possible we reunite them with their families and communities.

In addressing the issue we work through our three step change agenda to,

- Meet the immediate needs of children on the streets – we work with local organizations to provide shelter, education or vocational training, counselling and, if possible, reintegration to family life.
- Shift perception in the local context – we work with local stakeholders to ensure that street children are not viewed as commodities to be abused and exploited – but as children in need of care and protection.
- Hold Governments to account – if we are to see a long-term, sustainable change for the children with whom we work, we must influence key decision-makers, ensuring that provisions for safeguarding children are made within their policies and budgets.

Last year we reached over 27,000 children; 14,690 of these were in India where we reunited 2,820 with their families. In the UK we launched our research, "Off the Radar," which revealed the experiences of over 100 of the most detached children in the UK. Many of these children received no intervention either before leaving home or once they were on the streets. We have made recommendations that include emergency refuge for under 16s and a wrap-round of other services, such as Misper schemes, local helplines, outreach and family liaison, to allow children and young people to access interventions in a variety of ways.

To find out more about our work, or to help us support more vulnerable children, please go to www.railwaychildren.org.uk or call 00 44 1270 757596.

RAILWAY children

THE VOICE FOR STREET CHILDREN WORLDWIDE

1

The Psychology of Positivity and Strengths-Based Approaches at Work

Lindsay G. Oades, Michael F. Steger, Antonella Delle Fave, and Jonathan Passmore

Introduction

In this short introductory chapter, we aim to explore the nature of the psychology of positivity and how strengths-based approaches are used with individuals and organizations. We define positive psychology and describe strengths-based approaches and the relevance of both to work. Finally, we will briefly set out for the reader what follows in this edited handbook.

What Is Positive Psychology?

The science of positive psychology provides most of the empirical base for what is termed the "psychology of positivity" in the title of this handbook. Positive psychology has emerged as the scientific study of positive human functioning and flourishing intrapersonally (e.g., biologically, emotionally, cognitively), interpersonally (e.g., relationally), and collectively (e.g., institutionally, culturally, and globally) (Seligman & Csikszentmihalyi, 2000).

It may be considered to include three levels of research: the subjective level, the individual level, and the group level. Research at the *subjective level* includes valued subjective experiences and is broken down into past, present, and future constructs: the past involving well-being, contentment, and satisfaction; the present involving flow and happiness; and the future involving hope and optimism. The *individual level* involves research into individual traits that are positive, such as character strengths (including those that guide our interactions with others), talent, and the capacity for vocation. Finally, the *group level* involves research into "civic virtues and the institutions that move individuals towards better citizenship: responsibility, nurturance, altruism, civility, moderation, tolerance and work ethic" (Seligman & Csikszentmihalyi, 2000, p. 5). All three levels are relevant to the workplace, and we have attempted to represent each in the preparation

The Wiley Blackwell Handbook of the Psychology of Positivity and Strengths-Based Approaches at Work, First Edition. Edited by Lindsay G. Oades, Michael F. Steger, Antonella Delle Fave, and Jonathan Passmore.

of this handbook: Part I maps well onto the subjective and individual levels and Part II maps onto the group level. In particular, the established area of research in positive organizational scholarship has much relevance for research within Part II (Cameron & Dutton, 2003; Cameron & Spreitzer, 2012).

What Are Strengths-Based Approaches?

Well-being may be viewed as a key outcome of positive psychology endeavors. The use of strengths, and particularly character strengths, may be viewed as a key process of positive psychology. The concept of character strengths is based in a tradition that emphasizes virtues as inducements to behave well, in contrast with traditions that focus on rules to be followed. Peterson and Seligman (2004) developed a classification of strengths comprising 6 universal virtues and 24 character strengths. The Values in Action Inventory of Strengths Survey (VIA) identifies character traits expressed across all areas of life: home, family, social life, and work. For this title, work is the key area of focus.

In addition to exploration of specific character strengths and strengths-use, which is covered directly in Chapter 3, this guidebook is strengths-based more broadly. That is, the approaches taken across the chapters seek to approach individuals and organizations from a strengths perspective – looking for what is working well, how individuals are leveraging strengths, seeking optimal performance – compared to traditional approaches which may be diagnostic, problem-solving, seeking root causes, and so on. A strength-based approach is often contrasted with a deficit-based approach. It is an approach where one aims to approach the positive, rather than escape or avoid the negative. It is an approach where the presence of positive attributes is what is sought, not only the absence of negative attributes. It is one in which we guard against the negativity bias, one in which revenue is considered important and not only cost reduction, one in which human and environmental contribution becomes paramount. This is similar to the approach within positive organizational scholarship, as described by Professor Kim Cameron in the Foreword. Both the psychology of positivity and the related area of strengths provide a fertile theoretical and growing empirical base to understand the behavior of individuals and groups in an organizational context. The specific research developments are now introduced.

Research Developments in the Psychology of Positivity and Strengths-Based Approaches at Work

Our hope is that this handbook will be a useful resource for postgraduate researchers, students, and academics, who are looking for a comprehensive and critical review of the literature as a platform for their own research. Also scholar-practitioners can refer to this handbook to understand the depth and scope of the literature to enhance evidence-based practices and generate practice-based research. Importantly and more broadly, our hope is that the knowledge base described in this title will contribute to making workplaces more positive and meaningful places to work and developing organizations as contexts that can better leverage the strengths of their employees.

This book is structured using three parts focused on individual approaches to positive psychology at work, organizational approaches to positive psychology at work, and business or sector-based applications of positive psychology. Together these sections progress the reader through an ecological journey from the individual, to the organization, and then consider whole sectors on an international scale.

Part I comprises 12 chapters that describe classical positive psychological constructs and evidence in the workplace.

In Chapter 2 Green, McQuaid, Purtell and Dulagil set the foundation for this guide by reviewing the theories and evidence surrounding the psychology of positivity at work, including Fredrickson's broaden-and-build theory (Fredrickson, 2001; Fredrickson & Joiner, 2002). These authors assert that positive organizational scholars have become intrigued by the potential benefits that positive emotions (e.g., joy, gratitude, and hope) and "positivity" more broadly (encompassing emotions, thoughts, and behaviors), have to offer employees and organizations.

Biswas-Diener, Kashdan, and Lyubchik – Chapter 3 – explore the important area of psychological strengths at work. In addition to critically reviewing important literature, this chapter provides a useful comparison between well-known strengths frameworks of VIA, StrengthsFinder, and Realise2, and important exploration of the malleability of strengths (Linley, Nielsen, Wood, Gillett, and Biswas-Diener, 2010; Peterson & Seligman, 2004; Peterson, Stephens, Park, Lee, & Seligman, 2009).

Chapter 4 takes the reader to the future-oriented construct of hope. Wandeler, Marques, and Lopez provide a description of hope theory that addresses fundamental motivational, cognitive, and emotional components of human thinking, feeling, and action, and thus is well suited to be applied to the context of work. They assert that usually hope is considered as a characteristic of an individual, but organizations can also be considered hopeful (Wandeler, Baeriswyl, & Shavelson, 2011).

Steger – Chapter 5 – proposes that meaningful work holds the promise of being the 'next big thing' among organizations seeking a lever for improving organizational performance (Dik, Byrne, & Steger, 2013). Steger explores how meaningful work represents an opportunity to go beyond the standard maximization of effort and outcome to the improved well-being of the wider range of people associated with organizations. He suggests that not only is there meaning at work, but explores the idea of work itself as meaning (Steger & Dik, 2010). This chapter relates to the Good Work chapter – Chapter 14 – described below.

In Chapter 6, Niemiec and Spence introduce the archetypal workplace construct of motivation. Based particularly in self-determination theory (SDT), this chapter explores optimal motivation at work. The authors explain that optimal motivation – marked by volition and self regulation – is likely to be facilitated by contextual support for satisfaction of basic psychological needs: autonomy, competence, and relatedness (Baard, Deci, & Ryan, 2004). In addition to theoretical description, the chapter provides a critical review of recent empirical literature (Güntert, 2015).

In Chapters 7 and 8 the focus moves to issues of attention and absorption at work. In Chapter 7 Cziksentmihalyi, Khosla, and Nakamura describe flow theory (Csikszentmihalyi, 1990) and its relevance to the workplace and work itself. Based on a review of 10 years of literature, the chapter summarizes facilitators, inhibitors, and outcomes of flow.

In Chapter 8 Spence elucidates the recently popular area of mindfulness at work. Spence helps the reader wrestle with that considerable confusion that has arisen due to poorly defined approaches to mindfulness, which vary in its presentation as a state, trait, attentional process, mode of being, or committed lifestyle choice (Cavanagh & Spence, 2013). Notwithstanding these challenges, Spence reports how the positive impact of mindfulness on working adults is now being confirmed by meta-analytic studies, such as Sharma and Rush (2014) and Virgili (2015).

In Chapters 9 and 10 the notion of having something in reserve to deal with work challenges is addressed by exploring resilience and mental fitness respectively. Denovan, Crust, and Clough explore resilience at work in Chapter 9. These authors necessarily take the time to define the contested term resilience comparing it to other concepts including hardiness and mental toughness (Clough & Strycharczyk, 2012). The authors conclude by arguing for the need for future research with tighter ways of defining and measuring resilience.

Chapter 10 introduces the concept of mental fitness and its application at work. Robinson and Oades (Robinson, Oades, & Caputi, 2014) assert that mental fitness, based on an analogy to physical fitness, can make intentional efforts toward managing one's psychological well-being more accessible and more likely. They use strength, endurance, and flexibility as factors to achieve this. The chapter critiques related literature and provides workplace examples to elaborate this new empirical construct.

The final trio of chapters in this section involve relational concepts, positive relationships, and issues of humility and compassion at work. In Chapter 11 Roffey provides a critical overview of the broad and important issue of positive relationships at work. Quoting Reis and Gable's (2003) assertion that relationships may be the most important source of life satisfaction and well-being, Roffey covers how the changing nature of organizations has impacted upon relationships with work and relationships at work.

Davis, Hook, DeBlaere, and Placares – Chapter 12 – examine the interesting phenomenon of humility at work. They posit that we seem to struggle with narcissistic tendencies more so than in years past (Twenge & Campbell, 2009). Given this observation the chapter explores how humility may impact upon one's work life, and they note that since 2010 the scientific study of humility has grown considerably.

Chapter 13 examines compassion at work. Anstiss uses Jazaieri et al. (2013) to define compassion as 'a complex multidimensional construct that is comprised of four key components: (1) an awareness of suffering (cognitive component), (2) sympathetic concern related to being emotionally moved by suffering (affective component), (3) a wish to see the relief of that suffering (intentional component), and (4) a responsiveness or readiness to help relieve that suffering (motivational component)'. Anstiss argues that this research area now needs to progress from descriptive studies, theory building, and the development of plausible models to more rigorous and systematic model testing, single and multicomponent interventional studies, and research into casual pathways and mechanisms.

Part II comprises nine chapters that describe organizational approaches that involve positive psychology and well-being.

Wong, Itzvan, and Lomas commence the section – Chapter 14 – with exploration of the concept of good work based on a meaning-centered approach (Wong, 2006). These authors provide a critical review of previous approaches from positive psychology toward organizations. They argue that there is a somewhat unrecognized link between work and meaning in life.

In Chapter 15 Oades and Dulagil outline a three-level conceptualization of individual, group, and organizational well-being. They argue against the "individualist fallacy" in organizational research, which sometimes inadvertently reduces analysis to the level of the individual. They propose that systems thinking will be fruitful for future organizational research in workplace and organizational well-being (Schneider & Somers, 2006).

Cantore – Chapter 16 – examines the important area of organizational change. The author explores the role of pessimism and optimism in how people conceptualize organizations and change with them. He draws on concepts such as positive deviance from positive organizational scholarship (Cameron & Dutton, 2003) to outline the emergence of positive organizational development.

In Chapter 17 MacKie asserts that positive leadership development offers access to a range of new theoretical and evidence-based approaches that have the potential to refine and enhance how leaders and leadership are developed in organizations drawing on the works of writers such as Luthans and Avolio (2003).

Rothmann – Chapter 18 – addresses the growing interest in employee engagement from Kahn's (1990) notion of personal engagement of individuals in their work, represented by the person's investment of cognitive, physical, and emotional energy into their role performances. Schaufeli, Salanova, González-Romá, V., and Bakker (2002) claim that although engagement is negatively related to burnout, it is an independent and distinct concept characterized by three dimensions, namely vigor, dedication, and absorption at work. Rothmann critiques the current approaches to employee engagement calling for a new unifying model to support future empirical research.

In Chapter 19 Slemp summarizes and critiques the literature on job crafting – defined as "the physical and cognitive changes individuals make in the task or relational boundaries of their work" (Wrzesniewski & Dutton, 2001, p. 179). Slemp concludes that job crafting gives people a way to inject new organization into their work experiences, allowing them to steer their work tasks, relationships, and cognitions in a direction that is consistent with their intrinsic motives and preferences. He argues that this ultimately creates a different, more intrinsically driven experience of the job. Yoo and Lee – Chapter 20 – examine the interesting area of how people make career transitions at mid-stages of their career. These authors report that, for many, mid-career has been considered a plateaued period marked by the experience of mastery and maintenance (Slay, Taylor, & Williamson, 2004). To understand the nature of mid-career transition, Yoo and Lee review the evolution of the notion of mid-career, discussing the impact of environmental and individual factors on mid-career changes. They assert that future researchers need to move beyond the traditional approach to take into consideration the impacts of culture, gender, and types of work on the mid-career transition, as well as emerging new career patterns.

In Chapter 21 Cleveland, Fisher, and Walters explore the impact of the increasing length of our work life due to increased life expectancies (Phillips & Siu, 2012). These authors discuss positive aspects of aging in relation to work – particularly the benefits of aging, the positive contribution of older workers in the workplace, and implications of positive aging for human resource management in organizations.

Chapter 22 concludes this section, with Jarden and Jarden providing a critical analysis of existing well-being measures in the workplace. The chapter summarizes the benefits of well-being at work and the case for well-being assessments and the use of positive psychological assessment. Suggestions are provided as to what to assess in organizations, and how this should be assessed. The authors propose a new framework for conceptually evaluating organizational well-being research.

Part III, comprising five chapters, considers different sectors of business, and how specific typologies of job impact on work life. This section deliberately adopts an international focus.

In Chapter 23 Wiesmann investigates the well-being of health professionals – those professionals who have direct contact with patients. The World Health Organization defines the health workforce, as "all people engaged in actions whose primary intent is to enhance health" (World Health Organization, 2006, p. 1). Wiesmann provides a critical review of attempts to improve well-being in this context and asserts that, to date, positive psychology has given no theoretical input into "positive leadership" or "human resource management" in health institutions. Given the importance and size of this workforce worldwide, this represents a great opportunity.

Branand and Nakamura – Chapter 24 – move the context from health to education by examining the well-being of teachers and professors. These authors explore the concept of generativity as it relates to educators and serious challenges to persistence and well-being – burnout (Vailliant & Milofsky, 1980). A critical literature review of teacher and faculty well-being at work examines the impact of work on both hedonic and eudaimonic dimensions of well-being.

In Chapter 25 Singh and Junnarkar explore the well-being of information technology professionals (Diedericks & Rothmann, 2014). They open the chapter with an important fact: globally approximately a billion people work in information technology, however the sector still faces a shortfall of employees (Young, Marriott, & Huntley, 2008). Given the scope of this workforce, the promotion of workers' well-being in this sector will have broad importance.

Delle Fave and Zager Kocjan – Chapter 26 – examine the arts and crafts sector, summarizing studies focused on the challenges and benefits of creativity (Bille, Bryld Fjællegaard, Frey, & Steiner, 2013). As research into the well-being of people working in these domains has been largely neglected, the authors summarize the sparse studies investigating well-being among people who work as artists or skilled craftsmen, both in Western societies and in other countries and cultures. Importantly, these authors assert that findings derived from studies conducted on artists and craftsmen may provide useful suggestions for designing interventions aimed at increasing job satisfaction and work-related well-being among other professional categories more exposed to the risk of disengagement, repetitiveness, and lack of meaningful challenges.

In Chapter 27 Soosai-Nathan and Delle Fave examine the well-being of workers worldwide so essential to us all – farmers and personnel enrolled in the agricultural sector. Similar to information technology employees, it is estimated that approximately one billion people are officially employed in agriculture. Agriculture of course involves dealing with the unpredictability of climate, which has direct impact on work outcomes (Kennedy, Maple, McKay, & Brumby, 2014). While there is a limited number of studies on the well-being of workers in agriculture, there is evidence for the importance of positive relationships, mastery, self-efficacy, and connection with nature.

Conclusion

In this title we have taken a strongly academic approach to workplace applications of positive psychology including strengths and positivity. This is in contrast to popular texts such as Lyubomirsky (2008), which offers material for practitioners. The aim is to offer an up-to-date edited title, with leading international scholars providing comprehensive and importantly critical reviews of wide areas of literature related to the psychology of positivity and strengths in the workplace.

References

Baard, P. P., Deci, E. L., & Ryan, R. M. (2004). Intrinsic need satisfaction: A motivational basis of performance and well-being in two work settings. *Journal of Applied Social Psychology, 34*, 2045–2068.

Bille, T., Bryld Fjællegaard, C., Frey, B. S., & Steiner, L. (2013). Happiness in the arts: International evidence on artists' job satisfaction. *Economics Letters, 121*, 15–18.

Cameron, K., & Dutton, J. (Eds.) (2003). *Positive organizational scholarship: Foundations of a new discipline*. Oakland, CA: Berrett-Koehler Publishers.

Cameron, K., & Spreitzer, G. (Eds.) (2012). *The Oxford handbook of positive organisational scholarship*. New York, NY: Oxford University Press.

Cavanagh, M., & Spence, G. B. (2013). Mindfulness in coaching: Philosophy, psychology, or just a useful skill? In J. Passmore, D. Peterson, & T. Freire (Eds.), *The Wiley-Blackwell handbook of the psychology of coaching and mentoring* (pp. 112–134). Oxford, UK: Wiley-Blackwell.

Clough, P., & Strycharczyk, D. (2012). *Developing mental toughness: Improving performance, wellbeing and positive behaviours in others*. London, UK: Kogan Page.

Csikszentmihalyi, M. (1990). *Flow*. New York, NY: Harper & Row.

Diedericks, E., & Rothmann, S. (2014). Flourishing of information technology professionals: Effects on individual and organizational outcomes. *South African Journal of Business Management, 45*(1), 27–41.

Dik, B. J., Byrne, Z. S., & Steger, M. F. (2013). *Purpose and meaning in the workplace*. Washington, DC: APA Books.

Fredrickson, B. L. (2001). The role of positive emotions in positive psychology: The broaden-and-build theory of positive emotions. *American Psychologist, 56*, 218–226.

Fredrickson, B. L., & Joiner, T. (2002). Positive emotions trigger upward spirals toward emotional well-being. *Psychological Science, 13*(2), 172–175.

Güntert, S. T. (2015). The impact of work design, autonomy support, and strategy on employee outcomes: A differentiated perspective on self-determination at work. *Motivation and Emotion, 39*, 74–87.

Jazaieri, H., Jinpa, G. T., McGonigal, K., Rosenberg, E., Finkelstein, J., Simon-Thomas, E., ... Goldin, P. R. (2013). Enhancing compassion: A randomized controlled trial of a compassion cultivation training program. *Journal of Happiness Studies, 14*, 1113–1126.

Kahn, W. A. (1990). Psychological conditions of personal engagement and disengagement at work. *Academy of Management Journal, 33*, 692–724.

Kennedy, A., Maple, M. J., McKay, K., & Brumby, S. (2014). Suicide and accidental death in Australia's rural farming communities: A review of the literature. *Rural and Remote Health, 14*, 2517.

Linley, P. A., Nielsen, K. M., Wood, A. M., Gillett, R., & Biswas-Diener, R. (2010). Using signature strengths in pursuit of goals: Effects on goal progress, need satisfaction, and well-being, and implications for coaching psychologists. *International Coaching Psychology Review, 5*, 6–15.

Luthans, F., & Avolio, B. J. (2003). Authentic leadership: A positive developmental approach. In K. S. Cameron, J. E. Dutton, & R. E. Quinn (Eds.), *Positive organizational scholarship* (pp. 241–261). San Francisco, CA: Barrett-Koehler.

Lyubomirsky, S. (2008). *The how of happiness: A scientific approach to getting the life you want*. New York, NY: Penguin.

Peterson, C., & Seligman, M. (2004). *Character strengths and virtues: A handbook and classification*. New York, NY: Oxford University Press.

Peterson, C., Stephens, J. P., Park, N., Lee, F., & Seligman, M. E. P. (2009). Strengths of character and work. In P. A. Linley, S. Harrington, & N. Garcea (Eds.), *Oxford handbook of positive psychology and work* (pp. 221–234). Oxford, UK: Oxford University Press.

Phillips, D. R., & Siu, O. L. (2012). Global aging and aging workers. *The Oxford handbook of work and aging* (11–32). Oxford, UK: Oxford University Press.

Reis, H. T. and Gable, S. L. (2003). Toward a positive psychology of relationships. In C. L. M. Keyes & J. Haidt (Eds.), *Flourishing: Positive psychology and the life well lived* (pp. 129–159). Washington DC: American Psychological Association

Robinson, P. L., Oades, L. G., & Caputi, P. (2014). Conceptualising and measuring mental fitness: A Delphi study. *International Journal of Well-being, 5*(1), 53–73.

Schaufeli, W. B., Salanova, M., González-Romá, V., & Bakker, A. B. (2002). The measurement of engagement and burnout: A two sample confirmatory factor analytic approach. *Journal of Happiness Studies, 3*, 71–92.

Schneider, M., & Somers, M. (2006). Organizations as complex adaptive systems: Implications of complexity theory for leadership research. *The Leadership Quarterly, 17*, 351–365.

Seligman, M. E., & Csikszentmihalyi, M. (2000). Positive psychology: An introduction. *American Psychologist, 55*(1), 5–14.

Sharma, M., & Rush, S. E. (2014). Mindfulness-based stress reduction as a stress management intervention for healthy individuals: A systematic review. *Journal of Evidence-Based Complementary and Alternative Medicine, 19*, 271–286.

Slay, U. S., Taylor, M. S., & Williamson, I. O. (2004). *Midlife transition decision processes and career success: The role of identity, networks, and shocks*. Paper presented at the annual meeting of the Academy of Human Resource Development, Austin, TX.

Steger, M. F., & Dik, B. J. (2010). Work as meaning. In P. A. Linley, S. Harrington, & N. Page (Eds.), *Oxford handbook of positive psychology and work* (pp. 131–142). Oxford, UK: Oxford University Press.

Twenge, J. M., & Campbell, W. K. 2009. *The narcissism epidemic: Living in the age of entitlement.* New York, NY: Free Press.

Vailliant, G. E., & Milofsky, E. (1980). Natural history of male psychological health: IX. Empirical evidence for Erikson' s model of the life cycle. *The American Journal of Psychiatry, 137*, 1348–1359.

Virgili, M. (2015). Mindfulness-based interventions reduce psychological distress in working adults: A meta-analysis of intervention studies. *Mindfulness, 6*, 326–337.

Wandeler, C., Baeriswyl, F., & Shavelson, R. (2011). Hope at the workplace: A multilevel study. *Swiss Journal of Educational Research, 3*, 421–442.

Wong, P. T. P. (2006). Is your organization an obstacle course or a relay team? A meaning-centered approach to creating a collaborative culture. In S. Schuman (Ed.), *Creating a culture of collaboration: The International Association of Facilitators handbook* (pp. 229–256). San Francisco, CA: Jossey-Bass/Wiley.

World Health Organization. (2006). *The World Health Report 2006: Working together for health.* Geneva, Switzerland: WHO Press. Retrieved from http://www.who.int/whr/2006/whr06_en.pdf?ua=1

Wrzesniewski, A., & Dutton, J. E. (2001). Crafting a job: Revisioning employees as active crafters of their work. *Academy of Management Review, 26*, 179–201. doi: 10.5465/AMR.2001.4378011

Young, A., Marriott, I., & Huntley, H. (2008). *Offshoring IT services can cut costs: Options for a potential economic downturn.* Report Number G00155776, Gartner Inc., Stamford, CT.

Part I

Individual Approaches to Positive Psychology at Work

2

The Psychology of Positivity at Work

Suzy Green, Michelle McQuaid, Alicia Purtell, and Aylin Dulagil

Introduction

It has been reported that between 20 and 30% of business performance can be determined by the mood of employees (Goleman, 2000), however to date there has been limited evidence to support such a claim. There can be no denying, though, that contemporary organizations recognize that Taylor's (1911) once-popular scientific management practices of treating employees like machines overlooked emotion as one of the key drivers of human performance.

As organizations continue to grapple with ways to improve employee engagement, fuel collaboration and innovation, and find sustainable ways to maintain productivity, a growing body of research (Cameron, 2013; Dutton, 2014; Fredrickson, 1998, 2000, 2001, 2009; Isen, 2000, 2002; Tsai, Cheng & Cheng, 2009; Vacharkulksemsuk, Sekerka & Fredrickson, 2011) suggests that cultivating "heart-felt" positivity may be the means to achieving individual and organizational growth and optimal functioning over time.

Fredrickson (2009) proposes that positivity encompasses emotions like love, joy, gratitude, interest, and hope that improve our mindsets and biochemistry in synchrony. Vaillant (2012) notes that positivity is a state that emanates from our limbic mammalian brain and not only has an effect on how we feel, but also affects the way we function; while Scherer, Schorr, and Johnson (2001) point out that, in contrast to mere bodily pleasures, these positive emotions arise from how we interpret events and ideas as they unfold.

Consequently, positive psychologists and positive organizational scholars have become intrigued by the potential benefits that positive emotions, and "positivity" more broadly (encompassing emotions, thoughts, and behaviors), have to offer employees and organizations. Vacharkulksemsuk and Fredrickson (2013) state that the short and long-term outcomes of positive emotions can be beneficial in the workplace. They highlight that the "seemingly inconsequential" positive feelings that arise from small actions and acknowledgments in the workplace are associated with valuable workplace outcomes

The Wiley Blackwell Handbook of the Psychology of Positivity and Strengths-Based Approaches at Work, First Edition. Edited by Lindsay G. Oades, Michael F. Steger, Antonella Delle Fave, and Jonathan Passmore.

such as prosocial behavior, group development, established ethical cultures, and learning (Akrivou, Boyatzis, & McLeod, 2006; Arnaud & Sekerka, 2010; Luthans, Vogelgesang, & Lester, 2006; Triliva & Dafermos, 2008). This growing body of research shows and continues to demonstrate how experiences that foster positive emotions such as interest, joy, awe, and gratitude enable people to perform more effectively – individually and collectively.

This chapter aims to provide the reader, with a current and critical overview of the science of "positivity," with a specific focus on positive emotions where a large body of research already exists and continues to emerge. We also aim to provide an overview of current research that investigates more specifically the benefits of "positivity" at work. We begin with a review of representative research from social psychology and findings from organizational research, concluding with suggestions for further research into this promising area.

The Science of Positivity

While the founding fathers of modern psychology such as William James (1890), Carl Rogers (1959), and Abraham Maslow (1962) hinted at the potential of positive emotion, it wasn't until Alice Isen's ground-breaking work in the 1970s that we began to understand that positive emotions offered powerful benefits beyond the experience of simply pleasant and fleeting feelings.

Isen and her colleagues tested the effects of positive emotional states on a wide range of cognitive outcomes – from creativity puzzles to simulations of complex, life-or-death work situations. They found that positivity facilitated cognitive flexibility (Isen, Daubman, & Nowicki, 1987), promoted intrinsic motivation (Isen 2003), produced patterns of notably unusual thought (Isen, Johnson, Mertz, & Robinson, 1985), boosted receptivity to new information (Estrada, Isen, & Young, 1997) and creativity (Isen et al., 1987), and improved problem solving (Isen, Rosenzweig, & Young, 1991). Taken as a whole, Isen's research suggests that positive affect "gives rise to an enlarged cognitive context" (Isen, 1987, p. 222). Isen also found that positive affect impacted our social relationships by facilitating inclusion (Isen & Daubman, 1984), promoting generosity, helpfulness and social responsibility (Isen, 1987, 2003), and reducing conflict (Isen, 2001).

The potential benefits of positive emotional experiences were thrust further into the spotlight when Csikszentmihalyi (1990) began publishing his research on a psychological state identified as "flow." A positive emotion akin to interest, flow occurs when people have a clear goal, an appropriate level of challenge that matches their strengths to the tasks they're undertaking, and regular feedback. Inherently pleasurable and fulfilling, the experience of flow has been found to lead us to be more involved in life, to enjoy activities, to have a sense of control, and to feel a strong sense of self (Lyubomirsky, 2007), thus increasing positivity in individuals.

At the turn of the century, Seligman and Csikszentmihalyi established the field of positive psychology to increase the focus on the study of positive human functioning and a scientific understanding of the "good life" (Seligman & Csikszentmihalyi, 2000). Their efforts to highlight the legitimacy, value, and importance of positive emotions, states, and traits resulted in more than 200 citable publications appearing in the following decade (Rusk & Waters, 2013). To date the research on "happiness," or on its better-known scientific construct "subjective well-being" (Diener, Emmons, Larsen, & Griffin, 1985), has shown that happy individuals, or those who experience frequent positive affect, are successful across multiple life domains, including marriage, friendship, income, work performance, and health (Lyubomirsky, King, & Diener, 2005).

Diener, noted for his research over the past 25 years on subjective well-being/happiness, and his colleagues have suggested a conceptual model to account for these findings, arguing that the happiness–success link exists not only because success makes people happy, but also because positive affect engenders success. Three classes of evidence (cross-sectional, longitudinal, and experimental) were documented to test their model. Their meta-analysis of relevant studies revealed that happiness is associated with and precedes numerous successful outcomes, as well as behaviors paralleling success. Furthermore, they concluded that positive affect, which they refer to as the "hallmark of well-being," may be the cause of many of the desirable characteristics, resources, and successes correlated with happiness (Lyubomirsky et al., 2005).

Seligman (2009), however, notes that he "detests" the word happiness and suggests that the "topic of positive psychology is wellbeing" (p. 13). Seligman's (2012) PERMA model of well-being comprises the following elements: positive emotions, engagement, relationships, meaning and accomplishment. While there are other theories/models and approaches to understanding well-being (i.e., Deci & Ryan, 1985; Keyes, 2010; Ryff, 1999), and the debate continues as to its definition, positive emotions are often identified as a core component of well-being (Diener, 1984; Seligman, 2009).

There has since been a move toward the use of the terminology "wellbeing" to represent the full range of human emotions, rather than the sole pursuit of "happiness." The interest in the science and practice of positive psychology (i.e., positive organizational scholarship, positive education) continues together with a continued community and public interest in the field.

Broaden-and-Build Theory

Building on the work of Isen (1987), the research of Fredrickson (1998) asked the question: "What good are positive emotions?" Noting that traditional approaches to the study of emotions have tended to ignore positive emotions, squeeze them into purportedly emotion-general models, confuse them with closely related affective states, and describe their function in terms of generic tendencies to approach or continue, Fredrickson developed an alternative model for positive emotions that she believed better captured their unique effects. She called this the broaden-and-build theory of positive emotions because positive emotions appear to broaden peoples' momentary thought–action repertoires and build their enduring personal resources (Fredrickson, 1998; 2004).

While negative emotions have been shown to correspond with specific inclinations (e.g., fear moves us to escape or avoid the immediate context; anger moves us to attack or maintain a course of action; disgust moves us to expel or shun a stimulus), Fredrickson's research supported the idea that positive emotions also facilitate behavioral tendencies. However, she suggested that positive emotions are associated with diffuse rather than specific tendencies (e.g., joy moves us to experience contentment toward inaction or aimless interests [Frijda, 1986]).

Fredrickson (2009) suggests that with positivity, people are able to see new possibilities, bounce back from setbacks, connect more deeply with others, and reach their potential. In a comprehensive review (2013a) of her 15-year research program, Fredrickson describes 10 positive emotions and how they facilitate positivity (see Table 2.1).

Table 2.1 Fredrickson's 10 positive emotions.

	Impact and benefits
Joy	Joy emerges when one's current circumstances present unexpected good fortune. It creates the urge to play and get involved and allows us to accrue skills gained through experimental learning.
Gratitude	Gratitude emerges when people acknowledge another person as the source of their unexpected good fortune. It creates the urge to creatively consider new ways to be kind and generous and builds the skills for showing care, loyalty, and social bonds.
Serenity	Also called contentment, serenity emerges when people interpret their current circumstances as utterly cherished, right, or satisfying. It creates the urge to savor those current circumstances and integrate them into new priorities or values.
Interest	Interest arises in circumstances appraised as safe but offering novelty. It creates the urge to explore, to learn, to immerse oneself in the novelty and thereby expands the self.
Hope	Hope arises in dire circumstances in which people fear the worst yet yearn for better. It creates the urge to draw on one's own capabilities and inventiveness to turn things around and builds the resources of optimism and resilience.
Pride	Pride emerges when people take appropriate credit from some socially valued good outcome. It creates the urge to fantasize about even bigger accomplishments in similar arenas and leaves us feeling confident and self-assured.
Amusement	Amusement occurs when we appraise our current circumstances as involving some sort of non-serious social incongruity. It creates urges to share a laugh and find creative ways to continue the joviality helping us to build and solidify enduring social bonds.
Inspiration	Inspiration arises when people witness human excellence in some manner. It creates the urge to excel oneself, to reach one's own higher ground or personal best and builds the motivation for personal growth.
Awe	Awe emerges when people encounter goodness on a grand scale. The experience of awe compels people to absorb and accommodate this new vastness they have encountered and creates new worldviews.
Love	Love, which appears to be the positive emotion people feel most frequently, arises when any other of the positive emotions is felt in the context of a safe, interpersonal connection or relationship. It creates momentary perceptions of social connection and self-expansion and builds social bonds and community.

Source: Fredrickson (2013a).

The broaden effects of positive emotions

Drawing from multiple subdisciplines within psychology, ranging from work on cognition and intrinsic motivation, to attachment styles and animal behavior, empirical evidence suggests that positive emotions – relative to negative emotions and neutral states – broaden the scope of our attention, cognition, and action (Derryberry & Tucker, 1992; Fredrickson, 1998; Gasper & Clore, 2002; Isen, 1987; Johnson, Waugh, & Frederickson, 2010; Renninger, 1992). For example, Fredrickson and Branigan (2005) induced varied forms of emotions in people, followed with a separate task that asked participants to list all the things that they felt like doing right then, given their current emotional state. People induced to feel positive emotions listed more, and more varied, potential actions compared to those feeling no emotions or negative emotions.

Wadlinger and Isaacowitz (2006) have also supported the broaden hypothesis by randomly inducing various forms of emotions in people, who were then asked to view a slide show in which each screen was grouped to include three photographs, always arranged with one in the center and two at the periphery. They were instructed to look at whatever interested them as though watching TV, while sophisticated eye-tracking technology followed their gaze. The researchers found that under the influence of positivity, people looked around more and more frequently fixed their gaze on peripheral photos. Their finding that positivity expands our outlook by broadening our field of peripheral vision has been confirmed in numerous other studies (Fredrickson, 2008; Rowe, Hirsh, & Anderson, 2007; Schmitz, De Rosa, & Anderson, 2009; Trick, Brandigampola, & Enns, 2012).

Increased positive emotion has also been found to facilitate a greater sense of connectedness with others. Using a validated measure of connection in relationships (Aron, 1992), Fredrickson (2009) explored how positivity impacts our feelings about others. Participants were asked to convey how they felt about their relationship with their best friend. Positivity, negativity or neutrality was then randomly induced before they were asked again to describe how they felt about their best friend. The researchers found that a temporary boost in positivity allowed people to see more overlap between themselves and others, leading them to conclude that with positivity, people feel closer and more connected to the important people in their lives. Other studies have supported this finding with discoveries that positivity broadens social responses by expanding an individual's circles of trust (Dunn & Schweitzer, 2005), by forming common in-group identities reducing the distinction between "them" and "us" (Dovidio, Isen, Guerra, Gaertner, & Rust, 1998) and overcoming own-race bias (Johnson & Fredrickson, 2005).

As a result of these findings, Fredrickson (2009) contends that positivity does not just change one's bad thoughts for good ones, it changes the scope and boundaries of one's mind thereby impacting performance. Importantly, these changes have also been found to positively impact performance in the workplace. For example, a study examining medical decision-making among third-year medical students found that positive affect resulted in faster decision-making (that was as equally correct as the neutral affect control group) (Isen et al., 1991). In addition, subjects in the positive affect group were significantly more likely to go beyond the assigned task in considering the diagnosis. Positive affect subjects also showed better integration of diagnostic material and less confusion in diagnostic protocols (Isen et al., 1991).

Positive emotion in leaders has been found to have a significant impact on group performance and productivity. A study examining the effects of leaders' mood on group members' affect and group processes found that when leaders were in a positive mood (as opposted to a negative mood), individual group members experienced more positive moods (Sy, Cote, & Saavedra, 2005). The study also found that groups with leaders in a positive mood demonstrated better coordination among team members and required less effort to complete their work (Sy et al., 2005).

Positive emotion has also been found to impact the outcomes of complex business relationships. In a series of studies examining the impact of different emotional states (positive, negative, and neutral) on negotiation outcomes, it was found that negotiators who displayed positive emotion were more likely to build a future business relationship from the negotiation (Kopelman, Rosette, & Thompson, 2006). The second study in this series focused on ultimatum setting and found that managers displaying positive emotion were more likely to close a deal. In the final study, displaying positive emotion was found to be a more effective strategy for gaining concessions from other parties than displaying negative or neutral emotions, and negotiators made more extreme demands when faced with negotiations characterized by negative emotions (Kopelman et al., 2006).

These studies point to the importance of acknowledging and utilizing emotions in workplace settings to broaden the potential for positive and mutually beneficial outcomes.

The build effects of positive emotion

To the extent that positive emotions broaden the scope of attention and cognition, enabling flexible and creative thinking, researchers have argued that the expansive function of positive emotions is to spur the building of resources, placing people on positive trajectories of growth (Aspinwall 1998, 2001; Fredrickson, 1998; Fredrickson & Joiner, 2002; Isen 1990). A broadened mindset is the basis for discovery, discovery of new knowledge, new alliances and new skills (Fredrickson, 2013a).

These resources can emerge in several different forms, including cognitive (e.g., expert knowledge, intellectual complexity), social (e.g., friendships, social support networks), psychological (e.g., resilience, optimism), and physical (e.g., health, longevity) outcomes. Rather than merely signaling optimal functioning, enhanced resources can actually help to generate intrapersonal, interpersonal, and organizational growth (Lyubomirsky et al., 2005; Mauss et al., 2011; Vacharkulksemsuk et al., 2011).

For example, in a study comprising a seven-week "loving kindness" meditation, randomly assigned subjects were asked to complete daily web-based surveys describing a range of variables. Participants completed a diary reconstructing each day, pre- and post-intervention measures capturing their mental, psychological, social, and physical resources, as well as the extent to which they felt the ten positive emotions (Fredrickson, 2008). By the study's conclusion, participants practicing "loving kindness" meditation reported experiencing higher levels of heartfelt positivity and gaining mental, psychological, social, and physical resources that enabled them to become more accepting of themselves, feel a greater sense of purpose in their work, forge deeper and more trusting relationships with their colleagues, experience more support from others, and prove to be physically healthier.

Subsequent research replicated (Kok et al., 2013) and extended this initial evidence. A longitudinal study of secondary school teachers found positive emotions at work were reciprocally related to both personal resources and organizational resources (Salanova, Bakker, & Llorens, 2006). Bigger "boosts" in day-to-day positive emotion have also been found to forecast greater gains over time in the cognitive resource of mindfulness, which in turn predicts increased levels of flourishing in an upward spiral dynamic (Catalino & Fredrickson, 2011).

The empirical support for the broaden-and-build theory continues to grow and has sparked applications to improve both mental and physical health (Fredrickson, 2013a; Garland et al., 2010; Johnson et al., 2009) as well as organizational functioning (Sekerka, Vacharkulksemsuk, & Fredrickson, 2012).

Positivity Ratios

In 2004, researcher Marcial Losada and his colleagues during their studies of the characteristics of high-performing business teams observed more than 60 teams as they crafted their business missions and strategic plans and coded whether people's statements were positive or negative, self-focused or other focused, and based on inquiry or advocacy. He then compared this with independent business performance data. He believed that he had found that high-performing business teams stood out with their unusually high positivity ratios, at about 6:1 and this became known as the Losada Ratio (Losada & Heaphy, 2004).

In 2005, Losada and Fredrickson collaborated to explore the impact of positive to negative affect (P/N ratio) that distinguishes between a flourishing and non-flourishing state in individuals (Fredrickson & Losada, 2005). Applying the same non-linear mathematical modeling Losada had used in his research with business teams, their research suggested that the individuals who were flourishing experienced a mean ratio of 2.9:1 and this became known as the positivity ratio.

In 2013, Brown and his colleagues published an article disproving Losada's mathematical formulas and arguing that even if one takes the idea of the precise positivity/negativity ratio numbers seriously, there should exist not just a single ratio band in which "flourishing" should occur, but several "windows" of desirable and undesirable positivity/negativity ratios above a certain value (Brown, Sokal, & Friedman, 2013). Fredrickson responded (2013b) by acknowledging the fault in the mathematical computation and the ratio itself was withdrawn.

It is worth noting, however, that there is support for P/N ratios at the dyad level. P/N ratios have been used to discriminate distressed from non-distressed couples (Gottman, Markman, & Notarius, 1977). Lower P/N ratios (1:1) predicted a significantly greater risk for marital dissolution and lower marital satisfaction (Gottman & Levenson, 1992), whereas successful marriages are characterized by positivity ratios of about 5:1 (Gottman, 1994). Fredrickson (2013b) states that "considerable empirical work remains to be done to better understand the dynamic and nonlinear properties of positivity ratios as well as the most appropriate algorithms for computing them" (p. 7).

Positive Emotions, Well-being, and Health

As noted earlier, positive psychology's focus has evolved from happiness to well-being (Seligman, 2012), however positive emotions prevail as a key tenet of psychological flourishing, for example PERMA (Seligman, 2012). Researchers continue to find that feeling good is a key component of functioning effectively and engendering success (Huppert & So, 2013; Keyes, 2002; Kuppens, Realo, & Diener, 2008; Lyubomirsky et al., 2005).

Studies also suggest that positive emotions are relevant, not only when things are going well, but equally when life isn't going to plan. In particular, research highlights that resilient individuals use positive emotions in the face of adversity by finding positive meaning in ordinary events or within the adversity itself (Aspinwall, 2001; Cohn, Brown, Fredrickson, Mikels, & Conway, 2009; Folkman 1997; Tugade & Fredrickson, 2004).

It appears that positive emotions may also help undo the negative effects of stress. For example, where high-activation negative emotions that increased anxiety, heart rate, peripheral vasoconstriction, and systolic and diastolic blood pressure were induced in research participants, those who were then induced into a state of mild positivity – as opposed to neutrality or sadness – showed the fastest cardiovascular recovery (Fredrickson & Levenson 1998; Fredrickson et al., 2000).

In contrast to the literature that has found that depressed mood and the narrowed, pessimistic thinking it engenders leads to a downward spiral of well-being, Fredrickson et al. (2013) suggest that positive emotions and the broadened thinking they engender leads to an upward spiral in emotional well-being over time. The long-term consequences of such an effect can be seen in a 70-year longitudinal study of 180 Catholic nuns who agreed to give scientists access to their archived work (including autobiographies handwritten in their early twenties), medical records, and brain autopsies. Researchers recording instances of positive and negative emotions found that those subjects who expressed the most positive emotions lived on average 10 years longer than those who expressed the least positive emotions (Danner, Snowdon, & Friesen, 2001). Even when accounting for age, gender, health status, social class, and other confounding variables, researchers have found a link between feeling good and living longer (Ostir, Markides, Black, & Goodwin, 2000; Ostir, Markides, Peek, & Goodwin, 2001; Peterson, Seligman, & Vaillant, 1988; Richman et al., 2005).

Emerging evidence now suggests that people who cultivate more frequent positive emotions can shift their characteristic cardiovascular patterns toward better health, as indexed by increases in vagal tone (Kok et al., 2013). Researchers have hypothesized that the increased cognitive and behavioral repertoires created by positive emotions may produce biopsychosocial resources that support coping and flourishing mental health (Garland et al., 2010).

Fredrickson and colleagues are now testing whether people's efforts to increase their daily experience of positive emotions build other biological resources for health as well (Fredrickson, 2013b; Fredrickson et al., 2015). Drawing on the broaden-and-build theory, Fredrickson and colleagues (2015) posit that positive emotions resulting from physical activity may also create increases in resources such as environmental mastery, social support, and purpose in life. They claim that there is real benefit in focusing on physical activity because it is a behavior that is accessible to most individuals, requires no special training, and in one form or another appeals across strata of society.

The Downside of Positivity

While the evidence base exploring the benefits of positive emotion continues to grow, some in the field fear the psychological pendulum of practice risks swinging too far toward positivity. They suggest that too much positive emotion could potentially lead to people's downfall, and advocate that negative emotions are an essential mechanism to help us build distress tolerance and ensure we become stronger, more mentally agile, and ultimately happier (Kashdan & Biswas-Diener, 2014).

Similarly, researchers and practitioners of Acceptance and Commitment Therapy (ACT) suggest that our societal discourse idealizes positive emotions and looks for "quick fixes" to remove negative emotions. Hayes, Wilson, Gifford, Follette, and Strosahl (1996) claim that uncomfortable feelings are often seen as "bad" and are accompanied by efforts to avoid or stop them. Ironically, attempts to suppress distressing internal events may actually amplify them (e.g., Wegner, 1997), while other avoidance strategies (e.g., alcohol, drug use, procrastination) can have unhelpful long-term consequences. Indeed, research shows that avoidance of negative internal states can be associated with increased risk of psychopathology (Hayes & Gifford, 1997). Hence, ACT practitioners suggest that rather than labeling emotions "positive" or "negative," people are better served by simply accepting and observing that all emotions have a purpose in our lives (Harris, 2006). Positivity in the workplace is now discussed.

Positivity at Work

Scientific research has provided support for the tenet that "bad is stronger than good" Baumeister, Bratslavsky, Finkenauer, and Vohs (2001), whereby the tendencies toward protection and survival make negative events and negative stimuli extremely potent in affecting individual human emotions. It can be argued that this same tenet is powerfully at work within organizations and potentially impacting organizational performance (Alderfer, 1986; Maslow, 1968).

For this reason Cameron, one of the founders of the field of positive organizational scholarship (POS), and his colleagues (Cameron, Mora, Leutscher, & Calarco, 2011, p. 290) suggest that "extra emphasis is usually required on positive practices for positive effects to accrue in organizations, but most organizations remain focused on negative phenomena."

A range of organizational practices and theories has arisen to counteract the tendency to focus on negative stimuli in a range of organizational contexts (e.g., performance reviews, development planning, engagement strategies, change management, people strategies, leadership development). Whilst a detailed review of research within each of these contexts is beyond the scope of this chapter, we aim to examine some of the workplace positivity research that may apply to the aforementioned people practices.

It is important to note that measuring the relationship between employee emotions and workplace performance is not new. A study considering the role of emotions on workers' efficiency was reported as early as the 1930s (Hersey, 1932). Hersey found that workers who experienced positive emotional states demonstrated an 8% increase in efficiency compared with the output of workers in a negative emotional state. Despite these encouraging beginnings, it is only in the last decade that the science of positivity in the workplace has gained greater momentum.

Furthermore, an increasing body of research supports the idea that positive emotions are valuable in the workplace (Vacharkulksemsuk & Fredrickson, 2013). Building on the broader social psychological research, experienced daily positive emotions at work was found to mediate the relationship between an individual's job environment (e.g., autonomy, psychological climate of warmth and cooperation) and personal resources of optimism, self-efficacy, and self-esteem (Xanthopoulou, Bakker, Demerouti, & Schaufeli, 2012). Employees experiencing positive emotions are more helpful to customers, more creative, more attentive, and respectful to one another (George, 1998; Sharot, Riccardi, Raio, & Phelps, 2007). In addition, the daily experience of positive emotions influences an individual's readiness to engage in particular organizationally beneficial behaviors (Weiss, 2002).

While there may be a number of pathways for positivity to be researched and experienced in the workplace, we will focus on three key pathways: culture and engagement; employee practices that can be shaped and implemented at an individual level; and finally leadership practices that can impact on the performance and positivity of a team. Positivity at work will be discussed drawing on each of these pathways.

Culture and Engagement

Positive factors in organizations such as positive affect, subjective well-being, organizational citizenship and prosocial behavior, positive identity, engagement, psychological capital, and satisfaction (Harter, Schmidt, & Keyes, 2002; Luthans, Youseff, & Avolio, 2007) have received much attention in the organizational/industrial psychology literature. However, the majority of these studies focus on the individual level of analysis rather than on organizational performance (Cameron, et al., 2011; Moore & Beadle, 2006), highlighting the need to link employee well-being and positivity to organizational performance and effectiveness.

Organizational citizen behavior (OCB) is one way that a broader view of positivity can be attained, with OCB referring to employee behaviors that enhance task and organizational performance (Organ, 1997). OCB has been viewed as a critical component of job performance (Rotundo & Sackett, 2002) with a growing body of research finding that positive affect acts as a mediator between OCB and its various antecedents (Spence, Ferris, Brown, & Heller, 2011). For example, gratitude has been identified as a discrete positive emotion that may have specific relevance to OCB, primarily because it is hypothesized to generate helpfulness and positive feelings toward others (McCullough, Kilpatrick, Emmons, & Larson, 2001). State gratitude has been found to predict supervisor and co-worker directed OCBs (above and beyond generalized positive affect) and to contribute to within-person variation in enacting OCBs (Spence, Brown, Keeping, & Lian, 2014). Increasing gratitude may in turn increase collaboration, an important cultural facet which many organizations seek. Exploring a direct link between gratitude and collaboration is a future research area that could be considered.

While both positive psychology and positive organizational scholarship provide evidence for the benefits of positive emotions at the individual and team level, a promising complementary approach is Appreciative Inquiry (AI) (Cooperrider & Srivastva, 1987). This organizational change practice focuses on the existing and functioning positive aspects within an organization and uses employees' positive aspirations and organizational strengths as a platform for creating whole organizational positive cultural change. AI has been utilized and found to be successful in a variety of organization settings including schools (Dickerson & Helm-Stevens, 2011; Kozik, Cooney, Vinciguerra, Gradel, & Black, 2009), the British Broadcasting Corporation (Mishra & Bhatnagar, 2012), and the United Nations (https://appreciativeinquiry.case.edu/intro/commentFeb05.cfm).

Another area of focus within organizations is the study of employee engagement. Employee engagement has occupied the attention of leaders, human resource practitioners, and organizational/industrial psychologists, yet academic researchers continue to debate the definition of the construct (Shuck, Reio, & Rocco, 2011). Several definitions are worth discussing here. Employee engagement has been defined as "an individual employee's cognitive, emotional, and behavioural state directed toward desired organizational outcomes" (Shuck & Wollard, 2010, p. 15). Another conceptualization of employee engagement is that of "work engagement," defined as a "positive, fulfilling, work-related state of mind that is characterized by vigour, dedication, and absorption" (González-Romá, Schaufeli, Bakker, & Lloret, 2006; Schaufeli, Salanova, González-Romá, & Bakker, 2002). Bakker and Leiter (2010) define engagement as a psychological state, that is, as an individual and mediating factor between the antecedents and outcomes of engagement. Another definition of engagement is organizational commitment – an individual's psychological bond with the organization, defined as affective attachment and feelings of loyalty (Allen & Meyer, 1997; Judge & Kammeyer-Mueller, 2012; Meyer & Allen, 1997). It would seem that a common thread in these definitions is the affective component of employee engagement – the expression or demonstration of positive feelings toward aspects of the organization or task. Despite this confusion around the definition of engagement, there are compelling findings to support organizations' imperative to enhance employee engagement.

Employee engagement has been shown to relate to a range of organizational and performance outcomes such as discretionary effort, intention to leave (Shuck, 2010), overall performance (Rich, LePine, & Crawford, 2010), and well-being (Harter et al., 2002). Higher job satisfaction (a component of employee engagement) is related to greater employee cooperation, punctuality and efficiency, reduced absenteeism, and reduced turnover (Spector, 1997). Engaged employees are both cognitively and emotionally connected to their work and their workplace (Harter & Blacksmith, 2010) and consistently produce at high levels (Meere, 2005). Engaged employees are more likely to perform positive organizational behaviors (Meyer, Stanley, Herscovitch, & Topolnytsky, 2002) and to stay within an organization (Harter, Schmidt, Kilham, & Asplund, 2006). Higher levels of employee engagement are more likely to generate successful organizational outcomes (Rath & Harter, 2010). Employees who reported experiencing more positive emotions over negative emotions received higher performance ratings from supervisors (Wright & Bonett, 1997; Wright & Cropanzano, 2000).

Employee Practices

The implementation of positive practices within organizations has been found by the field of POS to have a significant impact on a range of organizational outcomes (Cameron, Dutton & Quinn, 2003). Positive practices include caring friendships, compassionate support for colleagues, fostering a culture of forgiveness, fostering respect, integrity and gratitude, inspiring each other at work, and an emphasis on meaningful work. Cameron and his colleagues (2011) have found that these positive practices are positively correlated with a range of reported business outcomes including reduced turnover, improved organizational effectiveness, better work environments, and better relationships with management. While positive workplace practices were found to have a significant effect on organizational-level effectiveness, no one positive practice stood out as the single most important factor, rather it was the combination of positive practices that appeared to have the most powerful impact.

Employee practices supporting the growth of positivity relate not only to single one-off behaviors, but also to a broader set of cognitive and emotional resources. The study of psychological capital, a positive psychological state of individual development, consisting of self-efficacy, optimism, hope, and resilience (Luthans, 2002a, 2002b; Luthans et al., 2007), offers practices that employees can apply to influence their thinking flexibility and improve their positivity.

For instance a recent cross-organizational study explored the link of psychological capital and creativity. The relationship between culture, psychological capital, and innovative behavior was measured through self report data of 781 employees from 16 organizations in Taiwan (Hsu & Chen, 2015). This study found that individual psychological capital levels had a greater impact on encouraging creative behavior than did organizational climate, with psychological capital acting as a mediator for innovation. Levels of optimism, hope, resilience, and creative self-efficacy operated as a protective buffer against creative failure, and provided a renewable personal resource for innovative thinking (Hsu & Chen, 2015).

The benefits of collective positive employee behaviors can be observed through a system perspective. Taking a system view through Social Network Analysis (SNA), a relatively new and developing methodology, provides support that shared positive employee behaviors could create an emotional contagion effect. For example, emotional states have been shown to transfer directly from one individual to another by mimicry and "emotional contagion," perhaps by the copying of emotionally relevant bodily actions, particularly facial expressions, seen in others (Fowler & Christakis, 2008). Research on "positive energizers" within organizations (Cross, Baker, & Parker, 2003) provides further evidence for the benefits of proactively training staff in the science of positivity with the aim of increasing their own well-being, which may provide a "ripple effect" within an organizational setting (O'Connor & Cavanagh, 2013). Furthermore, research on the use of developmental coaching in organizations that utilized SNA found significant increases in psychological well-being as a result of coaching, which has previously been shown to increase goal attainment and well-being (Green, Oades, & Grant, 2006; Linley, Willars, & Biswas-Diener, 2010; Spence & Grant, 2007).

An emerging positive employee practice to consider is current research about embodied cognition, the idea that information processing involves one's own motor experience, that is, one's motor movements are implicated in the affective and psychological experience of a situation (see Niedenthal, 2007; Havas, Glenberg, Gutowski, Lucarelli, & Davidson, 2010). For example, one's bodily expression when induced with feelings of joy and anger involves more shoulder, elbow, pelvis, and trunk motions, compared to feelings of sadness (Gross, Crane, & Fredrickson, 2012). It has been suggested that the intersection of broaden-and-build theory with evidence on embodied cognition may highlight the important role of entire bodily motions, beyond a simple focus on facial expressions, which may influence how one experiences emotions (Vacharkulksemsuk & Fredrickson, 2013).

Leadership

A leader's ability to generate or harness positive emotions in their teams is also crucial to organizational effectiveness. Research has found that leaders significantly impact how employees feel at work (Sy et al., 2005), indicating that emotions expressed from senior leaders can affect organizational climate, which contributes to organizational effectiveness (Ozcelik, Langton, & Aldrich, 2008). For example, positive emotions have been found to be more closely related with transformational leadership than with transactional leadership (Rowold & Rohmann, 2009). A five-day diary study found that daily transformational leadership behavior predicts employees' daily engagement at work, fully mediated by employees' daily levels of optimism (Tims, Bakker, & Xanthopoulou, 2011).

Leaders play a critical role in shaping the positive behavior of their team members. With significant organization change on the agenda within many organizations, it is valuable to reflect on how leaders influence the positive change behaviors of their team and in particular, to consider whether positive behaviors encourage greater employee openness to change. A recent study explored the importance of psychological capital in fostering change-orientated behaviors. Lin, Kao, Chen, and Lu (2015) studied two specific change-oriented behaviors (creative performance and taking charge), through 40 leader and 248 employee assessments. They found that positive leader and employee relationships were promoted through high levels of psychological capital. Psychological capital operated as a trigger for positive affect, in turn influencing higher levels of performance and taking charge. This research suggests that internal personal resources increase an individual's capacity to generate and implement novel and new ideas, but also lead to increased discretionary effort during change (Lin et al., 2015).

One of the most promising approaches to boosting positivity in the workplace is through the use of strengths at work. The application of strengths is multidimensional, and can be applied via many pathways. Managers can have a positive impact by focusing on the strengths of their employees. Employees who feel ignored by their managers are twice as likely to be actively disengaged at work, while managers who focus on their employees' weakness cut active disengagement to 22% (indicating that even negative attention is better than no attention) and managers who focus on their employees' strengths cut active disengagement to 1% (Gallup, 2013). When managers focus on the weaknesses of an employee, their average performance declines by up to 27%, whereas when they focus on the strengths of an employee, their average performance improves by up to 36% (Corporate Leadership Council, 2004). This research suggests that rather than following the natural 80:20 deficit-bias found in most organizations, managers reverse this ratio and spend more time, energy, and effort focused on building strengths (Cooperrider & Godwin, 2011).

The *2015 Strengths@Work Survey* (McQuaid & VIA Institute, 2015) also found that when managers had a meaningful discussion about employees' strengths, 78% of these employees reported feeling engaged and energized, and 65% of these employees described themselves as "flourishing" at work. Unfortunately the survey found that 68% of managers fail to have these conversations, with most providing minimal positive feedback, none at all, or pointing out the employee's faults without guidance for improvements.

While the positivity benefits of an individual using their strengths at work appear to be many, it is also important that both employees and managers are aware that people can occasionally feel disappointed, disengaged, or otherwise distressed as a result of strengths use. Because leveraging strengths at work is likely to make individuals feel more confident and optimistic of success, when failure occurs people who have been strongly anticipating an exceptional outcome may be more disappointed or self-punitive compared with those whose optimism is more cautious (Biswas-Diener, Kashdan, & Minhas, 2011). While tempering these risks with realistic expectations and reframing failure as an opportunity for learning can help, organizations and managers should be mindful that developing strengths might not be appropriate for every employee in every circumstance.

Explanations for Positive Effects

Given the outcomes associated with increased positive emotions and well-being, as outlined above, it is apparent that individuals would seek greater positivity in their workplace, and organizations would focus on increasing it. Below we explore an explanation of positivity's impact on organizational performance. According to positive organizational scholars, there are three sources that explain how and why positivity (specifically positive practices) elevate organizational performance: amplifying effects, buffering effects, and heliotropic effects (Cameron et al., 2011).

Amplifying effects

Amplification relates to the impact positive practices have on positive emotions, which in turn lead to elevated individual performance in organizations (Fineman, 1996; Fredrickson, 1998; Seligman, 2002; Staw, Sutton, & Pelled, 1994; Tutu, 1999; Wright & Staw, 1999). This effect is also well documented in social networks literature (Christakis & Fowler, 2009), which explores the ripple effect of emotional contagion (Baker, Cross, & Wooten, 2003). Research examining social capital in organizations (Baker et al., 2003; Coleman, 1988) highlights the benefits of enhanced relationships. Positive workplace practices such as the building of commitment, trust, and collaboration all work to create positive relationships and enhance social capital.

Buffering effects

Positive workplace practices buffer the organization from the negative effects of trauma or distress by enhancing resiliency in individuals (Cameron et al., 2011; Masten et al., 1999). Further, the cultivation of positive emotions such as compassion, courage, forgiveness, integrity, and optimism prevent psychological distress, addiction, and dysfunctional behavior (Seligman, Schulman, DeRubeis, & Hollon, 1999).

Heliotropic effects

Research suggests that positivity responds to the "heliotropic effect" whereby all living systems move toward positive energy and away from negative energy (D'Amato & Jagoda, 1962; Mrosovsky & Kingsmill, 1985; Smith & Baker, 1960). This is also posited to work within organizations as they serve a key organizing function and are intended to facilitate positive benefits for individual members (Cameron et al., 2011). Positive social processes are more likely to endure than negative social processes because they are more functional and beneficial for the group and its members (Cameron et al., 2011). Research has found that organizations characterized by positive practices foster positive energy among members, in turn producing elevated performance (Cameron et al., 2011; Dutton, 2003).

Future Research

While this chapter attests to a solid history and foundation of research supporting the benefits of positivity generally and more specifically at work, further research is required. In particular, future research needs to continue to build the "business case" for positivity at work with stronger links to overall organizational effectiveness using objective measurement.

It should be noted, though, that research in organizational/industrial psychology has already provided substantial evidence for the link between positive individual behavior (such as engagement, retention, organizational citizenship behavior) and organizational outcomes, such as profitability, customer relationships, and reduced turnover (Harter et al., 2002; Harter et al., 2006; Rotundo & Sackett, 2002; Salanova, Agut, & Peiro, 2005).

As such, further research is required to assist in understanding the direct relationship between positive affect and organizational performance. In particular, how positivity influences objective and external measures of success. The current focus is on studies that demonstrate that positive behaviors measurably improve engagement. To identify how positivity improves the bottom line, organizations must be willing to go further to test hypotheses and interventions. Leaders and their partnering organizational psychology practitioners need to commit to long-term interventions and measure their impact on both employee and financial performance.

There is an opportunity to explore further the benefits of positive affect within workplaces from a social network approach (Baker et al., 2003; Fowler & Christakis, 2008; O'Connor & Cavanagh, 2013). As discussed earlier, SNA explores the way in which network members are related (Scott, 2000). This practice can be applied in a wide variety of fields including management, anthropology, political science, and psychology (Hatala, 2006). SNA's potential use in exploring the interconnectivity of the interaction network could provide powerful understandings into the emotions and well-being of organizational members and their subsequent impact on overall organizational effectiveness.

We believe that as the research continues to mature, organizations will seek more informed analysis on how to navigate both positive and negative emotions to understand their impact on performance. While initial attempts have failed because of flawed methodologies and overly ambitious mathematical models (Fredrickson & Losada, 2005), this remains an important and worthy avenue of pursuit. We urge researchers to learn from past mistakes, but to continue searching for insights that will allow organizations, their leaders, and their employees to authentically and effectively manage their emotions for improved performance.

To support future research pursuits, connecting the study of positive affect and employee analytics could be an interesting partnership. The use of big data to identify trends and patterns in employee experiences is fast becoming the way to accelerate business performance and engage individuals (Davenport, Harris, & Shapiro, 2010). Analytics help to drive more effective decision-making, and to direct future people investment choices. Measuring the impact of positive emotions on human capital metrics such as talent acquisition, diversity, job success, and retention may result in organizations committing to practices that increase positive affect not just because it benefits individuals, but because it accelerates business performance.

Finally, given there are many paths to creating positive emotions in the workplace and a number of disciplines that are implicated in the research and practice – for example, positive psychology, positive organizational scholarship, appreciative inquiry – there is a need for interdisciplinary conversations and research, which as Vacharkulksemsuk and Fredrickson (2013, p. 56) conclude will be "key to determining effective and sustainable ways to extract short-term, long-term, and continued benefits of positive emotions" at work.

Conclusion

There is now a significant body of research to support the benefits of experiencing positive emotions and positivity more broadly (Lyubomirsky, King, & Diener, 2005). There is also research to support the individual benefits of engaging in positive psychology interventions (Bolier, Haverman, Riper, Smit, & Bohlmeijer, 2013; Sin & Lyubomirsky, 2009) that are aimed at increasing PERMA (Seligman, 2012). It has been suggested that the pattern of positivity and negativity that characterizes communications within an organization may have a significant influence over the experience of individual factors such as well-being, engagement, and satisfaction (Harter et al., 2006). However, there is a need for further research to prove the benefits of engaging in positive workplace practices that induce positive affect and heartfelt positivity that may impact broader organizational outcomes.

In conclusion, while the science continues to grow, we argue that the existing findings be given serious consideration as powerful tools for leaders, work-team members (and external consultants) to foster positive emotions, positive relationships, and positive performance within individuals. We envisage that this positivity may in turn create a positive upward spiral to the entire organization, resulting in improved organizational effectiveness (Vacharkulksemsuk, Sekerka, & Fredrickson, 2011).

References

Akrivou, K., Boyatzis, R. E., & McLeod, P. L. (2006). The evolving group: Towards a theory of prescriptive group development. *Journal of Management Development*, *25*(7), 689–706.

Alderfer, C. P. (1986). The invisible director on corporate boards. *Harvard Business Review*, *64*(6), 38.

Allen, N. J. & Meyer, J. P. (1997). *Commitment in the workplace: Theory, research, and application*. Thousand Oaks, CA: Sage.

Arnaud, A., & Sekerka, L. E. (2010). Positively ethical: The establishment of innovation in support of sustainability. *International Journal of Sustainable Strategic Management*, *2*, 121–137.

Aron, L. (1992). Interpretation as expression of the analyst's subjectivity. *Psychoanalytic Dialogues*, *2*(4), 475–507.

Aspinwall, L. G. (1998). Rethinking the role of positive affect in self-regulation. *Motivation and Emotion*, *22*, 1–32.

Aspinwall, L. G. (2001). Dealing with adversity: Self-regulation, coping, adaptation, and health. In A. Tesser & N. Schwarz (Eds.), *The Blackwell handbook of social psychology: Vol. 1. Intraindividual processes* (pp. 591–614). Malden, MA: Blackwell.

Baker, W., Cross, R., & Wooten, M. (2003). *Positive organizational network analysis and energizing relationships*. San Francisco, CA: Berrett-Kohler.

Bakker, A. B., & Leiter, M. P. (2010). *Work engagement: A handbook of essential theory and research* (1st ed.). Hoboken, NJ: Psychology Press.

Baumeister, R. F., Bratslavsky, E., Finkenauer, C., & Vohs, K. D. (2001). Bad is stronger than good. *Review of General Psychology*, *5*(4), 323–370.

Biswas-Diener, R., Kashdan, T. B., & Minhas, G. (2011). A dynamic approach to psychological strength development and intervention. *The Journal of Positive Psychology*, *6*(2), 106–118.

Bolier, L., Haverman, M., Westerhof, G. J., Riper, H., Smit, F., & Bohlmeijer, E. (2013). Positive psychology interventions: A meta-analysis of randomized controlled studies. *BMC Public Health*, *13*, 119–139.

Brown, N. J., Sokal, A. D., & Friedman, H. L. (2013). The complex dynamics of wishful thinking: The critical positivity ratio. *American Psychologist*, *68*(9), 801–813.

Cameron, K. (2013). *Practicing positive leadership: Tools and techniques that create extraordinary results*. San Francisco, CA: Berrett-Koehler.

Cameron, K., Dutton, J., & Quinn, R. (2003). *Positive organizational scholarship*. San Francisco, CA: Berrett-Koehler.

Cameron, K., Mora, C., Leutscher, T., & Calarco, M. (2011). Effects of positive practices on organizational effectiveness. *The Journal of Applied Behavioral Science*, *47*(3), 266–308.

Catalino, L. I., & Fredrickson, B. L. (2011). A Tuesday in the life of a flourisher: The role of positive emotional reactivity in optimal mental health. *Emotion*, *11*(4), 938–950.

Christakis, N. A., & Fowler, J. H. (2009). *Connected: The surprising power of our social networks and how they shape our lives*. New York, NY: Little, Brown, & Company.

Cohn, M. A., Brown, S. L., Fredrickson, B. A., Mikels, J. A., & Conway, A. M. (2009). Happiness unpacked: Positive emotions increase life satisfaction by building resilience. *Emotion*, *9*(3), 361–368.

Coleman, James, S. (1988). Social capital in the creation of human capital. *American Journal of Sociology*, *94*, Supplement: Organizations and institutions: Sociological and economic approaches to the analysis of social structure, S95–S120.

Cooperrider, D. L., & Godwin, L. (2011). Positive organization development: Innovation inspired change in an economy and ecology of strengths. In K. S. Cameron and G. Spreitzer (Eds.), *Oxford handbook of positive organizational scholarship* (pp. 737–750). Oxford, UK: Oxford University Press.

Cooperrider, D. L., & Srivastva, S. (1987). Appreciative inquiry in organizational life. In R. W. Woodman & W. A. Pasmore (Eds.), *Research in organizational change and development* (Vol. *1*, pp. 129–169). Stamford, CT: JAI.

Corporate Leadership Council. (2004). *Driving performance and retention through employee engagement*. Washington, DC: Corporate Executive Board.

Cross, R., Baker, W., & Parker, A. (2003). What creates energy in organizations? *MIT Sloan Management Review*, *Summer 2003*, 51–56.

Csikszentmihalyi, M. (1990). *Flow: The psychology of optimal experience*. New York, NY: Harper Perennial.

D'Amato, M. R., & Jagoda, H. (1962). Effect of early exposure to photic stimulation on brightness discrimination and exploratory behavior. *Journal of Genetic Psychology*, *101*(2), 267–271.

Danner, D., Snowdon, D., & Friesen, W. (2001). Positive emotions in early life and longevity: Findings from the nun study. *Journal of Personality and Social Psychology*, *80*(5), 804–813.

Davenport, T. H., Harris, J., & Shapiro, J. (2010). Competing on talent analytics. *Harvard Business Review*. Retrieved May 3, 2014 from http://www.harvardbusiness.org/sites/default/files/HBR_Competing_on_Talent_Analytics.pdf

Deci, E. L., & Ryan, R. M. (1985). The general causality orientations scale: Self-determination in personality. *Journal of Research in Personality*, *19*(2), 109–134.

Derryberry, D., & Tucker, D. M. (1992). Neural mechanisms of emotion. *Journal of Consulting and Clinical Psychology, 60*(3), 329–338.
Dickerson, M. S., & Helm-Stevens, R. (2011). Reculturing schools for greater impact: Using appreciative inquiry as a non-coersive change process. *International Journal of Business and Management, 6*, 66–74.
Diener, E. (1984). Subjective well-being. *Psychological Bulletin, 95*(3), 54 –575.
Diener, E., Emmons, R. A., Larsen, R. J., & Griffin, S. (1985). The Satisfaction With Life Scale. *Journal of Personality Assessment, 49*, 71–75.
Dovidio, J. F., Isen, A. M., Guerra, P., Gaertner, S. L., & Rust, M. (1998). Positive affect, cognition, and the reduction of intergroup bias. In C. Sedikides (Ed.), *Intergroup cognition and intergroup behavior* (pp. 337–366). Mahwah, NJ: Erlbaum.
Dunn, J. R., & Schweitzer, M. E. (2005). Feeling and believing: The influence of emotion on trust. *Journal of Personality and Social Psychology, 88*(5), 736–748.
Dutton, J. E. (2003). *Energize your workplace*. San Francisco, CA: Jossey-Bass.
Dutton, J. E. (2014). Build high quality connections. In J. E. Dutton & G. M. Spreitzer (Eds.), *How to be a positive leader: Small changes, big impact* (pp. 11–21). San Francisco, CA: Bettett-Koehler.
Estrada, C. A., Isen, A. M., & Young, M. J. (1997). Positive affect facilitates integration of information and decreases anchoring in reasoning among physicians. *Organizational Behavior and Human Decision Processes, 72*(1), 117.
Fineman, S. (1996). Emotion and organizing. In C. Hardy, S. Clegg, & W. Nord (Eds.), *Handbook of organization studies* (pp. 543–564). London, UK: Sage.
Fowler, J. H., & Christakis, N. A. (2008). Dynamic spread of happiness in a large social network: Longitudinal analysis over 20 years in the Framingham Heart Study. *British Medical Journal, 337*, 1–9.
Fredrickson, B. L. (1998). What good are positive emotions? *Review of General Psychology, 2*, 300–319.
Fredrickson, B. L. (2000). Cultivating positive emotions to optimize health and well-being. *Prevention and Treatment 3*. Retrieved April 26, 2015 from http://journals.apa.org/prevention/volume3/pre0030001a.html.
Fredrickson, B. L. (2001). The role of positive emotions in positive psychology: The broaden-and-build theory of positive emotions. *American Psychologist, 56*, 218–226.
Fredrickson, B. L. (2004). Gratitude, like other positive emotions, broadens and builds. In R. A. Emmons & M. E. McCullough (Eds.), *The psychology of gratitude* (pp. 145–166). New York, NY: Oxford University Press.
Fredrickson, B. L. (2008). Promoting positive affect. In M. Eid & R. J. Larsen (Eds), *The science of subjective well-being* (pp. 449–468). New York, NY: Guilford Press.
Fredrickson, B. L. (2009). *Positivity: Groundbreaking research reveals how to embrace the hidden strength of positive emotions, overcome negativity, and thrive*. New York, NY: Random House.
Fredrickson, B. L. (2013a). Positive emotions broaden and build. In E. Ashby Plant & P. G. Devine (Eds.), *Advances in experimental social psychology* (Vol. *47*, pp. 1–53). Burlington, VT: Academic Press.
Fredrickson, B. L. (2013b). Updated thinking on positivity ratios. *American Psychologist, 68*, 814–822.
Fredrickson, B. L., & Branigan, C. (2005). Positive emotions broaden the scope of attention and thought-action repertoires. *Cognition and Emotion, 19*(3), 313–332.
Fredrickson, B. L., Grewen, K. M., Algoe, S. B., Firestine, A. M., Arevalo, J. M. G., Ma, J., & Cole, S. W. (2015). Psychological well-being and the human conserved transcriptional response to adversity. *PLoS ONE, 10*(3): e0121839. doi:10.1371/journal.pone.0121839
Fredrickson, B. L., Grewen, K. M., Coffey, K. A., Algoe, S. B., Firestine, A. M., Arevalo, J. M. G., … Cole, S. M. (2013). A functional genomic perspective on human well-being. *Proceedings of the National Academy of Sciences, 110*, 13684–13689.
Fredrickson, B. L., & Joiner, T. (2002). Positive emotions trigger upward spirals toward emotional well-being. *Psychological Science, 13*(2), 172–175.
Fredrickson, B. L., & Levenson, R. W. (1998). Positive emotions speed recovery from the cardiovascular sequelae of negative emotions. *Cognition and Emotion, 12*(2), 191–220.

Fredrickson, B. L., & Losada, M. F. (2005). Positive affect and the complex dynamics of human flourishing. *American Psychologist, 60*(7), 678–686.

Fredrickson, B. L., Mancuso, R. A., Branigan, C., & Tugade, M. M. (2000). The undoing effect of positive emotions. *Motivation and Emotion, 24*(4), 237–258.

Frijda, N. H. (1986). *The emotions.* Cambridge, UK: Cambridge University Press.

Folkman, S. (1997). Positive psychological states and coping with severe stress. *Social Science Medicine, 45*, 1207–1221.

Gallup. (2013). *State of the American workplace.* Retrieved August 24, 2014, from: http://www.gallup.com/strategicconsulting/163007/state-american-workplace.aspx.

Garland, E. L., Fredrickson, B. L., Kring, A. M., Johnson, D. P., Meyer, P. S., & Penn, D. L. (2010). Upward spirals of positive emotions counter downward spirals of negativity: Insights from the broaden-and-build theory and affective neuroscience on the treatment of emotion dysfunctions and deficits in psychopathology. *Clinical Psychology Review, 30*, 849–864.

Gasper, K., & Clore, G. L. (2002). Attending to the big picture: Mood and global versus local processing of visual information. *Psychological Science, 13*(1), 34–40.

George, J. M. (1998). Salesperson mood at work: Implications for helping customers. *Journal of Personal Selling and Sales Management, 18*, 23–30.

Goleman, D. (2000). An EI-based theory of performance. In D. Goleman & C. Cherniss (Eds.), *The emotionally intelligent workplace: How to select for, measure, and improve emotional intelligence in individuals, groups, and organizations.* San Francisco, CA: Jossey-Bass.

González-Romá, V., Schaufeli, W. B., Bakker, A. B., & Lloret, S. (2006). Burnout and work engagement: Independent factors or opposite poles? *Journal of Vocational Behavior, 68*, 165–174.

Gottman, J. M. (1994). *What predicts divorce? The relationship between marital processes and marital outcomes.* Hillsdale, NJ: Lawrence Erlbaum.

Gottman, J. M., & Levenson, R. W. (1992). Marital processes predictive of later dissolution: Behavior, physiology, and health. *Journal of Personality and Social Psychology, 63*, 221–233.

Gottman, J., Markman, H., & Notarius, C. (1977). The topography of marital conflict: A sequential analysis of verbal and nonverbal behavior. *Journal of Marriage and the Family, 39*, 461–477.

Green, S., Oades, L., & Grant, A. M. (2006). Cognitive-behavioral, solution-focused life coaching: Enhancing goal striving, well-being, and hope. *The Journal of Positive Psychology, 1*(3), 142–149.

Gross, M. M., Crane, E. A., & Fredrickson, B. L. (2010). Methodology for assessing bodily expression of emotion. *Journal of Nonverbal Behavior, 34*, 223–248.

Harris, R. (2006). Embracing your demons: An overview of acceptance and commitment therapy. *Psychotherapy in Australia, 12*(4), 1–8.

Harter, J. K., & Blacksmith, N. (2010). Employee engagement and the psychology of joining, staying in, and leaving organizations. In P. A. E. Linley (Ed.), *Oxford handbook of positive psychology at work* (pp. 121–130). Oxford, UK: Oxford University Press.

Harter, J. K., Schmidt, F. L., & Keyes, C. L. (2002). Wellbeing in the workplace and its relationship to business outcomes: A review of the Gallup studies. In C. L. Keyes & J. Haidt (Eds.), *Flourishing: The positive person and the group life* (pp. 205–224). Washington, DC: American Psychological Association,

Harter, J. K., Schmidt, F. L., Kilham, E. A., & Asplund, J. W. (2006). *Q12 meta-analysis.* Omaha, NE: The Gallup Organization.

Hatala, J. P. (2006). Social network analysis in human resource development: A new methodology. *Human Resource Development Review, 5*(1), 45–71. doi:10.1177/1534484305284318

Havas, D. A., Glenberg, A. M., Gutowski, K. A., Lucarelli, M. J., & Davidson, R. J. (2010). Cosmetic use of botulinum toxin-a affects processing of emotional language. *Psychological Science, 21*(7), 895–900.

Hayes, S. C., & Gifford, E. V. (1997). The trouble with language: Experiential avoidance, rules, and the nature of verbal events. *American Psychological Society, 8*, 170–173.

Hayes, S. C., Wilson, K. W., Gifford, E. V., Follette, V. M., & Strosahl, K. (1996). Experiential avoidance and behavioral disorders: A functional dimensional approach to diagnosis and treatment. *Journal of Consulting and Clinical Psychology, 64*(6), 1152–1168.

Hersey, R. B. (1932). Rates of production and emotional state. *Personnel Journal, 10*, 355–364.

Hsu, M. A., & Chen, F. H. (2015). The cross-level mediating effect of psychological capital on the organizational innovation climate–employee innovative behavior relationship. *The Journal of Creative Behaviour*. doi:10.1002/jocb.90

Huppert, F. A., & So, T. T. (2013). Flourishing across Europe: Application of a new conceptual framework for defining well-being. *Social Indicators Research*, *110*(3), 837–861.

Isen, A. M. (1970). Success, failure, attention and reaction to others: The warm glow of success. *Journal of Personality and Social Psychology*, *15*(4), 294–301.

Isen, A. M. (1987). Positive affect, cognitive processes and social behaviour. In L. Berkowitz (Ed.), *Advances in experimental social psychology* (pp. 203–253). New York, NY: Academic Press.

Isen, A. M. (1990). The influence of positive and negative affect on cognitive organization: Some implications for development. In N. Stein, B. Leventhal, & T. Trabasso (Eds.), *Psychological and biological approaches to emotion* (pp. 75–94). Hillsdale, NJ: Erlbaum.

Isen, A. M. (2000). Positive affect and decision making. In M. Lewis & J. M. Haviland-Jones (Eds.), *Handbook of emotions* (pp. 417–432). New York, NY: Guilford Press.

Isen, A. M. (2001). An influence of positive affect on decision making in complex situations: Theoretical issues with practical implications. *Journal of Consumer Psychology*, *11*(2), 75–85.

Isen, A. M. (2002). A role of neuropsychology in understanding the facilitating influence of positive affect on social behaviour and cognitive processes. In C. R. Snyder & S. Lopez (Eds.), *Handbook of positive psychology* (pp. 528 – 540). New York, NY: Oxford University Press.

Isen, A. M. (2003). Positive affect as a source of human strength. In L.G. Aspinwall & U.M. Staudinger (Eds.), *A psychology of human strengths: fundamental questions and future directions for a positive psychology* (pp. 179–195). Washington, DC: American Psychological Association.

Isen, A. M., & Daubman, K. A. (1984). The influence of affect on categorization. *Journal of Personality and Social Psychology*, *47*, 1206–1217.

Isen, A. M., Daubman, K. A., & Nowicki, G. P. (1987). Positive affect facilitates creative problem solving. *Journal of Personality and Social Psychology*, *52*(6), 1122–1131.

Isen, A. M., Johnson, M. M. S., Mertz, E., & Robinson, G. F. (1985). The influence of positive affect on the unusualness of word associations. *Journal of Personality and Social Psychology*, *48*(6), 1413–1426.

Isen, A. M., Rosenzweig, A. S., & Young, M. J. (1991). The influence of positive affect on clinical problem solving. *Medical Decision Making: An International Journal of the Society for Medical Decision Making*, *11*, 221.

James, W. (1890). *The principles of psychology*. New York, NY: Holt & Company.

Johnson, K. J., & Fredrickson, B. L. (2005). "We all look the same to me": Positive emotions eliminate the own-race in face recognition. *Psychological Science*, *16*(11), 875–881.

Johnson, D. P., Penn, D. L., Fredrickson, B. L., Meyer, P. S., Kring, A. M., & Brantley, M. (2009). Loving-kindness meditation to enhance recovery from negative symptoms of schizophrenia. *Journal of Clinical Psychology*, *65*(5), 499–509. doi:10.1002/jclp.20591

Johnson, K. J., Waugh, C. E., & Fredrickson, B. L. (2010). Smile to see the forest: Facially expressed positive emotions broaden cognition. *Cognition and Emotion*, *24*(2), 299–321.

Judge, T. A., & Kammeyer-Mueller, J. D. (2012). Job attitudes. *Annual Review of Psychology*, *63*, 341–367.

Kashdan, T., & Biswas-Diener, R. (2014). *The upside of your darkside*. New York, NY: Hudson Street Press.

Keyes, C. L. M. (2002). The mental health continuum: From languishing to flourishing in life. *Journal of Health and Social Behavior*, *43*, 207–222.

Keyes, C. L. M. (2010). *Flourishing*. Oxford, UK: Wiley.

Kok, B. E., Coffey, K. A., Cohn, M. A., Catalino, L. I., Vacharkulksemsuk, T., Algoe, S. B., … Fredrickson, B. L. (2013). How positive emotions build physical health: Perceived positive social connections account for the upward spiral between positive emotions and vagal tone. *Psychological Science*, *24*, 1123–1132.

Kopelman, S., Rosette, A. S., & Thompson, L. (2006), The three faces of Eve: Strategic displays of positive, negative, and neutral emotions in negotiations. *Organizational Behavior and Human Decision Processes*, *99*, 81–101.

Kozik, P. L., Cooney, B., Vinciguerra, S., Gradel, K., & Black, J. (2009). Promoting inclusion in secondary schools through appreciative inquiry. *American Secondary Education, 38*(1), 77–91.

Kuppens, P., Realo, A., & Diener, E. (2008). The role of positive and negative emotions in life satisfaction judgement across nations. *Journal of Personality and Social Psychology, 95*(1), 66–75

Lin, C. C., Kao, Y. T., Chen, Y. L., & Lu, S. C. (2015). Fostering change oriented behaviors: A broaden and build model. *Journal of Business and Psychology*. doi:10.1007/s10869-015-9417-6

Linley, A., Willars, J., & Biswas-Diener, R. (2010). *The strengths book: What you can do, love to do, and find it hard to do – and why it matters*. Coventry, UK: CAPP Press.

Losada, M., & Heaphy, E. (2004). The role of positivity and connectivity in the performance of business teams: A nonlinear dynamics model. *American Behavioral Scientist, 47*(6), 740–765.

Luthans, F. (2002a). The need for and meaning of positive organizational behavior. *Journal of Organizational Behavior, 23*, 695–706.

Luthans, F. (2002b). Positive organizational behavior: Developing and managing psychological strengths. *The Academy of Management Executive, 16*, 57–75.

Luthans, F., Vogelgesang, G. R., & Lester, P. B. (2006). Developing the psychological capital of resiliency. *Human Resource Development Review, 5*(1), 25–44.

Luthans, F., Youssef, C. M., & Avolio, B. J. (2007). *Psychological capital*. New York, NY: Oxford University Press.

Lyubomirsky, S. (2007). *The how of happiness: A practical approach to getting the life you want*. New York, NY: Penguin.

Lyubomirsky, S. (2008). *The how of happiness: A scientific approach to getting the life you want*. New York, NY: Penguin.

Lyubomirsky, S., King, L., & Diener, E. (2005). The benefits of frequent positive affect: Does happiness lead to success. *Psychological Bulletin, 131*(6), 803–855.

Maslow, A. (1968). *Toward a psychology of being*. New York, NY: Van Nostrand.

Masten, A. S., Hubbard, J. J., Gest, S. D., Tellegen, A., Garmezy, N., & Ramirez, M. (1999). Competence in the context of adversity: Pathways to resilience and maladaptation from childhood to late adolescence. *Development and Psychopathology, 11*, 143–169.

Mauss, I. B., Shallcross, A. J., Troy, A. S., John, O. P., Ferrer, E., Wilhelm, F. H., & Gross, J. (2011). Don't hide your happiness! Positive emotion dissociation, social connectedness, and psychological functioning. *Journal of Personality and Social Psychology, 100*(4), 738–748.

McCullough, M. E., Kilpatrick, S. D., Emmons, R. A., & Larson, D. B. (2001). Is gratitude a moral affect? *Psychological Bulletin, 127*, 249–266.

McQuaid, M., & VIA Institute (2015). *The 2015 Strengths@Work Survey*. Retrieved March 1, 2015 from http://www.michellemcquaid.com/strengthssurvey

Meere, M. (Ed.) (2005). *The high cost of disengaged employees*. Hawthorne, Victoria: Swinburne University of Technology.

Meyer, J. P., & Allen, N. J., (1997). *Commitment in the workplace*. London, UK: Sage.

Meyer, J. P., Stanley, D. J., Herscovitch, L., & Topolnytsky, L. (2002). Affective, continuance, and normative commitment to the organization: A meta-analysis of antecedents, correlates, and consequences. *Journal of Vocational Behavior, 61*, 20–52.

Mishra, P., & Bhatnagar, J. (2012). Appreciative inquiry: Models and applications. *The Indian Journal of Industrial Relations, 47*(3), 543–558.

Moore, G., & Beadle, R. (2006). In search of organizational virtue in business: Agents, goods, practices, institutions and environments. *Organization Studies, 27*(3), 369–389.

Mrosovsky, N., & Kingsmill, S. F. (1985). How turtles find the sea. *Zeitschrift fur Tierpsychologie, 67*, 237–256.

Niedenthal, P. M. (2007). Embodying emotion. *Science, 316*, 1002–1005.

O'Connor, S., & Cavanagh, M. (2013). The coaching ripple effect: The effects of developmental coaching on wellbeing across organizational networks. *Psychology of Well-Being: Theory, Research and Practice, 3*(1), 1–23.

Organ, D. W. (1997). Organizational citizenship behavior: It's construct clean-up time. *Human Performance, 10*, 85–97.

Ostir, G. V., Markides, K. S., Black, S. A., & Goodwin, J. S. (2000). Emotional well-being predicts subsequent functional independence and survival. *Journal of the American Geriatrics Society, 48*, 473–478.

Ostir, G. V., Markides, K. S., Peek, K., & Goodwin, J. S. (2001). The associations between emotional well-being and the incidence of stroke in older adults. *Psychosomatic Medicine, 63*, 210–215.

Ozcelik, H., Langton, N., & Aldrich, H. (2008). Doing well and doing good: The relationship between leadership practices that facilitate a positive emotional climate and organizational performance. *Journal of Managerial Psychology, 22*(2), 186–203.

Peterson, C., Seligman, M., & Vaillant, G. (1988). Pessimistic explanatory style is a risk factor for physical illness: A thirty-five year longitudinal study. *Journal of Personality and Social Psychology, 55*, 23–27.

Rath, T., & Harter, J. (2010). *Wellbeing: The five essential elements*. New York, NY: Gallup Press.

Renninger, K. A. (1992). Individual interest and development: Implications for theory and practice. In K. A. Renninger, S. Hidi, & A. Krapp (Eds.), *The role of interest in learning and development* (pp. 361–395). Hillsdale, NJ: Erlbaum.

Rich, B. L., Lepine, J. A., & Crawford, E. R. (2010). Job engagement: Antecedents and effects on job performance. *Academy of Management Journal, 53*, 617–635.

Richman, L. S., Kubzansky, L., Maselko, J., Kawachi, I., Choo, P., & Bauer, M. (2005). Positive emotion and health: Going beyond the negative. *Health Psychology, 24*(4), 422–429.

Rogers, C. R. (1959). A theory of therapy, personality and interpersonal relationships, as developed in the client-centred framework. In S. Koch (Ed.) *Psychology: A study of science* (pp. 184–256). New York, NY: McGraw Hill.

Rotundo, M., & Sackett, P. R. (2002). The relative importance of task, citizenship, and counterproductive performance to global ratings of job performance: A policy-capturing approach. *Journal of Applied Psychology, 87*, 66–80.

Rowe, G., Hirsh, J. B., & Anderson, A. K. (2007). Positive affect increases the breadth of attentional selection. *Proceedings of the National Academy of Sciences of the United States of America, 104*, 383–388.

Rowold, J., & Rohmann, A. (2009). Transformational and transactional leadership styles, followers' positive and negative emotions, and performance in German nonprofit orchestras. *Nonprofit Management and Leadership, 20*, 41–59.

Rusk, D. E., & Waters, L. E. (2013). Tracing the size, reach, impact, and breadth of positive psychology. *The Journal of Positive Psychology, 8*, 207–221. doi:10.1080/17439760.2013.777766

Ryff, C. (1989). Happiness is everything, or is it? Explorations on the meaning of psychological well-being. *Journal of Personality and Social Psychology, 57*, 1069–1081.

Salanova, M., Agut, S., & Peiro, J. M. (2005). Linking organizational resources and work engagement to employee performance and customer loyalty: The mediation of service climate. *Journal of Applied Psychology, 90*(6), 1217–1227.

Salanova, M., Bakker, A. B., & Llorens, S. (2006). Flow at work: Evidence for an upward spiral of personal and organizational resources. *Journal of Happiness Studies, 7*(1), 1–22.

Schaufeli, W. B., Salanova, M., González-Romá, V., & Bakker, A. B. (2002). The measurement of engagement and burnout: A two sample confirmatory factor analytic approach. *Journal of Happiness Studies, 3*(1), 71–92.

Scherer, K. R., Schorr, A., & Johnstone, T. (Eds.) (2001). *Appraisal processes in emotion: Theory, methods, research*. Oxford, UK: Oxford University Press.

Schmitz, T. W., De Rosa, E., & Anderson, A. K. (2009). Opposing influences of affective state valence on visual cortical encoding. *The Journal of Neuroscience, 29*(22), 7199–7207.

Scott, J. (2000). *Social network analysis: A handbook*: London, UK: Sage.

Sekerka, L. E., Vacharkulksemsuk, T., & Fredrickson, B. L. (2012). Positive emotions: Broadening and building upward spirals of sustainable development. In K. Cameron & G. Spreitzer (Eds.), *Oxford handbook of positive organizational scholarship* (pp. 168–177). New York, NY: Oxford University Press.

Seligman, M. E. P. (2002). *Authentic happiness: Using the new positive psychology to realize your potential for lasting fulfillment*. New York, NY: Free Press.

Seligman, M. E. P. (2009). *What you can change … and what you can't*: The complete guide to successful self-improvement*. New York, NY: Vintage.

Seligman, M. E. P. (2012). *Flourish: A visionary new understanding of happiness and well-being*. New York, NY: Simon & Schuster.

Seligman, M. E. P., & Csikszentmihalyi, M. (2000). Positive psychology: An introduction. *American Psychologist*, *55*(1), 5–14.

Seligman, M. E. P., Schulman, P., DeRubeis, R. J., & Hollon, S. D. (1999). The prevention of depression and anxiety. *Prevention & Treatment*, *2*(1), 1–24.

Sharot, T., Riccardi, A. M., Raio, C. M., & Phelps, E. A. (2007). Neural mechanisms mediating optimism bias. *Nature*, *450*, 102–105.

Shuck, M. B. (2010). *Employee engagement: An examination of antecedent and outcome variables.* DEd dissertation, Florida International University. FIU Electronic Theses and Dissertations. Paper 235. http://digitalcommons.fiu.edu/etd/235

Shuck, B., Reio, T. G., & Rocco, T. S. (2011). Employee engagement: Aan examination of antecedent and outcome variables. *Human Resource Development International*, *14*, 427–445.

Shuck, B., & Wollard, K. (2010). Employee engagement and HRD: A seminal review of the foundations. *Human Resource Development Review*, *9*(1), 89–110.

Sin, N. L., & Lyubomirsky, S. (2009). Enhancing well-being and alleviating depressive symptoms with positive psychology interventions: A practice-friendly meta-analysis. *Journal of Clinical Psychology*, *65*, 467–487.

Smith, J. C., & Baker, H. D. (1960). Conditioning in the horseshoe crab. *Journal of Comparative and Physiological Psychology*, *53*, 279–281.

Spector, P. E. (1997). *Job satisfaction: Application, assessment, causes, and consequences.* Thousand Oaks, CA: Sage.

Spence, G. B., & Grant, A. M. (2007). Professional and peer life coaching and the enhancement of goal striving and well-being: An exploratory study. *The Journal of Positive Psychology*, *2*(3), 185–194.

Spence, J. R., Brown, D. J., Keeping, L. M., & Lian, H. (2014). Helpful today, but not tomorrow? Feeling grateful as a predictor of daily organizational citizenship behaviors. *Personnel Psychology*, *67*(3), 705–738. doi:10.1111/peps.12051

Spence, J. R., Ferris, D. L., Brown, D. J., & Heller, D. (2011). Understanding daily citizenship behaviors: A social comparison perspective. *Journal of Organizational Behavior*, *32*, 547–571.

Staw, B. M., Sutton, R. I., & Pelled, S. H. (1994). Employee positive emotions and favorable outcomes at the workplace. *Organization Science*, *5*, 51–71.

Sy, T., Cote, S., & Saavedra, R. (2005). The contagious leader: Impact of the leader's mood on the mood of group members, group affective tone, and group process. *Journal of Applied Psychology*, *90*, 295–305. 17.

Taylor, F. W. (1911). *The principles of scientific management.* New York, NY: Harper & Brothers.

Tims, M., Bakker, A. B., & Xanthopoulou, D. (2011). Do transformational leader enhance their followers' daily work engagement? *The Leadership Quarterly*, *22*, 121–131.

Trick, L. M., Brandigampola, S., & Enns, J. T. (2012). How fleeting emotions affect hazard perception and steering while driving: The impact of image arousal and valence. *Accident Analysis and Prevention*, *45*, 222–229.

Triliva, S., & Dafermos, M. (2008). Philosophical dialogues as paths to a more "positive psychology." *Journal of Community & Applied Social Psychology*, *18*(1), 17–38.

Tsai, W. C., Chen, H. W., & Cheng, J. W. (2009). Employee positive moods as a mediator linking transformational leadership and employee work outcomes. *The International Journal of Human Resource Management*, *20*(1), 206–219.

Tugade, M., & Fredrickson, B. (2004). Resilient individuals use positive emotions to bounce back from negative emotional experiences. *Journal of Personality & Social Psychology*, *86*(2), 320–333.

Tutu, D. (1999). *No future without forgiveness.* New York, NY: Doubleday.

Vacharkulksemsuk, T., & Fredrickson, B. L. (2013). Looking back and glimpsing forward: The broaden-and-build theory of positive emotions as applied to organizations. *Advances in Positive Organizational Psychology*, *1*, 45–60.

Vacharkulksemsuk, T., Sekerka, L. E., & Fredrickson, B. L. (2011). Establishing a positive emotional climate to create twenty-first century organizational change. In N. M. Ashkanasy, C. P. M. Wilderom, & M. F. Peterson (Eds.), *Handbook of organizational culture and climate* (2nd ed., pp. 101–118). Thousand Oaks, CA: Sage.

Vaillant, G. E. (2012). *Triumphs of experience: The men of the Harvard Grant study*. New York, NY: Belknap Press.

Wadlinger, H. A., & Isaacowitz, D. M. (2006). Positive mood broadens visual attention to positive stimuli. *Motivation and Emotion*, *30*(1), 87–99.

Wegner, D. M. (1997). When the antidote is the poison: Ironic mental control processes. *Psychological Science*, *8*, 148–150.

Weiss, H. M. (2002). Deconstructing job satisfaction: Separating evaluations, beliefs and affective experiences. *Human Resource Management Review*, *12*(2), 173–194.

Wright, T. A., & Staw, B. M. (1999). Affect and favorable work outcomes: Two longitudinal tests of the happy–productive worker thesis. *Journal of Organizational Behavior*, *20*, 1–23. doi:10.1002/(SICI)1099-1379(199901)20:1<1::AID-JOB885>3.0.CO;2-W

Wright, T. A., & Bonett, D. (2007). Job satisfaction and psychological well-being as nonadditive predictors of work-place turnover. *Journal of Management Development*, *33*, 141–160.

Wright, T. A., & Cropanzano, R. (2000). Psychological well-being and job satisfaction as predictors of job performance. *Journal of Occupational Health Psychology*, *5*, 84–94.

Xanthopoulou, D., Bakker, A. B., Demerouti, E., & Schaufeli, W. B. (2012). A diary study on the happy worker: How job resources generate positive emotions and personal resources. *European Journal of Work & Organizational Psychology*, *21*, 489–517.

3

Psychological Strengths at Work

Robert Biswas-Diener, Todd B. Kashdan, and Nadezhda Lyubchik

Introduction

In many ways, the topic of strengths is unique among all those that exist under the loose umbrella of positive psychology. Topics central to this emerging science, such as hope, subjective well-being, and resilience, are largely focused on specific psychological phenomena. In contrast, the topic of strengths is, instead, a category of phenotypes. Park, Peterson, and Seligman (2004) refer to strengths as "a family of positive traits" (p. 604). Thus, it is a large undertaking to write about strengths. A list of possible subtopics includes strengths assessment and identification, the correlates and consequences of strengths, and the notion of strengths development. Therefore, an in-depth discussion of these broad issues is beyond the scope of a single chapter. We will attempt here to highlight important points and offer practical suggestions, especially with regards to how strengths operate in work contexts.

An Overview of Strengths

We begin with a list of common scholarly approaches to understanding strengths. Most of these approaches are ensconced in formal assessment tools. The strengths approach that is the most researched and referred to in positive psychology journals and at associated conferences is the "character strength" approach embodied in the Values in Action (VIA) framework (Peterson & Seligman, 2004). The VIA itself is a list of 24 universal character strengths with face-valid labels such as bravery and forgiveness (Biswas-Diener, 2006). In this framework, strengths are trait-like features of personality that are valued in their own right (i.e., irrespective of what consequences might emerge from their usage). These positive traits are embodied in thought, feeling, and behavior and, when used, increase the likelihood of fulfilling outcomes. The VIA assessment has been used by approximately

The Wiley Blackwell Handbook of the Psychology of Positivity and Strengths-Based Approaches at Work, First Edition. Edited by Lindsay G. Oades, Michael F. Steger, Antonella Delle Fave, and Jonathan Passmore.

2.6 million people worldwide (www.viacharacter.org) and has been extensively studied. The foci of past research have ranged from self-esteem (Proctor, Maltby, & Linley, 2011) to academic achievement (Park & Peterson, 2009).

Another common approach has been developed by the Gallup Organization. Strengths, according to this approach, represent natural talents in combination with knowledge and skill (Buckingham & Clifton, 2001). The Gallup strengths framework is embodied in their assessment tool, the Clifton StrengthsFinder (Rath, 2007). The StrengthsFinder includes 34 strengths themes and is widely used in business and education with approximately 12.5 million people taking the assessment (www.gallupstrengthscenter.com). Although Gallup has published a technical report for this assessment (Asplund, Lopez, Hodges, & Harter, 2007) research on the correlates and consequences of this tool do not regularly appear in peer-reviewed academic journals. That said, Gallup publishes broad findings based on the StrengthsFinder in its self-published books (e.g., *Strengths based leadership*; Rath & Conchie, 2008).

A third approach to strengths, developed by Linley (2008), holds that strengths are "a capacity of thinking, feeling and behaving that allows for optimal functioning in the pursuit of desirable outcomes" (Linley & Harrington, 2007). Linley is the principal architect behind the R2 Strengths Profiler, an assessment that classifies 60 candidate attributes as strengths, weaknesses, or "learned behaviors" (Linley, Willars, & Biswas-Diener, 2010). The R2 Strengths Profiler has been more widely used as an applied instrument than as a tool of research. It is predominantly used as a tool for recruitment and placement, as well as for leadership development and teamwork (www.cappeu.com).

Despite differences in the vocabulary of strengths terms, these three approaches bear a common grounding in classic personality theory (see Table 3.1). That is, scholars generally agree that, to some extent, strengths represent personality traits that have a genetic component (they are "naturally occurring") and are associated with some degree of predictable

Table 3.1 Comparison of common strengths frameworks.

	VIA Institute/ VIA Survey	*Gallup/ StrengthsFinder 2.0*	*CAPP/R2 Strengths Profiler*
Key offering:	Common language	Talent themes	Performance categories
Intended domains	School, work, relationships	Work, School	Work
Relation to personality	Identity	Performance	Performance in context
Core question:	Who are you?	What do you do well?	What energizes you?
What is identified?	Core character	Talents/skills	Strengths, weaknesses, and learned behaviors
Basis for validity	Historical analyses, criteria, psychometrics	Polling, Psychometrics	Criteria, psychometrics
Focus	Signature strengths, but all 24 matter	Top 5 only, but all 34 matter	Varying lists from 4 conceptual categories
Technical report available	Yes	No	Yes
Number of attributes assessed	24	34	60

Source: Author.

performance or cross-situational consistency. What's more, there seems to be widespread agreement that strengths represent a combination of acquired knowledge and a disposition to act that involves good judgment and the pursuit of human excellence (see Schwartz & Sharpe, 2006, for a theoretical discussion of this issue). Perhaps the most important aspect of strengths work, directly rooted in the personality theory, is the idea of individual differences. It is assumed by virtually all scholars and practitioners that people will vary from one another in their unique leanings toward and away from specific strengths.

Since the inception of modern positive psychology, circa 1998, scholars have investigated the relation between strengths and well-being. In one early investigation, Park and colleagues (2004) found that strengths were correlated with life satisfaction in a sample of nearly 4,000 adults (average age 35–40). These correlations differed in magnitude from small (humility, $r = .05$) to large (hope, $r = .53$). Although researchers have conducted investigations of the relation to a wide range of variables – social relationships, physical health, and financial and career accomplishments – these areas of study are minimal compared with the attention given to indices of subjective well-being.

Although some research has focused on the relation between strengths and various well-being variables, much of the research has been conducted on strengths interventions. Interventions typically involve identifying strengths, using strengths in a novel way, or using strengths in the service of a goal. In one of the first randomized controlled trials, Seligman, Steen, Park, and Petersen (2005) found that identifying personal strengths and using strengths in a new or different way both led to subsequent gains in happiness at one week, one month, and three months after the intervention period; and at six months in the case of using strengths in a new way. Proyer, Ruch, and Buschor (2012) tested a wide range of strengths interventions against a wait-list control group and found that people who "trained" their strengths showed greater levels of life satisfaction. Subsequent studies have found strengths identification and use to be associated with fewer depressive symptoms (Seligman, Rashid, & Parks, 2006), lower perceived stress (Wood, Linley, Maltby, Kashdan, & Hurling, 2011), greater self-efficacy (Govindji & Linley, 2007), and greater ability to achieve goals (Linley, Nielson, Wood, Gillett, & Biswas-Diener, 2010). In the most recent research publication to date, Proyer, Gander, Wellenzohn, and Ruch (2015) conducted a randomized placebo-controlled trial of "signature" versus "lesser" strengths. Using happiness and depression as outcome measures, the Proyer research team found that strengths-based intervention, in general, was associated with increased well-being. Further, they found that participants who saw themselves as virtuous benefited more from working with lesser strengths, while those who saw themselves as low in virtue benefited from working with signature strengths. Taken together, these findings are suggestive that the identification, use, and development of strengths are worthwhile undertakings.

Despite the potential benefits of a focus on strengths, there is much about this process we do not know. In a review of the strengths intervention literature, Quinlan, Swain, and Vella-Brodrick (2012) argue that many strength interventions emphasize their use in the service of some goal and scholars would benefit from disentangling the role of goal planning from the actual development of strengths. In addition, Quinlan and her colleagues point out that many strengths interventions have a social component – sharing strengths, group learning, or employing strengths in a social way – and the extent to which the benefits of these interventions are a product of strengths use or of social processes remains unclear. To this list, we add that asking people to use strengths in a new or novel way (e.g., Proyer et al., 2015; Seligman et al., 2005) may obscure, rather than clarify, the purpose and consequences of the intervention. It is unclear whether the effects of such interventions are related to strengths use, or to the benefits of novelty (which has been shown to prevent hedonic adaptation; Sheldon & Lyubomirsky, 2012). To the best of our knowledge, no study has ensured that participants actually used strengths in a novel way (as opposed to simply using strengths in everyday life).

Among the most important issues related to strengths intervention – and one specifically relevant to work contexts – is the question of how much attention and energy a person should allocate toward strengths at the expense of focusing on weaknesses. Initial evidence provided by Rust, Diessner, and Reade (2009) suggests that concurrently addressing both personal strengths and weaknesses is as beneficial as working on strengths alone. van Woerkom and Meyers (2015) investigated potential differences between strengths versus deficiency interventions. They found that people who worked to develop strengths and those who worked to correct deficiencies both showed gains in personal growth; nonetheless, the strengths development group appeared to reap greater benefits. In another study conducted in 2012, researchers found that, when treating clinically depressed adults, use of an intervention that capitalized on people's strengths outperformed an intervention that compensated for deficits (Cheavens, Strunk, Lazarus, & Goldstein, 2012). As for how these benefits manifest, these researchers found that people in the strengths-based intervention experienced a faster drop in depressive symptoms in the first three weeks compared with people in the deficits-based interventions, and this improvement continued to widen over the course of the next 12 weeks. These studies provide an important reminder to those wanting to apply positive psychological science in general, and strengths specifically, at work. Namely, individuals may not need to focus exclusively on strengths to experience performance benefits or psychological benefits. More data is needed on the utility of strengths-based versus deficits-based versus combined interventions, and for whom each of these interventions works best. Importantly, practitioners who articulate their intention to attend to both strengths and weaknesses may be better received by both organizational and individual clients.

Strengths at Work

Of all possible topics related to positive psychology it is strengths, perhaps, that is the most relevant and applicable to work and organizations. In fact, there is a long history of attention to strengths in the workplace that pre-dates the advent of modern positive psychology (e.g., Clifton & Nelson, 1995; Drucker, 1967). One possible reason why the topic of strengths is seen favorably by people in organizations is the language associated with this concept. Unlike "forgiveness" or "happiness" – two examples of positive psychology topics – strengths is a familiar word in business culture and dovetails with longstanding workplace concerns like performance management and personnel selection. Strengths also suggests behavior and it might be that a focus on behavior is viewed in a more positive light in organizations because it is easier for non-psychologists to notice, evaluate, and train.

Research suggests that a strengths-oriented culture is directly associated with enhanced work performance (van Woerkom & Meyers, 2015). In a study by Dubreuil, Forest, and Courcy (2014) the researchers found that self-reported strengths use was significantly associated with and explained 16% of the variance in work performance. Subsequent analyses indicate that the personal strengths lead to healthy work outcomes by promoting increased vitality, concentration, and passionate dedication to work-related tasks. Other researchers have arrived at similar conclusions regarding the potential benefits of a strengths focus at work. In a review of Gallup work performance and strengths intervention data, Hodges and Asplund (2010) report that strengths interventions, compared with a waitlist control group, predicted enhanced engagement, lower turnover, higher productivity, and greater profitability. In a similar review, managers who focus on strengths have been shown to be nearly twice as likely to produce above median performance in their team as those who focus on weaknesses (Clifton & Harter, 2003). The findings regarding turnover dovetail with results from large organization case studies (Stefanyszyn, 2007). Finally, in a sample of over 7,000 Americans, the more that a person self-endorsed certain character strengths – most notably curiosity, zest, hope, gratitude, and spirituality – the greater their sense of work satisfaction (Peterson, Stephens, Park, Lee, & Seligman, 2009). Taken together, these findings on a strengths focus at work are suggestive of the potential of this approach for employee well-being, performance, and bottom line indicators.

One example of a "business friendly strengths oriented intervention" is appreciative inquiry (AI) (Cantore & Cooperrider, 2013; Cooperrider, Whitney, & Stavros, 2008). AI involves asking intact teams and work units to focus on what they do exceptionally well and to leverage this performance for a variety of goals: increased team cohesion, enhanced motivation and self-efficacy, and strategic planning for future goals. This facilitated conversation uses a variety of general positive psychology techniques (although not explicitly under that umbrella) to facilitate healthy work-related changes. Techniques embedded in this approach include an emphasis on affirming language, capitalizing on past success, stock-taking of strengths and resources, and the transformation of abstract values into concrete goals and behavioral efforts directed toward those goals. Case study research suggests that AI has been useful in helping organizations reach business performance milestones (Cooperrider et al., 2008).

An argument can be made that a strengths focus is most beneficial when it is *not* positioned as a one-off training or intervention (Linley, 2008). Specifically, strengths can best be seen as part of a larger philosophical mindset – what Linley calls the "abundance scenario" – that can guide the implementation of strengths in the workplace. Linley suggests that strengths can – and should – be plugged in to every aspect of the business cycle – recruitment and placement, team building, performance management, leadership development, and even outplacement. Finally, Linley admits that the abundance approach differs from traditional notions of management and that responses to strengths approaches fall on a continuum ranging from advocates to those who are undecided to those who are active resistors.

It is here that there is reason to offer caution to those hoping to apply positive psychology in general, and strengths practices specifically, in organizations. While these approaches can be useful, they lack attention to the larger cultural context and social dynamics. It seems likely that comprehensive strengths interventions that are embedded into the strategy and culture of a business will attain greater sustainability in their effectiveness. In the section below, we offer practical guidance regarding the actual use of strengths in the workplace, using a simply acronym – AID – which stands for Attitude, Identification, and Development.

Strengths Practice: The AID Method

In the past, we have discussed the most common strengths approach used by those who align themselves with positive psychology as "identify and use" (Biswas-Diener, Kashdan, & Minhas, 2011). As the name suggests, individuals are encouraged to first identify and then use personal strengths in an effort to enhance their performance or well-being. There is, in fact, some evidence that simply identifying strengths does lead to greater happiness (Seligman et al., 2005). Despite potential short-term gains, many practitioners are frustrated with the absence of a longer-term strategy for working with strengths.

We believe this concern can be ameliorated, in part, by using the AID (attitude, identification, development) approach to strengths intervention. This method treats strengths as capacities for excellence rather than personality traits and thereby assumes the possibility of ongoing development (Biswas-Diener et al., 2011). It also has the advantage of appreciating the ways that context can affect the use of strengths; even if strengths are of natural types, using them across situations is learned. Accordingly, AID begins with one's "attitude" about the very nature of strengths. According to Dweck (2008) people harbor self-theories in which they view their own personal qualities as either fixed (entity theories) or malleable (incremental theories). People who hold incremental theories – those attitudes that are the most conducive to ongoing strengths development – have been shown to be better at some business tasks such as negotiation (Kray & Haselhuhn, 2007); and in simulations they show high levels of self-efficacy and organizational performance (Wood & Bandura, 1989).

Further evidence for the potential benefits of seeing strengths as malleable rather than as being fixed comes from a study by Louis (2011). In it, Louis assigned 388 undergraduate students to either a talent identification group, a control group, or a strengths development group. Participants in the talent identification condition focused on labeling and using their own strengths while their counterparts in the development condition emphasized the cultivation of strengths. Louis found that a focus on talent identification (rather than development) led to significant decreases in growth mindset. Although this study was conducted in the context of higher education, its findings offer a preliminary caution for the workplace. Louis offers the following insight: "certain types of strengths interventions – specifically those focusing primarily or exclusively on labeling – may actually lead to unfavorable psychological or behavioral outcomes" (p. 212). Attitude, therefore, may be a precondition (and source of intervention) for effective strengths-based practice.

One of the most interesting and useful approaches to strengths development in organizations is provided by Meyers and van Woerkom (2014) in their discussion of attitudes toward talent. Although there may be conceptual differences between strengths and talent, we believe that there is sufficient overlap to warrant speaking about them as relatively interchangeable here. According to Meyers and van Woerkom there are beliefs about the source of talent (it is innate or malleable) and spread (it is exclusive or inclusive). Consider the simple 2 × 2 model shown in Figure 3.1 that illustrates the implications for talent development strategy. Interestingly, there is no suggestion that any one of these four

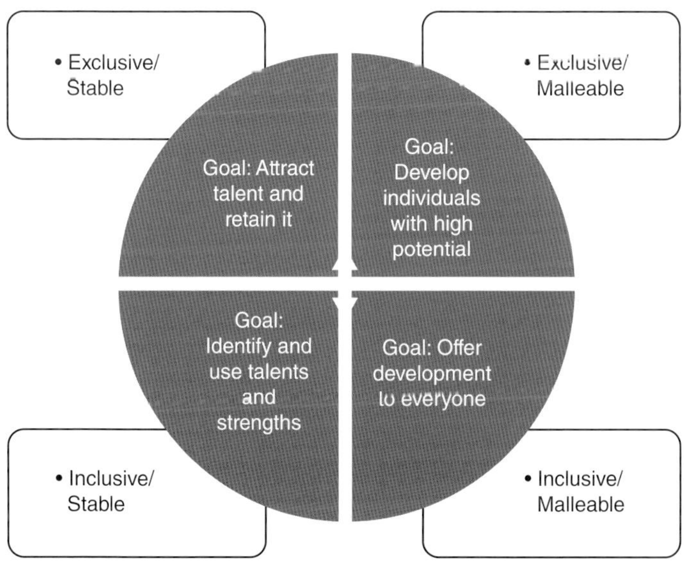

Figure 3.1 Common theories of talent. *Source*: Author.

common attitudes to talent is "correct." Rather, there is the suggestion that an individual's attitudes influence how they go about bringing strengths and talent into the workplace.

Looking at the 2 × 2 model of theories of talent, it is easy to see that whether a person believes that strengths are fixed or malleable must impact their strategy for bringing them into the workplace. People who are inclined to view strengths along the "fixed" side of the continuum are likely to emphasize the use rather than the development of strengths. This may be why a large number of practitioners who use the VIA (explicitly associated with personality; Peterson & Seligman, 2004) often focus on the use of strengths (e.g., Gander, Proyer, Ruch, & Wyss, 2012; Mongrain & Anslemo-Matthews, 2012; Seligman et al., 2005). People who see strengths on the "malleable" side of the continuum, on the other hand, are more likely to emphasize the development of strengths (Biswas-Diener et al., 2011).

A discussion of the malleability of strengths requires consideration of how we think and behave in the moment. That is, due consideration needs to be given to the powerful effects of situational influences and current circumstances. Take the example of courage: each of us has moments where we will be courageous and moments where we will be wary and unwilling to act in the presence of fearful thoughts, feelings, and sensations. When a claim is made that someone is a courageous person, what someone with a malleable attitude toward strengths is claiming is that during moments of fear a person tends to default toward courageous acts (Fleeson, 2007). This does not mean that they never avoid or disengage when afraid, but, rather, the bulk of their moments tilt toward an approach-oriented, courageous response. An individual can learn about strong situations that pull for particular behaviors over others. That is, an individual can learn what personal and environmental factors increase or decrease the probability that courage will be exemplified in a moment. In addition, with a malleable view of strengths, there is the belief that someone can be trained to engage in non-default behaviors in one context, and then another, and then soon the distribution of moments reaches a tipping point such that courageousness as a strength has been cultivated into their identity. Note that this entire chain of events is initiated by the theories held about strengths.

The second aspect of the AID method is "identify." Here, we focus on methods for identifying an individual's (or group's) strengths. It is necessary to identify strengths before one can appreciably use them as a means of intervention. There are both formal and informal methods of identifying strengths. Formal methods are principally embodied in strengths assessments such as the VIA, Gallup StrengthsFinder, R2 Strengths Profiler and similar instruments. Formal methods have the advantage of being able to be administered in larger scale, creating a common language for strengths, providing normative data for comparison purposes, and a greater emphasis on psychometric rigor (Asplund et al., 2007; Linley & Stoker, 2012; Peterson & Seligman, 2004). Indeed, formal approaches are, arguably, the most common methods of identifying strengths and frequently serve as the centerpiece of organizational trainings, team-building exercises, and management conversations.

There is also an informal method of identifying strengths known as "strengths spotting." Strengths spotting is an open-ended method of looking for strengths and using a wide range of potential labels for identifying them. Because strengths are associated with increased enthusiasm and physiological arousal, there are a wide range of physical and voice cues associated with strengths (see Table 3.2) (Linley, 2008). It is possible for managers, coaches, and others to pay close attention to these cues and use them as a potential signal indicating that a strength is being discussed. At this moment the observer can offer insights or ask questions about the potential strength at hand. This method has the advantage of being more organic, linked as it is to natural conversations. It can,

Table 3.2 Cues associated with strengths.

Physical
Better posture
More fluid hand gestures
More dramatic hand gestures
Leaning forward
Facial
Raised eyebrows
Eyes widening
Increased smiling
More sustained eye contact
Voice/Speech
Rising infection in voice
More rapid speech
Increased use of metaphor
More rapid speech or verbal fluency

Note: These cues vary by individual and by culture.
Source: Author.

therefore, be integrated into many business conversations ranging from job interviews to performance reviews. There is an advantage in going "off-script" from the language of formal assessments:

> some coaches prefer to use more open-ended approaches to the identification of assessment of strengths. The advantage of doing so is that the language and construction of the strengths is grounded firmly in the lived experience of the client, thereby feeling potentially more authentic and owned by them. (Linley, Garcea, et al., 2010, p. 167)

Crucially, Linley and colleagues (Linley, Garcea, et al., 2010) developed a strengths-spotting scale, a 20-item self-report assessment that parses strengths spotting into specific skills. These include (1) the ability to spot strengths, (2) the emotional reward when spotting strengths, (3) the frequency with which a person is vigilant for and spots strengths, (4) the motivation to spot strengths, and (5) the ability to apply the knowledge of a strength in real-world situations. All five dimensions are significantly correlated with higher optimism and positive affect, while higher rates of ability, application, and frequency predict lower negative affect. Therefore, strengths spotting may be a tool that is beneficial for the spotter as well as the spotted.

One final important note here with regards to identifying strengths. When using formal strengths assessments, but especially when using strengths spotting, it is crucial to check in with people to find out the extent to which they, themselves, identify with a particular strength. Key inquiries include questions about the specific strength language (Does this particular label make sense to you?), questions about accuracy (Can you point to examples of this strength in your own life?), and questions about evolution (How has your ability to wield this strength changed over time?). By checking in with a client or supervisee, strengths interventionists are better able to guard against possible assessment errors and increase buy-in and comprehension. We believe that strengths identification without a conversation regarding the degree to which a person incorporates strengths into their own identity is an incomplete intervention.

The third and final aspect of the AID approach to working with strengths is the development of strengths. As mentioned before, when strengths are viewed as malleable potentials there is the possibility of developing them. This stands in contrast to the view of strengths as personality traits. Dweck (2008) argues that that people's views of their own abilities – as either fixed traits or as developable potentials – affect performance. Unfortunately, there is a lack of research attention to the ways that Dweck's findings bear on specific strengths such as creativity or courage. Preliminary evidence suggests that it is advisable to proceed with the attitude that strengths can be developed, but further research is needed on the topic.

Crucially, the idea that strengths can be systematically developed is the answer to the "what now?" question that plagues many strengths interventionists and organizations for whom the initial excitement of strengths gives way to uncertainty about follow-up actions. We have argued that strengths are best viewed as existing in context, and that this view is suggestive of development strategies (Biswas-Diener et al., 2011). Specifically, we have pointed to the social context, situational context, and psychological context as three fruitful and distinct areas for exploration.

With regards to the social context, strengths development largely centers on honing the ability to deploy strengths in a way that has a net positive social impact. Because strengths and values are closely related, not everyone shares an equal appreciation for all strengths. People with a strength in planning and organization, for instance, sometimes find it difficult to appreciate or harness spontaneity, while those who are strong in the latter can find the structure of planning stifling. Developing strengths in a social context can be critical for team performance. This example cannot be understated because in American culture there is a greater appreciation of joviality, optimism, and sociability. For these reasons, people who are somber, defensive pessimists, and less interested in social attention (i.e., the core element of extraversion; Ashton, Lee, & Paunonen, 2002) are often underappreciated for their strength contributions to a team/organization. Defensive pessimists, unlike optimists, brace for the worst while simultaneously hoping for the best (Norem & Chang, 2002). Their tendency toward vigilance and anxiety, when harnessed, leads to superior problem-solving skills. This prevention-focused mindset, to avoid errors and failures, is crucial to organizational success. A culture that puts too much emphasis on positive emotions and optimism can ferret out defensive pessimism and other strengths. This example returns us to the importance of a flexible, inclusive attitude toward strengths to obtain the best possible individual and organizational outcomes (Kashdan & Biswas-Diener, 2014).

Cross-Cultural Research

There is a small research literature specifically addressing strengths across cultures. Research suggests that there are certain strengths that are more widely endorsed and more highly valued in certain countries and cultures such as religiosity (Park, Peterson & Seligman, 2006) or modesty and self-control (Biswas-Diener, 2006). Several studies surveying people from different parts of the world including Western, European, Middle-Eastern, African, and Asian nations have found that that all of these cultures have areas of strengths-focus and development and that they are valued and assessed similarly to the United States (Biswas-Diener, 2006; Park et al., 2006). Until there is greater research attention to culture as a possible factor in the use and development of strengths at work, it is advisable to attend to local cultural norms – both those of the organization and of the larger society – when creating strengths-based programs.

We also argue that strengths interventionists ought to pay special attention to situational contexts. It could be that the unique conditions have ramifications for *how* strengths should be deployed. Although counter-intuitive, it is possible to both over- and under-use strengths depending on situational requirements. When considering situational contexts it is helpful to ask "how can this strength best be used *right now*?" Even people who are proficient in a given strength can deploy it in a sub-optimal way. This can be seen in the example of humor: attempts at humor "work" to the extent that they are appropriate to the time and audience. Even people who are naturally funny will occasionally miss the mark with a joke. This does not mean that the strength is a weakness, but that it has simply been misused.

Finally, strengths exist within a psychological context. They are part of an internal framework that includes personal values, goals, attitudes, and preferences. Strengths and interests interact, for example, by guiding the way that a particular strength will manifest over time (Biswas-Diener et al., 2011). A person who is high in courage, for instance, may become a mountain climber if she also has a specific interest in nature, whereas she might be equally likely to become a legal advocate if her interests lie in the direction of social justice. There is also the issue of failure: occasionally people fail when deploying their top strengths and this typically carries more psychological sting because the failure happens in an area that is more closely associated with core identity. People who view strengths as malleable potentials are more likely to show resilience in that they assume, to some degree, that taking risks and occasional failure are not just unavoidable but are central to the strengths development process itself.

Creating a Strengths Context

Building on the idea that contexts of all sorts are important to the identification and development of strengths at work, it makes sense to spend time focusing here on issues related to creating a context favorable to strengths intervention. Importantly, some scholars have argued that strengths should not be a footnote in organizational culture but should, instead, be integrated into all aspects of business (Linley, 2008; Linley et al., 2010). By making strengths a central focus of business processes including performance reviews, succession planning, leadership development and recruitment – to name a few – interventionists are more likely to interact with people at all levels of the organization who are sympathetic to the potential of this focus. We argue that, while buy-in to a strengths focus is necessary at all levels of an organization, it is particularly important to have leadership model an openness to exploring and developing strengths.

This is consistent with the notion of culture as a meta-intervention that provides the context that supports or interferes with the effectiveness of specific strengths interventions. Biswas-Diener and Lyubchik (2013) suggest that "micro-cultures" – those that are temporary and involving a small number of people – can be engineered to support strengths interventions. Typically, this is done by having a conversation in which local roles and group norms are mutually agreed upon. For instance, teams whose weekly meeting includes a "positive 360" in which members receive small recognition for using strengths are more likely to be able to talk effectively about social impact, development, failure, and related strengths topics.

An emphasis on the way that cultural considerations might affect strengths discussion and development is especially germane to the broadest and most common conceptualization of culture; namely, culture as a shared set of norms held by members of a society. In particular, there are many cultures, such as those labeled as "collectivist" in which social harmony is the explicit norm (Triandis, 1993). As a result, these cultures are more likely to emphasize humility and de-emphasize uniqueness. It is here, in the context of such cultural leanings, that many individuals have a resistance to a focus on strengths. In fact, Wierzbicka (2008) argues that the language of positive psychology in general and – by extension – strengths concepts specifically are not easily translatable to other languages and have no common cultural ground. It is for this reason that care must be taken to be sensitive to cultural contexts when applying a strengths focus to the workplace. There are a number of ways to side-step the downsides associated with humility and similar reservations regarding strengths. For instance, strengths conversations can be held in private, can focus on collective (group-level) strengths, or can be prefaced with the disclaimer that attention to strengths is understood not to be synonymous with bragging or superiority.

Future Research

Although there is evidence that a strengths focus is a potentially beneficial approach to management and leadership, we should not treat it as either faddish or as a panacea. As with any helpful aspect of business – authenticity, strong communication, emotional intelligence, compensation – we should not assume that any one topic, alone, is a "secret" to success. Where strengths are concerned there are several considerations that ought to be taken into account. First, there is a certain danger that a strengths focus, if taken to an extreme, could lead people to overlook weaknesses, threats, or vulnerabilities. Indeed, some skeptics will use this more extreme position to argue that a strengths focus is by its very definition limited. For this reason it is important to state that we do not advocate the focus on strengths exclusively and believe that some attention should be given to weaknesses. Where a strengths focus stands apart, however, is in its emphasis on marshaling and developing strengths, side-stepping weaknesses where possible, and managing them where it is not.

There is also a certain danger in "pigeon-holing" people with strengths labels. Although strengths labels are often well intended, they can have the unintended consequence of creating fixed perception of individuals. Workers can come to be known as "the creative" or "the smooth talker" or "the planner" in ways that do not allow for more nuanced appreciation of other strengths or how these strengths fluctuate. In particular, so-called "top 5" approaches which take an artificial and myopic view of a narrow set of strengths are more likely to create the impression that strengths are traits and, therefore, less open to possible development. It is possible to guard against these rigid brands by occasionally opting for the informal method of strengths identification known as "strengths spotting." Here, it is possible to identify literally dozens of strengths using a wide range of locally appropriate and creative labels.

A third potential pitfall of a strengths focus is one particularly associated with stronger views of positive psychology; namely, there is a danger of too much positive reframing. Just as people are fond of reframing failures as "learning opportunities" there can be a tendency to filter all personal characteristics through the lenses of strengths. For example, chronic dissatisfaction can be recast as "improver," inappropriate risk-taking can be seen as "courage," and wasting resources on sunk costs looks shinier when labeled as "persistence." It can be difficult to distinguish between a strength misused and a weakness. In general, we suggest that people consider the following questions when determining whether a personal quality is actually a strength: Do I have a history of receiving positive feedback and compliments about this quality? Do I enjoy the quality and seek out opportunities to use it? Is my success directly attributable to this quality? When the quality is a legitimate strength there is a far higher likelihood of answering in the affirmative.

The final danger of a strengths focus lies in doing only those tasks at which you excel or clinging to processes that may have outlived their usefulness. Ibarra (2015) refers to this as the "competency trap" and argues that it is especially dangerous for leaders. She writes, "like athletes and companies, managers and professionals overinvest in their strengths under the false assumption that what produced their past successes will necessarily lead to future wins" (p. 29). She suggests that greater care needs to be taken to consider strengths in changing contexts and rapidly shifting business environments. This attitude leads to a fundamental shift in conversations – coaching or managerial – regarding strengths. Instead of asking "what do you do well?" there is an emphasis on "what is being called for right now?" and "how should you use your strength in this particular circumstance?" This is in line with the argument that wisdom is a meta-strength in that it can be used to optimally wield all other strengths (Schwartz & Sharpe, 2006).

Because strengths have long been a focus of workplace concern they may be viewed, as a topic, as less centrally the "property" of positive psychology than are other topics such as happiness or optimism. Even so, it should be noted that with the advent of positive psychology research, attention on strengths has experienced a renaissance. Positive psychological research has, inarguably, provided new theories, assessments, and interventions that are of use to professionals working in and with organizations.

The last two decades have seen a sea-change in focus on strengths. More traditional approaches to performance management are giving way to a more positive focus and an emphasis on employee engagement. As these trends continue, research must necessarily keep pace. Our field currently suffers from a lack of investigation on several important topics related to strengths. Future researchers should attend to potential cultural factors in strengths assessment and intervention. Similarly, more research is needed on the way that attitudes – especially "growth mindset" – might affect the effectiveness of strengths intervention. Finally, there is a need to parse apart specific strengths such as charisma, creativity, and emotional intelligence and investigate the unique roles that they might play in workplace success across roles and industries.

References

Ashton, M. C., Lee, K., & Paunonen, S. V. (2002). What is the central feature of extraversion? Social attention versus reward sensitivity. *Journal of Personality and Social Psychology*, *83*(1), 245–252.

Asplund, J., Lopez, S. J., Hodges, T., & Harter, J. (2007). *The Clifton StrengthsFinder® 2.0 technical report: Development and validation.* Princeton, NJ: The Gallup Organization.

Biswas-Diener, R. (2006). From the equator to the North Pole: A study of character strengths. *Journal of Happiness Studies*, *7*(3), 293–310.

Biswas-Diener, R., Kashdan, T. B., & Minhas, G. (2011). A dynamic approach to psychological strength development and intervention. *The Journal of Positive Psychology*, *6*(2), 106–118.

Biswas-Diener, R., & Lyubchik, N. (2013). Microculture as a contextual positive intervention. In T. Kashdan & J. Ciarrochi (Eds), *Bridging acceptance and commitment therapy and positive psychology: A practitioner's guide to a unifying framework.* (pp. 194–214). Oakland, CA: New Harbinger.

Buckingham, M., & Clifton, D. O. (2001). Now, discover your strengths. New York, NY: Free Press.

Cantore, S. P., & Cooperrider, D. L. (2013). Positive psychology and appreciative inquiry. In H. S. Leonard, R. Lewis, A. M. Freedman, & J. Passmore (Eds.), *The Wiley-Blackwell handbook of the psychology of leadership, change, and organizational development* (pp. 267–287). Oxford, UK: Wiley Blackwell. doi:10.1002/9781118326404

Cheavens, J. S., Strunk, D. R., Lazarus, S. A., & Goldstein, L. A. (2012). The compensation and capitalization models: A test of two approaches to individualizing the treatment of depression. *Behaviour Research and Therapy*, *50*(11), 699–706.

Clifton, D. O., & Harter, J. K. (2003). Investing in strengths. In A. K. S. Cameron, B. J. E. Dutton, & C. R. E. Quinn (Eds.), *Positive organizational scholarship: Foundations of a new discipline* (pp. 111–121). San Francisco, CA: Berrett-Koehler.

Clifton, D. O., & Nelson, P. (1995). *Soar with your strengths: A simple yet revolutionary philosophy of business and management.* New York, NY: Dell.

Cooperrider, D. L., Whitney, D., & Stavros, J. M. (2008). *Essentials of appreciative inquiry.* Brunswick, OH: Crown Custom Publications.

Drucker, P. F. (1967). *The effective executive.* London, UK: Heinemann.

Dubreuil, P., Forest, J., & Courcy, F. (2014). From strengths use to work performance: The role of harmonious passion, subjective vitality and concentration. *The Journal of Positive Psychology, 9*(4), 335–349.

Dweck, C. (2008). Can personality be changed? The role of beliefs in personality and change. *Current Directions in Psychological Science, 17*(6), 391–394.

Fleeson, W. (2007). Situation-based contingencies underlying trait-content manifestation in behavior. *Journal of Personality, 75*(4), 825–862.

Gander, F., Proyer, R. T., Ruch, W., & Wyss, T. (2012). The good character at work: An initial study on the contribution of character strengths in identifying healthy and unhealthy work-related behavior and experience patterns. *International Archives of Occupational and Environmental Health, 85*(8), 895–904.

Govindji, R., & Linley, A. P. (2007). Strengths use, selfconcordance and well-being: Implications For strengths coaching and coaching psychologists. *International Coaching Psychology Review, 2*(2), 143–153.

Hodges, T. D., & Asplund, J. (2010). Strengths development in the workplace. In P. A. Linley, S. Harrington, & N. Garcea (Eds.), *Oxford handbook of positive psychology and work* (pp. 213–220). New York, NY: Oxford University Press.

Ibarra, H. (2015). *Act like a leader, think like a leader.* Boston, MA: Harvard Business Review Press.

Kashdan, T. B., & Biswas-Diener, R. (2014). *The upside of your dark side: Why being your whole self – not just your "good" self – drives success and fulfillment.* New York, NY: Hudson/Penguin.

Kray, L. J., & Haselhuhn, M. P. (2007). Implicit negotiation beliefs and performance: Experimental and longitudinal evidence. *Journal of Personality and Social Psychology, 93*(1), 49.

Linley, A., & Stoker, H. (2012). *Technical manual and statistical properties for Realise2.* Coventry, UK: Centre of Applied Positive Psychology.

Linley, P. A. (2008). *Average to A+: Realizing strengths in yourself and others.* Coventry, UK: CAPP Press.

Linley, P. A., Garcea, N., Hill, J., Minhas, G., Trenier, E., & Willars, J. (2010). Strengthspotting in coaching: Conceptualization and development of the Strengthspotting Scale. *International Coaching Psychology Review, 5*(2), 165–176.

Linley, P. A., & Harrington, S. (2007). Playing to your strengths. *The Psychologist, 19*(2), 85–89.

Linley, P. A., Nielsen, K. M., Wood, A. M., Gillett, R., & Biswas-Diener, R. (2010). Using signature strengths in pursuit of goals: Effects on goal progress, need satisfaction, and well-being, and implications for coaching psychologists. *International Coaching Psychology Review, 5*(1), 6–15.

Linley, P. A., Willars, J., & Biswas-Diener, R. (2010). *The strengths book.* Coventry, UK: CAPP Press.

Louis, M. (2011). Strengths interventions in higher education: The effect of identification versus development approaches on implicit self-theory. *The Journal of Positive Psychology, 6*(3), 204–215.

Meyers, M. C., & van Woerkom, M. (2014). The influence of underlying philosophies on talent management: Theory, implications for practice, and research agenda. *Journal of World Business, 49*(2), 192–203.

Mongrain, M., & Anselmo-Matthews, T. (2012). Do positive psychology exercises work? A replication of Seligman et al., (2005). *Journal of Clinical Psychology, 68*(4), 382–389.

Norem, J. K., & Chang, E. C. (2002). The positive psychology of negative thinking. *Journal of Clinical Psychology, 58*(9), 993–1001.

Park, N., & Peterson, C. (2009). Character strengths: Research and practice. *Journal of College and Character, 10*(4), 1–11.

Park, N., Peterson, C., & Seligman, M. E. P. (2004). Strengths of character and well-being. *Journal of Social and Clinical Psychology, 23*(5), 603–619.

Park, N., Peterson, C., & Seligman, M. E. P. (2006). Character strengths in fifty-four nations and the fifty US states. *The Journal of Positive Psychology, 1*(3), 118–129.

Peterson, C., & Seligman, M. E. P. (2004). *Character strengths and virtues: A handbook and classification*. Oxford, UK: Oxford University Press.

Peterson, C., Stephens, J. P., Park, N., Lee, F., & Seligman, M. E. P. (2009). Strengths of character and work. In P. A. Linley, S. Harrington, & N. Garcea (Eds.), *Oxford handbook of positive psychology and work* (pp. 221–234). Oxford, UK: Oxford University Press.

Proctor, C., Maltby, J., & Linley, P. A. (2011) Strengths use as a predictor of well-being and health-related quality of life. *Journal of Happiness Studies*, *12*(1), 153–169.

Proyer, R. T., Gander, F., Wellenzohn, S., & Ruch, W. (2015). Strengths-based positive interventions: A randomized placebo-controlled online trial on long-term effects for a signature strengths – vs. a lesser strengths – intervention. *Frontiers in Psychology*, *6*, 1–14.

Proyer, R. T., Ruch, W., & Buschor, C. (2012). Testing strengths-based interventions: A preliminary study on the effectiveness of a program targeting curiosity, gratitude, hope, humor, and zest for enhancing life satisfaction. *Journal of Happiness Studies*, *14*(1), 275–292. doi 10.1007/s10902-012-9331-9

Quinlan, D., Swain, N., & Vella-Brodrick, D. A. (2012). Character strengths interventions: Building on what we know for improved outcomes. *Journal of Happiness Studies 13*(6), 1145–1163.

Rath, T. (2007). *StrengthsFinder 2.0*. New York, NY: Gallup Press.

Rath, T., & Conchie, B. (2008). *Strengths based leadership: Great leaders, teams, and why people follow*. New York, NY: Gallup Press.

Rust, T., Diessner, R., & Reade, L. (2009). Strengths only or strengths and relative weaknesses? A preliminary study. *The Journal of Psychology*, *143*(5), 465–476.

Schwartz, B., & Sharpe, K. E. (2006). Practical wisdom: Aristotle meets positive psychology. *Journal of Happiness Studies*, *7*(3), 377–395.

Seligman, M., Rashid, T., & Parks, A. C. (2006). Positive psychotherapy. *American Psychologist*, *61*(8), 774–788.

Seligman, M., Steen, T., Park, N., & Peterson, C. (2005). Positive psychology progress: Empirical validation of interventions. *American Psychologist*, *60*, 410–421.

Sheldon, K. M., & Lyubomirsky, S. (2012). The challenge of staying happier: Testing the hedonic adaptation prevention model. *Personality and Social Psychology Bulletin*, *38*(5), 670–680.

Stefanyszyn, K. (2007). Norwich Union changes focus from competencies to strengths. *Strategic HR Review*, *7*(1), 4–43.

Triandis, H. C. (1993). Collectivism and individualism as cultural syndromes. *Cross-Cultural Research*, *27*(3–4), 155–180.

van Woerkom, M., & Meyers, M. C. (2015). My strengths count! Effects of strengths-based psychological climate on positive affect and job performance. *Human Resource Management*, *54*(1), 81–103.

Wierzbicka, A. (2008). What makes a good life? A cross-linguistic and cross-cultural perspective. *Journal of Positive Psychology*, *4*(4), 260–272.

Wood, A. M., Linley, P. A., Maltby, J., Kashdan, T. B., & Hurling, R. (2011). Using personal and psychological strengths leads to increases in well-being over time: A longitudinal study and the development of the strengths use questionnaire. *Personality and Individual Differences*, *50*(1), 15–19.

Wood, R., & Bandura, A. (1989). Impact of conceptions of ability on self-regulatory mechanisms and complex decision making. *Journal of Personality and Social Psychology*, *56*(3), 407.

4

Hope at Work

Christian A. Wandeler, Susana C. Marques, and Shane J. Lopez

Introduction

Viewing the workplace with a positive lens has a long history, but the establishment of positive psychology created an agenda and stimulated positive approaches to the workplace. Creating a positive workplace requires human resources and leadership development (Youssef & Luthans, 2011). One of these positive psychological resources is hope (Snyder, 2000a). Hope theory addresses fundamental motivational, cognitive, and emotional components of human thinking, feeling, and action, and thus is well suited to be applied to the context of work. Usually hope is considered as a characteristic of an individual, but organizations can also be considered hopeful (Adams et al., 2002). Furthermore, results so far seem to indicate that hope at the workplace may help meet the significant challenges facing workplaces now and in the future.

This chapter starts with a brief introduction to hope theory, where we introduce what hope is and how it relates to people's goals, how it is being measured, and the relationships to related psychological theories and constructs. After having laid this foundation, we discuss hope research results documenting the various benefits of hope at the workplace ranging from performance, employee engagement, and job satisfaction to mental health and well-being. Afterward we provide interested readers with actionable information and practical approaches about how organizations and individuals can develop hope at the workplace at the individual, group, or organizational level. We conclude with recommendations for future research and conclusions.

The Wiley Blackwell Handbook of the Psychology of Positivity and Strengths-Based Approaches at Work, First Edition. Edited by Lindsay G. Oades, Michael F. Steger, Antonella Delle Fave, and Jonathan Passmore.

Hope Theory: Development, Measurement, and Distinctiveness of Hope

Seeking more paths to improved work performance, researchers commonly consider thoughts about the self (e.g., self-efficacy, self-concept) and about the future (e.g., hope, optimism) as important factors to successfully accomplish tasks and goals. The construct of hope as developed by Snyder et al. (1991) may be helpful in explaining which employees will strive toward tasks and goals in spite of setbacks and which will languish. (Hence, our chapter will emphasize scholarship spawned by Snyder's original work.) Snyder and his colleagues (Snyder, 1994; Snyder et al., 1991) developed a theory and associated measures of hope that have received much attention both within and outside the field of psychology (Edwards, Rand, Lopez, & Snyder, 2006), including (and more recently) vocational psychology (Juntunen & Wettersten, 2006) and organizational behavior (e.g., Luthans, 2002).

According to hope theory, hope reflects individuals' perceptions regarding their capacities to: (1) clearly conceptualize goals, (2) develop the specific strategies to reach those goals (pathways thinking), and (3) initiate and sustain the motivation for using those strategies (agency thinking). In contrast to goals as they are often conceptualized in the organizational literature (i.e., a "specific standard of proficiency on a given task, usually within a time limit"; Locke & Latham, 1990, p. 26), Snyder et al. (1991) considered goals as much more general and inclusive. Goals, whether short-term or long-term, provide the targets of mental action sequences and vary in the degree to which they are specified, but all goals must be of sufficient value to warrant sustained conscious thought about them (Snyder, 2002). Pathways thinking refers to a person's perceived ability to generate workable routes to desired goals (Snyder, Shorey, et al., 2002) and the production of several pathways is important when encountering impediments. Agency thinking is the motivational component in hope theory that reflects a person's cognitions about his or her ability to begin and sustain goal-directed behavior (Snyder, Lopez, Shorey, Rand, & Feldman, 2003), therefore it takes on special significance when people encounter impediments (Snyder, 2002). Pathways and agency thinking are positively related, additive and reciprocal, but neither component alone defines hope, nor are they synonymous.

Hope, however, is not only a goal-directed cognitive process. It is also a hierarchically organized system of beliefs regarding one's ability to successfully engage in such a thought process. These beliefs are organized into four specific levels of abstraction: global or trait hope; domain-specific hope; goal-specific hope; and state hope. Individuals' overall evaluation of their capacity to construct sufficient pathways and generate the agency thoughts necessary to achieve goals is known as global or trait hope (Snyder, Feldman, Shorey, & Rand, 2002). The Adult Hope Scale has been developed to measure such global hopes (Snyder et al., 1991). Furthermore, hope-related beliefs can be viewed as domain-specific, and at the same time connected to other domains (e.g., people who are high in global hope have the tendency to manifest high hope in most life domains. However, employees who, although they are quite hopeful about life in general, can display low hope in the work domain. To fill this need, the Domain Specific Hope Scale (Sympson, 1999) was developed to assess adults' hope in different life arenas: social relationships, romantic relationships, family life, work, and leisure.

A more concrete level in the hope belief hierarchy is the goal-specific level, manifested regarding a specific goal. Even when an individual's global and domain-specific hope levels are quite high, it is still possible that he or she will evidence low hope regarding a specific goal. The goal-specific level of analysis, then, may be important in understanding perceived deficits in specific goal pursuits. Additionally, Snyder et al. (1996) have developed and validated the State Hope Scale for tapping a person's hope in a specific context. Without identifying the goals, this State Hope Scale measures a person's momentary hopeful thinking, providing a snapshot of a person's current goal-directed thinking. That is to say, in contrast to the more enduring type of motivational set, the State Hope Scale is related to the ongoing events in people's lives. Both trait and state are operative and useful depending on one's focus. People probably have dispositional hope that applies across situations and times, but they also have state hope that reflects particular times and more proximal events. Theoretically, dispositional hope should relate to the intensity of state hope by setting a band or range within which state hope varies. For instance, strategies for enhancing both state and trait hope are recognized in the literature, such as practical approaches like setting "stretch" goals, contingency planning, and regoaling when necessary to avoid false hope (Snyder, 2000b).

It is therefore important to pay close attention not only to global hope, but also to domain- and goal-specific hope and state hope to understand the complex web of hope-related beliefs that individuals possess (Snyder, Feldman, et al., 2002).

Besides the commonalities, salient conceptual distinctions among hope and other positive psychology constructs such as goal theory (Covington, 2000; Dweck, 1999), optimism (Scheier & Carver, 1985), self-efficacy (Bandura, 1982), and problem-solving (Heppner & Petersen, 1982) exist. It is exactly the singularity and uniqueness of each of these capacities that makes an important contribution in today's workplace. Conceptually, the hope construct draws its singularity and uniqueness from the equal, additive, and interactive contributions of the goal-pursuit components: goal itself, agency and pathways components (Snyder, 1994). As such, pathways thinking leads employees to consider multiple alternative strategies when considering how to achieve a given goal and to pursue alternative strategies when one proves difficult. Together with pathways thinking, agency thoughts provide the motivation to pursue any of the strategies that might result in goal attainment. Under an additive, reciprocal and functionally inseparable relationship, the "will" and the "way" are the core ingredients to achieve goals. For detailed comparisons of the similarities and differences between hope theory and other theories (e.g., performance motivation, flow, mindfulness, optimism, resiliency, self-esteem), see Snyder (1994).

Hope and Desirable Outcomes at Work

Hope and performance at work

Empirical research suggests that hope is positively associated with performance at the workplace (Luthans, Avolio, Avey, & Norman, 2007; Luthans, Avolio, Walumbwa, & Li, 2005; Luthans, Norman, Avolio, & Avey, 2008). In three different U.S. samples of employees at different job levels and industries, hopeful people have been found to be higher performing than people lower in hope (using objective measures), even after controlling for their self-efficacy and cognitive ability (Peterson & Byron, 2008). Hope also has been found to predict performance in vocational training exit exams and the development of vocational competencies (Wandeler, Lopez, & Baeriswyl, 2011). The detailed dynamics of the effects hope has on performance have been theorized, expanded upon through individual studies (e.g., Curry, Snyder, Cook, Ruby, & Rehm, 1997; Peterson, Gerhardt, & Rode, 2006; Snyder, Shorey, et al., 2002), and summarized in a meta-analysis (Reichard, Avey, Lopez, & Dollwet, 2013). Reichard et al. (2013) examined 45 primary studies and found a moderate positive correlation between hope and overall work performance. (The effect size corrected for sampling error and unreliability of measure was mean $\rho = 0.27$, 95% CI: 0.24–0.31.)

Study location was a significant moderator – studies located in the United States reported significantly larger mean correlations between work performance and hope (USA mean $\rho = 0.34$, outside USA mean $\rho = 0.22$).

How does hope relate to performance?

Theoretical and empirical indications are that the relationship between hope and performance is reciprocal; therefore, performance experiences can also influence a person's levels of hope. Wandeler and Bundick (2011) tested a longitudinal autoregressive model over 3 years and found hope in Year 1 predicted self-perceived competency in Year 2, which in turn predicted hope in Year 3. Although the mechanisms through which hope impacts performance still warrant further investigation, five mechanisms appear plausible. First, high-hope individuals have strong agency thinking (Snyder, 2000a). Hopeful workers tend to have a strong belief that goals are attainable. When compared to other workers, they are more motivated, energized, and persist in the face of hindrances. Second, high-hope workers have strong pathways thinking, which reflects that they generally envision a variety of possible solutions to attain desired goals, and are able to develop alternative routes (Snyder, 2000a; Adams et al., 2002). Because they expect to apply alternative routes, obstacles are viewed as challenges. Consequently, high-hope workers should be more resilient in the face of obstacles at the workplace, and more creative in finding solutions. Third, hope contributes to self-regulation, self-determination, and proactive behavior (Snyder, 2002; Wandeler & Bundick, 2011). When framing goal pursuit at the workplace as a hierarchical structure of ever-smaller subgoals (Hacker, 2003), workers can be seen as coping with regulation problems in the goal attainment process. The goals at the workplace can range in time horizon and clarity. For example, goals can range from daily work tasks to overarching long-term goals, and from clearly defined to vague. Hopeful thinking plays an important role at all levels of goal pursuit. Fourth, high-hope individuals tend to set more demanding goals, which they strive to achieve (Snyder, Feldman, et al., 2002). Aspiring to more demanding goals at work should result in superior individual performance and overall organizational functioning. In rapidly changing work environments, high-hope workers are also more likely to choose learning goals instead of performance goals (Snyder, Feldman, et al., 2002), which should lead to mastery orientation and a growth mindset, rather than a helpless and fixed orientation (Dweck, 1986). Fifth, high-hope employees tend to be able to cope better with problems and stressors at work (Peterson & Byron, 2008; Snyder & Feldman, 2000).

Hope and other valued outcomes at work

Empirical research also suggests that hope is positively associated with various other valued outcomes at the workplace including employee satisfaction (Adams et al., 2002; Luthans et al., 2007; Luthans et al., 2008), job satisfaction (Hirschi, 2014), engagement at work (Ouweneel, Le Blanc, & Schaufeli, 2012), commitment (Adams et al., 2002; Luthans et al., 2008), supportive climate (Luthans et al., 2008), career exploration (Hirschi, Abessolo, & Froidevaux, 2015), and manager-rated employee creativity (Rego, Machado, Leal, & Cunha, 2009). In their meta-analysis, Reichard et al. (2013) examined 45 primary studies and found moderate positive effect sizes between hope and job satisfaction (mean $\rho = 0.37$, 95% CI: 0.33–0.42), hope and organizational commitment (mean $\rho = 0.31$, 95% CI: 0.24–0.39), and hope and health and well-being (mean $\rho = 0.44$, 95% CI: 0.37–0.50) and negative effect sizes between hope and burnout and stress (mean $\rho = -0.35$, 95% CI: −0.39 to −0.29).

Health, Hope, and Burnout at Work

Hope can also be viewed as an indicator of adjustment and optimal functioning, thus mental health. In addition to being concerned with increasing mental health such as work engagement, organizations also want to prevent potential negative effects of work such as burnout and stress. The mental processes associated with hope contribute to the individual's overall health, result in positive emotions, influence behavior related to prevention, and buffer negative effects in the occurrence of stressors (Snyder & Feldman, 2000; Stajkovic, 2006; Valle, Huebner, & Suldo, 2006). Reichard et al. (2013) found moderate positive effect sizes between hope and health and well-being mean $\rho = 0.44$, 95% CI: 0.37–0.50) and negative effect sizes between hope and burnout and stress (mean $\rho = -0.35$, 95% CI: −0.39 to −0.29).

Workplace research by Avey, Luthans, Smith, and Palmer (2010) showed that hope – as part of positive psychological capital – contributed to changes in the psychological well-being and general mental health of employees. Also, in an autoregressive cross-lagged structural equation model, Wandeler, Lopez, and Baeriswyl (2011) found a synchronous relationship between the same mental health indicator (GHQ-12) and hope, but hope did not predict mental health nine months later and neither did mental health predict hope, which suggested that the reciprocal influences are more short-term than nine months.

According to the second principle of the conservation of resources theory (Hobfoll, 1998), people with resources can increase and sustain their resources more easily than people with fewer resources who struggle to build up further resources and are more vulnerable to entering loss spirals. People with resources can enter gain spirals, where gains in resources lead to further gains (Hobfoll, 1998). Higher levels of hope, higher levels of professional performance, and higher levels of mental health are characteristics of healthy functioning persons and are resources. The interaction among these resources positively facilitates further increases and results in mutual stabilization when resources are lost or threatened. Beyond hope being generally related to better mental health, a specific relationship exists between hope and healthy behavior at work. For example, some techniques that have been found effective in lowering work stress (Hudson, Flannery-Schroeder, & Kendall, 2004), such as training in goal setting and problem resolution, could be seen as being directly related to increasing hope, while other techniques, including time management, aerobic exercise, relaxation techniques, and coping in general, can be viewed as facilitating and providing a basis for hopeful thinking. Two questions that arise from examining all these beneficial correlates of hope are how do people become hopeful and how does hope develop?

Development of Hope at the Workplace

Snyder (1994, 2000b, 2002) has extensively described a general theoretical process of development of hope and demonstrated numerous ways of raising hope in various domains of life (psychotherapy, education, health, work, etc.), and in diverse samples (children, elderly, athletes, students, etc.). Snyder (2000b) pointed out the relevance of hope for a fast-changing world and conceptualized hope as something that is learnable. Lack of hope is a result of not being taught to think in a hopeful manner or a consequence of intervening forces destroying such hopeful thought during childhood or later in life (Snyder, 2000a, 2002). The social environment plays a crucial role by modeling and coaching hopeful thinking and behavior (Snyder, 2000b).

Thus a triadic reciprocal deterministic approach seems useful (Bandura, 2008); the functioning of the individual is seen as a result of a reciprocal interplay between intrapersonal, behavioral, and environmental influences. Personality and work conditions can influence each other over time (Frese, Garst, & Fay, 2007; Kohn & Schooler, 1983); consequently, people's hope is influenced by and also influences the work environment. Second, the effects of job conditions on personality are viewed as a learning-generalization process (Kohn & Schooler, 1983), which entails learning from the job and generalizing those lessons to off-the-job realities. The implication is that workers experiencing hope at work transfer hope to other domains in their life. Along these lines Adams et al. (2002) assumed that high-hope employees are likely to be hopeful in their personal lives, because of the strong relation between purpose in life and hope, and work being a prominent source for sense of purpose.

In a diary study, Ouweneel, Le Blanc, Schaufeli, and van Wijhe (2012) found that daily positive emotions at the workplace built hope, which in turn was related to work engagement. On the other hand Snyder and Feldman (2000) discussed several consequences of working in a situation with low hope where employees are less motivated, less conscientious, and produce lower-quality results. These employees also tend to have lower self-esteem and engagement, higher absentee rates, and lower levels of respect demonstrated toward colleagues and management.

Practical Approaches for Developing Hope at Work

The presented research findings provide support for the beneficial effects of hope and at the same time lead to a question for organizations – how can hope be cultivated at the workplace? A shortsighted suggestion might be that organizations should consider levels of hope when they hire employees. However, what happens with the existing employees? Moreover, the validity of hope scales could be easily undermined once respondents understood the importance of their answers. Therefore, more constructive questions are needed. What can companies do to promote hope? What can leaders do to promote and also leverage the hope of their employees? We will discuss approaches at both the individual (e.g., one-on-one coaching, mentoring) and organizational (e.g., leadership, organizational structures, culture) levels.

Promoting hope at the individual level

Specific interventions have been developed to increase hope in individuals and teams (Lopez et al., 2004; Luthans & Jensen, 2002; Marques, Lopez, & Pais-Ribeiro, 2011; Marques, Lopez, Rose, & Robinson, 2014). In general, hope is promoted by encouraging individuals to develop their own ideas of how to overcome impediments, while adequate support should be made available for employees to learn how to cope with setbacks and gain experience in finding alternative solutions (McDermott & Hastings, 2000; Snyder, 2000b). The accumulation of experiences in an environment, which fosters these characteristics should eventually lead to a core self-belief that one is capable of generating pathways and sustaining the energy necessary to pursue goals. Leaders and mentors can serve as role models and help individuals to develop their own ideas for overcoming obstacles. Within a company these mentors could be managers or experienced colleagues. Snyder and Shorey (2004) described high-hope bosses who clearly identify work subgoals that are achievable, and in turn increase workers' motivations and chances of reaching the larger organizational goals. Also, high-hope bosses appreciate their social interactions with employees and tend to take an active interest in how the employees are doing at work and in their lives more generally.

Sheldon and Elliot (1999) showed that self-concordant goals – which are defined as goals consistent with a person's developing interests and core values – produce greater well-being benefits, are pursued with more sustained effort, and thus are more likely to be attained than other types of goals. Therefore, self-concordant goals are likely to be associated with deeply rooted, energizing agency thoughts, necessary to sustain action and spur the pathways thinking needed to overcome barriers in the goal-attainment process. Since hope is always goal-directed (Snyder, 2000), the goal structure underlying hope and the self-concordance of those goals should be crucial for the degree of agency that the goals fuel.

Furthermore, people's self-evaluative processes of their own performance can constitute an important intrinsic reward, bring them a sense of fulfillment, and create personal incentives for accomplishments (Bandura, 1997). These experiences of competencies interact with levels of hope and influence the development of hope at work (Wandeler & Bundick, 2011).

Promoting hope at the organizational level

Snyder and Feldman (2000) made recommendations for promoting hope by setting up work environments in a way that maximizes the workers' sense of pursuing meaningful goals while gaining satisfaction in doing tasks well. These recommendations about how to set up work environments and the characteristics of high-hope workplaces derived from Adams et al.'s (2002) qualitative survey research, in essence suggest promoting hope through the satisfaction of people's basic psychological needs. Adams et al. (2002) asserted that shared goals and tasks lead to an increased sense of social support and may help employees to internalize a sense of hope. Using this approach, employees are included in making company goals, and are given opportunities to make decisions and mistakes. They are given responsibility for finding solutions to problems and implementing new ideas. Environments with these characteristics should foster the needs for competence and autonomy, as well as infusing the workplace with greater meaning.

The characteristics of high-hope organizations are similar to those of companies using a high-involvement approach (Lawler, 1992). Adams et al. (2002) surveyed U.S. companies and identified common characteristics of companies with high hope levels. For example, employees were not afraid of anyone including management, everyone felt they had a chance to be successful, persons with lowest status were treated with the same respect as those with senior status, management's highest priority was to support employees and create an environment where they could do their work, employees and management practiced open communication, employees' feedback was valued and viewed as a way to improve the company, employees who did the work were delegated as much decision-making authority as possible, people were involved in goal setting, employees were given the responsibility to solve problems and implement solutions, and everyone understood the goal of establishing long-term relationships with customers instead of reaching certain sales targets.

These postulations about favorable environments for the development of hope converge to a great extent with the environmental conditions of self-determination theory (Deci & Ryan, 1985). Wandeler, Baeriswyl, and Shavelson (2011) used the theoretical and extensive empirical body of self-determination theory to enrich hope theory and empirically examine how certain favorable characteristics of workplace environments relate to levels of hope. Wandeler, Baeriswyl, et al. (2011) regressed hope in a multilevel model on individual level and group-level indicators of satisfaction of basic psychological needs and found supportive evidence that one of the characteristics of hope-nurturing workplaces is the satisfaction of basic psychological needs as described in self-determination theory (Deci & Ryan, 2000). Kenny, Walsh-Blair, Blustein, Bempechat, and Seltzer (2010) drew upon expectancy value, hope, and self-determination theories, and found that work hope of urban high school students evidenced a robust relationship with achievement-related beliefs and learning environments characterized by support and autonomy.

Since hope is about clearly defined goals, finding ways to achieve these goals (pathways), and motivating oneself to initiate and sustain action (agency), workplaces would benefit from involving employees in goal setting, developing clear goals, dividing larger goals into smaller goals, and developing capacity in the workers to problem solve and think creatively in order to find multiple routes to the goals. Organizations should also focus on why goals are pursued and the feelings of ownership in regards to goals (i.e., the self-concordance of goals; Sheldon & Elliot, 1999), because these elements can fuel agency. According to Lazarus (1991), hope is a seemingly goal-congruent emotion. Hope also is fostered when people are allowed the freedom to set their own goals, learn how to break large goals into smaller steps, experience the problems encountered in reaching goals, and make some mistakes, which should be seen as positive learning experiences (McDermott & Hastings, 2000). The accumulation of experiences in such an environment will eventually lead to a core self-belief that the individual is capable of generating pathways and can sustain the energy necessary to pursue goals.

People's affective self-reactions to the development of their competencies, their own performance, their professional pride, and positive emotional feedback in the process of goal pursuit at the workplace can favorably influence work related emotions, hope, and mental health. Positive emotions are not only associated with health, but produce health (Fredrickson, 2001). Experiences of problem solving and overcoming difficulties at work can be generalized to other domains of life and enhance pathways and agency thinking.

Future Research

The positive relationship between hope and positive work outcomes, and a negative relationship with undesirable work outcomes, has been well documented in various studies and Reichard et al. (2013) found some differences based on study location and conclude that future research should therefore examine different contexts and samples. In the current globalized workspace and global organizations it would indeed be helpful to have more information about the measurement and conceptualization of hope in different cultures, variation in the relationship with work outcomes, differences in the promotion of hope, and potential differences in the way hope works. This leads us to another gap in research, the understanding of how hope actually works in the workplace. Reichard et al. suggest "additional longitudinal and intervention studies … in order to understand which changes in workplace conditions, training, or management lead to increases in hope and corresponding improvement in outcomes" (p. 302). Furthermore, they recommend examining other moderators such as employee roles, employee autonomy, the type of hope measure (state vs. trait), and the developmental status of a company (start-up vs. established firms). The question is thus what organizations can do to promote hope among their members, and what organizations and their members are likely to get out of it.

Reichard et al. (2013) recommend that organizations identify low-cost strategies for raising employees' levels of hope. One aspect would be to increase trait hope, another focus would be to raise members' state hope. There are proven factors, such as leadership behavior, mentoring relationships, targeted interventions, so called 'micro-intervention' (Avey, Avolio, & Luthans, 2011), organizational structure, and the organizational culture. Future research can further explore how organizations can foster hope, or what organizations should avoid doing if they want to promote hope in their interactions. Wandeler, Baeriswyl, and Shavelson (2011) found that perceived competency, relatedness, and autonomy are positively related to hope. Experimental studies could examine how exactly these psychological needs relate to hope. Which organizational designs and characteristics are favorable to the development of hope in employees, customers, and other stakeholders? For example, organizational structures and strategies such as lean manufacturing, self-directed teams, or self-management provide a lot of opportunity for workers to be involved in the definition of goals, problem-solve, make autonomous decisions, and develop initiatives to overcome or anticipate obstacles. Taking initiative and thinking critically are highly valued in modern workplaces, and it would be of value to investigate how hope is intertwined with those desirable outcomes. In light of constant change it would also be of value to learn more about how transitions such as mergers, acquisitions, layoffs, and business growth affect levels of hope. Further research could explore whether there are elements of collective hope at various levels of organizations (e.g., whole organization, division, team), and what the effects of collective hope are. Can organizations develop it, and how? How much should organizations invest in developing individual and collective hope? How can hope be leveraged to facilitate difficult transitions? Finally, future research may uncover relevant information about the limits of hope in ameliorating the organizations. Can hope be maladaptative in certain circumstances? There still is a need to test these ideas empirically.

Conclusion

In summary, a review of the existing literature suggests that more hopeful employees do better in work and life (higher work performance, more desirable work behaviors and attitudes, less undesirable work outcomes, better scores in psychological indicators such as mental health) than less hopeful employees, and these findings remain true across countries, size of industry, and work setting. Hope, as a component of an individual's willingness to perform, provides the motivation ("agency") and the means ("pathways") for employees to persist at solving problems, completing their duties, and accomplishing their goals even when they encounter impediments. Organizations also can play an important role in fostering employees' levels of hope. This can occur through leadership behavior, mentoring relationships, targeted interventions, organizational structure, and the organizational culture.

References

Adams, V. H., Snyder, C. R., Rand, K. L., King, E. A., Sigman, D. R., & Pulvers, K. M. (2002). Hope in the workplace. In R. A. Giacolone & C. L. Jurkiewicz (Eds.), *Handbook of workplace spirituality and organization performance* (pp. 367–377). New York, NY: Sharpe.

Avey, J. B., Avolio, B. J., & Luthans, F. (2011). Experimentally analyzing the impact of leader positivity on follower positivity and performance. *Leadership*, *22*, 282–294.

Avey, J. B., Luthans, F., Smith, R. M., & Palmer, N. F. (2010). Impact of positive psychological capital on employee well-being over time. *Journal of Occupational Health Psychology*, *15*, 17–28.

Bandura, A. (1982). Self-efficacy mechanism in human agency. *American Psychologist, 37*, 122–147.

Bandura, A. (1997). *Self-efficacy: The exercise of control.* New York, NY: W. H. Freeman & Co.

Bandura, A. (2008). Toward an agentic theory of the self. In H. Marsh, R. G. Craven, & D. M. McInerney (Eds.), *Advances in self research: Vol. 3. Self-processes, learning, and enabling human potential* (pp. 15–49). Charlotte, NC: Information Age Publishing.

Covington, M. V. (2000). Goal theory, motivation, and school achievement: An integrative review. *Annual Review of Psychology, 51*, 171– 200.

Curry, L. A., Snyder, C. R., Cook, D. L., Ruby, B. C., & Rehm, M. (1997). The role of hope in student-athlete academic and sport achievement. *Journal of Personality and Social Psychology, 73*, 1257–1267.

Deci, E. L., & Ryan, R. M. (1985). *Intrinsic motivation and self-determination in human behavior.* New York, NY: Plenum.

Deci, E. L., & Ryan, R. M. (2000). The "what" and "why" of goal pursuits: Human needs and the self-determination of behavior. *Psychological Inquiry, 11*, 227–268.

Dweck, C. (1986). Motivational processes affecting learning. *American Psychologist, 41*, 1040–1048.

Dweck, C. S. (1999). *Self-theories: Their role in motivation, personality, and development.* Philadelphia, PA: Taylor & Francis.

Edwards, L. M., Rand, K., Lopez, S. J., & Snyder, C. R. (2006). Understanding hope: A review of measurement and construct validity research. In A. Ong & M. van Dulmen (Eds.), *Handbook of methods in positive psychology* (pp. 83–95). New York, NY: Oxford University Press.

Fredrickson, B. L. (2001). The role of positive emotions in positive psychology: The broaden-and-build theory of positive emotions. *American Psychologist, 56*, 219–226.

Frese, M., Garst, H., & Fay, D. (2007). Making things happen: Reciprocal relationships between work characteristics and personal initiative in a four-wave longitudinal structural equation model. *Journal of Applied Psychology, 92*, 1084–1102.

Hacker, W. (2003). Action regulation theory: A practical tool for the design of modern work processes? *European Journal of Work and Organizational Psychology, 12*, 105–130.

Heppner, P. P., & Petersen, C. H. (1982). The development and implications of a personal problem solving inventory. *Journal of Counseling Psychology, 29*, 66–75.

Hirschi, A. (2014). Hope as a resource for self-directed career management: Investigating mediating effects on proactive career behaviors and life and job satisfaction. *Journal of Happiness Studies, 15*, 1495–1512.

Hirschi, A., Abessolo, M., & Froidevaux, A. (2015). Hope as a resource for career exploration: Examining incremental and cross-lagged effects. *Journal of Vocational Behavior, 86*, 38–47.

Hobfoll, S. E. (1998). *Stress, culture, and community: The psychology and philosophy of stress.* New York, NY: Plenum.

Hudson, J. L., Flannery-Schroeder, E., & Kendall, P. C. (2004). Primary prevention of anxiety disorders. In J. A. Dozois and K. S. Dobson (Eds.), *The prevention of anxiety and depression: theory, research, and practice* (pp. 101–130). Washington, DC: American Psychological Association.

Juntunen, C. L., & Wettersten, K. B. (2006). Work hope: Development and initial validation of a measure. *Journal of Counseling Psychology, 53*, 94–106.

Kenny, M. E., Walsh-Blair, L. Y., Blustein, D. L., Bempechat, J., & Seltzer, J. (2010). Achievement motivation among urban adolescents: Work hope, autonomy support, and achievement-related beliefs. *Journal of Vocational Behavior, 77*, 205–212.

Kohn, M. L., & Schooler, C. (1983). *Work and personality: An inquiry into the impact of social stratification.* Norwood, NJ: Ablex.

Lawler, E. E. (1992). *The ultimate advantage: Creating the high involvement organization.* San Francsico, CA: Jossey-Bass.

Lazarus, R. S. (1991). Progress on a cognitive-motivational-relational theory of emotion. *American Psychologist, 46*, 819.

Locke, E. A., & Latham, G. P. (1990). *A theory of goal setting and task performance.* Upper Saddle River, NJ: Prentice Hall.

Lopez, S. J., Snyder, C. R., Magyar-Moe, J., Edwards, L. M., Pedrotti, J. T., Janowski, K., … Pressgrove, C. (2004). Strategies for accentuating hope. In P. A. Linley & S. Joseph (Eds.), *Positive psychology in practice*, (pp. 388–404). Hoboken, NJ: Wiley.

Luthans, F. (2002). The need for and meaning of positive organizational behavior. *Journal of organizational behavior, 23*, 695–706.

Luthans, F., Avolio, B. J., Avey, J. B., & Norman, S. M. (2007). Psychological capital: Measurement and relationship with performance and satisfaction. *Personnel Psychology, 60*, 541–572.

Luthans, F., Avolio, B., Walumbwa, F., & Li, W. (2005). The psychological capital of Chinese workers: Exploring the relationship with performance. *Management and Organization Review, 1*, 247–269.

Luthans, F., & Jensen, S. M. (2002). Hope: A new positive strength for human resource development. *Human Resource Development Review, 1*, 304–322.

Luthans, F., Norman, S. M., Avolio, B. J., & Avey, J. B. (2008). The mediating role of psychological capital in the supportive organizational climate–employee performance relationship. *Journal of Organizational Behavior, 29*, 219–238.

Marques, S. C., Lopez, S. J., & Pais-Ribeiro, J. L. (2011). "Building Hope for the Future" – A program to foster strengths in middle-school students. *Journal of Happiness Studies, 12*, 139–152.

Marques, S. C., Lopez, S. J., Rose, S., & Robinson, C. (2014). Measuring and promoting hope in schoolchildren. In R. Gilman, E. S. Huebner, & M. J. Furlong (Eds.), *A handbook of positive psychology in the schools* (2nd ed., pp. 35–50). Mahwah, NJ: Erlbaum.

McDermott, D., & Hastings, S. (2000). Children: Raising future hopes. In C. R. Snyder (Ed.), *Handbook of hope: Theory, measures, and applications* (pp. 25–57). San Diego, CA: Academic Press.

Ouweneel, E., Le Blanc, P. M., & Schaufeli, W. B. (2012). Don't leave your heart at home. *Career Development International, 17*, 537–556.

Ouweneel, E., Le Blanc, P. M., Schaufeli, W. B., & van Wijhe, C. I. (2012). Good morning, good day: A diary study on positive emotions, hope, and work engagement. *Human Relations, 65*, 1129–1154.

Peterson, S. J., & Byron, K. (2008). Exploring the role of hope in job performance: Results from four studies. *Journal of Organizational Behavior, 29*, 785–803.

Peterson, S. J., Gerhardt, M. W., & Rode, J. C. (2006). Hope, learning goals, and task performance. *Personality and Individual Differences, 40*, 1099–1109.

Rego, A., Machado, F., Leal, S., & Cunha, M. P. E. (2009). Are hopeful employees more creative? An empirical study. *Creativity Research Journal, 21*, 223–231.

Reichard, R. J., Avey, J. B., Lopez, S., & Dollwet, M. (2013). Having the will and finding the way: A review and meta-analysis of hope at work. *The Journal of Positive Psychology, 8*, 292–304.

Scheier, M. F., & Carver, C. S. (1985). Optimism, coping, and health: Assessment and implications of generalized outcome expectancies. *Health Psychology, 4*, 219–247.

Sheldon, K. M., & Elliot, A. J. (1999). Goal striving, need satisfaction, and longitudinal well-being: The self-concordance model. *Journal of Personality and Social Psychology, 76*, 482–497.

Snyder, C. R. (1994). *The psychology of hope: You can get there from here*. New York, NY: Free Press.

Snyder, C. R. (2000a). Hypothesis: There is hope. In C. R. Snyder (Ed.), *Handbook of hope: Theory, measures, and applications* (pp. 3–21). San Diego, CA: Academic Press.

Snyder, C. R. (2000b). Genesis: Birth and growth of hope. In C. R. Snyder (Ed.), *Handbook of hope: Theory, measures, and applications* (pp. 25–57). San Diego, CA: Academic Press.

Snyder, C. R. (2002). Hope: Rainbows in the mind. *Psychological Inquiry, 13*, 249–275.

Snyder, C. R., & Feldman, D. (2000). Hope for the many: An empowering social agenda. In C. R. Snyder (Ed.), *Handbook of hope: Theory, measures, and applications* (pp. 389–412). San Diego, CA: Academic Press.

Snyder, C. R., Feldman, D. B., Shorey, H. S., & Rand, K. L. (2002). Hopeful choices: A school counselor's guide to hope theory. *Professional School Counseling, 5*, 298–307.

Snyder, C. R., Harris, C., Anderson, J. R., Holleran, S. H., Irving, L. M., Sigmon, S. T., … Harney, P. (1991). The will and the ways: Development and validation of an individual-differences measure of hope. *Journal of Personality and Social Psychology, 60*, 570–585.

Snyder, C. R., Lopez, S. J., Shorey, H. L., Rand, K. L., & Feldman, D. B. (2003). Hope theory, measurements, and applications to school psychology. *School Psychology Quarterly, 18*, 122–139.

Snyder, C. R., & Shorey, H. (2004). Hope and leadership. In G. Goethals, J. Sorenson, & J. M. Burns (Eds.), *Encyclopedia of leadership* (673–675). Thousand Oaks, CA: Sage.

Snyder, C. R., Shorey, H., Cheavens, J., Pulvers, K. M., Adams, V. H., III, & Wiklund, C. (2002). Hope and academic success in college. *Journal of Educational Psychology, 94*, 820–826.

Snyder, C. R., Sympson, S. C., Ybasco, F. C., Borders, T. F., Babyak, M. A., & Higgins, R. L. (1996). Development and validation of the state hope scale. *Journal of Personality and Social Psychology, 70*, 321–335.

Stajkovic, A. (2006). Development of a core confidence – higher order construct. *Journal of Applied Psychology, 91*, 1208–1224.

Sympson, S. (1999). *Validation of the Domain Specific Hope Scale.* Unpublished doctoral dissertation, Department of Psychology, University of Kansas, Lawrence.

Valle, M., Huebner, E. S., & Suldo, S. (2006). An analysis of hope as a psychological strength. *Journal of School Psychology, 44*, 393–406.

Wandeler, C., Baeriswyl, F., & Shavelson, R. (2011). Hope at the workplace: A multilevel study. *Swiss Journal of Educational Research, 3*, 421–442.

Wandeler, C., & Bundick, M. J. (2011). Hope and self-determination of young adults in the workplace. *The Journal of Positive Psychology, 6*, 341–354.

Wandeler, C., Lopez, S. J., & Baeriswyl, F. (2011). Hope, mental health, and competency development in the workplace. *Empirical research in vocational education and training, 3*(2), 129–146.

Youssef, C. M., & Luthans, F. (2011). Positive psychological capital in the workplace: Where we are and where we need to go. In K. M. Sheldon, T. B. Kashdan, & M. F. Steger (Eds.), *Designing positive psychology: Taking stock and moving forward* (351–364). Oxford, UK: Oxford University Press.

5

Creating Meaning and Purpose at Work

Michael F. Steger

Introduction

Organizations frequently look to employee well-being as an engine for improved performance, motivated by the idea that a happy worker is a better worker and by data suggesting that work well-being delivers impressive return on investment. Every dollar an organization invests into its employees' well-being provides a return of roughly three to five dollars (Goetzel & Ozminkowski, 2008; Rath & Harter, 2010). Driven by an intuitive appeal and a growing body of research, meaningful work holds the promise of being the "next big thing" among organizations seeking a lever for improving organizational performance (Dik, Byrne, & Steger, 2013). Essentially, it may be time to move beyond engagement and commitment and strive for meaningful work.

The general public may have a ready, semantic grasp of what meaningful work should look like and feel like, but scholars have differed in how they have formally defined the construct. The common thread across all definitions is the idea that for work to be meaningful, an individual worker must be able to identify some personally meaningful contribution made by his or her effort. Beyond this, meaningful work speaks to people's subjective experience that their jobs, work, or careers are purposeful and significant, that their work is harmoniously and energetically synergistic with the meaning and purpose in their broader lives, and that they are enabled and empowered to benefit the greater good through their work. This chapter reviews current theory, assessment, and research on meaningful work with the hopes that a better understanding might enable meaningful work to be cultivated and harnessed to maximize performance, build strong brands, nurture innovation, and benefit both employees and their host communities while they are at it.

Meaningful work represents an opportunity to transition from organizational practices that seek simply to maximize effort and output – such as policies focused on incentives, engagement, and commitment – to practices that augment effort and output with improved welfare for a wide range of organizational stakeholders ranging from shareholders

The Wiley Blackwell Handbook of the Psychology of Positivity and Strengths-Based Approaches at Work, First Edition. Edited by Lindsay G. Oades, Michael F. Steger, Antonella Delle Fave, and Jonathan Passmore.

to employees to host communities. At its heart, meaningful work scholarship and application seeks to optimize occupational opportunities in such a way that employee motivation, effort, and productivity are enhanced, and that employees enthusiastically adopt attitudes of ownership, responsibility, and citizenship toward their organization, while simultaneously enjoying greater well-being, health, and belongingness. To access these qualities among its employees, organizations need to provide fertile conditions for the growth of meaningful work. This chapter draws on the relevant scholarship to review those qualities that characterize such meaning-friendly conditions. First, meaningful work theory is reviewed to identify the major themes and dimensions of meaningful work. Second, meaningful work assessment is reviewed. Third, correlates, predictors, and benefits of meaningful work are identified and discussed. Fourth, practical recommendations for fostering meaningful work are suggested to guide individual workers, leaders, and organizations.

Meaningful Work Theory

Theories of meaningful work could in some ways be said to draw their inspiration from Durkheim's (1897) sociological analysis of suicide. Durkheim argued that one cause of suicide was unemployment because it deprived people of their function and their opportunity to contribute to society. That a noted sociologist was so concerned with the damage unemployment could do to people may have been rooted in the massive changes wrought by the Industrial Revolution to the role of work in people's lives. In some ways, work was transformed from a predestined path trod by all members of a particular family lineage, where Shoemakers made shoes, Cartiers transported goods, and Breuers made beer. As machines replaced human labor and as assembly line techniques deconstructed work into a sequence of connected tasks, traditional occupations were uprooted and people became responsible not for production as *fait accompli* but rather for production in terms of incremental additions to a whole. More than 100 years after Durkheim's observations about the dire impact of losing one's place in society through the loss of work, we still see concerns about how quickly the world of work changes, how rapidly "human" jobs are outsourced or even replaced by robots or algorithms. As technology continues to change the shape of work in our lives, by increasing competition in the job market, increasing globalization, and increasing the reach of workplace communications into personal time, people struggle with the challenge of trying to balance work demands with life priorities.

Meaningful work is viewed as a way to bring harmony, if not balance, to the busy lives of workers, providing workers with well-being at the office and providing organizations with enhanced productivity, performance, and dedication. There are two primary families of meaningful work theories. The first is comprised of theories about either the meaning ascribed to work or the meaning people derive through their work; the second is comprised of theories about work as a calling.

Meaningful work theories

Simply put, meaningful work is any paid or unpaid work or occupational role people fulfill that is judged by them to possess meaning, purpose, or significance. This basic definition is similar to the definition offered through the influential Job Characteristics Model (JCM; Hackman & Oldham, 1976), where meaningful work is described in terms of employee perceptions that a particular job is meaningful, worthwhile, and valuable. Within the surveys that fleshed out the JCM, however, meaningful work was assessed by asking employees about their own personal opinions, and the opinions of their co-workers, regarding whether work done on a specific job is useless and trivial, or very meaningful (Hackman & Oldham, 1975). Accordingly, meaningful work is work that is not useless or trivial, but is instead meaningful. It is in elaborating this general sentiment that meaningful work should have some meaning to it that scholars recently have spent most of their efforts.

More recently, a formal multidimensional model of meaningful work has been proposed. Steger, Dik, and Duffy (2012) framed meaningful work in terms of three dimensions. Steger and colleagues drew upon the much larger body of scholarship on meaning in life as a whole to identify the important role of self-transcendence in meaningful work (for review, see Steger, 2009, 2012a, 2012b). It has been theorized and shown that as people transcend their own immediate and self-centered concerns to embrace the concerns of those beyond themselves they experience greater meaning in their lives (e.g., Dik, Duffy, & Steger, 2012; Reker, Peacock, & Wong, 1987; Schnell, 2009; Steger, Kashdan, & Oishi, 2008). The model Steger and colleagues developed can be displayed in terms of concentric circles indicating people's degree of transcendence from the basic qualities of a job. Meaningful work transcends simple job execution when workers perceive that their work is meaningful and has a point or purpose within the organization. The relationship of one's work to meaning in one's personal life as a whole is another step of transcendence away from simple job characteristics. Finally, the ability of work to surpass benefits to one's own life and provide broader impacts for the greater good represents yet another level of transcendence. Figure 5.1 displays the dimensions of meaningful work from this theory. In the central circle is the extent to which a worker judges her or his job to be meaningful and significant. In the next circle is the degree to which a job or work is harmonious with meaning and purpose in the worker's life as a whole, or alternatively, helps workers build more meaning in their lives. In the largest circle is the degree to which a job or work helps the worker contribute to or positively impact others or the greater good in prosocial ways.

Meanings of work An ancillary pursuit has grown around efforts to define the meaning of work to people, rather than what the experience of meaningful work is like for them. Although these two concepts – the meaning of work versus meaningful work – are distinct, their similar names warrant some explication. Whereas meaningful work, as discussed in the previous paragraphs, can be defined as the subjective experience that one's job, work, or career is meaningful, provides synergy with one's meaning in life, and benefits some greater good, the "meaning of work" pursues "the significance, beliefs, definitions and the value which individuals and groups attach to working as a major element of human activity" (Harpaz & Fu, 2002, p. 641). Another way of looking at the distinction is that meaningful work research seeks to understand the meaning and value work provides to people, and meaning of work research seeks to understand the role work plays in human life and society. Research in this tradition (e.g., Harpaz & Fu, 2002) has focused on the centrality of work in people's lives, their adoption of entitlement and obligation social norms, the value they place on common work outcomes, their work goals, and their identification with their work roles. An alternative approach to the meaning of work organized these concepts and many more into four categories: self-related variables such as values, beliefs, and motivation; other-related variables such as co-workers, leaders, communities, and families; work-context variables such as job design, financial considerations, and cultural work norms; and spiritual life variables such as spirituality, and sacred callings (Rosso, Dekas, & Wrzesniewski, 2010). One could argue that there are a few variables left out (physical work abilities, for example), but between these two approaches, it seems possible that nearly any aspect of a worker's life could impact the meaning she or he attaches to work. Thus, work will play an enormous variety of roles and be viewed in wide diversity

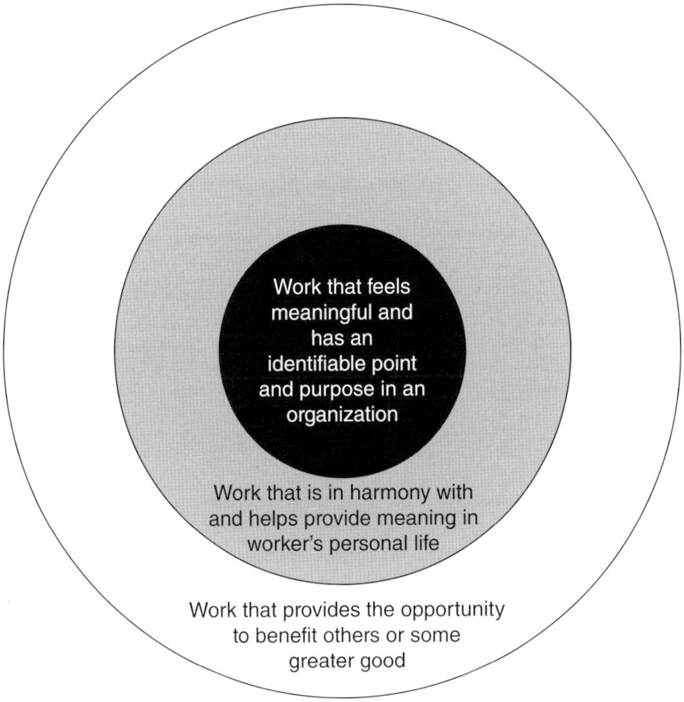

Figure 5.1 The three-level model of meaningful work proposed by Steger, Dik, & Duffy (2012). Each level represents a degree of transcendence from the worker's specific job. Meaningful work includes: (1) Workers' perceptions of meaning or purpose in job or career activities (in the center circle); (2) The capacity for work to be in harmony with and to help nurture meaning in the worker's broader life, which is one level of transcendence higher than the job itself (in the second circle); and (3) the opportunity to positively impact or benefit the greater good of stakeholders in the worker's community, society, or even planet, which is another level of transcendence higher (in the outer circle). *Source*: Steger et al. (2012). Reproduced with permission of Sage Publications, Inc.

of ways, but the question still remains, what factors make any give occupational pursuit more meaningful, purposeful, and significant?

Facilitators of meaningful work The most comprehensive accounting of mechanisms to create meaningful work organized the literature into seven pathways: authenticity, self-efficacy, self-esteem, purpose, belongingness, transcendence, and cultural and interpersonal sensemaking (Rosso et al., 2010). The origins of some of these pathways lie in the JCM. In the JCM, meaningful work results when workers engage in jobs that provide them with the necessity of using a variety of skills, talents, and activities; the opportunity to work on a job that results in a completed task such that they see a job progress from beginning to end; and the ability to work on a job that substantially impacts the lives or work of their co-workers or others outside of the organization (Hackman & Oldham, 1975). Thus, the JCM identifies elements that help people develop self-efficacy, self-esteem, belongingness, and perhaps cultural and interpersonal sensemaking. It can be seen that recent multidimensional models of meaningful work have incorporated and expanded the general idea of the third predictor of meaningful work. Rather than meaningful work arising because people view their job to impact the work or lives of others, meaningful work itself is composed in part of the desire and opportunity to tangibly help others or the greater good. The other two predictors of meaningful work articulated in the JCM, skill variety and completing a whole task, have been de-emphasized in recent models of meaningful work, in favor of organizational, social, and psychological characteristics.

In Steger and Dik's (2010) model of meaningful work, meaningful work is brought to life when people are able to develop a comprehensive and accurate cognitive understanding of themselves as a component of their working environment, as well as when they can discern a purpose or purposes in their lives that provides the fundamental motivation for their work efforts. Although not all aspects of this model were fully fleshed out, research and practice since the publication of that model has helped identify key aspects of how to help achieve meaningful work.

The multidimensional meaningful work model of Steger and colleagues (e.g., Steger & Dik, 2010; Steger et al., 2012) characterizes work as one of several important life domains in which people learn how to navigate, find their niche, and express their values, strengths, and aspirations. On the personal level, meaningful work is fostered by characteristics such as an honest appraisal of one's strengths and weaknesses, a desire to make a positive impact on others and on the greater good, authenticity, taking responsibility for and adopting an ownership mentality toward one's organization, knowledge of organizational policies and operations, a complete grasp of one's scope of work and responsibilities, and sufficient knowledge of the values and mission of an organization that one can ascertain fit with one's own purpose. On the interpersonal level, meaningful work is fostered by respectful relationships, a sufficient understanding of an organization's social and political landscape, and opportunities to help and be helped, or mentor and be mentored. On the leadership and organizational level, meaningful work is fostered by clear communication of the values and mission of the organization in conjunction with an authentic adoption of those characteristics in the operational culture and practice of the organization, authenticity and ethical behavior from leadership teams, a clear and articulated vision of how each employee contributes to the organization's functioning through his or her work, and the willingness to allow some degree of autonomy and personal expressiveness in how each worker fulfills his or her duties. All of the pathways to meaningful work identified by Rosso and colleagues (2010) are captured by this approach. In a later section, I will expand on how these many points of emphasis can be organized into a more user-friendly format to help individuals and organizations implement meaningful work programs.

Calling theories

In the broadest sense, calling in work is defined as work that is personally meaningful and holds some ability to pursue prosocial desires. For example, Dobrow and Tosti-Kharas (2011) define calling as "a consuming, meaningful passion people experience toward a domain" (p. 1003), and others similarly define calling in terms of purpose in life (Hall & Chandler, 2005) or meaning (Wrzesniewski, McCauley, Rozin, & Schwartz, 1997). This definition is the secular version of the calling construct, and is very similar to definitions of meaningful work, as we saw in the previous section of this chapter. The heritage of calling lies in its religious roots, however, and several modern theories of calling have adopted what is known as "neo-classical" or spiritually informed definitions. For example, Dik and Duffy (2009) define calling as "a transcendent summons, experienced as originating beyond the self, to approach a particular life role in a manner oriented toward demonstrating or deriving a sense of purpose or meaningfulness and that holds other-oriented values and goals as primary sources of motivation" (p. 427). Dik and Duffy fashioned their definition from an interdisciplinary review of relevant scholarly work.

A somewhat similar definition of calling emerged from qualitative research among working adults in Germany and the United States. Hagmaier and Abele (2012) found five dimensions in their interviews: sense and meaning, value-driven behavior, person–environment fit, identification with one's work, and transcendent guiding force. However, factor analysis of survey items derived from these dimensions resulted in three dimensions: transcendent guiding force (which is similar to transcendent summons, though it includes questions about inner voice, inner call, and destiny), identification with one's work (which assesses identifying with, feeling passionate about, and realizing full potential through one's work), and finally sense and meaning and value-driven behavior (which is very similar to the prosocial dimension of other calling theories, and includes items about serving a common goal, making the world a better place, and having high moral standards for one's work). This model of calling captures some sense that one is guided to work, that such work is personally expressive, and that one works with high moral standards to benefit others. It does not have an explicit dimension that assesses whether work is meaningful to the respondent. Thus, calling is work that is personally meaningful, is motivated by an interest in serving a prosocial benefit, and in addition is a response to a summons to work that comes from transcendent sources, such as religious Higher Powers, respected authorities, or perceived societal need.

The spiritual dimension of calling does seem to provide additional benefit in understanding the impact of a calling. A study of highly educated working mothers found that sanctification of work predicted higher positive emotions and job satisfaction, and lower life–work role conflict above and beyond other measures of religiosity (Hall, Oates, Anderson, & Willingham, 2012). Despite such results, several lines of research under the rubric of calling do not include transcendent summons or other spiritual content in their approach to calling. Because of this, most calling research is well aligned with meaningful work research and can be used to understand the predictors, correlates, and outcomes of meaningful work.

Calling as one among many work orientations Within the models of calling that are directly compatible with meaningful work theory, it is typical to draw upon a three-dimensional orientation toward work first presented by Bellah and colleagues (Bellah, Madsen, Sullivan, Swidler, & Tipton, 1985). People with a *job* orientation focus on work as an avenue toward financial or material compensation with little to no concern for whether work is meaningful or significant. People with a *career* orientation focus on work as an avenue for gaining a sense of achievement, mastery, status, or advancement within an organization, again with no particular interest in meaning. In contrast, however, people with a *calling* orientation focus on the fulfillment, prosocial benefits, and sense of purpose that work provides, particularly in terms of making the world a better place. The calling orientation is relevant to theories of meaningful work because of how scholars have relied upon it. For example, Wrzesniewski and colleagues (Wrzesniewski et al., 1997) framed their research in terms of calling.

Pratt and colleagues proposed that Bellah's classic calling orientation could itself be further understood as a combination of three independent dimensions (Pratt, Pradies, & Lepisto, 2013). Essentially, Pratt and colleagues suggest that work can be a calling for people because they can harvest different forms of fulfillment from their work: the *craftsmanship orientation* pertains to people who feel fulfilled by developing skills, mastery, and doing a job well; the *serving orientation* specifically captures the greater good aspect of calling and refers to people who feel fulfilled when their work helps other people; the *kinship orientation* applies to people who feel fulfilled in their work because of the quality of relationships people develop through their work, whether that pertains to co-workers, professional organizations, or customers. These dimensions may exist outside of the parameters of calling as well. For example, the craftsmanship orientation may be very similar to the career orientation if the worker's emphasis is upon mastery and execution more than on status and promotion.

Living a calling versus anticipating a calling One further distinction has been made in calling scholarship that has not been explored in the wider meaningful work literature. There appears to be a difference between having a calling and living a calling. Whereas the former refers to people's perception that they apprehend that there is a career out there that they would find to be meaningful, the latter refers to the realization of that career and that one is actively engaged in one's calling rather than simply feeling as if a calling awaits somewhere down the road (Duffy, Allan, Autin, & Bott, 2013). It may be well and good to feel that one's calling is coming, but theoretically, there should be greater benefits to be working one's calling (Duffy & Autin, 2013). From a conceptual standpoint, meaningful work most closely resembles living a calling; certainly the definition of meaningful work suggests that people are supposed to describe their current employment or volunteering. Because the difference between perceiving and living meaningful work has not been tested, it is difficult to say.

Calling theory, like meaningful work theory, emphasizes self-knowledge and self-understanding. There are few apparent ways to know if one has a calling that do not rely on comparing jobs and careers to how one wishes to work and what one desires to accomplish at work.

Meaningful Work Assessment

In part due to the theoretical efforts discussed above, meaningful work appears to be an increasingly important point of reference, both culturally and academically. Several international work and consulting firms have released surveys and recommendations about meaningful work, and the pace of research seems to have accelerated briskly. As one rough metric, a simple PsychINFO search was undertaken on May 17, 2015, using the search term "meaningful work," and limiting the results to journal articles and books. This search returned 225 results, of which more than 50% have been published since 2009 (110 citations) and *nearly 30% have been published between 2013 and mid-2015* (67 citations, 29.8%). There are much more rigorous ways of exploring just how active and growing this area of scholarship is, but this approximation corresponds well with anecdotal observations. In a field that marks publications from the 1940s, 1950s, and 1960s into the present, it is a testament to the rising prominence of meaningful work that almost one-third of papers and books published have appeared since 2012. It is also a testament to the amount of empirical exploration that is needed, given that we are talking about only a couple of hundred papers and books to date.

The backbone of any science is built upon theory, methods, and, ultimately, assessment. Meaningful work assessment spans a variety of efforts, from single items and ad hoc surveys to theoretically and psychometrically developed multidimensional questionnaires. The purpose of the following section is not to provide recommendations on which measures to use, but instead to bring together and review the most prominent and notable efforts in meaningful work assessment. Additional reviews of meaningful work and calling assessment are available as well (see Duffy, Autin, Allan, & Douglass, 2015; Steger, Dik, & Shim, in press).

Review of meaningful work assessment tools

Initial efforts to measure meaningful work, and also calling, have often focused on simply assessing the degree to which people report work as being meaningful or as being a calling. For example, meaningful work was measured as a simple, unidimensional construct in the JCM (Hackman & Oldham, 1975), and prominent early efforts to research calling relied on people to choose which of three paragraphs best described them, with one of the paragraphs standing as a definition of calling (Wrzesniewski et al., 1997). Implicit in each of these approaches were several qualities, however. In the JCM, meaningful work items assessed whether work was meaningful or whether it was useless and trivial. In calling measurement, the paragraph used as stimulus for calling measurement included descriptors of work being one of the most important parts of life, a vital part of who one is, taking work home with one, having the majority of friends at work, loving work, work making the world a better place, encouraging others to enter the same line of work, and being upset if forced to stop working (Wrzesniewski et al., 1997). Thus, particularly in the case of calling, a lot of concepts are packed into meaningful work.

The next major developments in assessing meaningful work continued to add content while still adhering to a unidimensional measurement strategy. For example, May, Gilson, & Harter (2004) assessed meaningful work as a component of workplace empowerment with six items assessing meaningfulness in terms of importance, value, worthwhileness, and significance of activities. All of these items essentially riffed on synonyms for "meaningful" and antonyms of "uselessness," which were the core components of meaningful work within JCM. In fact, most meaningful work assessment through the mid-2000s used various synonyms of meaningful work and antonyms of meaningless work to explore the construct. This includes a survey developed by Arnold, Turner, Barling, Kelloway, and McKee (2007), which added items assessing work as fulfilling, rewarding, and achieving important outcomes.

Ashmos and Duchon (2000) bucked this trend with the meaningful work subscale of their measure of workplace spirituality. In addition to assessing the personal meaningfulness of work, this scale focused on work's connection with important values as well as with greater social and community good. Unfortunately, it also added joy, energy, and positive anticipation of work to the list, clouding the issue of what the scale actually measures. For example, one person could obtain a high score on this scale primarily because her job enables her to make a personal contribution to a valued social cause, while another person could obtain a high score on this scale because she loves eating the free snacks, jumping on the trampoline, playing video games with her co-workers, and other trappings of work engagement campaigns. Despite, or perhaps because of, the fact that all of these meaningful work measures were unidimensional, scores tended to be quite reliable. In addition, they correlated in expected ways with other positive indicators of workplace adjustment, laying the initial groundwork for establishing that meaningful work is desirable. At the same time, they were less suited for helping determine what meaningful work actually is.

Part of the reason that these meaningful work measures may seem somewhat preliminary is that none of the assessment instruments were grounded in meaningful work theory but rather were developed according to the pragmatic needs of individual studies. More recently, measures of meaningful work and calling have been built on firmer theoretical foundations. For example, Dobrow and Tosti-Kharas (2011) sought to ameliorate the conceptual confusion they found around definitions of calling by defining it as "a consuming, meaningful passion people experience toward a domain" (p. 1005). They built a 12-item scale upon this definition, which logically asks about levels of passion, enjoyment, personal satisfaction, sense of destiny, constant presence in one's mind, being moved and gratified by one's calling, and even the degree of sacrifice people would accept and the obstacles people would overcome to pursue their calling. These items are summed to a single calling score, supported by confirmatory factor analysis. Calling scores showed large correlations with other ways of unidimensionally assessing calling. All of these unidimensional measures of calling also had large correlations with work engagement and job involvement. In fact, the largest correlate of both Dobrow and Tosti-Kharas' scale and Wrzesniewski and colleagues' (1997) calling measurement was with job involvement. The theory-driven unidimensional measurement of meaningful work thus seems to yield psychometrically robust scales, but may not do enough to differentiate meaningful work (and calling) from similar constructs.

Several recent efforts have consulted theory and developed psychometrically robust scales that assess multiple dimensions. The first is the Calling and Vocation Questionnaire (CVQ; Dik, Eldridge, Steger, & Duffy, 2012) which was developed to assess Dik and Duffy's (2009) theory of calling. The CVQ assesses a 2×3 array of calling subscales created by an overarching Searching For vs. Experiencing the Presence Of dimension laid over three content areas: Transcendent Summons, Purposeful Work, and Prosocial Orientation. The second is the Work and Meaning Inventory (WAMI; Steger et al., 2012) which was developed to assess Steger and Dik's multidimensional model of meaningful work (Steger & Dik, 2010; Steger et al., 2012). The WAMI uses three subscales to measure Positive Meaning, Meaning Making Through Work, and Greater Good Motivations. Both of these models are described earlier in this chapter. The resulting tools, the CVQ and the WAMI, correlate more highly with other measures of the same construct than with measures of related but distinct constructs and show patterns of differentiation among the subscales each assess. A third effort, the Multidimensional Calling Measure (MCM; Hagemeier & Abele, 2012) was developed psychometrically to have three subscales, each measured by three items. The subscales capture work identification/fit with job, sense of meaning as values-driven behavior, and transcendent guiding force. Scores converge with other measures of calling (Duffy et al., 2015). Finally, a fourth multidimensional measure was developed based on qualitative research. The Comprehensive Meaningful Work Scale has six subscales focused on assessing ways in which people view their work to help develop the self, promote unity with others, service to others, and developing potential (Lips-Wiersma & Wright, 2012). Although validity information for this scale was not presented, the psychometric properties and grounding theory are both compelling. Thus, using any of these three tools, meaningful work is measured with more specificity than simply using synonyms of the target construct. Further, hypotheses about which components of meaningful work are most central and important can be tested directly using subscales, which avoids the confusion caused by having diverse content included among the items.

Undoubtedly, further advances and refinements to the assessment of meaningful work will be forthcoming, but already there are a few theory-driven, psychometrically robust tools available, including unidimensional (Dobrow & Tosti-Kharas, 2011) and multidimensional (Dik, Eldridge, et al., 2012; Hagemeier & Abele, 2012; Steger et al., 2012) scales.

Correlates, Predictors, and Benefits of Meaningful Work

Not every study of meaningful work has used the best available measures. However, studies that have included multiple measures have all found high convergence among different measures of meaningful work (e.g., Dobrow & Tosti-Kharas, 2011; Duffy et al., 2015). Because of this, we can have some confidence that studies of the predictors and benefits of meaningful work are likely to pertain to a variety of meaningful work assessment tools. In addition, with the exceptions of the transcendence subscales of the CVQ and MCM, most measures of calling cover the same material as measures of meaningful work, so most research on calling is directly informative about meaningful work.

Correlates of meaningful work

The vast bulk of meaningful work research has used cross-sectional methods and correlation-based analyses. As would be expected from the meaningful work theories reviewed earlier in this chapter, meaningful work (and calling) positively correlates with a wide range of desirable well-being and work-related variables. In general, those who feel their work is meaningful also report higher levels of well-being (Arnold et al., 2007), including more frequent positive emotions (Steger, Littman-Ovadia, Miller, Menger, & Rothmann, 2013; Steger, Pickering, Shin, & Dik, 2010), more positive self-image (Torrey & Duffy, 2012), more satisfaction with life (Douglass, Duffy, & Autin, 2016; Steger et al., 2010; Steger et al., 2012), and more meaning in life (Dik, Sargent, & Steger, 2008; Dik & Steger, 2008; Douglass et al., 2016; Steger et al., 2010; Steger et al., 2012). People engaged in meaningful work also report lower levels of anxiety and depression (Steger et al., 2012). In addition to the personal well-being that those engaged in meaningful work enjoy, it appears that meaningful work adds significantly to the quality of home life as well. Those engaged in meaningful work reported a high degree of work-to-home enrichment such that their work helped them be a better member of their families (Tummers & Knies, 2013).

They also more highly value their work than other people do (Nord, Brief, Atieh, & Doherty, 1990) and believe their work to play a more central role in their lives (Harpaz & Fu, 2002). Although ambition, fear, or disempowerment also might drive work to be seen as valued and central, for people with meaningful work this does not seem to be the case. They are not more burned out at work (Creed, Rogers, Praskova, & Searle, 2014; Hagemeier & Abele, 2012). Rather they report greater job satisfaction (e.g., Douglass et al., 2016; Hagemeier & Abele, 2012; Kamdron, 2005; Littman-Ovadia & Steger, 2010; Lobene & Meade, 2013; Sparks & Schenk, 2001; Steger & Dik, 2009; Steger et al., 2012; Wrzesniewski et al., 1997) and work enjoyment (Steger et al., 2010). While at work, they are more engaged than others (Steger et al., 2013). They also appear to have greater certainty (Duffy & Sedlacek, 2007) and clarity about their career choices (Steger et al., 2010), and they feel greater self-efficacy about their careers (Dobrow & Tosti-Kharas, 2011; Domene, 2012). People who have meaningful work feel strongly positive about their careers and organizations, being more committed than others, having greater intrinsic motivation, and being less likely to have intentions to quit working for their organization (Duffy, Dik, & Steger, 2011; Fairlee, 2011; Lobene & Meade, 2013; Steger et al., 2012). Meaningful work is also positively correlated with self-reported supervisor performance ratings (Lobene & Meade, 2013), an indication that meaningful work pays off with better work.

People who experience meaningful work (and calling) may be profound social resources for organizations. For example, they are less hostile than other workers (Steger et al., 2012) and report greater work unit cohesion (Sparks & Schenk, 2001), greater faith in management and better work team functioning as rated by supervisors (Wrzesniewski et al., 1997). Further, they report engaging in more frequent organizational citizenship behaviors, meaning they are the ones who are turning off the lights before they go home, making the fresh pot of coffee, and leaving your lunch unmolested in the breakroom refrigerator (Rawat & Nadavulakere, 2015; Steger et al., 2012).

The seeds of meaningful work may be sown quite early. For example, within samples of American and Korean undergraduate students, those who reported that their academic majors were congruent with their eventual career aims reported significantly higher levels of meaningful work than those who perceived their academic majors to be a mismatch with the career they wanted to pursue (Shin, Steger, & Lee, 2014). This study suggests that knowing you are on the wrong career path diminishes meaningful work. Perceiving one's self to be overqualified for a job also appears to diminish meaningful work (Lobene & Meade, 2013).

Thus, research suggests a wide range of desirable correlates of meaningful work, such as life satisfaction, meaning in life, career commitment, and job satisfaction. These relationships appear to hold up over longitudinal analysis as well (Duffy, Allan, Autin, & Douglass, 2014). However, it should be noted that in this field, as in others within psychology, there has been some reliance on studying students, as well as on American samples. Exceptions to this trend are numerous. There are several examples of studies that have surveyed working samples, often using survey panel techniques, such as Mechanical Turk, which frequently yields a sample of workers from diverse occupations (e.g., Duffy et al., 2013). There also is no shortage of other studies that have recruited working samples from specific organizations from countries around the world (e.g., Steger et al., 2013), and some of those studies have been explicitly cross-cultural, comparing results with an eye to how nation of origin may moderate people's experiences (e.g., Douglass et al., 2016). The hope is that as meaningful work gains credibility and appeal, there will be expanded opportunities for using more sophisticated research methods in a wider range of working samples around the world.

Predictors of meaningful work

Predictors of meaningful work can be separated into three categories: individual-level predictors, interpersonal predictors, and workplace characteristic predictors. However, it should first be noted that most research on meaningful work has been correlational, so it is not generally possible to determine whether many of the variables that have been linked to meaningful work are predictors, benefits, or simply related variables. General correlates of meaningful work and calling were reviewed in the previous section. This section focuses on the minority of studies that generate plausible information about predictors and benefits of meaningful work.

Individual-level predictors of meaningful work The most commonly researched type of predictor for meaningful work seems to be individual-level variables, such as personality traits or other workplace variables (e.g., job satisfaction). Although they cannot unambiguously demonstrate causality, longitudinal studies suggest relationships between meaningful work and other variables across time. If early measures of some variables predict later meaningful work, but early meaningful work measures do not predict later variables, then it is not tenable to assert that meaningful work exerts causal influence over those other variables. In one example of this work, researchers assessed medical students twice in a two-year span, finding that changes in both meaning in life and vocational development predicted later changes in whether students felt they were living a calling, with no evidence supporting the reverse path (Duffy, Manuel, Borges, & Bott, 2014).

Some variables are thought to be predictors by their nature. A prime example is character strengths. Character strengths are theorized to be particular aspects of the self that are socially laudable, and generate positive experiences in the self and others when they are used. They are thought to be present from an early age, so they should precede meaningful work in development. Studies have found positive correlations between the degree to which people endorse their character strengths and the level of meaningful work they experience (Littman-Ovadia & Steger, 2010). There is no existing theoretical explanation for how meaningful work might create strengths, so logic suggests that cultivating strengths may be a way to facilitate meaningful work.

Studies also have shown that people who actually use their strengths in their work are more likely to view their work as meaningful (Hartzer & Ruch, 2012; Littman-Ovadia & Steger, 2010). Because one may use or stop using strengths on a daily, or even hourly, basis, there is less of a theoretical rationale for suggesting that strengths use creates meaningful work in favor of arguments that finding meaningful work encourages people to use their strengths. However, because of the flexibility of strengths use, this may be an important facet of programs designed to encourage meaningful work.

Interpersonal predictors of meaningful work There is very little research on interpersonal predictors of meaningful work, despite the importance of the social context to work experiences. Qualitative research on people who mentor others found that work becomes more meaningful for them because of their mentoring (Kennet & Lomas, 2015). Although the workers who were interviewed reported that mentoring was a way for them to obtain more meaning in their work, it is still possible that people who engage in mentoring (at least voluntarily) are precisely those who already find work to be meaningful. Despite the fact that research has not established causality in any way, mentoring is included as a potential predictor only because establishing a mentoring program is a potentially easy and concrete method that could be used to increase meaningful work.

Workplace characteristic predictors of meaningful work Perhaps the most logical place to start looking for workplace characteristic predictors of meaningful work is in the performance of leaders in organizations. A leader's behavior can have wide-ranging implications for employee performance, and set the tone for how workplaces function. Leadership provides an irresistible lever for models of how to foster meaningful work because of the potential to improve the working experience for multiple workers at a time through interventions with a much smaller number of leaders. There have not been any studies of the link between leadership and meaningful work that are able to speak directly to causality. Because of this it is perhaps not fully prudent to categorize leadership as a predictor of meaningful work simply because of assumptions that influence flows from leader to follower rather than from follower to leader. In the absence of more rigorous research methods, it is impossible to rule out alternative explanations, however. For example, people who view their work as more meaningful might be influenced by their meaningful work to view leaders through rose-colored glasses and transfer their positive feelings about work to leaders, whether the leaders have earned it or not. It is also possible that people engaged in meaningful work elicit better working relationships with their leaders because of the high value that those engaged in meaningful work bring to the workplace through increased commitment, enjoyment, engagement, effort, performance, and social contribution. There is reason to be cautious, therefore, in assuming that leadership automatically influences meaningful work.

With caveats in place, there is evidence that leadership and meaningful work are related. Because of the passion, authenticity, energy, and vision-setting emphasized in transformative leadership, it is expected that employees working for a transformational leader would connect those qualities with perceiving work to be worthwhile and to be rich in purpose.

Indeed, leaders who are more aligned with transformational leadership approaches have employees who find their work to be more meaningful (Judge & Piccolo, 2004). The provision of paths to meaningful work might be considered to be an important function of the best leaders, and their organizations may then harvest the benefits of having their employees engaged in meaningful work (Steger & Dik, 2010).

Beyond traditional leadership skills, helping employees feel supported also appears to help employees to find meaningful work. High-quality relations with one's supervisor include feeling supported, as well as feeling understood, cared for, and having mutually trusting working relationships. Such high-quality leadership relations are positively correlated with meaningful work (Tummers & Knies, 2013). Support from one's supervisor, as well as greater control over one's job, are both positively correlated with meaningful work. This research was correlational, so the possibility cannot be ruled out that people engaged in meaningful work are more likely to earn supervisor support and be given more control over their jobs. Nonetheless, both of these resources seem like compelling targets for improving the chances that employees will experience more meaningful work due to the fact that they are aspects of job design, which can be modified at the organizational level, rather than relying on individual workers enacting changes. This suggestion is bolstered by a longitudinal study among elder care workers that showed how active involvement of middle managers toward improving teamwork led to more positive perceptions of working conditions, a variable which included meaningful work in this study (Nielsen & Randall, 2009). Improvements in working conditions were further related to improvements in job satisfaction and well-being.

Finally, it appears important to meaningful work that organizations support the higher ideals of employees. People who volunteer are more likely to feel their work is meaningful, even if volunteering is completely separate from their job (Rodell, 2013). However, this does not mean that organizations should not encourage employees to volunteer. Actively supporting employees in their volunteering may be an important way for organizations to foster meaningful work not only because doing so clearly communicates an appreciation of something of importance to employees, but also because it communicates that the organization is willing to support actions that benefit the greater good, which is an important part of meaningful work. Supporting this claim is research showing that awareness of corporate social responsibility activities among employees is positively linked to their sense of meaningful work (labeled "task significance" but measured with items very similar to those on meaningful work questionnaires; Raub & Blunschi, 2014).

Despite the absence of large numbers of studies that have used research methods designed to shed light on causality, we might be able to extrapolate from existing longitudinal research and from correlational research focused on variables that are more or less out of the control of individual employees to form ideas about predictors of meaningful work. Fostering meaning in life, vocational identity, and the capacity to understand and use one's character strengths seem promising as predictors of meaningful work. Working in an organization led by a transformational leader who provides vision and support to employees, and provides opportunities for them to volunteer toward meaningful causes, also seems likely to predict meaningful work. As research continues to progress, we hope to gather more robust evidence about predictors, as well as become better at understanding how fostering meaningful work benefits individuals, organizations, and communities.

Benefits of meaningful work

In exploring the potential benefits of meaningful work, it is helpful to ask what kinds of benefits we should expect to see. According to the JCM, meaningful work helps produce high intrinsic work motivation, high job satisfaction, high-quality performance, and low levels of absenteeism and turnover. All of these relationships have been found within correlational research designs. However, more powerful causal research methods have not been widely deployed in the study of meaningful work to date. As has been the case with understanding the predictors of meaningful work, longitudinal research methods are the most common ones used to test thoughts about causality. Several studies have found that changes in meaningful work precede changes in job satisfaction and well-being, suggesting that these are potential benefits of meaningful work (Nielsen & Randall, 2009). One of the clearest benefits of meaningful work is reduced absenteeism. One study found that people with greater meaningful work were absent form work less often than others over a three-month span following initial assessment (Soane et al., 2013). Not only are those with meaningful work more physically present at work, they are also more psychologically, emotionally, and behaviorally present at work. Longitudinal research suggests that improving meaningful work benefits employees' engagement at work (Nakamura & Otsuka, 2013). Meaningful work also longitudinally predicted both job satisfaction and career commitment over 3- and 6-month time periods (Duffy, Allan, et al., 2014). Further, meaningful work and calling appear to foster a sense of perseverance, leading people to disregard negative career advice that contradicts their interest in following their calling (Dobrow & Heller, 2015). Of course, not all advice to quit a particular career is "bad" advice. Not everyone is cut out for success in a field just because they are passionate about it, and sometimes people's commitment to their calling can leave them exposed to potential exploitation (Bunderson & Thompson, 2009).

Thus, meaningful work provides benefits to employees both at work and in their broader lives. They are more committed, persistent, engaged, and satisfied at work, and enjoy greater well-being in life as a whole. To the degree that having happy and committed workers expending substantial effort in an organization is appealing to leaders and managers, then meaningful work warrants inclusion on the shortlist of any organization's programming.

Aside from the benefits to workers, however, there is some evidence that meaningful work provides a solid foundation for a better life. Perhaps the benefits of meaningful work also can be shown by what happens to people when they are unable to follow their desired path to meaningful work. One qualitative study focused on 31 people who said they were unable to follow their calling, whether because they chose another less fulfilling career path or because they followed one calling only to realize they had more than one. These people expressed regret that they missed their callings (Berg, Grant, & Johnson, 2010).

Fostering Meaningful Work

As employees and workplaces become increasingly sophisticated, they are likely to see advantages in transcending simplistic and mechanistic transactional approaches for retaining and motivating talent. It should be apparent that the root problem with simple transactional approaches to incentivizing workers to work harder and to stay with organizations longer is that it is easy for multiple marketplace entities to compete on salary and benefit terms. If the primary incentive a company is offering to a worker to work hard and stay with the company is monetary, then what is to prevent the worker from taking a better deal elsewhere? As both physical and virtual mobility of the workforce increases, companies need to offer more profound reasons for their best talent to stay. A further consideration is that employees appear to be seeking meaningful work, and may expect their employers to be able to provide it (Šverko & Vizek-Vidović, 1995). Of course, the hope of this chapter is that meaningful work is considered as an important cornerstone of talent retention, organizational optimization, and employee well-being. Workers themselves appear to be looking for meaningful work. The importance of meaningful work to workers is that many of them avow that finding meaning in one's work is as important as level of pay and job security (O'Brien, 1992). In fact, a more recent survey among the international workforce of temporary worker company Kelly Services found that a slight majority of their employees would choose a pay cut in order to have more meaningful work (Kelly Services, 2010).

This chapter has reviewed the theory, assessment, correlates, predictors, and benefits of meaningful work. In this section, efforts are made to pull together the many threads of meaningful work into a useful framework for fostering it within organizations. I have found it helpful to organize the theoretical and empirical predictors of meaningful work into two models. The first is the SPIRE model, which incorporates the most important personal-level predictors and correlates of meaningful work. The second is the CARMA model, which incorporates the most important leadership and organizational-level predictors and correlates of meaningful work. Figure 5.2 illustrates both models, along with brief descriptions of each of the components of SPIRE and CARMA.

Much of the meaningful work and calling literature has focused on providing motivation and inspiration to employees to craft more meaningful work for themselves (Berg, Dutton, & Wrzesniewski, 2013). I use the SPIRE model to focus on potentially important levers for building meaningful work: Strengths, Personalization, Integration, Resonance, and Expansion.

SPIRE Finding pathways to more meaningful work			CARMA Fostering meaningful work for your employees and followers		
S	Strengths	Know your unique strengths and talents, and use them in executing your work, even if that means going above and beyond your basic job duties	C	Clarity	Organizations need a vision and mission to be clearly shared across all levels, if a company lacks purpose, its workers might follow suit
P	Personalization	Bring more of yourself to work, align work with your values, take responsibility and adopt an ownership mentality for your work and your organization	A	Authenticity	Organizations must follow their own mission, leaders must behave ethically and honestly; phony purpose and exploitation kill meaning
I	Integration	Integrate the motivation of and execution of your job with other elements of your life, work in ways that bring meaning to the rest of your life	R	Respect	Building positive, effective relationships in an organization begins with leadership modeling respect and creating chances for beneficial interactions
R	Resonance	Learn your organization's core values and mission, find ways in which it resonates with your personal mission and meaning through your everyday work	M	Mattering	Leadership must convey to each worker exactly how their contribution is vital to the success and health of the organization and its mission
E	Expansion	Seek ways in which your work can be grown to benefit some greater good, expand your concerns to embrace broader interests beyond your self	A	Autonomy	Allow followers increased self-expression by providing opportunities for self-direction, trial and error, innovation, and idea interchange

Figure 5.2 One way of organizing theory and research on developing meaningful work at the personal and at the organizational/leadership level. The SPIRE model presents the most important theoretical and empirical predictors of meaningful work that individual workers are likely to have the ability to influence. The CARMA model presents the most important theoretical and empirical predictors of meaningful work that can be distributed organization-wide to increase the likelihood that workers and followers experience work at the organization to be meaningful. *Source*: Author.

As was reviewed above, recognizing one's personal and character strengths, and then finding opportunities to use them in the workplace has been related to perceiving greater meaning in one's work (e.g., Littman-Ovadia & Steger, 2010). Strengths reminds workers of the potential benefits of finding ways to actively and frequently use their strengths in their work.

Personalization refers to the relationship between meaningful work and both work centrality and organizational citizenship behavior, as well as the theorized importance of finding work that is personally expressive (e.g., Dik, Eldridge, et al., 2012; Dobrow & Tosti-Kharas, 2011; Steger et al., 2012; Wrzesniewski et al., 1997). Through personalization, people are encouraged to gain clarity regarding their values and to bring more of themselves to the kinds of work that are consistent with those values.

Integration builds on research showing reciprocal relationships over time between the meaning people find at work and the meaning they find in the rest of their lives (e.g., Duffy, Allan, et al., 2014; Steger & Dik, 2009). As meaning in life is thought to express in part a person's values (e.g., Steger, 2009), integration points to the potential importance of engaging in values-congruent activities while at work, both in terms of the actual tasks required and in terms of the overall values of the organization (Hoffman, Bynum, Piccolo, & Sutton, 2011). Work, then, can become an important path to meaning in life (e.g., Allan, Duffy, & Douglass, 2015; Steger & Dik, 2009).

Resonance builds on research showing that leaders who can express a vision and purpose for an organization make it easier for workers to find meaning in their efforts (Judge & Piccolo, 2004). Theoretically, being able to find similarities between one's own personal missions and purposes and those of one's employer should help workers feel more motivated to support organizational missions, and should help workers feel that their work makes their lives better overall by supporting their meaning in life (Nielsen & Randall, 2009; Steger et al., 2012).

Expansion builds on research and theory pointing to the importance of viewing one's work as benefitting others (e.g., Dik, Eldridge, et al., 2012; Grant, 2007; Steger et al., 2012). Longstanding theory (e.g., Dik et al., 2012) and psychometric factor analyses (e.g., Steger et al., 2012) demonstrate that the desire to serve some greater good or benefit others through one's effort is central to meaningful work. Through expansion, people are reminded that one path to meaningful work appears to be to transcend the demands and dynamics of the moment and of one's career ambitions to incorporate ways in which work can also be fashioned to help others.

The CARMA model was developed to light-heartedly remind managers, leaders, and their organizations that, as with properly spelled *karma*, we reap what we sow. If leaders can invest in making it easier for their followers to experience meaningful work, then they may reap the benefits. CARMA focuses on Clarity, Authenticity, Respect, Mattering, and Autonomy.

Clarity is in some ways the mirror image of Resonance from the SPIRE model, and builds on a similar body of research on transformational leadership and other leadership models in which a leader's ability to provide a clear sense of mission and purpose are important tools for inspiring greater performance (e.g., Judge & Piccolo, 2004). Clarity calls attention to the importance not only of setting and communicating a clear organizational purpose, but also the importance of having an apt purpose for an organization. An excellent example of clarity comes from a recent tumble in the U.S. stock market. The CEO of Starbucks, Howard Schultz, sent out a company-wide email very different than the typical emails that are sent out after plummeting stock prices. The email included assurances of the company's growth, its innovation, and competitive products, as well as its positive social impact and the centrality of its employees.

However, there were no stale references to defending shareholder returns, market capitalization, or initiatives to expand its sales force in developing markets. Instead, both modeling and reflecting upon Starbucks' core customer service message, Schultz reminded his employees that many of their customers would come into the store feeling worried and stressed out, so everyone on the Starbucks team should try harder than ever to give them a comforting experience. Imagine the cynical response if the CEO of a company that has a lip-service mission that no one believes tried to send out a similar email. When the mission is authentic and leaders buy in, the impact of mission messaging can be profound.

Authenticity also shares in the research and theory on new leadership models, such as transformational and authentic leadership (e.g., Judge & Piccolo, 2004). If leaders want their workers to bring the depths of dedication, commitment, engagement, and performance that are associated with meaningful work, they cannot repay employee efforts with unethical behavior, cynical manipulations, and disingenuous relationships. Authenticity also asserts that if organizations want followers to buy into their mission statements, leaders should act in accordance with them as well. People engaged in meaningful work appear to bring the best of their personal selves to work, and leaders who want to foster meaningful work should expect to do the same.

Respect builds on literature showing that the social environment of a workplace is important to workers' satisfaction. Leaders and managers play an important role, particularly in setting a supportive tone for a workplace (e.g., Tummers & Knies, 2013). Other people may be among the most influential workplace elements for creating meaningful work (Pratt et al., 2013), and creating a culture where people have fun, work hard and positively, look out for each other, provide support, and engage in caretaking for the organization (e.g., Steger et al., 2012) should be modeled and demonstrated by leaders interacting respectfully (e.g., Leape et al., 2012).

Mattering builds on JCM research and on the core theoretical aspect of meaningful work that job tasks must have a point within an organization, and should lead to recognizable and valued organizational outputs (e.g., Hackman & Oldham, 1976; Steger et al., 2012). Let's be honest, if an organization cannot express in no uncertain terms why a worker's efforts are important to the organization and how they contribute to a valued outcome, then how can we hope that a worker will discover such matters on her or his own? After all, the organization created the position and dedicated resources to it. To provide a sense of mattering to employees, organizations, and particularly leaders, managers, and supervisors, must take responsibility not only to outline what must be done and how it must be done, but also why it is valuable to everyone in the organization that it is being done.

Autonomy builds on extensive research on well-being (e.g., Ryan & Deci, 2001) and the theoretical importance of an employee being given enough authority and freedom to use strengths, engage in mentoring, and many other individualizations of their jobs that enable personalization of work (e.g., Littman-Ovadia & Steger, 2010; Rodell, 2013). There is risk inherent in granting autonomy to employees. Variations in job execution will emerge, and sometimes those variations will be to the detriment of performance. However, decentralization of responsibility for solving problems and improving organizational performance is a potentially rich source of ongoing innovation. Myriad opportunities for honing how tasks are executed exist within an organization, and the people who are directly encountering those tasks in their daily work are uniquely suited to experimenting with potential improvements. Autonomy is key for enabling employees to connect with their work, make the job their own, and take ownership over innovation and problem solving.

SPIRE and CARMA are intended to work together, and, on the one hand, they are structured to show leaders and organizations what they need to do (CARMA) to provide the seeds of meaningful work (SPIRE). On the other hand, they can be used to give prospective talent a lens (SPIRE) for evaluating whether an organization is capable of fostering meaningful work for them (CARMA). I suspect that opportunities for meaningful work will become a central evaluative tool that the best talent uses to consider job offers, as well as competing offers to leave a company. SPIRE and CARMA may help organizations become better recruiters for the best talent of the future.

Future Research

As the previous reviews of meaningful work assessment, and research on correlates, predictors, and benefits of meaningful work demonstrate, there is a great amount of potential for meaningful work to improve working, both for organizations and for individuals. However, as the review also showed, there are significant gaps in our knowledge of this important variable. Future research should prioritize three key areas. First, at the most fundamental level, most of what we know about meaningful work comes from research conducted in Europe and North America. Although far from perfect, these regions have mature, stable economies operating within democracies that provide employment for the vast majority of their people. Meaningful work is an important part of the picture in such economies for at least two reasons. Mature economies must invest in indirect, psychological means to motivate workers because coercive and exploitative labor practices are curtailed, and workers are usually educated, have access to information about working conditions and compensation, and can use residential mobility to access a wider employer base. In other words, it is generally true that workers in these regions normally cannot be abused and exploited indefinitely and the best of workers can be highly selective in choosing their employers. It is quite a bit less clear whether meaningful work is equally important to workers from countries with developing economies, high levels of unemployment, uneven labor rights, and less democratic governance. It is also unclear whether meaningful work is a similar concept with similar importance outside of North America and Europe. As one compelling example of what the future may hold for meaningful work research, scholars have increasingly incorporated meaningful work in research conducted South Africa, a country facing challenges around both education and raising employment levels (e.g., Rothmann, this volume; Van Zyl, Deacon, & Rothmann, 2010).

The second area of focus for future research should be on increasing the use of longitudinal and experimental research designs. The primary knowledge we have about meaningful work is that the best workers report that their work is meaningful. We are able to go beyond those statements to suggesting that meaningful work is fostered by certain characteristics and creates other benefits when we trace the development and impact of meaningful work over time. Following the reciprocal dynamics of meaningful work over time is not the only way in which the causal power of meaningful work can be tested. Experiments that pull the levers of meaningful work can also be used to assess how increasing or decreasing the meaningfulness of work aids or hamstrings work performance, productivity, and happiness. Such experiments do not always need to be conducted in organizations. For example, participants could be brought into a psychology lab to perform tasks under two conditions; the first would be a control condition in which instructions are given and nothing more, the second would be an experimental condition in which instructions are given alongside an explanation of how completing this task will help another group perform their work and will also benefit the greater good in some way. Comparisons then would be made in terms of performance, productivity, group dynamics, and participant happiness to see if adding qualities of meaningful work leads to benefits.

Although lab experiments can shed light on the essential promise of meaningful work, real-world research within active organizations is ultimately where the field needs to develop. Thus, the third area of focus for future research should be on building strong partnerships with organizations to enable the development and testing of meaningful work programs. Other partnerships should be created as well, especially between researchers and practitioners. Such partnerships would enable strategies and interventions executed by practitioners to inform future research, and allow the broader dissemination among practitioners of best practices as tested by researchers.

Conclusion

Building on a long tradition, recent years have been particularly exciting ones for meaningful work, with accelerating publication of research reports detailing the many desirable characteristics and outcomes linked to meaningful work. Certainly, more can be done to better understand the benefits of meaningful work and how to foster it on individual and organizational levels. As matters stand, we know quite a lot about the importance of meaningful work to individual and organizational health. Meaningful work is tied to greater personal well-being and meaning in life, more satisfaction and happiness at work, stronger work commitment and engagement, more positive social participation and mentoring, more conscientious caretaking and citizenship behavior, higher performance and more effective teams, and an investment by workers in the broader society that provides the homes for their organizations. Given the progress achieved already, there are compelling reasons to be enthusiastic about the potential for meaningful work to deliver value across multiple levels, encompassing the well-being of employees, the performance of organizations, and the health of communities and societies.

References

Allan, B. A., Duffy, R. D., & Douglass, R. (2015). Meaning in life and work: A developmental perspective. *The Journal of Positive Psychology*, *10*, 323–331.

Arnold, K. A., Turner, N., Barling, J., Kelloway, E. K., & McKee, M. C. (2007). Transformational leadership and psychological well-being: The mediating role of meaningful work. *Journal of Occupational Health Psychology*, *12*, 193–203.

Ashmos, D. P., & Duchon, D. (2000). Spirituality at work: A conceptualization and measure. *Journal of Management Inquiry*, *9*, 134–145.

Bellah, R. N., Madsen, R., Sullivan, W. M., Swidler, A., & Tipton, S. M. (1985). *Habits of the heart: Individualism and commitment in American life*. New York, NY: Harper & Row.

Berg, J., Dutton, J. E., & Wrzesniewski, A. (2013). Job crafting and meaningful work. In B. J. Dik, Z. S. Byrne, & M. F. Steger (Eds.), *Purpose and meaning in the workplace* (pp. 81–104). Washington, DC: APA Books.

Berg, J. M., Grant, A. M., & Johnson, V. (2010). When callings are calling: Crafting work and leisure in pursuit of unanswered occupational callings. *Organization Science*, *21*, 973–994.

Bunderson, J. S., & Thompson, J. A. (2009). The call of the wild: Zookeepers, callings, and the dual edges of deeply meaningful work. *Administrative Science Quarterly*, *54*, 32–57.

Creed, P. A., Rogers, M. E., Praskova, A., & Searle, J. (2014). Career calling as a personal resource moderator between environmental demands and burnout in Australian junior doctors. *Journal of Career Development*, *41*, 547–561.

Dik, B. J., Byrne, Z. S., & Steger, M. F. (2013). *Purpose and meaning in the workplace*. Washington, DC: APA Books.
Dik, B. J., & Duffy, R. D. (2009). Calling and vocation at work: Definitions and prospects for research and practice. *The Counseling Psychologist*, *37*, 424–450.
Dik, B. J., Duffy, R. D., & Steger, M. F. (2012). Enhancing social justice by promoting prosocial values in career development interventions. *Counseling and Values*, *57*, 31–37.
Dik, B. J., Eldridge, B. M., Steger, M. F., & Duffy, R. D. (2012). Development and validation of the Calling and Vocation Questionnaire (CVQ). *Journal of Career Assessment*, *20*, 242–263.
Dik, B. J., Sargent, A. M., & Steger, M. F. (2008). Career development strivings: Assessing goals and motivation in career decision-making and planning. *Journal of Career Development*, *35*, 23–41.
Dik, B. J., & Steger, M. F. (2008). Randomized trial of a calling-infused career workshop incorporating counselor self-disclosure. *Journal of Vocational Behavior*, *73*, 203–211.
Dobrow, S. R., & Tosti-Kharas, J. (2011). Calling: The development of a scale measure. *Personnel Psychology*, *64*, 1001–1049.
Dobrow Riza, S., & Heller, D. (2015). Follow your heart or your head? A longitudinal study of the facilitating role of calling and ability in the pursuit of a challenging career. *Journal of Applied Psychology*, *100*, 695–712.
Domene, J. F. (2012). Calling and career outcome expectations: The mediating role of self-efficacy. *Journal of Career Assessment*, *20*, 281–292.
Douglass, R. P., Duffy, R. D., & Autin, K. L. (2016). Living a calling, nationality, and life satisfaction: A moderated, multiple mediator model. *Journal of Career Assessment*, *24*, 253–269.
Duffy, R. D., Allan, B. A., Autin, K. L., & Bott, E. M. (2013). Calling and life satisfaction: It's not about having it, it's about living it. *Journal of Counseling Psychology*, *60*, 42–52.
Duffy, R. D., Allan, B. A, Autin, K. L., & Douglass, R. P. (2014). Living a calling and work well-being: A longitudinal study. *Journal of Counseling Psychology*, *61*, 605–615.
Duffy, R. D., & Autin, K. L. (2013). Disentangling the link between perceiving a calling and living a calling. *Journal of Counseling Psychology*, *60*, 219–227.
Duffy, R. D., Autin, K. L., Allan, B. A., & Douglass, R. P., (2015). Assessing work as a calling: An evaluation of instruments and practice recommendations. *Journal of Career Assessment*, *23*, 351–366.
Duffy, R. D., Dik, B. J., & Steger, M. F. (2011). Calling and work-related outcomes: Career commitment as a mediator. *Journal of Vocational Behavior*, *78*, 863–868.
Duffy, R. D., Manuel, R. S., Borges, N. J., & Bott, E. M. (2014). Calling, vocational development, and well being: A longitudinal study of medical students. *Journal of Vocational Behavior*, *79*, 361–366.
Duffy, R. D., & Sedlacek, W. E. (2007). The presence of and search for a calling: Connections to career development. *Journal of Vocational Behavior*, *70*, 590–601.
Durkheim, Emile (1897/1951). *Suicide: A study in sociology*. Glencoe, IL: The Free Press.
Fairlee, P. (2011). Meaningful work, employee engagement, and other key employee outcomes: Implications for human resource development. *Advances in Developing Human Resources*, *13*, 508–525.
Goetzel, R. Z., & Ozminkowski, R. J. (2008). The health and cost benefits of work site health-promotion programs. *Annual Review of Public Health*, *29*, 303–323.
Grant, A. M. (2007). Relational job design and the motivation to make a prosocial difference. *Academy of Management Review*, *32*, 393–417.
Hackman, J. R., & Oldham, G. R. (1975). Development of the Job Design Survey. *Journal of Applied Psychology*, *60*, 159–170.
Hackman, J. R., & Oldham, G. R. (1976). Motivation through the design of work: Test of a theory. *Organization Behavior and Human Decision Processes*, *16*, 250–279.
Hagmaier, T., & Abele, A. E. (2012). The multidimensionality of calling: Conceptualization, measurement and a bicultural perspective. *Journal of Vocational Behavior*, *81*, 39–51.
Hall, D. T., & Chandler, D. E. (2005). Psychological success: When the career is a calling. *Journal of Organizational Behavior*, *26*, 155–176.
Hall, M., Oates, K. L., Anderson, T. L., & Willingham, M. M. (2012). Calling and conflict: The sanctification of work in working mothers. *Psychology of Religion and Spirituality*, *4*, 71.

Harpaz, I., & Fu., X. (2002). The structure of the meaning of work: A relative stability amidst change. *Human Relations, 55*, 639–667.

Hartzer, C., & Ruch, W. (2012). When the job is a calling: The role of applying one's signature strengths at work. *The Journal of Positive Psychology, 7*, 362–371.

Hoffman, B. J., Bynum, B. H., Piccolo, R. F., & Sutton, A. W. (2011). Person–organization value congruence: How transformational leaders influence work group effectiveness. *Academy of Management Journal, 54*, 779–796.

Judge, T. A., & Piccolo, R. F. (2004). Transformational and transactional leadership: A meta-analytic test of their relative validity. *Journal of Applied Psychology, 89*, 755–768.

Kamdron, T. (2005). Work motivation and job satisfaction of Estonian higher officials. *International Journal of Public Administration, 28*(13/14), 1211–1240. doi:10.1080/01900690500241085

Kelly Services (2010). *Kelly global workforce report 2009*. Retrieved June 18, 2010 from https://issuu.com/michaelkirsten/docs/kelly_global_workforce_index_2009

Kennet, P., & Lomas, T. (2015). Making meaning through mentoring: Mentors finding fulfilment at work through self-determination and self-reflection. *International Journal of Evidence Based Coaching and Mentoring, 13*, 29–44.

Leape, L. L., Shore, M. F., Dienstag, J. L., Mayer, R. J., Edgman-Levitan, S., Meyer, G. S., & Healy, G. B. (2012). Perspective: A culture of respect, Part 2: Creating a culture of respect. *Academic Medicine, 87*, 853–858.

Lips-Wiersma, M., & Wright, S. (2012). Measuring the meaning of meaningful work: Development and validation of the Comprehensive Meaningful Work Scale (CMWS). *Group and Organization Management, 37*, 655–685.

Littman-Ovadia, H., & Steger, M. F. (2010). Character strengths and well-being among volunteers and employees: Towards an integrative model. *Journal of Positive Psychology, 5*, 419–430.

Lobene, E. V., & Meade, A. W. (2013). The effects of career calling and perceived overqualification on work outcomes for primary and secondary school teachers. *Journal of Career Development, 40*, 508–530.

May, D. R., Gilson, R. L., & Harter, L. M. (2004). The psychological conditions of meaningfulness, safety and availability and the engagement of the human spirit at work. *Journal of Occupational and Organizational Psychology, 77*, 11–37.

Nakamura, S., & Otsuka, Y. (2013). Job resources enhance work engagement through positive affect and meaningful work among Japanese employees. In F. Saraccino (Ed.), *The happiness compass* (pp. 141–151). Hauppage, NY: Nova Science Publishers.

Nielsen, K., & Randall, R. (2009). Managers' active support when implementing teams: The impact on employee well-being. *Applied Psychology: Health and Well-Being, 1*, 374–390.

Nord, W. R., Brief, A. P., Atieh, J. M., & Doherty, E. M. (1990). Studying meanings of work: The case of work values. In A. Brief & W. Nord (Eds.), *Meanings of occupational work: A collection of essays* (pp. 21–64). Lexington, MA: Lexington Books.

O'Brien, G. E. (1992). Changing meanings of work. In J. F. Hartley & G. M. Stephenson (Eds.), *Employment relations: The psychology of influence and control at work* (pp. 44–66). Oxford, UK: Blackwell.

Pratt, M. G., Pradies, C., & Lepisto, D. A. (2013). Doing well, doing good, and doing with: Organizational practices for effectively cultivating meaningful work. In B. J. Dik, Z. S. Byrne, & M. F. Steger (Eds.), *Purpose and meaning in the workplace* (pp. 173–196). Washington, DC: American Psychological Association.

Rath, T., & Harter, J. (2010). *The economics of wellbeing*. Washington, DC: Gallup Press.

Raub, S., & Blunschi, S. (2014). The power of meaningful work: How awareness of CSR initiatives fosters task significance and positive work outcomes in service employees. *Cornel Hospitality Quarterly, 55*, 10–18.

Rawat, A., & Nadavulakere, S. (2015). Examining the outcomes of having a calling: Does context matter? *Journal of Business Psychology, 30*, 499–512.

Reker, G. T., Peacock, E. J., & Wong, P. T. P. (1987). Meaning and purpose in life and well-being: A life-span perspective. *Journal of Gerontology, 42*, 44.

Rodell, J. B. (2013). Finding meaning through volunteering: Why do employees volunteer and what does it mean for their jobs? *Academy of Management Journal, 56*, 1274–1294.

Rosso, B. D., Dekas, K. H., & Wrzesniewski, A. (2010). On the meaning of work: A theoretical integration and review. *Research in Organizational Behavior, 30*, 91–127.

Ryan, R. M., & Deci, E. L. (2001). On happiness and human potentials: A review of research on hedonic and eudaimonic well-being. *Annual Review of Psychology, 52*, 141–166.

Schnell, T. (2009). The Sources of Meaning and Meaning in Life Questionnaire (SoMe): Relations to demographics and well-being. *Journal of Positive Psychology, 4*, 483–499.

Shin, J. Y., Steger, M. F., & Lee, K. (2014). Major incongruence and career development among American and South Korean college students. *Journal of Career Assessment, 22*, 433–450.

Soane, E., Shantz, A., Alfes, K., Truss, C., Rees, C., & Gatenby, M. (2013). The association of meaningfulness, well-being, and engagement with absenteeism: A moderated mediation model. *Human Resource Management, 52*, 441–456.

Sparks, J. R., & Schenk, J. A. (2001). Explaining the effects of transformational leadership: An investigation of the effects of higher-order motives in multilevel marketing organizations. *Journal of Organizational Behavior, 22*, 849–869. doi:10.1002/job.116

Steger, M. F. (2009). Meaning in life. In S. J. Lopez (Ed.), *Oxford handbook of positive psychology* (2nd ed., pp. 679–687). Oxford, UK: Oxford University Press.

Steger, M. F. (2012a). Experiencing meaning in life: Optimal functioning at the nexus of spirituality, psychopathology, and well-being. In P. T. P. Wong (Ed.), *The human quest for meaning* (2nd ed. pp. 165–184). New York, NY: Routledge.

Steger, M. F. (2012b). Making meaning in life. *Psychological Inquiry, 23*, 381–385.

Steger, M. F., & Dik, B. J. (2009). If one is searching for meaning in life, does meaning in work help? *Applied Psychology: Health and Well-Being, 1*, 303–320.

Steger, M. F., & Dik, B. J. (2010). Work as meaning. In P. A. Linley, S. Harrington, & N. Page, (Eds.), *Oxford handbook of positive psychology and work* (pp. 131–142). Oxford, UK: Oxford University Press.

Steger, M. F., Dik, B. J., & Duffy, R. D. (2012). Measuring meaningful work: The Work and Meaning Inventory (WAMI). *Journal of Career Assessment, 20*, 322–337.

Steger, M. F., Dik, B. J., & Shim, Y. (in press). Assessing meaning and satisfaction at work. In S. J. Lopez (Ed.), *The Oxford handbook of positive psychology assessment* (2nd ed.). Oxford, UK. Oxford University Press.

Steger, M. F., Kashdan, T. B., & Oishi, S. (2008). Being good by doing good: Eudaimonic activity and daily well-being correlates, mediators, and temporal relations. *Journal of Research in Personality, 42*, 22–42.

Steger, M. F., Littman-Ovadia, H., Miller, M., Menger, L., & Rothmann, S. (2013). Affective disposition, meaningful work, and work-engagement. *Journal of Career Assessment, 21*, 348–361.

Steger, M. F., Pickering, N. K., Shin, J. Y., & Dik, B. J. (2010). Calling in work: Secular or sacred? *Journal of Career Assessment, 18*, 82–96.

Šverko, B., & Vizek-Vidović, V. (1995). Studies of the meaning of work: Approaches, models, and some of the findings. In D. E. Super & B. Šverko (Eds.), *Life roles, values, and careers* (pp. 3– 21). San Francisco, CA: Jossey-Bass.

Torrey, C. L., & Duffy, R. D. (2012). Calling and well-being among adults: Differential relations by employment status. *Journal of Career Assessment, 20*, 415–425.

Tummers, L. G., & Knies, E. (2013). Leadership and meaningful work in the public sector. *Public Administrative Review, 73*, 859–866.

Van Zyl, L. E., Deacon, E., & Rothmann, S. (2010). Towards happiness: Experiences of work-role fit, meaningfulness and work engagement of industrial/organisational psychologists in South Africa. *SA Journal of Industrial Psychology, 36*, 1–10.

Wrzesniewski, A., McCauley, C. R., Rozin, P., & Schwartz, B. (1997). Jobs, careers, and callings: People's relations to their work. *Journal of Research in Personality, 31*, 21–33.

6

Optimal Motivation at Work

Christopher P. Niemiec and Gordon B. Spence

Introduction

Work is an integral part of the lives of most adults. Indeed, work-related activities occupy a substantial portion (from 25% to 33%; Harter, Schmidt, & Keyes, 2003) of employees' waking hours (U.S. Bureau of Labor Statistics, 2015) and facilitate the establishment and development of a personal identity (Doherty, 2009). As the nature of work has shifted toward an emphasis on psychological demands (rather than physical demands; Lundberg & Cooper, 2011), a burgeoning corpus of empirical evidence suggests that a variety of social-contextual factors exert influence on employees' health and functioning on the job (Schaufeli, Bakker, & Van Rhenen, 2009). At work, some employees have opportunities to pursue tasks that are self-endorsed and valued, to cultivate capabilities and strive for mastery, and to develop mutually supportive connections with important others. Yet other employees have experiences of pressure and coercion, inability, and disconnection from their supervisors, their co-workers, and their jobs. Highlighting the important impact that social-contextual factors have on employees' performance and wellness on the job, research has shown that the former set of affordances tends to be associated with health and functioning among employees, whereas the latter set of experiences tends to be associated with stress, somatic symptom burden, emotional exhaustion, turnover intention, and absenteeism (Gagné & Deci, 2005; Olafsen, Niemiec, Halvari, Deci, & Williams, 2015; Van den Broeck, Vansteenkiste, De Witte, Soenens, & Lens, 2010; Williams et al., 2014).

In this chapter, we apply self-determination theory to a discussion of optimal motivation in the workplace. From the perspective of self-determination theory, optimal motivation involves the organization, initiation, and direction of behavior through reflection on and coherence with abiding values and interests. To be sure, the proactive tendencies toward curiosity (Loewenstein, 1994), interest (Silvia, 2008), and coherence in knowledge and action (Ryan, 1995), which are so relevant to effective functioning among employees, are inherent in human nature (cf. Niemiec & Ryan, 2009).

The Wiley Blackwell Handbook of the Psychology of Positivity and Strengths-Based Approaches at Work,
First Edition. Edited by Lindsay G. Oades, Michael F. Steger, Antonella Delle Fave, and Jonathan Passmore.

Yet optimal motivation – marked by volition and self-regulation – is also likely to be facilitated by contextual support for satisfaction of basic psychological needs. To elucidate these ideas, this chapter is divided into five main sections. First, we discuss the metatheoretical and theoretical underpinnings of self-determination theory. Second, we review both theory and research on autonomous self-regulation as a form of optimal motivation in the workplace. Third, we review both theory and research on intrinsic life goals as a set of optimal aspirations in the workplace. Fourth, we reflect on how managerial support for basic psychological needs might facilitate autonomous self-regulation and the pursuit of intrinsic life goals among employees in the workplace. Fifth, we offer several directions for future research on optimal motivation in the workplace using the perspective of self-determination theory.

Metatheoretical and Theoretical Underpinnings of Self-Determination Theory

Self-determination theory (SDT; Deci & Ryan, 2000; Niemiec, Ryan, & Deci, 2010; Ryan & Deci, 2000b; Vansteenkiste, Niemiec, & Soenens, 2010) is a macro-theoretical approach to human motivation, emotion, and personality in social contexts that has direct applications in the workplace (Gagné & Deci, 2005). The philosophical starting point for SDT is its organismic-dialectic metatheory (Deci & Vansteenkiste, 2004; Ryan & Deci, 2002), which provides a set of assumptions about human nature that is used to guide subsequent theoretical development. In this view, humans are proactive organisms who seek out opportunities for choice, effectiveness, and connection with others, rather than passive organisms that are pushed around by contingencies of reinforcement in their environment. Thus, by nature, humans are oriented toward psychological and social integration (autonomy and homonomy, respectively; Angyal, 1965), yet they remain vulnerable to experiences of passivity and control, ineffectiveness, and alienation from others. In addition, humans are oriented toward differentiation and integration (Piaget, 1971), synthesis (Freud, 1923/1960), and realization of full potential (Rogers, 1963), yet they remain vulnerable to psychological fragmentation and disharmony that so typify burnout and other forms of non-optimal functioning in the workplace (Freudenberger, 1974). From the perspective of SDT, then, there exists a dialectic in which an inherent tendency toward full functioning and organismic wellness (cf. Niemiec & Ryan, 2013) stands in juxtaposition to social contexts that either support or thwart satisfaction of basic psychological needs.

The concept of basic psychological needs is a unifying principle within SDT. According to Deci and Ryan (2000, p. 229), basic psychological needs are defined as "innate psychological nutriments that are essential for ongoing psychological growth, integrity, and well-being." That is, satisfaction of the basic psychological needs for autonomy, competence, and relatedness is theorized to contribute to higher levels of psychological wellness, social integration, and physical health, as well as behavioral persistence and performance, across demographic categories, life domains, and cultures (Deci & Ryan, 2008). The need for autonomy (de Charms, 1968) refers to the experience of behavior as enacted with a sense of choice and personal endorsement, rather than heteronomy. The need for competence (White, 1959) refers to the experience of behavior as enacted with a sense of effectiveness and mastery, rather than inability. The need for relatedness (Baumeister & Leary, 1995; Ryan, 1995) refers to the experience of care for and support from important others, rather than disconnection.

As indicated above, SDT assumes that satisfaction of the basic psychological needs for autonomy, competence, and relatedness is a universal requirement for optimal functioning and wellness, although this perspective is not without critics (see Jordan, 1997; Markus & Kitayama, 2003; Stephens, Markus, & Townsend, 2007). To be sure, research conducted within SDT over the last 40 years has shown that need satisfaction confers functional benefits for all individuals, regardless of gender, age, social class, culture, or ambient values. Need satisfaction is associated with higher levels of psychological wellness, social integration, and/or physical health among men and women (Ryan, La Guardia, Solky-Butzel, Chirkov, & Kim, 2005); across the lifespan in infancy (Bernier, Carlson, & Whipple, 2010), in adolescence (Curran, Hill, & Niemiec, 2013), in young adulthood (Niemiec, Ryan, & Deci, 2009; Sheldon & Niemiec, 2006) and adulthood (Van den Broeck et al., 2010), and in old age (V. Kasser & Ryan, 1999); across countries and cultures (Deci et al., 2001; Quested et al., 2013; Vansteenkiste, Lens, Soenens, & Luyckx, 2006); and across social class (Williams, Niemiec, Patrick, Ryan, & Deci, 2009). More germane to our focus on the workplace, Baard, Deci, and Ryan (2004) found that need satisfaction is associated with higher levels of performance evaluation and adjustment, as well as somewhat lower levels of anxiety and depression, among employees.

Having outlined the metatheoretical and theoretical underpinnings of SDT, in the next section we review both theory and research on autonomous self-regulation as a form of optimal motivation in the workplace.

Autonomous Self-Regulation as a Form of Optimal Motivation in the Workplace

Motivation has been a longstanding topic of theoretical and empirical inquiry within psychology. At a broad level of analysis, motivation means to be moved or to be put into action. Historically, two distinct views on motivation have been prevalent within psychology. The so-called traditional view considers motivation to be a unitary concept – one that differs in amount rather than type. In the workplace, for instance, some employees have a high level of motivation and other employees have a low level of motivation. Indeed, performance and persistence in the workplace are presumed to follow from a high level of motivation. In this view, managers bear the responsibility for generating motivation in their subordinates, often by using contingencies of reinforcement (Skinner, 1953, 1971) through which engagement is presumed to derive in the workplace (Locke & Latham, 1990; Vroom, 1964). In contrast, the so-called differentiated view considers there to be distinct types of motivation that function in different ways, and SDT views motivation from a differentiated perspective.

One type of motivation is intrinsic motivation, which refers to doing an activity for its own sake (Deci, 1975; Ryan & Deci, 2000a). With intrinsic motivation, there are no separable outcomes or contingencies that reinforce the behavior. Rather, the activity is inherently satisfying and, as a result, such behavior occurs spontaneously and often manifests as exploration and play. Intrinsic motivation is perceived as emanating from the self (with an internal perceived locus of causality; de Charms, 1968) and is accompanied by affective experiences such as interest and excitement (Izard, 1977), enjoyment, and – at times – "flow" (Csikszentmihalyi, 1975). Intrinsic motivation is the embodiment of the proactive organism and plays an important role in healthy development (Flavell, 1999). As the prototype of volitional behavior, SDT posits that satisfaction of autonomy and competence is necessary for both the maintenance and enhancement of intrinsic motivation.

To be sure, research has shown that meaningful choice (Patall, Cooper, & Robinson, 2008) and competence (Vallerand & Reid, 1984) support intrinsic motivation, while controlling rewards (Deci, Koestner, & Ryan, 1999), along with other forms of pressure and coercion (Deci, Driver, Hotchkiss, Robbins, & Wilson, 1993; Ryan, 1982), undermine intrinsic motivation.

A second type of motivation is extrinsic motivation, which refers to doing an activity for the sake of a separable outcome or contingency, such as to obtain a reward or avoid punishment (Ryan & Deci, 2000a). Extrinsic motivation describes behavior that is not inherently satisfying or enjoyable. Some theorists (Harter, 1981) have viewed extrinsic motivation as antithetical to intrinsic motivation, and thus incompatible with volition. Yet, from the perspective of SDT, there are distinct types of extrinsic motivation that vary in their degree of self-determination (Ryan & Connell, 1989) and exist along an underlying continuum of relative autonomy, which reflects the extent to which extrinsic motivation has been internalized into the self.

According to SDT, through internalization people come to endorse the importance and value of extrinsic motivation (Ryan, 1993), and this natural, active process is necessary for self-initiation and maintenance of behavior that is important for effective social functioning yet is not done for its own sake. The least internalized type of extrinsic motivation is external regulation, in which the behavior is done to comply with external contingencies of reinforcement. For instance, an employee who is motivated by external regulation might complete tasks at work because of pressure from a manager or from co-workers. Such behavior is likely to be maintained only insofar as contingencies of reinforcement are in place in the environment (Vansteenkiste, Ryan, & Deci, 2008). The next type of extrinsic motivation is introjected regulation, in which the behavior is done to comply with internal (rather than external) contingencies of reinforcement. For instance, an employee who is motivated by introjected regulation might complete tasks at work to feel pride and self-aggrandizement for having worked hard enough, or to avoid guilt and shame for not having worked hard enough. Such behavior can manifest as ego involvement or as contingent self-esteem (Niemiec, Ryan, & Brown, 2008). From an attributional perspective, both external regulation and introjected regulation have an external perceived locus of causality (de Charms, 1968) and, therefore, are experienced as relatively controlled types of motivation.

As the process of internalization proceeds toward a higher level of autonomy, the next type of extrinsic motivation is identified regulation, in which the behavior is done because its value and relevance are understood. For instance, an employee who is motivated by identified regulation might complete tasks at work because doing so is of personal importance. The most internalized type of extrinsic motivation is integrated regulation, in which the behavior is self-endorsed and consistent with abiding values, beliefs, and other aspects of the self. For instance, an employee who is motivated by integrated regulation might complete tasks at work because doing so affords an opportunity for community contribution. From an attributional perspective, both identified regulation and integrated regulation have an internal perceived locus of causality (de Charms, 1968) and, therefore, are experienced as relatively autonomous types of motivation.

In line with SDT, correlational (Niemiec et al., 2006) and experimental (Deci, Eghrari, Patrick, & Leone, 1994) studies have shown that the process of internalization is facilitated by support for satisfaction of the basic psychological needs, including in the workplace (Williams et al., 2014). Also, past research from SDT in the work domain has shown that autonomous self-regulation is a form of optimal motivation in the workplace. That is, autonomous self-regulation confers functional benefits for psychological wellness, social integration, and physical health, as well as work-related experience, among employees. In what follows, we cite several illustrative examples of relevant research.

Senécal, Vallerand, and Guay (2001) examined 786 employees who lived with a romantic partner and had at least one child who lived at home, and found that autonomous self-regulation for work activities is associated with lower levels of family alienation and emotional exhaustion. Richer, Blanchard, and Vallerand (2002) examined 490 employees in the Greater Montreal area, and found that autonomous self-regulation for work activities is associated with lower levels of emotional exhaustion and turnover intention, and higher levels of work satisfaction. Williams et al. (2014) examined 287 employees from four leading companies in Norway, and found that autonomous self-regulation for work activities is associated with lower levels of somatic symptom burden, emotional exhaustion, turnover intention, and absenteeism. Güntert (2015) examined 201 employees from the Swiss insurance industry, and found that autonomous self-regulation for work activities is associated with lower levels of turnover intention, and higher levels of job satisfaction, civic virtue, and altruism. Taken together, the results of these studies suggest that employees with an experience of autonomous self-regulation at work tend to report less distance from their family, less desire to leave the company, less physical distress, and more organizational citizenship behavior.

Next, we consider research that has been conducted among professionals in the education domain. Fernet, Guay, and Senécal (2004) examined 398 faculty members from a large French-Canadian university, and found that autonomous self-regulation for work activities is associated with lower levels of emotional exhaustion and depersonalization, and higher levels of personal accomplishment. Lam and Gurland (2008) examined 160 non-faculty employees from a small liberal arts college in the United States, and found that autonomous self-regulation for work activities is associated with higher levels of job satisfaction and job commitment. Fernet, Gagné, and Austin (2010) examined 380 employees from a French-Canadian college, and found that autonomous self-regulation for work activities is associated with lower levels of emotional exhaustion and depersonalization, and higher levels of personal accomplishment and relationship quality. Fernet, Austin, and Vallerand (2012) examined 586 French-Canadian school principals, and found that autonomous self-regulation for work activities is associated with decreases in emotional exhaustion and increases in occupational commitment. Fernet, Guay, Senécal, and Austin (2012) examined 806 teachers in Canada, and found that increases in autonomous self-regulation for work activities is associated with decreases in depersonalization and emotional exhaustion, and increases in personal accomplishment. Trépanier, Fernet, and Austin (2012) examined 568 French-Canadian school principals, and found that autonomous self-regulation for work activities is associated with higher levels of transformational leadership – or, the perception of oneself as effective and able to inspire others by stimulating interest. Trépanier, Fernet, and Austin (2013) examined 356 employees of a school board in Canada, and found that autonomous self-regulation for work activities is associated with lower levels of role ambiguity, role conflict, role overload, and psychological distress – that is, anxiety, depression, irritability, and cognitive problems. Taken together, the results of these studies suggest that employees with an experience of autonomous self-regulation at work tend to report more success on the job, more relationship satisfaction, and more ability to promote success in others.

Last, we consider research that has been conducted among law enforcement personnel. Otis and Pelletier (2005) examined 122 police officers in Canada, and found that autonomous self-regulation for work activities is associated with lower levels of daily hassles and physical symptoms, and higher levels of future work intentions. In a first study, Gillet, Huart, Colombat, and Fouquereau (2013) examined 170 police officers in France, and found that autonomous self-regulation for work activities is associated with higher levels of job vigor, job dedication, and job absorption. In a second study, Gillet et al. found support for these associations over time among 147 police officers in France. Taken together, the results of these studies suggest that employees with an experience of autonomous self-regulation at work tend to report less psychological and physical distress, more desire to stay in their job, and more work engagement – even in a career such as law enforcement that is marked by high stress and job demands.

The aforementioned results suggest that autonomous self-regulation is a form of optimal motivation among employees from a variety of professions and in several countries. In the next section we review both theory and research on intrinsic life goals as a set of optimal aspirations in the workplace.

Intrinsic Life Goals as a Set of Optimal Aspirations in the Workplace

Life goals, or aspirations, are relatively stable motivational factors that bring organization and direction to behavior over extended periods of time and, therefore, may affect psychological wellness, social integration, and physical health. From the perspective of SDT, however, not all aspirations will contribute to full functioning and organismic wellness, even when the life goals are attained. Indeed, SDT distinguishes between two different categories of aspirations according to their association with satisfaction of the basic psychological needs for autonomy, competence, and relatedness (Ryan, Sheldon, Kasser, & Deci, 1996). Research on this distinction began with the work of Kasser and Ryan (1996; see also Kasser & Ryan, 1993), who used factor analysis to identify intrinsic aspirations for personal growth and development, community involvement and generativity, meaningful affiliation and close relationships, and physical health and wellness, as well as extrinsic aspirations for wealth and material possessions, having an appealing image and being physically attractive, and social recognition and fame. Theoretically, intrinsic aspirations are likely to be associated with satisfaction of autonomy, competence, and relatedness, whereas extrinsic aspirations are likely to be unassociated with satisfaction of the basic psychological needs (Kasser, 2002). Of importance, Grouzet et al. (2005) found evidence for the structural distinction between intrinsic aspirations and extrinsic aspirations across 15 cultures around the world.

Past research from SDT has examined correlates that are associated with the pursuit and attainment of intrinsic (relative to extrinsic) aspirations. Kasser and Ryan (1996) examined 100 community adults (in a first study) and 192 undergraduate students (in a second study) in the United States, and found that the centrality of intrinsic aspirations is associated with lower levels of depressive symptoms, narcissism, and physical symptoms, and higher levels of positive affect, vitality, and self-actualization. The reverse was true for the centrality of extrinsic aspirations. A similar pattern of results has been observed in Russia (Ryan et al., 1999), in Germany (Schmuck, Kasser, & Ryan, 2000), in South Korea (Kim, Kasser, & Lee, 2003), in Spain (Romero, Gómez-Fraguela, & Villar, 2012), in Hungary (Martos & Kopp, 2012), and in Iceland (Kasser et al., 2014), as well as with risky behaviors (Williams, Cox, Hedberg, & Deci, 2000), with long-term tobacco abstinence (Niemiec, Ryan, Deci, & Williams, 2009), with exercise (Sebire, Standage, & Vansteenkiste, 2009), and with bulimic symptoms (Verstuyf, Vansteenkiste, & Soenens, 2012). Taken together, the results of these studies suggest that pursuit of intrinsic (relative to extrinsic) aspirations tends to be associated with health in several countries as well as across behaviors and life domains.

Research has examined the association between pursuit of intrinsic (relative to extrinsic) aspirations and social attitudes and interpersonal behaviors, as well. Sheldon and Kasser (1995) examined 161 undergraduate students from a private university in the United

States, and found that the centrality of intrinsic aspirations is associated with higher levels of cognitive empathy. McHoskey (1999) examined 70 undergraduate students from a public university in the United States, and found that the centrality of intrinsic aspirations is associated with lower levels of alienation, normlessness, antisocial behavior, and Machiavellianism (the tendency to manipulate others), and higher levels of prosocial behavior. Duriez, Vansteenkiste, Soenens, and De Witte (2007) examined 905 high school students in Belgium, and found that the centrality of extrinsic aspirations is associated with increases in social dominance orientation and racial and ethnic prejudice. Sheldon and McGregor (2000) examined 152 undergraduate students in the United States, and found that the centrality of extrinsic aspirations is associated with higher levels of acquisitiveness yet lower levels of profit in a simulated resource management game. Taken together, the results of these studies suggest that pursuit of intrinsic (relative to extrinsic) aspirations tends to be associated with a more healthy interpersonal orientation that may impact "the bottom line" (profit) in the workplace.

Other research from SDT has examined the association between attainment of intrinsic (relative to extrinsic) aspirations and health. In two samples of college students, Kasser and Ryan (2001) found that attainment of intrinsic aspirations is associated with lower levels of depression and anxiety, and higher levels of self-actualization, vitality, self-esteem, and relationship quality. Attainment of extrinsic aspirations was unassociated with these indices of health. In a sample of elderly citizens, Van Hiel and Vansteenkiste (2009) found that attainment of intrinsic aspirations is associated with lower levels of ill-being, despair, and death anxiety, and higher levels of well-being, ego integrity, and death acceptance. Attainment of extrinsic aspirations was associated with lower levels of death acceptance, and higher levels of despair. In a sample of recent college graduates in the United States, Niemiec, Ryan, and Deci (2009) found that attainment of intrinsic aspirations is associated with lower levels of anxiety, physical symptoms, and negative affect, and higher levels of life satisfaction, self-esteem, and positive affect. Attainment of extrinsic aspirations was unassociated with these indices of well-being, and predicted higher levels of ill-being. It is important to note that the associations between attainment of intrinsic aspirations and both well-being and ill-being were explained by satisfaction of the basic psychological needs for autonomy, competence, and relatedness. Taken together, the results of these studies question the belief that goal attainment (regardless of content) is conducive to psychological health (Carver & Scheier, 1990; Locke & Latham, 1990). It is primarily when people attain intrinsic (rather than extrinsic) aspirations that they tend to experience higher levels of well-being and lower levels of ill-being.

Last, we consider research that has been conducted among business students and working adults. Kasser and Ahuvia (2002) examined 92 business students in Singapore, and found that the centrality of extrinsic aspirations is associated with higher levels of anxiety, and lower levels of self-actualization and vitality. Vansteenkiste, Duriez, Simons, and Soenens (2006) examined 248 undergraduate students in Belgium who were majoring in business or studying to become teachers, and found that the centrality of intrinsic aspirations is associated with lower levels of internal distress and substance use, and higher levels of well-being. The centrality of extrinsic aspirations was associated with lower levels of well-being, and higher levels of internal distress and substance use. Of importance, this pattern of results was observed among business students and education students alike. Vansteenkiste et al. (2007) examined 119 employees in Belgium, and found that the centrality of an extrinsic work value orientation is associated with lower levels of job dedication, job vitality, and job satisfaction, and higher levels of short-lived satisfaction with success, work–family conflict, emotional exhaustion, and turnover intention. It is important to note that the associations between holding an extrinsic work value orientation and the work-related outcomes were explained by satisfaction of the basic psychological needs for autonomy, competence, and relatedness at work. Taken together, the results of these studies underscore the benefit of intrinsic aspirations and the detriment of extrinsic aspirations, even in educational and contextual environments that tend to emphasize money, fame, and an appealing image.

The aforementioned results suggest that intrinsic life goals are a set of optimal aspirations among business students and working adults in several countries. In the next section we reflect on how managerial support for basic psychological needs might facilitate autonomous self-regulation and the pursuit of intrinsic life goals among employees in the workplace.

Managerial Need Support and Optimal Motivation in the Workplace

A recent meta-analysis across 184 studies in the health domain provided strong support for the association between perceptions of need support from the social context and autonomous self-regulation (Ng et al., 2012), and research from SDT has also shown that perceptions of need support from the social context are associated with the centrality of intrinsic aspirations (Kasser, Ryan, Zax, & Sameroff, 1995; Williams et al., 2000). Therefore, it is important to consider some specific ways in which managers can provide support for satisfaction of autonomy, competence, and relatedness so as to facilitate optimal motivation in the workplace.

As discussed in more detail elsewhere (Niemiec & Coulson, in press; Niemiec, Soenens, & Vansteenkiste, 2014; Williams et al., 2011), support for satisfaction of the basic psychological needs begins with an authority figure (for instance, a manager) or peer (for instance, a colleague) who assumes the phenomenological perspective of another person (for instance, an employee). From this perspective, a need-supportive manager works to elicit, acknowledge, and accept the employee's thoughts and feelings about a particular occurrence in the workplace. The manager may initiate a conversation by saying, "I wonder how you understand [the occurrence] at work." This statement is neither judgmental nor accusatory, but rather is intended to convey interest in the employee's experience. It is important for the manager to relate to the employee in a direct and respectful way so as to develop a clear understanding of the employee's point of view. With such an understanding, the manager may encourage the employee to reflect on personal values or aspirations, and to consider how what occurs at work may help or hinder the attainment of life goals. Throughout this conversation and moving forward, the manager encourages self-initiation, provides a desired amount of choice for the employee, and offers meaningful rationales for limits that are set on behavior and for other relevant requests. In addition, the manager refrains from using controlling and/or manipulative language ("should," "have to"), which can undermine depth of processing, persistence, and performance (Vansteenkiste, Simons, Lens, Sheldon, & Deci, 2004). Taken together, these strategies are intended to provide support for satisfaction of autonomy.

A need-supportive manager provides structure by communicating clear, consistent norms for appropriate practice in the workplace, and it is important that structure is communicated in an autonomy-supportive way (Curran et al., 2013; Jang, Reeve, & Deci, 2010). When the employee is having difficulty at work, the manager remains positive that the employee can succeed, works to identify barriers to success, and helps with building skills and learning to solve problems. The manager creates optimal challenges for the employee, which refer to interesting experiences that require attention and skill for successful completion (Deci & Ryan, 1985). Under conditions of autonomy support, adults tend to prefer activities that test their capacities and expand their skills (Shapira, 1976). The manager also offers immediate and accurate feedback on how the employee is performing on work tasks. Taken together, these strategies are intended to provide support for satisfaction of competence.

A need-supportive manager creates a warm, empathic, and non-judgmental interpersonal climate in the workplace, and communicates unconditional positive regard (Rogers, 1957) to the employee especially vis-à-vis adversity at work. Taken together, these strategies are intended to provide support for satisfaction of relatedness.

Past research from SDT has examined whether managers can learn to be need supportive toward their subordinates. Among managers in a Fortune 500 company, Deci, Connell, and Ryan (1989) designed and implemented an organizational development intervention with a focus on providing support for subordinates' autonomy. Results showed that managers who received need support training had an increase in their orientation toward providing support for subordinates' autonomy, relative to managers who did not receive need support training. In addition, the effect of need support training radiated to the employees, who reported higher levels of trust in the corporation and satisfaction with the potential for advancement after the intervention. In a similar way, Hardré and Reeve (2009) found that managers who received need support training had a more autonomy-supportive style than managers who did not receive need support training, and their employees reported higher levels of autonomous self-regulation and engagement at work. Taken together, the results of these studies suggest that it is possible for managers to become more need supportive toward their subordinates, and such a shift in orientation among managers has associated benefits for the employees.

Other research from SDT has examined whether organizational coaches who are trained to be need supportive can facilitate internalization of motivation for important work goals among managers and supervisors. Broadly speaking, organizational coaching is an interpersonal activity that is designed to facilitate goal setting (Grant & Cavanagh, 2011) and to optimize functioning and wellness (Spence & Grant, 2013). With a focus on the enhancement of human functioning and the realization of human potential, research has shown that coaching is associated with lower levels of anxiety and workplace stress (Gyllensten & Palmer, 2005), and higher levels of self-efficacy and ability to set personal goals (Evers, Brouwers, & Tomic, 2006). It is interesting to note, though, that the academic literature on coaching has advanced in a largely atheoretical way. Recently, Spence and Oades (2011) and Spence and Deci (2013) have advocated for SDT as a theoretical framework that can be used to understand the processes and outcomes associated with coaching and to guide empirical investigations into dynamics relevant to the coaching enterprise.

Among managers and supervisors of a national provider of integrated building systems, Spence and Niemiec (2016) designed and implemented an organizational coaching intervention with a focus on training organizational coaches to be need supportive in their coaching practice. The intervention consisted of a half-day training workshop in which coaches became familiar with the principles of SDT and their applications to coaching, as well as a series of supervision sessions that were designed to maximize fidelity. Results showed that at the end of the 10-week coaching period, managers and supervisors whose organizational coaches were trained to be need supportive had an increase in their autonomous self-regulation for important work goals, relative to managers and supervisors in a control condition. Also, an increase in autonomous self-regulation was associated with an increase in perceived competence for important work goals, which in turn was associated with an increase in work engagement, a decrease in somatic symptom burden, and a decrease in mental health problems. Taken together, these results suggest that optimal motivation in the workplace is born out of interpersonal contexts that offer support for autonomy, competence, and relatedness.

Directions for Future Research

In this chapter, we developed a conceptual model based on SDT in which managerial need support is associated with optimal motivation (autonomous self-regulation and pursuit of intrinsic life goals) among employees, which in turn is associated with psychological wellness, social integration, physical health, behavioral persistence, and performance in the workplace. In this section, we offer several directions for future research.

First, it is important for future research to test all components of this conceptual model simultaneously and in various types of organizations, among various types of employees within organizations, and across gender, age, social class, and culture. SDT assumes that satisfaction of the basic psychological needs for autonomy, competence, and relatedness is a universal condition for optimal functioning and wellness. Accordingly, we speculate that the strength of association among the various components of this conceptual model will be invariant across different types of organizations, across different types of employees within organizations, and across delimiting factors associated with demographic categories. To be sure, mean-level differences in managerial need support, optimal motivation, functioning, and wellness may exist across different types of organizations and their employees, yet we predict that the functional significance of support for autonomy, competence, and relatedness will be invariant across such categories.

Second, it is important for future research to theorize on and examine other processes by which managerial need support is associated with optimal functioning and wellness among employees. We speculate that support for the basic psychological needs will be associated with higher levels of cognitive flexibility (McGraw & Fiala, 1982; McGraw & McCullers, 1979), depth of processing (Vansteenkiste et al., 2004), creativity (Amabile, 1979), optimal challenge (Deci & Ryan, 1985), and flow (Csikszentmihalyi, 1990). We also speculate that support for the basic psychological needs will be associated with higher levels of integrative emotion regulation (Roth, Assor, Niemiec, Ryan, & Deci, 2009), mindfulness (Schultz, Ryan, Niemiec, Legate, & Williams, 2015), and interest taking (Deci, Ryan, Schultz, & Niemiec, 2015). Of course, most – if not all – of these cognitive, affective, and self-regulatory factors are associated with optimal motivation and experience.

Third, it is important for future research to develop interventions that enhance managerial need support and examine their effects on autonomous self-regulation, pursuit of intrinsic life goals, psychological wellness, social integration, physical health, behavioral persistence, and performance among employees in the workplace. Past research from SDT has shown that it is possible for managers to become more need supportive toward their subordinates (Deci et al., 1989; Hardré & Reeve, 2009). We speculate that interventions will be "successful" to the extent that they emphasize to managers the importance of assuming the phenomenological perspective of their subordinates, offering immediate and accurate feedback, and building a non-judgmental interpersonal climate in the workplace. It is also important to examine the short-term and the long-term effects of such interventions on employees' motivation, functioning, and wellness, as benefits associated with need support in the workplace are likely to continue to accrue over time.

Conclusion

From the perspective of SDT, optimal motivation in the workplace can take the forms of autonomous self-regulation and pursuit of intrinsic life goals among employees. The experiences of autonomous self-regulation and pursuit of intrinsic life goals are facilitated by satisfaction of the basic psychological needs for autonomy, competence, and relatedness. Nonetheless, even in the most need-supportive workplace settings employees can experience periodic setbacks in their motivation with associated consequences for their performance and wellness on the job. At these times, it is important that managers maintain trust in their employees' organismic development, or the belief that movement toward optimal motivation is most likely to occur in need-supportive social contexts (Landry et al., 2008). With trust, managers are more likely to create conditions in the workplace that are conducive to full functioning and organismic wellness among employees.

References

Amabile, T. M. (1979). Effects of external evaluations on artistic creativity. *Journal of Personality and Social Psychology*, *37*, 221–233.

Angyal, A. (1965). *Neurosis and treatment: A holistic theory*. New York, NY: Wiley.

Baard, P. P., Deci, E. L., & Ryan, R. M. (2004). Intrinsic need satisfaction: A motivational basis of performance and well-being in two work settings. *Journal of Applied Social Psychology*, *34*, 2045–2068.

Baumeister, R. F., & Leary, M. R. (1995). The need to belong: Desire for interpersonal attachments as a fundamental human motivation. *Psychological Bulletin*, *117*, 497–529.

Bernier, A., Carlson, S. M., & Whipple, N. (2010). From external regulation to self-regulation: Early parenting precursors of young children's executive functioning. *Child Development*, *81*, 326–339.

Carver, C. S., & Scheier, M. (1990). Principles of self-regulation: Action and emotion. In E. T. Higgins & R. M. Sorrentino (Eds.), *Handbook of motivation and cognition: Foundations of social behavior* (Vol. 2, pp. 3–52). New York, NY: Guilford Press.

Csikszentmihalyi, M. (1975). *Beyond boredom and anxiety*. San Francisco, CA: Jossey-Bass.

Csikszentmihalyi, M. (1990). *Flow: The psychology of optimal experience*. New York, NY: HarperCollins.

Curran, T., Hill, A. P., & Niemiec, C. P. (2013). A conditional process model of children's behavioral engagement and behavioral disaffection in sport based on self-determination theory. *Journal of Sport & Exercise Psychology*, *35*, 30–43.

de Charms, R. (1968). *Personal causation*. New York, NY: Academic Press.

Deci, E. L. (1975). *Intrinsic motivation*. New York, NY: Plenum.

Deci, E. L., Connell, J. P., & Ryan, R. M. (1989). Self-determination in a work organization. *Journal of Applied Psychology*, *74*, 580–590.

Deci, E. L., Driver, R. E., Hotchkiss, L., Robbins, R. J., & Wilson, I. M. (1993). The relation of mothers' controlling vocalizations to children's intrinsic motivation. *Journal of Experimental Child Psychology*, *55*, 151–162.

Deci, E. L., Eghrari, H., Patrick, B. C., & Leone, D. (1994). Facilitating internalization: The self-determination theory perspective. *Journal of Personality*, *62*, 119–142.

Deci, E. L., Koestner, R., & Ryan, R. M. (1999). A meta-analytic review of experiments examining the effects of extrinsic rewards on intrinsic motivation. *Psychological Bulletin*, *125*, 627–668.

Deci, E. L., & Ryan, R. M. (1985). *Intrinsic motivation and self-determination in human behavior*. New York, NY: Plenum.

Deci, E. L., & Ryan, R. M. (2000). The "what" and "why" of goal pursuits: Human needs and the self-determination of behavior. *Psychological Inquiry*, *11*, 227–268.

Deci, E. L., & Ryan, R. M. (2008). Facilitating optimal motivation and psychological well-being across life's domains. *Canadian Psychology*, *49*, 14–23.

Deci, E. L., Ryan, R. M., Gagné, M., Leone, D. R., Usunov, J., & Kornazheva, B. P. (2001). Need satisfaction, motivation, and well-being in the work organizations of a former Eastern Bloc country. *Personality and Social Psychology Bulletin, 27*, 930–942.

Deci, E. L., Ryan, R. M., Schultz, P. P., & Niemiec, C. P. (2015). Being aware and functioning fully: Mindfulness and interest taking within self-determination theory. In K. W. Brown, J. D. Creswell, & R. M. Ryan (Eds.), *Handbook of mindfulness: Theory, research, and practice* (pp. 112–129). New York, NY: Guilford Press.

Deci, E. L., & Vansteenkiste, M. (2004). Self-determination theory and basic need satisfaction: Understanding human development in positive psychology. *Ricerche di Psicologia, 27*, 23–40.

Doherty, M. (2009). When the working day is through: The end of work as identity? *Work, Employment and Society, 23*, 84–101.

Duriez, B., Vansteenkiste, M., Soenens, B., & De Witte, H. (2007). The social costs of extrinsic relative to intrinsic goal pursuits: Their relation with social dominance and racial and ethnic prejudice. *Journal of Personality, 75*, 757–782.

Evers, W. J. G., Brouwers, A., & Tomic, W. (2006). A quasi-experimental study on management coaching effectiveness. *Consulting Psychology Journal: Practice and Research, 58*, 174–182.

Fernet, C., Austin, S., & Vallerand, R. J. (2012). The effects of work motivation on employee exhaustion and commitment: An extension of the JD-R model. *Work & Stress, 26*, 213–229.

Fernet, C., Gagné, M., & Austin, S. (2010). When does quality of relationships with coworkers predict burnout over time? The moderating role of work motivation. *Journal of Organizational Behavior, 31*, 1163–1180.

Fernet, C., Guay, F., & Senécal, C. (2004). Adjusting to job demands: The role of work self-determination and job control in predicting burnout. *Journal of Vocational Behavior, 65*, 39–56.

Fernet, C., Guay, F., Senécal, C., & Austin, S. (2012). Predicting intraindividual changes in teacher burnout: The role of perceived school environment and motivational factors. *Teaching and Teacher Education, 28*, 514–525.

Flavell, J. H. (1999). Cognitive development: Children's knowledge about the mind. *Annual Review of Psychology, 50*, 21–45.

Freud, S. (1923/1960). *The ego and the id*. New York, NY: Norton. (Original work published 1923.)

Freudenberger, H. J. (1974). Staff burn-out. *Journal of Social Issues, 30*, 159–165.

Gagné, M., & Deci, E. L. (2005). Self-determination theory and work motivation. *Journal of Organizational Behavior, 26*, 331–362.

Gillet, N., Huart, I., Colombat, P., & Fouquereau, E. (2013). Perceived organizational support, motivation, and engagement among police officers. *Professional Psychology: Research and Practice, 44*, 46–55.

Grant, A. M., & Cavanagh, M. J. (2011). Coaching and positive psychology. In K. M. Sheldon, T. B. Kashdan, & M. F. Steger (Eds.), *Designing positive psychology: Taking stock and moving forward* (pp. 293–309). Oxford, UK: Oxford University Press.

Grouzet, F. M. E., Kasser, T., Ahuvia, A., Dols, J. M. F., Kim, Y., Lau, S., ... Sheldon, K. M. (2005). The structure of goals across 15 cultures. *Journal of Personality and Social Psychology, 89*, 800-816.

Güntert, S. T. (2015). The impact of work design, autonomy support, and strategy on employee outcomes: A differentiated perspective on self-determination at work. *Motivation and Emotion, 39*, 74–87.

Gyllensten, K., & Palmer, S. (2005). Can coaching reduce workplace stress? A quasi-experimental study. *International Journal of Evidence Based Coaching and Mentoring, 3*, 75–85.

Hardré, P. L., & Reeve, J. (2009). Training corporate managers to adopt a more autonomy-supportive motivating style toward employees: An intervention study. *International Journal of Training and Development, 13*, 165–184.

Harter, J. K., Schmidt, F. L., & Keyes, C. L. M. (2003). Well-being in the workplace and its relationship to business outcomes: A review of the gallup studies. In C. L. M. Keyes & J. Haidt (Eds.), *Flourishing: The positive person and the good life* (pp. 205–224). Washington, DC: American Psychological Association.

Harter, S. (1981). A new self-report scale of intrinsic versus extrinsic orientation in the classroom: Motivational and informational components. *Developmental Psychology, 17*, 300–312.

Izard, C. E. (1977). *Human emotions.* New York, NY: Plenum.

Jang, H., Reeve, J., & Deci, E. L. (2010). Engaging students in learning activities: It is not autonomy support or structure but autonomy support and structure. *Journal of Educational Psychology, 102*, 588–600.

Jordan, J. V. (1997). Do you believe that the concepts of self and autonomy are useful in understanding women? In J. V. Jordan (Ed.), *Women's growth in diversity: More writings from the Stone Center* (pp. 29–32). New York, NY: Guilford Press.

Kasser, T. (2002). *The high price of materialism.* London, UK: MIT Press.

Kasser, T., & Ahuvia, A. (2002). Materialistic values and well-being in business students. *European Journal of Social Psychology, 32*, 137–146.

Kasser, T., Rosenblum, K. L., Sameroff, A. J., Deci, E. L., Niemiec, C. P., Ryan, R. M., ... Hawks, S. (2014). Changes in materialism, changes in psychological well-being: Evidence from three longitudinal studies and an intervention experiment. *Motivation and Emotion, 38*, 1–22.

Kasser, T., & Ryan, R. M. (1993). A dark side of the American dream: Correlates of financial success as a central life aspiration. *Journal of Personality and Social Psychology, 65*, 410–422.

Kasser, T., & Ryan, R. M. (1996). Further examining the American dream: Differential correlates of intrinsic and extrinsic goals. *Personality and Social Psychology Bulletin, 22*, 280–287.

Kasser, T., & Ryan, R. M. (2001). Be careful what you wish for: Optimal functioning and the relative attainment of intrinsic and extrinsic goals. In P. Schmuck & K. M. Sheldon (Eds.), *Life goals and well-being: Towards a positive psychology of human striving* (pp. 116–131). Seattle, WA: Hogrefe & Huber Publishers.

Kasser, T., Ryan, R. M., Zax, M., & Sameroff, A. J. (1995). The relations of maternal and social environments to late adolescents' materialistic and prosocial values. *Developmental Psychology, 31*, 907–914.

Kasser, V. G., & Ryan, R. M. (1999). The relation of psychological needs for autonomy and relatedness to vitality, well-being, and mortality in a nursing home. *Journal of Applied Social Psychology, 29*, 935–954.

Kim, Y., Kasser, T., & Lee, H. (2003). Self-concept, aspirations, and well-being in South Korea and the United States. *The Journal of Social Psychology, 143*, 277–290.

Lam, C. F., & Gurland, S. T. (2008). Self-determined work motivation predicts job outcomes, but what predicts self-determined work motivation? *Journal of Research in Personality, 42*, 1109–1115.

Landry, R., Whipple, N., Mageau, G., Joussemet, M., Koestner, R., DiDio, L., ... Haga, S. M. (2008). Trust in organismic development, autonomy support, and adaptation among mothers and their children. *Motivation and Emotion, 32*, 173–188.

Locke, E. A., & Latham, G. P. (1990). *A theory of goal setting and task performance.* Englewood Cliffs, NJ: Prentice-Hall.

Loewenstein, G. (1994). The psychology of curiosity: A review and reinterpretation. *Psychological Bulletin, 116*, 75–98.

Lundberg, U., & Cooper, C. L. (2011). *The science of occupational health: Stress, psychobiology and the new world of work.* Oxford, UK: Wiley-Blackwell.

Markus, H. R., & Kitayama, S. K. (2003). Models of agency: Sociocultural diversity in the construction of action. In V. Murphy-Berman & J. J. Berman (Eds.), *Nebraska symposium on motivation: Cross-cultural differences in perspectives on self* (Vol. *49*, pp. 1–57). Lincoln, NE: University of Nebraska Press.

Martos, T., & Kopp, M. S. (2012). Life goals and well-being: Does financial status matter? Evidence from a representative Hungarian sample. *Social Indicators Research, 105*, 561–568.

McGraw, K. O., & Fiala, J. (1982). Undermining the Zeigarnik effect: Another hidden cost of reward. *Journal of Personality, 50*, 58–66.

McGraw, K. O., & McCullers, J. C. (1979). Evidence of a detrimental effect of extrinsic incentives on breaking a mental set. *Journal of Experimental Social Psychology, 15*, 285–294.

McHoskey, J. W. (1999). Machiavellianism, intrinsic versus extrinsic goals, and social interest: A self-determination theory analysis. *Motivation and Emotion, 23*, 267–283.

Ng, J. Y. Y., Ntoumanis, N., Thøgersen-Ntoumani, C., Deci, E. L., Ryan, R. M., Duda, J. L., & Williams, G. C. (2012). Self-determination theory applied to health contexts: A meta-analysis. *Perspectives on Psychological Science, 7*, 325–340.

Niemiec, C. P., & Coulson, J. C. (in press). Need-supportive parenting and its role in the well-being and recovery of individuals: A self-determination theory perspective. In M. Slade, L. Oades, & A. Jarden (Eds.), *Wellbeing, recovery and mental health*. Cambridge, UK: Cambridge University Press.

Niemiec, C. P., Lynch, M. F., Vansteenkiste, M., Bernstein, J., Deci, E. L., & Ryan, R. M. (2006). The antecedents and consequences of autonomous self-regulation for college: A self-determination theory perspective on socialization. *Journal of Adolescence, 29*, 761–775.

Niemiec, C. P., & Ryan, R. M. (2009). Autonomy, competence, and relatedness in the classroom: Applying self-determination theory to educational practice. *Theory and Research in Education, 7*, 133–144.

Niemiec, C. P., & Ryan, R. M. (2013). What makes for a life well lived? Autonomy and its relation to full functioning and organismic wellness. In S. A. David, I. Boniwell, & A. C. Ayers (Eds.), *The Oxford handbook of happiness* (pp. 214–226). Oxford, UK: Oxford University Press.

Niemiec, C. P., Ryan, R. M., & Brown, K. W. (2008). The role of awareness and autonomy in quieting the ego: A self-determination theory perspective. In H. A. Wayment & J. J. Bauer (Eds.), *Transcending self-interest: Psychological explorations of the quiet ego* (pp. 107–115). Washington, DC: APA Books.

Niemiec, C. P., Ryan, R. M., & Deci, E. L. (2009). The path taken: Consequences of attaining intrinsic and extrinsic aspirations in post-college life. *Journal of Research in Personality, 43*, 291–306.

Niemiec, C. P., Ryan, R. M., & Deci, E. L. (2010). Self-determination theory and the relation of autonomy to self-regulatory processes and personality development. In R. H. Hoyle (Ed.), *Handbook of personality and self-regulation* (pp. 169-191). Malden, MA: Blackwell.

Niemiec, C. P., Ryan, R. M., Deci, E. L., & Williams, G. C. (2009). Aspiring to physical health: The role of aspirations for physical health in facilitating long-term tobacco abstinence. *Patient Education and Counseling, 74*, 250–257.

Niemiec, C. P., Soenens, B., & Vansteenkiste, M. (2014). Is relatedness enough? On the importance of need support in different types of social experiences. In N. Weinstein (Ed.), *Human motivation and interpersonal relationships: Theory, research and applications* (pp. 77–96). Dordrecht, the Netherlands: Springer.

Olafsen, A. H., Niemiec, C. P., Halvari, H., Deci, E. L., & Williams, G. C. (2015). *On the dark side of work: A longitudinal analysis using self-determination theory*. Unpublished manuscript, Buskerud and Vestfold University College, Hønefoss, Norway.

Otis, N., & Pelletier, L. G. (2005). A motivational model of daily hassles, physical symptoms, and future work intentions among police officers. *Journal of Applied Social Psychology, 35*, 2193–2214.

Patall, E. A., Cooper, H., & Robinson, C. (2008). The effects of choice on intrinsic motivation and related outcomes: A meta-analysis of research findings. *Psychological Bulletin, 134*, 270–300.

Piaget, J. (1971). *Biology and knowledge*. Chicago, IL: University of Chicago Press.

Quested, E., Ntoumanis, N., Viladrich, C., Haug, E., Ommundsen, Y., Hoye, A. V., … Duda, J. L. (2013). Intentions to drop-out of youth soccer: A test of the basic needs theory among European youth from five countries. *International Journal of Sport and Exercise Psychology, 11*, 395–407.

Richer, S. F., Blanchard, C., & Vallerand, R. J. (2002). A motivational model of work turnover. *Journal of Applied Social Psychology, 32*, 2089–2113.

Rogers, C. R. (1957) The necessary and sufficient conditions of therapeutic personality change. *Journal of Consulting Psychology, 21*, 95–103.

Rogers, C. R. (1963). The actualizing tendency in relation to "motives" and to consciousness. In M. R. Jones (Ed.), *Nebraska symposium on motivation* (Vol. *11*, pp. 1–24). Lincoln, NE: University of Nebraska Press.

Romero, E., Gómez-Fraguela, J. A., & Villar, P. (2012). Life aspirations, personality traits and subjective well-being in a Spanish sample. *European Journal of Personality, 26*, 45–55.

Roth, G., Assor, A., Niemiec, C. P., Ryan, R. M., & Deci, E. L. (2009). The emotional and academic consequences of parental conditional regard: Comparing conditional positive regard, conditional negative regard, and autonomy support as parenting practices. *Developmental Psychology, 45*, 1119–1142.

Ryan, R. M. (1982). Control and information in the intrapersonal sphere: An extension of cognitive evaluation theory. *Journal of Personality and Social Psychology*, *43*, 450–461.

Ryan, R. M. (1993). Agency and organization: Intrinsic motivation, autonomy and the self in psychological development. In J. Jacobs (Ed.), *Nebraska symposium on motivation: Developmental perspectives on motivation* (Vol. *40*, pp. 1–56). Lincoln, NE: University of Nebraska Press.

Ryan, R. M. (1995). Psychological needs and the facilitation of integrative processes. *Journal of Personality*, *63*, 397–427.

Ryan, R. M., Chirkov, V. I., Little, T. D., Sheldon, K. M., Timoshina, E., & Deci, E. L. (1999). The American dream in Russia: Extrinsic aspirations and well-being in two cultures. *Personality and Social Psychology Bulletin*, *25*, 1509–1524.

Ryan, R. M., & Connell, J. P. (1989). Perceived locus of causality and internalization: Examining reasons for acting in two domains. *Journal of Personality and Social Psychology*, *57*, 749–761.

Ryan, R. M., & Deci, E. L. (2000a). Intrinsic and extrinsic motivations: Classic definitions and new directions. *Contemporary Educational Psychology*, *25*, 54–67.

Ryan, R. M., & Deci, E. L. (2000b). Self-determination theory and the facilitation of intrinsic motivation, social development, and well-being. *American Psychologist*, *55*, 68–78.

Ryan, R. M., & Deci, E. L. (2002). Overview of self-determination theory: An organismic dialectical perspective. In E. L. Deci & R. M. Ryan (Eds.), *Handbook of self-determination research* (pp. 3–33). Rochester, NY: University of Rochester Press.

Ryan, R. M., La Guardia, J. G., Solky-Butzel, J., Chirkov, V., & Kim, Y. (2005). On the interpersonal regulation of emotions: Emotional reliance across gender, relationships, and cultures. *Personal Relationships*, *12*, 145–163.

Ryan, R. M., Sheldon, K. M., Kasser, T., & Deci, E. L. (1996). All goals are not created equal: An organismic perspective on the nature of goals and their regulation. In P. M. Gollwitzer & J. A. Bargh (Eds.), *The psychology of action: Linking cognition and motivation to behavior* (pp. 7–26). New York, NY: Guilford Press.

Schaufeli, W. B., Bakker, A. B., & Van Rhenen, W. (2009). How changes in job demands and resources predict burnout, work engagement, and sickness absenteeism. *Journal of Organizational Behavior*, *30*, 893–917.

Schmuck, P., Kasser, T., & Ryan, R. M. (2000). Intrinsic and extrinsic goals: Their structure and relationship to well-being in German and U.S. college students. *Social Indicators Research*, *50*, 225–241.

Schultz, P. P., Ryan, R. M., Niemiec, C. P., Legate, N., & Williams, G. C. (2015). Mindfulness, work climate, and psychological need satisfaction in employee well-being. *Mindfulness*, *6*, 971–985.

Sebire, S. J., Standage, M., & Vansteenkiste, M. (2009). Examining intrinsic versus extrinsic exercise goals: Cognitive, affective, and behavioral outcomes. *Journal of Sport & Exercise Psychology*, *31*, 189–210.

Senécal, C., Vallerand, R. J., & Guay, F. (2001). Antecedents and outcomes of work–family conflict: Toward a motivational model. *Personality and Social Psychology Bulletin*, *27*, 176–186.

Shapira, Z. (1976). Expectancy determinants of intrinsically motivated behavior. *Journal of Personality and Social Psychology*, *34*, 1235–1244.

Sheldon, K. M., & Kasser, T. (1995). Coherence and congruence: Two aspects of personality integration. *Journal of Personality and Social Psychology*, *68*, 531–543.

Sheldon, K. M., & McGregor, H. A. (2000). Extrinsic value orientation and "the tragedy of the commons." *Journal of Personality*, *68*, 383–411.

Sheldon, K. M., & Niemiec, C. P. (2006). It's not just the amount that counts: Balanced need satisfaction also affects well-being. *Journal of Personality and Social Psychology*, *91*, 331–341.

Silvia, P. J. (2008). Interest – the curious emotion. *Current Directions in Psychological Science*, *17*, 57–60.

Skinner, B. F. (1953). *Science and human behavior*. New York, NY: Macmillan.

Skinner, B. F. (1971). *Beyond freedom and dignity*. New York, NY: Knopf.

Spence, G. B., & Deci, E. L. (2013). Self-determination theory within coaching contexts: Supporting motives and goals that promote optimal functioning and well-being. In S. David, D. Clutterbuck, & D. Megginson (Eds.), *Beyond goals: Effective strategies for coaching and mentoring* (pp. 85–108). Farnham, UK: Gower.

Spence, G. B., & Grant, A. M. (2013). Coaching and well-being: A brief review of existing evidence, relevant theory, and implications for practitioners. In S. A. David, I. Boniwell, & A. C. Ayers (Eds.), *The Oxford handbook of happiness* (pp. 1009–1025). Oxford, UK: Oxford University Press.

Spence, G. B., & Niemiec, C. P. (2016). *Coaching for employee engagement: Using self-determination theory to predict engagement, turnover intention, and well-being among employees.* Unpublished manuscript, University of Wollongong, Sydney, Australia.

Spence, G. B., & Oades, L. G. (2011). Coaching with self-determination theory in mind: Using theory to advance evidence-based coaching practice. *International Journal of Evidence Based Coaching and Mentoring, 9*, 37–55.

Stephens, N. M., Markus, H. R., & Townsend, S. S. M. (2007). Choice as an act of meaning: The case of social class. *Journal of Personality and Social Psychology, 93*, 814–830.

Trépanier, S-G., Fernet, C., & Austin, S. (2012). Social and motivational antecedents of perceptions of transformational leadership: A self-determination theory perspective. *Canadian Journal of Behavioural Science, 44*, 272–277.

Trépanier, S-G., Fernet, C., & Austin, S. (2013). The moderating role of autonomous motivation in the job demands–strain relation: A two sample study. *Motivation and Emotion, 37*, 93–105.

U.S. Bureau of Labor Statistics (2015). *American Time Use Survey – 2014 Results.* Available online at http://www.bls.gov/news.release/pdf/atus.pdf

Vallerand, R. J., & Reid, G. (1984). On the causal effects of perceived competence on intrinsic motivation: A test of cognitive evaluation theory. *Journal of Sport Psychology, 6*, 94–102.

Van den Broeck, A., Vansteenkiste, M., De Witte, H., Soenens, B., & Lens, W. (2010). Capturing autonomy, competence, and relatedness at work: Construction and initial validation of the Work-related Basic Need Satisfaction scale. *Journal of Occupational and Organizational Psychology, 83*, 981–1002.

Van Hiel, A., & Vansteenkiste, M. (2009). Ambitions fulfilled? The effects of intrinsic and extrinsic goal attainment on older adults' ego-integrity and death attitudes. *International Journal of Aging and Human Development, 68*, 27–51.

Vansteenkiste, M., Duriez, B., Simons, J., & Soenens, B. (2006). Materialistic values and well-being among business students: Further evidence of their detrimental effect. *Journal of Applied Social Psychology, 36*, 2892–2908.

Vansteenkiste, M., Lens, W., Soenens, B., & Luyckx, K. (2006). Autonomy and relatedness among Chinese sojourners and applicants: Conflictual or independent predictors of well-being and adjustment? *Motivation and Emotion, 30*, 273–282.

Vansteenkiste, M., Neyrinck, B., Niemiec, C. P., Soenens, B., de Witte, H., & Van den Broeck, A. (2007). On the relations among work value orientations, psychological need satisfaction and job outcomes: A self-determination theory approach. *Journal of Occupational and Organizational Psychology, 80*, 251–277.

Vansteenkiste, M., Niemiec, C. P., & Soenens, B. (2010). The development of the five mini-theories of self-determination theory: An historical overview, emerging trends, and future directions. In T. C. Urdan & S. A. Karabenick (Eds.), *Advances in motivation and achievement, v. 16A – The decade ahead: Theoretical perspectives on motivation and achievement* (pp. 105–165). London, UK: Emerald Group Publishing.

Vansteenkiste, M., Ryan, R. M., & Deci, E. L. (2008). Self-determination theory and the explanatory role of psychological needs in human well-being. In L. Bruni, F. Comin, & M. Pugno (Eds.), *Capabilities and happiness* (pp. 187–223). Oxford, UK: Oxford University Press.

Vansteenkiste, M., Simons, J., Lens, W., Sheldon, K. M., & Deci, E. L. (2004). Motivating learning, performance, and persistence: The synergistic effects of intrinsic goal contents and autonomy-supportive contexts. *Journal of Personality and Social Psychology, 87*, 246–260.

Verstuyf, J., Vansteenkiste, M., & Soenens, B. (2012). Eating regulation and bulimic symptoms: The differential correlates of health-focused and appearance-focused eating regulation. *Body Image, 9*, 108–117.

Vroom, V. H. (1964). *Work and motivation.* New York, NY: Wiley.

White, R. W. (1959). Motivation reconsidered: The concept of competence. *Psychological Review, 66*, 297–333.

Williams, G. C., Cox, E. M., Hedberg, V. A., & Deci, E. L. (2000). Extrinsic life goals and health-risk behaviors in adolescents. *Journal of Applied Social Psychology*, *30*, 1756–1771.

Williams, G. C., Halvari, H., Niemiec, C. P., Sørebø, Ø., Olafsen, A. H., & Westbye, C. (2014). Managerial support for basic psychological needs, somatic symptom burden and work-related correlates: A self-determination theory perspective. *Work & Stress*, *28*, 404–419.

Williams, G. C., Niemiec, C. P., Patrick, H., Ryan, R. M., & Deci, E. L. (2009). The importance of supporting autonomy and perceived competence in facilitating long-term tobacco abstinence. *Annals of Behavioral Medicine*, *37*, 315–324.

Williams, G. C., Patrick, H., Niemiec, C. P., Ryan, R. M., Deci, E. L., & Lavigne, H. M. (2011). The *Smoker's Health Project*: A self-determination theory intervention to facilitate maintenance of tobacco abstinence. *Contemporary Clinical Trials*, *32*, 535–543.

7

Flow at Work

Mihaly Csikszentmihalyi, Sonal Khosla, and Jeanne Nakamura

Introduction: What Is Work?

Work is not a stable, unchanging entity. Under favorable conditions it can be the best part of life, under badly designed social conditions it can be an almost unendurable burden. The work of anthropologists who have observed contemporary groups of hunter-gatherers have often remarked that in these societies men and women seem to enjoy whatever work they have to do to survive – and that for them, the distinction between what we would call "work" and what we would call "leisure" – such as dancing, playing music, telling stories around the campfire – was practically non-existent (Evans-Pritchard, 1956; Sahlins, 1972; Turnbull, 1961). It took a long time for work to become an alienating experience. What made it so was the evolution of technology that allowed people to accumulate food like grains and cereals, that could be stored without spoilage; in turn, this allowed some sections of the population to become full-time soldiers, others to farm full-time, or to become masons, carpenters, servants, and scribes. Society turned from a democratic group made of people who all did the same thing for a living, to an increasingly differentiated workforce ruled by the armies of despotic tyrants.

Despite the many negative changes in the conditions surrounding work, some of the most satisfying and meaningful moments of life still happen when we are working (Csikszentmihalyi, 2003; Csikszentmihalyi & LeFevre, 1989). The reason for this is not difficult to find. Living organisms are built for extracting energy from the environment, and when they are allowed to do it well, they usually feel a deep sense of satisfaction, or even enjoyment. Bees living in a mountain meadow full of flowers might lazily flit in the sun, while still filling their hive with fine nectar. But no matter how hard an animal has to work, it is difficult to say that it finds the struggle stressful or boring. In fact, most animals – at least those that are close enough to us to observe and interpret – are at their best when engaged in what we would call "work," that is, when they practice the activity that makes it possible for them to survive.

The Wiley Blackwell Handbook of the Psychology of Positivity and Strengths-Based Approaches at Work, First Edition. Edited by Lindsay G. Oades, Michael F. Steger, Antonella Delle Fave, and Jonathan Passmore.

Thinkers across the ages have remarked that living beings are at their best when they do what they are specifically adapted to do. The recently developed discipline of positive psychology is reaching similar conclusions. Individuals have different strengths – 24 according to Peterson and Seligman (2004) – and when they are using their strengths they are not only more efficient, but also feel more positive moods. A good example was quoted in the obituary of Richard Grossman, a physician specializing in the treatment of burn victims, whose "fierce dedication" to his work and the new techniques he developed for alleviating the pain of his patients had become legendary. When he was asked what led him to become so addicted to such grueling work, he did not mention the good he was accomplishing, but simply answered: "You develop a skill, and you want to use it" (Nelson, 2014). But this is not true only of professionals or other fortunate individuals. Assembly-line workers, service workers, people who apparently would have very little to enjoy about their work, are often as eloquent about what they do for a living as a poet or a physician. "I still take care of the cows and tend the orchard," said a 62-year-old woman living in the Italian Alps. "I feel special satisfaction in caring for the plants: I like to see them grow day by day. It is very beautiful" (Delle Fave & Massimini, 1988, pp. 197, 199).

And yet, surveys around the world show that "work" is often disliked and rarely found engaging by most adults (Gallup, 2013). Despite improved working conditions, something is still clearly lacking. It is still very rare for workers to feel that their job is an expression of their best qualities, that it is a personally meaningful activity, that it is *fun*. Where can we look for ideas that can change this state of affairs? In this chapter, we are going to review the concept of flow – a psychological state in which a person feels completely engaged with what he or she is doing, and which is experienced as some of the most rewarding and worthwhile moments of life; discuss how flow can be experienced at work; and then review the recent literature on the topic of flow at work to determine what some of the convergent findings have been, and what might be missing in the studies that have been conducted so far.

Reconstructing Enjoyable Work

What we, and other researchers who have studied enjoyment of work have found, is that when a person is deeply engaged in his or her work, they begin to find the work intrinsically rewarding, and the phenomenology they report is in many ways indistinguishable from the phenomenology reported by artists, musicians, and athletes describing how it feels when their performance goes well. For instance, in describing how it feels to do an operation that is very engaging, surgeons say that it is "like skiing down a slope," "like sailing with the wind," or "like body contact sport" (Csikszentmihalyi, 1975). These common elements of experiences that are enjoyable by themselves, even when they do not result in any conventional gain, characterize what has been referred to as the *flow experience* (Csikszentmihalyi, 1975, 1990; Csikszentmihalyi & Csikszentmihalyi, 1988).

In this chapter we will present a short summary of the flow model of optimal experience, and then summarize what psychologists and other social scientists have written about how it feels, what causes it, and what are the consequences of experiencing it in a work environment.

The development of flow

The concept of flow was developed in a series of studies aimed at understanding "optimal experiences," or those moments in life when people claim to have been feeling at their best. Contrary to expectations, it was found that these optimal experiences were described in much the same way whether they occurred when the person was composing or playing music, forging a sculpture, writing a poem, scaling a mountain, swimming across the British Channel, or having a good conversation. As the research progressed, it was found that this kind of optimal experience could happen also at work – in elite professions such as surgery or poetry, but also in apparently menial jobs like working on an assembly line, or making sandwiches in a delicatessen.

Respondents who described how it felt when they had this kind of experience generally mentioned eight characteristics they could remember feeling at the time. What was unexpected is that the same phenomenological profile of optimal experiences emerged regardless whether the activity was a game, a sport, or involved making music, or poetry, or work – ranging from computer programming and surgery to farming and building machinery. And when our studies in the United States were replicated in Italy, Germany, South Korea, Japan, and many other cultures, the same phenomenological profile emerged.

The first surprise was that the accounts focused a great deal on a challenge that started the process that led to the optimal experience. The challenge could have been to play Chopin for an aspiring violinist, or to climb a particularly difficult pitch of rock in Yosemite for a climber; for a scientist it was to prove a hypothesis by running the most relevant experiment, or to develop the most satisfying theory to explain hitherto unrelated facts. For a mother the challenge could be to teach important issues to her child, and for the child it could be to learn how to use a key to open a door. The point is, contrary to popular opinion, the most memorable moments in people's lives do not seem to occur when they experience comfort, relaxation, or external success based on financial gains or popular acclaim; but they occur when a person has been able to meet a challenge that he or she had thought to be difficult and daunting.

Which means, of course, that optimal experience depends not only on challenges but on the availability of skills to meet them. When the challenges far outpace skills, the person feels worried and anxious; when the skills are higher than the challenges, one feels bored. When both challenges and skills are low, the best word to describe the phenomenology is apathy. Later studies suggest that flow is at its peak when the challenges are a few percentage points above the person's skills; it is still almost as high when the two variables are matched exactly, but it drops very quickly when the skills are even slightly higher than the challenges (Abuhamdeh & Csikszentmihalyi, 2012).

The challenge one takes on determines the goals that a person must reach in the activity. In a chess game, each move has a particular goal within the overall goal of winning the game. The goal might be to defend one's territory, or one's king, and it might have short-term or overall strategic purposes. Or the goal might be to capture one of the opponent's pieces, or to establish control of one side of the board. During a game hundreds of decisions must be made, each requiring the best solution to the problem presented by the opponent's moves. Winning the game is the overall purpose of the game, but what makes the game enjoyable is the fact that it offers hundreds of opportunities for solving problems, each presenting a goal that when solved provides a moment of rewarding accomplishment.

What makes singing or playing music enjoyable is not to finish the song; it is to get every chord, every note as well expressed as possible in the process of playing. A rock climber is attracted not so much by the reward of reaching the top of the wall, but by the ability to make each of the hundreds – or thousands – of moves required to complete the ascent, each providing a different problem, a different goal that must be solved for the overall challenge of reaching the top to be met.

The next characteristic common to optimal experiences is that one knows moment by moment what one needs to do, and how well one is performing. Games, whether physical or mental, have built-in rules that make it clear "what's the score"; the tennis player knows at each moment whether the ball is going where she intends it to go; the musician monitors the stream of sound she produces and can tell when it is not what she would like it to be; the rock climber can see he is a few feet higher up after each move, and that he has still not fallen into the void … Physicians say that one of the reasons surgery is so satisfying is that "you always know when you made a mistake – there is blood in the cavity, you have cut an artery …"

When these conditions are present – a matching of skills with slightly higher challenges in an activity that provides a chain of clear goals, and that provides immediate feedback – the activity will require focusing of attention; a degree of concentration that excludes irrelevant distractions, the usual existential worries that take up our attention in normal life. If the climber indulges in worrying about himself, or the future of mankind, he is likely to fall off the rock face; the pianist will hit a wrong note, the chess player sacrifice her Queen unwittingly. With the unwanted distractions of everyday life temporarily removed, one can experience the fullness of life by engaging with challenges that will bear witness to one's skills. And this is the ultimate reason for engaging in such activities: one feels what the Greeks called an *autotelic experience*, that is, an experience that is its own reward.

It seems that, in the course of evolution, some of our ancestors established a connection between effortful engagement with challenges, and the pleasure centers of the brain. How this happened is a mystery, and it must have been accidental; however, those individuals whose brains were rewired this way were likely to benefit from this neurophysiological accident, because they would be more likely to be curious, experimental, more willing to take risks in the pursuit of new challenges. Although this inference must remain speculative, there is evidence that supports it. For example, neurophysiologists at the Karolinska Institute in Stockholm have shown that individuals who experience flow more often tend to release dopamine to areas of the brain that are involved in effortful pursuits; whereas those who report fewer flow experiences release dopamine almost exclusively to the centers of the brain involved in producing passive pleasure (de Manzano, Cervenka, Jucaite, Hellenäs, Farde, & Ullén, 2013). This connection between effort and pleasure could be entirely genetic, or it could be that the potential for experiencing flow is present in everyone's brain, but needs to be activated by exercise to become habitual. In any case, it seems that enjoying challenges is part of our nature, and it should be something that we can experience in work as well as in activities that exist for the purpose of providing enjoyment, such as sports, games, music, and art. But what can organizations do to make it more likely that their workers will experience flow?

The implications of flow for the workplace

To start, this could be accomplished simply by providing professional development opportunities to teach employees about how to find enjoyment in their work. The first step toward employees finding more flow in work is increasing their understanding of what flow is and how to find it. Secondly, organizations can explicitly support employees by talking about flow-inducing and flow-blocking components of the work during performance reviews and other opportunities where managers or leaders can hear from employees. In documented cases of introducing flow as a corporate priority, managers have helped employees to figure out ways to overcome the parts of their job that seem to be resulting in boredom, anxiety, or other negative states; and then help them to give them more responsibilities for aspects of the job they enjoy doing (e.g., Marsh, 2005).

Finally, organizations can provide the resources to allow employees the opportunity to develop their skills and provide more challenging opportunities. Recently the CEO of one of the major Asian technological companies employing over 80,000 workers showed

Csikszentmihalyi the balance sheets for the company through the past 25 years. He pointed to an inflection point a dozen years earlier, when the profits of the company, which had been stagnant for the last dozen years despite steadily increasing revenues, had taken a sudden surge upwards. He then said that from that point, where flow was introduced into the management system, the company made 6.5 billion dollars more profit than had been projected on the basis of past performance. Not an important reason for taking flow seriously, perhaps, but not entirely insignificant, either.

A likely consequence of being in flow is that the skills of employees will constantly grow. In order to remain in flow, employees need to have greater challenges on which they can utilize their increasing skills. Organizations that fail to provide for the growth of their employees will likely experience an unmotivated workforce as boredom and apathy set in. And they are likely to face an exodus of their best employees, who will move to jobs where their skills are recognized and used, and where they can grow.

These suggestions derive directly from flow theory. To complement this, what is needed is a synthetic review of the empirical basis for translating flow theory to applied recommendations that extend earlier (e.g., Delle Fave, Massimini, & Bassi, 2011) and briefer (e.g., Nakamura & Dubin, 2015) reviews of the literature on flow at work. Given the changing face of work, these recommendations should be relevant to current work conditions. Toward this end, we conducted a focused review of recent research on flow at work to determine what is known that can inform practitioners, and where the gaps lie that future research might address.

A Short Review of the Literature on Flow and Work for the Past Decade

Many recent studies on flow in work settings have focused on the factors that facilitate or inhibit flow in employees. Some studies have also emphasized the outcomes generated as a result of flow experiences at work. Because the literature on flow and work has been expanding rapidly, we decided to focus on a subset of studies that would indicate the trends and gaps in the research base. For the purpose of this chapter, studies related to flow and work that were published from 2005 to mid-2015 were considered to give as updated a view of trends as possible. Most of the studies taken into consideration involved discussion of either facilitators or inhibitors of flow at work, or mentioned quantifiable outcomes of flow; 28 studies met these criteria, with 25 studies focusing on the antecedents of the flow experience, 9 studies focusing on inhibiting factors, and 13 on the outcomes of the flow experience. Apart from these studies, there was one article that investigated the experience of flow at work, but did not contribute to the understanding of flow at work in terms of facilitators, inhibitors and outcomes of flow.

Findings

Facilitators Of the 25 studies that mentioned one or more factors that facilitate flow at work, many examined characteristics of the person. There were 11 related to personal-cognitive factors. Salanova, Bakker, & Llorens (2006) asserted that personal resources such as self-efficacy beliefs of an individual act as facilitators for work-related flow. The studies that emphasized perceptions as facilitators of flow in work settings are also coded as cognitive. One of the studies that associated perceptions with flow emphasized factors such as "seeing difficulty," for example, planning analytical problem solving, and task focus (Baumann & Scheffer, 2010). There were 8 studies that examined personal-behavioral influences (e.g., approach coping). In a study by Tobert and Moneta (2013), approach coping, which involves planning and active coping, was found to be a predictor of flow. There were 6 studies that focused on personal-emotional factors (e.g., positive affect and emotion). In the same study by Tobert and Moneta, positive affect was also found be a positive predictor of flow. There were 5 studies that mentioned personal-motivational factors as facilitators of flow. According to Moneta (2012), the higher the trait of intrinsic motivation, the higher the probability of experiencing flow in work. Personality dispositions are coded as emotional, cognitive, motivational, and/or behavioral. Far fewer studies deal with factors involving other people (e.g., the social network). An interpersonal factor was mentioned 2 times out of 25 as facilitator of flow. One the studies that mentions interpersonal factors found out that flow in music teachers can facilitate flow in subordinates (Bakker, 2005).

Apart from personal and interpersonal factors, some studies looked into situational factors. Situational factors have been categorized as work related and nonwork related in this chapter. Work-related situational factors include job characteristics (e.g., high skill variety, low strain) and job resources (e.g., social support). Jobs that provide room for employee autonomy and professional development have been found to have direct and significant impact on flow experience (Kuo & Ho, 2010). Moreover, job characteristics such as emotional demands, job pressure and autonomy have also been associated with flow (Bakker, 2008). Situational factors related to work were mentioned 13 times, while a nonwork-related situational factor was only mentioned in one study according to which working at home is flow-inducing (Peters, Poutsma, Van der Heijden, Bakker, & De Bruijn, 2014).

Inhibitors Of the 9 studies that mentioned factors that inhibit flow, 8 mentioned factors that could be categorized as personal-emotional. Negative affect has been found to be negatively related with flow (Tobert & Moneta, 2013). There were 7 studies that mentioned personal-cognitive influences. Mental exhaustion has been linked with lower levels of flow in several studies (Demerouti, Bakker, Sonnentag & Fullagar, 2012; Mäkikangas, Bakker, Aunola, & Demerouti, 2010). Moreover, 3 studies focused on personal-behavioral factors. Maladaptive coping, which involves avoidance and self-punishment, is one of the behavioral factors that negatively predicts flow (Tobert & Moneta, 2013). Many studies had an overlap of more than one category of personal factors. According to Peters et al. (2014), work-related flow is not achieved "when employees do not experience being empowered, and when they do not use and experience their working conditions as job resources" (p. 271). None of the studies dealt with inhibiting factors involving other people.

Apart from personal and interpersonal factors, situational factors related to work were mentioned in only one study (Fagerlind, Gustavsson, Johansson, & Ekberg, 2013). According to Fagerlind et al., high-strain jobs, that is, jobs imposing high demand and high control, were inhibitors of flow. On the other hand, nonwork-related situational factors were not mentioned in any study (see Figure 7.1).

It is important to note that factors related to the working situation have been given more attention by flow researchers as facilitators, rather than inhibitors. It appears that when considering the flow experiences of employees, ways of improving the work environment have been given greater importance. Interpersonal factors are much less often reported as having importance for either facilitation or inhibition of flow.

Outcomes Of the 13 studies that mentioned outcomes of experiencing flow at work, there were 7 that considered personal-cognitive factors. Flow was seen to result in creativity at work (Yan, Davison, & Mo, 2013). Experiencing flow at work was also related to lower burnout or exhaustion after work (Demerouti et al., 2012; Lavinge, Forest, & Crevier-Braud, 2011).

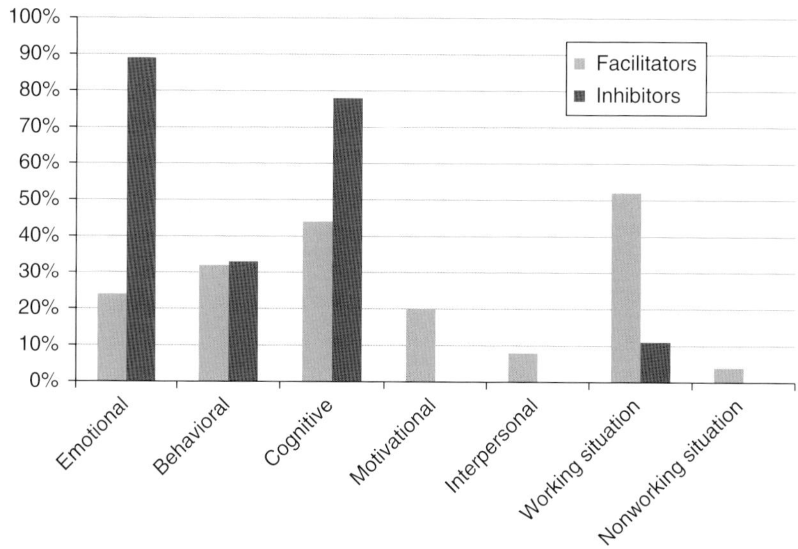

Figure 7.1 Percentages of studies (2005–2015) examining facilitators and inhibitors of flow at work (Facilitators, $n=25$; Inhibitors, $n=9$). *Source*: Author.

There were 6 studies that considered factors related to personal-emotional factors. In many studies, presence of flow was said to lead to positive affect (Demerouti et al., 2012; Eisenberger, Jones, Stinglhamber, Shanock, & Randall, 2005; Fullagar & Kelloway, 2009). Moreover, personal-behavioral outcomes were studied only 3 times. Working on a task with more spontaneity and interest was one of the behavioral outcomes found, as a result of flow (Eisenberg et al., 2005). There were also 3 studies in which flow was seen as an outcome of interpersonal factors. In one such study, flow in subordinates was generated by flow in supervisors (Bakker, 2005).

Work-related situational outcomes were examined in 4 studies. Flow led to in role and extra-role performance at work (Demerouti, 2006), and better quality of service to clients (Kuo & Ho, 2010). Only one study addressed outcomes in nonwork-related situations (i.e., higher energy level in situations outside of work, Demerouti et al., 2012). Also, of the studies reviewed, 3 gathered evidence for short-term outcomes (e.g., less exhaustion at work during the particular workday), while only 2 studies reported outcomes that were long-term in nature (e.g., subsequent personal resources). In many of the studies it was not possible to determine whether outcomes were short-term or long-term. The counts reflect significant results only.

Summary and suggestions

Of the 28 studies that were reviewed, almost all discussed at least one factor that facilitates or inhibits flow at work. Of the 25 studies that discussed *facilitators* of flow, 17 considered personal factors. Most of these are cognitive factors, broadly defined, with fewer emotional and behavioral factors studied as facilitating flow. Motivational factors have also been examined as facilitators of flow. On the other hand, for *inhibition* of flow, addressed in only 9 studies, cognitive and emotional factors were examined almost the same number of times, or a factor was both cognitive and emotional in nature. Many more studies have

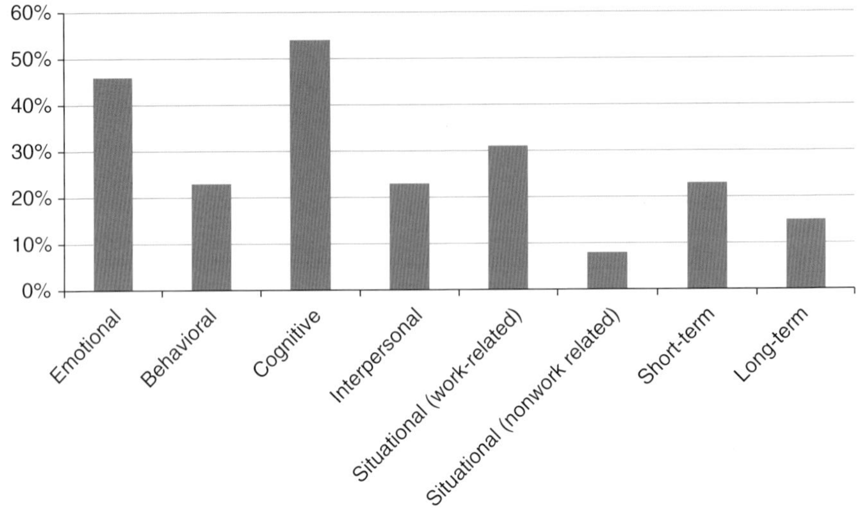

Figure 7.2 Percentages of studies (2005–2015) examining outcomes of flow at work ($n = 13$). *Source*: Author.

examined situational factors that facilitate flow at work than inhibit it. Very few studies discuss nonwork situational factors.

Of the studies that discuss outcomes of work-related flow, most include emotional and cognitive outcomes. Not much has been done to study behavioral or interpersonal outcomes. Only a few studies discuss work-related outcomes, and even fewer discuss nonwork-related outcomes. Finally, some of the studies differentiated outcomes as short-term, and very few as long-term effects of experiencing flow at work.

As observed, factors related to working environment have been given more importance for facilitating flow, while personal factors tend to be held responsible for inhibiting flow. It is of course the case that studies of job resources often include social support, but interpersonal processes are rarely studied; thus more studies should be carried out which aim to find out the role of interpersonal factors in flow at work.

Similarly, only one study discussed non-workplace situational factors that facilitate flow and none of the studies reviewed examined how such factors might inhibit flow; thus studies which aim to find out nonwork situational factors that facilitate and inhibit flow should also be carried out.

Finally, as most of the studies are cross-sectional or very short-term longitudinal, there is a great need to begin trying to find out what the long-term consequences of experiencing flow at work are. There is no question that the issues discussed here point to a very rich intellectual and socio-economic lode that should yield many important findings in the future. We hope that this short introduction will help researchers to recognize the issues, and to get involved in resolving the questions they pose.

Future Research

Even though many studies have focused on flow, relatively few have dealt with flow in work. Even fewer have studied factors that facilitate or inhibit flow, or have measured the results of experiencing flow at work. Based on the studies above, a few suggestions for future research can be recommended. First, more studies should be carried out to find out interpersonal facilitators and inhibitors of flow. There were few studies that mentioned the influence of other people in facilitation of flow; there was no study of whether other people play a role in inhibiting flow or not. For example, one study found that presence of flow in supervisors accounted for presence of flow in the subordinates (Bakker, 2005). Similarly, more such studies could be carried out in the interpersonal and social domain, to explain how the presence of other people influences the flow experiences.

Second, work-related situational factors, which have mostly been studied as facilitators of flow, should also be studied to find out how they inhibit flow. Work-related situational factors that inhibit flow, such as job demands, structure of job, job resources, and so on, should be studied in more detail. Third, nonworking situational factors such as home environment, cultural factors, societal influences, should be studied in order to understand their influence on flow. From the studies that were reviewed, only one outlined the influence of nonwork situation as a facilitator of flow (Demerouti et al., 2012) and no studies attempted to understand the the influence of such factors to inhibit flow. Fourth, most studies that focus on outcomes of flow emphasize personal outcomes such as emotional, behavioral, or cognitive changes, but few studies have attempted to find out situational outcomes that result because of flow experienced at work. Thus, there is a lack of studies that help us understand how flow leads to situational outcomes, whether work related or nonwork related. Finally, it is important to explain whether the outcomes that result because of flow are short-term in nature, or long-term.

Conclusions

This chapter aimed to summarize several factors related to flow, based on a literature review of studies carried out in the last 10 years. The observed factors can be categorized as facilitators of flow, inhibitors of flow, and outcomes of flow. While most studies focused on facilitators of flow, fewer focused on inhibitors and outcomes. Of the studies that outlined facilitators, most considered personal-cognitive factors (e.g., self-efficacy beliefs), personal-emotional (e.g., positive affect and emotion) and personal-behavioral (e.g., approach coping) influences, factors involving other people (e.g., the social network), motivational factors (e.g., trait-intrinsic motivation), and situational factors (e.g., design of work). Factors that inhibit flow were mostly personal, in comparison to situational, such as personal-emotional (e.g., negative affect) personal-cognitive influences (e.g., mental exhaustion), and personal-behavioral factors (e.g., self-punishment). For outcomes of flow, factors such as personal-emotional (e.g., well-being at work), personal-cognitive (e.g., cognitive involvement), personal-behavioral (e.g., spontaneity in tasks) were studied. While work-related situational outcomes (e.g., better service at work) were reported in a few studies, only one study addressed outcomes in nonwork-related situations (i.e., higher energy levels in situations outside of work).

References

Abuhamdeh, S., & Csikszentmihalyi, M. (2012). The importance of challenge for the enjoyment of intrinsically motivated, goal-directed activities. *Personality and Social Psychology Bulletin*, *38*, 317–330.

Bakker, A. (2005). Flow among music teachers and their students. The cross-over of peak experiences. *Journal of Vocational Behavior*, *66*, 26–44.

Bakker, A. (2008). The work-related flow inventory: Construction and initial validation of the WOLF. *Journal of Vocational Behavior, 75*, 400–414.

Bassi, M., & Delle Fave, A. (2012). Optimal experience among teachers: New insights into the work paradox. *The Journal of Psychology: Interdisciplinary and Applied, 146*, 533–557.

Baumann, N., & Scheffer, D. (2010). Seeing and mastering difficulty: The role of affective change in achievement flow. *Cognition and Emotion, 24*, 1304–1328.

Ceja, L., & Navarro, J. (2012). 'Suddenly I get into the zone': Examining discontinuities and nonlinear changes in flow experiences at work. *Human Relations, 65*, 1101–1127.

Csikszentmihalyi, M. (1975). *Beyond boredom and anxiety.* San Francisco, CA: Jossey-Bass.

Csikszentmihalyi, M. (1990). *Flow.* New York, NY: Harper & Row.

Csikszentmihalyi, M. (2003). *Good business.* New York, NY: Viking.

Csikszentmihalyi, M., & Csikszentmihalyi, I. (Eds.) (1988). *Optimal experience.* Cambridge, UK: Cambridge University Press.

Csikszentmihalyi, M., & LeFevre, J. (1989). Optimal experience in work and leisure. *Journal of Personality and Social Psychology, 56*, 815–822.

de Manzano, Ö., Cervenka, S., Jucaite, A., Hellenäs, O., Farde, L., & Ullén, F. (2013). Individual differences in the proneness to have flow experiences are linked to dopamine D2-receptor availability in the dorsal striatum. *Neuroimage, 67*, 1–6.

Delle Fave, A., & Massimini, F. (1988). Modernization and the changing contexts of flow in work and leisure. In M. Csikszentmihalyi & I. Csikszentmihalyi (Eds.), *Optimal experience* (pp. 193–213). Cambridge, UK: Cambridge University Press.

Delle Fave, A., Massimini, F., & Bassi, M. (2011). *Psychological selection and optimal experience across cultures: Social empowerment through personal growth.* Dordrecht, the Netherlands: Springer.

Demerouti, E. (2006). Job characteristics, flow, and performance. The moderating role of conscientiousness. *Journal of Occupational Health Psychology, 11*, 266–280.

Demerouti, E., Bakker, A. B., Sonnentag, S., & Fullagar, C. (2012). Work-related flow and energy at work and at home: A study on the role of daily recovery. *Journal of Organizational Behavior, 33*, 276–295.

Eisenberger, R., Jones, J. R., Stinglhamber, F., Shanock, L., & Randall, A. T. (2005). Flow experiences at work: For high need achievers alone? *Journal of Organizational Behavior, 26*, 755–775.

Evans-Pritchard, E. E. (1956). *Nuer religion.* Oxford, UK: Clarendon Press.

Fagerlind, A-C., Gustavsson, M., Johansson, G., & Ekberg., K. (2013). Experience of work related flow: Does high decision latitude enhance benefits gained from job resources? *Journal of Vocational Behavior, 83*, 161–170.

Fullagar, C. J., & Kelloway, E. K. (2009). "Flow" at work: An experience sampling approach. *Journal of Occupational and Organizational Psychology, 82*, 595–615.

Gallup. (2013). *State of the global workplace.* Washington, DC: Gallup.

Kuo, T.-H., & Ho, L.-A. (2010). Individual differences and performance: The relationship between personal traits, job characteristics, flow experience, and service quality. *Social Behavior and Personality, 38*, 531–552.

Lavigne, G. L., Forest, J., & Crevier-Braud, L. (2012). Passion at work and burnout: A two-study test of the mediating role of flow experiences. *European Journal of Work and Organizational Psychology, 21*, 518–546.

Mäkikangas, A., Bakker, A. B., Aunola, K., & Demerouti, E. (2010). Job resources and flow at work: Modelling the relationship via latent growth curve and mixture model methodology. *Journal of Occupational and Organizational Psychology, 83*, 795–814.

Marsh, A. (2005, August). The art of work. *Fast Company, 97*, 77–79.

Moneta, G. B. (2012). Opportunity for creativity in the job as a moderator of the relation between trait intrinsic motivation and flow in work. *Motivation and Emotion, 36*, 491–503.

Nakamura, J., & Dubin, M. (2015). Flow in motivational psychology. In J. D. Wright (Ed.), *International encyclopedia of the social and behavioral sciences* (2nd ed., pp. 260–265). Oxford, UK: Elsevier.

Nelson, V. J. (2014, March 14). A. Richard Grossman dies at 81; surgeon founded burn-treatment center. *Los Angeles Times.* Retrieved January 2, 2015 from http://www.latimes.com

Peters, P., Poutsma, E., Van der Heijden, B. I. J. M., Bakker, A. B., & De Bruijn, T. (2014). Enjoying new ways to work: An HRM process approach to study flow. *Human Resource Management*, *53*, 271–290.

Peterson, C., & Seligman, M. E. P. (2004). *Character strengths and virtues: A handbook and classification*. Washington, DC: American Psychological Association.

Sahlins, M. D. (1972). *Stone age economics*. New York, NY: de Gruyter.

Salanova, M., Bakker, A. B., & Llorens, S. (2006). Flow at work: Evidence for an upward spiral of personal and organizational resources. *Journal of Happiness Studies*, *7*, 1–22.

Tobert, S., & Moneta, G. B. (2013). Flow as a function of affect and coping in the workplace. *Individual Differences Research*, *11*, 102–113.

Turnbull, C. M. (1961). *The forest people*. New York, NY: Simon & Schuster.

Yan, Y. L., Davison, R. M., & Mo, C. Y. (2013). Employee creativity formation: The roles of knowledge seeking, knowledge contributing and flow experience in Web 2.0 virtual communities. *Computers in Human Behavior*, *29*, 1923–1932.

8

Mindfulness at Work

Gordon B. Spence

Introduction

To date the workplace mindfulness literature has been dominated by questions related to the role of mindfulness in the successful management of work stress, the cultivation of adaptive coping, and the enhancement of well-being (Aikens et al., 2014; Brown & Ryan, 2003; Michel, Bosch, & Rexroth, 2014; Reb, Narayanan, & Ho, 2013; Shonin, Van Gordon, Dunn, Singh, & Griffiths, 2014; van Berkel, Boot, Proper, Bongers, & van der Beek, 2014; van Gordon, Shonin, Zangeneh, & Griffiths, 2014; Vindholmen, Høigaard, Espnes, & Seiler, 2014). The positive impact of mindfulness on working adults is now being confirmed by meta-analytic studies, such as Sharma and Rush (2014) and Virgili (2015). Extending beyond work stress, researchers are also examining the relationship between mindfulness and work performance (Dane, 2010; Dane & Brummel, 2014; Reb et al., 2013; Shonin et al., 2014; Van Gordon et al., 2014), its impact on team dynamics and interpersonal relationships (Krishnakumar & Robinson, 2015; Vallabh & Singhal, 2014), as well as its implications for leadership (Reb, Narayanan, & Chaturvedi, 2014; Roche & Haar, 2013; Roche, Haar, & Luthans, 2014).

This chapter will focus on the contribution that this emerging work is making to the current understanding of mindfulness at work. It will begin by acknowledging that scholarly work in the area has been strongly influenced by an "epidemic" of work stress (Wainwright & Calnan, 2002) and the desire to find systematic ways to ameliorate its harmful effects. After presenting some work-oriented definitions of the construct, the focus will shift to summarizing what is known about the beneficial effects of mindfulness. Here particular attention will be paid to well-being and work-related outcomes for working adults, along with collective and social effects. At this point the discussion will turn to an examination of how sociocultural factors might influence the cultivation, and maintenance, of mindfulness and work. Self-determination theory (SDT; Deci & Ryan, 1985) will be used to theoretically anchor this part of the discussion and argue that employee mindfulness can be powerfully influenced

The Wiley Blackwell Handbook of the Psychology of Positivity and Strengths-Based Approaches at Work,
First Edition. Edited by Lindsay G. Oades, Michael F. Steger, Antonella Delle Fave, and Jonathan Passmore.

by the extent to which managers (and organizations more broadly) provide support for basic psychological needs. The discussion is then extended to consider the question: Do workers in unsupportive environments derive different benefits from mindfulness than workers in supportive environments? The chapter concludes by recommending that some empirical attention be given to this question, along with several others, as directions for future research.

The "Violence" of Work and How Mindfulness Helps

In a dynamic, unpredictable and complex world, the modern workplace is a reliable source of constant and unrelenting stress. Despite the many positive properties of work (Dutton, Roberts, & Bednar, 2010), the "violence" of modern work has long been noted (e.g., Terkel, 1974) and large numbers of employees seem to experience it in a profoundly negative way (Nixon, Mazzola, Bauer, Krueger, & Spector, 2011; Wainwright & Calnan, 2002). It is easy to bring to mind stressors that profoundly challenge business leaders, managers, and employees. Simple examples include the frustration felt by a CEO upon reviewing a fourth consecutive quarter of declining sales; the dread felt by a Human Resources manager before giving a salesperson a "poor" performance rating; the confusion felt by that salesperson upon receiving it. It is natural to conclude that these scenarios are all "negative" insofar as they would most likely result in strong reactive responses for those involved (e.g., fury for the CEO; passivity for the manager; demotivation for the salesperson).

Transactional models of stress and coping (e.g., Lazarus & Folkman, 1984) suggest that our responses to stressors are mediated by how they are appraised. As such, viewing a negative work outcome as a personal failure, as opposed to a personal challenge, is likely to result in two different responses. Critically it is the transaction between the objective environmental stressor (e.g., the performance rating) and the subjective personal appraisal (e.g., challenge or failure) that determines the quality of the coping response (Garland, 2007; Garland, Gaylord, & Fredrickson, 2011). This, for many Western scholars and practitioners, is the starting point for discussions about mindfulness. Indeed, Mindfulness-Based Stress Reduction (MBSR; Kabat-Zinn, 1990), Acceptance and Commitment Therapy (ACT; Hayes, Strosahl, & Wilson, 1999), and other formalized, structured mindfulness programs (e.g., Linehan, Cochran, & Kehrer, 2001; Teasdale, 2004) all seek to change the way people *relate* to a variety of life stressors, such that they are able to generate healthy, adaptive coping responses.

These programs tend to promote the idea that difficult experiences become more manageable when a person can: (1) appraise stressors with a vivid awareness of the prevailing context, (2) be open to perceiving and reframing events in different ways, and (3) fully attend to his or her own reactions as they unfold moment by moment. For the CEO confronted with poor performance, this could mean: (1) acknowledging the constraints of broader market factors, (2) searching for signs of recovery amid a disappointing outcome, and (3) noticing feelings of frustration and signs of possible ego-involvement. As this example suggests, mindfulness can be helpful for changing how one relates to life events by fundamentally altering the way one views them.

Defining Mindfulness for the Workplace

The rapid growth in mindfulness research over the past 15 years has been accompanied by a deepening of the definitional debate that surrounds the construct, with heightened scholarly interest doing little to improve conceptual clarity (Mikulas, 2011). Rather, considerable confusion seems to have arisen because authors have not adequately distinguished different understandings of mindfulness, which vary from its presentation as a state, trait, attentional process, mode of being, or committed lifestyle choice (Cavanagh & Spence, 2013; Reb et al., 2013). According to Brown, Ryan and Creswell (2007), much of the confusion is related to the prevailing concerns of Western clinicians, whose applied interests (in cultivating mindfulness for clients) have resulted in conceptualizations that include *attitudinal* qualities (Shapiro, Carlson, Astini, & Feedman, 2006), *labeling* of thoughts (Baer, 2003), *purposeful* attention (Kabat-Zinn, 1990), and *goal-directedness* (Rapgay & Bystrisky, 2009). For proponents of more parsimonious definitions (e.g., Brown & Ryan, 2003; Mikulas, 2011), infusing the construct with a mixture of attitudes, cognitive operations, and personal intentions is incompatible with the core experience of mindfulness (something more akin to bare awareness). One such definition is offered by Niemiec et al. (2010) who state that mindfulness is "a receptive state of mind wherein attention, informed by awareness of present experience, simply observes what is taking place" (p. 345). Leaving aside conceptual variations, Dane (2010) has noted that most definitions refer to mindfulness being (1) a mental state, focused on (2) present-moment realities, which may be (3) internal and/or external nature.

Workplace definitions

While the search for a consensual definition of mindfulness is sure to continue, recent theorizing has begun to address how the concept occurs within work and organizational contexts. For example, Dane and Brummel (2014) introduced the term *workplace mindfulness* to reflect the different degrees to which employees are mindful on the job. In doing so they also made three observations. First, that some individuals are predisposed toward greater levels of mindfulness than others (by virtue of their generic endowment and environmental influences). Second, despite its trait-like qualities, all people possess the ability to cultivate mindfulness through committed training and practice. Third, mindful attention is profoundly influenced by the working environment. According to this view, any consideration of mindfulness at work should encompass a combination of dispositional, experiential, and contextual factors.

While mindfulness is usually construed as an intrapersonal, individual-level phenomenon, it is not always conceived of in this way. For example, constructs like *organizational mindfulness* (OM; Ray, Baker, & Plowman, 2011) and *mindful organizing* (MO; Vogus & Sutcliffe, 2007; Vogus & Sutcliffe, 2012) construe mindfulness at work to be more of an interpersonal and collective-level construct. According to Vogus and Sutcliffe (2012), OM and MO are complementary constructs that exist at different levels of abstraction. Unlike most definitions of mindfulness, they are not construed as an intrapsychic process of individuals or collectives. Rather, they are understood as being an attribute of an organization (OM) and an active social process (MO). A notable feature of these constructs is that they are generally framed in terms of organizational survival. For Weick and Sutcliffe (2001), OM is a hallmark of a "high-reliability organisation," or an organization capable of functioning consistently well in risky, highly complex environments. As shown in Table 8.1, it is akin to a form of collective attunement to the success of an organization, one where the actions of managers and employees are galvanized by their tendency: (1) to be preoccupied with failure, (2) to be reluctant to simplify, (3) to be sensitive to operations, (4) to be committed to resilience, and (5) to show deference to expertise. According to its proponents, this form of mindfulness is top-down, with its five facets endorsed and embodied at the highest levels of authority (i.e., CEO, senior leaders), thereby creating a context for adaptive thought and action throughout all layers of the organization (Weick & Sutcliffe, 2001).

Table 8.1 Definitions, characteristics, and examples of organizational mindfulness and mindful organizing.

	Definition	*Characteristics*	*Practical examples*
Organizational mindfulness (OM)	Strategic and attitudinal. A top-down, enduring capability of an organization to foster acute awareness of discriminatory detail about emerging threats, along with the capacity to respond appropriately. Creates a context for adaptive thought and action on the "front line."	A set of shared attitudes that shapes organizational culture through valuing: • Preoccupation with failure • Reluctance to simplify • Sensitivity to operations • Commitment to resilience • Deference to expertise	Examples of • Preoccupation with failure – open discussion of problems; supported reporting of mistakes • Reluctance to simplify – seeking out divergent views; refusal to opt for easy answers • Sensitivity to operations –closely attending to work processes; looking for ways to mitigate risk • Commitment to resilience – prompt recovery from errors; learning from mistakes • Deference to expertise – valuing knowledge over hierarchical positions or roles; utilizing best resource for task at hand
Mindful organizing (MO)	Operational and behavioral. An operational state that emerges (bottom-up) when organizational members consistently act upon information about emerging threats. "Front-line" action supported by the context that *Organizational Mindfulness* creates.	Emerges from the collective action of organizational members, whose behavior displays a: • Preoccupation with failure • Reluctance to simplify • Sensitivity to operations • Commitment to resilience • Deference to expertise	

Source: Definitions in this table are composites derived from Ray, Baker, & Plowman (2011), Vogus & Sutcliffe (2012), and Weick & Sutcliffe (2001).

In contrast, MO is a state that emerges through the enactment of the collective attunement just outlined. Stated differently, it emerges out of the accumulated actions of organizational members, most noticeably when they are (1) openly discussing problems (i.e., showing a preoccupation with failure), (2) seeking out divergent views (i.e., being reluctant to simplify), (3) paying close attention to work processes (i.e., showing sensitivity to operations), (4) taking prompt action to recover from errors (i.e., being committed to resilience), and (5) seeking task-relevant information or resources from those with the most knowledge, rather than those with the most power (i.e., showing deference to expertise).

The conceptual contributions outlined in this section should help to further research into mindfulness at work. However, due to the time-lagged nature of the empirical process, it is likely to be a while before the research agenda proposed by Vogus and Sutcliffe (2012) is converted into published work. Nonetheless, the scientific investigation of mindfulness continues to advance in many domains of life (including work and organizations) and will now be briefly reviewed.

The Beneficial Effects of Mindfulness

Mindfulness has received a considerable amount of research attention in the past decade and led to the development of a vast literature. Indeed, the literature now boasts numerous meta-analytic and systematic reviews on the use of mindfulness within an array of contexts. Table 8.2 presents a sample of these studies, with key findings noted for each. Given that much of this work has been published since 2010, the empirical literature has been developing at a pace. However, as noted by Dane and Brummel (2014), the study of mindfulness in work contexts has lagged well behind the level of research interest displayed in other domains, such as those listed in Table 8.2. Of the work-related research that has been conducted, most has tended to focus on the effect of mindfulness on individual-level outcomes, using an array of well-being and work-related variables.

Individual well-being-related outcomes

Mindfulness is increasingly associated with a range of beneficial outcomes in samples of working adults. For example, the use of mindfulness-based interventions (MBIs) have been found to increase dispositional mindfulness in employees (Aikens et al., 2014; Flook, Goldberg, Pinger, Bonus, & Davidson, 2013; Malarkey, Jarjoura, & Klatt, 2013), successfully lower levels of work-related stress, depression, and burnout (e.g., Flook et al., 2013; Geary & Rosenthal, 2011; Gold et al., 2010; Kang, Choi, & Ryu, 2009; Krasner et al., 2009; Manocha, Black, Sarris, & Stough, 2011; Spence, Cavanagh, & Grant, 2008; Warnecke, Quinn, Ogden, Towle, & Nelson, 2011), as well as increasing levels of resiliency and vigor (Aikens et al., 2014), work–life satisfaction and psychological detachment from work (Michel et al., 2014), general health (Bazarko, Cate, Azocar, & Kreitzer, 2013; Foureur, Besley, Burton, Yu, & Crisp, 2013), self-compassion (Flook et al., 2013), while also assisting workers in emotionally demanding roles (like health care) to maintain high levels of service quality (Krasner et al., 2009).

Other studies have added more depth to the workplace mindfulness literature by investigating how trait mindfulness relates to work recovery processes. In one study, Allen and Kiburz (2012) found that mindfulness correlated with work–life balance and vitality levels for employed individuals. Interestingly, trait mindfulness and sleep quality were also found to be positively related (Allen & Kiburz, 2012), a relationship that Hülsheger et al. (2014)

Table 8.2 Systematic reviews and meta-analyses published in the mindfulness literature.

Area of Investigation	*Author*	*Type*	*N*	*Key findings*
Substance abuse and addiction	Zgierska et al. (2009)	SR	25	Evidence supporting general efficacy of meditation-based interventions for SUDs although significant methodological limitations noted (e.g., small sample sizes).
	Chiesa & Serretti (2014)	SR	24	Evidence suggests MBIs reduce substance consumption (e.g., alcohol, cocaine) compared to controls, while also reducing craving and increasing mindfulness.
Mental health and psychotherapy	Khoury et al. (2013)	MA	209	MBTs effective for a variety of psychological problems (especially anxiety, depression and stress); did not significantly differ from CBT or drug treatments.
	Strauss, Cavanagh, Oliver, & Pettman (2014)	MA	12	MBIs lowered depressive symptom severity (but not anxiety). Effects also noted in MBCT studies (but not MBSR) and studies with inactive (but not active) controls.
Children and adolescents	Black (2015)	SR	41	High-quality evidence for MBI use with youth is sparse but is strengthening in areas like executive function and aspects of mental and physical health.
	Zoogman, Goldberg, Hoyt, & Miller (2014)	MA	20	Small to moderate effect sizes found for MBIs over active controls, with larger effect sizes for psychological symptoms and clinical samples.
Health behavior modification	Godfrey, Gallo, & Afari (2015)	SR/MA	19	Medium to large effect sizes found for MBIs on binge eating, although findings were limited due to substantial heterogeneity observed across the study sample.
	Olson & Emery (2015)	SR	19	Significant weight loss was observed in 13 out of 19 studies, although studies could not assign a causal role to changes in mindfulness.
Clinical conditions:				
multiple sclerosis (MS)	Simpson et al. (2014)	SR	3	MBIs may benefit some MS patients in terms of quality of life, mental health, and some physical health measures.
HIV/AIDS	Riley & Kalichman (2015)	SR	11	MBSR found to produce small to moderate effect sizes for emotional distress, with mixed effects for disease progression.
fibromyalgia	Lauche, Cramer, Dobos, Langhorst, & Schmidt (2013)	SR/MA	6	Weak evidence found for MBSR as an approach with fibromyalgia syndrome, with short-term improvements noted for quality of life and pain.
sleep disturbance	Winbush, Gross, & Kreitzer (2007)	SR	38	Some evidence to suggest that MBSR is associated with improved sleep and a decrease in sleep-interfering cognitive processes.
gastrointestinal disorders	Aucoin, Lalonde-Parsi, & Cooley (2014)	MA	7	Weak evidence found for efficacy of MBT to reduce symptom severity of irritable bowel syndrome and improve quality of life.
vascular disease	Abbott et al. (2014)	SR/MA	8	Whilst MBSR/MBCT interventions appear to produce a range of psychological benefits, studies have yet to clarify their effects on physical aspect of disease.
cancer (various)	Piet, Wurtzen, & Zachariae (2012)	SR/MA	22	Good-quality evidence was found that MBT improves mindfulness skills and reduces anxiety and depression in adult cancer patients and survivors.

Note: SR = systematic review; MA = meta-analysis; SUD = substance use disorders; MBI = mindfulness-based interventions; MBT = mindfulness-based therapy; CBT = cognitive-behavioral therapy; MBCT = Mindfulness-based cognitive therapy; MBSR = mindfulness-based stress reduction.
Source: Author.

later found was mediated by psychological detachment after work. In a subsequent study, Hülsheger, Feinholdt, and Nübold (2015) reported that a simple, "low-dose" mindfulness intervention positively impacted both sleep quality and sleep duration, but not psychological detachment.

As always, care should be taken when considering these findings. While a meta-analysis of 19 studies found support for the use of MBIs within organizational settings (Virgili, 2015), it was also noted that they were no more effective than other stress management interventions (such as relaxation and yoga). In addition, MBIs do not always result in the outcomes expected. For example, in a controlled study van Berkel et al. (2014) investigated the impact of a worksite MBI and assessed its impact on lifestyle behaviors (such as physical activity and fruit intake). Despite being provided with eight weeks of in-company sponsored mindfulness training, health foods and e-coaching (to embed new behaviors), no significant pre/post differences were found in either lifestyle behaviors or the determinants of such behaviors (e.g., intention to act; perceived barriers to action). As such, some doubt has been cast over the efficacy of formal, structured workplace interventions and more research is still needed to tease out their unique impact and contribution (Virgili, 2015).

Individual work-related outcomes

Organizations and businesses are interested in what employees can do, not just in how well they feel. Not surprisingly then, organizational scholars (like Dane & Brummel, 2014) are showing increasing interest in the relationship between mindfulness and an array of work-related variables (such as job performance). However, as work performance cannot sensibly be decoupled from its subjective determinants (e.g., self-efficacy), these strands of enquiry are likely to occur in tandem, such as studies that have examined variables related to both mindfulness and sleep (i.e., Allen & Kiburz, 2012; Hülsheger et al., 2014; Hülsheger et al., 2015).

From the perspective of work outcomes, findings that mindfulness impacts the quality and duration of sleep are interesting because of the strong empirical links that exist between sleep and work performance (Pilcher & Huffcutt, 1996; Swanson et al., 2011). Until research begins to clarify the links between mindfulness and work-outcome variables, researchers and practitioners may need to rely upon the robustness of other strands of research (e.g., sleep and performance) for making claims about the impact that mindfulness may have on performance in the workplace.

These observations notwithstanding, more direct explorations into the mindfulness–performance relationship have been reported. In one of the first studies, Shao and Skarlicki (2009) investigated the academic performance of 149 MBA students and found that mindfulness interacted with gender to predict performance for women (but not for men). While this was not a workplace study per se, the data was collected from adults with a strong work orientation (i.e., MBA students) and showed no direct relationship between mindfulness and performance. However, given the complex relationship that is likely to exist between mindfulness and performance, such a finding does not seem unsurprising. Fortunately, several recent theoretical contributions have advanced scholarship in the area (e.g., Dane, 2010; Rees, Breen, Cusack, & Hegney, 2015; Vallabh & Singhal, 2014). For example, Dane (2010) argues that mindfulness may not always be useful for workplace performance. Rather, its value should be dependent upon the type of environment that one is working within (i.e., dynamic or static) and/or what level of task expertise one has (i.e., expert or novice). In amongst several theoretical propositions, Dane argues that the "wide attentional breadth" conferred by mindfulness should facilitate task performance in dynamic environments, but inhibit it in static environments (Proposition 1; Dane, 2010,

p. 1007). He also argues that it should facilitate task performance for those with high task expertise, while inhibiting it for task novices (Proposition 2, p. 1009). Such propositions are useful because they introduce context into considerations about the utility of mindfulness for performance.

In a test of Dane's (2010) first proposition, Dane and Brummel (2014) studied restaurant workers and found support for the hypothesis that workplace mindfulness was positively related to job performance in a dynamic customer service environment. They concluded that (in the pressurized reality of a busy restaurant) highly mindful staff did better than less mindful colleagues, because they could attend to an array of competing stimuli and still situate their minds in present-moment time. While only a few other studies have explored similar links (Ho, 2011; Shonin et al., 2014), the testing of research hypotheses derived from theoretical proposals such as Dane's (2010) seem a useful empirical pathway to explore.

Collective and social-level outcomes

As outlined earlier, mindfulness has been defined in ways that extend it beyond simply being a quality of individual consciousness. While articulating facets of *organizational mindfulness* and *mindful organizing* (Ray et al., 2011; Vogus & Sutcliffe, 2012) opens up new opportunities for researching mindfulness in work settings, these opportunities have yet to translate into empirical publications. Nonetheless, the conceptual value of constructs like organizational mindfulness continues to be explored in relation to a broad range of collective-level outcomes and behaviors. Examples include its role in the global market performance of firms (Nwankpa & Roumani, 2014), its influence as an antecedent of enterprise resource planning system use (Bayraktar & Oly Ndubisi, 2014), and its role in the emergence (or non-emergence) of bandwagoning decision-making (Fiol & O'Connor, 2003).

Other strands of mindfulness research focus on outcomes that are more sociocultural in nature (using individual-level measures). For example, in a study of hostile work behaviors, Krishnakumar and Robinson (2015) found that mindful people were less Machiavellian and engaged in less counterproductive work behavior. According to the authors, this represented further evidence that mindfulness operates like a protective factor for organizations, by allowing people to circumvent strong feelings before they occur. Similar conclusions have been drawn from studies that have investigated leader/manager mindfulness (Roche et al., 2014) and the impact of supervisor mindfulness on employee well-being and performance (Reb et al., 2014).

While this review of the workplace mindfulness literature has revealed some substantial theorizing on what mindfulness *is* within the domain of work, there does not appear to have been much discussion about what helps to support workplace mindfulness, beyond advocacy for MBIs that rely primarily on meditation as the major agent of change. In the next section the focus switches to an examination of the sociocultural forces that exist within organizations and that are likely to powerfully shape both individual and collective mindfulness at work.

Impact of Organizational Support on Mindfulness at Work

Several authors have argued recently that individual mindfulness is influenced by cultural or environmental factors (Reb et al., 2013; Wolff, 2014). For example, Dane and Brummel (2014) suggest that:

> The contextual elements of one's workplace may exert a rather profound influence on how one behaves at work and, indeed, how one focuses attention within one's work setting. It is

therefore possible that, for some individuals, certain features of the work environment "cue" mindfulness. (p. 108)

The suggestion that employee mindfulness is triggered by cultural or environmental forces raises questions about the role that leaders and managers play in this process. Two recent studies reported by Reb and colleagues offer some guidance. In the first study, Reb et al. (2013) found that supervisor support predicted self-awareness amongst employees. As self-awareness is central to most definitions of mindfulness (Baer, 2003), this study suggests that employee mindfulness may indeed be enhanced by the presence of a supportive authority figure. In the other study, Reb et al. (2014) found that the trait mindfulness of leaders was negatively related to employee deviance and emotional exhaustion, and positively related to work–life balance and employee performance. In addition, these authors also found that basic psychological need satisfaction (i.e., autonomy, competence, relatedness) meditated the relationship between leader mindfulness and work outcomes. From this it was concluded that "leaders who are fully present when interacting with subordinates may derive a better understanding of their employees' needs [allowing] them to more effectively support employees" (p. 43) and generate positive work-related outcomes.

From an attentional perspective, the findings reported by Reb et al. (2014) make some sense. That is, employees who consistently enjoy support for their basic needs (enabled by levels of leader mindfulness) will be unlikely to direct much attention toward having their views and opinions acknowledged (autonomy), their worthiness and value confirmed (competence), or seeking more secure, nourishing connections (relatedness). Put differently, with these psychological prerequisites met, employees should be free to fully deploy attentional resources toward work tasks and responsibilities.

A Self-Determination Theory (SDT) View of Mindfulness at Work

As mentioned several times in the preceding review, the study of mindfulness at work has focused primarily on its ability to counteract the harmful effects of an array of cognitive, affective, and behavioral dysfunctions. Indeed, much of the published research has concentrated on the beneficial effects of MBIs for individuals, most particularly the intrapersonal changes they seem to produce. However, as research reviewed in the previous section suggests, there is a social psychology associated with mindfulness that warrants attention. This involves the observation that sociocultural factors, such as manager behaviors, have the power to either sharpen or dull the conscious experience of workers and, with it, their levels of psychological well-being and productive performance. A useful theory for exploring this aspect of mindfulness at work is SDT (Deci & Ryan, 1985) because it provides an explanation of how social contexts effect the emergence of mindfulness in people, while also proposing a link between mindfulness and motivational phenomena that are salient to work settings (principally autonomous motivation).

SDT: Key conceptual ideas

SDT (Deci & Ryan, 1985) is a macro-theory of human motivation and personality development. Whilst the six mini-theories that comprise SDT address different aspects of motivational and personality processes (for a summary, see Spence & Deci, 2013, p. 91), at its core is the proposition that human beings have a set of universal, fundamental psychological needs, the satisfaction of which are essential for healthy development, vital engagement, effective behaving, and psychological well-being. More specifically, the theory proposes that a person's level of functioning and well-being depends upon the degree of satisfaction of three basic psychological needs: autonomy, competence, and relatedness (Deci & Ryan, 2008). It predicts that people will do well and feel their best when the sociocultural conditions of their lives (i.e., family relationships, friendships, workplace culture, political systems, cultural norms) support the inherent needs for experiencing their behavior as owned and choiceful (i.e., autonomy), producing valued outcomes through the use of their strengths and abilities (i.e., competence), and feeling closely and securely connected to significant others (i.e., relatedness).

Intrinsic and extrinsic motivation SDT asserts the importance of differentiating between types of motivation for understanding and predicting different qualities of human behavior and psychological well-being. A primary distinction is made between autonomous motivation and controlled motivation. Autonomous motivation involves acting with a full sense of choice, willingness, and volition. When autonomous, people concur with that which they are doing, and they are more likely to experience positive affect, endorsement, and satisfaction. Autonomous motivation comprises two specific types of motivation – intrinsic motivation and well-internalized extrinsic motivation. Intrinsic motivation means engaging in an activity because the activity itself is interesting and enjoyable. Intrinsic motivation is the prototype of autonomous motivation (e.g., children at play), where the motivation is internal and inherent, and the satisfaction most significant. By contrast, extrinsic motivation refers to acting in order to get some separate consequence. As will shortly be explored, mindfulness seems to play a role in the internalization of extrinsic motivation, which represents a movement toward greater levels of autonomous motivation.

Internalization and integration According to Deci and Ryan (2008) internalization refers to the process whereby people "take in" an external value or regulation but may or may not accept it as their own. The process of organismic integration, which is the fundamental developmental process, involves fuller internalization in which people accept the value and regulation of an extrinsically motivated behavior and integrate it with their own sense of self. More specifically, there are four types of extrinsic motivation that vary in the degree of internalization and in the degree of autonomy of resulting behaviors (see Table 8.3).

As previously mentioned, *external regulation* is extrinsic motivation for which there has been no internalization of the regulation and no value ascribed to an activity or task. Rather, people are impelled into action through the presence of an inducement (e.g., financial incentive) or some coercive factor (e.g., the threat of reprimand). Introjection results when people take in a controlling contingency (i.e., "I must help or others will see me as a lazy person") and maintain it in a similar form such that they are then using it to control themselves. Within SDT the terms "self-control" and "internal control" refer to pressuring oneself to behave with ego-involved contingencies of self-esteem and guilt. This is very different from true self-regulation in which one acts with volition and choice rather than pressure and tension. Thus, and importantly, *introjected regulation* is not autonomous but is one of the two types of controlled motivation, the other being external regulation.

According to SDT, people can internalize a regulation more fully by identifying with its importance for their own needs and self-selected goals. When this has occurred, they have accepted the regulation as their own and are relatively autonomous when enacting it.

Table 8.3 Varying levels of integration and ownership associated with extrinsic motivation.

Reason	*Type*	*Motivation*	*Example*
External	Controlled	Striving because somebody else wants you to and you'll get some reward for doing it or get into trouble for not.	"I'll mentor my staff because it'll help my chances of promotion."
Introjected	Controlled	Striving because you would feel ashamed, guilty, or anxious if you didn't, or self-aggrandized if you did. You strive for this because you think you should and use internal sanctions to motivate the striving.	"I'll mentor my staff because that's what a good manager should do."
Identified	Autonomous	Striving because you personally accept the value of the behavior for yourself. Although the behavior or goal may have been acquired from others, you now endorse its utility for your own needs and goals.	"I'll mentor my staff because it's a good, inexpensive way to develop potential."
Integrated	Autonomous	Striving because of the importance of the behavior as an integrated aspect of who you are. This motivation is not about the activity being interesting or fun, but rather about it being deeply important for behaving with integrity and respect.	"I'll mentor my staff because it means a lot to me to see other people develop."

Source: Adapted from Deci and Ryan (2000).

This type of extrinsic motivation is referred to as *identified regulation*. Finally, when people take this one step further and integrate an identification into their sense of self, the extrinsic motivation is referred to as *integrated regulation*, which is the most mature form of extrinsic motivation and successful type of socialization. As shown in Table 8.3, identified regulation and integrated regulation are both considered types of autonomous motivation. It should be noted that fully internalized extrinsic motivation is different from intrinsic motivation because intrinsic motivation is about people's inherent interest in behaviors. In contrast, integrated regulation is about the internalized importance of the behaviors for their plans, goals, or values.

As indicated in the examples presented in Table 8.3, the same activity or goal can be underpinned by quite different motivations. Importantly SDT stipulates that all motivations would be present (to varying degrees) in the goal striving of workers. It also argues that the strength of these motives will be influenced by the presence of appropriately supportive sociocultural conditions. Within the present discussion this means that sources of organizational need support (e.g., managers, mentors, coaches) can assist individuals to move toward more autonomous (identified and integrated) goal selection, to the extent that those supports facilitate the satisfaction of autonomy, competence, and relatedness. As will shortly be explained, this is more likely to occur when high levels of mindfulness are present in the manager, mentor, coach or other salient people in the social network of workers.

The organismic dialectic and basic psychological needs As mentioned, the SDT perspective views humans as proactive and growth-oriented, manifest in their intrinsic motivation and organismic integration. From that perspective, the self is viewed as an active processor of experience, a set of dynamic psychic processes and structures that continuously seeks to make meaning of the myriad internal and external events that comprise a person's life and to integrate them into a coherent, unified sense of self. As such it represents an inherently positive view of human nature. Nonetheless, SDT explicitly acknowledges, and focuses much of its empirical attention, on the organismic dialectic of human experience (Deci and Ryan, 1985). Simply put, a dialectic is the juxtaposition of conflicting forces or ideas. The dialectic that is central to SDT is the conflict that exists between people's natural orientation toward growth and development in interaction with the potentially disruptive power of various socio-contextual forces (e.g., parental control, peer pressure, restrictive legislation) that can block, impair, or stall these positive developmental tendencies and autonomous motivations.

Internalization and integration, which represent one aspect of the organismic dialectic, are developmental processes that can be either helped or hindered by the presence of different sociocultural conditions (the other aspect of the dialectic). It is this nexus where the basic psychological needs once again become salient. An enormous body of SDT research confirms that the satisfaction of autonomy, competence, and relatedness serves to maintain intrinsic motivation and to facilitate internalization and integration of extrinsic motivation (e.g., Baard, Deci, & Ryan, 2004; Deci, Eghrari, Patrick, & Leone, 1994). This implies that social agents (such as managers) who in some way supervise, advise, or guide others (such as employees) are likely to more effectively motivate others to the degree that they can facilitate the satisfaction of basic psychological needs. Accordingly, SDT research examines the degree to which individuals experience their environments as satisfying or thwarting of these basic needs. To the degree that their basic needs are thwarted, the darker side of the human experience becomes evident in the form of negative affect, aggressive behaviors, and/or, more specifically in the workplace, active employee disengagement.

Motivating Style, Autonomy Support, and the Role of Mindfulness

Consistent with these core SDT predictions, several studies have reported on the importance of need-supportive environments for surfacing autonomous motivation in employees (Gillet, Gagné, Sauvagère, & Fouquereau, 2013; Hardre & Reeve, 2009; Schultz, Ryan, Niemiec, Legate, & Williams, 2014). Also known as "autonomy-supportive social contexts" (Schultz et al., 2014, p. 4), these contexts are powerfully shaped in the workplace by the actions and behaviors of managers and leaders (Gillet et al., 2013; Roche & Haar, 2013). These behaviors include the provision of meaningful rationales (for work tasks), the use of non-controlling language, the provision of real choice (when it exists), the encouragement of self-initiation, and most fundamentally, the willingness to engage, and genuinely acknowledge, employee perspectives (such as a negative reaction to a work decision, or a creative idea for service improvement).

For Hardre and Reeve (2009) these behaviors reflect the *motivating style* of a manager, which is defined as "the characteristic way that a manager seeks to motivate employees in the workplace" (p. 167). In an intervention study designed to examine this subset of management style, the researchers found evidence for the overall malleability of motivating styles, while noting that some behaviors were easier to change than others. In particular they noted that managers were generally successful at becoming less controlling (by using more non-controlling language, providing rationales for action, and acknowledging negative affect), but not necessarily at becoming highly autonomy supportive (by better nurturing employees' inner motivational resources). Based on their data, Hardre and Reeve (2009) concluded that this facet of autonomy support seems to require extensive training because it involves becoming aware of employee interests, values, and preferences, and then finding ways to align these inner resources to their workplace roles and responsibilities.

A manager's capacity for mindfulness seems central to being able to nurture the inner motivational resources of employees. This is simply because it is extremely difficult to develop a decent understanding of others if one does not have a decent understanding of oneself. To do this, one must develop a secure attachment to oneself (Bruce, Manber, Shapiro, & Constantino, 2010), which involves maintaining an open, curious stance toward the full range of personal experience. Cavanagh and Spence (2013) elaborate this point via the observation that "the security afforded by an affirming and curious relationship with oneself enables the individual to engage with their ongoing experience and derive important insights from it. This leads to better self-understanding and, ultimately, better understanding of others" (p. 121). Stated differently, *intrapersonal attunement* seems to play an important role in *interpersonal attunement* (Bruce et al., 2010), which Cavanagh and Spence (2013) argue are first-order and second-order effects that flow from the development of mindfulness (see Figure 7.2, p. 120 and Figure 7.4, p. 126).

While mindfulness would seem to enhance employee autonomy support through better manager–employee relations, it is likely to assist in at least two other important ways. First, as summarized by Schultz et al. (2014), the non-evaluative nature of mindfulness enhances emotional regulation by helping troublesome thoughts and feelings to be seen for what they are (impermanent), while its enhanced awareness provides individuals with "a small interval of time" (Martin, 1997) that enables them to choose from a range of possible responses. Put differently, mindfulness lowers behavioral reactivity by creating a psychological "space" between one's appraisals and ensuing reactions, which increases personal reflectivity and softens the impact of negative stimuli (Schultz et al., 2014). Second, the cultivation of reflective capacity helps individuals become more sensitive to important aspects of the self (e.g., values, interests, intuitions) and more likely to select behaviors that accord well with them (Brown & Ryan, 2015). From this a sense of choicefulness and self-direction can emerge, forming the basis of authentic personality development.

The preceding discussion has suggested that high levels of mindfulness are closely related to self-understanding, interpersonal attunement, and low behavioral reactivity. When well represented within a workplace, these qualities are likely to result in the emergence of a proactive, supportive environment that seeks to work in the best interests of the organization and those that comprise it.

The Interaction of Mindfulness and Workplace Perceptions

As suggested in the preceding review, the effects of mindfulness on individual workers would appear to depend upon the quality of the work climate they are working within. This prompts the question: do workers in unsupportive environments derive different benefits from mindfulness than workers in supportive environments? Recent empirical evidence suggests they might, with Schultz et al. (2014) reporting that highly mindful workers experienced less basic psychological need frustration in controlling environments, compared to those that were less mindful. Contrary to other SDT studies reviewed so far, this study is notable because it examined perceptions of active need thwarting (or frustration) in the workplace, rather than perceptions of the relative presence or absence of need support. See Table 8.4 for a description of these different workplace perceptions.

Table 8.4 Features of need-satisfying and need-frustrating workplaces.

	Need-satisfying	*Need-frustrating*
Autonomy	Promotes self-initiation and subjective ownership of work goals by acknowledging the perspective of workers, providing choice (where it exists) and rationales for requested tasks.	Seeks to control and/or manipulate employee activity levels by employing a variety of reinforcements, punishments or other coercive tactics (e.g., ultimatums).
Competence	Provides workers with an array of support for effective action such as information-rich feedback, recognition of effort and achievements, and good working conditions.	Engenders a sense of hopelessness and/ or failure in workers via either an absence of feedback, constant criticism, lack of appreciation or inadequate resourcing.
Relatedness	Creates interpersonal context in which workers are able to communicate openly, can trust (and feel trusted), and experience warm, genuine relationships with work colleagues.	Creates interpersonal context in which workers are disinclined to communicate freely and/or experience relational exclusion or ostracism within their work role.

Source: Adapted from Chen et al. (2015).

Table 8.5 The interaction of mindfulness and work climate for individual workers.

	Unsupportive work climate	*Supportive work climate*
High mindfulness	• Managed reactivity • Frequent interpersonal challenge • Social connectivity retained • Stablized work engagement • Manageable psychological distress	• High proactivity • Harmonious interpersonal relationships • High social connectivity • Full work engagement • Flourishing mental health
Low mindfulness	• High reactivity • Volatile interpersonal relationships • Low social connectivity • Active work disengagement • Acute psychological distress	• Moderate to low proactivity • Stable interpersonal relationships • Moderate social connectivity • Partial work engagement • Languishing mental health

Source: Author.

Prompted by the findings published by Schultz et al. (2014), some consideration of the interaction between mindfulness and work climate seem warranted. Accordingly, Table 8.5 speculates on the impact that *high* and *low* levels of employee mindfulness might have within *unsupportive* and *supportive* work climates. Each will now be briefly described.

Unsupportive work climate/High mindfulness: In line with findings reported by Schultz et al. (2014), high levels of mindfulness are likely to have protective qualities for workers in unsupportive work climates. Given that the frustration of autonomy, competence, and relatedness needs tends to predict an array of negative outcomes (including stress biomarkers; Bartholomew, Ntoumanis, Ryan, Bosch, & Thøgersen-Ntoumani, 2011), it is useful to know that mindfulness helps to mitigate the costs associated with exposure to toxic workplaces (Roche et al., 2014) and reassuring to have several evidence-based MBIs available for use (Virgili, 2015).

Unsupportive work climate/Low mindfulness: In contrast, employees with low levels of mindfulness are likely to cope poorly in situations where there has been a break in the psychological contract, either due to toxic organizational principles (e.g., profits before people), poor work conditions, or intra-office conflicts (Harder, Rash, & Wagner, 2014). Faced with a constant dissatisfaction or frustration of basic needs, these employees will feel under relentless psychological attack but lack the self-awareness and self-understanding to make sense of their experiences or respond adaptively to them. As such they will be most likely to experience acute psychological distress, struggle to maintain healthy social connections, and be very reactive, responding to stressors in ways that vary from overt aggression to passive withdrawal.

Supportive work climate/Low mindfulness: In supportive work climates, employees with low levels of mindfulness are likely to have a satisfactory experience but may well be a source of great frustration to others. This is because these individuals will lack the metacognitive skills needed to optimize the opportunities these environments will afford them (potentially resulting in significant unrealized potential). For example, a junior manager purposefully avoids delivering a board presentation (because of performance anxiety), despite having the full support and backing of her department head. Whilst these employees are likely to show a strong disinclination to take on any personally challenging work tasks or assignments, research reviewed earlier (e.g., Reb et al., 2014; Reb et al., 2013) suggests that the presence of a highly mindful manager can influence the employees' own levels of mindfulness (through support for basic needs, role modeling, etc.).

Supportive work climate/High mindfulness: For employees with high levels of self-awareness and self-understanding, a work environment that honors the psychological contract (Harder et al., 2014) is likely to provide a context that promotes optimal functioning (Spence & Deci, 2013) and flourishing mental health (see Grant & Spence, 2010). In these environments, employees are likely to approach (rather than avoid) their professional challenges because they (1) will be encouraged to do so by their immediate manager(s) and other contextual supports (such as "safe-to-fail" experiments or psychologically safe environments; Edmondson, 2011), and (2) will feel able to manage the psychological reactions associated with extending themselves.

From Basic Need Support to Organizational Mindfulness and Mindful Organizing

In this chapter a variety of conceptualizations of mindfulness have been considered, with a particular focus given to workplace mindfulness (Dane & Brummel, 2014; Vogus & Sutcliffe, 2012). These have been accompanied by an exploration of sociocultural factors (elucidated by SDT) that may explain how mindfulness at work can be cultivated and maintained outside the use of standard MBIs. Some final thoughts will now be offered on how these concepts are related.

As previously outlined in Table 8.1, organizational mindfulness (OM) and mindful organizing (MO) are complementary constructs insofar as one, OM, represents an attitude and general preoccupation with collective success that is endorsed at the highest levels of management and creates a context for adaptive thought and action throughout the entire organization. The other, MO, is an emergent property of the system, one that stems from the accumulated action of employees who are working to safeguard the best interests of the organization.

At the core of these constructs is a fundamental concern that the organization function reliably and sustainably. The key to this, its proponents suggest, is to attune acutely to how the organization is operating and, when problems arise, think expansively about them and respond promptly using all available sources of expert knowledge (Vogus & Sutcliffe, 2012). From an SDT perspective, these qualities reflect a high degree of work proactivity, a level one could expect to see from autonomously motivated employees. As has been indicated many times already, the support and satisfaction of basic psychological needs is intimately tied to autonomous motivation and the extent to which employees freely engage in work tasks and activities. As Schultz et al. (2014) illustrate:

> When a manager takes an employee's perspective, that employee is likely to feel competent, as his/her opinions matter, feel connected with the manager, and experience greater volition, given the manager is listening to his/her opinion or seeing things through his/her frame of reference rather than pressuring him/her to a particular outcome. (pp. 4–5)

Given that autonomy support in the workplace directly involves canvassing and understanding alternative viewpoints (autonomy/reluctance to simplify), accessing tacit knowledge and latent abilities (competence/deference to expertise), and seeking collective solutions to problems (relatedness/commitment to resilience), it would seem to have a vital role to play in both the establishment of collective forms of mindfulness. That is, autonomy support may provide the foundational mindset for OM, one that can be embodied by senior leaders and that helps to create the "context for thinking and action on the front line" (Vogus & Sutcliffe, 2012, p. 724). In contrast, autonomy support may help to scaffold the social process that underpins MO, which relies on "continuous real time communication and interactions that occur in briefings, meetings, updates, and in teams' ongoing work" (Vogus & Sutcliffe, 2012, pp. 724–725). Given the untested nature of these speculations, future research will be needed to confirm such relationships.

Future Research

As just outlined, one avenue for future research would be to investigate whether autonomy support is an important contributor to collective-level mindfulness, using constructs such as OM and MO. If such a relationship were to be established (using cross-sectional designs), attention would naturally be drawn toward seeking to understand how, and to what extent, the support of basic psychological needs within workplaces impacts mindfulness within those environments.

As reviewed earlier, research into the link between mindfulness and work performance is still developing and requires more attention (Dane & Brummel, 2014). An interesting focal point for future research would be the link between mindfulness, sleep, and performance, given emerging evidence of a link between mindfulness and sleep quality and duration (Hülsheger et al., 2015), and the more well-established links between sleep and several aspects of human performance (Pilcher & Huffcutt, 1996; Swanson et al., 2011). Research designs that permit simultaneous testing of these variables (using structural equation modeling or mediation/moderation analyses) would be helpful for teasing out the combined, and relative, contributions of mindfulness and sleep to performance at work.

Finally, the research reported in this chapter on manager motivating style (Hardre & Reeve, 2009) seems worthy of further attention. One approach would be to assess whether the use of formal, structured mindfulness training for managers leads to greater autonomous motivation in their employees. More specifically, this link could be examined through the mechanism identified by Hardre and Reeve (2009) – a manger's capacity to nurture employees' inner motivational resources. As reasoned earlier, nurturing the inner motivational resources of others requires a capacity to understand others, which is extremely difficult without an understanding of oneself. Studies of this type would both help to illuminate little-known linkages between mindfulness and work outcomes, and may provide managers and leaders with compelling reasons to engage in professional development practices (e.g., MBIs) that could benefit their employees, their organizations, and, ultimately, themselves.

Conclusion

Theoretical and empirical investigations into mindfulness at work have tended to focus disproportionately on the use of MBIs for managing stress and a range of occupational dysfunctions. While numerous studies have confirmed the utility of mindfulness training for such purposes, other studies indicate that MBIs may not be as effective as widely believed (Virgili, 2015). When considered in the context of complex modern workplaces, such findings seem unsurprising. This is because most workplace stressors are socially and culturally derived, and MBIs may be insufficient for helping employees to psychologically adjust to their effects.

In this chapter, SDT has been used to present a sociocultural account of mindfulness at work. In effect it has argued that, from a stress management perspective, autonomy supportive management and organizational practices may render MBIs largely irrelevant for many workers. This is because worker outcomes seem to depend as much on one's sociocultural circumstances (e.g., need satisfaction or need frustration), as one's intrapersonal circumstances (e.g., the ability to maintain a state of decentered awareness). As such, the ability to create a mindful workplace would seem to require more attention to organizational, cultural-level interventions than personal, individual-level interventions.

References

Abbott, R. A., Whear, R., Rodgers, L. R., Bethel, A., Coon, J. T., Kuyken, W., … Dickens, C. (2014). Effectiveness of mindfulness-based stress reduction and mindfulness based cognitive therapy in vascular disease: A systematic review and meta-analysis of randomised controlled trials. *Journal of psychosomatic research*, *76*(5), 341–351.

Aikens, K. A., Astin, J., Pelletier, K. R., Levanovich, K., Baase, C. M., Park, Y. Y., & Bodnar, C. M. (2014). Mindfulness goes to work: Impact of an online workplace intervention. *Journal of Occupational and Environmental Medicine*, *56*(7), 721–731.

Allen, T. D., & Kiburz, K. M. (2012). Trait mindfulness and work–family balance among working parents: The mediating effects of vitality and sleep quality. *Journal of Vocational Behavior*, *80*(2), 372–379.

Aucoin, M., Lalonde-Parsi, M. J., & Cooley, K. (2014). Mindfulness-based therapies in the treatment of functional gastrointestinal disorders: A meta-analysis. *Evidence-Based Complementary and Alternative Medicine*, *2014* (Article ID 140724, 11 pages). doi: 10.1155/2014/140724

Baard, P. P., Deci, E. L., & Ryan, R. M. (2004). Intrinsic need satisfaction: A motivational basis of performance and well-being in two work settings. *Journal of Applied Social Psychology*, *34*(10), 2045–2068.

Baer, R. A. (2003). Mindfulness training as a clinical intervention: A conceptual and empirical review. *Clinical Psychology: Science and Practice*, *10*(2), 125–143.

Bartholomew, K. J., Ntoumanis, N., Ryan, R. M., Bosch, J. A., & Thøgersen-Ntoumani, C. (2011). Self-determination theory and diminished functioning: The role of interpersonal control and psychological need thwarting. *Personality and Social Psychology Bulletin*, *37*, 1459–1473.

Bayraktar, A., & Oly Ndubisi, N. (2014). The role of organizational mindfulness in firms' globalization and global market performance. *Journal of Research in Marketing and Entrepreneurship*, *16*(1), 26–46.

Bazarko, D., Cate, R. A., Azocar, F., & Kreitzer, M. J. (2013). The impact of an innovative mindfulness-based stress reduction program on the health and well-being of nurses employed in a corporate setting. *Journal of Workplace Behavioral Health*, *28*(2), 107–133.

Black, D. S. (2015). Mindfulness training for children and adolescents. In K. Brown, D. Creswell, & R. Ryan (Eds.), *Handbook of mindfulness: Theory, research, and practice* (pp. 283–310). New York, NY: Guilford Press.

Brown, K. W., & Ryan, R. M. (2003). The benefits of being present: Mindfulness and its role in psychological well-being. *Journal of Personality and Social Psychology*, *84*, 822–848.

Brown, K. W., & Ryan, R. M. (2015). A self-determination theory perspective on fostering healthy self-regulation from within and without. In S. Joseph (Ed.), *Positive psychology in practice: Promoting human flourishing in work, health, education and everyday life* (pp. 139–157). Hoboken, NJ: Wiley.

Brown, K. W., Ryan, R. M., & Creswell, J. D. (2007). Mindfulness: Theoretical foundations and evidence for its salutary effects. *Psychological Inquiry*, *18*(4), 211–237.

Bruce, N. G., Manber, R., Shapiro, S. L., & Constantino, M. J. (2010). Psychotherapist mindfulness and the psychotherapy process. *Psychotherapy: Theory, Research, Practice, Training*, *47*(1), 83–97.

Cavanagh, M., & Spence, G. B. (2013). Mindfulness in coaching: Philosophy, psychology, or just a useful skill? In J. Passmore, D. Peterson, & T. Freire (Eds.), *The Wiley-Blackwell handbook of the psychology of coaching and mentoring* (pp. 112–134). Oxford, UK: Wiley-Blackwell.

Chen, B., Vansteenkiste, M., Beyers, W., Boone, L., Deci, E. L., Van der Kaap-Deeder, J., … & Ryan, R. M. (2015). Basic psychological need satisfaction, need frustration, and need strength across four cultures. *Motivation and Emotion*, *39*(2), 216–236.

Chiesa, A., & Serretti, A. (2014). Are mindfulness-based interventions effective for substance use disorders? A systematic review of the evidence. *Substance Use & Misuse*, *49*(5), 492–512.

Dane, E. (2010). Paying attention to mindfulness and its effects on task performance in the workplace. *Journal of Management*, *37*(4), 997–1018.

Dane, E., & Brummel, B. J. (2014). Examining workplace mindfulness and its relations to job performance and turnover intention. *Human Relations*, *67*(1), 105–128.

Deci, E. L., Eghrari, H., Patrick, B. C., & Leone, D. (1994). Facilitating internalization: The self-determination theory perspective. *Journal of Personality*, *62*, 119–142.

Deci, E. L., & Ryan, R. M. (1985). *Intrinsic motivation and self-determination in human behavior*. New York, NY: Plenum.

Deci, E. L., & Ryan, R. M. (2000). The "what" and "why" of goal pursuits: Human needs and the self-determination of behavior. *Psychological Inquiry*, *11*(4), 227–268.

Deci, E. L., & Ryan, R. M. (2008). Facilitating optimal motivation and psychological well-being across life's domains. *Canadian Psychology*, *49*, 14–23.

Dutton, J. E., Roberts, L. M., & Bednar, J. (2010). Pathways for positive identity construction at work: Four types of positive identity and the building of social resources. *Academy of Management Review*, *35*(2), 265–293.

Edmondson, A. C. (2011). Strategies for learning from failure. *Harvard Business Review*, *89*(4), 48–55.

Fiol, C. M., & O'Connor, E. J. (2003). Waking up! Mindfulness in the face of bandwagons. *Academy of Management Review*, *28*(1), 54–70.

Flook, L., Goldberg, S. B., Pinger, L., Bonus, K., & Davidson, R. J. (2013). Mindfulness for teachers: A pilot study to assess effects on stress, burnout, and teaching efficacy. *Mind, Brain, and Education*, *7*(3), 182–195.

Foureur, M., Besley, K., Burton, G., Yu, N., & Crisp, J. (2013). Enhancing the resilience of nurses and midwives: Pilot of a mindfulness-based program for increased health, sense of coherence and decreased depression, anxiety and stress. *Contemporary Nurse*, *45*(1), 114–125.

Garland, E. L. (2007). The meaning of mindfulness: A second-order cybernetics of stress, metacognition, and coping. *Journal of Evidence-Based Complementary & Alternative Medicine, 12*(1), 15–30.

Garland, E. L., Gaylord, S. A., & Fredrickson, B. L. (2011). Positive reappraisal mediates the stress-reductive effects of mindfulness: An upward spiral process. *Mindfulness, 2*(1), 59–67.

Geary, C., & Rosenthal, S. L. (2011). Sustained impact of MBSR on stress, well-being, and daily spiritual experiences for 1 year in academic health care employees. *Journal of Alternative and Complementary Medicine, 17*(10), 939–944.

Gillet, N., Gagné, M., Sauvagère, S., & Fouquereau, E. (2013). The role of supervisor autonomy support, organizational support, and autonomous and controlled motivation in predicting employees' satisfaction and turnover intentions. *European Journal of Work and Organizational Psychology, 22*(4), 450–460.

Godfrey, K. M., Gallo, L. C., & Afari, N. (2015). Mindfulness-based interventions for binge eating: A systematic review and meta-analysis. *Journal of Behavioral Medicine, 38*(2), 348–362.

Gold, E., Smith, A., Hopper, I., Herne, D., Tansey, G., & Hulland, C. (2010). Mindfulness-based stress reduction (MBSR) for primary school teachers. *Journal of Child and Family Studies, 19*(2), 184–189.

Grant, A. M., & Spence, G. B. (2010). Using coaching and positive psychology to promote a flourishing workforce: A model of goal-striving and mental health. In P. A. Linley, S. Harrington, & N. Garcea (Eds.), *Oxford handbook of positive psychology and work* (pp. 175–188). New York, NY: Oxford University Press.

Harder, H. G., Rash, J., & Wagner, S. (2014). *Mental illness in the workplace: Psychological disability management.* Farnham, UK: Gower.

Hardre, P. L., & Reeve, J. (2009). Training corporate managers to adopt a more autonomy-supportive motivating style toward employees: An intervention study. *International Journal of Training and Development, 13*(3), 165–184.

Hayes, S. C., Strosahl, K. D., & Wilson, G. (1999). *Acceptance and commitment therapy: An experiential approach to behavior change.* New York, NY: Guilford Press.

Ho, L. (2011). Meditation, learning, and organisational innovation and performance *Industrial Management and Data Systems, 111*, 113–131.

Hülsheger, U. R., Feinholdt, A., & Nübold, A. (2015). A low-dose mindfulness intervention and recovery from work: Effects on psychological detachment, sleep quality, and sleep duration. *Journal of Occupational and Organizational Psychology, 88*(3), 464–489. doi:10.1111/joop.12115

Hülsheger, U. R., Lang, J. W., Depenbrock, F., Fehrmann, C., Zijlstra, F. R., & Alberts, H. J. (2014). The power of presence: The role of mindfulness at work for daily levels and change trajectories of psychological detachment and sleep quality. *Journal of Applied Psychology, 99*(6), 1113–1128.

Kabat-Zinn, J. (1990). *Full catastrophe living: Using the wisdom of your body and mind to face stress, pain, and illness.* New York, NY: Bantam Books.

Kang, Y. S., Choi, S. Y., & Ryu, E. (2009). The effectiveness of a stress coping program based on mindfulness meditation on the stress, anxiety, and depression experienced by nursing students in Korea. *Nurse Education Today, 29*(5), 538–543.

Khoury, B., Lecomte, T., Fortin, G., Masse, M., Therien, P., Bouchard, V., … Hofmann, S. G. (2013). Mindfulness-based therapy: A comprehensive meta-analysis. *Clinical Psychology Review, 33*(6), 763–771.

Krasner, M. S., Epstein, R. M., Beckman, H., Suchman, A. L., Chapman, B., Mooney, C. J., & Quill, T. E. (2009). Association of an educational program in mindful communication with burnout, empathy, and attitudes among primary care physicians. *Journal of American Medical Association, 302*(12), 1284–1293.

Krishnakumar, S., & Robinson, M. D. (2015). Maintaining an even keel: An affect-mediated model of mindfulness and hostile work behavior. *Emotion, 15*(5), 579–589.

Lauche, R., Cramer, H., Dobos, G., Langhorst, J., & Schmidt, S. (2013). A systematic review and meta-analysis of mindfulness-based stress reduction for the fibromyalgia syndrome. *Journal of Psychosomatic Research, 75*(6), 500–510.

Lazarus, R. S., & Folkman, S. (1984). *Stress, appraisal and coping*. New York, NY: Springer.

Linehan, M. M., Cochran, B. N., & Kehrer, C. A. (2001). Dialetical behavior therapy for borderline personality disorder. In D. H. Barlow (Ed.), *Clinical handbook of psychological disorders: A step-by-step treatment manual* (pp. 470–522). New York, NY: Guilford Press.

Malarkey, W. B., Jarjoura, D., & Klatt, M. (2013). Workplace based mindfulness practice and inflammation: A randomized trial. *Brain, Behavior, and Immunity, 27*, 145–154.

Manocha, R., Black, D., Sarris, J., & Stough, C. (2011). A randomized, controlled trial of meditation for work stress, anxiety and depressed mood in full-time workers. *Evidence-Based Complementary and Alternative Medicine, 2011* (Article ID 960583, 8 pages). doi: 10.1155/2011/960583

Martin, J. R. (1997). Mindfulness: A proposed common factor. *Journal of Psychotherapy integration, 7*(4), 291.

Michel, A., Bosch, C., & Rexroth, M. (2014). Mindfulness as a cognitive-emotional segmentation strategy: An intervention promoting work–life balance. *Journal of Occupational and Organizational Psychology, 87*(4), 733–754.

Mikulas, W. L. (2011). Mindfulness: Significant common confusions. *Mindfulness, 2*(1), 1–7.

Niemiec, C. P., Brown, K. W., Kashdan, T. B., Cozzolino, P. J., Breen, W. E., Levesque-Bristol, C., & Ryan, R. M. (2010). Being present in the face of existential threat: The role of trait mindfulness in reducing defensive responses to mortality salience. *Journal of Personality and Social Psychology, 99*(2), 344–365.

Nixon, A. E., Mazzola, J. J., Bauer, J., Krueger, J. R., & Spector, P. E. (2011). Can work make you sick? A meta-analysis of the relationships between job stressors and physical symptoms. *Work & Stress, 25*(1), 1–22.

Nwankpa, J. K., & Roumani, Y. (2014). The influence of organizational trust and organizational mindfulness on ERP systems usage. *Communications of the Association for Information Systems, 34*(1), 1469–1492.

Olson, K. L., & Emery, C. F. (2015). Mindfulness and weight loss: A systematic review. *Psychosomatic Medicine, 77*(1), 59–67.

Piet, J., Würtzen, H., & Zachariae, R. (2012). The effect of mindfulness-based therapy on symptoms of anxiety and depression in adult cancer patients and survivors: A systematic review and meta-analysis. *Journal of Consulting and Clinical Psychology, 80*(6), 1007–1020.

Pilcher, J. J., & Huffcutt, A. I. (1996). Effects of sleep deprivation on performance: A meta-analysis. *Sleep, 19*(4), 318–326.

Rapgay, L., & Bystrisky, A. (2009). Classical mindfulness: An introduction to its theory and practice for clinical application. *Annals of the New York Academy of Sciences, 1172*(1), 148–162.

Ray, J. L., Baker, L. T., & Plowman, D. A. (2011). Organizational mindfulness in business schools. *Academy of Management Learning & Education, 10*(2), 188–203.

Reb, J., Narayanan, J., & Chaturvedi, S. (2014). Leading mindfully: Two studies on the influence of supervisor trait mindfulness on employee well-being and performance. *Mindfulness, 5*(1), 36–45.

Reb, J., Narayanan, J., & Ho, Z. W. (2013). Mindfulness at work: Antecedents and consequences of employee awareness and absent-mindedness. *Mindfulness, 6*(1), 111–122.

Rees, C. S., Breen, L. J., Cusack, L., & Hegney, D. (2015). Understanding individual resilience in the workplace: The international collaboration of workforce resilience model. *Frontiers in Psychology, 6*. doi:10.3389/fpsyg.2015.00073

Riley, K. E., & Kalichman, S. (2015). Mindfulness-based stress reduction for people living with HIV/AIDS: Preliminary review of intervention trial methodologies and findings. *Health Psychology Review, 9*(2), 224–243. doi:10.1080/17437199.2014.895928

Roche, M., & Haar, J. M. (2013). A metamodel approach towards self-determination theory: A study of New Zealand managers' organisational citizenship behaviours. *International Journal of Human Resource Management, 24*(18), 3397–3417.

Roche, M., Haar, J. M., & Luthans, F. (2014). The role of mindfulness and psychological capital on the well-being of leaders. *Journal of Occupational Health Psychology, 19*(4), 476–489.

Schultz, P. P., Ryan, R. M., Niemiec, C. P., Legate, N., & Williams, G. C. (2014). Mindfulness, work climate, and psychological need satisfaction in employee well-being. *Mindfulness, 6*(5), 971–985.

Shao, R., & Skarlicki, D. P. (2009). The role of mindfulness in predicting individual performance. *Canadian Journal of Behavioural Science, 41*(4), 195–201.

Shapiro, S. L., Carlson, L., Astini, J. A., & Freedman, B. (2006). Mechanisms of mindfulness. *Journal of Clinical Psychology, 62*(3), 373–386.

Sharma, M., & Rush, S. E. (2014). Mindfulness-based stress reduction as a stress management intervention for healthy individuals: A systematic review. *Journal of Evidence-Based Complementary and Alternative Medicine, 19*(4), 271–286.

Shonin, E., Van Gordon, W., Dunn, T. J., Singh, N. N., & Griffiths, M. D. (2014). Meditation awareness training (MAT) for work-related wellbeing and job performance: A randomised controlled trial. *International Journal of Mental Health and Addiction, 12*(6), 806–823.

Simpson, R., Booth, J., Lawrence, M., Byrne, S., Mair, F., & Mercer, S. (2014). Mindfulness based interventions in multiple sclerosis-a systematic review. *BMC Neurology, 14*(1), 15.

Spence, G. B., Cavanagh, M. J., & Grant, A. M. (2008). The integration of mindfulness training and health coaching: An exploratory study. *Coaching: An International Journal of Theory, Research and Practice, 1*(2), 145–163.

Spence, G. B., & Deci, E. L. (2013). Self-determination with coaching contexts: Supporting motives and goals that promote optimal functioning and well-being. In S. David, D. Clutterbuck, & D. Megginson (Eds.), *Beyond goals: Effective strategies for coaching and mentoring* (pp. 85–108). Padstow, UK: Gower.

Strauss, C., Cavanagh, K., Oliver, A., & Pettman, D. (2014). Mindfulness-based interventions for people diagnosed with a current episode of an anxiety or depressive disorder: A meta-analysis of randomised controlled trials. *PloS one, 9*(4), e96110.

Swanson, L. M., Arnedt, J., Rosekind, M. R., Belenky, G., Balkin, T. J., & Drake, C. (2011). Sleep disorders and work performance: Findings from the 2008 National Sleep Foundation Sleep in America poll. *Journal of Sleep Research, 20*(3), 487–494.

Teasdale, J. D. (2004). Mindfulness-based cognitive therapy. In J. Yiend (Ed.), *Cognition, emotion and psychopathology: Theoretical, empirical and clinical directions* (pp. 270–289). New York, NY: Cambridge University Press.

Terkel, S. (1974). *Working: People talk about what they do all day and how they feel about what they do.* New York, NY: The New Press.

Vallabh, P., & Singhal, M. (2014). Buddhism and decision making at individual, group and organizational levels. *Journal of Management Development, 33*, 763–775.

van Berkel, J., Boot, C. R. L., Proper, K. I., Bongers, P. M., & van der Beek, A. J. (2014). Effectiveness of a worksite mindfulness-based multi-component intervention on lifestyle behaviors. *International Journal of Behavioral Nutrition and Physical Activity, 11*(1).

van Gordon, W., Shonin, E., Zangeneh, M., & Griffiths, M. D. (2014). Work-related mental health and job performance: Can mindfulness help? *International Journal of Mental Health and Addiction, 12*(2), 129–137.

Vindholmen, S., Høigaard, R., Espnes, G. A., & Seiler, S. (2014). Return to work after vocational rehabilitation: Does mindfulness matter? *Psychology Research and Behavior Management, 7*, 77–88.

Virgili, M. (2015). Mindfulness-based interventions reduce psychological distress in working adults: A meta-analysis of intervention studies. *Mindfulness, 6*(2), 326–337.

Vogus, T. J., & Sutcliffe, K. M. (2007, October). *Organizational resilience: Towards a theory and research agenda. I.* Paper presented at the IEEE International Conference, Montreal, Canada.

Vogus, T. J., & Sutcliffe, K. M. (2012). Organizational mindfulness and mindful organizing: A reconciliation and path forward. *Academy of Management Learning & Education, 11*(4), 722–735.

Wainwright, D., & Calnan, M. (2002). *Work stress: The making of a modern epidemic.* Buckingham, UK: Open University.

Warnecke, E., Quinn, S., Ogden, K., Towle, N., & Nelson, M. R. (2011). A randomised controlled trial of the effects of mindfulness practice on medical student stress levels. *Medical Education, 45*(4), 381–388.

Weick, K., & Sutcliffe, K. (2001). *Managing the unexpected: Assuring high performance in an age of uncertainty.* San Francisco, CA: Jossey-Bass.

Winbush, N. Y., Gross, C. R., & Kreitzer, M. J. (2007). The effects of mindfulness-based stress reduction on sleep disturbance: A systematic review. *EXPLORE: The Journal of Science and Healing, 3*(6), 585–591.

Wolff, S. B. (2014). Emotion and mindfulness: Using emotion as information to raise collective performance. In N. M. Ashkanasy, W. J. Zerbe, & C. E. J. Härtel (Eds.), *Emotions and the organizational fabric* (pp. 367–395). Bingley, UK: Emerald.

Zgierska, A., Rabago, D., Chawla, N., Kushner, K., Koehler, R., & Marlatt, A. (2009). Mindfulness meditation for substance use disorders: A systematic review. *Substance Abuse*, *30*(4), 266–294.

Zoogman, S., Goldberg, S. B., Hoyt, W. T., & Miller, L. (2014). Mindfulness interventions with youth: A meta-analysis. *Mindfulness*, *6*(2), 290–302.

9

Resilience at Work

Andrew Denovan, Lee Crust, and Peter J. Clough

Introduction

Resilience at work continues to be a major focus of both research and applied work. Often it is viewed in isolation from other perspectives and is rarely linked to positive psychology. In this chapter the concept of resilience will be briefly described, discussed, and placed in the context of other theoretical models. The final part of the chapter deals with mental toughness, providing one specific approach to linking resilience and positive psychology to the world of work.

Positive Psychology

The positive psychology movement, spearheaded by the seminal work of Seligman and Csikszentmihayli (2000), offers perhaps the best framework to understand psychological well-being. These researchers argued for greater attention to be given to the study of positive human functioning and flourishing. The message and approach presented by Seligman and Csikszentmihayli, as they freely acknowledged, was nothing particularly new. Nevertheless, given the scant knowledge of positive human functioning at the time, the timing of their "call to arms" was crucial in highlighting that research efforts in psychology had tended to focus upon alleviating negative psychological states such as anxiety and depression, and that the absence of such states alone was not indicative of well-being. After all, achieving good mental health comprises not only the absence of illness, but also self-satisfaction, independence, capability and competency, and coping well with stress and adversity (Bird, 2007). While accepting the importance of understanding and treating psychological conditions and remediating deficits, these researchers encouraged greater efforts to understand concepts such as enjoyment, authentic happiness, and well-being. In short, past research efforts primarily focused upon returning those suffering from negative psychological conditions back

The Wiley Blackwell Handbook of the Psychology of Positivity and Strengths-Based Approaches at Work, First Edition. Edited by Lindsay G. Oades, Michael F. Steger, Antonella Delle Fave, and Jonathan Passmore.

to normal functioning (however defined); but beyond normal functioning the positive half of the continuum of human experience remains less well understood.

Within the foundations of humanistic psychology, the *positive psychology* movement is concerned with three important concepts. First, the *life of enjoyment* concerns savoring positive emotions and feelings. The work of Fredrickson (2001), which is described elsewhere in this chapter, has led to better understanding of how positive emotions such as joy and interest can create broader thinking, help to build personal resources, and facilitate personal growth through positive or adaptive spirals of emotion.

Second, the *life of engagement* reflects being immersed and absorbed in what one is doing. Flow is one important positive psychological concept associated with engagement and is described as an intrinsically motivating experience involving an altered state of awareness which typically occurs when high levels of skill are matched with high levels of challenge (Jackson & Csikzentmihalyi, 1999). Third, the *life of affiliation* concerns how positive relationships can help people to derive a sense of well-being, belonging, meaning, and purpose. These central themes from positive psychology might be contrasted against most research that has focused on understanding negative emotional states and illness.

Psychological well-being represents "the achievement of one's full psychological potential" (Carr, 2004, p. 36). While different opinions still exist concerning the exact conceptualization of psychological well-being, it is generally agreed to be a multidimensional construct. The work of Carol Ryff and colleagues provides perhaps the most accepted and theory-driven approach to the study of psychological well-being. Ryff (1989) identified six distinct components that represent the six-factor model of psychological well-being. The breadth of wellness identified by Ryff consists of: (1) self-acceptance (positive evaluations of oneself and one's past life), (2) personal growth (sense of development and continued growth as an individual), (3) purpose in life (belief that one's life is meaningful), (4) positive relations with others (existence of meaningful relationships with others), (5) environmental mastery (capacity to effectively manage one's life and the surrounding world), and (6) autonomy (a sense of self-determination).

Until recently, most research efforts in psychology, often linked to the financial support of research councils, have been based around a medical or deficit model. Simply put, the focus has been upon understanding psychological problems and developing and testing treatments that facilitate the return to normal states of functioning. In light of evidence that one in four people will experience psychological problems within their lifetime (e.g., Layard & Clark, 2014), this is of course an important endeavor. Nevertheless, the predominant focus upon remediating deficits and treating illness has meant that much less attention has been devoted to understanding positive human functioning and flourishing. It would seem reasonable that one of the best ways of understanding more about resilience is to study and learn from those individuals who have demonstrated resilience in challenging circumstances. If we can understand the processes and mechanisms that highly resilient people use, then it should be possible to apply this knowledge to help others become more resilient. To aid this understanding, this chapter will place resilience within the context of other related concepts including hardiness and mental toughness.

Hardiness

Suzanne Kobasa and colleagues (Kobasa, 1979; Kobasa, Maddi, & Khan, 1982) identified an important protective characteristic called psychological hardiness that distinguishes between people who cope more and less successfully when facing potentially stressful circumstances. Given that numerous studies predicted high correlations between stress and illness, but actually found low to moderate associations, it became apparent that the relationship was more complex than first thought. While continued exposure to stressful situations has been linked to illness and serious stress-related disorders, not all people succumb, even in highly stressful environments. Kobasa identified that individual differences were important in understanding the stress–illness relationship. Hardiness was presented as an important variable that could help buffer the potential negative consequences of stress.

Kobasa (1979) initially found that three attitudes or dispositions of commitment, control, and challenge, known as "the three Cs," were crucial in understanding the differences between managers and executives who became ill, and those who remained healthy when faced with stressful circumstances. Commitment reflected being deeply involved and interested in what one is doing as opposed to feeling alienated or disinterested. Control concerns a tendency to believe and act as if one is influential rather than passively accepting circumstances. Challenge involves the perceptions or evaluations of potential stressors with hardy individuals most likely to view these as challenges and opportunities for personal growth rather than being overly threatening. These findings posited hardiness as an important personal resource that enabled the potential negative effects of stress to be resisted. Since this initial work, a body of evidence has supported the role of hardiness as a stress-buffer when individuals are exposed to increasingly adverse and challenging circumstances across a broad range of domains (i.e., business, education, military). In terms of coping, it appears that hardy individuals are adept at maintaining optimistic appraisals by placing stressors into perspective, and employing what is termed "transformational coping" to downplay any stressors and limit any negative effects upon health and performance.

Following initial research efforts to understand hardiness, Maddi (2004) emphasized the combined importance of the three Cs of hardiness and provided examples of how conceptually no one of the three was enough to provide the courage and motivation to turn stressful circumstances into advantage. In short, hardiness was a reflection of the three Cs operating together and an expression of existential courage.

Maddi, like other existential psychologists, is primarily concerned with the ongoing search for meaning in life – a process that involves making decisions that can be of low (e.g., choice of meal) to high (e.g., changing career) importance. According to Maddi, all decisions have an invariant form; to either choose the future or the past. In the ongoing search for meaning, choosing the past would seem like an odd choice, given it is primarily about holding on to what is familiar, and remaining within a comfort zone. Choosing the past can lead to stagnation and is not regarded as a pathway to learning and personal growth. The main reason that some people regularly choose the past, is that by so doing they avoid the uncomfortable experience of ontological anxiety. By choosing the future, individuals are likely to face challenges and uncomfortable feelings, but it is this route that involves learning, development, and the building of personal resources. For some, the fear and risk involved with change outweighs the possible advantages of choosing the future, but ultimately the downside of choosing the past is a process that progresses from boredom to a painful sense of meaninglessness. In order to choose the future, to embrace change and experience personal growth in the process, individuals need to have courage. To Maddi, hardiness is an operationalization of existential courage, with the three Cs facilitating decision-making that embraces change and the future rather than the past. In the following section, the synergies, and differences, between hardiness and resilience will be further explored.

Resilience

Resilience is a rather amorphous concept, but the various definitions do agree that it is the ability to deal with stressors and setbacks and has become an essential part of human existence that is associated with both successful outcomes and well-being. Psychological resilience has been defined in several ways, but perhaps most usually as flexibility in response to changing situational demands and the ability to bounce back after negative emotional experiences (see Tugade, Fredrickson, & Barrett, 2004). Nevertheless, several theorists such as Neenan (2009) have criticized definitions and conceptualizations of resilience that emphasize "bouncing back" because it creates the perception of quickly and effortlessly returning to a previous state, when resilience often develops over longer periods of time and can involve significant struggles, pain, and reorganization for the individual. While definitions of resilience have been numerous and varied, it is generally agreed that resilience concerns positive adaptation despite the presence of risk or adversity (Luthar & Cicchetti, 2000).

To add to the lack of agreement over the definition of resilience, the mechanisms implicit in the construct have been the subject of debate, with some researchers advocating a process approach, and others a trait approach (Jacelon, 1997). Popular process models include those of Wilson, Friedman, and Lindy (2001) and Richardson, Neiger, Jensen, and Kumpfer (1990; and Richardson, 2002). Wilson et al. (2001) developed a trauma model of resilience. Here, a traumatic event impacts on personality, self-structure, and ego processes which influence activation of the allostatic stress reaction (behavioral or physiological efforts to maintain homeostasis) (Sterling & Eyer, 1988), which influences the continuum of resilience and adaptation. The stress response is characterized by a culmination of interactive factors of personality, ego defences, coping style, modulation of affect, and use of protective factors. The product of the stress reaction to the event is the measure of adaptation and resilience.

Richardson et al. (1990; and Richardson, 2002) developed a biopsychospiritual balance model. Here, internal and external stressors threaten biopsychospiritual homeostasis (mind, body, and spirit), and the ability to cope is influenced by successful and unsuccessful past attempts at dealing with disruptions. Response to disruption is a reintegrative process which is viewed to influence one of several possible outcomes: one being growth and increased resilience, with adaptation leading to a higher threshold of homeostasis; another being recovery with loss, which leads to a lower level of homeostasis. A third outcome is a return to homeostasis and just getting past the disruption. The fourth is a dysfunctional state where maladaptive coping is practiced (e.g., self-destructive conduct).

Resilience as a trait was defined by Wagnild and Young (1993) as the characteristic of an individual which facilitates adaptation and moderates the negative impacts of stress. This is viewed as consisting of stable personal factors including reflectiveness, positive responsiveness to others, above average intelligence, equanimity, self-reliance, meaningfulness, a wide range of personal and social activities and interests, perseverance, and an optimistic and energetic approach to life. In contrast to the trait approach is the process approach. This tries to provide a better understanding of how resilience is developed and operates, whereas the trait approach takes a simpler perspective – basically resilience is present or not. Among researchers the process approach lacks agreement on an appropriate model, and lacks clarity regarding the steps in the process. Furthermore, it emphasizes that resilience is learned, and although this intuitively makes sense, the time required to develop resilience is unclear (Jacelon, 1997).

Resilience has attracted considerable research attention. One key focus of the myriad of investigations has been the development of resilience. The majority of developmental research has investigated resilience among children growing up in the midst of unfavorable circumstances (parental illness, poverty), and traumatic experience research has investigated the role of resilience in recovery from traumatic events (Bonanno, 2004). Werner and Smith (2001) conducted a landmark longitudinal study of children born into poverty on the island of Kauai. Two thirds of the 505 children developed serious problems. The remaining third developed into "healthy" adults, who demonstrated various protective factors including having a good-natured and affectionate temperament, having many friends and interests at school, and a good attachment to a carer. Masten et al. (2005) conducted a 20-year study and found that children who developed healthily in the midst of unfavorable circumstances had more available internal and external resources, including good parenting and good cognitive abilities. Children with less of these resources became more vulnerable, underwent more stressful incidents, and had less ability to cope as adults. Masten (1994) reviewed research on resilience and found various important protective factors, including good parenting, good intellectual ability, self-reliance, self-worth, hope, and good performance at school.

Research on resilience as a recovery process following trauma has shown various protective factors which help to maintain a stable equilibrium (Bonanno, 2004). Examples include repressive coping such as emotional dissociation (Weinberger, Schwartz, & Davidson, 1979), self-enhancement where people with an over-high view of themselves are more resistant to stressful events (Bonanno, Rennicke, & Dekel, 2005), and positive emotion and humor (Ong & Bergeman, 2004).

Some research has investigated academic resilience among economically disadvantaged adolescents. Gordon (1995, 1996) found resilient African-American students were more motivated by material gain, cognitive, and extra-curricular pursuits than non-resilient African-American students. Gordon-Rouse (2001) discovered among 170 high school students from a stressful, economically deprived background that resilient students displayed more positive motivational behavior than non-resilient students, in particular more belief and tenacity regarding their cognitive ability, which was linked with better academic performance (measured by Grade Point Average).

Luthar (1991) found resilient adolescent students to have an internal locus of control and possess excellent social skills. However, intelligence was found to be a vulnerability factor, which was attributed to the higher levels of sensitivity that are linked with higher intelligence. Garmezy and Rutter (1983) found resilient schoolchildren were academically and cognitively superior and more independent than non-resilient students. Such evidence is interesting given the trend of research associating economic disadvantage with poor academic performance and ability (Hanusek, 1997). Initially, positive adaptation in response to adversity was viewed to be characteristic of extraordinary individuals, inferring a sense of "invincibility." However, Masten's research suggests that resilience is a relatively common phenomenon which emerges not from extraordinary qualities, but rather from "ordinary magic" (Masten, 2001).

Resilience has long been associated with stress and coping, which are to an extent embedded in definitions of the construct (Maluccio, 2002). This has clear links with the previously reported work on hardiness. However, consistent with a positive psychology emphasis, more research is now concerned with well-being and adaptation in response to stress as a function of resilience. For example, some studies have investigated the role of positive emotion, experience of which is viewed to have adaptive benefits for coping with stress (Folkman & Moskowitz, 2004). Research supports this via demonstrating that resilient individuals utilize positive emotion producing coping techniques to minimize negative emotional experiences, such as problem-focused, goal-oriented coping (Billings, Folkman, Acree, & Moskowitz, 2000), positive reappraisal and benefit finding (Affleck & Tennen, 1996), and humor (Ong, Bergeman, & Bisconti, 2004). This will be discussed in more detail later in this chapter.

Also, individual differences in resilience are associated with greater recovery from stressful experiences. Fredrickson, Tugade, Waugh, and Larkin (2003) discovered that higher trait resilience correlated with less depressive symptomology. Tugade, Fredrickson, and Barrett (2004) found that quicker cardiovascular recovery from a laboratory stressor (speech preparation task) was associated with higher trait resilience. Importantly, depressive symptoms and cardiovascular response were mediated by the experience of positive emotion. Ong, Bergeman, Bisconti, and Wallace (2006) found the experience of positive emotion to be common among resilient individuals and served to assist their ability to rebound from stress. Low-resilient individuals exhibited greater reactivity to daily stressors and had greater difficulty controlling negative emotions. Interestingly, this study found trait resilience was relevant not only to individuals under extreme trauma, but also to individuals experiencing daily stressors (hassles). This infers that resilience is a common phenomenon (Bonanno, 2004), and is to some extent an important trait which can aid individuals in dealing with stress transactions on a daily basis.

Martin and Marsh (2008) focused on resilience among undergraduates in relation to daily hassles, specifically academic setbacks and challenges including exam pressure, deadlines, and poor marks. This study labeled resilience differently as buoyancy, suggesting it was an everyday type of resilience. Although the term used was different, the concept is essentially the same. Higher academic resilience was linked with higher self-efficacy and student engagement and lower anxiety. Campbell-Sills, Cohan, and Stein (2006) investigated the relationship of resilience to personality traits, coping styles, and psychiatric symptoms in young adulthood (undergraduates). Resilient students had higher levels of conscientiousness and extraversion, lower neuroticism, and utilized problem-focused coping whereas emotion-focused coping was utilized by students low in resilience.

In terms of research, Richardson (2002) makes the important distinction between what is termed first and second wave resiliency. First wave resiliency research coheres around the identification of resilient qualities and has been much in evidence within sports mental toughness literature (i.e., identifying the component parts of mental toughness). Second wave resilience research is more concerned with understanding how individuals acquire such qualities to allow them to adapt and successfully move past adverse circumstances. One conceptualization (Lepore & Revenson, 2006) is particularly useful in understanding how individuals acquire resilience, with three dimensions being held as important. First, *resistance* reflects being undisturbed by adversity. Second, *recovery* involves disturbance but an eventual return to pre-stress levels of functioning. Third, *reconfiguration* refers to being disturbed, but rather than returning to pre-stress functioning, a new worldview is formed that can result in more or less adaptive outcomes. The potential for resilience to develop appears to occur when homeostasis is disturbed due to stressful conditions, and the individual finds him/herself outside of their comfort zone. When this happens, the return to homeostasis can occur through four possible routes. The first of these is termed *dysfunctional reintegration* and sees the individual deal with adversity through destructive means such as violence. In contrast, *reintegration with loss* reflects overcoming the adversity but at some cost, often in terms that deplete personal resources (i.e., confidence, motivation). *Homeostatic reintegration* reflects moving beyond the adversity unchanged (with nothing lost or gained). The final and most desirable form of reintegration is termed *resilient reintegration*, and involves successfully moving beyond the adversity and in the process acquiring new personal resources that make the individual better prepared for future confrontations with stress.

It is interesting to note that positive outcomes have been reported following stressful, adverse, and at times traumatic encounters in several other domains. It has been consistently shown that trauma initially exerts a negative influence upon perceptions of psychological well-being (Board, Arrighi, & Thatcher, 2003), but before-and-after studies have shown stress-related growth (Calhoun & Tedeschi, 1999; Joseph, 2012; Peterson & Seligman, 2003). Stress-related growth is known to occur following a period of reflection and contemplation (Helgeson, Reynolds, & Tomich, 2006) and occurs through (1) changes in views of the self, such as greater self-acceptance, (2) increasing value of personal relationships, and (3) changes in life philosophy, such as re-evaluating what really matters (Joseph, 2012). However, according to Joseph one of the challenges in studying stress-related growth is the reliance on retrospective accounts from participants, and the potential difference between perceptions of growth and actual growth. It would also be wrong to assume that traumatic events always lead to positive outcomes such as personal growth. Unfortunately, some people constantly relive traumatic events, experience powerful negative emotions, and remain unable to move on successfully. This highlights some important differences between those who survive and those who thrive. Only resilient individuals are able, usually after significant struggle and hardship, to obtain positive outcomes like personal growth and new perspectives on life following trauma (Neenan, 2009).

Resilience, Positive Emotions, and Well-being

Research has demonstrated the ability of hardy and mentally tough individuals to remain positive and calm, and to think flexibly in adverse circumstances. Studies have demonstrated that certain coping strategies (i.e., approach rather than avoidance) are indicative of more resilient individuals (Nicholls et al., 2008). The underlying processes of how hardy or mentally tough individuals develop resistance resources are still being examined, but one theory that has emerged within a positive psychology framework holds some promise. The broaden-and-build theory of positive emotions (Fredrickson, 2001) was developed from work examining the long-held view that experiencing positive emotions is good for health (e.g., the role of laughter, humor) and is linked to approach type behaviors. While negative emotions serve to heighten sympathetic nervous system activity, narrow attentional processing, and support action tendencies such as fight or flight, Fredrickson theorized that positive emotions have a somewhat different function. For example, joy sparks the urge to play, interest triggers the urge to explore, and contentment creates the urge to savor and integrate.

A significant body of evidence has supported the broaden-and-build theory (e.g., Fredrickson & Levenson, 1998), which proposes that positive emotions produce patterns of thought that are flexible, creative, and open to information. This broadening effect is also accompanied by physiological processes that reduce sympathetic nervous system functioning and increase momentary thought–action repertoires. Experiencing positive emotions in the aftermath of negative experiences also appears to produce an "undoing effect." For example, Fredrickson and colleagues (Fredrickson & Levenson, 1998; Fredrickson, Mancuso, Branigan, & Tugade, 2000) reported the findings of three experiments that initially induced high arousal and negative emotions, and followed this by having participants view an emotionally stimulating film that induced joy, contentment, neutrality, or sadness. Films that contained positive emotions were found to elicit faster cardiovascular return to baseline measures compared with neutral or sad films.

Furthermore, and perhaps of most significance, is that the broaden-and-build theory proposes that repeatedly experiencing positive emotions can build lasting resources.

Evidence identifies resilient individuals as being characterized by positive emotionality, but also as cultivating positive emotions in others through providing appropriate support within close relationships. According to Tugade et al. (2004), positive emotions are not merely the by-product of psychological resilience, but serve an important function in enabling people to recover following stressful encounters. A broad range of evidence including self-report, observational, and longitudinal studies has supported a relationship between positive emotions and resilience (see Fredrickson, 2004). Indeed, Cohn, Fredrickson, Brown, Mikels, and Conway (2009) found that positive emotions were significantly related to ego-resilience in students, and during the month-long study where emotions were reported daily, positive emotions also predicted increases in reported resilience. More recent work (Stamp et al., 2015) involving students from several UK universities found moderate to strong significant and positive relationships between mental toughness and psychological well-being across all three years of undergraduate study. Previous work had already established mental toughness as a significant and positive predictor of achievement and progression in first-year university students (Crust, Earle, et al., 2014). It is very likely that these findings would be repeated in an occupational setting. University students are now very likely to work while studying and often view their degree studies as a job. In addition, they soon enter the world of work and it is very unlikely that the links identified would not be present.

Research supports the notion that participants who experience frequent positive emotions build resources that helped them deal with life challenges. For example, positive emotions such as interest and contentment may lead to the building of personal resources as the individual grows and develops through approach rather than avoidance behaviors, and using creativity and/or reflection as a result of positive emotional experiences. As Fredrickson (2004, p. 1367) acknowledges:

> The bottom-line message is that people should cultivate positive emotions in themselves and in those around them, not just as end-states in themselves, but also as a means to achieving psychological growth and improved psychological and physical well-being over time.

In contrast, the effects of negative emotions on resilience have generally been found to be weak or null. In times of stress, resilient individuals report similar levels of negative emotions to other participants but more positive emotions. Consistent with this, recent studies have found that in demanding circumstances that are often associated with negative feelings and emotions, mentally tough individuals were able to draw upon humor and previous positive experiences to help maintain perspective and cope effectively (Crust et al., 2010). Evidence has shown that mentally tough athletes are more successful and effective at coping with adverse circumstances (Nicholls, Levy, Polman, & Crust, 2011).

As mentioned earlier, research also indicates that higher levels of resilience are associated with greater use of specific coping strategies which elicit positive affect in response to stress, such as positive reappraisal and problem-focused coping (Affleck & Tennen, 1996; Billings et al., 2000; Folkman, Acree, & Moskowitz, 2000). Greater access to and the ability to use positive emotional resources can buffer the impact of stress and offer respite from ongoing stressful experiences (Zautra, Johnson, & Davis, 2005). Vulpe and Dafinoiu (2012) suggest that positive and negative emotions can co-occur in response to stressful episodes, and importantly that positive emotion could dominate under any of the following circumstances: when an individual feels they are in control of a situation; when the experience is viewed to be an opportunity for growth; or when the individual utilizes adaptive coping. Positive affect is important for resilience because it has been linked with coping styles which can help buffer and lessen potential negative effects of stress (see, e.g., Folkman et al., 2000). Chen et al. (1996) found positive affective responses predicted engaged coping among women undergoing a biopsy for suspected breast cancer, and following breast cancer surgery, pre-existing levels of positive mood predicted the tendency to cope through active engagement (Carver et al., 1993).

In terms of the mechanisms relating to how positive affect may foster resilience and the building of lasting resources, the broaden-and-build theory posits that experience of positive emotion is associated with a growth in coping resources which facilitate greater resilience in response to stress and future experience of positive affect (Reschly, Huebner, Appleton, & Antaramian, 2008). Such a process is suggested to operate in a "virtuous circle," with positive affect catalyzing a growth in coping and resilience over time. A recent study by Gloria, Faulk, and Steinhardt (2013) found evidence for the building effect of positive emotion in relation to work stress, as positive emotions predicted lower work stress and greater levels of psychological resilience in public school teachers. Moreover, the study found support for positive emotion acting as a mediator in relation to work stress and resilience.

Vulpe and Dafinoiu (2012) also found direct support for the building function of the broaden-and-build theory in that positive emotion mediated the relationship between adaptive coping strategies (approach coping, self-help coping, and accommodation coping) and ego-resiliency. This study suggested that individuals who utilize adaptive coping experience positive emotion, which in turn facilitates ego-resiliency. Importantly, positive emotions are seen to be the cause and consequence of broad-minded and adaptive coping. Fredrickson and Joiner (2002) found that experience of positive emotion at one time period was associated with more effective coping (broad-minded coping) and greater positive affect five weeks later in 138 university students, indicating a reciprocal enhancing effect. Mediational analyses provided support for the spiralling effects of positive affect and coping over time. Broad-minded coping and positive emotions were found to mutually build on one another: positive emotions not only enabled individuals to feel good in the present, but through their effect on broadened thinking they increase the likelihood that people will feel good in the future and recruit effective coping for difficult situations, thus enhancing resiliency over time.

Positive emotions are important factors for developing resilience and in turn psychological well-being. The relationship of psychological well-being and positive emotions has been reported in a good number of studies (Greenglass & Fiksenbaum, 2009). For example, Affleck and Tennen (1996) discovered that women who were able to find benefits from a stressful experience (complicated child delivery and prolonged stay at hospital) reported higher levels of well-being, which extended to their children's developmental well-being. A longitudinal study reported that women displaying more positive emotion in their college photographs achieved more desirable outcomes in marriage and well-being 30 years on (Freese, Meland, & Irwin, 2006). Furthermore, positive affect is associated with developing satisfying social relationships, as optimistic and self-confident individuals (qualities related with positive affect) receive and seek out more social support and utilize other adaptive coping strategies in response to stress (for example problem-focused coping) (Aspinwall & Taylor, 1992; Chemers, Hu, & Garcia, 2001). Thus, positive affect is associated with the promotion of psychological well-being.

Lyubomirsky, King, and Diener (2005) reported positive affect to be the hallmark of physical and psychological health. The influence of positive affect on physical and psychological well-being has been frequently discussed (Bartram & Boniwell, 2007; Dockray & Steptoe, 2010; Pressman & Cohen, 2005). The influence of positive affect on psychological resilience has also been documented (Fredrickson et al., 2003; Tugade & Fredrickson, 2004), and resilience has been identified to have a key role in the relationship of positive affect with psychological and physical health (Aspinwall, 2001; Folkman et al., 2000; Tugade & Fredrickson, 2004). For example, Cohn et al. (2009) found that resilience mediated the relation between positive affect and increased life satisfaction, suggesting that happy people become more satisfied not simply because they feel better, but because they develop resources for living well. Furthermore, Tugade and Fredrickson (2004) discovered that positive affect contributed to psychological and physical health via psychological resilience. Specifically, when participants were given a time-pressured speech preparation task, those higher in resilience experienced greater levels of life satisfaction and positive emotion (such as interest) along with high levels of anxiety during the task.

The broaden-and-build theory posits that resilience and positive affect mutually build on one another and trigger an upward spiral of resource building that leads to physical and psychological well-being over time (Fredrickson, 1998, 2001). Being resilient and able to find positive meaning in general and in adverse life situations encourages proactive coping, which facilitates an initial increase in positive affect. This increase in positive affect then leads to increases in psychological resilience. As this cycle repeats itself, an upward spiral of positive emotion occurs, which results in long-term well-being (Fredrickson, 2001; Fredrickson & Joiner, 2002). Therefore, it is suggested that positive affect leads to long-term physical and psychological well-being with psychological resilience as a mediator. Nath and Pradhan (2012) found support for the mediating role of psychological resilience in the positive emotion–health relationship in a sample of 146 university students. Thus, a person's level of psychological resilience in turn informs their ability to maintain positive affect and cultivate physical and psychological growth.

Cohn et al. (2009) found momentary experiences of positive emotion catalyze growth and change over time, helping to build resources and, with regard to resilience, skills for bouncing back from adversity. Positive emotions predicted growth in ego-resilience, a psychological resource useful for handling mild and severe stressors (Ong et al., 2006; Tugade & Fredrickson, 2004). Ego-resilience is a multidimensional skill which consists of problem solving, emotion regulation, and the capacity to change perspective, an ability that extends beyond the discrete positive emotions that promote it. Cohn et al. (2009) found ego-resilience was a key factor that promoted happiness and well-being over time due to its positive influence on life satisfaction, indicating the presence of an upward spiral where positive emotion and ego-resilience maintain and build on one another.

The relationship of positive affect with ego-resilience implies that the higher the levels of positive affect the higher the ability to find positive meaning in times of adversity because of the flexible thinking that results from positive emotions. Such flexible thinking typifies psychological resilience and leads to improved physical health and psychological well-being (Waugh & Fredrickson, 2006). Importantly, experience of positive emotions such as joy, enthusiasm, and interest are responsible for catalyzing the process of learning, connecting, exploring, and ultimately building new resources such as resilience (Cohn et al., 2009). In other words, positive affect forecasts an individual's psychological well-being and physical health via psychological resilience.

Positive emotions are suggested to extend beyond hedonic experience and momentary broadening, and eventually build resources that enable survival and flourishing. Flourishing refers to optimal functioning, which consists of growth, generativity, and resilience (Diener et al., 2010), and is the hallmark of the "good life." Resilience is suggested to be a key ingredient of flourishing, and research shows that positive affect and coping are associated with the promotion of flourishing (Fredrickson & Joiner, 2002). Reschly et al. (2008) discovered that greater experience of positive affect and resilience was predictive of adaptive coping and flourishing in high school students. Faulk, Gloria, and Steinhardt (2013) found that coping influences the tendencies of individuals to either flourish or languish in life.

Specifically, individuals who used more adaptive methods of coping (which are typically used by resilient individuals) were more likely to be flourishing, whereas individuals who used maladaptive coping were more likely to be languishing in life. Therefore, it appears that positive affect and resilience are not only key for psychological and physical well-being in terms of the regulation of distress, but extend beyond this and help to improve one's life, providing opportunities for growth and leading to a flourishing and fulfilling life.

Mental Toughness: An Example of the Application of Resilience to Positive Psychology

Throughout this chapter, the causes and consequences of resilience have been discussed. However, it is important to tie some of these ideas to more applied settings. In this section two areas will be briefly examined: sport and work. Both areas are central to the psychological health of those involved in them. It is important to avoid creating "psychological silos." We strongly believe that resilience and positive psychology are not domain-specific. They are at the core of the human condition. Lessons can be drawn from all aspects of applied psychology. The purpose of this section is simply to provide the reader with a slightly more practical perspective.

Mental toughness in sport

Work by Clough, Earle, and Sewell (2002) first reported mental toughness as a construct that was related yet distinct from hardiness. Clough et al. (2002) studied elite athletes, coaches, and sport psychologists, before producing a model and measure of mental toughness that emphasized six components (confidence in abilities, interpersonal confidence, emotional control, life control, commitment, and challenge). Since 2002, several other competing models and perspectives on mental toughness have been presented (i.e., Gucciardi, Gordon, & Dimmock, 2009; Jones, Hanton, & Connaughton, 2007), but in line with general resilience literature, these tend to cohere around adaptation to changing situational factors and effective coping. While much of the initial research on mental toughness focused upon elite athletes, there are some noteworthy exceptions that take a similar view to Neenan (2009) that resilience is not some superhuman attribute but something that is ordinarily in evidence during daily confrontations with stress, adversity, and challenge. Many of the findings from sport have a direct relevance to the world of work. Sport offers an ideal test bed for resilience research as it is clearly a high-pressure, performance-driven environment. This crossover is well illustrated by the work of Crust, Swann, Allen-Collinson, Breckon, and Weinberg (2014).

Crust et al. (2014) interviewed exercise leaders, and frequent/regular exercisers that leaders identified as epitomizing mental toughness in an exercise setting. The focus of the research, in line with positive psychology, was to understand more about those exercisers who have embedded exercise within their lifestyle and managed to maintain this behavior. The authors argued that given high dropout rates from formal exercise programs, mental toughness should be one of a number of important determinants that differentiate between participants that stick with the program through the challenging journey of behavior change, and those who withdraw. Exercise leaders reported mentally tough exercisers could be identified within group or individual sessions, by their work rate, competitiveness, preference for intense and demanding exercise, high commitment (e.g., attending frequently), positive responses to setbacks, thirst for knowledge, sense of purpose, limited emotional expression, and tendency to embrace rather than avoid challenges.

The construct of mental toughness was readily identifiable within exercise settings and the findings were largely consistent with previous conceptualizations of mental toughness in sport (Clough et al., 2002). The exercisers reported being focused, committed (to the point of being selfish), and highly competitive with self and others, which on some occasions led to more risky behaviors such as over-training and continuing to train with injuries. These participants reported approaching others for support and advice when necessary, which demonstrated a commitment to learning and growth but also highlights that developing mental toughness is seldom about "going it alone." These findings highlighted exercisers who were focused upon improvement and personal growth, and could manage their emotions and remain positive when setbacks occurred or progress was slow (similar to the findings of Crust & Azadi, 2010). One of the potential limitations of this work is, however, that a major reason for maintained participation was enjoyment of exercise – although there were some reports that this was not always the case. It is likely to be easier to adhere to something that is enjoyable rather than something aversive. Perhaps a better account of exercise mental toughness could be achieved by studying those participants who don't enjoy exercise but still maintain this behavior over long periods of time, perhaps for health-related reasons.

The world of work

The mental toughness in the workplace perspective has stressed the importance of contentment and fulfillment. Clough and Strycharcyk (2012, p. 227) write: "Mental toughness is about opening doors to opportunity and contentment and then having the psychological equipment to go through them." In a broader sense, the concept of mental toughness can be linked to some of the key concepts that underpin occupational and other areas of applied psychology. Three key concepts will be briefly discussed:

- Motivation
- Stress
- Working with others

All these need to be "right" in an organization if the workforce is to be fully content and satisfied. Motivational theories are clearly a source of linkage between mental toughness and positive psychology. The seminal work of Maslow (1943) highlighted the importance of self-actualization, but without resilience and toughness it is difficult to see how this would be achieved. Setbacks are part of development, but without a foundation of resilience setbacks often mean the end of development and a retreat into compliance.

Stress is a significant cause of health problems. It is important that organizations reduce the levels of stress where possible, but it is not always a real option. Stress can be destructive to physical and psychological well-being, as well as having an invidious impact on other aspects of applied functioning such as cognition. There is a truly vast array of stressors in the workplace. At the individual level these include job demands, role conflict, role ambiguity, and workload. At the group level there are such things as lack of team cohesiveness and intra-group conflict, and the organization itself produces many stressors from its structures, culture, and technologies. Mentally tough individuals not only survive the pressure, they actually thrive on it. The more sensitive individuals often have to battle to function, greatly reducing their potential for happiness and contentment. Therefore, resilience is a precursor to psychological health and fulfillment. It may be the case that, without this solid foundation, contentment is an impossible dream.

Finally, in this section we will make brief mention of "other people." These others are both a cause of stress and a solution to stress. It is interesting to note that more sensitive individuals are perhaps far more dependent on others for their well-being. Research using the Clough et al. (2002) model of mental toughness has shown that tough individuals tend to adopt active coping styles whereas more sensitive individuals tend to adopt a more passive, emotional approach (e.g., Nicholls, Polman, Levy, & Backhouse, 2008). Organizations are perhaps better able to deal with, and reward, active copers than they are emotional copers.

A key player in all relationships at work is the leader, who tends to be tougher than the average (e.g., Marchant et al., 2009). This could mean they are liable to bruise their sensitive colleagues. Whilst this no doubt does happen, the idea that tough and resilient individuals are unable to understand and take care with people does not seem to be the case. Research has looked at the link between emotional intelligence and mental toughness (e.g., Nicholls et al., 2015). They showed a positive relationship between mental toughness and emotional intelligence. An intriguing research study was carried out by Onley, Veselka, Schermer, and Vernon (2013). They investigated the relationship between the dark triad of personality (Machiavellianism, narcissism, and psychopathy) and toughness. They reported that there was a small positive correlation with narcissism, but negative associations with psychopathy and Machiavellianism.These findings, taken in conjunction with the recent findings by Nicholls et al. relating to emotional intelligence, may go some way to dispel the very unfair stereotype of the uncaring and manipulative boss.

Future Research

There are at least three significant omissions in the existing research literature on resilience and positive psychology. These relate to: (1) definitions; (2) the centrality of resilience to the experiencing of positive psychology and (3) possible interventions. The conceptual space representing the link between resilience and positive psychology is a complex and messy area to research. Perhaps the biggest causes of the "fog" are the many definitions and conceptualizations of resilience and resilience-related models and theories. We have tried to outline these. We have focused on mental toughness, as we have considerable experience of this particular concept. However, we are not suggesting that this is the only appropriate concept, but rather we have used it to illustrate some of the linkages. One pressing need is therefore to identify and agree on a "gold standard" model when trying to research in this domain. We would of course argue the merits of mental toughness, but we are not blind to the merits of the broader resilience concept (e.g., Putwain, Nicholson, Connors, & Woods, 2013), grit (Duckworth, Peterson, Matthews, and Kelly, 2007) and mindset (Dweck, 2006) among others.

A key research question that needs further investigation is the apparent dependence on resilience for people to experience the happiness and contentment that are central to positive psychology. Time and time again, mentally tough individuals appear to be happier and healthier (e.g., Brand et al., 2014; Brand et al., in press).

Finally, as applied psychologists we are interested in changing the status quo. Unfortunately, few studies have examined the impact of resilience training on the long-term positive outlook of the individuals involved. We need to identify what tools and techniques, if any, can be employed to enhance the core well-being of people and evaluate these with care and rigor. The extent to which resilience can be developed is far from clear. It has been viewed as both a trait and a state, and there is evidence that both biological and environmental factors can have a significant effect on it. Again, mental toughness provides a specific example. Horsburgh, Schermer, Veselka, and Vernon (2009) found that mental toughness is influenced by both genetics and features of the environment, and as such behaves, "in the same manner as virtually every personality trait that has ever been investigated in behavioural genetic study" (p. 104). In establishing significant correlations between the Mental Toughness Questionnaire (MTQ48) and the so-called big five personality factors (extraversion, openness, agreeableness, conscientiousness, and neuroticism), Horsburgh et al. suggest that mental toughness is strongly influenced by genetics and as such may not be easy to modify. However, these researchers did contend that the aspects of mental toughness that showed least heritability (i.e., commitment or control) may be easier to strengthen. Practical guidance for mental toughness development has been suggested by Crust and Clough (2011).

Conclusion

The relationship of resilience with positive psychology is a complex one. They are clearly integral, but at some points appear to be in opposition with each other. Issues are created by the diversity of the models and theories that relate to resilience. It is seen as a trait, a state, and all points in between. However, while clarity is a far distant ambition, research findings do strongly suggest that resilience is related to well-being and personal development. Without it, it might not be possible to build the three core pillars of "a life of enjoyment," "a life of engagement," and "a life of affiliation" which are central objectives to the positive psychology movement (Seligman & Csikszentmihayli, 2000). This brings into sharp focus the importance of individual differences in positive psychology. There is no blanket solution or underpinning model. It depends, as does most of psychology, on the person.

It is fair to conclude that resilience is very important to well-being and the enjoyment of life, but just how important is not yet known. It is also relatively clear that some of us are born resilient, some of us become resilient, some of us become less resilient, and some of us start and finish with low levels of resilience. It seems to be the case that developing resilience for some people would help them engage in the ideal world postulated by positive psychology. However, it is unclear how, and if, resilience can be truly developed. We do believe that it is possible to develop it, and that it would be a good thing to do. Much more research is needed before our beliefs can be reported as fact. Resilience and its impact on the well-being of individuals is not domain-specific. It has a role in work settings, sport, leisure, and education. It is an area that is both vibrant and intriguing and in our opinion well worth researching.

References

Affleck, G., & Tennen, H. (1996). Construing benefits from adversity: Adaptational significance and dispositional underpinnings. *Journal of Personality*, *64*, 899–922.

Aspinwall, L. G. (2001). Dealing with adversity: Self-regulation, coping, adaptation, and health. In A. Tesser & N. Schwarz (Eds.), *The Blackwell handbook of social psychology: Vol 1. Intrapersonal processes* (pp. 159–614). Malden, MA: Blackwell.

Aspinwall, L. G., & Taylor, S. E. (1992). Modelling cognitive adaptation: A longitudinal investigation of the impact of individual differences and coping on college adjustment and performance, *Journal of Personality and Social Psychology*, *63*, 989–1003.

Bartram, D., & Boniwell, I. (2007). The science of happiness: Achieving sustained psychological wellbeing. *In Practice*, *29*, 478–82.

Billings, D. W., Folkman, S., Acree, M., & Moskowitz, J. T. (2000). Coping and physical health during caregiving: The roles of positive and negative affect. *Journal of Personality and Social Psychology, 79*, 131–142.

Bird, W. (2007). *Natural thinking: Investigating the links between the natural environment, biodiversity and mental health.* Sandy, UK: RSPB.

Board, E., Arrighi, C., & Thatcher, J. (2003). Effectiveness of a multidisciplinary cardiac rehabilitation programme on the psychological wellbeing of myocardial infaction survivors. *British Journal of Sports Medicine, 37*, 467.

Bonanno, G. A. (2004). Loss, trauma, and human resilience: Have we underestimated the human capacity to thrive after extremely aversive events? *American Psychologist, 59*, 20–28.

Bonanno, G. A., Rennicke, C., & Dekel, S. (2005). Self-enhancement among high-exposure survivors of the September 11th terrorist attack: Resilience or social maladjustment? *Journal of Personality and Social Psychology, 88*, 984–998.

Brand, S., Gerber, M., Kalak, N., Kirov, R., Lemola, S., Clough, P. J., & Pühse, U. (2014). Adolescents with greater mental toughness show higher sleep efficiency, more deep sleep and fewer awakenings after sleep onset, *Journal of Adolescent Health, 54*, 109–113.

Brand, S., Kalak, N., Gerber, M., Clough, P. J., Lemola, S., Pühse U. and Holsboer-Trachsler, E. (in press). During early and mid-adolescence, greater mental toughness is related to increased sleep quality and psychological functioning, *Journal of Health Psychology.*

Calhoun, L. G., & Tedeschi, R. G. (1999). *Facilitating posttraumatic growth: A clinician's guide.* Mahwah, NJ: Erlbaum.

Campbell-Sills, L., Cohan, S., & Stein, M. (2006). Relationship of resilience to personality, coping and psychiatric symptoms in young adults. *Behaviour Research and Therapy, 44*, 585–599.

Carr, A. (2004). *Positive psychology: The science of happiness and human strengths.* New York, NY: Brunner-Routledge.

Carver, C. S., Pozo, C., Harris, S. D., Noriega, V., Scheier, M. F., Robinson, D. S., ... Clark, K. C. (1993). How coping mediates the effect of optimism on distress: A study of women with early stage breast cancer. *Journal of Personality and Social Psychology, 65*, 375–390.

Chemers, M. M., Hu, L., & Garcia, B. (2001) Academic self-efficacy and first-year college student performance and adjustment. *Journal of Educational Psychology, 93*, 55–65.

Chen, C., David, A., Thompson, K., Smith, C., Lea, S., & Fahy, T. (1996). Coping strategies and psychiatric morbidity in women attending breast assessment clinics. *Journal of Psychosomatic Research, 40*, 265–270.

Clough, P. J., Earle, K., & Sewell, D. (2002). Mental toughness: The concept and its measurement. In I. Cockerill (Ed.), *Solutions in sport psychology* (pp. 32–43). London, UK: Thomson.

Clough, P. J., & Strycharczyk, D. (2012). *Developing mental toughness: Improving performance, wellbeing and positive behaviours in others.* London, UK: Kogan Page.

Cohn, M., Fredrickson, B., Brown., S., Mikels, J., & Conway, A. (2009). Happiness unpacked: Positive emotions increase life satisfaction by building resilience. *Emotion, 9*, 361–368.

Crust, L. & Azadi, K. (2010). Mental toughness and athletes' use of psychological strategies. *European Journal of Sport Science, 10*, 43–51.

Crust, L., & Clough, P. J. (2011) Developing mental toughness: From research to practice, *Journal of Sport Psychology in Action, 2*, 21–32

Crust, L., Earle, K., Perry, J., Earle, F., Clough, A., & Clough, P. (2014). Mental toughness in higher education: Relationships with achievement and progression in first-year university sport students. *Personality and Individual Differences, 69*, 87–91.

Crust, L., Swann, C., Allen-Collinson, J., Breckon, J., & Weinberg, R. (2014). A phenomenological exploration of exercise mental toughness: Perceptions of exercise leaders and regular exercisers. *Qualitative Research in Sport, Exercise, & Health, 6*, 441–461.

Diener, E., Wirtz, D., Tov, W., Kim-Prieto, C., Choi, D., Oishi, S., & Biswas-Diener, R. (2010). New measures of wellbeing: Flourishing and positive and negative feelings. *Social Indicators Research, 97*, 143–156.

Dockray, S., & Steptoe, A. (2010). Positive affect and psychobiological processes. *Neuroscience and Biobehavioral Reviews, 35*, 69–75.

Duckworth, A. L., Peterson, C., Matthews, M. D., & Kelly, D. R. (2007). Grit: Perseverance and passion for long-term goals. *Journal of Personality and Social Psychology, 92*, 1087–1101.

Dweck, C. (2006). *Mindset*. New York, NY: Random House.

Faulk, K. E., Gloria, C. T., & Steinhardt, M. A. (2013). Coping profiles characterize individual flourishing, languishing, and depression. *Anxiety, Stress, & Coping, 26*, 378–390.

Folkman, S., Acree, M., & Moskowitz, J. T. (2000). Positive affect and the other side of coping. *American Psychologist, 55*, 647–654.

Folkman, S., & Moskowitz, J. T. (2004). Coping: Pitfalls and promise. *Annual Review of Psychology, 55*, 745–774.

Fredrickson, B. L. (1998). What good are positive emotions? *Review of General Psychology, 2*, 300–319.

Fredrickson, B. (2001). The role of positive emotions in positive psychology: The broaden-and-build theory of positive emotions. *American Psychologist, 56*, 218–226.

Fredrickson, B. (2002). Positive emotions. In C. Snyder, and S. Lopez (Eds.), *Handbook of positive psychology* (pp. 120–134). New York, NY: Oxford University Press.

Fredrickson, B. (2004). The broaden-and-build theory of positive emotions. *Philosophical Transactions of the Royal Society: Biological Sciences, 359*, 1367–1377.

Fredrickson, B., & Joiner, T. (2002). Positive emotions trigger upward spirals toward emotional wellbeing. *Psychological Science, 13*, 172–175.

Fredrickson, B., & Levenson, R. (1998). Positive emotions sped recovery from the cardiovascular sequelae of negative emotions. *Cognition and Emotion, 12*, 191–220.

Fredrickson, B., Mancuso, R., Branigan, C., & Tugade, M. (2000). The undoing effect of positive emotions. *Motivation and Emotion, 24*, 237–258.

Fredrickson, B. L., Tugade, M. M., Waugh, C. E., & Larkin, G. (2003). What good are positive emotions in crises? A prospective study of resilience and emotions following the terrorist attacks on the United States on September 11th, 2001. *Journal of Personality and Social Psychology, 84*, 365–376.

Freese, J., Meland, S., & Irwin, W. (2006). Expressions of positive emotion in photographs, personality, and later-life marital and health outcomes, *Journal of Personality and Social Psychology, 70*, 349–361.

Garmezy, N., & Rutter, M. (1983). *Stress, coping and development in children*. New York, NY: McGraw-Hill.

Gloria, C. T., Faulk, K. E., & Steinhardt, M. A. (2013). Positive affectivity predicts successful and unsuccessful adaptation to stress. *Motivation and Emotion, 37*, 185–193.

Gordon, K. A. (1995). Self-concept and motivational patterns of resilient African American high school students. *Journal of Black Psychology, 21*, 239–255.

Gordon, K. A. (1996). Resilient Hispanic youths' self-concept and motivational patterns. *Hispanic Journal of Behavioural Sciences, 18*, 63–73.

Gordon-Rouse, K. (2001). Resilient students' goals and motivation. *Journal of Adolescence, 24*, 461–472.

Greenglass, E. R., & Fiksenbaum, L. (2009). Proactive coping, positive affect and wellbeing: Testing for mediation using path analysis. *European Psychologist, 14*, 29–39.

Gucciardi, D., Gordon, S., & Dimmock, J. (2009). Advancing mental toughness research and theory using personal construct psychology. *International Review of Sport and Exercise Psychology, 2*, 54–72.

Hanusek, E. A. (1997). Applying performance incentives to schools for disadvantaged populations. *Education and Urban Society, 29*, 296–316.

Helgeson, V., Reynolds, K., & Tomich, P. (2006). A meta-analytic review of benefit finding and growth. *Journal of Consulting and Clinical Psychology, 74*, 797–816.

Horsburgh, V., Schermer, J., Veselka, L., & Vernon, P. (2009). A behavioral genetic study of mental toughness and personality, *Personality and Individual Differences, 46*, 100–105

Jacelon, C. S. (1997). The trait and process of resilience. *Journal of Advanced Nursing, 25*, 123–129.

Jackson, S., & Csikszentmihalyi, M. (1999). *Flow in sports*. Champaign, IL: Human Kinetics.

Jones, G., Hanton, S., & Connaughton, D. (2007). A framework of mental toughness in the world's best performers. *The Sport Psychologist, 21*, 243–264.

Joseph, S. (2012). What doesn't kill us … the psychology of post-traumatic growth. *The Psychologist, 25*, 816–819.

Kobasa, S. (1979). Stressful life events, personality, and health: An inquiry into hardiness. *Journal of Personality and Social Psychology, 37*, 1–11.

Kobasa, S., Maddi, S., & Khan, S. (1982). Hardiness and health: A prospective study. *Journal of Personality and Social Psychology, 42*, 884–890.

Layard, R., & Clark, D. M. (2014). *Thrive: The power of psychological therapy*. London, UK: Penguin.

Lepore, S., & Revenson, T. (2006). Resilience and posttraumatic growth: Recovery, resistance, and reconfiguration. In L. Calhoun & R. Tedeschi (Eds.), *Handbook of posttraumatic growth: Research and practice* (pp. 24–46). Mahwah, NJ: Erlbaum.

Luthar, S. (1991). Vulnerability and resilience: A study of high-risk adolescents. *Child Development, 62*, 600–616.

Luthar, S., & Cicchetti, D. (2000). The construct of resilience: Implications for interventions and social policies. *Development & Psychopathology, 12*, 857–885.

Lyubomirsky, S., King, L., & Diener, E. (2005). The benefits of frequent positive affect: Does happiness lead to success? *Psychological Bulletin, 131*, 803.

Maddi, S. (2004). Hardiness: An operationalization of existential courage. *Journal of Humanistic Psychology, 44*, 279–298.

Maluccio, A. N. (2002). Resilience: A many-splendored construct? *American Journal of Orthopsychiatry, 72*, 596–599.

Marchant, D., Polman, R., Clough, P., Jackson, J., Levy, A., & Nicholls, A. (2009). Mental toughness: Managerial and age differences, *Journal of Managerial Psychology, 24*, 428–437.

Martin, A. J., & Marsh, H. W. (2008). Academic buoyancy: Towards an understanding of students' everyday academic resilience. *Journal of School Psychology, 46*, 53–83.

Maslow, A. (1943). A theory of human motivation, *Psychological Review, 50*, 370–396.

Masten, A. S. (1994). Resilience in individual development: Successful adaptation despite risk and adversity. In M. C. Wang, & E. Gordon (Eds.), *Educational resilience in inner-city America: Challenges and prospects* (pp. 3–26). Hillsdale, NJ: Erlbaum.

Masten, A. S. (2001). Ordinary magic: Resilience processes in development. *American Psychologist, 56*, 227.

Masten, A. S., Roisman, G. I., Long, J. D., Burt, K. B., Obradović, J., Riley, J. R., … Tellegen, A. (2005). Developmental cascades: Linking academic achievement and externalizing and internalizing symptoms over 20 years. *Developmental Psychology, 41*, 733.

Nath, P., & Pradhan, R. K. (2012). Influence of positive affect on physical health and psychological wellbeing: Examining the mediating role of psychological resilience. *Journal of Health Management, 14*, 161–174.

Neenan, M. (2009). *Developing resilience: A cognitive behavioural approach*. London, UK: Routledge.

Nicholls, A., Levy, A., Polman, R., & Crust, L. (2011). Mental toughness, coping self-efficacy, and coping effectiveness among athletes. *International Journal of Sport Psychology, 42*, 513–524.

Nicholls, A. R., Perry, J. L., Jones, L., Sanctuary, C., Carson, F., & Clough, P. J. (2015). The mediating role of mental toughness in sport, *Journal of Sports Medicine and Physical Fitness, 55*, 824–834.

Nicholls, A. R., Polman, R., Levy, A., & Backhouse, S. (2008). Mental toughness, optimism, and coping among athletes. *Personality and Individual Differences, 44*, 1182–1192.

Ong, A. D., & Bergeman, C. S. (2004). The complexity of emotions in later life. *Journals of Gerontology, Series B: Psychological Sciences and Social Sciences, 59*, 117–P122.

Ong, A. D., Bergeman, C. S., & Bisconti, T. L. (2004). The role of daily positive emotions during conjugal bereavement. *Journal of Behavioural, Psychological, and Social Sciences, 59*, 68–176.

Ong, A. D., Bergeman, C. S., Bisconti, T. L., & Wallace, K. A. (2006). The contours of resilience and the complexity of emotions in later life. *Journal of Personality and Social Psychology, 91*, 730–749.

Onley, M., Veselka, L., Shermer, J. A., & Vernon, P. A. (2013). Survival of the scheming: A genetically informed link between the dark triad and mental toughness, *Twin Research and Human Genetics, 16*, 1087–1093.

Peterson, C., & Seligman, M. (2003). Character strengths before and after September 11th. *Psychological Science, 14*, 381–384.

Pressman, S. D., & Cohen, S. (2005). Does positive affect influence health? *Psychological Bulletin, 131*, 925–971.

Putwain, D. W., Nicholson, L. J., Connors, L., & Woods, K. (2013). Resilient children are less test anxious and perform better in tests at the end of primary schooling. *Learning and Individual Differences, 28*, 41–46.

Reschly, A. L., Huebner, E. S., Appleton, J. J., & Antaramian, S. (2008). Engagement as flourishing: The role of positive emotions and coping in student engagement at school and with learning. *Psychology in the Schools, 45*, 419–431.

Richardson, G. E. (2002). The metatheory of resilience and resiliency. *Journal of Clinical Psychology, 58*, 307–321.

Richardson, G. E., Neiger, B. L., Jenson, S., & Kumpfer, K. L. (1990). The resiliency model. *Health Education, 21*, 33–39.

Ryff, C. (1989). Happiness is everything, or is it? Explorations on the meaning of psychological wellbeing. *Journal of Personality and Social Psychology, 57*, 1069–1081.

Seligman, M., & Csikszentmihalyi, M. (2000). Positive psychology: An introduction. *American Psychologist, 55*, 5–14.

Stamp, E., Crust, L., Swann, C., Clough, P., Perry, J., & Marchant, D. (2015). Relationships between mental toughness and psychological wellbeing in undergraduate university students. *Personality and Individual Differences, 75*, 170–174.

Sterling, P., & Eyer, J. (1988). Allostasis: A new paradigm to explain arousal pathology. In S. Fisher, & J. T. Reason (Eds.), *Handbook of life stress, cognition and health* (pp. 629–649). Chichester, UK: Wiley.

Tugade, M., & Fredrickson, B. (2004). Resilient individuals use positive affect to bounce back from negative emotional experiences, *Journal of Personality and Social Psychology, 86*, 320–333.

Tugade, M., Fredrickson, B., & Barrett, L. (2004). Psychological resilience and positive emotional granularity: Examining the benefits of positive emotions on coping and health. *Journal of Personality, 72*, 1161–1190.

Vulpe, A., & Dafinoiu, I. (2012). Positive emotions, coping strategies, and ego-resiliency: A mediation model. *Procedia – Social and Behavioral Sciences, 33*, 308–312.

Wagnild, G. M., & Young, H. M. (1993). Development and psychometric evaluation of the resilience scale. *Journal of Nursing Measurement, 1*, 165–178.

Waugh, C. E., & Fredrickson, B. (2006). Nice to know you: Positive emotions, self–other overlap, and complex understanding in the formation of a new relationship. *The Journal of Positive Psychology, 1*, 93–106.

Weinberger, D. A., Schwartz, G. E., & Davidson, R. J. (1979). Low-anxious, high-anxious, and repressive coping styles: Psychometric patterns and behavioural and physiological responses to stress. *Journal of Abnormal Psychology, 88*, 369–380.

Werner, E., & Smith, R. (2001). *Journeys from childhood to midlife: Risk, resilience, and recovery.* Ithaca, NY: Cornell University Press.

Wilson, J. P., Friedman, M. J., & Lindy, J. D. (2001). *Treating psychological trauma and PTSD.* New York, NY: Guilford.

Zautra, A., Johnson, L., & Davis, M. (2005). Positive affect as a source of resilience for women in chronic pain. *Journal of Consulting and Clinical Psychology, 73*, 212–20.

10

Mental Fitness at Work

Paula Robinson and Lindsay G. Oades

Introduction

This chapter introduces the concept of mental fitness and its association to mental health and well-being, particularly in the workplace. The burden of mental illness is significant, accounting for between 3% and 16% of total health expenditure across many countries (Organisation for Economic Co-operation and Development; OECD, 2011). The increasing levels of mental illness are a significant concern; for example, the World Health Organization (WHO, 2012) estimates that almost half of the world's population are affected in some way by a mental illness. Bloom et al. (2011), in his report to the The World Economic Forum, cites the global cost of mental illness at nearly $2.5 trillion in 2010, with a projected increase to over $6 trillion by 2030. This increase is also affecting organizations as is evidenced in a report by the OECD (2015) suggesting that mental illness is responsible for a significant loss of labor supply, high rates of unemployment, and a high incidence of illness, absence, and decreased productivity at work.

Since 2000 the focus has been shifting toward a proactive, preventative approach as the most obvious way to reduce the burden of mental illness, for example the European Union's (2008) *European Pact for Mental Health and Well-Being* and the WHO Report *Prevention of Mental Disorders* (2004). Keyes (2007) suggests there are economic and social advantages for a paradigm shift toward well-being and mental health promotion to work in conjunction with mental illness prevention. He argues that if the strategies of governments and indeed organizations continue to focus on diagnosed mental illness alone, the best they can hope for is to reduce levels of diagnosed mental illness. Moreover, this approach does not assure a mentally healthy population or workplace. Keyes argues that mental health is a separate continuum whereby a languishing individual can function at levels similar to someone with a major depressive episode – that is, there is no diagnosed mental illness but they are not mentally healthy either.

The Wiley Blackwell Handbook of the Psychology of Positivity and Strengths-Based Approaches at Work,
First Edition. Edited by Lindsay G. Oades, Michael F. Steger, Antonella Delle Fave, and Jonathan Passmore.

Huppert (2009) concurs with Keyes that the primary aim should be to enhance well-being instead of just reducing disorder, and in recent years positive psychology has made great strides forward within the well-being paradigm (Seligman & Csikszentmihalyi, 2000; Peterson, Park, & Castro, 2011). Seligman (2002) emphasizes that prevention is a primary purpose of positive psychology research.

In this chapter, after outlining mental health and well-being issues at work, the concept of fitness is then described before introducing the emerging concept of mental fitness. A critical review of literature, which led to the development of mental fitness, is provided before focusing on the conceptual application of mental fitness to work. The chapter concludes with the significant future research required to further develop the empirical bases for mental fitness at work.

Mental Health and Well-Being at Work

Given the previous statistics, providing a safe and healthy *psychological* workplace is becoming a big issue for organizations. Before taking into account those languishing individuals at work, research suggests that at any given time, at least 1 in 5 employees are likely to be experiencing a mental health condition (Australian Human Rights Commission, 2010). Consequently mental illness is a costly component of organizational life and may be considered in terms of risk assessment, for example, costs risk, key staff risk, and work health and safety risk as follows:

1 *Costs risk: failure to manage costs within budget*: Insurance premium increases, backup staff costs, retraining, medical bills, counseling costs, employee assistance program costs
2 *Key staff risk: failure to attract, retain and develop key staff*: Loss of staff, loss of knowledge, use of consultants, inability to recruit the best people, absenteeism, lack of staff development, reputation issues
3 *Work health and safety risk: failure to comply with work health and safety legislation/regulation*: Bullying and harassment claims, mentally injured workers, unsafe workplace, regulatory sanctions, legal proceedings

Given the steady increase of mental illness and the burgeoning associated costs, the workplace is an important context when considering population-based mental health and well-being. Therefore, promoting a proactive approach to mental illness, particularly targeting prevention and well-being, is becoming increasingly crucial to organizations not only as part of corporate governance and social responsibility strategies but as part of cost reduction, risk mitigation, and increasing engagement.

However, while there is evidence that positive psychology interventions reduce depression and improve well-being (e.g., Pietrowsky & Mikutta, 2012), these interventions are more difficult to implement in an organizational setting. In today's highly competitive business environment, companies have to go beyond fixing problems to promoting excellence. It is no longer simply a matter of getting employees to *do* their work, but rather how to get them to do *good* work, or their *best* work (Davis, 2010). Therefore, the management of human capital and the relationship between employee well-being and business outcomes is a crucial area of research and practice. Boards, senior/frontline managers and leaders are only gradually becoming aware that employee well-being and business performance are complementary components of a financially and psychologically healthy workplace.

Therefore, organizations and individuals need to allocate time, energy, and resources to well-being research and interventions as a serious strategy to reduce mental illness and improve engagement. Research supports the notion that creating a mentally healthy workplace is good business. Examples of research to support this proposition are now described below:

1 In the USA, employees ranked "senior management interest in employee well-being" as the top driver of engagement. A Gallup Workplace Audit was analyzed using approximately 200,000 respondents in over 8,000 business units, with results suggesting that employee turnover, customer loyalty, productivity, profitability, and higher turnover of sales were all influenced by the way managers address the issues of employee well-being and engagement (see Harter, Schmidt & Keyes, 2003; Judge, Thoresen, Bono, & Patton, 2001).
2 Data from a global workplace study of 90,000 employees across 18 countries suggesting that only 1 out of every 5 employees feel fully engaged by their work, with 40% reporting being *actively disengaged*. This translates directly to the bottom line. The companies with the most engaged employees reported a 19% year-to-year increase in operating income and 28% growth in earnings per share, with 90% of their employees reporting having no plans to leave. Conversely, companies with the lowest levels of engagement reported a 32% year-to-year decline in operating income while their earnings dropped more than 11%, with 50% of employees saying they were considering leaving during the coming year (Towers Watson Global Workforce Study, 2012).
3 The positive mental health and well-being of leaders and staff can have measurable, positive effects on individual, team, and organizational outcomes, in relation to reduced costs, and also by improving productivity, creativity, work–life integration, and other important indicators (e.g., Cameron & Spreitzer, 2012; Hillier, Fewell & Shephard, 2005; Linley, Harrington & Garcia, 2010; Mental Health Commission, 2010; Robertson & Cooper, 2010).
4 Well-being can provide a buffering effect; Wills and Isasi (2007) suggest that buffering is a process whereby a psychological resource reduces the impact of stress on psychological well-being.
5 Return on investment (ROI) analysis by Price Waterhouse Coopers (2014) suggests that every dollar spent on effective workplace mental health actions can generate $2.30 in benefits to an organization. These benefits are derived from a reduction in presenteeism, absenteeism, and compensation claims. This report also suggests ROI is likely to be increased from implementing multiple targeted actions.
6 The Sloan Center for Aging and Work (2014) suggests that organizations of the 21st century would like to be and remain employers of choice and so must consider what will motivate employees to come to work, work hard while they are at work, and want to stay rather than work for a competitor. Meaning at work, autonomy, and inclusion (all positive mental health predictors) were found to be crucial components of retaining older employees in the workplace.
7 Fairlie and Svergun (2015) surveyed more than 700 Canadians and Americans working at a variety of organizations. The study focused on traditional Corporate Social Responsibility (CSR) and additionally the concept of *positive* CSR (i.e., discretionary, proactive social initiatives for the betterment of the world and not necessarily associated to business outcomes). Results further supported positive CSR perceptions being associated with levels of stress, engagement, commitment, and intention to leave.
8 Cameron (2013) highlights the importance of the positive energy of leaders by studying various business units and found performance to be four times better if an employee is at the centre of a positive energy network. Youssef and Luthans (2007) found hope, optimism, and resilience had a positive effect on job performance, job satisfaction, work happiness, and organizational commitment.

If the objective of the organizational intervention is positive mental health and well-being outcomes, then it becomes similar to any other change initiative in that the design, effective implementation, measurement, and sustainability rely first and foremost on leader and employee participation and buy-in. This is not easily achieved, as many people still primarily view the main role of mental health interventions as one of curing psychological pathology rather than preventing it. Further to this, the conceptual and empirical evaluation and development of well-being outcomes are to date not well understood by organizations. Well-being is often perceived to be associated with "soft skills" and/or issues of mental health and illness. As a result, the design, delivery, and maintenance of mental illness prevention, positive mental health promotion, and well-being strategies and practices are often sporadic and tokenistic within government and organizations.

Barriers to Well-Being at Work

Stigma and conceptual confusion surrounding mental health are significant barriers to mental illness prevention, mental health promotion, and engagement in positive mental health activities and practices. For example, a comprehensive review by Cheverton (Cheverton & The Queensland Alliance for Mental Health, 2009) suggests that the stigma attached to mental ill health prevents most people from disclosing. Lawyers are a notable example. Research in the United States by Benjamin, Darling, and Sales (1990) on over 11,000 participants and across 100 occupations revealed that lawyers had the highest prevalence of depression of all the workers. There are estimates that the incidence of chemical dependency is between 15% and 18% in the legal profession, compared to 8–10% of the general population (Resner, 2006). The nature of the legal profession is cited as being adversarial and conflict-driven, with attributes shared by lawyers including perfectionism and pessimism. However, it is difficult not to see these and other negative attributes present in many 21st-century organizations.

Cheverton emphasizes that the longer people leave seeking help, the more significant their ultimate call on health and associated services will be. They note that because of stigma and conceptual confusion, a broader *prevention* and *promotion* agenda is required to assist in advising the steps that individuals, organizations, governments, and communities can take to build the resources and competencies to keep them mentally healthy.

The barriers of stigma and conceptual confusion exemplify the clear and urgent need for mental health and well-being interventions, and for programs that are easy to understand, have overarching community acceptability and face validity, and that cut through multiple contexts. Theoretical and empirical innovation is required to ensure that positive mental health research and practice is understood and adopted. New, inventive approaches and conceptual frameworks are now more than ever essential to capture the attention of individuals, organizations, and governments to decrease the incidence of mental illness and increase positive mental health education and activities. Keyes (2007) emphasizes that promotion of positive mental health strategies and activities is a crucial component of any mental health initiative. Seligman (2002) emphasizes that there is very little focus on *how* to educate, promote, and engage people in proactive positive mental health activities to prevent mental illness. Luthans (2002, 2012) argues that there is a need for new positive core concepts, provided they have good theoretical and empirical foundations, that particularly lend themselves to development and application in multiple settings. The question is how to promote and engage individuals to be proactive and enjoy the development of their own positive mental health and well-being and to get involved in their own regular, targeted intentional activities, without the stigma of mental ill health? The concept of fitness is now discussed as one possible way forward.

Fitness

WHO use the term *fitness* in their evidence paper on mental health promotion (see Naidoo & Wills, 2000) by stating that "health can mean the absence of disease or disability but, just as often, may refer to a state of *fitness* and ability or to a reservoir of personal resources that can be called on when needed" (p. 17). There is no dissection of mental and physical fitness in the meaning of fitness in the above definition, suggesting fitness is a holistic term that encompasses both mental and physical components.

"Physical fitness is a combination of qualities that enable individuals to be at their full potential in performing vigorous physical activities and involve (but are not limited to) *endurance, strength & flexibility*" (Physical fitness, 2004). This definition suggests that physical fitness activities are an enabler toward realizing one's potential by way of performing a range of intentional physical activities. Physical fitness interventions have, over recent years, been utilized by governments, organizations, and the medical profession as an invaluable *preventative* measure in the fight against disease. For example, individuals are able to go to a medical practitioner or a reputable assessment center to ascertain their general physical fitness level and then be advised about options for improving it; governments and organizations too have many and varied physical fitness interventions to improve the health of their citizens, leaders, and staff.

While obviously physical illness is still treated after it occurs, the concept of physical fitness has provided a proactive and preventative strategy to support higher levels of physical health. Physical fitness is also a simple concept to promote. Most would be aware that millions of dollars are already spent on promoting fitness and the average person already understands this term. Primarily, fitness promotion focuses on assessment and intervention programs and healthy exercise routines utilizing equipment, fitness centers, books, apps, and so on. Additionally, personal trainers and coaches who come from a range of fields, for example, medicine, sport, psychology and health, offer to improve your fitness using an array of frameworks and methodologies, some scientifically validated and some not.

Why Mental Fitness?

The concept of fitness is a term that has central meaning and understanding within the wider community and emphasizes the dynamic nature of levels of optimal functioning, competitive edge, and the understanding that achieving fitness requires effort and motivation over time and is based on regular activities and practices. This is the communication that needs to be conveyed for mental fitness too so that it becomes part of a total fitness strategy. The term mental fitness aligned to physical fitness can create a total fitness approach for individuals, organizations, governments, and the wider community. By using the term "mental" prior to fitness, mental fitness can be seen as analogous to physical fitness. Physical fitness is a better-known domain and it can be used to enable people to grasp potential meanings of mental fitness.

The alignment of positive mental health assessment, activities, and practices to a fitness analogy can assist in mental health promotion because fitness is proactive, preventative, and easily understood, without stigma. Individuals already understand fitness and know that it is essential to engage in regular and targeted exercises with the primary goal of improving their physical health and well-being.

A mental fitness strategy aligned to the concept of physical fitness is already recognized as part of a positive health approach. For example, from 1948 to the present day WHO's definition of health has had a holistic approach by including physical and mental indicators together: "health is a state of complete physical, mental and social well-being and not merely the absence of disease or infirmity" (1948, p. 1). The American College of Sports Medicine (ACSM, 2000) supports the definition of "health-related fitness" developed by Pate (1988), who defines fitness as the demonstration of capacities that help prevent disease and promote health. Seligman (2008) argues that a scientific discipline of total health barely exists despite the fact that the fields of biology, chemistry, and medicine have validated many of the physical and mental health improvements obtained from regular physical exercise.

There is already growing evidence that mental and physical health work together to create positive outcomes (e.g., Richards, Campania, & Muse-Burke, 2010). Further, the benefit of regular physical exercise activities on mental health is supported by numerous studies, for example, exercise alters the brain to become more resistant to stress (Schoenfeld, Rada, Pieruzzini, Hsueh, & Gould, 2013), it has a protective effect against anxiety (Smith, 2013), and is associated with relief from depression (Cooney et al., 2013).

The promotion of fitness activities and practices to increase adoption and in turn positive economic and health outcomes is a big challenge. For example, there is an increase in sedentary lifestyle behaviors and most mental health professionals will admit that one of their greatest challenges is to motivate their clients to regularly practice their prescribed mental health activities for longer periods of time. Therefore, an urgent need exists for more cooperative and integrated approaches between the physical and mental health domains by organizations and governments (e.g., Ory, Smith, Mier, & Wernicke, 2010).

Fitness requires intentional activities

Just as the physical fitness literature indicates, there is also growing evidence that specific activities and practices have a beneficial effect on well-being outcomes. Positive psychology and neural plasticity research has become a promising area for positive mental health activities across multiple contexts, with evidence suggesting that throughout the lifespan individuals are able to learn and grow (Greenwood & Parasuraman, 2010; Shaw & McEachern, 2001; Sin and Lyubormirsky, 2009).

While twin studies by Lykken and Tellegen (1996) suggest that a stable part of happiness is accounted for by heredity, the amount of variance would decide the extent to which happiness is changeable. Lyubomirsky, Sheldon and Schkade (2005) examined the role of heredity and found that three major factors may govern a person's chronic happiness level: set point or potential range (i.e., genetic predisposition, heredity), life circumstances (e.g., race, age, disability), and intentional activities, which are defined as voluntary activities that you choose to participate in. Intentional activities include a wide variety of activities that involve how people think, feel, and behave. Approximate percentage breakdown of the variance of each factor in cross-sectional well-being suggests around 40% of the variance is related to intentional activities. This 40% would be the target for mental fitness activities.

Sheldon and King (2001) highlighted the need for positive psychology to reconsider how to engage "the average person to find out what is right and what needs improving" (p. 216). A meta-analysis by Sin and Lyubomirsky (2009) suggests one of the most promising areas of research to improve one's well-being is the use of intentional activities to decrease depressive symptoms and to improve well-being. However, they also comment that although happiness for a population can be increased, it remains unclear how long the increase would last, that is, motivation of the individual to engage in these activities for longer period of time is a challenge. Diener and Biswas-Diener (2008) also include engaging activities as part of the process of improving happiness. The challenge for researchers and practitioners is to identify which intentional activities to target and to discover how to motivate people to engage in these activities. The question is, as Haidt (2006) comments "how to push a person up to the top of his/her potential range" (p. 91).

The motivation to participate in intentional psychological activities regularly and over long periods of time would be advantageous to advance theory, research, and practice. This concept and practice of intentional activities aligns well with the physical fitness analogy, given the wider community already understands that to become fit, one must engage in regular and targeted activities and practices that "fit" with the person's goals, for example, lifting weights (building strength) and running (building endurance).

The concept of mental fitness aligns well with this research on intentional activities because it is structured in a similar way to physical fitness (i.e., regular and varied intentional exercises designed to "fit" the specific criteria of each person). Moreover, the concept of mental fitness helps to address the problem of motivating people to work on their mental fitness as part of their life activities,given the analogy of physical fitness suggests that fitness is not stored – that is, fitness dissipates without the frequency and duration of workouts.

To summarize, mental fitness can be one effective solution to assist in mental health initiatives in community and workplace contexts because (1) it can utilize language already known and understood that is easy to relate to concepts such as strength, flexibility, endurance; (2) it assists in reducing stigma and conceptual confusion that exists around the concept of mental health; (3) it helps to address the need for more proactive, preventative, and holistic approaches to improved mental health that have consumer acceptability; (4) the term progresses the idea that a fit mind and body are equally important and need regular, intentional activities and practices to build sustainable habits of mind; (5) mental fitness is viewed as a *process* (a series of assessment and regular activities) to achieve a particular outcome, that is, improved levels of mental health and well-being.

Although the concept of mental fitness can provide a way of explaining positive mental health theory, research, and activities in a non-threatening, parsimonious, and proactive way, until recently the psychological literature did not have a scientific term that corresponded to physical fitness. There were no consistent theoretical foundations or standardized measures to research and replicate or for mental health practitioners to apply.

What Is Mental Fitness?

To commence the process of scientifically developing a mental fitness concept, Robinson, Oades, and Caputi (2014) examined three questions:

1 What is mental fitness and how should it be defined?
2 What are the components of mental fitness?
3 What are the factors underlying current published measures that can be used to operationalize mental fitness?

To examine these research questions a conceptual review and two studies were conducted: the preliminary construction of mental fitness was supported by a conceptual and critical literature review; a Delphi study assisted in formulating a definition and underlying principles by way of an international expert panel; and an empirical study revealed a multifactorial model of mental fitness underpinned by 73 items (Robinson, Oades, & Caputi, 2014). Results from this body of work are now summarized.

The term *mental fitness* is not new to the psychological literature. The concept was proposed by McCarthy (1964) who suggested it would "serve psychology well through the many gradations represented by the various nosological categories of clients served by community mental-health clinics, to the well-adjusted, spontaneous, natural, creative individuals who are coping with reality, making effective contributions to society and realising their intellectual, emotional and social potential" (p. 202). McCarthy also suggested that mental fitness formed an excellent counterpart for the late President Kennedy's population-based program for physical fitness, that is, a total fitness initiative combining mental and physical fitness together. In a more recent example, Seligman (2011) has incorporated the concept of fitness in a military resiliency training context known as comprehensive solider fitness.

The historical use of the term fitness commenced from the 14th century (e.g., "Fitness," 2012). The term fitness continued through time to be viewed developmentally, suggesting it is a function and that individuals are active agents in the process by achieving the ability or capacity to change, develop, adapt, and respond to enable them to move toward a successful fit between themselves and their environment (e.g., Darwin, 1869). The term physical fitness by way of exercises was not explicitly referred to until the 1920s and then, moving into the 21st century, the term fitness became more focused on regular exercise (practice) as an enabler to achieve good health and physical fitness. There was no reference to the term mental fitness during this period.

Modern meaning and use of the term fitness

Following the examination of the more historical meaning and use of the term fitness, the next step was to investigate and further understand the contemporary meaning and use of the term. To achieve this, Robinson, Oades, and Caputi (2014) analyzed how the English-speaking Internet users of the 21st century view the terms fitness, physical fitness, and, specifically, mental fitness by undertaking a Google search (carried out in 2013) via their web browser. While it was virtually impossible to examine every entry, results from this search revealed a plethora of hits: fitness, 461 million; physical fitness, 86 million; mental fitness, over 17 million; and physical/mental fitness together revealed 6 million hits. These initial search results strongly suggested that the concept of mental fitness has meaning and utility in modern-day society.

Results revealed five primary categories where the term was being utilized. The first category was coded as providing creditable information from websites that reflected a reputable genre, for instance health and psychological services; the second category contained more unreliable sources, such as individuals without qualifications, private blogs, social media, and so on; the third category was specifically advertising courses and programs from multiple sources; the fourth category contained either government or non-government organizations; and finally there was a media category where the term appeared in published material, such as magazines.

In summary, the search clearly indicated that the concept of fitness (both mental and physical) is now widely used and suggested that the meaning still, to some degree, reflects its historical roots. For example, mental fitness (like physical fitness) requires practice and suggests that those who participate in improving their mental fitness are functioning at an optimal level and are more capable; mental fitness is a process that can be learned, indeed the primary focus across all categories was exercises and training across multiple settings, such as work, life, school. Additionally, personal trainers and coaches who came from a range of fields, for example, medicine, sport, psychology, and health, offered to improve physical and/or mental fitness using a vast array of frameworks and methodologies including fitness centers, DVDs, and self-help books. Moreover, it was evident that considerable amounts of money and time are spent on promoting mental fitness in much the same way as physical fitness.

Essentially the analysis revealed the primary focus was assessment and intervention programs and tools across multiple contexts. The search also indicated that, by way of private blogs and social websites dedicated to sharing information and experiences of mental fitness, there is a growing level of interest in the concept among Google users. However, while there were commonalities between the historical and popular interpretations of mental fitness, the five categories showed differing usage of the term with no evidence of a scientifically generated definition, measure, or evidence-based development activities.

Psychological literature

The next phase of the analysis was to search the psychological literature to ascertain if this reflected the historical and popular conceptualizations. The search was carried out in 2013 in the database PsycInfo. Results suggest mental fitness is not a robust scientific endeavor in the psychological literature (only 60 results in total). However, salient themes suggested some congruence with the historical and popular searches, specifically: (1) mental and physical health and fitness often appear together and involve learned, changeable skills and regular exercises to practice; (2) evolutionary theory, the process of adaptation, is prominent; (3) mental fitness includes cognitive, affective behavioral components; (4) mental fitness can be domain-specific, that is, work, life, and social; (5) mental fitness is a process with well-being outcomes; (6) mental fitness involves psychological resources, such as resilience; (7) mental fitness also assists in the reduction of some mental illnesses, such as anxiety, anger, and depression – there are treatment and prevention components; (8) mental fitness can be intentional and goal-directed; (9) there are numerous mental fitness tests and indicators but they vary in explanation and content. Consistent with the popular literature search, there were no reliable and valid measures nor a consistent definition.

In summary, the above review explored the concept of mental fitness within the historical, popular, and psychological literatures. Based on these findings, an initial definition and four guiding principles were formulated to influence future research and practice (see the results of the Delphi study below).

Experts' views of mental fitness

Following the conceptual review of the term mental fitness, Robinson, Oades, and Caputi (2015) conducted a Delphi study to engage an international expert panel ($n = 25$) to evaluate the proposed definition and four guiding principles of mental fitness; expert consensus was achieved. Results provided a definition of mental fitness as being "the modifiable capacity to utilize resources and skills to flexibly adapt to challenges or advantages, enabling thriving." Results for the four guiding principles were: (1) fitness is a positive term without connotations of illness implied by mental health or mental illness; (2) mental fitness could be understood by the wider community in a similar way to physical fitness; (3) mental fitness is measurable; and (4) mental fitness can be improved, in a similar way to physical fitness. The panel also offered valuable, qualitative input and recommendations for future research and practice.

Below is a brief summary of the four guiding principles supported by the expert panel.

(1) Fitness is a positive term without connotations of illness implied by mental health or mental illness Principle 1 is based on the assumption that the term *physical health* is understood by individuals and the wider community as absence of physical disease and is without stigma. However, the term *mental health* is understood as absence of mental illness and is largely stigmatized. The conceptual review of the literature by Robinson, Oades, and Caputi, (2014) suggested that the term mental fitness is not stigmatized.

(2) Mental fitness can be understood by the wider community in a similar way to physical fitness As previously stated, *Microsoft Encarta Reference Library* (Physical fitness, 2004) suggests *physical fitness* involves (but is not limited to) *endurance*, *strength*, and *flexibility*. The term mental fitness could transpose components from one context to another (psychological strength, flexibility, and endurance) as they already have meaning and relevance for the wider community.

The expert panel also suggested the formulation of individual definitions for the components of a mental fitness resource index (strength, flexibility, endurance). These were drawn from the *Merriam-Webster Online Dictionary* ("Endurance," 2014; "Flexibility," 2014; "Strength," 2014) to reflect a broad, "layman's" understanding of the labels. *Strength* is defined as "the quality or state of being strong: capacity for exertion or endurance"; *Flexibility* is defined as "a ready capability to adapt to new, different, or changing requirements". *Endurance* is defined as "the ability to withstand prolonged hardship or adversity."

(3) Mental fitness is measurable Principle 3 suggests that a *mental fitness* model would be helpful in generating items by synthesizing key theories, research, and practices that remain largely disconnected within the psychological literature relating to positive mental health. For example, meaning, purpose, strengths knowledge and use, resiliency, positive emotions, mindfulness, acceptance are all related to well-being and featured prominently in the positive mental health research.

(4) Mental fitness can be improved in a way similar to physical fitness Principle 4 suggests that *mental fitness* can be learned via developmental intentional activities, exercises, and regular practice to "fit" the assessed needs, thus creating positive psychological habits or rituals.

The Delphi study expert panel concurred that an alignment of the physical fitness paradigm is easy to understand, preventative, and proactive and has good face validity that provides a way of explaining positive mental health theory, research, and activities that could be easily understood by the wider community, without stigma. The panel endorsed development of a holistic model of mental fitness as a worthy field of study. The panel also advocated that a mental fitness strategy creates the opportunity to develop workplace community-based programs and suggested that mental fitness activities could be developed to simultaneously work on mental and physical fitness, but must be targeted based on accurate assessment.

A multifactorial model of mental fitness

Peterson and Seligman (2004) emphasized the need for more conceptual and empirical tools to craft and evaluate interventions. There is also growing interest in the investigation of a smaller set of higher-order constructs that examine, within a single study, multiple components that are enablers of well-being outcomes (Sheldon & Hoon, 2007; Staats, 1999). Although there are several multidimensional models that measure multiple positive mental health variables together in different contexts (e.g., Luthans, 2012; Ryff, 1985; Ryff & Keyes, 1995) more research is needed given that the majority of past research on positive mental health has predominantly measured the correlates and predictors of well-being in isolation.

Robinson, Oades, and Caputi (2014) have developed a theoretical model to underpin empirical investigation of mental fitness. The aim has been to (1) ascertain whether a smaller set of higher-order dimensions would emerge from the analysis to validate a structure that best represents mental fitness, and (2) to determine whether there is an overarching factor of mental fitness that subsumes the dimensions. Results from this study are now being finalized for publication.

The theoretical construction of mental fitness must be supported by psychological literature encompassing items reflecting important psychological resources that research suggests are developmental. There are many published psychological theories, constructs, and measures related to positive mental health outcomes that could be considered as an important psychological resource for inclusion in a mental fitness model. The Delphi study had several suggestions, as does previous multi-measure research: for example, the variables must be identified in peer review literature and be measurable, and they must be developmental and have associated interventions and intentional activities that can be utilized across multiple contexts. These variables would then be incorporated into a preliminary conceptual framework analogous to that for physical fitness – that is, strength, flexibility, and endurance – to ensure a familiar language that is easy to explain.

Given the holistic nature of mental fitness and the interest in examining multiple variables together in a single study, several examples of proposed higher-order theories and methodologies are provided below. The combining in one study of the items associated to these variables offers the opportunity to simplify and categorize a large number of variables into a more manageable resource index. This would be particularly beneficial to the concept of mental fitness and the guiding principles, and relevant to the workplace and community contexts.

Self-determination theory (SDT) SDT is a theory of motivation that has evolved over the past three decades (Deci & Ryan, 1985, 2000; Sheldon, 2002). SDT is an approach to human motivation driven by the assumption that humans are inherently proactive and have the potential to master their inner forces (drives and emotions) and the external forces (environment). A review of SDT research and application supports the theory that the mental fitness concept given autonomous motivation would be crucial to engagement and sustainability. SDT also supports the premise that individuals are active participants intrinsically interested in their own development via autonomous self-regulation.

Theories of emotion The regulation of emotion has been defined as the ability to respond to the ongoing demands of experience with a range of emotions in a manner that is socially tolerable and sufficiently flexible to permit spontaneous reactions and to delay spontaneous reactions as needed (Cole, Michel, & Teti, 1994). For example, broaden-and-build theory asserts that positive emotions evolved as psychological adaptations that increased our human ancestors' odds of survival and reproduction (Fredrickson, 1998, 2001). Research suggests positive emotions widen the array of thoughts and actions compared to negative emotions. The benefits of broadened mindsets is that they build a variety of personal resources – for example, social connections, coping strategies, environmental knowledge, creativity, and innovation – reserves that can also be drawn on to manage threats or stressors. There is growing scientific evidence in relation to interventions that reliably increase positive emotions and overall happiness and well-being. Longitudinal studies suggest that positive emotions are important in the development of long-term psychological and personal resources, for example resilience (Cohn, Fredrickson, Brown, Mikels, & Conway, 2009; Fredrickson, 2004). Further, Kok et al. (2013) showed that cardiovascular health improved by increasing positive emotions.

Social support theories There are a number of theories that are linked to the importance of social support; for example, coping theory, social exchange theory, and social comparison theory (see Williams, Barclay, & Schmied, 2004). Positive relationships are associated with numerous positive mental and physical health outcomes (e.g., Dutton & Ragins, 2007; Uchino, 2009). A review of cross-national studies found that positive relationships were the one factor that consistently predicted subjective well-being in every country studied (Diener, 2005).

Stress and coping theory suggests that social support fosters adaptive appraisal and coping. Evidence for this is found in studies that observe stress-buffering effects following perceived social support. Relational regulation theory suggests that the link between social support and mental health is driven by individuals regulating their emotions via conversations and shared activities. Given the plethora of research on social support and its developmental opportunities, it is viewed as an essential component of mental fitness.

Resiliency theories Psychological resilience has a large number of theoretical frameworks and definitions. For example, The American Psychological Association (2014) generally defined resilience as an individual's ability to properly adapt to stress and adversity. It is further defined as "good outcomes in spite of serious threats to adaptation or development" (Masten, 2001, p. 238). Resilience is thought to promote protective factors that support positive outcomes. In the past resilience was viewed as a trait, however, more recently it is also considered to be a process defined by two factors: (1) exposure to stressors or risks, and (2) demonstration of competence and successful adaptation (Luthar & Cicchetti, 2000).

Seligman and Matthews (2011) suggest resilience can be enhanced and developed within an individual. Well-being research also suggests positive emotions are more common among high-resilient individuals (Ong, Bergeman, Bisconti, & Wallace, 2006). A comprehensive literature review on resilience suggests resilience needs to be put into action with the focus not on resilience per se, but on the capabilities and assets that are associated to the outcome of resilience (Martin-Breen & Anderies, 2011). There is evidence to support that individuals are able to learn and develop resilience (e.g., Connor & Davidson, 2003; Luthans, Norman, & Hughes, 2006).

Attention and awareness theories One of the most prominent of this array of attention and awareness theories is mindfulness. There has been much research on the benefits of cultivating mindfulness which is defined as "the state of being attentive to and aware of what is taking place in the present" (Brown and Ryan, 2003, p. 822). Research suggests that training in mindfulness techniques enables a number of positive mental and physical health and well-being outcomes (Kabat-Zinn, 1990; Piet & Hougaard, 2011).

Evidence supports physiological and psychological benefits of self-regulating human functioning for those who practice mindfulness by way of intervening with habitual, automatic thoughts and evaluating them in relation to the best response for an individual's primary goals and objectives (Alexander, Langer, Newman, Chandler, & Davies, 1989;

Levesque & Brown, 2007; Rosch, 1997). Thus, the self-awareness and self-regulating nature of mindfulness and its well-documented interventions suggest mindfulness would be an important component of mental fitness.

Theories of acceptance The emergence of acceptance is prominent in the psychological literature (e.g., Hayes, Strosahl, & Wilson, 2011; Linehan, 1993; Segal, Teasdale, & Williams, 2002). Hayes (1994) has defined psychological acceptance as one of the most crucial contextual change strategies. Wong (1998) concurs in his implicit theory of the good life, but argues that the adaptive value of acceptance is not widely recognized in positive psychology. Ryff (1985) features self-acceptance in her psychological well-being scale, as do Keyes and Magyar-Moe (2003) in their model of social well-being. Kashdan and Ciarrochi (2013) provided a rare and integrated review of mindfulness, acceptance, and positive psychology, and consider how these concepts are utilized via a number of effective intervention strategies.

Theories of meaning and purpose in life The prominence of the concepts and development of meaning and purpose in life and positive human functioning have become a core element within traditional and positive psychology (e.g., Crumbaugh & Maholick, 1964; Frankl, 1963) and therefore highly congruent with mental fitness. Damon (2008) suggests that purpose in life forms the answer to the "why" question, McKnight and Kashdan (2009) suggest purpose is a protective factor for well-being. Purpose in life also relates to creating authentic life goals. (See King, Hicks, Krull, & Del Gaiso, 2006; Schulenberg, Hutzell, Nassif, & Rogina, 2008; Wong & Fry, 1998.)

The concept of meaning in life has been positively associated with hope, faith, love, health, happiness, resilience, coping skills and empowerment, and inversely related to depression, anxiety, posttraumatic stress, drug and alcohol use, materialism and experiential avoidance (see Morgan & Farsides, 2009; Schulenberg, Baczwaski, & Buchanan, 2013; Schulenberg, Schnetzer & Buchanan, 2011; Steger, Frazier, Oishi, & Kaler, 2006; Wong 2012). Meaning research suggests meaning is developmental and that stability is important (e.g., Kim, Sun, Park, Kubzansky, & Peterson, 2013; Steger & Kashdan, 2013).

Social learning theory The concept of self-efficacy is central to Albert Bandura's influential and highly researched social learning theory. According to Bandura, self-efficacy is an individual's belief in their ability to succeed in a particular situation; it is an essential part of Bandura's self-system and can be learned and developed. As Bandura and other researchers have demonstrated, self-efficacy can have an impact on psychological states, behavior, and motivation (see Bandura, 1977, 1992, 1994, 1995, 2006). Conner and Norman (2005) found that decisions affecting health are associated with the level of self-efficacy, for example, smoking and physical exercise. Gist and Mitchell (1992) found that individuals with high levels of self-efficacy deal better with difficulties and are more likely to persist in the face of failure, a valuable asset for achieving mental fitness.

In summary, the strength, endurance, and flexibility conceptual dimensions of the mental fitness model are drawn from existing theories, research, and associated measures. As the concept of mental fitness is innovative and exploratory, the formation of a nomological network as identified by Cronbach and Meehl (1955) at this stage of development would be premature. However, the conceptual framework in Table 10.1 shows examples of the previously reviewed concepts as part of a mental fitness resource index and their relevance to a workplace context. The term "resource index" is used, as it suggests that

Table 10.1 Mental fitness domains and workplace relevance.

	Subdomain	*Utility in a work context*
Strength	Meaning	People feel more connected when there is congruence between their role and their work values and the organizational contribution to the greater good.
	Purpose	People understand their life goals and how these relate to their work.
	Social support	People like good relationships with work colleagues and in their teams.
	Strengths	Knowing and using one's strengths at work can help people feel more engaged and assist with recruitment, role clarity, and task delegation.
Flexibility	Mindfulness	Being able to focus attention for longer and choosing work distractions mindfully can be valuable to people in a multi-tasking work environment that requires agility.
	Positive emotions	Positive emotions can assist to improve creativity, innovation, and team performance, important attributes in a 21st-century workplace.
Endurance	Self-efficacy	Individuals and teams who have confidence and belief in themselves and their colleagues can do what is required of them/their team.
	Competence	People at work are more motivated when they feel mastery over what they do.
	Autonomy	People in a work environment that offers and supports as much choice as possible are more motivated.
	Resilience	Resilient people can adjust and adapt better when experiencing challenging work conditions such as change initiatives.

Source: Author.

each domain of mental fitness (e.g., strength) has a set of resources. This example resource index shows how the subcomponents might be categorized and map onto intentional activities/practices under the physical fitness analogy. It provides an exploratory framework for empirical modeling.

The examples in Table 10.1 suggest that individuals who are functioning well psychologically would have the capacity to utilize one or more of the previously reviewed psychological resources. While there is growing interest from researchers and practitioners to simultaneously measure a more comprehensive range of positive mental health determinants, there is a paucity of studies examining multiple variables together within a single study (e.g., Sheldon & Hoon, 2007; Staats, 1999).

Examples of published models and constructs that do measure multiple variables together in a single study are the Psychological Well-being Scale, a generic measure containing six subscales of eudaimonic well-being (e.g., Ryff, 1985); PsyCap, primarily developed for the organizational context, which measures four aspects of positive mental health – self-efficacy, resiliency, optimism, and hope (e.g., Luthans, 2002); and The Global Assessment Tool, currently being used in resilience training for the U.S. Military, which measures four dimensions of positive mental health, emotional, social, spiritual, and family (Peterson, Park, & Castro, 2011). These are examples of multiple component measures that have offered valuable research and insights into positive mental health utilizing several variables within a single study. While there are similarities and differences between these and other models, more research is needed to understand how these multiple variables interrelate and predict positive mental health outcomes. In relation to the criteria of mental fitness, which variables together would (or would not) constitute an overarching construct of mental fitness is yet to be finalized empirically.

The concept and model of mental fitness provides a conceptual framework analogous to physical fitness to engage and promote to individuals, organizations, and the wider community as a proactive and preventative approach to mental health, without the stigma sometimes associated with terms like mental health. In addition, it can promote an understanding that mental fitness, as with physical fitness, requires the motivation to regularly practice intentional activities to create positive psychological habits predicting positive outcomes that can be scientifically investigated, for example, well-being, engagement, hope, social/emotional intelligence, and flow.

Future Research

There are many possibilities and a great need for future research on a mental fitness model. Future research in mental fitness at work is needed across the following domains:

- *Language*: Examining employee and manager perceptions of mental fitness as a "term" to assist promotion of mental health and well-being in the workplace. For example, exploring the proposition that leaders and employees could not only view mental fitness without the constraint and stigma associated to mental health but could perceive it as a way of gaining a type of competitive work–life advantage as is the case with physical fitness.
- *Measurement*: Developing workplace-specific measures of mental fitness, that address common workplace challenges of individuals. Moreover, expanding measurement to performance-based measures, not only self-report measurement. For example, there are objective performance-based measures of physical fitness – what do these look like for mental fitness, applied to contemporary workplaces, that is, "fit to work"?
- *Interventions*: Developing evidence-informed mental fitness interventions at work with specific protocols to enable rigorous experimental and longitudinal empirical investigation. The interventions may target individuals (e.g., does the intervention improve the mental fitness of individuals?) or organizational practices (e.g., does the intervention improve how the practices, policies, and culture of the organization assist the promotion of mental fitness of those associated with the organisation?). Further, examining the ROI of mental fitness interventions would be an ultimate organizational and research aim.

Conclusion

The concept, measurement, and development of mental fitness can assist individuals, schools, organizations, communities, and governments to understand that the road to optimal mental health requires engagement, motivation, commitment, self-awareness, and self-management based on reliable and valid measures and intentional activities performed on a regular basis and tailored to individual needs. Physical fitness regimes at work guide and assist the employees toward optimal levels of physical health and mental fitness regimes could do the same for mental health if designed and delivered utilizing scientific rigor together with evidence-based engaging practices and activities.

References

ACSM (2000). *ACSM's guidelines for exercise testing and prescription* (6th ed.). Baltimore, MD: Lippincott, Williams, Watkins.

Alexander, C. N., Langer, E. J., Newman, R. I., Chandler, H. M., & Davies, J. L. (1989). Transcendental meditation, mindfulness, and longevity: An experimental study with the elderly. *The Journal of Personality and Social Psychology*, *57*, 950–964.

American Psychological Association (APA) (2014). *Road to resilience*. Retrieved from http://www.apa.org/helpcenter/road-resilience.aspx

Australian Human Rights Commission (2010). *Workers with mental illness: A practical guide for managers*. Retrieved from https://www.humanrights.gov.au/sites/default/files/document/publication

Bandura, A. (1977). Self-efficacy: Toward a unifying theory of behavioral change. *Psychological Review*, *84*, 191–215.

Bandura, A. (1992) Exercise of personal agency through the self-efficacy mechanisms. In R. Schwarzer (Ed.), *Self-efficacy: Thought control of action* (pp. 3–38). Washington, DC: Hemisphere.

Bandura, A. (1994). Self-efficacy. In V. S. Ramachaudran (Ed.), *Encyclopedia of human behavior* (Vol. *4*, pp. 71–81). New York, NY: Academic Press.

Bandura, A. (1995). *Self-efficacy in changing societies*. Cambridge, UK: Cambridge University Press.

Bandura, A. (2006). Toward a psychology of human agency. *Perspectives on Psychological Science*, *1*, 2.

Benjamin G. A. H., Darling, E. J., & Sales, B. (1990). The prevalence of depression, alcohol abuse, and cocaine abuse among United States lawyers. *International Journal of Law and Psychiatry*, *13*, 233–246.

Bergman, A., Bosconti, T., & Wallace K. (2006). *Journal of Personality and Social Psychology*, *91*(4), 730-749.

Bloom, D. E., Cafiero, E. T., Jané-Llopis, E., Abrahams-Gessel, S., Bloom, L. R., Fathima, S., … Weinstein, C. (2011). *The global economic burden of noncommunicable diseases*. Geneva, Switzerland: World Economic Forum.

Brown, K. W., & Ryan, R. M. (2003). The benefits of being present: Mindfulness and its role in psychological well-being. *Journal of Personality and Social Psychology*, *84*, 822–848.

Cameron, K. (2013). *Practicing positive leadership: Tools and techniques that create extraordinary results*. San Francisco, CA: Berrett-Kohler.

Cameron, K. S., & Spreitzer, G. M. (2012). *Oxford handbook of positive organizational scholarship*. New York, NY: Oxford University Press.

Cheverton, J., & The Queensland Alliance for Mental Health (2009). *From discrimination to social inclusion A review of the literature on anti stigma initiatives in mental health*. Retrieved from http://qldalliance.org.au/resources/discrimination-social-inclusion/

Cohn, M. A., Fredrickson, B. L. Brown, S. L., Mikels, J. A., & Conway, A. M. (2009). Happiness unpacked: Positive emotions increase life satisfaction by building resilience. *Emotion*, *9*, 361–368.

Cole, P. M., Michel, M. K., & Teti, L. O. (1994). *Emotion regulation and dysregulation: A clinical perspective*. In N. A. Fox (Ed.), *Monographs of the Society for Research in Child Development: Vol. 59 (2–3). The development of emotion regulation: Biological and behavioral considerations* (pp. 73–100). Chicago, IL: University of Chicago Press.

Conner, M., & Norman, P. (Eds.) (2005). *Predicting health behaviour* (2nd ed., rev.). Buckingham, UK: Open University Press.

Connor, K. M., & Davidson, J. R. T. (2003). Development of a new resilience scale: The Connor-Davidson Resilience Scale (CD-RISC). *Depression and Anxiety*, *18*, 76–82.

Cooney, G. M., Dwan, K., Greig, C. A., Lawlor, D. A., Rimer, J., Waugh, F. R., … Mead G. E. (2013). Exercise for depression. *Cochrane Database of Systematic Reviews*, *9*.

Cronbach, L., & Meehl, P. (1955). Construct validity in psychological tests. *Psychological Bulletin*, *52*, 281–302.

Crumbaugh, J. C., & Maholick, L. T. (1964). An experimental study in existentialism: The psychometric approach to Frankl's concept of *noogenic* neurosis. *Journal of Clinical Psychology 20*(2), 200–207.

Damon, W. (2008). *The path to purpose: Helping children find their calling in life.* New York, NY: Free Press.

Darwin, C. (1869). *On the origin of species by means of natural selection* (5th ed.). London, UK: John Murray.

Davis, O. C. (2010, April). *Microflow: An experience worth waiting for.* Retrieved from: http://www.cgu.edu/pages/8582.asp

Deci, E. L., & Ryan R. M. (1985). *Intrinsic motivation and self-determination in human behavior.* New York, NY: Plenum.

Deci, E. L., & Ryan. R. M. (2000). The "what" and "why" of goal pursuits: Human needs and the self-determination of behavior. *Psychological Inquiry, 4,* 227–268.

Diener, E. (2005, November). Guidelines for national indicators of subjective well-being and ill-being. *SINET,* pp. 4–6.

Diener, E., & Biswas-Diener, R. (2008). *The science of optimal happiness.* Boston, MA: Blackwell.

Dutton, J., & Ragins, B. (2007). Moving forward: Positive relationships at work as a research frontier. In J. Dutton & B. Ragins, *Exploring positive relationships at work: Building a theoretical and research foundation* (pp. 387–400). Mahwah, NJ: Erlbaum.

Endurance. (2014). *Merriam-Webster online dictionary.* Retrieved from http://www.merriam-webster.com/dictionary/endurance

European Union (2008). *Pact for mental health.* Retrieved from http://ec.europa.eu/health/ph_determinants/life_style/mental/docs/pact_en.pdf

Fairlie, P., & Svergun, O. (2015, May 6–12). *The interrelated roles of CSR and stress in predicting employee outcomes.* Paper presented at the 11th International Conference on Occupational Stress and Health, Atlanta, GA.

Fitness. (2012). In *Online etymology dictionary.* Retrieved from http://www.etymonline.com/index

Flexibility. (2014). *Merriam-Webster online dictionary.* Retrieved from http://www.merriam-webster.com/dictionary/flexibility

Frankl, V. E. (1963). *Man's search for meaning: An introduction to logotherapy.* New York, NY: Washington Square Press.

Fredrickson, B. L. (1998). What good are positive emotions? *Review of General Psychology, 2,* 300–319.

Fredrickson, B. L. (2001). The role of positive emotions in positive psychology: The broaden-and-build theory of positive emotions. *American Psychologist, 56,* 218–226.

Fredrickson, B. L. (2004). The broaden-and-build theory of positive emotions. *Philosophical Transactions: Biological Sciences, 359,* 1367–1377.

Gist, M. E., & Mitchell, T. R. (1992). Self-efficacy: A theoretical analysis of its determinants and malleability. *Academy of Management Review, 17,* 183–211.

Greenwood, P. M., & Parasuraman, R. (2010). Neuronal and cognitive plasticity: A neurocognitive framework for ameliorating cognitive aging. *Aging Neuroscience 2,* 150.

Haidt, J. (2006). *The happiness hypothesis.* New York, NY: Basic Books.

Harter, J. K., Schmidt, F. L., & Keyes, C. L. M. (2003). *Well-being in the workplace and its relationship to business outcomes: A review of the Gallup Studies.* In C. L. M. Keyes & J. Haidt (Eds.), *Flourishing: The positive person and the good life* (pp. 205–224). Washington, DC: American Psychological Association.

Hayes, S. C. (1994). *Content, context, and the types of psychological acceptance.* In S. C. Hayes, N. S. Jacobson, V. M. Follette, & M. J. Dougher (Eds.), *Acceptance and change: Content and context in psychotherapy* (pp. 13–32). Reno, NV: Context Press.

Hayes, S. C., Strosahl, K. D., & Wilson, K. G. (2011). *Acceptance and commitment therapy: The process and practice of mindful change.* New York, NY: Guilford Press.

Hillier, D., Fewell, F., & Shephard (2005). Wellness at work: Enhancing the quality of our working lives. *International Review of Psychiatry, 17*(5), 419–431

Huppert, F. A. (2009). A new approach to reducing disorder and improving well-being. *Perspectives in Psychological Science, 4,* 108–11.

Judge, T. A., Thoresen, C. J., Bono, J. E., & Patton, G. K. The job satisfaction–job performance relationship: A qualitative and quantitative review. *Psychological Bulletin, 127* (3), 376.

Kabat-Zinn, J. (1990). *Full catastrophe living: Using the wisdom of your body and mind to face stress, pain, and illness.* New York, NY: Delacourt.

Kashdan, T. B., & Ciarrochi, J. (2013). *Mindfulness, acceptance, and positive psychology: The seven foundations of well-being.* Oakland, CA: New Harbinger Publications.

Keyes, C. L. M. (2007). Promoting and protecting mental health as flourishing: A complementary strategy for improving national mental health. *American Psychologist, 62*, 95–108.

Keyes, C. L. M., & Magyar-Moe, J. L. (2003). *The measurement and utility of adult subjective well-being.* S. J. Lopez & C. R. Snyder (Eds.), *Positive psychological assessment: A handbook of models and measures* (pp. 411–425). Washington, DC: American Psychological Association.

Kim, E. S., Sun, J. K., Park, N., Kubzansky, L. D., & Peterson, C. (2013). Purpose in life and reduced risk of myocardial infarction among U.S. adults with coronary heart disease: A two-year follow-up. *Journal of Behavioral Medicine, 36*(2), 124–133.

King, L. A., Hicks, J. A., Krull, J. L., & Del Gaiso, A. K. (2006). Positive affect and the experience of meaning in life. *Journal of Personality and Social Psychology, 90*, 179–196.

Kok, B. E., Coffey, K. A., Cohn, M. A., Catalino, L. I., Vacharkulksemsuk, T., Algoe, S. B., … Fredrickson, B. L. (2013). How positive emotions build physical health: Perceived positive social connections account for the upward spiral between positive emotions and vagal tone. *Psychological Science, 24*, 1123–1132.

Levesque, C., & Brown, K. W. (2007). Mindfulness as a moderator of the effect of implicit motivational self-concept on day-to-day behavioral motivation. *Motivation and Emotion, 31*, 284–299.

Linehan, M. M. (1993). Dialectical behavior therapy for treatment of borderline personality disorder: Implications for the treatment of substance abuse. *NIDA Research Monograph, 137*, 201–216.

Linley, P. A., Harrington, S., & Garcea, N. (Eds.) (2010). *Oxford handbook of positive psychology and work.* New York, NY: Oxford University Press.

Luthans, F. (2002). Positive organizational behavior: Developing and managing psychological strengths. *Academy of Management Executive, 16*, 57–72.

Luthans, F. (2012). Psychological capital: Implications for HDR, retrospective analysis, and future directions. *Human Resource Development Quarterly, 23*, 1–8. doi: 10.1002/hrdq.21119

Luthans, F., Norman, S., & Hughes, L. (2006). Authentic leadership: A new approach for a new time. In R. J. Burke and C. L. Cooper (Eds.), *Inspiring leaders* (pp. 84–104). New York, NY: Routledge.

Luthar, S. S., & Cicchetti, D. (2000). The construct of resilience: Implications for interventions and social policies. *Development and Psychopathology, 12*, 857–885.

Lykken, D., & Tellegen, A. (1996). Happiness is a stochastic phenomenon. *Psychological Science, 7*, 186–189.

Lyubomirsky, S., Sheldon, K., & Schkade, D. (2005). Pursuing happiness: The architecture of sustainable change. *Review of General Psychology, 9*(2), 111–131.

Martin-Breen, P., & Anderies, J. M. (2011, September). *Resilience: A literature review.* Unpublished paper prepared for the Rockefeller Foundation.

Masten, A. S. (2001). Ordinary magic: Resilience processes in development. *American Psychologist, 56* (3), 227–238.

McCarthy, D. (1964). Mental fitness. *American Psychologist, 19*(3), 201–202.

McKnight, P. E., & Kashdan, T. B. (2009). Purpose in life as a system that creates and sustains health and well-being: An integrative, testable theory. *Review of General Psychology, 13*, 242–251.

Mental Health Commission and the Mentally Healthy Workplace Alliance (November, 2010). *Developing a mentally healthy workplace: A review of the literature.* Retrieved from http://www.mentalhealthcommission.gov.au/our-work/mentally-healthy-workplace-alliance

Morgan, J., & Farsides, T.(2009). Measuring meaning in life. *Journal of Happiness Studies, 10* (2), 197–214.

Naidoo J., & Wills, J. (2000). *Health promotion: Foundations for practice.* Edinburgh, Scotland: Harcourt Publishers.

OECD (2011). *Health at a glance 2011: OECD indicators.* Paris: OECD Publishing. Retrieved from http://dx.doi.org/10.1787/health_glance-2011-en

OECD (2015). *Fit mind, fit job: From evidence to practice in mental health and work.* Paris, France: OECD Publishing.

Ong, A. D., Bergeman, C. S., Bisconti, T. L., & Wallace, K. A. (2006). The contours of resilience and the complexity of emotions in later life. *Journal of Personality and Social Psychology, 91*(4), 730–749.

Ory, M. G., Smith, M. L, Mier, N., & Wernicke, M. M. (2010). The science of sustaining health behavior change: The health maintenance consortium. *American Journal of Health Behavior, 34*(6), 647–659.

Pate, R. (1988). The evolving definition of physical fitness. *Quest, 40*(3), 174–179.

Peterson, C., Park, N., & Castro, C. A. (2011). Assessment for the U.S. Army Comprehensive Soldier Fitness program: The Global Assessment Tool. *American Psychologist, 66*(1), 8–10.

Peterson, C., & Seligman, M. E. P. (2004). *Character strengths and virtues: A handbook and classification.* New York, NY: American Psychological Association/Oxford University Press.

Physical fitness (2004). In *Microsoft encarta reference library* (Version 2.1) [Computer Software]. Redmond, WA: Microsoft Corporation.

Piet, J., & Hougaard, E. (2011). The effect of mindfulness-based cognitive therapy for prevention of relapse in recurrent major depressive disorder: A systematic review and meta-analysis. *Clinical Psychology Review, 31*(6), 1032–1040.

Pietrowsky, R., & Mikutta, J. (2012). Effects of positive psychology interventions in depressive patients: A randomized control study. *Psychology, 3*, 1067–1073.

Price Waterhouse Coopers. (2014, March). *Creating a mentally healthy workplace: Return on investment analysis.* The Mentally Healthy Workplace Alliance, beyondblue, Final report, p. 4.

Resner, R. D. (2006, December). *Addiction and the Legal Profession*, in California MCLE Marathon. (PLILitig. and Admin. Practice, Course Handbook Series No. 9012.)

Richards, K. C., Campania, C., & Muse-Burke, J. L. (2010). Self-care and well-being in mental health professionals: The mediating effects of self-awareness and mindfulness. *Journal of Mental Health Counseling, 32* (3), 247.

Robertson, I. T., & Cooper, C. L. (2010). Full engagement: The integration of employee engagement and psychological well-being. *Leadership & Organization Development Journal, 31*, 4, 324–336

Robinson, P. L., Oades, L. G., & Caputi, P. (2014). *Conceptualising and measuring mental fitness.* PhD dissertation, University of Wollongong, Australia.

Robinson, P. L., Oades, L. G., & Caputi, P. (2015). Conceptualising and measuring mental fitness: A Delphi study. *International Journal of Wellbeing, 5*(1), 53–73.

Rosch, E. (1997). Mindfulness meditation and the private (?) self. In U. Neisser & J. A. Jopling (Eds), *The conceptual self in context: Culture experience self understanding* (pp. 185–202). Cambridge, UK: Cambridge University Press.

Ryff, C. D. (1985). Adult personality development and the motivation for personal growth. In D. Kleiber & M. Maehr (Eds.), *Advances in motivation and achievement: Vol. 4. Motivation and adulthood* (pp. 55–92). Greenwich, CT: JAI Press.

Ryff, C. (1989). Happiness is everything, or is it? Explorations on the meaning of psychological well-being. *Journal of Personality and Social Psychology, 57*, 1069–1081.

Ryff, C., & Keyes, C. (1995). The structure of psychological well-being revisited. *Journal of Personality and Social Psychology, 69*, 719–727.

Schoenfeld, T. J., Rada, P., Pieruzzini, P. R., Hsueh, B., & Gould, E. (2013). Physical exercise prevents stress-induced activation of granule neurons and enhances local inhibitory mechanisms in the dentate gyrus. *The Journal of Neuroscience, 33*(18), 7770–7777.

Schulenberg, S. E., Baczwaski, B. J., & Buchanan, E. M. (2013). Measuring search for meaning: A factor-analytic evaluation of the Seeking of Noetic Goals test (SONG). *Journal of Happiness Studies, 15*, 693–715. doi:10.1007/s10902-013-9446-7

Schulenberg, S. E., Hutzell, R. R., Nassif, C., & Rogina, J. M. (2008). Logotherapy for clinical practice. *Psychotherapy: Theory, Research, Practice, Training, 45*, 447–463.

Schulenberg, S. E., Schnetzer, L. W., & Buchanan, E. M. (2011). The Purpose in Life test – short form: Development and psychometric support. *Journal of Happiness Studies, 12*, 861–876.

Segal, Z., Teasdale, J., & Williams, M. (2002). *Mindfulness-based cognitive therapy for depression*. New York, NY: Guilford Press.

Seligman, M. E. P., (2002). *Positive psychology, positive prevention, positive therapy*. In C. R. Snyder & S. J. Lopez (Eds.), *Handbook of positive psychology* (pp. 3–9). New York, NY: Oxford University Press.

Seligman, M. E. P. (2008), Positive health. *Applied Psychology: An International Review*, *57*, 3–18.

Seligman, M. E. P. (2011). *Flourish: A visionary new understanding of happiness and well-being*. New York, NY: The Free Press.

Seligman, M. E. P., & Csikszentmihalyi, M. (Eds.) (2000). Positive psychology: An introduction. *American Psychologist*, *55*, 5–14.

Seligman, M. E. P., & Matthews, M. D. (2011). Comprehensive soldier fitness [Special issue]. *American Psychologist*, *66*(1).

Shaw, C., & McEachern, J. (Eds.) (2001). *Toward a theory of neuroplasticity*. London, UK: Psychology Press.

Sheldon, K. M. (2002). The self-concordance model of healthy goal-striving: When personal goals correctly represent the person. In E. L. Deci & R. M. Ryan (Eds.), *Handbook of self-determination research* (pp. 65–86). Rochester, NY: University of Rochester Press.

Sheldon, K. M., & Hoon, T. H. (2007). The multiple determination of well-being: Independent effects of positive traits needs goals, selves, social support and cultural context. *Journal of Happiness Studies*, *8*, 565–592

Sheldon, K. M., & King, L. (2001). Why positive psychology is necessary. *American Psychologist*, *56*, 216–217.

Sin, N. L., & Lyubomirksy, S. (2009). Enhancing well-being and alleviating depressive symptoms with positive psychology interventions: A practice-friendly meta-analysis. *Journal of Clinical Psychology*, *65*(5),467–487.

Smith, J. C. (2013). Effects of emotional exposure on state anxiety after acute exercise. *Medicine and Science in Sports and Exercise*, *45*, 372–378. doi:10.1249/MSS.0b013e31826d5ce5

Staats, A. W. (1999). Uniting psychology requires new infrastructure, theory, method, and a research agenda. *Review of General Psychology*, *3*, 3–13.

Steger, M. F., Frazier, P., Oishi, S., & Kaler, M. (2006). The Meaning in Life Questionnaire: Assessing the presence of and search for meaning in life. *Journal of Counseling Psychology*, *53*, 80–93.

Steger, M. F., & Kashdan, T. B. (2013). The unbearable lightness of meaning: Well-being and unstable meaning in life. *The Journal of Positive Psychology*. doi:10.1080/17439760.2013.771208

Strength. (2014). *Merriam-Webster online dictionary*. Retrieved from http://www.merriam-webster.com/dictionary/strength

Sloan Center on Aging and Work at Boston College. (2014). *Quality of employment*. Retrieved from http://www.bc.edu/research/agingandwork/about/qualityEmploy.html

Towers Watson Global Workforce Study. (2012). Retrieved from https://www.towerswatson.com/assets/pdf/2012-Towers-Watson-Global-Workforce-Study.pdf

Uchino, B. (2009). Understanding the links between social support and physical health: A life-span perspective with emphasis on the separability of perceived and received support. *Perspectives on Psychological Science*, *4*, 236–255.

WHO (1948). *Preamble to the Constitution of the World Health Organization as adopted by the International Health Conference, New York, 19–22 June, 1946*. Retrieved from http://www.who.int/about/definition/en/print.html

WHO (2004). *Prevention of mental disorders: Effective interventions and policy options*. A Report of the World Health Organization, Department of Mental Health and Substance Abuse in collaboration with the Prevention Research Centre of the Universities of Nijmegen and Maastricht. Retrieved from http://www.who.int/mental_health/evidence/en/prevention_of_mental

WHO (2012). *World health statistics 2012*. Geneva, Switzerland: WHO. Retrieved from http://www.who.int/gho/publications/world_health_statistics/EN_WHS2012_Full.pdf

Williams, P., Barclay, L., & Schmied, V. (2004). Defining social support in context: A necessary step in improving research, intervention and practice. *Qualitative Health Research*, *14*, 942–960.

Wills, T., & Isasi, C. (2007). Buffering effect. In R. Baumeister & K. Vohs (Eds.), *Encyclopedia of social psychology* (pp. 128–129). Thousand Oaks, CA: Sage. doi: http://dx.doi.org/10.4135/9781412956253.n76

Wong. P. T. P. (1998). Implicit theories of meaningful life and the development of the Personal Meaning Profile (PMP). In P. T. P. Wong & P. S. Fry (Eds.), *The human quest for meaning: A handbook of psychological research and clinical applications* (pp. 111–140). Mahwah, NJ: Erlbaum.

Wong, P. T. P. (2012). From logotherapy to meaning-centered counseling and therapy. In *The human quest for meaning: Theories, research, and applications* (2nd ed., pp. 619–647). New York, NY: Routledge.

Wong, P. T. P., & Fry, P. S. (1998). *The human quest for meaning: A handbook of psychological research and clinical applications.* Mahwah, NJ: Erlbaum.

Youssef, C. M., & Luthans, F. (2007). *Positive organizational behavior in the workplace: The impact of hope, optimism, and resilience.* Management Department Faculty Publications, University of Nebraska-Lincoln, Paper 36. Retrieved from http://digitalcommons.unl.edu/managementfacpub/36

11

Positive Relationships at Work

Sue Roffey

Introduction

Reis and Gable (2003) consider that relationships may be the most important source of life satisfaction and well-being. The quality of our relationships at work matters not only for our ability to flourish personally, but is also likely to enhance our sense of achievement. Proactive interventions to promote high levels of social capital across all levels of an organization can add value to business outcomes and embed the economic success of enterprises.

Our lives at work have changed dramatically, especially since the advent of digital communications. What people do, how they do it, the influence of technology, globalization, and female education have altered both our relationship with work and consequently relationships at work. The first section of this chapter sets the scene by addressing this changing nature of work: What does work now mean in the context of people's lives? There are cultural differences but also many global similarities. The chapter then examines the multiple relationships people have at work – with colleagues, clients, and management – and how the changing relationship with work is influencing a new paradigm for relationships at work. The section concludes with a summary of well-being in the workplace and how positive psychology research is defining practices that enable people to flourish at work.

The second section provides a rationale for the development of positive practices. Why is it valuable for both individuals and for the organization? What motivates people to give of their best, to work collaboratively with others? What is the place of positive relationships in the bigger picture of productivity?

The third section describes the practices of positive relationships. How can we grow social capital in an organization and what is the place of relational values and emotional literacy? What enables people to feel they belong and their contributions are valued? How do people learn to work effectively together and deal constructively with difference and conflict?

The chapter concludes by exploring what further research is needed to help better understand positive relationships at work.

The Wiley Blackwell Handbook of the Psychology of Positivity and Strengths-Based Approaches at Work, First Edition. Edited by Lindsay G. Oades, Michael F. Steger, Antonella Delle Fave, and Jonathan Passmore.

Setting the Scene

People's relationship with work

Following the industrial revolution many individuals in the "developed" world would have been defined by what they did to earn a living. You were perhaps a miner, a policeman, a teacher, or a banker – and that is what you did for most of your working life. You entered a certain profession and for the most part stayed put. Your workmates were a fixed feature and there was a clear delineation between work and home. Before the middle of the 20th century you were only likely to be in paid professional employment if you were a man; women certainly worked, but rarely with the status afforded by a higher education. What many people do every day and the conditions under which they do it has changed almost out of recognition in the last 50 years. There has been a significant decline in both agriculture and manufacturing jobs in many Western countries. Between 1940 and 2002 the percentage of the U.S. working population in manufacturing declined from 48% to 28% (Employment Policy Foundation, 2003) and in Australia between 1983 and 1999 it dropped from 18.1% to 12.8% (Pusey, 2003). This is, however, the opposite of other countries, such as Korea, where it has increased by similar margins and China now has the highest number of employees in manufacturing across the world.

The decrease in manufacturing and agricultural employment in Europe, the USA, and Australasia has been replaced by a need for more professional, technical, and administrative work together with service-related occupations such as tourism, education, and hospitality. Unskilled work is still needed, but these jobs are particularly vulnerable to shifting demand.

In the second half of the 20th century most working people in the developed world belonged to their trade union or professional association, who negotiated with employers on their behalf. Governments in the UK and USA have successfully reduced the power of the unions and there has been a steady decline in union membership (Department for Business Innovation and Skills, 2014). This has implications for both pay and working conditions that impact on a sense of security in the workplace (WHO, 1999). Some countries, however, such as Germany, Belgium, and the Nordic countries, continue to have unions for specific trades affiliated to strong national confederations.

Incomes Data Service in the UK (2014) found that between 2000 and 2014 the median total earnings for FTSE 100 bosses rose by 278%, while the corresponding rise in total earnings for full-time employees was 48%. Gender differentials also remain a concern in many but not all countries. In 2014 the average gender pay gap in the UK was 19.1%, with the gap in the private sector larger than in the public (Office for National Statistics, 2014a). In Australia the differential is 18.8% (Australian Government, 2015) and in the USA 21.7% (National Committee on Pay Equity, 2015). As the well-being research consistently finds that equality matters (Huppert & So, 2011; Wilkinson & Pickett, 2010), these figures are likely to impact on both relationships and well-being at work.

Since the 1980s work has become a more fluid activity (HSE, 2006). Some individuals will be working full-time, but part-time and job shares are increasingly common. Companies increasingly employ people on short-term contracts or as agency workers. Relationships at work might become more functional and role driven as people come and go.

In the past one often stayed in one location, not only working one's way up the same organization but probably staying in the same town and keeping the same network of friends and family. Today people may go where the work is – and this may not only be another town but even another country. Mobility for work across Europe has become a political issue. By contrast, families in the USA are more likely to live and work in the same town, or at least the same state, in which they were born. Mobility there appears to be decreasing rather than increasing (Cohn & Morin, 2008). Relationships at work may take on greater significance when there is no access to socialization with an established local network. Loyalty will be less toward a particular company than in the relationships that people form there (Ragins & Kram, 2007). The social and relational dimensions of work may therefore have more influence than economic considerations in retention of staff.

Career paths can take twists and turns and there are blurred boundaries around the working day for many. The culture of an organization still matters but will depend less on history than on current processes of engagement and management.

According to Landy and Conte (2010), workplaces are far more diverse than ever. In most organizations there will be a range of social and cultural backgrounds. Also, many people do not go "out" to work but carry out tasks in a "virtual" environment, such as telemarketers. Across the board, industries engaged in manufacturing, retail, service provision, financial and artisan services use technology – even landscape designers use computer programs in their creative endeavors – so our primary communication at work may be with a computer: it is where we find information, record data, play with ideas, connect remotely with colleagues and clients, and even manage human resources. All these changes in people's relationships *with* work have implications for relationships *at* work. The next section addresses some of these implications.

Relationships at work

When individuals travel away to work, their primary relationships as an adult are less likely to be with the people they knew in childhood including their original family. For some, work itself is away from home, perhaps for weeks at a time. Those in the military, working on oilfields or in mines, employed as international consultants or as entertainers "on tour" may leave children and spouses behind. This can put family relationships at risk (Green & Canny, 2003) and is particularly hard for maintaining positive contact with children after family breakdown – an issue for the well-being of young people (Dowling & Elliot, 2012). Primary relationships may be at work rather than at home – and even these may be short-term as people move on or out.

On the other hand, the location of work has become much more flexible. In the UK 13.5% of those in work are based at home (Office for National Statistics, 2014b) and many employees work from home at least a few days a week. Initial research on working remotely (telecommuting) is mixed: there are positive outcomes for family relationships and a sense of autonomy but collegial relationships may not fare well when there is little chance for face-to-face interaction (Gajendran & Harrison, 2007).

An individual in an organization will have relationships with line managers, colleagues, team members, mentors, clients/customers, trainees/apprentices, and other employees such as cleaners and caterers. Although each of these roles will differ, some of the basic premises for a positive relationship are common across all of them. Knowing how to establish a positive relationship, use emotional literacy in everyday communications, and address difficulties with a thoughtful "win–win" approach can make all the difference to the working environment, even where communications are primarily conducted via technology. Although a strong industry-specific knowledge base is still relevant in the workplace, personality and interpersonal skills are having more attention than ever. How people relate to each other matters, not only for personal well-being but also for meeting company goals.

Relational quality in an organization is ecological – it does not depend solely on the micro level, which focuses on interactions between individuals, but also on management, organizational culture, and expectations across the workplace. Leadership style, communication practices, strengths-based approaches, and human services policies all contribute. This ranges from how diversity is valued, what happens when a female employee returns after maternity leave, how meetings are run, the norms for interaction and teamwork, consultation procedures, induction practices, and how someone is acknowledged for long service. All these things – and more – matter to whether or not the working environment is healthy or toxic.

The nature of interactions can either promote trust, respect, and collegiality, enabling mutually agreed goals to be met, or do the opposite. Dutton and Heaphy (2003) discuss "relational micro-moments" and how the experience of a high-quality connection can leave people feeling more energized. Individuals seek out interactions that make them feel energized and avoid those that deplete them. This can mean that someone will approach a less knowledgeable colleague because that person feels more accessible (Casciaro & Lobo, 2008). Relational energy (Owens, Baker, Sumpter, & Cameron, 2015) is a construct that captures how interactions impact on motivation and are positively associated with job performance.

Leadership

It is the executive group in an organization that usually determines the goals and sets the tone for the quality of the working environment. It is the values of leaders, either overt or covert, that predominate in the development of organizational culture. The literature sometimes distinguishes those who are leaders from those who are managers (e.g., Channer & Hope, 2001). It has been said that managers are concerned with doing things right, while leaders are concerned about doing the right thing: managers control, while leaders facilitate, managers work in the organization, whereas leaders work on the organization (Ellyard, 2001). Managers focus on rules, leaders on relationships.

> A leader sets the vision but doesn't stop there. A leader listens, understands, motivates, reinforces and makes the tough decisions. A leader passes out praise when things go well and takes responsibility and picks up the pieces when things fall apart. Leadership is about relationships. (Hoerr, 2006)

Armstrong (2012) argues for a new paradigm for future leadership – one that does not see a leader as a superhero or hero-innovator or someone who has more knowledge than anyone else. She asserts that effective leadership is based less on technical expertise and hierarchical power, and more on relational understanding and facilitative skills. These are sometimes denigrated as "soft skills" but comprise complex social and emotional intelligences that enable leaders to engage, motivate, and stimulate people – both individually and in teams. This approach recognizes that no one is a "born" leader but that leadership is a social endeavor, a leader does not exist without a follower, and that the ability to connect well with others is paramount.

Wolff, Pescosolido, and Druskat (2002) claim that leadership often emerges when someone is able to influence and manage emotions within a group, providing direction in times of ambiguity. This involves both empathy and modeling of emotional responses that increase solidarity and help others make meaning of a situation.

When Scott (2003) asked school principals about the most challenging aspects of their job, they were primarily concerned with relationships. They ranked the qualities of effective school leaders as:

1 *Emotional intelligence*. This included staying calm, keeping things in perspective and maintaining a sense of humor. Resilience and bouncing back from adversity, learning from errors, and being able to take a hard decision also came under this category – along with wanting to achieve the best outcome possible.

2 *Social intelligence.* This included dealing effectively with conflict situations, being able to empathize and work productively with people from a wide range of backgrounds, respecting and honoring people's values, a willingness to listen to different points of view before making decisions, and contributing positively to team projects.
3 *Intellectual abilities.* These included identifying priorities and being flexible. Generic and specific skills covered having a clear justified vision for the school and being able to organize and manage time effectively.

Like Dutton and Spreitzer (2014), Armstrong highlights the minutiae of interactions – the everyday conversations that make a difference. Whether those connections are public or private, formal or informal, the feelings engendered by them are critical. Dutton (2014) refers to high-quality connections (HQCs) as those that: (a) show willingness to listen attentively to what others have to say; (b) are constructively responsive; (c) make requests rather than demands; (d) are task enabling; (e) show trust by relying on others to meet their commitments; and (f) encourage playfulness!

Cameron (2014) says that the key tasks of effective leaders are to model and foster HQCs among all their employees. They can do this by providing professional development in relational skills, acknowledging and rewarding those who demonstrate HQC, and embedding good practice in meetings, induction programs and conversations around values such as kindness, compassion, acceptance, honesty and forgiveness.

Even when difficult decisions have to be made, such as downsizing leading to job loss, a high level of trust in the executive can limit the adverse reactions of this from employees (Brockner, Seigel, Daley, Tyler, & Martin, 1997). The effects of what we do depend on how we do it. Brockner's research suggests that if downsizing is done with fairness, justice, and compassion it can lead to significantly more positive outcomes for both those who leave and those who stay.

Well-being at work

The New Economics Foundation in the UK (2014) summarized the literature on well-being at work, and concluded that people's personal lives and working lives are inextricably intertwined and that there is a need for a more well-rounded approach to fostering well-being at work. Their specific findings and recommendations include:

- People who achieve good standards of well-being at work are likely to be more creative, more loyal, more productive, and provide better customer satisfaction than those who have lower standards of well-being.
- The different features of working lives have varying degrees of influence over different aspects of well-being – a sense of purpose, positive emotions, motivation, morale, job satisfaction, and life satisfaction.
- There is a strong association between good health and well-being – employers could encourage physical activity and healthy eating and ensure that work does not get in the way of good sleep.
- Getting the right work–life balance reduces stress and its negative outcomes.
- Organizational well-being is promoted by fair pay structures and job security.
- Employee morale is heightened when employees feel tasks are achievable.
- By taking steps to improve relationships at work – with a particular focus on relationships between staff and managers and by encouraging positive feelings – it appears to be possible to improve not only job satisfaction but also life satisfaction.

Why Promote Positive Relationships?

A meta-analysis of research appears to indicate that when people experience high levels of job satisfaction there is lower absenteeism, higher retention rate, and better performance (Judge, Thorensen, Bono, & Patton, 2001).

The following are specific but inter-related reasons for the promotion of positive relationships in the workplace. Some are primarily concerned with the individual and others with the quality of interactions among individuals. All contribute to promoting the effectiveness of the organization. They include:

- enhancing subjective well-being – the ability of the individual to flourish and thrive
- the reduction of stress and promotion of mental health
- the promotion of good physical health and consequent reduction of absenteeism
- retention of staff
- the promotion of effective collaboration and teamwork
- reducing conflict and resolution of difference
- motivation
- the development of conditions that maximize creative innovation
- optimal client and customer interactions

Flourishing at work is a complex construct including engagement, motivation, growth, and learning. Dutton, Roberts, and Bednar (2011) talk about how work-related identities are formed in the workplace, and that when they become more positive there is enhanced psychological and social functioning and more positive feelings. Work engagement promotes greater adaptive behavior and innovation that consequently affects productivity, profits, and customer satisfaction.

There have been a number of studies (e.g., Twenge, 2000) illustrating that the focus on economic prosperity and growth has not been matched by an increase in people's well-being. The World Health Organization (WHO) estimates that over 400 million people worldwide experience mental health difficulties (WHO, 2001) although only a small proportion have complex and debilitating conditions.

Czabala, Charzynska, and Mroziak (2011) reviewed studies published between 1988 and 2009 that addressed mental health promotion in the workplace. The authors identified 4,865 studies and selected 315 for abstract screening and 79 for final detailed review. They found that interventions were still predominantly focused on stress reduction rather than mental health promotion and also that strategies were overwhelmingly individual, including education programs, relaxation techniques, coping skills, and mindfulness. Others were concerned with organizational structure such as guaranteed breaks, but few addressed social dynamics.

Positive relationships not only improve psychological well-being, they also impact on physical health. Positive emotions and a consequent reduction in stress affect our hormonal, cardiovascular, and immune systems (Lewis, 2011). One principal who actively promotes healthy relationships throughout his school has enough in his budget to pay for a high level of professional development for staff – he says that this is because of a routine under-spend on sickness cover (Roffey, 2007). Teacher attrition is a concern in many parts of Europe, Australia, Canada, and the USA. Buchanan et al. (2013) explored the experiences of 329 early career teachers and identified six factors that made a difference. These included collegiality and support and how this impacted on their own self-worth and levels of isolation.

Fay, Shipton, West, and Patterson (2014) analyzed data from 45 UK organizations in the manufacturing sector and discovered that the more widespread the use of teamwork, the more innovation there was in the organization. However, putting people together does not necessarily form an effective team. Stewart's (2006) meta-analysis of the relationship between team design features and performance found that factors that correlated with higher performance were autonomy, intra-team coordination, and transformational leadership.

According to Richardson and West (2010), an effective team needs to have a task that inspires and engages team members, be able to both value and use diverse strengths of individuals, and ensure clarity of expectation and that roles evolve as the task progresses. Positive team relationships and a sense of belonging are encouraged by frequent interaction, quick successes, appreciation of each person's efforts, and shared rewards.

Quick, Gavin, Cooper, and Quick (2004) summarize the pros and cons of a competitive versus a collaborative working environment, believing that each has a place in the achievement of excellence. They come to the conclusion that a win–lose paradigm can lead to a lose–lose one and that a balance between both paradigms can be found in competition between teams. Intergroup competition has better outcomes for both.

Poor-quality connections can leave people feeling "diminished, frustrated, demotivated, demoralised, disrespected or worse – this can lead to being revengeful, despairing or annihilated" (Lewis, 2011, p. 180). Not only do poor relationships cost individuals in terms of their psychological well-being, they also cost organizations in lack of collaboration, reduced innovation, wasted time, and absenteeism. Conflict is normal – differences between people are inevitable in any relationship; it is how this difference is managed that matters. Both intra- and interpersonal skills are needed to reduce the frequency, intensity, and destructiveness of conflict (Edmund, 2012). Effective approaches include acknowledging interdependence, exploring intention, and analyzing communication – especially how misunderstandings might have developed. The promotion of positive feelings and behaviors can also mitigate the more unpleasant and undesirable aspects of conflict.

Restorative approaches to address conflict in schools and courts are familiar to many, but there is now interest in how such approaches might be integrated into the workplace. This is a way of addressing behaviors that are seen as undermining community connectedness, and acknowledges the ripple effect of the impact on those who might not be directly involved. In seeking to repair harm and resolve conflict, relationships and feelings are paramount. Lambert, Johnstone, Green, and Shipley (2011) carried out action research in an organization in Hull, UK, and found that although there were challenges, and the process of implementation and training were critical, there were some promising developments over time. These included an understanding by staff of how to address problematic issues themselves, usually before they were referred to management; and increased engagement in team meetings and decision-making. The restorative approach resolved some poor communication practices between departments and integrated restorative approaches and language throughout organizational culture. This saved time, greatly reduced grievance procedures, and freed managers for more constructive tasks.

Pink (2009) challenged the idea that people were mostly motivated by extrinsic rewards and that the more you paid someone the more productive they would be. He summarizes motivation at work as a combination of purpose, meaning, and mastery. Once you pay people enough – and fairly – they give of their best for intrinsic reasons. Dik, Byrne, and Steger (2013) distinguish between meaning in work (how meaningful is your work?) and meaning of work (what makes it so?). For many, the source of meaning is those with whom you work, whether these are your co-workers, clients, or the community you serve (Wrzesniewski, Dutton, & Debebe, 2003). Khan and Fellows (2013) outline four dimensions that describe people who are fully engaged in what they are doing: they are fully present and attending closely to what is happening; they are connected either with others working toward the same ends or to the bigger picture or purpose; they are integrated so that they bring their thoughts, intuitions, energies, and feelings to the work; and they are absorbed – fascinated and focused – the opposite of being distant or standing apart. This brings to mind Csikszentmihalyi's construct of "flow" (1990). Relationships at work can enable or inhibit the conditions that promote such engagement.

In a competitive global environment, creativity and innovation are a foundation of competitive advantage. Saccheti and Tortia (2013) explored the organizational features that favor the accomplishment of creativity and creativity-related satisfaction with work. They define creativity as the ability to see and enact in new ways. Self-determination theory (Ryan & Deci, 2000) suggests that such fulfillment relies on specific contextual conditions that allow individuals to pursue ends harmoniously with their own needs and aspirations. Saccheti and Tortia, however, found that satisfaction with creativity is supported by teamwork, autonomy, domain-relevant competences, and inclusive, fair processes and relationships. Janssen, Van De Vliert, and West (2004) reviewed the factors that contributed to innovative teamwork. These include knowledge sharing and job rotation, a climate of trust and reciprocal respect, support and backing from management, and participation in decision-making.

Seybold, Marshak, and Lewis (2001) suggest that customers now have greater control in how they choose and use services. They have access to many sources of information giving them both options and a level of expertise. The relationship with clients and their experience therefore matters even more than it used to (Gillies, 2012). Brand loyalty in the market depends on customer satisfaction and this includes both price and service. Hanif, Hafeez, and Riaz (2010) concluded in their study of mobile phone providers that "if customers are provided with courteous behavior of sales person or complaint officer then they feel emotional attachment with their brand of cellular company. Similarly, if their complaints are solved promptly and commitments are fulfilled then it would provide a sense of belongingness to the brand" (p. 50).

Those companies who encourage staff to respond to queries promptly, take clients, views seriously, and are clear and courteous at all times are likely to have a competitive advantage. In an ecological model it is easier to relate well to customers if that is modeled within the organization and everyone feels valued by managers and colleagues.

Positive Relational Values and Practices

What makes people want to get up, go to work, and give of their best? What feelings do they have about themselves, their colleagues, and what they are doing? What do we know helps to promote the positive in the workplace?

As Dutton and Ragins (2007) acknowledge, there is no overarching consensus on the definition of a positive relationship at work. It is a complex and multifaceted construct with differing emphases depending on specific perspectives and positions.

The relational beliefs and behavior of everyone in an organization, however, matter in the creation of a relational culture, and each affects the other in a bi-directional ecological model (Bronfenbrenner, 1979; Roffey, 2008). The way teachers are treated in a school by the executive, for instance, has impact on how they relate to students (Roffey, 2012).

There are, however, commonalities for positive relationships that apply across various contexts and together lead to an increase in social capital. A toxic environment develops where people are silenced, intimidated, unvalued, and demotivated. Social capital is the opposite of this, but requires awareness and active intervention to promote in the workplace.

Lewis (2011) defines social capital as the quality of relationships and interactions within organizations, and that the key to building good reserves of social capital is an affirmative bias within organizational life. Social capital facilitates respectful communication and cooperation and enhances employee commitment. According to Lewis, a high level of social capital has benefits for individuals in that it can inoculate against a range of dysfunctional behaviors and promote the factors that enhance both psychological resilience (Werner & Smith, 2001), and optimal physical well-being (Baker & Dutton, 2007; Heaphy & Dutton, 2008). At an organizational level, social capital helps organizations be connected, optimistic, proactive, and effective.

Positive relationships are imbued with positive feelings about the self and others. Positive feelings lead to behaviors that grow social capital. So how can we enhance the relationships that promote both the behaviors and feelings that enable people to give of their best in the workplace and have an optimal working experience? The list below summarizes key findings from the literature on positive relationships at work.

- When people feel respected they are more likely to listen to what others have to say.
- When people feel included they are more likely to actively participate.
- When people feel valued and their efforts acknowledged they are more likely to seek opportunities to contribute and are more able to value others.
- When people feel cared for they are more likely to have consideration and compassion for others.
- When people feel a sense of belonging they are more likely to be committed to the group that includes them.
- When people laugh together they are less stressed and more resilient.
- When people feel accepted they are likely to be motivated to develop their strengths for the benefit of the organization.
- When negative feeling and concerns are acknowledged and heard they are more likely to be addressed so there is less need to maintain and increase the negativity.

The ASPIRE principles for positive relationship building

The ASPIRE principles have provided a framework for the development of positive relationships and group interaction in educational contexts (Dobia et al., 2014; Roffey, 2013), but are applicable across a range of organizational settings. ASPIRE is an acronym for Agency, Safety, Positivity, Inclusion, Respect, and Equality. This section explores how these relational values are validated in the research, incorporate relevant constructs such as self-determination, trust, compassion and fairness, and how these might be translated into relational practices in the working environment. There is overlap between these principles and they foster each other in a virtuous cycle.

Agency This principle in a relationship refers to the amount of control someone has over actions and decision-making. Empowerment of employees in a work context gives them encouragement to take initiative, take pride in their work, and experience ownership (Wagner et al., 2010). It would appear to be beneficial to both the individual and the organization (Seibert, Wang, & Courtright, 2011).

Agency incorporates one of the determinants of well-being – self-determination. Those who see themselves as choosing to engage in a task rather than being controlled by demands or being externally regulated are more likely to see meaning in what they do. Those who are given some choice in the way a task is undertaken, and find that task both challenging within their sphere of competence and in line with their goals, will experience a degree of autonomous motivation. This contrasts with pressure that comes from external non-negotiable demands and extrinsic rewards. These are insufficient to enhance motivation and work performance (Gagne & Deci, 2005). Deci, Connell, and Ryan (1989) found that managers supported autonomy when they acknowledged subordinates' perspectives, provided relevant information in a non-controlling way, offered choice, and encouraged self-initiation. This was associated with employees being more satisfied with their jobs, having a higher level of trust in corporate management, and displaying other positive work-related attitudes. An example of agency/autonomy in practice is Google, who give their employees one day a week to work on whatever they choose. The outcomes have been a range of new ideas and solutions (Pink, 2009).

Safety A hallmark of a healthy relationship is where people feel physically and emotionally safe. This does not happen in workplaces imbued with a culture of bullying and intimidation. Workplace bullying occurs where an employee is subjected to systematic and negative behaviors that cause humiliation and distress (Trepanier, Fernet, & Austin, 2015). This can include persistent criticism, belittling competencies, unreasonable deadlines, exclusion, excessive teasing, and shouting and threatening behaviors. The outcomes of workplace bullying include absenteeism, poor retention of staff, psychological stress, and physical ill health. It is associated with poor employee functioning, expressed through disengagement, job dissatisfaction, and symptoms of anxiety, depression, and burnout. As organizations can condone, and even reward, bullying behaviors there is a need to rethink organizational culture to promote collaboration over rivalry, enhance social support, and foster a safe environment (Yamada, 2010). Workplace safety is exemplified where there are high levels of trust in which people are able to acknowledge vulnerability and ask for guidance.

Trust is a critical facet of a strong relationship. This multidimensional construct is being given increasing attention in the literature on well-being at work (e.g., Helliwell & Huang, 2011). Mayer, Davis, and Schoorman (1995) suggest that components include trust in someone's ability and competence to carry out a task, trust in their benevolence and goodwill, and in their integrity – a belief that they will act within a set of ethical principles. According to Frost and Moussavi (1992), having power without being trusted diminishes a person's influence within the workplace. Church and Waclawski (1999) go on to say that, in today's less authoritarian environment, individuals must work within relationships that require trust and the ability to influence others in both lateral and hierarchical relationships.

Helliwell and Huang (2011) report on studies that found that trust in management has a value in terms of life satisfaction of more than a 30% increase in monetary income. There is a significant gender difference across the USA, Canada, and the UK with women rating social relationships at work more highly than men. When someone is trusted, their actions are seen as predictable and dependable. There is a tension in many workplaces between levels of trust and the need for accountability (Ammeter, Douglas, Ferris, & Goka, 2004) and a suggestion that formal mechanisms for accountability that ignore the social and value dimensions of work have undermined trust, initiative, and well-being in the workplace (Berryhill, Linney, & Fromewick, 2009). As Lee and Teo (2005) found in their study in Singapore, trust is under threat when significant changes are required of employees. This can be mitigated by involving personnel in restructuring.

Positivity Relationships and emotions exist within the workplace all day and every day, impacting on both human and social capital. It makes sense to actively promote the positive, both for the individual and the effectiveness of the organization. Relationships are enhanced by both the experience and expression of positive emotions (Barsade & Gibson, 2007), whereas negativity undermines the ability to "think straight." Fredrickson (2001) found that positive emotions promote problem-solving and creative thinking. This can help organizations come up with fresh ideas that give them the edge over competitors (Caruso & Salovey, 2004). Positive emotions also facilitate collaboration, reduce conflict, raise resilience, promote socially responsible and helpful behavior, increase the ability to learn and integrate complex information, enhance more thorough decision-making, and enable change (Isen, 2005). But positive emotion is a broad term: what do we mean by this? Some aspects are addressed in other sections of this chapter so our focus here is on the specific emotions generated by presence, playfulness, kindness, gratitude, and celebration.

The Fish philosophy, initiated originally in the Pike Place Fish Market in Seattle, is a framework for developing more positive relationships at work – both within the organization and in providing customer service. The four pillars below summarize much of the literature on positive organizational practice, especially that developed by Dutton (2014) on high-quality connections.

- *Be there.* Being present in the moment in order to get the most out of it. This means focusing and paying attention; being fully engaged with the person that you are with rather than responding to interruptions or paying attention to other things.
- *Make their day.* Turning an everyday interaction, whether this is with a colleague or a client, into a more pleasant experience – a smile, a small kindness, courtesy, or acknowledgment. Kindness is not a passive state but an active practice. According to Lyubomirsky (2007), kindness not only changes self-perception leading to more confidence and self worth, it can also jumpstart a range of positive social consequences.
- *Play.* Injecting a sense of fun into the working day can put problems into a different perspective and enhance both creativity and resilience. The act of laughing together releases oxytocin into the body. Oxytocin is the "feel-good" neurotransmitter that is often implicated in social attitudes and behaviors such as couple bonding, relaxation, trust, and cooperativeness (Olff et al., 2013). Not all tasks in the workplace are inherently engaging, sometimes it is helpful to approach something creatively so that it becomes challenging or fun. Organizations can promote opportunities for play in the workplace, from team-building activities to social events and celebrations. This needs careful introduction as individuals with a negative social bias may find playfulness threatening rather than rewarding.
- *You can choose your attitude.* If you look for the positive you will identify factors that energize and engage you. Both are self-fulfilling prophecies in that the person is not passive in fulfilling expectations but acts to make it happen. Part of this strategy is to not only mindfully identify individual strengths and engage these in the workplace, but also acknowledge and utilize the diverse strengths of others. In appreciative inquiry and solution-focused thinking, it is the difference between thinking "this always happens" and looking at what happens in those times when it doesn't, and beginning to build small steps to a solution by looking at what already works.

Positivity and gratitude: Grateful people feel better about themselves and the world they are in; they feel more support from others and give more support. Studies on the efficacy of gratitude-related exercises have shown that noticing what you can be thankful for promotes a sense of optimism and reduces depression (Seligman, Parks, & Steen, 2005). Rather than gratitude simply being a way of thinking, Howells (2012) suggests that it is relational: her work, based within educational settings, turns gratitude into action to impact on organizational culture. Buote (2014) cites an American study that found 29% of respondents never thank a co-worker and 35% of respondents never thank their boss. Gratitude begins by noticing – one of the five ways to well-being suggested by the New Economics Foundation (2014). Noticing a clean office, contributions by colleagues, a supportive gesture by a manager needs to be followed by an expression of gratitude. "A simple 'thank you for …' can have a spiral of positive consequences for promoting pro-social behavior and a sense of connection" (Grant & Gino, 2010).

Celebration is one step on from gratitude. Couple research indicates that active constructive responses when one person has been successful strengthens relationships (Gable, Reis, Impett, & Asher, 2004). This contrasts with disinterest, envy, or pointing out the negatives. Acknowledgment and celebration of team success bonds people together, shares the good feelings in accomplishment, and reinforces expectations for the future. We are not as good at celebration in the workplace as we might be – the term is absent from much of the literature.

The neurology of emotion: Mirror neurons in our brains make us hard wired to respond and replicate the emotions of others. This has major implications for the emotional climate of the workplace (Mukamel, Ekstrom, Kaplan, Iacoboni, & Freid, 2010). As all emotions are contagious, an emotionally literate leader will know that their emotional presence will have an impact on the team and will do what they can to promote the positive. Our experiencing of emotion and the embodiment of this is bi-directional. This means that not only do we smile when we feel good – the very act of smiling increases our sense of well-being (Wenner, 2009). The opposite is also true – frowning increases our negative mood and can affect the demeanor of others. Anyone who injects gentle humor into the workplace, greets others as valued colleagues, or celebrates another's success is not only doing a service to individuals, they are promoting a more successful organization.

Inclusion A sense of connectedness is increasingly recognized as a basic psychological need (Baumeister & Leary, 1995) and a protective factor in resilience and well-being (Werner & Smith, 2001).

Putnam (2000) extends the concept of social capital into bonding capital, that relates to in-group connections, and bridging capital, that relates to intergroup connections. He illustrates this with a vivid metaphor: bonding social capital constitutes a kind of sociological superglue, whereas bridging social capital provides a "sociological WD-40" (Putnam, 2000, p. 23).

Healthy relationships require both but the former can lead to "exclusive" belonging where those who are not part of the "in-group" can be demonized and scapegoated (Roffey, 2013).

In order to feel we belong, others must act in a certain way (Baumeister & Leary, 1995). We are unlikely to experience a deep sense of belonging if others are simply pleasant but do not put themselves out in any way. They need to be positively welcoming and not distant or indifferent to our presence. When they attend to what we say and treat us an ally then we will feel we are significant to the organization and it matters that we are there. We also need to be able to rely on others to be supportive and committed to our welfare. Catalano, Haggerty, Oesterle, Fleming, and Hawkins (2004) say something similar about connectness in the school environment: a safe, supportive environment is essential for belonging, but organizations also need to be places where strengths are identified and each individual sees themselves as progressing, achieving, and contributing.

There are particular challenges for promoting a sense of belonging in an organization when employees work remotely or on restricted hours.

Respect "We have discovered that in order to get respect you have to give respect" (Feedback from the Aboriginal Girls Circle, Dobia et al., 2014). The first pathway to building high-quality connections at work (Dutton & Spreitzer, 2014) is to "respectfully engage with others." Respect is no longer a "given" that comes with authority: it is demonstrated by giving messages that the people with whom you are engaging are important. Both verbal and non-verbal messages can be subtle but powerful: they can make people feel acknowledged, heard, and valued or the opposite. Being fully attentive to another is hard for busy people – especially leaders – as it is assumed that this will take up valuable time that could be better spent. Relationships can be built, however not by doing more but by small changes in how interactions take place and with a greater sense of awareness of the longer-term benefits. Simply greeting someone by name and with a smile can promote feelings of value (Roffey, 2005). Acknowledging a mistake, poor judgment, or lateness and offering an apology prioritizes the relationship rather than the ego. The seating arrangements in a meeting can give messages of power and position in the same way that the depth of a bow in Japan lets everyone know who is most important. Egan (2002) defines a respectful interaction as one in which one person does not overwhelm the other with her or his own agenda and does not rush to judgment. Active listening means turning off your phone, tuning into what is being said, asking for clarification, and building on ideas. Respect means showing interest in the other person and what they can offer. Beginning both conversations and emails with a positive comment or query personalizes the interaction, shows value to the individual, and makes it easier to focus on what comes next.

Appreciative inquiry (Cooperrider, Sorenson, Yaegar, & Whitney, 2001) is a way of putting respect into practice and is congruent with positive psychology approaches by building on strengths, focusing on an imagined ideal future and making meaning within a collaborative framework. It is particularly valuable when work environments are undergoing changes (Lewis, 2011). As the name suggests, it is more about asking, finding out and collaboratively crafting ways forward, than making statements and demands.

Chinese working practices are imbued with the principle of Guanxi - which acknowledges the centrality of relationships. Business transactions can only proceed once a level of trust and familiarity has been established. Multinational companies need to understand how this operates in order to conduct successful discussions that the Chinese regard as respectful (Gold, Guthrie, & Wank, 2004).

Equality "The leaders who work most effectively, it seems to me, never say 'I' … they don't think 'I'. They think 'we'; they think 'team'. They accept responsibility and don't sidestep it, but 'we' gets the credit" (Peter Drucker, cited in Collins & Thompson, 2008).

McCashen (2005) talks about the essence of the strengths-based approach as being "power with," rather than "power over". It is about having a high regard for uniqueness and diversity and also respect for the commonalities between people. An inclusive and democratic work culture needs opportunities to discover commonalities in values and goals.

Such activities can acknowledge shared vulnerability and this can promote empathy. Everyone makes mistakes occasionally and we all face adversity and challenges from time to time. There is often a denial of this in the workplace where people have to be seen to be on top of everything.

Equal access to information enhances trust. McCashen refers to this as transparency. It enables personnel to be open and honest about both possibilities and challenges and not engaging in cliques and secret agendas. Such "empire-building" undermines ownership of organizational development and can foster a toxic environment.

The human need for fairness is hard-wired. The brain's reward center is activated when fairness and cooperation are experienced (Tabibnia & Leiderman, 2007).

Fairness does not, however, mean rigid sameness – it means acknowledgment of different circumstances and flexibility in response to these. This includes recognition and understanding for those who have young families or aging parents who may be on call at any time. Supervisors who model good home–life balance have employees who feel they are able to do the same and are consequently less exhausted and more engaged in the workplace (Koch & Binnewies, 2015).

Effective communication

Communication in an organization covers a number of functions, some of which overlap. These include information giving and seeking, sharing ideas, decision-making, persuading, directing, motivating and supporting, resolving difficulties, and otherwise relationship building.

Communication is, however, not an event so much as an unending social and emotional process of sense-making (Lewis, 2011). It takes place within a context of history, relationships, expectations, and the present setting. And communication is not merely verbal or written – it exists in timing, gestures, and settings. Effective communication processes require a level of emotional literacy that enables the participants to tune into their own reactions to what is being discussed, the emotional context in which interactions are taking place, and to be able to read and take account of the responses of others. The quality of communication at work can create or destroy relationships (Langley, 2012). The language used can either expand or contract conversation and not only does this have an outcome on the generation of ideas but it also promotes or inhibits the ASPIRE principles described above. Expansive communication includes acknowledging the value of what someone has said and asking others their views. It is putting into operation the "no put-down" rule, which does not denigrate or dismiss someone but engages with "personal positives" instead.

Losada and Heaphy (2004) found that high-performing teams had a ratio of five positive interactions to each negative one. They also had an equal balance of inquiry to advocacy statements and the same for self- to other-oriented comments. Poorly performing teams had a ratio of 20 to 1 for advocacy and self-orientation, indicating a lack of collaboration or connectivity. Lewis (2011) makes the observation that high performance does not depend on public criticism when someone underperforms but on generosity, forgiveness, appreciation, encouragement, and positive feedback – especially when times are tough.

People need to disagree, but how this takes place matters. Giving critical feedback is challenging for some supervisors, which is why some may go at this with all guns blazing, but ignoring rather than addressing poor practices just condones and increases them. Negative feedback needs to be on actions, never on personalities and blame must be fairly apportioned – what could you have done differently, what could others have done differently, and what part did chance play. Listen to what the other person says, but getting into arguments or going on the defensive does not help. Importantly, ensure that the person knows what future expectations are and the rationale for these, linked to organizational values and goals.

Future Research

There are many challenges for the future of relationships at work as the nature of working lives continues to change. Among the issues that have arisen in this chapter are the balance of relationships at work with those at home as boundaries become increasingly blurred, the dichotomy between competitive and collaborative cultures in a world were work is increasingly focused on economic advantage, new paradigms for leadership, the nature of high-quality connections and how these are perceived and promoted, and how to understand and work with relational differences across cultures.

The vast majority of studies on positive psychology at work are based in the developed world, within a Western and capitalist ideology. We therefore do not know so much about the working lives of those in the developing world. There also appears to be a preponderance of studies related to professional, white-collar occupations.

Positive psychology at work is a broadening field and needs to be able to keep pace with a rapidly changing world. The values and beliefs within a positive psychology paradigm, however, are not always congruent with those often espoused in a business environment. A positive psychology approach may need to address these bigger issues, such as: How do you continue to maintain a focus on the well-being of those who work across a wide range of roles when economic imperatives undermine this? How can people continue to be treated as valuable human beings when their role becomes redundant?

Many of the constructs within the field such as empowerment, gratitude, and emotional literacy have traction in the evidence for relationships at work although contextual factors matter to their impact and sustainable efficacy (Mills, Fleck, & Koziowski, 2013). You cannot impose a positive psychology intervention without taking account of organizational culture. This is exemplified in many studies within education where a whole school approach for well-being is advocated (Noble, McGrath, Roffey, & Rowling, 2008). Organization culture is ecological and combines the structural with the psychological – what part do relationships have to play in the changes that lead to both individual well-being and flourishing enterprises and what is the interplay between them?

The ASPIRE framework addresses how relational values might impact on behaviors. Although not specific to the workplace this takes account of the multiple interactive factors that support high-quality connections across contexts. As an entity, however, it requires empirical validity.

Although the literature on positive relationships has offered significant insights, there are still questions to be answered on how to identify, deconstruct, and maintain the positive across time and place. Relationships are complex, bi-directional, and fluctuating: how people feel about themselves and others is embedded in an ecological and often chronological framework. Measuring outcomes of specific interventions does not guarantee efficacy across contexts or time. More information about people's lived experiences would be valuable. Much of the data is positivistic and linear, so does not capture the narratives that illuminate the minutiae of difference.

There is much evidence on what works for well-being in relationships, but how does this translate into policy and practice holistically across large institutions and at the macro socio-political level? On the one hand, for instance, we have evidence for positive outcomes for a flatter organizational structure and more equality, but hierarchical cultures and management behaviors persist. How do we address power issues in relationships at work and what is the impact of individual psychologies on organizational systems (Case & Maner, 2014). How can we make the evidence of what enables both individuals and organizations to flourish become a reality for everyday working lives?

Conclusions

In this chapter I have reviewed the role of positive relationships within the changing environment of work. While there are some interestingly cultural differences, a number of key characteristics can enhance the experience of work. These characteristics have been summarized by the ASPIRE framework. The area of positive relations is a relatively new and emerging area within positive psychology and thus further research is required to deepen and broaden our understanding.

References

Ammeter, A. P., Douglas, C., Ferris, G. R., & Goka, H. (2004). A social relationship conceptualisation of trust and accountability in organisations. *Human Resource Management Review*, *14*(1), 47–65.

Armstrong, H. B. (2012). Spirited leadership: Growing leaders for the future. In S. Roffey (Ed.), *Positive relationships: Evidence based practice across the world* (pp. 215–226). Dordrecht, the Netherlands: Springer.

Australian Government (2015). *Workplace Gender Equality*. Retrieved March 30, 2015 from https://www.wgea.gov.au/

Baker, W., & Dutton, J. E. (2007). Enabling positive social capital in organisations. In J. E. Dutton and B. R. Ragins (Eds.), *Exploring positive relationships at work: Building a theoretical and research foundation* (pp. 325–345). Mahwah, NJ: Erlbaum.

Barsade, S. G., & Gibson, D. E. (2007). Why does affect matter in organisations? *Academy of Management Perspectives*, *2* (1), 36–59.

Baumeister, R. F., & Leary, M. R. (1995). The need to belong: Desire for interpersonal attachments as a fundamental human motivation. *Psychological Bulletin*, *117*(3), 497–529.

Berryhill, J., Linney, J. A., & Fromewick, J. (2009). The effects of education accountability on teachers: Are policies too stress provoking for their own good? *International Journal of Education Policy & Leadership*, *4* (5), 1–14.

Brockner, J., Seigel, P. A., Daley, J. P., Tyler, T., & Martin, C. (1997). When trust matters: The moderating effect of outcome favourability. *Administrative Science Quarterly*, *42*, 558–583.

Bronfenbrenner, U. (1979). *The ecology of human development: Experiences by nature and design*. Cambridge, MA: Harvard University Press.

Buchanan, J., Prescott, A., Schuck, S., Aubusson, P., Burke, P., & Louviere, J. (2013). Teacher retention and attrition: Views of early career teachers. *Australian Journal of Teacher Education*, *38*(3). doi:10.14221/ajte.2013v38n3.9

Buote, V. (2014). *Gratitude at Work: its Impact on Job Satisfaction and Sense of Community*. Plasticity Labs. Retrieved from http://www.plasticitylabs.com/wp-content/uploads/2014/04/Gratitude-At-Work-Final.pdf

Case, C. R., & Maner, J. K. (2014). Divide and conquer: When and why leaders undermine the cohesive fabric of their group. *Journal of Personal and Social Psychology*, *107* (6), 1033–1050.

Cameron, K. (2014). Activate virtuousness. In J. E. Dutton and G. M. Spreitzer (Eds.), *How to be a positive leader: Small actions big impact* (pp. 79–89). San Francisco, CA: Berrett-Khoeler.

Caruso, D., & Salovey, P. (2004). *The emotionally intelligent manager*. San Francisco, CA: Jossey-Bass.

Casciaro, T., & Lobo, M. S. (2008). When competence is irrelevant. The role of interpersonal affect in task-related ties. *Administrative Science Quarterly*, *53*, 655–684.

Catalano, R. F., Haggerty, K. P., Oesterle, S., Fleming, C. B., & Hawkins, J. D. (2004). The importance of bonding to school for healthy development: Findings from the social development research group. *Journal of School Health*, *74*(7), 252–261.

Channer, P., & Hope T. (2001). *Emotional impact: Passionate leaders and corporate transformation*. Basingstoke, UK: Palgrave.

Church, A. H., & Waclawski, J. (1999). Influence behaviours and managerial effectiveness in lateral relations. *Human Resource Development Quarterly*, *10*, 3–34.

Cohn, D. V., & Morin, R. (2008). *American mobility: Who moves, who stays put, where's home?* Social & Demographic Trends report. Washington, DC: Pew Research Center.

Collins, D., & Thompson, D. (2008). *Trust unwrapped: A story of ethics, integrity and chocolate.* Ware, UK: Fresh Publishing.

Cooperrider, D., Sorenson. Jnr., P. F., Yaegar, T., & Whitney, D. (Eds.) (2001). *Appreciative inquiry: An emerging direction for organizational development.* Champaign, IL: Stipes.

Csikszentmihalyi, M. (1990). *Flow: The psychology of optimal experience.* New York, NY: Harper & Row.

Czabala, C., Charzynska, K., & Mroziak, B. (2011). Psycho-social intervention in workplace mental health promotion. *Health Promotion International*, *26*(1), 170–184.

Deci, E. L., Connell, J. P., & Ryan, R. M. (1989). Self-determination in a work organisation. *Journal of Applied Psychology*, *74*(4), 580–590.

Department for Business Innovation and Skills. (2014). *Trade Union Membership 2013 Statistical Bulletin.* Retrieved from https://www.gov.uk/government/uploads/system/uploads/attachment_data/file/313768/bis-14-p77-trade-union-membership-statistical-bulletin-2013.pdf

Dik, B. J., Byrne, Z. S., & Steger, M. F. (2013). *Purpose and meaning in the workplace.* Washington, DC: American Psychological Association.

Dobia, B., Bodkin-Andrees, G., Parada, R., O'Rourke, V., Gilbert, S., Daley, A., & Roffey. S. (2014). *Aboriginal girls circle enhancing connectedness and promoting resilience for aboriginal girls. Final pilot report.* University of Western Sydney, Australia.

Dowling, E., & Elliot, D. (2012). *Understanding children's needs when parents separate.* Milton Keynes, UK: Speechmark Books.

Dutton, J. E. (2014). Build high quality connections. In J. E. Dutton & G. M. Spreitzer (Eds.), *How to be a positive leader: Small actions big impact* (pp. 11–21). San Fransisco, CA: Berrett-Khoeler.

Dutton, J. E., & Heaphy, E. (2003). The power of high quality connections. In K. Cameron, J. Dutton, & R. Quinn (Eds.), *Positive organisational scholarship: Foundations of a new discipline* (pp. 263–278). San Francisco, CA: Berrett-Keohler.

Dutton, J. E., & Ragins, B. R. (2007). *Exploring positive relationships at work: Building a theoretical and research foundation.* Mahwah, NJ: Erlbaum.

Dutton, J. E., Roberts, L. M., & Bednar, J. (2011). Pro-social practices, positive identity and flourishing at work. In S. I. Donaldson, M. Csikszentmihalyi, & J. Nakamura (Eds.), *Applied positive psychology. Improving everyday life, health, work, schools and society* (pp. 155–170). New York, NY: Psychology Press.

Dutton, J. E., & Spreitzer, G. M. (Eds.) (2014). *How to be a positive leader: Small actions big impact.* San Francisco, CA: Berrett-Koehler.

Edmund, L. (2012). Conflict and confrontation. In S. Roffey (Ed.), *Positive relationships: Evidence-based practice across the world* (pp. 261–276). Dordrecht, the Netherlands: Springer.

Egan, G. (2002). *The skilled helper: A problem management and opportunity development approach to helping* (7th ed.). Pacific Grove, CA: Brooks Cole.

Ellyard, P. (2001). *Ideas for the new millennium* (2nd ed.). Carlton South, Australia: Melbourne University Press.

Employment Policy Foundation. (2003). *An economic primer to white collar reform.* Washington, DC: Employment Policy Foundation.

Fay, D., Shipton, H., West, M. A., & Patterson, M. (2014). Teamwork and organisational innovation: The moderating effect of the HRM context. *Creativity and Innovation Management*, *24*(2), 261–277. doi:10.1111/caim.12100

Fredrickson, B. L. (2001). The role of positive emotions in positive psychology: The broaden-and-build theory of positive emotions. *American Psychologist*, *56*(3), 218–226.

Frost, T. F., & Moussavi, F. (1992). The relationship between leader power base and influence: The moderating role of trust. *Journal of Applied Business Research*, *8*, 9–14.

Gable, S. L., Reis, H. T., Impett, E. A., & Asher, A. R. (2004). What do you do when things go right? The intrapersonal and interpersonal benefits of sharing positive events. *Journal of Personality and Social Psychology*, *87*(2), 228–245.

Gagne, M., & Deci, E. L. (2005). Self-determination theory and work motivation. *Journal of Organizational Behaviour*, *26*, 331–362.

Gajendran, R. S., & Harrison, D. A. (2007). The good, the bad and the unknown about telecommuting: Meta-analysis of psychological mediators and individual consequences. *Journal of Applied Psychology*, *92*(6), 1524–1541.

Gillies, E. (2012). Positive professional relationships. In S. Roffey (Ed.), *Positive relationships, evidence based practice across the world* (pp. 181–196). Dordrecht, the Netherlands: Springer.

Gold, T., Guthrie, G., and Wank, D. (Eds.) (2004). *Social connections in China: Institutions, culture and the changing nature of Guanxi*. Cambridge, UK: Cambridge University Press.

Grant, A.M., & Gino, F. (2010). A little thanks goes a long way; Explaining why gratitude expressions motivate pro-social behavior. *Journal of Personality and Social Psychology*, *98*(6), 946–955.

Green, A. E., & Canny, A. (2003). *Geographical mobility, family impacts*. Bristol, UK: Policy Press and Joseph Rowntree Foundation.

Hanif, M., Hafeez, S., & Riaz, A. (2010). Factors affecting customer satisfaction. *International Research Journal of Finance and Economics*, *60*, 44–52.

HSE (Health and Safety Executive) Horizon Scanning Intelligence Group. (2006). *Short report flexible working and employment patterns*. Retrieved March 16, 2015 from http://www.hse.gov.uk/horizons/current-issues/workplace/precariousworking.htm

Heaphy, E. D., & Dutton, J. E. (2008). Positive social interactions and the human body at work: Linking organisation and physiology. *Academy of Management Review*, *33*(1), 137–162.

Helliwell, J. F., & Huang, H. (2011). Wellbeing and trust in the workplace. *Journal of Happiness Studies*, *12*, 747–767.

Hoerr. T. (2006). *The art of school leadership*. Alexandria, VA: Association for Supervision and Curriculum Development.

Howells, K. (2012), *Gratitude in education: A radical view*. Rotterdam, the Netherlands: Sense Publishers.

Huppert, F. A., & So, T. T. C. (2011). Flourishing across Europe: Application of a new conceptual framework for defining wellbeing. *Social Indicators Research*, *110*(3), 837–861.

Incomes Data Service. (2014, October). Retrieved March 28, 2015 from http://www.incomesdata.co.uk/wp-content/uploads/2014/10/IDS-FTSE-100-directors-pay-20141.pdf

Isen, A. (2005). A role for neuropsychology in understanding the facilitating influence of positive affect on social behaviour and cognitive affect. In C. R Snyder & S. J. Lopez (Eds.), *Handbook of positive psychology* (pp. 528–540). Oxford, UK: Oxford University Press.

Janssen, O., Van De Vliert, E., & West, M. (2004). The bright and dark sides of individual and group innovation: A special issue introduction. *Journal of Organizational Behavior*, *25*(2), 129–145.

Judge, T. A., Thorensen, C. J., Bono, J. E., & Patton, G. K. (2001). The job-satisfaction–job performance relationship: A qualitative and quantitative review. *Psychological Bulletin*, *127*(3), 376–407.

Kahn, W. A. & Fellows, S. (2013). Employee engagement and meaningful work. In B. J. Dik, Z. S. Byrne, & M. F. Steger (Eds.), *Purpose and meaning in the workplace* (pp. 105–126). Washington, DC: American Psychological Association.

Koch, A. R., & Binniewies, C. (2015). Setting a good example: Supervisors as good work-life-friendly role models within the context of boundary management. *Journal of Occupational Health Psychology*, *20*(1), 82–92.

Lambert, C., Johnstone, G., Green, S., & Shipley, R. (2011). *Building restorative relationships for the workplace*. University of Hull, UK. Retrieved April 2, 2015 from http://bit.ly/1FahbAu

Landy, F. J., & Conte, J. M. (2010). *Work in the 21st century: An introduction to industrial and organisational psychology* (3rd ed.). Hoboken, NJ: Wiley.

Langley, S. (2012). Positive relationships at work. In S. Roffey (Ed), *Positive relationships: Evidence based practice across the world* (pp. 163–180). Dordrecht, the Netherlands: Springer.

Lee, G., & Teo, A. (2005). Organisational restructuring: Impact on trust and work satisfaction. *Asia Pacific Journal of Management*, *22*(1), 23–39.

Lewis, S. (2011). *Positive psychology at work*. Chichester, UK: Wiley-Blackwell.

Losada, M., & Heaphy, E. (2004). The role of positivity and connectivity in the performance of business teams: A non-linear dynamics model. *American Behavioural Scientist, 47*, 740–765.

Lyubomirsky, S. (2007). *The how of happiness.* London, UK: Sphere.

Mayer, R. C., Davis, J. H., & Schoorman, F. D. (1995). An integrative model of organisational trust. *Academy of Management Review, 20*, 709–734.

McCashen, W. (2005). *The strengths approach: A strengths based resource for sharing power and creating change.* Bendigo, Australia: St Luke's Innovative Resources.

Mills, M. J., Fleck, C. R., & Koziowski, A. (2013). Positive psychology at work: A conceptual review, state-of-practice assessment and a look ahead. *Journal of Positive Psychology, 8*(2), 153–164.

Mukamel, R., Ekstrom, A. D., Kaplan, J., Iacoboni, M., & Freid, I. (2010). Single neuron responses in humans during execution and observation of actions, *Current Biology, 20*, 750–756.

National Committee on Pay Equity. (2015). Retrieved March 30, 2015 from http://www.pay-equity.org/

New Economics Foundation. (2014). *Well-being at work: A review of the literature.* Retrieved April 6, 2015 from http://b.3cdn.net/nefoundation/71c1bb59a2ce151df7_8am6bqr2q.pdf

Noble, T., McGrath, H., Roffey, S., & Rowling, L. (2008). *Scoping study into approaches to student wellbeing.* Canberra, Australia: Australian Federal Government, Department of Education, Employment and Workplace Relations.

Office for National Statistics. (2014a). *Annual survey of hours and earnings.* Retrieved March 23, 2015 from http://www.ons.gov.uk/ons/rel/ashe/annual-survey-of-hours-and-earnings/2014-provisional-results/stb-ashe-statistical-bulletin-2014.html

Office for National Statistics. (2014b). *Characteristics of home workers.* Retrieved from www.ons.gov.uk/ons/dcp171776_365592.pdf

Olff, M., Friiling, J. L., Kubansky, L. D., Bradley, B., Ellenbogen, M. A., Cardoso, ... van Zuiden, M. (2013). The role of oxytocin in social bonding, stress regulation and mental health: An update on the moderating effects of context and interindividual differences. *Psychoneuroendocrinology, 38*(9), 1883–1894.

Owens, B. P., Baker, W. E., Sumpter, D. M., & Cameron, K. S. (2015). Relational energy at work: Implications for job engagement and job performance. *Journal of Applied Psychology*, online publication. Retrieved July 17, 2015 from http://dx.doi.org/10.1037/apl0000032

Pink, D. H. (2009). *Drive: The surprising truth about what motivates us.* New York, NY: Riverhead Books.

Pusey, M. (2003). *The experience of middle Australia.* Cambridge, UK: Cambridge University Press.

Putnam, R. D. (1995). Bowling alone: America's declining social capital. *Journal of Democracy, 6*(1), 65–78.

Putnam, R. D. (2000) *Bowling alone: The collapse and revival of American community.* New York, NY: Simon & Schuster.

Quick, J. C., Gavin, J. H., Cooper. C. L., & Quick, J. D. (2004). Working together: Balancing head and heart. In R.H. Rozensky, N. D. Johnson, C. D. Goodheart, & W. R. Hammond (Eds.), *Psychology builds a healthy world: Opportunities for research and practice* (pp. 219–232). Washington, DC: American Psychological Association.

Ragins, B. R., & Kram, K. E. (2007). *The handbook of mentoring at work: Theory, research and practice.* London: Sage.

Reis, H. T., & Gable, S. L. (2003). Toward a positive psychology of relationships. In C. L. M. Keyes & J. Haidt (Eds.), *Flourishing: Positive psychology and the life well lived* (pp. 129–159). Washington, DC: American Psychological Association.

Richardson, J., & West, M. (2010). Dream teams: Towards a positive psychology of team working. In P. A. Linley, S. A. Harrington, & N. Garcea (Eds.), *Oxford handbook of positive psychology and work* (pp. 235–250). Oxford, UK: Oxford University Press.

Roffey, S. (2005). *Respect in practice: The challenge of emotional literacy in education.* Conference paper for the Australian Association for Research in Education. Retrieved from http://www.aare.edu.au/data/publications/2005/rof05356.pdf

Roffey, S. (2007). Transformation and emotional literacy: The role of school leaders in developing a caring school community. *Leading and Managing, 13*(1), 16–30.

Roffey, S. (2008), Emotional literacy and the ecology of school wellbeing. *Educational and Child Psychology, 25(2).*

Roffey, S. (2012). Teacher wellbeing, pupil wellbeing: Two sides of the same coin. *Educational and Child Psychology, 29(4),* 8–17.

Roffey, S. (2013). Inclusive and exclusive belonging: The impact on individual and community wellbeing. *Educational and Child Psychology, 30*(1), 38–49.

Ryan, R. M., & Deci, E. L. (2000). Self-determination theory and the facilitation of intrinsic motivation, social development, and well-being. *American Psychologist, 55*(1), 68–78.

Saccheti, S., & Tortia, E. C. (2013). Satisfaction with creativity: A study of organisational characteristics and individual motivation. *Journal of Happiness Studies, 14,* 1789–1811.

Scott, G. (2003). *Learning principals: Leadership capability and learning research.* Sydney, Australia: NSW Department of Education and Training.

Seibert, S., Wang, G., Courtright, S. (2011). Antecedants and consequences or psychological and team empowerment in organisations: A meta-analytic review. *Journal of Applied Psychology, 96,* 981–1003.

Seligman, M. E. P. (2011). *Flourish: A visionary new understanding of happiness and wellbeing.* London, UK: William Heinemann.

Seligman, M. E. P., Parks, A. C., & Steen, T. (2005). A balanced psychology and a full life. In F. A. Huppert, N. Baylis, & B. Keverne (Eds.), *The science of wellbeing* (pp. 275–283). Oxford, UK: Oxford University Press.

Seybold, P. B., Marshak, R. T., & Lewis, J. M. (2001). *The customer revolution.* New York, NY: Crown Business.

Stewart, G. A. (2006). A meta-analytic review of relationships between team design features and team performance. *Journal of Management, 32*(1), 29–55.

Tabibnia, G., & Leiderman, M. D. (2007). Fairness and cooperation are rewarding: Evidence from social cognitive neuroscience. *Annals of the New York Academy of Sciences, 1118,* 90–101.

Trepanier, S. G., Fernet, C., & Austin, S. (2015). A longitudinal investigation of workplace bullying: Basic need satisfaction and employee functioning. *Journal of Occupational Health Psychology, 20*(1), 105–116.

Twenge, J. M. (2000). The age of anxiety: Birth cohort change in anxiety and neuroticism 1952–1993. *Journal of Personality and Social Psychology, 79*(6), 1007–1021.

Wagner, J., Cummings, G., Smith, D., Olson, J., Anderson, L., & Warren, S. (2010). The relationship between structural empowerment and psychological empowerment for nurses: A systematic review. *Journal of Nursing Management, 18,* 448–462.

Wenner, M. (2009, September 1). Smile! it could make you happier! *Scientific American.* Retrieved April 6, 2015 from http://www.scientificamerican.com/article/smile-it-could-make-you-happier

Werner, E., & Smith, R. (2001). *Journeys from childhood to the midlife: Risk, resilience, and recovery.* New York, NY: Cornell University Press.

Wilkinson, R., & Pickett, K. (2010). *The spirit level: Why equality is better for everyone.* London, UK: Penguin.

Wolff, S. B., Pescosolido, A. T., & Druskat, V. U. (2002). Emotional intelligence as the basis of leadership emergence in self-managing teams. *The Leadership Quarterly, 13*(5), 505–522.

WHO. (1999). *Labour market changes and job insecurity: A challenge for social welfare and health promotion.* Retrieved June 29, 2015 from http://www.euro.who.int/__data/assets/pdf_file/0005/98411/E66205.pdf

WHO. (2001). *Mental health 2001: Report by the Secretariat.* Retrieved April 1, 2015 from http://apps.who.int/iris/bitstream/10665/78668/1/ee27.pdf?ua=1

Wrzesniewski, A., Dutton, J. E., & Debebe, G. (2003). Interpersonal sensemaking and the meaning of work. *Research in Organisational Behaviour, 25,* 93–135.

Yamada, D. C. (2010). Workplace bullying and the law: Emerging global responses. In S. Einarsen, H. Hoel, D. Zapf, & Cooper, C. L. (Eds.), *Bullying and harassment in the workplace: Developments in theory, research and practice* (2nd ed., pp. 469–484). London, UK: Taylor & Francis.

12

Humility at Work

Don E. Davis, Joshua N. Hook, Cirleen DeBlaere, and Vanessa Placeres

Introduction

We live in a society and world that is focused on the self. Children are encouraged to have high levels of self-esteem. Young adults are encouraged to find a career that fits their unique set of gifts and talents. Adults are encouraged to maximize their potential. One drawback of these cultural foci is that individuals in today's society might struggle with humility. Indeed, some writers have noted that we seem to struggle with narcissistic tendencies more than in years past (Twenge & Campbell, 2009).

In light of those struggles, in the current chapter we explore how humility might impact one's work life. Relative to other constructs important to the study of positive psychology, such as subjective well being, gratitude, and forgiveness, the scientific study of humility had a slow start. For the first decade after the positive psychology movement began, the study of humility did not receive much empirical attention from psychologists (Davis, Worthington, & Hook, 2010). A major issue was that humility appeared to be mired in seemingly intractable measurement problems. The main concern was the validity of self-report measures in operationalizing humility. Indeed, claiming to be "very humble" seems akin to bragging, which directly contradicts what one might expect a humble person to do. People worried that individuals with very high levels of humility might temper their responses on self-report measures, whereas narcissistic individuals might self-enhance their responses.

However, since 2010 the scientific study of humility has grown considerably. Given the original concerns about measurement, researchers have inundated the literature with new measures of humility. For example, a recent review of measures found 14 published measures of humility (Davis & Hook, 2014). In addition to working on measurement issues, researchers have also explored various contexts in which humility might be important. In this chapter, we review one of the more promising contexts – humility at work. Specifically, we explore the role of humility in organizational leadership. First, we provide an overview

The Wiley Blackwell Handbook of the Psychology of Positivity and Strengths-Based Approaches at Work, First Edition. Edited by Lindsay G. Oades, Michael F. Steger, Antonella Delle Fave, and Jonathan Passmore.

of definitions and measures of humility in the work context. Second, we review theory and empirical research on the benefits of humility in organizations. Third, we look forward and describe several exciting areas of future research.

Sprawling Definitions

As with many emerging research areas, definitions and measures of humility have expanded rather than consolidated. Several strategies to assess and measure humility, including self-report surveys, other-report surveys, observational measures, and implicit measures, have been used by researchers (for a review, see Davis, Worthington, & Hook, 2010). Although initial writing on humility questioned the validity of self-report measures, empirical studies that have examined the accuracy of self-report measures of humility have not found reason for grave concern (e.g., Davis et al., 2013). In fact, self-report measures of humility show (a) strong self–other agreement when completed by well-known others and (b) evidence of predictive validity (e.g., Cohen, Panter, Turan, Morse, & Kim, 2013). These multi-method strategies align with a rich history in the study of personality of triangulating traits using self-reports, other-reports, and observation of actual behavior (Baumeister, Vohs, & Funder, 2007; Dorn, Hook, Davis, Van Tongeren, & Worthington, 2014). Thus, although researchers have historically bemoaned measurement difficulties (e.g., Tangney, 2000), we believe that the primary challenge currently facing humility scholars is the need for conceptual refinement.

Definitions of humility almost always involve both intrapersonal and interpersonal elements, with more shared consensus about the intrapersonal aspects of humility than the interpersonal facets. With regard to the intrapersonal aspects, humility involves having an accurate view of the self. Many researchers stress the importance of having an accurate view of one's limitations, although some researchers also propose that humility involves having an accurate view of one's strengths. For example, a humble leader does not overestimate or underestimate his or her ability relative to other team members, but rather has a "just right" view of self.

There is less agreement about the interpersonal or relational aspects of humility. For some researchers, having an interpersonal stance that is other-oriented, rather than self-focused, is an important aspect of humility (e.g., Davis et al., 2011). Likewise, humility likely involves interpersonal modesty, teachability, and/or a willingness to express appreciation to others (Owens, Johnson, & Mitchell, 2013). In contrast, some researchers view interpersonal characteristics as correlative to rather than constitutive of the definition of humility – meaning that the intrapsychic qualities are the essence of humility, and the interpersonal characteristics are related to (but not the core of) humility.

From a personality perspective, for someone to accurately judge a trait they have to be able to observe trait-relevant behavior (Funder, 1995). Thus, we consider interpersonal behavior to be essential to our definition of humility, and people are only able to infer intrapsychic qualities of others indirectly through observing their own or others' behavior. Just as accurately judging courage requires a person to see how someone responds in the context of danger, accurately judging humility requires the ability to observe how someone responds to situations that tend to evoke egotism and defensiveness (e.g., Davis et al., 2013). One reason the interpersonal aspect of humility may be so difficult to define is that humility likely refers to a very broad range of contexts relative to other virtues, such as forgiveness (i.e., how one deals with an offense) or gratitude (i.e., how one handles receiving benefits). Both these situations – and many others – pertain to humility. An offender who refuses to accept responsibility and apologize will be labeled arrogant. The target of the offense, if he or she refuses to offer any mercy, even after the offender apologizes far beyond what would be expected for the offense, might also be labeled arrogant. Someone who fails to say "thank you" may be characterized as entitled. Someone who gives gifts in order to put others in their debt could be regarded as exploitative. Consequently, there are a wide range of situations that are highly pertinent to one's humility, including how one handles conflict, negotiates ideas, deals with power differentials, uses wealth, receives honor, or engages with cultural differences.

To further complicate the issue, individuals and groups may not understand or evaluate humility in the same way. Viewing someone as arrogant in a specific context often involves appraising that a person has committed an interpersonal offense and then refused to repair the relationship after the violation of a personal boundary or social norm. As such, people's perceptions of humility are tied to values and cultural norms. For example, one study found that liberal communities, humility might be more associated with values such as self-transcendence or openness; whereas in conservative communities, humility may be more associated with respecting authority (Schwartz et al., 2012). Humility scholars have yet to offer a strong theory for integrating the ways in which culture and interpersonal context affect perceptions of humility.

Attempting to circumscribe the various interpersonal qualities that are essential to humility, researchers have developed complex, multifaceted definitions and measures. For example, Davis and Hook (2014) identified six themes in the content of existing scales, including (1) being other-oriented or unselfish, (2) openness/lack of superiority, (3) interpersonal modesty, (4) willingness to admit mistakes/teachable, (5) regulation of the need for status, and (6) spiritual or existential humility.

Another recently proposed strategy for conceptual refinement involves theorizing that different forms of humility may exist and vary based on the contexts that might strain the practice of humility (McElroy et al., 2014). In other words, some scholars have begun to contextualize the conceptualization and measurement of humility into particular subdomains, such as intellectual humility or cultural humility. From this perspective, just as self-efficacy can be domain-specific, we might also consider the humility behaviors associated with particular contexts. This theorizing makes the question of whether subdomains of humility are sufficiently correlated to support a general humility construct, or whether the subdomains tend to be relatively independent of one another, an empirical rather than just a conceptual one. This subdomain conceptualization provides another approach to reconcile the seemingly disparate conceptualizations of humility present within broader scholarship on humility.

Measuring Humility in Organizational Leaders

As it relates to studies of organizational leadership, there are two prominent measures of humility (see Davis, Worthington, & Hook, 2010 and Davis & Hook, 2014, for reviews of other humility measures): The Honesty-Humility (HH) subscale of the HEXICO-PI-R (Lee & Ashton, 2004) and the Expressed Humility Scale (EHS; Owens et al., 2013).

The Honesty-Humility (HH) subscale

The HH is by far the most widely used measure of humility in general and within the study of humility in organizational leadership literature. The HH is part of a six-factor model of personality (i.e., humility–honesty, emotionality, extraversion, agreeableness, conscientiousness, and openness) that has emerged as a formidable competitor to the five-factor model of personality. This model has shown incremental predictive validity over the five-factor model (for a review, see Ashton, Lee, & deVries, 2014).

Some humility scholars have reflexively rejected the HH as a strong measure of humility, but we challenge that conclusion in the current chapter. The typical critique of the HH is that, although it includes items associated with humility, it also includes content that does not align well with existing definitions of humility. The HH has four subscales: Fairness (e.g., "If I want something from a person I dislike, I will act very nicely toward that person in order to get it"), Sincerity (e.g., "If I knew that I could never get caught, I would be willing to steal a million dollars"), Modesty (e.g., "I would not want people to treat me as though I were superior to them"), and Greed-Avoidance (e.g., "I would like to live in a very expensive, high-class neighborhood").

We agree that Fairness and Sincerity are less related to existing definitions of humility, but we think a reasonable case can be made for considering the Modesty and Greed-Avoidance facets as measures of humility subdomains. Conceptually, we view interpersonal modesty as a subdomain that involves moderating one's self-presentation to others in order to avoid envy and jealousy. The Modesty subscale of the HH correlates strongly with other measures of humility (Davis et al., 2011). Greed-Avoidance taps into a perhaps less often considered aspect of humility related to one's ability to regulate motives for status, especially materialism and wealth. Without a stronger guiding framework, we certainly see no reason to exclude these subdomains over other valued aspects of humility, such as spiritual humility (Davis, Hook, et al., 2010) or cultural humility (Hook, Davis, Owen, Worthington, & Utsey, 2013).

Expressed Humility Scale (EHS)

The other prominent measure of humility among leaders is the Expressed Humility Scale (EHS; Owens et al., 2013). One practical feature of the EHS for the study of humility at work is that the three EHS subscales are particularly contextualized within the organizational context. Another strength of this measure is the rigorous qualitative approach used to inform the development of item content (Owens & Hekman, 2012). Based on interviews with executives, Owens et al. (2013) developed a conceptualization of humility that involved (1) having an accurate view of self, (2) appreciating the strengths of others, and (3) being teachable. In a series of studies on undergraduate and community samples, Owens et al. (2013) established the scale using exploratory and confirmatory factor analyses and provided initial evidence of construct validity. Specifically, in their first study, expressed humility was strongly related to modesty, narcissism, honesty–humility, and learning goal orientation in the anticipated directions; moderately and positively related to openness, emotional stability, and core self-evaluation; and weakly related to conscientiousness and extraversion.

In a second study, using undergraduate management students ($N = 144$) working in teams for 10 weeks, expressed humility was associated with individual and team performance. Expressed humility positively predicted individual and team performance controlling for demographic variables (i.e., age, gender, race, work experience, openness, core self-evaluation), self-efficacy, conscientiousness, and mental ability. In addition, expressed humility showed a strong, positive relationship with performance at lower levels of mental ability. This finding suggests that humility may be especially important as a way of compensating for lower intelligence, perhaps because it is interpersonally offensive for leaders to overestimate their abilities in a leadership role, or perhaps because one pathway to effective leadership for individuals with lower cognitive abilities involves acknowledging one's limitations and drawing on the strengths of others.

In a third field study, using employees (N=704) from health service organizations, expressed humility was related to job engagement (r=.25), job satisfaction (r=.44), team learning goal-orientation (r=.35), and voluntary turnover (r=-.14). Importantly, expressed humility predicted these constructs controlling for covariates (i.e., gender, race, tenure, and tenure under the leader).

A potential disadvantage of the EHS is that, because items were developed based on leader–subordinate relationships, these behaviors may be less relevant to assessing humility in other relationship contexts (e.g., marriage), which may explain why additional researchers have continued to add interpersonal subdomains – there are many contexts in which we might study humility, such as health care (Baughman, Aultman, Ludwick, & O'Neill, 2014; Beagan & Chacala, 2012; Brown et al., 2011; Carter & Swan, 2012; Griswold, Zayas, Kernan, & Wagner, 2007; Mahant, Jovcevska, & Wadhwa, 2012; Varkey, Peloquin, Reed, Lindor, & Harris, 2009), schools (Theoharis, 2008), couples (Farrell et al., 2015), religion (Boyatzis, Brizz, & Godwin, 2011), cross-cultural relationships (Hook et al., 2013) – and thus many subdomains from which we might sample behaviors.

Theory and Research on Humility in Organizational Leadership

In the early years of research on humility in the context of organizational leadership, researchers focused on the potential benefits of humility for organizations and individuals within those organizations (see Table 12.1 for a summary of the method and results of studies). We organize initial research under the domain of four theories that address the importance of humility within the organizational leadership context: (1) humility and social bonds, (b) humility and morality, (3) humility contagion, and (4) humility as social oil.

Humility and Social Bonds

The social bond hypothesis suggests that perceptions of humility regulate social bonds. Social bonds cause people in interdependent relationships to react to others' needs as their own. Davis et al. (2013) argued that one aspect of perceiving someone to be humble involves perceiving that their motives are other-oriented, rather than selfish. Put simply, humble individuals transcend selfishness by emphasizing "we" over "me." Humility involves integrity of thought, action, and motivation. A humble person not only has an accurate view of the self and portrays modest behavior, but also cultivates other-oriented motives when engaging with others. Davis et al. (2013) built on theories of altruism to describe relationship factors that can promote humility (e.g., perceptions of interdependence) as well as how perceptions of humility help regulate social bonds. They suggested that appraisals of another person's humility help to regulate the strength of social bonds. Although social bonds facilitate cooperation and close relationships, they can make people vulnerable to exploitation to the extent that someone feels a strong bond within a relationship, but that commitment and loyalty are not reciprocated by the other person. Thus, social bonds require precise regulation. According to their theorizing, seeing another person act arrogantly and selfishly should cause one to view that person as less humble and weaken a social bond; whereas seeing a person act unselfishly and in an other-oriented way should strengthen a social bond.

These ideas converge with Stanley's work on commitment and sacrifice (Stanley, Rhoades, & Whitton, 2010). Commitment involves one's psychological awareness of a social bond. It involves the desire to persist in a relationship and maintain an emotional

Table 12.1 Description of method of studies included in review.

Article	*Sample*	*Measure of humility*	*Outcome measures*	*Main finding*
Basford, Offermann, & Behrend (2014)	511 employees	Owens' (2009) 9-item scale of humility	Source credibility, transformational leadership, apology, apology sincerity, forgiveness, relational humility, trust in/loyalty to the supervisor, satisfaction with the supervisor, leader–member exchange, affective organizational commitment, and contextual variables	• Credibility factors –trustworthiness and caring/goodwill – demonstrated positive relationship with leader apology • Followers' assessment of a leaders' apology sincerity significantly impacted the followers' reaction to the leader and enhanced trust in the leadership
Bourdage, Lee, Lee, & Shin (2012)	262 Korean employees	HH	Organizational citizenship behavior motives; worker-rated organizational citizenship behavior	• HH related to impression management, but not other motives
Cohen, Panter, Turan, Morse, Kim (2014; Study 1)	1,020 employees; 215 co-workers	HH	Demographic characteristics, personality, moral character, and work environment	• Found three groups with latent profile analysis, corresponding to high, medium, and low morality • HH was one of the stronger measures to distinguish class
Cohen et al. (2014; Study 2)	494 employees; 126 co-workers	HH	Emotions, work experience, and behaviors	• Replicated three groups • Class predicted self- and employee-ratings of harmful and helpful behaviors at work
Cohen et al. (2014; Study 3)	553 employees	HH	Personality and social behavior	• Replicated three groups • Class predicted delinquent behavior and attitudes toward unethical negotiating tactics
de Vries (2012)	113 leaders; 201 subordinates	HH	Ethical leadership, charismatic leadership, supportive leadership, task oriented leadership, controls	• Controlling for bias related to method artifacts, HH was strongly and positively related to ethical leadership and strongly, negatively related to task-oriented leadership
Effelsberg, Solga, & Gurt(2014)	321 employees	HH	Transformational leadership, organizational identification and selfless pro-organizational behavior	• Transformational leadership enhances employees' willingness to sacrifice their personal gain for the benefit of the company

Grahek, Thompson, & Toliver (2014)	274 participants of leadership programs	Own scale	Behavioral ratings, importance ratings, and California Psychological Inventory	• Humility strongly related to other ratings of character on the same measure; showed weak relationships with various subscales of the California Psychological Inventory
Jonason & McCain (2012)	269 employees	HH	Big five, supervisor ratings of job skills	• HH predicted job skills above and beyond the five-factor model
Lee, Ashton, Morrison, Cordery, & Dunlop (2008; Study 1)	1,105 job applicants	HH	HEXACO	• HH can be distinguished from other personality factors even in the high-stakes setting of personnel selection
Lee et al. (2008; Study 2)	326 undergraduates	HH	Demographics, big five, integrity, ethical decision-making	• HH predicted scores on an integrity test and a business ethical decision-making task
Marcus, Lee, & Ashton (2007)	853 employees and students from Germany and Canada	HH	Counterproductive work behavior; counterproductive academic behavior; integrity	• HH more important for overt integrity tests; big five more important for personality-based integrity tests
McElroy, Rice, Davis, Hook, Hill, Worthington, & Van Tongeren (2014; Study 1)	213 community sample	Intellectual Humility Scale, 60-item version (own scale)	n/a	• Developed a measure of intellectual humility • Used exploratory factor analysis to winnow items • Final version was a two-factor, 12-item measure
McElroy et al. (2014; Study 2)	213 community sample	Intellectual Humility Scale	n/a	• Two-factor structure replicated well in a second sample
McElroy et al. (2014; Study 3)	139 undergraduates	Intellectual Humility Scale	Dyadic trust and the big five	• Perceiving leaders as more intellectually humble was related to greater trust; intellectual humility related to agreeableness and openness

(Continued)

Table 12.1 (Continued)

Article	*Sample*	*Measure of humility*	*Outcome measures*	*Main finding*
McElroy et al. (2014; Study 4)	105 undergraduates	Intellectual Humility Scale	Desecration, positive and negative attitudes toward God, forgiveness	• Intellectual humility was positively related to positive attitudes toward God and negatively related to anger toward God
Mittal & Dorfman (2012)	12,681 managers across 59 societies	Own scale of servant leadership	Power distance, uncertainty avoidance, humane orientation, collectivism, assertiveness, gender egalitarianism, future orientation, performance orientation	• Found that humility was more strongly endorsed as part of servant leadership in Asian cultures than in European cultures; humility was related to values of uncertainty avoidance, collectivism, assertiveness, future orientation, and performance orientation
Ogunfowora (2014; Study 1)	111 career fair attendees	Ethical leadership scale	Organizational reputation, job pursuit intentions, job pursuit behavior, ethical leadership	• Job seekers at a career fair are more likely to apply to a job with an ethical CEO's (including humility) company • Perceived organizational reputation mediated the relationship between CEO ethicality and job pursuit
Ogunfowora (2014; Study 2)	335 undergraduates	HH	Personality, perception of value congruence, value congruence, organizational reputation, ethical leadership	• Perceived value congruence with the CEO also mediated the link between CEO ethicality and job pursuit • This effect was conditional on the HH personality of the prospective job applicant
Ogunfowora & Bourdage (2014)	237 undergraduates	HH	Personality, moral disengagement, leadership emergence	• HH did not have a significant direct effect on leadership emergence • Individuals with low levels of HH were more likely to utilize moral disengagement, which led to lower self-peer evaluations of leadership emergence

Ogunfowora, Bourdage, & Nguyen (2013; Study 1)	258 undergraduates	HH	Self-monitoring	• High self-monitors are more likely to score low on HH based on a tendency to be dishonest and driven by self-gain
Ogunfowora et al. (2013; Study 2)	215 undergraduates	HH	Big five, liveliness, social boldness, and self monitoring	• High self-monitors are likely to engage in unethical business decision-making, which is mediated by the propensity to engage in moral disengagement • This effect disappeared when controlling for HH
Oh, Ashton, & de Vries (2014)	217 Korean military candidates	HH	Cognitive ability, contextual performance, task performance	• HH showed some incremental validity for contextual performance but not task performance
Ou et al. (2014; Study 1)	276 Chinese undergraduates	Own scale	n/a	• Exploratory factor analysis with three factors
Ou et al. (2014; Study 2)	286 MBA students in China	Own scale	Core self-evaluation, learning goal orientation, modesty, and narcissism	• Confirmatory factor analysis showed adequate fit • Initial evidence of construct validity
Ou et al. (2014; Study 3) 3	130 CEOs; 645 middle managers	Own scale	CEO humility, empowering leadership, TMT (Top Management Team) integration, and empowering organizational climate; middle managers' work engagement, affective commitment, and job performance	• Humility of CEO related to empowering leadership behaviors, which is related to greater TMT integration • Greater TMT integration is related to a more empowering organizational climate, which is related to greater work engagement, affective commitment, and job performance

(*Continued*)

Table 12.1 (Continued)

Article	*Sample*	*Measure of humility*	*Outcome measures*	*Main finding*
Owens, Johnson, & Mitchell (2013; Study 1)	165 business students; 236 business students; 124 business students; 511 health employees; 263 full-time employees	EHS (own scale)	Modesty, narcissism, conscientiousness, extraversion, openness to experience, emotional stability, core self-evaluation, HH, learning goal orientation	• Exploratory factor analysis suggested three factors • CFA results replicated well in two additional samples • Evidence of temporal stability • Evidence of discriminant validity
Owens et al. (2013; Study 2)	144 business students	EHS	Openness, core self-evaluation, self-efficacy, conscientiousness, general mental ability, team contribution, individual performance	• Evidence of incremental predictive validity • Humility helps compensate for lower intelligence
Owens et al. (2013; Study 3)	704 employees of health services organization	EHS	Job engagement, job satisfaction, team leader growth orientation, voluntary turnover	• Humility predicts job engagement, job satisfaction, team growth orientation, and voluntary turnover
Owens & Heckman (2015; Study 1)	89 undergraduates	EHS	Team collective promotion focus	• Leader humility, rated by team, positively predicted team collective promotion focus through collective humility
Owens & Heckman (2015; Study 2)	192 undergraduates	EHS	Team collective promotion focus, team performance	• Collective promotion focus mediated the relationship between collective humility and team performance
Owens & Heckman (2015; Study 3)	362 health services employees	EHS	Team collective promotion focus, team performance	• Leader humility is important to overall team performance and influence through the two-stage process of collective humility and collective promotion focus • Task allocation effectiveness mediated the effect of leader humility and team performance

Owens, Wallace, & Walkman (2015)	876 employees	EHS	Leader narcissism, perceived leader effectiveness, follower job engagement, follower subjective performance, follower objective performance, controls	• Humility buffered the negative effect of narcissism on workplace outcomes
Schneider & Goffin (2012)	213 undergraduates	HH	Ability to deceive, self-deception, impression management, anxiety, test-taking motivation, five-factor model, counterproductive work behavior	• HH related to perceived ability to deceive and impression management, but not self-deception, test-taking motivation, or anxiety
Toorenburg, Oostrom, & Pollet (2015)	73 recruiters	HH	Cognitive ability and hirability	• Informal email address associated with lower hirability ratings, and this relationship was mediated by perceptions of humility
Wiltshire, Bourdage, & Lee (2014)	368 employees	HH	Perception of organizational politics, personality, counterproductive work behavior, impression management behavior, job stress, job satisfaction, control variables	• Humility–honesty amplifies the relationship between perceived organizational politics and counterproductive work behavior

Source: Author.

attachment (Rusbult, 1980); a decision to give up other choices or alternatives for relationship partners; and a future-orientation for a relationship (Stanley et al., 2010). Theorizing on commitment also aligns with our premise that humility is most accurately judged while it is strained. Some situations, more than others, help clarify the strength of a social bond and degree of commitment. Diagnostic situations that strain humility help people judge commitment clearly: They contrast one's self interest with the needs of the relationship (Holmes & Rempel, 1989; Wieselquist, Rusbult, Foster, & Agnew, 1999). In such a situation, if a person forgoes her or his immediate self-interest for the good of the relationship, this serves as a clear signal of her or his commitment to the relationship. This is called a *sacrifice-behavior*, which we also conceptualize as a humility-relevant behavior.

In highly committed relationships, a transformation of motivation occurs wherein individuals adopt their partner's interests as their own (Rusbult, 1980). Such dyads not only sacrifice for each other, but they enjoy it, which can initiate positive, iterative dynamics that continue to strengthen commitment (see Stanley et al., 2010, for a review). In this context, humility is relationship-specific, but some people may cultivate greater humility across all their relationships. In other words, they may generally negotiate relationships that optimize interdependence and commitment.

This assertion about the importance of humility in relationships dovetails nicely with theorizing on leadership qualities that promote trust and commitment in employees. Namely, because of the power differential inherent in leadership–subordinate relationships, there is a need for continual monitoring of possible exploitation. According to the social bond hypothesis, when leaders violate expectations and offend subordinates, shifts in how subordinates view the character – particularly the humility of – the leader are anticipated to occur.

Several empirical studies have reported findings consistent with the social bonds hypothesis. For example, in a community sample, de Vries (2012) examined the relationship between humility, measured with the HH, and several leadership styles hypothesized to be related to the six-factor model of personality, including ethical leadership, charismatic leadership, supportive leadership, and task-oriented leadership. As predicted, self-reported humility was strongly and positively related to self-reported ethical leadership, controlling for covariates as well as method variance using other-reports. Likewise, humility was strongly and negatively related to task-oriented leadership. Another study demonstrated that applicants at a career fair were more attracted to working for a CEO with a reputation for being ethical, relative to a CEO with a reputation for being unethical or with an unknown reputation, and this preference was especially strong for applicants higher in humility (Ogunfowora, 2014).

In addition to helping develop social bonds through increased commitment, humility helps repair social bonds after offenses. Two studies have offered initial evidence for this hypothesis within an organizational context (Basford, Offermann, & Behrend, 2014; McElroy et al., 2014). With a community sample of employees, Basford et al. (2014) found that perceived humility was strongly and positively associated with forgiveness as well as several other relational outcomes, such as trust and commitment. McElroy et al. (2014) found that perceived humility was correlated with forgiveness of a religious leader in a sample of undergraduates. Both of these studies are limited by cross-sectional designs, so experimental or longitudinal designs are needed to test the causal inferences implied by the hypothesis.

The studies we have reviewed thus far have focused on how employees perceive leaders. However, there is also evidence that humility affects social bonds among colleagues. For example, in a community sample, humility (measured with the HH) was associated with self-reported selfless pro-organizational behavior ($r = .28$) and a behavioral task ($r = .15$)

involving allocating lottery tickets for personal or organizational benefit (Effelsberg, Solga, & Gurt, 2014). With another community sample of employees, participants completed measures of office politics and other work outcomes (job satisfaction, job stress, impression management behavior, counterproductive work behavior; Wiltshire, Bourdage, & Lee, 2014). The authors found a consistent pattern in which humility, measured with HH, buffered the relationship between perceiving office politics and negative work outcomes, such that the association between perceived office politics and negative work outcomes was stronger at higher levels of HH.

Humility and morality

A second prominent line of work in humility is based on the premise that humility is closely linked with morality. If this assertion is accurate, then being able to predict humble behaviors might have critical implications for personnel selection, to the degree that humility is consistently linked with integrity-related outcomes in the workplace such as greater ethical behavior and lower counterproductive work behavior such as retaliation, irresponsible use of company resources, or dishonesty behavior. For decades, researchers have called for a strong measure of integrity, and some initial work has explored the promise of the HH subscale for predicting behaviors associated with integrity (Ashton et al., 2014). We briefly review several recent studies that pertain to the humility–morality theory.

Across two studies using latent profile analysis, Cohen, Panter, Turan, Morse, and Kim (2014) found three groups associated with high, medium, and low morality. These groups predicted key work outcomes, including harmful work behaviors, helpful work behaviors, delinquent behaviors, and attitudes toward unethical negotiation tactics. Among a variety of measures of morality, the HH subscale and a measure of conscientiousness were the two scales that most strongly distinguished among the high-, medium-, and low-morality groups.

The HH subscale has also been linked with other variables associated with morality. For example, in a sample of college students, HH (self-reports and other-reports) predicted integrity and ethical decision-making above and beyond the big five personality variables (Lee, Ashton, Morrison, Cordery, & Dunlop, 2008). In graduate students studying business, the HH subscale was negatively related to moral disengagement ($r = -.40$) and unethical decision making ($r = -.47$; Ogunfowora, Bourdage, & Nguyen, 2013). In two samples of small groups assessed three times while working together on a course project, HH scores were indirectly related to greater leadership emergence via lower moral disengagement (Ogunfowora & Bourdage, 2014).

Although these initial results are promising, the value of the HH subscale has not been fully explored within the context of personnel selection. One study did replicate the six-factor structure of the HEXICO-PI-R within a selection context (Lee et al., 2008), but it is important to evaluate the predictive validity of the HH in longitudinal studies, relative to other predictors of performance.

Humility Contagion

Another promising idea, called *humility contagion*, states that when leaders model humility, it can in turn cause their work teams to relate to each other in more humble ways, exemplified through greater willingness to accurately self-evaluate, appreciate the strengths of team members, and learn from others (Owens & Hekman, 2015). Specifically, in three studies, the authors explored a model in which leader humility was hypothesized to lead to greater collective humility, which in turn was posited to cause members to strive to help the team reach its true potential (i.e., collective promotion focus), resulting in enhanced team performance.

In the first study, participants ($N = 89$) were assigned to work in teams. The teams included confederate leaders in order to experimentally manipulate leader humility. As predicted, leader humility was associated with an increase in collective humility, which in turn affected collective promotion focus. These analyses controlled for average team size, gender, and age.

In the second study, participants ($N = 192$ undergraduate business students) were assigned to teams for a project designed to simulate the automobile industry. The simulation provides a realistic portrayal of how management decisions affect market share and stock value within the automobile industry. At six weeks into the simulation, participants completed team variables, including collective humility, promotion focus, cohesion, and psychological safety. As predicted, collective humility was positively associated with collective promotion focus, which in turn was associated with higher team performance. These analyses controlled for team size, gender, and age, as well as stock price after the third round of competition and degree of competition (i.e., number of teams).

In the third study, participants (326 health service employees on 77 work teams) completed measures of leader humility and transformational leadership (i.e., a leadership style that involves motivating greater performance through inspirational values and vision) at Time 1. Employees rated collective humility and team collective promotion focus one month later (Time 2). In addition, leaders rated team performance at Time 2. As hypothesized, leader humility was associated with greater collective humility, which in turn predicted greater collective promotion focus and thereby increased team performance. These analyses again controlled for team size, gender, age, and transformational leadership (correlated .53 with leader humility). Taken together, results from these three studies provide promising initial evidence that humble behaviors by leaders can influence how individuals on a team relate to one another.

Humility as Social Oil

The final theory is admittedly more speculative than the others. The benefits of humility may be somewhat paradoxical and concealed. For example, research has demonstrated how narcissism is on the rise in the United States (e.g., Twenge & Campbell, 2009) and humility is consistently ranked low among other virtues in a variety of samples (Linley et al., 2007; Park, Peterson, & Seligman, 2004; Shimai, Otake, Park, Peterson, & Seligman, 2006). This hypothesis is designed to elucidate the contexts where humility ought to be especially helpful.

According to the social oil theory, humility acts as "social oil," preventing relational wear-and-tear in the way that oil prevents the machinations of an engine from causing overheating. In his groundbreaking research, Collins (2001) found that humility and drive were two qualities of exceptional leaders who not only guided their companies into eras of high productivity, but whose companies also continued to thrive after they left their leadership post. The social oil theory is one way to understand these results. It is perhaps unsurprising that successful CEOs were driven – ambition is a character trait that is highly valued in potential leaders – but the same qualities that lead to high achievement can also cause wear-and-tear on relationships. For example, CEOs have higher rates of depression and divorce than the general population (e.g., Meers & Strober, 2009). We theorize that humility buffers the potential drawbacks of competitive traits by promoting an optimal balance of competition and cooperation. Providing initial evidence for this hypothesis in an organizational context, Owens, Wallace, and Waldman (2015) measured the degree to which subordinates ($N = 876$) perceived leaders within a health care organization as being humble (expressed humility). Narcissism and expressed humility interacted to predict perceptions of leader effectiveness, job engagement, and subjective and objective performance. Therefore, initial studies provide promising evidence for the social bonds hypothesis in leaders. It is important to explore this hypothesis across a range of relationships and contexts in which competitive traits may cause wear-and-tear on relationships and strain cooperation.

Future Research

There are several exciting areas for future research focused on the importance of humility in organizational leadership. First, measurement issues persist. Researchers should continue to work to clarify optimal strategies for operationalizing humility in various contexts. Researchers need to advance theoretical arguments for consolidating definitions of humility and its various subdomains. Some humility measures that are focused on the organizational context may be poorly suited for comparing the influence of humility across a variety of relationships (e.g., work and family life). Most studies have examined humility as a trait, but we might also explore humility as a state. For example, researchers might explore particular appraisal styles associated with humility in the context of transition or stress, such as being more willing to examine existential assumptions and reconfigure cherished beliefs when challenged. In addition, researchers might explore specific behaviors that are indicative of low humility in high-pressure situations. Initial work has found low self–other agreement for humility ratings at minimal levels of acquaintance, but perhaps observing how people respond to certain diagnostic situations for leaders could increase the accuracy of such brief judgments. Just as accurately assessing courage requires seeing how someone responds to danger, getting a good read on a leader's humility likely requires seeing how he or she responds to interpersonal situations that are likely to lead to interpersonal conflict. Assessing humility would be especially helpful for subsequent applications regarding hiring decisions. For example, perhaps researchers could develop standardized interview questions that would help provide accurate judgments of a leader's humility.

Furthermore, it is critical to evaluate measurement invariance of humility measures across different groups. It seems plausible that the construct of humility could vary by gender, race/ethnicity, and nationality identities, to name a few. Thus, a second area for future research involves the need to investigate how cultural identity might impact humility norms and the benefits of humility. A potential dark side of humility is that groups may apply different standards for evaluating humility to individuals. For instance, the social, cultural, and political experiences of women could lead to intrapersonal and interpersonal interpretations of humility that differ from those of men. For instance, if women are held to a higher standard when it comes to displaying humility, then men may receive greater social recognition and benefits for exhibiting equivalent (or even less) behavior as women. Research has only begun to explore how cultural norms influence perceptions of humility and its relationship with other variables (e.g., Hook et al., 2013; Kim & Lee, 2014).

A third area for future research involves exploring the robustness of humility as a predictor of various benefits. Given that many of the studies we reviewed may capitalize on mono-method bias, a critical reader might question whether it is humility – or perhaps just general likeability or approval – that is associated with positive outcomes. Thin-slice approaches (i.e., behavioral observation based on diagnostic situations) as described above would provide stronger evidence that humility behaviors in key situations (e.g., high potential for conflict) could predict subsequent outcomes. In addition, experimental designs that actually manipulate humble behavior (e.g., Owens & Hekman, 2015) will help address this concern.

A fourth area for future research involves exploring moderators of the link between humility and various outcomes. The social oil hypothesis is one example. Humility may be especially critical and related to positive outcomes in certain situations, such as highly competitive contexts. Having the ability to soften one's interpersonal relationships might allow one to engage in a highly competitive way without the typical wear-and-tear that can accompany competition. Furthermore, it is important to explore contexts for which humility may be especially ill suited. For example, in qualitative interviews, executives identified high-pressure situations as a potential weakness of humility (Owens & Heckman, 2012). Consequently, the pressured nature of a situation could moderate the link between humility and work-related outcomes (e.g., team performance, collective promotion focus).

Finally, a fifth area of future research involves the need for intervention studies (Lavelock et al., 2014). Despite the fact that basic research focused on humility, both generally and in work contexts, is still in an early stage, we do not think it is premature to begin considering strategies to facilitate the practice and development of humble behaviors in certain contexts. Given the advantages of experimental designs, brief interventions can complement basic research on humility and help refine developing theory.

Conclusion

Given rapid changes in the economy in the United States and the world, as well as shifts in humility-related traits (Twenge & Campbell, 2009), it has become increasingly important to understand how humility affects organizational leadership. The breadth of this virtue makes it a theme that cuts across a variety of prominent theories within organizational leadership, and recent advances in measurement now make it possible for rapid progress in our understanding of the importance of humility in relationships between leaders and their fellow leaders and teammates.

References

Ashton, M. C., Lee, K., & de Vries, R. E. (2014). The HEXACO Honesty-Humility, Agreeableness, and Emotionality factors: A review of research and theory. *Personality and Social Psychology Review*, *18*, 139–152.

Basford, T. E., Offermann, L. R., & Behrend, T. S. (2014). Please accept my sincerest apologies: Examining follower reactions to leader apology. *Journal of Business Ethics*, *119*, 99–117.

Baughman, K. R., Aultman, J. M., Ludwick, R., & O'Neill, A. (2014). Narrative analysis of the ethics in providing advance care planning. *Nursing Ethics*, *21*, 53–63.

Baumeister, R. F., Vohs, K. D., & Funder, D. C. (2007). Psychology as the science of self-reports and finger movements: Whatever happened to actual behavior? *Perspectives on Psychological Science*, *2*, 396–403.

Beagan, B. L., & Chacala, A. (2012). Culture and diversity among occupational therapists in Ireland: When the therapist is the "diverse" one. *The British Journal of Occupational Therapy*, *75*, 144–151.

Bourdage, J. S., Lee, K., Lee, J.-H., & Shin, K.-H. (2012). Motives for organizational citizenship behavior: Personality correlates and coworker ratings of OCB. *Human Performance*, *25*, 179–200.

Boyatzis, R., Brizz, T., & Godwin, L. (2011). The effect of religious leaders' emotional and social competencies on improving parish vibrancy. *Journal of Leadership & Organizational Studies*, *18*, 192–206.

Brown, J., Lewis, L., Ellis, K., Stewart, M., Freeman, T. R., & Kasperski, M. J. (2011). Conflict on interprofessional primary health care teams: Can it be resolved? *Journal of Interprofessional Care*, *25*, 4–10.

Carter, B. S., & Swan, R. (2012). Pediatric palliative care instruction for residents: An introduction to IPPC. *American Journal of Hospice & Palliative Medicine*, *29*, 375–378.

Cohen, T. R., Panter, A. T., Turan, N., Morse, L., & Kim, Y. (2013). Agreement and similarity in self–other perceptions of moral character. *Journal of Research in Personality*, *47*, 816–830.

Cohen, T. R., Panter, A. T., Turan, N., Morse, L., & Kim, Y. (2014). Moral character in the workplace. *Journal of Personality and Social Psychology*, *107*, 943–963.

Collins, J. (2001). *Good to great*. New York, NY: HarperCollins.

Davis, D. E., & Hook, J. N. (2014). Humility, religion, and spirituality: An endpiece. *Journal of Psychology and Theology*, *42*, 111–117.

Davis, D. E., Hook, J. N., Worthington, E. L., Jr., Van Tongeren, D. R., Gartner, A. L., & Jennings, D. J., II. (2010). Relational spirituality and forgiveness: Development of the Spiritual Humility Scale (SHS). *Journal of Psychology and Theology*, *38*, 91–100.

Davis, D. E., Hook, J. N., Worthington, E. L., Jr., Van Tongeren, D. R., Gartner, A. L., Ii, D. J. J., & Emmons, R. A. (2011). Relational humility: Conceptualizing and measuring humility as a personality judgment. *Journal of Personality Assessment*, *93*, 225–234.

Davis, D. E., Worthington, E. L., Jr., & Hook, J. N. (2010). Humility: Review of measurement strategies and conceptualization as personality judgment. *The Journal of Positive Psychology*, *5*, 243–252.

Davis, D. E., Worthington, E. L., Jr., Hook, J. N., Emmons, R. A., Hill, P. C., Bollinger, R. A., & Van Tongeren, D. R. (2013). Humility and the development and repair of social bonds: Two longitudinal studies. *Self and Identity*, *12*, 58–77.

de Vries, R. E. (2012). Personality predictors of leadership styles and the self–other agreement problem. *The Leadership Quarterly*, *23*, 809–821.

Dorn, K., Hook, J. N., Davis, D. E., Van Tongeren, D. R., & Worthington, E. L., Jr. (2014). Behavioral methods of assessing forgiveness. *Journal of Positive Psychology*, *9*, 75–80.

Effelsberg, D., Solga, M., & Gurt, J. (2014). Getting followers to transcend their self-interest for the benefit of their company: Testing a core assumption of transformational leadership theory. *Journal of Business and Psychology*, *29*, 131–143.

Farrell, J. E., Hook, J. N., Ramos, M., Davis, D. E., Van Tongeren, D. R., & Ruiz, J. M. (2015). Humility and relationship outcomes in couples: The mediating role of commitment. *Couple and Family Psychology: Research and Practice*, *4*, 14–26.

Funder, D. C. (1995). On the accuracy of personality judgment: A realistic approach. *Psychological Review*, *102*, 652–670.

Grahek, M. S., Thompson, A. D., & Toliver, A. (2010). The character to lead: A closer look at character in leadership. *Consulting Psychology Journal: Practice and Research*, *62*, 270–290.

Griswold, K., Zayas, L. E., Kernan, J. B., & Wagner, C. M. (2007). Cultural awareness through medical student and refugee patient encounters. *Journal of Immigrant and Minority Health*, *9*, 55–60.

Holmes, J. G., & Rempel, J. K. (1989). Trust in close relationships. In C. Hendrick (Ed.), *Review of personality and social psychology* (Vol. *10*, pp. 187–220). London, UK: Sage.

Hook, J. N., Davis, D. E., Owen, J., Worthington, E. L., Jr., & Utsey, S. O. (2013). Cultural humility: Measuring openness to culturally diverse clients. *Journal of Counseling Psychology*, *60*, 353–366.

Jonason, P. K., & McCain, J. (2012). Using the HEXACO model to test the validity of the Dirty Dozen measure of the Dark Triad. *Personality and Individual Differences*, *53*, 935–938.

Kim, P. Y., & Lee, D. (2014). Internalized model minority myth, Asian values, and help-seeking attitudes among Asian American students. *Cultural Diversity and Ethnic Minority Psychology*, *20*, 98–106.

Lavelock, C. R., Worthington, E. L., Jr., Davis, D. E., Griffin, B. J., Reid, C. A., Hook, J. N., & Van Tongeren, D. R. (2014). The quiet virtue speaks: An intervention to promote humility. *Journal of Psychology and Theology*, *42*, 99–110.

Lee, K., & Ashton, M. C. (2004). Psychometric properties of the HEXACO personality inventory. *Multivariate Behavioral Research*, *39*, 329–358.

Lee, K., Ashton, M. C., Morrison, D. L., Cordery, J., & Dunlop, P. D. (2008). Predicting integrity with the HEXACO personality model: Use of self- and observer reports. *Journal of Occupational and Organizational Psychology*, *81*, 147–167.

Linley, P. A., Maltby, J., Wood, A. M., Joseph, S., Harrington, S., Peterson, C., … Seligman, M. E. P. (2007). Character strengths in the United Kingdom: The VIA Inventory of Strengths. *Personality and Individual Differences*, *43*, 341–351.

Mahant, S., Jovcevska, V., & Wadhwa, A. (2012). The nature of excellent clinicians at an academic health science center: A qualitative study. *Academic Medicine*, *87*, 1715–1721.

Marcus, B., Lee, K., & Ashton, M. C. (2007). Personality dimensions explaining relationships between integrity tests and counterproductive behavior: Big five, or one in addition? *Personnel Psychology*, *60*, 1–34.

McElroy, S. E., Rice, K. G., Davis, D. E., Hook, J. N., Hill, P. C., Worthington, E. L., Jr., & Van Tongeren, D. R. (2014). Intellectual humility: Scale development and theoretical elaborations in the context of religious leadership. *Journal of Psychology and Theology*, *42*, 19–30.

Meers, S., & Strober, J. (2009). *Getting to 50/50: How working couples can have it all by sharing it all*. New York, NY: Bantam Dell.

Mittal, R., & Dorfman, P. W. (2012). Servant leadership across cultures. *Journal of World Business*, *47*, 555–570.

Ogunfowora, B. (2014). The impact of ethical leadership within the recruitment context: The roles of organizational reputation, applicant personality, and value congruence. *The Leadership Quarterly*, *25*, 528–543.

Ogunfowora, B., & Bourdage, J. S. (2014). Does honesty–humility influence evaluations of leadership emergence? The mediating role of moral disengagement. *Personality and Individual Differences*, *56*, 95–99.

Ogunfowora, B., Bourdage, J. S., & Nguyen, B. (2013). An exploration of the dishonest side of self-monitoring: Links to moral disengagement and unethical business decision making. *European Journal of Personality*, *27*, 532–544.

Oh, I., Lee, K., Ashton, M., & de Vries. (2014). Are dishonest extraverts more harmful than dishonest introverts? The interaction effects of honesty-humility and extraversion in predicting workplace deviance. *Applied Psychology*, *60*, 496–516.

Ou, A., Tsui, A., Kinicki, A., Waldman, D., Xiao, Z., & Song, L. (2014). Humble chief executive officers' connections to top management team integration and middle managers' responses. *Administrative Science Quarterly*, *59*, 34–72.

Owens, B. P., & Hekman, D. R. (2012). Modeling how to grow: An inductive examination of humble leader behaviors, contingencies, and outcomes. *Academy of Management Journal*, *55*, 787–818.

Owens, B., & Hekman, D. R. (2015). How does leader humility influence team performance? Exploring the mechanisms of contagion and collective promotion focus. *Academy of Management Journal*. doi:10.5465/amj.2013.0660

Owens, B. P., Johnson, M. D., & Mitchell, T. R. (2013). Expressed humility in organizations: Implications for performance, teams, and leadership. *Organization Science*, *24*, 1517–1538.

Owens, B. P., Wallace, A., & Waldman, D. A. (2015). Leader narcissism and follower outcomes: The counterbalancing effect of leader humility. *Journal of Applied Psychology*, *100*, 1203–1213.

Park, N., Peterson, C., & Seligman, M. E. P. (2004). Strengths of character and well-being. *Journal of Social and Clinical Psychology*, *23*, 603–619.

Rusbult, C. E. (1980). Commitment and satisfaction in romantic associations: A test of the investment model. *Journal of Experimental Social Psychology*, *16*, 172–186.

Schneider, T. J., & Goffin, R. D. (2012). Perceived ability to deceive and incremental prediction in pre-employment personality testing. *Personality and Individual Differences*, *52*, 806–811.

Schwartz, S. H., Cieciuch, J., Vecchione, M., Davidov, E., Fischer, R., Beierlein, C., … Demirutku, K. (2012). Refining the theory of basic individual values. *Journal of Personality and Social Psychology*, *103*, 663–688.

Shimai, S., Otake, K., Park, N., Peterson, C., & Seligman, M. E. P. (2006). Convergence of character strengths in American and Japanese young adults. *Journal of Happiness Studies*, *7*, 311–322.

Stanley, S. M., Rhoades, G. K., & Whitton, S. W. (2010). Commitment: Functions, formation, and the securing of romantic attachment. *Journal of Family Theory & Review*, *2*, 243–257.

Tangney, J. P. (2000). Humility: Theoretical perspectives, empirical findings and directions for future research. *Journal of Social and Clinical Psychology*, *19*, 70–82.

Theoharis, G. (2008). Woven in deeply: Identity and leadership of urban social justice principals. *Education and Urban Society*, *41*, 3–25.

Toorenburg, M., Oostrom, J., & Pollet, T. (2015). What a difference your e-mail makes: Effects of informal e-mail addresses on online resume screening. *Cyberpsychology, Behavior, and Social Networking*, *18*, 135–140.

Twenge, J. M., & Campbell, W. K. (2009). *The narcissism epidemic: Living in the age of entitlement*. New York, NY: Free Press.

Varkey, P., Peloquin, J., Reed, D., Lindor, K., & Harris, I. (2009). Leadership curriculum in undergraduate medical education: A study of student and faculty perspectives. *Medical Teacher*, *31*, 244–250.

Wieselquist, J., Rusbult, C. E., Foster, C. A., & Agnew, C. R. (1999). Commitment, pro-relationship behavior, and trust in close relationships. *Journal of Personality and Social Psychology*, *77*, 942–966.

Wiltshire, J., Bourdage, J. S., & Lee, K. (2014). Honesty-humility and perceptions of organizational politics in predicting workplace outcomes. *Journal of Business and Psychology*, *29*, 235–251.

13

Compassion at Work

Tim Anstiss

Introduction

There is a growing interest in the field of compassion: its evolutionary origins; the underpinning neuroscience; its determinants, benefits, and its cultivation. We are also seeing a growth in research studies, journal articles, initiatives, policy documents, strategies, conferences, groups, and organizations focusing on the topic of compassion and compassion at work, for instance: The Centre for Compassion and Altruism Research (http://ccare.stanford.edu/), The Compassionate Mind Foundation (http://www.compassionatemind.co.uk/), The Charter for Compassion (http://www.charterforcompassion.org/).

In the first section of the chapter I will explore what compassion is, why it matters for individuals and organizations, and the evidence that it can be increased. In the second section I look at some of the factors known or thought to be associated with the appearance and unfolding of compassion at work. In the final section I make some theory driven and evidence-informed suggestions about how organizations might go about increasing compassion at work, and explore where research into the topic might best focus in the future.

What Is Compassion, and Why Does It Matter?

The word "compassion" comes from the Latin *compati*, meaning "to suffer with." There is no universally agreed definition of compassion. The Compassion Cultivation Training approach of Stanford University (Jazaieri et al., 2010) defines compassion as: "a process that unfolds in response to suffering. It begins with the recognition of suffering, which gives rise to thoughts and feelings of empathy and concern. This, in turn, motivates action to relieve that suffering."

The Wiley Blackwell Handbook of the Psychology of Positivity and Strengths-Based Approaches at Work,
First Edition. Edited by Lindsay G. Oades, Michael F. Steger, Antonella Delle Fave, and Jonathan Passmore.

Jazaieri et al. (2013) define compassion as:

> a complex multidimensional construct that is comprised of four key components: (1) an awareness of suffering (cognitive component), (2) sympathetic concern related to being emotionally moved by suffering (affective component), (3) a wish to see the relief of that suffering (intentional component), and (4) a responsiveness or readiness to help relieve that suffering (motivational component).

A shorter and commonly used definition within the literature is that compassion is: "a sensitivity to suffering in self and others with a commitment to try to alleviate and prevent it" (Germer & Siegel, 2012; Gilbert & Choden, 2013).

These three definitions emphasize two key aspects of compassion:

1 the intention and act of turning toward and engaging with suffering in self and/or others – rather than avoiding or dissociating from it; and
2 the intention to acquire the wisdom to learn how to alleviate and prevent suffering and act on that wisdom.

Compassion is rooted in our ancient caring motivations and is enabled by a range of competencies, abilities, skills, and strengths including empathy, sympathy, generosity, openness, distress tolerance, commitment. and courage (Gilbert, 1989, 2005, 2009; Gilbert & Choden, 2013; Goetz, Keltner, & Simon-Thomas, 2010). It is important to note that compassion is not one thing – for example, it is not just an emotion (see Figure 13.1). It is related to – but not the same as – sympathy, empathy and empathic concern, kindness, caring, and altruism. It can also be considered a motivation involving feeling, thinking, behavioral readiness, physiological preparedness, and action components. It also requires or builds on such character strengths as bravery and wisdom (Peterson & Seligman, 2004).

To better understand what compassion is and what it isn't, it may be helpful to explore some of these related terms.

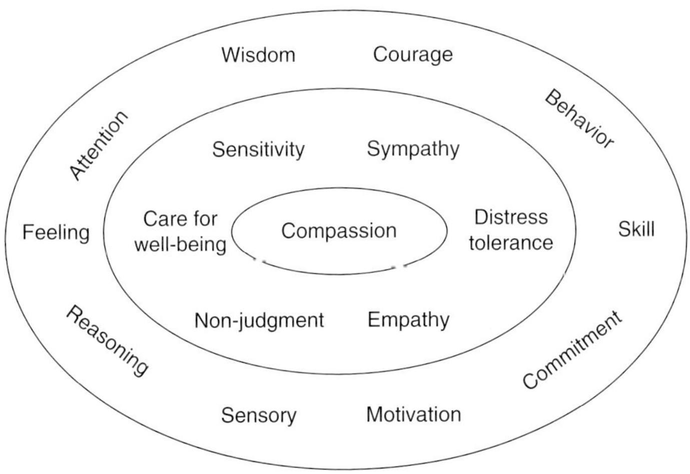

Figure 13.1 Attributes and aspects of compassion. *Source*: Adapted from Gilbert (2009).

"Sympathy" is the distress we feel when we encounter suffering – for example, concern, distress, or sorrow. However, what the sympathetic person feels may be different from what the suffering person is actually feeling. For instance, a person with a certain kind of brain injury may have become relatively indifferent to what is going on around them, but we may feel very sad for what has happened to them. Loewenstein and Small (2007) consider sympathy as caring, but immature and irrational.

"Empathy" comes from the Greek *empatheria* meaning "to feel into" or "to enter into the experience of another." It links to abilities to feel a similar emotion to the other person (sometimes called emotional contagion) and to have insight into the nature of their emotional *and* motivational state. The latter skill is called cognitive perspective-taking or mentalizing. This means we can understand not only *what* somebody might be feeling but *why* they might be feeling as they do, and hence why they might act in the way that they do. Sometimes these different aspects of empathy are called emotional empathy (the feeling of similar feelings) and cognitive empathy (the less emotionally involved sense of perspective-taking; Decety & Cowell, 2014; Decety & Ickes, 2011). Empathy, of course, does not have to be about someone else's suffering – it could be about their feelings of joy, achievement, confusion, delight, surprise, or any one of several other emotions and experiences.

We have a growing understanding of the neural basis of empathy and its fundamental importance for good social functioning (Singer & Lamm, 2009). Empathy is necessary but not sufficient for compassion. It is necessary in that one needs to be able to imagine what it might be like for the other person in order to identify that they might be suffering. It is insufficient in that it one might empathize with another person, identify that they may be suffering, but not be moved to act to alleviate or prevent their suffering. In fact, some people might even use empathy in order to increase the suffering of another – for instance, a bully, a torturer, a kidnapper, or an advertiser wishing to sell more beauty products by inducing feelings of shame over appearance. When the focus of empathy is on another's suffering or distress and this is combined with a desire to alleviate this suffering or distress, then this is sometimes referred to as empathic concern (Decety & Cowell, 2014).

Compassion can thus be thought of as an innate, multicomponent, and very human process (and motivation) which appears and unfolds in certain situations and circumstances. The unfolding of compassion is thought to take place via the stages illustrated in Figure 13.2 (Kanov, Maitlis, Worline, Dutton, & Lilius, 2004; Miller, 2007).

The first step in the unfolding of compassion is the noticing of suffering in another (or in oneself in the case of self-compassion). Then there is the arising of a feeling of "empathic concern" – a desire to act so as to alleviate the noticed suffering, and/or prevent future suffering. Then there is the taking of action to alleviate the suffering and/or prevent future suffering.

The unfolding of compassion in response to noticed suffering shows considerable individual variation, and this variation may be partly explained by various appraisal processes taking place rapidly, automatically, and outside of conscious awareness in the person noticing the suffering of another. In fact, these appraisal processes may also influence whether or not suffering is noticed in the first place. Variables the brain may assess in

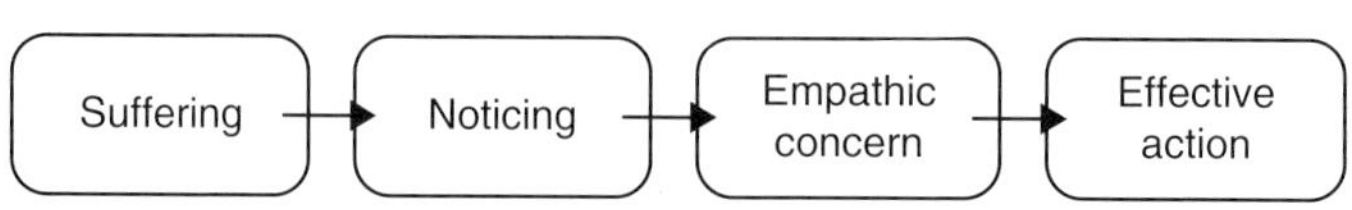

Figure 13.2 Compassion as a process which unfolds. *Source*: Author.

its calculation of whether or not to act may include: level of similarity with the person suffering; the extent to which the person suffering was complicit or caused his or her own suffering; whether or not the suffering is in some way "good" for him or her; whether or not the skills are present to help him or her; whether or not the distress involved in helping can be tolerated (Goetz et al., 2010; Loewenstein & Small, 2007).

The skills which may be required for compassionate responding are not just immediate helping skills (first aid, advocacy, swimming, counseling, pain relief, befriending, reassuring, etc.), but also management and planning skills, listening skills (to learn about what the suffering person may want for themselves, including whether they want help at all), and skills related to the ability to tolerate the distress which may arise in the face of being close to someone with, for example, disfiguring injuries or an unpleasant disease.

Compassionate action may also require courage – for instance when the responder needs to put herself or himself in harm's way, such as when trying to save someone from drowning in rough seas, or rescue them from an angry mob or from a high ledge. Intention is also key to compassion. The same behavior – such as caring for other human beings when they are suffering – can be performed for both compassionate and non-compassionate motivations. Caring for others, for example, can be done for pay, out of fear, or because a person is following a moral code. The caring would only be considered to be coming from a place of compassion if the responder felt moved by the noticed suffering – if there was empathic concern. When empathic concern is absent, so is compassion.

Skillful action is also essential for compassion. For instance, a person might notice a child getting into difficulty in a river, feel empathic concern, and jump into the river to try and save the child from drowning. But if that person could not swim, it might not be considered a wise compassionate action. Some people spend decades improving their skills at being able to respond to suffering with compassion – for instance, neurosurgeons, social workers, and cancer researchers.

Compassion evolved over millions of years from the mammalian reproductive strategies of caring for infants. Mammals differ from most reptiles in being orientated to stay close to their infants, to feed and provide for them – including providing them with protection and being sensitive to and responding to their distress calls. Thus our ability to be attentive to the needs and distress of others is evolutionarily very old and predates the emergence of humans as a distinct species. Humans have developed this capacity for compassion to a very high degree, not least because human infants are born prematurely compared to other animals (due to our large brain size), which makes human infants significantly more dependent on maternal and paternal care than the newborn infants of other animals (Dunsworth & Ecclestone, 2015). The underpinning neural and behavioral mechanisms for noticing and responding to actual or potential suffering in our own infants was then extended to kin, non-kin members of the tribe (Barrett, Dunbar, & Lycett, 2002; Gilbert, 1989; Preston, 2013), and eventually to strangers and non-humans (Geary, 2000; Gilbert, 1989, 2015; Loewenstein & Small, 2007; MacLean, 1985; Penner, Dovidio, Piliavin, & Schroeder, 2005; Preston, 2013).

Why does compassion at work matter?

Compassion is thus a very important contributor to prosocial behavior, which in turn is one of the main drivers of human evolution and human intelligence (Carter, 2014; Dunbar, 2007, 2010; Porges, 2007). Without this complex and innate motivational, interpersonal, and behavioral process it is unlikely humans would ever have been able to form the many cooperative alliances and enterprises we notice all around us – including teams and organizations. Viewed in this way, compassion can be considered to be at the very heart of organizations. It helps and enables groups of unrelated humans cooperate, flourish, and thrive.

Compassion is linked to a wide range of benefits for a wide range of people: the sufferer; the person acting compassionately; witnesses to compassionate responding; work units; organizations, and society more generally.

Compassion and self-compassion have been shown to be associated with increases in prosocial motivation and helping (Leiberg, Klimecki, & Singer, 2011; Weng et al., 2013), as well as being linked to a range of health and well-being outcomes (Arch et al., 2014; Barnard & Curry, 2011; Brach, 2003; Breines et al., 2015; Raque-Bogdan, Ericson, Jackson, Martin, & Bryan, 2011; Salzberg, 1997; Seppala, Rossomando, & Doty, 2013).

In a prosocial game experiment, Leiberg et al. (2011) showed that participants who had received short-term compassion training increased their helping behavior between pre-training and post-training measures ($p=.05$) whereas participants receiving short-term memory training did not ($p=.24$).

Weng et al. (2013) examined whether compassion could be systematically trained by testing whether short-term compassion training increased altruistic behavior outside the training context, and whether any individual differences in altruism were associated with induced changes in neural responses to suffering. Individuals were randomly allocated to either compassion training ($n=20$) or reappraisal training ($n=21$). Firstly, examining all participants together, they observed a positive correlation between trait levels of empathic concern and the level of money distributed ($r=.43$, $p<.001$). Secondly, after 2 weeks of training, the mean level of money distributed to a victim was higher in participants who received the compassion training compared to participants who received the reappraisal training ($t=2.09$, $p<.05$). They also found that such behavior was associated with altered activation in the parts of the brain associated with understanding suffering in others, executive and emotional control, and reward processing.

Breines et al. (2015) exposed 33 healthy volunteers to a standardized laboratory stressor on 2 separate days and found that scores on a self-compassion rating scale were a significant negative predictor of salivary-amylase levels (a marker of sympathetic nervous system activity) on both days (day 1, $p=.007$; day 2, $p=.03$).

Self-compassionate individuals may experience better psychological health than those lacking self-compassion, and experience lower levels of anxiety and depression (Neff, Hsieh, & Dejitterat, 2005), lower cortisol levels, increased heart-rate variability (Rockliff, Gilbert, McEwan, Lightman, & Glover, 2008), less rumination, less perfectionism, less fear of failure (Neff, 2003; Neff, Hsieh, & Dejitterat, 2005), less suppression of unwanted thoughts, and a greater willingness to accept negative emotions as valid and important (Leary, Tate, Adams, Allen, & Hancock, 2007; Neff, 2003).

Self-compassion is also associated with psychological strengths such as happiness, optimism, wisdom, curiosity and exploration, personal initiative, and emotional intelligence (Heffernan, Griffin, McNulty, & Fitzpatrick, 2010; Hollis-Walker & Colosimo, 2011; Neff, Rude, & Kirkpatrick, 2007). People with higher levels of self-compassion also seem better able to cope with such adversities as academic failure (Neff et al., 2005); divorce (Sbarra, Smith, & Mehl, 2012); childhood maltreatment (Vettese, Dyer, Li, & Wekerle, 2011); and chronic pain (Costa & Pinto-Gouveia, 2011), and may be more likely to exhibit healthier behavior patterns, such as: persistence with dietary changes (Adams & Leary, 2007); smoking reductions (Kelly, Zuroff, Foa, & Gilbert, 2009); seeking appropriate medical care (Terry & Leary, 2011); and physical activity (Magnus, Kowalski, & McHugh, 2010). They may also experience improved relationship functioning (Neff & Beretvas, 2012; Yarnell & Neff, 2012); empathetic concern for others; altruism; perspective taking; and forgiveness (Neff & Pommier, 2012). For these reasons, and others, compassion has become the focus for psychotherapeutic interventions with increasing evidence for their effectiveness (Gilbert, 2010; Hofmann, Grossman, & Hinton, 2011; Hofman, Sawyer, Witt, & Oh, 2010).

In two studies involving 222 undergraduates, Neff at al. (2005) explored the relationship between self-compassion, academic achievement goals, and coping with perceived academic failure. They found self-compassion negatively predicted fear of failure ($B = -.54$, $p < .001$) and positively predicted perceived competence ($B = .33$, $p < .001$), as well as being positively correlated with mastery goals, and negatively associated with performance-avoidance goals.

The person suffering (or at risk of suffering) may benefit from compassion in a number of ways, for instance by: being cared for; being protected; being listened to, heard, and understood; being reassured; being rescued; being helped to escape from a dangerous situation; being helped with task they are struggling with; being helped to reduce their risk of poor health or injury risk; being helped to find a new job; receiving material assistance in the form of goods or money, shelter, transportation, and so on. They may also benefit from the feeling of being supported, cared for, and protected by others. Compassion has also been associated with improved healing and recovery (Bento, 1994; Brody, 1992; Doka, 1989), as well as communicating dignity and feelings of being valued (Clarke, 1987; Dutton, Debebe, & Wrzesniewski, 2012; Frost, 2003).

The person acting compassionately can benefit from: taking effective action in line with their values of what matters in life; seeing the person suffering respond to their efforts; being appreciated by the other person; and being able to maintain or improve their self-concept as a caring and effective person. Acting with compassion is also something that people can enjoy. Of course they may not enjoy engaging with the suffering and might even feel bad and distressed themselves – hence the need for distress tolerance. But they may enjoy the consequences of being helpful, which can also provide meaning and job satisfaction (Graber & Mitcham, 2004; Kim & Flaskerud, 2007; Pearson, 2006; Youngson, 2008), a positive work identity (Moon, Hur, Ko, Kim, & Yoon, 2012), and perceptions of being a leader (Melwani, Mueller, & Overbeck, 2012).

Moon et al. (2012) studied 338 employees from 10 firms in South Korea, and used structural equation modeling and bootstrapping statistical methods to discover that positive work identity mediated the relationship between compassion and affective organizational commitment ($B = .45$, 95% confidence intervals .36, .58).

People witnessing compassion at work may experience feelings of pride about the way that work colleagues are behaving (Dutton et al., 2006) as well as the positive emotion of elevation which may in turn encourage people to act more for the common good (Haidt, 2002). Condon and DeSteno (2011) have also suggested that when people witness compassionate action, punitive action against transgressors unrelated to the compassion episode may be reduced.

Work units and organizations may benefit from the appearance and unfolding of compassion at work by noticing improved levels of positive emotions such as pride and gratitude (Dutton, Worline, Frost, & Lilius, 2006), improved health and well-being, improved collective commitment, lower turnover rates (Grant, Dutton, & Rosso, 2008; Lilius et al., 2008), improved levels of collaboration (Dutton et al., 2006), improved reputation, and an improved ability to attract and retain needed human resources. Compassionate acts may also reduce costs that arise due to injuries, ill-health, sickness absence, and damage.

Grant et al. (2008) used qualitative date from 40 interviews with employees of a Fortune 500 retail company, from 20 stores across the USA. The interviews focused on understanding employees' relationships with their employer, especially accounts of exchange when they gave something to or received something from the company, as well as accounts of organizational commitment. They found that contributing to the company's internal charitable Employee Support Foundation initiated a process of "prosocial sensemaking," leading to employees judging personal and company actions and identities as caring, and strengthening affective commitment to the employer.

Failure to act with compassion at work can also be very costly. Reducing staffing levels and pay levels without sufficient compassion may increase the probability of lawsuits (Lind, Greenberg, Scott, & Welchans, 2000), disengagement, and unwanted behavior (Greenberg, 1990). In the UK there have been incidents where poor levels of compassion have resulted in organizational failure and even breakup of the offending organization (Francis, 2013).

Can compassion be increased?

A number of approaches have been developed to help people experience an increased sensitivity to suffering in themselves and others, as well as an increase in their empathic concern and ability or readiness to act on their own or other people's suffering, including: Compassion-Focused Therapy and Compassionate Mind Training (Gilbert, 2009, 2010); Compassion Cultivation Training (Jazaieri et al., 2010); and Mindful Self-Compassion (MSC; Neff & Germer, 2012).

Neff and Germer (2012) evaluated the effectiveness of an 8-week Mindful Self-Compassion program designed to train people to be more self-compassionate, in which only one of the 8 sessions specifically focused on mindfulness. They found significant pre/post gains in self-compassion, mindfulness, and various well-being outcomes, with gains maintained at 6- and 12-month follow-up.

Jazaieri et al. (2013) examined the effects of a 9-week Compassion Cultivation course taught by trained instructors in a randomized control trial using a community sample of 100 adults assigned to either intervention ($n = 60$) or a waiting-list control group ($n = 40$). Within-group t-tests demonstrated significant improvement in all three domains of compassion – compassion for others (effect size .44, $p < .001$), receiving compassion (effect size .27, $p < .001$), and self-compassion (effect size .34, $p < .001$). They concluded that specific domains of compassion can be intentionally cultivated in a training program.

Klimecki, Leiberg, Ricard, and Singer (2014) investigated the functional neural plasticity underlying increases in empathy in training, and the impact of compassion on any negative affect associated with empathizing with someone in pain. They found empathy training increased activation in anterior insula and anterior midcingulate cortex regions of the brain, areas known to be associated with empathy for another person's pain. Subsequent compassion training attenuated this negative affect ($t = 3.04$, $p < 0.01$) and increased self-reports of positive emotions ($t = 4.25$, $p < 0.001$). They concluded that training in compassion can help overcome empathic distress and strengthen resilience.

Engen and Singer (2015) investigated the effects of an emotional regulation technique based on compassion meditation on experiential and neural affective responses to images of people in distress. They found the technique increased positive emotions relative to control groups, and also that compassion increased activation in brain regions previously associated with affiliative types of positive affect such as maternal love (Bartels & Zeki, 2004).

Rosenberg et al. (2015) also examined the impact of meditation training on emotional responses to scenes of human suffering. Sixty participants were randomly allocated to either meditation or waiting-list control. Training comprised daily practice in techniques to improve attention and compassionate regard toward others. After 12 weeks of training and upon viewing film scenes depicting human suffering, participants in the meditation group were more likely than controls to show facial displays of sadness ($B = 0.783$, $p < 0.001$), with fewer facial displays of rejection emotions such as anger, contempt, or disgust. Rosenberg et al. felt this result suggested that intensive mindfulness training encouraged enhanced empathic concern for, and reduced aversion to, suffering in others.

As previously discussed, compassion involves more than noticing and experiencing empathic concern – it also involves skillful action to alleviate current suffering and prevent future suffering. This skillful responding to noticed suffering can be improved with training – after all, that is why we educate, train, and assess people in various helping professions such as doctors, nurses, therapists, social workers, first-aiders, emergency relief workers, disaster response planners, medical researchers, fire-fighters, and so on.

What we know less about is whether or not we can increase compassion at work. We will return to this issue later.

What Factors Shape the Appearance and Unfolding of Compassion at Work?

Compassion at work arises in response to the noticing of suffering and the desire to prevent future suffering. Suffering in the workplace may result both from things happening in the workplace and things happening outside of the workplace which then result in the person suffering while at work. Workplace causes of suffering include, but are not limited to: work-related stress; redundancy; relocation; bullying; discrimination; accidents and injuries; occupational diseases; missing out on promotion; job insecurity; isolation; working unwanted hours; physical discomfort; verbal abuse from customers; assault (Ashford, Lee, & Bobko, 1989; Dutton et al., 2014; Driver, 2007; HSE, 2011; Lilius, Kanov, Dutton, Worline, & Maitlis, 2012). Non-workplace causes of suffering which may result in suffering at work include: financial worries; injury; ill-health; death and grieving; loss; relationship breakup; being a victim of crime; hunger; loneliness; natural and man-made disasters.

Suffering in the workplace is costly to individuals, work teams, and organizations. Individuals who suffer may find it hard to perform their work tasks to their usual standard and may need to take time away from work. Suffering can result in absence, staff turnover, disengagement, bad workplace reputation, and an organization finding it hard to attract and retain talent (EUOSH, 2014; Rosch 2001; Zaslow, 2002).

It should be noted, however, that there is significant variation in the extent to which people suffer when faced with the same situation or circumstance, as well as how they communicate their suffering (if at all), whether or not they want to be helped, and how they would like to be helped or cared for (Beck, 1970; Ellis, 1980; Lazarus & Folkman, 1984; Lin & Peterson, 1990; NHS England, 2015).

Since compassion is an innate human motivational system, compassion at work will be arising all the time in response to noticed suffering. Compassion at work has been studied: in a range of different workplaces and sectors – for example, banks, schools, airlines, call centers, healthcare organizations, care homes, universities, financial services, the criminal justice system, and so on; as it unfolds between two people, as well as more collectively in groups, departments and organizations; and using a range of different research methods and designs, including interviews, surveys, case studies, action learning, appreciative inquiry, and interventions. Researchers have examined: when, where, and how compassion arises and unfolds, and its impact on the principal actors and others; as well as which work-related factors might increase or inhibit the appearance and unfolding of compassion at work. Factors that have been examined include: values, beliefs, norms, practices, quality of relationships, aspects of leadership, and patterns of internal organization. (For a comprehensive review, see Dutton et al., 2014.)

Shared values

Shared values refer to what people in an organization believe is important. They shape "sensemaking" (Smircich 1983), the communication of what is significant, and what gets noticed (Dutton et al., 2006). They provide motivation for certain actions and behaviors (O'Reilly & Chatman, 1996). In a detailed case study describing and analyzing how compassion at work unfolded in response to a student house fire on a university campus, Dutton et al. (2006) suggested that the shared value of treating individuals as whole persons affected both the noticing of suffering, the sharing of the news about the students' experience, and the legitimization of their painful circumstances as something worthy of attention, responding, and resources.

In workplaces where such a shared value (of treating people as whole people) is less present, Bento (1994) argued that emotional suffering such as grief may be stifled and thus compassion at work less likely to flow and unfold. Similarly the rise of financial performance as a value together with the need to meet targets may result in a decline in caring and compassion in health care workplaces (Crawford, Gilbert, Gilbert, & Harvey, 2013; Maben, Latter, & Clark, 2007).

Shared beliefs

In the previously mentioned detailed case study of a university fire, Dutton et al. (2006), suggested that the shared belief that it was acceptable to "put one's humanity on display" made sharing the circumstances of the three students involved more likely, which in turn facilitated the speed and scope of compassionate responding. Similarly, Ashforth, Kreiner, and Fugate (2000) have suggested that when people at work share the belief that it is acceptable and desirable to know about a colleague's personal life outside of work and act on that knowledge, then people are more likely to express that they may be suffering at work, and colleagues in turn may be more likely to respond compassionately.

In contrast, some shared beliefs may reduce the likelihood of compassion unfolding at work. Martin et al. (2015) examined the relationship between competitive, hierarchical belief systems and empathy in business school students. They measured Social Dominance Orientation (Pratto, Sidanius, Stallworth, & Malle, 1994; Sidanius et al., 2012) – the belief in the world as a competitive, dog-eat-dog environment of winners and losers with the strong wish that one's in-group dominate and be superior to out-groups – and found that students having strong social dominance beliefs were more fearful of expressing compassion for others, of receiving compassion from others, and of expressing kindness and compassion toward themselves (self-compassion). Molinksy, Grant, and Margolis (2012), in a series of experiments, primed or activated beliefs about economic efficiency, rationality, and self-interest and found that this resulted in a dampening of the empathy people experienced along with heightened concerns about the unprofessionalism of expressing emotion in the workplace. Similarly, Darley and Batson (1973) manipulated beliefs about the urgency of a task (including, ironically, giving a short talk on the parable of the good Samaritan), and found people in more of a hurry were less likely to stop and help someone who appeared to be suffering.

Organizational norms

Organizational norms reflect expected behaviors – including the way things are done and what is not permitted (Schein, 1985). They may shape whether and how suffering at work is expressed as well as how colleagues are expected to respond. Goodrum (2008) commented that in a study of employees' grief reactions after losing a family member to murder, grief displayed at the wrong time, in the wrong place, or to the wrong person represented a norm violation and brought negative reactions from others. Grant and Patil (2012) explored how helping norms can emerge in workplaces to support caring and compassion, and examined how norms of self-interest (which may inhibit helping) can be changed by a single team member who consistently models, advocates, and enquires about helping behavior. They also explored how a person's ability to shape work unit norms is likely to be influenced by their status, similarity, work unit agreeableness, openness, and timing considerations.

Organizational practices

Organizational practices are repeated patternings of actions (Orlikowski, 1992). Three detailed case studies (Dutton et al., 2006; Lilius, Worline, Dutton, Kanov, & Maitlis, 2011; McClelland, 2012) have shown how various organizational practices seem to influence the appearance and unfolding of compassion in the workplace during both single incidents of suffering and across a range of episodes of suffering. For instance, selection practices such as selecting people on the basis of their relational skills may influence the extent to which a workplace contains people more likely to act compassionately toward noticed suffering. Research by McClelland (2012) showed how some hospitals used behavioral interviewing techniques and responses to prompts about compassion to select people they thought were more likely to behave compassionately at work. Once employed, assistance and support practices that help employees in need are both manifestations of compassion and may also help people behave more compassionately toward others at work. Grant et al. (2008) found that donating a dollar a week to a workplace fund for helping struggling colleagues also helped strengthen workers' identities as prosocial, caring people, and McClelland (2012) found that the existence of formal employee support practices in turn helped to foster compassion toward hospital patients. There are also "notification" practices which let key people know about the occurrence of harm, pain, and suffering at work. Such practices contribute to the appearance and unfolding of compassion in the workplace by strengthening the first step in the process, the noticing of suffering. Dutton, Frost, Worline, Lilius, and Kanov (2002) mention John Chambers, the CEO of Cisco, establishing an HR communication practice to inform him when anyone in the company experiences a severe loss, such as a serious illness or the death of a family member, so he may contact them personally. Another organizational practice likely to influence the prevalence of compassionate responding at work is recognizing and rewarding people for their helping and compassionate responding (McClelland, 2012).

Quality of relationships

Being an innate and interpersonal process (influenced by appraisal processes including similarity, see previously), levels of compassion at work will also be influenced by the structure and quality of people's relationships at work. When relationships at work are characterized by mutual respect and positive regard (Dutton & Heaphy, 2003), people will be more emotionally attached to each other (Kahn, 1998), which in turn will likely facilitate compassionate responding to incidents of suffering (Lilius et al., 2012). News of episodes of suffering is also more likely to spread when ties are strong (Dutton et al., 2006).

Leadership

The quality and style of leadership is another contextual factor likely to influence the emergence and unfolding of compassion at work. Leaders can notice suffering, draw attention it, shape its meaning, and model compassionate responding (Boyatzis & McKee, 2005; Dutton et al., 2002). Furthermore, leaders' formal power and status help them shape the previously mentioned contextual factors of shared values, shared beliefs, organizational practices, and the structure and quality of relationships – thus multiplying their personal impact on the amount of compassion at work. The fact that people often attribute leadership traits to people acting compassionately (Melwani et al., 2012) suggests leadership practices and compassion responding may work in harmony to deliver superior outcomes for multiple stakeholders – customers, employees, teams, managers, leaders, and the organization as a whole.

Patterns of Internal Organization

Much of the research into compassion at work has looked at how compassion arises and unfolds in dyads, but there has also been research and theory building into how compassion arises and unfolds at the group and organizational level, and how an organization's capacity for compassion might be improved over time. Dutton et al. (2006) explored how individual responses to suffering in organizations can become socially coordinated through a process they term "compassion organizing," which they define as "a collective response to a particular incident of human suffering that entails the coordination of individual compassion in a particular organizational context." They describe how the contextual enabling factors of attention, emotion, and trust interact with the social architecture, improvised structures, and processes of symbolic enrichment to shape and influence the generation, mobilization, and coordination of resources for compassionate responding, and hope their insights can help organizations wishing to build their capacity to act and respond compassionately.

Madden, Duchon, Madden, and Plowman (2012) explored how an organization's capacity for compassion can be seen as an emergent property, arising without formal direction. Using the lens of complexity science (Anderson, Mayer, Esienhardt, Carley, & Pettigrew, 1999; Axelrod & Cohen, 2000; Beeson & Davis, 2000; Stacey, 2005), they explored the conditions under which an emergent organizational compassionate response to a pain trigger is more likely to happen – including conditions of diversity, having interdependent roles, and the right social interactions. They also looked at how the process of compassionate responding may over time change the structure, culture, routines, roles, and scanning mechanisms within the organization and thereby improve the organization's capacity for compassionate responding in the future. They believe a tipping point may occur when an organization internalizes compassion as an organizational value and incorporates it into its structures and norms.

Evolutionary psychology and aspects of work climate

Organizations can be viewed as groups of social living primates, and ethologists have recognized two quite separate modes of social interaction in social primates: agonic and hedonic (Chance, 1977, 1998; Gilbert, 1989; Price, 1992). The agonic mode is based on threat, power, and anxiety; the hedonic mode is based on reassurance, safeness, play, and affiliation. When levels of threat, dominance, and urgency are high, these can act to suppress compassionate responding (Darley & Batson, 1973; Martin et al., 2015; Molinsky, Grant, & Margolis, 2012).

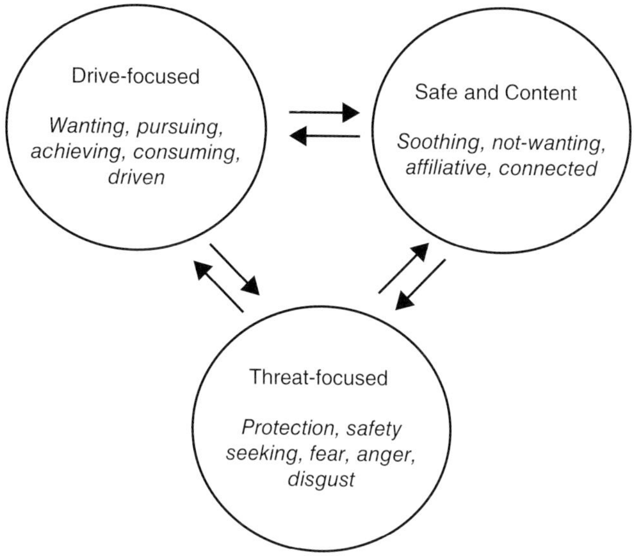

Figure 13.3 The three circles model of emotional regulation. *Source*: Adapted from Gilbert (2009).

These findings can be explained by the social neuroscience-informed three circles model of emotional regulation (Gilbert, 2009; see Figure 13.3). The threat-focused and the drive-focused motivational-emotional systems are both associated with sympathetic drive, while the safe, calm, affiliative, prosocial motivational-emotional system involves parasympathetic activation. All three motivational systems can be activated very rapidly and outside our awareness, and they shape what we pay attention to, how we feel, and how we behave (Gilbert, 2009; Kahneman, 2011; Lazarus & Folkman, 1984). They can also compete with each other for control of the organism.

Excessive activation of the threat and drive systems at work may inhibit activity in the more prosocial, caring system, and activation of threat based emotional states may interfere with our ability to mentalize, be reflective, and integrate information (Liotti & Gilbert, 2011). The excessive emphasis on financial performance with an associated culture of fear may also have contributed to the high-profile failure of care and compassion at the Mid Staffordshire Hospital NHS Foundation Trust (Francis, 2013).

This ability of high levels of threat in the workplace to undermine performance is the reason why Deming (1982) emphasized the importance to leaders and managers of "Driving out Fear" in his 14 points for managers.

In order to increase the appearance, flow, and benefits of compassion at work – including aspects of performance – organizations may wish to temper hierarchical and authoritarian management styles and cultures, and create feelings of safeness, connection, and affiliation in the workplace.

Leading with and for compassion at work

Since 1990 we have seen the emergence and exploration of several leadership models and frameworks emphasizing different aspects of leadership (Day, Fleenor, Atwater, Sturm, & McKee, 2014). They tend to agree that leadership involves bringing about change and improvement for and with others.

Table 13.1 Actions and rationale for increasing compassion at work.

Potential action	*Rationale and detail*
Creating the right conditions for compassion to appear and unfold at work.	Compassion is an innate human capacity and process which emerges when the conditions are right. Things managers and others can do to create the right conditions include: creating shared values around treating people as whole people at work; promoting shared beliefs about it being acceptable to be fully human at work; reducing authoritarian management styles, fear, and feelings of threat; selecting people on the basis of their relational skills; creating opportunities for people to act compassionately at work (e.g., volunteering, donating to workplace charitable funds, etc.); establishing notification systems and processes which can detect and communicate episodes of employee suffering; modeling compassionate responding; recognizing and rewarding compassion at work; building and maintaining positive workplace relationships characterized by mutual respect and positive regard; making changes to roles to make it easier for people to notice and respond to suffering; making policy changes to better protect people's health and well-being at work.
Providing opportunities for people to learn about and develop their skills around empathy and compassion – including self-compassion	Compassion is an innate human processes, but a growing body of evidence suggests both compassion and its constituent elements (e.g., empathy, empathic concern, distress tolerance, helping skills, etc.), can be increased with training.
Developing and implementing a strategy to bring about the desired change.	Piecemeal action can be helpful but large-scale culture change toward more compassion at work is more likely with a well-designed and well-executed strategy. Appelbaum, Habashy, Malo, and Shafiq (2012) reviewed 15 years of literature on change management for each of the steps outlined in Kotter's 1996 book *Leading Change* (Kotter, 1996) and found support for most of the steps, with no evidence found against this change-management model. They recommended its use as an implementation tool, in combination with other tools to adapt for contextual factors or obstacles. The eight steps they examined were: establish a sense of urgency about the need to achieve change; create a guiding coalition; develop a vision and strategy; communicate the change vision; empower broad-based action; generate short-term wins; consolidate gains and produce more change; and anchor the new approaches in the corporate culture. One complementary approach that has been used and evaluated as a tool for increasing levels of compassion at work is appreciative inquiry (Dewar, 2011; Youngson, 2014).

Source: Author.

Empathy and perspective taking – the ability to feel and think what others are or might be feeling and thinking – is thus a core element of leadership, sometimes subsumed under the topic of emotional intelligence. So too is empathic concern – the ability to be moved by other people's struggle, frustration, and suffering – together with taking firm action to bring about a reduction in other people's suffering and/or an improvement in their well-being and flourishing. Viewed like this, good leadership is very much based on compassion.

To the extent that compassion involves noticing, being moved by, and acting to reduce or prevent suffering, it helps to reduce levels of negative emotion in an organization. To the extent that receiving compassion from others, being compassionate toward others, and witnessing compassion can help people experience such states as commitment, achievement, friendship, job satisfaction, uplift, and positive workplace identity, it can be seen as increasing positive emotional states. In this way, compassion can be seen as helping to increase the ratio of positive to negative emotions and thus contributing to human thriving and flourishing at work (Fredrickson, 2013).

Leaders can therefore draw upon the emerging science of compassion and compassion at work in their efforts to being about improved levels of health, well-being, engagement, and performance for themselves, their teams, their employees, and their organizations. In acting compassionately, leaders also increase the extent to which they are judged as leaders by others (Melwani et al., 2012).

While we await high-quality, repeatable studies showing how compassion at work can be reliably increased, based on the current scientific knowledge outlined in this chapter and elsewhere (Dutton et al., 2014; Gilbert, 2005, 2009; Lilius et al., 2011; Madden et al., 2012; Ricard, 2013), people seeking to increase compassion at work may wish to consider the actions in Table 13.1.

Future Research

Scientific interest in the topic of compassion is growing. For instance, the result of a recent search of Medline using the search term "compassion" is illustrated in Figure 13.4.

Since around 2000 there have been growing calls for more research in this area (Frost, 1999). This chapter helps illustrate how far the field has come in that period.

The field is truly multidisciplinary, touching as it does upon leadership, management, organizational development, evolutionary biology, social neuroscience, economics, physical and mental health, and well-being. But it is still an emerging science.

Much of the research on compassion at work to date has been of a descriptive, exploratory and theory-building nature, using case studies, observational studies, interviews, surveys, action research, and a few experimental studies to better understand when and how compassion appears, the consequences of compassion at work for various stakeholders, and the contextual factors which encourage or inhibit its appearance and flow.

While continuing with observational and model-building work, for the field to progress it now needs to focus much more on experimental tests and interventional studies, preferably experimental design, exploring the impact of well-described and reproducible interventions on both compassion at work and the downstream effects of compassion at work on individuals, teams, work units, services, organizations, and local communities.

For instance, what is the impact, if any, of educating and training leaders, managers, and employees in compassion and compassion-related skills and competencies (including self-compassion) on dependent variables such as: engagement; well-being and thriving; positive emotions; prosocial behaviors; creativity; ethical behaviors; job performance; health outcomes; service quality; customer care; attendance, and so on. And what are the precise pathways and mechanisms through which any beneficial effects are realized?

Beyond the individual level, what is the impact of manipulating the previously mentioned contextual factors on compassion and related variables, for example, job roles;

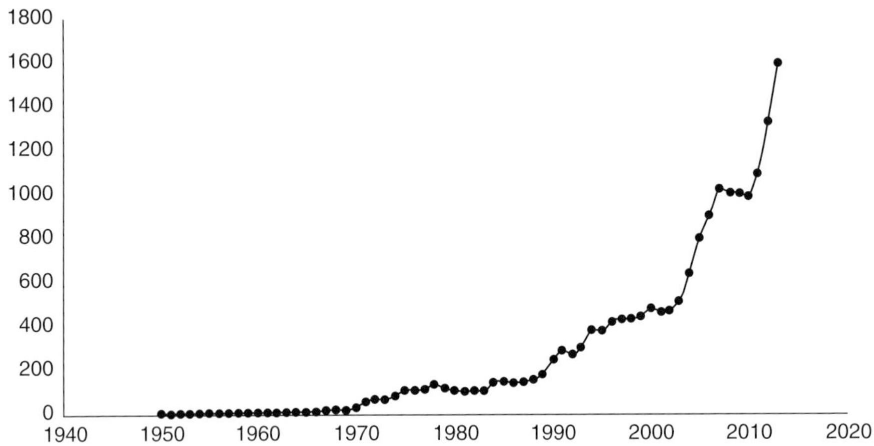

Figure 13.4 Medline citations for the term "compassion," 1950–2013. *Source*: Author.

volunteering opportunities; modeling of compassionate action by leaders and managers; stories celebrating compassionate actions at work; values clarification exercises and activities; compassionate coaching and mentoring activities; incorporating information about the importance of compassion at work in new employee induction and socialization processes; providing feedback to managers about compassion-related aspects of the work climate they have helped create – including feeling of being cared for, respected, affiliation, and safeness?

While single interventions to improve compassion at work do need to be developed and tested, future researchers should also develop and test multicomponent interventions that target several variables at once, using Medical Research Council (MRC) guidelines for evaluating the impact of complex interventions (MRC, 2006).

Other questions suggested by researchers in the field of compassion at work include: how a single compassion episode unfolds and affects the likelihood of compassion in the future; which types of pain trigger stimulate compassion at the individual level, and which stimulate more collective forms of responding; how sufferers communicate that they are in pain; how the personal context of the sufferer – for instance, individual differences and role characteristics – influences their experience of, or even desire for, compassion from another, and how they shape and respond to the compassionate acts of others; how national–cultural differences may influence compassion at work, including how suffering is expressed and responded to; the experience and perceptions of employees when compassion might have been expected but was not forthcoming; circumstances when compassionate responding is considered unwelcome and even harmful by the person suffering; how, during a single or a series of acts of compassion, the thoughts, feelings and behaviors of the sufferer, responder and any third parties interact; how the power of the focal actors affects the range and nature of compassionate actions; whether and how an organization's capacity for compassion affects future responses to suffering; whether or not organizations that have internalized compassion into their value and belief structures notice suffering more often, or notice different types of pain; whether or not, and how, the mission and structure of an organization might increase or decrease compassion at work; whether an internal focus on compassion at work translates to, or correlates with, corporate social responsibility, and/or a sensitivity to suffering outside of the organization; whether or not organizations that say they value compassion are less likely to harm external stakeholder groups; how an organization decides which internal and external pain triggers to respond to; when and how the presence of compassion can have negative repercussions; how compassion can be best institutionalized; the links between compassion at work and the neuroscience of emotions; and how insights from compassion at work might inform compassion at a more global or macro level – that is, how best to cultivate a more compassionate society

Conclusion

Compassion at work is an important field of study. It is a multi- and interdisciplinary topic, informed by evolutionary biology, physiology, neuroscience, and positive, organizational and performance psychology, as well as philosophy and economics.

Compassion itself is a complex, innate, motivational system or process built on the mammalian caring system and involving noticing suffering, being moved by the suffering, and acting so as to alleviate and prevent suffering. Research into both compassion and compassion at work is increasing, and we now have a growing understanding of the circumstances in which compassion appears and unfolds in the workplace, the benefits to different stakeholders, and how levels of compassion at work might be increased over time.

The research area now needs to progress from descriptive studies, theory building, and the development of plausible models to more rigorous and systematic model testing, single- and multicomponent interventional studies, and research into causal pathways and mechanisms. Research investigating compassion at work is thriving but still in its infancy. If we can discover and develop reliable, repeatable, and scalable methods for increasing the appearance, unfolding, and benefits of compassion at work, then we will have taken a big step forward in understanding how to increase levels of compassion in general society and the world.

Acknowledgment

I would like to thank Paul Gilbert, Chris Irons, Neil Clapton, and Jane Dutton for their helpful comments during the preparation of this chapter.

References

Adams, C. E., & Leary, M. R. (2007). Promoting self-compassionate attitudes toward eating among restrictive and guilty eaters. *Journal of Social and Clinical Psychology*, *26*, 1120–1144.

Anderson, P., Mayer, A., Esienhardt, K., Carley, K., & Pettigrew, A. (1999). Introduction to the Special Issue: Applications of complexity theory to organization science. *Organization Science*, *10*, 223–236.

Appelbaum, S. H., Habashy, S., Malo, J.-L., & Shafiq, H. (2012). Back to the future: Revisiting Kotter's 1996 change model. *Journal of Management Development*, *31*, 764–782.

Arch, J. J., Brown, K. W., Dean, D. J., Landy, L. N., Brown, K., & Laudenslager, M. L. (2014). Self-compassion training modulates alpha-amylase, heart rate variability, and subjective responses to social evaluative threat in women. *Psychoneuroendocrinology*, *42*, 49–58.

Appelbaum, S. H., Habashy, S., Malo, J.-L., & Shafiq, H. (2012). Back to the future: Revisiting Kotter's 1996 change model. *Journal of Management Development*, *31*, 764–782.

Ashford, S. J., Lee, C., & Bobko, P. (1989). Content, causes, and consequences of job insecurity: A theory-based measure and substantive test. *Academy of Management Journal*, *32*(4), 803–829.

Ashforth, B. E., Kreiner, G. E., & Fugate, M. (2000). All in a day's work: Boundaries and micro role transitions. *Academy of Management Review*, *25*, 472–491.

Axelrod, R., & Cohen, M. D. (2000). *Harnessing complexity: Organizational implications of a scientific frontier*. New York, NY: The Free Press.
Barnard, K. L., & Curry, J. F. (2011). Self-compassion: Conceptualizations, correlates, and interventions. *Review of General Psychology, 5*, 289–303.
Barrett, L., Dunbar, R., & Lycett, J. (2002). *Human evolutionary psychology*. London, UK: Palgrave.
Bartels, A. & Zeki, S. (2004). The neural correlates of maternal and romantic love. *Neuroimage, 21*, 1155–1166.
Beck, A. T. (1970). Cognitive therapy: Nature and relation to behaviour therapy. *Behaviour Therapy, 1*, 184–200.
Beeson, I., & Davis, C. (2000). Emergence and accomplishment in organizational change. *Journal of Organizational Change Management, 13*, 178–189.
Bento, R. F. (1994). When the show must go on: Disenfranchised grief in organizations. *Journal of Managerial Psychology, 9*(6), 35–44.
Boyatzis, R. E., & McKee, A. (2005). *Resonant leadership: Renewing yourself and connecting with others through mindfulness, hope, and compassion*. Boston, MA: Harvard Business School Press.
Brach, T. (2003). *Radical acceptance: Embracing your life with the heart of a Buddha*. New York, NY: Bantam.
Breines, J. G., McInnis, C., Kuras, Y., Thoma, M., Gianferante, D., Hanlin, L., ... Rohleder, N. (2015). Self-compassionate young adults show lower salivary alpha-amylase responses to repeated psychosocial stress. *Self and Identity, 14*, 390–402.
Brody, H. (1992). *The healer's power*. New Haven, CT: Yale University Press.
Carter, C. S. (2014). Oxytocin pathways and the evolution of human behavior. *Annual Review of Psychology, 65*, 17–39.
Chance, M. (1977). The infrastructure of mentality. In M. T. McGuire & L. A. Fairbanks (Eds.), *Ethological psychiatry* (pp. 180–195). New York, NY: Grune & Stratton.
Chance, M. (1998). *Social fabrics of the mind*. London, UK: Psychology Press.
Clarke, C. (1987). *Misery and company: Sympathy in everyday life*. Chicago, IL: University of Chicago Press.
Condon, P., & DeSteno, D. (2011). Compassion for one reduces punishment for another. *Journal of Experimental Social Psychology, 47*, 698–701.
Costa, J., & Pinto-Gouveia, J. (2011). Acceptance of pain, self-compassion and psychopathology: Using the chronic pain acceptance questionnaire to identify patients' subgroups. *Clinical Psychology and Psychotherapy, 18*, 292–302.
Crawford, P., Gilbert, P., Gilbert, J., & Harvey, K. (2013). The language of compassion in acute mental healthcare. *Qualitative Health Research, 23*, 719–727.
Darley, M., & Batson, D. (1973). "From Jerusalem to Jericho": A study of situational and dispositional variables in helping behavior. *Journal of Personality and Social Psychology, 27*, 100–108.
Day, D., Fleenor, J., Atwater, L., Sturm, R., & McKee, R. (2014). Advances in leader and leadership development: A review of 25 years of research and theory. *The Leadership Quarterly, 25*, 63–82.
Decety, J., & Cowell, J. M. (2014). Friends or foes: Is empathy necessary for moral behavior? *Perspectives on Psychological Science, 9*, 525–537.
Decety, J., & Ickes, W. (2011). *The social neuroscience of empathy*. Cambridge, MA: MIT Press.
Deming, W. E. (1982). *Out of the crisis*. Cambridge, MA: MIT Press.
Dewar, B. J. (2011). Caring about caring: An *appreciative inquiry about compassionate relationship-centred care*. PhD thesis, Edinburgh Napier Univesity, Scotland.
Doka, K. (1989). Disenfranchised grief. In K. Doka (Ed.), *Disenfranchised grief: Recognising hidden sorrow* (pp. 3–11). New York, NY: Lexington Books.
Driver, M. (2007). Meaning and suffering in organizations. *Journal of Organizational Change Management, 20*, 611–632.
Dunbar, R. I. M. (2007). Mind the bonding gap: Or why humans aren't just great apes. *Proceedings of the British Academy, 154*, 403–433.
Dunbar, R. I. M. (2010). The social role of touch in humans and primates: Behavioral function and neurobiological mechanisms. *Neuroscience and Biobehavioral Reviews, 34*, 260–268.
Dunsworth, H., & Ecclestone, L. (2015). The evolution of difficult childbirth and helpless hominin infants. *Annual Review of. Anthropology, 44*, 55–69.

Dutton, J., Debebe, G., & Wrzesniewski, A. (2012). Being valued and devalued at work: A social valuing perspective. In A. Beth, B. A. Bechky, & K. D. Elsbach (Eds.), *Qualititative organisational research: Best papers from the Davis Conference on Qualitative Research* (Vol. *3*). Greenwich, CT: Information Age Publishing.
Dutton, J. E., Frost, P. J., Worline, M. C., Lilius, J. M., & Kanov, J. M. (2002). Leading in times of trauma. *Harvard Business Review*, *80*(1), 54–61.
Dutton, J. E., & Heaphy, E. D. (2003). The power of high-quality connections. In K. S. Cameron, J. E. Dutton, & R. E. Quinn (Eds.), *Positive organizational scholarship: Foundations of a new discipline* (pp. 263–78). San Francisco, CA: Berrett-Koehler.
Dutton, J. E., Workman, K. M., & Hardin, A. E. (2014). Compassion at work. *Annual Review of Organizational Psychology and Organizational Behavior*, *1*, 277–304.
Dutton, J. E., Worline, M. C., Frost, P. J., & Lilius, J. M. (2006). Explaining compassion organizing. *Administrative Science Quarterly*, *51*, 59–96.
Ellis, A. (1980). Rational-emotive therapy and cognitive behaviour therapy: Similarities and differences. *Cognitive Therapy and Research*, *4*, 325–340.
Engen, H. G., & Singer, T. (2015). Compassion-based emotion regulation up-regulates experienced positive affect and associated neural networks. *Social, Cognitive and Affective Neuroscience*, *10*(9), 1291–1301.
EUOSH (European Agency for Safety and Health at Work) (2014). *Calculating the cost of work related stress and psychosocial risks* (European Risk Observatory Literature Review). Retrieved from https://osha.europa.eu/en/publications/literature_reviews/calculating-the-cost-of-work-related-stress-and-psychosocial-risks/view
Francis, R. (2013). Mid Staffordshire NHS Foundation Trust Public Inquiry. Retrieved from http://webarchive.nationalarchives.gov.uk/20150407084003/http://www.midstaffspublicinquiry.com/report
Fredrickson, B. L. (2013). Updated thinking on positivity ratios. *American Psychologist*, *68*, 814–822.
Frost, P. J. (1999). Why compassion counts! *Journal of Management Inquiry*, *8*(2), 127–133.
Frost, P. J. (2003). *Toxic emotions at work: How compassionate managers handle pain and conflict.* Boston, MA: Harvard Business School Press.
Geary, D. C. (2000). Evolution and proximate expression of human parental investment. *Psychological Bulletin*, *126*, 55–77.
Germer, C. K., & Siegel, R. D. (2012). *Wisdom and compassion in psychotherapy.* New York, NY: Guilford.
Gilbert, P. (1989). Human nature and suffering. Hove, UK. Erlbaum.
Gilbert, P. (2005). Compassion and cruelty: A biopsychosocial approach. In P. Gilbert (Ed.), *Compassion: Conceptualisations, research and use in psychotherapy* (pp. 3–74). London, UK: Routledge.
Gilbert, P. (2009). The compassionate mind: A new approach to the challenge of life. London, UK: Constable & Robinson.
Gilbert, P. (2010). Compassion focused therapy: The CBT distinctive features series. London, UK: Routledge
Gilbert, P. (2015). The evolution and social dynamics of compassion. *Social and Personality Psychology Compass*,*9*, 1–16.
Gilbert, P., & Choden. (2013). *Mindful compassion*. London,UK: Constable & Robinson.
Goetz, J. E., Keltner, D., & Simon-Thomas, E. (2010). Compassion: An evolutionary analysis and empirical review. *Psychological Bulletin*, *136*, 351–374.
Goodrum, S. (2008). When the management of grief becomes everyday life: The aftermath of murder. *Symbolic Interaction*, *31*, 420–441.
Graber, D. R., & Mitcham, M. D. (2004). Compassionate clinicians: Take patient care beyond the ordinary. *Holistic Nursing Practice*, *18*, 87–94.
Grant, A. M., Dutton, J. E., & Rosso, B. D. (2008). Giving commitment: Employee support programs and the prosocial sensemaking process. *Academy of Management Journal*, *51*, 898–918.
Grant, A. M., & Patil, S. V. (2012). Challenging the norm of self-interest: Minority influence and transitions to helping norms in work units. *Academy of Management Review*, *37*, 547–568.

Greenberg, J. (1990). Employee theft as a reaction to underpayment inequity: The hidden cost of pay cuts. *Journal of Applied Psychology, 75*, 561–568.

Haidt, J. (2002). The moral emotions. In R. J. Davidson, K. R. Scherer, & H. H. Goldsmith (Eds.), *Handbook of affective sciences* (pp. 852–870). New York, NY: Oxford University Press.

Heffernan, M., Griffin, M., McNulty, S., & Fitzpatrick, J. J. (2010). Self-compassion and emotional intelligence in nurses. *International Journal of Nursing Practice, 16*, 366–373.

Hofmann, S. G., Grossman, P., & Hinton D. E. (2011). Loving-kindness and compassion meditation: Potential for psychological intervention. *Clinical Psychology Review, 13*, 1126–1132.

Hofmann, S. G., Sawyer, A. T., Witt, A. A., & Oh, D. (2010). The effect of mindfulness-based therapy on anxiety and depression: A meta-analytic review. *Journal of Consulting and Clinical Psychology, 78*, 169–183.

Hollis-Walker, L., & Colosimo, K. (2011). Mindfulness, self-compassion, and happiness in non-meditators: A theoretical and empirical examination. *Personality and Individual Differences, 50*, 222–227.

HSE (Health and Safety Executive) (2011). *Work-related stress*. Topic Inspection Pack, Human Factors, Ergonomics & Psychology Unit. Retrieved from www.hse.gov.uk/foi/internalops/fod/inspect/stress.pdf

Jazaieri, H., Jinpa, G. T., McGonigal, K., Rosenberg, E. L., Finkelstein, J., Simon-Thomas, E., … Jinpa, T. (2010). *Compassion cultivation training (CCT): Instructor's manual*. Unpublished manuscript, Stanford, CA.

Jazaieri, H., Jinpa, G. T., McGonigal, K., Rosenberg, E., Finkelstein, J., Simon-Thomas, E., … Goldin, P. R. (2013). Enhancing compassion: A randomized controlled trial of a compassion cultivation training program. *Journal of Happiness Studies, 14*, 1113–1126.

Kahn, W. A. (1998). Relational systems at work. *Research in Organizational Behavior, 20*, 39–76.

Kahneman, D. (2011). *Thinking, fast and slow*. London, UK: Penguin.

Kanov, J., Maitlis, M., Worline, J., Dutton, P., & Lilius, J. (2004). Compassion in organisational life. *American Behavioural Scientist, 47*, 808–827.

Kelly, A. C., Zuroff, D. C., Foa, C. L., & Gilbert, P. (2009). Who benefits from training in self-compassionate self-regulation? A study of smoking reduction. *Journal of Social and Clinical Psychology, 29*, 727–755.

Kim. S., & Flaskerud, J. H. (2007). Cultivating compassion across cultures. *Issues in Mental Health Nursing, 28*, 931–934.

Klimecki, O. M., Leiberg, S., Ricard, M., & Singer, T. (2014). Differential pattern of functional brain plasticity after compassion and empathy training. *Social Cognitive and Affective Neuroscience, 9*(6), 873–879.

Kotter, P. (1996). *Leading change*. Cambridge, MA: Harvard Business School Press.

Lazarus, & Folkman,(1984). *Stress, appraisal and coping*. Dordrecht, the Netherlands: Springer.

Leary, M. R., Tate, E. B., Adams, C. E., Allen, A. B., & Hancock, J. (2007). Self-compassion and reactions to unpleasant self-relevant events: The implications of treating oneself kindly. *Journal of Personality and Social Psychology, 92*, 887–904.

Leiberg, S., Klimecki, O., & Singer, T. (2011). Short-term compassion training increases prosocial behavior in a newly developed prosocial game. *PLoS ONE, 6*(3): e17798.

Lilius, J. M., Kanov, J. M., Dutton, J. E., Worline, M. C., & Maitlis, S. (2012). Compassion revealed: What we know about compassion at work (and where we still need to know more). In K. S. Cameron & G. Spreitzer (Eds.), *The handbook of positive organizational scholarship* (pp. 273–287). New York, NY: Oxford University Press.

Lilius, J. M., Worline, M. C., Dutton, J. E., Kanov, J. M., & Maitlis, S. (2011). Understanding compassion capability. *Human Relations, 64*, 873–899.

Lilius, J. M., Worline, M. C., Maitlis, S., Kanov, J. M., Dutton, J. E., & Frost, P. J. (2008). The contours and consequences of compassion at work. *Journal of Organizational Behavior, 29*, 193–218.

Lin, E., & Peterson, C. (1990). Pessimistic explanatory style and response to illness. *Behaviour Research and Therapy*, 28, 243–248.

Lind, E. A., Greenberg, J., Scott, K. S., & Welchans, T. D. (2000). The winding road from employee to complainant: Situational and psychological determinants of wrongful termination claims. *Administrative Science Quarterly*, *45*, 557–590.

Liotti, G., & Gilbert, P. (2011). Mentalizing, motivation and social mentalities: Theoretical considerations and implications for psychotherapy. *Psychology and Psychotherapy: Theory, Research and Practice*, *84*, 9–25.

Loewenstein, G., & Small, D. A. (2007). The scarecrow and the tin man: The vicissitudes of human sympathy and caring. *Review of General Psychology*, *11*, 112–126.

Maben, J., Latter., S., & Clark, J. M. (2007). The sustainability of ideals, values and the nursing mandate: Evidence from a longitudinal qualitative study. *Nursing Inquiry*, *14*, 99–113.

MacLean, P. (1985). Brain evolution relating to family, play and the separation call. *Archives of General Psychiatry*, *42*, 405–417.

Madden, L. T., Duchon, D., Madden, T. M., & Plowman, D. A. (2012). Emergent organizational capacity for compassion. *Academy of Management Review*, *37*, 689–708.

Magnus, C. M. R., Kowalski, K. C., & McHugh, T. L. F. (2010). The role of self-compassion in women's self-determined motives to exercise and exercise-related outcomes. *Self and Identity*, *9*, 363–382.

Martin, D., Seppala, E., Heineberg, Y., Rossomando, T., Doty, J., Zimbardo, P., … Zhou, Y. Y. (2015). Multiple facets of compassion: The impact of social dominance orientation and economic systems justification. *Journal of Business Ethics*, *129*, 237–249.

McClelland, L. E. (2012). *From compassion to satisfaction: Examining the relationship between routines that facilitate compassion and quality of service*. PhD thesis, Emory University, Atlanta, USA.

Melwani, S., Mueller, J. S., & Overbeck, J. R. (2012). Looking down: The influence of contempt and compassion on emergent leadership categorizations. *Journal of Applied Psychology*, *97*, 1171–1185.

Miller, K. (2007). Compassionate communication in the workplace: Exploring processes of noticing, connecting and responding. *Journal of Applied Communication Research*, *35*, 223–245.

Molinsky, A., Grant, A., & Margolis, J. (2012). The bedside manner of homo economicus: How and why priming and economic schema reduces compassion. *Organizational Behavior and Human Decision Processes*, *119*, 27–37.

Moon, T.-W., Hur, W.-M., Ko, S.-H., Kim, J-.W., & Yoon, S.-W. (2012). Positive work-related identity as a mediator of the relationship between compassion at work and employee outcomes. *Human Factors and Ergonomics in Manufacturing & Service Industries*, *26*(1), 84–94.

MRC (Medican Research Council) (2006). *Developing and evaluating complex interventions: New guidance*. Retrieved from www.mrc.ac.uk/complexinterventionsguidance

Neff, K. D. (2003). The development and validation of a scale to measure self-compassion. *Self and Identity*, *2*, 223–250.

Neff, K. D., & Beretvas, S. N. (2012). The role of self-compassion in romantic relationships. *Self and Identity*, *12*, 79–98

Neff, K. D., & Germer, C. (2012). A pilot study and randomised controlled trial of the Mindful Self-Compassion Programme. *Journal of Clinical Psychology*, *69*, 28–44.

Neff, K. D., Hsieh, Y., & Dejitterat, K. (2005). Self-compassion, achievement goals and coping with academic failure. *Self and Identity*, *4*, 263–287.

Neff, K. D., & Pommier, E. (2012). The relationship between self-compassion and other-focused concern among college undergraduates, community adults, and practicing meditators. *Self and Identity*, *12*, 160–176.

Neff, K. D., Rude, S. S., & Kirkpatrick, K. (2007). An examination of self-compassion in relation to positive psychological functioning and personality traits. *Journal of Research in Personality*, *41*, 908–916.

NHS England (2015). *Personalised care and support planning handbook*. Retrieved from https://www.england.nhs.uk/wp-content/uploads/2016/04/core-info-care-support-planning-1.pdf

O'Reilly, C. A., & Chatman, J. A. (1996). Culture as social control: Corporations, cults, and commitment. *Research in Organizational Behavior*, *18*, 157–200.

Orlikowski, W. J. (1992). The duality of technology: Rethinking the concept of technology in organizations. *Organization Science*, *3*, 398–427.

Pearson, A. (2006). Powerful caring. *Nursing Standard, 20*(48), 20–22.

Penner, L. A., Dovidio, J. F., Piliavin, J. A., & Schroeder, D. A. (2005). Prosocial behavior: Multilevel perspectives. *Annual Review of Psychology, 56*, 1–28.

Peterson, C., & Seligman, M. E. P. (2004). *Character strengths and virtues: A handbook and classification*. Oxford, UK: Oxford University Press.

Porges, S. W. (2007). The polyvagal perspective. *Biological Psychology, 74*, 116–143.

Pratto, F., Sidanius, J., Stallworth, L. M., & Malle, B. F. (1994). Social dominance orientation: A personality variable predicting social and political attitudes. *Journal of Personality and Social Psychology, 67*, 741–763.

Preston, S. D. (2013). The origins of altruism in offspring care. *Psychological Bulletin, 139*, 1305–1341.

Price, J. (1992). The agonic and hedonic modes: Definition, usage, and the promotion of mental health. *World Future, 35*, 87–113.

Rague-Bogdan, T., Ericson, S., Jackson, J., Martin, H., & Bryan, A. (2011). Attachment and mental and physical health: Self-compassion and mattering as mediators. *Journal of Counseling Psychology, 58*, 272–278.

Ricard, M. (2015). *Altruism: The power of compassion to change yourself and the world*. London, UK: Atlantic Books.

Rockliff, H., Gilbert, P., McEwan, K., Lightman, S., & Glover, D. (2008). A pilot exploration of heart rate variability and salivary cortisol responses to compassion-focussed imagery. *Clinical Neuropsychiatry, 5*(3), 132–139.

Rosch, P. (2001). The quandary of job stress compensation. *Health Stress, 3*, 1–4.

Rosenberg, E. L., Zanesco, A. P., King, B. G., Aichele, S. R., Jacobs, T. L., Bridwell, D. A., ... Saron, C. D. (2015). Intensive meditation training influences emotional responses to suffering. *Emotion, 15*, 775–790.

Salzberg, S. (1997). *Lovingkindness: The revolutionary art of happiness*. Boston, MA: Shambala.

Sbarra, D. A., Smith, H. L., & Mehl, M. R. (2012). When leaving your Ex, love yourself: Observational ratings of self-compassion predict the course of emotional recovery following marital separation. *Psychological Science, 23*, 261–269.

Schein, E. H. (1985). *Organizational culture and leadership*. San Francisco, CA: Jossey-Bass.

Seppela, E., Rossomando, T., & Doty, R. (2013). Social connection and compassion: Important predictors of health and well-being. *Social Research, 80*(2), 411–430.

Sidanius, J., Kteily, N., Sheehy-Skeffington, J., Ho, A. K., Sibley, C., & Duriez, B. (2012). You're inferior and not worth our concern: The interface between empathy and social dominance orientation. *Journal of Personality, 81*, 313–323.

Singer, T., & Lamm, C. (2009). The social neuroscience of empathy. *Annals of the New York Academy of Sciences, 1156*, 81–96.

Smircich, L. (1983). Concepts of culture and organizational analysis. *Administrative Science Quarterly, 28*, 339–358.

Stacey, R. D. (2005). *Experiencing emergence in organisations: Local interactions and the emergence of global pattern*. New York, NY: Routledge.

Terry, M. L., & Leary, M. R. (2011). Self-compassion, self-regulation, and health. *Self and Identity, 10*, 352–362.

Vettese, L. C., Dyer, C. E., Li, W. L., & Wekerle, C. (2011). Does self-compassion mitigate the association between childhood maltreatment and later emotional regulation difficulties? *International Journal of Mental Health and Addiction, 9*, 480–491.

Weng, H., Fox, A., Shackman, A., Stodola, S., Caldwell, J., Olson, G., ... Davidson, R. (2013). Compassion alters altruism and neural responses to suffering. *Psychological Science, 24*,1171–1180.

Yarnell, M. & Neff, (2012). Self-compassion, interpersonal conflict resolutions and wellbeing. *Self and Identity, 12*, 146–159.

Youngson, R. (2008) *Compassion in healthcare: The missing dimension of healthcare reform?* London, UK: NHS Confederation.

Youngson, R. (2014). Re-inspiring compassionate caring: the reawakening purpose workshop. *Journal of Compassionate Heath Care, 1*, 1.

Zaslow, J. (2002, November 20). Putting a price tag on grief. *Wall Street Journal*, section D, 1.

Part II

Organizational Approaches to Positive Psychology at Work

14

Good Work

The Meaning-Centered Approach (MCA)

Paul T. P. Wong, Itai Ivtzan, and Tim Lomas

Introduction

This chapter focuses on the notion of good work from a meaning-centered approach (MCA). MCA views good work at three levels: the individual, the organization, and society. At the individual level, good work means that employees are empowered through intrinsic motivation to make the optimal use of their strengths, resulting in a high level of job satisfaction and productivity. At the organizational level, a virtuous servant style of leadership (Wong, 2004) unleashes the full potential of employees and provides a positive culture (Wong, 2005). At the societal level, good organizations assume their social responsibilities to contribute to the greater good beyond the bottom line. Thus, a good organization is not only a good place to work for, but also an agent of positive social change.

MCA, which is informed by existential positive psychology (EPP; Wong, 2010), is an example of an emergent branch of scholarship labeled as PP "2.0" (Wong, 2011), also referred to as the "second wave" of positive psychology (Ivtzan, Lomas, Hefferon, & Worth, 2015; Lomas & Ivtzan, 2015). When positive psychology (PP) first emerged in 1998, in what we could refer to as its "first wave" incarnation, its stated prerogative was to explore "positive" aspects of human functioning (Seligman & Csikszentmihalyi, 2000). This was in apparent contrast to "psychology as usual," which was characterized as taking a deficit-based approach to human beings. However, as valuable as this emphasis on positive functioning was, critics suggested that this focus on positivity could potentially be problematic, in various ways. For instance, positioning ostensibly positive qualities (e.g., optimism) as desirable, and conversely other seemingly negative qualities (e.g., pessimism) as undesirable, means that people experiencing the latter quality might feel additionally burdened or even chastised for doing so (see, e.g., Held, 2002, 2004). Moreover, focusing on "positive" aspects of functioning has paradoxically meant that PP has tended to insufficiently engage with the "darker" side of humanity (e.g., negative emotions or humankind's potential for causing harm). In recognition of this point, PP 2.0 takes a more

The Wiley Blackwell Handbook of the Psychology of Positivity and Strengths-Based Approaches at Work, First Edition. Edited by Lindsay G. Oades, Michael F. Steger, Antonella Delle Fave, and Jonathan Passmore.

dialectical approach, recognizing that optimal functioning comes from the dynamic interplay between positive and negative factors.

At the heart of PP 2.0 is a focus on the centrality of meaning to human flourishing (Wong, 2011; Wong, 2012a). This is especially the case with MCA, which originates from the application of Frankl's (1985) logotherapy paradigm to organizations. MCA has several advantages over alternative models, such as positivity, character strengths, or virtuousness, because it is capable of incorporating all these major themes of PP without the problems associated with the first wave of PP. Consistent with existential philosophy, MCA embraces human beings in their entirety, with their potentials for both goodness and "evil." (While evil could be regarded as a somewhat metaphysically loaded term [Allison, 2002], it is used here to vividly capture the range of hateful and destructive acts that people are capable of undertaking.) In practice, MCA allows individuals greater openness and readiness for positive change within the organization (Burger, Crous, & Roodt, 2008).

A Critical Review of PP and Its Approach to Organizations

The first wave of PP could be characterized as the scientific study of positive emotions, positive traits, and positive institutions (Seligman & Csikszentmilahlyi, 2000). Applied PP in particular is concerned with the applications of PP research findings to enable people to flourish at home, at work, and in school (Donaldson, 2011). As this first wave unfolded, a considerable literature emerged highlighting the beneficial effects of PP variables such as positive affect, psychological capital, signature strengths, flow and engagement, and meaning and purpose (see, e.g., Bolier et al., 2013; Sin & Lyubomirsky, 2009).

However, while PP has attracted enormous interest and enthusiasm, it has not been without its critics. For instance, Wong (2007a, 2007b) argued that the field's emphasis on "happiness-oriented" outcomes like subjective well-being rendered PP guilty of encouraging people to pursue a futile hedonic quest instead of helping people to seek a meaning-orientation that would enable them to find a more "authentic" and socially responsible form of happiness. Similarly, scholars such as Held (2002, 2004) critiqued PP's role in helping create and sustain a busy "happiness industry," involving government and big business selling people happiness and well-being. More damagingly, it has even been suggested empirically that the pursuit of happiness may not always be good for us (e.g., Gruber, Mauss, & Tamir, 2011; Mauss, Tamir, Anderson, & Savino, 2011); for instance, Mauss et al. found that people who valued happiness more strongly actually experienced lower levels of happiness under conditions of low life stress than people who valued happiness less strongly. Finally, scholars such as McNulty and Fincham (2011) have argued that if PP only focuses on ostensibly positive qualities and topics, this is liable to lead to a truncated and incomplete understanding of well-being (e.g., one that fails to appreciate the potential beneficial role of ostensibly negative emotions and experiences).

As a result of these types of criticisms, scholars within PP are more alert to the risks of simply focusing on the "positive," and are engaging more critically with the very notions of positive and negative. With these developments, the field could be said to be moving into a "second wave" phase, labeled here as PP 2.0. In this, while there is still a focus on topics such as happiness, there is also a recognition of the potential challenges that are involved in such a pursuit. Moreover, from a dialectical perspective, it is seen that these challenges may actually be an integral part of eudaimonic happiness, where negative emotions, for example, could be part of the experience of happiness. While this might sound paradoxical (how could happiness and negative emotions go hand in hand?), if we shift from the understanding of happiness as simply a positive emotion, into the more complex understanding of it as a fulfilling way of being, negative emotions become an important dimension of happiness. When embraced and accepted, negative emotions can be a powerful catalyst to positive change in one's life and can lead to deeper feeling of meaning and authenticity.

From the perspective of PP 2.0, Wong (2012a) has proposed the "deep-and-wide" hypothesis to highlight the positive benefits of negative emotions, thus complementing Fredrickson's (2001) broaden-and-build theory of positive emotions. According to Wong (1995, 2006), frustration and other negative experiences can motivate us to dig deeper into our inner resources and expand our horizons for new possibilities. For example, research on possible benefits of negative affect show improved memory performance, reduced judgmental errors, improved motivation, and increased effectiveness of interpersonal strategies (Forgas, 2013; Storbeck & Clore, 2005). There are indeed numerous empirical findings based on the dialectical notion of flourishing arising from the integration and transcendence of negative and positive. From Wong's own research alone, these include the benefits of death acceptance (Wong & Tomer, 2011), transformative coping (Wong, Reker, & Peacock, 2006), and tragic optimism (Wong, 2009). Similarly, Cozzolino's (2006) research on death awareness and acceptance shows that when individuals are exposed to the personal realization of their death, their reaction tends to be intrinsic and growth orientated. These studies indicate that direct experience with death enhances intrinsic life changes, such as renewed appreciation for life, concern for others, and higher levels of meaning.

Perhaps because first wave PP has tended toward a rather binary and restricted notion of happiness (one centered around ostensibly "positive" topics, as explored above), applications of PP to the workplace have been similarly limited. For instance, Ko and Donaldson (2011) conducted an extensive review of the literature in PP in relation to work, and found that this was dominated by such positive topics as organizational virtuousness, psychological capital, flow, positive emotions, and work engagement. While these are of course valuable and important areas of enquiry, it has meant that in the first 12 years of research on positive organizational psychology, the key topic of meaning has been largely ignored, in spite of the fact that meaning at work has been shown in research to increase job satisfaction (Kamdron, 2005), well-being (Arnold, Turner, Barling, Kelloway, & McKee, 2007), and the value employees place on their work (Nord, Brief, Atieh, & Doherty, 1990). Therefore, the MCA seeks to redress this balance by focusing on the importance of meaning at work.

An Existential Paradigm Shift

According to Kuhn (1962), a paradigm shift occurs when there are enough problems that question the basic assumptions of a dominant conceptual framework. The first wave of PP represented a paradigm shift from the deficit model of "psychology as usual," with its preoccupation with disorder and dysfunction, to a focus on happiness and strengths, driven by a recognition that the deficit model failed to adequately cover human potentialities (Seligman & Csikszentmihalyi, 2000). Similarly, the more recent shift to a second wave paradigm has been prompted by the recognition that "first wave" PP tended to overlook the "dialectical" nature of flourishing, including a focus on inescapable existential aspects of human existence and the central role of meaning in surviving and thriving. It acknowledges that the world is full of hardships and yet full of meaning potentials (Frankl, 1985).

When we discover the hidden opportunities for meaningful engagement and act with responsibility and ethics, we will find our lives more fulfilling.

The important insight of PP 2.0 – and indeed of EPP (Wong, 2010), as PP 2.0 is thoroughly existential in character – is that suffering is both inevitable and potentially beneficial; it is through engaging with painful situations that we dig deeper into ourselves and become open to new possibilities which will enrich our lives, as per Wong's (2012b) "deep-and-wide" hypothesis. PP 2.0 also addresses the fundamental paradoxes and dilemmas of human existence. For instance, here is one of the fundamental paradoxes of human nature: Whenever we draw attention to ourselves, be it making ourselves happier or more virtuous, we end up defeating our own purpose. Whenever we direct our attention to others, be it helping others or contributing to society, we end up both happy and virtuous. This paradox is rooted in human nature, just as Viktor Frankl (1988) has said: "Self-transcendence is the essence of existence. Being human is directed to something other than itself" (p. 50).

There are encouraging signs that positive organizational psychology is beginning to take on board this existential perspective. For example, the latest publication of *Positive Psychology in Practice* edited by Joseph (2015) includes Bretton's (2015) chapter on the existential dimensions of PP, and Pauwels' (2015) chapter on the uneasy but necessary role of negativity in PP. The fact that this chapter on MCA is part of the present volume is another indication. In sum, PP 2.0 – and MCA, which is emblematic of this second wave paradigm – is meaning-oriented rather than happiness-oriented in pursuing the good life. Informed by existential psychology and philosophy, it recognizes the dark side of the human condition as well as the bright side of fulfilling human potentials. It is based on both scientific findings and time-tested wisdom on healing and flourishing.

The MCA to Positive Organizations

Since a large part of adult life is work, it follows that research findings on the benefits of meaning in life are most likely applicable to work life. We have found that meaning is the foundation for well-being (Hicks & Routledge, 2013; Park, Park, & Peterson, 2010; Ryff & Keyes, 1995) and psychosocial adaptation (Reker & Wong, 2012). However, so far, this natural connection between work and meaning in life has not been widely recognized. The meaning hypothesis posits that when we value and pursue what really matters and what is intrinsically worthwhile, we will experience authentic happiness. Meaning is not only inherently virtuous and satisfying, but is also closely connected with the other two terminal values – virtue and happiness. Thus, a meaning-centered theory of good life and good work is based on three overlapping pillars – meaning, virtue, and happiness.

MCA is based on the application of Frankl's logotherapy (1985) to the workplace. MCA believes that every person is unique and has intrinsic value, but it also recognizes the dark side of human nature – greed, pride, prejudice, egotistic tendencies, and the potential for destructive acts. MCA benefits from the increasing interest in integrating PP with existential psychology, as per PP 2.0 (Wong, 2011). Meaning as a major source of intrinsic motivation both inspires and energizes workers, particularly if one's career is regarded as a "calling" (Wrzesniewski, McCauley, Rozin, & Schwartz, 1997), and good work as an achievement of excellence and ethics (Gardner, Csikszentmihalyi, & Damon, 2001). MCA capitalizes on the innate human capacity for meaning making (Wong & Weiner, 1981) and the universal accessibility of meaning (Frankl, 1985). More specifically, MCA is based around a novel conceptual model of meaning making, known as the PURE way of flourishing, as the next section elucidates.

The PURE Way to Flourishing

PURE stands for Purpose, Understanding, Responsibility, and Enjoyment/Evaluation, and serves both as a complete definition of meaning and as a conceptual framework for implementing MCA in the context of work.

The imperative of purpose

A sense of purpose within an organization can be assessed on five key dimensions, and moreover can be applied to seven areas of organizational functioning. In terms of the five dimensions, it can be asked whether a sense of purpose is: (1) absent or present; (2) clear; (3) compelling; (4) consistent; and (5) collaborative. These five dimensions reflect the recognition of the need for: (1) a present vision and mission in order for people to be motivated and united behind a common goal; (2) the team members and partners to share the same clearly articulated purpose and objectives, with the clarity aided by this purpose being concise, concrete, focused, and measurable; (3) the purpose to be compelling, which occurs when it resonates with the needs and values of all stakeholders; (4) a consistency of purpose, which refers to the practice of making decisions according to the same core values across departments and over time; and (5) the purpose being collaborative, which occurs when it emphasizes teamwork, cooperation, and partnership. Moreover, this sense of purpose can be considered in terms of seven different areas of organizational functioning: (1) the overall vision and mission of the company; (2) the company's societal concerns and broader sense of civic responsibility; (3) the company's systemic functioning, that is, the quality of its organizational operation; (4) human resources (e.g., its regard for employees); (5) the company's service or product; (6) efficiency; and (7) overall quality.

Thus, in practical terms, purpose can be assessed using Table 14.1, in which each of the seven dimensions of organizational functioning can be rated from 1 to 10 on the five key dimensions of purpose. The total score, aggregated from all 70 individual scores on the matrix, reflects the strength and scope of the organization's purposefulness. We can predict that the higher the score, the greater the morale and productivity.

Bridges of understanding

Understanding is the key to assessing the real situation in order to find solutions to an organizational problem. Facing up to the challenge requires that we understand and accept the seriousness of an existing problem. Understanding also involves making sense

Table 14.1 Assessment of different levels of purpose in five dimensions across seven areas of organizational functioning.

	Absent or present?	*Clear?*	*Compelling?*	*Consistent?*	*Collaborative?*
1. Vision/mission					
2. Societal concerns					
3. Organization					
4. Human resources					
5. Service/product					
6. Efficiency					
7. Quality					

Source: Author.

of what happens and knowing oneself. Having a sense of coherence and a clear concept of self-identity are essential for meaningful employment and optimal functioning. All kinds of barriers can prevent effective teamwork and slow down the production process. These gulfs can come from cultural differences, miscommunication, personal biases, and the built-in walls in a highly hierarchical organization. Territorial instincts, tribal mentalities, and power struggles can further cripple an organization. No organization can survive and flourish without building bridges of understanding that connect people.

The power of responsible action

Responsibility has always been considered as an important area in leadership and management (Bass & Bass, 2008). More recently, Cameron (2011) defined responsible leadership as virtuous leadership. Responsible action will include making the right decision, hiring the right people, developing the right product, and eliminating wasteful practices. Sometimes, it takes courage to do restructuring and retooling in order to survive turbulent times. Recent years have seen an emerging literature on the value of responsible leadership, not only to the success of organizations themselves (see, e.g., Berger, Choi, & Kim, 2011), but to the quality and coherence of wider civic society (Szekely & Knirsch, 2005).

Enjoyment or evaluation

Enjoyment refers to the intrinsic and deep satisfaction from both active engagement in a worthwhile task and experiencing progress. Feeling good from doing good is a common experience known for ages, arguably reflecting the innate moral nature of humanity (Hitlin, 2007). It is less known that doing good can also mean good business as Cameron (2011) has argued. For instance, ethical behavior by organizations can be rewarded via ethical consumer decision-making: in the UK, The Cooperative (2012) assessed the ethical market to be worth £47.2 billion in 2012 (up from £13.5 billion in 1999), with 50% of consumers avoiding products based on a company's responsible reputation (up from 44% in 2000).

The PURE model predicts that both extrinsic and intrinsic sources of satisfaction are important for well-being and productivity. However, at both the low and high end of salary scales, intrinsic motivation becomes most important. Figure 14.1 and Figure 14.2 describe both intrinsic and extrinsic sources of work satisfaction at the workplace. We

Figure 14.1 Levels of intrinsic motivation. *Source*: Author.

Figure 14.2 Levels of extrinsic motivation. *Source*: Author.

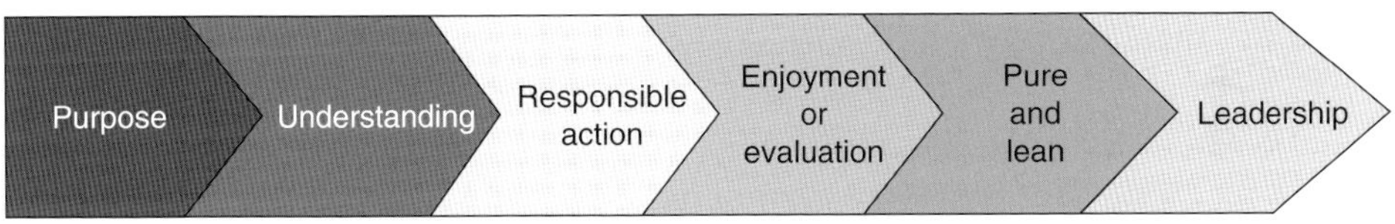

Figure 14.3 The PURE way to move forward. *Source*: © Paul T. P. Wong.

could give a score of 1 to 10 for each level of intrinsic and extrinsic satisfaction. These scores provide important information about areas for continuous improvement. A low level of enjoyment is sufficient ground for re-evaluation of purpose, understanding, and responsible action to determine areas that need radical change or gradual improvement. Higher scores, particularly in terms of intrinsic motivation, can be regarded as reflective of a person experiencing greater depth of meaning.

Applications of the PURE Strategy

The four components of PURE can be taught through workshops, modeling, and coaching. They can also be measured qualitatively and quantitatively. More importantly, the benefits of MCA can be measured by increased profit, productivity, and morale as well as decreased waste and absenteeism. Figure 14.3 shows how the PURE model moves an organization forward in good times and bad. As mentioned earlier, leadership is a key to organizational excellence. Effective leaders set the standard of competence and integrity. They are also able to inspire and motivate others, and develop the right strategies to move the company forward.

Positive Corporate Culture

MCA entails creating a positive culture because of its emphasis on human resources development and meaning at work. Schein (1990) defines corporate culture as "the unique and essential function of management" (p. 317). Organizations need a positive culture in order to keep their best workers, motivate their workforce, and grow their business.

When you walk into a positive and successful organization, you can feel the difference the moment you step inside the door. The atmosphere is inviting, and there is a distinct sense of dedication and energy about the people working there. Ultimately, a positive cooperative culture is essential for sustainable growth. MCA has been applied to transforming culture (Wong, 2002, 2005; Wong & Gupta, 2004), restoring integrity (Wong, 2002, 2004), and improving teamwork and cooperation (Wong, 2005, 2006). It would be difficult to transform a corporate culture without a leadership totally committed to positive change.

Wong and Gupta (2004) identify four types of positive cultures: (1) progressive–adaptive culture, (2) purpose-driven culture, (3) community-oriented culture, and (4) people-centered culture. The above cultures contribute to intrinsically motivated high performance because they meet people's deepest needs for meaning, community, spirituality, and agency. The ideal company should possess the attributes of all four types of healthy corporate cultures. Wong and Gupta (2004) also identify five negative cultures: (1) authoritarian–hierarchical culture, (2) competing–conflictive culture, (3) laissez-faire culture, (4) dishonest–corrupt culture, and (5) rigid–traditional culture. The above five negative cultures are not mutually exclusive. Negative cultures can be transformed through MCA. But the most urgent task is to weed out toxic elements and transform negative cultures through the PURE strategy.

The PURE Way to Reduce Wasteful Spending

The fastest ship will not go very far if there is a leak in the hull. The PURE model not only improves the speed, but also repairs the leakage. A systematic implementation of the PURE strategy will greatly reduce toxic elements, such as nepotism, cronyism, fraud, and mismanagement, while increasing efficiency, productivity, innovation, and job satisfaction. The PURE model provides a strategic and systematic way to reduce waste in financial and human resources in connection with the pruning of toxic elements. Here is a brief guideline of a meaningful way of cutting costs.

Firstly, every organizational department could be asked to come up with a clear mission statement. The purpose assessment tool (Table 14.1) can be used to prioritize the purpose, objectives, and projects of each operational unit. Anything not essential to the stated mission would warrant closer scrutiny. Of course, no organization can survive on purpose alone; a sound business model is also essential. Thus, both purposefulness and profitability need to be included in the equation. The challenge is to develop a workable formula to reduce waste and enhance productivity of each unit. This formula will yield a *Value Index* involving appropriate weightings of *Mission Value* and *Financial Value*. Some departments may load heavily in Mission Value because of their contribution to the mission and purpose of the organization, but contribute little financially. The reverse may be true for some other departments. Any unit with an overall negative Value Index does not deserve to exist.

The second step is to consult and communicate with all stakeholders to ensure that everyone in the organization understands the need to cut spending and the due process of reducing waste. It will take negotiation and compromise to develop fair, transparent procedures to eliminate non-essential operational processes and potentially reduce the contribution of non-productive members. The third step is that all levels of the organization, from the CEO to the most junior employees, take personal responsibility to ensure that due process is being carried out fairly and effectively. Great care is taken so that people who may face a reduction in their working hours or even lose their job entirely will be fairly compensated and given the opportunity for career counseling and assistance to secure another job. Finally, the benefits of reducing waste and reviving a struggling organization will be enjoyed by all stakeholders. More importantly, the result of reducing wasteful spending may have a positive rippling effect on society. In developing this type of positive culture, in which a model like PURE can flourish, effective leadership is needed. One such model of good leadership in this regard is that of servant leadership, as the next section explores.

Servant Leadership

Servant leadership is an ideal model for implementing MCA generally, and the PURE approach specifically, because it emphasizes such qualities as integrity, humility, serving a higher purpose, fulfilling a mission, and the need to develop and release the creative potential of all workers. Servant leadership is of ultimate importance in the PURE way of organizational transformation (Wong, 2004). The leader sets the tone and provides a role model. Only the leader can ensure that the PURE principles are being implemented systematically at all levels of the organization.

Servant leadership emphasizes such qualities as integrity, humility, virtue, higher purpose, responsibility, and the need to develop the potentials of all workers. In terms of the identification and assessment of the construct of servant leadership, Wong and colleagues have developed two relevant instruments: a self-assessment of servant leadership (Page & Wong, 2000); and the 360-degree assessment of leadership (Rude, 2004). From a more practical perspective, Page (2009) has provided a detailed hands-on guide to transforming management to servant leadership. In terms of empirical validation of the concept, Searle and Barbuto (2010) reported that servant leadership could impact organizational virtuousness at all three levels of good work and increase productivity.

In sum, the PURE way is humane and virtuous. PURE provides a conceptual framework and procedures to eliminate waste and toxic elements, and build up the full potentials of both individuals and the organization. Before looking at future directions for research and implementation of the PURE model, we shall examine a case study of organizational excellence that fully embodies this approach.

A Case Study in Organizational Excellence

Synovus Financial Corporation (www.synovus.com), listed as one of the best companies to work for by *Fortune* magazine for many years, is a good example of the benefits of MCA and servant leadership. Synovus employees find meaning and satisfaction through serving customers, fulfilling their potentials, and working under caring servant-leaders. The PURE principles are clearly at work throughout this organization.

Synovus' culture of "people first" is a key to its success. The value inherited from the early pioneers of the company and forged down through the years remains unchanged. It emphasizes the imperative of treating each worker, stakeholder, and customer with kindness and respect because every person matters. Such unwavering commitment to serving others generates stability, loyalty, and enduring success.

Its relationship-based philosophy dictates its values and defines its future. Its culture of service over self is clearly reflected in its customer covenant. The same philosophy is also applied to each team member. It wants each employee to feel that they have an opportunity to contribute, grow, and benefit from the company's success. It aspires to "become the employer of choice in every market we serve. Creating a great workplace is the foundation of every Synovus strategy. Team member enthusiasm yields higher productivity and profitability" (Page, 2000, p. 1).

It does not take much stretch of imagination to understand why servant leadership is the best model for a corporation devoted to serving others. "I am convinced," writes William Turner, as chairman of the Executive Committee of Synovus Financial Corporation, "that servant leadership will be the way to manage in the future, not only because it brings personal fulfillment to everyone in the organization, including the boss, but also because it can deal with change quickly and effectively" (Turner, 2000). "The vision must have meaning," Turner continues, "because man cannot live without meaning. The vision must be holistic and congruent, encompassing the church, the family, the community, and the institution. If it doesn't, values and priorities will conflict" (p. 83).

Given Synovus' meaning-centered vision, one can readily detect the PURE principles in their policies and operations. The purpose of serving customers with enthusiasm and excellence is so ingrained in all workers that it has become a habitual practice. Likewise, the company's interest in the professional and personal growth of its team members has led to a variety of career development programs. The focus on facilitating individual development and coaching for optimum performance further enhances the meaning of work, because employees feel that they are able to grow and fulfill their potential within the organization.

In addition to taking care of its customers and employees, Synovus is also unabashedly dedicated to the higher purpose of improving the quality of life in the communities it serves. Community service is entrenched as an integral part of the company. In 1996, it formally codified its community outreach projects under an umbrella effort called REACH: Recognizing and Encouraging an Atmosphere of Community and of Hope. REACH encourages and enables team members to give back to the communities. "The creation of the foundations [for community service] was the beginning of servant-leadership in our company," writes Turner (2000), "I believe a servant leader should meet the needs of the people who work with him – at work, at home, and in the community" (p. 139).

It is hard not to value the principles of serving when the culture of the heart permeates everything the company does, from the top management to each and every employee. All the policies and decisions convey the same message of "people first." Explicit understanding of the values and purpose of Synovus is reinforced by its customer covenant which reads in part:

> We pledge to serve every customer with the highest levels of sincerity, fairness, courtesy, respect and gratitude, delivered with unparalleled responsiveness, expertise, efficiency and accuracy. We are in the business to create lasting relationships, and we will treat our customers like we want to be treated.

The consistent message is to treat people right, to do the right thing, and to give your best in everything you do. There is no exception, no excuse. The ethos of Synovus is conducive to responsible actions. When the work is intrinsically motivating and meaningful, people are more likely to be engaged and passionate about what they do.

The philosophy of serving the community rather than maximizing short-term financial gains empowers Synovus to do what is right and what is in the best interest of the customers and communities. It should be noted that this is not at the expense of sound financial analysis: it is constantly improving its policies and procedures of risk management to reduce bad loans, and it also makes sure that it builds up sufficient capital asset in order to be prepared for the unexpected. By being proactive, it is able to protect its customers against future losses. Synovus thus provides an example of how one can create a positive and virtuous company by following the PURE principles and servant leadership.

Future Research

MCA is a case of value-centered and virtuous leadership. It offers a promising framework for positive management research with the dialectical framework of PP 2.0. However, more research is needed on how best to promote meaning at work, given that Gallup-Healthways' (2015) *State of Global Well-Being* report also indicates that 52% of all adults are struggling in purpose-related well-being, and these people are consequently less likely to be engaged in their jobs. This high rate of disengagement may be due to a variety of reasons, such as work stress, emotional disorders, mismatch between the individual and work, or a lack of meaning. Schawbel's (2015) recent observation that "millennials" are the least engaged generation suggests that they may have difficulty finding jobs that meet their high expectations for meaningful work; thus, how to increase engagement through meaningful work remains a research challenge (Cartwright & Holmes, 2006). Similarly, from an assessment perspective, while there are already valid and reliable measures of general meaning in life (Steger, Frazier, Oishi, & Kaler, 2006; Wong, 2012b) and meaning in work (Steger, Dik, & Duffy, 2012), future research needs to further elucidate the substantive content of meaning in life (McDonald, Wong, & Gingras, 2012; Peterson & Park, 2014; Wong, 1998). Likewise, there is a need for quantitative and qualitative meaning-centered audits with respect to a sense of meaning at work.

From a critical perspective, we also need research on the potential downsides and risks of promoting meaning at work; for instance, PP 2.0 also directs our attention to the potential abuse of power by leaders. Passion and talents could be used by some ambitious individuals to manipulate and con stakeholders for personal gain; similarly, even too much of character strengths, such as confidence and optimism, could become vices (Chang & Sanna, 2003). MCA may shed new light on the role of personality factors in organizations. Likewise, it is possible that management may use dedication to mission as a way to exploit employees; leaders may justify their unkind treatment of others in the name of serving a higher purpose (McGregor et al., 1998; Peterson, 2012). PP 2.0 also provides a fertile ground for research on how to integrate both the positive and negative in creating an optimal organization. More research should be directed to increasing intrinsic motivation while reducing waste. Similarly, we need to find ways to reduce/remove toxic elements and, at the same time, transform negative emotions and experiences into positive motivation.

Conclusions

This chapter defines good work as work that is beneficial at three levels: individual, organization, and society. It then critiques the limitations of the first wave of PP and positive organization research, primarily because it generally fails to engage with the dark side of the human condition. Consequently, it argues for a paradigm shift to the existentially-toned PP 2.0 as an ideal synthesis between the thesis of "psychology as usual" (which did pay attention to this darker side) and its antithesis (the strength-based approach of "first wave" PP); such integration will greatly expand the scope of PP 2.0 research and applications.

The chapter then introduced the meaning-centered approach (MCA) to positive management and organizational excellence, and in particular the PURE approach to organizational functioning. MCA provides a deeper and richer understanding of work because it is informed by existential psychology regarding the reality of human existence. MCA incorporates management processes with servant leadership as practical ways to reduce waste and at the same time enhance virtuousness, creativity, and productivity. This chapter also introduces practical guidelines on how to implement servant leadership and capitalize on our innate capacity for meaning making.

Since no existing method has succeeded in completely liberating us from human foibles and baser aspirations, MCA represents a promising and workable framework to keep these destructive forces in check, while cultivating personal responsibility for good work and higher aspiration. The most attractive aspect of MCA is that it does not require exceptional virtue and talents; it only requires a shift in attitude and motivation from self-centeredness to self-transcendence. With an appreciative attitude, even mundane or low-paying work can become meaningful. In sum, MCA not only provides a healthy relationship with the dark side of the human condition, but also empowers us to achieve human excellence and create good work to the benefit of all stakeholders.

References

Allison, H. E. (2002). On the very idea of a propensity to evil. *The Journal of Value Inquiry, 36*(2), 337–348.

Arnold, K., Turner, N., Barling, J., Kelloway, E., & McKee, M. (2007). Transformational leadership and psychological well-being: The mediating role of meaningful work. *Journal of Occupational Health Psychology, 12*, 193–203.

Bass, B. M., & Bass, R. (2008). *The Bass handbook of leadership: Theory, research, and managerial applications.* New York, NY: Free Press.

Berger, R., Choi, C., & Kim, J. (2011). Responsible leadership for multinational enterprises in bottom of pyramid countries: The knowledge of local managers. *Journal of Business Ethics, 101*(4), 553–561.

Bolier, L., Haverman, M., Westerhof, G. J., Riper, H., Smit, F., & Bohlmeijer, E. (2013). Positive psychology interventions: A meta-analysis of randomized controlled studies. *BMC Public Health, 13*, 119.

Bretton, R. (2015). The existential dimensions of positive psychology. In S. Joseph (Ed.), *Positive psychology in practice: Promoting human flourishing in work, health, education and everyday life* (2nd ed., pp. 47–60). Chichester, UK: Wiley.

Burger, D. H., Crous, F., & Roodt, G. (2008). Logo-OD: The application of logotherapy as an organization development intervention. *SA Journal of Industrial Psychology, 34*(3), 68–80.

Cameron, K. (2011). Responsible leadership as virtuous leadership. *Journal of Business Ethics, 98*(1), 25–35.

Cartwright, S., & Holmes, N. (2006). The meaning of work: The challenge of regaining employee engagement and reducing cynicism. *Human Resource Management Review, 16*(2), 199–208.

Chang, E. C., & Sanna, L. J. (Eds.) (2003). *Virtue, vice, and personality: The complexity of behavior.* Washington, DC: American Psychological Association.

Cooperative, The (2012). *Ethical Consumer Markets Report 2012.* London, UK: Author.

Cozzolino, P. J. (2006). Death contemplation, growth, and defense: Converging evidence of dual-existential systems? *Psychological Inquiry, 17*(4), 278–287.

Donaldson, S. I. (2011). Determining what works, if anything, in applied positive psychology. In S. I. Donaldson, M. Csikszentmihalyi, & J. Nakamura (Eds.), *Applied positive psychology: Improving everyday life, health, schools, work, and society* (pp. 3–11). London, UK: Routledge.

Forgas, J. P. (2013). Don't worry, be sad! On the cognitive, motivational and interpersonal benefits of negative mood. *Current Directions in Psychological Science, 22*, 225–232.

Frankl, V. E. (1985). *Man's search for meaning: An introduction to logotherapy* (Revised & updated ed.). New York, NY: Pocket Books.

Frankl, V. E. (1988). *The will to meaning: Foundations and applications of logotherapy.* New York, NY: Penguin.

Fredrickson, B. L. (2001). The role of positive emotions in positive psychology: The broaden-and-build theory of positive emotions. *American Psychologist, 56*, 218–226.

Gallup-Healthways (2015, October 14). *Gallup-Healthways state of global well-being final report.* Retrieved from http://info.healthways.com/hs-fs/hub/162029/file-1634508606-pdf/WBI2013/Gallup-Healthways_State_of_Global_Well-Being_vFINAL.pdf?t=1427897436886Page

Gardner, H., Csikszentmihalyi, M., & Damon, W. (2001). *Good work: How excellence and ethics meet.* New York, NY: Basic Books.

Gruber, J., Mauss, I. B., & Tamir, M. (2011). A dark side of happiness? How, when, and why happiness is not always good. *Perspectives on Psychological Science, 6*(3), 222–233.

Held, B. S. (2002). The tyranny of the positive attitude in America: Observation and speculation. *Journal of Clinical Psychology, 58*(9), 965–991.

Held, B. S. (2004). The negative side of positive psychology. *Journal of Humanistic Psychology, 44*(1), 9–46.

Hicks, J. A., & Routledge, C. (Eds.) (2013). *The experience of meaning in life: Classical perspectives, emerging themes, and controversies.* Dordrecht, the Netherlands: Springer.

Hitlin, S. (2007). Doing good, feeling good: Values and the self's moral center. *The Journal of Positive Psychology, 2*(4), 249a–259.

Ivtzan, I., Lomas, T., Hefferon, K., & Worth, P. (2015). *Second wave positive psychology: Embracing the dark side of life.* London, UK: Routledge.

Joseph, S. (Ed.). (2015). *Positive psychology in practice: Promoting human flourishing in work, health, education and everyday life* (2nd ed.). Chichester, UK: Wiley.

Kamdron, T. (2005). Work motivation and job satisfaction of Estonian higher officials. *International Journal of Public Administration, 28*(13/14), 1211–1240.

Ko, I., & Donaldson, S. I. (2011). Applied positive organizational psychology: The state of the science and practice. In S. I. Donaldson, M. Csikszentmihalyi, & J. Nakamura (Eds.) *Applied positive psychology: Improving everyday life, health, schools, work, and society* (pp. 137–154). London, UK: Routledge.

Kuhn, T. (1962). *The Structure of scientific revolutions* (50th anniversary ed.). Chicago, IL: University of Chicago Press.

Lomas, T., & Ivtzan, I. (2015). Second wave positive psychology: Exploring the positive-negative dialectics of wellbeing. *Journal of Happiness Studies.* doi: 10.1007/s10902-015-9668-y

Mauss, I. B., Tamir, M., Anderson, C. L., & Savino, N. S. (2011). Can seeking happiness make people unhappy? Paradoxical effects of valuing happiness. *Emotion, 11*, 807–815.

McDonald, M. J., Wong, P. T. P., & Gingras, D. T. (2012). Meaning-in-life measures and development of a brief version of the Personal Meaning Profile. In P. T. P. Wong (Ed.), *The human quest for meaning: Theories, research, and applications* (2nd ed., pp. 357–382). New York, NY: Routledge.

McGregor, H. A., Lieberman, J. D., Greenberg, J., Solomon, S., Arndt, J., Simon, L., & Pyszczynski, T. (1998). Terror management and aggression: Evidence that mortality salience motivates aggression against worldview-threatening others. *Journal of Personality and Social Psychology, 74*(3), 590–605.

McNulty, J. K., & Fincham, F. D. (2011). Beyond positive psychology? Toward a contextual view of psychological process and well-being. *American Psychologist, 67*(2), 101–110.

Nord, W. R., Brief, A. P., Atieh, J. M., & Doherty, E. M. (1990). Studying meanings of work: The case of work values. In A. Brief, & W. Nord (Eds.), *Meanings of occupational work: A collection of essays* (pp. 99–100). Lexington, MA: Lexington Books.

Page, D. (2000). *Finding meaning through servant leadership in the workplace.* Paper presented at the International Conference on Searching for Meaning in the New Millennium, Vancouver, BC, Canada.

Page, D. (2009). *Servant empowered leadership: A hands-on guide to transforming you and your organization.* Langley, Canada: Power to Change.

Page, D., & Wong, P. T. P. (2000). A conceptual framework for measuring servant leadership. In S. Adjibolooso (Ed.), *The human factor in shaping the course of history and development* (pp. 69–110). Washingdon, DC: American University Press.

Park, N., Park, M., & Peterson, C. (2010). When is the search for meaning related to life satisfaction? *Applied Psychology: Health and Well-Being, 2*(1), 1–13.

Pauwels, B. G. (2015). The uneasy – and necessary – role of negative in positive psychology. In S. Joseph (Ed.), *Positive psychology in practice: Promoting human flourishing in work, health, education and everyday life* (2nd ed., pp. 807–822). Chichester, UK: Wiley.

Peterson, C., & Park, N. (2014). Meaning and positive psychology. *International Journal of Existential Psychology and Psychotherapy, 5*, 2–8.

Peterson, J. B. (2012). The meaning of meaning. In P. T. P. Wong, L. C. J. Wong, M. J. McDonald, & D. W. Klaassen (Eds.), *The positive psychology of meaning and spirituality.* (pp. 11–32). Birmingham, AL: Purpose Research.

Reker, G. T., & Wong, P. T. P. (2012). Personal meaning in life and psychosocial adaptation in the later years. In P. T. P. Wong (Ed.), *The human quest for meaning: Theories, research, and applications* (2nd ed., pp. 433–456). New York, NY: Routledge.

Rude, W. (2004). *The connection between servant leadership and job burnout.* Unpublished master's thesis, Trinity Western University, Langley, Canada.

Ryff, C. D., & Keyes, C. I. M. (1995). The structure of psychological well-being revisited. *Journal of Personality and Social Psychology, 69*(4), 719–727.

Schawbel, D. (2015, October 14). The 4 things millennials want most from employers may surprise you. *Business Insider.* Retrieved from http://www.businessinsider.com/what-millennials-want-most-from-employers-2015-4

Schein, E. H. (1990). *Organizational culture and leadership.* San Francisco, CA: Jossey-Bass.

Searle, T. P. & Barbuto, J. E. (2010). Servant leadership, hope, and organizational virtuousness: A framework exploring positive micro and macro behaviors and performance impact. *Journal of Leadership & Organizational Studies.* doi:10.1177/1548051810383863

Seligman, M. E. P., & Csikszentmihalyi, M. (2000). Positive psychology: An introduction. *American Psychologist, 55*, 5–14.

Sin, N. L., & Lyubomirsky, S. (2009). Enhancing well-being and alleviating depressive symptoms with positive psychology interventions: A practice-friendly meta-analysis. *Journal of Clinical Psychology, 65*(5), 467–487.

Steger, M. F., Dik, B. J., & Duffy, R. D. (2012). Measuring meaningful work: The work and meaning inventory (WAMI). *Journal of Career Assessment, 20*, 322–337.

Steger, M. F., Frazier, P., Oishi, S., & Kaler, M. (2006). The Meaning in Life Questionnaire: Assessing the presence of and search for meaning in life. *Journal of Counseling Psychology, 53*(1), 80–93.

Storbeck, J., & Clore, G. L. (2005). With sadness comes accuracy; with happiness, false memory. *Psychological Science, 16*(10), 785–791.

Szekely, F., & Knirsch, M. (2005). Responsible leadership and corporate social responsibility: Metrics for sustainable performance. *European Management Journal, 23*(6), 628–647.

Turner, W. B. (2000). *Learning of love: A journey toward servant leadership.* Macon, GA: Smyth & Helwys.

Wong, P. T. P. (1995). A stage model of coping with frustrative stress. In R. Wong (Ed.), *Biological perspectives on motivated activities* (pp. 339–378). Norwood, NJ: Ablex.

Wong, P. T. P. (1998). Implicit theories of meaningful life and the development of the personal meaning profile. In P. T. P. Wong & P. S. Fry (Eds.), *The human quest for meaning: A handbook of psychological research and clinical applications* (pp. 111–140). Mahwah, NJ: Erlbaum.

Wong, P. T. P. (2002). Creating a positive, meaningful work climate: A new challenge for management and leadership. In B. Pattanayak & V. Gupta (Eds.), *Creating performing organizations: International perspectives for Indian management.* New Delhi, India: Sage.

Wong, P. T. P. (2004). The paradox of servant leadership. *Leadership Link, Spring, 2004*, 3–5. Ohio State University, Leadership Research Center.

Wong, P. T. P. (2005). Creating a positive participatory climate: A meaning-centered counselling perspective. In S. Schuman (Ed.), *The IAF Facilitation Handbook* (pp. 171–190). San Francisco, CA: Jossey-Bass.

Wong, P. T. P. (2006). Is your organization an obstacle course or a relay team? A meaning-centered approach to creating a collaborative culture. In S. Schuman (Ed.), *Creating a culture of collaboration: The International Association of Facilitators handbook* (pp. 229–256). San Francisco, CA: Jossey-Bass/Wiley.

Wong, P. T. P. (2007a). Positive psychology: A quiet revolution. In P. T. P. Wong, L. C. J. Wong, M. J. McDonald, & D. W. Klaassen (Eds.), *The positive psychology of meaning and spirituality* (pp. 17–27). Abbotsford, Canada: INPM Press.

Wong, P. T. P. (2007b). Perils and promises in the pursuit of happiness [Review of *In search of happiness: Understanding an endangered state of mind*]. *PsycCRITIQUES, 52*(49), 2.

Wong, P. T. P. (2009). An existential vision of the good life: Toward an international psychology and psychotherapy based on meaning. [Review of L. Hoffman, M. Yang, F. J. Kaklauskas, & A. Chan (Eds.), *Existential psychology East-West.* Colorado Springs, CO: University of the Rockies Press, 2009.] *PsycCRITIQUES, 54.*

Wong, P. T. P. (2010). What is existential positive psychology? *International Journal of Existential Psychology and Psychotherapy, 3*(1), 1–10.

Wong, P. T. P. (2011). Positive psychology 2.0: Towards a balanced interactive model of the good life. *Canadian Psychology, 52*(2), 69–81.

Wong, P. T. P. (2012a). Toward a dual-systems model of what makes life worth living. In P. T. P. Wong (Ed.), *The human quest for meaning: Theories, research, and applications* (2nd ed., pp. 3–22). New York, NY: Routledge.

Wong, P. T. P. (Ed.) (2012b). The meaning mindset: Measurement and implications. *International Journal of Existential Psychology and Psychotherapy, 4*(1), 1–3.

Wong, P. T. P., & Gupta, V. (2004). The positive psychology of transformative organizations: A fresh perspective and evidence from the Anglo context. In V. Gupta (Ed.), *Transformative organizations* (pp. 341–360). New Delhi, India: Sage.

Wong, P. T. P., Reker, G. T., & Peacock, E. (2006). The resource-congruence model of coping and the development of the Coping Schema Inventory. In P. T. P. Wong & L. C. J. Wong (Eds.), *Handbook of multicultural perspectives on stress and coping* (pp. 223–283). New York, NY: Springer.

Wong, P. T. P., & Tomer, A. (2011). Beyond terror and denial: The positive psychology of death acceptance. *Death Studies, 35*(2), 99–106.

Wong, P. T. P., & Weiner, B. (1981). When people ask "Why" questions and the heuristic of attributional search. *Journal of Personality and Social Psychology, 40*, 650–663.

Wrzesniewski, A., McCauley, C. R., Rozin, P., & Schwartz, B. (1997). Jobs, careers, and callings: People's relations to their work. *Journal of Research in Personality, 31*(1), 21–33.

15

Workplace and Organizational Well-Being

Lindsay G. Oades and Aylin Dulagil

Introduction

The notion of the happy and productive worker has long fascinated organizational scientists and practitioners alike. According to this thesis, happy employees exhibit higher levels of job-related performance behaviors than do unhappy employees. The happy worker hypothesis has typically been operationalized by correlating employee self-ratings of job satisfaction with supervisory ratings of performance (Wright & Cropanzano, 2000).

However, the happy worker hypothesis (and individual well-being) does not address the contextual or emergent issues associated with organizations. In addition, the current approach in well-being puts the onus on an individual to enhance his or her own well-being. Organizations are made up of individuals and teams, as well-being dynamic entities in their own right. It is important for researchers and practitioners to focus on both individual well-being and organizational performance (Cotton & Hart, 2003). However, we argue that there are intrinsic, conceptual differences between variables at the individual, group, and organizational level that need to be taken into account when defining and examining the contribution of individual well-being to organizational well-being and vice versa (Loney & Nagelkerke, 2014). This chapter proposes that organizational theory needs to move beyond the happy worker hypothesis and in so doing avoid the individualist fallacy. That is, there is a need to not always conceptualize well-being, or reduce conceptualization to the individual level.

Researchers have historically conceptualized well-being at the individual level and this has influenced the conceptualization of well-being of people at work within organizations. In this chapter, we use the term "individualist fallacy" to refer to the phenomenon of conflating group or organization-level constructs with individual-level analysis. The individualist fallacy has been pervasive in the understanding of organizational well-being. The understanding of the complexities of an organization, in terms of well-being, needs necessarily to be a multilevel conceptualization.

The Wiley Blackwell Handbook of the Psychology of Positivity and Strengths-Based Approaches at Work, First Edition. Edited by Lindsay G. Oades, Michael F. Steger, Antonella Delle Fave, and Jonathan Passmore.

A three-level conceptualization of well-being is proposed. The workplace and organizational well-being model (WOWM) proposes that well-being exists at the individual level, at the team/group level, and at the organizational level and that there is a reciprocal impact at each of these three levels. After defining well-being, a review of relevant literature at each three levels is provided, demonstrating significantly more evidence at the first level. The chapter concludes with discussion of the need for future research, including systems science and systems thinking that explore well-being at different levels of the organization, and the interaction between these levels.

Workplace Well-Being at the Individual Level

We define individual well-being using Ryff and Singer's (2008) definition of eudaimonic well-being, as living a meaningful life steeped in self-truth and self-responsibility, and striving toward excellence by realizing our unique potential and achieving the best within us. The well-being perspective enhances the happy worker hypothesis and suggests that the presence of positive emotional states and positive appraisals accentuates worker performance and quality of life. These, in turn lead to more productive, profitable, and successful organizations.

Individual well-being can be divided into two distinct constructs. Hedonic (or subjective) well-being is defined by maximizing pleasure and minimizing pain. It is also characterized by high positive affect, low negative affect, and happiness. Eudaimonic well-being defines well-being as a derivative of personal fulfillment and expressiveness. There is evidence that these two constructs are distinct (Keyes, Shmotkin, & Ryff, 2002). A full critical review of differences between eudaimonic well-being, emotional well-being, and psychological well-being is beyond the scope of this chapter. For current purposes in organizational contexts it is useful to consider Ryff and Singer's (2008) six dimensions of psychological well-being. These are:

1 Growth – ongoing personal change, development, and psychological growth
2 Relatedness – positive, warm, affectionate relationships with others
3 Autonomy – self-determination and freedom, the ability to resist the influence of social norms
4 Purpose in life – goals, meaningfulness, and a sense of direction in life, creating meaning and direction, zest – actively engaging, clear comprehension of purpose
5 Environmental mastery – a sense of mastery over the environment and everyday affairs
6 Self-acceptance – positive view of oneself and one's current and past life.

Ryff and Singer's psychological well-being model applies at the individual level and provides a useful starting point for expanding definitions of well-being to the team, organization, and environment. It is also important to note that Ryff and Singer's model includes the three basic psychological needs inherent in self-determination theory (autonomy, relatedness, and competence [environmental mastery and growth]; Deci & Ryan, 1985).

Job satisfaction

A key tenet of the individually focused happy worker hypothesis is that high job satisfaction leads to high productivity. According to this thesis, happy employees exhibit higher levels of job-related performance behaviors than do unhappy employees (Spector, 1997). The happy worker hypothesis has typically been operationalized by correlating employee self-ratings of job satisfaction with supervisory ratings of performance (Wright & Cropanzano, 2000).

Job satisfaction is a state in which an individual expresses contentment with and positive feelings about her or his jobs (Judge & Kammeyer-Mueller, 2012). Job satisfaction is an important variable because it has been linked to performance (Iaffaldano & Muchinsky, 1985; Judge, Thoresen, Bono, & Patton, 2001). Job satisfaction may be diminished by the workplace context and by events that may elicit emotions and attitudes that cause an employee to consider leaving the organization (Mitchell, Holtom, Lee, Sablynski, & Erez, 2001).

Organizations with happy and satisfied employees fare better in a number of ways, including on the stock market (Edmans, 2012). Research on the job satisfaction–productivity connection has typically yielded very low correlations (from $r = .17$ to $r = .30$; Judge et al., 2001; Laffaldano & Muchinsky, 1985). Judge et al. (2001) conducted a meta-analysis on the relationship between job satisfaction and job performance and found a correlation of .30 between these variables, only weakly supporting the happy worker hypothesis.

Some researchers suggest that focusing on the relationship between productivity and employee well-being is likely to be more productive than focusing on job satisfaction alone (Cotton & Hart, 2003). Further research during the 1990s supported the contention that a "happy worker" is better described through the concept of employee well-being than through job satisfaction (Cropanzano & Wright, 1999; Wright & Bonett, 1997; Wright & Cropanzano, 1997). However, the results were no better than the job satisfaction–job performance correlation, leading researchers to question whether the equivocal findings to support this relationship are due to the inconsistent operationalization of employee "happiness" (Cropanzano & Wright, 2001). Subsequent research provides some support for the relationship between employee well-being and employee productivity. Despite the significant research done in this area, general skepticism regarding the satisfaction–performance relationship has led to a decline in research, notwithstanding the fact that causality between these two concepts is yet to be determined (Cropanzano & Wright, 2001).

Employee engagement

Another incarnation of the happy worker hypothesis has been the recent focus on employee engagement. Employee engagement has received much attention in the popular human resources and management literature; however, it remains a construct requiring further conceptualization and clarification (Macey & Schneider, 2008a; Robinson, Perryman, & Hayday, 2004; Saks, 2006). There are many existing definitions of employee engagement, for example as a specific concept (Bakker & Leiter, 2010), or an umbrella term (to include a multitude of conceptualizations, e.g., trait, state, behavioral, attitudinal; Christian, Garza, & Slaughter, 2011; Kahn, 1990; Macey & Schneider, 2008b). This lack of unified conceptualization makes it difficult to draw general conclusions regarding employee engagement and organizational outcomes. While a comprehensive review of the employee engagement constructs is not within the scope of this chapter, we will examine it in the context of well-being at work.

An early conceptualization of engagement was the job demands-resources (JD-R) model (Bakker, 2011). Job demands and resources trigger two different psychological processes that are the roots of work engagement and burnout. Job resources such as feedback, autonomy, and supervisory support are posited as the major antecedents of work engagement (Hakanen, Bakker, & Schaufeli, 2006), and they appear to enhance engagement especially when job demands are high (Bakker, Hakanen, Demerouti, & Xanthopoulou, 2007). In addition to job resources, personal resources have also been found to predict work engagement (Xanthopoulou, Bakker, Demerouti, & Schaufeli, 2007). Thus, according to the JDR model, work engagement is impacted by both the individual and the work environment, supporting the notion of a reciprocal relationship between these levels.

In a meta-analysis of the Gallup studies investigating the relationship between employee well-being and business outcomes such as customer service, productivity, Harter, Schmidt, & Keyes (2003) found a moderate correlation between employee engagement and performance (covering approximately 8,000 business units and 200,000 individuals).

Job satisfaction is one of several important job attitudes that have been studied by organizational psychologists and researchers. Job attitudes are evaluations of one's job that express one's feelings toward, beliefs about, and attachment to one's job (Judge & Kammeyer-Mueller, 2012). Job attitudes are closely related to global measures of life satisfaction (Judge & Watanabe, 1993) and are important in industrial/organizational psychology because they are thought to predict important behaviors that contribute to organizational productivity and culture (Harrison, Newman, & Roth, 2006). The three primary job attitudes are organizational commitment, job satisfaction, and intention to stay. Job attitudes have been found to predict behavioral engagement (Langford, 2010; Langford & Demirian, 2007; Langford, Parkes, & Metcalf, 2006; Newman, Joseph, & Hulin, 2010) and to outperform behavioral measures in correlating with organizational outcomes (Langford, 2010). It is still unclear whether employee engagement is the same (Macey & Schneider, 2008a) as, or different from, job attitudes (Little & Little, 2006).

Job satisfaction and organizational commitment substantially overlap, yet differ in their conceptual targets (role versus organization; Newman et al., 2010). Researchers have argued, however, that while they are correlated, they are distinguishable constructs (Meyer & Allen, 1991). Organizational commitment is an individual's psychological bond with the organization, defined as an affective attachment and feeling of loyalty to the organization (Judge & Kammeyer-Mueller, 2012; Meyer & Allen, 1997). A three-component model of organizational commitment has been proposed incorporating affective, normative, and continuance commitment (Meyer & Allen, 1984). However, affective commitment was found to have the strongest relationship with positive organizational behaviors and perceived organizational support (Meyer, Stanley, Herscovitch, & Topolnytsky, 2002). Sung and Choi (2014) investigated the effects of various human resource development (HRD) dimensions on organizational performance, using path analyses to confirm that both qualitative and quantitative dimensions of HRD initiatives improved employee commitment, in turn determining the financial performance of the organization.

In a study examining the job satisfaction of teachers, salary and length of service were found not to be correlated with job satisfaction, whereas relationships with co-workers and supervisors did affect job satisfaction (Tillman & Tillman, 2008; suggesting support for the relationship between the psychological need of relatedness and job satisfaction).

An early study determined that teachers perceive their needs and measure their job satisfaction by considering factors such as participation in decision-making, use of valued skills, freedom and independence, challenge, expression of creativity, and opportunity for learning (Pastor, 1982). These findings have been supported in more recent research, for example in research findings that an employee empowerment climate is associated with higher levels of job satisfaction (Seibert, Silver, & Randolph, 2004). Opportunity to use strengths is, arguably, closely related to the above factors that contribute to job satisfaction. If particular expectations have been established (e.g., that the organization will encourage individual strengths use through the provision of a strengths assessment tool at induction), then these unmet expectations may impact on job satisfaction.

Research has shown that measures of employee turnover, intention to quit, or retention are a reliable indicator of employee attitudes to their workplace (Langford, 2010; Little & Little, 2006; Steel and Ovalle, 1984) or level of engagement (Harter & Blacksmith, 2010). For example, individuals are more likely to leave an organization if their expectations are not met (Cotton & Tuttle, 1986). Such expectations have been found to include "interest in the type of job," "quality of manager," "opportunity to learn and grow," and an expectation of engagement (Harter & Blacksmith, 2010). Managing turnover in order to retain valuable organizational knowledge and skills is a key outcome for organizations.

Another conceptualization of employee engagement is "work engagement," defined as a "positive, fulfilling, work-related state of mind that is characterized by vigor, dedication, and absorption" (González-Romá, Schaufeli, Bakker, & Lloret, 2006; Schaufeli, Salanova, González-Romá, & Bakker, 2002). Work engagement has been found to predict a higher level of service climate, which in turn predicts employee performance and customer loyalty (a clear and desired organizational outcome; Salanova, Agut, & Peiró, 2005).

Attempts have been made to define engagement more comprehensively within the positive psychology paradigm. For example, Stairs, Galpin, Page, and Linley (2006) define engagement as the extent to which employees thrive at work, are committed to their employer, and are motivated to do their best for their own benefit and that of the organization. Such a definition incorporates the notion of well-being, organizational commitment, and motivational states for both the individual and the organizational outcomes.

Employee well-being

There is substantial research to show that individual well-being has positive outcomes for individuals, is good for organizations, and contributes to organizational well-being. Since the advent of the field of positive psychology, the notion of the happy worker has moved toward a conceptualization of employee well-being rather than employee engagement or job satisfaction (Cropanzano & Wright, 1999; Wright & Bonett, 1997; Wright & Cropanzano, 1998, 2000). The well-being perspective incorporates job satisfaction with the presence of positive emotional states and positive appraisals to accentuate worker performance and quality of life (Cotton & Hart, 2003).

While employee well-being and engagement have overlapping elements (Robertson & Cooper, 2011, pp. 33–35), well-being is different from engagement because it implies a more comprehensive approach that focuses on enabling employees to maximize their personal resources as well as creating an organizational structure that enables employees to flourish. Another key difference between the well-being and engagement literature is that the engagement literature focuses on outcomes for employers and organizations at the expense of positive outcomes for employees (Robertson & Cooper, 2010). The well-being literature, on the other hand, has focused on individual outcomes. These differences in approach reflect the originating paradigms within which each construct has arisen – engagement from the management and organizational development literature, and well-being from the psychological literature. While psychological well-being is not usually positioned as a key component of employee engagement (Harter et al., 2002; Schaufeli et al., 2006), Robertson et al. (2012) propose that including well-being in the construct of employee engagement would lead to more positive business outcomes, as well as a more comprehensive employee engagement definition for individuals (Meyer & Maltin, 2010) and organizations alike (Robertson & Cooper, 2010).

Higher well-being is associated with positive self-perceptions and judgments of others, higher performance on complex mental tasks, greater creativity, flexibility, and originality – behaviors and psychological processes linked to work success (Lyubomirsky, Sheldon, & Schkade, 2005). These, in turn lead to more productive, profitable, and successful organizations. Using meta-analysis, Harter et al. (2002) investigated the relationship between well-being in the workplace and organizational outcomes and found that positive workplace perceptions and positive emotions were associated with higher business-unit customer loyalty, higher profitability, higher productivity, and lower turnover.

High levels of psychological well-being among employees translate into good news for the organization – including lower sickness/absence levels, attraction and retention of talented people, and more satisfied customers, clients or service users. People with higher levels of psychological well-being work better, live longer, and have happier lives. Engagement and well-being can sustain each other and lead to a healthier and more productive organization – a win–win for employees and employer (Langford, 2010). Higher satisfaction among employees leads to greater discretionary effort that contributes to the customer satisfaction of the organization (Harter et al., 2002).

Workers who experience poor health and well-being in the workplace have been found to be less productive, make poorer decisions, be more prone to being absent from work, and make diminishing contributions to the organization (Price & Hooijberg, 1992). In service organizations where staff well-being is higher, members of staff are more likely to provide extra-role customer service (Moliner, Martinez-Tur, Ramos, Peiro, & Cropanzano, 2008); customer satisfaction and service quality have also been shown to be linked to employee well-being (Leiter, Harvie, & Frizzell, 1998; Robertson & Cooper, 2011).

Page and Vella-Brodrick (2009) proposed a model that goes beyond job satisfaction to define well-being and its importance to organizations, and to explore how it can be enhanced. This model comprises three elements of employee well-being: subjective well-being (high levels of positive affect, low levels of negative affect, life satisfaction); workplace well-being (work-related affect and job-satisfaction); and psychological well-being (based on Ryff's [1995] six healthy psychological dimensions). Wright and colleagues found that job satisfaction was a valid predictor of performance, moderated by employee well-being (Wright et al., 2007; Wright & Bonett, 2007). These results provide preliminary support for the inclusion of job satisfaction as a core element of employee well being (Page & Vella-Brodrick, 2009).

The New Economic Foundation produced a model of well-being at work which takes into account an individual's experience at work (how they feel), their personal resources (who they are), their functioning at work (what they do), and the organizational systems they work within. Reciprocal relationships and feedback loops exist between these four levels of the model, highlighting the interaction between individual experience and resources and organizational context and structure (New Economic Foundation, 2014). Such a model hints at the complexity that lies beneath the relationship between employee well-being and organizational success.

A comprehensive study examined 16,000 employees across 15 different organizations in a wide range of workplaces and varying roles. They found generally that higher employee productivity was associated with better psychological well-being (Donald et al., 2005). Further research has established the relationship between psychological well-being on the one hand, and job performance and productivity on the other, in many different settings (Robertson & Cooper, 2011). In another meta-analysis Ford, Cerasoli, Higgins, and Decesare (2011) examined 111 studies (87,634 respondents) from a range of countries, concluding that psychological health (i.e., psychological well-being, depression, general anxiety, and life satisfaction) was moderately to strongly correlated with work performance.

However, focusing on individual work performance does not provide a comprehensive framework for organizational success as a whole, as it fails to take into account team and organizational context that may impact on the value of individual output and effort.

Further, the complex nature of these potentially reciprocal relationships is highlighted by research that has found that people with higher well-being are better equipped to deal with life generally and to be successful (Robertson & Cooper, 2011). There is evidence that people high in well-being (and thus experiencing more positive emotions) have a reciprocal impact on organizational context and group environments, and create positive upward spirals in their organizations (Fredrickson, 2001).

Factors that contribute to individual well-being in the workplace

Workplace factors that drive individual well-being at work include the individuals' degree of control and autonomy and the extent to which they feel their workload is unmanageable. Employee welfare is a climate factor that has shown a strong relationship with productivity – that is, when employees feel that the organization is concerned about their welfare they are more likely to be productive (Patterson, Warr, & West, 2004). Such research supports the relatedness aspect of well-being, underlining the importance of warm, positive, affectionate relationships with others in the workplace (Dutton & Heaphy, 2003).

Positive organizational behavior fosters positive characteristics in individuals, such as hope (Snyder, 2002) and gratitude (Emmons & McCullough, 2003). An individual's psychological capital (i.e., levels of hope, resilience, optimism, and self-efficacy) is related to his or her level of financial performance, referrals within the firm, and manager-rated performance (Avey, Nimnicht, & Nancy, 2010). And it is related to his or her well-being?

Mental fitness is defined as the flexible capacity to utilize resources and skills to adapt to challenges or opportunities (Robinson, Oades, & Caputi, 2015). The three elements of mental fitness – strengths, flexibility, and endurance – are measurable and can be improved through targeted development and intervention. To date, there is little research linking mental fitness to organizational outcomes; however, there is significant overlap between mental fitness and well-being with the former providing potential for the investigation of specific relationships. For a more detailed coverage of mental fitness, see Chapter 10, this volume.

The impact of positive emotions themselves on individual well-being at work is worth noting. Research has shown that when individuals experience positive emotions they are better able to perform flexible cognitive processing (Fredrickson, 2001) that extends creativity and allows them to make the most of their situation (Isen, 2003). Well-being and the experience of positive emotions provide opportunities for growth, self development, and environmental mastery in the workplace. An employee's involvement in meaningful work is believed to improve work motivation and performance (Steger & Dik, 2010). The extent to which a person considers her or his work as a vocation and a calling is viewed as an important quality of that person's work experiences (Steger & Dik, 2010). Meaningfulness at work can be defined as understanding one's fit within an organization and as a sense of belonging (Pratt & Ashforth, 2003). Further, meaning making occurs in a social context, therefore enabling the development of relationships and a sense of identity (Steger & Dik, 2010). Organizational practices may foster meaningfulness by enriching role tasks and membership within the organization (Pratt & Ashforth, 2003). However, in organizations which do not focus on fostering meaningfulness for individuals, the onus falls on individual workers to create meaning (Pratt & Ashforth, 2003).

Mindfulness has a range of physiological and psychological benefits for individuals which have been extensively reported elsewhere (Marianetti & Passmore, 2010). Mindfulness at work has been shown to impact several areas that are linked to business performance including safety, conflict resolution, creativity, and decision-making (Marianetti & Passmore, 2010). Mindfulness can also be applied collectively at an organizational level (Weick & Sutcliffe, 2001).

Self-determination theory (SDT) is a motivational framework comprising a set of related theories (Deci & Ryan, 2002). One of these (basic needs theory) posits that humans have three basic psychological needs (autonomy, competence, and relatedness), the fulfillment of which is related to increased well-being. The extent to which an environment, such as a workplace, provides fulfillment and expression of these three needs is the extent to which it can be described as autonomy supportive. SDT proposes that the more autonomy supportive an environment is, the more intrinsically motivated an individual will be within that environment. This proposition has important implications for organizations, as many desirable employee behaviors are based around directing intrinsic motivation toward organizational goals, for example engagement and organizational citizenship behavior. Indeed, Meyer and Gagne (2008) state that SDT can be readily applied to a wide range of engagement-related measures. The reciprocity of this construct resides in the provision of autonomy-supportive environments that allow individuals to enhance their own levels of motivation in the pursuit of organizationally beneficial goals.

Psychological ownership, a construct somewhat similar to autonomy, is positively related to extra-role or organizational citizenship behaviors (Vandewalle, Van Dyne, & Kostova, 1995) and organizational financial performance (Wagner, Parker, & Christiansen, 2003). Psychological ownership is defined as an individual feeling responsible for a particular target and feeling concerned about that target (which may be a job or their organization; Parker et al., 2003). It differs from the SDT definition of autonomy, in that the individual has not necessarily chosen the target, but displays ownership and responsibility toward it regardless.

It is important to note the reciprocal relationship between individual and organizational well-being here. In Langford's university example, as performance improves, facilities are built or upgraded, for example a library, common staff areas, parking, and a university pub. Langford (2010) notes evidence that higher-performing organizations provide more recognition for employees, thereby potentially enhancing individual well-being. Conversely, low-performing organizations are marked by a lack of individual progression opportunities (Langford, 2010). This reciprocal relationship between individual and organizational well-being is key to the argument we are making.

Workplace Well-Being at the Group or Team Level

In this chapter we propose that group and organizational well-being are different constructs from individual level well-being. Organizational level well-being must take into account tangible organizational outcomes that define the sustainability and well-being of the organization as a separate entity (e.g., productivity, financial performance, customer loyalty, growth and assets). Group-level well-being has not received much attention in the literature and below we pull together the existing research on group and team well-being and related constructs.

New organizational contexts such as globalization, technology, and changing boundaries continually redefine what it is to be a team (Wageman, Gardner, & Mortensen, 2012). A team has previously been defined as having a bounded and stable membership and a being focused on a shared collaborative task (Wageman et al., 2012). Hackman (2012) defines a team as a social system, collectively perceived as an entity by both members and non-members. Working in a team is distinct from working alone. Team members need to coordinate their actions and the success of teams is dependent on how team members interact with each other (Marks, Mathieu, & Zaccaro, 2001).

Using Ryff's six psychological well-being dimensions as a starting point, we define a group high in well-being as one that is growing and developing, that experiences more positive relationships than conflict, that has clarity of purpose, acts with autonomy, has a strong capacity to manipulate its environment in order to achieve its goals, and is characterized by self-acceptance, empathy, and belonging. As well-being at the group level has not received much attention in recent research, we have included other related constructs in our review of group-level well-being. One conceptualization of well-being at the group level is that of group morale. Group morale has been posited as an important indicator of group-level well-being (Peterson, Park, & Sweeney, 2008) and performance outcomes (Armstrong, Hart, & Fisher, 2003).

Group morale can be defined as including the following: confidence in the group's ability; enthusiasm for the tasks of the group; optimism for group success; belief in the group's capability, resilience, and leadership; mutual trust and respect between group members and leaders; loyalty to the group and its members; social cohesion; common purpose; sacrifice of individual needs for the group; and a compelling group history (Peterson et al., 2008). Apart from the last of these, however, they are all individual constructs which reside in individual group members, thereby demonstrating the individualistic fallacy. Peterson et al. (2008) identify that there is a conflation between individual and group descriptions of morale, however they do point out that individual-level analysis that is then aggregated to a group level does not comprehensively measure true group-level morale. While Peterson et al. recommend the inclusion of methodologically independent group-level measures, they offer few suggestions to counteract this approach.

Group morale in the workplace is enhanced by effective leadership, job security, safety, good salary and benefits, opportunities for advancement, sufficient resources to do the work, the status of the work, and the value associated with the goals of the organization (Hart & Cooper, 2001). Group well-being can also be described as effective teamwork – that is, working together to produce synchronized, collaborative outcomes (Paris, Salas, & Cannon-Bowers, 2000).

Research on group morale within organizations has often focused on unhealthy work environments marked by group conflict, harassment, prejudice, and poor communication problems, and rarely on healthy work environments that encourage well-being and flourishing (Cameron & Caza, 2004). Group morale is thought to be motivating, leading to perseverance and presumably success at group tasks, especially under trying circumstances (Manning, 1991). The lack of research into the antecedents and consequences of high morale is surprising. Peterson et al. (2008) maintain that morale has positive outcomes at both the individual and group levels.

Constructs that have been considered at the individual level may operate differently at the group or team level. For example, self-efficacy has a different mediating effect on the relationship between transformational leadership and either job satisfaction or well-being, at the individual or team level. In addition to both self- and team efficacy fully mediating the relationships between transformational leadership and well-being, team efficacy also partially meditates the relationship between transformational leadership and job satisfaction (Nielsen, Yarker, Randall, & Munir, 2009).

Alongside the individual study of work engagement at the individual level, researchers have also started to explore the construct at the team level (Costa, Passos, & Bakker, 2014). Team-level work engagement is associated with task and team performance, group positive affect and efficacy, as well as with individual work engagement (Costa et al., 2014).

Bakker, Albrecht, and Leiter (2011) propose that team engagement (team vigor, team dedication, and team absorption) is perceived by individual employees and might exist due to emotional contagion (Hatfield, Cacioppo, & Rapson, 1994) among team members. This perspective on team-work engagement highlights the affective dimension of the team construct, and not a cognitive or motivational one. Torrente, Salanova, Llorens, and

Schaufeli (2012a) also state that emotional contagion could be the mechanism underlying team-work engagement. Through structural equation modeling, and using 62 teams from 13 organizations, they reported evidence for a mediation role of team-work engagement between social resources (supportive team climate, coordination, and team-work) and team performance. This model builds on the individual JD-R model (Bakker, 2011) to account for team-level variables in explaining the existence of team-work engagement and its relationship with team performance (Costa et al., 2014).

A group that is high in well-being is characterized by positive relationships. A culture of psychological safety moderates the relationship between task conflict and performance in teams (Bradley, Postlethwaite, Klotz, Hamdani, & Brown, 2012).The reciprocal relationship between group- and individual-level well-being becomes apparent when examining the impact of team factors on individual outcomes. For example, a study examining team-based working, team structure, and job design on employee job satisfaction and work stress found that team structure and job design were associated with employee satisfaction and lower stress (So, West, & Dawson, 2011).

There is also a reciprocal relationship evident between group-level well-being and individual level well-being. Groups with high levels of morale enable positive traits like optimism, gratitude, and love that in turn contribute to individual well-being (Park, Peterson, & Seligman, 2004). Positive groups (i.e., those with good morale) allow people to be more engaged and to find meaning (Peterson, Park, & Seligman, 2005). Furthermore, researchers posit that it is in social participation that people find pleasure and savoring of the good things that happen (Bryant & Veroff, 2006). Such findings highlight the limitations of adopting the individualistic fallacy to multiple-level conceptualizations of organizational well-being and emphasize the value of examining the reciprocity that may occur between levels. Individual and contextual factors in the psychosocial work environment (e.g., quality of leadership, influence at work, team climate, role ambiguity, and work pace) require multilevel models in order to understand complex organizational phenomena and outcomes (such as affective organizational commitment; Clausen & Borg, 2010).

Potential pathways to build teamwork and develop successful teams come from correlational research finding that team optimism predicts outcomes for teams that are newly formed, and that team resiliency and team efficacy predict outcomes for established teams (West, Patera, & Carsten, 2009).

Social network analysis provides an opportunity to examine relationships within groups (Baker, Cross, & Wooten, 2003; Cross, Baker, & Parker, 2003). However, the relationships examined tend to be based on individuals or dyads, not on the social network analysis of the group as a whole. This highlights, again, the lack of methodological tools to measure group-level well-being.

In examining team-level engagement, Richardson and West (2010b) suggest that team engagement arises from the combined allocation of individual team members' resources and the interaction processes that move the group toward their objectives. Richardson and West (2010a) propose a positive inputs–process–outputs model that identifies team inputs, team engagement, and team outcomes at the micro level. The key inputs to a positive team are: an inspiring team task (such that it encourages creative achievement through intrinsic motivation and meaningful purpose); valued team diversity (to enable the development of psychological safety, creativity and team learning [Edmondson, 1999; Hoffman & Maier, 1961]); clear and evolving roles (to promote growth and task engagement); positive team relationships (to meet the innate need in humans for positive social interaction); and positive team attachment (further generating a shared sense of belonging; Sparrow & West, 2002). Richardson and West (2010a) also discuss the macro level: organizational factors that include organizational climate, alignment of values and goals, and transformational leadership. Their model embraces the reciprocity that exists between the levels of team engagement and organizational factors. Indeed, researchers have found considerable evidence that social groups are important psychological resources that have the capacity to protect individual health and well-being (Jetten, Haslam, Haslam, Dingle, & Jones, 2014) and to motivate individuals to achieve organizational outcomes (Haslam, Powell, & Turner, 2000), providing further support for the reciprocity of the multiple-layered well-being approach.

Group-level analysis can be described as the difference between saying "I have a lot of energy and enthusiasm" versus "There is a lot of energy and enthusiasm in my workgroup" (Cotton & Hart, 2003). However, even this description talks of individual constructs *within* a workgroup, thereby relying on the individualistic fallacy, and not giving ontological status to a group. Rather this approach relies on aggregating individual-level constructs (in this instance, energy). Here we are considering the collective energy of individuals rather than the group as a whole. A better descriptive statement might be "My workgroup has a lot of energy and enthusiasm." An analogy to consider here is the family unit: How do we say that a family is functioning well? There are different constructs that apply to the family unit as a whole, rather than to individuals, within a family.

The research described above demonstrates some of the key criticisms of group-level research and analysis of the well-being construct. Most of the research purporting to examine group-level constructs relies on individual responses that have been aggregated to a group. Few researchers discuss the reciprocity of well-being elements between the individual and group contexts. We see this as a key area for future research, elucidating the reciprocal relationships and impacts that the three levels of well-being (individual, group, and organizational) can have on each other.

Well-Being at the Organizational Level

There is a deal of confusion regarding the term "well-being" at the organizational or workplace level. Some definitions refer specifically to the well-being of individuals within organizations – such as the definition put forward by the Chartered Institute of Personnel and Development. In this definition, organizational well-being is defined as providing employees with meaningful and challenging work, and giving them an opportunity to apply their skills and knowledge in effective working relationships with colleagues and managers, in a safe and healthy environment (Chartered Institute of Personnel and Development, 2007). The term "organizational well-being" is also often used to refer to an employer-sponsored program to increase individual well-being within an organization. In this chapter we define organizational well-being as addressing the overall well-being of the organization as an entity itself. Nevertheless, a discussion of organizational well-being must also look at the organizational impact and outcomes of individual well-being.

Organizations with happier employees demonstrate better outcomes, including on key financial indicators (Edmans, 2012). Harter and colleagues demonstrated that employees' positive workplace perceptions and emotions were associated with higher customer loyalty, higher profitability and productivity, and lower turnover (Harter et al, 2002). As far back as 1958, researchers have sought to explore the concept of a psychologically healthy organization and have questioned the value of traditional indices such as absenteeism, turnover, and productivity in measuring organizational health (Argyris, 1958). Various frameworks and models have been proposed to describe the relationship between individual and organizational elements and characteristics.

Danna and Griffin (1999) proposed a framework examining health and well-being in the workplace. In their framework they described three antecedent factors – the work setting, personality traits, and occupational stress – and two sets of consequences – individual physical, psychological, and behavioral consequences; and organizational consequences (including health insurance costs, productivity, absenteeism, and litigation costs). They pointed out that organizational consequences are not orthogonally related to individual consequences, flagging the complexity of the relationships between the three different levels of well-being and highlighting the need for a more nuanced examination of these relationships.

The Organizational Health Framework (OHF) was proposed as an alternative theoretical perspective to the stressors and strains approach to occupational stress, which typically fails to take into account the broader organizational context (Cotton & Hart, 2003). The stressors and strains approach tends to reinforce the view that stress is an individual employee issue rather than an organizational one that should be addressed systematically (Hurrell, 1995). In addition, occupational stress has rarely been linked to organizational performance outcomes, resulting in the further marginalization of stress in the broader management and organizational behavior literature (Hart & Cooper, 2001; Wright & Cropanzano, 2000).

The OHF has as its starting point a systematic focus on the dynamic interactions between people and their environment. It is a theory-based approach delineating how individual and organizational factors interact to determine employee well-being and organizational performance (Cotton & Hart, 2003). Well-being must be linked to outcomes that affect organizational performance, for example job satisfaction leads to higher discretionary effort that contributes to customer satisfaction (Hart et al., 2002). One way in which the OHF extends organizational theory beyond the "happy worker hypothesis" is that it recognizes that the relationship between individual and organizational characteristics occurs in a broader context depending on the level of analysis applied. One aspect of this relationship between individual and organizational characteristics can be found in discussions of organizational climate.

Organizational climate is a subset of organizational culture. Schein (1990) defined culture as "a pattern of basic assumptions … that are … invented, discovered, or developed by a given group, as it learns to cope with its problems of external adaptation and internal integration" (p. 111). Schein added that these assumption had to have worked well enough to be considered valid and "therefore be taught to new members as the correct way to perceive, think, and feel in relation to those problems" (p. 111). Organizational climate refers to employees' perceptions about how their workplace functions and the policies and practices that guide behavior. Research has found that organizational climate exerted the strongest influence on morale (group-level construct) and occupational well-being among a sample of police officers and teachers (Hart, 1999; Hart & Cotton, 2003; demonstrating the key role of organizational climate in influencing occupational well-being). Further evidence that there is a reciprocal link between organizational and individual-level well-being includes the finding that organizational climate is the strongest indicator of individual overall well-being, whereas personality is the strongest determinant of employee withdrawal behavior intentions (Cotton & Hart, 2003). The impact that organizational climate has on occupational well-being is found across different occupational groups and has been found to be more important than job-specific stressors (Cotton & Hart, 2003).

According to De Smet, Loch, and Schaninger (2007), conceptualizing the health of organizations emerges out of a metaphor of "performance and health." This metaphor symbolizes the health of the organization as improving when cared for and deteriorating when ignored, thus signifying the importance of employees' well-being for business profitability. Adkins (1999) proposed the organizational health concept as an extension of occupational health psychology with a clear organizational focus, and Danna and Griffin (1999) related employee well-being to organizational effectiveness and functioning. Lowe (2003, 2010) defines a healthy organization as one whose culture, climate, and practices create an environment that promotes employee health and safety as well as organizational effectiveness. However, this definition does not refer to possible measures of organizational health such as profitability, productivity, or shareholder value.

Traditionally, good financial performance and productivity measures have been deemed indicators of a healthy organization (Raya & Panneerselvam, 2013). However, writers have argued that accounting-based financial measurements are insufficient to measure the health of organizations (e.g., Schneider, Hanges, Smith, & Salvaggio, 2003). Schneider et al. (2003) also raised the issue of using individual-level measures to analyze group- or organizational-level constructs. Schneider et al. cite several studies that provide preliminary evidence that aggregated employee attitudes are related to organizational performance (operationalized as customer satisfaction), productivity (Ryan, Schmitt, & Johnson, 1996), teacher turnover and student academic achievement (Ostroff, 1992), and short-term financial performance (Denison, 1990).

In a review of employee well-being and the human resource management (HRM)–organizational performance relationship, Van De Voorde, Paauwe, and Van Veldhoven (2012) made the distinction between two indicators of organizational performance: operational outcomes (such as productivity and quality) and financial outcomes (such as returns on invested capital and shareholder return). They posited that the effects of HRM interventions targeting employee well-being might show a greater impact on operational performance indicators than on financial performance indicators, characterizing these as proximal and distal outcomes respectively. A range of stressors may affect employee well-being – job control, role overload, social support, and supervisor behavior. Researchers have long argued that human resources practices and HRD professionals can improve employees' well-being and contribute to organizational effectiveness by focusing on these concerns (Gilbreath & Montesino, 2000). Clarke and Hill (2012) explored the relationship between employee well-being and service quality and suggest that both can be improved with targeted HRM strategies such as learning and development, employee voice, and involvement in workplace health and safety. In a study examining the effects of HRM practices on employee well-being at work and performance in the public sector, Baptiste (2008) found that line management support and trust were pivotal to good relations between managers and employees, and that these factors subsequently promoted employee well-being at work.

De Smet et al. (2007) describe a healthy organization as one which demonstrates five overarching characteristics: resilience (proactively putting the organization into a bracing position to be able to withstand disasters; Burnard & Bhamra, 2011), execution (ability to make sound and timely decisions, forecasting skills, employee who understand their roles and responsibilities), alignment (cohesiveness of purpose), renewal (expanding into well-chosen markets where existing assets and competencies provide leverage, ability to generate ideas and adapt to change), and complementarity (of organizational practices, such as hiring policies and "consistent and mutually reinforcing behavioral incentives").

Another concept related to organizational autonomy is that of dynamic capabilities. Teece, Pisano, and Shuen (1997) define a dynamic capability as the ability to integrate, build, and reconfigure internal and external competences to address changing environments

(Helfat, 2007). Dynamic capabilities are different from operational capabilities, which pertain to the current operations of an organization. This definition of dynamic capabilities draws on an organization's environmental mastery and autonomy and the extent to which an organization demonstrates dynamic capabilities may indicate organizational well-being.

Further evidence that there is a reciprocal link between organizational and individual level well-being includes the finding that organizational climate is the strongest indicator of individual overall well-being whereas personality is the strongest determinant of employee withdrawal behavior intentions (Cotton & Hart, 2003). The impact that organizational climate has on occupational well-being is found across different occupational groups and is more important than job-specific stressors (Cotton & Hart, 2003).

Positive organizational scholarship (POS) theorists propose the concept of organizational virtuousness as a way of thinking about positive activities and deviance within organizations. Organizational virtuousness is characterized by three key principles: human impact (actions are undertaken to ensure positive human impact), moral goodness (virtuousness possesses inherent goodness), and social betterment (creates social value that produces benefits to others without expectation of reciprocity or reward) (Cameron, 2003). POS differentiates between virtuousness in organizations (relating to the behavior of individuals), and virtuousness through organizations (relating to enablers within organizations that foster and perpetuate virtuousness [Cameron, 2003]). While Cameron predicts that virtuousness through organizations is likely to be associated with positive performance, he admits little empirical evidence has been conducted to test this hypothesis at the organizational level (Cameron, 2003).

Much has been written in the management literature and popular press of the need for organizations to define and communicate a purpose to their stakeholders in order to galvanize action toward achieving that purpose. Organizational purpose links to individual employee well-being, for example staff training and retention is an important step along the way of reaching organizational goals (Steger & Dik, 2010). The more visibility and alignment there are between organizational and individual goals and purpose, the more effectively they will be achieved. Individual well-being is linked to feeling a sense of contribution toward meaningful goals (e.g., Chalofsky & Krishna, 2009). Organizations that focus on promoting their goals, values, and purpose are more likely to foster meaningfulness in employees (Pratt & Ashforth, 2003). Similarly, visionary leadership practices that foster idealistic organizational goals create meaning for employees by appealing to and resonating with the individual's sense of identity and belonging (Pratt & Ashforth, 2003). Meaning can be created by organizations that build organizational communities either through developing family-like dynamics at work, or emphasizing a mission based on values beyond mere profit (Pratt & Ashforth, 2003). A further concept is that of the learning organization.

A learning organization is one whose individuals continually increase their capacity to learn new patterns of thinking and behaving in order that the organization can continue to transform itself, adapt, and create results (Senge, 1990). The concept of the learning organization relates to growth as one of Ryff's six psychological well-being dimensions (2008).

In keeping with the positive psychology movement, "amplition" is based on the principle of improvement, rather than fixing what appears to be broken (the traditional problem-based psychological model). Within an organizational context, amplition also refers to positive interventions that promote and increase employee well-being (Schaufeli & Salanova, 2010). Amplition is based on the notion that improving employee well-being is a long-term goal requiring sustained and conscious effort. Schaufeli and Salanova

(2010) argue that organizations need to focus on both positive individual- and organizational-based interventions to ensure their ongoing profitability and sustainability, thereby recognizing the reciprocity between these two levels within organizations.

Future Research

While understanding the well-being of individuals in the workplace is an appropriate approach, supported by increasing empirical evidence, multilevel conceptualizations are needed to understand the complexity of well-being in and of organizations. Complex adaptive systems (CAS) theory (see Anderson 1999; Miller & Page, 2009) offers a fertile conceptual, methodological, and empirical foundation within which to consider workplace well-being and organizational well-being.

CAS theory suggests that a process that appears to occur by chance when examined at the individual level can be predictable at the whole society level (e.g., rates of suicide). This phenomenon is known as "emergence." If we move beyond causality at the individual level to the behavior of the system as a whole, global patterns of behavior may become apparent. However, this eliminates the ability to understand causality at the individual level (Lansing, 2003). Thinking about organizations as complex adaptive systems (Dooley, 1997; Schneider & Somers, 2006) allows us to become aware of more global patterns of behavior at the system, or organizational, level.

In addition to further research of well-being at the individual level in the workplace, complex and adaptive approaches combined with tools such as system dynamics, agent-based simulation modeling (see Borshchev & Filippov, 2004; Sterman, 2000, 2001) allow the modeling of interactions across individual, team, and whole of organization functioning. Future individual and organizational well-being research will be well served by moving beyond the individualist fallacy – that is, the organization, and more specifically organizational well-being, is more than the aggregate of the well-being of happy workers.

For example, if an employee has high levels of individual well-being, within a team that has a moderate level of well-being, what is the likely impact on organizational well-being? Is organizational well-being an emergent property of the other levels? These are key guiding questions for future well-being related research in the workplace and for the organization writ large.

Conclusion

This chapter proposed that organizational theory needs to move beyond the happy worker hypothesis and conceptualize well-being beyond the individual level. A three-level conceptualization of well-being referred to as the workplace and organizational well-being model (WOWM) was examined: (1) well-being at the individual level, (2) well-being at the team/group level, and (3) well-being at the organizational level. Systems theory and methods were recommended to explore the interaction of well-being at different levels of the organization, and can enable the discovery of new places to intervene and leverage points to improve organizational functioning. Table 15.1 illustrates the many different constructs of well-being at the three different levels within organizations, underscoring the importance of adopting a multilevel approach to well-being.

Table 15.1 Existing constructs relevant to different levels of well-being in an organizational context.

Individual-level well-being constructs

- Flow at work (Csikszentmihalyi, 1990)
- Job crafting (Wrzesniewski & Dutton, 2001)
- Job satisfaction (Locke, 1976)
- Mindfulness (Roche, Haar, & Luthans, 2014)
- Mental fitness (Robinson et al., 2015)
- PsyCap (psychological capital: hope, optimism, resilience, self-efficacy) (Luthans, Avolio, Avey, & Norman, 2007)
- Openness to experience (Revised Neo Personality Inventory; NEO-PIR) (Costa & McRae, 1992)
- STD theory – basic psychological needs (autonomy, competence, relatedness) (Baard, Deci, & Ryan, 2004)
- Sense of meaning and purpose (Ryff, 2008; Steger & Dik, 2010)
- Strengths knowledge and use (Crossan, Mazutis, Seijts, & Gandz, 2013)

Team-level well-being constructs

- Group's capacity to manipulate and control their environment
- Group psychological safety (Kahn, 1990)
- Group reputation (Kimbrough & Rubin, 2015)
- Group understanding of common purpose and working together to achieve this (Kurtzman, 2010)
- Positive relationships in team, fostered in empathy and appreciation for each other's strengths (Dutton & Ragins, 2007)
- Self-managing teams, autonomy to do job (Campion, Medsker, & Higgs, 1993; Spreitzer, 1995)
- Team achievement, progress, and recognition (McClelland & Burnham, 2003)
- Team cohesion (Paskevich, Brawley, Dorsch, & Widmeyer, 1999)
- Team diversity and appreciation for different perspectives (Horwitz & Horwitz, 2007)

Organizational-level well-being constructs

- Ability to manipulate and control complex environments (Boisot & Child, 1999)
- Amplition (Schaufeli & Salanova, 2010)
- Appreciative inquiry (Cooperrider & Srivastva, 1987)
- Change management (Todnem, 2005)
- Clear vision and purpose, defining strategy, vision, and values (McClelland & Burnham, 2003)
- Clear understanding of organizational strengths, weaknesses, and target clients in order to define core business (Porter, 2008)
- Dynamic capabilities (Teece et al., 1997; Helfat, 2007)
- Freedom from over-regulation, freedom from over-reliance on shareholder value, union intervention (Andrews, Boyne, Law, & Walker, 2008)
- Leadership (Alimo-Metcalfe, Alban-Metcalfe, Bradley, Mariathasan, & Samele, 2008; Hunter, 2009; McMurray, Pirola-Merlo, Sarros, & Islam, 2010)
- Learning organization – ability to learn from feedback and change (Senge, 1990)
- Strategic alliances, good supplier relationships (Austin, 2010; Hamel, 1991)
- Organizational culture (Schein, 1990)
- Organizational resilience (Burnard & Bhamra, 2011; Parsons, 2010)
- Organizational success and progress (Cotton & Hart, 2003)
- Organizational virtuousness (Cameron, 2003)
- Positive ethics (Stansbury & Sonenshein, 2012)
- Positive institutions (Cameron, Mora, Leutscher, & Calarco, 2011)
- Positive organizational scholarship (Cameron, 2003)
- Strategic decision-making (Schwenk, 1995)
- Strategic execution (Sheehan, 2006)

Source: Author.

References

Adkins, J. A. (1999). Promoting organizational health: The evolving practice of occupational health psychology. *Professional Psychology: Research and Practice*, *30*(2), 129.

Alimo-Metcalfe, B., Alban-Metcalfe, J., Bradley, M., Mariathasan, J., & Samele, C. (2008). The impact of engaging leadership on performance, attitudes to work and wellbeing at work: A longitudinal study. *Journal of Health Organization and Management*, *22*(6), 586–598.

Anderson, P. (1999). Perspective: Complexity theory and organization science. *Organization Science*, *10*(3), 216–232.

Andrews, R., Boyne, G. A., Law, J., & Walker, R. M. (2008). Organizational strategy, external regulation and public service performance. *Public Administration*, *86*, 185–203.

Argyris, C. (1958). The organization: What makes it healthy? *Harvard Business Review*, *36*, 107–116.

Armstrong, K., Hart, P. M., & Fisher, P. (2003). *Integrating climate, emotions, and contextual and task performance into a coherent managerial framework.* Paper submitted to the 2003 Academy of Management Meeting, Seattle, Washington.

Austin, J. E. (2010). *The collaboration challenge: How nonprofits and businesses succeed through strategic alliances.* Hoboken, NJ: Wiley.

Avey, J. B., Nimnicht, J. L., & Nancy, G. P. (2010). Two field studies examining the association between positive psychological capital and employee performance. *Leadership & Organization Development Journal*, *31*(5), 384–401.

Baard, P. P., Deci, E. L., & Ryan, R. M. (2004). Instrinsic need satisfaction: A motivational bias of performance and well-being in two work settings. *Journal of Applied Social Psychology*, *34*(10), 2045–2068.

Baker, W., Cross, R., & Wooten, M. (2003). Positive organizational network analysis and energizing relationships. In K. S. Cameron, J. E. Dutton, & R. E. Quinn (Eds.), *Positive organizational scholarship: Foundations of a new discipline* (pp. 328–342). San Francisco, CA: Berrett-Koehler.

Bakker, A. B. (2011). An evidence-based model of work engagement. *Current Directions in Psychological Science*, *20*(4), 265–269.

Bakker, A. B., Albrecht, S. L., & Leiter, M. P. (2011). Key questions regarding work engagement. *European Journal of Work and Organizational Psychology*, *20*(1), 4–28.

Bakker, A. B., Hakanen, J. J., Demerouti, E., & Xanthopoulou, D. (2007). Job resources boost work engagement, particularly when job demands are high. *Journal of Educational Psychology*, *99*(2), 274.

Bakker, A. B., & Leiter, M. P. (2010). *Work engagement: A handbook of essential theory and research* (1st ed.). Hoboken, NJ: Psychology Press.

Baptiste, N. R. (2008). Tightening the link between employee wellbeing at work and performance: A new dimension for HRM. *Management Decision*, *46*(1–2), 284–309.

Boisot, M., & Child, J. (1999). Organizations as adaptive systems in complex environments: The case of China. *Organization Science*, *10*(3), 237–252.

Borshchev, A., & Filippov, A. (2004, July). From system dynamics and discrete event to practical agent based modeling: Reasons, techniques, tools. In *Proceedings of the 22nd international conference of the system dynamics society*, Oxford, UK.

Bradley, B. H., Postlethwaite, B. E., Klotz, A. C., Hamdani, M. R., & Brown, K. G. (2012). Reaping the benefits of task conflict in teams: The critical role of team psychological safety climate. *Journal of Applied Psychology*, *97*(1), 151.

Bryant, F. B., & Veroff, J. (2006). *The process of savouring: A new model of positive experience.* Mahwah, NJ: Erlbaum.

Burnard, K., & Bhamra, R. (2011). Organizational resilience: Development of a conceptual framework for organizational responses. *International Journal of Production Research*, *49*(18), 5581–5599.

Cameron, K. (2003). Virtuousness and performance. In K. Cameron, J. Dutton, & R. Quinn (Eds.), *Positive organizational scholarship* (pp. 48–65). San Francisco, CA: Berrett-Koehler.

Cameron, K. S., & Caza, A. (2004). Contributions to the discipline of positive organizational scholarship. *American Behavioral Scientist*, *47*(6), 731–739.

Cameron, K., Mora, C., Leutscher, T., & Calarco, M. (2011). Effects of positive practices on organizational effectiveness. *The Journal of Applied Behavioral Science, 47*, 266–308.

Campion, M. A., Medsker, G. J., & Higgs, A. C. (1993). Relations between work group characteristics and effectiveness: Implications for designing effective work groups. *Personnel Psychology, 46*(4), 823–847.

Chalofsky, N., & Krishna, V. (2009). Meaningfulness, commitment, and engagement: The intersection of a deeper level of intrinsic motivation. *Advances in Developing Human Resources, 11*(2), 189–203.

Chartered Institute of Personnel Development. (2007). *What's happening with well-being at work?* London, UK: Author.

Christian, M. S., Garza, A. S., & Slaughter, J. E. (2011). Work engagement: A quantitative review and test of its relations with task and contextual performance. *Personnel Psychology, 64*(1), 89–136.

Clarke, M. A., & Hill, S. R. (2012). Promoting employee wellbeing and quality service outcomes: The role of HRM practices. *Journal of Management and Organization, 18*(5), 702–713.

Clausen, T., & Borg, V. (2010). Do positive work-related states mediate the association between psychosocial work characteristics and turnover? A longitudinal analysis. *International Journal of Stress Management, 17*(4), 308.

Cooperrider, D. L., & Srivastva, S. (1987). Appreciative inquiry in organizational life. *Research in organizational change and development, 1*(1), 129–169.

Costa, P. L., Passos, A. M., & Bakker, A. B. (2014). Team work engagement: A model of emergence. *Journal of Occupational and Organizational Psychology, 87*, 414–436.

Costa, P. T., & McCrae, R. R. (1992). The five-factor model of personality and its relevance to personality disorders. *Journal of Personality Disorders, 6*, 343–359.

Cotton, J. L., & Tuttle, J. M. (1986). Employee turnover: A meta-analysis and review with implications for research. *Academy of Management Review, 11*(1), 55–70.

Cotton, P., & Hart, P. M. (2003). Occupational wellbeing and performance: A review of organizational health research. *Australian Psychologist, 38*(2), 118–127.

Cropanzano, R., & Wright, T. A. (1999). A 5-year study of change in the relationship between well-being and job performance. *Consulting Psychology Journal: Practice and Research, 51*(4), 252.

Cropanzano, R., & Wright, T. A. (2001). When a "happy" worker is really a "productive" worker: A review and further refinement of the happy productive worker thesis. *Consulting Psychology Journal: Practice and Research, 53*(3), 182.

Cross, R., Baker, W., & Parker, A. (2003). What creates energy in organizations? *MIT Sloan Management Review, 44*(4), 51–56.

Crossan, M., Mazutis, D., Seijts, G., and Gandz, J. (2013). Developoing leadership character in business programs. *Academy of Management Learning & Education, 12*(2), 285–305.

Csikszentmihalyi, M. (1990). *Flow: The psychology of optimal experience.* New York, NY: Harper & Row.

Danna, K., & Griffin, R. W. (1999). Health and well-being in the workplace: A review and synthesis of the literature. *Journal of Management, 25*, 357–384.

Deci, E. L., & Ryan, R. M. (1985). The general causality orientations scale: Self-determination in personality. *Journal of Research in Personality, 19*, 109–134.

Deci, E. L., & Ryan, R. M. (2002). *Handbook of self-determination research.* Rochester, NY: University of Rochester Press.

Denison, D. R. (1990). *Corporate culture and organizational effectiveness.* New York, NY: Wiley.

De Smet, A., Loch, M., & Schaninger, B. (2007, May). Anatomy of a healthy corporation. *The McKinsey Quarterly*, 1–11.

Donald, I., Taylor, P., Johnson, S., Cooper, C., Cartwright, S., & Robertson, S. (2005). Work environments, stress, and productivity: An examination using ASSET. *International Journal of Stress Management, 12*(4), 409–423.

Dooley, K. J. (1997). A complex adaptive systems model of organization change. *Nonlinear Dynamics, Psychology, and Life Sciences, 1*(1), 69–97.

Dutton, J. E., & Heaphy, E. D. (2003). The power of high-quality connections. In K. S. Cameron, J. E. Dutton, & R. E. Quinn (Eds.), *Positive organizational scholarship: Foundations of a new discipline* (pp. 263–278). San Francisco, CA: Berrett-Koehler.

Dutton, J. E., & Ragins, B. R. E. (2007). *Exploring positive relationships at work: Building a theoretical and research foundation*. Mahwah, NJ: Erlbaum.
Edmans, A. (2012). The link between employee satisfaction and firm value, with implications for corporate social responsibility. *The Academy of Management Perspectives 26*(4), 1–19.
Edmondson, (1999). Psychological safety and learning behavior in work teams. *Administrative Science Quarterly, 44*(2), 350–383.
Emmons, R. A., & McCullough, M. E. (2003). Counting blessings versus burdens: An experimental investigation of gratitude and subjective well-being in daily life. *Journal of Personality and Social Psychology, 84*(2), 377.
Ford, M. T., Cerasoli, C. P., Higgins, J. A., & Decesare, A. L. (2011). Relationships between psychological, physical, and behavioural health and work performance: A review and meta-analysis. *Work and Stress: An International Journal of Work, Health and Organizations, 25*(3), 185–204.
Fredrickson, B. L. (2001). The role of positive emotions in positive psychology: The broaden-and-build theory of positive emotions. *American Psychologist, 56*(3), 218.
Gilbreath, B., & Montesino, M. U. (2000). Expanding the HRD role: Improving employee well-being and organizational performance. *Human Resource Development International, 9*, 563–571.
González-Romá, V., Schaufeli, W. B., Bakker, A. B., & Lloret, S. (2006). Burnout and work engagement: Independent factors or opposite poles? *Journal of Vocational Behavior, 68*, 165–174.
Hackman, J. R. (2012). From causes to conditions in group research. *Journal of Organizational Behavior, 33*(3), 428–444.
Hakanen, J. J., Bakker, A. B., & Schaufeli, W. B. (2006). Burnout and work engagement among teachers. *Journal of School Psychology, 43*(6), 495–513.
Hamel, G. (1991). Competition for competence and inter-partner learning within international strategic alliances. *Strategic Management Journal, 12*(4), 83–103.
Harrison, D. A., Newman, D. A., & Roth, P. L. (2006). How important are job attitudes? Meta-analytic comparisons of integrative behavioral outcomes and time sequences. *Academy of Management Journal, 49*, 305–325.
Hart, P. M. (1999). Predicting employee life satisfaction: A coherent model of personality, work, and nonwork experiences, and domain satisfactions. *Journal of Applied Psychology, 84*(4), 564–584.
Hart, P. M., & Cooper, C. L. (2001). Occupational stress: Toward a more integrated framework. In N. Anderson, D. S. Ones, H. K. Sinangil, & C. Viswesvaran *Handbook of industrial, work and organizational psychology: Vol. 1. Personnel psychology* (pp. 93–114). London, UK: Sage.
Harter, J., & Blacksmith, N. (2010). Employee engagement and the psychology of joining, staying in, and leaving organizations. In P. A. E. Linley (Ed.), *Oxford handbook of positive psychology at work* (pp. 121–130). Oxford, UK: Oxford University Press.
Harter, J. K., Schmidt, F. L., & Hayes, T. L. (2002). Business unit level outcomes between employee satisfaction, employee engagement and business outcomes: A meta-analysis. *Journal of Applied Psychology, 87*, 268–279.
Harter, J. K., Schmidt, F. L., & Keyes, C. L. M. (2003). Well-being in the workplace and its relationship to business outcomes. A review of the Gallup studies. In C. L. M. Keyes & J. Haidt (Eds.), *Flourishing: The positive person and the good life* (pp. 205–224). Washington, DC: American Psychological Association.
Haslam, S. A., Powell, C., & Turner, J. (2000). Social identity, self-categorization, and work motivation: Rethinking the contribution of the group to positive and sustainable organizational outcomes. *Applied Psychology: An International Review, 49*, 319–339.
Hatfield, E., Cacioppo, J. T., & Rapson, R. L. (1994). *Emotional contagion*. Cambridge, UK: Cambridge University Press.
Helfat, C. E. (2007). Stylized facts, empirical research and theory development in management. *Strategic Organization, 5*(2), 185–192.
Hoffman, L. R., & Maier, N. R. (1961). Quality and acceptance of problem solutions by members of homogeneous and heterogeneous groups. *The Journal of Abnormal and Social Psychology, 62*(2), 401.
Horwitz, S. K., & Horwitz, I. B. (2007). The effects of team diversity on team outcomes: A meta-analytic review of team demography. *Journal of Management, 33*(6), 987–1015.

Hunter, D. J. (2009). Leading for health and wellbeing: The need for a new paradigm. *Journal of Public Health, 32*(2), 202–204.

Hurrell, J. J. (1995). Police work, occupational stress and individual coping. *Journal of Organizational Behaviour, 16*, 27–28.

Iaffaldano, M. T., & Muchinsky, P. M. (1985). Job satisfaction and job performance: A meta-analysis. *Psychological Bulletin, 97*, 251–273.

Isen, A. M. (2003). Positive affect as a source of human strength. In L. G. Aspinwall & U. M. Staudinger (Eds.), *A psychology of human strengths: Fundamental questions and future directions for a positive psychology* (pp. 179–195). Washington, DC: American Psychological Association.

Jetten, J., Haslam, C., Haslam, S. A., Dingle, G., & Jones, J. M. (2014). How groups affect our health and well-being: The path from theory to policy. *Social Issues and Policy Review, 8*, 103–130.

Judge, T. A., & Kammeyer-Mueller, J. D. (2012). Job attitudes. *Annual Review of Psychology, 63*, 341–367.

Judge, T. A., Thoresen, C. J., Bono, J. E., & Patton, G. K. (2001). The job satisfaction–job performance relationship: A qualitative and quantitative review. *Psychological Bulletin, 127*, 376–407.

Judge, T. A., & Watanabe, S. (1993). Another look at the job satisfaction–life satisfaction relationship. *Journal of Applied Psychology, 78*, 939–948.

Kahn, W. A. (1990). Psychological conditions of personal engagement and disengagement at work. *Academy of Management Journal, 33*(4), 692–724.

Keyes, C. L., Shmotkin, D., & Ryff, C. D. (2002). Optimizing well-being: The empirical encounter of two traditions. *Journal of Personality and Social Psychology, 82*(6), 1007.

Kimbrough, E. O., & Rubin, J. (2015). Sustaining group reputation. *Journal of Law, Economics, & Organization*. doi:10.1093/jleo/ewu019

Kurtzman, J. (2010). *Common purpose: How great leaders get organizations to achieve the extraordinary*. San Francisco, CA: Jossey-Bass.

Langford, P. H. (2010). Benchmarking work practices and outcomes in Australian universities using an employee survey. *Journal of Higher Education Policy and Management, 32*(1), 41–53.

Langford, P., & Demirian, S. (2007). The effect of organizational performance on employee engagement. In M. Dollard, T. Winefield, M. Tuckey, & P. Winwood (Eds.),*Proceedings of the 7th Industrial and Organisational Psychology Conference/1st Asia Pacific Congress on Work and Organisational Psychology* (pp. 180–184). Melbourne, Australia: Australian Psychological Society.

Langford, P. H., Parkes, L. P., & Metcalf, L. (2006). *Developing a structural equation model of organizational performance and employee engagement*. Paper presented at the 2006 Joint Conference of the Australian Psychological Society and the New Zealand Psychological Society, Auckland, New Zealand.

Lansing, J. S. (2003). Complex adaptive systems. *Annual Review of Anthropology, 32*, 183–204.

Leiter, M. P., Harvie, P., & Frizzell, C. (1998). The correspondence of patient satisfaction and nurse burnout. *Social Science & Medicine, 47*(10), 1611–1617.

Little, B., & Little, P. (2006). Employee engagement: Conceptual issues. *Journal of Organizational Culture, Communications and Conflict, 10*, 111–120.

Locke, E. A. (1976). The nature and causes of job satisfaction. In M. D. Dunnette (Ed.), *Handbook of industrial and organizational psychology* (pp. 1297–1349). Chicago, IL: Rand McNally.

Loney, T., & Nagelkerke, N. J. (2014). The individualistic fallacy, ecological studies and instrumental variables: A causal interpretation. *Emerging Themes in Epidemiology, 19*(11), 18.

Lowe, W. H. (2003). Linking dispersal to local population dynamics: A case study using a headwater salamander system. *Ecology, 84*(8), 2145–2154.

Lowe, W. H. (2010). Explaining long-distance dispersal: Effects of dispersal distance on survival and growth in a stream salamander. *Ecology, 91*(10), 3008–3015.

Luthans, F., Avolio, B. J., Avey, J. B., & Norman, S. M. (2007). Positive psychological capital: Measurement and relationship with performance and satisfaction. *Personnel Psychology, 60*(3), 541–572.

Lyubomirsky, S., Sheldon, K. M., & Schkade, D. (2005). Pursuing happiness: The architecture of sustainable change. *Review of General Psychology, 9*, 111–131.

Macey, W. H., & Schneider, B. (2008a). Engaged in engagement: We are delighted we did it. *Industrial and Organizational Psychology, 1*, 76–83.

Macey, W. H., & Schneider, B. (2008b). The meaning of employee engagement. *Industrial & Organizational Psychology, 1*, 3–30.

Manning, F. J. (1991). Morale, unit cohesion, and esprit de corps. In R. Gal & D. Mangelsdorff (Eds.), *Handbook of military psychology* (pp. 453–470). New York, NY: Wiley.

Marianetti, O., & Passmore, J. (2010). Mindfulness at work: Paying attention to enhance wellbeing and performance. In P. A. Linley, S. Harrington, & N. Garcea (Eds.), *Oxford handbook of positive psychology and work* (pp. 189–200). Oxford, UK: Oxford University Press.

Marks, M. A., Mathieu, J. E., & Zaccaro, S. J. (2001). A temporally based framework and taxonomy of team processes. *Academy of Management Review, 26*(3), 356–376.

McClelland, D. C., & Burnham, D. H. (2003). Power is the great motivator. *Harvard Business Review, 81*(1), 117–126.

McMurray, A. J., Pirola-Merlo, A., Sarros, J. C., & Islam, M. M. (2010). Leadership, climate, psychological capital, commitment, and wellbeing in a non-profit organization. *Leadership & Organization Development Journal, 31*(5), 436–457.

Meyer, J. P., & Allen, N. J. (1984). Testing the "side-bet theory" of organizational commitment: Some methodological considerations. *Journal of Applied Psychology, 69*, 372.

Meyer, J. P., & Allen, N. J. (1991). A three-component conceptualization of organizational commitment. *Human Resource Management Review, 1*, 61–89.

Meyer, J. P., and Allen, N. J. (1997). *Commitment in the workplace: Theory, research and application.* Thousand Oaks, CA: Sage.

Meyer, J. P., & Gagné, M. (2008). Employee engagement from a self-determination theory perspective. *Industrial and Organizational Psychology, 1*(01), 60–62.

Meyer, J. P., & Maltin, E. R. (2010). Employee commitment and well-being: A critical review, theoretical framework and research agenda. *Journal of Vocational Behavior, 77*(2), 323–337.

Meyer, J. P., Stanley, D. J., Herscovitch, L., & Topolnytsky, L. (2002). Affective, continuance, and normative commitment to the organization: A Meta-analysis of antecedents, correlates, and consequences. *Journal of Vocational Behavior, 61*, 20–52.

Miller, J. H., & Page, S. E. (2009). *Complex adaptive systems: An introduction to computational models of social life: an introduction to computational models of social life.* Princeton, NJ: Princeton University Press.

Mitchell, T. R., Holtom, B. C., Lee, T. W., Sablynski, C. J., & Erez, M. (2001). Why people stay: Using job embeddedness to predict voluntary turnover. *Academy of Management Journal, 44*, 1102–1121.

Moliner, C., Martinez-Tur, V., Ramos, J., Peiro, J. M., & Cropanzano, R. (2008). Organizational justice and extra-role customer service: The mediating role of well-being at work. *European Journal of Work and Organizational Psychology, 17*, 327–348.

New Economics Foundation Consulting. (2014). *Wellbeing at work: A review of the literature.* Retrieved March 30, 2015 from http://www.neweconomics.org/publications/entry/well-being-at-work

Newman, D. A., Joseph, D. L., & Hulin, C. L. (2010). Job attitudes and employee engagement: Considering the attitude "A-factor." In S. L. Albrecht (Ed.), *Handbook of employee engagement: Perspectives, issues, research and practice* (pp. 43–61). Cheltenham, UK: Edward Elgar.

Nielsen, K., Yarker, J., Randall, R., & Munir, F. (2009). The mediating effects of team and self-efficacy on the relationships between transformational leadership, and job satisfaction and psychological wellbeing in healthcare professionals: A cross-sectional questionnaire survey. *International Journal of Nursing Studies, 46*, 1236–1244.

Ostroff, C. (1992). The relationship between satisfaction, attitudes, and performance: An organizational level analysis. *Journal of Applied Psychology, 77*, 963–974.

Page, K. M., & Vella-Brodrick, D. A. (2009). The "what," "why" and "how" of employee well-being: A new model. *Social Indicators Research, 90*(3), 441–458.

Paris, C. R., Salas, E., & Cannon-Bowers, J. A. (2000). Teamwork in multi-person systems: A review and analysis. *Ergonomics, 43*(8), 1052–1075.

Park, N., Peterson, C., & Seligman, M. E. P. (2004). Strengths of character and well-being. *Journal of Social and Clinical Psychology, 23*, 603–619.

Parsons, D. (2010). Organizational resilience. *Australian Journal of Emergency Management, (25)*2, 18–20.

Paskevich, D. M., Brawley, L. R., Dorsch, K. D., & Widmeyer, W. N. (1999). Relationship between collective efficacy and team cohesion: Conceptual and measurement issues. *Group Dynamics: Theory, Research, and Practice, 3*(3), 210.

Pastor, M. C. (1982). A study of higher order needs strength and job satisfaction in secondary public school teachers. *Journal of Educational Administration, 20*, 172–183.

Patterson, M., Warr, P., & West, M. (2004). Organizational climate and company productivity: The role of employee affect and employee level. *Journal of Occupational and Organizational Psychology, 77*, 193–216.

Peterson, C., Park, N., & Seligman, M. E. (2005). Orientations to happiness and life satisfaction: The full life versus the empty life. *Journal of Happiness Studies, 6*(1), 25–41.

Peterson, C., Park, N., & Sweeney, P. J. (2008). Group well-being: Morale from a positive psychology perspective. *Applied Psychology, 57*(Suppl. s1), 19–36.

Porter, M. E. (2008). The five competitive forces that shape strategy. *Harvard Business Review, 86*(1), 78–93.

Pratt, M. G., & Ashforth, B. E. (2003). Fostering meaningfulness in working and at work. In K. S. Cameron, J. E. Dutton, & R. E. Quinn (Eds.), *Positive organizational scholarship: Foundations of a new discipline* (pp. 309–327). San Francisco, CA: Berrett-Koehler.

Price, R. H., & Hooijberg, R. (1992). Organizational exit pressures and role stress: Impact on mental health. *Journal of Organizational Behavior, 13*(7), 641–651.

Raya, R. P., & Panneerselvam, S. (2013). The healthy organization construct: A review and research agenda. *Indian Journal of Occupational and Environmental Medicine, 17*(3), 89–93.

Richardson, J., & West, M. (2010a). Dream teams: A positive psychology of team working. In P. A. Linley, S. Harrington, & N. Garcea (Eds.), *Oxford handbook of positive psychology and work* (pp. 235–250). Oxford, UK: Oxford University Press.

Richardson, J., & West, M. (2010b). Engaged work teams. In S. L. Albrecht (Ed.), *Handbook of employee engagement: Perspectives, issues, research and practice* (pp. 323–340). Cheltenham, UK: Edward Elgar.

Robertson, I. T., Birch, A. J., & Cooper, C. L. (2012). Job and work attitudes, engagement and employee performance: Where does psychological well-being fit in? *Leadership & Organization Development Journal, 33*(3), 224–232.

Robertson, I. T., & Cooper, C. L. (2010). Full engagement: The integration of employee engagement and psychological well-being. *Leadership & Organization Development Journal, 31*(4), 324–336.

Robertson, I. T., & Cooper, C. (2011). *Well-being, productivity and happiness at work.* Basingstoke, UK: Palgrave Macmillan.

Robinson, D., Perryman, S., & Hayday, S. (2004). *The drivers of employee engagement.* Brighton, UK: Institute for Employment Studies.

Robinson, P., Oades, L. G., & Caputi, P. (2015). Conceptualising and measuring mental fitness: A Delphi study. *International Journal of Wellbeing, 5*(1), 53–73.

Roche, M., Haar, J. M., & Luthans, F. (2014). The role of mindfulness and psychological capital on the well-being of leaders. *Journal of Occupational Health Psychology, 19*(4), 476.

Ryan, A. M., Schmitt, M. J., & Johnson, R. (1996). Attitudes and effectiveness: Examining relations at an organizational level. *Personnel Psychology, 49*, 853–882.

Ryff, C. D. (1995). Psychological well-being in adult life. *Current Directions in Psychological Science, 4*(4), 99–104.

Ryff, C. D. (2008). Challenges and opportunities at the interface of aging, personality, and well-being. In O. P. John, R. W. Robins, & L. A. Pervin (Eds.), *Handbook of personality: Theory and research* (pp. 399–418). New York, NY: Guildford Press.

Ryff, C. D., & Singer, B. H. (2008). Know thyself and become what you are: A eudaimonic approach to psychological well-being. *Journal of Happiness Studies, 9*(1), 13–39.

Saks, A. M. (2006). Antecedents and consequences of employee engagement. *Journal of Managerial Psychology, 21*, 600–619.

Salanova, M., Agut, S., & Peiró, J. M. (2005). Linking organizational resources and work engagement to employee performance and customer loyalty: The mediation of service climate. *Journal of Applied Psychology*, *90*(6), 1217.

Schaufeli, W. B., Bakker, A. B., & Salanova, M. (2006). The measurement of work engagement with a short questionnaire a cross-national study. *Educational and Psychological Measurement*, *66*(4), 701–716.

Schaufeli, W. B., & Salanova, M. (2010). How to improve work engagement? In S. L. Albrecht (Ed.), *Handbook of employee engagement: Perspectives, issues, research and practice* (pp. 399–415). Cheltenham, UK: Edward Elgar.

Schaufeli, W. B., Salanova, M., González-Romá, V., & Bakker, A. B. (2002). The measurement of engagement and burnout: A two sample confirmatory factor analytic approach. *Journal of Happiness Studies*, *3*, 71–92.

Schein, E. H. (1990). Organizational culture. *American Psychologist*, *45*(2), 109–119.

Schneider, B., Hanges, P. J., Smith, D. B., & Salvaggio, A. N. (2003). Which comes first: employee attitudes or organizational financial and market performance? *Journal of Applied Psychology*, *88*(5), 836.

Schneider, M., & Somers, M. (2006). Organizations as complex adaptive systems: Implications of complexity theory for leadership research. *The Leadership Quarterly*, *17*(4), 351–365.

Schwenk, C. R. (1995). Strategic decision making. *Journal of Management*, *21*(3), 471–493.

Seibert, S. E., Silver, S. R., & Randolph, W. A. (2004). Taking empowerment to the next level: A multiple-level model of empowerment, performance, and satisfaction. *Academy of Management Journal*, *47*, 332–349.

Senge, P. (1990). *The fifth discipline: The art and practice of the learning organization*. London, UK: Random House.

Sheehan, N. T. (2006). Want to improve strategic execution? Simons says levers. *Journal of Business Strategy*, *27*(6), 56–64.

Snyder, C. R. (2002). Hope theory: Rainbows in the mind. *Psychological inquiry*, *13*(4), 249–275.

So, T. T. C., West, M. A., & Dawson, J. F. (2011). Team-based working and employee well-being: A cross-cultural comparison of United Kingdom and Hong Kong health services. *European Journal of Work and Organizational Psychology*, *20*(3), 305–325.

Sparrow, P. R., & West, M. (2002). Psychology and organizational effectiveness. In I. T. Robertson, M. Callinan, & D. Bartram (Eds.), *Organizational effectiveness: the role of psychology* (pp. 13–44). Chichester, UK: Wiley.

Spector, P. E. (1997). *Job satisfaction: Application, assessment, causes, and consequences*. Thousand Oaks, CA: Sage.

Spreitzer, G. M. (1995). An empirical test of a comprehensive model of intrapersonal empowerment in the workplace. *American Journal of Community Psychology*, *23*(5), 601–629.

Stairs, M., Galpin, M., Page, N., & Linley, A. (2006). Retention on a knife edge: The role of employee engagement in talent management. *Selection and Development Review*, *22*(5), 19.

Stansbury, J. M., & Sonenshein, S. (2012). Positive business ethics: Grounding and elaborating a theory of good works. In K. S. Cameron & G. M. Spreitzer (Eds.), *Oxford handbook of positive organizational scholarship* (pp. 340–352). New York, NY: Oxford University Press.

Steel, R. P., & Ovalle, N. K. (1984). A review and meta-analysis of research on the relationship between behavioral intentions and employee turnover. *Journal of Applied Psychology*, *69*, 673–686.

Steger, M. F., & Dik, B. J. (2010). Work as meaning. In P. A. Linley, S. Harrington, & N. Garcea (Eds.), *Oxford handbook of positive psychology and work* (pp. 131–142). Oxford, UK: Oxford University Press.

Sterman, J. D. (2000). *Business dynamics: Systems thinking and modeling for a complex world* (Vol. *19*). Boston, MA: Irwin/McGraw-Hill.

Sterman, J. D. (2001). System dynamics modeling: Tools for learning in a complex world. *California Management Review*, *43*(4), 8–25.

Sung, S. Y., & Choi, J. N. (2014). Multiple dimensions of human resource development and organizational performance, *Journal of Organizational Behavior*, *35*, 851–870.

Teece, D. J., Pisano, G., & Shuen, A. (1997). Dynamic capabilities and strategic management. *Strategic Management Journal*, *18*(7), 509–533.

Tillman, W. R., & Tillman, C. J. (2008). And you thought it was the apple: A study of job satisfaction among teachers. *Academy of Educational Leadership Journal, 12*, 1–18.
Todnem, R. (2005). Organizational change management: A critical review. *Journal of Change Management, 5*(4), 369–380.
Torrente, P., Salanova, M., Llorens, S., & Schaufeli, W. B. (2012). Teams make it work: How team work engagement mediates between social resources and performance in teams. *Psicothema, 24*(1), 106–112.
Van De Voorde, K., Paauwe, J., & Van Veldhoven, M. (2012). Employee well-being and the HRM–organizational performance relationship: A review of quantitative studies. *International Journal of Management Reviews, 14*, 391–407.
Vandewalle, D., Van Dyne, L., & Kostova, T. (1995). Psychological ownership: An empirical examination of its consequences. *Group & Organization Management, 20*(2), 210–226.
Wageman, R., Gardner, H., & Mortensen, M. (2012). The changing ecology of teams: New directions for teams research. *Journal of Organizational Behavior, 33*(3), 301–315.
Wagner, S. H., Parker, C. P., & Christiansen, N. D. (2003). Employees that think and act like owners: Effects of ownership beliefs and behaviors on organizational effectiveness. *Personnel Psychology, 56*(4), 847–871.
Weick, K., & Sutcliffe, K. (2001). *Managing the unexpected: Assuring high performance in an age of uncertainty*. San Francisco, CA: Jossey-Bass.
West, B. J., Patera, J. L., & Carsten, M. K. (2009). Team level positivity: Investigating positive psychological capacities and team level outcomes. *Journal of Organizational Behavior, 30*(2), 249–267.
Wright, T. A., & Bonett, D. G. (1997). The contribution of burnout to work performance. *Journal of Organizational Behavior, 18*(5), 491–499.
Wright, T. A., & Bonett, D. G. (2007). Job satisfaction and psychological well-being as nonadditive predictors of workplace turnover. *Journal of Management, 33*(2), 141–160.
Wright, T. A., & Cropanzano, R. (1997, August). Wellbeing, satisfaction and job performance: Another look at the happy/productive worker thesis. In J. B. Keys & L. N. Dosier (Eds.), *Academy of Management Proceedings 1997* (Vol. *1*, pp. 364–368). New York, NY: Academy of Management.
Wright, T. A., & Cropanzano, R. (1998). Emotional exhaustion as a predictor of job performance and voluntary turnover. *Journal of Applied Psychology, 83*(3), 486
Wright, T. A., & Cropanzano, R. (2000). Psychological well-being and job satisfaction as predictors of job performance. *Journal of Occupational Health Psychology, 5*(1), 84.
Wright, T. A., Cropanzano, R., & Bonett, D. G. (2007). The moderating role of employee positive well being on the relation between job satisfaction and job performance. *Journal of Occupational Health Psychology, 12*(2), 93.
Wrzesniewski, A., & Dutton, J.E. (2001). Crafting a job: Revisioning employees as active crafters of their work. *Academy of Management Review, 26*, 179–201.
Xanthopoulou, D., Bakker, A. B., Demerouti, E., & Schaufeli, W. B. (2007). The role of personal resources in the job demands-resources model. *International Journal of Stress Management, 14*(2), 121.

16

Positive Approaches to Organizational Change

Stefan P. Cantore

Introduction

The period since 2000 especially has seen a growing interest in positive approaches to organizational change. This has been generated by both academic researchers and organizational change practitioners.

One reason for this is undoubtedly the growth in popularity of positive psychology. Much of the research in this allied field, as it relates to work, has been concerned with a diverse range of topics including, for example, the value of identifying and using employee strengths (Rath & Conchie, 2009), optimizing work experiences (Csikszentmihalyi, 2014), and the value of positive emotions (Fredrickson, 2001). The chapters in this book reflect this wide range.

On the other hand, some organizational development/change practitioners and organizational leaders have been searching for meaningful and effective new ways in which whole organizational change efforts can benefit from a generally more positive and engaging approach to change. Here the use of dialogical approaches to change have made an impact and been identified as new and different, in a similar way perhaps to how positive psychology has marked itself as new and different when contrasted with more established humanistic psychological approaches (e.g., Bushe & Marshak, 2009; Grant & Marshak, 2011; Marshak & Bushe 2013; Oswick, 2009).

This chapter begins with a context-setting discussion concerned with what may lie behind the felt need for "new" approaches to organizational change and the disillusionment with what are perceived to be the "old" approaches. Given that it is particularly concerned with "the positive," brief consideration is given to the philosophical notions of pessimism and optimism. The aim is to draw attention to some of the fundamental, and frequently under-reflected upon, assumptions behind organizational change theorizing and practice with a view to signposting their potential influence on the development of positive approaches to organizational change.

The Wiley Blackwell Handbook of the Psychology of Positivity and Strengths-Based Approaches at Work, First Edition. Edited by Lindsay G. Oades, Michael F. Steger, Antonella Delle Fave, and Jonathan Passmore.

Making the connection between psychological insights, which essentially begin with individual behavior, to whole organizational efforts is an intellectual and practice development process. The content and structure of this chapter reflects this and in the later sections key strands of theory and practice are followed by critical reflections. The intention is to contribute to the learning process with which scholars, practitioners, and scholar-practitioners are currently engaged. Furthermore the research base is still relatively "thin," which means that philosophical perspectives, theorizing, some relevant research findings combined with self-reported case studies form much of the literature. The penultimate section identifies areas for further research and the chapter concludes with a summary.

Background

In this chapter a very broad definition of organization is adopted to include its many forms. An organization is "an organised group of people with a particular purpose" (Stevenson, 2010, p. 1240). The implicit, and optimistic, belief is usually that organizations can accomplish much more than individuals. Likewise "change" as a construct, in organizational management contexts, invariably seems to be defined as any effort intended to bring some measure of improvement. Change is therefore also perceived optimistically, at least by those charged with designing and leading organizational change processes! This chapter is concerned with approaches to organization-wide change that make this positive, or optimistic, dimension explicit and assume it to be a sustaining force behind effective change processes.

By contrast, and arguably particularly since the global financial crisis of 2008, there has been a steady diminution in the belief in the intrinsic goodness or positivity of organizations and their ability to marshal resources and people in a way that leads to a better world. Instead people across the globe have become more suspicious of organizations, both doubting what they can achieve, and concerned about how they treat individuals and whether or not they are amenable to planned change (Roth, 2009). This section considers some of the meta-thought trends in which thinking about organizations and organizational change is located.

You do not have to look very hard to find evidence of organizations that are perceived to have let down the people they were originally conceived to serve. In a global context the 2008 banking crisis left a bitter taste in the mouth as people who trusted their investments and house mortgages with large prestigious organizations found that banks' public relations assertions did not match the reality of poor governance, and unethical business practices and cultures that rewarded greed while ignoring the needs of the investor. Even high-reputation, value-driven organizations, like Apple Inc., have been accused of poor employment and supply-chain management in China ("Stark reality of iPod's Chinese factories," 2006).

In the UK an inquiry into the Mid Staffordshire Hospitals Foundation Trust (Francis, 2010) found a widespread disengagement of professionals, a negative culture, patients' needs and concerns being ignored, poor governance, and lack of effective external scrutiny. The consequence of poor organization, although contended, is said to have resulted in avoidable deaths. Two of the main outcomes, however, were both a reduction in trust by the local community and an urgent call by Sir Robert Francis, the chair of the inquiry, for the hospital to "make its visible first priority the delivery of a high-class standard of care to all its patients by putting their needs first" (2010, p. 403). This is how far away from its original purpose this health care organization had drifted.

Alongside these narratives of disappointment sit narratives of frustration that organizational change efforts seem to not be sufficient to make the much-needed difference. Academic researchers have made their own contributions to this sense of despondency. For example, the notion that 70% of organizational change efforts fail has become folklore frequently referred to by academics and change practitioners. This figure, originally estimated by Hammer and Champy (1993), has subsequently been cited by Beer and Nohria (2000), Kotter (1995), and many others. Even though Hughes (2011) has helpfully pointed out that the 70% is an unsupported figure with no empirical evidence behind it, the end result is a pessimistic sense that it might not even be worth making the effort to help organizations change.

Philosophical Perspectives

This chapter works from the premise that behind this somewhat depressing context sits a deeper, more pervasive and often unspoken set of philosophical and cultural beliefs about the nature of reality, organizations, and change. Without exploring the broader discourses of optimism and pessimism within which organizations exist it is not easy to fully appreciate the current apparent attractiveness of explicitly positive, uplifting, and optimistic approaches to change. Also, given that positive organizational change is an emerging construct, academics, and to an extent practitioners, are keen to locate its philosophical positions as a way of differentiating it from the rest of the field. This also perhaps begins to explain the imbalance between the amount of empirical research material available and theory and practitioner narratives.

Dienstag (2006) makes the thought-provoking point that the dominant discourse in Western philosophical thinking is inherently an optimistic one. He argues that optimistic philosophies encourage us to believe that improvement is always our trajectory and that human rational thought is sufficient to solve our problems.

If Dienstag's perspective is accepted then it is not a step too far to conclude that when those tasked with organizational change talk about it they are usually assuming that the intentions they hold behind such change efforts will be an improvement or positive, even if people might experience them initially as negative. A brief consideration of the language used by those involved in theorizing about organization development (OD) support this view. French and Bell (1999) speak of *increasing* individual and organizational effectiveness, while Margulies and Raia (1978), along with others, speaks about the focus on *improvement*. Schein (2010) changes the metaphor as he talks about *building* and *maintaining* the health of the organization (emphasis added).

Alongside the optimistic voices of change agents and positive change literature are the voices of those who take a pessimistic viewpoint. The philosophical literature is rich in examples of such perspectives. Defining pessimism, however, is a challenge in itself. Bailey (2013), for example, suggests that we separate out our emotional responses to pessimism and optimism and consider that they are simply terms referring to "people's shared judgements about the supposed direction of social (or organizational) change on criteria which can be made explicit" (p. 5). Bertrand Russell (1945/2013), on the other hand, takes an opposing perspective, arguing that both optimism and pessimism are to do with personal temperament and not related to any rational judgments. Arguably, whatever position is taken there is always an underlying assumption that organizations can be better places. This philosophy drives those with an interest in organizational change.

Understanding the philosophical assumptions that sit beneath positive organizational change will help make sense of both the theories and practices which follow as well as offering a basis upon which to critique the constructs. There is no right or wrong position, but rather an evident co-existence of optimism and pessimism combined with an aspiration for better organizations.

This chapter makes the case for positive organizational change, not just because of an apparently attractive philosophical and values-based stance, but also because the emerging evidence, in its many forms, is supporting effective practice and the development of useful theory.

Organizational Change Trends and Emerging Positive Approaches to Organizational Change

This section briefly considers recent trends in organizational change theory and uses these as a lens by which to understand the terminology and constructs of positive approaches to organizational change.

The last two decades have seen shifts in how organizational change is to be understood and enacted in practice. Oswick, Grant, Michelson, & Wailes (2005) draw attention to a number of key ones, arguing that from the 1950s until the 1990s the focus had been on centrally managed top-down change (OD), organized in an, apparently, predictable world. Subsequently they suggest the trend has been to perceive and talk about organizational change as turbulent and involving employees dispersed across the organization. The change process is now considered more emergent and less amenable to being carefully pre-planned.

They go on to argue that OD, which once claimed to be the repository of much organizational change wisdom alongside expert OD consultants, is now being replaced by change management literatures and practices given that "the management of change has become more localized and, hence, the responsibility of in situ managers through direct engagement with employees as part of an unfolding and emergent everyday process of instigating new actions and formulating responses to issues, concerns and opportunities that arise" (2005, p. 386).

Since Oswick et al. made their observations there has been resurgence in the field of OD which Marshak and Grant (2008) call the emergence of "New OD." From their perspective, the hallmarks of "Old OD" included an acceptance of a classical science-based approach to thinking about change – that is, that there is a single objective truth about an organization, that analysis and reason will lead to discovering the truth, and that using valid data and rationality will enable leaders to problem-solve. In contrast, "New OD" is shaped by post-modern thought, especially social constructionism – there is no one truth or reality but one that emerges from the collective, power and political processes are integral to change negotiation, and the intention is to shift thinking rather than just behavior. Change in the "New OD" construct is continuous and can be self-organizing, hence the greater emphasis on change management rather than pure OD, which tends to see change as linear and requiring special effort.

An interesting critique they offer of "New OD" is that they perceive "power has been neglected in favour of less confronting and more 'optimistic' or 'positive' approaches" (2008, p. S18). In relation to this point Marshak and Grant reference the work of Cameron and colleagues, who since the early 2000s have been publishing extensively on the theme of positive organizational scholarship (POS) (e.g., Cameron & Dutton, 2003).

In this initial work Cameron et al. (2003) explain that for them POS is a focus on organizational dynamics that can be described as representing "excellence, thriving, flourishing, abundance, resilience, or virtuousness" (p. 4). It distinguishes itself from other types of organizational studies in that it aims to research those things that are best about people in the way they organize together. Cameron et al. are careful to say that they don't reject considering dysfunction, but that it is not the primary lens through which they consider organizational behavior. What can be considered to be "positive" is undoubtedly a value judgment. Fineman, in his extensive critique of POS, suggests that one of the consequences of positivity is "a convincing case that positiveness closes important doors, excluding opportunities that could well serve its own aims. Positive experiences, learning, and change are tied to negative occurrences and events, as well as to positive ones" (2006, p. 275).

Since that critique, defining what is meant by "positive" has occupied the work of scholars in the field. More recently Cameron and Spreitzer have acknowledged that the term positive is so broad it is very hard to define accurately. Instead they have categorized what they mean by positive in relation to organization studies under the following four headings:

1 "Positive" is a unique lens looking primarily for opportunities and strengths in organizational contexts.
2 "Positive" highlights extraordinary or unexplained positively deviant performance.
3 "Positive" seeks to affirm that which fosters growth in the capacity and capability of individuals and organizations.
4 "Positive" means looking at how organizations can, as human systems, achieve their very highest potential, state of virtuousness, and ultimate human satisfaction. (2012, adapted from pp. 2–3).

Even these, they acknowledge, do not give a particularly precise definition, but do give a flavor of the stance taken by scholars in this field.

Parallel to the development of POS is the emergence and growth of interest in positive psychology. Boniwell (2008), reflecting the perspective of the founding fathers of this discipline Seligman and Csikszentmihalyi, defines positive psychology as "a science of positive aspects of human life" (2000, p. 1). Broadly speaking, positive psychology has not particularly focused on organizational change, although it has offered the construct of positive institutions which enable individuals to move toward altruism, civility, and a better work ethic.

In the 2000s a research domain developed to incorporate positive psychology within the field of organization studies which Luthans called positive organizational behavior (POB) and defined as "the study and application of positively orientated human resource strengths and psychological capacities that can be measured, developed, and effectively managed for performance improvement in today's workplace" (Wright, 2003, p. 437). The focus is on research that considers positive personality traits as they relate to work performance, core self-evaluations (self-esteem, generalized self-efficacy, locus of control, and emotional stability), and positive psychological traits (Luthans & Youssef, 2007).

What this suggests is that positive psychology as a subdiscipline within psychology has, over the past decade or so, contributed to the body of research and theory concerned with individual development and performance within an organizational context. The development of POB is one example within the field where the focus is on what needs to be done to help individuals perform positively in organization contexts (Bakker & Schaufeli, 2008; Luthans, 2002; Luthans & Youssef, 2007). However, arguably it has not added significant understanding about how extensive organizational change can be enacted if a positive psychology frame of reference is adopted.

In the discourse about positive approaches to human psychology and to organizational change the term "strengths" is often used alongside, or instead of, the term "positive." Again, there is some difficulty in defining precisely what is meant by the terminology in the context of organizations. Martin Seligman and his colleague Christopher Peterson compiled a character and strengths handbook which classifies positive human strengths (Peterson & Seligman, 2004).This classification is based on assumptions that human strengths are not secondary to weaknesses, that they can be understood scientifically, that they differentiate people, and are similar to traits but can be influenced by the environment. They concluded that there are six prime virtues against which strengths may be categorized. These are wisdom and knowledge, courage, love and humanity, justice, temperance, and transcendence.

Debate continues about the validity and measurability of strengths and Boniwell (2006) argues that there may be some sense in working with both weaknesses and strengths at an individual level

Combining a focus on both strengths and the positive in the field of organizational and system change since the late 1980s has been the development and application of appreciative inquiry (AI). This process and its overtly social constructionist philosophical stance is covered in more detail in a later section, but it is worth mentioning in this discussion since it has made a profound impact on thinking about the nature of positive organizational change.

A straightforward definition of AI is "the study and exploration of what gives life to human systems when they function at their best" (Whitney & Trosten-Bloom, 2010, p. 1). However, a number of texts elaborate on this in order to try and capture something of the philosophy and practices encapsulated by the term. So, for example, Cooperrider, Whitney, and Stavros (2008, p. 3) comment that AI is "the co-operative co-evolutionary search for the best in people, their organizations, and the world around them … it involves the art and practice of asking questions that strengthen a system's capacity to apprehend, anticipate and heighten positive potential."

A more recent development has been the attempt to integrate positive psychological approaches with what Cooperrider and Godwin (in Cameron & Spreitzer, 2012) have called innovation-inspired positive organization development (IPOD). Interestingly they argue that this new discipline is a return to the optimistic philosophical stance taken by the early founders of OD and the work of Bennis in particular (1969). This concept will be explored later in greater depth. However, what is relevant here is their argument that positive approaches to organizational change are being manifested in three key trends. Firstly, the emergence of a "rich vocabulary of the positive" (Cameron & Spreitzer, 2012, p. 742). Secondly, the development by Cameron, Bright, & Caza (2004) of a framework in which to discuss negatively deviant and positively deviant performance; and thirdly, a growing body of research into positive deviancy.

To summarize, the field of positive organizational change:

- Is emerging out of a diverse range of historic strands of thought and practice that relate to both individual and organizational change
- Uses language to create a positive "feel" that sits in contradistinction to the language of problem-solving and apparently rational scientific approaches
- Often adopts a social constructionist stance by proposing that social realities within an organization are co-created and re-created by all the participants
- Explicitly distances itself from positivistic and problem-solving approaches adopted by other change methods
- Provokes a critical response from academics and people living in cultural contexts in which positivity is viewed with skepticism
- Tends to be more future-orientated than retrospective
- Inherently privileges an optimistic perspective that change will lead to a better life
- Lacks clear definitions and agreed frameworks as it continues to develop and change.

Positive Approaches to Organizational Change

Given the diverse and emergent nature of the field, this section covers a broad range of related topic areas. The criteria for inclusion and the amount of space spent on each area are dependent on the degree to which the topic explicitly relates to organizational change. Other chapters in this book focus on areas of positive psychology, which are complementary but often have the development of the individual or team as their prime interest. Here the aim is to expand the description, consider the practices, and critique the approaches that have been alluded to in earlier sections.

A further aim is to illustrate and signpost the research literature associated with each approach. This is easier said than done for a number of reasons. Firstly, for some processes, like World Café, Open Space, and Future Search, very little written formal research has been published. This does not mean that nothing is available. On the contrary there are plenty of self-reported case study materials, as well as books and practitioner guides. This reflects the nature of the field that has, until relatively recently, been perceived as the domain primarily of practitioners rather than academics. Bartunek and Woodman comment that "it might seem like the academic/scholarly side of the field is trying to 'kill off' OD but OD practitioners persist in keeping it alive through practicing it" (2012, p. 730). One result of this tension is a bias in the literature toward the reporting *of* practice rather than research *on* practice.

Secondly, positive organizational change is an under-researched area, particularly with respect to the interconnections between positive psychology and positive organizational change. Higgs comments cautiously that, in an organizational context "positive psychology may be valuable in developing an understanding of how we can implement change much more effectively" (2013, p. 74). There is, however, an assumption in the wider organizational change literature that a generally positive approach is going to be more successful than more negative, fear-based approaches. Examples of this literature include peer-reviewed evidence for the value of readiness for change, organizational commitment and well-developed social relationships (Madsen, Miller, & John 2005), supportive change leadership behaviors (Caldwell, Chatman, O'Reilly, Ormiston, & Lapiz, 2008; Higgs and Rowland 2011), change and trust (Saunders & Thornhill, 2003), and emotional intelligence (Higgs, 2002).

Finally, and more provocatively, there is the argument by Gergen that to use scientific assumptions in order to analyze human social activity is neither fruitful nor relevant. Instead he suggests the creation of a new social science that is primarily future-orientated and with a generative capacity. This he defines as the "capacity to challenge the guiding assumptions of the culture, to raise fundamental questions regarding contemporary social life, to foster reconsideration of that which is 'taken for granted' and thereby furnish new alternatives for social actions" (1978, p. 1346). Arguably Gergen's approach has been taken to heart and much of the literature relating to positive organizational change tends toward theorizing about generative organizational change processes. Cooperrider's construct of Innovation-inspired Positive Organization Development, considered later in this chapter, is a good example.

In summary, what follows seeks both to describe the approaches and to augment the descriptions with relevant examples of the research literature that is currently available.

Appreciative inquiry (AI)

AI is probably the first positive organizational change process both to fully elucidate its philosophy and offer a framework for practice. Its focus on working with strengths and social constructionist philosophy made a break from old-style OD and change management techniques with their positivistic approach to diagnosis and problem-solving by experts.

Taking all the definitions together, AI can be summarized as "as a living research process engaging with human systems and based upon a set of philosophical understandings about the way the social world in which we live is being continually co-constructed between us" (Cantore & Cooperrider, 2013, p. 271).

AI is philosophically grounded in social constructionism and particularly the approach developed by Gergen, who argued that our sense of who we are and the knowledge we hold is generated within and between our social relationships (Gergen, 1997a, 1997b). He applied these ideas to both organizational science (Gergen & Thatchenkery, 1996) and social psychology (Gergen, 1997b).

Of particular interest in considering the positive nature of AI is the optimistic aspiration Gergen voices in his earlier key paper "Toward generative theory" (Gergen, 1978). Gergen sees social constructionist practices as a means to build what he called "generative capacity," which, by Gergen's definition, is the "capacity to challenge the guiding assumptions of the culture, to raise fundamental questions regarding contemporary social life, to foster reconsideration of that which is taken for granted and thereby furnish new alternatives for social actions" (1978, p. 1346).

Cantore and Cooperrider note that "AI picks up the notion of generative capacity and incorporates it into its methodology and language. Whilst not explicitly positive in its definition, it is implicitly, and often explicitly, positive in its practice" (2013, p. 272). The method is usually described as a five-"D" process, beginning with the definition of the focus for change followed by discovery, dream, design, and destiny stages. Each element is intended to be co-designed by participants and usually involves extensive conversational group work. There is no exact protocol, since each organization is expected to craft a process that meets its needs and respects its context.

AI perspectives

Research on the effectiveness or otherwise of AI needs to be drawn from a wide range of sources which may not necessarily be specifically solely focused on AI. For example, Choi (2007) notes that with regard to change-oriented Organizational Citizenship Behavior (OCB), strong collective vision and an innovative climate, both of which AI explicitly encourages, support both individual and collective psychological empowerment to effect change. Interestingly, in his study of a large Korean company, it was the focus on organization-wide approaches that offered most promise for change, rather than group work. AI, of course focuses on the whole organization rather than individuals or groups. This organization-wide finding is supported by Powley, Fry, Barrett, and Bright in research on a large AI process in a U.S. Navy organization. They comment that AI processes appeared to "create spaces that intrinsically motivate people to assume more task responsibility for the incorporation of change" (2004, p. 77). They also noted that AI encouraged what they called normative consciousness, holistic collegiality, and communal conviction, not just for the duration of the process but continuing well after the intervention had formally concluded.

Looking at AI through a community psychology "lens," Boyd and Bright conclude, following a piece of case study research, that AI is "consistent with ecological analysis and the concept of person–environment fit" (2007, p. 1033). They argue that, given the transactional nature of the relationship between people and their environments, AI supports an alteration in the perceived environment which enhances the psychological "fit" between individuals and the organizational context in which they work. Interestingly, they also observed that AI enhances the toleration of individual differences between organization members. Furthermore, they make the link between the concept of learned optimism (Seligman, 1991) and AI, arguing that participants in their research demonstrated the avoidance of "negative psychological states," creating a sense of greater control over the process of change (p. 1034).

From yet another perspective, the research literature around the organizational impact of positive emotions adds weight to the usefulness of AI. Fredrickson argues that positive emotions "serve to broaden an individual's momentary thought–action repertoire which in turn, over time, has the effect of building that individual's physical, intellectual and social resources" (1998, p. 300). Subsequent research by Sekerka and McCraty links what goes on physiologically for people when they experience appreciation (2004). This supports the earlier work of Staw, Sutton, and Pelled (1994), who reported connections between work outcomes and positive emotions. Work by Fredrickson and others has linked positive emotions with resilience (Fredrickson, Tugade, Waugh, & Larkin, 2003), indicating that creating organizational spaces where positive emotions can flourish is likely to support change processes which, by their nature, require resilience.

In an interesting study, initially focused on exploring the gender aspects of AI, Sekerka, Brumbaugh, Rosa, and Cooperrider concluded that "Appreciative Inquiry with a self-focus engenders more favorable emotional responses than diagnostic approaches, makes salient positive aspects of participants self-concepts, and enhances engagement and creativity among men who might exhibit lower levels of each in a more traditional change exercise" (2006, p. 474). This does not preclude benefits from other approaches to organizational change, but does strengthen the case for links between positive emotion and positive approaches to change.

Using this and other examples of positive psychology research, Sekerka and Fredrickson have concluded that there is a case to be made for an evidence-based theory of positive organizational change with AI being one example among a growing number of change approaches (2013). This theory links strengths-based approaches, positive emotions, positive organizational emotional climates, organizational relational strengths, and organizational growth and development.

The question remains: Does AI actually effect positive organizational change? As with many organizational change processes, verifiable evidence of effectiveness is hard to find especially in empirical research literature. It is the case-study, qualitative research literature that offers most material. Carter (2006) describes and positively critiques the use of AI in supporting the development of excellent nursing practice and research in a UK context. Richer, Ritchie, and Marchionni (2009) confirm similar beneficial findings in a Canadian context. Bright, Cooperrider, and Galloway (2006) record the impact of using AI to strengthen the collaborative capacity of a large department of the U.S. Environment Protection Agency. Ryan, Soven, Smither, Sullivan, and VanBuskirk (1999) outline how AI was used to support school reform, while Giles and Alderson (2008) report on a similar project in a New Zealand adult learning institution and More (2011) describes the value of AI in a school improvement program in India. Calabrese and Cohen (2013) relate how AI was used to transform the culture of a U.S. Drug Offenses court.

In a commercial context, Vanstone and Dabliez (2008) outline how AI was used to revitalize the corporate values of a very large multinational company, while Stavros and Sprangel (2008) illustrate the use of AI to develop a new company strategy. Higgs (2013) offers a case of AI being used in a professional services firm illustrating specifically how leadership behaviors that support the expression of positive emotions can have a significant impact on creativity and organizational citizenship behavior, at least in the short term. Case-study literature continues to grow in scale and an up-to-date repository can be found at http://appreciativeinquiry.case.edu/

Bushe and Kassam (2005) take an overview and ask the question: When is AI transformational? This is the only meta-case analysis available in the literature. The authors examine 20 published cases where AI was adopted as a process for change, some transactional and others transformational of culture in intention. In summary, their findings are that if AI is used as a transactional change process then it is as effective as any other conventional change process. However, where the process was intentionally transformational, AI supported the emergence of new thinking and generative images and led to desired shifts that the organizations themselves would consider transformational.

Taken together, the evidence base linking positive psychology knowledge and positive organizational change approaches, including AI, is available but not as extensive as it might be. However, this should only encourage further research and development in organizational change practice.

As indicated earlier in the chapter, given its longevity, AI has by far the most extensive evidence base compared to other positive organizational change processes. This is reflected in the comparatively fewer cases cited in the sections that follow. It is also fair to say that evidence used in support of AI is often also relevant in support of other positive approaches where the focus on inquiry, strengths, positive emotions, and transformational change in thinking is also prevalent.

Dialogic organization development (DOD)

Frequently linked with AI is the emerging field of DOD. Providing a definitive definition of DOD is a challenge, given its ongoing development as an approach. Bushe and Marshak (2009, p. 362) describe it as a paradigm in which:

- The change process emphasizes changing the conversations that normally take place in the system.
- The purpose of inquiry is to surface, legitimate, and/or learn from the variety of perspectives, cultures, and/or narratives in the system.
- The change process results in new images, narratives, texts, and socially constructed realities that affect how people think and act.
- The change process is consistent with traditional organization development values of collaboration, free and informed choice, and capacity building in the client system.

Given the focus it places on socially constructed realities and generative imagery, it fits within an understanding of positive approaches to organizational change. This is underscored by the sense of inclusivity suggested by the definition which is a hallmark of positive approaches. Change management is not perceived as vested in elite managers, but becomes a wholly collective effort.

The paper from which the above definition is taken argued that OD was, at that point, experiencing a bifurcation. The field was splitting into two branches. The first is characterized as a focus on diagnosis and problem-solving, while the other is conversationally or dialogically oriented and implicitly more positive in orientation. AI is cited as one of these positive, future-orientated approaches. Subsequently practitioners and academics who align themselves with this new development have developed the literature in support of the theory (e.g., Bushe & Marshak, 2009, 2014, 2015; Cantore & Passmore, 2012; Lewis, Passmore, & Cantore, 2008; Marshak, 2013; Marshak & Bushe, 2013; Rothwell, Stavros, Sullivan, & Sullivan, 2010).

In presenting the case for DOD, Bushe and Marshak sense that they are pulling away from the "old" way of doing and thinking about organizational change:

> The term *dialogic organization development* will become, we hope, a generative image that will allow OD scholars and professionals to reimagine and reinvigorate the theory and practice of OD. In offering the image of Dialogic OD, we hope to create a space where conversations can take place about the nature of organizations and organizing, about the nature of change processes and change agentry, and about the nature of leadership and consulting, that adhere to OD values but fall outside the traditional diagnostic mind-set. (2015, p. 3)

In positioning DOD in this manner, they align with positive organizational change, which can appear not be fully able to articulate what it does do or think but is clearer about its contention that it wants to be perceived as significantly different from what has come before. It is this sense of newness and a break from the past that is a key characteristic.

Oswick adds a cautionary note about the dangers of giving primacy to DOD. Firstly he suggests that many forms of change, like outsourcing and downsizing, rely less on OD and are the result of economic pressures. In these circumstances OD is perhaps seen as less relevant to organizations. Secondly, he sees a danger in ignoring the material aspects of both convening conversations and enacting the outcomes with the risk that "tangible, material outcomes are overlooked or underplayed in favour of a preoccupation with, or predisposition towards, intangible, discursive content" (2013, p. 374). The minutiae and perhaps the materiality of organizational change tend to be viewed as those management activities that will work themselves out and need not be of significant concern in the meta-change effort. It is an interesting point and one that draws attention to the large scale transformative focus of DOD in particular and positive organizational change in general.

DOD perspectives

Bushe suggests that there are three broad phases to working with DOD (2013): firstly, the reframing of concerns and problems in a manner that is optimistic about the future; secondly, intentionally convening conversations across the organization to stimulate the emergence of generative images; and thirdly, encouraging people to speak, think, and act differently to enable the emergence of a new shared social reality. Enacted within this framework are a series of conversational processes. These have been, and continue to be, developed by consulting practitioners who use them with organizational clients. This highlights one of the notable characteristics of positive organizational change, which is the emergence in the field of both theory and practice through the continuing interplay of learning between practitioners and academics. Bartunek and Woodman argue and evidence the criticality of these scholar and practitioner links, making the case that "Organisation Development lives because it effectively bridges the scholar–practitioner gap" (2012, p. 731).

Cantore and Hick (2013) offer a detailed description of both the design and implementation of a DOD intervention in a UK primary school. The intention in this case is to demonstrate how creating spaces for people to engage in conversation can be combined with intentionality around transforming the images people hold about the organization and their role in it. In this case creating a coaching culture was seen as critical in addressing the needs of both the school as an organization and individuals as practitioners. The result was a school whose rate of performance improvement outstripped virtually every other school in the UK using external inspection ratings. Baldwin recounts a very similar experience in leading the performance transformation of a school in Florida, USA (in Lewis, Passmore, & Cantore, 2008, pp. 112–114). In this instance AI was the primary framework adopted and other change processes like World Café and Open Space were incorporated as needed. Gordezky (2015) cites work with a social enterprise to reclaim contaminated land. DOD processes enabled a sense of relatedness between stakeholders and in so doing encouraged the emergence of a new shared identity and core narrative. The work they were called to do was therefore enabled to move forward.

Of interest in these examples is that often in the background to DOD change processes is a felt need in the system for a transformational change. The implicit and often explicit assumption is therefore that there will emerge a widespread commitment to organizational change by most, if not all members of the organization. Jaros (2010) noted that there is a growing body of research literature concerned with employee commitment to change. In his critical review of the empirical literature he observed that commitment to change is dependent on the extent to which: employees' values are in some way aligned with the proposed change; managers exhibit empowering behaviors; people are familiar with the change process adopted; and groups or teams preceive the impact of change on their role/work. Jaros also observed that across the literature there is recognition that positive feelings play a role in commitment to change however this construct may be defined. He suggests that "maybe feelings of commitment to a change effort cause the formation of a behavioral intent to act, which leads to actual change-supportive behaviors. This implies a causal ordering among the concepts, testable by structural path analysis" (p. 325).

Interestingly the 2015 handbook of *Dialogic Organization Development* (Bushe & Marshak) makes just one explicit mention the role of emotions in change commitment. However, implicit in the practice and theory of DOD is that emotions do play a fundamental role as people engage in conversations both with their reason (dialogue) and emotionally (conversing) (Cantore, 2014). This suggests that further research in the affective aspects of change commitment is required to contribute to the further development of the theory and practice of DOD.

Since DOD is focused on enabling participation of employees and consequently transformational change, it is worth considering research that links the two constructs together. Lines and Selart (2013) draw attention to the literatures that apply to both participation and organizational commitment, and participation and organizational change. The first domain, they argue, is most investigated and includes empirical studies relating to high-involvement work processes, team empowerment, and employee participation in decision-making. They conclude that "generally the main-effect relationship has been hypothesized to be a positive one, a relationship that has been supported by the findings from a number of empirical studies" (p. 290). The inference is therefore that DOD is likely to impact positively on organizational commitment. But does it impact on transformational change? Lines and Selart found that it is difficult to differentiate in the literature between participation in organizations and participation in change (2013). In their review of the evidence they found that participation in change leads to lower levels of resistance to change (Hideg, Michela, & Ferris, 2011), reduced levels of cynicism (Brown & Cregan, 2008), and higher levels of commitment to the change (Neubert & Cady, 2001). This supports the potential of DOD as an effective approach to supporting change given the extensive participation it encourages.

Perhaps the most significant conclusion Lines and Selart come to is the view that if the degree of radical (or in DOD terminology "transformational") change grow, then the implications of the change as perceived by employees grows and their psychological need to exert control also grows. As a result they conclude "it is likely that employees' willingness to participate in change-related activities increases as change becomes more radical. Furthermore we believe that the positive emotions, cognitions, attitudes and behaviors that are often associated with participative processes will be more pronounced during radical compared to evolutionary change" (p. 299).

The research appears to signpost a set of linkages between the individual psychology of participation, the experience of collective commitment to change through participation, and the proposed degree of change. The greater the scale and extent of organizational transformation, the greater the likelihood of active participation. DOD is therefore potentially a useful set of constructs and practices when transformational change is needed. Researchers agree that this remains an underexplored area in organization studies.

DOD practices

Some of the most well-known examples of DOD practice are outlined below.

World Café By recreating a café atmosphere, anywhere between 12 and 1,500 people can feel relaxed and encouraged to have a series of 20- to 30-minute conversations around a question that matters. Volunteer table hosts remain at the tables to connect conversations while participants move twice or three times to new tables. At the end of each round of conversations the café host facilitates a whole café conversation that surfaces underlying themes and key insights. The process can then be repeated with a new question. When the café concludes there is an opportunity for participants to share their sense of emerging themes (Brown & Isaacs, 2005). This process is often incorporated into an AI event when people need encouragement and the space and time to engage with one another in some depth. The approach encourages the mutual ownership of the generative images and discourses that emerge.

Ward, Borawski, & Brown (2008) describe in some detail both the design, delivery, and impact of a large World Café intervention in the American Society for Quality. Reported outcomes include the use of dialogue across the organization as an integral aspect of business processes, leading to more meaningful engagement with stakeholders, and reduced internal politics as a result of greater trust and transparency.

Bastien (2005) recounts how World Café processes enabled Sanofi-Synthelabo to generate new business ideas and an image of community impact that has successfully shaped relationships with significant stakeholders. Others relate similar successes when using the World Café process (e.g., Burke & Sheldon, 2010; Delaney, Daley, & Lajoie, 2006; Fouché & Light, 2011; Fullarton & Palermo, 2008; Hechenbleikner, Gilburg, & Dunnell, 2008; Prewitt, 2011; Ritch & Brennan, 2010).

Open Space Open Space begins with self-selected participants meeting in a circle invited to consider a pre-determined theme, moves onto working with a community bulletin board, and then a market place that helps participants structure their own agendas and meetings. A series of self-managed conversations, usually lasting about one and a half hours, then follows and the event concludes with participants back in a circle, each given an opportunity to make a closing comment. An Open Space event can last half a day or as long as three days dependent on the issues being considered (Owen, 2008a).

As its name implies Open Space has a loose structure and relies on people taking their own responsibility for hosting conversations on subjects that matter to them. The interventions by the facilitator are very minimal. Their prime role is to "hold the space," thereby allowing participants to enjoy the freedom to converse. This enables free-flowing and usually energized conversations which open up themes previously not considered within the change process (Cantore & Passmore, 2012).

What is the impact of Open Space on organizational change? Alongside the benefits of participation outlined in an earlier section of this chapter there are numerous case studies published in support of this process. Thakadipuram and Stevenson (2013), for example, use an interpretive case-study method to analyze the process and its reported effectiveness. They conclude that Open Space offers a simple process that creates the conditions for complex self-organization to take place. Responsibility for design of the process is largely handed over to all involved to maximize the potential for participation. Owen (2008b) describes the use of Open Space for American Telephone and Telegraph Company (AT&T) in which a highly complex set of design and planning changes were agreed in 2 days rather than the 10 months such a process would normally be expected to take. The focus here is on the perceived time efficiency of the process. Elenurm (2012) evaluates the use of Open Space as both a change metaphor and a process for supporting knowledge-sharing across a very diverse range of participants in a large-scale civic society project in Estonia. Owen, the designer of the Open Space, offers a free download book containing a very wide variety of case studies (1995), while Hallgren (2009) explores the use of Open Space as a means to engage people in participating in an innovation audit and research project.

Future Search A Future Search conference typically involves 25–100+ people focused on joint action toward a desired future for a community, organization, or issue. Its structure is designed to explore the past and present and then, using these, to help create ideal future scenarios. The conditions for success identified by Weisbord and Janoff (2010) include an invitation to the whole system to be present and the exploration through conversation of common ground. During a Future Search event a wide range of processes will be used to surface knowledge and support learning. These include small group work, brainstorming, mapping, and dialogue sessions that bear a strong resemblance to Open Space in design (Lewis et al., 2008). Again the notable emphasis is on the future and generative images that inspire action. Weisbord (2004) outlines a major transformation of work processes at the furniture company Ikea as a good example of the ability of Future Search processes to enable rapid change. Further case studies and details of how Future Search can be used can found through the dedicated website: http://www.futuresearch.net

Summary These are but three examples of DOD processes. Bushe and Marshak (2015) identify no fewer than 40 distinctive conversational processes that are available to those who plan to use a DOD approach to organizational change. This is 17 more that they described in 2013, such is the growth in the field (Bushe & Marshak, 2013).

Evidence in support of the effectiveness of each process is often available in the form of practitioner-authored case-study material. Empirical evidence in relation to the deeper, psychological and organizational change processes is available to a limited but growing extent. However, such material is distributed across a range of academic domains and is rarely connected directly with practitioner practice and theorizing. This of course makes evaluation and critical review of both research and practice a considerable challenge.

Positive organizational scholarship (POS)

As mentioned previously in this chapter, POS is a broad and evolving meta-construct encompassing a whole range of ideas and research related to positivity and strengths. To illustrate this point, Cameron and Spreitzer (2012) in the *Oxford Handbook of Positive*

Organizational Scholarship review positive individual attributes, positive emotions, strengths and virtues, positive relationships, positive human resource practices, positive organizational practices, positive leadership and change, and a positive lens on problems and challenges. A significant number of these are referenced elsewhere in this volume. Of particular interest here is what POS has to say about the nature of organizational change.

Several different themes are evident: Firstly, recognition that OD and POS are different but that there is a congruency between them in terms of their aspirations to develop human potential and fulfillment (Bartunek & Woodman, 2012). Secondly, the potential to fully integrate OD with POS (Cooperrider & Godwin 2012). Thirdly, the potential to develop deeper understanding of the links between the positive approach to organizational change and encouraging positive change behaviors and mindsets in individuals (Quinn & Wellman, 2012). What is apparent is a degree of caution expressed by most authors that POS and positive organizational change are a perfect fit.

One reason for this may be the still underexplored differences between the philosophies held by those who adopt a psychological stance and those who take an organizational change perspective. Psychology, including positive psychology as a discipline, takes as its starting point that psychology is the "scientific study of the human mind and its functions especially those affecting behaviour in a given context" (Stevenson, 2010, p. 1420). It is important here to note that the starting point is the individual mind combined with a belief that the mind can be subject to scientific study. This study is presumed then to link the individual mind with behavior. This may or may not be possible and "true," but it is not the starting point for those who adopt a positive organizational change lens on the field. Their starting point tends to be not the individual mind but rather the collective sense-making and new realities that emerge from multiple conversations and narratives. In their groundbreaking work on positive psychology, Seligman and Csikszentmihalyi (2000) clearly identified "Positive Institutions" as a construct that would need to be given attention. It is fair to say, as evidenced by the volume of published papers, that compared with individual well-being, institutional well-being has received much less attention from experimental psychologists. It is possible that one reason for this is that the social constructionist perspective taken by those with an interest in positive organizational change does not always fit easily with a scientific perspective intending to analyze change through an experimental or scientific lens.

Cantore and Cooperrider suggest that positive psychology and social constructionist theory are

> answering two different but allied questions from two different change paradigms. Appreciative Inquiry (in this instance) answers the question what people can do to create new ways of working by suggesting the use of a co-designed relational inquiry process that will enable them to make the future happen as they inquire together. Positive psychology answers the question of what makes for the greatest satisfaction, happiness and effectiveness in the workplace by offering the use of formal scientific methods to test theories on sample groups. (2013, p. 280)

So while POS and positive approaches to organizational change share a positive, optimistic, and strengths-based stance, when it comes to adopting them both in a change effort there are evident differences to be either overcome or actively worked with. One approach that aims to do just this is IPOD (Cooperrider & Godwin, 2012).

IPOD practice

IPOD draws upon AI and positive psychology for its inspiration, but adds to them the constructs of design and biomimicry. Cooperrider and Godwin argue that at the intersections of these different domains is "a breakthrough moment in the field of organization development and change" (2012, p. 743).

IPOD consists of three principal areas or "pillars" of activity that, when acted upon together, build momentum toward a positive trajectory for the organization:

1. *Elevation of strengths.* The focus at this level is on individuals and groups. Positive psychology and POS more generally are used to help make people aware of their strengths and in so doing begin to build a climate of interest and excitement around a positive approach to development. So, for example, the Strengths Finder tool (Rath, 2007) might be used alongside emotionally intelligent leadership development (Boyatzis & Mckee, 2005). Appreciative coaching methodologies may also be useful (Orem, Binket, & Clancy, 2007).
2. *Configuration and magnification of strengths.* The idea at this stage is to amplify "individual strengths into a symphony of the whole" (Cooperrider & Godwin, 2012, p. 745). AI is cited as one of the key approaches alongside business and strategy development with the aim of securing the active involvement of everyone in the process of organization design (Stavros & Hinrichs, 2011).
3. *Refraction of strengths.* Cooperrider and Godwin emphasize that this stage is the most innovative. At this point the aim is to discover and design positive institutions that magnify the characteristics of the best strengths we can identify, whether these are found in human institutions and design or in nature itself. POS is judged to be a helpful set of resources to support this phase (Cameron & Spreitzer, 2012). The authors also cite the work of Benyus (1997) in biomimicry, McDonough & Braungart (2010) in relation to sustainability, and the work of Laszlo (2003) in relation to sustainable value creation.

IPOD does not offer a step-by-step methodology, but rather suggests a blending of approaches with some, like positive psychology, more useful at some points than others. The authors describe the three pillars generating a significant amount of positive energy as they combine in a double helix of positive development and change. There is little research to support the effectiveness of the model.

IPOD perspectives

In common with all positive organizational change approaches, IPOD sets itself apart from the "old" and, according to Cooperrider and Cameron, "problem-centered and negative orientation in OD" (2012, p. 748). IPOD can be characterized as having a significant degree of optimism about the nature of change, becoming almost poetic in style: "change is all about strengths; we live in a universe of strengths, in which the appreciable world is profoundly larger than our normal appreciative eye, and positive change is a powerful, self-renewing and clean resource – much like an energy source that is abundant and renewable" (p. 746). This almost evangelical belief in the importance of positive change opens up IPOD and other similar processes to significant critiques explored in the next section.

However, it is worth noting that in IPOD interesting connections are made with both the purpose of change and the ethical underpinnings of change. These are not made so explicitly in other POS organizational change approaches. For the Cooperrider and Godwin, the opportunity to bring about an environmentally sustainable world is integral to the reason for practicing IPOD – for example, they ask how will it be possible to implement a green solar economy and shift away from oil dependency? They also express a concern about the ethics of using fear as a means to prompt change, citing Kotter's work

(1995) as typical of this approach, and instead suggest that positive psychology should be harnessed to prompt strong positive feelings which readily embrace change.

Critiquing Positive Approaches to Organizational Change

This chapter has illustrated a range of approaches to organizational change that proponents argue have a bias toward the positive. Because of the difficulty in defining what "positive" actually means there remains some confusion and ambiguity, although the implication is always that the positive is better than what has come before it. In turn there can be a tendency to define what is "positive" by referencing what is deemed to be less so, or even "negative."

Of all the elements of positive organizational change that have been subject to critical comment, positive psychology has been pre-eminent. McDonald & O'Callaghan take a Foucauldian perspective and suggest that "positive psychology needs to acknowledge its limitations, and that, far from liberating psychology from the negative and pathological, it has instituted a new set of governmental and disciplinary mechanisms by means of defining what is 'positive' in human existence via a prescriptive set of constructs (Peterson & Seligman, 2004), and in its attempts to silence critical reflexivity and alternative perspectives" (2008, p. 128). Using Foucault's concept of the intimate relationship between power and knowledge, they argue that a dominant discourse around positive psychology has been formed and normalized in a way that controls and coerces other voices. They go on to suggest that those promoting positive psychology, as a part of this process, deliberately discredit and disengage from humanistic psychology arguing that the "old" and "negative" psychology failed in being sufficiently scientific in its experiments. Space here precludes a more detailed look at the supporting argument, but if at least this aspect of their argument is accepted then it is possible to critique positive organizational change approaches as follows in a similar manner.

DOD advocates, for example, say that:

> The assumption that there are objective data that can be used in a process of social discovery, therefore, is a central aspect of the change process in Diagnostic ("old") OD. ... these bedrock premises and practices are now being challenged by newer OD practices operating implicitly or explicitly from other assumptions. (Bushe & Marshak, 2009, p. 351)

The implication is that there is something fundamentally wrong with the old and of greater significance in the new. Whether these new practices are or are not more effective is not the principal issue being commented upon. What is the issue, if we follow McDonald and O'Callaghan's line of thinking, is the way new OD is being positioned and promoted as likely to be the most hopeful and optimistic or positive means to the end of developing better organizations.

In a similar vein, IPOD originators Cooperrider and Godwin juxtapose IPOD against what they call the "storehouse of problem-focused interventions and diagnostic methods of analysis" while at the same time saying that they are enabling OD to "surpass this deficit-based detour and come full circle back to its positive roots" (2012, p. 740).

This mirrors to an extent the claims of positive psychology to recapture the true science of psychology from the mistaken ways of the past. They go even further when they claim that the most effective transformational change, an implicitly positive construct, is "really about establishing the new and eclipsing the old" (2012, p. 746).

This is an ideological position rather than one based on careful judgment and evidence. What if the "old" offers the most effective processes or even the most "positive" for all involved? These considerations do not have space for being voiced if the "new" is considered superior to all that has gone before. Oswick observes that one of the implications of this apparent shift to new OD is that "Forward-facing interventions are undoubtedly a valuable addition to the OD repertoire of techniques. However, one of the unfortunate consequences of this temporal turn is the unanticipated and unintended marginalization and stifling of 'backward-facing' forms of OD" (2013, p. 375).

From the perspective of McDonald and O'Callaghan, the unintended consequence is to "unwittingly support subjectivities tied to a neo-liberal political and economic discourse" (2008, p. 129). As Oswick observes, in the day-to-day practice and experience of organizational change efforts "this is deeply problematic because the highly contingent nature of organizations and organizational situations means that there are likely to be circumstances in which a problem-centred OD approach is particularly pertinent, but may be overlooked in favour of an alluring, projectively oriented, alternative" (2013, p. 375). The implication is that there is, alongside positive organizational change theory and practice, a shadow side encouraging, either knowingly or unknowingly, a discourse that privileges the "new" and the "positive" while relegating the "old" to the sidelines regardless of potential usefulness.

The positive turn in psychology and organizational change has further been critiqued by a number of academics and commentators. Fineman (2006), for example, highlights concerns that these approaches:

- Demonstrate partisanship and lack definitional clarity
- Fail to make linkages between their key concepts and specific outcomes in organizational contexts
- Manifest beliefs that human beings are essentially morally good and that virtue can be found in positive attitudes and behavior; this creates a normative moral agenda
- Hold to the view that all people ultimately wish to self-realize – to express their capacities to the greatest possible extent
- Falsely separate out certain feelings as positive and leading to good outcomes while other feelings are labeled as negative and therefore to be rejected as having any value
- Tend to be culturally located particularly within the USA where individualism and self-promotion are woven into the culture; this contrasts with societies shaped by Confucianism where emotional restraint and concern for familial and social relationships play a greater role
- Promote a social orthodoxy about how people *should* behave in organizations and as a consequence stigmatize those who do not behave or speak in a positive manner

Miller (2008) supports Fineman's critique, emphasizing the error of distinguishing between optimism and pessimism and suggesting that people are more complex in their perspectives and moods than positive psychology allows for. Sundararajan argues that there exists within positive psychology a hidden moral map that needs to be surfaced through self-reflexivity and critical thinking (2005). The critique here is that positive psychology is not ideologically neutral, but ought to be honest and strong enough to bring to the surface the beliefs that drive its development and promotion. More recently, Ríos and Pérez go further by suggesting that the whole positive psychology endeavor is based on ignorance:

> Positive Psychology has attempted to become a new paradigm in the theory and practice of Psychology but is not. A thorough analysis of the history of knowledge on the struggle to live

> leads to the conclusion that Positive Psychology is neither original nor as promising as many researchers believe. It has not contributed anything new from a theoretical point of view. (2012, p. 342).

This illustrates the antipathy that positive psychology can stir up, alongside concerns that there is relatively little evidence of critical thinking by scholars and scientists in the field.

How much of this critique can be translated across to the domain of organizational change is an interesting question. Given recent developments in theoretical frameworks, with IPOD for example making specific reference to the significant role of positive psychology, it seems reasonable to take careful note of the issues raised by critics. There remains also a continuing concern that, in the field of organizational change, evidence of effectiveness is very hard to come by. Indeed, at a very fundamental level Sturdy and Grey (2003) suggest that the notion of "organizational change" itself should not be beyond challenge. They argue that consideration also needs to be given to the idea of organizational stability and that the pro-change bias of organizational literature forms part of a dominant, but not necessarily an evidenced-based nor balanced, discourse.

Future Research

To develop the field of positive organizational change and respond to the concerns of critics, a number of avenues for future research and theorizing open up. Firstly, there is a need to encourage both theorists and practitioners to engage in critical reflection both in respect of the positive organizational change constructs themselves but also in respect of how the discourse is being developed and engaged with. One potentially fruitful area to consider is an exploration of the intersections between social constructionism and critical realism in both theory and change practice (Cantore, 2014). Currently these philosophical positions can be portrayed as "either/or." It may ultimately not be a case of "both/and" but rather a question of how to move with agility between them. Whatever the process or positions held by different groupings, ultimately the need is to create spaces for exploration of ideas without one discourse being privileged over another.

Bartunek and Woodman (2012) argue for the inclusion of practitioners in this process, since this historically has been one of the major strengths of OD. The call here is not just for abstract research, but research processes and relationships that build both scholarly and practitioner understandings and practices. An example of this is recent research by Cantore into the behaviors and attitudes of change practitioners using collaborative action research methods (2014). Furthermore a view that there is a lack of reflexivity apparent in the field is a critique that warrants some response. Is there a dominant organizational change discourse that excludes other voices and perspectives? If so, what might be done to open up the inquiry?

Secondly, if the construct of positive approaches to organizational change is to be further developed then probably more attention needs to be given to the organizational dimension. Cameron and Spreitzer make this point when they comment that "we still have much to learn about the 'O' in Positive Organizational Scholarship" (2012, p. 1040). This is particularly important given the changing nature of organizations and organizing in both local and global contexts. Questions remain about what is actually meant when people talk about change. There are plenty of typologies of change found in the change management texts (e.g., Carnall, 2007; Cummings and Worley, 2014; Hayes, 2014; Myers, Hulks, & Wiggins, 2012), but are these sufficient for the tasks facing both researchers and practitioners? Avenues for future research are likely to be through collaborative thinking and action that enables high levels of reflexivity and engagement. Without collective effort, the research and discourse around positive organizational change have the potential to become narrow and potentially unfruitful.

A question which remains to be asked is: Why concern ourselves with organizational change, positive or negative, at all? Perhaps it is time to consider afresh the purposes of organizing together in the 21st century. Why is it worth working together and what end purposes have we in mind in doing so? This opens philosophical, ethical, economic, moral, and spiritual questions for all to explore.

Conclusions

The field of positive approaches to organizational change is a broad collection of ideas and practices drawing upon a range of philosophical perspectives. It demonstrably is itself subject to development and debate. Theory and research, particularly in the domain of positive psychology, continue to have significant influence on the conversation around the future direction of the field with advocates like Cooperrider arguing that a blended approach that meshes positive psychology with organizational change is not only possible but the obvious way forward (Cooperrider & Godwin, 2012).

Recent critiques, however, call for caution and a careful consideration of the value of past learning alongside some questioning of the language and power strategies used by proponents of positivity. The explicit connection made between ideological positions about how positivity can change the world and organizations deserves more reflection and shared explorations between practitioners and scholars.

Behind organizational change efforts is an implicit and optimistic assumption that change inevitably will lead to improvement. Recognizing such beliefs and how they shape those who engage in organizational change efforts is an area for further inquiry. Similarly, the scholarly discourses that risk falling into a trap of dichotomous thinking – positing either negative or positive, new or old, and change or stability – need recognizing and careful handling to avoid missing wisdom that often emerges from "both/and" thinking.

References

Bailey, J. (2013). *Pessimism*. London, UK: Routledge.

Bakker, A. B., & Schaufeli, W. B. (2008). Positive organizational behaviour: Engaged employees in flourishing organizations. *Journal of Organizational Behavior*, *29*(2), 147–154.

Bartunek, J., & Woodman, R. (2012). The spirits of organisation development, or why OD lives despite its pronounced death. In K. S. Cameron & G. Spreitzer (Eds.), *The Oxford handbook of positive organizational scholarship* (pp. 727–737). New York, NY: Oxford University Press.

Bastien, Y. (2005). It's win-win all the way. In J. Brown & D. Isaacs (Eds.), *The World Café: Shaping our futures through conversations that matter* (pp. 31–33). Oakland, CA: Berrett-Koehler.

Beer, M., & Nohria, N. (2000). Cracking the code of change. *Harvard Business Review*, *78*(3), 133–141.

Bennis, W. G. (1969). Organization development: Its nature, origins, and prospects. Reading, MA: Addison-Wesley.

Benyus, J. M. (1997). *Biomimicry*. New York, NY: William Morrow.

Boniwell, I. (2008). *Positive psychology in a nutshell: A balanced introduction to the science of optimal functioning* (2nd ed.). London, UK: Personal Well-Being Centre.

Boyatzis, R. E., & Mckee, A. (2005). *Resonant leadership: Renewing yourself and connecting with others through mindfulness, hope, and compassion*. Watertown, MA: Harvard Business Press.

Boyd, N. M., & Bright, D. S. (2007). Appreciative inquiry as a mode of action research for community psychology. *Journal of Community Psychology, 35*(8), 1019–1036.

Bright, D. S., Cooperrider, D. L., & Galloway, W. B. (2006). Appreciative inquiry in the Office of Research and Development: Improving the collaborative capacity of organization. *Public Performance & Management Review, 29*(3), 285–306.

Brown, J., & Isaacs, D. (2005). *The World Café: Shaping our futures through conversations that matter.* Oakland, CA: Berrett-Koehler.

Brown, M., & Cregan, C. (2008). Organizational change cynicism: The role of employee involvement. *Human Resource Management, 47*(4), 667.

Burke, C., & Sheldon, K. (2010). Encouraging workplace innovation using "World Café" model. *Nursing Management, 17*(7), 14–19.

Bushe, G. R. (2013). Dialogic OD: A theory of practice. *OD Practitioner, 45*(1), 11–17.

Bushe, G. R., & Kassam, A. F. (2005). When is appreciative inquiry transformational? A meta-case analysis. *Journal of Applied Behavioral Science, 41*(2), 161–181.

Bushe, G. R., & Marshak, R. J. (2009). Revisioning organization development diagnostic and dialogic premises and patterns of practice. *Journal of Applied Behavioral Science, 45*(3), 348–368.

Bushe, G. R., & Marshak, R. J. (2014). The dialogic mindset in organization development. *Research in Organizational Change and Development, 22*, 55–97.

Bushe, G. R., & Marshak, R. J. (Eds.) (2015). *Dialogic organization development: The theory and practice of transformational change.* Oakland, CA: Berrett-Kohler.

Calabrese, R. L., & Cohen, E. (2013). An appreciative inquiry into an urban drug court: Cultural transformation. *Qualitative Report, 18*, 2.

Caldwell, D. F., Chatman, J., O'Reilly III, C. A., Ormiston, M., & Lapiz, M. (2008). Implementing strategic change in a health care system: The importance of leadership and change readiness. *Health Care Management Review, 33*(2), 124–133.

Cameron, K. S., Bright, D., & Caza, A. (2004). Exploring the relationships between organizational virtuousness and performance. *American Behavioral Scientist, 47*(6), 766–790.

Cameron, K., & Dutton, J. (Eds.). (2003). *Positive organizational scholarship: Foundations of a new discipline.* Oakland, CA: Berrett-Koehler.

Cameron, K. S., & Spreitzer, G. (Eds.) (2012). *The Oxford handbook of positive organizational scholarship.* New York, NY: Oxford University Press.

Cantore, S. (2014). *A practitioner inquiry project to develop an emerging framework for conversational consulting.* Unpublished DProfS project report: Middlesex University, UK.

Cantore, S., & Cooperrider, D. (2013). Positive psychology and appreciative inquiry. In H. S. Leonard, R. Lewis, A. M. Freedman, & J. Passmore (Eds.), *The Wiley-Blackwell handbook of the psychology of leadership, change and organizational development* (pp. 267–289). Oxford, UK: Wiley-Blackwell.

Cantore, S., & Hick, W. (2013). Dialogic OD in practice. *OD Practitioner, 45*(1), 5–10.

Cantore, S., & Passmore, J. (2012). *Top business psychology models.* London, UK: Kogan Page.

Carnall, C. A. (2007). *Managing change in organizations.* London, UK: Pearson Education.

Carter, B. (2006). "One expertise among many": Working appreciatively to make miracles instead of finding problems; using appreciative inquiry as a way of reframing research. *Journal of Research in Nursing, 11*(1), 48–63.

Choi, J. N. (2007). Change-oriented organizational citizenship behavior: Effects of work environment characteristics and intervening psychological processes. *Journal of Organizational Behavior, 28*(4), 467.

Cooperrider, D. L., & Godwin, L. N. (2012). Positive organisation development. In K. Cameron & G. Spreitzer (Eds.), *The Oxford handbook of positive organizational scholarship* (pp. 737–751). New York, NY: Oxford University Press.

Cooperrider, D. L., Whitney, D., & Stavros, J. M. (2008). *Appreciative inquiry handbook: For leaders of change.* Oakland, CA: Berrett-Koehler.

Csikszentmihalyi, M. (2014). *Flow.* Dordrecht, the Netherlands: Springer.

Cummings, T. G., & Worley, C. G. (2014). *Organization development and change.* Andover, UK: Cengage Learning.

Delaney, C., Daley, K., & Lajoie, D. (2006). Facilitating empowerment and stimulating scholarly dialogue using the World Café model. *Journal of Nursing Education*, *45*(1), 46.

Dienstag, J. F. (2006). *Pessimism: Philosophy, ethic, spirit*. Princeton, NJ: Princeton University Press.

Elenurm, T. (2012). Open space as a knowledge metaphor and a knowledge sharing intervention. *Knowledge Management Research & Practice*, *10*(1), 55–63.

Fineman, S. (2006). On being positive: Concerns and counterpoints. *Academy of Management Review*, *31*(2), 270–291.

Fouché, C., & Light, G. (2011). An invitation to dialogue: "The World Café" in social work research. *Qualitative Social Work*, *10*(1), 28–48.

Francis, R. (2010). *Independent Inquiry into care provided by Mid Staffordshire NHS Foundation Trust January 2005–March 2009*. London, UK: The Stationery Office.

Fredrickson, B. L. (1998). What good are positive emotions? *Review of General Psychology*, *2*(3), 300–319.

Fredrickson, B. L. (2001). The role of positive emotions in positive psychology: The broaden-and-build theory of positive emotions. *American Psychologist*, *56*(3), 218.

Fredrickson, B. L., Tugade, M. M., Waugh, C. E., & Larkin, G. R. (2003). What good are positive emotions in crises? A prospective study of resilience and emotions following the terrorist attacks on the United States on September 11th, 2001. *Journal of Personality and Social Psychology*, *84*(2), 365–376.

French, W., & Bell, C. (1999). *Organizational development: Behavior science interventions for organizational improvement*. London, UK: Prentice Hall.

Fullarton, C., & Palermo, J. (2008). Evaluation of a large group method in an educational institution: The World Café versus large group facilitation. *Journal of Institutional Research*, *14*(1), 109–117.

Gergen, K. J. (1978). Toward generative theory. *Journal of Personality and Social Psychology*, *36*(11), 1344.

Gergen, K. J. (1997a). *Realities and relationships: Soundings in social construction*. Boston, MA: Harvard University Press.

Gergen, K. J. (1997b). Social psychology as social construction: The emerging vision. In C. McGarty & A. Haslam (Eds.), *The message of social psychology: Perspectives on mind in society* (pp. 113–128). Oxford, UK: Blackwell.

Gergen, K. J., & Thatchenkery, T. J. (1996). Organization science as social construction: Postmodern potentials. *The Journal of Applied Behavioral Science*, *32*(4), 356.

Giles, D., & Alderson, S. (2008). An appreciative inquiry into the transformative learning experiences of students in a family literacy project. *Australian Journal of Adult Learning*, *48*(3), 466–478.

Gordezky, R. (2015). From them to us. In G. R. Bushe & R. J. Marshak (Eds.), *Dialogic organisation development: The theory and practice of transformational change* (pp. 305–325). Oakland, CA: Berrett-Kohler.

Grant, D., & Marshak, R. J. (2011). Toward a discourse-centered understanding of organizational change. *The Journal of Applied Behavioral Science*, *47*(2), 204–235.

Hallgren, E. W. (2009). How to use an innovation audit as a learning tool: A case study of enhancing high-involvement innovation. *Creativity and Innovation Management*, *18*(1), 48–58.

Hammer, M., & Champy, J. (1993). *Reengineering the corporation: A manifesto for business revolution*. London, NY: Nicholas Brealey.

Hayes, J. (2014). *The theory and practice of change management*. Basingstoke, UK: Palgrave Macmillan.

Hechenbleikner, P., Gilburg, D., & Dunnell, K. (2008). Reading's World Café: Increasing community engagement in planning for the future. *Public Management*, *90*(10), 6–12.

Hideg, I., Michela, J. L., & Ferris, D. L. (2011). Overcoming negative reactions of nonbeneficiaries to employment equity: The effect of participation in policy formulation. *Journal of Applied Psychology*, *96*(2), 363.

Higgs, M. (2002). Do leaders need emotional intelligence? A study of the relationship between emotional intelligence and leadership of change. *International Journal of Organisational Behaviour*, *5*(6), 195–212.

Higgs, M. (2013). Change and its leadership: The role of positive emotions. In P. A. Linley, S. Harrington, & N. Garcea (Eds.), *Oxford handbook of positive psychology and work* (pp. 67–81). Oxford, UK: Oxford University Press.

Higgs, M., & Rowland, D. (2011). What does it take to implement change successfully? A study of the behaviors of successful change leaders. *The Journal of Applied Behavioral Science*, *47*(3), 309–335.

Hughes, M. (2011). Do 70 per cent of all organizational change initiatives really fail? *Journal of Change Management*, *11*(4), 451–464.

Jaros, S. (2010). Commitment to organizational change: A critical review. *Journal of Change Management*, *10*(1), 79–108.

Kotter, J. P. (1995). Leading change: Why transformation efforts fail. *Harvard Business Review*, *73*(2), 59–67.

Laszlo, C. (2003). *The sustainable company: How to create lasting value through social and environmental performance*. Washington, DC: Island Press.

Lewis, S., Passmore, J., & Cantore, S. (2008). *Appreciative inquiry for change management: Using AI to facilitate organizational development*. London, UK: Kogan Page.

Lines, R., & Selart, M. (2013). Participation and organisational commitment during change. In H. S. Leonard, R. Lewis, A. M. Freedman, & J. Passmore (Eds.), *The Wiley-Blackwell handbook of the psychology of leadership, change and organizational development* (pp. 289–313). Oxford, UK: Wiley-Blackwell.

Luthans, F. (2002). The need for and meaning of positive organizational behavior. *Journal of Organizational Behavior*, *23*(6), 695–706.

Luthans, F., & Youssef, C. M. (2007). Emerging positive organizational behavior. *Journal of Management*, *33*(3), 321–349.

Madsen, S. R., Miller, D., & John, C. R. (2005). Readiness for organizational change: Do organizational commitment and social relationships in the workplace make a difference? *Human Resource Development Quarterly*, *16*, 213–234.

Margulies, N., & Raia, A. P. (1978). *Conceptual foundations of organizational development*. London, UK: McGraw-Hill College.

Marshak, R. J. (2013). Leveraging language for change. *OD Practitioner*, *45*(2), 49–55.

Marshak, R. J., & Bushe, G. R. (2013). An introduction to advances in dialogic organization development. *OD Practitioner*, *45*(1), 1–4.

Marshak, R. J., & Grant, D. (2008). Organizational discourse and new organization development practices. *British Journal of Management*, *19*(Issue Supplement s1), S7–S19.

McDonald, M., & O'Callaghan, J. (2008). Positive psychology: A Foucauldian critique. *The Humanistic Psychologist*, *36*(2), 127–142.

McDonough, W., & Braungart, M. (2010). *Cradle to cradle: Remaking the way we make things*. Basingstoke, UK: MacMillan.

Miller, A. (2008). A critique of positive psychology – or "the new science of happiness." *Journal of Philosophy of Education*, *42*(3–4), 591–608.

More, C. (2011). The effect of Appreciative Inquiry as organizational development intervention on organizational planning and service quality improvement in St. Francis School (ECSE). *Revista de cercetare și intervenție socială*, *33*, 27–43.

Myers, P., Hulks, S., & Wiggins, L. (2012). *Organizational change: Perspectives on theory and practice*. Oxford, UK: Oxford University Press.

Neubert, M. J., & Cady, S. H. (2001). Program commitment: A multi-study longitudinal field investigation of its impact and antecedents. *Personnel Psychology*, *54*(2), 421–448.

Orem, S., Binket, J., & Clancy, A. (2007). *Appreciative coaching: A positive process for change*. San Francisco, CA: Jossey Bass.

Oswick, C. (2009). Revisioning or re-versioning? A commentary on diagnostic and dialogic forms of organization development. *The Journal of Applied Behavioral Science*, *45*(3), 369–374.

Oswick C. (2013). Reflections: OD or not OD that is the question! A constructivist's thoughts on the changing nature of change. *Journal of Change Management*, *13*(4), 371–381.

Oswick, C., Grant, D., Michelson, G., & Wailes, N. (2005). Looking forwards: Discursive directions in organizational change. *Journal of Organizational Change Management*, *18*(4), 383–390.

Owen, H. (1995). *Tales from open space.* Potomac, MD: Abbott Publishing.
Owen, H. (2008a). Open space technology: A user's guide. Oakland, CA: Berrett-Koehler.
Owen, H. (2008b). Wave rider: Leadership for high performance in a self-organizing world. Oakland, CA: Berrett-Koehler.
Peterson, C., & Seligman, M. E. P. (2004). *Character strengths and virtues: A handbook and classification.* New York, NY: Oxford University Press.
Powley, E. H., Fry, R. E., Barrett, F. J., & Bright, D. S. (2004). Dialogic democracy meets command and control: Transformation through the appreciative inquiry summit. *The Academy of Management Executive, 18*(3), 67–80.
Prewitt, V. (2011). Working in the café: Lessons in group dialogue. *The Learning Organization, 18*(3), 189–202.
Quinn, R., & Wellman, N. (2012). Seeing and acting differently. In K. S. Cameron & G. Spreitzer (Eds.), *The Oxford handbook of positive organizational scholarship* (pp. 751–763). New York, NY: Oxford University Press.
Rath, T. (2007). *Strengths Finder 2.0.* New York, NY: Gallup Press.
Rath, T., & Conchie, B. (2009). *Strengths based leadership.* New York, NY: Gallup Press.
Richer, M. C., Ritchie, J., & Marchionni, C. (2009). "If we can't do more, let's do it differently!": Using appreciative inquiry to promote innovative ideas for better health care work environments. *Journal of Nursing Management, 17*(8), 947–955.
Ríos, L. F., & Pérez, M. N. (2012). Positive pychology: "Zeigeist"(or spirit of the times) or ignorance (or disinformation) of history? *International Journal of Clinical and Health Psychology, 12*(2), 333–344.
Ritch, E. L., & Brennan, C. (2010). Using World Café and drama to explore older people's experience of financial products and services. *International Journal of Consumer Studies, 34*(4), 405–411.
Roth, F. (2009). The effect of the financial crisis on systemic trust. *Intereconomics, 44*(4), 203–208.
Rothwell, W. J., Stavros, J. M., Sullivan, R. L., & Sullivan, A. (Eds.). (2010). *Practicing organization development: A guide for leading change.* Chichester, UK: Wiley.
Russell, B. (1945/2013). *History of Western philosophy: Collectors edition.* London, UK: Routledge.
Ryan, F. J., Soven, M., Smither, J., Sullivan, W. M., & VanBuskirk, W. R. (1999). Appreciative inquiry: Using personal narratives for initiating school reform. *The Clearing House, 72*(3), 164–167.
Saunders, M. N., & Thornhill, A. (2003). Organisational justice, trust and the management of change: An exploration. *Personnel Review, 32*(3), 360–375.
Schein, E. (2010). *Organizational culture and leadership.* San Francisco, CA: Jossey-Bass.
Sekerka, L. E., Brumbaugh, A. M., Rosa, J. A., & Cooperrider, D. (2006). Comparing appreciative inquiry to a diagnostic technique in organizational change: The moderating effects of gender. *International Journal of Organization Theory and Behavior, 9*(4), 449.
Sekerka, L., & Fredrickson, B. (2013). Working positively toward transformative cooperation. In P. A. Linley, S. Harrington, & N. Garcea (Eds.), *Oxford handbook of positive psychology and work* (pp. 81–95). Oxford, UK: Oxford University Press.
Sekerka, L., & McCraty, R. (2004). The psychophysiology of appreciation in the workplace. In D. L. Cooperrider & M. Avital (Eds.), *Constructive discourse and human organization advances in appreciative inquiry* (Vol. 1, pp. 217–239). Bingley, UK: Emerald.
Seligman, M. E. P. (1991). *Learned optimism.* New York, NY: Knopf.
Seligman, M. E. P., & Csikszentmihalyi, M. (2000). Positive psychology: An introduction. *American Psychological Association 55*(1), 5–14.
Stavros, J. M., & Hinrichs, G. (2011). *The thin book of® SOAR: Building strengths-based strategy.* Bend, OR: Thin Book Publishing.
Stavros, J. M., & Sprangel, J. R. (2008). Applying Appreciative Inquiry to deliver strategic change: Orbseal Technology Center. In S. Lewis, J. Passmore, & S. Cantore (Eds.), *Appreciative Inquiry for change management: Using AI to facilitate organizational development* (pp. 185–199). London, UK: Kogan Page.
Staw, B. M., Sutton, R. I., & Pelled, L. H. (1994). Employee positive emotion and favorable outcomes at the workplace. *Organization Science, 5*(1), 51–71.

Stevenson, A. (Ed.). (2010). *Oxford dictionary of English*. London, UK: Oxford University Press.

Sturdy, A., & Grey, C. (2003). Beneath and beyond organizational change management: Exploring alternatives. *Organization, 10*(4), 651–662.

Sundararajan, L. (2005). Happiness donut: A Confucian critique of positive psychology. *Journal of Theoretical and Philosophical Psychology, 25*(1), 35–60.

Thakadipuram, T., & Stevenson, L. (2013). Turnaround: From breakdown to breakthrough with Open Space Technology. *Human Resource Development International, 16*(1), 116–127.

Vanstone, C., & Dabliez, B. (2008). Case study revitalising corporate values in Nokia. In S. Lewis, J. Passmore, & S. Cantore (Eds.), *Appreciative Inquiry for change management: Using AI to facilitate organizational development* (pp. 161–171) London, UK: Kogan Page.

Ward, A., Borawski, P., & Brown, J. (2008). Case study: World Café. In S. Lewis, J. Passmore, & S. Cantore (Eds.), *Appreciative Inquiry for change management: Using AI to facilitate organizational development* (pp. 172–184). London, UK: Kogan Page.

Weisbord, M. R. (2004). *Productive workplaces revisited: Dignity, meaning, and community in the 21st century*. New York, NY: Wiley.

Weisbord, M. R., & Janoff, S. (2010). *Future search: Getting the whole system in the room for vision, commitment, and action*. San Francisco, CA: Berrett-Koehler.

Whitney, D., & Trosten-Bloom, A., (2010). *The power of appreciative inquiry: A practical guide to positive change*. San Francisco, CA: Berrett-Koehler.

Wright, T. A. (2003). Positive organizational behavior: An idea whose time has truly come. *Journal of Organizational Behavior, 24*(4), 437–442.

17

Positive Approaches to Leadership Development

Doug MacKie

Introduction

Positive leadership development (PLD) offers access to a range of new theoretical and evidence-based approaches that have the potential to refine and enhance how leaders and leadership are developed in organizations. To date there is no grand unifying theory of leadership, studies on leadership development vary significantly in their efficacy (Avolio, Reichard, Hannah, Walumbwa, & Chan, 2009), and the evidence base continues to lag behind practitioner applications (Aguinis & Cascio, 2008). Leadership development consumes an estimated $50 billion annually (Bolden, 2007) in the USA alone and yet many programs lack a substantial evidence base or coherent theoretical rationale (Brinner, 2012). This review aims to outline some of the potential contributions that the emerging field of PLD can make to enhancing leadership development effectiveness.

The rationale for this approach is clear and compelling. Firstly, the focus on strengths seeks to redress the traditional deficit reduction focus in leadership development (Luthans & Avolio, 2003). Secondly, meta-analytic outcome studies show that current leadership models are unable to explain significant amounts of variance, suggesting there are many more critical variables to be discovered in the field of leadership development (Avolio, Reichard et al., 2009). Thirdly, practitioner application of the positive, and especially strength-based, approaches appears to be significantly ahead of the research evidence making it an opportune time to review the status of the current evidentiary base (Donaldson & Ko, 2010). Finally, applied positive psychology constructs have been successfully translated to other domains, including clinical psychology, suggesting the assessment of their cross-domain application is warranted and timely (Seligman, Steen, Park, & Petersen, 2005).

The chapter is divided into four broad and interconnected areas considered foundational to the development of the construct and evidence base for positive leadership development. Firstly, existing positive leadership theories will be reviewed, including theories of readiness for development and change as well as positive theories like authentic leadership that have

The Wiley Blackwell Handbook of the Psychology of Positivity and Strengths-Based Approaches at Work,
First Edition. Edited by Lindsay G. Oades, Michael F. Steger, Antonella Delle Fave, and Jonathan Passmore.

evolved under the positive leadership domain. Theories can be either implicit (e.g., mindsets) or explicit, and both are relevant and formative in the PLD field. Secondly, the areas of positive leadership assessment will reviewed, as the reliable and valid assessment of positive models and constructs is a common and necessary precursor to PLD (McCauley & Wakefield, 2006). Positive constructs related to leadership have traditionally been evaluated and categorized across the state–trait continuum from positive emotions to psychological capital and character strengths. The concept of strengths in particular will be reviewed, as this is one of the more developed criteria in positive leadership assessment.

Thirdly, the evidence for the effectiveness of PLD will be reviewed. There are broadly two competing methodologies that place differential emphasis on both the constructs to be developed and whether the development is conducted in a traditional group training format or a more individualized coaching design. As coaching is increasingly becoming a key delivery mechanism for executive and leadership development (Day, 2001), its alignment with positive organizational psychology is potentially critical to applying these concepts in practice. Finally, the limitations of PLD will be discussed along with suggestions for future research. Thus the aim of the review is to survey the landscape of PLD and articulate both the strengths and the limitations of this developing approach to enhancing leadership effectiveness.

Origins of PLD

Despite the focus on positive organizational psychology found in the work of humanistic psychologists (Maslow, 1954), including the attention to peak experiences and human potential, this approach failed to gain traction in organizations partly due to the lack of empiricism and development of a supportive evidence base (Wright & Quick, 2009). Positive constructs resurfaced again as part of the positive psychology movement pioneered by Martin Seligman as part of his presidency of the American Psychological Association. The resurgence of interest in positive leadership development can, in part, be traced to the paradigm shift that occurred in applied psychology at the start of the new millennium (Seligman & Csikszentmihalyi, 2000). Positive psychology originally called for a radical change in perspective away from the reduction of psychological distress and disease and toward the identification and enhancement of what made life engaging and meaningful (Seligman & Csikszentmihalyi, 2000). Positive psychology focused on three pillars of inquiry including positive subjective experiences, trait-like character strengths, and positive institutions. Originally aimed at redressing the negative bias in clinical psychology, some have argued that the positive psychology paradigm has been slower to influence organizational issues (Wright & Quick, 2009). However, it may be that with its focus toward optimizing performance, industrial psychology has always adopted a more positive approach to individuals than other aspects of psychology and lacked the overtly negative bias that prevailed in the disease models of clinical psychology (Hackman, 2009) and its uneasy alignment with biological psychiatry. As well as the success of the positivist paradigm in other areas of applied psychology, a related but independent shift in the field of talent management provided additional support for PLD. Specifically beliefs about the origin of talent in general and of leadership capability in particular began to shift from being trait-like and infrequent to state-like and much more commonly found in individuals within organizations (Meyers & Van Woerkom, 2014; Meyers, Van Woerkom, & Dries, 2013). This prompted a more inclusive perspective on leadership development where the focus on developable states would lead to the unlocking of as yet unrealised leadership potential. Positive and strengths-based approaches to leadership development offered an immediate conceptual verification and coherent methodology to assist organizations in exploiting this unrealized leadership resource (MacKie, 2014).

Positive organizational psychology (POP) has been slow to evolve as a distinct research paradigm for a number of reasons. Firstly, the three pillars of positive psychology did not align that well with organizational psychology's need for the identification of developable constructs that had explicit links to organizational effectiveness (Money, Hillenbrand, & da Camara, 2009). Secondly, evidence emerged that many individuals were unaware of their strengths (Kaplan & Kaiser, 2010), removing one of the key potential foci of positive organizational interventions. Thirdly, much of the positively orientated research conducted in organizations was cross-sectional and heavily reliant on self-report data (Mills, Fleck, & Kozikowski, 2013), limiting conclusions to correlational inferences and promoting a focus on individual well-being over organizational performance.

There are other, more enduring, reasons for the resilience of the deficit focus in organizations. There is strong and converging evidence for an evolutionary preparedness toward negativity that means it is much easier to learn to be fearful and acquire aversions than it is to develop positive associations (Rozin & Royzman, 2001). This evolutionary perspective, which explains the adaptive nature of negative emotions to deal with threat and loss and their necessary over-estimation, suggests a functional adaptation to identify and focus on the negative and over-estimate its probability. This unifying model explains a number of otherwise disconnected observations, including the lopsided taxonomy of emotional descriptors and the ease with which we learn to fear and avoid ancestral challenges (Nesse, 2005). Developing a positive focus in organizations requires overcoming these significant, adaptive, and enduring biases.

However, POP has progressed in terms of taxonomy to the point where two distinct research approaches have emerged in the field. Positive organizational behavior (POB) is construed as a research-based, measurable, and state-like approach whose constructs could consequently be targeted for further development (Luthans & Youssef, 2007). A contrasting approach to this has been defined as positive organizational scholarship (POS), which focuses on positive behavior from a more trait-like perspective. The POS focus on the classification and identification of virtues like compassion and gratitude (Boyatzis, Smith, & Blaize, 2006) in organizations lends itself more to selection than development processes. The POB approach has supported the development of research on positive psychological states, such as "PsyCap" where positive states like confidence, hope, optimism, and resilience are seen as essential prerequisites to developing a positive leadership style (Avolio & Luthans, 2006). PLD is the logical extension of this trend in POB.

Psychological capital (PsyCap) has developed as a model of the underlying positive psychological states that can be developed in followers as a result of positive leadership behaviors (Luthans, Avolio, Avey, & Norman, 2007). There is evidence that suggests that PsyCap mediates the impact of transformational leadership on follower performance (Gooty, Gavin, Johnson, Frazier, & Snow, 2009), building their capacities in motivation and goal perseverance. The PsyCap model differs from other strengths models in that it is much more circumscribed, with only one domain and four constructs, demonstrates good reliability and validity, is explicitly state-like, and has been found to be easily developed with specific interventions (Luthans, Avey, Avolio, Norman, & Combs, 2006).

The separation of POP into these two separate and conceptually distinct research domains –those that chose to focus on positive organizational behavior (POB) and those that preferred to focus on positive institutions (Positive Organizational Scholarship or POS) – has caused some challenges in the development of positive models in organizations. The distinction may appear somewhat arbitrary and more reflective of research group interests than a useful taxonomic divide (Hackman, 2009). Nonetheless, it matters as the assumptions, level of analysis, and models behind each approach are significantly different and have led to different research programs that have contrasting models for organizational, including leadership, development.

Despite these taxonomic challenges, several strands of research have emerged and are developing significant empirical support. These include the investigation of psychological capital, and its links with emotional contagion, follower positivity, and performance, (Meyers, van Woerkom, & Bakker, 2013; Meyers, Van Woerkom, de Reuver, Bakk, & Oberski, 2015). Research on strengths identification and development has resulted in novel taxonomies of strengths and virtues being developed, as well as methodologies for developing them (Biswas-Diener, Kashdan, & Minhas, 2011; Petersen & Seligman, 2004). Research on positive organizations has included the identification and development of high-performing teams (Cohn & Fredrickson, 2010). In addition, the identification and development of positive leadership, including authentic, transformational, altruistic, and servant leadership, appears to be generating significant interest and research impact (Donaldson & Ko, 2010). In terms of operationalizing these constructs into a leadership development methodology, POB is increasingly aligned with leadership coaching as an individualized methodology to deliver the positive interventions to leaders and their organizations (Linley, Woolston, & Biswas-Diener, 2009).

Positive Leadership Theory

Although there are many leadership theories, to be categorized as truly positive leadership theories, three elements must be included. Firstly, a positive leadership theory should focus on the strengths (both situational and dispositional) of the leader (Linley et al., 2009). When are they at their best and why is it so? Secondly, positive leadership needs to have a positive impact on followers, proximately in the form of greater confidence and discretionary effort and distally in the form of superior individual and organizational performance (Avey, Avolio, & Luthans, 2011). Thirdly, the purpose of the positive leadership theory is to enable the pursuit of goals and objectives that are self-transcendent and not complicit in the manipulation of others for personal benefit (Fambrough & Hart, 2008). Authenticity has been suggested as the core construct on which positive models of leadership like transformational, ethical, and servant leadership are based (Avolio & Gardner, 2005). There are now a variety of theoretical domains that are providing support for PLD. These can be classified as theories or models (e.g., authentic leadership; Avolio, Walumba, & Weber, 2009), or underlying psychological constructs (e.g., psychological capital; Luthans et al., 2007). In addition, models of PLD can be moderated by implicit leadership theories (ILTs); that is, what are the underlying assumptions about leadership and its development in an organization. Implicit leadership models such as developmental readiness and mindsets are of interest in PLD as they contain within them elements of both motivation and capability that signal a readiness and belief in successful leadership development that are seen as essential precursors of a successful positive leadership development process (Avolio, 2011).

Implicit leadership theories and positive leadership

Implicit models of leadership have been implicated in the veracity of managers' perceptions of the performance of their reports and beliefs about the malleability of behaviors, ability, and personality (Heslin & VandeWalle, 2008). Growth or incremental mindsets are those conducive to development, as they assume an inherent capacity in self and others for developing and enhancing abilities (Dweck, 2006). In contrast, fixed managerial mindsets assume abilities are relatively stable over time and do not support investment in developing the capability of others (Heslin & VandeWalle, 2008). The concept of developmental readiness as a precursor to successful PLD has emerged from this focus on the leader's underlying assumptions of the malleability of leadership competence (Avolio & Hannah, 2008).

Developmental readiness is a potentially key precursor of successful leadership development that seeks to identify key positive states and traits in the individual that are suggestive of a readiness to constructively engage in enhancing leadership capacity. Developmental readiness has been defined as "both the ability and the motivation to focus on, make meaning of and develop new and more complex ways of thinking that position you to more effectively assume leadership roles" (Avolio & Hannah, 2008). Emerging from the clinical literature on change readiness (Prochaska & DiClemente, 1983), the construct was supported by empirical evidence that suggested both the low heritability of leadership (Ilies, Gerhardt, & Lee, 2004) and meta-analytic studies on leadership effectiveness that suggested significant levels of the variance in predicting leadership effectiveness were still unaccounted for (Avolio, Reichard, et al., 2009).

Developmental readiness sits squarely within the POB tradition in that it assumes readiness is a state-like construct that can be positively inflated with the right intervention (Hannah & Avolio, 2010). The construct was conceptualized as having both a motivational and ability higher-order construct with supporting subdomains nesting underneath. Motivation was comprised of interest and goals, goal orientation, and developmental efficacy, whereas the ability factor was comprised of self-awareness and self-concept clarity, leader complexity, and metacognitive ability. The supporting subdomains of both the ability and the motivational readiness factors were not new but instead drawn from pre-existing theories of change. Goal orientation drew on the implicit theories of self (Dweck & Leggett, 1988) that proposed that leaders could either adopt an incremental view of their own development where their growth mindset encouraged exploration and assimilation of new experiences, or an entity model where a relatively fixed mindset encouraged self-limiting beliefs about their potential to develop. Developmental efficacy too had a long history and is conceptualized as the level of confidence the leader possesses in the development and application of new knowledge, skills, and abilities (Luthans, Luthans, Hodgetts, & Luthans, 2001).

The ability to develop was also predicated on existing theoretical constructs including self-awareness, self-concept clarity, and the complexity of the leader's self-image and the capacity to reflect on one's own thinking (metacognitive ability). Much of the evidence comes from studies on the individual subdomains including goal-setting (Locke & Latham, 1990), mindsets (Dweck, 2006), metacognitive ability (Hannah, 2006), and self-awareness (Avolio, Wernsing, Chan, & Griffeth, 2007), but it remains to be seen if the construct of developmental readiness in its totality adds anything more than the sum of its parts to the prediction of who will benefit most from leadership development. Despite the apparent face and concurrent validity of the construct of developmental readiness, the concept remains to be operationalized in the form of a reliable and valid psychometric that will facilitate the demonstration of its incremental validity beyond that of its subdomains.

Explicit theories of positive leadership

There is a variety of positive leadership theories that have emerged as a response to the shift to a more positive strengths-based conceptualization of leaders and leadership. These include authentic leadership (Luthans & Avolio, 2003), servant leadership (Liden, Wayne,

Zhao, & Henderson, 2008), and positive global leadership (Youseff & Luthans, 2012). In addition, existing models of leadership – including transformational leadership (Bass, 1999), with its emphasis on the instillation of positive affect in followers, and Greenleaf's servant leadership model (1977), with its focus on stewardship – qualify to be included in the positive leadership domain. Of the newly emerged theories, it is authentic leadership that has generated the greatest empirical and research evidence base (e.g., Avolio & Gardner, 2005; Gardner et al., 2011).

Authentic leadership is defined by Luthans and Avolio (2003, p. 243) as "a process that draws from both positive psychological capacities and a highly developed organizational context which results in both greater self-awareness and self-regulated positive behaviors." Consequently the development of authentic leaders involves the identification and enhancement of positive psychological states and the integration of a moral element into leadership development to further develop the purpose as well as the process of leadership (Avolio & Gardner, 2005). Authentic leadership arose out of the concept of transformational leadership when a distinction was made between pseudo-transformational leaders, who manipulated followers for their own ends, and genuine transformational leaders (Avolio, Walumbwa, & Weber, 2009). Transformational leadership emphasized the leader's impact on followers in terms of inspiring them toward enhancing their performance toward a shared vision for the benefit of the organization and its values (Bass, 1999). Bass integrated the five transformative elements of leadership into his full range leadership model (FRLM) that, in addition, included two transactional elements that focused on rewarding followers' behaviors and two laissez-faire elements that described the less functional, passive, and avoidant leadership styles. There have been a variety of attempts to operationalize the transformational leadership construct, the most prolific of those being the Multifactor Leadership Questionnaire (MLQ; Bass & Avolio, 1997). There is now a substantial amount of evidence supporting the construct validity of the FRLM, and the MLQ is one of the most commonly used leadership instruments by both researchers and practitioners in the field (Alban-Metcalfe & Mead, 2010).

The concept of authentic leadership also capitalized on the increasing influence of positive organizational behavior and offered a way to integrate this into a more strengths-orientated leader development process (Avolio & Luthans, 2006). Authentic leadership was seen to contain four key elements: balanced processing in decision-making, an internalized moral perspective, relational transparency with others, and self-awareness (Walumbwa, Avolio, Gardner, Wernsing, & Peterson, 2008). These four scales appeared to load onto a higher-order factor of authenticity that was distinguishable from the concept of transformational leadership. Authentic leadership is closely aligned to the concept of psychological capital in that the goal of the authentic expression of beliefs and values is the elevation of trust, hope, and optimism in one's followers (Hernandez, Eberly, Avolio, & Johnson, 2011).

Emerging models of positive leadership

Mindfulness and the related field of Acceptance and Commitment Therapy (ACT) have been described as the third wave of cognitive-behavioral theories that have emerged to manage the epidemic of disorders related to negative moods (Hayes, 2004). Both of these traditions focus less on efforts made to challenge, refute, and eliminate negative experiences, and more on encouraging full awareness and non-judgmental acceptance of them in order to identify beliefs and actions that are aligned with one's values. There is a long history of interchange and innovation between clinical and organizational psychology (MacKie, 2007; Smither, 2011), and the wave of mindfulness and acceptance-based techniques is now lapping at the shores of leadership development. The reason these processes relate to positive leadership is that there is now acknowledgment that these techniques not only assist in the management of negative emotions but also promote positivity, well-being, and psychological flexibility (Kashdan & Ciarrochi, 2013). Given that positive leadership models like authentic leadership actively promote greater self-regulation as a pathway to enhanced leadership effectiveness (Avolio & Gardner, 2005), and that both mindfulness and acceptance have been found to enhance self-regulation (Kinsler, 2014), there is a promising and exploratory link between these techniques and PLD.

Mindfulness has been suggested to mediate leadership development by helping leaders differentiate from their thoughts and beliefs through a process known as *cognitive defusion* (Atkins, 2008). Cognitive defusion in turn facilitates the taking and holding of multiple perspectives that can be explored in the decision-making process of the leader. Mindfulness also promotes self-compassion in the leader and engagement through a focus on present moment attention (Reb, Narayanan, & Ho, 2013). However, the majority of the research on workplace mindfulness is focused on the intrapersonal domain, such as reducing burnout (Narayanan, Chaturvedi, Reb, & Srinivas, 2011), rather than the interpersonal where leaders impact on their followers. Nevertheless, one study that did focus on the interpersonal impact of mindfulness found significant correlations between leader mindfulness and employee performance, employee organizational citizenship behaviors, and job satisfaction (Reb, Narayanan, & Chaturvedi, 2014). Despite these encouraging exploratory findings and their apparent alignment with positive leadership models like authentic leadership, there are no current between-subject longitudinal studies that demonstrate the added value of mindfulness techniques in PLD.

Whereas mindfulness has a heritage steeped in millennia of spiritual practices, ACT originally developed within the context of clinical therapies. ACT is a set of related techniques that focus on a combination of mindfulness and acceptance processes and values-based behavioral activation (Flaxman, Bond, & Livheim, 2013). ACT training has been shown to enhance work performance (Bond & Flaxman, 2006) and has been suggested to develop resilience in managers (Moran, 2010) through enhancing psychological flexibility. This decoupling from habitual patterns and reflexive reactions promotes balanced decision-making, and greater self-regulation has been shown to positively impact on followers' well-being and positivity (Avey et al., 2011). However, ACT has yet to be shown to have an additive and significant empirical impact on PLD in organizations.

Positive Leadership Assessment

Assessment in PLD is intimately related to the underlying theory and philosophy of leadership and in particular whether state-like or traitlike constructs are the focus of assessment (Biswas-Diener et al., 2011). Assessment can focus on both the individual's capacity in the underlying positive leadership model, such as authentic leadership, and the assessment of the underlying positive constructs like strengths that are hypothesized to moderate and even mediate enhanced leadership effectiveness (Gooty et al., 2009; MacKie, 2014). Due to the recency of the strength-based approach in leadership development, there is yet no consensus on how to define, assess, or develop strengths (Roarty & Toogood, 2014). However, it is apparent that what you assess can significantly determine how you develop positive leaders. Thus a focus on traits can lead to an "identify and use" approach,whilst a focus on states leads to an emphasis on strengths development (Biswas-Diener et al., 2011).

One of the cornerstones of the applied positive psychology paradigm has been the focus on strengths (Luthans & Youseff, 2007). Understanding how strengths are defined, identified, utilized, and leveraged is key if they are to be successfully applied to positive leadership development. In order to test the effectiveness of a strengths-based approach, it is necessary both to be consistent in the definitions and classification of strengths, and also to demonstrate that adherence to a strengths-based leadership development protocol is predictive of enhanced leadership effectiveness (MacKie, 2014).

Strengths-based leadership psychometrics

There have been a number of attempts to define strengths in the context of individual and organizational development. The Gallup StrengthsFinder (Rath & Conchie, 2008) attempts to describe four domains of leadership, namely: executing, influencing, relationship building, and strategic thinking, which are themselves clusters of the 34 strengths identified in the StrengthsFinder instrument. Despite being assessed on all 34 strengths, subjective self-assessment routinely only produces a list of the participant's top five relative strengths. The scoring is ipsative rather than normative, limiting its utility as a dependent variable, and Gallup's own internal research reports reliabilities of the 34 strengths ranging from 0.52 to 0.79 (Asplund, Lopez, Hodges, & Harter, 2007). The model defines strengths as "the ability to consistently produce near-perfect performance on a specific task" (Rath, 2007), with the performance predicated on a combination of elements of skill, knowledge, and naturally occurring talents that cannot be acquired through development. This trait-based approach and the focus on identifying underlying talents makes it more aligned with leadership assessment than development.

The Values in Action (VIA) questionnaire (Peterson, Stephens, Park, & Seligman, 2010) was explicit in its intention to develop a model designed to assess and measure strength of character and virtues. A review of the world's most influential religious and philosophical texts by the authors of the inventory led to the identification of six domains (wisdom, courage, humanity, justice, temperance, and transcendence), all underpinned by specific signature strengths. The VIA then aimed to identify 24 character strengths from these domains, that individuals recognize and apply to achieve fulfillment. Again, like the StrengthsFinder, the VIA depends on the veracity of the self-assessment to produce a relative ranking of the top five signature strengths. In terms of the construct validity, there is evidence to suggest it more closely fits the big five model of personality than a discrete construct of six independent virtues (MacDonald, Bore, & Munro, 2008). Unlike the Gallup StrengthsFinder, there is no overt connection between the VIA and leadership behavior. However,there are some implicit links to leadership with character strengths like authenticity, teamwork, and leadership identified in the assessment (Money et al., 2009).

The Realise2 model (Linley & Stoker, 2010) attempted to take a broader approach to the process of strengths assessment by including development areas and relative weaknesses in the model. The Realise2 model requires participants to rate 60 attributes according to how energizing they find them, how competently they display them, and how frequently they use them. The model then divides the responses into four quadrants: realized strengths that are known and used, unrealized strengths that are known but underutilized, learned behaviors where performance has been acquired but is not energizing, and weaknesses where both competence and energy are low. Accordingly, the greatest developmental opportunity is found in unrealized strengths as these are underutilzed areas of interest and competence. The mean reliability scores across all 60 attributed item groupings was reported to be 0.82 (Linley & Stoker, 2012).

There is clearly a degree of equivocation about what the construct of strengths encompasses, with significant apparent overlap with personality traits, competencies, and virtues. In addition, the lack of normative comparisons, reliance on subjective assessment, absence of peer reviewed publications, and the utilization of opaque proprietary scoring systems makes this domain fraught with difficultly for comparative research. Future research needs to conclusively establish the construct and discriminant validity of this concept (Hackman, 2009).

Strengths and performance

Using strengths as a mechanism for positive leadership development requires some understanding of how strengths relate to performance. Specifically, data on whether this relationship is curvilinear or linear will inform how strengths are developed in the pursuit of enhanced leadership effectiveness. There is evidence for a curvilinear relationship between assertiveness and leadership effectiveness (Ames & Flynn, 2007), between conscientiousness and emotional stability and job performance (Le et al., 2011), and between ethical leadership and organizational citizenship behavior (Stouten, van Dijke, Mayer, De Cremer, & Euwema, 2013). In addition, the leadership derailment literature suggests that, when overdone, strengths become weaknesses and this can be in the form of excessive leverage or contextual misapplication (Kaiser, 2009). This suggests that the unregulated leverage of strengths, independent of intensity or context, could adversely impact on leadership performance (Kaiser & Overfield, 2010).

Positive Leadership Development (PLD)

Recent reviews of the leadership development literature have provided convincing data that leadership can be developed over time via a variety of methods and processes (Day, 2001; Day, Harrison, & Halpin, 2012). Leadership development occurs and is evaluated in both formal training approaches and, increasingly, in individualized and team coaching contexts (Carey, Philippon, & Cummings, 2011).

Training in PLD

There have been several meta-analyses that have examined the combined effectiveness of leadership development interventions. Collins and Holton (2004) examined 83 formal leadership training studies that looked at enhancing leadership performance at the individual, team, and organizational level. Of these, 19 studies used a longitudinal controlled design to assess objective outcomes at the level of increased leadership expertise and found an overall effect size of 1.01. However the range of effect sizes was from −0.28 to 1.66, suggesting the significant variation in the efficacy of different leadership development methodologies.

Avolio, Reichard, et al. (2009) reviewed 200 laboratory and field studies of leadership development. They found an overall small effect size of leadership change after the development intervention of 0.65 (versus 0.35 for control groups) and could find no significant difference depending on the theory utilized in the intervention. Despite this relatively small combined effect size, the standard deviation of outcomes was 0.80, suggesting significant variation in the effectiveness of the studies assessed. Overall they concluded that despite the heterogeneous mix of theory, dependent variables, developmental processes, and outcomes, leadership could be enhanced over a short period of time using a variety of methodologies. In this study positive leadership theories were combined with other models, making it impossible to be specific about the relative value of transformational or authentic approaches.

These meta-analyses provide convincing evidence that leadership ratings can change significantly over time, but tell us little about the impact of those changes on subsequent work performance criteria. However, the performance impacts and outcomes of transformational leadership have been extensively studied. Wang, Oh, Courtright, and Colbert (2011) performed a meta-analysis of 113 studies investigating the impacts of transformational leadership on task, contextual, and creative performance outcomes. They reported a mean correlation between individual-level performance and transformational leadership of 0.25 using non-self-report measures.

This meta-analytic evidence suggests that leadership is state-like and malleable in its ability to be enhanced by specific development interventions and that improved leadership impacts directly on objective performance criteria and beyond the level of self-report. However, because of a lack of consistency in outcome measurement, the absence of measures of methodological adherence, and an over-reliance on self-report measures, the identification of specific active components in leadership development has been problematic (MacKie, 2014). The specific literature on PLD is not as advanced as the generic leadership development literature reviewed above. This is partly a function of the relative recency of the construct and partly a function of the complexity in training leaders in ethical decision-making and relational transparency, as in the case of authentic leadership development (Cooper, Scandura, & Schriesheim, 2005). However, the literature on the trainability of transformational leadership is substantial and positive (Avolio, Reichard, et al., 2009; Day, Fleenor, Atwater, Sturm, & McKee, 2014; Kelloway & Barling, 2010). In addition, the effects of transformational leadership (TL) on followers have been empirically investigated with evidence that TL builds PsyCap in followers, which in turn positively links to performance (Gooty et al., 2009). Precisely which aspects of transformational leadership build PsyCap in followers is unclear, but one option is that followers are inspired through emotional contagion from the leader (Walumbwa, Peterson & Avolio, & Hartnell, 2010).

There have been a variety of theoretical papers that have laid the groundwork for positive and especially authentic leadership development (Avolio & Gardner, 2005; Cooper et al., 2005; Spreitzer, 2006). However, the performance link between the underlying subscales including relational transparency and an internalized moral perspective have yet to be demonstrated and may prove challenging to develop in leaders (Cooper et al., 2005). There is also the question of how much authenticity is desired in leadership development, given that its relationship is likely to be curvilinear with performance and the potential coercive nature of unregulated self-disclosure (Tourish, 2013).

Coaching in PLD

Individualized coaching has become an increasingly popular alternative to a standardized training methodology for developing leaders (Carey et al., 2011). Coaching has been used in a leadership development context in a number of ways, including building and transferring skills, raising self-awareness, and enhancing motivation (Hernez-Broome & Boyce, 2011; Passmore, 2010). It has been noted that coaching was traditionally content-neutral in its approach (Grant, Green, & Rynsaardt, 2010). As coaching has developed, specialist coaching models, including leadership coaching, have begun to emerge in the literature (Elliot, 2005). Coaching aligns well as a key methodology for PLD due to their mutual focus on performance enhancement and strengths-based methodology (Biswas-Diener & Dean, 2007; Linley & Harrington, 2005; Seligman, 2007).

Recently two meta-analytic studies of coaching outcomes have provided some support for the effectiveness of coaching as a leadership development methodology. Theeboom,

Beersma, and van Vianen (2014) found 18 studies of sufficient rigor to be included in their analysis. Unfortunately, only 4 of these studies were conducted in the workplace, used a between-subject design and collected data beyond the level of self-report, and only one study used transformational leadership as the independent variable (Cerni, Curtis, & Colmar, 2010). The average effect size (using Hedges' g, a more conservative index of change) for these 4 studies was $g = 0.08$ to 0.36, which would be considered small- to medium-sized effects. A more recent meta-analysis (Jones, Woods, & Guillaume, 2016) focused specifically on workplace coaching and found 17 studies of sufficient rigor to be included in the analysis. In addition they only looked at outcomes relevant to organizations like skill acquisition and individual performance results. Their analysis found effect sizes of coaching and outcome criteria ranging from $d = 0.28$ to 1.24 with individual-level results achieving the biggest impact. However, in terms of measuring outcomes, there was no distinction made between self-ratings of outcomes and feedback sourced from other raters including managers, peers, and direct reports, so the broader impact of these coaching studies is not known. Interestingly they also reported that coaching without multisource feedback (MSF) had a stronger effect size. This is a concerning finding given the ubiquity of MSF in leadership development programs. While there remains no agreed outcome criterion for executive coaching, it is difficult to compare studies reporting a self-reported improvement in well-being after coaching with those that report significant positive multi-rater changes in leadership behaviors (MacKie, 2014). This is in part due to the tendency of individuals to overestimate their performance when compared to more objective performance criteria (Kruger & Dunning, 1999).

Studies that examine the specific impact of workplace coaching on leadership outcomes remain relatively uncommon. McColl-Kennedy and Anderson (2002) did examine the link between coaching and leadership and found that frustration and optimism fully mediated the link between leadership style and subordinate performance in a study of 139 sales representatives. However, the study used a survey design with existing performance criteria so the trainability of the optimistic explanatory style and its capacity to predict future performance were not assessed.

Cilliers (2011) used a qualitative methodology to investigate the effects of a positive psychological approach to leadership coaching. Defining positive psychology leadership coaching as a focus on the people aspects of learning, growth, and change in order to positively impact on the intrapersonal and interpersonal aspects of leadership, the study examined the impacts of positive leadership coaching on 11 leaders in a financial organization. Participants engaged in 10 experiential coaching sessions that focused on work engagement, coherence, values, resourcefulness, and locus of control. Using discourse analysis in a series of single-case designs, 6 emergent themes were identified. These included engagement in the role, role complexity, emotional self-awareness, self-authorization, and facilitating the growth of others. No quantitative data were reported and no post-intervention outcomes evaluated, so the broader impact of this intervention is difficult to ascertain.

Studies have also begun to examine the efficacy of specific strengths-based leadership development methodologies in a coaching context (MacKie, 2014). Using the MLQ360 as the dependent variable, a between subject non-randomized design was used with 37 leaders and managers from an international not-for-profit (NFP) organization. Strengths were assessed using a combination of interview (peak experiences), psychometric (Realise2 Inventory), and multi-rater data (the MLQ360). The study used a manualized strengths-based coaching protocol that focused on developing both fully and partially utilized strengths and addressing weaknesses where relevant. Participants received 6 sessions of strengths-based coaching over a 3-month period. The results showed that the coaching cohort experienced highly significant changes in transformational leadership (as rated by all others on the MLQ360).

In addition to the significant changes in transformational leadership after strengths-based leadership coaching, significant positive changes in leadership outcomes were also reported. Leadership outcomes are what other raters report in terms of extra effort, effectiveness, and satisfaction with the coachee's leadership style before and after coaching. So after coaching the raters of the coachee were willing to provide additional discretionary effort as a function of positive changes in the coachee's leadership style. This is another critical finding as positive leadership is ultimately trying to unlock additional resources from others in the organization, including peers and direct reports. Finally, adherence to the strengths-based coaching manual from both the coach and the coachee perspective was also rated and found to be predictive of positive changes in transformational leadership. This result indicates that it was the strengths-based component of the program that was influential in achieving positive leadership change in the coachees (MacKie, 2014).

PLD in teams

So far we have only discussed PLD as an individual phenomenon, but it also occurs in teams (Zaccaro, Heinen, & Shuffler, 2009). This distinction between leader development, for example enhancing intrapersonal skills like self-regulation, and leadership development, for example enhancing relational skills like team orientation, is a development predicated on the recognition of the complexity of the interaction between a leader and her or his organizational context (Day, 2001). It has been argued elsewhere that individual theories of leadership, for instance transformational leadership, can form the basis of effective team leadership, but in addition team leadership focuses on integration, interconnectivity, and coherence (Marks, Zaccaro, & Mathieu, 2000). Team leadership models tend to see team leadership as a moderator of team effectiveness and tend to involve more collective or shared models of leadership that involve the harnessing of the synergies of individual leaders' strengths (Yammarino, Salas, Serban, Shirreffs, & Shuffler, 2012). Promoting leadership development at the group or team level is not new and has been disseminated through concepts like action learning (Day, 2001; Marquardt, 2000). However, team-based PLD is more explicit in its focus on relational, distributed, and shared models of leadership that support the concept of identifying and leveraging individual leader strengths in the pursuit of facilitating more flexible and adaptive team leadership systems (Gordon & MacKie, 2016). Existing meta-analytic team research has found a significant correlation between person-focused transformational leadership behaviors and both team effectiveness and productivity (Burke et al., 2006). In addition, team-level positivity, especially optimism and efficacy, has been found to be predictive of subsequent team performance (West, Patera, & Carsten, 2009). However, the exact ratio of positive affect in high-performing teams remains the source of some controversy (Brown, Sokal, & Friedman, 2013).

Limitations of PLD

The positive leadership framework is in its early stages of development and has been challenged by a number of critics on a variety of criteria including the theoretical, conceptual, and political grounds. Conceptual criticisms have included the risk of promoting lopsided leadership (Kaiser & Overfield, 2011), ignoring the benefits of negative emotions (Gilbert, 2006), encouraging an entity or fixed theory of leadership, and ignoring the situational context to positive leadership development (Biswas-Diener et al., 2011). Building on this theme, Collinson (2012) has cautioned against "Prozac leadership," where the reluctance to anticipate and prepare for anything other than a positive outcome can result in insufficient risk assessment and poor anticipation of negative consequences of decision-making.

There are also concerns about one of the core constructs of positive leadership – authentic leadership. In particular, the construct and discriminant validity of authenticity has been challenged (Cooper et al., 2005), suggesting that there has been insufficient qualitative exploration of this construct prior to converging on models of its psychometric measurement and methods of authentic leadership development. Others have challenged the construct from an identity perspective, arguing for the impossibility of knowing the core self (Ford & Harding, 2011) or questioning the assumption that the core authentic self will be universally positive (Tourish, 2013). Clearly this is both a potential limitation and a fruitful area for future research.

In addition, there is also an ongoing concern regarding the application of strengths-based approaches with the realization that strengths can be overdone and that all strengths, if leveraged without regard to context or impact, will become derailers (Kaiser, 2009; MacKie, 2008). Given that many people already overestimate their competence on a wide variety of tasks (Dunning, Johnson, Ehrlinger, & Kruger, 2003), there is also the risk that an unrelenting focus on the positive further distorts intrapersonal perceptions and reaffirms pre-existing positive biases. Furthermore, there is the risk that a focus on strengths becomes just another trait-based approach to developing individuals and organizations, and ignores the complex interplay of personal qualities with team, group, and dyadic and situational variables (Hernandez et al., 2011).

Finally, criticisms emanating from critical leadership studies include the assertion that positive leadership theories including transformational and authentic models over-attribute agency to leaders and concurrently diminish the contributions that followers make (Collinson, 2011). Thus they can be construed as the continuation of a trend that has focus on leaders, not leadership, and a trend that has yet to fully explore the potential downside of coercive power in leader–follower relationships where power is so clearly imbalanced (Tourish, 2013). There is also the concern of the promotion of excessive positivity where low mood or a less effusive style can be construed as misaligned with the prevailing organizational culture and even pathological (Fineman, 2006). This individualization of the responsibility for well-being at work has been challenged by those emphasizing more social explanations for positive mood and well-being (Wilkinson & Pickett, 2009), but this tension between individual and social attributions has yet to be fully explored in positive organizational research.

These criticisms in their totality clearly argue for a balanced and considered approach to the application of positive organizational behavioral constructs to the leadership development domain where the limitations of a blinkered and partial approach to positivity are clearly recognized and avoided.

Future Research

This purpose of this review was to identify the advances made in the field of positive leadership development since its emergence around 2000. Despite the significant advances made in the conceptualization of positive leadership theories and their application to leader and leadership development, there remain several areas of research that require the application of scholarly rigor if the movement is to advance. Firstly, there needs to be greater homogeneity of organizationally relevant outcome variables to allow cross study comparisons, (Day et al., 2014). Following on from this there is a need to investigate outcomes beyond the level of self-report so that the data of followers, in particular, is included in outcome analysis. In terms of further investigating the efficacy of positive leadership studies, it is necessary to employ active comparison studies where authentic leadership development, for example, is contrasted with a strengths development approach (Barling, 2014). To augment this approach, there needs to be greater transparency in positive leadership coaching with manualization one option to test adherence to the protocol. Research also needs to continue into the concept of strengths, clarifying whether the discriminant validity is sufficient to justify their status as a stand-alone construct. Finally, it is time to close the gap on the research–practitioner divide and subject some well-developed practitioner approaches (e.g,. Zenger, Folkman, & Edinger, 2011) to independent empirical substantiation.

In terms of developing the organizational research base in the emergent theories like mindfulness and ACT, consideration needs to be given as to how these constructs may mediate or moderate PLD. ACT, for example, promotes the pursuit of valued goals despite the potential presence of negative emotions, so measuring subsequent changes in well-being or positive affect may not be a fair test of the model. However, the enhancement of psychological flexibility following ACT-based leadership development would be a critical finding as leadership flexibility has been identified as a predictor of leader emergence and effectiveness (Good & Sharma, 2010). Equally, longitudinal studies on the impact of leaders' mindfulness on follower engagement, positivity, and performance would be foundational in the support of the integration of this construct into the PLD process (Kinsler, 2014). Research on leader mindfulness is a priority, as it is yet another domain in which practice is significantly ahead of the evidence and there are emerging methodological concerns about existing mindfulness research including the unreliability of self-reports of practice, challenges to construct validity of mindfulness inventories, and a lack of convergent validity around different mindfulness scales (Grossman, 2011).

There are also opportunities for cultural extensions of PLD, given that the vast majority of research to date has been conducted in the USA and UK and is imbued with the values of positive individualism (Collinson, 2011). Does the individual identity focus implicit in authentic leadership have meaning in more collective cultures that favor social responsibility over individual attainment (Wong, 2011) or in societies that advocate restraint and temperance over personal advancement and gratification (Hofstede, 1991)?

Finally, at the team level of analysis there are opportunities to examine the moderating role of strengths and their development on team effectiveness as well the effects of a positive team process on task and process outcomes. There is also preliminary evidence to suggest that team stage or maturity also moderates the effectiveness of PLD interventions, (Burke et al., 2006). Identifying the stages of team development, and the concomitant evolution of positive leadership behaviors within, would be a significant addition to the literature.

Conclusion

The positive approach to leadership development is both a process of the identification of positive states and traits and a method of aligning the individual's strengths and weaknesses against the challenges of the organization. Strengths development is a complicated and nuanced process that requires taking a systemic view of strengths profiles in the context of the environment in which they are applied (Zenger & Folkman, 2011). Given the current challenges in enhancing the discriminant validity of strengths as a construct, it seems likely that progress in integrating strengths into PLD will depend on the refinement and testing of strengths-development methodologies. Leadership coaching offers the natural vehicle for the delivery of PLD, but exactly how to integrate a strengths-based process into a coaching methodology, with its multiplicity of variables, processes and models, can only be clarified by further research. Longitudinal controlled studies with alternative positive leadership coaching methodologies that target malleable positive constructs are most suited to answering this comparative question (Mills et al., 2013).

Existing models of positive leadership including authentic and developmental readiness are insightful additions that offer the opportunity to streamline delivery and enhance effectiveness to those most ready to engage in the leadership development process. However, these need to be incorporated alongside the existing multifactor full-range models such as transformational leadership (Bass & Bass, 2008) to avoid repeating the bias in perspective and partial focus that they were designed to redress. Finally, PLD needs to move beyond the trait-based approach and consider under what situations and in what contexts the considered and mindful application of positive states, mindsets, and strengths are able to facilitate optimal leader and leadership development.

References

Aguinis, H., & Cascio, W. F. (2008). Narrowing the science–practice divide: A call to action. *The Industrial-Organizational Psychologist*, *2*, 27–36.

Alban-Metcalfe, J., & Mead, G. (2010). Coaching for transactional and transformational leadership. *Leadership Coaching: Working with Leaders to Develop Elite Performance*, 211–228.

Ames, D. R., & Flynn, F. J. (2007). What breaks a leader: The curvilinear relation between assertiveness and leadership. *Journal of Personality and Social Psychology*, *92*(2), 307.

Asplund, J., Lopez, S. J., Hodges, T., & Harter, J. (2007). *The Clifton StrengthsFinder® 2.0 technical report: Development and validation*. Princeton, NJ: Gallup.

Atkins, P. (2008). Leadership as response not reaction: Wisdom and mindfulness in public sector leadership. In P. 't Hart & J. Uhr (Eds.), *Public leadership: Perspectives and practices* (pp. 73–82). Canberra: ANU E-Press.

Avey, J. B., Avolio, B. J., & Luthans, F. (2011). Experimentally analyzing the impact of leader positivity on follower positivity and performance. *The Leadership Quarterly*, *22*, 282–294.

Avolio, B. J. (2011). *Full range leadership development* (2nd ed.). London, UK: Sage.

Avolio, B. J., & Gardner, W. L. (2005). Authentic leadership development: Getting to the root of positive forms of leadership. *The Leadership Quarterly*, *16*, 315–338.

Avolio, B. J., & Hannah, S. T. (2008). Developmental readiness: Accelerating leader development. *Consulting Psychology Journal: Practice and Research*, *60*, 331–347.

Avolio, B. J., & Luthans, F. (2006). *The high impact leader*. New York, NY: Mcgraw-Hill.

Avolio, B. J., Reichard, R. J., Hannah, S. T., Walumbwa, F. O., & Chan, A. (2009). A meta-analytic review of leadership impact research: Experimental and quasi-experimental studies. *The Leadership Quarterly*, *20*, 764–784.

Avolio, B. J., Walumbwa, F. O., & Weber, T. J. (2009). Leadership: Current theories, research, and future directions. *Annual Review of Psychology*, *60*, 421–449.

Avolio, B. J., Wernsing, T., Chan, A., & Griffeth, J. (2007). *A theory of developing leader self-awareness*. Unpublished manuscript, University of Nebraska–Lincoln.

Barling, J. (2014). *The science of leadership*. Oxford, UK: Oxford University Press.

Bass, B. M. (1999). Two decades of research and development in transformational leadership. *European Journal of Work and Organizational Psychology*, *8*, 9–32.

Bass, B. M., & Avolio, B. J. (1997). *Full range leadership development: Manual for the Multifactor Leadership Questionnaire*. Palo Alto, CA: Mind Garden.

Bass, B. M., & Bass, R. (2008). *The Bass handbook of leadership: Theory, research, and managerial applications* (4th ed.). New York, NY: The Free Press.

Biswas-Diener, R., & Dean, B. (2007). *Positive psychology coaching: Putting the science of happiness to work for your clients.* Hoboken, NJ: Wiley.

Biswas-Diener, R., Kashdan, T. B., & Minhas, G. (2011). A dynamic approach to psychological strength development and intervention. *Journal of Positive Psychology, 6*, 106–118.

Bolden, R. (2007). Trends and perspectives in management and leadership development. *Business Leadership Review, 4*, 1–13.

Bond, F. W., & Flaxman, P. E. (2006). The ability of psychological flexibility and job control to predict learning, job performance, and mental health. *Journal of Organizational Behavior Management, 26*(1–2), 113–130.

Boyatzis, R. E., Smith, M. L., & Blaize, N. (2006). Developing sustainable leaders through coaching and compassion. *Academy of Management Learning & Education, 5*, 8–24.

Brinner R. B. (2012). Does coaching work and does anyone really care? *OP Matters, 17*, 4–12.

Brown, N. J. L., Sokal, A. D., & Friedman, H. L. (2013). The complex dynamics of wishful thinking: The critical positivity ratio. *American Psychologist, 68*(9), 801–813.

Burke, C. S., Stagl, K. C., Klein, C., Goodwin, G. F., Salas, E., & Halpin, S. M. (2006). What type of leadership behaviors are functional in teams? A meta-analysis. *The Leadership Quarterly, 17*, 288–307.

Carey, W., Philippon, D. J., & Cummings, G. G. (2011). Coaching models for leadership development: An integrative review. *Journal of Leadership Studies, 5*, 51–69.

Cerni, T., Curtis, G. J., & Colmar, S. (2010). Increasing transformational leadership by developing leaders' information-processing systems. *Journal of Leadership Studies, 4*(3), 51–65.

Cilliers, F. (2011). Positive psychology leadership coaching experiences in a financial organisation. *SA Journal of Industrial Psychology, 37*, 1–14.

Cohn, M. A., & Fredrickson, B. L. (2010). In search of durable positive psychology interventions: Predictors and consequences of long-term positive behavior change. *The Journal of Positive Psychology, 5*, 355–366.

Collins, D. B., & Holton, E. F. (2004). The effectiveness of managerial leadership development programs: A meta-analysis of studies from 1982 to 2001. *Human Resource Development Quarterly, 15*, 217–248.

Collinson, D. (2011). Critical leadership studies. In A. Bryman, D. Collinson, K. Grint, & B. Jackson (Eds.), *The Sage handbook of leadership* (pp. 179–192). London, UK: Sage.

Collinson, D. (2012). Prozac leadership and the limits of positive thinking. *Leadership, 8*(2), 87–107.

Cooper, C. D., Scandura, T. A., & Schriesheim, C. A. (2005). Looking forward but learning from our past: Potential challenges to developing authentic leadership theory and authentic leaders. *The Leadership Quarterly, 16*, 475–493.

Day, D. V. (2001). Leadership development: A review in context. *The Leadership Quarterly, 11*, 581–613.

Day, D. V., Fleenor, J. W., Atwater, L. E., Sturm, R. E., & McKee, R. A. (2014). Advances in leader and leadership development: A review of 25 years of research and theory. *The Leadership Quarterly, 25*, 63–82.

Day, D. V., Harrison, M. M., & Halpin, S. M. (2012). *An integrative approach to leader development: Connecting adult development, identity, and expertise.* London, UK: Routledge.

Donaldson, S. I., & Ko, I. (2010). Positive organizational psychology, behavior, and scholarship: A review of the emerging literature and evidence base. *The Journal of Positive Psychology, 5*(3), 177–191.

Dunning, D., Johnson, K., Ehrlinger, J., & Kruger, J. (2003). Why people fail to recognize their own incompetence. *Current Directions in Psychological Science, 12*, 83–87.

Dweck, C. S. (2006). *Mindset: The new psychology of success.* New York, NY: Random House.

Dweck, C. S., & Leggett, E. L. (1988). A social-cognitive approach to motivation and personality. *Psychological Review, 95*, 256–273.

Elliott, R. (2005). The parameters of specialist professional leadership coaching. *Evidence-based coaching: Contributions from the behavioral sciences, 1*, 111–126.

Fambrough, M. J., & Hart, R. K. (2008). Emotions in leadership development: A critique of emotional intelligence. *Advances in Developing Human Resources, 10*(5), 740–758.

Fineman, S. (2006). On being positive: Concerns and counterpoints. *Academy of Management Review*, *31*(2), 270–291.

Flaxman, P. E., Bond, F. W., & Livheim, F. (2013). *The mindful and effective employee: An acceptance and commitment therapy training manual for improving well-being and performance*. Oakland, CA: New Harbinger.

Ford, J., & Harding, N. (2011). The impossibility of the "true self" of authentic leadership. *Leadership*, *7*(4), 463–479.

Gardner, W. L., Cogliser, C. C., Davis, K. M., & Dickens, M. P. (2011). Authentic leadership: A review of the literature and research agenda. *The Leadership Quarterly*, *22*(6), 1120–1145.

Gilbert, P. (2006). Evolution and depression: Issues and implications. *Psychological Medicine*, *36*, 287–297.

Good, D. J., & Sharma, G. (2010). A little more rigidity: Firming the construct of leader flexibility. *Journal of Change Management*, *10*(2), 155–174.

Gooty, J., Gavin, M., Johnson, P. D., Frazier, M. L., & Snow, D. B. (2009). In the eyes of the beholder: Transformational leadership, positive psychological capital, and performance. *Journal of Leadership & Organizational Studies*, *15*(4), 353–367.

Gordon, S., & MacKie, D. (2016). Team coaching. In S. Palmer & A. Whybrow (Eds.), *Handbook of coaching psychology: A guide for practitioners* (2nd ed.). London, UK: Routledge.

Grant, A. M., Green, S. L., & Rynsaardt, J. (2010). Developmental coaching for high school teachers: Executive coaching goes to school. *Consulting Psychology Journal: Practice and Research*, *62*, 151–168.

Greenleaf, R. K. (1977). *Servant leadership*. New York, NY: Paulist Press.

Grossman, P. (2011). Defining mindfulness by how poorly I think I pay attention during everyday awareness and other intractable problems for psychology's (re)invention of mindfulness: Comment on Brown et al. (2011). *Psychological Assessment*, *23*(4), 1034–1040.

Hackman, R. J. (2009). The perils of positivity. *Journal of Organisational Behaviour*, *30*, 309–319.

Hannah, S. T. (2006). *Agentic leadership efficacy: Test of a new construct and model for development and performance*. Unpublished doctoral dissertation, University of Nebraska–Lincoln.

Hannah, S. T., & Avolio, B. J. (2010). Ready or not: How do we accelerate the developmental readiness of leaders? *Journal of Organisational Behaviour*, *31*, 1181–1187.

Hayes, S. C. (2004). Acceptance and commitment therapy, relational frame theory, and the third wave of behavioral and cognitive therapies. *Behavior therapy*, *35*(4), 639–665.

Hernandez, M., Eberly, M. B., Avolio, B. J., & Johnson, M. D. (2011). The loci and mechanisms of leadership: Exploring a more comprehensive view of leadership theory. *The Leadership Quarterly*, *22*, 1165–1185.

Hernez-Broome, G., & Boyce, L. A. (Eds.) (2011). *Advancing executive coaching: Setting the course for successful leadership coaching*. San Francisco, CA: Jossey-Bass.

Heslin, P. A., & VandeWalle, D. (2008). Managers' implicit assumptions about personnel. *Current Directions in Psychological Science*, *17*(3), 219–223.

Hofstede, G. (1991). *Cultures and organizations – software of the mind: Intercultural cooperation and its importance for survival*. New York, NY: McGraw-Hill.

Ilies, R., Gerhardt, M. W., & Le, H. (2004). Individual differences in leadership emergence: Integrating meta-analytic findings and behavioral genetics estimates. *International Journal of Selection and Assessment*, *12*, 207–219.

Jones, R. J., Woods, S. A., & Guillaume, Y. R. (2016). The effectiveness of workplace coaching: A meta-analysis of learning and performance outcomes from coaching. *Journal of Occupational and Organizational Psychology*, *89*(2), 249–277.

Kaiser, R. B. (Ed.). (2009). *The perils of accentuating the positive*. Tulsa, OK: Hogan Press.

Kaiser, R. B., & Overfield, D. V. (2010). Assessing flexible leadership as a mastery of opposites. *Consulting Psychology Journal: Practice and Research*, *62*, 105–118.

Kaiser, R. B., & Overfield, D. V. (2011). Strengths, strengths overused, and lopsided leadership. *Consulting Psychology Journal: Practice and Research*, *63*, 89–109.

Kaplan, R. E., & Kaiser, R. B. (2010). Towards a positive psychology for leaders. In P. A. Linley, S. Harrington, & N. Garcea (Eds.), *Oxford handbook of positive psychology and work* (pp. 107–120). Oxford, UK: Oxford University Press.

Kashdan, T., & Ciarrochi, J. (2013). *Mindfulness, acceptance, and positive psychology: The seven foundations of well-being*. Oakland, CA: New Harbinger.

Kelloway, E. K., & Barling, J. (2010). Leadership development as an intervention in occupational health psychology. *Work and Stress*, *24*, 260–279.

Kinsler, L. (2014). Born to be me … who am I again? The development of authentic leadership using evidence-based leadership coaching and mindfulness. *International Coaching Psychology Review*, *9*(1), 92–105.

Kruger, J., & Dunning, D. (1999). Unskilled and unaware of it: How difficulties in recognizing one's own incompetence lead to inflated self-assessments. *Journal of Personality and Social Psychology*, *77*(6), 1121.

Le, H., Oh, I. S., Robbins, S. B., Ilies, R., Holland, E., & Westrick, P. (2011). Too much of a good thing: Curvilinear relationships between personality traits and job performance. *Journal of Applied Psychology*, *96*, 113–133.

Liden, R. C., Wayne, S. J., Zhao, H., & Henderson, D. (2008). Servant leadership: Development of a multidimensional measure and multi-level assessment. *The Leadership Quarterly*, *19*, 161–177.

Linley, P. A., & Harrington, S. (2005). Positive psychology and coaching psychology: Perspectives on integration. *The Coaching Psychologist*, *1*(1), 13–14.

Linley, P. A., & Stoker, H. (2012). *Technical manual and statistical properties for Realise2*. Coventry, UK: Centre of Applied Positive Psychology.

Linley, P. A., Woolston, L., & Biswas-Diener, R. (2009). Strengths coaching with leaders. *International Coaching Psychology Review*, *4*, 37–48.

Locke, E. A., & Latham, G. P. (1990). Work motivation and satisfaction: Light at the end of the tunnel. *Psychological Science*, *1*, 240–246.

Luthans, F., Avey, J. B., Avolio, B. J., Norman, S. M., & Combs, G. M. (2006). Psychological capital development: Toward a micro-intervention. *Journal of Organizational Behavior*, *27*(3), 387–393.

Luthans, F., & Avolio, B. J. (2003). Authentic leadership: A positive developmental approach. In K. S. Cameron, J. E. Dutton, & R. E. Quinn (Eds.), *Positive organizational scholarship* (pp. 241–261). San Francisco, CA: Berrett-Koehler.

Luthans, F., Avolio, B. J., Avey, J. B., & Norman, S. M. (2007). Positive psychological capital: Measurement and relationship with performance and satisfaction. *Personnel Psychology*, *60*(3), 541–572.

Luthans, F., Luthans, K. W., Hodgetts, R. M., & Luthans, B. C. (2001). Positive approach to leadership (PAL) implications for today's organizations. *Journal of Leadership Studies*, *8*(2), 3.

Luthans, F., & Youssef, C. M. (2007). Emerging positive organizational behavior. *Journal of Management*, *33*, 321–349.

Macdonald, C., Bore, M., & Munro, D. (2008). Values in action scale and the Big 5: An empirical indication of structure. *Journal of Research in Personality*, *42*, 787–799.

MacKie, D. (2007). Evaluating the effectiveness of executive coaching: Where are we now and where do we need to be? *Australian Psychologist*, *42*, 310–318.

MacKie, D. (2008). Leadership derailment and psychological harm. *InPsych: The Bulletin of the Australian Psychological Society*, *30*, 12–13.

MacKie, D. (2014). The effectiveness of strength-based executive coaching in enhancing full range leadership development: A controlled study. *Consulting Psychology Journal: Practice and Research*, *66*(2), 118–137.

Marks, M. A., Zaccaro, S. J., & Mathieu, J. E. (2000). Performance implications of leader briefings and team-interaction training for team adaptation to novel environments. *Journal of Applied Psychology*, *85*(6), 971.

Marquardt, M. J. (2000). Action learning and leadership. *The Learning Organization*, *7*(5), 233–241.

Maslow, A. H. (1954). *Motivation and personality*. New York, NY: Harper & Row.

McCauley, C., & Wakefield, M. (2006). Talent management in the 21st century: Help your company find, develop, and keep its strongest workers. *The Journal for Quality and Participation*, *29*(4), 4.

McColl-Kennedy, J. R., & Anderson, R. D. (2002). Impact of leadership style and emotions on subordinate performance. *The Leadership Quarterly*, *13*, 545–559.

McKenna, D., & Davies, S. L. (2009). Hidden in plain sight: The active ingredients of executive coaching. *Industrial and Organisational Psychology, 2*, 244–260.

Meyers, M. C., & van Woerkom, M. (2014). The influence of underlying philosophies on talent management: Theory, implications for practice, and research agenda. *Journal of World Business, 49*(2), 192–203.

Meyers, M. C., van Woerkom, M., & Bakker, A. B. (2013). The added value of the positive: A literature review of positive psychology interventions in organizations. *European Journal of Work and Organizational Psychology, 22*(5), 618–632.

Meyers, M. C., Van Woerkom, M., & Dries, N. (2013). Talent – innate or acquired? Theoretical considerations and their implications for talent management. *Human Resource Management Review, 23*(4), 305–321.

Meyers, M. C., van Woerkom, M., de Reuver, R. S., Bakk, Z., & Oberski, D. L. (2015). Enhancing psychological capital and personal growth initiative: Working on strengths or deficiencies. *Journal of Counseling Psychology, 62*(1), 50.

Mills, J. M., Fleck, R. C., & Kozikowski, A. (2013). Positive psychology at work: A conceptual review, state-of-practice assessment, and a look ahead. *The Journal of Positive Psychology, 8*, 153–164.

Money, K., Hillenbrand, C., & da Camara, N. (2009). Putting positive psychology to work in organisations. *Journal of General Management, 34*, 21–36.

Moran, D. J. (2010). ACT for leadership: Using acceptance and commitment training to develop crisis-resilient change managers. *International Journal of Behavioral Consultation and Therapy, 6*(4), 341.

Narayanan, J., Chaturvedi, S., Reb, J., & Srinivas, E. (2011). *Examining the role of trait mindfulness on turnover intentions and job performance: The mediating role of emotional exhaustion.* Working paper, National University of Singapore.

Nesse, R. (2005). Evolutionary psychology and mental health. In D. Buss (Ed.) *The handbook of evolutionary psychology* (pp. 903–927). Hoboken, NJ: Wiley & Sons, Inc.

Passmore, J. (Ed.). (2010). *Leadership coaching: Working with leaders to develop elite performance.* London, UK: Kogan Page.

Peterson, C., & Seligman, M. E. P. (2004). *Character strengths and virtues: A handbook and classification.* Oxford, UK: Oxford University Press.

Peterson, C., Stephens, J. P., Park, N., Lee, F., & Seligman, M. (2010). Strengths of character and work. In P. A. Linley, S. Harrington, & N. Garcea (Eds.), *Oxford handbook of positive psychology and work* (pp. 221–231). New York, NY: Oxford University Press.

Prochaska, J. O., & DiClemente, C. C. (1983). Stages and processes of self-change of smoking: Toward an integrative model of change. *Journal of Consulting and Clinical Psychology, 51*, 390–395.

Rath, T. (2007). *StrengthsFinder 2.0.* New York, NY: Gallup.

Rath, T., & Conchie, B. (2008). *Strengths based leadership: Great leaders, teams, and why people follow.* New York, NY: Gallup.

Reb, J., Narayanan, J., & Chaturvedi, S. (2014). Leading mindfully: Two studies on the influence of supervisor trait mindfulness on employee well-being and performance. *Mindfulness, 5*(1), 36–45.

Reb, J., Narayanan, J., & Ho, Z. W. (2013). Mindfulness at work: Antecedents and consequences of employee awareness and absent-mindedness. *Mindfulness, 6*(1), 111–122.

Roarty, M., & Toogood, K. (2014). *The strengths-focused guide to leadership: Identify your talents and get the most from your team.* Harlow, UK: Pearson.

Rozin, P., & Royzman, E. B. (2001). Negativity bias, negativity dominance, and contagion. *Personality and Social Psychology Review, 5*(4), 296–320.

Seligman, M. E. P. (2007). Coaching and positive psychology. *Australian Psychologist, 42*, 266–267.

Seligman, M. E. P., & Csikszentmihalyi, M. (2000). Positive psychology: An introduction. *American Psychologist, 55*, 5–14.

Seligman, M. E. P., Steen, T. A., Park, N., & Petersen, C. (2005). Positive psychology progress: Empirical validation of interventions. *American Psychologist, 60*, 410–421.

Smither, J. W. (2011). Can psychotherapy research serve as a guide for research about executive coaching? An agenda for the next decade. *Journal of Business and Psychology, 26*(2), 135–145.

Spreitzer, G. M. (2006). Leading to grow and growing to lead: Leadership development lessons from positive organizational studies. *Organizational Dynamics*, *35*(4), 305–315.

Stouten, J., van Dijke, M., Mayer, D. M., De Cremer, D., & Euwema, M. C. (2013). Can a leader be seen as too ethical? The curvilinear effects of ethical leadership. *The Leadership Quarterly*, *24*, 680–695.

Theeboom, T., Beersma, B., & van Vianen, A. E. (2014). Does coaching work? A meta-analysis on the effects of coaching on individual level outcomes in an organizational context. *The Journal of Positive Psychology*, *9*(1), 1–18.

Tourish, D. (2013). *The dark side of transformational leadership: A critical perspective*. New York, NY: Routledge.

Walumbwa, F. O., Avolio, B. J., Gardner, W. L., Wernsing, T. S., & Peterson, S. J. (2008). Authentic leadership: Development and validation of a theory-based measure. *Journal of Management*, *34*, 89–126.

Walumbwa, F. O., Peterson, S. J., Avolio, B. J., & Hartnell, C. A. (2010). An investigation of the relationships among leader and follower psychological capital, service climate, and job performance. *Personnel Psychology*, *63*(4), 937–963.

Wang, G., Oh, I. S., Courtright, S. H., & Colbert, A. E. (2011). Transformational leadership and performance across criteria and levels: A meta-analytic review of 25 years of research. *Group & Organization Management*, *36*, 223–270.

West, B. J., Patera, J. L., & Carsten, M. K. (2009). Team level positivity: Investigating positive psychological capacities and team level outcomes. *Journal of Organizational Behavior*, *30*(2), 249–267.

Wilkinson, R., & Pickett, K. (2009). *The spirit level. Why more equal societies almost always do better*. London, UK: Penguin.

Wright, T. A., & Quick, J. C. (2009). The emerging positive agenda in organizations: Greater than a trickle, but not yet a deluge. *Journal of Organizational Behavior*, *30*(2), 147–159.

Wong, P. T. P. (2011). Reclaiming positive psychology: A meaning-centered approach to sustainable growth and radical empiricism. *Journal of Humanistic Psychology*, *51*(4), 408–412.

Yammarino, F. J., Salas, E., Serban, A., Shirreffs, K., & Shuffler, M. L. (2012). Collectivistic leadership approaches: Putting the "we" in leadership science and practice. *Industrial and Organizational Psychology*, *5*(4), 382–402.

Youssef, C. M., & Luthans, F. (2012). Positive global leadership. *Journal of World Business*, *47*(4), 539–547.

Zaccaro, S. J., Heinen, B., & Shuffler, M. (2009). Team leadership and team effectiveness. In E. Salas, G. F. Goodwin, & C. S. Burke (Eds.), *Team effectiveness in complex organizations: Cross-disciplinary perspectives and approaches* (pp. 83–111). New York, NY: Routledge.

Zenger, J. H., Folkman, J. R., & Edinger, S. K. (2011). Making yourself indispensable. *Harvard Business Review*, *89*, 84–92.

18

Employee Engagement

Sebastiaan Rothmann

Introduction

The notion of personal engagement of individuals in their work (investing cognitive, physical, and emotional energy into their role performances) was first introduced by Kahn (1990). Since then, interest in employee engagement has grown gradually for various reasons. First, the focus in psychology shifted from weaknesses, malfunctioning, and damage toward happiness, human strengths, and optimal functioning (Seligman & Csikszentmihalyi, 2000; Strümpfer, 2005). Seligman (2003) regarded the study and promotion of happiness as important goals of psychology and suggested three routes to happiness, namely pleasure, engagement, and meaning. Engagement entails that individuals pursue gratification by applying their strengths. In a follow-up book, Seligman (2011) regarded engagement as one of the dimensions of human flourishing. In the burnout literature (Maslach & Leiter, 1997), interest arose in engagement as the direct opposite of burnout. According to Bakker, Schaufeli, Leiter, and Taris (2008), research on burnout has stimulated research on employee engagement. Maslach and Leiter (1997, p. 23) define burnout as "an erosion of engagement with the job." The view of these authors is that employee engagement is characterized by energy, involvement, and efficacy (i.e., direct opposites of exhaustion, cynicism, and low professional efficacy, which were identified as the dimensions of burnout). In contradiction to this view, Schaufeli, Salanova, González-Romá, and Bakker (2002) point out that although engagement is negatively related to burnout, it is an independent and distinct concept characterized by three dimensions, namely vigor, dedication, and absorption at work.

Second, the needs of businesses to maximize the inputs of employees have contributed to the interest in engagement. The satisfaction–engagement approach, which was developed by Gallup, showed that employee engagement enhances organizational outcomes, such as customer satisfaction, return on assets, profits, and shareholder value (Harter, Schmidt, & Hayes, 2002; Harter, Schmidt, & Keyes, 2002; May, Gilson, & Harter, 2004). Third, it

The Wiley Blackwell Handbook of the Psychology of Positivity and Strengths-Based Approaches at Work, First Edition. Edited by Lindsay G. Oades, Michael F. Steger, Antonella Delle Fave, and Jonathan Passmore.

was found that personal engagement at work has positive effects on the psychological well-being of employees (Robertson & Cooper, 2009). Engagement affects the mindset of employees, and relates to personal initiative and learning (Sonnentag, 2003). Furthermore, it fuels discretionary efforts and concerns for quality (Salanova, Llorens, Cifre, Martinez, & Schaufeli, 2003). Fourth, the multidimensional approach to engagement, associated with the work of Saks (2006), distinguished between job engagement and organizational engagement (Shuck, 2011).

Employee engagement has caught the imagination of academics and practitioners in the disciplines of psychology, industrial/organizational psychology, nursing, education, human resource management, and business (Truss, Delbridge, Alfes, Shantz, & Soane, 2014). Bargagliotti (2011) notes that engagement of more than one million employees has been studied by scientists. Furthermore, it is predicted that employee engagement will become an increasingly important concern for organizations and countries seeking to increase labor productivity as the global economy continues its rapid pace of change (Gallup, 2013). However, engagement research has been plagued by inconsistent definitions and measurement of the construct (Schaufeli, 2014) and inconsistent views of antecedents and consequences of employee engagement by academics and practitioners (Truss et al., 2014).

This chapter provides an overview of the research regarding employee engagement. First, employee engagement is conceptualized and current knowledge regarding the measurement and prevalence thereof is reported. Second, an overview of the theories and models which explain employee engagement is given. Third, drivers and outcomes of employee engagement are identified. Finally, future research regarding employee engagement is discussed.

Conceptualization, Measurement, and Prevalence of Employee Engagement

Conceptualization of employee engagement

Confusion exists about the definition of employee engagement: it occasionally refers to states, traits, and behavior, and even to antecedents and outcomes thereof. Variations are evident in the terms used to refer to the concept, such as "work engagement" and "employee engagement" (Truss et al., 2014). Schaufeli (2014) argues that the term *work engagement* refers to an individual's relationship with his or her job, while *employee engagement* refers to the individual's relationship with his or her job as well as organization. However, in this chapter the term employee engagement is used to cover both work engagement and employee engagement.

Employee engagement has been conceptualized from various perspectives, namely individual versus organizational engagement, academic versus practitioner perspectives, "hard" versus "soft" perspectives, fluctuating versus enduring engagement, and employee engagement versus well-being perspectives.

Individual versus organizational perspectives Concerning the *individual perspective* on employee engagement, Macey and Schneider (2008) distinguished three types of definitions of employee engagement, namely engagement as a psychological state (indicated by involvement, commitment, and attachment), a trait (e.g., positive affect and conscientiousness), and direct observable behavior in the work context (putting forth discretionary effort, i.e., extra time, brainpower, and energy). Engaged employees will not only do more; they also demonstrate innovative behaviors and initiative, proactively seek opportunities to contribute and go beyond what is typically expected in their roles (Macey & Schneider, 2008).

Definitions of engagement which focus on its state-like nature include those of Kahn (1990) and Schaufeli et al. (2002):

- Kahn (1990, p. 694) defined engagement as the "harnessing of organizational members' selves to their work role by which they employ and express themselves physically, cognitively and emotionally during role performance." Kahn (1990) argues that people can use varying degrees of their selves, physically, cognitively, and emotionally in the work they perform. The more people draw on their selves to perform their roles, the more stirring their performances. Furthermore, engagement is the simultaneous employment and expression of a person's preferred self in task behaviors that promote connections to work and to others.
- Schaufeli et al. (2002), on the other hand, defined employee engagement as a positive, fulfilling, work-related state of mind characterized by vigor, dedication, and absorption. Schaufeli (2014) states that sufficient evidence exists to claim that employee engagement is a psychological state.

According to Rothbard and Patil (2012), engagement has its roots in the concept authenticity, which results in individuals investing personal energies into role behaviors and expressing their selves in roles by exhibiting authenticity. They criticize definitions of employee engagement that equate it with positive affect (e.g., Bakker & Oerlemans, 2012; Schaufeli et al., 2002) and point out that engagement can be associated with both positive and negative affect.

Based on the perspectives of Kahn (1990) and Schaufeli et al. (2002), it can be stated that employee engagement comprises three dimensions, namely a physical dimension (being physically involved in a task and showing vigor and a positive affective state), a cognitive dimension (being alert at work and experiencing absorption and involvement), and an emotional dimension (being connected to job/others while working and showing dedication and commitment).

Macey and Schneider (2008) combine psychological state and behavior when they define engagement as a state signifying high levels of involvement (passion, absorption) in the work and the organization (pride, identity), affective energy (enthusiasm, alertness), and a sense of self presence in work. Rich, LePine, and Crawford (2010) suggested that antecedents of employee engagement, the psychological state (i.e., cognitive, physical, and emotional dimensions), and behavior (i.e., performance-related outcomes) should be considered in the definition of employee engagement. Therefore engagement refers to how employees experience and interpret the context around them and how they behave (Shuck, Ghosh, Zigarmi, & Nimon, 2012). Employee engagement entails an intense focus on a task, and a decision to invest personal resources (Christian, Garza, & Slaughter, 2011). Shuck et al. (2012) argue that focus on the tasks related to the immediate work of employees is a fundamental characteristic of engagement. This is followed by a decision to invest personal resources into work, depending on specific psychological conditions (e.g., meaningfulness, safety, and availability).

Studies showed that employee engagement is a construct distinct from job attitudes (Christian et al., 2011), job involvement, job satisfaction, and organizational commitment (Rich et al., 2010; Shuck et al., 2012). Employee engagement also has predictive value above antecedents, such as work role fit (Shuck, Reio, & Rocco, 2011).

Concerning the *organizational perspective*, Harter, Schmidt, and Hayes (2002) suggested that organization-level engagement might be a way in which organizations are able to affect engagement at that level. However, few studies focused on employee engagement at an organizational level. Saks (2006, p. 601), included the organizational level when defining engagement as "to be psychologically present when occupying and performing an organizational role." Saks (2006) included an individual perspective on engagement, but argued that a stronger focus on employee engagement with an organization is necessary. In the long term organizational arrangements may have a stronger effect on employees' propensity to engage, because transitions in organizational ownership have become frequent. MacLeod and Clarke (2009, p. 9) defined engagement as "a workplace approach designed to ensure that employees are committed to their organization's goals and values, motivated to contribute to organizational success, and are able at the same time to enhance their own sense of well-being." This definition views engagement in terms of an approach to manage a workforce rather than a psychological state.

Barrick, Thurgood, Smith, and Courtright (2015) developed a concept of employee engagement on organizational level, called collective organizational engagement. Organizational engagement is distinct from aggregated individual-level engagement and is defined as "shared perceptions of organizational members that members of the organization are, as a whole, physically, cognitively, and emotionally invested in their work (Barrick et al., 2015, p. 114). Three factors contribute to collective organizational engagement, namely motivating work designs, human resource management practices, and transformational leadership behaviors of the chief executive officer. The effects of these variables are moderated by strategic implementation.

Academic versus practitioner perspectives Different perspectives regarding the definition of employee engagement resulted in a divide between academics and practitioners: Academics have been wary of practitioners' focus on engagement strategies and perceived lack of interest in theories, while practitioners question the relevance of definitions and theories for fostering high levels of engagement at work (Truss, 2014).

In their study of employee engagement, Jenkins and Delbridge (2013) contrasted academic and practitioner perspectives. The academic perspective is strongly drawn from psychology (e.g., Bakker & Demerouti, 2008) and has provided very useful information regarding employee engagement, its antecedents and outcomes. Management's role in promoting engagement of employees is central within the practitioner perspective, for example managers' role in establishing and maintaining a constructive organizational culture, management approaches which value employees' contributions, employee voice mechanisms, trust and organizational integrity are regarded as important in the practitioner's perspective. However, within the practitioner agenda the "dark" side of engagement (e.g., its association with stress and burnout) are often not considered.

"Hard" versus "soft" approaches to employee engagement The "soft" approach to employee engagement is centered on positive workplace conditions and relationships between management and employees, designing a work environment conducive to employee engagement, while increasing productivity was not the primary aim. The "hard" approach aims at gaining a competitive advantage by focusing on employee engagement to improve organizational performance. Research by Jenkins and Delbridge (2013) showed that the "soft" approach was associated with high levels of engagement, while the "hard" approach was associated with high levels of disengagement. However, they found that organizations implementing these approaches faced contextual factors which provided opportunities and constraints for management's abilities to provide internal contexts supportive of employee engagement.

Employee engagement versus employee well-being Robertson and Cooper (2009) introduced the concept of *full engagement*, which integrates employee engagement and well-being. Full engagement is in contrast with a narrow definition of engagement which exclusively focuses on employee commitment, attachment, and citizenship and not on psychological well-being of employees. A longitudinal study by Cropanzano and Wright (1999) found that psychological well-being is related to employee performance. Their results showed that the relationship between employee well-being in the first year and performance in the subsequent five years deteriorated, which supports the importance of well-being for performance.

The concept of *thriving* (Porath, Spreitzer, Gibson, & Garnett, 2012) integrates dimensions of engagement (i.e., vitality) with learning in a bidimensional model of well-being. The importance of a bidimensional perspective is evident when its two dimensions (vitality and learning) are combined to understand behavior. For example, if an employee is learning but feels depleted, he or she does not thrive. Diedericks and Rothmann (2013) reported strong relationships between employee engagement and flourishing (defined as emotional, psychological, and social well-being).

Various theories and models of engagement include dimensions of well-being. For example, psychological meaningfulness, safety, and availability are included in the personal engagement model (Kahn, 1990; Kahn & Heaphy, 2014). Burnout, physical ill health, psychological well-being, and organizational commitment are part of the job demands-resources (JD-R) model (Demerouti, Bakker, Nachreiner, & Schaufeli, 2001). Rothmann (2013) integrated employee engagement in a model of *flourishing* at work. This model includes emotional well-being (i.e., job satisfaction and positive affect balance), psychological well-being (absorption, vitality, dedication, meaning, purpose, autonomy satisfaction, competence satisfaction, and relatedness satisfaction at work), and social well-being.

By investing in programs that promote individual well-being, organizations can enhance the engagement of employees. Physical health of employees relates positively to their engagement at work. Engaged employees have healthier habits and lower incidences of chronic health problems (e.g., high blood pressure, diabetes, high cholesterol, obesity, depression, and heart problems) than actively disengaged employees (Gallup, 2013).

Fluctuating versus enduring engagement The concept of engagement was initially developed to refer to an enduring affective-motivational state of employees regarding their work (Schaufeli et al., 2002), or psychological presence in a role (Rothbard & Patil, 2012). However, engagement has also been defined as fluctuating intra-individual experiences of the work and environment in which it occurs (Bakker, 2014). Diary studies make it possible to study how and why employee engagement states and behaviors vary over time. Furthermore, they allow researchers to examine psychological processes in more detail, on a real-time basis, in field settings. Third, they prevent problems with inaccuracies that arise when employees have to recall experiences and behaviors (Sonnentag, 2003). Bakker (2014) supported the use of diary studies given that a considerable amount of variance in employee engagement can be attributed to within-person fluctuations. Furthermore, daily fluctuations in job resources explain daily fluctuations in employee engagement.

Measurement of employee engagement

Utrecht Work Engagement Scale (UWES) Studies have shown that engagement can be measured in a valid and reliable way using the UWES (Bakker et al., 2008; Barkhuizen & Rothmann, 2006; Burke, Koyuncu, Tekinkus, Bektas, & Fiksenbaum 2012; Schaufeli et al., 2002; Storm & Rothmann, 2003). Either a three-factor (i.e., absorption, vigor, and dedication) or a one-factor model was reported in most studies. Although a one-factor model of employee engagement might be preferable to use across cultures (Shimazu, Schaufeli, Miyanaka, & Iwata 2010), the dimensions of engagement (e.g., the emotional versus the cognitive component) might show differential predicting value of individual and organizational outcomes.

Measurement invariance of the UWES was reported for different cultural groups in a sample of police members in South Africa (Storm & Rothmann, 2003), emergency medical technicians from different cultural groups (Naudé & Rothmann, 2004), employees in the Netherlands and Italy (Balducci, Fraccaroli, & Schaufeli, 2010), and teachers in Australia, Canada, China, Indonesia, and Oman (Klassen et al., 2012). Klassen and colleagues found that a three-factor model of employee engagement (consisting of vigor, dedication, and absorption) was acceptable in countries such as Australia and Indonesia, while a one-factor model (where all the items of the UWES formed part of a single employee engagement factor) was acceptable within countries such as Canada and China. Furthermore, the UWES was invariant for Western and non-Western groups, but not across Western and non-Western groups. However, the UWES is not without problems, especially when it is used in multicultural or cross-cultural contexts (Naudé & Rothmann; 2004; Shimazu et al., 2010).

Engagement Inventory (EI) The EI was developed by May et al. (2004). The inventory measures three components of employee engagement, namely cognitive, physical, and emotional engagement. These components shows overlap with the three dimensions used in the UWES, namely absorption (cognitive), vigor (physical), and dedication (emotional). Rothmann and Rothmann (2010) found that the psychometric properties of the EI are problematic. In follow-up studies (e.g., Diedericks & Rothmann, 2013), the items used in the inventory were adapted to improve its construct validity and reliability. A subsequent study by Fouché (2015) supports the construct validity of the EI and reliability of the subscales.

Intellectual, Social, Affective (ISA) Engagement Scale The ISA Engagement Scale was developed by Soane et al. (2013). The scale is based on the personal engagement model of Kahn (1990). It measures three components of employee engagement, namely intellectual engagement (absorption in work), social engagement (the extent to which employees are socially connected with the working environment), and affective engagement (the extent to which employees experience positive affect relating to their work roles).

Gallup Survey Gallup (2013) classified the satisfaction–engagement causes in terms of four dimensions, namely (1) whether primary needs of employees are satisfied (e.g., do they know what is expected of them in their roles, and do they have the materials and equipment for doing their jobs properly); (2) evaluating their contributions and assessing whether others value their contributions (e.g., do they have the opportunity to use their strengths, do they receive recognition and praise, do their supervisors care about them as persons, and does someone at work encourage their development); (3) whether they belong (e.g., do their opinions count at work, does the mission of the company make them feel that their jobs are important, are their fellow workers committed to doing good work, and do they have a best friend at work); (4) whether they can make improvements, learn, grow, innovate, and apply new ideas (e.g., does someone talk to them about their progress, and do they have opportunities to learn and grow).

Prevalence of engagement

It is difficult to evaluate what the global employee engagement levels are. Comparison of employee engagement in different contexts requires that measurement invariance exists before scores on a single measuring instrument can be compared. However, given the different conceptualizations and measures of employee engagement used by academic researchers and practitioners throughout the world, such studies have been done on a small scale.

Rothmann (2005) reported a measurement invariance study of employee engagement in different occupations in South Africa. The UWES was used in the study and measurement invariance was found for two subscales (vigor and dedication) in samples of employees in different occupations in South Africa. Employee engagement in different occupations was divided into three categories, namely low (pharmacists, emergency health technicians, correctional officers, administrative staff at higher educational institutions, and secondary school teachers), medium (police officers, nurses, and call-center operators), and high (non-professional counselors and train drivers).

Gallup (2013) report results of engagement of employees according to their definition thereof on a bi-annual basis (see Table 18.1 for the results of 2011–2012). Research shows that only 13% of employees across 142 countries are engaged in their work, 63% are not

Table 18.1 Employee engagement in selected countries.

	Engagement category		
Country	*Engaged*	*Not engaged*	*Actively disengaged*
United States	30%	52%	18%
Philippines	29%	63%	8%
Qatar	28%	62%	10%
Brazil	27%	62%	12%
Australia	24%	60%	16%
New Zealand	23%	62%	15%
Denmark	21%	69%	10%
Russia	19%	63%	19%
United Kingdom	17%	57%	26%
Argentina	16%	56%	28%
Germany	15%	61%	24%
Pakistan	15%	68%	16%
Egypt	13%	55%	32%
Nigeria	12%	65%	23%
Mexico	12%	60%	28%
South Korea	11%	67%	23%
Malaysia	11%	81%	8%
Saudi Arabia	9%	80%	11%
India	9%	60%	31%
South Africa	9%	46%	45%
Iran	7%	56%	38%
Japan	7%	69%	24%
China	6%	68%	26%
Iraq	6%	63%	31%
Israel	5%	73%	22%

Source: Author.

engaged, and 24% are actively disengaged (Gallup, 2013). However, these results vary among different global regions. Among 26 countries in the Sub-Saharan Africa region included in the 2011–2012 Gallup survey, only 19% of the respondents overall indicated that they work for an employer. South Africa had the highest percentage of actively disengaged employees in the world. One factor contributing to this state is the destabilizing labor unrest in the mining sector. In most cases, actively disengaged employees outnumbered engaged employees by 3 to 1. In South Korea, cultural norms pose challenges to increasing employee engagement. For example, tenure, rather than performance, is used when pay and promotion decisions are made. Talent development is undermined by a "group" mentality. In countries in South Asia, poor education and a lack of high-level talent undermine employee engagement. In Western Europe, low levels of confidence in local job markets may lead employees to remain in workplaces that do not engage them. In Russia, management and leadership, trust and integrity are areas which have to be addressed to promote employee engagement.

Theories and Models of Employee Engagement

Various models and theories of employee engagement, including the personal engagement model of Kahn (1990), the JD-R model (Schaufeli & Bakker, 2004), self-determination theory (SDT; Deci et al., 2001), and social exchange theory have been used to understand and predict employee engagement. The personal engagement model has been developed to understand employee engagement.

The personal engagement model

The personal engagement model of Kahn (1990) is classified as a need-satisfying approach (Shuck, 2011; Truss, Shantz, Soane, Alfes, & Delbridge, 2013). According to this model, various antecedents contribute to individuals attaching themselves to their work roles. The perception of job context affects employees' psychological responses, which affect their engagement. Kahn (1990) concluded from a qualitative study that various job contextual factors impact employee engagement via the experience of three psychological conditions, namely psychological meaningfulness, psychological availability, and psychological safety. Kahn and Heaphy (2014) refer to this model as a "relational model" of employee engagement.

Psychological meaningfulness refers to "a feeling that one is receiving a return on investment of one's self in a currency of physical, cognitive, or emotional energy" (Kahn, 1990, pp. 703–704). Kahn and Heaphy (2014) argued that deepened purposes (resulting from collective efforts in groups, transformational leadership, belongingness, and contact with beneficiaries) result in psychological meaningfulness and employee engagement. Studies (May et al., 2004; Olivier & Rothmann, 2007; Pratt & Ashforth, 2003; Rothmann & Welsh, 2013; Steger & Dik, 2010), showed that work role fit, the inherent task characteristics, and the nature of relations with co-workers are strongly associated with psychological meaningfulness at work. Psychological meaningfulness predicts a large percentage of the variance in employee engagement (May et al., 2004; Rothmann & Buys, 2011; Rothmann & Rothmann, 2010). Steger, Littman-Ovadia, Miller, Menger, and Rothmann (2013) found that when work was not perceived as meaningful, employees characterized by high scores on affective disposition (i.e., positive affect) were more strongly engaged compared to employees characterized by low scores on affective disposition. However, when work was perceived to be meaningful, no difference in level of engagement was found between those with high or low scores on affective disposition.

Psychological safety entails feeling able to show and employ one's self without fear of negative consequences to self-image, status, or career (Kahn, 1990). Individuals working in a safe environment will understand the boundaries surrounding acceptable behaviors. According to Kahn and Heaphy (2014), "holding" environments characterized by leaders and co-workers who are accessible and who show respect and empathy contribute strongly to psychological safety. Psychological safety will lead to engagement, because it reflects one's belief that a person can employ him-/herself without fear of negative consequences. The opposite would occur in a work environment that is ambiguous, unpredictable, and threatening. Employees in unsafe environments with ambiguous, unpredictable, and threatening conditions are likely to disengage from the work and would be more cautious to try new things (May et al., 2004).

Psychological availability is defined by Kahn (1990) as the ability to engage as a result of having the cognitive, emotional, and physical resources. Energizing interactions and emotional relief affect psychological availability and employee engagement positively, while cognitive, emotional, and/or physical depletion affect these outcomes negatively Factors such as the individual's work-role insecurities might influence an individual's beliefs, which might have a direct influence on his or her psychological availability (Vinarski-Peretz & Carmeli, 2011). May et al. (2004) and Olivier and Rothmann (2007) confirmed that psychological availability is positively associated with employee engagement.

The JD-R model

Research on engagement as an experience of work activity has utilized the JD-R model (Demerouti et al., 2001; Hakanen, Schaufeli, & Ahola, 2008; Jackson, Rothmann, & Van de Vijver, 2006; Schaufeli &, Bakker, 2004).

The JD-R model assumes that it is possible to model work characteristics associated with well-being in two broad categories, namely job demands and job resources (Demerouti et al., 2001). Job demands refer to the physical, psychological, social, or organizational aspects of the job that require sustained physical and/or psychological effort and are therefore associated with certain physiological and/or psychological costs (e.g., work pressure, role overload, and emotional demands). Job resources refer to the physical, psychological, social, or organizational aspects of the job that may be functional in achieving work goals, reducing job demands, and stimulating personal growth and development. Resources may be located at the level of the organization (e.g., salary, career opportunities, job security), interpersonal and social relations (e.g., supervisor support, co-worker support, and team climate), the organization of work (e.g., role clarity, and participation in decision-making), and the level of the task (e.g., performance feedback, skill variety, task significance, task identity, and autonomy).

Rothmann, Strydom, and Mostert (2006) confirmed the measurement invariance of a measure of job demands and resources in a sample of 2,717 employees representing five different types of organizations in South Africa. Various studies have shown that job resources, including social support from supervisors and colleagues, and the intrinsic nature of the job (e.g., skill variety, autonomy, and learning opportunities) are positively associated with employee engagement (Bakker et al., 2008; Schaufeli & Bakker, 2004). In a longitudinal study, Mauno, Kinnunen, and Ruokolainen (2007) found that job resources predicted employee engagement better than did job demands. Hakanen et al. (2008) conducted a longitudinal study and found that job resources predicted future engagement. Rothmann and Pieterse (2007) studied the relationship between job resources and employee engagement and found that growth opportunities in the job (i.e., variety, learning opportunities, and autonomy) best predicted employee engagement. Rothmann and Joubert (2007) found that organizational support and growth opportunities in the job were strong predictors of employee engagement in the mining industry. High job resources, such as social support and feedback, may reduce the effects of job demands (Demerouti et al., 2001).

Van den Broeck, Vansteenkiste, De Witte, and Lens (2008) found that job demands and resources indirectly affect employee engagement via satisfaction of the psychological needs for autonomy, competence, and relatedness. Furthermore, using the model of Spreitzer (1995), Mendes and Stander (2011) found that leadership and role clarity indirectly affect employee engagement via psychological empowerment (i.e., meaningfulness, self-determination, and impact). However, most studies (e.g., Bakker, Hakanen, Demerouti, & Xanthopoulou, 2007; Saks, 2006; Schaufeli & Bakker, 2004) did not empirically test the mediating effects of these conditions on employee engagement.

In a study of eight European countries, Taipale, Selander, Anttila, and Nätti (2011) found that job demands reduced employee engagement, while autonomy and support increased employee engagement. Regarding the role of the organization and the supervisor, Mone, Eisinger, Guggenheim, Price, and Stine (2011) showed that performance management activities contribute to employee engagement. More specifically, setting performance and development goals in a collaborative way, providing ongoing feedback and recognition, managing employee development, discussing performance with employees, and building a climate of trust and empowerment contribute to employee engagement.

The role of personal resources in the JD-R model has also been studied. Personal resources were seen to determine the way people perceive and react to build a comprehensible, manageable, and meaningful environment (e.g., Feldt, Kivimäki, Rantala, & Tolvanen, 2004; Judge, Bono, & Locke, 2000; Xanthopoulou, Bakker, Demerouti, & Schaufeli, 2009), which results in employee well-being and engagement. Barkhuizen, Rothmann, and Van de Vijver (2014) found that dispositional optimism, defined as "a relatively stable, generalized expectation that good outcomes will occur across important life domains" (Wrosch & Scheier, 2003, p. 64), had a strong direct effect on perceptions of job resources as well as strong indirect effects (via job resources) on employee engagement.

Social exchange theory

Social exchange is the basic underpinning of relationships between individuals, groups, and organizations. Social exchange theory (Blau, 1964) can be used to explain why employees respond to these conditions with various degrees of engagement (Saks, 2006). According to this theory, obligations are generated through a series of interactions between parties that are in a state of reciprocal interdependence. Using social exchange theory, Saks (2006) states that social relationships and organizational support are crucial for the development of employee engagement. Reissner and Pagan (2013) found that organizational communication activities, which promote a coherent strategic message and enhance employees' knowledge of the organization and its culture, strongly contributed to engagement at organizational level.

Specific drivers of employee engagement (e.g., providing effective leadership and/or role clarity) might be perceived as evidence of organizational support, which can instill a sense of trust and justice (Meyer, 2013). Employees that experience organizational support reciprocate by increased commitment to organizational goals and increased discretionary efforts. Employees feel obliged to engage as repayment for the resources they receive from their organization. Employees are likely to disengage from their roles when the organization fails to provide resources.

Trust seems to be central to the development of employee engagement (Macey & Schneider, 2008). Employees that are engaged invest their energy, time, and resources trusting the investment will be rewarded (intrinsically or extrinsically) in a meaningful way. From the perspective of social exchange theory, employees make investments for reasons of reciprocity (Coyle-Shapiro & Conway, 2004). Employees could also make investments for reasons of social identity (Moorman & Byrne, 2005). Hence trust in the leader, team, and/or organization increases the likelihood that employees will be more engaged.

The satisfaction–engagement approach

It is important to note that although Harter et al. (2002, p. 269) defined engagement as the involvement and satisfaction with, and enthusiasm for, work, the construct has not been measured in line with this definition in Gallup surveys. Based on 12 items (which can be seen as antecedents of engagement), surveys by Gallup classify employees into three categories (Gallup, 2013):

1. *Engaged employees*: They work with passion and feel connected to their organizations. They drive innovation and move their organizations forward.
2. *Not engaged employees*: They are difficult to spot because they are not hostile or disruptive. They have little concern for customers, productivity, profitability, waste, safety, and mission and purpose of their teams.
3. *Actively disengaged employees*: They are out to damage the organization, have more accidents, account for more quality defects, are sicker, are more absent from work, and more often think of quitting their jobs.

The Gallup survey measures conditions that are required for employees to be satisfied rather than engaged (Schaufeli, 2014). However, the results of Gallup surveys made an impact on research and practice because they have linked employee engagement with business unit outcomes (Harter et al., 2002).

Self-determination: The role of psychological need satisfaction

Deci and Ryan (1985, 2011) developed the SDT, which postulates that human behavior is motivated by three innate, essential, and universal needs: namely autonomy, competence, and relatedness (Deci & Ryan, 2008). Psychological needs provide the energy and direction for people to engage in activities that influence need satisfaction, allow observers to understand whether people will be subjectively well, and enable interventionists to determine which social contextual aspects should be changed to promote need satisfaction (Deci & Ryan, 2011).

Within the SDT framework, it is the satisfaction of the three needs rather than the strength of the desire that is important in predicting employee engagement. The needs for autonomy, competence, and relatedness are universal, but individuals differ in terms of the degree to which they are able to satisfy the needs (Deci & Ryan, 2011). SDT differentiates between autonomous and controlled motivation. Autonomous motivation predicts perseverance and adherence (Deci & Ryan, 2008) and relates to psychological well-being. The psychological needs for autonomy, competence, and relatedness complement autonomous motivation. Autonomous motivation elicits behavior by choice and volition; whereas controlled motivation acts via forces external to the self, under pressure and demand.

The need for *autonomy* is defined as the desire to experience freedom and choice when carrying out an activity. The need for *competence* refers to individuals' inherent desire to feel effective in interacting with the environment. The need for *relatedness* concerns the innate need of individuals to feel connected to others, to love and care for others, and to be loved and cared for. This need is satisfied when individuals experience a sense of communion and develop close and intimate relationships with others. Psychological needs that are unmet (deficiency needs) as well as needs that are satisfied (growth needs) have motivational value across life domains (Sheldon & Gunz, 2009). Individuals therefore want more autonomy, competence, and relatedness experiences if their basic psychological needs have been satisfied.

If a work environment provides adequate support for the satisfaction of the three needs, it should generate more participation from employees as it will be associated with more autonomous motivation. Satisfaction of the basic needs for autonomy, competence, and relatedness leads to autonomous motivation (Milyavskaya & Koestner, 2011). Employees setting themselves autonomous goals attain more goals, which then motivate them to set and attain more autonomous goals in the future and in so doing enhance their own well-being (Sheldon & Houser-Marko, 2001). The degree to which goals are autonomous will determine individuals' energy in achieving their goals. Goals that are achieved relate to psychological need satisfaction for autonomy, competence, and relatedness, which in turn is essential for optimal human development and integrity (Gagné & Deci, 2005), and prompts positive organizational outcomes (Greguras & Diefendorff, 2010).

The self-determination literature acknowledges the role of the leader in affecting psychological need satisfaction and autonomous motivation of employees (Gagné & Deci, 2005). More specifically, Baard, Deci, and Ryan (2004) have demonstrated the beneficial effects of autonomy-support in a work context. Furthermore, a study by Graves and Luciano (2013) showed how leader–member exchange theory evokes psychological need satisfaction. Studies by Hetland, Hetland, Andreassen, Pallesen, and Notelaers (2011), Kovjanic, Schuh, Jonas, Van Quaquebeke, and van Dick (2012), and Kovjanic, Schuh, and Jonas (2013) focused on the positive effects of transformational leadership on psychological need satisfaction, work engagement, and performance. Specific leader behaviors elicit satisfaction of employees' psychological needs, which in turn promotes their work engagement.

Van den Broeck et al. (2008) found that job demands and resources indirectly affect employee engagement via satisfaction of the psychological needs for autonomy, competence, and relatedness. Findings of a study by Fouché (2015) showed that leader support (for autonomy, competence, and relatedness) was positively related to employees' psychological need satisfaction and engagement. Leader support affected engagement positively via employees' autonomy satisfaction.

Drivers of Employee Engagement

The relational context: The role of the leader, co-workers, and customers

Leaders (including managers and supervisors) play a critical role in creating an environment conducive to employee engagement in organizations (Kahn & Heaphy, 2014; Soane, 2014). Leader behaviors that support, encourage, and develop people play a significant role in the engagement of employees (Harter & Adkins, 2015; May et al., 2004; Rothmann & Rothmann, 2010; Schaufeli & Bakker, 2004). Porath (2014) found that employees were 55% more engaged when leaders treated them with respect. Half of employees in her study did not feel respected by their leaders. According to Harter and Adkins (2015), managers account for up to 70% of the variance in employee engagement scores.

Leader–follower relationships can offer a sense of connectedness and opportunities to attach to a purpose (Kahn & Heaphy, 2014), individualized consideration (Soane, 2014), and opportunities to promote psychological meaningfulness, availability, and safety (Crawford, Rich, Buckman, & Bergeron, 2014). Macey and Schneider (2008) argued that transformational leadership will unlock employee engagement. Barrick et al. (2015) found that transformational leadership of the chief executive officer of an organization is positively related to collective employee engagement.

Trust in a leader, which is affected by authentic leadership, leads to employee engagement (Wang & Hsieh, 2013). Leader trustworthiness can be linked to five categories of behavior, namely behavioral consistency, behavioral integrity, sharing and delegation of control, accurate and open communication, and a demonstration of concern (May et al., 2004). Reluctance on the part of managers to loosen their control can send a message to their employees that they are not trusted, which might cause employees to be afraid of taking any chances or of overstepping their boundaries. This fear will be strengthened when managers behave unpredictably, inconsistently, or hypocritically (Kahn, 1990; May et al., 2004). Trustworthy leader and manager behaviors should lead to feelings of psychological safety as well as willingness among employees to invest themselves at work (Edmondson, 2004). Interpersonal trust can either have cognitive or affective bases (McAllister, 1995). The reliability and dependability of others are related to cognitive-based trust, whereas the emotional relationships between individuals impact on affective trust.

May et al. (2004) found that supportive co-worker relations that create camaraderie and a sense of belonging predict psychological meaningfulness and employee engagement. Rewarding co-worker relations can create an experience of belonging and care, which can lead to feeling psychologically safer at work (Olivier & Rothmann, 2007). In addition, Wrzesniewski, Dutton, and Debebe (2003) suggest that employees receive cues from interaction with co-workers to deduce meaning from their work. According to Kahn and Heaphy (2014), employees will experience a sense of meaningfulness from their interactions when they are treated with respect and dignity and are valued for their contributions.

Strategic implementation by the senior management team in organizations enhances the relationship between organizational resources and collective organizational engagement because of greater psychological meaningfulness, safety, and availability experienced by employees (Barrick et al., 2015). Strategic implementation by the senior management team is characterized by the following behaviors: ensuring the employees understand the goals and strategies of the organization, relying on clearly defined metrics to assess progress on organizational goals and strategies, linking senior management team goals to the strategic direction of the organization, monitoring events outside the organization that might affect progress on goals and strategies, and seeking timely feedback from stakeholders about how well the team meets organizational goals and strategies.

Participation

Rees, Alfes, and Gatenby (2013) found that employee voice is positively related to employee engagement. Their study found that only 1 in 8 Chinese employees strongly agrees with an item which asks whether their opinions count at work. Voice is defined as verbal communication of ideas, suggestions and/or opinions with the intent to improve organizational functioning. Employee voice indirectly affected engagement via employee trust in senior management and the employee–manager relationship. Yoerger, Crowe, and

Allen (2015) found that participation in decision-making is related to employee engagement. Meeting participation had a stronger effect on employee engagement when meeting load was high and when the supervisor was supportive.

Human resource management practices

Human resource management practices that affect the collective engagement of employees can be categorized along two dimensions, namely practices that focus on an organization's expectations of employees, and practices that enhance employees' expected rewards and outcomes (Barrick et al., 2015). Employees vary in their engagement as a function of their perceptions of the benefits they receive from a role, for example a pay raise, job security, a promotion, freedom and opportunities, respect from co-workers, praise from supervisors, training and development opportunities, challenging work assignments, and public recognition. According to Barrick et al. (2015), human resource investments and expectation-enhancing practices (e.g., pay equity, job security, developmental feedback, and pay for performance) are positively related to organizational engagement.

Person–environment fit

Building on theories such as self-concordance theory (Sheldon & Elliot, 1999), self-determination theory (Ryan & Deci, 2000), and self-concept-based theory (Shamir, House, & Arthur, 1993), Bono and Judge (2003) argue that individuals will be engaged if their work is consistent with their personal values. Therefore person–environment fit, rather than specific environmental demands and/or resources, lead to employee engagement. In line with the personal engagement model of Kahn (1990), the interaction between individual and organization explains employee engagement.

Individuals seek work roles in which they can express their authentic selves fully in creative ways. Fit between an individual's self-concept and his or her work role will lead to a sense of meaning due to the ability of the individual to express his or her values and beliefs (Shamir, 1991). When people perceive their work as an opportunity to express their beliefs and values, they will experience meaning at work, because they will perceive a work role fit (May et al., 2004). Human beings are creative and self-expressive and therefore they will look for work roles that will help them express their true self. Individuals will feel more effective in a job that helps them express their true self-concept; where they experience a work role fit. The identity their work gives will be readily assumed by employees if it fits how they see themselves when they perceive a work role fit (Kahn, 1990; May et al., 2004).

Individuals will experience more psychological meaningfulness, and invest more of the self in achieving the goals set out for them by the organization, when they experience greater congruence between the self and the requirements of their work role (May et al., 2004). Van Zyl, Deacon, and Rothmann (2010) found that work role fit predicted psychological meaningfulness and work engagement in a sample of industrial psychologists. This is because such individuals see their work as not only a means to an end but as an end in itself; they will see their work as a calling (Dik & Duffy, 2008). When the work roles are not fitting their self-concepts, such individuals will recraft their work to match how they perceive the self (Wrzesniewski, 2012). Lu, Wang, Lu, Du, and Bakker (2013) found that engaged employees craft their work in physical and relational ways, which creates a better person–job fit. Rothmann and Hamakangandu (2013) confirmed that work role fit and work orientation predicted experiences of psychological meaningfulness and employee engagement of teachers in Zambia.

Strengths use

An engaged life results from knowing what your signature strengths are and recrafting your life to use them at work or in other life contexts (Peterson, Park, & Seligman, 2005). Building on strengths creates more engagement than identifying weaknesses and trying to correct them (Linley, Woolston, & Biswas-Diener, 2009). Strength is defined as "a pre-existing capacity for a particular way of behaving, thinking or feeling that is authentic and energising to the user" (Linley, 2008, p. 9). The *identify-and-use* approach to strengths assumes that strengths can and should be used more than they currently are. About one-third of people can identify their own strengths, and only 17% say that they use their strengths most of the time each day (Buckingham, 2007). The identify-and-use approach assumes that people are competent, and focus on employing strengths in the pursuit of personal achievement. The *strengths development* approach assumes that strengths interventions should not primarily be about the use of strengths, but rather about strengths development. This approach emphasizes building strengths competency. While the identify-and-use approach can influence individuals' happiness and depression, strengths development focuses also on motivation, effort, interpersonal effectiveness, and other aspects of psychological functioning.

Employees experience engagement when they use their strengths. Employees will be 2.5 times more likely to be engaged than people whose supervisors focus on their weaknesses. Intentions to leave were 14.9% lower for employees that received feedback on their strengths (rather than their weaknesses). Units where the strengths-based approach was implemented were 12.5% more productive after the intervention than before it was implemented (Lewis, 2011).

Organizational factors

The organization itself, especially its goals and values, can be a source of engagement. Work conditions not only have a main effect on state and behavioral engagement – they also may moderate the relationships between trait engagement and state engagement as well as relationships between state and behavioral engagement (Macey & Schneider, 2008).

Perceived organizational support is defined as a general belief that an organization cares about and supports its employees (Rhoades & Eisenberger, 2002). An organization serves as a source of socio-emotional resources, including respect, satisfactory wages, and medical benefits. Therefore perceived organizational support contributes to satisfaction of employees' needs for approval, esteem, and affiliation. Organizational support includes giving information to enable employees to plan their schedules, enabling access to useful training on the job, providing rewards, considering the goals and values of employees, showing concern for employees, caring about the employees' opinions, being willing to help the employees when they experience problems, and not taking advantage of them. Saks (2006) found that perceived organizational support is a significant predictor of employee engagement. Employees that perceive the organization to be supportive of them become more engaged as part of the reciprocity norm of social exchange theory. Therefore, when employees believe that their organization is concerned about them and cares about them, they are likely to respond by attempting to fulfill their obligations to the organization by becoming more engaged.

Work design

The significance and purposefulness of tasks contribute to experiences of psychological meaningfulness. Five dimensions of a task, namely skill variety, task identity, task significance, autonomy, and feedback, may affect psychological meaningfulness and employee engagement (Hackman & Oldham, 1980; May et al., 2004). Barrick et al. (2015) found that collective employee engagement at organizational level was related to the implementation of these job characteristics at an organizational level. Skill variety refers to the assortment of diverse skills employees have to apply in order to complete their task. Task identity relates to the degree to which a specific piece of work is identifiable, in other words, where it is clear to see what piece of work has been completed. Task significance is defined as the importance of a piece of work against the backdrop of the overall organizational goal. Autonomy in a task relates to the degree of freedom with which employees can choose what tasks to complete and and how to complete them. The last component of job enrichment relates to the feedback from the job itself. Studies (e.g., May et al., 2004; Rothmann & Buys, 2011) confirmed the positive relationship between work design, psychological meaningfulness, and employee engagement.

The role of the context

Context seems to matter for employee engagement and its antecedents. Firstly, cultures in different countries might differ, which makes it difficult to generalize findings concerning employee engagement and its antecedents (Rothmann, 2014). Secondly, broader organizational factors (e.g., industry sector, market conditions, ownership and governance arrangements, organizational size, and internal structures) might affect employee engagement (Jenkins & Delbridge, 2013). Therefore a one-size-fits-all approach will be doomed to failure.

Rothmann (2014) argued that it is necessary to take a combined etic and emic approach toward the assessment and promotion of employee engagement. This will combine the scientific rigor of an etic approach with the cultural sensitivity of an emic approach (Cheung, Van de Vijver, & Leong, 2011). Unique cultural behavior can be detected when an emic approach is used. Cultural or measurement artifacts may contribute to constructs not being invariant between cultures. Therefore measurement invariance should be assessed when measuring instruments are applied in different contexts. Various methodological questions should be attended to when assessing employee engagement, namely whether respondents understood the items of measures, whether translation of measures was done accurately, whether the translated measure is equivalent to the original measure, whether there are cross-cultural differences in the means and distributions of scores, and how cross-cultural differences in scores could be interpreted.

It is crucial for employers expanding their operations around the world to find the drivers of employee engagement in culturally diverse workforces. The cultural dimensions (individualism, power distance, uncertainty avoidance, masculinity, and long-term orientation) identified by Hofstede, Hofstede, and Minkov (2010) could be analyzed to understand the factors driving employee engagement. Drivers of engagement in different countries might differ (Sanchez & McCauley, 2006). Drivers of employee engagement in the United Kingdom and China included a sense of personal accomplishment, confidence in senior management, training opportunities, fair pay, and receiving performance feedback. In the United Kingdom and the United States, respect matters; in France and India, employees care about the type of work that they are doing; while in Germany, the type of people employees work with matters (Sanchez & McCauley, 2006). Lu, Siu, Chen, and Wang (2011) found that family mastery strongly affected the work engagement of nurses in China, especially when their job demands were high, presumably because the family is a major source of ego strength for individuals in collectivistic cultures.

Klassen et al. (2012) reported that educators' work-related beliefs vary with cultural beliefs (i.e., level of collectivism) and country. Widely shared cultural values within a country influence the ways workplace motivation beliefs operate for educators and other workers. Motivation beliefs that focus on the individual (e.g., engagement) would show lower levels of reliability and construct validity in collectivist settings compared to individualistic settings. In their study of employee engagement Burke et al. (2012) cautioned against the application of Western human resource practices to Turkish organizations. The Gallup report (2013) shows how conventions undermine employee engagement in the Middle East and the North Africa region. For example, "who you know" plays an important role in gaining employment and advantages in the workplace, resulting in poor fit for roles and negative perceptions about organizations.

Outcomes of employee engagement

Employee engagement has been associated with various positive and negative outcomes. Concerning individual well-being outcomes, the Gallup report (2013) shows that engaged employees are more likely to be thriving, that is, they experience higher satisfaction with life and more positive emotions than do actively disengaged employees.

- Engaged employees are 1.6 times as likely as actively disengaged employees to be thriving. In South Asia, engaged employees are 5.5 times as likely to be thriving as actively disengaged employees.
- Engaged employees in East Asia are half as likely to experience stress the previous day as actively disengaged employees.
- Two thirds of engaged employees in Latin America are thriving, while it is the case with only 42% of actively disengaged employees.

Results of meta-analyses showed that engaged employees make a difference to their organizations. Conducting 263 studies across 192 organizations and in 34 countries, Gallup (2013) showed that employee engagement has effects on 9 performance outcomes, namely customer ratings (10%), profitability (22%), productivity (21%), turnover (65%), safety incidents (48%), shrinkage (28%), absenteeism (37%), patient safety incidents (41%), and quality (41%) (the percentages in brackets reflect median differences between top- and bottom-quartile units).

- Work units in the top 25% of the employee engagement scores have significantly higher productivity, profitability, customer ratings, low intentions to leave and absenteeism, and fewer safety incidents than those in the bottom 25%.
- Organizations with 9.3 engaged employees for every actively disengaged employee in 2010–2011 experienced 147% higher earnings per share compared to their competition in 2011–2012. Furthermore, organizations with 2.6 engaged employees for every actively disengaged employee experienced 2% lower earnings per share compared to their competition during the same time.
- In the United States, active disengagement costs the economy up to $550 billion per year; in Germany it costs up to $186 billion per year, and in the United Kingdom up to $112 billion per year.

Future Research

Various questions remain unanswered pertaining to the development, implementation, and experience of engagement initiatives (Truss, 2014).

First, to increase the usefulness of the engagement concept, research is needed that includes the psychological state and behavior it implies simultaneously. In the absence of such a model (which has to include potential antecedents and moderators), it will be difficult to make meaningful scientific progress in terms of measurement and interventions to increase employee engagement. Psychological state engagement could be modeled as an antecedent of behavioral engagement (e.g., discretionary effort and in-role or extra-role behavior). Utilizing a broader definition of employee engagement that includes the psychological state as well as behavior, questions such as the following should be answered: What are the consequences of low employee engagement? Are individual and organizational outcomes of employee engagement always positive? How can selection tools be used to select engaged employees? How can employee engagement best be promoted? Multilevel research designs should be implemented to study employee engagement at an individual level and at a collective organizational level.

Second, research on employee engagement has taken place from a psychological perspective and with micro-level attitudinal variables (Truss et al., 2014). Research is needed on how managers and human resource professionals could develop and embed employee engagement programs and to evaluate lived experiences of such programs. New research themes will emerge that bring together the concerns of practitioners with those of researchers regarding employee engagement.

Third, a gap exists in current knowledge in that no information is available regarding cultural conventions that might explain *why* individuals are engaged. Future research should pay more attention to the contextual factors which affect employee engagement. The literature has not given sufficient attention to the complexity of the environments employees find themselves in. Scientific information is also needed regarding diversity (e.g., in terms of culture and gender) and employee engagement. It is also necessary to study the interplay between internal and external contextual environments, managerial constraints, and employee engagement. Poortinga (2011) points out that individuals' motives behind behavior might be based on constraints on the one hand, and on affordances referring to those options open to an individual from which he or she can choose on the other. These affordances or options and constraints or rules are what inform decisions on how to act, think, and feel. An individual's cognition, behavior, and affect again crystallize into practices and mentalities which are often unique to a particular community of people. Conventions refer to agreements in a society about how things should be done (Poortinga, 2011). Cultural conventions will have a large impact on how individuals cope with or are motivated to act on, think about, and feel about their work and organization.

Fourth, it is necessary to study employee engagement at group or team level. For example, information is needed concerning the contagiousness of engagement at group or team level.

Conclusion

The interest in employee engagement can be attributed to the increased interest in positive psychological states and the growing realization of the importance of human factors in employee well-being and business performance. Employee engagement can be regarded as a state, a behavior, or a trait. To advance knowledge, the definition of employee engagement should include consequential behavior in line with organizational goals in addition to the psychological state. Employees might experience the psychological state of engagement, but might not contribute to organizational goals. While differences in approaches of academic researchers and practitioners might be reduced if such a definition is used, it might threaten the distinctiveness of the concept (Schaufeli, 2014). Research on collective organizational engagement (Barrick et al., 2015) has shown that employee engagement also matters on a collective level.

A unique theoretical framework for employee engagement does not exist. The personal engagement model of Kahn (1990), the recent relational model of employee engagement (Kahn & Heaphy, 2014), and the JD-R model made important contributions to understanding and predicting aspects of employee engagement. However, there is a lack of an overarching model of employee engagement. Research and practice could benefit by the development of a comprehensive theory of employee engagement. Research will be needed to ensure the validity of the constructs (i.e., the empirical foundation). However, it is also necessary to ensure that employee engagement is grounded in theory (so that findings can be explained). More scientific information is needed to explain the relationships among employee engagement and its antecedents (e.g., drivers and psychological processes and conditions).

Despite more than two decades of research on the topic, research shows that engagement levels remain low in many countries. The question arises whether researchers focus on all relevant psychological processes and conditions which might explain employee engagement. Kahn and Heaphy's (2014) model of employee engagement focuses on psychological meaningfulness, safety, and availability as mediators in the relationships between context-specific variables and employee engagement. Furthermore, SDT (Deci & Ryan, 2011) focuses on psychological need satisfaction as a possible mediating variable in the relationships between job demands/resources and employee engagement. However, longitudinal research is necessary to investigate the contribution that such psychological conditions and processes make to predicting employee engagement.

The utility of employee engagement has always been emphasized by practitioners. Various positive individual and organizational outcomes have been attributed to employee engagement. Successful application of existing employee engagement models supports the utility thereof.

Employee engagement in organizations could be influenced by contextual factors. This has various implications for managers and human resource practitioners. Increased contact between people of different cultures, wealth, and education reduces cross-cultural differences. While the importance of culture should not be overstated, some aspects of cultures could be unique and should be considered to understand and affect employee engagement. Measurement invariance of engagement measures should be tested when differences in scores could be attributed to cultural and/or contextual influences in terms of item meaning and understanding, rather than differences resulting from the measuring of the constructs. If cultural and contextual influences are not accounted for, invalid conclusions could be drawn regarding the constructs under study.

References

Baard, P. P., Deci, E. L., & Ryan, R. M. (2004). Intrinsic need satisfaction: A motivational basis of performance and well-being in two work settings. *Journal of Applied Social Psychology*, *34*, 2045–2068.

Bakker, A. B. (2014). Daily fluctuations in work engagement: An overview and current directions. *European Psychologist*, *19*, 227–236.

Bakker, A. B., & Demerouti, E. (2008). Towards a model of work engagement. *Career Development International*, *13*, 209–223.

Bakker, A. B., Hakanen, J. J., Demerouti, E., & Xanthopoulou, D. (2007). Job resources boost work engagement, particularly when job demands are high. *Journal of Educational Psychology, 99*, 274–284.

Bakker, A. B., & Oerlemans, G. M. (2012). Subjective well-being in organizations. In K. S. Cameron & G. M. Spreitzer (Eds.), *The Oxford handbook of positive organizational scholarship* (pp. 178–189). New York, NY: Oxford University Press.

Bakker, A. B., Schaufeli, W. B., Leiter, M. P., & Taris, T. W. (2008). Work engagement: An emerging concept in occupational health psychology. *Work & Stress, 22*, 187–200.

Balducci, C., Fraccaroli, F., & Schaufeli, W. B. (2010). Psychometric properties of the Italian version of the Utrecht Work Engagement Scale: A cross-cultural analysis. *European Journal of Psychological Assessment, 26*, 143–149.

Bargagliotti, A. (2011). Work engagement in nursing: A concept analysis. *Journal of Advanced Nursing, 68*, 1414–1428.

Barkhuizen, N., & Rothmann, S. (2006). Work engagement of academic staff in South African higher education institutions. *Management Dynamics, 15*(1), 38–48.

Barkhuizen, N., Rothmann, S., & Van de Vijver, A. J. R. (2014). Burnout and engagement of academics in higher education institutions: Effects of dispositional optimism. *Stress and Health, 30*(4), 322–332.

Barrick, M. R., Thurgood, G. R., Smith, T. A., & Courtright, S. H. (2015). Collective organizational engagement: Strategic implementation and firm performance. *Academy of Management Journal, 58*, 111–135.

Blau, P. (1964). *Exchange and power in social life*. New York, NY: Wiley.

Bono, J. E., & Judge, T. A. (2003). Self-concordance at work: Toward understanding the motivational effects of transformational leaders. *Academy of Management Journal, 46*, 554–571.

Buckingham, M. (2007). *Go put your strengths to work: Six powerful steps to achieve outstanding performance*. New York, NY: Free Press.

Burke, R. J., Koyuncu, M., Tekinkus, M., Bektas, C., & Fiksenbaum, L. (2012). Work engagement among nurses in Turkish hospitals: Potential antecedents and outcomes. *IS GUC: Industrial Relations and Human Resources Journal, 14*(1), 7–24.

Cheung, F. M., Van de Vijver, F. J. R., & Leong, F. T. L. (2011). Toward a new approach to the study of personality in culture. *American Psychologist, 66*, 593–603.

Christian, M. S., Garza, A. Z., & Slaughter, J. E. (2011). Work engagement: A quantitative review and test of its relations with task and contextual performance. *Personnel Psychology, 64*(1), 89–136.

Coyle-Shapiro, J. A., & Conway, N. (2004). The employment relationship through the lens of social exchange. In J. A. Coyle-Shapiro, L. M. Shore, S. Taylor, & L. Tetrick (Eds.), *The employment relationship: Examining psychological and contextual perspectives* (pp. 5–28). Oxford, UK: Oxford University Press.

Crawford, E. R., Rich, B. L., Buckman, B., & Bergeron, J. (2014). The antecedents and drivers of employee engagement. In C. Truss, R. Delbridge, E. Soane, K. Alfes, & A. Shantz (Eds.), *Employee engagement in theory and practice* (pp. 57–81). Abingdon, UK: Routledge.

Cropanzano, R., & Wright, T. A. (1999). A 5-year study of change in the relationship between well-being and job performance. *Consulting Psychology Journal: Practice and Research, 51*, 252–265.

Deci, E. L., & Ryan, R. M. (1985). *Intrinsic motivation and self-determination in human behavior*. New York, NY: Plenum Books.

Deci, E. L., & Ryan, R. M. (2008). Self-determination theory: A macro-theory of human motivation, development, and health. *Canadian Psychology, 49*(3), 182–185.

Deci, E. L., & Ryan, R. M. (2011). Levels of analysis, regnant causes of behavior and well-being: The role of psychological needs. *Psychological Inquiry, 22*, 17–22.

Deci, E. L., Ryan, R. M., Gagné, M., Léone, D. R., Usunov, J., & Kornazheva, B. P. (2001). Need satisfaction, motivation, and well-being in the work organizations of a former Eastern Bloc country. *Personality and Social Psychology Bulletin, 27*, 930–942.

Demerouti, E., Bakker, A. B., Nachreiner, F., & Schaufeli, W. B. (2001). The job demands-resources model of burnout. *Journal of Applied Psychology, 86*, 499–512.

Diedericks, E., & Rothmann, S. (2013). Flourishing of information technology professionals: The role of work engagement and job satisfaction. *Journal of Psychology in Africa*, *23*, 225–234.

Dik, B. J., & Duffy, R. D. (2008). Calling and vocation at work: Definitions and prospects for research practice. *The Counselling Psychologist*, *8*, 48–61.

Edmondson, A. (2004). Psychological safety and learning behavior in work teams. *Administrative Science Quarterly*, *44*, 350–383.

Feldt, T., Kivimäki, M., Rantala, A., & Tolvanen, A. (2004). Sense of coherence and work characteristics: A cross-lagged structural equation model among managers. *Journal of Occupational and Organizational Psychology*, *77*, 323–342.

Fouché, E. (2015). *Well-being of teachers in secondary schools.* Unpublished doctoral dissertation, North-West University, Vanderbijlpark, South Africa.

Gagné, M., & Deci, E. L. (2005). Self-determination theory and work motivation. *Journal of Organizational Behavior*, *26*, 331–362.

Gallup. (2013). *State of the global workplace: Employee engagement insights for business leaders worldwide.* Washington, DC: Gallup.

Graves, L. M., & Luciano, M. M. (2013). Self-determination at work: Understanding the role of leader–member exchange. *Motivation and Emotion*, *37*, 518–536.

Greguras, G. J., & Diefendorff, J. M. (2010). Why does proactive personality predict employee life satisfaction and work behaviors? A field investigation in the mediating role of the self-concordance model. *Personnel Psychology*, *63*, 539–560.

Hackman, J. R., & Oldham, G. R. (1980). *Work redesign.* Reading, MA: Addison-Wesley.

Hakanen, J. J., Schaufeli, W. B., & Ahola, K. (2008). The Job Demands-Resources model: A three-year cross-lagged study of burnout, depression, commitment, and work engagement. *Work & Stress*, *22*, 224–241.

Harter, J., & Adkins, A. (2015, April). What great managers do to engage employees. *Harvard Business Review.* Retrieved from: https://hbr.org/2015/04/what-great-managers-do-to-engage-employees

Harter, J. K., Schmidt, F. L., & Hayes, T. L. (2002). Business-unit-level relationship between employee satisfaction, employee engagement and business outcomes: A meta-analysis. *Journal of Applied Psychology*, *87*, 268–279.

Harter, J. K., Schmidt, F. L., & Keyes, C. L. (2002). Well-being in the workplace and its relationship to business outcomes: A review of the Gallup studies. In C. L. Keyes & J. Haidt (Eds.), *Flourishing: The positive person and the good life* (pp. 205–224). Washington, DC. American Psychological Association.

Hetland, H., Hetland, C., Andreassen, C. S., Pallesen, S., & Notelaers, G. (2011). Leadership and fulfillment of the three basic psychological needs at work. *Career Development International*, *16*, 507–523.

Hofstede, G., Hofstede, G. J., & Minkov, M. (2010). *Cultures and organizations: Software of the mind* (3rd ed.). New York, NY: McGraw-Hill.

Jackson, L. T. B., Rothmann, S., & Van de Vijver, A. J. R. (2006). A model of work-related well-being for educators in South Africa. *Stress and Health*, *22*, 263–274.

Jenkins, S., & Delbridge, R. (2013). Context matters: Examining "soft" and "hard" approaches to employee engagement in two workplaces. *International Journal of Human Resource Management*, *24*, 2670–2691.

Judge, T. A., Bono, J. E., & Locke, E. A. (2000). Personality and job satisfaction: The mediating role of job characteristics. *Journal of Applied Psychology*, *85*, 237–249.

Kahn, W. A. (1990). Psychological conditions of personal engagement and disengagement at work. *Academy of Management Journal*, *33*, 692–724.

Kahn, W. A., & Heaphy, E. D. (2014). Relational context of personal engagement at work. In C. Truss, R. Delbridge, E. Soane, K. Alfes, & A. Shantz (Eds.), *Employee engagement in theory and practice* (pp. 163–179). London, UK: Routledge.

Klassen, R. M., Aldhafri, S., Mansfield, C. F., Purwanto, E., Siu, A. F. Y., Wong, M. W., & Woods-McConney, A. (2012). Teachers' engagement at work: An international validation study. *The Journal of Experimental Education*, *80*, 317–337.

Kovjanic, S., Schuh, S. C., & Jonas, K. (2013). Transformational leadership and performance: An experimental investigation into the mediating effects of basic needs and work engagement. *Journal of Occupational and Organizational Psychology*, *86*, 543–555.

Kovjanic, S., Schuh, S. C., Jonas, K., Van Quaquebeke, N., & van Dick, R. (2012). How do transformational leaders foster positive employee outcomes? A self-determination based analysis of employees' needs as mediating links. *Journal of Organizational Behavior*, *33*, 1031–1052.

Lewis, S. (2011). *Positive psychology at work: How positive leadership and appreciative inquiry create inspiring organizations*. Oxford, UK: Wiley-Blackwell.

Linley, P. A. (2008). *Average to A+: Realising strengths in yourself and others*. Coventry, UK: CAPP Press.

Linley, P. A., Woolston, L., & Biswas-Diener, R. (2009). Strengths coaching with leaders. *International Coaching Psychology Review*, *4*(1), 20–41.

Lu, C., Sui, O., Chen, W., & Wang, H. (2011). Family mastery enhances work engagement in Chinese nurses: A cross-lagged analysis. *Journal of Vocational Behavior*, *78*, 100–109.

Lu, C., Wang, H., Lu, J., Du, D., & Bakker, A. B. (2014). Does work engagement increase person–job fit? The role of job crafting and job insecurity. *Journal of Vocational Behavior*, *84*, 142–152.

Macey, W. H., & Schneider, B. (2008). The meaning of employee engagement. *Industrial and Organizational Psychology*, *1*, 3–30.

MacLeod, D., & Clarke, N. (2009). *Engaging for success: Enhancing performance through employee engagement*. London, UK: Department of Business, Innovation and Skills.

Maslach, C., & Leiter, M. P. (1997). *The truth about burnout: How organizations cause personal stress and what to do about it*, San Francisco, CA: Jossey-Bass.

Mauno, S., Kinnunen, U., & Ruokolainen, M. (2007). Job demands and resources as antecedents of work engagement: A longitudinal study. *Journal of Vocational Behavior*, *70*, 149–171.

May, D. R., Gilson, R. L., & Harter, L. M. (2004). The psychological conditions of meaningfulness, safety and availability and the engagement of the human spirit at work. *Journal of Occupational and Organizational Psychology*, *77*, 11–37.

McAllister, D. J. (1995). Affect- and cognition-based trust as foundations for interpersonal cooperation in organizations. *Academy of Management Journal*, *38*, 24–59.

Mendes, F., & Stander, M. W. (2011). Positive organisation: The role of leader behaviour in employee engagement and turnover intention. *SA Journal of Industrial Psychology*, *37*(1). doi:10.4102/sajip.v37i1.900

Meyer, J. P. (2013). The science–practice gap and employee engagement: It's a matter of principle. *Canadian Psychology*, *54*, 235–245.

Milyavskaya, M., & Koestner, R. (2011). Psychological needs, motivation, and well-being: A test of self-determination theory across multiple domains. *Personality and Individual Differences*, *50*, 387–391.

Mone, E., Eisinger, C., Guggenheim, K., Price, B., & Stine, C. (2011). Performance management at the wheel: Driving employee engagement in organizations. *Journal of Business and Psychology*, *26*, 205–212.

Moorman, R. H., & Byrne, Z. S. (2005). What is the role of justice in promoting organizational citizenship behavior? In J. Greenberg & J. A. Colquitt (Eds.), *Handbook of organizational justice: Fundamental questions about fairness in the workplace* (pp. 355–380). Mahwah, NJ: Erlbaum.

Naudé, J. L. P., & Rothmann, S. (2004). The validation of the Utrecht Work Engagement Scale for emergency health technicians in Gauteng. *South African Journal of Economic and Management Sciences*, *7*, 459–468.

Olivier, A. L., & Rothmann, S. (2007). Antecedents of work engagement in a multinational oil company. *SA Journal of Industrial Psychology*, *33*(3), 49–56.

Peterson, C., Park, N., & Seligman, M. E. P. (2005). Orientations to happiness and life satisfaction: The full life versus the empty life. *Journal of Happiness Studies*, *6*, 25–41.

Poortinga, Y. H. (2011). Research on behaviour and culture: Current ideas and future projections. In F. J. R. van de Vijver, A. Chasiotis, & S. Breugelmans (Eds.), *Fundamental questions in cross-cultural psychology* (pp. 545–578). Cambridge, UK: Cambridge University Press.

Porath, C. (2014). Half of employees don't feel respected by their bosses. *Harvard Business Review*. Retrieved from https://hbr.org/2014/11/half-of-employees-dont-feel-respected-by-their-bosses

Porath, C., Spreitzer, G., Gibson, C., & Garnett, F. G. (2012). Thriving at work: Toward its measurement, construct validation, and theoretical refinement. *Journal of Organizational Behavior*, *33*, 250–275.

Pratt, M. G., & Ashforth, B. E. (2003). Fostering meaningfulness in work and working. In K. S. Cameron, J. E. Dutton, & R. E. Quinn (Eds.), *Positive organizational scholarship: Foundations of a new discipline* (pp. 309–327). San Francisco, CA: Berrett-Koehler.

Rees, C., Alfes, K., & Gatenby, M. (2013). Employee voice and engagement: Connections and consequences. *The International Journal of Human Resource Management*, *24*, 2780–2798.

Reissner, S., & Pagan, V. (2013). Generating employee engagement in public–private partnership: Management communication and employee experiences. *The International Journal of Human Resource Management*, *24*, 2741–2759.

Rhoades, L., & Eisenberger, R. (2002). Perceived organizational support: A review of the literature. *Journal of Applied Psychology*, *87*, 698–714.

Rich, B. L., LePine, J. A., & Crawford, E. R. (2010). Job engagement: Antecedents and effects on job performance. *The Academy of Management Journal*, *53*, 617–635.

Robertson, I. T., & Cooper, C. L. (2009). Full engagement: The integration of employee engagement and psychological well-being. *Leadership and Organization Development Journal*, *31*, 324–336.

Rothbard, N. P., & Patil, S. V. (2012). Being there: Work engagement and positive organizational scholarship. In K. S. Cameron & G. M. Spreitzer (Eds.), *The Oxford handbook of positive organizational scholarship* (pp. 56–68). New York, NY: Oxford University Press.

Rothmann, S. (2005, June). *Work engagement in South African organisations*. Paper presented at the 8th Annual Conference of the Society for Industrial and Organisational Psychology, Pretoria, South Africa.

Rothmann, S. (2013). From happiness to flourishing at work: A southern African perspective. In M. P. Wissing (Ed.), *Well-being research in South Africa: Cross-cultural advances in positive psychology* (Vol. 4, pp. 123–152). Dordrecht, the Netherlands: Springer.

Rothmann, S. (2014). Employee engagement in a cultural context. In C. Truss, R. Delbridge, E. Soane, K. Alfes, & A. Shantz (Eds.), *Employee engagement in theory and practice* (pp. 163–179). Abingdon, UK: Routledge.

Rothmann, S., & Buys, C. (2011). Job demands and resources, psychological conditions, religious coping, and work engagement of reformed church ministers. *Journal of Psychology in Africa*, *21*(2), 173–185.

Rothmann, S., & Hamukangandu, L. (2013). Psychological meaningfulness and work engagement among educators of Zambia. *SA Journal of Education*, *33*(2), 1–16.

Rothmann, S., & Joubert, J. H. M. (2007). Job demands, job resources, burnout and work engagement of management staff at a platinum mine in the North West Province. *South African Journal of Business Management*, *38*(3), 49–61.

Rothmann, S., & Pieterse, A. J. H. (2007). Predictors of work-related well-being in Sector Education and Training Authorities. *South African Journal of Economic and Management Sciences*, *10*, 298–312.

Rothmann, S., & Rothmann, S. (Jr). (2010). Factors associated with employee engagement in South Africa. *SA Journal of Industrial Psychology*, *36*(1), 1–12.

Rothmann, S., Strydom, M., & Mostert, K. (2006). A psychometric evaluation of the Job Demands-Resources Scale in South Africa. *SA Journal of Industrial Psychology*, *32*(4), 76–86.

Rothmann, S., & Welsh, C. (2013). Employee engagement in Namibia: The role of psychological conditions. *Management Dynamics*, *22*(1), 14–25.

Ryan, R. M., & Deci, E. L. (2000). Self-determination theory and the facilitation of intrinsic motivation, social development, and well-being. *American Psychologist*, *55*, 68–78.

Saks, A. M. (2006). Antecedents and consequences of employee engagement. *Journal of Managerial Psychology*, *21*, 600–619.

Salanova, M., Llorens, S., Cifre, E., Martinez, I., & Schaufeli, W. B. (2003). Perceived collective efficacy, subjective well-being and task performance among electronic work groups: An experimental study. *Small Group Research, 34*, 43–73.

Sanchez, P., & McCauley, D. (2006). Measuring and managing engagement in a cross-cultural workforce: New insights for global companies. *Global Business and Organizational Excellence, 26*(1), 41–50.

Schaufeli, W. B. (2014). What is engagement? In C. Truss, R. Delbridge, E. Soane, K. Alfes, & A. Shantz (Eds.), *Employee engagement in theory and practice* (pp. 15–35). London, UK: Routledge.

Schaufeli, W. B., & Bakker, A. B. (2004). Job demands, job resources and their relationship with burnout and engagement: A multi-sample study. *Journal of Organizational Behavior, 25*, 293–315.

Schaufeli, W. B., Salanova, M., González-Romá, V., & Bakker, A. B. (2002). The measurement of engagement and burnout: A two-sample confirmatory factor analytic approach. *Journal of Happiness Studies, 3*, 71–92.

Seligman, M. E. P. (2003). *Authentic happiness*. New York, NY: The Free Press.

Seligman, M. E. P. (2011). *Flourish: A new understanding of happiness and well-being – and how to achieve them*. London, UK: Nicolas Brealey.

Seligman, M. E. P., & Csikszentmihalyi, M. (2000). Positive psychology: An introduction. *American Psychologist, 55*, 5–14.

Shamir, B. (1991). Meaning, self and motivation in organizations. *Organization Studies, 12*, 405–424.

Shamir, B., House, R. J., & Arthur, M. B. (1993). The motivational effects of charismatic leadership: A self-concept based theory. *Organization Science, 4*, 577–593.

Sheldon, K. M., & Elliot, A. J. (1999). Goal striving, need satisfaction, and longitudinal well-being: The self-concordance model. *Journal of Personality and Social Psychology, 76*, 546–557.

Sheldon, K. M., & Gunz, A. (2009). Psychological needs as basic motives, not just experiential requirements. *Journal of Personality, 77*, 1467–1492.

Sheldon, K. M., & Houser-Marko, L. (2001). Self-concordance, goal attainment, and the pursuit of happiness: Can there be an upward spiral? *Journal of Personality and Social Psychology, 80*, 152–165.

Shimazu, A., Schaufeli, W. B., Miyanaka, D., & Iwata, N. (2010). Why Japanese workers show low work engagement: An item-response theory analysis of the Utrecht Work Engagement Scale. *BioPsychoSocial Medicine, 4*(17), 1–6.

Shuck, B. (2011). Integrative literature review: Four emerging perspectives of employee engagement: An integrative literature review. *Human Resource Development Review, 10*, 304–328.

Shuck, B., Ghosh, R., Zigarmi, D., & Nimon, K. (2012). The jingle jangle of employee engagement: Further exploration of the emerging construct and implications for workplace learning and performance. *Human Resource Development Review, 12*, 11–35.

Shuck, B., Reio, T., & Rocco, T. (2011). Employee engagement: An antecedent and outcome approach to model development. *Human Resource Development International, 14*, 427–445.

Soane, M. (2014). Leadership and employee engagement. In C. Truss, R. Delbridge, E. Soane, K. Alfes, & A. Shantz (Eds.), *Employee engagement in theory and practice* (pp. 149–162). London, UK: Routledge.

Soane, E., Truss, C., Alfes, K., Schantz, A., Rees, C., & Gatenby, M. (2013). Development and application of a new measure of employee engagement: The ISA Engagement Scale. *Human Resource Development International, 15*, 529–547.

Sonnentag, S. (2003). Recovery, work engagement, and proactive behavior: A new look at the interface between non-work and work. *Journal of Applied Psychology, 88*, 518–528.

Spreitzer, G. M. (1995). Psychological empowerment in the workplace: Dimensions, measurement and validation. *Academy of Management Journal, 38*, 1442–1465.

Steger, M. F., & Dik, B. J. (2010). Work as meaning. In P. A. Linley, S. Harrington, & N. Garcea (Eds.), *Oxford handbook of positive psychology and work* (pp. 131–142). Oxford, UK: Oxford University Press.

Steger, M. F., Littman-Ovadia, H., Miller, M., Menger, L., & Rothmann, S. (2013). Engaging in work even when it is meaningless: Positive affective disposition and meaningful work interact in relation to work-engagement. *Journal of Career Assessment, 21*, 348–361.

Storm, K., & Rothmann, S. (2003). The validation of the Utrecht Work Engagement Scale in the South African Police Services. *SA Journal of Industrial Psychology, 29*(4), 62–70.

Strümpfer, D. J. W. (1995). The origins of health and strength: From salutogenesis to fortigenesis. *South African Journal of Psychology, 25*(2), 81–89.

Strümpfer, D. J. W. (2005). Standing on the shoulders of giants: Notes on early positive psychology. *South African Journal of Psychology, 35*, 21–44.

Taipale, S., Selander, K., Anttila, T., & Nätti, J. (2011). Work engagement in eight European countries: The role of job demands, autonomy and social support. *International Journal of Sociology and Social Policy, 31*, 486–504.

Truss, K. [C.] (2014). The future of research in employee engagement. In D. Robinson & J. Gifford (Eds.), *The future of engagement: Thought piece collection* (pp. 80–87). Brighton, UK: Institute for Employment Studies.

Truss, C., Delbridge, R., Alfes, K., Shantz, A., & Soane, E. (2014). Introduction. In C. Truss, R. Delbridge, E. Soane, K. Alfes, & A. Shantz (Eds.), *Employee engagement in theory and practice* (pp. 1–11). London, UK: Routledge.

Truss, C., Shantz, A., Soane, E., Alfes, K., & Delbridge, R. (2013). Employee engagement, organisational performance and individual well-being: Exploring the evidence, developing the theory. *International Journal of Human Resource Management, 24*, 2657–2669.

Van den Broeck, A., Vansteenkiste, M., De Witte, H., & Lens, W. (2008). Explaining the relationships between job characteristics, burnout, and engagement: The role of basic psychological need satisfaction. *Work & Stress, 22*, 277–294.

Van Zyl, L., Deacon, E., & Rothmann, S. (2010). Towards happiness: Work–role fit, meaningfulness and engagement of industrial/organisational psychologists in South Africa. *SA Journal of Industrial Psychology, 36*(1), Art. #890. 10 pages.

Vinarski-Peretz, H., & Carmeli, A. (2011). Linking care felt to engagement in innovative behaviors in the workplace: The mediating role of psychological conditions. *Psychology of Aesthetics, Creativity, and the Arts, 5*(1), 43–53.

Wang, D., & Hsieh, C. (2013). The effect of authentic leadership on employee trust and employee engagement. *Social Behavior and Personality, 41*, 613–624.

Wrosch, C., & Scheier, M. F. (2003). Personality and quality of life: The importance of optimism and goal adjustment. *Quality of Life Research, 12*, 59–72.

Wrzesniewski, A. (2012). Callings. In K. S. Cameron & G. M. Spreitzer (Eds.). *The Oxford handbook of positive organizational scholarship* (pp. 45–55). New York, NY: Oxford University Press.

Wrzesniewski, A., Dutton, J. E., & Debebe, G. (2003). Interpersonal sensemaking and the meaning of work. *Research in Organizational Behaviour, 25*, 93–135.

Xanthopoulou, D., Bakker, A. B., Demerouti, E., & Schaufeli, W. B. (2009). Reciprocal relationships between job resources, personal resources, and work engagement. *Journal of Vocational Behavior, 74*, 235–244.

Yoerger, M., Crowe, J., & Allen, J. A. (2015). Participate or else! The effect of participation in meetings on employee engagement. *Consulting Psychology Journal: Practice and Research, 67*, 65–80.

19
Job Crafting

Gavin R. Slemp

Introduction

Paid employment is viewed and is indeed experienced in a variety of ways (Gini, 1998). For some people, it is a curse to which they are condemned, a burden imposed on them, an unfortunate obligation that takes their time away from the things that *really* matter in life. Perhaps not surprisingly, evidence suggests that for many the thought of going to work is accompanied by chronic stress and worrying (Scholtz, Hellhammer, Schulz, & Stone, 2004), an indication that for these people their jobs are unlikely to generate feelings of gleeful anticipation. Yet, evidence also suggests that for some people the opposite experience reflects their reality of work (Wrzesniewski, 2003; Wrzesniewski, McCauley, Rozin, & Schwartz, 1997). These people do not typically experience the pain, the drudgery, or the daily "grind" of work. Instead, they see it is a source of joy, something to look forward to because it provides a context to pursue and achieve goals, learn new skills, experience challenge, efficacy, and contribution, and to develop relationships with others. For these people, working often forms a central feature in their concept of self, and helps shape their understanding of who they are and why their lives matter. And for many others still, their experience of work lies between these two polar realities.

Irrespective of one's subjective quality of work experiences, working is typically a non-negotiable reality of adult living and research shows that paid employment has significant implications for adult psychological and physical health (Linn, Sandifer, & Stein, 1985; Repetti, Matthews, & Waldron, 1989; Steger & Dik, 2010). Despite working often being a significant source of worry and stress (Scholtz et al., 2004), one only has to examine the relationship between unemployment and ill health to understand the significance that work has in healthy living (see Jin, Shah, & Svoboda, 1995; Murphey & Athanasou, 1999). Further, research shows that even though humans are innately resilient and tend to positively adapt to negative or painful circumstances in life (e.g., Brickman, Coates, & Janoff-Bulman, 1978; Frederick & Lowenstein, 1999), a sustained period of unemployment

The Wiley Blackwell Handbook of the Psychology of Positivity and Strengths-Based Approaches at Work, First Edition. Edited by Lindsay G. Oades, Michael F. Steger, Antonella Delle Fave, and Jonathan Passmore.

is one of the few life circumstances to which humans have difficulty adapting and from which they often fail to return to their baseline psychological state (Clark, Diener, Georgellis, & Lucas, 2008; Lucas, Clark, Georgellis, & Diener, 2004). Hence, working and employment matter for a healthy adult life.

Once employed, the nature of the job has further implications for mental health and well-being (O'Brien & Feather, 1990). Accordingly, the last three decades have seen substantial scholarly inquiry into the employees' experience of work and what makes work enjoyable, meaningful, and engaging. While much of this research was guided by the theoretical assumption that employees are passive recipients of their work tasks and contexts (Fried & Ferris, 1987; Hackman & Oldham, 1976, 1980; Loher, Noe, Moeller, & Fitzgerald, 1985), more recently the perspective has shifted from the design of jobs to the job incumbents, suggesting that they take a more active role in shaping their tasks, their environment, and their overall experience of work (Wrzesniewski & Dutton, 2001; Wrzesniewski, LoBuglio, Dutton, & Berg, 2013).

One of these more recent theoretical perspectives is *job crafting*, which is defined as "the physical and cognitive changes individuals make in the task or relational boundaries of their work" (Wrzesniewski & Dutton, 2001, p. 179). Rather than making formal changes to position descriptions and the structural characteristics of jobs, job crafting is an agentic and informal process whereby employees take initiative to shift and push the task and relational boundaries of their jobs, potentially introducing a new understanding of what may be considered the entity of work (Wrzesniewski & Dutton, 2001).

It is the aim of this chapter to explore the concept of job crafting and to review the theoretical underpinnings about how it predicts relevant outcomes in the workplace, such as well-being, engagement, and mental health – focusing on self-determination theory (SDT) and the job demands-resources (JD-R) model. This chapter will also explore how the application of job crafting can potentially create greater coherence between the individual and the working environment, such that employees might create better alignment between their natural preferences and dispositions and the broader contexts in which they work. It will finish with some suggestions for future research.

Job Crafting and Its Subcomponents

Job crafting fits within the literature on employee proactivity, which suggests that employees do not just let their work happen to them, but instead they have an active role in shaping the nature of their work (Grant & Ashford, 2008). Some job redesign concepts that are related to job crafting, though conceptually distinct, are those such as expressing voice (Van Dyne & LePine, 1998), task revision (Staw & Boettger, 1990), role innovation (Van Maanen & Schein, 1979), or making idiosyncratic deals (Rousseau, 2005; see Tims & Bakker, 2010 for a description and review). While these concepts are about the proactive changes employees make to aid the redesign of their work roles, they are distinct from job crafting in that they are generally focused on resolving organizational problems and improving organizational effectiveness. Hence they do not necessarily contribute to a higher-quality work experience for employees, which some scholars have argued is a central feature of job crafting (e.g., Tims & Bakker, 2010). Job crafting also differs from concepts such as job enlargement and job enrichment (Parker, 1998), which are mediums through which the amount of work or the nature of work, respectively, are generally altered in a top-down way from management in order to enhance the quality of the work experience for employees. Hence, employee proactivity does not necessarily form a central feature of this type of job redesign.

Wrzesniewski and Dutton's (2001) original theoretical position on job crafting was that employees can proactively craft their jobs in three distinct ways, which they referred to as task, relational, and cognitive crafting. *Task crafting* involves shifting the "physical or temporal" qualities (Wrzesniewski et al., 2013, p. 283) that make up the job. Employees might add new tasks to (or remove tasks from) the job such that the physical nature of the work is changed. Similarly, employees might invest their time and effort more exclusively on a particular part of their job, such that the overall nature of the job is altered. Opting for additional challenge or complexity in one's role, placing an emphasis on those tasks that are more enjoyable, adding or reducing one's responsibility for different tasks, or perhaps embracing new tasks that do not naturally form part of one's work role are just some of the activities that have been suggested that might constitute task crafting. *Relational crafting* involves initiating changes to the social features of working and pushing the schematic relational boundaries of the job (Wrzesniewski & Dutton, 2001; Wrzesniewski et al., 2013). It might involve creating new relationships, limiting or ending toxic interactions or relationships, or taking steps to cultivate and strengthen positive relationships at work – all possible actions that alter the way in which the job is experienced. Further, employees might even just *think* about their work connections in a new way, potentially developing a greater sense of meaning and appreciation for the role that other people have in their work life (Wrzesniewski et al., 2013). Finally, *cognitive crafting* refers to shifting the cognitive boundaries that attribute meaning or significance to the tasks or relationships within the job. This can involve altering how one thinks about the job, such as by viewing it as a set of discrete tasks or as an integrated whole (Wrzesniewski & Dutton, 2001), or it can also involve ascribing purpose or significance to the work itself (Wrzesniewski et al., 2013). Cognitive crafting is the facet of job crafting that most closely aligns with work identity, which can be broadly characterized as a work-based "self-definition" that facilitates an understanding of the actions needed to be performed within a given occupation and the corresponding ways to effectively perform those actions (Ashforth & Kreiner, 1999; Wrzesniewski & Dutton, 2001). It also includes a stable idea of who one is at work, including both the personal attributes (e.g., assertiveness, ambition) and the social identities (e.g., male/female, manager) one holds (Ashforth & Kreiner, 1999; Walsh & Gordon, 2008). Through shaping the cognitions employees have about work, they are able to shift the meaning and significance they derive from their work experiences and potentially create a more positive or self-congruent work identity.

The three types of job crafting can overlap and it is quite plausible that one form of activity or agency in an organization might encompass multiple types of job crafting, potentially all three (see Wrzesniewski, Berg, & Dutton, 2010; Wrzesniewski & Dutton, 2001; Wrzesniewski et al., 2013 for a deeper discussion about the three components of job crafting with several examples). The temporal span of job crafting is also not fixed, but instead it can occur quickly, whereby employees craft their more immediate, day-to-day work experiences; it might also develop over longer periods of time (Wrzesniewski et al., 2013) and potentially be integrated into goal setting and other longer-term development planning.

Much of the theorizing on job crafting has placed the emphasis on individual agency and has thus focused on the individual level of analysis (to be explored shortly). However, there is also some evidence that job crafting occurs among workgroups who collectively modify how their work is to be organized and enacted. In one of the early empirical studies Leana, Appelbaum, and Shevchuck (2009) extended job crafting theory to incorporate both individual and "collaborative" job crafting – the latter described as team-members jointly determining how to modify their work to meet shared objectives. Using modified scales to capture the collaborative aspect of job crafting in a sample of 232 teachers and teaching aides, these authors found that individual and collaborative crafting are empirically distinct constructs. Further, collaborative crafting positively related with job performance, particularly for the less experienced teachers. The authors concluded that both collaborative and individual job crafting are distinct and important constructs that could be incorporated into future research.

The following section will explore the research findings on job crafting in more detail by exploring the possible consequences of job crafting and how it potentially benefits employees. This discussion will include a review of two theoretical models through which job crafting might create these valued outcomes in employees.

The Theoretical Underpinnings and Possible Consequences of Job Crafting

Job crafting, environmental integration, and self-determination

SDT (Deci & Ryan, 1985; Ryan & Deci, 2000a) is a metatheory of human motivation that posits that humans hold an innate drive to behave in self-directed, intrinsically motivated ways. It suggests that people are active, growth-oriented beings who seek a synthesis with their environment and to integrate themselves into larger social systems (Deci & Ryan, 2000). Through this process of integration, individuals pursue challenge and opportunities to use their natural talents and dispositions, thus acting in accordance with their internally driven, "true" selves (Ryan & Deci, 2002). Self-actualization, vitality, and integrity tend to occur when individuals successfully integrate and behave in accordance with their true selves, thus allowing for intrinsically motivated, self-determined, pursuits and behaviors (Deci & Ryan, 2008a, 2008b).

One subtheory of SDT – based on decades of research on intrinsic motivation and well-being (Deci & Ryan, 2008b) – suggests that humans contain a set of universal psychological needs that must be satisfied in order to attain optimal functioning and psychological health. These are the needs to feel autonomous, competent, and related to others. *Autonomy* requires a sense of volition and the perception that one's behavior is self-directed (Deci, 1975; Deci & Ryan, 1995). *Competence* requires feelings of mastery, attaining desired outcomes, and succeeding at challenging tasks (Deci & Ryan, 1980). *Relatedness* requires an ability to develop meaningful relationships with others and a sense of mutual respect and reliance with others (Baumeister & Leary, 1995). SDT defines the three needs as fundamental nutriments for human functioning, growth, and integrity. Accordingly, research has largely supported the importance of need satisfaction for psychological health and vitality, as well as vice versa – thwarting need satisfaction is related to various indices of ill-being (see Deci & Ryan, 2000; Ryan & Deci, 2000b; Vansteenkiste & Ryan, 2013).

The needs have also been explored within several different contexts, such as sport (e.g., Gagné, Ryan, & Bargmann, 2003; Reinboth & Duda, 2006; Reinboth, Duda, & Ntoumanis, 2004; Wilson, Rodgers, Blanchard, & Gessell, 2003), everyday life (e.g., Reis, Sheldon, Gable, Roscoe, & Ryan, 2000; Sheldon, Ryan, & Reis, 1996), and, importantly, at work. This latter body of research has generally shown that need satisfaction at work predicts enhanced work-related outcomes, such as motivation, engagement, well-being, and performance. Baard, Deci, and Ryan (2004), for example, investigated intrinsic need satisfaction as a motivational basis for performance and well-being in two different organizations. They showed that those employees who were generally higher in need satisfaction received higher performance evaluations and were higher in psychological adjustment.

Graves and Luciano (2013) supported these results and showed that psychological need satisfaction predicts autonomous motivation at work, which in turn predicts higher vitality, job satisfaction, and affective organizational commitment. Deci et al. (2001) found similar results but also included different cultures in the analysis. Specifically, they found support for a "self-determination model" in both U.S. and Bulgarian participants, whereby need satisfaction predicted enhanced engagement and self-esteem, as well as lower anxiety. Further research with European samples shows consistent patterns with Deci et al. (2001) (e.g., Van den Broeck, Vansteenkiste, De Witte, & Lens, 2008), showing that need satisfaction predicts low levels of exhaustion as well as enhanced vigor. Overall, research has largely supported these findings, suggesting that intrinsic need satisfaction is an important potential antecedent to workplace well-being (see Gagné & Deci, 2005; Van den Broeck, Vansteenkiste, & De Witte, 2008).

Job crafting presents opportunities for employees to integrate and meaningfully organize their experience of work into an authentic sense of self. By crafting their jobs, employees can better align their work experiences with their internally driven, true sense of self, potentially fostering and enabling more intrinsically motivated behaviors. In line with this view, Wrzesniewski and Dutton (2001) suggested that the impetus to engage in job crafting (though task, relational, or cognitive forms of crafting) arises from three important human motivations. First, humans are motivated to maintain control over their environment (see Bandura, 1989; Leotti, Lyengar, & Ochsner, 2010) and job crafting helps employees to attain a greater sense of control over their jobs and hence to avoid alienation from their work. Second, humans are driven to create a positive self-image in their own eyes (see Pyszczynski, Greenberg, Solomon, Arndt, & Schimel, 2004) and job crafting aids the striving toward self-enhancement through the creation of a more positive work identity. Finally, humans are driven by the need to belong and feel interpersonal connection (see Baumeister & Leary, 1995) and job crafting provides a way for employees to forge and foster connections with others.

While Wrzesniewski and Dutton (2001) did not explicitly link these three motivations with SDT, their conceptual similarity with the needs for autonomy, competence, and relatedness, respectively, is quite evident (Slemp & Vella-Brodrick, 2014). Hence, employees are perhaps motivated to craft their work experiences toward need-satisfying activities, which potentially allows for the better utilization of natural talents, dispositions, and work preferences. This process, in turn, likely enables progress toward more advanced integration and synthesis with the working environment and thus allows for the application of self-determined behaviors and pursuits. The pursuit of need-satisfying experiences at work should also have corresponding influences on employee functioning and well-being. This theoretical model was recently explored by Slemp and Vella-Brodrick (2014) in a sample of 253 working adults. Using structural equation modeling, their results showed that, as hypothesized, job crafting predicted intrinsic need satisfaction at work, which in turn predicted hedonic (e.g., pleasure, satisfaction) and eudaimonic (e.g., growth, mastery, fulfillment, etc.) well-being – measured with the Mental Health Continuum, Short Form (MHCSF; Keyes et al., 2008). Although this finding needs to be replicated with longitudinal or experimental data where the temporal ordering of the variables can be established more clearly, this study is consistent with the notion that job crafting is a potential mechanism through which employees satisfy their fundamental psychological needs at work, which enhances their experience of work, including their well-being.

This study is also consistent with research showing that job crafting potentially contributes to employee perceptions of person–job fit, typically defined as the perceived compatibility between the individual and their job characteristics (Kristof-Brown, Zimmerman, & Johnson, 2005). Lu, Wang, Lu, Du, and Bakker (2014), for example, explored the relation between job crafting and person–job fit in a two-wave longitudinal study of 246 Chinese employees in a technology firm. Specifically, these authors found support for a model in which engagement predicted job crafting, which in turn predicted demands–abilities fit (i.e., whether an employee's skills match the requirements of the job) and needs–supplies fit (i.e., whether the job represents what the employee is "looking for" in their work). A very similar finding was recently found in a sample of 246 Taiwanese hotel employees (Chen, Yen, & Tsai, 2014). Specifically, this study found that both individual and collaborative crafting were related to job engagement, and this relation was mediated by person–job fit. Hence, there is some evidence that job crafting is an antecedent to perceptions of person–job fit, and a possible reason for this is that job crafting allows employees to align the job with their intrinsic needs and preferences. However, it is worth noting that an important discrepancy between the Chen et al. (2014) and Lu et al. (2014) studies was where engagement was placed in the model – the former study hypothesized engagement as the antecedent whereas in the latter it was the outcome variable. Accordingly, there are some conflicting results about whether job crafting is an antecedent or outcome of work engagement and future research is obviously needed to better establish the causal ordering of the variables.

Qualitative research has also shown some support for these findings, suggesting that job crafting is a method employees use to align the job with their motivations for working. Berg, Grant, and Johnson (2010) conducted a qualitative investigation of 31 employees across a variety of sectors and found that various forms of agency associated with job crafting (e.g., adding tasks to the job, altering one's perception of one's role) were used to pursue "unanswered occupational callings" – which they defined as unrealized potential occupations that employees strongly desire because they expect to find them intrinsically enjoyable, meaningful, and consistent with their work identity. This finding suggests that job crafting may be a process employees use to facilitate the pleasurable psychological states that come with aligning the job they have with the job they expect to find more intrinsically enjoyable and meaningful.

In short, the evidence provides preliminary support for a theoretical process where employees engage in job crafting to align their work experiences with their intrinsically driven needs, motives, and preferences. By creating more advanced integration and alignment between themselves and the working context, employees are able to exercise more internally driven, intrinsically motivated pursuits and behaviors – potentially increasing their work engagement, well-being, and person–job fit.

Job crafting and the shaping of job demands and resources

At present there are two contrasting models that explain how employees engage in job crafting. As described above, Wrzesniewski and Dutton's (2001) original theoretical model posits that employees can craft their jobs in three distinct ways: through initiating changes to the tasks, the relationships, or the cognitions they have about their work. By initiating changes to these three features of the job, employees alter how the work is experienced and can shift the job toward more desired preferences, needs, and motives. Wrzesniewski and Dutton's (2001) model of job crafting contrasts with a more recent theoretical position put forward by proponents of the JD-R model of stress and engagement (Bakker & Demerouti, 2007; Bakker, Demerouti, & Schaufeli, 2003; Demerouti, Bakker, Nachreiner, & Schaufeli, 2000, 2001). As most of the empirical work on job crafting has focused on the JD-R model, it will be reviewed here before addressing how it relates to job crafting.

JD-R scholars describe the JD-R model as a balance theory of employee well-being, positing that exhaustion or engagement can arise from a disturbance in the equilibrium between two competing forces on employee health: the demands or resources experienced on the job. *Job demands* refers to the physical, psychological, social, and organizational features of a job that require sustained physical and mental effort, and are thus associated with corresponding physiological or psychological costs. A high-pressure job, for example, may lead employees to exercise sustained cognitive effort for longer working hours. Such a sustained effort depletes energy and can therefore lead to a range of costs, both physiological (e.g., fatigue, tiredness, tension) and psychological (e.g., disengagement, depression, burnout, anxiety). Other possible examples of job demands include changes in work tasks, emotional stresses, or computer problems. While this *strain* process explains the relationship between job demands and outcomes such as exhaustion and disengagement, a separate *motivational* process explains what helps individuals to maintain their physical and psychological health while under the pressure of job demands. *Job resources* refers to the physical, psychological, social, and organizational features of a job that offer employees any of a range of benefits, including (1) aiding the attainment of work goals; (2) stimulating learning, growth or development; or (3) reducing or "buffering" the experience of job demands and their associated psychological and physiological costs. Examples of job resources are autonomy, task feedback or advice, and role clarity.

Proponents of the JD-R model suggest that its dual processes play a role in the development of job strain and motivation both directly and through an interaction effect (see Bakker & Demerouti, 2007). Some studies offer some support for the dual process hypothesis. Bakker, Demerouti, and Schaufeli (2003), for example, examined job demands and resources in 447 Dutch call-center employees. They found that job demands (e.g., workload, computer problems) predicted health problems, which in turn predicted absenteeism – offering some support for the strain process. They also found that job resources (e.g., social support, feedback) predicted job involvement, which in turn predicted turnover intentions – offering some support for the motivational process. Hakanen, Bakker, and Schaufeli (2006) found similar results in a sample of 2,038 Finnish teachers. Specifically, this study found that job demands (e.g., pupil misbehavior) predicted burnout, and in turn ill health, whereas job resources (e.g., job control) predicted work engagement, and in turn organizational commitment. Other cross-sectional studies have largely shown similar results, offering support of the JD-R model across a variety of occupational groups (e.g., Bakker, Demerouti, Taris, Schaufeli, & Schreurs, 2003; Hakanen, Bakker, & Demerouti, 2005).

Tests of the JD-R model using longitudinal research designs are less common. However, the longitudinal studies to date have generally provided at least some support for its theoretical propositions. Hakanen, Schaufeli, and Ahola (2008) used cross-lagged tests of two waves of data over a 3-year period from a sample of 2,555 Finnish dentists. They found that job demands predicted future burnout, which in turn predicted depression. Although job resources predicted future work engagement, and in turn organizational commitment, the correlations in support of the motivational process were quite small in this study (e.g., $\gamma = .08$, $p < .01$ for job resources → work engagement). Schaufeli, Bakker, and van Rhenen (2009) examined the dual processes in a sample of 201 Dutch managers and executives and found stronger correlations for both processes in the model, though their data spanned only one year. Therefore, although longitudinal evidence shows some support for the dual processes, the relationships are generally much smaller than the cross-sectional evidence.

Although some research has provided support for the demands × resources interaction – suggesting that employee well-being is highest when job demands are low and job resources are present – the findings are more mixed. Xanthopoulou et al. (2007) used a cross-sectional design with 747 Dutch home care employees. Using moderated structural equation modeling, as well as synergistic tests, they found that high job demands coincided with high levels of exhaustion and cynicism, but only when job resources (i.e., feedback and opportunities for professional development) were low. The authors concluded that job resources buffer the effect of job demands on burnout. Bakker, Hakanen, Demerouti, and Xanthopoulou (2007) found support for 14 of 18 interaction tests in a sample of 805 Finnish teachers. Specifically, they largely found that job resources coincide with work engagement, particularly when job demands are high – concluding that job resources become more salient when demands are high.

Other studies have found more mixed results. Hu, Schaufeli, and Taris (2011) examined the additive and moderating effects of job demands and resources on burnout and engagement in two Chinese samples: 625 blue-collar employees and 761 health care professionals. While these authors found support for the strain and motivational processes in the model, they found only weak support for the relationship between the demands × resources interaction and burnout ($\gamma = -.08$, $p < .05$) in the health care sample, and in the blue-collar sample it was not significant. Moreover, the interaction failed to predict engagement in either sample. This is consistent with more recent research using cross-cultural comparisons between Australia and China, where the interaction tests largely failed to reach statistical significance (Brough et al., 2013). Overall, while the dual processes of the JD-R model have received relatively robust support with cross-sectional evidence, and to an extent the longitudinal evidence, the support for the demands × resources interaction is more mixed.

Although JD-R scholars were originally interested in the role of demands and resources as they were experienced through the design of jobs – hence taking the view that employees were passive recipients of their work context – more recent inquiry has adopted the view that employees take a more active role in shaping the demands and resources they experience on the job (e.g., Tims & Bakker, 2010; Tims, Bakker, & Derks, 2012). Hence, these authors frame their conceptualization of job crafting[1] within the JD-R model by suggesting that employees craft their jobs through actions that shift the levels of job demands and resources in desired directions. More specifically, this model posits that employees craft their work in four possible ways: (1) increasing their structural job resources (e.g., taking opportunities to learn new things, taking steps to develop themselves): (2) increasing social job resources (e.g., requesting feedback and advice, taking opportunities to be mentored); (3) decreasing hindering job demands (e.g., minimizing contact with people whose expectations are unrealistic, avoiding difficult decisions); or (4) increasing challenging job demands (e.g., starting new projects when time allows for it, volunteering to work on projects that aid learning or promote a sense of challenge) (Tims & Bakker 2010; Tims et al., 2012).

Through shaping the demands and resources experienced at work, employees are able to drive changes to their job characteristics and, in turn, contribute to work engagement, less burnout, and increased performance. This theoretical model has received some empirical support. Tims, Bakker, and Derks (2013), for example, conducted a longitudinal investigation on 288 chemical plant employees. They showed that employees who crafted

[1] The term "job demands-resources crafting" (JD-R crafting) is used hereafter to describe this conceptualization of job crafting that is based on the JD-R model, theorized as self-initiated modifications specifically to one's job demands and resources. Although scholars within this literature refer to this process as "job crafting," this theoretical approach conceptually differs from the original job crafting theory model by Wrzesniewski and Dutton (2001) – consisting of the task, relational, and cognitive crafting subcomponents. Hence, to avoid confusion the two approaches to job crafting are distinguished in this chapter.

their work such that they increased their job resources during the first month of the study experienced enhanced well-being (i.e., increased engagement and job satisfaction, and less burnout) over the course of the study than those who did not engage in JD-R crafting. More recently, Petrou, Demerouti, and Schaufeli (2015, March 23) examined two-wave longitudinal data from 580 police officers undergoing organizational change over a 1-year period. They found that seeking job resources and job challenges at Time 1 predicted higher task performance and lower exhaustion at Time 2 (after the organizational change was implemented). The findings suggest that JD-R crafting is a potential strategy for employees to cope with organizational change. These findings have been extended to the team level, where it has been found that collaborative JD-R crafting predicts team-level performance and engagement (McClelland, Leach, Clegg, & McGowan, 2014; Tims, Bakker, Derks, & van Rhenen, 2013).

Nielsen and Abildgaard (2012) modified the JD-R crafting model to capture further elements of job demands that are more relevant for blue-collar employees. These authors found that some aspects of JD-R crafting (i.e., increasing challenging job demands and quantitative job demands) predicted work engagement 12 months later. Although increasing quantitative job demands and social job resources predicted job satisfaction after 12 months, none of the JD-R crafting facets predicted burnout at follow-up (all p's > .05). More recent research has largely supported these findings, suggesting that JD-R crafting is related to work engagement (e.g., Brenninkmeijer & Hekkert-Koning, 2015).

While the vast majority of the empirical research on job crafting and JD-R crafting is correlational, recently a study was conducted to test the potential individual consequences of a JD-R crafting intervention in a sample of Dutch police ($n = 39$) (van den Heuvel, Demerouti, & Peeters, 2015). The intervention consisted of a full-day training where participants learned about the JD-R model and subsequently generated work goals based on crafting their work by seeking resources (e.g., asking a colleague for feedback), reducing hindering demands (e.g., making use of travel time to type up reports), and seeking challenging demands (e.g., participating in a negotiation to build negotiation skills). Participants then worked on their goals over a 4-week period which focused on making these self-initiated modifications to their job demands and resources. Results indicated some preliminary support for the efficacy of the intervention. For example, at post-test, the intervention group recorded enhanced opportunities for development, leader–member exchange, and self-efficacy, as well as lower negative affect. While none of these differences were observed in the control group, the time × group interaction (which considers the intervention and control groups simultaneously) failed to reach statistical significance on any of the outcomes. While further work is clearly needed using larger samples, the study presents promising results for the efficacy of interventions in enhancing work outcomes for employees.

In sum, proponents of the JD-R model suggest that people craft their jobs by shaping the job demands and job resources they face at work. While this view offers a unique theoretical perspective, a limitation is that it does not account for the role that cognitions have in shaping work identity (Slemp & Vella-Brodrick, 2013). Another potential limitation is that it offers a somewhat prescriptive view of how employees might shape their experience of work for the better. Accordingly, it is unclear whether actions that conform to the original theoretical model of job crafting (e.g., people who craft their job by *decreasing* their social interactions at work – such as hairdressers who "fire clients," Wrzesniewski & Dutton, 2001, p. 191) might fall outside the conceptual space of the JD-R model. Nonetheless, the literature on the whole suggests that JD-R crafting might be a promising method for employees to potentially enhance their work engagement and performance, as well as reduce levels of burnout.

Job Crafting in an Organizational Context: Contextual Correlates and Undesired Potential Outcomes

Contextual correlates of job crafting

Job crafting is typically viewed as a form of proactive behavior or intentional agency that has positive implications for both individuals and organizations. Yet few studies have explored contextual variables that potentially impede, limit, or, conversely, enable employees' capacity to craft their jobs in organizations. Consistent with several studies showing that job autonomy is a contextual antecedent to agentic behavior in organizations (Crant, 2000; Parker, Williams, & Turner, 2006), the extent to which employees have the autonomy, or perceived autonomy, to initiate changes to their experience of work is likely to influence their ability to implement job crafting. Petrou, Demerouti, Peeters, Schaufeli, & Hetland (2012) found preliminary support for this using a daily diary measure of job autonomy and JD-R crafting. These authors found that in "active jobs" – defined as jobs that are not only highly demanding but also provide high job control – employees typically engage in more JD-R crafting. More specifically, using moderated structural equation modeling, they found that the combination of day-level work pressure and day-level job autonomy predicted day-level seeking resources and day-level reducing demands. Within the SDT literature, a similar social-contextual factor that has received some research attention is autonomy support (Baard et al., 2004; Deci, Connell, & Ryan, 1989), which is defined as an interpersonal orientation by those in positions of leadership or authority that supports the inner motivational resources of their employees. For example, autonomy supportive managers take steps to acknowledge and understand subordinates' perspectives, offer opportunities for choice and volition, and encourage self-initiation (Deci et al., 2001). Conversely, managers with a controlling style – generally considered the antipode of an autonomy supportive style – will tend to place pressure on their staff to think, feel, or behave in a particular way.

As job crafting is a form of proactive behavior self-initiated by employees, autonomy-supportive work contexts are theoretically more likely to enable this type of workplace agency. In other words, employees will craft their jobs to the extent to which they feel they have the autonomy and scope to initiate changes to their experience of work. Yet at the same time research shows that the work context is not stable and fixed, but rather is malleable to change (Berg, Wrzesniewski, & Dutton, 2010), suggesting that employees can initiate changes to produce more autonomy supportiveness into their roles. Berg, Wrzesniewski, and Dutton (2010) coined the term "adaptive moves" to describe the cognitive or behavioral responses that employees make to overcome perceived challenges to initiating job crafting. In this study, one adaptive move relevant for lower-ranked employees in particular, who might typically experience lower levels of autonomy support, was to change others' expectations and behaviors toward their work environments in order to enable more scope for job crafting.

Taken together, these findings suggest a possible reciprocal relationship between job crafting and autonomy support – where employees can engage in more job crafting in contexts in which they enjoy a high-level of perceived autonomy supportiveness, and vice versa; the work context is malleable and employees can craft more autonomy supportiveness into their roles. This process was supported by a recent cross-sectional study that found job crafting and autonomy support were reciprocally related (Slemp, Kern, & Vella-Brodrick, 2015). This study also found a synergistic relationship between job crafting and autonomy support with employee well-being. The synergistic relationship suggests that even though job crafting and autonomy support independently predicted employee well-being, well-being tended to be highest when both autonomy support and job crafting were present. Although it needs to be replicated with longitudinal data, these findings offer preliminary evidence of a process in organizations where both job crafting and autonomy support may reciprocally enable one another, which potentially has promising effects for employee well-being.

Some research also suggests that job crafting might be an employee-driven response to the experience of work-related boredom. For example, while certain personality factors (e.g., boredom proneness; Vodanovich, 2003) predict boredom, research also suggests that boredom is created through social-contextual factors (e.g., too little work, repetition, monotony; Loukidou, Loan-Clarke, & Daniels, 2009). To examine the relationship between work-related boredom and self-regulatory behaviors such as job crafting (which they operationalized as JD-R crafting), van Hooff and van Hooft (2014) conducted a 1-month longitudinal investigation among a sample of 189 Dutch employees. They found that employees who were experiencing higher boredom at work were more likely to seek to increase their challenging job demands and their structural job resources. Accordingly, JD-R crafting is a potential coping mechanism employees might use to manage work-related boredom and its adverse potential consequences.

In sum, the literature supports a set of relationships where autonomy-supportive work climates predict job crafting, and indicates that employees can also take action to craft more autonomy supportiveness into their roles. Moreover, work contexts that are likely to produce work-related boredom may drive employees to craft the job in order to lessen the negative experience of boredom at work.

Is there a downside to job crafting?

While much of the research on job crafting has been conducted under the assumption that it has positive consequences for employees and organizations, recent research is beginning to emerge showing that it also has a potential downside. Much of this research has focused on JD-R crafting. For example, one study examined JD-R crafting within dyads, focusing on whether crafting by one team member was related to the job characteristics and well-being of his or her partner (Tims, Bakker, & Derks, 2015,). The study found that when one team member sought to reduce their hindering job demands, the partner was more likely to report a higher workload and conflict, which in turn predicted partner burnout. While the findings are correlational, they are consistent with the pattern that some types of JD-R crafting might consist of shifting responsibility for particular tasks to team members, which may have a corresponding impact on partner workload and burnout. Other recent studies have found similar undesirable potential correlates. Demerouti, Bakker, and Halbesleben (2015), for example, conducted a daily diary study over a period of 5 days to determine whether daily JD-R crafting was related to daily job performance (which they operationalized with measures of self-reported task performance, altruism, and counterproductive work behavior). They found that daily reportings of seeking job resources was positively related to daily task performance, which was potentially explained by employee autonomy and work engagement correspondingly increasing over the 5 days. However, on days where employees sought to reduce their job demands, their daily task performance was *lower* – perhaps explained by employee workloads and work engagement decreasing over the 5 days. Interestingly, on days where employees sought more challenges they also tended to show more counterproductive work behavior (e.g., hiding mistakes, gossiping, etc.). Hence, this study shows a potential negative side effect of both reducing job demands and increasing challenges. One further study has shown an unfavorable potential outcome of JD-R crafting (Petrou et al., 2015). These authors found that seeking to reduce job demands is positively related to employee exhaustion one year later. While the correlation was quite small, a possible explanation for this effect is that employees who seek to reduce their workload might put less effort into their tasks, which potentially increases their workload and aggravates their exhaustion.

Overall, while much of the research on job crafting indeed shows that it has valued correlates and empirical outcomes, some studies have shown that there are also unfavorable potential consequences. In particular, it appears that when employees craft their job by seeking to reduce their job demands, they may do so by transferring their tasks to their colleagues. Moreover, it is possible that during the process of reducing their job demands they also put less effort into their own tasks, which potentially increases their exhaustion.

Methods of Job Crafting: An SDT Approach

There are various models available that offer accounts about how employees might craft their jobs in order to alter their experience of work for the better. Some authors have offered suggestions that align with the facets of task, relational, and cognitive crafting (e.g., Berg, Dutton, & Wrzesniewski, 2013; Wrzesniewski et al., 2010). Similarly, much of the empirical literature thus far has focused on the JD-R model, suggesting that employees should focus their attention on shifting their job demands and resources in desired directions (Tims et al., 2012; Tims, Bakker, & Derks, 2013). As these theoretical applications have been extensively covered elsewhere, this section will focus on possible methods of job crafting that align with SDT. Accordingly, it will focus primarily on ways job crafting could aid employees to integrate their natural preferences and dispositions into their work experiences, potentially enabling greater alignment between the individual and the working environment. Some scholars have made a useful start toward this end. The Job Crafting Exercise (Berg Dutton, Wrzesniewski, & Baker, 2008), for example, is a practical tool that aims to assist employees to identify and use their inner motives, passions, and strengths at work, which, theoretically, should help employees better integrate with the work environment. This section will further explore relevant concepts in the literature that, if enacted on the job, might help employees craft their tasks, relationships, or cognitions to align with their intrinsic preferences and dispositions.

Task crafting

Pursuing self-concordance Goal setting forms an important function in most jobs and careers, as well as being a useful way for employees to push their task boundaries in the pursuit of personal aspirations. Several goal-setting models and frameworks exist (see Locke & Latham, 2002), but the goal self-concordance approach (Sheldon, 2014; Sheldon & Elliot, 1998, 1999) is a useful goal-setting framework for aligning the experience of work with the needs of the self. The model suggests that goals that originate from the deepest point of human agency – the integrated self where one's most inner and authentic interests, values, needs, and motives lie – are where employees can craft a more integrated and intrinsically motivating experience of work. Further, self-concordant goals are more likely to be attained because they lead to more persistent goal effort (Koestner, Lekes, Powers, & Chicoine, 2002; Sheldon & Elliot, 1998, 1999). Similarly, evidence suggests that self-concordant goals help to enable optimal psychological functioning, including motivation, satisfaction, and well-being (Sheldon, 2014; Sheldon & Houser-Marko, 2001; Sheldon, Ryan, Deci, & Kasser, 2004). For goals to be self-concordant, they must be (1) autonomous and volitional, and (2) intrinsically motivating and rewarding, presumably because the goals reflect innate psychological needs such as those for autonomy, competence, and relatedness (Deci & Ryan, 2000).

Although much of the self-concordant motivation literature has focused on students, goal self-concordance is very relevant to the workplace, which offers individuals a context for goal pursuits. Therefore, consistent with the notion that job crafting can develop over long periods of time (Wrzesniewski et al., 2013), it is possible that employees can craft their task boundaries in the pursuit of self-concordant work goals. Self-concordant goals represent people's interests and passions, as well as their central values and beliefs. By generating and pursuing objectives that reflect this but are also are relevant to the job, employees can potentially reshape their work toward a more meaningful, engaging, and intrinsically driven experience. In particular, self-concordant goals offer employees a way to integrate activities that are deeply enjoyable, interesting, and intrinsically valuable – areas of passion (Vallerand et al., 2003) – into their work. Supporting this, studies have found that self-concordant goal pursuits at work predict life satisfaction and self-reported goal attainment (Judge, Bono, Erez, & Locke, 2005; study 2). Ultimately, pursuing self-concordance may help employees craft new organization into their work tasks and allow them to steer their work in desired and meaningful directions (Sheldon, 2014).

Using strengths and talents While proponents of self-concordant goals are concerned with sources of motivation for work, employees might also craft their tasks by re-orienting their attention toward leveraging what they are naturally "good at" in relation to their work. Put simply, employees might look for ways to use areas of strength – defined broadly as the individual characteristics that allow people to perform well or at their personal best (Wood, Linley, Maltby, Kashdan, & Hurling, 2011). By doing so, employees are able to push their task boundaries by focusing their energy on doing what they naturally do well and that which they find energizing. As an example, a qualitative study found that a customer service representative who was very skilled and talented with computers took steps to become the "go-to person" for his colleagues when they required computer-related assistance (Berg, Wrzesniewski, & Dutton, 2010). While being expert with computers is a useful but perhaps unnecessary skill for a customer service assistant, offering his expertise to colleagues enabled this individual to add desirable tasks to his job and was a way in which he was able to exercise an area of strength at work.

There is now a strong literature on the mental health correlates and outcomes that follow from using strengths (Peterson & Seligman, 2004; Seligman, Steen, Park, & Peterson, 2005), and Gallup strengths data suggest that using strengths at work may help employees to become more engaged (see Clifton & Harter, 2003; Harter, Schmidt, & Hayes, 2002; Hodges & Clifton, 2004). Moreover, evidence suggests that using strengths predicts intrinsic need satisfaction (Linley, Nielsen, Gillett, & Biswas-Diener, 2010), suggesting that, similar to self-concordant goals, strengths perhaps reflect inner preferences or dispositions and that using strengths at work is a way to better integrate with the work context. Accordingly, identifying tasks and opportunities to use strengths at work is a promising way in which employees can re-orient their jobs toward the use of their natural talents and dispositions, which may help them to integrate what they naturally do well into their working environment.

Relational crafting

Aligning work with preferences for sociality Humans are strongly and deeply driven by the need to feel belongingness and connection with others (see Baumeister & Leary, 1995). Given the workplace provides a context for people to exist in close proximity for extended periods of the day (or night), it offers an important medium through which they can satisfy this fundamental need. Yet the way in which people develop and cultivate relationships is idiosyncratic and, through relational crafting, people can potentially tailor how they cultivate work-based connections based on individual needs and preferences. As an example, the workplace generally offers people the opportunity to invest and integrate into larger spheres of social relationships as well as the opportunity to develop and foster more dyadic, personal, and nurturing relationships with others (see Baumeister & Sommer, 1997), such as those experienced in high-quality connections (Dutton & Heaphy, 2003). Depending on individual needs and preferences, employees might craft their jobs so that they can orient toward larger spheres of social relations (e.g., joining, chairing, or creating committees; joining or leading large project, cross-functional, or hierarchical teams), whereas others might craft their jobs toward smaller numbers of close relationships (e.g., opting to coach or mentor others, opting to receive coaching or mentoring; collaborating on smaller project teams).

Personality and dispositional characteristics may also influence preferences about how employees relate to others. Perhaps one of the more obvious personality characteristics to potentially influence relational preferences, given sociality is one of its central features, is introversion–extraversion. Although introverts and extraverts both tend to be happier when they have solid social connections (Hotard, McFatter, McWhirter, & Stegall, 1989), they may opt to forge connections in different ways. Eysenck's (1967) early view of the trait suggested that extraverted people require more social stimulation to satisfy their higher threshold for arousal, while introverts, endowed with a lower arousal threshold, perhaps require less social interaction. Such a view would suggest that for some people it may make more sense to deepen and strengthen the quality of their existing relationships than to take opportunities to establish new relationships with broad networks and wide groups of people. A more recent perspective suggests that a central feature of extraversion is agency – a more general disposition encompassing factors such as ambition, dominance, assertiveness, efficacy, achievement, and exhibitionism (Depue & Collins, 1999). This perhaps suggests that employees high on extraversion might enjoy crafting leadership activities into their roles, or pursuing situations where their skills can be put on display. Such factors might also be considered during career mobility. For example, whereas some people could strive for positions that involve leading or managing large groups of people, others may be more suited to progress their career in different ways (e.g., opting to extend their skills and expertise).

Cognitive crafting

Crafting meaningful cognitions about work Despite few empirical studies having explored cognitive crafting, theorizing by organizational scholars has uncovered a variety of ways in which people can craft more meaningful and positive cognitions about their work, potentially more congruent with their work identity. This is particularly revealing within the literature on "dirty work," which refers broadly to occupations that are necessary for a functional society, but are considered low-status, stigmatized, degrading, or "tainted" in either a physical, social, or moral sense (Ashforth & Kreiner, 1999; Ashforth, Kreiner, Clark, & Fugate, 2007). Ashforth and Kreiner (1999, 2013) suggest that occupations can be physically tainted if they are associated with garbage, death, or human waste (e.g., funeral director, janitor) or if they are dangerous (e.g., soldier, miner). Occupations can be socially tainted if they involve regular contact with stigmatized groups (e.g., prison guard, psychiatric ward attendant) or if the worker appears to adopt a subservient role to others (e.g., shoe-shiner, butler, maid). Finally, jobs can be morally tainted if they are regarded as sinful and/or appear to be devoid of moral principle or virtue (e.g., exotic dancer, sex worker, abortion worker). Yet even though many of these occupations are stigmatized, research suggests that employees within them develop strong workgroup cultures as particular ideologies become shared among the groups' members (see Ashforth & Kreiner, 1999).

Ashforth and Kreiner (1999, 2013) describe three cognitive strategies through which "dirty workers" are able to transform the meaning of the work by negating its negative attributions and instead associating it with positive qualities. First, workers can engage in *reframing*, which involves flooding the stigma of the work with positive value, ultimately wearing it as a "badge of honor" (e.g., a funeral director might see that they are facilitating the grieving process for the bereaved rather than profiting from their loss). Second, workers can use a technique known as *recalibrating*, which involves adjusting the evaluative standards against which the work tasks are assessed. By utilizing this technique, seemingly insignificant and unimportant tasks can be recalibrated as necessary and even fundamental for human kind (Ashforth & Kreiner, 1999, 2003; Dik, Duffy, & Eldridge, 2009). For example, a hospital cleaner might note the importance of their role for the safe delivery of routine and complicated medical procedures (Dutton, Debebe, & Wrzesniewski, 2012). While reframing involves transforming the stigmatized properties of a job into positive qualities, workers can also shift their attention from the stigmatized features of the job to its non-stigmatized features – a cognitive strategy called *refocusing* (Ashforth & Kreiner, 1999, 2013). This can involve shifting attention to positive extrinsic features of the job (such as high pay or flexible hours) or it can involve shifting attention to its positive intrinsic qualities (such as the pleasantness associated with working outdoors). The three cognitive shaping strategies allow employees to further appreciate the features of the job that are enjoyable, beneficial, or that serve to make the job worthy of their time, energy, and motivation.

While these three cognitive shaping strategies were initially conceptualized as ways in which "dirty workers" create a more positive work identity, it is quite easy to envisage how they could also be useful for other occupational groups that are not considered in the domain of dirty work. For example, employees within high-stress occupations (e.g., teachers/social workers; Johnson et al., 2005) might choose to redirect their attention and reflect on those parts of the job that are less stressful or more enjoyable (*refocusing*). Men or women working in traditionally gender-imbalanced occupations might see their minority status as a source of pride and inspiration for others with similar aspirations in that line of work, hence wearing it as a badge of honor (*reframing*; e.g., Eisenberg, 1999; O'Lynn, 2007). Commercial aircraft pilots might spend some time reflecting on their vital function for global businesses heavily reliant on international travel for the successful operations of geographically distributed subsidiaries (*recalibrating*; Beaverstock, Derudder, Faulconbridge, & Witlox, 2009). Ultimately, such cognitive crafting strategies give employees a way to ascribe greater meaning and purpose to the tasks and to their job more broadly, which may also help to align it with their intrinsic motives for doing such work.

Future Research

Until recently, most of the inquiry into job crafting provided a theoretical review or a qualitative investigation into the construct (e.g., Berg, Grant, & Johnson, 2010; Berg, Wrzesniewski & Dutton, 2010; Fried, Grant, Levi, Hadani & Slowik, 2007; Lyons, 2008; Wrzesniewski & Dutton, 2001). While this research was particularly important to help consolidate what constitutes job crafting and how it potentially differs from similar forms of proactive workplace behavior (Tims et al., 2012), only a few studies had made attempts to study it using quantitative methods (e.g., Ghitulescu, 2006; Leana et al., 2009). The empirical research showed promising desired potential correlates and outcomes of job crafting, including job satisfaction, commitment, performance, and absenteeism. However, the scales used were context-specific (manufacturing and education, respectively) and hence were not appropriate for use with the general working population. Consequently, recent attempts have been made to address this deficiency and thus produce scales that are more applicable and relevant for general working populations (e.g., Slemp & Vella-Brodrick, 2013; Tims et al., 2012). Accordingly, empirical research on job crafting has increased substantially over the past three years.

Nonetheless, there are still some significant limitations with much of the existing literature and future research is needed to address these. First, many studies have used cross-sectional methods (Slemp & Vella-Brodrick, 2014; Slemp et al., 2015; Tims, Bakker, Derks, & van Rhenen, 2013), longitudinal self-report data (Nielsen & Abildgaard, 2012; Tims, Bakker, & Derks, 2013), or daily diary methods (e.g., Demerouti et al., 2015; Petrou et al., 2012; Tims, Bakker, & Derks, 2014) and we still need to better understand whether job crafting is a causal factor in creating enhanced employee engagement and well-being, or merely a by-product. While a recent study has made a promising start with a quasi-experimental field intervention (van den Heuvel et al., 2015), the results are preliminary and future research efforts can extend this study by using larger samples, randomization, and longer follow-up periods. Such methods will better establish whether job crafting is a causal factor in enhancing the employee experience of work. Second, the existing measures are quite prescriptive about the types of activities that constitute job crafting (e.g., Ghitulescu, 2006; Leana et al., 2009; Slemp & Vella-Brodrick, 2013; Tims et al., 2012). Accordingly, they are only capable of capturing a limited range of information and are thus restricted in their ability to fully capture the breadth of activities that might constitute job crafting within the working environment. Future studies might consider moving beyond self-report survey data and instead exploring potentially more rigorous indicators of job crafting and well-being within naturalistic settings. For example, day reconstruction (Kahneman, Krueger, Schkade, Schwarz, & Stone, 2004) or experience sampling (Csikszentmihalyi & Larson, 1987) would provide useful and rich insight into the potential situational or temporal predictors of job crafting, as well as its real-time correlates and potential consequences. In particular, it would potentially account for a fuller range of agency that might constitute job crafting rather than the comparatively limited range that can be captured through the current self-report tools.

Third, future research should also further explore the situational, contextual, or "top-down" variables that moderate job crafting in organizations. Indeed, a possible criticism of job crafting is its emphasis on individual responsibility in creating a more optimal experience of work, potentially at the expense of those factors that are often beyond the employee's direct control but clearly affect the subjective quality of the working experience. While the concept of job crafting is promising because it suggests individuals can play a role in shaping how they approach their job – individual agency in organizations, including job crafting, is typically influenced by a variety of contextual factors within organizations (e.g., management, job design, climate) (see Johns, 2006). Future research needs to explore the variety of "top-down" or contextual factors that may interact with the employee's ability to enact job crafting and the consequent effect on employee mental health outcomes. Such a line of research will strengthen our understanding of how the organizational context shapes workplace behavior and employee mental health, ultimately informing best practices in management to better enable job crafting in organizations.

Finally, most of the current research on job crafting has studied its positive correlates and consequences and we still need a better understanding of its potential negative consequences or possible side effects. More recent studies are beginning to explore these questions (as reviewed earlier), and future studies need to continue this line of research, exploring more distal potential consequences of job crafting (e.g., organizational performance). Furthermore, research needs to incorporate the use of more objective data (e.g., absenteeism, performance review metrics) to better establish its correlates beyond self-report data.

Conclusions

Job crafting offers employees a novel way in which they can alter their subjective experience of work. Two theoretical processes explain how this might occur. First, job crafting offers a potential process employees can use to better align the job with their intrinsic preferences, potentially enabling greater coherence and consistency between their internally driven, authentic selves and their working context. This process of alignment potentially allows for the satisfaction of intrinsic psychological needs and enhanced employee well-being. Goal self-concordance, using strengths and talents, aligning work with idiosyncratic preferences for sociality, and crafting meaningful cognitions about work are just some of the ways employees might align their work with their intrinsic interests and needs. A second theoretical model is that it presents an opportunity for employees to change the job demands and resources they face at work, which may ultimately aid their ability to shape their job characteristics and, in turn their work engagement and well-being. Job crafting is correlated with autonomy-supportive work environments and employees are more likely to use job crafting when they work in environments where they feel bored. Further, while job crafting generally has positive consequences, it can have unfavorable potential outcomes – particularly when employees seek to reduce their job demands by transferring tasks to their team members or placing less effort into their tasks. Nonetheless, job crafting gives people a way to inject new organization into their work experiences, allowing them to steer their work tasks, relationships, and cognitions in a direction that is consistent with their intrinsic motives and preferences, ultimately creating a different, more intrinsically driven experience of the job.

References

Ashforth, B. E., & Kreiner, G. E. (1999). "How can you do it?": Dirty work and the challenge of constructing a positive identity. *Academy of Management Review*, *24*, 413–434. doi:10.5465/AMR.1999.2202129

Ashforth, B. E., & Kreiner, G. E. (2013). Profane or profound? Finding meaning in dirty work. In B. J. Dik, Z. S. Byrne, & M. F. Steger (Eds.), *Purpose and meaning in the workplace* (pp. 127–150). Washington, DC: American Psychological Association.

Ashforth, B. E., Kreiner, G. E., Clark, M. A., & Fugate, M. (2007). Normalizing dirty work: Managerial tactics for countering occupational taint. *Academy of Management Journal*, *50*, 149–174. doi:10.5465/AMJ.2007.24162092

Baard, P. P., Deci, E. L., & Ryan, R. M. (2004). Intrinsic need satisfaction: A motivational basis of performance and weil-being in two work settings. *Journal of Applied Social Psychology*, *34*, 2045–2068. doi:10.1111/j.1559-1816.2004.tb02690.x

Bakker, A. B., & Demerouti, E. (2007). The job demands-resources model: State of the art. *Journal of Managerial Psychology*, *22*, 309–328. doi:10.1108/02683940710733115

Bakker, A. B., Demerouti, E., & Schaufeli, W. B. (2003). Dual processes at work in a call centre: An application of the job demands-resources model. *European Journal of Work and Organizational Psychology, 12*, 393–417. doi:10.1080/13594320344000165

Bakker, A. B., Demerouti, E., Taris, T. W., Schaufeli, W. B., & Schreurs, P. J. G. (2003). A multi-group analysis of the Job Demands-Resources model in four home care organizations. *International Journal of Stress Management, 10*, 16–38. doi: 10.1037/1072-5245.10.1.16

Bakker, A. B., Hakanen, J. J., Demerouti, E., & Xanthopoulou, D. (2007). Job resources boost work engagement, particularly when job demands are high. *Journal of Educational Psychology, 99*, 274–284. doi:10.1037/0022-0663.99.2.274

Bandura, A. (1989). Human agency in social cognitive theory. *American Psychologist, 44*, 1175–1184. doi:10.1037/0003-066X.44.9.1175

Baumeister, R. F., & Leary, M. R. (1995). The need to belong: Desire for interpersonal attachments as a fundamental human motivation. *Psychological Bulletin, 117*, 497–529. doi:10.1037/0033-2909.117.3.497

Baumeister, R. F., & Sommer, K. L. (1997). What do men want? Gender differences and two spheres of belongingness. *Psychological Bulletin, 122*, 38–44. doi:10.1037/0033-2909.122.1.38

Beaverstock, J. V., Derudder, B., Faulconbridge, J. R., & Witlox, F. (2009). International business travel: Some explorations. *Geografiska Annaler: Series B, Human Geography, 91*, 193–202. doi:10.1111/j.1468-0467.2009.00314.x

Berg, J. M., Dutton, J. E., & Wrzesniewski, A. (2013). Job crafting and meaningful work. In B. J. Dik, Z. S. Byrne, & M. F. Steger (Eds.), *Purpose and meaning in the workplace* (pp. 81–104). Washington, DC: American Psychological Association.

Berg, J. M., Dutton, J. E., Wrzesniewski, A., & Baker, W. E. (2008). *Job Crafting Exercise*. University of Michigan: Center for Positive Organizations.

Berg, J. M., Grant, A. M., & Johnson, V. (2010). When callings are calling: Work and leisure in pursuit of unanswered occupational callings. *Organization Science, 21*, 973–994. doi:10.1287/orsc.1090.0497

Berg, J. M., Wrzesniewski, A., & Dutton, J. E. (2010). Perceiving and responding to challenges in job crafting at different ranks: When proactivity requires adaptivity. *Journal of Organizational Behavior, 31*, 158–186. doi:10.1002/job.645

Brenninkmeijer, V., & Hekkert-Koning, M. (2015). To craft or not to craft: The relationships between regulatory focus, job crafting and work outcomes. *Career Development International, 20*, 147–162. doi:10.1108/CDI-12-2014-0162

Brickman, P., Coates, D., & Janoff-Bulman, R. (1978). Lottery winners and accident victims: Is happiness relative? *Journal of Personality and Social Psychology, 36*, 917–927. doi:10.1037/0022-3514.36.8.917

Brough, P., Timms, C., Siu, O-L., Kalliath, T., O'Driscoll, M. P., Sit, C. H. P., ... Lu, C-Q. (2013). Validation of the job demands-resources model in cross-national samples: Cross-sectional and longitudinal predications of psychological strain and work engagement. *Human Relations, 66*, 1311–1335. doi:10.1177/0018726712472915

Chen, C-Y., Yen, C-H., & Tsai, F. C. (2014). Job crafting and job engagement: The mediating role of person–job fit. *International Journal of Hospitality Management, 37*, 21–28. doi:10.1016/j.ijhm.2013.10.006

Clark, A. E., Diener, E., Georgellis, Y., & Lucas, R. E. (2008). Lags and leads in life satisfaction: A test of the baseline hypothesis. *The Economic Journal, 118*, 222–243. doi:10.1111/j.1468-0297.2008.02150.x

Clifton, D. O., & Harter, J. K. (2003). Investing in strengths. In K. S. Cameron, B. J. E. Dutton, & C. R. E. Quinn (Eds.), *Positive organizational scholarship: Foundations of a new discipline* (pp. 111–121). San Francisco, CA: Berrett-Koehler.

Crant, J. M. (2000). Proactive behavior in organizations. *Journal of Management, 26*, 435–462. doi:10.1177/014920630002600304

Csikszentmihalyi, M., & Larson, R. (1987). Validity and reliability of the Experience-Sampling Method. *The Journal of Nervous and Mental Disease, 175*, 526–535.

Deci, E. L. (1975). *Intrinsic motivation*. New York, NY: Plenum.

Deci, E. L., Connell, J. P., & Ryan, R. M. (1989). Self-determination in a work organization. *Journal of Applied Psychology, 74*, 580–590. doi:10.1037/0021-9010.74.4.580

Deci, E. L., & Ryan, R. M. (1980). *The psychology of self-determination.* Lexington, MA: Heath (Lexington Books).
Deci, E. L., & Ryan, R. M. (1985). *Intrinsic motivation and self-determination in human behavior.* New York, NY: Plenum.
Deci, E. L., & Ryan, R. M. (1995). Human autonomy: The basis for true self-esteem. In M. H. Kernis (Ed.), *Efficacy, agency, and self-esteem* (pp. 31–49). New York, NY: Springer.
Deci, E. L., & Ryan, R. M. (2000). The "what" and "why" of goal pursuits: Human needs and the self-determination of behavior. *Psychological Inquiry, 11,* 227–268. doi:10.1207/S15327965PLI1104_01
Deci, E. L., & Ryan, R. M. (2008a). Facilitating optimal motivation and psychological well-being across life's domains. *Canadian Psychology, 49,* 14–23. doi:10.1037/0708-5591.49.1.14
Deci, E. L., & Ryan, R. M. (2008b). Self-Determination Theory: A macrotheory of human motivation, development, and health. *Canadian Psychology, 49,* 182–185. doi:10.1037/a0012801
Deci, E. L., Ryan, R. M., Gagné, M., Leone, D. R., Usunov, J., & Kornazheva, B. P. (2001). Need satisfaction, motivation, and well-being in the work organizations of a former Eastern Bloc country: A cross-cultural study of self-determination. *Personality and Social Psychology Bulletin, 27,* 930–942. doi:10.1177/0146167201278002
Demerouti, E., Bakker, A. B., Halbesleben, J. R. B. (2015). Productive and counterproductive job crafting: A daily diary study. *Journal of Occupational Health Psychology, 20,* 457–469. doi:http://dx.doi.org/10.1037/a0039002
Demerouti, E., Bakker, A. B., Nachreiner, F., & Schaufeli, W. B. (2000). A model of burnout and life satisfaction among nurses. *Journal of Advanced Nursing, 32,* 454–464. doi:10.1046/j.1365-2648.2000.01496.x
Demerouti, E., Bakker, A. B., Nachreiner, F., & Schaufeli, W. (2001). The job demands-resources model of burnout. *Journal of Applied Psychology, 86,* 499–512. doi:10.1037/0021-9010.86.3.499
Depue, R. A., & Collins, P. F. (1999). Neurobiology of the structure of personality: Dopamine, facilitation of incentive motivation, and extraversion. *Behavioral and Brain Sciences, 22,* 491–569.
Dik, B. J., Duffy, R. D., & Eldridge, B. M. (2009). Calling and vocation in career counselling: Recommendations for promoting meaningful work. *Professional Psychology: Research and Practice, 40,* 625–632. doi:10.1037/a0015547
Dutton, J. E., Debebe, G., & Wrzesniewski, A. (2012). Being valued and devalued at work: A social valuing perspective. In K. Elsbach & B. Betchky (Eds.), *Qualitative organizational research: Best papers from the davis conference on qualitative research.* Charlotte, NC: Information Age Processing.
Dutton, J. E., & Heaphy, E. D. (2003). The power of high-quality connections. In K. S. Cameron, J. E. Dutton, & R. E. Quinn (Eds.), *Positive organizational scholarship: Foundations of a new discipline* (pp. 263–278). San Francisco, CA: Berrett-Koehler.
Eisenberg, S. (1999). *We'll call you if we need you: Experiences of women working construction.* NY: ILR Press.
Eysenck, H. J. (1967). *The biological basis of personality.* Springfield, IL: Charles C. Thomas.
Frederick, S., & Loewenstein, G. (1999). Hedonic adaptation. In D. Kahneman, E. Diener, & N. Schwarz. (Eds.), *Well-being: The foundations of hedonic psychology* (pp. 302–309). New York, NY: Russell Sage Foundation.
Fried, Y., & Ferris, G. R. (1987). The validity of the job characteristics model: A review and meta-analysis. *Personnel Psychology, 40,* 287–322. doi:10.1111/j.1744-6570.1987.tb00605.x
Fried, Y., Grant, A. M., Levi, A. S., Hadani, M., & Slowik, L. H. (2007). Job design in temporal context: A career dynamics perspective. *Journal of Organizational Behavior, 28,* 911–927. doi:10.1002/job.486
Gagné, M., & Deci, E. L. (2005). Self-determination theory and work motivation. *Journal of Organizational Behavior, 26,* 331–362. doi:10.1002/job.322
Gagné, M., Ryan, R. M., & Bargmann, K. (2003). Autonomy support and need satisfaction in the motivation and well-being of gymnasts. *Journal of Applied Sport Psychology, 15,* 372–390. doi:10.1080/714044203
Ghitulescu, B. E. (2006). *Shaping the tasks and relationships at work: Examining the antecedents and consequences of employee job crafting.* Unpublished doctoral dissertation, University of Pittsburgh, USA.

Gini, A. (1998). Work, identity, and self: How we are formed by the work we do. *Journal of Business Ethics, 17*, 707–714.

Grant, A. M., & Ashford, S. K. (2008). The dynamics of proactivity at work. *Research in Organizational Behavior, 28*, 3–34. doi:10.1016/j.riob.2008.04.002

Graves, L. M., & Luciano, M. M. (2013). Self-determination at work: Understanding the role of leader–member exchange. *Motivation and Emotion, 37*, 518–536. doi:10.1007/s11031-012-9336-z

Hackman, J. R., & Oldham, G. R. (1976). Motivation through the design of work: Test of a theory. *Organizational Behavior and Human Performance, 16*, 250–279. doi:10.1016/0030-5073(76)90016-7

Hackman, J. R., & Oldham, G. R. (1980). *Work redesign*. Reading, MA: Addison-Wesley.

Hakanen, J. J., Bakker, A. B., & Demerouti, E. (2005). How dentists cope with their job demands and stay engaged: The moderating role of resources. *European Journal of Oral Science, 113*, 479–487.

Hakanen, J. J., Bakker, A. B., & Schaufeli, W. B. (2006). Burnout and work engagement among teachers. *Journal of School Psychology, 43*, 495–513. doi:10.1016/j.jsp.2005.11.001

Hakanen, J. J., Schaufeli, W.B., & Ahola, K. (2008). The job demands-resources model: A three year cross-lagged study of burnout, depression, commitment, and work engagement. *Work & Stress, 22*, 224–241. doi:10.1080/02678370802379432

Harter, J. K., Schmidt, F. L., & Hayes, T. L. (2002). Business-unit level relationship between employee satisfaction, employee engagement, and business outcomes: A meta-analysis. *Journal of Applied Psychology, 87*, 268–279. doi:10.1037/0021-9010.87.2.268

Hodges, T. D., & Clifton, D. O. (2004). Strength-based development in practice. In P. A. Linley & S. Joseph (Eds.), *International handbook of positive psychology: From research to application* (pp. 256–268). Hoboken, NJ: Wiley.

Hotard, S. R., McFatter, R. M., McWhirter, R. M., & Stegall, M. E. (1989). Interactive effects of extraversion, neuroticism, and social relationships on subjective well-being. *Journal of Personality and Social Psychology, 57*, 321–331. doi:10.1037/0022-3514.57.2.321

Hu, Q., Schaufeli, W. B., & Taris, T. W. (2011). The job demands-resources model: An analysis of additive and joint effects of demands and resources. *Journal of Vocational Behavior, 79*, 181–190. doi:10.1016/j.jvb.2010.12.009

Jin, R. L., Shah, C. P., & Svoboda, T. J. (1995). The impact of unemployment on health: A review of the evidence. *Canadian Medical Association Journal, 153*, 529–540.

Johns, G. (2006). The essential impact of context on organizational behavior. *The Academy of Management Review, 31*, 386–408. doi:10.5465/AMR.2006.20208687

Johnson, S., Cooper, C., Cartwright, S., Donald, I., Taylor, P., & Millet, C. (2005). The experience of work-related stress across occupations. *Journal of Managerial Psychology, 20*, 178–187. doi:10.1108/02683940510579803

Judge, T. A., Bono, J. E., Erez, A., & Locke, E. A. (2005). Core self-evaluations and job and life satisfaction: The role of self-concordance and goal attainment. *Journal of Applied Psychology, 90*, 257–268. doi:0.1037/0021-9010.90.2.257

Kahneman, D., Krueger, A. B., Schkade, D. A., Schwarz, N., & Stone, A. A. (2004). A survey method for characterizing daily life experience: The Day Reconstruction Method. *Science, 306*, 1776–1780. doi:10.1126/science.1103572

Keyes, C. L. M., Wissing, M., Potgieter, J. P., Temane, M., Kruger, A., & van Rooy, S. (2008). Evaluation of the Mental Health Continuum-Short Form (MHC-SF) in Setswana-speaking South Africans. *Clinical Psychology and Psychotherapy, 15*, 181–192. doi:10.1002/cpp.572

Koestner, R., Lekes, N., Powers, T. A., & Chicoine, E. (2002). Attaining personal goals: Self-concordance plus implementation intentions equals success. *Journal of Personality and Social Psychology, 83*, 231–244. doi:10.1037//0022-3514.83.1.231

Kristof-Brown, A. L., Zimmerman, R. D., & Johnson, E. C. (2005). Consequences of individuals' fit at work: A meta-analysis of person–job fit. *Personnel Psychology, 58*, 281–342. doi: 10.1111/j.1744-6570.2005.00672.x

Leana, C., Appelbaum, E., & Shevchuck, I. (2009). Work process and the quality of care in early childhood education: The role of job crafting. *Academy of Management Journal, 52*, 1169–1192. doi:10.5465/AMJ.2009.47084651

Leotti, L. A., Lyengar, S. S., & Ochsner, K. N. (2010). Born to choose: The origins and value of the need for control. *Trends in Cognitive Sciences, 14*, 457–463. doi:10.1016/j.tics.2010.08.001

Linley, P. A., Nielsen, K. M., Gillett, R., & Biswas-Diener, R. (2010). Using signature strengths in the pursuit of goals: Effects on goal progress, need satisfaction, and well-being, and implications for coaching psychologists. *International Coaching Psychology Review, 5*, 6–15.

Linn, M. W., Sandifer, R., & Stein, S. (1985). Effects of unemployment on mental and physical health. *American Journal of Public Health, 75*, 502–506. doi:10.2105/AJPH.75.5.502

Locke, E. A., & Latham, G. P. (2002). Building a practically useful theory of goal setting and task motivation: A 35-year odyssey. *American Psychologist, 57*, 705–717. doi:10.1037//0003-066X.57.9.705

Loher, B. T., Noe, R. A., Moeller, N. L., & Fitzgerald, M. P. (1985). A meta-analysis of the relation of job characteristics to job satisfaction. *Journal of Applied Psychology, 70*, 280–289. doi:10.1037/0021-9010.70.2.280

Loukidou, L., Loan-Clarke, J., & Daniels, K. (2009). Boredom in the workplace: More than monotonous tasks. *International Journal of Management Reviews, 11*, 381–405. doi:10.1111/j.1468-2370.2009.00267.x

Lu, C., Wang, H-J., Lu, J., Du, D., & Bakker, A. B. (2014). Does work engagement increase person-job fit? The role of job crafting and job insecurity. *Journal of Vocational Behavior, 84*, 142–152. doi:10.1016/j.jvb.2013.12.004

Lucas, R. E., Clark, A. E., Georgellis, Y., & Diener, E. (2004). Unemployment alters the set point for life satisfaction. *Psychological Science, 15*, 8–13. doi:10.1111/j.0963-7214.2004.01501002.x

Lyons, P. (2008). The crafting of jobs and individual differences. *Journal of Business and Psychology, 23*, 25–36. doi:10.1007/s10869-008-9080-2

McClelland, G. P., Leach, D. J., Clegg, C. W., & McGowan, I. (2014). Collaborative crafting in call centre teams. *Journal of Occupational and Organizational Psychology, 87*, 464–486. doi:10.1111/joop.12058

Murphey, G. C., & Athanasou, J. A. (1999). The effect of unemployment on mental health. *Journal of Occupational Health Psychology, 72*, 83–89. doi:10.1348/096317999166518

Nielsen, K., & Abildgaard, J. S. (2012). The development and validation of a job crafting measure for use with blue-collar workers. *Work & Stress: An International Journal of Work, Health, & Organisations, 26*, 365–384. doi:10.1080/02678373.2012.733543

O'Brien, G. E., & Feather, N. T. (1990). The relative effects of unemployment and quality of employment on the affect, work values and personal control of adolescents. *Journal of Occupational and Organizational Psychology, 63*, 151–165. doi:10.1111/j.2044-8325.1990.tb00517.x

O'Lynn, C. E. (2007). Preface. In C. E. O'Lynn & R. E. Tranbarger (Eds.), *Men in nursing: history, challenges, and opportunities* (pp. xv–xx). New York, NY: Springer.

Parker, S. K. (1998). Enhancing role breadth self-efficacy: The roles of job enrichment and other organizational interventions. *Journal of Applied Psychology, 83*, 835–852. doi:10.1037/0021-9010.83.6.835

Parker, S. K., Williams, H. M., & Turner, N. (2006). Modeling the antecedents of proactive behavior at work. *Journal of Applied Psychology, 91*, 636–652. doi:10.1037/0021-9010.91.3.636

Peterson, C., & Seligman, M. E. P. (2004). *Character, strengths and virtues: A handbook and classification*. New York, NY: Oxford University Press.

Petrou, P., Demerouti, E., Peeters, M. C. W., Schaufeli, W. B., & Hetland, J. (2012). Crafting a job on a daily basis: Contextual correlates and the link to work engagement. *Journal of Organizational Behavior, 33*, 1120–1141. doi:10.1002/job

Petrou, P., Demerouti, E., & Schaufeli, W. B. (2015). Job crafting in changing organizations: Antecedents and implications for exhaustion and performance. *Journal of Occupational Health Psychology, 20*, 470–480. doi:10.1037/a0039003

Pyszczynski, T., Greenberg, J., Solomon, S., Arndt, J., & Schimel, J. (2004). Why do people need self-esteem? A theoretical and empirical review. *Psychological Bulletin, 130*, 435–468. doi:10.1037/0033-2909.130.3.435

Reinboth, M., & Duda, J. L. (2006). Perceived motivational climate, need satisfaction and indices of well-being in team sports: A longitudinal perspective. *Psychology of Sport and Exercise*, *7*, 269–286. doi:10.1016/j.psychsport.2005.06.002

Reinboth, M., Duda, J. L., & Ntoumanis, N. (2004). Dimensions of coaching behavior, need satisfaction, and the psychological and physical welfare of young athletes. *Motivation and Emotion*, *28*, 297–313. doi:10.1023/B:MOEM.0000040156.81924.b8

Reis, H. T., Sheldon, K. M., Gable, S. L., Roscoe, J., & Ryan, R. M. (2000). Daily well-being: The role of autonomy, competence, and relatedness. *Personality and Social Psychology Bulletin*, *26*, 419–435. doi:10.1177/0146167200266002

Repetti, R. L., Matthews, K. A., & Waldron, I. (1989). Employment and women's health: Effects of paid employment on women's mental and physical health. *American Psychologist*, *44*, 1394–1401. doi:10.1037/0003-066X.44.11.1394

Rousseau, D. M. (2005). *I-deals: Idiosyncratic deals employees bargain for themselves*. Armonk, NY: Sharpe.

Ryan, R. M., & Deci, E. L. (2000a). Self-Determination Theory and the facilitation of intrinsic motivation, social development, and well-being. *American Psychologist*, *55*, 68–78. doi:10.1037/0003-066X.55.1.68

Ryan, R. M., & Deci, E. L. (2000b). The darker and brighter sides of human existence: Basic psychological needs as a unifying concept. *Psychological Inquiry*, *11*, 319–338.

Ryan, R. M., & Deci, E. L. (2002). Overview of Self-Determination Theory: An organismic dialectical perspective. In E. L. Deci & R. M. Ryan (Eds.), *Handbook of self-determination research* (pp. 3–33). New York, NY: University of Rochester Press.

Schaufeli, W. B., Bakker, A. B., & van Rhenan, W. (2009). How changes in job demands and resources predict burnout, work engagement, and sickness absenteeism. *Journal of Organizational Behavior*, *30*, 893–917. doi:10.1002/job.595

Scholtz, W., Hellhammer, J., Schulz, P., & Stone, A. A. (2004). Perceived work overload and chronic worrying predict weekend–weekday differences in the cortisol awakening response. *Psychosomatic Medicine*, *66*, 207–214. doi:10.1097/01.psy.0000116715.78238.56

Seligman, M. E. P., Steen, T. A., Park, N., & Peterson, C. (2005). Positive psychology progress: Empirical validation of interventions. *American Psychologist*, *60*, 410–421. doi:10.1037/0003-066X.60.5.410

Sheldon, K. M. (2014). Becoming oneself: The central role of self-concordant goal selection. *Personality and Social Psychology Review*, *18*, 349–365 doi:0.1177/1088868314538549

Sheldon, K. M., & Elliot, A. J. (1998). Not all goals are personal: Comparing autonomous and controlled reasons for goals as predictors of effort and attainment. *Personality and Social Psychology Bulletin*, *24*, 546–557. doi:10.1177/0146167298245010

Sheldon, K. M., & Elliot, A. J. (1999). Goal striving, need satisfaction, and longitudinal well-being: The Self-Concordance Model. *Journal of Personality and Social Psychology*, *76*, 482–497. doi:10.1037/0022-3514.76.3.482

Sheldon, K. M., & Houser-Marko, L. (2001). Self-concordance, goal attainment, and the pursuit of happiness: Can there be an upward spiral? *Journal of Personality and Social Psychology*, *80*, 152–165. doi:10.1037/0022-3514.80.1.152

Sheldon, K. M., Ryan, R. M., Deci, E. L., & Kasser, T. (2004). The independent effects of goal contents and motives on well-being: It's both what you pursue and why you pursue it. *Personality and Social Psychology Bulletin*, *30*, 475–486. doi:10.1177/0146167203261883

Sheldon, K. M., Ryan, R. M., & Reis, H. T. (1996). What makes for a good day? Competence and autonomy in the day and in the person. *Personality and Social Psychology Bulletin*, *22*, 1270–1279. doi: 10.1177/01461672962212007

Slemp, G. R., Kern., M. L., & Vella-Brodrick, D. A. (2015, 5 August). Workplace well-being: The role of job crafting and autonomy support. *Psychology of Wellbeing: Theory, Research, and Practice*. doi:10.1186/s13612-015-0034-y

Slemp, G. R., & Vella-Brodrick, D. A. (2013). The job crafting questionnaire: A new scale to measure the extent to which employees engage in job crafting. *International Journal of Wellbeing*, *3*, 126–146. doi:10.5502/ijw.v3i2.1

Slemp, G. R., & Vella-Brodrick, D. A. (2014). Optimising employee mental health: The relationship between intrinsic need satisfaction, job crafting, and employee well-being. *Journal of Happiness Studies, 15*, 957–977. doi:10.1007/s10902-013-9458-3

Staw, B. M., & Boettger, R. D. (1990). Task revision: A neglected form of work performance. *Academy of Management Journal, 33*, 534–559. doi:10.2307/256580

Steger, M. F., & Dik, B. J. (2010). Work as meaning: Individual and organizational benefits of engaging in meaningful work. In P. A. Linley, S. Harrington, & N. Garcea (Eds.), *Oxford handbook of positive psychology and work* (pp. 131–142). Oxford, UK: Oxford University Press.

Tims, M., & Bakker, A. B. (2010). Job crafting: Towards a model of individual job redesign. *SA Journal of Industrial Psychology, 36*, 1–9.

Tims, M., Bakker, A. B., & Derks, D. (2012). Development and validation of the job crafting scale. *Journal of Vocational Behavior, 80*, 173–186. doi:10.1016/j.jvb.2011.05.009

Tims, M., Bakker, A. B., & Derks, D. (2013). The impact of job crafting on job demands, job resources, and well-being. *Journal of Occupational Health Psychology, 18*, 230–240. doi:10.1037/a0032141

Tims, M., Bakker, A. B., & Derks, D. (2014). Daily job crafting and the self-efficacy–performance relationship. *Journal of Managerial Psychology, 29*, 490–507. doi:10.1108/JMP-05-2012-0148

Tims, M., Bakker, A. B., & Derks, D. (2015, 2 March). Examining job crafting from an interpersonal perspective: Is employee job crafting related to the well-being of colleagues? *Applied Psychology: An International Review*. Advanced online publication. doi:10.1111/apps.12043

Tims, M., Bakker, A. B., Derks, D., & van Rhenen, W. (2013). Job crafting at the team and individual level: Implications for work engagement and performance. *Group & Organization Management, 38*, 427–454. doi:10.1177/1059601113492421

Vallerand, R. J., Blanchard, C., Mageau, G. A., Koestner, R., Ratelle, C., Léonard, M., … Marsolais, J. (2003). Les passions de l'Âme: On obsessive and harmonious passion. *Journal of Personality and Social Psychology, 85*, 756–767. doi:10.1037/0022-3514.85.4.756

Van den Broeck, A., Vansteenkiste, M., & De Witte, H. (2008). Self-determination theory: A theoretical and empirical overview in occupational health psychology. In J. Houdmont & S. Leka (Eds.), *Occupational health psychology: European perspectives on research, education, and practice* (pp. 63–88). Nottingham, UK: Nottingham University Press.

Van den Broeck, A., Vansteenkiste, M., De Witte, H., & Lens, W. (2008). Explaining the relationships between job characteristics, burnout, and engagement: The role of basic psychological need satisfaction. *Work & Stress, 22*, 277–294. doi:10.1080/02678370802393672

van den Heuvel, M., Demerouti, E., & Peeters, M. C. W. (2015). The job crafting intervention: Effects on job resources, self-efficacy, and affective well-being. *Journal of Occupational and Organizational Psychology, 88*, 511–532. doi:10.1111/joop.12128

Van Dyne, L., & LePine, J. (1998). Helping and extra-role behaviors: Evidence of construct and predictive validity. *Academy of Management Journal, 41*, 108–109. doi:10.2307/256902

van Hooff, M. L. M., & van Hooft, E. A. J. (2014). Boredom at work: Proximal and distal consequences of affective work-related boredom. *Journal of Occupational Health Psychology, 19*, 348–359. doi:10.1037/a0036821

Van Maanen, J., & Schein, E. H. (1979). Towards a theory of organizational socialization. In B. M. Staw (Ed.), *Research in organizational behavior* (pp. 209–264). Greenwich, CT: JAI Press.

Vansteenkiste, M., & Ryan, R. M. (2013). On psychological growth and vulnerability: Basic psychological need satisfaction and need frustration as a unifying principle. *Journal of Psychotherapy Integration, 23*, 263–280. doi:10.1037/a0032359

Vodanovich, S. J. (2003). Psychometric measures of boredom: A review of the literature. *Journal of Psychology: Interdisciplinary and Applied, 137*, 569–595. doi:10.1080/00223980309600636

Xanthopoulou, D., Bakker, A. B., Dollard, M. F., Demerouti, E., Schaufeli, W. B., Taris, T. W., & Schreurs, P. J. G. (2007). When do job demands particularly predict burnout? The moderating role of job resources. *Journal of Managerial Psychology, 22*, 766–786. doi:10.1108/02683940710837714

Walsh, K., & Gordon, J. R. (2008). Creating an individual work identity. *Human Resource Management Review, 18*, 46–61. doi:10.1016/j.hrmr.2007.09.001

Wilson, P. M., Rodgers, W. M., Blanchard, C. M., & Gessell, J. (2003). The relationship between psychological needs, self-determined motivation, exercise attitudes, and physical fitness. *Journal of Applied Social Psychology*, *33*, 2373–2392. doi:10.1111/j.1559-1816.2003.tb01890.x

Wood, A. M., Linley, P. A., Maltby, J., Kashdan, T. B., & Hurling, R. (2011). Using personal and psychological strengths leads to increases in well-being over time: A longitudinal study and the development of the strengths use questionnaire. *Personality and Individual Differences*, *50*, 15–19. doi:10.1016/j.paid.2010.08.004

Wrzesniewski, A. (2003). Finding positive meaning in work. In K. S. Cameron, J. E. Dutton, & R. E. Quinn (Eds.), *Positive organizational scholarship: Foundations of a new discipline* (pp. 297–308). San Francisco, CA: Berrett-Koehler.

Wrzesniewski, A., Berg, J. M., & Dutton, J. E. (2010). Turn the job you have into the job you want. *Harvard Business Review, June*, 114–117.

Wrzesniewski, A., & Dutton, J. E. (2001). Crafting a job: Revisioning employees as active crafters of their work. *Academy of Management Review*, *26*, 179–201. doi:10.5465/AMR.2001.4378011

Wrzesniewski, A., LoBuglio, N., Dutton, J. E., & Berg, J. M. (2013). Job crafting and cultivating positive meaning and identity in work. In A. B. Bakker (Ed.), *Advances in positive organizational psychology* (pp. 281–302). Bingley, UK: Emerald Group.

Wrzesniewski, A., McCauley, C., Rozin, P., & Schwartz, B. (1997). Jobs, careers, and callings: People's relations to their work. *Journal of Research in Personality*, *31*, 21–33. doi:10.1006/jrpe.1997.2162

20

Positive Approaches to Mid-Life Careers

Sung-Kyung Yoo and Hyjin Lee

Introduction

Traditionally, mid-career has been considered a plateaued period marked by the experience of mastery and maintenance (Slay, Taylor, & Williamson, 2004). However, with the increase in career changes due to shifting economic conditions and organizational structures, mid-career is now considered a time of transition and continued growth. Although career transitions occur throughout the lifespan, the transition around the age of 45, termed mid-life career transition, is considered the most prevalent and critical. The purpose of this chapter is to discuss positive approaches to mid-career or mid-life career transition. To this end, three themes are specified and covered in depth.

The first theme is the overview of mid-career transition. To understand mid-career transition, we review the evolution of the notion of mid-career from a time of maintenance to a time of transition. While discussing the key features of mid-career transition, we try to differentiate the mid-career transition and the mid-life transition. In spite of the substantial overlap between the two concepts, the experiences of the mid-career transition and the mid-life career transition are distinct. The second theme is the review of the relevant theories that contribute to the understanding of mid-career transition. Classical theories on mid-life crisis provide an important framework to approach mid-career as a time to simultaneously look back and look forward. Also, the recent models of the boundaryless and protean career provide critical importance of self-directed and value-driven attitude for individual initiated career transition. The last theme of the chapter is the promotion of a positive approach to mid-career transition at both individual and organizational levels. Based on suggestions from the recent career models, we discuss the important roles of career adaptability and self-awareness in facilitating positive mid-career transition. In addition, a positive approach to mid-career transition cannot be achieved without sufficient support from organizations. Due to the unpredictable fluctuation in the economy and rapid changes in employees' needs, organizations are required to constantly

The Wiley Blackwell Handbook of the Psychology of Positivity and Strengths-Based Approaches at Work, First Edition. Edited by Lindsay G. Oades, Michael F. Steger, Antonella Delle Fave, and Jonathan Passmore.

align the characters of each employee with the requirements of each job, while also taking the situational context into consideration. Through this alignment process, a proper level of adaptability for mid-career transition can be reached. Recent trends in organizational psychology practice are also discussed in this section.

Understanding Mid-Career Transition

Mid-career was initially considered a time to maintain the career one had established in early adulthood (Super, 1957). However, the maintenance notion of mid-career contrasts with the well-known crisis notion of mid-life, which views mid-life as a critical developmental phase characterized by change points, or periods of transition (Jaques, 1965; Jung, 1966). This apparent disagreement between the notions of mid-career and mid-life can be explained by the fact that career researchers made overly specific distinction between "career" and "personal issues" in addressing career development (Hackett, 1993; Swanson & Holton, 2001). However, since the beginning of the 21st century, there has been an increased appreciation of the mobility and potential for continued growth in mid-career. Such change was possible due to dramatic shifts in the economy and in organizations, as well as individuals' increasing need for integration of work and nonwork experiences. This change of perspectives is reflected in the contemporary notion of mid-career as a time for transition, in which individuals both look back and look forward (Vander Zanden, 2000). The concept of mid-career transition appears to adequately incorporate the characteristics of mid-life. We will discuss the issue of mid-career transition as a way of integrating career and personal issues and as a phenomenon reflecting emerging changes in contemporary societies. In our discussion of mid-career transition, we will use the terms "mid-life career transition" and "mid-career transition" distinctively, in spite of many commonalities between them. The term mid-life career transition emphasizes career reevaluation and change that emerge as a reaction to mid-life crisis, regardless of the person's stage in his or her career. In contrast, mid-career transition is defined as expeditions and changes undertaken at the midpoint of one's working life, regardless of one's biological age. Although there appears to be a substantial overlap between the two experiences, we will address their disparate psychological aspects.

Changing Views on Mid-Career: From a Time of Maintenance to a Time of Transition

To take a closer look at the phenomenon of mid-career, we need to first explore the meaning of "mid." When is mid-career? The concept of mid-career is based on the classical notion of mid-life. Mid-life, sometimes referred to as middle adulthood or middle age, is defined as the period between the ages of 35 and 65 (Dacey & Travers, 2004; Vander Zanden, 2000). Super (1957) defined the mid-life career stage as a maintenance stage (ages 45–64), with preceding stages of growth stage (birth to age 14), exploration stage (ages 15–24), and establishment stage (ages 25–44), and followed by decline stage (age 65 and on). Since mid-career issues were addressed within the career development stage model based on chronological ages, initially the term mid-career was used interchangeably with mid-life career.

Recognizing the limitation of proposing strict linearity and distinctiveness across career stages, Super (1980) later acknowledged that people who do not wish to continue their established career may recycle through various career stages, which may ramify into career change. Super, Savickas, & Super (1996) also questioned whether people want to continue their career for the rest of their working lives. They suggested that the developmental tasks of the maintenance stage (ages 45–65) are "holding on, keeping up, and innovating" (p. 134). The notion that mid-career is not a time to merely hold onto the previously established career, but rather a time to generate career innovations, reflects the more active stance of contemporary mid-career workers. Along with the expansion of Super's life-span, life-space (LSLS) theory (1957, 1990; Super et al., 1996), which included the concepts of recycling and self-concept implementation, other models of adult development (e.g., Golan, 1986; Levinson, 1980) also recognized that many college-educated mid-lifers reevaluated and changed their careers in relation to their personal lives and goals (Arbona, 2003). Similarly, scholars such as Sheehy (1976), Vaillant (1977), Gould (1978), and Levinson, Darrow, Klein, Levinson, & McKee (1978) began to argue that mid-life can be a time of considerable transition, reshaping the view on mid-life career as a time for potential continued growth (Wang, Olson, & Shultz, 2013). According to the revised view on mid-career, individuals in middle adulthood are required to recycle through earlier career stages and crystallize a new choice (Savickas, 1990) through navigating new life situations and role transitions.

Career change may take place at any age across the lifespan; however, people often seek new career opportunities around the age of 45 (Guerrier & Philpot, 1978). Middle adulthood in general can be considered a critical time for change (Barclay, Stoltz, & Chung, 2011; Bobek & Robbins, 2005; Heppner, Multon, & Johnston, 1994). Researchers examining older people in organizations often put the threshold at 40 or 45, seeing "old" as referring to obsolete knowledge, skills, and attitudes (Kooij, De Lange, Jansen, & Dikkers, 2008). Therefore, the choices and experiences individuals make and have around the age of 45 significantly influence how people evaluate their present choices and options, as well as the risks they are willing to take. Whereas career reevaluation during mid-career may emerge as a reaction to mid-life crisis, individuals must also respond to rapid shifts in economic situations. With globalization and the intensified economic competition in the 21st century, individuals are required to proactively change their career more frequently.

As Hall (1996) suggested, the concept of one career in one life is not valid or realistic any more. A lifelong stationary career is not a norm in the 21st century. With higher demands for learning experiences and voluntary efforts by employees to change career, career transitions have escalated significantly. As a result, the career transition is not delayed until middle adulthood, and mid-career transition may occur even before mid-life. As a response to the dramatic changes in the 21st century, mid-career workers, not limited to mid-life workers, are now more mobile and less secure than in the past, and are expected to take greater responsibility in shaping their own career.

Background of Mid-Career Transition

More recent career models (e.g., the protean career model [Hall, 1996, 2002], and the boundaryless career model [Arthur & Rousseau, 1996]) suggest the need for individual-initiated career change in contemporary societies. To understand the background of mid-career transition, we need to consider both macro- and micro-level approaches, as Swanson & Holton (2001) and Ng, Sorensen, and Yim (2009) suggested. At macro-level, we will focus on two conditions, economic changes and population aging. First, globalization and intensified economic competition have become increasingly apparent in the past 10 years (Power & Rothausen, 2003; Sullivan, 1999), and they are rapidly changing the shape of organizations. Power and Rothausen (2003) acknowledged a set of contemporary problems, such as the flattening of organizational structure that leads to fewer opportunities for individuals to move beyond the middle management level via vertical corporate ascension. Since there is no guarantee for promotion in developing organization-specific skills and knowledge, more individuals are challenged to engage in multiple careers and to reinvent their career trajectories. Changes in economy and organizational systems are profoundly altering the way people live and relate to others (Carnoy, 2001; Liu, Englar-Carlson, & Minichiello, 2012). Exposed to the turbulent and unpredictable contemporary workplace (Bauman, 1998; Beck, 1992; Giddens, 1991), people need to assume full responsibility for their career paths. As a result, careers are customized according to one's needs, circumstances, and abilities. In other words, organization-owned career paths are now replaced with individual-initiated career paths.

In addition to the rapid changes in economic situations and organizational structures, population aging is another macro-level contextual factor that affects the mid-career transition. The population is aging and the workforce is "graying" (Alley & Crimmins, 2007). Especially, as the baby boomers – those born between 1957 to 1964 – age, most countries encounter the issue of an aging population and workforce. As individuals are living longer and more healthily, they are expected to spend about a third of their lives in retirement after leaving their main jobs (Owen & Flynn, 2004). Many studies show that middle-age or elderly workers often wish to remain in the labor force and delay retirement. A survey in the USA found that approximately 80% of baby boomers anticipated working past the traditional retirement age, at least as part-time employees (Harris Interactive, 2005). To remain in the labor force, mid-career workers are required to be flexible in planning their future worklife. To help middle-age and elderly workers delay retirement and remain in the workforce, the OECD countries (2015) argued for a new agenda of age-friendly employment policies and practices. Also, the European Union has set targets to increase the labor market participation of workers between the ages of 50 and 69 by 50%. In addition to the macro-level policies that accommodate the aging workforce, individuals are responsible for planning how and when to exit from the labor market. More recent career models promote more proactive and agentic attitudes in approaching career transition, which are highly applicable to mid-career workers in their preparation for gradual retirement or career renewal (Bejian & Salomone, 1995; Murphy & Burck, 1976; Williams & Savickas, 1990). We will discuss means to help mid-career workers prepare for career transition in the next section.

In addition to the macro-level factors (e.g., economic conditions and industry differences), researchers on career mobility have also considered micro-level factors (e.g., individual differences: dispositional attributes; Ng, Sorensen, Eby, & Feldman, 2007). A person's career is not just "blowing in the wind in a world without boundaries" (Feldman 2002, p. 4), but is anchored by factors such as one's interests, needs, abilities, values, and personality. Among these individual psychosocial variables influencing mid-career transition, values and meaning of work have been identified as especially salient factors (Hall, Feldman, & Kim, 2013). Based on their reflection on why they work and what needs they want to fulfill through work, individuals prepare for and make decisions on mid-career transition. Living in the 21st century, an era of well-being, individuals care more about the integration of work and personal lives than ever before (Greenhaus & Allen, 2011). One recent meta-analysis found that supporting work–family issues has become a major part of a supervisor's role expectation at work (Kossek, Pichler, Bodner, & Hammer, 2011), showing how both employers and employees consider work and family integration important. The increasing concern for work–life integration among workers is an important background to mid-career transition in the modern society.

When the career change is negative, the purpose and value of work play critical roles in fostering the meaningfulness of work. It is especially true for people who are highly self-directed and value-driven (Hall et al., 2013). As a person ages, the focus of his or her work and career plans subtly shifts from personal goals to the amount of time left to work (Smyer & Pitt-Catsouphes, 2007). Recognizing the limited time left for work, mid-career workers tend to seek meaning in work that is compatible with their meaning in life, and want to fulfill their life values through their career. Empirical studies show a certain connection between the meaning of work and the overall meaning of life (Holbeche & Springett, 2004). Steger and Dik (2009) recognized the importance of meaning in work by finding that meaning in work might make a lager contribution to meaning in life than meaning in life makes to meaningful work. It shows the importance of having meaning in one's work during mid-life for living up to one's ideas of meaning in life.

The macro-level changes in economic and employment conditions and the micro-level changes in values and meanings related to work affect the experiences of mid-career transition in certain ways. Now we will explore the key features of mid-career transition that are distinct from mid-life career transition.

Mid-Life Career Transition and Mid-Career Transition

With dramatic changes in the economy and in employment structure, a continuous and logically coherent working life is now less available (Carnoy, 1999), and career changes are becoming more prominent in contemporary societies. Career transition is marked by the "entry [to] a new occupation which requires fundamentally different skills, daily routines, and work environment from the present one" (Feldman, 2002, p. 76). Career change is defined as a shift from one job to another, or a complete change of career. Any career change, whether it is negative or positive, is disruptive (Farjoun, 2010). Especially, career changes in mid-life are more prevalent and salient as they intermingle with biological, psychological, and social changes during mid-life. As a subtype of mid-career transition, mid-life career transitions are a reaction to both experience and mortality (Zemon, 2002). Consequentially, the features of mid-life career transition are different from mid-career transition, although there are many commonalities. In this section, we will discuss the distinct features and focuses of mid-life career transition and mid-career transition.

Mid-life career transition

Although chronological age is not equivalent to career age, chronological age is still a salient factor in career transition (David, 2005). As employees are getting more self-driven, "age" plays a key role in mid-life. Older individuals are less motivated to learn (Inceoglu, Segers, Bartram, & Vloeberghs, 2008; Maurer, 2001; Warr, 2001; Warr & Birdi, 1998). To put it more concretely, older employees are less motivated by extrinsically rewarding job features but more by intrinsically rewarding job features. Inceoglu, Segers, and Bartram's empirical research (2012) through a motivation questionnaire over 9,388 employees showed that intrinsically rewarding job features such as interesting tasks, working with other people, and having autonomy over one's own tasks tend to have stronger effects when employees are older. In contrast, extrinsically rewarding job features such as status, financial rewards, praise and outward signs of recognition, and a pleasant work environment tend to have weaker effect when employees are older. Kanfer and Ackerman (2004) also noticed that the need to achieve and meet the performance requirements tends to decline with age. Reasons for such decline include lower energy levels, habituation effects, and reduced expected values of the required effort (Warr, 2001).

Owen and Flynn (2004) noted that people in early adulthood change jobs due to more career-related reasons. However, when people reach their mid-thirties, they become less likely to experience positive change. Owen and Flynn (2004) empirically explored the types of career change during mid-to-late life transitions in employment, and found that only 28% of the research participants were choosers, those who would enjoy a new phase of life, or the "third age"; 40% were survivors, who made their career transitions for reasons beyond their control; and 32% were jugglers between work and nonwork. That only a limited percentage of mid-life workers were choosers of their work implies that career changes in mid-to-late life are quite negative, marked by a decreased sense of control.

Other research results also negatively portray involuntary mid-life career transition. For example, according to a report by Ilg (2010), in 2009 in the USA, only 18% of workers aged 25–54 were able to find another job after being laid off. This shows that although most mid-life workers want to continue working either full- or part-time, the chances of remaining in the workforce are reduced. Research also indicates significant negative effects of unemployment on middle-aged workers (Murphy & Shillingford, 2012), which were especially evident and severe among men (Goodman, Schlossberg, & Anderson, 2006; Jeon & Jin, 2011; Levinson, 1978, 1990). Simmelink (2006) compared the negative psychological effects of a job loss or an involuntary career change to that of a grieving process, conveying the negative impact of losing one's job. Research highlights that losing a job may result in lower self-esteem, shame, isolation, and depression. And if depression does become worse, the ability to seek reemployment can be impaired (Guindon & Smith, 2002). Considering the negative effects of unprepared, mandated career transition during mid-life, research and practice on facilitating positive career transition during mid-life is imperative.

In spite of the vulnerability of mid-life career transition, Huebner and Royal (2013) argued that voluntary mid-life career changes could sometimes be attributed to self-actualization concerns. It is not uncommon for a middle-aged adult to ask himself why he is doing what he does for a living. In a serious reflection on this question, some workers realize that the original reasons for their career choices are no longer valid (Super & Bohn, 1970). Some workers may not be willing to sustain the personal sacrifice that they endured in their twenties and thirties. Changing careers in mid-life is not always a rational decision; emotion often plays a strong role (Huebner & Royal, 2013). However, while the mid-life workers reevaluate what they have accomplished, they also explore alternatives through seeking new information about the world of work (Super, 1980) or search for meaning in life. Some successfully attain this latter quest through discovering their calling (Huebner & Royal, 2013).

There are many reasons for voluntary mid-life career change (Barclay et al., 2011). Some of these include occupational dissatisfaction (Brown, 1995; Donohue, 2007), lack of challenge (Vander Zanden, 2000), lack of career-related identity (Dacey & Travers, 2004), stress and anxiety related to job insecurity (Donohue, 2007; Tivendell & Bourbonnais, 2000), workplace bullying (Donohue, 2007), and conflicts between work and other life roles (Brown, 1995). The reasons behind job changes and the specific transition processes they choose are incorporated in individuals' experience of mid-career transition.

Mid-career transition

As workers are constantly required to consider career changes to adapt to the dynamic shifts in the economy and globalized competition, frequent career changes and early exit are noticeable phenomena in the labor market. For example, the U.S. Department of Labor (2008) reported that a person born between 1957 and 1964 held 10.8 jobs between the ages of 19 and 42 on average (Barclay et al., 2011). Another survey with 724 Korean employers reported that the average number of career changes during working life was about 2.8 (Career, 2013). In terms of early exit phenomena, according to OECD, the average effective age of retirement from 2007 to 2012 in Korea was 71.1 for men and 69.8 for women. However, one recent survey conducted in 2015 reported that the Korean employees' expected retirement age is 52, and that younger workers expect to retire at an earlier age than older workers do. In addition, the survey result showed that 82.8% of the participants expressed anxiety about being laid off unprepared (Job Korea, 2015). The early exit phenomenon is one of the worldwide concerns in the labor market (HayGroup, 2013).

To adapt to the frequent career changes and early exit, individuals have to prepare for and plan career changes much earlier than mid-life. Whereas the mid-life career transition is based on psychological development with an assumption of a stable world of work, the mid-career transition needs a more strategic approach. More proactive initiation of career transitions can be found in mid-career transitions than in mid-life career transitions. The focus of mid-career transition is to enhance the work value of potential employees, whereas the focus of mid-life career transition is to prepare for a better exit from labor force. However, both types of transitions require self-directed and value-driven reflection on what individuals have done and what they want to fulfill in the future. In the rest of the chapter, we will use mid-career transition as a term that incorporates mid-life career transition, since the concept of mid-career transition is not limited to the chronological developmental stage.

Relevant Theories on Mid-Career Transition

As reviewed above, the world of work demands employees to be increasingly adaptable, imposing greater pressure on them. Consequently, those who are at the midpoint of their career path need support from the organization and from people outside the workplace, including family, friends, or even professionals. However, as Peake and McDowall (2012) stated, noticeably little research exists on mid-career transitions, especially on the impacts of mid-career occupational transitions. In this section, we review the theories that have contributed to our understanding of mid-career transition. Based on the review of relevant theories, we will draw important implications on how to facilitate mid-career workers approach their career transition positively.

Mid-life crisis theory

To understand the core features of mid-career transition, we first begin with the mid-life crisis theory. Although career change is a salient phenomenon throughout career development in contemporary society, it happens more frequently in mid-life. Also, "mid," either in life journey or in career trajectory, implies the notion of crisis, in that it leads to both rigorous examination of what has been done and anxious projection on what should be done. The mid-life crisis theory provides insights on what people experience as they stand in the midway between the half gone and the half to come.

Mid-life crisis is a term first coined by Jaques (1965), referring to a critical phase in human development during the thirties to early sixties, which is characterized by change points, or periods of transition. It is a time to simultaneously look back and to look forward (Vander Zanden, 2000), in which a person experiences doubt and anxiety, uncomfortable with the realization that his or her "life is half over" (Weaver, 2009). Mid-life transition is considered a "crisis" requiring an examination of the self and life. Such reflection often conjures up feelings of panic (Bell, 1982), which are necessary for mid-life renewal.

Mid-lifers in contemporary society are destined to face more intensified pressure of "now or never" (Blanton & Gordon, 1967). Thus, psychological theories of mid-life crisis indicate that the major characteristics of mid-life changes are self-awareness and crisis.

Super's extended life-span, life-space model

Super's (LSLS) model extended Super's original life-span approach asserting very specific age ranges and employing the notions of "maturity" and "planfulness." However, the theory has been extended to include the concepts of "recycling" and "self-concept implementation," recognizing the cyclic feature of career changes that contributes to identity implementation. The LSLS model first recognized the importance of the mid-career stage. However, although Super's LSLS approach to career development is useful for exploring one's needs and expectations in specific stages of the lifespan, LSLS has been criticized for its limited, narrow, and linear perspective (Peake & McDowall, 2012). In addition, the LSLS approach does not address the underlying processes that actually lead to one's career change. Some career researchers have attempted to develop or extend Super's LSLS approach to mid-career transition.

Barclay et al. (2011) further extended Super's LSLS model by explaining how the career transition processes occur. They integrated the transtheoretical model of change (TTM) with the LSLS theory in order to outline the processes of mid-career changes (the integration of LSLS and TTM is summarized in Table 20.1). TTM is a well-researched theory of behavior change that explains the process of change, addressing its cognitive,

Table 20.1 Model integrating the TTM and Super's LSLS approach to career development.

Stage	*Mid-life career changer*
Precontemplation/ Disengagement	• Experience of discouragement (although not fully aware of the reason) • Loss of interest in work tasks/industry • Letting go of work and old work identity
Contemplation/Growth	• Growing awareness of job dissatisfaction • Concerns for the future • Initial thoughts of a possible career change • Expressions of doubt regarding career change • Weighing pros/cons of a career change • Emotional expressions • Increasing personal control/self-efficacy
Preparation/Exploration	• Increased motivation to change careers • Willingness to explore interests/skills through assessments • Willingness to explore educational opportunities • Crystallizing, specifying, and implementing
Action/Establishment	• Management of stress • Redefinition of self • New life roles (e.g., student, new employee/trainee) • Determining/committed • Stabilizing, consolidating, and advancing
Maintenance/Maintenance	• Building co-worker relationships • End of formal educational pursuits • Completion of career change • Holding on, keeping up, and innovating

Source: Barclay et al. (2011, p. 391). Reproduced with permission of John Wiley & Sons.

emotional, and behavioral aspects. By integrating Super's model with the change process model, the researchers showed how mid-career workers make voluntary transitions, starting with a lack of awareness of their dissatisfaction with their present career and ending with voluntary career transition. As shown in Table 20.1, those who change careers in mid-life experience gradual shifts in their cognitions, emotions, and behaviors. This model was developed with the purpose of providing guidelines for counseling services for mid-career workers.

Boundaryless and protean career models

As individuals assume more responsibility in reshaping their career, and as career transition becomes more salient, contemporary career models such as the boundaryless career model (Arthur & Rousseau, 1996) and the protean career model (Hall, 1996, 2002) are replacing the traditional models. The boundaryless career highlights seemingly infinite possibilities of the career and individual competencies in recognizing and utilizing the opportunity (Arthur, Inkson, & Pringle, 1999). The protean career emphasizes a self-directed approach to the career, and a career that is managed by one's own values (Hall, 2002). In this section we will explore the boundaryless and protean career separately, and then we will discuss the individual competencies suggested by the boundaryless and protean career models.

The boundaryless career The concept of boundaryless career is useful in describing the prevalent career transitions in contemporary society. Arthur and Rousseau (1996) described boundaryless careers as the opposite of organizational careers and careers that are expected to unfold in a single employment setting. The boundaryless career model has stimulated career research (Wang et al., 2013), and has evolved to include other areas related to boundary issues, such as work/nonwork conflict, retirement transitions, and mentoring (Sullivan & Baruch, 2009). Sullivan and Arthur (2006) solidified the concept of boundaryless career by delineating the interdependence between physical mobility and psychological mobility. They suggested that the boundaryless career is a multifaceted phenomenon that encompasses and transcends various boundaries and levels of analysis, both physical and psychological, objective and subjective.

The boundaryless career highlights "being motivated by autonomy," which tends to increase with age (Inceoglu et al., 2008; Ryff, 1995). In the middle stage of work life or personal life, individuals are expected to reshape the boundaries of their work or personal life according to their changing roles and identities. Thus, the core idea of the boundaryless career, which states that the boundary is not given but created by the individual, provides important implications in understanding mid-career or mid-life career transition. Also, the individual competencies required in the boundaryless career offer a useful framework in approaching issues of mid-career transition. In the next section, we will explore ways to promote the individual competencies that are required for positive mid-career transitions in the boundaryless career environment.

The protean career The concept of protean career is defined as a career in which the person is (1) value-driven, in the sense that his or her internal values provide the guidance and measure of success for his or her career; and (2) self-directed in personal career management (Briscoe & Hall, 2002). Here, self-direction implies autonomy and self-determination, and value-driven behavior indicates reliance on personal values to evaluate choices and career success (Briscoe & Hall, 2003). The protean career is not a particular career behavior

Table 20.2 Comparison between the characteristics of the protean career perspective and those of the traditional career perspective.

Perspectives	*Protean career*	*Traditional career*
Driver	Individual	Organization
Core values	Freedom, growth	Promotion
Movability	High	Low
Type of success	Psychological success	Position, salary
Core attitudes	Job satisfaction, job commitment	Commitment to organization

Source: Briscoe, Hall, and DeMuth (2006).

but an attitude or orientation that affects career behavior. A summary of the characteristics of the protean career in comparison to those of the traditional career is presented in Table 20.2. Briscoe and Hall (2006) suggested four primary categories based on two core aspects, self-directedness and value-drivenness. People who are neither self-directed nor value-driven are labeled as "dependent," those who are self-directed but not value-driven as "reactive," those who are not self-directed but value-driven as "rigid," and those who are both self-directed and value-driven as "protean" (Briscoe & Hall, 2006).

The protean career model is particularly relevant to mid-career workers, as the two metacompetencies, adaptability and identity growth, are required to survive in a boundaryless environment (Hall & Mirvis, 1995). Individuals are required to develop skills and learn ways to enhance their adaptability and self-reflection to facilitate identity growth. One of the difficulties mid-career workers encounter is that they have to change their learning skills. They have already accumulated a set of skills and knowledge required in their main job, but they have to acquire a different set of learning skills to become adaptable and able to engage in continuous learning. Hall and colleagues (2013) noted that when the career change is positive, people may rely on increased self-worth and self-efficacy to find meaningfulness in work. However, when the change is negative, individuals with high protean career orientation find meaningfulness in work based on their purpose in life and value.

Since the boundaryless and protean careers assume that individuals take full responsibility in the context of limitless opportunities presented by their career, individual competencies in self-directedness and self-awareness regarding their own values are considered pivotal. In the boundaryless and protean career models, the importance of "individual competencies" outside the boundary of organization is emphasized (Briscoe et al., 2006). DeFillippi and Arthur (1994) suggested that the individual competencies of "knowing why," "knowing how," and "knowing whom" are required in the boundaryless career. The "knowing why" competency is the meaning that gives direction, identity, and motivation for work. The "knowing how" competency includes tacit knowledge and explicit knowledge necessary for work. The "knowing whom" competency comprises interpersonal and networking skills. Workers are responsible for developing these individual competencies to adapt to the boundaryless career environment. Based on the individual competencies, the boundaryless career explicates individuals' physical and psychological mobility between different occupations and organizations. In this perspective, individuals are seen as independent, driven by inner-directed choices, and capable of crossing organizational boundaries (Chin & Rasdi, 2014).

Two metacompetencies are central to the protean career: *self-awareness*, which is a clear sense of one's personal identity, and *adaptability*, which is the capacity to change (Hall et al., 2013). Hall and colleagues (2013) noted that possessing one metacompetency without the other can be highly problematic, and stressed the importance of balanced development between self-awareness and adaptability. The two metacompetencies are comparable to the individual competencies of "knowing why," "knowing how," and "knowing whom." These metacompetencies are necessary conditions for successful transition, especially when the labor market, organization of work, and underlying occupational knowledge bases are all subject to considerable change.

Gubler, Arnold, and Coombs (2014) reviewed the empirical literature published between 2006 and 2013 using the key words "protean career," "self-directed," or "values-driven," and "boundaryless" or "boundaries." With a comprehensive literature review, they found a consistent positive relationship between protean career orientation and various career outcomes including career satisfaction (e.g., Gasteiger & Briscoe, 2007; Volmer & Spurk, 2010), and job satisfaction (e.g., Baruch & Quick, 2007: Jung & Takeuchi, 2011). Also, career insight mediated the positive relationship between protean career attitude and perceived employability and career satisfaction (De Vos & Soens, 2008). More recently, Herrmann, Hirschi, and Baruch (2015) conducted a study with 526 German employees showing that a protean career orientation predicts proactive behaviors and career satisfaction beyond a proactive disposition and core self-evaluation. Also, they found a significant mediating role of protean career orientation between proactive personality and positive career outcomes. For future studies, more clarity of the constructs and measures are required.

Facilitating a Positive Approach to Mid-Career Transition

There are different forms of mid-career transitions: voluntary or involuntary, planned or reactive. However, not all career transitions are positive. Research findings on the negative impact of unplanned and mandated mid-career transition suggest that a proactive approach to mid-career transition is not an option but rather a necessity in contemporary society. What should individuals and employers do to facilitate the positive approach to mid-career transition? Recent career models reviewed in the previous section – that is, the mid-career development model, extensions of the LSLS model, the protean career model, and the boundaryless career model – commonly emphasize the importance of self-directed and value-driven approaches to career transition. If mid-career workers direct the transition themselves and have personal values to guide the change process, they will experience enhanced meaningfulness in both their work and personal lives. Considering the crisis notion of the "middle stage" in career and life that incorporates both danger and opportunity, the restoration of personal agency and goals through meaningful work can be considered the most positive approach to mid-career transition. Therefore, we will next discuss ways to promote a self-directed and value-driven attitude in mid-career transition, which can in turn lead to meaningfulness in work.

Facilitating a positive approach to mid-career transition at the individual level

Hall et al.'s (2013) notion of two critical metacompetencies, self-awareness and adaptability, has useful implications for the facilitation of positive approach to mid-career transition. They emphasized that the balanced development of the two metacompetences is crucial in achieving meaningful work. The roles of adaptability and self-awareness have also been recognized in the boundaryless and protean career models. As career development has become cyclical instead of linear, and mobility has become a standard feature of careers, individuals' responsibility to initiate their career transition is becoming more emphasized.

To assume full responsibility in their mid-career transition, individuals first need to be equipped with the adaptability to cope with changing roles and workforce. In addition, to reevaluate their past and future career, awareness of their own values and meaning in life is essential. Sullivan and Emerson (2000) and Hall (1996) noted that, in contemporary society which is moving toward the boundaryless career, the focus is shifting from extrinsic to intrinsic rewards, and self-reliance is becoming increasingly more important. Facing growing insecurity and mobility, mid-career workers are required to be self-determined and self-directed, guided by their values and meanings in life.

Career adapt-abilities Deriving from Super's (1980) work on career maturity, Savickas (1997, 2005, 2008) coined the term "career adapt-ability" as a psychosocial construct that denotes an individual's readiness and resources for coping with current and anticipated tasks, transitions, and traumas in their occupational roles, and that alters their social integration to a certain degree. Furthermore, career adapt-ability is related to the individual capability to make successful transitions in the labor market. Research suggests that those with a high level of career adapt-ability can easily adjust themselves to changing occupational situations. Generally, career adaptability has been suggested as a key competency in career success (O'Connel, McNeely, & Hall, 2008; Omar, & Noordin, 2013).

The "five-fold career adapt-abilities competency framework" (see Table 20.3) was developed from a cross-cultural quantitative study on career counseling. Savickas and colleagues (2009) proposed a life design approach to career development with the five competencies, or five Cs, as focal points (Bimrose, Brown, Barnes, & Hughes, 2011). The five Cs stand for control, curiosity, commitment, confidence, and concern. These five separate but interrelated competencies are crucial factors in increasing individuals' adaptive responses to career transitions (Bimrose et al., 2011).

Researchers suggest that this framework can be used to motivate workers in mid-career to adopt behaviors that can promote positive career changes. Recent study on career adaptability evidenced the relationship between career adaptability and job satisfaction in a sample of 577 older workers from Australia (Zacher & Griffin, 2015). The result indicated that older workers' chronological age was positively related to motivation to continue working, and motivation to continue working was also related to career adaptability and job satisfaction. Furthermore, counselors can focus on career adapt-ability with the goal of supporting clients to become more resilient and capable of managing risk and uncertainty in the rapidly changing and unpredictable education, training, and employment contexts (Brown, Bimrose, Barnes, & Hughes, 2012). Brown and colleagues (2012) emphasized

Table 20.3 The five-fold career adapt-abilities competency framework.

Competencies	*Definition*
Control	Learning through challenging work, increasing influence on one's career situations, updating a substantive knowledge base
Curiosity	Experimenting with a wider set of new and different activities and projects; exploring a wider range of opportunities and possibilities; learning through interactions at work
Commitment	Learning through interactions at work; how individuals should experiment with new and different activities and projects, rather than being focused narrowly on getting into a particular job, so that new possibilities can be generated
Confidence	Belief in self and own ability to achieve what is necessary to achieve one's career goal
Concern	Stimulating or developing a positive and optimistic attitude toward the future

Source: Author.

the role of "learning." They stated that adults in employment who do not engage in substantive up-skilling or re-skilling through either formal learning or training at work for periods of 5–10 years, are at increasing risk of being locked in particular ways of working. Because of their low adaptability, these workers become vulnerable in the labor market, especially if their jobs or circumstances change (Brown et al., 2010, p. 754). Career adaptability, one particular type of competency, can be seen as a combination of working experience, continuous learning, and proactive self-development.

The importance of lifelong learning to enhance career adaptability has been constantly emphasized. Power and Rothausen (2003) addressed the need for a strategic and proactive approach to maintain future employability, through continuous honing of skills and accumulation of knowledge that are applicable across various jobs. In the boundaryless career, professional loyalty instead of organizational loyalty receives greater respect (Sullivan & Emerson, 2000), and experience and expertise are valued (Wang et al., 2013). Thus, the learning for career adaptability is not limited to learning skills and knowledge for promotion within a specific organization. However, one of the problems with middle-aged or elderly workers is that they do not have a clear view on their skills and know-how. Also, learning opportunities for skill development in either formal or informal settings are not easily accessible for these individuals (Cedefop, 2011). If mid-career workers are not provided with adequate learning opportunities, they may experience frustrations in career transition. In addition, potential misplacement and lack of preparation can lead to low levels of job performance and job satisfaction.

Self-awareness Although there is a rising need for lifelong learning to enhance career adaptability, some workers display a lack of commitment to learn in preparation for any future career change. The lack of commitment to enhance adaptability may be a signal of career stagnation, indicating the need to be more adventurous in one's current career path. Traditionally, workers placed value primarily on their work performance. However, today people value intrinsic reward or psychological success more than they do extrinsic values, and they are more aware of their own psychological standards. Mid-career workers in particular have the need to develop personal value and purpose at work. When mid-career workers realize the gap between their career identity and personal identity, they begin to consider career changes. Even when they are well established in their career and experience mastery in mid-career, they may change their attitudes toward or perceptions of their career (Slay et al., 2004). Power and Rothausen (2003) suggested that as an individual accumulates experience, a personalized definition of work – answers to the questions of what he or she does, for whom, and why – evolves. In mid-career, workers tend to rely on their own subjective definition of work, which includes the personal meaning of the work, or what they personally want to achieve as the result of their efforts.

In developing self-awareness, self-reflection on personal values and meaning is vital. Values are core beliefs that serve as standards against which individuals judge their and others' daily performance (Rokeach, 1973). Thus, "for a job to be satisfying, it must allow individuals to engage in activities that they believe are worthwhile, which in turn allows them to compare themselves favorably with others" (Brown, 1995). Noon and Blyton (1997) suggested that the majority of people, regardless of their jobs, would continue to work even if there is no financial need, in order to gain social contact and sustain their identities. Confirmation of personal value and meaning of work is especially important when the career change is negative (Hall et al., 2013). When individuals reflect on their career, they need an overarching value system to provide orientation and direction against which they examine their career trajectory.

Research in meaning shows a certain connection between the meaning of work and the overall meaning of life (Steger & Dik, 2009). In the face of the unstable and dynamic nature of modern society, individuals tend to make career transitions in such a way that their meaning in work corresponds with their meaning in life. Through an arduous process of exploring the meaning of their work and duty, they reform their perspectives on meaning, and ultimately discover their greatest value (Briscoe et al., 2006). In the same context, Erikson and Peck noted that through searching for meaning, people achieve personal growth, discover new possibilities, and enter the next developmental stage (Weaver, 2009). According to Weaver (2009), people can move closer to achieving their individuation through creative work, experience of love and fortitude, and acceptance and "owning" of the whole self. Furthermore, this allows them to deepen the meaning of their existence and continue their process of personal growth.

Thus, through a training of perspective change and intervention that promotes positive attitude, which turns a crisis into an opportunity, successful mid-career transition can be achieved. Individuals should be encouraged to utilize transition as an opportunity for change and a steppingstone for the exploration of their ideal jobs.

Facilitating a Positive Approach to Mid-Career Transition at Organizational Level

We will now look at the "organizational-level" factors that facilitate mid-career transitions. Generally speaking, in the perspective of business management, "Human Resources" (HR) or "Human Capital" is viewed as a crucial factor that determines performance output in organizations. Thus, the HR department is responsible for the balanced management of strategies, organizational climate, systematic processes, as well as "people," or the human resources.

HR departments typically consist of two divisions: Human Resource Management (HRM), and Human Resource Development (HRD). Although each division has unique purposes and responsibilities, they are not separate entities. There is growing support for the integration of HRM and HRD to increase the effectiveness of HR practices in organizations.

Human Resource Management (HRM)

Scholars have emphasized the importance of gaining competitive advantage through employees, and identified several HR practices necessary to obtain this advantage (Pfeffer, 1998; Vermeeren et al., 2014). First of all, the HRM department, through processes such as screening and placement, can assist workers during the challenging period of mid-career transition. For example, individually tailored jobs can improve workers' productivity, which is the ultimate goal of HRM itself as well. Based on the old-fashioned notion of the organization as director and employees as the passive follower, it is hard to find a fit between the job and individual. It is even more so in the contemporary world, where there is a constant fluctuation in external environments and in the characteristics required of workers. In the case of the mid-life career crisis, individuals have a higher tendency to experience low motivation toward work; thus, the expected performance level becomes harder to reach.

Therefore, we can state that HRM has a responsibility to align the characters of each employee and the requirements of each job, while taking continuous changes in the environment and individuals in consideration. Through this alignment process, a proper level of adapt-ability for mid-career transition can be achieved.

Strategic HRM practices also affect the employee–organization relationship. Since every employee has different needs, strategic HRM practices are required for the establishment and maintenance of a positive relationship between the employee and organization. For example, as Wang et al. (2013) stated, "employees in their early career stages will have different needs compared to employees in their mid and late career stages. Therefore, differentiated systems of HR practices are needed to address both the needs of various constituents within the organization and the contingencies posed by the organization's strategy and environment." In particular, health care and retirement benefits are the two most important employee benefits for mid- and late-career workers. Institutional support that utilizes individually tailored HRM strategies is expected to be particularly effective in assisting individuals about to retire (Kim & Jin, 2013).

Human Resource Development (HRD)

HRD is an important research area that has received much research attention. Theorists have been actively defining HRD from a global perspective (Khan, Khan, & Mahmood, 2012). From the perspective of HRM, HRD is a "set of systematic and planned activities designed by an organization to provide its members with the opportunities to learn necessary skills to meet current and future job demands" (Werner & DeSimone, 2006, p. 5). Traditionally, HRD was regarded as a subdiscipline of HRM. However, the definition and scope of HRD have evolved from the narrow definition limited to training. HRD is now considered a "process of developing and unleashing expertise for the purpose of improving individual, team, work process, and organizational system performance" (Khan et al., 2012). Broadly speaking, HRD has been defined as a "process for developing and unleashing human expertise through organization development and personnel training and development for the purpose of improving performance" (Swanson & Holton, 2001).

Scholars have argued that training enhances innovation through promoting a learning climate in the organization (Sung & Choi, 2014). Recent business studies suggest that the capacity for constant learning is a condition for organizational survival, in addition to individuals' self-directed learning (Mansour, Chik, & Mohamad, 2014; Senge, 1997). Organizations should pay attention to creating a learning climate in order to facilitate the learning process of employees, especially those who are in need of organizational support. According to Al-Kahtani and Khan (2013), HR plays an active role in the modern economic scenario of every country, and its development in the organization context is a process through which the employees are helped in a continuous and planned manner. Through HRD, workers develop their general capabilities as individuals, and discover and harness their inner potentials for personal and/or organizational development. Since HRD is a key factor of an HR system, it is important to review recent HRD programs that aim to positively change employees' perspectives to enhance their performance. In the same vein, HRD practices in the organization can contribute to the creation of a "learning and facilitating environment" at the workplace for mid-career workers.

Slay et al. (2004) provided several important suggestions for HRD practices for mid-life career transition. First, they noted that HRD should increase the use of professional growth plans for mid-life employees who often experience fewer advancement opportunities as they age. Although mid-life employees need to upskill or reskill their abilities in order to increase their career adapt-abilities, they often lack support from the organization. Another suggestion from Slay and colleagues (2004) is job crafting. Job crafting is a "creative and improvised process that captures how individuals locally adapt their jobs in ways that create and sustain a viable definition of the work they do and who they are at work" (Wrzesniewski & Dutton, 2001). Other researchers have also offered several recommendations for HRD practices. One of them is to provide training programs to help managers recognize that "individuals [define] the same work differently as well as how to affirm and create opportunities for individuals as strengths and career desires become evident." As employees learn to see their own work in a different light, they realize the significance of their work. In other words, they find their meaning of work. In the same vein, organizations can encourage employees to "redesign" their jobs in ways that mirror their "reflected best self" (Roberts, Dutton, Spreitzer, Heaphy, & Quinn, 2005).

So far, we have reviewed the effects of HR practices for employees, especially those undergoing mid-career transition. Another important message is that constant investment in HR is not optional. During times of economic difficulties, organizations often reduce the budget for training and development. For instance, in a survey on HRM in Irish enterprises, more than half of the firms reported a decrease in their budget for training and development (Mulhall, 2014; Roche, Teague, Coughlan, & Fahy, 2011). In another survey in Romanian enterprises, 82% of companies reduced spending on HR in 2009 after the global recession (Daedalus Millward Brown, 2010). In addition, scholars should pay greater attention to the interpersonal relation competencies of each employee, as the performance of members in any organization depends on the members' ability to effectively interact with their superiors, subordinates, and co-workers within the organization, as well as with customers, suppliers, and the general public (Hullamani, & Ramakrishna, 2013). In the case of mid-career transitioners, HRD can extend the scope of developmental programs to help with not only "self-awareness" but also "interpersonal relations," so that the workers can establish their career goals according to their future plans. In this way, HRD will be able to broaden individuals' views on their capabilities, which will guide their career paths in a positive direction.

Future Research

The mid-career transition began to receive research attention in the late 1990s. The recent theoretical and empirical studies on careers indicate that career development has gone beyond the traditional, linear, male-oriented, and organizationally based career (Sullivan & Baruch, 2009). Career research is now paying increasing attention to the cultural, work, personal, and environmental contexts of the contemporary society. The issue of mid-career is related to the individual developmental task, and is affected by changes in the organizational and global environments. Therefore, future research should focus on the effects of diverse psychosocial factors across multiple levels on mid-career transition. However, there has been a lack of an integrative approach that incorporates multiple factors across multiple levels and shows how these factors together contribute to the mid-career transition. Future research need to develop an integrative framework to explain how various factors facilitate or impede the mid-career transition. To do so, researchers should take a multidisciplinary approach and utilize advanced analytical methods such as multilevel analysis.

Future research also needs to recognize that most mid-career transition in the real world is temporal and dynamic, as opposed to static and cross-sectional. Thus, researchers are encouraged to pay closer attention to longitudinal changes. For example, do workers with high levels of self-awareness predict better performance and subjective job satisfaction in the future? Does a specific mentoring approach facilitate career adaptabilities with time? Does a high level of involvement in learning in the initial career phase predict later voluntary career changes? Longitudinal studies may provide answers to these potential research questions.

Recent studies consistently suggest that future researchers should consider societal culture as an important context in examining the experience of mid-career transition (Wang, et al., 2013). In different cultures, mid-career workers may develop disparate needs and values. For example, Li, Tsui, and Weldon (2000) showed that in Confucian culture older age is typically associated with seniority and higher social hierarchies. Therefore, older workers in those societies may particularly value opportunities to participate in company policy making, even if such practice is only an act of formality. In addition, in Confucian culture, more rigid gender roles are ascribed to each gender, assigning breadwinning to men and family chores to women. Although increasing numbers of women are entering the workforce, the gender roles are still rigid in many aspects. Consequently, men in mid-career transition in Confucian culture may experience greater anxiety about career changes.

As continuous learning has been shown to be crucial in career adaptability, future research should examine and identify the characteristics of effective career strategies and actions. Also, further research is needed to clarify how mid-career workers transfer knowledge attained through training or mentoring to on-the-job performance. Specifically, future research should identify whether there are certain training processes or mentoring approaches that facilitate the successful transfer of knowledge. In addition, we need to understand the source of low motivation among mid-career workers who may be forced to retire earlier than they desire. Since self-directedness is the key factor in managing self-initiated career transition, understanding the source of low motivation would provide valuable insights for effective interventions to enhance self-directedness.

Sense of purpose and meaning is found to be an important drive for mid-life and mid-career transition. With a high level of protean career orientation, the meaningfulness of work is expected to lead to better job performance and greater satisfaction at work. Considering that the mid-career transition and mid-life career transition have negative connotations, it would be interesting to see how the protean career orientation and the sense of meaningfulness interact with each other. Future studies also need to identify individual and organizational factors related to the high level of protean career orientation and sense of meaningfulness during mid-career transition.

Finally, future researchers need to acknowledge that career patterns that are considered deviant from traditional career perspectives appear in the modern society. For example, contingent workers, who make up a growing portion of the workforce, may be stigmatized as "temporary" and less likely to receive the necessary mentoring and/or training to make progress in their career (Wang et al., 2013). Due to the devastating economic situation in several countries, these nontraditional career patterns have evolved rapidly. The concept of mid-career transition may be too traditional to apply to these career patterns. Future researchers need to expand their research interest to include these evolving career patterns.

Conclusion

In this chapter, we have reviewed the theoretical and empirical literature relevant to mid-career transition. The notion of mid-career is rooted in mid-life career, but the concept of mid-career has been revised due to worldwide economic and organizational changes. To understand the nature of mid-career transition, we have reviewed the evolution of the notion of mid-career and the impact of environmental and individual factors on mid-career changes. During our discussion, we have differentiated between the concepts of mid-career transition and mid-life career transition. Next, we have provided the theoretical context for understanding the key features of mid-career transition in contemporary society. Super's initial model of mid-career development was expanded to include recycling based on self-concept implementation. In addition, we have discussed recent career models, that is boundaryless and protean career models, and their emphasis on individual-initiated career transition as opposed to organization-owned career transition. Lastly, we have discussed ways to facilitate a positive approach to mid-career transition both at the individual and organizational levels. To achieve successful individual-initiated career transition, self-directed and value-driven attitudes toward career transition are critical. Although the mid-career transition is recognized as an insecure and vulnerable experience, individuals can approach it positively if they are prepared to be self-directed and value-driven. Also, organizations need to take an active role in the balanced management of strategies, organizational climate, and systematic process, as well as human resources. Future studies on mid-career transition should integrate multiple factors across multiple levels. In addition, future researchers need to move beyond the traditional approach to take into consideration the impacts of culture, gender, and types of work on the mid-career transition, as well as emerging new career patterns.

References

Al-Kahtani, N. S., & Khan, N. A. (2013). Human resource development practices in telecom sector in Saudi Arabia: An empirical presentation. *World Applied Sciences Journal, 28*, 1567–1578.

Alley, D., & Crimmins, E. (2007). The demography of aging and work. In K. S. Shultz & G. A. Adams (Eds.), *Aging and work in the 21st century* (pp. 7–24). London, UK: Erlbaum.

Arbona, C. (2003). Work-oriented midcareer development: A commentary. *The Counseling Psychologist, 31*, 198–204.

Armstrong, M., & Taylor, S. (2014). *Armstrong's handbook of human resource management practice.* London, UK: Kogan Page.

Arthur, M. B., & Rousseau, D. M. (1996). *The boundaryless career: A new employment principle for a new organizational era.* Oxford, UK: Oxford University Press.

Arthur, M. B., Inkson, K., & Pringle, J. K. (1999). *The new careers. Individual action and economic change.* London, UK: Sage.

Barclay, S. R., Stoltz, K. B., & Chung, Y. B. (2011). Voluntary midlife career change: Integrating the transtheoretical model and the life-span, life-space approach. *Career Development Quarterly, 60*, 386–399.

Baruch, Y., & Quick, J. C. (2007). Understanding second careers: Lessons from a study of U.S. Navy admirals. *Human Resource Management, 46*, 471–491.

Bauman, Z. (1998). *Globalization: The human consequences.* Cambridge, UK: Polity Press.

Beck, U. (1992). *Risk society: Towards a new modernity.* London, UK: Sage.

Bejian, D. V., & Salomone, P. R. (1995). Understanding midlife career renewal: Implications for counseling. *The Career Development Quarterly, 44*, 52–63.

Bell, J. E. (1982, August). Mid-life transition in career men. *AMA Management Digest*, 8–10.

Bimrose, J., Brown, A., Barnes, S-A., & Hughes, D. (2011). The role of career adaptability in skills supply, *Evidence report 35. Main Report.* Wath-upon-Dearne, UK: UK Commission for Employment and Skills.

Blanton, S., & Gordon, A. (1967). *Now or never: The promise of the middle years.* Englewood Cliffs, NJ: Prentice Hall.

Bobek, B., & Robbins, S. (2005). Counseling for career transition: Career pathing, job loss, and reentry. In S. D. Brown & R. W. Lent (Eds.), *Career development and counseling: Putting theory and research to work* (pp. 625–650). Hoboken, NJ: Wiley.

Briscoe, J., & Hall, D. (2002, August). *The protean orientation: Creating the adaptable workforce necessary for flexibility and speed.* Paper presented at the annual meeting of the Academy of Management, Denver.

Briscoe, J., & Hall, D. (2003). *Being and becoming protean: Individual and experiential factors in adapting to the new career.* Unpublished technical report. Department of Management, Northern Illinois University, DeKalb.

Briscoe, J. P., & Hall, D. T. (2006). The interplay of boundaryless and protean careers: Combinations and implications. *Journal of Vocational Behavior, 69*, 4–18.

Briscoe, J. P., Hall, D. T., & DeMuth, R. L. F. (2006). Protean and boundaryless careers: An empirical exploration. *Journal of Vocational Behavior, 69*, 30–47.

Brown, A., Bimrose, J., Barnes, S. A., & Hughes, D. (2012). The role of career adaptabilities for mid-career changers. *Journal of Vocational Behavior, 80*, 754–761.

Brown, A., Bimrose, J., Barnes, S. A., Kirpal, S., Grønning, T., & Dæhlen, M. (2010). *Changing patterns of working, learning and career development across Europe.* Brussels, Belgium: Education, Audiovisual, Culture Executive Agency.

Brown, D. (1995). A values-based approach to facilitating career transitions. *The Career Development Quarterly, 44*, 4–11.

Career (2013). How often do employees change jobs?? [Press release.] Retrieved from http://www.careernet.co.kr/prcenter/media_data_view.asp?rid=2072&page=16

Carnoy, M. (1999). The great work dilemma. In J. Ahier & G. Esland (Eds.), *Education, training and the future of work: Vol. 1. Social, political and economic contexts of policy development* (pp. 62–75). London, UK: Routledge.

Carnoy, M. (2001). Work, society, family and learning for the future. In *What schools for the future? Schooling for tomorrow.* Paris: OECD.

Cedefop (2011). *Learning while working: Success stories on workplace learning in Europe.* Luxembourg: Publications Office of the European Union. Retrieved from http://www.cedefop.europa.eu/EN/Files/3060_en.pdf

Chin, W. S., & Rasdi, R. M. (2014). Protean career development: Exploring the individuals, organizational and job-related factors. *Asian Social Science, 10*, 203–215.

Dacey, J. S., & Travers, F. F. (2004). *Human development across the lifespan.* New York, NY: McGraw Hill.

David, R. (2005). Mid-career entrepreneurial learning. *Education and Training, 47*, 562–574.

Daedalus Millward Brown (2010). *HR approach in recession.* Retrieved from http://www.hr-club.ro/portalhrclub/bibliotecavirtuala/HR%20Approach%20in%20%20Recession.pdf

DeFillippi, R. J., & Arthur, M. B. (1994). The boundaryless career: A competency-based perspective. *Journal of Organizational Behavior, 15*, 307–324.

De Vos, A., & Soens, N. (2008). Protean attitude and career success: The mediating role of self-management. *Journal of Vocational Behavior, 73*, 449–456.

Donohue, W. A. (2007). Methods, milestones, and models: State of the art in conflict analysis research. *Negotiation Journal, 23*, 487–497.

Farjoun, M. (2010). Beyond dualism: Stability and change as a duality. *Academy of Management Review, 35*, 202–225.

Feldman, D. C. (2002). Stability in the midst of change: A developmental perspective on the study of careers. In D. C. Feldman (Ed.), *Work careers: A developmental perspective* (pp. 3–26). San Francisco, CA: Jossey-Bass.

Gasteiger, R. M., & Briscoe, J. P. (2007, August). *What kind of organization do protean people prefer? The case of Germany and the United States.* Paper presented at the Academy of Management Conference, Philadelphia.

Giddens, A. (1991). *Modernity and self-identity: Self and society in the late modern age.* Stanford, CA: Stanford University Press.

Golan, N. (1986). *The perilous bridge.* New York, NY: The Free Press.

Goodman, J., Schlossberg, N. K., & Anderson, M. L. (2006). *Counseling adults in transition: Linking practice with theory* (3rd ed.). New York, NY: Springer.

Gould, R. (1978). *Transformations: Growth and change in adult life.* New York, NY: Simon & Schuster.

Greenhaus, J., & Allen, T. (2011). Work–family balance: A review and extension of the literature. In J. Campbell Quick & L. E. Tetrick (Eds.), *Handbook of occupational health psychology* (2nd ed., pp. 165–183). Washington, DC: American Psychological Association.

Gubler, M., Arnold, J., & Coombs, C. (2014). Reassessing the protean career concept: Empirical findings, conceptual components, and measurement. *Journal of Organizational Behavior*, *35*, S23–S40.

Guerrier, Y., & Philpot, N. (1978). *The British manager: Careers and mobility*. Windsor, UK: British Institute of Management.

Guindon, M. H., & Smith, B. (2002). Emotional barriers to successful reemployment: Implications for counselors. *Journal of Employment Counseling*, *39*, 73–82.

Hackett, G. (1993). Career counseling and psychotherapy: False dichotomies and recommended remedies. *Journal of Career Assessment*, *1*, 105–196.

Hall, D. T. (1996). Protean careers of the 21st century. *The Academy of Management Executive*, *10*, 8–16.

Hall, D. T. (2002). *Protean careers in and out of organizations*. Thousand Oaks, CA: Sage.

Hall, D. T., Feldman, E., & Kim, N., (2013). *Meaningful work and the protean career: Purpose and meaning in the workplace*. Washington, DC: American Psychological Association.

Hall, D. T., & Mirvis, P. H. (1995). The new career contract: Developing the whole person at midlife and beyond. *Journal of Vocational Behavior*, *47*, 269–289.

Harper, M. C. (2005). *Retirement modeling: An exploration of the effects of retirement role model characteristics on retirement self-efficacy in middle worker*. Unpublished doctorial dissertation, University of North Carolina at Greensboro.

Harris Interactive (2005, May). *Pulte homes baby boomer study*. Retrieved March, 25, 2015 from http://www.corporate-ir.net/media_files/irol/77/77968/BabyBoomerStudy.pdf

HayGroup (2013). *Global employee engagement and enablement trends*. Retrieved April 30, 2015, from http://www.haygroup.com/downloads/sg/2013%20global%20employee%20engagement%20and%20enablement%20trends.pdf

Heppner, M. J., Multon, K. D., & Johnston, J. A. (1994). Assessing psychological resources during career change: Development of the Career Transitions Inventory. *Journal of Vocational Behavior*, *44*, 55–74.

Herrmann, A., Hirschi, A., & Baruch, Y. (2015). The protean career orientation as predictor or career outcomes: Evaluation of incremental validity and mediation effects. *Journal of Vocational Behavior*, *88*, 205–214.

Holbeche, L., & Springett, N. (2004). *In search of meaning at work*. Horsham, UK: Roffey Park Institute.

Huebner, E., & Royal, C. (2013). Beyond self-actualization: Voluntary midlife career transitions and implications for career counselors. *Career Planning and Adult Development Journal*, *29*, 37–44

Hullamani, R. M., & Ramakrishna, H. (2013). A empirical study on interpersonal behavior skills and its effect on organization – HR Consulting Firm. *Elixir Human Res. Mgmt.*, *5*, 12751–12753.

Ilg, R. (2010, June). *Long-term unemployment experience of the jobless*. BLS Summary 10-05, U. S. Bureau of Labor Statistics.

Inceoglu, I., Segers, J., Bartram, D., & Vloeberghs, D. (2008, April). *Age differences in work motivation*. Paper presented at the 23rd Annual Conference of the Society for Industrial and Organizational Psychology, San Francisco.

Inceoglu, I., Segers, J., & Bartram, D. (2012). Age-related differences in motivation. *Journal of Occupational and Organizational Psychology*, *85*, 300–329.

Jaques, E. (1965). Death and the mid-life crisis. *The International Journal of Psycho-analysis*, *46*, 502.

Jeon, C. H., & Jin, S. M. (2011). A study of motivation in learning of mid-career baby-boomer men in career development. *The Korean Journal of Human Resource Development Quarterly*, *13*, 21–43.

Job Korea (2015). *Expected retirement age, "52," 54 for men, 49 for women* [Press release]. Retrieved from http://company.jobkorea.co.kr/cyber_pr/default.asp#news

Jung, C. G. (1966). *The collected works of C. G.Jung: Vol. 7. Two essays on analytical psychology*. London: Routledge.

Jung, Y., & Takeuchi, N. (2011, July). *Relationships among protean career, organizational support, and subjective career success in early and mid-career stages*. Paper presented at the EGOS Colloquium, Gothenburg.

Khan, M. T., Khan, N. A., & Mahmood, K. (2012). An organizational concept of human resource development: How human resource management scholars view "HRD." *Universal Journal of Management and Social Sciences*, *2*(5), 36–47.

Kanfer, R., & Ackerman, P. L. (2004). Aging, adult development, and work motivation. *Academy of Management Review*, *29*, 440–458.

Kim, N. H., & Jin, S. M. (2013). Career adaptabilities as experienced by mid-career adults in career transition. *Journal of Korean HRD Research*, *8*, 28–53.

Kooij, D., De Lange, A., Jansen, P., & Dikkers, J. (2008). Older workers' motivation to continue to work: Five meanings of age. *Journal of Managerial Psychology*, *23*, 364–394.

Kossek, E. E., Pichler, S., Bodner, T., & Hammer, L. B. (2011). Workplace social support and work–family conflict: A meta-analysis clarifying the influence of general and work–family specific supervisor and organizational support. *Personnel Psychology*, *64*, 289–313.

Levinson, D. J. (1978). Eras: The anatomy of the life cycle. *Psychiatric Opinion*, *15*, 39–48.

Levinson, D. J. (1980). Toward a conception of the adult life course. In N. Smelser & E. Erikson (Eds.), *Themes of work and love in adulthood* (pp. 265–289). Cambridge, MA: Harvard University Press.

Levinson, D. J. (1990). A theory of life structure development in adulthood. In C. N. Alexander & E. J. Langer (Eds.), Higher stages of human development (pp. 35–54). Oxford: Oxford University Press.

Levinson, D. J., Darrow, C. N., Klein, E. B., Levinson, M. H., & McKee, B. (1978). *The seasons of a man's life*. New York, NY: Knopf.

Li, J. T., Tsui, A. S., & Weldon, E. (2000). *Management and organizations in the Chinese context*. Basingstoke, UK: Macmillan.

Liu, Y., Englar-Carlson, M., & Minichiello, V. (2012). Midlife career transitions of men who are scientists and engineers: A narrative study. *The Career Development Quarterly*, *60*, 273–288.

Mansour, N., Chik, S. B., & Mohamad, Z. (2014). Strengthening staff competency through organizational learning and group differences. *Journal of Applied Environmental and Biological Sciences*, *4*, 90–100.

Mattihijs, B. P., Kleef, M. V., & Jansen, P. G. (2015). The impact of career customization on work outcomes: Boundary conditions of manager support and employee age. *Journal of Organizational Behavior*, *36*, 421–440.

Maurer, T. J. (2001). Career-relevant learning and development, worker age, and beliefs about self-efficacy for development. *Journal of Management*, *27*, 123–140.

Mulhall, S. (2014). Careers and career development. In B. Harney & K. Monks (Eds.), *Strategic HRM: Research and practice in Ireland* (pp. 211–229). Dublin, Ireland: Orpen Press.

Mumford, A., & Gold, J. (2004). *Management development: Strategies for action*. London, UK: Chartered Institute of Personnel and Development.

Murphy, C. M., & Shillingford, M. (2012). Supporting unemployed, middle-aged men: A psychoeducational group approach. *Journal of Employment Counseling*, *49*, 85–96.

Murphy, P. P., & Burck, H. D. (1976). Career development of men at mid-life. *Journal of Vocational Behavior*, *9*, 337–343.

Ng, T. W., Sorensen, K. L., Eby, L. T., & Feldman, D. C. (2007). Determinants of job mobility: A theoretical integration and extension. *Journal of Occupational and Organizational Psychology*, *80*, 363–386.

Ng, T. W. J., Sorensen, K. L., & Yim, F. H. K. (2009). Does the job satisfaction–job performance relationship vary across cultures? *Journal of Cross-Cultural Psychology*, *40*, 761–796.

Noon, M., & Blyton, P. (1997). *The realities of work*. London, UK: Macmillan.

O'Connel, D. J., McNeely, E., & Hall, D. T. (2008). Unpacking personal adaptability at work. *Journal of Leadership & Organizational Studies*, *14*, 248–259.

OECD (2013). *Pensions at a glance 2013: OECD and G20 indicators*. Paris, France: OECD Publishing.

OECD (2015). OECD Review from 2011 to 2014. Retrieved March 25, 2015, from http://www.oecd.org/employment/livelongerworklonger.htm

Omar, S., & Noordin, F. (2013). Career adaptability and intention to leave among ICT professionals: An exploratory study. *Turkish Online Journal of Educational Technology*, *12*(4), 11–18.

Owen, L., & Flynn, M. (2004). Changing work: Mid-to-late life transitions in employment. *Ageing International*, *29*, 333–350.

Peake, S., & McDowall, A. (2012). Chaotic careers: A narrative analysis of career transition themes and outcomes using chaos theory as a guiding metaphor. *British Journal of Guidance & Counselling*, *40*, 395–410.

Pfeffer, Jeffrey (1998). *The human equation: Building profits by putting people first.* Boston, MA: Harvard Business School Press.

Power, S. J., & Rothausen, T. J. (2003). The work-oriented midcareer development model: An extension of Super's maintenance stage. *The Counseling Psychologist, 31*, 157–197.

Roberts, L. M., Dutton, J. E., Spreitzer, G. M., Heaphy, E. D., & Quinn, R. E. (2005). Composing the reflected best-self portrait: Building pathways for becoming extraordinary in work organizations. *Academy of Management Review, 30*, 712–736.

Roche, W. K., Teague, P., Coughlan, A., & Fahy, M. (2011). *Human resources in the recession: Managing and representing people at work in Ireland.* Dublin, Ireland: Labour Relations Commission.

Rokeach, M. (1973). *The nature of human values* (Vol. *438*). New York, NY: The Free Press.

Ryff, C. D. (1995). Psychological well-being in adult life. *Current Directions in Psychological Science, 4*, 99–104.

Savickas, M. L. (1990). The use of career choice measures in counseling practice. In E. Watkins & V. Campbell (Eds.), *Testing in counseling practice* (pp. 373–417). Hillsdale, NJ: Erlbaum.

Savickas, M. L. (1997). Career adaptability: An integrative construct for life-span, life-space theory. *The Career Development Quarterly, 45*, 247–259.

Savickas, M. L. (2005). The theory and practice of career construction. In S. D. Brown & R. W. Lent (Eds.), *Career development and counseling: Putting theory and research to work* (2nd ed., pp. 42–70). Hoboken, NJ: Wiley.

Savickas, M. L. (2008). Helping people choose jobs: A history of the guidance profession. In J. A. Athanasou & R. Van Esbroeck (Eds.), *International handbook of career guidance* (pp. 97–113). Dordrecht, the Netherlands: Springer.

Savickas, M. L., Nota, L., Rossier, J., Dauwalder, J.-P., Duarte, M. E., Guichard, J., & Van Vianen, A. E. (2009). Life designing: A paradigm for career construction in the 21st century. *Journal of Vocational Behavior, 75*, 239–250.

Segers, J., Inceoglu, I., Vloeberghs, D., Bartram, D., & Henderickx, E. (2008). Protean and boundaryless careers: A study on potential motivators. *Journal of Vocational Behavior, 73*, 212–230.

Senge, P. M. (1990). *The fifth discipline: The art and practice of the learning organization.* London, UK: Doubleday.

Senge, P. M. (1997). The fifth discipline. *Measuring Business Excellence, 1*, 46–51.

Sheehy, G. (1976). *Passages: Predictable crises of adult life.* New York, NY: Button.

Simmelink, M. N. (2006, September). *Understanding grief in the context of job loss and lifestyle adjustment.* National Career Development Association News. Retrieved from http://www.ncda.org/aws/NCDA/pt/sd/news_article/5232/_PARENT/layout_details_cc/false

Slay, U. S., Taylor, M. S., & Williamson, I. O. (2004, March). *Midlife transition decision processes and career success: The role of identity, networks, and shocks.* Paper presented at the Annual Meeting of the Academy of Human Resource Development. Austin, TX.

Smyer, M. A., & Pitt-Catsouphes, M. (2007). The meanings of work for older workers. *Generations, 31*(1), 23–30.

Steger, M. F., & Dik, B. J. (2009). If one is looking for meaning in life, does it help to find meaning in work? *Applied Psychology: Health and Well-Being, 1*, 303–320.

Sullivan, S. E. (1999). The changing nature of careers: A review and research agenda. *Journal of Management, 25*, 457–484.

Sullivan, S. E., & Arthur, M. B. (2006). The evolution of the boundaryless career concept: Examining physical and psychological mobility. *Journal of Vocational Behavior, 69*, 19–29.

Sullivan, S. E., & Baruch, Y. (2009). Advances in career theory and research: Critical review and agenda for future exploration. *Journal of Management, 35*, 1452–1571.

Sullivan, S. E., & Emerson, R. (2000), *Recommendations for successfully navigating the boundaryless career: From theory to practice.* Paper presented at the Academy of Management 2000 Annual Conference, Chicago.

Sung, S. Y., & Choi, J. N. (2014). Do organizations spend wisely on employees? Effects of training and development investments on learning and innovation in organizations. *Journal of Organizational Behavior, 35*, 393–412.

Super, D. E. (1957). *The psychology of careers* (Vol. *195*). New York, NY: Harper & Row.

Super, D. E. (1980). A life-span, life-space approach to career development. *Journal of Vocational Behavior, 16*, 282–298.

Super, D. E. (1990). A life-span, life-space approach to career development. In D. Brown & L. Brooks (Eds.), *Career choice and development: Applying contemporary theories to practice* (2nd ed., pp. 197–269). San Francisco, CA: Jossey-Bass.

Super, D. E., & Bohn, M. J., Jr. (1970). *Occupational psychology*. Belmont, CA; Brookes Cole.

Super, D. E., Savickas, M. L., & Super, C. M. (1996). The life-span, life-space approach to careers. In D. Brown & L. Brooks (Eds.), *Career choice and development: Applying contemporary theories to practice*, (3rd ed., pp. 121–178). San Francisco, CA: Jossey-Bass.

Swanson, R. A., & Holton, E. F. (2001). *Foundations of human resource development*. San Francisco, CA: Berrett-Koehler.

Tivendell, J., & Bourbonnais, C. (2000). Job insecurity in a sample of Canadian civil servants as a function of personality and perceived job characteristics. *Psychological Reports, 87*, 55–60.

U.S. Department of Labor (2008). *Number of jobs held, labor market activity, and earnings growth among the youngest baby boomers: Results from a longitudinal survey*. Retrieved from http://www.bls.gov/news.release/pdf/nlsoy.pdf

Vaillant, G. E. (1977). *Adaptation to life: How the best and the brightest came of age*. Boston, MA: Little, Brown.

Vander Zanden, J. W. (2000). *Human development* (7th ed.). Boston, MA: McGraw-Hill.

Volmer, J., & Spurk, D. (2010). Protean and boundaryless career attitudes: Relationships with subjective and objective career success. *Journal for Labour Market Research, 43*, 207–218.

Vermeeren, B., Steijin, B., Tummers, L., Lankhaar, M., Poerstamper, R.-J., & Beek, S. (2014). HRM and its effect on employee, organizational and financial outcomes in health care. *Human Resources for Health, 12*, 35.

Wang, M., Olson, D. A., & Shultz, K. S. (2013). *Mid and late career issues: An integrative perspective*: London, UK: Routledge.

Warr, P. (2001). Age and work behaviour: Physical attributes cognitive abilities, knowledge, personality traits and motives. *International Review of Industrial and Organizational Psychology, 16*, 1–36.

Warr, P. B., & Birdi, K. (1998). Employee age and voluntary development activity. *International Journal of Training and Development, 2*, 190–204.

Weaver, Y. (2009). Mid-life: A time of crisis or new possibilities? *Existential Analysis: Journal of the Society for Existential Analysis, 20*, 69–78.

Werner, J. M., & DeSimone, R. L. (2006). *Human resource development* (4th ed.). London, UK.

Williams, C. P., & Savickas, M. L. (1990). Developmental tasks of career maintenance. *Journal of Vocational Behavior, 36*, 166–175.

Wrzesniewski, A., & Dutton, J. E. (2001). Crafting a job: Revisioning employees as active crafters of their work. *Academy of Management Review, 26*, 179–201.

Zacher, H., & Griffin, B. (2015). Older workers' age as a moderator of the relationship between career adaptability and job satisfaction. *Work, Aging and Retirement,1*(2), 227–236.

Zemon, C. (2002). Midlife career choices: How are they different from other career choices? *Library Trends, 50*, 665–672.

21

Positive Organizations and Maturing Workers

Jeanette N. Cleveland, Gwenith G. Fisher, and Kevin M. Walters

Introduction

Within the 21st century, approximately 30 years have been added onto our average life expectancies. Unlike any previous times, significant numbers of individuals will live until old age. A new age (i.e., the "fourth stage") has been added to our lifespan and life cycle (Charles & Carstensen, 2003), which represents a significant period of time when people have outlived the traditional definitions of "old." Importantly, health and well-being within our lives have been enhanced and extended such that individuals remain active and contribute as members of society longer, often reaching into their eighties and beyond (Phillips & Siu, 2012). Coupled with the evolution of technology, along with more complex and engaging service- and information-based work and less physically demanding tasks or workplaces, healthy individuals are choosing to work longer beyond traditional government-supported retirement ages to obtain financial resources, remain active, or maintain health. Increasingly among some occupations, working enhances or helps maintain one's physical, cognitive, and emotional health rather than draining vital human resources. Further, with the advent of global acknowledgment of equal rights, diversity management, and inclusion, together with the development of worklife programs, organizations have incorporated a number of norms, cultures, and practices that stand to benefit not only the intended targets (e.g., historically underrepresented groups and peoples), but *all* workers including employees as they mature.

Paralleling the dual views of aging, one of decline and another of awe or optimism, psychological and organizational research on employees historically has focused on both the identification and methods of overcoming obstacles faced by older workers. Research and practice are increasingly focusing on high functioning behaviors or performance and on ways of controlling and managing barriers to effective performance in a range of environments, including the workplace. With the emergence and growth of positive

The Wiley Blackwell Handbook of the Psychology of Positivity and Strengths-Based Approaches at Work, First Edition. Edited by Lindsay G. Oades, Michael F. Steger, Antonella Delle Fave, and Jonathan Passmore.

psychology and positive organizational scholarship (POS), it is increasingly important to study the challenges and limitations associated with work organizations and aging individuals as well as the positive contributions and the achievements of older workers. This dual focus parallels emerging trends in the aging literature, which has moved from an almost exclusive focus on decline, loss, decay, and weakness to include the identification of aspects of maturity and aging that are positive and beneficial to prevention of loss/decline (e.g., intellectual development, etc.; Baltes, 1987).

The purpose of this chapter is to discuss positive aspects of aging in relation to work – particularly the benefits of aging, benefits of older workers in the workplace, and implications of positive aging for human resource (HR) management in organizations. First, we describe what it means to become old or older. Although chronological age is widely used to make both economic and political decisions, its limitations provide creative alternative and meaningful measures of ages. Many of these alternative age conceptualizations have emerged from multidisciplinary theories of aging itself. In the next section of the chapter, we introduce a brief discussion of the primary features of POS and link them with aspects of four theories that reflect socio-emotional/motivational theories of aging, including lifespan development theories that especially focus on the perspectives of successful aging, such as selection-optimization-compensation theory (SOC), socio-emotional selectivity theory (SST), Kanfer and Ackerman's (2004) age and work motivation theory, and the job demands-resources (JD-R) model. We then describe resources and organizational practices that can be integrated and applied to maintain and enhance workers' contributions for as long as possible, so that older workers can continue to lead meaningful careers that positively impact and benefit their organization(s) and co-workers. We identify ways that organizations can adapt to provide opportunities for older workers to flourish and continue to contribute to organizations as their capabilities, strengths, and limitations change.

What does it mean to be old?

The concept of an "older worker" is multidimensional such that chronological age only provides a narrow approach to this construct (Cleveland & Lim, 2007). Chronological age is linked with predictable changes across a number of domains that involve health, work, family, and life, including changes in eyesight, reductions in muscular mass, slowing of cognitive processing speed, and so forth. But the perception on the part of workers of whether or not a particular individual is "older" does not depend solely on chronological age. It is possible for two workers with the same chronological age to be different enough that one may be considered to be an older worker while the other one is not. Because there are significant individual variations associated with age-related changes in abilities and other characteristics, chronological age reflects only one general marker of becoming "older" (Barak & Schiffman, 1981; Beier & Gilberto, 2015; Borkan & Norris, 1980; Kleinspehn-Ammerlahn, Kotter-Grühn, & Smith, 2008; Kooij, De Lange, Jansen, & Dikkers, 2008). Because it is difficult to concretely classify the age at which someone becomes old at work, it is important for us to also use alternative age measures aside from chronological age in order to further understand the concept of age (McCarthy, Heraty, Cross, & Cleveland, 2014).

Biological age is defined in terms of where a person stands in relation to the number of years that they will live or their longevity (Jackson, Weale, & Weale, 2003). Because it is difficult to predict the length of a person's life with great accuracy due to vast individual differences, biological age is typically assessed in terms of the body's organ systems and physical appearance, especially in comparison to others of the same chronological age (e.g., one's peers). Functional age refers to a person's competence in performing certain tasks (Anstey, Lord, & Smith, 1996). Like biological age, functional age involves a comparison with age peers. Further, functional age can vary within the same individual (Siegler, 1995) depending upon the functional capabilities involved. Functional age then is often assessed in relation to a specific context or set of activities or jobs.

Psychological age refers to how well a person functions and adapts to changing situations, the extent to which the person can tap a range of skills – including cognitive, personal, or social – to adapt, and the ability to remain flexible (Kooij et al., 2008). Social age consists of views held by most members of a society regarding expectations for a particular age group in terms of what they should do and how they should behave at a particular age (e.g., at what age to marry, have children, move out from one's parents' home, etc.). For example, a person who is 45 years old and is just having a first child is considered socially younger than one who is having a first child at age 28. Neugarten and Reed (1997) referred to this as a social clock that people use to assess whether their own life stage or progress or the progress of others is "on-time" or "off-time" (Binstock, 2002). Subjective age refers to the age at which an individual is seen as entering middle age or older age. Standards for defining subjective age depend in part on an individual's own chronological age. For example, people in their twenties tend to believe middle and older age begin at a lower chronological age than do older individuals, whereas people in their sixties often consider themselves to be middle-aged. The gap between chronological age and social age becomes wider as individuals become older such that older individuals feel younger (Goldsmith & Heiens, 1992). In addition, the gap between subjective age and chronological age is wider for middle-aged and older women than it is for middle-aged and older men (Montepare & Lachman, 1989).

Work-based age measures

Research on older workers has placed substantial emphasis on Sterns and Doverspike's (1989) five conceptualizations of age: chronological, functional, psychosocial, organizational, and lifespan age. Their definitions of chronological, functional, and psychosocial age correspond substantially with the age constructs discussed in the previous paragraphs (see McCarthy et al., 2014; Segers, Inceoglu, and Finkelstein, 2014; Sterns & Miklos, 1995). Organizational age refers to the length of time (i.e., tenure) that the individual has spent in their current job or organization. Lifespan age takes into account one's chronological age, cohort/generational variables, and unique career and life circumstances, which collectively are responsible for life changes throughout age. This age measurement emphasizes how a person's lifespan age is unique and behavior may change during any point in the life cycle. In a review of recent European literature, Schalk et al. (2010) provide a highly useful representation of Sterns and Doverspike's (1989) categories, incorporating a number of suggested indicators for each age category (e.g., chronological age = calendar age; functional age = health; or psychosocial age = social or self-perceived age).

Consistent with Sterns and Doverspike (1989), Cleveland and colleagues (e.g., Cleveland & Shore, 1992; Cleveland, Shore & Murphy, 1997) suggested that approaches to defining workers' age can be categorized into two distinct types of perceptual age measures: person-based (i.e., within-person focused) age measures, and context-based age measures (i.e., between-person comparisons). These measures are broadly similar to the perceptual age measures outlined by Sterns and Doverspike (1989).

Prism of age, age matrix, and age cube of work In order to provide organizational dimensions to several of these age measure alternatives, the researchers at the Sloan Center for Aging and Work developed the prism of age (Pitt-Catsouphes, Matz-Costa, & Brown, 2010).

This work further extended Sterns and Doverspike's (1989) and Cleveland and Shore's (1992) models to include generational age, tenure age, and career-stage age. Generational age refers to individuals born within a certain time period (e.g., traditionalists, born before 1946; baby-boomers, born 1946–1964; Generation X, born 1965–1980; and Generation Y, born after 1980 and sometimes referred to as "the millennials"; Johnson & Lopes, 2008), whereas tenure age refers to the number of years an individual has worked for an employer, and career stage age refers to an individual's stage in their respective career. Both the age matrix and the age cube provide variations on the Prism of Age (Segers et al., 2014). Lawrence (1984, 1987, 1988) found that age in organizations is linked to beliefs about an individual's career, or indeed, their career opportunities. There is also some evidence to suggest that the gender of a worker has a bearing on how they are defined as "older." For example, a review of research (National Centre for the Protection of Older People, 2009) found that some employers consider females to be older workers at younger ages than males. As such, older women may therefore be more susceptible to ageist attitudes in the workplace than older men.

Navigating the maze of alternative age measures Although recent work in the USA has successfully yielded multiple alternative work-linked and relevant age conceptualizations, both the age prism and the age cubes or matrix models have yet to be empirically tested (Allen et al., 2012; Finkelstein, 2015). Further, it is unlikely that except in extremely narrowly defined settings, all configurations of context-dependent age (e.g., Segers et al., 2014) or age perspectives make independent contributions for understanding most important work challenges faced by older workers. Kooij et al. (2008) stated a need for additional research addressing the psychometric relations among organizational and individual age measures.

Responding to this need, McCarthy et al. (2014) surveyed organizational decision-makers to determine (1) at what chronological age organizational decision-makers consider a worker to be "older," and, importantly, (2) how they arrived at that decision. Using the Sterns and Doverspike (1989) conceptualization jointly with the age indicators provided by Schalk et al. (2010), McCarthy et al. (2014) found that the average age of older workers ranged from 28 to 75 years with a mean of 52.4 years ($SD=6.95$) and a median age of 55 years old. Further, younger decision-makers (i.e., those less than 35 years old) categorized a worker as older at a younger chronological age ($M=50.91$) than did middle-aged decision-makers ($M=53.11$) or decision-makers over 50 years old ($M=53.46$). No differences were found among decision-makers' age assessments by gender, position, organizational tenure, or industry type. More recently, Cleveland and Hanscom (2015) extended the findings of McCarthy et al. (2014) and also surveyed employees to determine at what chronological age a man, a woman, and a worker are considered "older."

The concept of an "older worker" is one that is defined in terms of multiple indicators, some objective (e.g., chronological age), some perceptual (e.g., subjective age), and some context-dependent (e.g., age compared to peers or to expectations for a particular job or occupation). It is important to consider multiple conceptualizations of age when discussing the challenges and opportunities confronting older workers because these challenges and opportunities are influenced by both the biological changes associated with age and the way people are perceived and treated as they are seen to enter different phases of the lifespan. Workers who are chronologically older but who are *seen* as younger might face very different situations in the workplace than those who are chronologically younger but who are *seen* as older.

Positive (Organizational) Psychology and Theories of Age

There are a number of theoretical perspectives in the psychology literature which can provide insight into the experience of working until later ages, one of which is positive psychology. Seligman and Csikszentmihalyi (2000) were among the early pioneers of positive psychology, which emphasizes a focus on building positive traits and enabling people and communities to thrive, rather than on repairing negative aspects of one's life experiences (Seligman & Csikszentmihalyi, 2000). Within positive psychology, there are a number of mechanisms of interest (i.e., extra-psychological factors) that facilitate or impede the pursuit of positive life experiences (Alex-Linley, Joseph, Harrington, & Wood, 2006). Among other mechanisms (e.g., personal relationships), one such cluster of mechanisms involves working environments, organizations, and institutions (Alex-Linley et al., 2006). In other words, our individual lives are embedded in organizational systems that can affect the pursuit of "the good life," with older workers as no exception to this general rule. With that in mind, this section serves as a brief overview of key features of positive psychology that are relevant to work and working longer.

In general, research and application of positive psychology to the work environment orient toward creating a healthy and positive work experience and actualizing job-related well-being (Turner, Barling, & Zacharatos, 2002). For example, Turner et al. (2002), although primarily focused on people at work, identified the potential for job-related well-being to translate into other mental health outcomes and indirectly affect employees' life satisfaction. In other words, work and nonwork domains are related, and positive experiences at work can potentially carry over into personal nonwork lives (Turner et al., 2002). In fostering and creating work environments for workers (including older workers) to thrive, a number of key positive psychology features are relevant and applicable.

One relevant concept common in positive psychology literature is "positive organizational behavior" (POB), which partially overlaps with the aforementioned POS (Bakker & Schaufeli, 2008). Luthans (2002) described POB as emphasizing a focus on theory building, research, and application of positive behaviors, states, and traits of employees in organizations. POB generally involves an emphasis on employee well being and performance improvement (Bakker & Schaufeli, 2008). Whereas POB emphasizes the individual-level influences of employee performance (i.e., a positive individual perspective), POS focuses on the organizational context and positive aspects therein which can influence employees' thriving and work-related outcomes (i.e., a positive organizational perspective; Bakker & Schaufeli, 2008; Cameron, 2005). This focus on both positive organizational and positive individual perspectives resonates throughout the positive psychology and work literature; previous research and applications often focus on behaviors and practices at various levels of organizations.

At the individual level, Luthans (2002) identified specific inclusion criteria for POB, including a basis in theory and research, and the ability to measure, develop, and effectively manage the behavior to impact and improve performance in the workplace. With these criteria, Luthans (2002) identified three capacities of POB: hope (a cognitive set based on a sense of successful determination toward goals and planning to meet those goals; Snyder et al., 1991), confidence (or self-efficacy; see Bandura, 1982), and resiliency (the capability to successfully cope in the face of change, adversity, or risk; Stewart, Reid, & Mangham, 1997).

These capacities appear elsewhere in the positive psychology literature as well, such as in discussions on a "positive approach to leadership" (PAL), which Luthans, Luthans, Hodgetts, and Luthans (2001) identified as more proactive than transformational leadership (see Avolio & Bass, 1988) and composed of the following criteria: Realistic optimism, Intelligence, Confidence, and Hope (i.e., RICH). Similar capacities appear in Luthans, Luthans, and Luthans' (2004) discussion of "positive psychological capital," which Luthans et al. (2004) identified as including the capacities of confidence, hope, optimism, and resilience. Luthans et al. (2004) describe positive psychological capital as consisting of these four capacities which identify "who you are" rather than who you know (i.e., social capital) or what you know (i.e., human capital).

C. Peterson (2006) elaborated on the definition of positive organizational psychology and included (1) positive subjective experience, (2) positive traits, and (3) positive institutions which includes families, schools, businesses, communities, and societies (Donaldson & Dollwet, 2013). Workplaces and organizations are considered part of institutions and therefore POS is a subset of positive psychology. POS is the scientific study of positive subjective experience, positive traits, and positive organizations with the application to improve both quality of life and effectiveness in organizations (Donaldson & Ko, 2010). There are a number of ways that positive psychology has been applied to the workplace including areas of leadership, organizational development and change, emotions, relationships, HR practices, flow, work engagement and well-being. In general, the approach in these areas is to understand how and when employees will thrive at work. As Donaldson and Dollwet (2013) indicate, thriving refers to humans feeling "vigorous" and performing at their optimal levels. At work, thriving can result from the acquisition of new knowledge and finding meaning at work (Niessen, Sonnentag, & Sach, 2012). POS differs from positive psychological research as it focuses on organizational dynamics including both the positive factors and processes within organizations as well as the positive organizational contexts (Cameron & Dutton, 2003). These include highlighting or making visible positive states, positive processes, and positive relationships that are usually ignored or hidden at work. For example, this approach includes practices that enhance work meaningfulness (Berg, Wrzesniewski, & Dutton, 2010) or empowerment processes that enhance inclusion of employees (Feldman & Khademian, 2003).

Cameron and Dutton (2003) explain the term "positive" in POS is controversial. The meaning of the term is emerging after about a decade of research and can be summarized in terms of four approaches. First is that "positive" refers to adopting a unique way or alternative perspective on approaching an issue or situation. Here a problem or phenomenon is altered, and challenges or obstacles are reinterpreted and framed as opportunities or growth experiences (Gittell, Cameron, Lim, & Rivas, 2006). When reframed in this positive way, other factors can then be drawn in for consideration (e.g., compassion, inspiration, and/or energy). Thus, the phenomenon is not different, but the perspective on what the phenomenon implies is. A second approach to "positive" is to focus on unusually positive outcomes that exceed expectations. The focus here is on exceptional behaviors and exceptional performance. A third area features a focus on an "affirmative" bias that enhances resourcefulness (Cameron & Dutton, 2003, p. 26). This perspective focuses on the amplifying effect of positivity resulting in greater resources and capacity. A fourth approach to the concept of "positive" is the examination of the best in humans or their virtuousness. This includes a focus on individual behaviors in organizations that reflect character strengths and help others flourish as well, including hope, courage, wisdom, gratitude, and forgiveness (Grant & Schwartz, 2011).

S. J. Peterson and Spiker (2005), who were among the first to take a clearly positive psychology view of older workers, focus on the idea that human capital can accumulate as people age. Citing data collected from HR directors and meta-analyses, Peterson and Spiker (2005) indicated that older workers learn and perform as well as, if not better than, younger workers. Furthermore, Peterson and Spiker (2005) argue that the collective psychological, intellectual, emotional, and social capital of older workers combine to create unique positive contributory value of older workers which, in turn, leads to beneficial organizational outcomes, such as the creation and retention of institutional memory, increased productivity, decreased turnover, and increased loyalty.

Age Theories Using a Positive Psychology Lens

Workers change as they age, gaining some skills and capabilities and losing others over time. Different theories of age and aging focus on quite different types of changes, and no single theory fully captures the full range or extent of these changes. The lifespan development perspective of aging theory is concerned with the development of changes across the lifespan. This is a large theoretical perspective and is not one particular theory; many orientations are connected with these ideas and encompass the approach. For example, as we will discuss next, the "useful organizing structure" (Hansson, DeKoekkoek, Neece, & Patterson, 1997, p. 209; Zacher, 2015) for research on aging in the workplace is the construct of successful aging. Further, one theoretical framework for this construct is the selection-optimization-compensation (SOC) model. We will describe each of these two frameworks as ones that actually predate the formal positive psychology movement in the USA. In addition, we present Kanfer's lifespan model of motivation which is a more targeted and work-centric application of both of these approaches. Finally, we also describe socio-emotional selectivity theory, the convoy model of social relations, and the job demands-resources model as more specific aging and work theories that incorporate a number of the facets of positive psychology.

Successful aging

Prior to the positive psychology movement, the term successful aging was introduced in the 1950s by Birren (1958), Havighurst & Orr (1955), and others (e.g., Gumpert, 1954). Within the gerontology and lifespan development literature, successful aging research reflected a new, alternative orientation and perspective on old age and the aging process. Until this time, gerontological research largely focused upon the negative consequences of growing old, including cognitive and physical declines, social withdrawal and depression, dependency, and negative economic impacts (Zacher, 2015).

In order to understand successful aging, aging in general may involve three conditions or levels (Baltes, 1997; Friedrich, 2001; Rowe & Kahn, 1987): (1) normal "usual" aging which describes how the average individual usually scores on any given age measure; (2) pathological aging (or below average), which refers to the rate of aging when either acute or chronic disease is altering the normal aging patterns (e.g., Alzheimer's disease); and (3) successful aging, which describes persons living a long, productive, satisfactory life and aging above average in comparison to relevant physical, psychological, and/or social domains. Some individual might not fully or accurately fit into any of these three conditions; however, other individuals may fit into several of the conditions. Recently Zacher (2015) reviewed and integrated prior research on successful aging and offered a framework of successful aging at work. This framework suggests a number of personal and contextual variables that serve to moderate the relation between workers' age and work-related outcomes. Altogether, we believe that the increased attention given in the aging and work literature to theory development surrounding successful aging has the potential to have significant contributions to our knowledge on older workers.

The SOC theory of aging

The SOC model conceptualizes how people cope with age-related changes, adapt throughout their lives, and use strategies to maximize potential for successful aging. The theory emerged from the gain–loss dynamic within lifespan development. This is the process of how we both grow (gain) and decline throughout the aging process (Baltes, 1987). For example, as we age, our declarative knowledge can continue to evolve (i.e., growth) and fluid cognitive functioning might decline. SOC theory has three main components that encompass the gain–loss relationship for successful aging. First, the theory suggests that it is useful to examine the process of strategic selection of focusing one's resources and adapting in terms of contexts, outcomes, and goal structures. This process is important because it directs a person's behavior based on their hierarchy of goals, which is necessary because one's resources are often limited. There are multiple selection strategies (e.g., elective, loss-based, etc.), for optimizing potential by maximizing the gains possible, and compensating for losses (Baltes, 1997; Baltes & Baltes, 1990; Freund & Baltes, 2002). We can provide an illustration of the SOC process for the work setting: First, selection may occur when older employees can redesign or restructure work to emphasize tasks that require knowledge, skills, and/or abilities that remain strong and pursue goals that have become more important to them (e.g., mentoring others, utilizing experience, or tapping co-worker networks), and can give up other activities that are less desirable. Next, optimization could occur through the stimulating opportunities presented to the individuals at work, such as a continued learning course, group- or team-based training, or pairing with a younger co-worker. Last, compensation could be considered in terms of the availability of programs or technology to maintain the health of the individuals in the work setting, such as onsite gyms, midday walkabouts, or vertical sit/stand desks.

A lifespan approach to work motivation and age

Using similar functions to other expectancy theories of work motivation and facets of both SOC and positive psychology, Kanfer (1987) described a model showing how age-related changes and development may influence one's motivation at work. Kanfer (1987) stated that the effort that a person allocates to a particular task or job is based upon their perceptions of three factors: (1) effort to performance function; (2) performance to utility function; and (3) effort to utility function. The effort–performance function is largely based upon the task demands and the requisite cognitive abilities, knowledge, and skills necessary to performance them. Although it is a perceptual function, it reflects an individual's assessment or perception of the amount of effort needed to reach a given level of performance (e.g., by maintaining a given adequate level of effort to ramp up performance levels). Both the performance–utility and the effort–utility functions of the model are influenced by such non-ability factors as self-concept, motives, and interests (Kanfer & Ackerman, 2004).

As such, age development throughout life influences each of these three functions. For example, work situations that require significant demands of general fluid intelligence (*Gf*) may require a more mature worker to at least initially increase their efforts on the job in order to attain a previous level of job performance. That is, the individual is motivated to compensate for the decline in cognitive ability in order to sustain performance. However, with increasing loss of *Gf*, this increase in one's effort–performance function will be less effective with time for the aging employee in high *Gf*-demanding jobs. On the other hand, Kanfer (1987) states that in other job contexts where the tasks require demands on general crystalized intelligence (*Gc*), the mid-life or older worker will be more experienced and will have greater job knowledge to compensate for losses in *Gf* abilities. That is, the mid-life or older worker gains greater *Gc* with age which can, in these latter jobs, compensate for *Gf* loss such that the worker may not need to increase effort–performance function in order to maintain performance levels. This has a number of implications for employee supervisors as well as organizations in terms of supportive work climates/cultures and work design/job crafting.

Historically, much of the study of performance and success at work has been defined primarily in terms of task and technical performance. It is in these areas where *Gf* loss may be most apparent. However, with organizations and HR professionals embracing non-technical performance, including contextual performance or organizational citizenship behaviors and positive work behaviors (e.g., safety, customer service, etc.), it is likely that mature and older adults will thrive in these occupational contexts. Where greater supervisory or managerial roles are reflected in the performance criterion rather than solely technical performance, older adults may perform better and with greater effort–utility as well as performance–utility functions.

Socio-emotional selectivity theory (SST)

SST focuses greatly on the fact that as we age, our perception of time shifts (e.g., Carstensen, Isaacowitz, & Charles, 1999). Among younger individuals, the future seems more distal than among those who are older; therefore, motivations and goal-seeking are quite different between older and younger individuals. There are three presumptions of the theory: first, that social interactions are of deep importance to our lives; second, that humans act in ways that are guided by goals; and third, that we often hold many goals, so prioritizing by choice is often necessary (Carstensen et al., 1999). Coming from these presumptions, SSC recognizes that not only will these goals shift throughout the lifespan due to the distinct time limitations at hand, but the selection of goals will change as well. For example, people will be more motivated to have knowledge-related goals earlier in life and more emotion-related goals later in life. It would be more likely for an older person to reduce their social interactions to people who are more emotionally meaningful to them and weight goals accordingly to satisfying emotional needs rather than preparing for the future.

Convoy model of social relations

The convoy model emphasizes the interaction between individual development throughout the lifespan and social relations (Kahn & Antonucci, 1980). One's convoy – or the social relationships and interpersonal interactions that surround an individual – influences a person's life experiences, perceptions and development, and gives them social support, and more. For example, the convoy model explains how social relations influence both psychological and physical health as someone moves across the lifespan (Antonucci, Birditt, & Akiyama, 2009). A convoy can provide three broad types of support: aid (e.g., concrete assistance like money or advice), affect (e.g., emotional support), and affirmation (e.g., communication to the person of interest regarding values, norms, goals, and aspirations; Kahn & Antonucci, 1980). It is likely that a person's social network will vary depending on their personal characteristics (e.g., age, gender, and race) and situational characteristics (e.g., environment, culture).

JD-R model

A final model that we will describe is not an aging model but rather a job context and stress model with processes that parallel both the work motivation model and the SOC model of aging (Demerouti, Bakker, Nachreiner, & Schaufeli, 2001) which has been applied to understanding aging and work (Fisher, Ryan, & Sonnega, 2015). According to this model, job demands refer to "physical, social, or organizational aspects of a job that require sustained physical or mental effort and are therefore associated with certain physiological or psychological costs" (Demerouti et al., 2001, p. 501). Examples of job demands include physical demands, emotional demands, and work pressure. Job resources refer to physical, psychological, social, or organizational aspects of the job that facilitate achieving work goals or serve to reduce job demands and the associated physiological and psychological costs, such as supervisor support, having clear expectations of what to do at work, and autonomy or control of one's work and/or work schedule. The JD-R model is consistent with Karasek's (1979) job demands/control model, which indicates that job strain is likely to result from working in a job characterized by high levels of demands (e.g., workload, time pressure) and low levels of job control (i.e., autonomy and decision latitude). However, the JD-R model is broader and describes aspects of one's job that facilitate work motivation and achievement of work goals beyond just job control. Based on the JD-R model, workers are less likely to experience deleterious effects of work and more likely to benefit from work if job demands are low or resources are available to buffer against negative job demands (Fisher et al., 2015).

There are a number of ways of thinking about what it means to become an "older worker." This categorization is probably influenced by chronological, social, and contextual factors, and the implications of becoming older in the workplace are similarly complex. There are clear declines in some physical and psychological functions as workers get older, but there is increasing evidence of concomitant gains. Historically, research on aging and work has focused more on the challenges faced by workers and organizations as the workforce ages, but it is increasingly clear that a more nuanced perspective is needed. The recent growth of interest in positive psychology provides a useful lens for thinking about how to recognize and maximize the gains workers accrue as they age and how to leverage these gains to compensate for the physical and psychological changes that create barriers to effective performance and satisfying experiences in the workplace.

In summary, there are a number of features from positive psychology that can be applied to the workplace as well as the experiences and contributory value of older workers, such as POB, POS, positive approaches to leadership, and positive psychological capital. Generally speaking, these features are built upon a foundation of certain capacities, including confidence, hope, optimism, resilience, and intelligence. Through this common foundation, researchers have developed these key positive psychology features that apply to individual, group, and organizational levels.

Application of Positive Psychology to Workplace Practices

In an exceptional review of HR practices and implications for an aging workforce, Truxillo, Cadiz, and Rineer (2012) provide a review of what organizations can do within the framework of traditional HR practice to keep employees productive, engaged, and healthy at work as they age. We will not attempt to replicate this review here; rather we will highlight some of the key areas where positive psychology and aging theories converge in such a way as to inform both organizations and HR experts on practices to enhance the quality and longevity of working life for both current and future mature workers.

HR practices can be grouped into three general categories that reflect various stages of attachment or engagement with the organization, including moving into the organization, moving onward, and then moving out. In the first stage, practices that attract and select employees to enter into the organization are central. In the second stage, performance evaluation, training, and challenging work as well as job design and career development are emphasized. Finally, a number of informal norms and practices can influence the decisions of older workers to either leave or continue within the organization, including organizational climate, supervisor and co-worker support, mentoring, and valuing diversity.

Entry to organizations: Attraction and selection of older workers

According to Truxillo et al. (2012a), although there is little research on what attracts older and younger people to organizations, there is evidence that some older workers may have a future time perspective that may be associated with socio-emotional fulfillment and continuance commitment (Bal, De Lange, Zacher, & Van der Heijden, 2013). Further, older individuals are less likely to leave an organization when it values and develops them and when practices are fairly applied by supervisors. Positive age-diverse organizational climates tend to have greater organizational commitment and lower turnover (Kunze, Böhm, & Bruch, 2011). A positive diversity climate is also associated with whether an organization actively recruits older workers and then actually hires them for full-time employment (Goldberg, Perry, Finkelstein, & Shull, 2013; Karpinska, Henkens, & Schippers, 2013).

More research has been devoted to the potential for bias in the selection of older workers, especially into specific jobs or occupations that are more often held by younger workers. The presence of negative age stereotypes may prohibit the entry of qualified older individuals from being considered for employment, particularly in these jobs. Age stereotypes operate in numerous ways: (1) stereotypic and negative characteristics are associated with lower perceptions of success; (2) older workers may be stereotypically perceived as overqualified; and (3) older workers may be perceived as stereotypically not appropriate for certain jobs (i.e., job-age stereotype) (Cleveland & Landy, 1983). It is important to keep in mind that age stereotypes include both negative and positive characteristics as reflected in items (1) and (2). Older workers may be viewed as slower and less willing to learn new technologies, yet they may also be viewed as more emotionally stable, even-tempered, conscientious, and reliable. A key issue in this area is reflected in point (3) above, regarding one's occupation. The relative influence of inaccurate or positive/negative age perceptions may vary considerably across occupations. Therefore it is critical to examine this salient contextual variable.

Another issue concerning organizational entry involves the types of selection assessment methods used and the utility of the information provided regarding older applicants. Although not empirically tested, research suggests that any selection test that weighs *Gf* heavily will result in outcomes and decisions that place older individuals at a distinct disadvantage due to the steady decline of *Gf* beginning in one's mid-twenties. If a selection system is designed such that prior experience, practice, and personality factors are not considered, potentially high-performing and adaptable mature workers may be overlooked.

Importantly, most recruitment and selection methods and objectives focus upon the assessment of task-related abilities, skills, and capacity for acquisition or learning. A person must be capable, for example sufficiently intelligent, and have sufficient task knowledge to successfully perform required job tasks. However, performance (or success) is a function of three factors: job-related ability (i.e., is a person able to do the job?), motivation (will a person do the job?), and the opportunity to perform (is a person allowed to do the job?), and assessment that focuses solely on ability may lead to selection errors. Consistent with Kanfer's motivation model, the SOC, and application of positive psychology, a substantial portion of variance in successful performance at work may reflect motivation-based components; whereas many HR practices focus upon ability-related components of performance. As we will describe in the section that follows, the role of motivational components may increase in importance as employees age and move through their careers. It behooves organizations to then shift the lens of positive employee management toward understanding and strengthening linkages among HR motivation-based practices and employee behavior.

Moving on within the organization: Performance evaluation, feedback, training, and career development

A number of HR practices are available to provide performance feedback to and evaluate employees, and to assess employee readiness for advancement and promotion, challenging career opportunities, and development, as well as opportunities to lead and mentor others. As employees acquire experience and knowledge in performing their work, they may be able to focus more upon performing facets of the job that tax them less (both cognitively and physically) which may in turn result in performance returns for both the employee and the organization.

Performance appraisal and feedback are widely used HR practices which are intended to address multiple purposes, including improving individual and organizational effectiveness. One purpose of appraisal includes the supervisory evaluation of how well or poorly an employee is performing various aspects of his or her work. Although older employees may be incorrectly perceived to have lower ability, motivation, and productivity as compared to younger employees (Hedge, Borman, & Lammlein, 2006), a recent meta-analysis provided an empirical basis for refuting negative age-performance stereotypes (Ng & Feldman, 2012). To the contrary, specific performance types are positively related to age, including contextual performance or organizational citizenship behavior (Ng & Feldman, 2012). Further, older employees may engage in more citizenship behavior as discretionary behaviors to compensate for task-skill loss. Other job-skill behaviors, such as networking, positive affect, and experience, may also offset slight skill losses. These tradeoffs are important because of the age-related decline in the performance of tasks that depend upon *Gf*. Further, significant and sharp declines in *Gc* often only become evident at older ages than those of most working adults (e.g., after 75–80 years of age).

There is little applied evidence outside of somewhat artificial laboratory studies of age bias in performance ratings by supervisors (Cleveland, Festa, & Montgomery, 1988; Ng & Feldman, 2008). However, this finding can vary by occupation stereotype and by the age composition of jobs, co-workers, and supervisor–employee dyads (Cleveland & Landy, 1983; Cleveland & Shore, 1992; Cleveland, Shore & Murphy, 1997; Murphy & Cleveland, 1995). The possibility that older workers might be perceived as less effective suggests the need to develop compensatory strategies and mechanisms to offset this perception.

Performance feedback, development, and employee motivation One critical area where SOC, SST, and positive psychology can make a significant impact on employees is in the area of performance feedback and employee development. Feedback is intended to convey to employees their areas of performance strengths as well as where they need to improve or increase performance. However, supervisory feedback research shows that improvements or changes in performance with such information is at best mixed with approximately one third of research indicating performance improvement, one third indicating performance declines, and another one third indicating no change (Kluger & DeNisi, 1996). One outcome of these findings is that some organizations and feedback researchers redoubled or tripled their efforts and implemented multisource feedback practices in which employees receive performance information from co-workers and subordinates (or direct reports) in addition to their supervisors (Atwater, Brett, & Charles, 2007). Although the presumed effectiveness of these practices is not clear, the assumption underlying multisource feedback is the same as that underlying single, supervisory feedback: if the employee believes that the feedback is accurate and fair, then the employee will change his or her behavior and (presumably) increase performance. However, the SOC theory and SST suggest that this assumption may be false. As employees mature they may devote more of their energy and attention to those performance areas in which they excel or use performance in these areas to compensate for their weaknesses, rather than directing resources toward areas that will yield lower payoff (i.e., their developmentally weaker areas). The assumption here then is that consistent with Kanfer and Ackerman's (2004) prediction that employees will be motivated to devote more efforts to skills and performance areas that they believe have higher expectancies for success.

Further, this perspective suggests that employees will not have high expectancies for success in those performance areas where they are given negative or developmental feedback. This is likely true for all employees, but may be especially relevant for mature workers who are likely to have received similar feedback on their relative strengths and weaknesses repeatedly. Even the most motivated and skilled employee will have limited success in significantly improving some performance limitations, and it is likely that especially experienced employees will behave in ways that maximize their payoffs and highlight and utilize skill strengths and resources. One implication for performance feedback research and practice is that greater attention might be given to the effectiveness of identifying strengths of employee behavior, focusing upon enhancing and maximizing these individual strengths, and that less emphasis is devoted to employee limitations or weaknesses (i.e., areas where individuals may be less able and motivated to devote resources). For example, employees in jobs that primarily require experience-based knowledge may be more successful than employees in jobs with significant cognitive requirements (Kanfer & Ackerman, 2004). Further, these perspectives suggest that the focus of feedback should shift toward the identification of employee strengths in ways such that individuals are motivated to realize their potential to enhance strengths rather than to expend effort to address areas with little payoff or hope of significant improvements or rewards. This shift in assumption – that employees are motivated to change their performance in areas that reflect their strengths – is an outcome that is highly consistent with research on aging. Other research suggests that, among older workers, satisfaction with older co-workers was strongly correlated with work engagement (Avery, McKay, & Wilson, 2007).

Work attitudes Research on work attitudes indicates that age is positively associated with more favorable work attitudes and this holds for most job attitudes (Ng & Feldman 2010). Specifically, for 27 out of 35 job and organizational attitudes, older employees reported more positive and less negative attitudes than younger employees. Using the lifespan perspective consistent with positive psychology, Truxillo, Cadiz, Rineer, Zaniboni, and Fraccaroli (2012) proposed that a combination of positive person factors (e.g., work experience, health, personality) combined with a number of job-related resources (e.g., job autonomy, social support, etc.) may assist employees in maintaining positive attitudes including job satisfaction, engagement, and performance.

Job characteristics, especially job control and employee need–supplies lack of fit, and broader organizational factors also influence older employee attitudes. For example, feedback and opportunity for work recovery were more positively related to work attitudes among older employees (Bos, Donders, Schouteten, & Van der Gulden, 2013). At the organizational level, a breach in psychology contract (Bal, De Lange, Jansen, & Van Der Velde, 2008) as well as the the perceived effectiveness or use of certain HR practices (e.g., teamwork, flexwork) are more strongly related to job satisfaction and commitment among older employees than among younger employees.

Training Training and career development are activities designed to promote sustainable changes in behavior and cognition so that employees possess the competencies they need to perform their work and advance either inside or outside of an organization throughout their career (Maurer, 2007; Salas, Tannenbaum, Kraiger, & Smith-Jentsch, 2012; Sterns & Kaplan, 2003). Consistent with both SST and SOC theory, older workers may select goals related to mentoring or generativity which tap experience and *Gc* (Kanfer & Ackerman, 2004). Older workers, known for having more seniority and experience, may derive a sense of meaningfulness or satisfaction from sharing their knowledge or experiences with others, known as generativity (Kanfer & Ackerman, 2004; Templer, Armstrong-Stassen, & Cattaneo, 2010). Therefore, older workers may benefit from engaging in social interactions, such as organizational socialization and training, and may contribute to the design of such learning situations. For example, older workers can participate in the development of training content by providing examples and scenarios where they can apply their accumulated knowledge and experience to benefit other employees in the organization.

One consistent finding in the training literature is that older workers are less likely to be offered or recommended for training or for challenging tasks/opportunities (Maurer, 2001; 2007). One reason for this may be that traditional training focuses on information acquisition for core work tasks, which are more heavily linked with *Gf* rather than the strengths of older employees. It is unclear what types of training are motivating to older learners that will increase their engagement in work (Truxillo et al., 2012a).

In addition to lower access and opportunity for training, older workers are less likely to obtain or receive career counseling and developmental opportunities for advancement (Cleveland & Shore, 1992), often resulting in lower ratings of perceived promotability (Shore, Cleveland, & Goldberg, 2003) and actual promotions (Goldberg, Finkelstein, Perry, & Konrad, 2004). This has problematic implications in both the short term and the long term. First, having fewer opportunities leads to a downward spiraling effect of older worker skills in acquiring and developing new skills, thus leading to continued negative perceptions. In the longer term, lower career and development opportunities can lead to lower mobility and stability. Career mobility and stability reflect an employee's motivation and ability to adapt and change jobs/careers (Feldman 2007). The notion of career embeddedness is related to both the motivation and ability to adapt to specific career paths. When employees have high embeddedness, they have extensive ties with other people in their area of expertise, their work fits with their work life, it would be effortful to leave the job, and there are significant barriers to pursuing a new career (Feldman, 2007). When employees have high embeddedness supported by developmental opportunities, career counseling, and support, they are less likely to leave or retire from the organization (Wang & Shultz, 2010) and more likely to continue to be engaged and productive contributors.

Deciding to continue, retire, or exit the organization

Health, safety, and feeling valued are key factors in decisions to retire (Wang & Shi, 2014) as well as antecedents to engagement and well-being at work. Recent and increasing research on occupational health psychology reflects a positive confluence of work psychology, health psychology, and positive psychology which benefits all workers regardless of age. However, there are negative age stereotypes suggesting that older workers experience greater health problems. While there may be health concerns specific to occupations, older employees do not have greater self-reported physical or somatic health complaints nor do they have poorer mental health than younger workers (Ng & Feldman, 2013). Further, greater age-strain-stress variations appear to occur for certain types of jobs or occupations, especially physically demanding jobs, than variations for age alone (Rauschenbach, Krumm, Thielgen, & Hertel, 2013). One of the most promising areas for research according to Truxillo and others is to understand how work environments can provide support for workers throughout the lifespan so they can adapt to age-related changes, sustain their work ability, and contribute productively (Ilmarinen, Tuomi, & Klockars, 1997; McGonagle, Fisher, Barnes-Farrell, & Grosch, 2015). Two critical factors to the continued engagement, health, and striving/thriving of the mature worker are work design and an inclusive organizational climate.

Work design

Organizational psychology literature has described multiple theories relevant to understanding psychological aspects of job design. One of the first, most widely known and well-supported theories is the job characteristics model (Hackman & Oldham, 1976). The job characteristics model identified five intrinsic job characteristics – skill variety, task identity, task significance, autonomy, and feedback – which lead to psychological states such as meaningfulness of work, responsibility, and knowledge of results which then lead to important positive outcomes at work including motivation, satisfaction, and performance. With regard to age, Truxillo and colleagues (Truxillo, Cadiz, & Rineer, 2012; Truxillo, Cadiz, Rineer, Zaniboni, & Fraccaroli, 2012) suggested that autonomy and task significance are more important for older workers. Truxillo and Zaniboni (2015) also suggested that older workers may also benefit from autonomy so that they may craft their jobs to be more meaningful. Moghimi, Scheibe, and Van Yperen (2015) indicated that older workers may be more interested in or benefit from job crafting compared to younger workers in order to enhance person–job fit (i.e., the extent to which the demands of their job match their knowledge, skills, abilities, and interests).

Organizational climate for age diversity and inclusion

Establishing a climate for age diversity and inclusion includes team diversity and strengths for working with others and valuing within-person changes over time. Although there is evidence that age bias is still a persistent and serious problem in the workplace, there are also some reasons for optimism. Some types of discrimination or bias can be mitigated through careful monitoring and enforcement of existing laws. Hirsh (2009) examined the relationship of racial discrimination charges formally filed with the U.S. Equal Employment Opportunity Commission (EEOC) to changes in occupational segregation by race. Three factors were examined as predictors, including direct equal employment opportunity (EEO enforcement, industry environment, and organizational characteristics). Results indicated that EEO enforcement resulted in few changes, while organizational factors were linked to changes in occupational desegregation. Additionally, greater media coverage of racial discrimination within an industry led to greater desegregation of occupations.

In addition to legal factors, there are social factors that can mitigate bias. For example, Cleveland and Landy (1983) found that older-behaving employees were rated lower in performance regardless of chronological age than employees who behaved in ways less consistent with negative age stereotypes. Further, workplace characteristics (e.g., level of supervisory control, percentage of minority managers, occupation segregation) can mitigate potentially biased perceptions (e.g., race, Hirsh & Kornrich, 2008). Finally, when employees believed that the organization was making efforts to support diversity by using fair practices, they were less influenced by individual acts of discrimination at work and more likely to perceive that their treatment by the organization as a whole had been fair (Triana & García, 2009; Triana, García, & Colella, 2010).

Building on Ferdman's (2014) thematic depiction of the literature, Shore, Cleveland, and Sanchez (2015) synthesized and expanded upon Ferdman's (2014) ideas for a more fully developed framework that can be useful for theory building, empirical testing, and practical application. There are at least seven factors or elements that contribute to an inclusion organizational climate. The first inclusion element is "feeling safe" and includes both psychological and physical safety associated with sharing different opinions and views from others. Such safety can be for individuals or for the identity groups of particular employees (e.g., mature worker). For example, an older person who expresses views that are associated with her female identity (e.g., the need for better health care or elder care benefits) would feel safe in doing so. More subtle expressions could involve an older person in a younger-dominated team comfortably expressing views that may differ from others in the team. Satisfaction of this inclusion element would be associated with fulfilling needs for uniqueness (Shore et al., 2010).

The second factor refers to "involvement in the work group," and refers to the individual or identity group feeling like an insider with access to critical information and resources, opportunity to succeed, conflict management, and organizational promotion of teamwork. Satisfaction of this inclusion element would be associated with fulfilling needs for belongingness (Shore et al., 2010). A third element, "feeling respected and valued," involves being treated with respect as a valued and esteemed member of the group and organization. As an example, when disparaging remarks are made by co-workers about "over-the-hill" or "tech-challenged" employees, older individuals may view this as a sign of disrespect toward a key identity group. Some relevant HR practices may include mentoring and recognizing and rewarding managers for promoting inclusionary practices (Shore et al., 2010).

The fourth inclusion element is "influence on decision-making," in which employees believe that their ideas and perspectives are heard (or they are listened to) and influential. Satisfaction of this inclusion element would be associated with fulfilling needs for belongingness (Shore et al., 2010). "Authenticity" is the fifth inclusion element, and refers to transparency and sharing of valued identities. An example of this element is when a middle-aged or older employee shares events or "stories" related to generativity, such as grandchildren events or eldercare. Satisfaction of this inclusion element would be associated with fulfilling needs for uniqueness (Shore et al., 2010). A sixth inclusion element is when "diversity is recognized, attended to, and honored," referring to fair treatment, sharing differences for mutual learning and growth, and top management showing their value for diversity through words and actions (e.g., employee survey results that show increasingly positive views of diversity climate and inclusion climate). Satisfaction of this inclusion element would be associated with fulfilling needs for uniqueness (Shore et al., 2010). The final inclusion element is "policies and practices that support inclusion" and refers to the elimination of structural and other impediments to success for older workers and other diverse people. Satisfaction of this inclusion element would be associated with fulfilling needs for both belongingness and uniqueness (Shore et al., 2010).

Consequences for Individuals

There are likely to be both positive and negative consequences for individuals and organizations associated with work at later ages. Because the focus of this chapter is to discuss the positive aspects of aging and work, here we focus on the benefits of continued work. Some benefits (e.g., psychological and economic) may be the direct result of work, whereas others may be derived through job resources based on the JD-R model. Individual-level benefits include psychological well-being, social support, cognitive activity, and economic benefits. Next we describe each of these further.

Psychological well-being

One benefit of work among older adults is better health and well-being. For example, Calvo (2006) found that working appears to be associated with higher life satisfaction and health. He examined work and well-being in the Health and Retirement Survey between 1998 and 2002 and sought to determine whether health resulted in cessation of work or whether continuing to work resulted in better health and well-being. After controlling for baseline health in 1998, he found that being employed 4 years later is associated with a 6% reduction in the report of fair or poor health. Reports of negative mood were 2% lower for those who were working compared to those not working. Results were moderated by type of work, such that working in undesirable jobs was not associated with the positive effects of paid work on mood indicators and mortality. Results also indicated that, in some cases, working in later life is associated with many benefits and helps individuals maintain their level of well-being.

Social support

Work can serve as an important source of social connection or social support (Elovainio et al., 2003; Moen, Fields, Quick, & Hofmeister, 2000). Engagement in productive and social activities has been found to be beneficial to physical health and psychological well-being. Part of the enhanced well-being observed in those who continue to work may be a result of maintaining social relationships with people at work. Although retirement offers the prospect of spending more time in leisure pursuits that may involve social connections, such as volunteering or socializing, formal social connections associated with work may offer a "built-in" network for those with fewer informal connections (Lancee & Radl, 2012). In addition, the U.S. Bureau of Labor Statistics reports that only 24.4% of adults aged 65 and older engaged in volunteer work in 2012, indicating that the potential loss of a social network from retirement is likely for the majority older adults.

Cognitive activity

Work can also provide a source of cognitive activity. Rohwedder and Willis (2010) compared measures of cognitive functioning in relation to labor force participation among people in their fifties and sixties cross-nationally at a country-aggregate level and concluded that early retirement has a significant negative impact on cognitive functioning. Other studies have demonstrated that doing work characterized as having a higher level of cognitive complexity is related to higher levels of cognitive functioning in older adulthood and protective against cognitive decline post-retirement (Finkel, Andel, Gatz, & Pedersen, 2009; Fisher et al., 2014). For example, even after controlling for education and social economic status, working in occupations characterized by high levels of cognitive complexity is associated with not only higher levels of cognitive functioning in later life, but also a slower rate of cognitive decline both before and after retirement. Although individuals with higher levels of cognitive abilities are more likely to select occupations characterized by being cognitively complex, empirical evidence is mounting to suggest that such work may be protective to some degree against cognitive decline. Moreover, empirical research to date regarding the relationship between age and job performance has not found empirical support for the notion that older workers perform their jobs any worse than younger workers (Ng & Feldman, 2008).

Identity

Continued work participation, either based on paid or volunteer work, serves to provide an individual with a source of identity with a work role. For individuals whose identity is strongly associated with their work (i.e., who have a high level of job involvement), this may be particularly important. Another way in which identity comes into play is in regard to a worker's self-concept or identity. For example, Barnes-Farrell (2003) pointed out that individuals are motivated to maintain a positive self-image or identity, which may have an impact on their retirement intentions. Zaniboni, Sarchielli, and Fraccaroli (2010) found that having work identity was negatively related to intentions to retire fully from one's job. Taylor and Shore (1995) studied predictors of planned retirement age among a sample of workers from a multinational firm. They found that in addition to age and health, workers' belief in their ability to adjust to retirement was a significant predictor of planned retirement age. Specifically, individuals who doubted their ability to adjust to retirement planned to retire at a later age. These results are consistent with the notion that individuals with a high level of job involvement may wish to retire later.

Economic benefits

In addition to the psychological benefits just described, there is a clear economic benefit to working, including earned wages, and possibly contributions to retirement savings accounts and/or employer-provided health insurance. For example, R. W. Johnson (2005) showed that the average unmarried man could nearly double his annual income at age 75 by retiring at age 70 instead of age 62. Furthermore, with changes to Social Security that essentially removed the penalty to work imposed by the Earning Test, there is no longer a loss to benefits by earning other income. The percentage increase for delaying benefits beyond normal retirement age to age 70 has increased in a way that makes the policy more age-neutral (Burtless & Quinn, 2002). Working longer provides additional financial resources so that individuals do not need to fund a lengthy retirement. Those who retire in their early sixties but live until their mid-eighties (based on current life expectancy tables) may be at risk for not having enough income in their older age (Burtless & Quinn, 2002). Thus, working longer confers a financial advantage through benefits workers receive for delaying Social Security claiming, the longer amount of time for potential savings to grow, and the shorter amount of time retirement savings must last.

Consequences for the Organization

In addition to benefits at the individual level, there are also organizational benefits to having and retaining older workers in the workforce. These benefits/opportunities are to have experienced workers on staff and to have resources for training and mentoring more junior workers. Each of these issues is described further below.

Retention of experienced workers

There is currently a large proportion of older workers in the global workforce, and at the same time lower birth rates mean fewer workers entering the workforce. Many organizations have been trying to identify the best human resources to accomplish the work to be done. One solution is to retain older workers in the workplace (Hanson & Lesser, 2009). A key benefit to retaining these workers is that they often have a great deal of knowledge and experience to contribute that is not easily replaced by a much younger employee entering the workforce. In some cases, workers' knowledge may include institutional knowledge – a long history of who, what, where, when, why, and how business practices or procedures have been conducted in an organization. As described earlier, older workers often have very positive characteristics that are attractive and beneficial to organizations (Peterson & Spiker, 2005).

Mentoring for younger or more junior workers

Another way in which having older workers in the workforce can benefit organizations is by mentoring and training more junior employees. Earlier in the chapter we described training and indicated that one source of motivation for workers may be generativity. First, it is important to consider work motivation (Kanfer, Beier, & Ackerman, 2013), as prior research has suggested that there is variability regarding the extent to which employees have generativity motives. For example, Arnold and Clark (2015) found that among men a forward career orientation was positively related to generativity motives and personal growth. However, preoccupation with career maintenance was negatively related to generativity and personal growth.

Future Research

Based on our review and synthesis of positive psychology and aging at work, we have a number of recommendations for future research. First, additional empirical research is needed to further examine successful aging (Zacher, 2015). Zacher presented a useful framework for guiding future research that examines person and contextual factors, as well as multiple work-related outcome variables (e.g., work motivation, job performance, job attitudes, and health and well-being). We also recommend extending empirical work beyond successful aging at work to examine other criteria of successful aging more generally, such as well-being, and physical and mental health. Second, as an increasing proportion of workers globally remain in the workforce until older ages, we need additional research to examine individual and organizational consequences of working until later ages and perhaps later than one may have expected. Third, because aging is a process that unfolds over time, we recommend longitudinal research for examining intra-individual trajectories over time. For example, are there personal characteristics and positive aspects of the work environment that benefit older workers? Are there ways in whch work can be effectively structured and designed to not only retain older workers and benefit organizations, but protect and promote health and well-being even after retirement? Lastly, we call for field research in organizations to better understand benefits of industrial/organizational psychology and HR management practices. This recommendation is consistent with De Lange, Kooij, and van der Heijden (2015), who called for the development of more theory to better understand why certain industrial/organizational psychology and HR management practices are beneficial for older workers, and empirical research to examine outcomes of such practices among older workers.

Conclusion

Increases in longevity as well as recent economic trends have resulted in a significantly larger proportion of the population remaining in the workforce until later ages. In this chapter we reviewed theories of positive psychology and aging, and industrial/organizational psychology to increase our understanding of aging and work as viewed through a positive psychology lens. Research and application of positive psychology to the work environment orient toward creating a healthy and positive work experience and actualizing job-related well-being. Additional literature regarding HR practices increases our understanding of how workers and the organizations that employ them can capitalize on strengths that come with age to establish positive work environments.

Workers change as they age, and the best organizations and business practices will take this into account in a way that facilitates work and well-being for aging workers. Examples include selection practices that do not lead to age discrimination (e.g., stereotypes, disparate treatment of adverse impact), training delivered in ways that take into account differences in preferences and learning styles, feedback and reward systems that are compatible with the notion that aging workers are more likely to work in ways that capitalize on their strengths rather than seek development to overcome weaknesses. SOC theory, the JD-R model, and a growing empirical literature suggest that workers should have autonomy, and organizational, supervisor, and co-worker support to facilitate their work. Workers are also more likely to thrive when they have opportunities to engage in meaningful work. Those with generativity motives would benefit from formal and informal mentoring relationships with younger or less-experienced workers. Taken together, there are many ways in which organizations can create positive and successful work environments. Our hope is that any HR practices that benefit older workers may in fact benefit workers of *any* age by contributing toward worker well-being across the lifespan.

References

Alex-Linley, P., Joseph, S., Harrington, S., & Wood, A. M. (2006). Positive psychology: Past, present, and (possible) future. *The Journal of Positive Psychology, 1*(1), 3–16.

Allen, T., Finkelstein, L., Kanfer, R., Müller, A., Weigl, M., Vuuren, T., van, … Wang, M. (2012). *White Paper for EAWOP Small Group Meeting on Age Cohorts in the Workplace: Understanding and Building Strength through Differences.* Retrieved from http://www.researchgate.net/profile/Justin_Marcus/publication/264116308_White_Paper_for_EAWOP_Small_Group_Meeting_on_Age_Cohorts_in_the_Workplace_Understanding_and_Building_Strength_through_Differences/links/546f25bd0cf2d67fc0301990.pdf

Anstey, K. J., Lord, S. R., & Smith, G. A. (1996). Measuring human functional age: A review of empirical findings. *Experimental Aging Research, 22*(3), 245–266.

Antonucci, T. C., Birditt, K. S., & Akiyama, H. (2009). Convoys of social relations: An interdisciplinary approach. In V. L. Bengston, D. Gans, N. M. Pulney, M. Silverstein, V. L. Bengston, D. Gans, … M. Silverstein (Eds.), *Handbook of theories of aging* (2nd ed., pp. 247–260). New York, NY: Springer.

Arnold, J., & Clark, M. (2015). Running the penultimate lap of the race: A multi-method analysis of growth, generativity, career orientation and personality amongst men in mid/late career. *Journal of Occupational and Organizational Psychology, 89*(2), 308–329.

Atwater, L. E., Brett, J. F., & Charles, A. C. (2007). Multisource feedback: Lessons learned and implications for practice. *Human Resource Management, 46*(2), 285–307.

Avery, D. R., McKay, P. F., & Wilson, D. C. (2007). Engaging the aging workforce: The relationship between perceived age similarity, satisfaction with coworkers, and employee engagement. *Journal of Applied Psychology, 92*(6), 1542.

Avolio, B. J., & Bass, B. M. (1988). Transformational leadership, charisma, and beyond. In J. G. Hunt, B. R. Baliga, H. P. Dachler, & C. A. Schriesheim (Eds.), *Emerging leadership vistas* (pp. 29–49). Lexington, MA: Lexington Books.

Bakker, A. B., & Schaufeli, W. B. (2008). Positive organizational behavior: Engaged employees in flourishing organizations. *Journal of Organizational Behavior, 29*(2), 147–154.

Bal, P. M., De Lange, A. H., Jansen, P. G., & Van Der Velde, M. E. (2008). Psychological contract breach and job attitudes: A meta-analysis of age as a moderator. *Journal of Vocational Behavior, 72*(1), 143–158.

Bal, P. M., De Lange, A. H., Zacher, H., & Van der Heijden, B. I. (2013). A lifespan perspective on psychological contracts and their relations with organizational commitment. *European Journal of Work and Organizational Psychology, 22*(3), 279–292.

Baltes, P. B. (1987). Theoretical propositions of life-span developmental psychology: On the dynamics between growth and decline. *Developmental Psychology, 23*(5), 611–626.

Baltes, P. B. (1997). On the incomplete architecture of human ontogeny: Selection, optimization, and compensation as foundation of developmental theory. *American Psychologist, 52*(4), 366–380.

Baltes, P. B., & Baltes, M. M. (1990). Psychological perspectives on successful aging: The model of selective optimization with compensation. In P. B. Baltes & M. M. Baltes (Eds.), *Successful aging: Perspectives from the behavioral sciences* (pp. 1–34). Cambridge, UK: Cambridge University Press.

Bandura, A. (1982). Self-efficacy mechanism in human agency. *American Psychologist, 37*(2), 122.

Barak, B., & Schiffman, L. G. (1981). Cognitive age: A nonchronological age variable. *Advances in Consumer Research, 8*(1), 602–606.

Barnes-Farrell, J. L. (2003). Beyond health and wealth: Attitudinal and other influences on retirement decision making. In G. A. Adams & T. A. Beehr (Eds.), *Retirement: Reasons, processes, and results* (pp. 159–187). New York, NY: Springer.

Beier, M. E., & Gilberto, J. M. (2015). Age-related changes in abilities. In N. A. Pachana (Ed.), *Encyclopedia of geropsychology* (pp. 1–8). Singapore: Springer Singapore. Retrieved from http://link.springer.com/10.1007/978-981-287-080-3_26-1

Berg, J. M., Wrzesniewski, A., & Dutton, J. E. (2010). Perceiving and responding to challenges in job crafting at different ranks: When proactivity requires adaptivity. *Journal of Organizational Behavior, 31*(2–3), 158–186.

Binstock, R. H. (2002). In memoriam Bernice L. Neugarten. *The Gerontologist, 42*(2), 149–151.

Birren, J. E. (1958). Chapter X: Aging and psychological adjustment. *Review of Educational Research, 28*, 475–490. doi:http://www.jstor. org/stable/1168974

Borkan, G. A., & Norris, A. H. (1980). Assessment of biological age using a profile of physical parameters. *Journal of Gerontology, 35*(2), 177–184.

Bos, J. T., Donders, N. C. G. M., Schouteten, R. L. J., & Van der Gulden, J. W. J. (2013). Age as a moderator in the relationship between work-related characteristics, job dissatisfaction and need for recovery. *Ergonomics, 56*(6), 992–1005.

Burtless, G., & Quinn, J. F. (2002, December). *Is working longer the answer for an aging workforce?* Issue in Brief no. 11. Chestnut Hill, MA: Center for Retirement Research at Boston College.

Calvo E. (2006, February). *Does working longer make people healthier and happier?* Issue in Brief series 2. Chestnut Hill, MA: Center for Retirement Research at Boston College.

Cameron, K. (2005). Organizational effectiveness: Its demise and re-emergence through positive organizational scholarship. In K. G. Smith & Michael A. Hitt (Eds.), *Great minds in management: The process of theory development* (pp. 304–330). Oxford, UK: Oxford University Press.

Cameron, K., & Dutton, J. (Eds.). (2003). *Positive organizational scholarship: Foundations of a new discipline.* San Francisco, CA: Berrett-Koehler.

Carstensen, L. L., Isaacowitz, D. M., & Charles, S. T. (1999). Taking time seriously: A theory of socioemotional selectivity. *American Psychologist, 54*(3), 165.

Charles, S. T., & Carstensen, L. L. (2003). A life span view of emotional functioning in adulthood and old age. *Advances in Cell Aging and Gerontology, 15*, 133–162.

Cleveland, J. N., Festa, R. M., & Montgomery, L. (1988). Applicant pool composition and job perceptions: Impact on decisions regarding an older applicant. *Journal of Vocational Behavior, 32*(1), 112–125.

Cleveland, J. N., & Hanscom, M. (2015, September). *Age and gender variations in perceptions of older workers, ageism, sexism, associated threats, and perceived employability.* Paper presented at the Irish Academy of Management, NUI Galway.

Cleveland, J. N., & Landy, F. J. (1983). The effects of person and job stereotypes on two personnel decisions. *Journal of Applied Psychology*, *68*(4), 609.

Cleveland, J. N., & Lim, A. (2007). Employee age and performance in organisations. In K. Shultz and G. Adams (Eds.), *Aging and work in the 21st century* (pp. 109–138). Mahwah, NJ: Erlbaum.

Cleveland, J. N., & Shore, L. M. (1992). Self- and supervisory perspectives on age and work attitudes and performance. *Journal of Applied Psychology*, *77*(4), 469–484.

Cleveland, J. N., Shore, L. M., & Murphy, K. R. (1997). Person-and context-oriented perceptual age measures: Additional evidence of distinctiveness and usefulness. *Journal of Organizational Behavior*, *18*(3), 239–251.

De Lange, A. H., Kooij, D., & van der Heijden, B. I. J. M. (2015). Human resource management and sustainability at work across the lifespan: An integrative perspective. In L. M. Finkelstein, D. M. Truxillo, F. Fraccaroli, & R. Kanfer (Eds.), *Facing the challenges of a multi-age workforce: A use-inspired approach* (pp. 50–79). New York, NY: Routledge.

Demerouti, E., Bakker, A. B., Nachreiner, F., & Schaufeli, W. B. (2001). The job demands-resources model of burnout. *Journal of Applied Psychology*, *86*(3), 499–512.

Donaldson, S. I., & Dollwet, M. (2013). Taming the waves and wild horses of positive organizational psychology. In A. B. Bakker (Ed.), *Advances in Positive Psychology* (pp. 1–21). Bingley, UK: Emerald.

Donaldson, S. I., & Ko, I. (2010). Positive organizational psychology, behavior, and scholarship: A review of the emerging literature and evidence base. *The Journal of Positive Psychology*, *5*(3), 177–191.

Elovainio, M., Kivimäki, M., Vahtera, J., Ojanlatva, A., Korkeila, K., Suominen, S., ... Koskenvuo, M. (2003). Social support, early retirement, and a retirement preference: A study of 10,489 Finnish adults. *Journal of Occupational and Environmental Medicine*, *45*(4), 433–439.

Feldman, D. C. (2007). Career mobility and career stability among older workers. In K. Shultz and G. Adams (Eds.), *Aging and work in the 21st century* (pp. 179–198). Mahwah, NJ: Erlbaum.

Feldman, M. S., & Khademian, A. M. (2003). Empowerment and cascading vitality. In K. Cameron & J. Dutton (Eds.), *Positive organizational scholarship: Foundations of a new discipline* (pp. 343–358). San Francisco, CA: Berrett-Koehler.

Ferdman, B. M. (2014). The practice of inclusion in diverse organizations. In B. M. Ferdman and B. R. Deane (Eds.), *Diversity at work: The practice of inclusion* (pp. 3–54). San Francisco, CA: Jossey-Bass.

Finkel, D., Andel, A., Gatz, M., & Pedersen, N. L. (2009). The role of occupational complexity in trajectories of cognitive aging before and after retirement. *Psychology and Aging*, *24*(3), 563–573.

Finkelstein, L. M. (2015). Older workers, stereotypes, and discrimination in the context of the employment relationship. In P. M. Bal, D. T. A. M. Kooij, & D. M. Rousseau (Eds.), *Aging workers and the employee–employer relationship* (pp. 13–32). Dordrecht, the Netherlands: Springer.

Fisher, G. G., Ryan, L. H., & Sonnega, A. (2015). Prolonged working years: Consequences and directions for interventions. In J. Vuori, R. Blonk, & R. H. Price (Eds.) *Sustainable working lives: Managing work transitions and health throughout the life course* (pp. 269–288.). Dordrecht, the Netherlands: Springer.

Fisher, G. G., Stachowski, A., Infurna, F. J., Faul, J. D., Grosch, J., & Tetrick, L. E. (2014). Mental work demands, retirement, and longitudinal trajectories of cognitive functioning. *Journal of Occupational Health Psychology*, *19*(2), 231.

Freund, A. M., & Baltes, P. B. (2002). Life-management strategies of selection, optimization and compensation: Measurement by self-report and construct validity. *Journal of Personality and Social Psychology*, *82*(4), 642.

Friedrich, D. D. (2001). *Successful aging: Integrating contemporary ideas, research findings, and intervention strategies.* Springfield, IL: Charles C. Thomas.

Gittell, J. H., Cameron, K., Lim, S., & Rivas, V. (2006). Relationships, layoffs, and organizational resilience airline industry responses to September 11. *The Journal of Applied Behavioral Science*, *42*(3), 300–329.

Goldberg, C. B., Finkelstein, L. M., Perry, E. L., & Konrad, A. M. (2004). Job and industry fit: The effects of age and gender matches on career progress outcomes. *Journal of Organizational Behavior*, *25*(7), 807–829.

Goldberg, C. B., Perry, E. L., Finkelstein, L. M., & Shull, A. (2013). Antecedents and outcomes of targeting older applicants in recruitment. *European Journal of Work and Organizational Psychology*, *22*(3), 265–278.

Goldsmith, R. E., & Heiens, R. A. (1992). Subjective age: A test of five hypotheses. *The Gerontologist*, *32*(3), 312–317.

Grant, A. M., & Schwartz, B. (2011). Too much of a good thing: The challenge and opportunity of the inverted U. *Perspectives on Psychological Science*, *6*(1), 61–76. doi:10.1177/1745691610393523

Gumpert, M. (1954). Old age and productive loss. Pastoral Psychology, 5, 37–44. doi:10.1007/BF01570566

Hackman, J. R., & Oldham, G. R. (1976). Motivation through the design of work: Test of a theory. *Organizational behavior and human performance*, *16*(2), 250–279.

Hanson, V. L., & Lesser, E. (2009). Implications of an aging workforce: An industry perspective. In S. J. Czaja, & J. Sharit (Eds.), *Aging and work: Issues and implications in a changing landscape* (pp. 90–104). Baltimore, MD: Johns Hopkins University Press.

Hansson, R. O., DeKoekkoek, P. D., Neece, W. M., & Patterson, D. W. (1997). Successful aging at work: Annual review, 1992–1996: The older worker and transitions to retirement. *Journal of Vocational Behavior*, *51*(2), 202–233.

Havighurst, R. J., & Orr, B. E. (1955). Chapter VI: Aging and psychological adjustment. *Review of Educational Research*, *25*, 477–486. doi:10.3102/00346543025005477

Hedge, J. W., Borman, W. C., & Lammlein, S. E. (2006). *The aging workforce: Realities, myths, and implications for organizations.* Washington, DC: American Psychological Association.

Hirsh, C. E. (2009). The strength of weak enforcement: The impact of discrimination charges, legal environments, and organizational conditions on workplace segregation. *American Sociological Review*, *74*(2), 245–271.

Hirsh, C. E., & Kornrich, S. (2008). The context of discrimination: Workplace Conditions, institutional environments, and sex and race discrimination charges. *American Journal of Sociology*, *113*(5), 1394–1432.

Ilmarinen, J., Tuomi, K., & Klockars, M. (1997). Changes in the work ability of active employees over an 11-year period. *Scandinavian Journal of Work, Environment & Health*, *23*, 49–57.

Jackson, S. H., Weale, M. R., & Weale, R. A. (2003). Biological age: What is it and can it be measured? *Archives of Gerontology and Geriatrics*, *36*(2), 103–115.

Johnson, J. A., & Lopes, J. (2008). The intergenerational workforce, revisited. *Organization Development Journal*, *26*(1), 31–36.

Johnson, R. W. (2005, September). Working longer to enhance retirement security. *Older Americans' Economic Security, The Retirement Project, 1.*

Kahn, R. L., & Antonucci, T. C. (1980). Convoys over the life course: Attachment, roles, and social support. In P. B. Baltes & O. Brim (Eds.), *Life-span development and behavior* (Vol. *3*, pp. 254–283). New York, NY: Academic Press.

Kanfer, R. (1987). Task-specific motivation: An integrative approach to issues of measurement, mechanisms, processes, and determinants. *Journal of Social and Clinical Psychology*, *5*, 237–264.

Kanfer, R., & Ackerman, P. L. (2004). Aging, adult development, and work motivation. The *Academy of Management Review*, *29*(3), 440.

Kanfer, R., Beier, M. E., & Ackerman, P. L. (2013). Goals and motivation related to work in later adulthood: An organizing framework. *European Journal of Work and Organizational Psychology*, *22*(3), 253–264.

Karasek, R. A., Jr. (1979). Job demands, job decision latitude, and mental strain: Implications for job redesign. *Administrative Science Quarterly*, *24*(2), 285–308.

Karpinska, K., Henkens, K., & Schippers, J. (2013). Retention of older workers: Impact of managers' age norms and stereotypes. *European Sociological Review*, *29*(6), 1323–1335.

Kleinspehn-Ammerlahn, A., Kotter-Grühn, D., & Smith, J. (2008). Self-perceptions of aging: Do subjective age and satisfaction with aging change during old age? *The Journals of Gerontology Series B: Psychological Sciences and Social Sciences, 63*(6), 377–385.

Kluger, A. N., & DeNisi, A. (1996). The effects of feedback interventions on performance: A historical review, a meta-analysis, and a preliminary feedback intervention theory. *Psychological Bulletin, 119*(2), 254–284.

Kooij, D., de Lange, A., Jansen, P., & Dikkers, J. (2008). Older workers' motivation to continue to work: Five meanings of age: A conceptual review. *Journal of Managerial Psychology, 23*(4), 364–394.

Kunze, F., Böhm, S. A., & Bruch, H. (2011). Age diversity, age discrimination climate and performance consequences: A cross organizational study. *Journal of Organizational Behavior, 32*(2), 264–290.

Lancee, B., & Radl, J. (2012). Social connectedness and the transition from work to retirement. *Journals of Gerontology: Series B: Psychological Sciences and Social Sciences, 67*(4), 481–490.

Lawrence, B. S. (1984). Age grading: The implicit organizational timetable. *Journal of Occupational Behaviour, 5*(1), 23–35. doi:10.1002/job.4030050104

Lawrence, B. S. (1987). An organizational theory of age effects. *Research in the Sociology of Organizations, 5*(3), l.

Lawrence, B. S. (1988). New wrinkles in the theory of age: Demography, norms, and performance ratings. *Academy of Management Journal, 31*(2), 309–337.

Luthans, F. (2002). The need for and meaning of positive organizational behavior. *Journal of Organizational Behavior, 23*(6), 695–706.

Luthans, F., Luthans, K. W., Hodgetts, R. M., & Luthans, B. C. (2001). Positive approach to leadership (PAL) implications for today's organizations. *Journal of Leadership & Organizational Studies, 8*(2), 3–20.

Luthans, F., Luthans, K. W., & Luthans, B. C. (2004). Positive psychological capital: Beyond human and social capital. *Business Horizons, 47*(1), 45–50.

Maurer, T. J. (2001). Career-relevant learning and development, worker age, and beliefs about self-efficacy for development. *Journal of Management, 27*(2), 123–140.

Maurer, T. J. (2007). Employee development and training issues related to the aging workforce. In K. Shultz and G. Adams (Eds.), *Aging and work in the 21st century* (pp. 163–178). Mahwah, NJ: Erlbaum.

McCarthy, J., Heraty, N., Cross, C., & Cleveland, J. N. (2014). Who is considered an "older worker"? Extending our conceptualisation of "older" from an organisational decision maker perspective. *Human Resource Management Journal, 24*(4), 374–393.

McGonagle, A. K., Fisher, G. G., Barnes-Farrell, J. L., & Grosch, J. W. (2015). Individual and work factors related to perceived work ability and labor force outcomes. *Journal of Applied Psychology, 100*(2), 376–398.

Moen, P., Fields, V., Quick, H., & Hofmeister, H. (2000). A life-course approach to retirement and social integration. In K. Pillemer, P. Moen, E. Wethington, & N. Glasgow (Eds.), *Social integration in the second half of life* (pp. 75–107). Baltimore, MD: Johns Hopkins.

Moghimi, D., Scheibe, S., & Van Yperen, N. W. (2015). Job crafting in aging employees. In N. A. Pachana & N. Thapa (Eds.), *Encyclopedia of geropsychology*. Singapore: Springer.

Montepare, J. M., & Lachman, M. E. (1989). "You're only as old as you feel": Self-perceptions of age, fears of aging, and life satisfaction from adolescence to old age. *Psychology and Aging, 4*(1), 73.

Murphy, K. R., & Cleveland, J. N. (1995). Understanding performance appraisal: Social, organizational, and goal-oriented perspectives. Newbury Park, CA: Sage.

National Centre for the Protection of Older People (2009, November). *Public perceptions of older people and ageing: A literature review*. Dublin, Ireland: Author. Retrieved from www.ncpop.ie

Neugarten, B. L., & Reed, S. C. (1997). Social and psychological characteristics. In C. K. Cassel, H. J. Cohen, E. B. Larson, D. E. Meier, N. M. Resnick, L. A. Rubinstein, & L. B. Sorensen (Eds.), *Geriatric medicine* (pp. 45–53). New York, NY: Springer.

Niessen, C., Sonnentag, S., & Sach, F. (2012). Thriving at work: A diary study. *Journal of Organizational Behavior, 33*(4), 468–487.

Ng, T. W. H., & Feldman, D. C. (2008). The relationship of age to ten dimensions of job performance. *Journal of Applied Psychology, 93*, 392–423.

Ng, T. W. H., & Feldman, D. C. (2010). The relationships of age with job attitudes: A meta-analysis. *Personnel Psychology, 63*(3), 677–718.

Ng, T. W. H., & Feldman, D. C. (2012). Employee voice behavior: A meta-analytic test of the conservation of resources framework. *Journal of Organizational Behavior, 33*(2), 216–234.

Ng, T. W. H., & Feldman, D. C. (2013). How do within-person changes due to aging affect job performance? *Journal of Vocational Behavior, 83*(3), 500–513.

Peterson, C. (2006). *A primer in positive psychology*. Oxford, UK: Oxford University Press.

Peterson, S. J., & Spiker, B. K. (2005). Establishing the positive contributory value of older workers: A positive psychology perspective. *Organizational Dynamics, 34*(2), 153–167.

Phillips, D. R., & Siu, O. I. (2012). Global aging and aging workers. In W. C. Borman & J. W. Hedge (Eds.), *The Oxford handbook of work and aging* (pp. 11–32). Oxford, UK: Oxford University Press.

Pitt-Catsouphes, M., Matz-Costa, C., & Brown, M. (2010). The prism of age: Managing age diversity at the 21st century workplace. In S. Tyson and E. Parry (Eds.), *Managing an age diverse workforce* (pp. 80–94). London, UK: Palgrave Macmillan.

Rauschenbach, C., Krumm, S., Thielgen, M., & Hertel, G. (2013). Age and work-related stress: A review and meta-analysis. *Journal of Managerial Psychology, 28*(7/8), 781–804.

Rohwedder, S., & Willis, R. J. (2010). Mental retirement. *Journal of Economic Perspectives, 24*, 119–138.

Rowe, J. W., & Kahn, R. L. (1987). Human aging: Usual and successful. *Science, 237*(4811), 143–149.

Salas, E., Tannenbaum, S. I., Kraiger, K., & Smith-Jentsch, K. A. (2012). The science of training and development in organizations: What matters in practice. *Psychological Science in the Public Interest, 13*(2), 74–101.

Schalk, R., Van Veldhoven, M., De Lange, A. H., De Witte, H., Kraus, K., Stamov-Rossnagel, C., … Zacher, H. (2010). Moving European research on work and ageing forward: Overview and agenda. *European Journal of Work and Organizational Psychology, 19*(1), 76–101.

Segers, J., Inceoglu, I., & Finkelstein, L. (2014). The age cube of work. In E. Parry (Ed.), *Generational Diversity at Work: New Research Perspectives* (pp. 11–36). London, UK: Routledge.

Seligman, M. E., & Csikszentmihalyi, M. (2000). Positive psychology: An introduction. *American Psychologist, 55*(1), 5–14.

Shore, L. M., Cleveland, J. N., & Goldberg, C. B. (2003). Work attitudes and decisions as a function of manager age and employee age. *Journal of Applied Psychology, 88*(3), 529–537.

Shore, L. M., Cleveland, J. N., & Sanchez, D. (2015). *Inclusive workplaces: Moving beyond inequality and diversity management*. Colorado State University: Manuscript under review.

Shore, L. M., Randel, A. E., Chung, B. G., Dean, M. A., Ehrhart, K. H., & Singh, G. (2010). Inclusion and diversity in work groups: A review and model for future research. *Journal of Management, 37*(4), 1262–1289. doi:0149206310385943

Siegler, R. S. (1995). How does change occur? A microgenetic study of number conservation. *Cognitive Psychology, 28*(3), 225–273.

Snyder, C. R., Harris, C., Anderson, J. R., Holleran, S. A., Irving, L. M., Sigmon, S. T., … Harney, P. (1991). The will and the ways: Development and validation of an individual-differences measure of hope. *Journal of Personality and Social Psychology, 60*(4), 570.

Sterns, H. L., & Doverspike, D. (1989). Aging and the training and learning process in organizations. In I. Goldstein & R. Katzell (Eds.), *Training and development in work organizations* (pp. 299–322). San Francisco, CA: Jossey-Bass.

Sterns, H. L., & Kaplan, J. (2003). Self-management of career and retirement. In G. G. Adams & T. A. Beehr (Eds.), *Retirement: Reasons, processes, and results* (pp. 188–213). New York, NY: Springer.

Sterns, H. L., & Miklos, S. M. (1995). The aging worker in a changing environment: Organizational and individual issues. *Journal of Vocational Behavior, 47*(3), 248–268.

Stewart, M., Reid, G., & Mangham, C. (1997). Fostering children's resilience. *Journal of Pediatric Nursing, 12*(1), 21–31.

Taylor, M. A., & Shore, L. M. (1995). Predictors of planned retirement age: An application of Beehr's model. *Psychology and Aging, 10*(1), 76.
Templer, A., Armstrong-Stassen, M., & Cattaneo, R. J. (2010). Antecedents of older workers' motives for continuing to work. *Career Development International, 15*(5), 479–500.
Triana, M. D. C., & García, M. F. (2009). Valuing diversity: A group-value approach to understanding the importance of organizational efforts to support diversity. *Journal of Organizational Behavior, 30*(7), 941–962.
Triana, M. D. C., García, M. F., & Colella, A. (2010). Managing diversity: How organizational efforts to support diversity moderate the effects of perceived racial discrimination on affective commitment. *Personnel Psychology, 63*(4), 817–843.
Truxillo, D. M., Cadiz, D. A., & Rineer, J. R. (2012). Designing jobs for an aging workforce: An opportunity for occupational health. In J. Houdmont, S. Leka, & R. R. Sinclair (Eds.), *Contemporary occupational health psychology: Global perspectives on research and practice* (Vol. 2, pp. 109–125). Oxford, UK: Oxford University Press.
Truxillo, D. M., Cadiz, D. M., Rineer, J. R., Zaniboni, S., & Fraccaroli, F. (2012). A lifespan perspective on job design: Fitting the worker to the job to promote job satisfaction, engagement, and performance. *Organizational Psychology Review, 2*(4), 340–360.
Truxillo, D. M., & Zaniboni, S. (2015). Work design and aging. In N. A. Pachana (Ed.), *Encyclopedia of Geropsychology* (pp. 1–9). Singapore: Springer. Retrieved from: http://link.springer.com/10.1007/978-981-287-080-3_19-1
Turner, N., Barling, J., & Zacharatos, A. (2002). Positive psychology at work. In C. R. Snyder & S. J. Lopez (Eds.), *Handbook of positive psychology* (pp. 715–728). Oxford, UK: Oxford University Press.
U.S. Bureau of Labor Statistics (2016, February 25). Volunteering in the United States – 2015, Usdl16-0363 [News release]. Retrieved from bls.gov
Wang, M., & Shi, J. (2014). Psychological research on retirement. *Annual Review of Psychology, 65*, 209–233.
Wang, M., & Shultz, K. S. (2010). Employee retirement: A review and recommendations for future investigation. *Journal of Management, 36*(1), 172–206.
Zacher, H. (2015). Successful aging at work. *Work, Aging and Retirement, 1*(1), 4–25.
Zaniboni, S., Sarchielli, G., & Fraccaroli, F. (2010). How are psychosocial factors related to retirement intentions? *International Journal of Manpower, 31*(3), 271–285.

22

Positive Psychological Assessment for the Workplace

Aaron Jarden and Rebecca Jarden

Introduction

The workplace is rapidly and dramatically changing. This change is underpinned by accelerating technological advancement such as the influence of social media, and the desire for better working experiences. Recent books such as *Reinventing Organizations* (Laloux, 2014) and case studies of positive organizational practices (e.g., David, Boniwell, & Ayers, 2012; Dutton & Spreitzer, 2014) further fuel the desire for a "good day at work." Increasing public debate regarding National Accounts of Well-being (Diener, Oishi, & Lucas, 2015; Weijers & Jarden, 2013) also contribute on a broader level to the desire for a better way of living and working.

Against this backdrop of increasing demand for positive change sit the related fields of Positive Organizational Scholarship (Cameron, Dutton, & Quinn, 2003) and Positive Organizational Behavior (Luthans, 2002a; Nelson & Cooper, 2007). Research stemming from these fields, as well as from organizational (e.g., Luthans, 2002b) and positive psychologists (e.g., Steger, Dik, & Shim, in press) beginning to focus on well-being at work, has demonstrated that work well-being is good for the individual, the organization, and for society as a whole. Work well-being is also good fiscally, with every organizational dollar invested into organizational well-being providing a return of approximately 3 to 5 times the original investment (Goetzel & Ozminkowski, 2008; Rath & Harter, 2010).

Such findings, particularly at the organizational level, are driving organizations to investigate and then further invest in Workplace Well-being Programs (henceforth WWPs).[1] With such activity it is important to know how organizations and organizational consultants implementing WWPs assess the well-being of employees, and how they evaluate the WWPs they implement in relation to their impacts on employee well-being and important organizational performance indicators.

The Wiley Blackwell Handbook of the Psychology of Positivity and Strengths-Based Approaches at Work, First Edition. Edited by Lindsay G. Oades, Michael F. Steger, Antonella Delle Fave, and Jonathan Passmore.

This chapter firstly summarizes the benefits of well-being at work, and the case for well-being assessments and the use of positive psychological assessment measures is made. Following this, we appraise current workplace well-being assessment practices, drawing on various related literature. Then suggestions are provided as to both what should be assessed in organizations, and how this should be assessed. Lastly, a new framework for conceptually evaluating organizational well-being research is briefly outlined, which is also a practically useful framework when obtaining commitment for WWPs and implementing them within organizations. The chapter ends with some suggestions for further research and conclusions.

The Benefits of Well-Being at Work

Workplace stress is a chronic and pressing issue for organizations (Nixon, Mazzola, Bauer, Kruger, & Spector, 2011). Particularly in Western countries, there is a stark contrast between knowledge of the benefits of work well-being for both the employee and the organization (see Harter, Schmidt, & Keyes, 2002; or Lewis, 2011) and the high rates of unhappiness at work (e.g., 50%; Mercer, 2011). However, employees with high well-being provide many benefits. For example, happier employees are healthier (Waddell & Burton, 2006), have fewer sick days (Bertera, 1990), earn more (Koo & Suh, 2013), and get promoted sooner (Boehm & Lyubomirsky, 2008). They are more effective (George & Bettenhausen, 1990) and productive (Bockerman & Ilmakunnas, 2012; Page & Vella-Brodrick, 2009), display better organizational citizenship behaviors (Organ, 1988), inspire customer loyalty (Harter, Schmidt, & Hayes, 2002), increase the well-being of other employees (Christakis & Fowler, 2009; Totterdell, Kellett, Teuchmann, & Briner, 1998), stay in their jobs longer (Judge, 1993; Rusbult & Farrell, 1983), and can even increase an organization's stock market value (Edmans, 2012). Of course happy employees have a place in society beyond their organizations as they spread their well-being influence; happy employees are good for societal well-being (Graham, 2010). The benefits of work well-being are thus relatively well established. On the whole it is better for employees to be happier and satisfied at work than not, and these benefits accrue from the individual, to the organization, and to society.

The Potential Benefits of Well-Being Assessment at Work

There are benefits beyond the results of the assessments themselves in conducting organizational well-being assessments; the wider context of these assessments matters also. These benefits include aspects such as (1) the organization being perceived as caring towards employees (improving recruitment), (2) the organization being seen as an attractive place to work (making retention easier), (3) that the information obtained can be used to make important management decisions (e.g., how and when to restructure a division), or (4) that well-being information can assist with managing both psychological and physical health more specifically and constructively (Lewis, 2011; Lopez & Snyder, 2003; Nelson & Cooper, 2007). However, more research on the impact of these more contextual factors is needed.

Current Workplace Well-Being Assessment Practice

There is growing evidence that work well-being is part of a bigger picture of better functioning individuals, organizations, and societies, and should be a priority target for organizations. How might organizations track progress toward well-being targets though?

That is, if work well-being and knowledge of well-being is a valued goal for employees and organizations, what do current workplace well-being assessment practices look like?

Poor assessments in, and of, workplaces

Unfortunately there is scant data available on current positive psychological assessment practices in workplaces.[2] There is, as such, no critical review or study of well-being assessment practice presently available. In addition, as Spence (2015) notes, what data there are suggest that (1) very little assessment of organizational well-being happens in practice, and (2) when it does happen, this assessment is typically superficial.

Regarding Spence's first point, anecdotal reports from organizational consultants suggest that well-being assessments usually happen in the context of an intended WWP. It does not seem to be the case that employee or organizational well-being assessments are undertaken without any view toward increasing levels of employee or organizational well-being. This point is important, because in countries such as Australia as few as 1,500 organizations (3.6% of the total workforce) provide formal, structured workplace health and well-being programs (HAPIA, 2009). So, if very few workplace health and well-being programs happen in the first instance, there is very little opportunity for well-being assessments to occur if they only exist in the context of these programs. In addition, McCarthy, Almeida, and Ahrens (2011) reported that 46% of organizations implementing WWPs (in a sample of 319 Human Resources professionals) did not evaluate their WWPs. Of the remainder that did evaluate their WWPs, these assessments were largely limited to the usage of the program and overall satisfaction with the program, rather than the impacts of the program per se. Similar results have been reported elsewhere (e.g., in the UK: McGillivray, 2002). Such findings suggest that very little positive psychological assessment happens in workplaces.

Regarding Spence's second point, when well-being assessments do happen, they are not as psychometrically sound, rigorous, or appropriately focused as they should be, according to standard psychological assessment processes (see Shum, O'Gorman, Myors, & Creed, 2013). Instead well-being assessments are more commonly limited by their small scale, with few questions asked (e.g., on overall job satisfaction), and they fail to measure the multidimensional nature of well-being (Diener et al., 2015; Hone, Jarden, Schofield, & Duncan, 2014). So when they do happen, they seem to lack appropriate and rigorous evaluation.

These points concerning the lack of well-being assessment, and lack of rigor in assessments, add to the finding that WWPs themselves vary in quality. As a report by PriceWaterhouseCoopers mentions, WWPs when delivered are usually "a patchwork of uncoordinated programmes, often delivered by multiple vendors, with limited consistency or integration" (PriceWaterhouseCoopers, 2010, p. 21), which makes high-quality, sound psychometric assessment even more challenging. Such diversity in programs delivered may then lead to insufficient or inappropriate measurement, as Mills, Fleck, and Kozikowski recently mentioned:

> the operationalization of positive constructs has lurched forward so rapidly that their measurement in the workplace has proceeded without a proper foundation and with an insufficient assessment as to the appropriateness of the various measurement instruments used to assess such constructs. (2013, p. 160)

In other words, the choice of construct measure used may not be fit for purpose on all occasions, and this may be related to the quality of the WWP being delivered and then evaluated. More research, including a study and review of workplace well-being assessment practice, is needed in order to fully understand the scale and scope of current well-being assessments in organizations.[3] At this point it is hard to draw any firm conclusions about current well-being assessment practices in workplaces beyond the above points. Given that scant assessment practice data is available, and it seems that very little sound, rigorous, or multidimensional assessment of psychological well-being happens in organizations when assessments do happen, it is beneficial then to investigate what positive psychological and well-being assessment measures are used in well-being promotion research, what measures are used in workplace well-being research, and what measures are suggested by positive psychological assessment experts.

Assessment measures in applied research

Currently, it is difficult to identify, or even categorize, what measures are used in workplaces to assess employee and organizational well-being and the impacts of WWPs, or the extent to which they are used at all. It is possible that organizations are using a myriad of idiosyncratic and proprietary measures, severely limiting what can be learned from organizationally embedded measures. We can more easily investigate research using published positive psychological assessment measures by focusing on research that tests interventions that aim to increase well-being (similarly to the aims of WWPs), and with research on work well-being in particular.

Well-being promotion research

In 2015, Hone, Jarden, and Schofield identified 40 positive psychological intervention effectiveness trials targeting adults in real-world settings, involving a total of 10,664 participants. These 40 articles reported which assessment measures (including positive psychological assessment measures) they used to assess the effectiveness of their positive psychological intervention programs. All studies needed to meet eight selection criteria (see Hone et al., 2015, p. 3), one of which was that: "Pre-intervention and post-intervention assessment using psychometrically sound measures of positive variables must be reported (such as positive emotions, subjective well-being, psychological, optimism and/or resilience)." For the purpose of this chapter we explored further the assessment measures used in these 40 effectiveness trials,[4] and this highlighted both which assessment measures, and to what extent those measures, are used in positive psychology intervention effectiveness trials. These results are displayed in Table 22.1, and sorted by most frequent use.

Across these 40 trials, 34 measures (e.g., Satisfaction with Life Scale, Scales of Psychological Well-being) were used to capture 17 constructs (e.g., positive affect and negative affect, well-being). This review of measures used in positive psychological intervention research highlights that:

1. There are only a few relatively frequently used measures (e.g., only 6 measures were used 4 or more times), and 20 of the 34 measures were only used once.
2. Many of the measures used are not traditional "positive measures," nor do they assess "positive variables," but rather measure more clinical type variables (e.g., depression, anxiety, stress).
3. Only one specific workplace well-being measure was used.
4. Many hedonic measures of emotions and affect were used.

Table 22.1 Assessment measures used in 40 positive psychological intervention effectiveness trials.

No.	*Measure*	*Measure authors*	*Construct/s*	*Times used*
1	Satisfaction with Life Scale (SWLS)	Diener, Emmons, Larsen, & Griffin (1985)	Life satisfaction	11
2	Scales of Psychological Well-being (SPW)	Ryff & Singer (1998)	Well-being	9
3	Positive Affect and Negative Affect Schedule (PANAS)	Watson, Clark, & Tellegan (1988)	Positive affect and negative affect	8
4	Centre for Epidemiological Studies Depression Scale (CES-D)	Radloff (1977)	Depressed mood	6
5	Depression Anxiety Stress Scale (DAS-21)	Lovibond & Lovibond (1995)	Depression/ Anxiety/Stress	5
6	Quality of Life Inventory (QoLI)	Frisch (2004)	Life satisfaction, life domains	4
7	Profile of Mood States (POMS)	McNair, Lorr, & Droppelman (1981)	Emotions	3
8	Workplace Well-being Index (WWI)	Page (2005)	Workplace well-being	3
9	Cognitive Hardiness Scale (CHS)	Nowack (1990)	Cognitive hardiness	2
10	Warwick-Edinburgh Mental Well-being Scale (WEMWBS)	Tennant, Fishwick, Platt, Joseph, & Stewart-Brown (2006)	Well-being	2
11	Clinical Interview for Depression (CID)	Paykel (1985)	Depression	2
12	SPF-Index Level Scale (SPF-IL)	Nieboer, Lindenberg, Boomsma, & Van Bruggen (2005)	Well-being	2
13	Steen Happiness Index (SHI)	Seligman, Steen, Park, & Peterson (2005)	Happiness	2
14	Mental Health Continuum – Short Form (MHC-SF)	Keyes (2005)	Well-being	1
15	Authentic Happiness Inventory (AHI)	Peterson (2005)	Happiness	1
16	Subjective Happiness Scale (SHS)	Lyubomirsky & Lepper (1999)	Happiness	1
17	Life Orientation Test-Revised (LOT-R)	Scheier, Carver, & Bridges (1994)	Optimism	1
18	Short Happiness and Affect Research Protocol (SHARP)	Stones et al. (1996)	Happiness	1
19	Job-related Affective Well-being S scale (JAWS)	Van Katwyk, Fox, Spector, & Kelloway (2000)	Work affect	1
20	Self-developed self-efficacy scale based on Bandura (2012)	Ouweneel, Le Blanc, & Schaufeli (2013)	Self-efficacy	1
21	Utrecht Work Engagement Scale (UWES)	Schaufeli, Bakker, & Salanova (2006)	Work engagement	1
22	EuroQol Group 5-Dimension Self-Report Questionnaire (EQ-5D)	EuroQol Group (1990)	Health outcome	1

(*Continued*)

Table 22.1 (Continued)

No.	*Measure*	*Measure authors*	*Construct/s*	*Times used*
23	Generalized Anxiety Disorder 7-item scale (GAD-7)	Spitzer, Kroenke, Williams, & Löwe (2006)	Anxiety	1
24	SF-36 Health Survey (SF-36)	Ware & Sherbourne (1992)	Health status	1
25	Hopkins Symptom Checklist-25 (HSCL-25)	Derogatis, Lipman, Rickels, Uhlenhuth, & Covi (1974);	Anxiety/ Depression	1
26	Self-Management Ability-Scale (SMAS-30)	Schuurmans et al. (2005)	Self-management ability	1
27	PsyCap Questionnaire (PCQ)	Luthans, Avolio, Avey, & Norman (2007)	Psychological capital	1
28	World Health Organization Quality of Life Inventory – Brief (WHOQOL-BREF)	WHOQOL Group (1998)	Quality of life	1
29	Flourishing Scale (FS)	Diener et al. (2009)	Flourishing	1
30	WHO-5 Well-being Index (WHO-5)	Primack (2003)	Quality of life/ Well-being	
31	Personal Well-being Index (PWI-A)	International Wellbeing Group (2006)	Well-being	1
32	Assessing Emotions Scale (AES)	Schutte et al. (1998)	Emotions	1
33	Affective Well-being Scale (AWS)	Daniels (2000)	Emotions	1
34	Orientations to Happiness Questionnaire (OTHQ)	Peterson, Park, & Seligman (2005)	Well-being	1

Source: Author.

Workplace well-being research

Next, for the purpose of this chapter we conducted a systematic review to investigate which positive psychological measures are used to evaluate the effectiveness of a workplace well-being intervention. Electronic databases (OVID: psych INFO, psych TESTS, Cochrane library, AMED, Health and psychosocial instruments, MEDLINE; EBSCO Health Databases: MEDLINE, CINHAL Plus with Full Text; Scopus; Proquest) were searched without date limiters up to December 2015 to identify primary research studies that investigated which positive psychological measures are used to evaluate the effectiveness of a workplace intervention. Database search terms included "positive psych*" OR well-being OR "well being" AND assessment OR measure* AND worker OR workplace OR organi* AND intervention AND effect* OR effic* OR outcome* OR evaluat*. Forward and backward citation searches were carried out on any studies included following the electronic database searches. Studies were eligible if they measured the efficacy[5] of a workplace positive psychological intervention using an assessment measure. The two chapter authors independently screened the reports for inclusion, looking first at title and abstracts. Full text articles were obtained for studies that appeared to meet the inclusion criteria, or studies where a definite decision could not be made. Studies were then individually reviewed and each assessment tool used to measure efficacy of a workplace positive

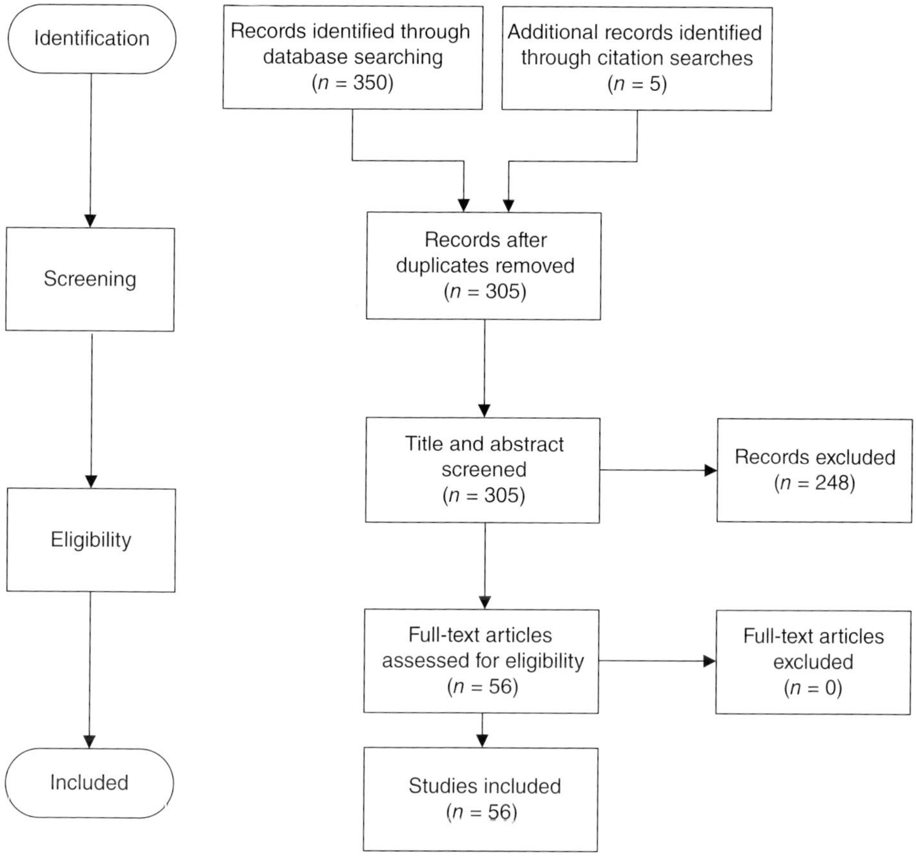

Figure 22.1 PRISMA diagram showing the selection process for articles in the review. *Source*: Author.

psychological intervention was identified. Database searches identified 350 articles, with 5 additional records from citation searches. Following removal of duplicates and title and abstract screening, 56 full text articles were assessed and met the selection criteria: see the PRISMA diagram in Figure 22.1. This process identified 56 articles that utilized 111 measures in total (or selected a subset of questions from an established measure). Of these 111 measures, 17 were used in 2 or more of the 56 studies and are displayed in Table 22.2, and sorted by most frequent use.

This review of measures used in workplace well-being research highlights that:

1 There are only a few relatively frequently used measures (e.g., only 8 of the 111 measures were used 4 or more times) with most ($n = 94$) of the 111 measures only used once.
2 Many of the measures used are not traditional "positive measures," nor do they assess "positive variables," but rather measure clinical type variables (e.g., depression, anxiety, stress), or health variables.
3 The Satisfaction with Life Scale, the most used measure in the review of effectiveness trials, was only used in 4 of the 56 studies.

Table 22.2 Assessment measures used 2 or more times in 56 workplace well-being research articles.

No.	*Measure*	*Authors*	*Construct/s*	*Times used*
1	General Health Questionnaire (GHQ-12)	Goldberg & Hillier (1979)	Health	10
2	Perceived Stress Scale (PSS)	Cohen & Williamson (1988)	Stress	8
3	Job Satisfaction Scale (JSS)	Warr, Cook, & Wall (1979)	Job satisfaction	7
4	Malach Burnout Scale (MBS)	Malach-Pines (2005)	Burnout	6
5	Utrecht Work Engagement Scale (UWES)	Schaufeli, Bakker, & Salanova (2006)	Work engagement	5
6	Satisfaction with Life Scale (SWLS)	Diener et al. (1985)	Life satisfaction	4
7	Positive Affect and Negative Affect Schedule (PANAS)	Watson et al. (1988)	Positive affect and negative affect	4
8	Centre for Epidemiological Studies Depression Scale (CES-D)	Radloff (1977)	Depressed mood	4
9	Pittsburgh Sleep Quality Index (PSQI)	Buysse, Reynolds, Monk, Berman, & Kupfer (1989)	Sleep	3
10	Mindfulness Attention Awareness Scale (MAAS)	Brown & Ryan (2003)	Mindfulness	3
11	Copenhagen Psychosocial Questionnaire (CPQ)	Kristensen, Hannerz, Hogh, Borg (2005)	Psychosocial work environment	3
12	Vitality Scale (VS)	Ryan & Frederick (1997)	Vitality	3
13	Job Demands (JD)	Wall, Jackson, & Mullarkey (1995)	Job demands	2
14	Organizational Commitment Scale (OCS)	Cook & Wall (1980)	Organizational commitment	2
15	State/Trait Anxiety Inventory (STAI)	Spielberger (1972, 1983)	Anxiety	2
16	SF-12 Health Survey (SF-12)	Ware, Kosinski, & Keller (1996)	Health	2
17	Work Ability Index (WAI)	Ilmarinen (2007)	Work ability	2

Source: Author.

Measures suggested by positive psychological assessment experts

In their 2015 paper, Owens, Magyar-Moe, and Lopez suggested a list of 23 areas of positive psychological assessment (e.g., emotions, gratitude, strengths, well-being, optimism, mindfulness, etc.) and 58 specific measures (e.g., Flourishing Scale, Mindfulness Attention Awareness

Scale) capturing constructs in these areas of positive psychological assessment. These authors are experts in practice and in positive psychological assessment. For example, Lopez was one of the editors of the key text on positive psychological assessment (Lopez & Snyder, 2003), and Owens and Magyar-Moe have both published on positive assessment in particular (e.g., Keyes & Magyar-Moe, 2003). These 58 measures are presented as "standardised positive psychological measures" for children, adolescents, and adults which are "an extensive, but not exhaustive, list of measures available, largely from the 1990s to the present" (Owens et al., 2015, p. 649). The measures which overlap with Owens et al.'s recommended list of 58 and with either the above 34 that have been used in well-being promotion research (Table 22.1) *or* with the 17 measures used two or more times in workplace well-being research (Table 22.2) include the following nine:

1 Satisfaction with Life Scale (SWLS)
2 Scales of Psychological Well-being (SPW)
3 Positive Affect and Negative Affect Schedule (PANAS)
4 Quality of Life Inventory (QoLI)
5 Steen Happiness Index (SHI)
6 Subjective Happiness Scale (SHS)
7 Life Orientation Test-Revised (LOT-R)
8 Flourishing Scale (FS)
9 Mindfulness Attention Awareness Scale (MAAS)

In other words, these nine include one of the measures suggested by Owens et al. that was also relatively popular in well-being promotion research *or* workplace well-being research. Taking this one step further, including measures that were popular in both well-being promotion research (Table 22.1) *and* with the 17 measures used two or more times in workplace well-being research (Table 22.2), this list would then include two more:

10 Utrecht Work Engagement Scale (UWES)
11 Centre for Epidemiological Studies, Depression Scale (CES-D)

For further detail of how these were identified, see Appendix A. Psychometric properties aside,[6] these 11 measures, because of their popularity across two of the three data sources, are likely good candidates for potential use in positive psychological assessment practices in workplaces.

Ideal Organizational Well-Being Assessments

The case that well-being should be assessed in the workplace relies on employees and organizations first realizing the benefits and value of high well-being in a work context. If it is the case that well-being is a goal for employees and organizations (i.e., it is seen as a commodity that should be developed and increased as the research suggests), then well-being should be assessed soundly. The management adage that "you can only manage what you measure" applies equally well to psychological well-being in organizations. As Nobel Prize-winning economist Joseph Stiglitz mentioned, "What we measure affects what we do; and if our measurements are flawed, decisions may be distorted" (Stiglitz, Sen, & Fitoussi, 2009, p. 7). If organizations do not assess well-being rigorously, it is difficult for employees, organizational consultants, and organizations to then determine the need, appropriate type, scale, and effectiveness over time of WWPs. Assuming that sound well-being assessments are the first step toward considering WWPs, the important questions then become, "*What* should be assessed?" and "*How* should it be assessed?"

In addressing these two questions it is of foremost importance to be mindful of the goals of assessment (at least from the perspective of management), which usually includes the obtainment of high-quality information that directly leads to actionable decisions. For example, a finding that employees are highly stressed may lead to investment in a stress-reduction program or workload changes, or the finding that employees are not utilizing their strengths may lead to investment in a strengths program or team reconfigurations.

What should be assessed? Putting together a dream list of measures

Although the nature and conceptualization of psychological well-being itself is contentious (Diener, 2009; Warr, 2013), the field of positive psychological assessment (see Lopez & Snyder, 2003) is reaching consensus that a dashboard of metrics are needed to capture the multidimensional nature of well-being (Diener et al., 2015; Hone et al., 2014). As such, this chapter proposes 11 measures that have been identified by a review of research and by experts, and in addition we propose an additional 16 measures. Together these 27 assessment measures provide both global and evaluative well-being information (i.e., they largely address the question "What is the level of well-being in our organization?") as well as information on more specific drivers and enablers of work well-being (i.e., they largely address the question "What are the contributing factors to our organization's level of well-being?").[7] These additional 16 measures suggested by us are to fill exactly this balance gap between global well-being and well-being drivers. Nonetheless, the correct battery of assessment measures for each specific organization will depend on that organization's situation and requirements, and in addition organizations are likely to want to assess relevant indicators related to employee well-being (e.g., turnover, sick days, performance). The 16 measures listed below were chosen according to the following eight criteria:[8]

1 They are not included in the 11 measures identified above.
2 They provide information that is actionable.
3 They provide a mixture of assessing what is going right (e.g., hope, self-efficacy) and what is going wrong (e.g., resilience), at both global and well-being driver levels.
4 They are relatively short and quick to administer.
5 Some are work-specific (e.g., the Work and Meaning Inventory) and some global (e.g., the Meaning in Life Questionnaire).
6 Some are free to use, and for the rest permission is relatively affordable and accessible.
7 They all have acceptable and validated psychometric properties (some slightly better than others) and are well utilized in practice and/or research.[9]
8 They align well with likely WWPs (e.g., a hope program is aptly assessed with the Adult Hope Scale, a meaning program is aptly assessed with the Work and Meaning Inventory).

Thus the two well-being outcome and 14 well-being driver measures listed below are proposed as potentially valuable components of an organizational well-being assessment, although they are by no means definitive or exhaustive, and in conjunction with consideration of the above 11 represent a "good first step" in the direction of better organizational well-being assessment and toward capturing the multidimensional nature of organizational well-being:

Global outcome measures:
1 Warwick-Edinburgh Mental Well-being Scale (Tennant et al., 2007)
2 Workplace Well-being Index (Page, 2005)

Measures of drivers of well-being:

3 Adult Hope Scale (Snyder et al., 1991)
4 Work and Meaning Inventory (Steger, Dik, & Duffy, 2012)
5 Meaning in Life Questionnaire (Steger, Frazier, Oishi, & Kaler, 2006)
6 Subjective Vitality Scale (Ryan & Frederick, 1997)
7 Strengths Use and Knowledge Scale (Govindji & Linley, 2007)
8 Gratitude Scale (McCullough, Emmons, & Tsang, 2002)
9 Curiosity and Exploration Inventory – II (Kashdan et al., 2009)
10 General Self-Efficacy Scale (Schwarzer & Jerusalem, 1995)
11 Brief Resilience Scale (Smith et al., 2008)
12 General Health Questionnaire (Goldberg & Hillier, 1979)
13 Perceived Stress Scale (Cohen & Williamson, 1988)
14 Job Satisfaction Scale (Warr, Cook, & Wall, 1979)
15 Malach Burnout Scale (Malach-Pines, 2005)
16 VIA (Values In Action) strengths (Peterson & Park, 2009; Peterson & Seligman, 2004)

It should also be pointed out that some drivers are more apt to drive global well-being, and some drivers more apt to drive work well-being. For example, Hamling, Jarden, and Schofield (2016) found that different occupational groups (e.g., managers vs. sales workers vs. laborers etc.) had different drivers for global well-being (i.e., flourishing) than for aspects of work well-being (e.g., job satisfaction). Here aspects such as "work–life balance" and "engagement" were large drivers of work well-being, whereas aspects such as a sense of "meaning and purpose" and "self-esteem" were larger drivers of global well-being.

In summary, measuring global well-being outcomes provides valuable information to decision-makers, especially if the outcomes are sensitive enough to be tracked over time (although some constructs, such as cognitive judgments of life satisfaction, are relatively stable over time, other constructs, such as emotions, are much less so; e.g., see Sheldon, Jose, Kashdan, & Jarden, 2015). In addition, measuring drivers and enablers of well-being also provides valuable information toward decisions if they are sensitive enough to be tracked over time. The research literature indicates that increasing aspects of any of these drivers is good not only for organizational performance, but also for employees' well-being. For example, the strength of curiosity is not only beneficial for goal attainment (e.g., reaching key performance indicators at work), but also provides increased well-being benefits from goal attainment per se (Sheldon et al., 2015).

Given these 16 assessment measures covering a range of constructs, what is missing from this battery of suggested measures? What else might an organization wish to measure in a well-being assessment? Firstly, there is no good measure (according to the eight criteria we listed earlier) of positive leadership (see also MacKie, this volume).[10] Secondly, given the emerging and important relationship between physical health and subjective well-being (Seligman, 2008), a more detailed measure of employee health indicators than the GHQ-12 may be beneficial (e.g., such as health conditions).[11] These, positive leadership and health, are two areas organizations are likely to want to assess.

In summary, a variety of methods (i.e., review of well-being promotion research, review of workplace well-being research, expert opinion) have been used to identify possible assessment measures for use in well-being assessment in organizations. In addition, we have suggested additional measures based on rational criteria and that fill the balance gap between global well-being and well-being driver measures. In making such suggestions we believe this above dream list of 27 measures is a good battery to draw from in the first instance, depending on each organization's particular context.

Once "What should be assessed?" has been addressed, the question then becomes "How should well-being be assessed?," that is, what is the best way to conduct an organizational well-being assessment?

Implementing well-being assessment in organizations

There are many methods one can use in work well-being assessment (e.g., Juniper, White, & Bellamy, 2009) and psychological assessment (see Shum et al., 2013) including both paper-based and online psychometric tests, self-monitoring, direct observation, physiological measures (e.g., heart rate, skin conductivity), interviews, and using existing records. In regard to well-being specifically, there are also the Experience Sampling Method (ESM: Larson & Csikszentmihalyi, 1983) and the Day Reconstruction Method (DRM: Kahneman, Krueger, Schkade, Schwarz, & Stone, 2004). However, by far the most popular are psychometric tests, mostly due to the increased cost, level of experience, specialist equipment, and time associated with other methods. When comparing paper-based and online tests, research indicates that there are no significant differences in the psychometric properties of measures completed online compared to paper-based versions (Lewis, Watson, & White, 2009; Riva, Teruzzi, & Anolli, 2003), which is one reason why the use of web-based research methods is increasing (Reips, 2006). Online testing is also quicker, provides greater confidentiality, and scoring is automated (Shum et al., 2013). For all of the above reasons we advocate the use of online assessment methods.

Although a selection of the 27 measures listed above can be self-administered by organizations via standard web-based survey software (e.g., survey monkey, survey gizmo, survey pro), two currently available online well-being assessment tools are now briefly highlighted, both capturing a combination of outcome- and driver-level well-being indicators.

Work on Wellbeing[12] (www.workonwellbeing.com) is an online assessment tool specifically developed to assess and track employee well-being over time in organizations. The assessment comprises 50 questions and takes on average nine minutes to complete. Consisting of a collection of validated psychometric measures from the psychology literature, the assessment has four main modules: an assessment of Global Well-being (e.g., life satisfaction); an assessment of Domain Well-being (e.g., satisfaction with intimate relationships); an assessment of Workplace Well-being (e.g., autonomy at work); and an assessment of Component Well-being factors underpinning well-being that are related to a workplace context (e.g., physical health indicators, resilience). In addition, organizations can add their own specific questions to the assessment, and select to add further construct measures from a list of 50 additional validated measures (such as work engagement, burnout, stress, hope, meaning, mindfulness). At the end of the assessment, employees are presented with real-time, benchmarked and contextualized well-being reports. Both organizational account holders and employees are provided with aggregate, anonymous organizational-level well-being reports at the end of the organization's assessment period. These reports can also be tailored for subgroup-level reporting (i.e., teams).

The *Happiness at Work Survey* (www.happinessatworksurvey.com) is an online work well-being assessment tool comprised of 48 questions which takes on average 10 minutes to complete. The survey measures four dynamic and interrelated categories that impact happiness at work: (1) personal resources, (2) the organization itself, (3) the work itself, and (4) thoughts and emotions at work. Employees receive real-time reports, and results identify highlights and lowlights in a dynamic model that encourages discovery. Organizational-level results are aggregated and anonymous, and available at subgroup levels (i.e., teams). Questions are benchmarked against national samples, and presented so that participants can take action to increase their happiness at work.

In addition to these two well-being assessment tools, other options may include Moodscope (www.moodscope.com), Tiny Pulse (www.tinypulse.com), or the Gallup Wellbeing Finder (www.gallup.com), and there are many others (although very few that easily allow the tracking of well-being over time). Regardless of survey tool, it is important to note that (1) assessments should use multiple methods (e.g., survey plus observation) rather than just one piece of information, (2) assessments should be undertaken regularly (e.g., pre, during, and post WWPs), and (3) regular conversations regarding well-being are one key pathway to increasing workplace well-being, and frequent assessment points provide the opportunity to instigate these conversations (Dutton & Spreitzer, 2014).

So given this outline of both what should be assessed and how, we now briefly outline a new framework – the Me, We, Us framework – for conceptually evaluating organizational well-being which is, importantly, also a practically useful framework when obtaining commitment for WWPs and implementing them within organizations. This model provides organizations with a rationale and reminder that multiple levels of assessment and intervention may be needed to maximize performance and well-being across an organization, and thus a focus on assessing constructs at an individual level may not be sufficient. The previously suggested measures that provide a "good first step" are almost exclusively at the individual level.

The 'Me, We, Us' Framework

Although the benefits of high psychological well-being impact individuals, organizations, and the whole of society, WWPs largely target the organization (i.e., individuals at work), and to a lesser extent the individual (i.e., individuals outside of work). When focusing specifically on organizational well-being, well-being assessments and WWPs can happen at three distinct levels regardless of organizational structure or size. These three levels include the individual level (Me), group level (We), and the organizational level (Us), as depicted in Figure 22.2.

Individual-level well-being initiatives include strategies and tasks that employees can do by themselves, such as learning about and utilizing their strengths mindfully (Niemiec, 2013), or undertaking a mindfulness program (Kabat-Zinn, 2005). Such "Me" initiatives do not require the involvement of others within the organization. Group-level well-being initiatives include strategies and tasks that involve an employee working on their

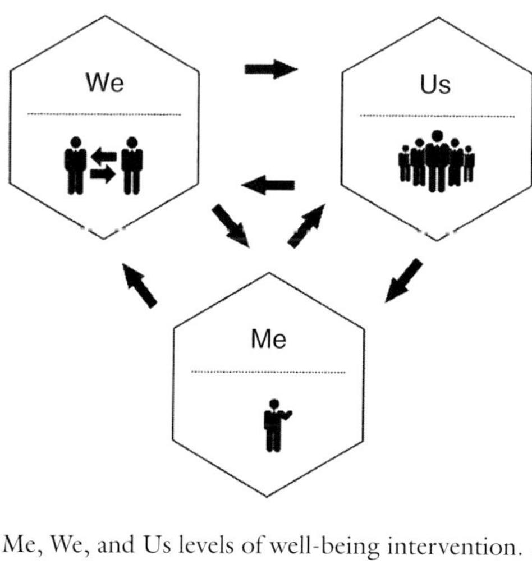

Figure 22.2 Me, We, and Us levels of well-being intervention. *Source*: Author.

well-being with either their manager, their direct team, or other employees with whom they are in frequent contact within the work setting. These activities either have influence on a small group or are undertaken in a group format, and cannot be undertaken by employees themselves as they require cooperation and input from others, for example the employee's manager or team members. Examples of "We" initiatives include strategies and tasks such as job crafting (Wrzesniewski, 2014) or building high-quality connections (Dutton & Heaphy, 2003). Organizational-level well-being initiatives include strategies and tasks that aim to have an impact over the whole of the organization, or are designed to trickle down from the top of the organization (ideally to all employees). Examples of such "Us" initiatives include strategies and tasks such as creating an organizational well-being policy (HAPIA, 2009), directing resources toward one-off or smaller scale well-being initiatives, or whole of organization well-being assessments or WWPs such as appreciative inquiry summits (Cooperrider & Whitney, 2005). Additionally, these levels of Me, We, and Us can also be integrated. For example, an employee (Me) can choose to work on their strengths, a team (We) can choose to focus on team members' strengths in the deployment of team projects, and the organization (Us) can choose to invest in a strengths program for all employees.

On the whole, at all levels of Me, We, and Us, high well-being from a positive psychology perspective is about employees and organizations shifting their perspective from predominately focusing on what is wrong, to building on what is going right and working, to capitalizing on the good and building and seeding the enabling conditions for high well-being (Jarden & Jarden, 2015; Lewis, 2011). Workplace well-being programs across these three levels are about helping employees to use their strengths, enhance their relationships, and find more meaning and engagement at work so that both employees and the organization as a whole can achieve their, and its, true potential.[13]

To date, arguably, well-being assessments and WWPs have focused on the individual (Me) level. However, well-being activities at the group (We) level (e.g., soft relationship and communication skills for managers) are a prime target for WWPs, and well-being assessment metrics at the We level are largely non-existent. While there is no measure, scale, or tool which holistically accounts adequately for all three Me, We, and Us levels at present (including tools like Work on Wellbeing, Happiness at Work Survey, and others), further consideration of the We and Us levels is needed – both in practice, and from a research intervention and assessment perspective. This recommendation is based on the realization that the vast majority of work well-being research to date has been on the benefits at the individual level. Obviously research and validation of the Me, We, Us framework per se, and its integrated levels, is needed.

Future Research

To maximize the potential of positive psychological assessment for workplace well-being and health promotion, various avenues of research are now suggested.

Firstly, there is a need for expanded reporting on current assessment practice. A study and review of current workplace well-being assessment practice and reporting across countries is needed that isolates what specific assessment measures are used, when, why, by whom, and how they are used. This will also highlight aspects such as whether the current choice of measures is fit for purpose, or whether well-being assessment is commonly aligned with yearly engagement surveys, with specific health and wellness initiatives, or with a particular additional organizational objective (e.g., restructure) rather than as a primary objective in itself. More research is needed in order to fully understand the scale and scope of current well-being assessments in organizations and to establish firmer baseline usage and characteristics as a basis for change.

Secondly, the potential barriers and challenges to undertaking well-being assessment at work need further exploration. For example, from the chapter authors' perspective these can include aspects such as: (1) employees feeling burnout from many and various types of assessments or surveys within the organization; (2) previous bad experiences of engagement surveys where information is embargoed or results withheld, or lack of subsequent commitment or change associated with the results; (3) fear that sensitive and personal well-being data will not be anonymous or secure; or (4) practicalities of implementing the assessments (e.g., obtaining experts in positive psychological assessment, or with the technology or research expertise to deliver them appropriately). These challenges span and apply to the employee, the organization, and to society, and are likely different in every context. However, we currently do not know the extent to which these barriers and challenges impact well-being assessments. More research is needed in order to substantiate such contextual aspects which may limit positive psychological assessment practices.

Thirdly, more research is needed into the potential benefits, beyond the results of the assessments themselves, of conducting organizational well-being assessments. These wider contextual benefits can include aspects such as the beneficial impacts of the organization being perceived as caring toward employees, the organization being seen as a great place to work, that well-being assessment information can be used to make important management decisions, or that well-being information can assist with managing both psychological and physical health more constructively. We simply do not know the full extent of the influence of these more contextual aspects that are related to well-being assessments. More research is needed in order to substantiate such contextual aspects.

Lastly, further investigation of the Me, We, Us framework and its utility, and in particular the 'We' and 'Us' levels is needed – from a research intervention and assessment perspective. This recommendation is based on the realization that the vast majority of work well-being research to date has been on the benefits at the individual level.

Conclusions

The business case for organizational well-being is accruing, both academically and fiscally. It is therefore only a matter of time before knowledge of the benefits of high work well-being become widespread, and WWPs and positive psychological assessments become common. Although it seems as if very little positive psychological assessment happens in workplaces at present, now is the opportunity to gather more information on current organizational well-being practices, particularly of the positive psychological assessment measures used and how they are used, to take a "good first step" toward improving organizational well-being assessments, and think more conceptually about levels of well-being intervention and assessment. It is also the time to establish firmer guidelines and recommendations regarding what these assessments should include, what they should accomplish, and how they should happen if they are to be the basis for change, consistency, and comparability. Further research is needed to inform such recommendations.

It is our view that high-quality psychological well-being information can be used to create positive workplaces where employees are able to do meaningful and enjoyable work that taps into their greatest strengths and their most important goals. With such assessment information organizations can capitalize on the unique intellectual and personal strengths of each employee. It is possible to focus less on getting employees to do their work, but rather on how to enable them to do good work; their best work. Organizations can go beyond fixing problems and into promoting excellence. Advances such as these are under way, and will start addressing employee's desires for better working experiences, helping to create a "good day at work," and moving society toward a better way of living.

Appendix A: Positive psychological measures used in two or more data sources

We have identified 11 measures that are popular in research and that are recommended by positive psychology assessment experts.

Assessment measures used in two or more data sources.

No.	*Measure*	*Measure authors*	*Construct/s*	*Well-being promotion research (Table 22.1)*[a]	*Work well-being research (Table 22.2)*[b]	*Expert recommends*[c]
1	Satisfaction with Life Scale (SWLS)	Diener et al. (1985)	Life satisfaction	✓	✓	✓
2	Scales of Psychological Well-being (SPW)	Ryff & Singer (1998)	Well-being	✓		✓
3	Positive Affect and Negative Affect Schedule (PANAS)	Watson, Clark, & Tellegan (1988)	Positive affect and negative affect	✓	✓	✓
4	Centre for Epidemiological Studies Depression Scale (CES-D)	Radloff (1977)	Depressed mood	✓	✓	
5	Quality of Life Inventory (QoLI)	Frisch (2004)	Life satisfaction, life domains	✓		✓
6	Steen Happiness Index (SHI)	Seligman, Steen, Park, & Peterson (2005)	Happiness	✓		✓
7	Subjective Happiness Scale (SHS)	Lyubomirsky & Lepper (1999)	Happiness	✓		✓
8	Life Orientation Test-Revised (LOT-R)	Scheier, Carver, & Bridges (1994)	Optimism	✓		✓
9	Flourishing Scale (FS)	Diener et al. (2010)	Flourishing	✓		✓
10	Utrecht Work Engagement Scale (UWES)	Schaufeli et al. (2006)	Work engagement	✓	✓	
11	Mindfulness Attention Awareness Scale (MAAS)	Brown & Ryan (2003)	Mindfulness		✓	✓

[a] Used one or more times.
[b] Used two or more times.
[c] Owens et al. (2015).

Notes

1 "Well-being" is the most popular identifiable subfield within the field of positive psychology, and is also the term most often used in a business context. As such there is no positive workplace assessment program per se, the more widely used term being workplace well-being program.
2 The relationship between positive psychology and well-being is often discussed. Well-being is considered a key outcome of positive psychological interventions and a hence a key area to assess, including in the workplace. The assessments evaluated in this chapter represent a sample of key well-being assessments for the workplace and do not represent the full range of positive psychological assessments.
3 A similar point could equally be made about the scale and scope of well-being assessments in academic research, especially across disciplines.
4 With the assistance of the co-author Lucy Hone.
5 Note the difference between the focus on efficacy here and the previous focus on effectiveness trials.
6 We note that the psychometric quality of some of these scales has been well identified in the literature – for example, that the 18-item version of the SPW has particularly low alphas, or that the MAAS has issues related to construct validity, or that the PANAS has inferior psychometric properties compared to more contemporary measures such as the SPANE. Just because they are popular does not necessarily mean they are psychometrically sound.
7 We note that it is also subjective and arguable as to what may be considered an outcome or input variable, and many may be easily conceived of as both (e.g., burnout may be both an outcome of interest to an organization, and an input to well-being). The purpose of this chapter is not to debate this specific point, so this list represents the authors' perspective.
8 Criteria for selection are also debatable; these eight criteria were deemed important to the current authors for both practical and theoretical reasons.
9 As mentioned in note 6 above, this is not the case for all of the previously identified 11 measures.
10 Although it is acknowledged that there are good measures of aspects of positive leadership, such as measures of Authentic Leadership (see the Authentic Leadership Inventory: Neider & Schriesheim, 2011).
11 There are many other constructs such as virtuousness, mindsets, psychological capital, positive identity, etc., that would also be beneficial to assess.
12 We note that one chapter author is a Director of Work on Wellbeing Ltd, and the other chapter author is a senior scientist for Work on Wellbeing Ltd.
13 We are not suggesting an exclusive focus on happiness and well-being (which can be bad – see Caza & Cameron, 2008), just a more inclusive approach to both what is going right and what is going wrong.

References

Antony, M. M., Bieling, P. J., Cox, B. J., Enns, M. W., & Swinson, R. P. (1998). Psychometric properties of the 42-item and 21-item versions of the Depression Anxiety Stress Scales (DASS) in clinical groups and a community sample. *Psychological Assessment*, *10*, 176–181.

Bandura, A. (2012). On the functional properties of self-efficacy revisited. *Journal of Management*, *38*, 9–44.

Bertera, R. L. (1990). Du Pont: The effects of workplace health promotion on absenteeism and employment costs in a large industrial population. *American Journal of Public Health*, *80*(9), 1101–1105.

Bockerman, P., & Ilmakunnas, P. (2012). The job satisfaction–productivity nexus: A study using matched survey and register data. *Industrial and Labor Relations Review*, *65*, 244–262.

Boehm, J. K., & Lyubomirsky, S. (2008). Does happiness lead to career success? *Journal of Career Assessment*, *16*(1), 101–116.

Brown, K., & Ryan, R. M. (2003). The benefits of being present: Mindfulness and its role in psychological well-being. *Journal of Personality and Social Psychology, 84*(4), 822–848. doi:10.1037/0022-3514.84.4.822

Buysse, D. J., Reynolds, C. F., Monk, T. H., Berman, S. R., & Kupfer, D. J. (1989). The Pittsburgh Sleep Quality Index: A new instrument for psychiatric practice and research. *Psychiatry Research, 28*, 193–213. doi:10.1016/0165-1781(89)90047-4

Cameron, K., Dutton, J., & Quinn, R. (2003). *Positive organizational scholarship: Foundations of a new discipline*. San Francisco, CA: Berrett-Koehler.

Caza, A., & Cameron, K. (2008). Positive organizational scholarship: What does it achieve? In S. Clegg, & C. Cooper (Eds.), *The Sage handbook of organizational behavior: Vol. 2. Macro approaches* (pp. 99–117). London, UK: Sage. doi:10.4135/9781849200455.n6

Christakis, N., & Fowler, J. (2009). *Connected: The amazing power of social networks and how they shape our lives*. New York, NY: Little, Brown & Company.

Cohen, S., & Williamson, G. (1988). Perceived stress in a probability sample of the United States. In S. Spacapan & S. Oskamp (Eds.), *The social psychology of health: Claremont Symposium on applied social psychology* (pp. 31–67). Newbury Park, CA: Sage.

Cook, J., & Wall, T. (1980). New work attitude measures of trust, organizational commitment and personal need non-fulfillment. *Journal of Occupational Psychology, 53*, 39–52.

Cooperrider, D., & Whitney, D. (2005). *Appreciative inquiry: A positive revolution in change*. San Francisco, CA: Berrett-Koehler.

Daniels, K. (2000). Measures of five aspects of affective well-being at work. *Human Relations, 53*, 275–294.

David, S. A., Boniwell, I., & Ayers, A. C. (Eds.) (2012). *The Oxford handbook of happiness*. Oxford, UK: Oxford University Press.

Derogatis, L. R., Lipman, R. S., Rickels, K., Uhlenhuth, E. H., & Covi, L. (1974). The Hopkins Symptom Checklist (HSCL): A self-report symptom inventory. *Behavioral Science, 19*(1), 1–15.

Diener, E. (2009). *Assessing well-being: The collected works of Ed Diener* (Vol. 3). New York, NY: Springer.

Diener, E., Emmons, R. A., Larsen, R. J., & Griffin, S. (1985). The Satisfaction with Life Scale. *Journal of Personality Assessment, 49*, 71–75.

Diener, E., Oishi, S., & Lucas, R. E. (2015). National accounts of subjective well-being. *American Psychologist, 70*(3), 234–242.

Diener, E., Wirtz, D., Tov, W., Kim-Prieto, C., Choi, D., Oishi, S., & Biswas-Diener, R. (2010). New measures of well-being: Flourishing and positive and negative feelings. *Social Indicators Research, 39*, 247–266.

Dutton, J., & Heaphy, E. (2003). The power of high quality connections. In K. Cameron, J. Dutton, & R. Quinn (Eds.), *Positive organizational scholarship: Foundations of a new discipline* (pp. 263–278). San Francisco, CA: Berrett-Koehler.

Dutton, J. E., & Spreitzer, G. (Eds.) (2014). *How to be a positive leader: Small actions, big impacts*. San Francisco, CA: Berrett-Koehler.

Edmans, A. (2012). The link between job satisfaction and firm value, with implications for corporate social responsibility. *The Academy of Management Perspectives, 26*, 1–19. doi:10.5465/amp.2012.0046

EuroQol Group (1990). EuroQol: A new facility for the measurement of health-related quality of life. *Health Policy, 16*, 199–208.

Frisch, M. B. (2004). Use of the QoLI or quality of life inventory in quality of life therapy and assessment. In M. R. Maruish (Ed.), *The use of psychological testing for treatment planning and outcome assessment: Vol 3. Instruments for adults* (pp. 749–798). Mahwah, NJ: Erlbaum.

George, J. M., & Bettenhausen, K. (1990). Understanding prosocial behavior, sales performance, and turnover: A group level analysis in a service context. *Journal of Applied Psychology, 75*, 698–709.

Goetzel, R. Z., & Ozminkowski, R. J. (2008). The health and cost benefits of work site health-promotion programs. *Annual Review of Public Health, 29*, 303–323.

Goldberg, D. P., & Hillier, V. F. (1979). A scaled version of the General Health Questionnaire. *Psychological Medicine, 9*, 139–145.

Govindji, R., & Linley, P. A. (2007). Strengths use, self-concordance and well-being: Implications for strengths coaching and coaching psychologists. *International Coaching Psychology Review, 2*(2), 143–153.

Graham, C. (2010). *Happiness around the world: The paradox of happy peasants and miserable millionaires.* Oxford, UK: Oxford University Press.

Hamling, K., Jarden, A., & Schofield, G. (2016). Recipes for occupational wellbeing: An investigation of the associations with wellbeing in New Zealand workers. *New Zealand Journal of Human Resource Management, 12*(2), 151–173.

HAPIA. (2009). *Best practice guidelines: Workplace health in Australia.* Sydney: Health and Productivity Institute of Australia.

Harter, J. K., Schmidt, F. L., & Hayes, T. L. (2002). Business-unit-level relationship between employee satisfaction, employee engagement, and business outcomes: A meta-analysis. *Journal of Applied Psychology, 87*, 268–279. http://dx.doi.org 10.1037/0021-9010.87.2.268

Harter, J. K., Schmidt, F. L., & Keyes, C. L. M. (2002). Well-being in the workplace and its relationship to business outcomes: A review of the Gallup studies. In C. L. M. Keyes & J. Haidt (Eds.), *Flourishing: The positive person and the good life* (pp. 205–224). Washington, DC: American Psychological Association.

Hone, L., Jarden, A., & Schofield, G. (2015). An evaluation of positive psychology intervention effectiveness trials using the re-aim framework: A practice-friendly review. *Journal of Positive Psychology, 10*(4), 303–322.

Hone, L., Jarden, A., Schofield, G. M., & Duncan, S. (2014). Measuring flourishing: The impact of operational definitions on the prevalence of high levels of wellbeing. *International Journal of Wellbeing, 4*(1), 62–90. doi:10.5502/ijw.v4i1.1

Ilmarinen, J. (2007). The Work Ability Index (WAI). *Occupational Medicine, 57*, 160.

International Wellbeing Group (2006). *Personal Wellbeing Index.* Melbourne, Australia: Australian Centre on Quality of Life, Deakin University.

Jarden, A., & Jarden, R. (2015). Applied positive psychology in higher education. In M. Henning, C. Krägeloh, & G. Wong-Toi (Eds.), *Student motivation and quality of life in higher education* (pp. 37–44). London, UK: Routledge.

Judge, T. A. (1993). Does affective disposition moderate the relationship between job satisfaction and voluntary turnover? *Journal of Applied Psychology, 78*, 395–401.

Juniper, B., White, N., & Bellamy, P. (2009). Assessing employee wellbeing: Is there any other way? *International Journal of Workplace Health Management, 2*(3), 220–230.

Kabat-Zinn, J. (2005). *Guided mindfulness mediation* [audiobook]. Louisville, CO: Sounds True.

Kahneman, D., Krueger, A. B., Schkade, D., Schwarz, N., & Stone, A. A. (2004). A survey method for characterizing daily life experience: The Day Reconstruction Method (DRM). *Science, 306*, 1776–1780.

Kashdan, T. B., Gallagher, M. W., Silvia, P., Breen, W. E., Terhar, D., & Steger, M. F. (2009). The Curiosity and Exploration Inventory-II: Development, factor structure, and initial psychometrics. *Journal of Research in Personality, 43*, 987–998.

Keyes, C. L. M. (2005). Mental illness and/or mental health? Investigating axioms of the complete state model of health. *Journal of Consulting and Clinical Psychology, 73*, 539–548.

Keyes, C. L. M., & Magyar-Moe, J. L. (2003). The measurement and utility of adult subjective well-being. In S. J. Lopez & C. R. Snyder (Eds.), *Positive psychological assessment: A handbook of models and measures* (pp. 411–426). Washington, DC: American Psychological Association.

Koo, J., & Suh, E. M. (2013). The influence of happiness on future income and job performance. *Korean Journal of Social and Personality Psychology, 27*, 17–36.

Kristensen, T. S., Hannerz, H., Hogh, A., & Borg, V. (2005). The Copenhagen Psychosocial Questionnaire: A tool for the assessment and improvement of the psychosocial work environment. *Scandinavian Journal of Work and Environmental Health, 31*(6), 438–449.

Laloux, F. (2014). *Reinventing organizations.* Brussels, Belgium: Nelson Parker.

Larson, R., & Csikszentmihalyi, M. (1983). The experience sampling method. *New Directions for Methodology of Social and Behavioral Science, 15*, 41–56.

Lewis, I., Watson, B., & White, K. M. (2009). Internet versus paper-and-pencil survey methods in psychological experiments: Equivalence testing of participant responses to health-related messages. *Australian Journal of Psychology, 61*(2), 107–116.

Lewis, S. (2011). *Positive psychology at work: How positive leadership and appreciative inquiry create inspiring organizations.* Oxford, UK: Wiley-Blackwell.

Lopez, S. J., & Snyder, C. R. (2003). *Positive psychological assessment: A handbook of models and measures.* Washington, DC: American Psychological Association.

Lovibond, S. H., & Lovibond, P. F. (1995). *Manual for the Depression Anxiety Stress Scales* (2nd ed.). Sydney, Australia: Psychology Foundation.

Luthans, F. (2002a). Positive organizational behavior: Developing and managing psychological strengths. *Academy of Management Executive, 16*, 57–72.

Luthans, F. (2002b). The need for and meaning of positive organizational behavior. *Journal of Organizational Behavior, 23*, 695–706.

Luthans, F., Avolio, B. J., Avey, J. B., & Norman, S. M. (2007). Psychological capital: Measurement and relationship with performance and job satisfaction. *Personnel Psychology, 60*, 541–572.

Lyubomirsky, S., & Lepper, H. (1999). A measure of subjective happiness: Preliminary reliability and construct validation. *Social Indicators Research, 46*, 137–155.

Malach-Pines, A. (2005). The burnout measure, short version. *International Journal of Stress Management, 12*, 78–87.

McCarthy, G., Almeida, S., & Ahrens, J. (2011). Understanding employee wellbeing practices in Australian organizations. *International Journal of Health, Wellness and Society, 1*(1), 181–197.

McCullough, M. E., Emmons, R. A., & Tsang, J. (2002). The grateful disposition: A conceptual and empirical topography. *Journal of Personality and Social Psychology, 82*, 112–127.

McGillivray, D. (2002). Health promotion in the workplace: A missed opportunity? *Health Education, 102*(2), 60–67.

McNair, D. M., Lorr, M., & Droppleman, L. (1981). *Manual for the profile of mood states.* San Diego, CA: Educational and Industrial Testing Service.

Mercer. (2011). *"What's Working" survey.* Retrieved from http://www.hreonline.com/pdfs/07012012Extra_Mercer.pdf

Mills, M. J., Fleck, C. R., & Kozikowski, A. (2013). Positive psychology at work: A conceptual review, state-of-practice assessment, and a look ahead. *The Journal of Positive Psychology, 8*, 153–164. doi:10.1080/17439760.2013.776622

Neider, L. L., & Schriesheim, C. A. (2011). The Authentic Leadership Inventory (ALI): Development and empirical tests. *The Leadership Quarterly, 22*(6), 1146–1164. doi:10.1016./j.leaqua.2011.09.008

Nelson, D. L., & Cooper, C. L. (Eds.) (2007). *Positive organizational behavior.* London, UK: Sage.

Nieboer, A., Lindenberg, S., Boomsma, A., & Van Bruggen, A. C. (2005). Dimensions of well-being and their measurement: The SPF-IL Scale. *Social Indicators Research, 73*, 313–353.

Niemiec, R. (2013). *Mindfulness and character strengths: A practical guide to flourishing.* Göttingen, Germany: Hogrefe Publishing.

Nixon, A. E., Mazzola, J. J., Bauer, J., Kruger, J. R., & Spector, P. E. (2011). Can work make you sick? A meta-analysis of the relationships between job stressors and physical symptoms. *Work and Stress, 25*(1), 1–22.

Nowack, K. (1990). Initial development of an inventory to assess stress and health risk. *American Journal of Health Promotion, 4*, 173–180.

Organ, D. W. (1988). *Organizational citizenship behavior: The good soldier syndrome: Issues in organization and management series.* Lexington, MA: Lexington Books.

Ouweneel, E., Le Blanc, P. M., & Schaufeli, W. B. (2013). Do-it-yourself: An online positive psychology intervention to promote positive emotions, self-efficacy, and engagement at work. *Career Development International, 18*(2), 173–195. doi:10.1108/CDI-10-2012-0102

Owens, R. L., Magyar-Moe, J. L., & Lopez, S. J. (2015). Finding balance via positive psychological assessment: Recommendations for practice. *The Counseling Psychologist, 43*(5), 634–670.

Page, K. (2005). *Subjective wellbeing in the workplace.* Unpublished honours thesis, Deakin University, Melbourne, Australia.

Page, K., & Vella-Brodrick, D. (2009). The "what," "why" and "how" of employee wellbeing: A new model. *Social Indicators Research, 90*, 441–458.

Paykel, E. S. (1985). The clinical interview for depression. *Journal of Affective Disorders, 9*, 85–96.
Peterson (2005). *Authentic Happiness Inventory (AHI)*. Philadelphia, PA: University of Pennsylvania Press.
Peterson, C., & Park, N. (2009). Classifying and measuring strengths of character. In S. J. Lopez & C. R. Snyder (Eds.), *Oxford handbook of positive psychology* (2nd ed., pp. 25–33). New York, NY: Oxford University Press.
Peterson, C., Park, N., & Seligman, M. E. P. (2005). Orientations to happiness and life satisfaction: The full life versus the empty life. *Journal of Happiness Studies, 6*, 25–41.
Peterson, C., & Seligman, M. E. P. (2004). *Character strengths and virtues: A handbook and classification*. New York, NY: Oxford University Press; and Washington, DC: American Psychological Association.
PriceWaterhouseCoopers. (2010). *Workplace wellness in Australia: Aligning action with aims: Optimising the benefits of workplace wellness*. Sydney, Australia: Author.
Primack, B. (2003). The WHO-5 wellbeing index performed the best in screening for depression in primary care. *Evidence Based Medicine, 8*, 155. doi:10.1136/ebm.8.5.155
Radloff, L. S. (1977). The CES-D scale: A self-report depression scale for research in the general population. *Applied Psychological Measurement, 1*, 385–401.
Rath, T., & Harter, J. (2010). *The economics of wellbeing*. Washington, DC: Gallup.
Reips, U. D. (2006). Web-based methods. In M. Eid & E. Diener (Eds.), *Handbook of multi-method measurement in psychology* (pp. 73–85). Washington, DC: American Psychological Association.
Riva, G., Teruzzi, T., & Anolli, L. (2003). The use of the internet in psychological research: Comparison of online and offline questionnaires. *CyberPsychology & Behavior, 6*(1), 73–80.
Rusbult, C. E., & Farrell, D. (1983). A longitudinal test of the investment model: The impact on job satisfaction, job commitment, and turnover of variations in rewards, costs, alternatives, and investments. *Journal of Applied Psychology, 68*, 429–438. doi:10.1037/0021-9010.68.3.429
Ryan, R. M., & Frederick, C. M. (1997). On energy, personality and health: Subjective vitality as a dynamic reflection of well-being. *Journal of Personality, 65*, 529–565.
Ryff, C. D., & Singer, B. (1998). The contours of positive human health. *Psychological Inquiry, 9*, 1–28.
Schaufeli, W. B., Bakker, A. B., & Salanova, M. (2006). The measurement of work engagement with a short questionnaire. A cross-national study. *Educational and Psychological Measurement, 66*(4), 701–716.
Scheier, M. F., Carver, C. S., & Bridges, M. W. (1994). Distinguishing optimism from neuroticism (and trait anxiety, self-mastery, and self-esteem): A re-evaluation of the Life Orientation Test. *Journal of Personality and Social Psychology, 67*, 1063–1078.
Schutte, N. S., Malouff, J. M., Hall, L. E., Haggerty, D. J., Cooper, J. T., Golden, C. J., & Dornheim, L. (1998). Development and validation of a measure of emotional intelligence. *Personality and Individual Differences, 25*, 167–177.
Schuurmans, H., Steverink, N., Frieswijk, N., Buunk, B. P., Slaets, J. P. J., & Lindenberg, S. (2005). How to measure self-management abilities in older people by self-report? The development of the SMAS-30. *Quality of Life Research, 14*, 2215–2228.
Schwarzer, R., & Jerusalem, M. (1995). Generalized Self-Efficacy scale. In J. Weinman, S. Wright, & M. Johnston, *Measures in health psychology: A user's portfolio. Causal and control beliefs* (pp. 35–37). Windsor, UK: Nfer-Nelson.
Seligman, M. E. P. (2008). Positive health. *Applied Psychology: An International Review, 57*, 3–18.
Seligman, M. E. P., Steen, T., Park, N., & Peterson, C. (2005). Positive psychology progress: Empirical validation of interventions. *American Psychologist, 60*, 410–421.
Sheldon, K. M., Jose, P. E., Kashdan, T. B., & Jarden, A. (2015). Personality strengths, effective goal-striving, and enhanced well-being: Comparing 12 candidate keystone constructs. *Personality and Social Psychology Bulletin, 41*(4), 575–585. doi:10.1177/0146167215573211
Shum, D., O'Gorman, J., Myors, B., & Creed, P. (2013). *Psychological testing and assessment* (2nd ed.). Oxford, UK: Oxford University Press.

Smith, B. W., Dalen, J., Wiggins, K., Tooley, E., Christopher, P., & Bernard, J. (2008). The brief resilience scale: Assessing the ability to bounce back. *International Journal of Behavioral Medicine, 15*(3), 194–200.

Snyder, C. R., Harris, C., Anderson, J. R., Holleran, S. A., Irving, L. M., Sigmon, S. T., ... Harney, P (1991). The will and the ways: Development and validation of an individual-differences measure of hope. *Journal of Personality and Social Psychology, 60*, 570–585.

Spence, G. (2015). Workplace wellbeing programs: If you build it they may NOT come ... because it's not what they really need! *International Journal of Wellbeing, 5*(2), 109–124.

Spielberger, C. D. (1983). *Manual for the State–Trait Anxiety Inventory.* Palo Alto, CA: Mind Garden.

Spielberger, C. D. (1972). Conceptual and methodological issues in anxiety research. In C. D. Spielberger (Ed.), *Anxiety: Current trends in theory and research* (pp. 481–492). New York, NY: Academic Press.

Spitzer, R., Kroenke, K., Williams, J., & Löwe, B. (2006). A brief measure for assessing generalized anxiety disorder: The GAD-7. *Internal Medicine, 166*, 1092–1097.

Steger, M. F., Dik, B. J., & Duffy, R. D. (2012). Measuring meaningful work: The Work as Meaning Inventory (WAMI). *Journal of Career Assessment, 20*, 322–337. doi:10.1177/1069072711436160

Steger, M. F., Dik, B. J., & Shim, Y. (in press). Assessing meaning and satisfaction at work. In S. J. Lopez (Ed.), *The Oxford handbook of positive psychology assessment* (2nd ed.). Oxford, UK: Oxford University Press.

Steger, M. F., Frazier, P., Oishi, S., & Kaler, M. (2006). The Meaning in Life Questionnaire: Assessing the presence of and search for meaning in life. *Journal of Counseling Psychology, 53*, 80–93.

Stiglitz, J. E., Sen, A., & Fitoussi, J. P. (2009). *Report by the commission on the measurement of economic performance and social progress.* Paris, France. Retrieved from http://www.stiglitzsen-fitoussi.fr/en/index.htm

Stones, M. J., Kozma, A., Hirdes, J., Gold, D., Arbuckle, T., & Kolopack, P. (1996). Short Happiness and Affect Research Protocol (SHARP). *Social Indicators Research, 37*, 75–91.

Tennant, R., Fishwick, R., Platt, S., Joseph, S., & Stewart-Brown, S. (2006). *Monitoring positive mental health in Scotland: Validating the Affectometer 2 scale and developing the Warwick-Edinburgh Mental Well-being Scale for the UK.* Edinburgh, Scotland: NHS Health Scotland.

Tennant, R., Hiller, L., Fishwick, R., Platt, P., Joseph, S., Weich, S., ... Stewart-Brown, S. (2007). The Warwick-Edinburgh Mental Well-being Scale (WEMWBS): Development and UK validation. *Health and Quality of Life Outcomes, 5*(63), 1–13.

Totterdell, P., Kellett, S., Teuchmann, K., & Briner, R. R. (1998). Evidence of mood linkage in work groups. *Journal of Personality and Social Psychology, 74*(6), 1504–1515.

Van Katwyk, P. T., Fox, S., Spector, P. E., & Kelloway, E. K. (2000). Using the Job-related Affective Well-being Scale (JAWS) to investigate affective responses to work stressors. *Journal of Occupational Health Psychology, 5*, 219–230.

Waddell, G., & Burton, A. K. (2006). *Is work good for your health and well-being?* London, UK: The Stationery Office.

Wall, T. D., Jackson, P. R., & Mullarkey, S. (1995). Further evidence on some new measures of job control, cognitive demand and production responsibility. *Journal of Organizational Behavior, 16*, 431–455.

Ware, J. E., Kosinski, M., & Keller, S. D. (1996). A 12-Item Short-Form Health Survey: Construction of scales and preliminary tests of reliability and validity. *Medical Care, 34*, 220–223.

Ware, J. E., & Sherbourne, C. D. (1992). The MOS 36-item Short-Form Health Survey (SF-36): Conceptual framework and item selection. *Medical Care, 30*, 473–83.

Warr, P. B. (2013). How to think about and measure psychological well-being. In R. R. Sinclair, M. Wang, & L. E. Tetrick (Eds.), *Research methods in occupational health psychology* (pp. 76–90). New York, NY: Routledge.

Warr, P. B., Cook, J., & Wall, T. (1979). Scales for the measurement of some work attitudes and aspects of psychological well-being. *Journal of Occupational Psychology, 52*, 129–148.

Watson, D., Clark, L. A., & Tellegan, A. (1988). Development and validation of brief measures of positive and negative affect: The PANAS scales. *Journal of Personality and Social Psychology*, *54*(6), 1063–1070.

Weijers, D., & Jarden, A. (2013). The science of happiness for policymakers: An overview. *Journal of Social Research & Policy*, *4*(2), 21–40.

WHOQOL Group (1998). Development of the World Health Organization WHOQOL-BREF Quality of Life Assessment. *Psychological Medicine*, *28*, 551–558.

Wrzesniewski, A. (2014). Engage in job crafting. In Jane Dutton and Gretchen Spreitzer (Eds.), *How to be a positive leader: Insights from leading thinkers on positive organizations*. San Francisco, CA: Berrett-Koehler.

Part III

International Business Applications of Positive Psychology

23

Well-Being in Health Professionals: Positive Psychology at Work

Ulrich Wiesmann

Introduction

Until recently, positive psychology identified members of the health workforce as a target group for promoting well-being at work. Formally, the job of a health professional is to systematically provide preventive, curative, promotional, or rehabilitative health care services (Wikipedia, 2015). In this respect, they represent human resources that people can make use of to improve their health or overcome diseases. The World Health Organization speaks of a health workforce, which is defined as "all people engaged in actions whose primary intent is to enhance health" (World Health Organization, 2006, p. 1). Of course, the complex task of health care is an interdisciplinary endeavor, which brings together health workers from different backgrounds such as physicians, dentists, nurses, psychotherapists, community health workers, social health workers, and other providers (including health management, health support personnel, and others). This chapter is specifically focused on those health professionals who are directly involved with patients, that is, who are in face-to-face contact with patients.

Members of the health workforce are committed to a high standard of excellence in different areas. Due to their professional training, they hold particular competencies – knowledge, skills, abilities, and behaviors – which enable them to successfully enhance the health of others. In doing so, they acknowledge duties and responsibilities for the people whom they care for. In other words, delivering health care is focused on the benefit of patients, or clients, and thus implies ethical and moral considerations. Health professionals should attend to the best interest of their patients and not to self-interest, showing respect to people entrusted to their care. Remarkably, many health professionals consider the focus on self-care as rather a private matter, not a professional one. The culture of medicine implies a self-image of a physician as an invincible caregiver (Wallace & Lemaire, 2009).

The Wiley Blackwell Handbook of the Psychology of Positivity and Strengths-Based Approaches at Work, First Edition. Edited by Lindsay G. Oades, Michael F. Steger, Antonella Delle Fave, and Jonathan Passmore.

In principle, the idea of caring for one's own health and well-being should apply to all health professionals who are directly involved with patients, or clients (Figley & Beder, 2012; Figley, Huggard, & Rees, 2013). Health professionals are directly and indirectly confronted with potentially traumatizing events, such as severely injured and dying patients or histories of violence and sexual abuse. These cumulative experiences may result in a secondary trauma (Canfield, 2005; Collins & Long, 2003; Figley, 1995), end up in burnout (Maslach, Schaufeli, & Leiter, 2001), and impair subjective well-being (Diener, Lucas, & Oishi, 2002).

With respect to the process of giving health care services, professionals' negative mental conditions would be detrimental to the intentional enhancement of patients'/clients' health. An emotionally unbalanced and mentally unstable physician or nurse would set a bad example. Therefore, workers enrolled in the health sector owe it to their clients to take care of themselves as professionals (Hantke & Görges, 2012; Larsen & Stamm, 2008).

In practice, the quality of life health professionals experience at work has been largely neglected. At first glance, the question of how these workers can enhance their own health, well-being and professional fulfillment (Brown & Gunderman, 2006) appears to be a weird focus against a background of patients' suffering. Personal well-being seems to naturally emerge if a health professional does a good job. What can be more professionally rewarding than a patient who has been healed, or a client who has overcome a life-threatening disease? For sure, this is important, too. But at a second glance it becomes evident that health professionals are no longer genuine human resources for health if they are burned out or sick. If their resources are depleted, the quality of health care they deliver will become poor (e.g., Scheepers, Boerebach, Arah, Heineman, & Lombarts, 2015).

In this chapter, research on well-being among health professionals is reviewed and evaluated. First, a positive psychology framework is suggested, based on both a hedonic and eudaimonic well-being perspective (Ryff, 1989, 1995), which may serve as a positive psychology guideline for research in the health care setting. Before turning to positive psychology approaches, research on occupational stress and its threat to the well-being of health professionals is summarized. Studies in this domain have explored detrimental work-related and individual factors that predict a broad scope of negative mental conditions. Subsequently, research is presented substantiating that the absence of these negative factors, as well as the presence of their "positive" opposites, respectively (e.g., lack of autonomy and autonomy/self-determination), predict an alleviation of negative outcomes (e.g., burnout).

Subsequently, some core concepts in positive psychology will be discussed, that reflect a new model of human being and a new understanding of well-being. Researchers are taking increasing interest in resources, potentials, competencies and positive states of health personnel. In this section, research on issues such as job satisfaction, work engagement, self-determination, or autonomy, job crafting, mindfulness, resilience, and empowerment is presented. Next, "positive" intervention studies are scrutinized which were designed to improve subjective well-being in health personnel. The chapter ends with an outlook on future research and conclusions.

A Positive Psychology Framework for Studying Well-Being among Health Professionals

The question how to maintain or to enhance the well-being of health professionals is an imperative topic. Hence, it is important to get an idea what well-being as a positive psychology concept is about. Prominent researchers such as Diener, Oishi, and Lucas

(2003, p. 404) suggest the following definition, which captures certain specific aspects of this phenomenon:

> The field of subjective well-being (SWB) comprises the scientific analysis of how people evaluate their lives – both at the moment and for longer periods such as for the past year. These evaluations include people's emotional reactions to events, their moods, and judgments they form about their life satisfaction, fulfillment, and satisfaction with domains such as marriage and work. Thus, SWB concerns the study of what lay people might call happiness or satisfaction.

Researchers have further distinguished between *hedonic well-being* and *eudaimonic well-being* (Ryan & Deci, 2001; Ryff, 1989, 1995). The former refers to the above-reported definition of SWB, and it includes the affective component of hedonic balance (the prominence of positive emotions in daily experience) and the cognitive component of life satisfaction (as a global evaluation). The latter instead refers to the fulfillment of psychological needs and the idea of a fully functioning person. In other words, hedonic well-being encompasses the phenomenon of "feeling good", reflecting pleasant experiences and positive evaluations, and eudaimonic well-being puts emphasis on "functioning well" and on developing one's resources and potentials. The latter therefore includes elements of a good life that go beyond pleasant affect and life satisfaction. "The main themes of eudaimonia revolve around the ideas of flourishing, true self, actualizing potential, and personal expressiveness. In essence, who are you and are you living that out?" (Kimiecik, 2011, p. 776).

Relying on classical psychological works (e.g., Allport, 1961; Erikson, 1982; Maslow, 1968; Rogers, 1961), Ryff (1989, 1995) distinguished six dimensions of psychological well-being (PWB) that can be understood as facets of positive psychological functioning: self-acceptance, positive relations with others, autonomy, environmental mastery, purpose in life, and personal growth. These dimensions represent six qualities of human wellness.

Self-acceptance is a main criterion of mental health as well as self-actualization (Abraham Maslow, 1968), the fully functioning person (Carl Rogers, 1961) and maturity (Gordon Allport, 1961). Holding positive attitudes toward oneself and toward one's past life, and accepting both one's good and bad characteristics are a central characteristic of positive psychological functioning. *Positive relations with others* are also vital for mental health. Many theories and models in positive psychology emphasize the importance of warm, trusting interpersonal relations reflecting genuine social interests (having strong feelings of empathy and affection for others), close connection with others (intimacy), and guidance and direction of others (generativity). *Autonomy* is also emphasized as an integral part of positive psychological functioning. Self-determination, independence from others, and inner regulation of behavior characterize this facet of well-being. *Environmental mastery* reflects the individual's ability to choose or create environments based on his or her needs and ideas. It is a characteristic of mental health in that individuals are able to advance in the world and shape complex environments creatively. *Purpose in life* or meaning in life is also an integral part of mental health. The fully functioning individual has goals, intentions, and a sense of direction that nurture the feeling that life is meaningful. *Personal growth* goes beyond the achievement of the other characteristics of optimal psychological functioning. It refers to the individual's striving to develop his or her potential, grow, and expand as a person. Personal growth implies an intrinsic motivational force in the direction of self-realization.

Well-being researchers argue that it is important to study both aspects. From the positive psychology point of view, the eudaimonic approach is a good reference model for exploring well-being in the health workforce, because it is linked with professional personality development. The hedonistic "feeling good" aspect might often be misplaced, for example, when an oncologist has to break serious news to her patient, while having developed a patient-oriented style in delivering serious news might nurture the six facets of PWB. So far, the eudaimonic approach has not been fully applied. A main reason is that this is a general view of well-being which is not focused on specific life domains, such as the occupational context. Nevertheless, with respect to work-related well-being, the theoretically derived components of PWB cover the realization of one's true potential as a human being working as a health professional. In trying to find out if health professionals are working in accordance to their true selves, it would be interesting to invite them to address the following eudaimonic questions.

Reflecting on experiences as a health practitioner, can I hold a positive attitude to myself, or do I despise what I am doing in my job (*self-acceptance*)? Are my relations with patients and their families, and with my colleagues, rewarding, supportive, sincere and genuine/authentic (*positive relations with others*)? Can I do my work in a self-determined way, or am I heteronomous in that I cannot make decisions (*autonomy*)? Can I participate in the creation of my working site, or am I not allowed to design the place where I am working with patients (*environmental mastery*)? Can I find a meaning in life in what I am professionally doing, or does my caring for others make no sense (*purpose in life*)? Can I develop my professional potential and can I expand as a person in my work-site, or do I waste away (*personal growth*)?

The review of the literature on well-being in health personnel shows that the majority of studies investigate hedonic aspects of well-being, using different measures of happiness, life satisfaction and job satisfaction, or health and quality of life indicators. As already mentioned, most of these studies also evaluate occupational stress, in an attempt to elucidate the consequences of stressful conditions, such as depression, suicidal ideations, psychological distress, burnout. Publications on these topics are abundant.

In the following sections, determinants of work-related stress that threaten the well-being of health personnel and instigate habitual stress reactions are reviewed. Then, well-being enhancing factors are examined, taking the perspective of positive psychology (Seligman & Csikszentmihalyi, 2000).

Occupational Stress and Its Threat to Well-Being in Health Professionals

When talking about occupational stress of health professionals, it is important to have a look at the macro-social conditions and economic-political context that determine their work life. Nowadays, multinational health care companies that are listed on the stock exchange earn their money by employing members of the health workforce. Due to shortage of financial resources and a rising competitive pressure in the health care system, the workload of health professionals is increasing tremendously. At the same time, the commercialization of public health care systems is taking place all over the world, which means that health care services are provided for those able to pay. Working conditions reflect the maxim "health care for profit," which conflicts with the professionals' ethical responsibilities. As a consequence of this economic-political development, and in addition to the emotional strain and pressure resulting from working with patients, the quality of life conditions of health professionals are alarmingly worsening.

Huge empirical evidence highlights that health professionals are an occupational group at risk of a wide range of psychological impairments (Humphries et al., 2014; Moreau & Mageau, 2012). About one third of physicians report to be dissatisfied with their work, a similar percentage of residents are not contented with their career choice, and the situation for nurses is comparable (Brown & Gunderman, 2006; Djukic, 2011; Lu, Barriball, Zhang, & While, 2012; Lu, While, & Barriball, 2005; Utriainen & Kyngäs, 2009; Van Ham, Verhoeven, Groenier, Groothoff, & De Haan, 2006). Physicians, especially female medical practitioners and nurses, are vulnerable to committing suicide (Hem et al., 2005a, 2005b; Schernhammer & Colditz, 2004). Health professionals experience high levels of stress and psychological distress, which often manifest as fatigue, depression, insomnia, and substance abuse (Firth-Cozens, 2001; Hegney et al., 2014; Mohammed, Ali, Youssef, Fahmy, & Haggag, 2014; Oyane, Pallesen, Moen, Akerstedt, & Bjorvatn, 2013; Pereira-Lima & Loureiro, 2015; Smith-Miller, Shaw-Kokot, Curro, & Jones, 2014). Secondary trauma and compassion fatigue are also widespread problems, as health professionals are continuously confronted with adverse events such as death and dying, and severely injured and ill persons (e.g., Fernando & Consedine, 2014; Mathieu, 2014; Rossi et al., 2012; Sprang, Clark, & Whitt-Woosley, 2007; Wentzel & Brysiewicz, 2014). A vast number of empirical studies show that they suffer from job burnout, "a psychological syndrome in response to chronic interpersonal stressors on the job. The three key dimensions of this response are an overwhelming exhaustion, feelings of cynicism and detachment from the job, and a sense of ineffectiveness and lack of accomplishment" (Maslach et al., 2001, p. 399). Burnout is a state of depletion of resources that has been shown to be contagious. The burnout syndrome was detected in different health professional groups, as reported in Table 23.1.

Table 23.1 Burnout studies across health professional groups.

Professional group	*Evidence*
1 Emergency nurses	Adriaenssens, De Gucht, & Maes (2015)
2 Intensive/critical care nurses	Bakker, Le Blanc, & Schaufeli (2005), Epp (2012)
3 Oncology/hematology nurses	Sherman, Edwards, Simonton, & Mehta (2006), Toh, Ang, & Devi (2012)
4 Hospital nurses	Sahraian, Fazelzadeh, Mehdizadeh, & Toobaee (2008), Wang, Kunaviktikul, & Wichaikhum (2013)
5 Mental health nurses	Edwards, Burnard, Coyle, Fothergill, & Hannigan (2000)
6 Palliative care personnel	Pereira, Fonseca, & Carvalho (2011)
7 Residents	Ishak et al. (2009), N. K. Thomas (2004), West, Shanafelt, & Kolars (2011)
8 U.S. medical students, residents, and early career physicians	Dyrbye et al. (2014)
9 Physicians/surgeons	Arora, Asha, Chinnappa, & Diwan (2013), Klein, Frie, Blum, & von dem Knesebeck (2010), Roberts, Cannon, Wellik, Wu, & Budavari (2013)
10 Dentists	Hakanen & Schaufeli (2012), Hakanen, Schaufeli, & Ahola (2008)
11 Human service workers	Thomas, Kohli, & Choi (2014)
12 Dietitians	Gingras, de Jonge, & Purdy (2010)
13 Paediatric oncology staff	Mukherjee, Beresford, Glaser, & Sloper (2009)
14 Cancer professionals	Trufelli et al. (2008)
15 Oncologists	Sherman et al. (2006)
16 Health professionals from other clinical settings	Bohmert, Kuhnert, & Nienhaus (2011), Hyman et al. (2011), Kareaga, Exeberria, & Smith (2009)

Source: Author.

The condition of burnout has both somatic consequences (Kakiashvili, Leszek, & Rutkowski, 2013) and negative economic outcomes, such as absenteeism, job terminations, and turnovers (e.g., Adriaenssens et al., 2015; Davey, Cummings, Newburn-Cook, & Lo, 2009; Flinkman, Leino-Kilpi, & Salantera, 2010; Hayes et al., 2006).

A review of the scientific literature from PsycINFO and Medline reveals a myriad of studies exploring the factors that cause occupational stress and impair the well-being of health professionals. These studies refer to very heterogeneous theories (if any) and are empirically focused. They primarily investigate the working conditions and psycho-social characteristics of nurses and physicians, who are also heterogeneous with respect to work setting and specialty. The majority of the studies are focused on deficits in health-related quality of life, investigated through negative indicators of well-being. Their main objective is to evaluate different aspects of negative mental health, while no space is left for the evaluation of the idea of hedonic and eudaimonic well-being components.

When asked about stressful working conditions, health professionals report heavy workload, huge administrative tasks, financial issues, limited amount of personal time, exposure to patients' suffering and death, the possibility of making professional mistakes, and the threat of lawsuits (e.g., Moreau & Mageau, 2012). Most of these working conditions can be summarized under the global concept of *job demands*. Recent reviews of studies on health professionals' work stress have identified several causes of psychological strain (e.g., Adriaenssens et al., 2015; Arora et al., 2013; Gurman, Klein, & Weksler, 2012; Hyman et al., 2011; Pereira et al., 2011; Sherman et al., 2006; Trufelli et al., 2008). Following Adriaenssens et al.'s (2015) taxonomy, a distinction is made between work-related factors and individual factors. Among work-related factors, researchers discuss eight categories of detrimental forces in the work setting of health professionals: traumatic events, job characteristics, heavy workload/high work demands, lack of autonomy, low social support, organizational factors, staffing issues, and organizational culture.

In oncology and emergency settings, health professionals are particularly exposed to *traumatic events*, which can cause tremendous emotional stress. Health professionals in these specialties are often confronted with severe injuries, life-threatening diseases, suffering and dying patients, desperate families, suicidal ideation or suicide, and are the target of aggressive behaviors. Witnessing such an event is a trauma if this event involves (1) witnessing actual or threatened death or serious injury, or a threat to the physical integrity of others, *and* (2) if the health professional reaction involves intense fear, helplessness, or horror. Such a vicarious traumatization may lead to post-traumatic stress disorder among health personnel (Canfield, 2005).

Furthermore, three classes of *job characteristics* represent influential occupational risk factors: job demands, low decision latitude, and low social support. In this context, the demand control model developed by Karasek and Theorell (1990) has been one of the most used theoretical models explaining work stress. As the authors state, "elevation of risk with a demanding job appears only when these demands are in interaction with low control on the job" (p. 9). As a consequence, heavy workload should be irrelevant unless the decision latitudes of health professionals are large. It is questionable that this assumption applies to health care services, because of emotional costs and ethical/moral pressure when caring for suffering patients. Later, social support was added to this model, and it was re-named as the demand control support model. Social support received by supervisors and colleagues has been shown to reduce the job strain caused by high job demands and low job control.

Heavy workload or *high work demands* represent important clinical stressors that lead to job burnout. This also involves the problem of time pressure: having only a limited amount of time available for a patient and/or the problem of lack of variety can mean that work is heteronomous and incongruent with self-endorsed values and interests. Health professionals often have to work overtime to sufficiently care for their patients due to a high patient-to-health professional ratio. These pressures are further exaggerated through sickness and absenteeism, resulting in compulsory overtime and further pressure and fatigue. A closely related problem is lack of breaks and its effect on reduced recreational space during the work period. A consequence of all of these factors is that work demands interfere with family life and may lead to conflicts in private life, and, vice versa, conflicts at home may enter the work site: stressors in personal life impair the working atmosphere. Finally, a particular job demand of health professionals is the complexity of treatments and concerns about treatment toxicity (e.g., in oncology). "The combination of increasingly complex cancer treatments with higher demands from patients and the 'downsizing' of hospital services for patients with cancer put oncology staff at particular risk of work stress and burnout" (Jones, Wells, Gao, Cassidy, & Davie, 2013, p. 46). In witnessing patients' extreme suffering and dying, health professionals are more likely to feel a failure (in terms of committing a fundamental attribution error, overemphasizing internal and overlooking external conditions).

Lack of autonomy in health care decisions is a severe problem in health care. Medical systems are hierarchic organizations. The lower the position in the hierarchy, the lower the individual health professional's self-determination. Administrative and financial issues can also restrict decision latitudes and (sometimes) dictate health care interventions or confine them to the absolutely necessary, but not sufficient. This autonomy issue will re-appear in the next section of this chapter.

Health care service is delivered in an interpersonal context. *Low social support* means that there is no teamwork in that staff members do not help each other. There is no mutual trust, no work group cohesion, little social or emotional exchange. It also means that one's work is not recognized and appreciated by one's colleagues or superiors. In its most malicious form, low social support manifests itself as bullying (Johnson, 2009).

Organizational factors have been identified as work-stress factors. Health professionals often feel that their work environment is unfavorable, for example, ward architecture, room size, no space for confidential conversations with patients, lack of privacy settings, small locker rooms, and so on. Moreover, interdisciplinary communication and collaboration may be strenuous, due to the factors previously discussed. As a consequence, intra- and interprofessional information provision may be poor, and both the individual health professional and patient can be left at a disadvantage.

Furthermore, *staffing issues* – which are closely connected to heavy workload – increase the occupational stress level, such as low quality of staffing, understaffing (high patient-to-health workers ratio), inequitable working schedules, and inadequacy of shift work. With respect to the latter, permanent night shift is detrimental to long-term quality of life. In addition to little personal manpower, lack of material resources also seems to be a crucial factor.

Finally, aspects of the *organizational culture* might also yield stress. A low degree of innovation and change, a lack of interest in quality assurance initiatives, and low financial reward (in combination with high workload and individual efforts) increase job dissatisfaction and burnout. The latter point is central to the effort–reward theory of work stress (Siegrist & Peter, 1994), which has also inspired a lot of occupational stress researchers. An imbalance between efforts and rewards, also known as inequity (van Dierendonck, Schaufeli, & Buunk, 2001), causes emotional distress.

Among individual factors, researchers distinguish between demographic characteristics, personality characteristics, deficits in patient-centered communication skills, and role stress/role ambiguity. The reviews show a mixed picture with respect to *demographic characteristics* such as age, gender, or health profession. Systematic effects of these variables on health-related quality of life or burnout are not convincingly documented.

Investigations into the role of *personality characteristics* elaborated low resilience (Epstein & Krasner, 2013; Taku, 2014), low hardiness and its constituents (low commitment, low engagement, low control), high neuroticism, high perfectionism, low self-criticism, an external locus of control, and passive-avoidant and emotional coping styles. The problem is that these personality variables overlap as regards content with outcome measures of burnout and psychological distress. Therefore, it is unclear what a high correlation between a personality trait and a burnout measure really means.

Deficits in patient-centered communication skills and lack of empathy are associated with job burnout. These deficits lead to dissatisfying doctor–patient relationships, especially when patients behave in a "difficult" way. From the perspective of the health professional, difficult patients display traits or behavioral dispositions such as being depressive, dependent, manipulative, self-destructive, noncompliant, or aggressive/hostile. Difficult patients are time- and attention-consuming, and health professionals often experience feeling of frustration and exhaustion. At the same time, burned out health professionals become "difficult" for their patients, because burnout impedes critical self-reflection and creates biases toward patients, perceiving them as "difficult."

Role stress reflects a disparity between a health professional's perception of the characteristics of his or her job and what is actually being accomplished when caring for patients. *Role ambiguity* may emerge, that is, the lack of clear consistent information about the behavior expected in a role as a member of a particular health profession. If expectations, objectives, and responsibilities have not been clearly explicated, health professionals become ambivalent in appraising their supervisor's or colleagues' responses to their work as success or as failure. There is empirical evidence of the negative impact of role stress and role ambiguity on subjective well-being and burnout in nurses (e.g., Brunetto, Farr-Wharton, & Shacklock, 2011; Chen, Chen, Tsai, & Lo, 2007; Iliopoulou & While, 2010; Ruel, 2010; Tunc & Kutanis, 2009).

Which of the two broad categories – work-related factors or individual factors – has a deeper impact on well-being? Jones et al. (2013) argue that the organizational culture, the health care setting, and the nature of the health care work have been largely underestimated. This means that individual factors have been overestimated. This is reflected in the fact that most intervention concepts have a focus on modifying individuals' stress reactions and coping strategies, not on the characteristics of the work setting (see below). For example, acute settings such as oncology or emergency are supposed to be more demanding than palliative care settings or rehabilitative settings (see Prins et al., 2010). As Jones et al. note, "… the theoretical basis of studies in this area needs to be strengthened and … future work should focus more on organizational factors" (2013, p. 46).

In the aftermath of identifying stress-enhancing conditions, focusing on deficits in working conditions and individual characteristics of health professionals, the interest in stress-lowering factors (resources) such as work engagement, commitment, psychological growth, resilience, and empowerment have been explored. These issues will be presented in the next section.

The Discovery of Resources and Positive States in Health Personnel

Recapitalizing the "negative" psychology findings, Sherman et al. (2006, Table 5, p. 76) specify in their review "positive" organizational and individual factors that minimize caregiver stress and burnout in oncology. From a positive psychology point of view, these

Table 23.2 Positive organizational and individual resources.

Organization
Adequate staffing, reduced work hours or patient contact
Increased staff autonomy and decision latitude
Flexibility in scheduling or assignment to work setting
Enhanced teamwork, reduced interdisciplinary conflict
Adequate space, facilities
Reallocation of selected tasks or conflicting responsibilities
Individual staff member
Increased personal days/vacation time
Communication and management skills training
Training courses in interpersonal skills
Recognition and appreciation of staff, feedback to staff
Support groups
Grief/bereavement workshops
Stress management programs, healthful lifestyle
Enhanced sense of meaningfulness of work, Logo-therapy
Humor

Source: Adapted from Sherman et al. (2006, Table 5, p. 76).

strategies do represent organizational and individual assets for enhancing well-being, and not merely for reducing psychological distress. Sherman et al.'s compilation is a useful summary about which resources could represent well-being enhancing factors for health professionals (see Table 23.2).

These assets fit perfectly in positive psychology as a science of positive subjective experience, positive individual traits, *and* positive institutions. Whereas "negative psychology" gives attention exclusively to repairing damage (e.g., burnout) caused by pathological conditions (located in the individual and/or institution), positive psychology focuses on "the fulfilled individual and the thriving community" (Seligman & Csikszentmihalyi, 2000, p. 5):

> The field of positive psychology at the subjective level is about valued subjective experiences: well-being, contentment, and satisfaction (in the past); hope and optimism (for the future); and flow and happiness (in the present). At the individual level, it is about positive individual traits: the capacity for love and vocation, courage, interpersonal skill, aesthetic sensibility, perseverance, forgiveness, originality, future mindedness, spirituality, high talent, and wisdom. At the group level, it is about the civic virtues and the institutions that move individuals toward better citizenship: responsibility, nurturance, altruism, civility, moderation, tolerance, and work ethic. (Seligman & Csikszentmihalyi, 2000, p. 5)

It is exactly the merit of positive psychology that it puts an emphasis on resources, potentials and strengths of individuals and their working environment. Positive occupational psychology research primarily scrutinizes the experience of nurses and physicians, and it includes heterogeneous measures of well-being referring to different theories and constructs, such as job satisfaction, work engagement, self-determination/autonomy, job crafting, mindfulness, resilience, and empowerment. The concept of eudaimonic well-being (Ryff, 1989, 1995), which has been suggested as a possible theoretical guideline for positive psychology research, has not been fully applied yet in the health care setting.

Job satisfaction

Recent research discovered job satisfaction as a central outcome variable in positive psychology. Van Ham et al. (2006) assert that job satisfaction is an ambiguous term that can be operationalized in different ways considering a number of dimensions. Job satisfaction implies "all the feelings that an individual has about his/her job" (Lu et al., 2005, p. 211). This definition illustrates that subjective interpretation and expectations play a major role in evaluating job satisfaction. Following Spector (1997), several areas of job satisfaction can be distinguished: "appreciation, communication, co-workers, fringe benefits, job conditions, nature of the work itself, the nature of the organization itself, an organization's policies and procedures, pay, personal growth, promotion opportunities, recognition, security and supervision" (p. 212). The list is very long and presumably not exhaustive. Identifying the contents of job satisfaction is thus a complicated topic as they might be easily confounded with determinants of job satisfaction.

In their pioneering work, Herzberg and Mausner (1959) postulated a two-factor theory of job satisfaction, assuming a positive and a negative dimension – job satisfaction and job dissatisfaction. These are supposed to be distinct phenomena which feed upon different sources. Job satisfaction is energized by intrinsic factors labeled as "motivators" such as achievement, recognition, work itself and responsibility; whereas job dissatisfaction is largely determined by extrinsic factors they called "hygiene factors," for example, company policy, administration, supervision, salary, interpersonal relations and working conditions (see Lu et al., 2005, p. 212).

In a review including 1,157 studies conducted among U.S. physicians, Scheurer, McKean, Miller, and Wetterneck (2009) identified three basic types of satisfaction: overall satisfaction, career/professional satisfaction, and practice/job/work satisfaction. Overall, they revealed relative stability in repeated cross-sectional surveys, documenting a rate of 80% satisfied physicians. However, the proportion of "very satisfied" general practitioners declined – as compared to other specialists. Contrasting findings were detected in another review (Williams and Skinner, 2003), showing a decline in physician job satisfaction from the 1960s to 2002. Van Ham et al. (2006) recognized three factors that increase physicians' job satisfaction: variety in the job, relationships and contact with colleagues, and lecturing to medical students. Factors impeding job satisfaction were low income, too many working hours, administrative burdens, heavy workload, lack of time, and lack of recognition. Haggerty, Fields, Selby-Nelson, Foley, and Shrader (2013) concede that especially rural doctors are disadvantaged.

With respect to nurses, a review of 1,189 research papers (Lu et al., 2005) described a mixed picture of job satisfaction, highlighting the impact of organizational, professional, and personal variables. These variables include working conditions, interaction (with patients, co-workers, managers), work itself (including workload, scheduling, challenging work, routinization, task requirements), remuneration (pay, salary), self-growth and promotion, praise and recognition, control and responsibility, job security, leadership styles, and organizational policies. Again, this empirically based list is extensive. As a consequence, a comprehensive theory or model that can explain and predict job satisfaction satisfactorily is still lacking.

Most importantly, job satisfaction is not only an outcome variable in positive psychology. Williams and Skinner (2003) found in their narrative review that job satisfaction is strongly associated with vital outcomes of both physician and patient. Physician outcomes are turnover, mental and physical health, nonwork satisfactions and work-related issues, and patient outcomes imply quality of care and patient relationships (2003, see Figure 1, p. 129).

Work engagement

In the realm of occupational health psychology, the idea of positive psychology has been incorporated into the job demands-resources model (e.g., Hakanen et al., 2008), which extends the aforementioned demand control model. As reflected in the name of the model, psychosocial work characteristics can be categorized as either job demands or *job resources*. The former are aspects of a job that require effort and are associated with costs. The latter represent the physical, psychological, social, or organizational aspects of a job that may reduce job demands and associated costs, are functional in achieving work goals, and stimulate personal benefits such as personal growth, learning, and development. Job resources are both extrinsically and intrinsically motivating. Intrinsic motivation is nurtured by satisfying basic needs of autonomy, belongingness and competence (Hakanen et al., 2008, p. 225). In this approach, three of the six facets of Ryff's PWB are affected – autonomy, positive relations with others, and personal growth. The three basic needs are also the core components of self-determination (Deci & Ryan, 2000; Ryan & Deci, 2000; Ryan, Huta, & Deci, 2008, see below).

Job resources are supposed to foster *work engagement* – a permanent state which is conceptualized as the opposite of job burnout. Schaufeli, Salanova, González-Romá, and Bakker (2002, pp. 74) define work engagement as follows:

> A positive, fulfilling, work-related state of mind that is characterized by vigor, dedication, and absorption. Rather than a momentary and specific state, engagement refers to a more persistent and pervasive affective-cognitive state that is not focused on any particular object, event, individual, or behavior. Vigor is characterized by high levels of energy and mental resilience while working, the willingness to invest effort in one's work, and persistence even in the face of difficulties. Dedication refers to being strongly involved in one's work and experiencing a sense of significance, enthusiasm, inspiration, pride, and challenge … The final dimension of engagement, absorption, is characterized by being fully concentrated and happily engrossed in one's work, whereby time passes quickly and one has difficulties with detaching oneself from work.

According to the demands-resources model, work engagement is a kind of job-related well-being (van Beek, Hu, Schaufeli, Taris, & Schreurs, 2012). If so, it seems to be a special facet of hedonic well-being – feeling good at work and feeling happy to do this kind of work. Work engagement is linked with positive outcomes such as *organizational commitment*, which is the counterpart of turnover intentions. Put in positive terms, it is a health professional's identification with and involvement in his or her health institution or with his or her health profession, respectively.

Simpson's (2009) review of antecedents and/or consequences of work engagement in the nurse workforce provided consistent evidence of the primary role of organizational predictors, and to a lesser extent individual predictors. Work engagement, in its turn, has a positive impact on productivity and performance. In a Dutch study involving residents, highly engaged young physicians reported fewer errors (Prins et al., 2009). In an Italian study involving different health professions, both organizational and personal factors were profoundly linked with work engagement (Fiabane, Giorgi, Sguazzin, & Argentero, 2013).

Self-determination, or autonomy

Recently, research on well-being in health personnel has been inspired by self-determination theory (SDT; Deci & Ryan, 2000; Ryan & Deci, 2000; Ryan et al., 2008), which assumes that human beings are inherently active and growth-oriented organisms. The working environment either promotes, stimulates, and encourages this disposition or blocks, suppresses, and eliminates it. This means that the interplay between health professional and his or her working environment is important to understand the achievement of subjective well-being or personal growth.

SDT distinguishes between intrinsic and extrinsic motivation. Health professionals who are intrinsically motivated to work on a task see that experience as fascinating, pleasing, and satisfying. In other words, they are engaged in their work for its own sake, and act in a deliberate way. This means that intrinsically motivated work activity is autonomous or self-determined. In contrast, health professionals who are extrinsically motivated to work on a task do so because of its instrumental value. In general, intrinsic motivation of health professionals is very high, because choosing this career is associated with pro-social attitudes and values. For example, in a study involving surgeons, anesthesiologists, and gynecologists, about one third reported that work affords flow experience (see Chapter 7, this volume). Performing surgery, doing research and communicating with patients were the work activities prominently associated with flow. Intrinsic motivation to work as a physician was important for the vast majority of the respondents (Delle Fave, 2006).

The work environment can facilitate or undermine intrinsic motivation and its consequences by fulfilling or frustrating three innate psychological needs: relatedness, competence, and autonomy (Ryan & Deci, 2000). Relatedness refers to the search for positive relationships with patients and colleagues, as well as mutual respect, caring, and trust; competence represents the need for accomplishing challenging tasks at work successfully and to care for patients and their families professionally; autonomy is the need to experience freedom of choice and the opportunity to initiate health care activities (see van Beek et al., 2012, p. 34)

Referring to Gagné and Deci's (2005) article, van Beek et al. (2012) summarized results from studies outside of the health care setting: "Satisfaction of the three psychological needs, autonomous motivation, and the possibility of satisfying one's innate growth tendency are associated with optimal functioning and well-being. With respect to the work context, research has shown that satisfaction of psychological needs and autonomous motivation are associated with positive outcomes, such as task persistence, superior performance, job satisfaction, positive work attitudes, organizational commitment" (p. 34). In their study involving Chinese health professionals, van Beek et al. (2012) showed that intrinsic motivation was positively linked with work engagement, which was also in line with the job demands-resources model. At the same time, a positive relationship was detected between extrinsic motivation and work engagement, suggesting that health professionals engage in their health care activities for their instrumental value as well. In a study of Canadian nurses, Trépanier, Fernet, and Austin (2015) found that basic need satisfaction promotes work engagement and reduces turnover intentions.

Job crafting

The concept of job crafting focuses on how employees redraft or restyle their job. "Job crafting captures what employees do to redesign their own jobs in ways that can foster job satisfaction, as well as engagement, resilience and thriving at work" (Berg, Dutton, & Wrzesniewski, 2008, p. 1). By independently modifying aspects of their job, employees can improve the fit between job characteristics and their own needs, abilities, and preferences (Tims, Bakker, & Derks, 2013). In principle, they can apply three types of customizing strategies. First, they can change the scope of their sphere of action. For example, a resident may ask for different tasks that require new skills because performing colonoscopies day in and day out is too monotonous, which means that this person is definitely underchallenged in his or her job. Second, employees can change their relationships at work by modifying the nature or extent of interactions. For example, a nurse may intensify contact with a colleague her or she finds to be inspiring. Third, they can use cognitive strategies by changing the ways they perceive and think about their job tasks. For example, a resident performing colonoscopies may consider this task as boring but could reframe it as important (Berg et al., 2008; Tims et al., 2013).

According to Slemp and Vella-Brodrick (2014), job crafting has to be distinguished from job enlargement or job enrichment. Whereas the latter terms allude to making changes with respect to structural job characteristics, job crafting represents a series of individual strategies in shaping and molding job experiences according to individual needs and desires. In accordance with SDT, job crafting satisfies the basic psychological needs – relatedness, competence, and autonomy – that that lead to optimal functioning and subjective well-being. Indeed, job crafting reflects exerting control over work, creating a positive self-image, and connecting with others in the workplace. Job crafting could also be a means for cultivating positive meaning and identity in work over time (Wrzesniewski, LoBuglio, Dutton, & Berg, 2013).

The literature review suggests that job crafting has not yet been explored in the health workforce. Only one U.S. study investigates how nurses deal with adversity at the worksite (Caza, 2008). Using narrative interviews, the researcher explored the role of work identity and found out that job crafting was one out five identity-based response moves (the others being disengagement, stoic coping, switching jobs, and identity customization).

Mindfulness

According to K. W. Brown, Ryan, and Creswell (2007), mindfulness is rooted in the fundamental activities of consciousness: *awareness* of stimuli which can be perceived with one or more of the five physical senses, and *attention* in terms of turning toward a stimulus in a focused way. Mindfulness "is most commonly defined as the state of being attentive to and aware of what is taking place in the present" (Brown & Ryan, 2003, p. 822) and can be conceived of as "*a receptive attention to and awareness of present events and experience*" (Brown et al., 2007, p. 212). Empirical evidence shows that mindfulness has beneficial effects on psychological well-being and physical health.

Shapiro and Carlson (2009) argue that mindfulness is particularly appropriate for members of the health workforce. Given the emotional burden and ethical-moral responsibilities when caring for suffering and dying patients, mindful health care professionals can explore their own suffering, affliction, fatigue, anxiety, or depressive reactions, and put these experiences in a personal context. First and foremost, it helps to understand the causes and consequences of these experiences. As a medium-term effect, mindfulness generates well-being. "It teaches us to become interested in the inner workings of our own minds, bodies, and hearts, with kindness, and in this way discover what it means to be human" (Shapiro & Carlson, 2009, p. 107). In line with SDT, mindful persons are happier because they choose options for themselves that are consistent with their needs, values, and interests.

Richards, Campenni, and Muse-Burke (2010) showed that mindfulness mediates the relationship between self-care importance and well-being in mental health care workers. Mindfulness-based intervention programs designed for different health professional groups seem to promote employees' well-being (e.g., Boellinghaus, Jones, & Hutton, 2014; Byron et al., 2014; Cohen-Katz, Wiley, Capuano, Baker, & Shapiro, 2004) and decrease negative mental states such as burnout, depression, anxiety, and stress (Cohen-Katz et al., 2005; Fortney, Luchterhand, Zakletskaia, Zgierska, & Rakel, 2013; Goodman & Schorling, 2012; Krasner et al., 2009; Moody et al., 2013). The only randomized controlled study in positive psychology will be described in the section on interventions below.

Resilience

Zwack and Schweitzer (2013) explicitly investigated the work experience of health professionals from a positive psychology perspective revolving around the concept of resilience: If around 20% of physicians are affected by burnout, what about the other 80%? How can physicians stay healthy and maintain or enhance their well-being despite facing adversities in delivering health care services? The authors identified three dimensions of (1) general sources of gratification (e.g., from the doctor–patient relationship, medical efficacy), (2) behavioral routines and practices (e.g., leisure time activity to reduce stress, quest for and cultivation of contact with colleagues, proactive engagement with limits, self-demarcation), and (3) attitudes and mental strategies (e.g., acceptance and realism, self-awareness and reflexivity, appreciating good things).

In their review, Jackson, Firtko, and Edenborough (2007) identified similar personal resilience or self-development strategies nurses used to bolster resilience: (1) *Building positive nurturing professional relationships and networks*. This strategy underscores the importance of social support for resilience. The institutional network becomes a support system nurses can fall back on in case of need. (2) *Maintaining positivity*. This orientation emphasizes the positive effects of drawing on some form of positive emotion in the midst of stress and adversity. With respect to future prospects, maintaining positivity implies optimism and a positive outlook on things to come, and appreciating potentially positive aspects and benefits. (3) *Developing emotional insight*. This strategy encompasses emotional intelligence and understanding one's own emotional needs, with respect to both negative and positive emotions, and getting to know the emotional conditions and needs of co-workers. (4) *Achieving life balance and spirituality*. Resilient individuals possess a philosophical, religious, or other spiritually based belief system that provides a purpose in life, a coherent life narrative, and a positive understanding of oneself as a unique human being. Moreover, regular practice of healthy habits outside of work acts as a counterbalance against work-related stress. It is important to find a balance between demanding work/tension and necessary recreation/relaxation. The final strategy is (5) *becoming more reflective*. Self-reflection is an important prerequisite for learning and positive change. It implies developing insights into concrete experiences. This increase in level of knowledge can be applied in future situations.

Empowerment

Cicolini, Comparcini, and Simonetti (2014) reviewed empirical studies investigating the role of *empowerment* for job satisfaction in nurses. Two aspects of empowerment emerged. *Structural empowerment* denotes nurses' access to four different organizational empowerment structures, or applications (Kanter, 1977): information (data, technical knowledge, expertise), resources (money, material, time, equipment), support (leadership, guidance, feedback), and opportunity (for autonomy, self-determination, challenge, personal growth). *Psychological empowerment* "deals with ways in which these applications are experienced and understood by workers … and occurs when there is a sense of motivation in relation to the workplace environment" (Cicolini et al., 2014, p. 856). These authors found substantial relationships between empowerment, job satisfaction, and other organizational outcomes. Structural empowerment proves to be a prerequisite for psychological empowerment. In other words, the combination of the two is a strong predictor of job satisfaction. As a conclusion, "removing disempowering structures from the work setting leads to a strong sense of autonomy among employees, who have a strong belief that they have an impact at work" (Cicolini et al., 2014, p. 867). Concordantly, Pearson et al. (2006) backed up in their review the importance of structural requirements such as adequate workload and staffing for creating and maintaining healthy work environments.

Interventions Aimed at Improving Subjective Well-Being in Health Personnel

It is not surprising to find that intervention research on both the promotion of well-being and the prevention of work-related stress and its consequences is very heterogeneous. Before presenting the few positive psychology interventions aimed at enhancing well-being in health personnel, reviews will be summarized that examined the alleviation of negative outcomes such as burnout, anxiety, or psychological distress. These works are interesting from a positive psychology point of view because the interventions addressed positive factors related to both the organization and the individual.

Prevention of work-related stress through positive psychology interventions

Some studies explored the effectiveness of a positive psychology intervention on alleviating negative states, such as stress symptoms. Awa, Plaumann, and Walter (2010) reviewed intervention programs published between 1995 and 2007 aimed at preventing *burnout*. They identified 25 studies that included, among other workers, health care professionals, dentists, interdisciplinary care workers, and social workers. About two thirds (68%) of the interventions were person-directed, as they aimed at changing factors located within the individual staff member. Participants were offered individual or group sessions of "cognitive-behavioral training, psychotherapy, counseling, adaptive skills training, communication skills training, social support, relaxation exercises or recreational music making amongst others" (p. 187). Only few studies (8%) were organization-directed, measuring "work process structuring, work performance appraisals, work shift readjustments, and job evaluations" (p. 187). About one quarter (24%) implemented a combination of both person- and organization-directed interventions. The duration of interventions and assessment points in time varied to a high degree. In about two thirds of the studies, interventions lasted less than 6 months. The time span between pre-test and post-tests also differed from study to study.

Bearing this diversity in mind, this review highlighted that the majority of person-directed studies (82%) backed up a significant reduction in burnout and associated negative indicators such as "state anxiety, psychological distress, depression, moods, fear, perceived stress, self-esteem, feelings of guilt, feeling of deprivation, effort-reward imbalance, and emotional job demands amongst others" (Awa et al., 2010, p. 187). Results concerning organization-directed interventions were inconclusive, due to the limited number of studies with such a focus. Finally, the authors found evidence that combined interventions delivered better results than separate person- or organization-directed interventions.

In their recent Cochrane review (an update of Marine, Ruotsalainen, Serra, & Verbeek, 2006), Ruotsalainen, Verbeek, Mariné, and Serra (2015) scrutinized 58 studies that aimed at preventing *occupational stress* in healthcare workers. They categorized interventions as cognitive-behavioral training (24%), mental and physical relaxation (36%), a combination of cognitive behavioral training and relaxation (10%), and organizational interventions (34%). Outcomes were classified as stress, anxiety, or general health. The authors conclude that there is only low-quality evidence concerning psychological interventions, and that there is no evidence that organizational interventions would have an effect. However, the latter finding is based on a very small number of studies.

Positive psychology interventions: Promoting positive consequences

In their short programmatic paper, Muha and Manion (2010) proposed 6 *positive psychology principles*, summarized in the acronym PROPEL. These are *passion* (creating a compelling and detailed vision of how health professionals can live a valuable life); *relationships* (positive interactions must outweigh negative ones with a 5:1 ratio at least); *optimism* (getting an idea that mutually satisfying solutions can be found); *proactivity* (consistently focusing on strengths rather than deficits); *energy* (making and taking opportunities to routinely recharge and recover), and *legacy* (enabling health professionals to make a difference in the lives of their patients and families). All principles aim at instigating positive emotions in health professional leaders and staff, which is a prerequisite for optimal organizational functioning. Unfortunately, the PROPEL approach has not been subjected to empirical interventional research. Essentially, it is striking to see that there are only a few intervention studies inspired by positive psychological *theory*.

Ouweneel, Le Blanc, and Schaufeli (2013) developed an online positive psychology intervention program to instigate and reinforce positive emotions, self-efficacy, and work engagement. However, it is unclear from the study if their sample included health professionals. Nevertheless, their person-directed approach is very appealing. They compared a self-enhancement group with a control group that only monitored their well-being. The self-enhancement interventions included happiness activities, goal setting at work, and resource building assignments. They demonstrated that the intervention had a significant impact on positive emotions and self-efficacy, but not on work engagement. Only initially unengaged individuals had a benefit in increase of work engagement.

An employer-provided intervention program with protected time to promote physician well-being was also recently developed (West et al., 2014). This program took place every 2 weeks for 1 hour of paid time over a period of 9 months. This group-based program included elements of mindfulness, reflection, exchange of experiences, and group learning intended to promote group cohesiveness. In their randomized controlled trial, the authors showed that the intervention group significantly improved in meaning, empowerment, and engagement in work. Most importantly, these changes were sustained over a period of 12 months. However, no differences could be found in overall quality of life and job satisfaction. The same was true for stress levels and depressive symptoms.

Bolier and her colleagues (2014) conducted an online intervention study aimed at promoting the well-being of nurses and other health professionals. In the experimental condition, the authors offered screening, personalized feedback and a tailored offer of online self-help interventions. Five programs consisting of different modules were available: *Psyfit* (aimed at enhancing well-being and mental fitness); *Colour Your Life* (a cognitive-behavioral program for alleviating [subclinical] depressive conditions); *Strong at work* (aimed at reducing work stress and improving coping strategies); *Don't Panic Online* (a cognitive-behavioral program for alleviating [subclinical] panic conditions and mild cases of panic disorder); and *Drinking Less* (aimed at changing risky drinking). The control condition was a waitlist group, getting the same intervention after the 6-month follow-up assessment. The authors were able to demonstrate that the intervention effectively enhanced especially psychological well-being, disclosing a medium-effect size after 3 months and 6 months follow-up. However, this pattern should be interpreted cautiously because of high attrition rates, especially in the intervention group.

Future Research

An important future research task for positive work psychology in the health domain would be the formulation of a meta-theoretical conception that might integrate positive phenomena such as job satisfaction, work engagement, self-determination/autonomy, job crafting, mindfulness, resilience, and empowerment. Moreover, it would be important to expand the person-centered perspective in positive psychology by embedding it into a positive organizational psychology framework (e.g., Bakker, 2013) and by applying it to different health care settings. It would be interesting to investigate to what extent hedonic and eudaimonic facets of well-being could represent central organizational goals (among others).

One rather unexplored research avenue should address the relative influence of individual and work-related factors on the hedonic and eudaimonic well-being of health professionals. In this respect, it would be also important to compare different professional groups of the health workforce in different health care areas, or sectors (e.g., oncology, emergency, psychiatry).

The majority of positive psychology studies providing evidence of health professionals' well-being so far is limited by its cross-sectional design. Therefore, an interpretation of cause–effect relations is not possible. Consequently, positive psychology needs prospective studies with longitudinal designs to explore changes, developments, and continuity. Such research designs would allow for more analysis of determinants, mediators/moderators, and consequences of well-being.

Positive psychology lacks intervention studies, preferably randomized controlled trials, in health care institutions/settings. Goldenhar, LaMontagne, Katz, Heaney, and Landsbergis (2001) described the intervention research process as consisting of three phases, which can be understood as a research circle: development, implementation, and effectiveness. Whereas mainstream intervention research focuses on short-term program effectiveness (in terms of effect sizes), little attention has been devoted to the theory-driven development of a program and how to successfully implement it permanently and sustainably. Thus, the connection between interventional research and organizational change seems to be the key.

Conclusions

Positive psychology for health professionals is a new field of research that is gradually developing. Started at the end of the last century as a science of positive subjective experience, positive individual traits, and positive institutions (Seligman & Csikszentmihalyi, 2000), positive psychology has raised important research questions and provided interesting answers. But still a vast research field lies ahead. On the one hand, we already seem to know detrimental work-related and individual factors that lead to burnout, depression, suicidal ideation, anxiety, and other forms of psychological distress. We also have an idea of what could be positive outcomes of caring for people and their families, learning something about job satisfaction, work engagement, self-determination/autonomy, job crafting, mindfulness, resilience, and empowerment. On the other hand, these positive concepts stem from different theoretical perspectives, and sometimes, one and the same term is explored from different theoretical backgrounds.

One integrative starting point could be the concept of eudaimonic well-being (or PWB). As already foreshadowed at the beginning of this chapter, the significance of eudaimonia in occupational positive psychology, the fulfillment of individual needs and the idea of a fully functioning person in a fully functioning organization, should be explored systematically and in more detail. Recent empirical work on work engagement (including vigor, dedication, and absorption), self-determination, and organizational commitment (identification with and involvement in a health institution, identification with a health profession) are all steps in the right direction. With respect to the investigation of well-being, a theoretically derived research agenda would be imperative. The classical six facets of positive psychological functioning in the health workforce should be of special interest: self-acceptance, positive relations with others, autonomy, environmental mastery, purpose in life, and personal growth. As Ruotsalainen et al. (2015) ascertained, there is a lack of studies exploring the well-being (both SWB and PWB) of physicians.

Positive psychology has not yet developed a footprint of a positive health care setting or institution. Instead of having worked out a theoretically driven concept, there is a loose list of positive work-related factors. It starts with the claim for "adequate" space and facilities such as "favorable" ward architecture, "adequate" size of locker room and work rooms (including space for confidential conversations with patients). Researchers also suggested that "adequate" staffing (including quality of staffing) and reduced work hours or patient contact would be important (in view of the documented huge workload for the individual health professional). The question would be how to operationalize adequacy, and who should have the power to define and to realize it. The question of adequacy or sufficiency is also connected with issues of increased staff autonomy and decision latitude. The question arises who determines autonomy or decision latitudes (with respect to functions, techniques, professional work, economy), for example, in a commercial enterprise such as a hospital: the provider, the management board, the operative and strategic controlling division, the head physician, the head nurse, or the individual health professional directly involved with the patient? The same holds true for flexibility in scheduling or assignment to work setting. Other researchers emphasize enhanced teamwork and social support to be important, having an impact on increasing mutual trust, good cooperation, and a culture of resolving conflicts. To sum up, positive psychology has given no theoretical input on "positive leadership" or "human resource management" in health institutions, that is, how to let human resources for health thrive.

There is a lack of evidence concerning the main characteristics of a positive organizational culture and their significance for bringing about hedonic and eudaimonic well-being (SWB and PWB) among health professionals as an organizational goal. In this respect, positive organizational psychology has not yet initiated a value-driven discourse on ethics for institutions in which preventive, curative, promotional, or rehabilitative health care services are provided. In this context, the nature of the health care work would be a significant determinant that influences different aspects of well-being for different health professional groups.

Consequently, there is little research on creating healthy institutions for health professionals. In this context, an empowerment and participation perspective would be of special interest (Cicolini et al., 2014). This is a political issue, too. The intervention research conducted so far has focused on modifying individuals' stress reactions and coping strategies, not on the characteristics of the work setting itself. As already delineated, the organizational culture, the health care setting, and the nature of the health care work have been largely underestimated in relation to health professionals' well-being. Clinics are run by analogy with industrial units of health care products. Economic issues add more weight to organizational decisions than moral–ethical arguments. Staff health matters are directed by economic principles and profit interests. Persons in need of health care treatments are treated like customers, not like patients. This means that the nature of the classical doctor–patient relationship has become ambivalent and hesitant. Especially in oncology and emergency units, caring for severely injured, severely ill, and dying patients is extremely straining, also because of the complexities of treatments and concerns about treatment toxicity. This means that the nature of health care work can push health professionals to their individual limits. As a consequence, evidence-based structural solutions are necessary.

References

Adriaenssens, J., De Gucht, V., & Maes, S. (2015). Determinants and prevalence of burnout in emergency nurses: A systematic review of 25 years of research. *International Journal of Nursing Studies*, *52*(2), 649–661.

Allport, G. W. (1961). *Pattern and growth in personality*. New York, NY: Holt, Rinehart & Winston.

Arora, M., Asha, S., Chinnappa, J., & Diwan, A. D. (2013). Review article: Burnout in emergency medicine physicians. *Emergency Medicine Australasia*, *25*(6), 491–495.

Awa, W. L., Plaumann, M., & Walter, U. (2010). Burnout prevention: A review of intervention programs. *Patient Education and Counseling*, *78*(2), 184–190.

Bakker, A. B. (2013). *Advances in positive organizational psychology* (Vol. *1*). Bingley, UK: Emerald Group.

Bakker, A. B., Le Blanc, P. M., & Schaufeli, W. B. (2005). Burnout contagion among intensive care nurses. *Journal of Advanced Nursing*, *51*(3), 276–287.

Berg, J. M., Dutton, J. E., & Wrzesniewski, A. (2008). *What is job crafting and what does it matter?* Available from http://positiveorgs.bus.umich.edu/wp-content/uploads/What-is-Job-Crafting-and-Why-Does-it-Matter1.pdf

Boellinghaus, I., Jones, F. W., & Hutton, J. (2014). The role of mindfulness and loving-kindness meditation in cultivating self-compassion and other-focused concern in health care professionals. *Mindfulness*, *5*(2), 129–138.

Bohmert, M., Kuhnert, S., & Nienhaus, A. (2011). Psychological stress and strain in dialysis staff: A systematic review. *Journal of Renal Care*, *37*(4), 178–189.

Bolier, L., Ketelaar, S. M., Nieuwenhuijsen, K., Smeets, O., Gärtner, F. R., & Sluiter, J. K. (2014). Workplace mental health promotion online to enhance well-being of nurses and allied health professionals: A cluster-randomized controlled trial. *Internet Interventions*, *1*(4), 196–204.

Brown, K. W., & Ryan, R. M. (2003). The benefits of being present: Mindfulness and its role in psychological well-being. *Journal of Personality and Social Psychology*, *84*(4), 822–848.

Brown, K. W., Ryan, R. M., & Creswell, J. D. (2007). Mindfulness: Theoretical foundations and evidence for its salutary effects. *Psychological Inquiry*, *18*(4), 211–237.

Brown, S., & Gunderman, R. B. (2006). Viewpoint: Enhancing the professional fulfillment of physicians. *Academic Medicine*, *81*(6), 577–582.

Brunetto, Y., Farr-Wharton, R., & Shacklock, K. (2011). Supervisor–nurse relationships, teamwork, role ambiguity and well-being: Public versus private sector nurses. *Asia Pacific Journal of Human Resources*, *49*(2), 143–164.

Byron, G., Ziedonis, D. M., McGrath, C., Frazier, J. A., deTorrijos, F., & Fulwiler, C. (2014). Implementation of mindfulness training for mental health staff: Organizational context and stakeholder perspectives. *Mindfulness*, *6*(4), 861–872.

Canfield, J. (2005). Secondary traumatization, burnout, and vicarious traumatization: A review of the literature as it relates to therapists who treat trauma. *Smith College Studies in Social Work*, *75*(2), 81–101.

Caza, B. B. (2008). *Experiences of adversity at work: Toward an identity-based theory of resilience. Dissertation Abstracts International: Section B: The Sciences and Engineering*, *68*(8-B), 5621.

Chen, Y.-M., Chen, S.-H., Tsai, C.-Y., & Lo, L.-Y. (2007). Role stress and job satisfaction for nurse specialists. *Journal of Advanced Nursing*, *59*(5), 497–509.

Cicolini, G., Comparcini, D., & Simonetti, V. (2014). Workplace empowerment and nurses' job satisfaction: A systematic literature review. *Journal of Nursing Management*, *22*(7), 855–871.

Cohen-Katz, J., Wiley, S. D., Capuano, T., Baker, D. M., Kimmel, S., & Shapiro, S. (2005). The effects of mindfulness-based stress reduction on nurse stress and burnout, Part II: A quantitative and qualitative study. [Erratum appears in *Holistic Nursing Practice, 19*(2), 78: Note: Kimmel, Sharon [added].] *Holistic Nursing Practice, 19*(1), 26–35.

Cohen-Katz, J., Wiley, S. D., Capuano, T., Baker, D. M., & Shapiro, S. (2004). The effects of mindfulness-based stress reduction on nurse stress and burnout: A quantitative and qualitative study. *Holistic Nursing Practice, 18*(6), 302–308.

Collins, S., & Long, A. (2003). Working with the psychological effects of trauma: Consequences for mental health-care workers – a literature review. *Journal of Psychiatric & Mental Health Nursing, 10*(4), 417–424.

Davey, M. M., Cummings, G., Newburn-Cook, C. V., & Lo, E. A. (2009). Predictors of nurse absenteeism in hospitals: A systematic review. *Journal of Nursing Management, 17*(3), 312–330.

Deci, E. L., & Ryan, R. M. (2000). The "what" and "why" of goal pursuits: Human needs and the self-determination of behavior. *Psychological Inquiry, 11*(4), 227–268.

Delle Fave, A. (2006). The impact of subjective experience on the quality of life: A central issue for health professionals. In M. Csikszentmihalyi & I. S. Csikszentmihalyi (Eds.), *A life worth living: Contributions to positive psychology* (pp. 165–181). New York, NY: Oxford University Press.

Diener, E., Lucas, R. E., & Oishi, S. (2002). Sujective well-being: The science of happiness and life satisfaction. In C. R. Snyder and S. J. Lopez (Eds.), *Handbook of positive psychology* (pp. 463–473). London, UK: Oxford University Press.

Diener, E., Oishi, S., & Lucas, R. E. (2003). Personality, culture, and subjective well-being: Emotional and cognitive evaluations of life. *Annual Review of Psychology, 54*, 403–425.

Djukic, M. (2011). Review: Job satisfaction and intentions to leave of new nurses. *Journal of Research in Nursing, 16*(6), 549–550.

Dyrbye, L. N., West, C. P., Satele, D., Boone, S., Tan, L., Sloan, J., & Shanafelt, T. D. (2014). Burnout among U.S. medical students, residents, and early career physicians relative to the general U.S. population. *Academic Medicine, 89*(3), 443–451.

Edwards, D., Burnard, P., Coyle, D., Fothergill, A., & Hannigan, B. (2000). Stress and burnout in community mental health nursing: A review of the literature. *Journal of Psychiatric & Mental Health Nursing, 7*(1), 7–14.

Epp, K. (2012). Burnout in critical care nurses: A literature review. *Dynamics, 23*(4), 25–31.

Epstein, R. M., & Krasner, M. S. (2013). Physician resilience: What it means, why it matters, and how to promote it. *Academic Medicine, 88*(3), 301–303.

Erikson, E. H. (1982). *The life cycle completed: A review*. New York, NY: Norton.

Fernando, A. T., III, & Consedine, N. S. (2014). Beyond compassion fatigue: The transactional model of physician compassion. *Journal of Pain & Symptom Management, 48*(2), 289–298.

Fiabane, E., Giorgi, I., Sguazzin, C., & Argentero, P. (2013). Work engagement and occupational stress in nurses and other healthcare workers: The role of organisational and personal factors. *Journal of Clinical Nursing, 22*(17–18), 2614–2624.

Figley, C. R. (Ed.) (1995). *Compassion fatigue: Secondary traumatic stress disorders from treating the traumatized*. New York, NY: Brunner/Mazel.

Figley, C. R., & Beder, J. (2012). The cost of caring requires self care. In J. Beder (Ed.), *Advances in social work practice with the military* (pp. 278–286). New York, NY: Routledge/Taylor & Francis.

Figley, C. R., Huggard, P., & Rees, C. E. (2013). *First do no self-harm: Understanding and promoting physician stress resilience*. New York, NY: Oxford University Press.

Firth-Cozens, J. (2001). Interventions to improve physicians' well-being and patient care. *Social Science & Medicine, 52*(2), 215–222.

Flinkman, M., Leino-Kilpi, H., & Salantera, S. (2010). Nurses' intention to leave the profession: Integrative review. *Journal of Advanced Nursing, 66*(7), 1422–1434.

Fortney, L., Luchterhand, C., Zakletskaia, L., Zgierska, A., & Rakel, D. (2013). Abbreviated mindfulness intervention for job satisfaction, quality of life, and compassion in primary care clinicians: A pilot study. *Annals of Family Medicine, 11*(5), 412–420.

Gagné, M., & Deci, E. L. (2005). Self-determination theory and work motivation. *Journal of Organizational Behavior, 26*(4), 331–362.

Gingras, J., de Jonge, L. A., & Purdy, N. (2010). Prevalence of dietitian burnout. *Journal of Human Nutrition and Dietetics, 23*(3), 238–243.

Goldenhar, L. M., LaMontagne, A. D., Katz, T., Heaney, C., & Landsbergis, P. (2001). The intervention research process in occupational safety and health: An overview from the national occupational research agenda intervention effectiveness research team. *Journal of Occupational & Environmental Medicine, 43*(7), 616–622.

Goodman, M. J., & Schorling, J. B. (2012). A mindfulness course decreases burnout and improves well-being among healthcare providers. *International Journal of Psychiatry in Medicine, 43*(2), 119–128.

Gurman, G. M., Klein, M., & Weksler, N. (2012). Professional stress in anesthesiology: A review. *Journal of Clinical Monitoring & Computing, 26*(4), 329–335.

Haggerty, T. S., Fields, S. A., Selby-Nelson, E. M., Foley, K. P., & Shrader, C. D. (2013). Physician wellness in rural America: A review. *International Journal of Psychiatry in Medicine, 46*(3), 303–313.

Hakanen, J. J., & Schaufeli, W. B. (2012). Do burnout and work engagement predict depressive symptoms and life satisfaction? A three-wave seven-year prospective study. *Journal of Affective Disorders, 141*(2–3), 415–424.

Hakanen, J. J., Schaufeli, W. B., & Ahola, K. (2008). The job demands-resources model: A three-year cross-lagged study of burnout, depression, commitment, and work engagement. *Work & Stress, 22*(3), 224–241.

Hantke, L., & Görges, H.-J. (2012). *Handbuch Traumakompetenz. Basiswissen für Therapie, Beratung und Pädagogik [Handbook of trauma competence. Basic knowledge for therapy, counseling and pedagogics]*. Paderborn, Germany: Junfermann.

Hayes, L. J., O'Brien-Pallas, L., Duffield, C., Shamian, J., Buchan, J., Hughes, F., … North, N. (2006). Nurse turnover: A literature review. *International Journal of Nursing Studies, 43*(2), 237–263.

Hegney, D. G., Craigie, M., Hemsworth, D., Osseiran-Moisson, R., Aoun, S., Francis, K., & Drury, V. (2014). Compassion satisfaction, compassion fatigue, anxiety, depression and stress in registered nurses in Australia: Study 1 results. *Journal of Nursing Management, 22*(4), 506–518.

Hem, E., Haldorsen, T., Aasland, O. G., Tyssen, R., Vaglum, P., & Ekeberg, Ø. (2005a). Suicide among physicians. *The American Journal of Psychiatry, 162*(11), 2199–2200.

Hem, E., Haldorsen, T., Aasland, O. G., Tyssen, R., Vaglum, P., & Ekeberg, Ø. (2005b). Suicide rates according to education with a particular focus on physicians in Norway 1960–2000. *Psychological Medicine, 35*(6), 873–880.

Herzberg, F., & Mausner, B. (1959). *The motivation to work* (2nd ed.). New York, NY: Wiley.

Humphries, N., Morgan, K., Conry, M. C., McGowan, Y., Montgomery, A., & McGee, H. (2014). Quality of care and health professional burnout: Narrative literature review. *International Journal of Health Care Quality Assurance, 27*(4), 293–307.

Hyman, S. A., Michaels, D. R., Berry, J. M., Schildcrout, J. S., Mercaldo, N. D., & Weinger, M. B. (2011). Risk of burnout in perioperative clinicians: A survey study and literature review. *Anesthesiology, 114*(1), 194–204.

Iliopoulou, K. K., & While, A. E. (2010). Professional autonomy and job satisfaction: Survey of critical care nurses in mainland Greece. *Journal of Advanced Nursing, 66*(11), 2520–2531.

Ishak, W. W., Lederer, S., Mandili, C., Nikravesh, R., Seligman, L., Vasa, M., …Bernstein, C. (2009). Burnout during residency training: A literature review. *Journal of Graduate Medical Education, 1*(2), 236–242.

Jackson, D., Firtko, A., & Edenborough, M. (2007). Personal resilience as a strategy for surviving and thriving in the face of workplace adversity: A literature review. *Journal of Advanced Nursing, 60*(1), 1–9.

Johnson, S. L. (2009). International perspectives on workplace bullying among nurses: A review. *International Nursing Review, 56*(1), 34–40.

Jones, M. C., Wells, M., Gao, C., Cassidy, B., & Davie, J. (2013). Work stress and well-being in oncology settings: A multidisciplinary study of health care professionals. *Psycho-Oncology, 22*(1), 46–53.

Kakiashvili, T., Leszek, J., & Rutkowski, K. (2013). The medical perspective on burnout. *International Journal of Occupational Medicine and Environmental Health, 26*(3), 401–412.

Kanter, R. M. (1977). *Men and women of the corporation*. New York, NY: Basic Books.
Karasek, R., & Theorell, T. (1990). *Healthy work: Stress, productivity and the reconstruction of working life*. New York, NY: Basic Books.
Kareaga, A. A., Exeberria, S. A., & Smith, J. C. (2009). Assessment of burnout and psychological wellbeing among health professionals in the Basque country. *Psychology in Spain, 13*(1), 62–71.
Kimiecik, J. (2011). Exploring the promise of eudaimonic well-being within the practice of health promotion: The "how" is as important as the "what." *Journal of Happiness Studies, 12*(5), 769–792.
Klein, J., Frie, K. G., Blum, K., & von dem Knesebeck, O. (2010). Burnout and perceived quality of care among German clinicians in surgery. *International Journal for Quality in Health Care, 22*(6), 525–530.
Krasner, M. S., Epstein, R. M., Beckman, H., Suchman, A. L., Chapman, B., Mooney, C. J., & Quill, T. E. (2009). Association of an educational program in mindful communication with burnout, empathy, and attitudes among primary care physicians. *JAMA: Journal of the American Medical Association, 302*(12), 1284–1293.
Larsen, D., & Stamm, B. H. (2008). Professional quality of life and trauma therapists. In S. Joseph & P. A. Linley (Eds.), *Trauma, recovery, and growth: Positive psychological perspectives on posttraumatic stress* (pp. 275–293). Hoboken, NJ: Wiley.
Lu, H., Barriball, K. L., Zhang, X., & While, A. E. (2012). Job satisfaction among hospital nurses revisited: A systematic review. *International Journal of Nursing Studies, 49*(8), 1017–1038.
Lu, H., While, A. E., & Barriball, K. L. (2005). Job satisfaction among nurses: A literature review. *International Journal of Nursing Studies, 42*(2), 211–227.
Marine, A., Ruotsalainen, J. H., Serra, C., & Verbeek, J. H. (2006). Preventing occupational stress in healthcare workers. *Cochrane Database of Systematic Reviews, 4*. Art. No.: CD002892
Maslach, C., Schaufeli, W. B., & Leiter, M. P. (2001). Job burnout. *Annual Review of Psychology, 52*, 397–422.
Maslow, A. H. (1968). *Toward a psychology of being* (2nd ed.). New York, NY: Van Nostrand.
Mathieu, F. (2014). Occupational hazards: Compassion fatigue, vicarious trauma and burnout. *Canadian Nurse, 110*(5), 12–13.
Mohammed, K. A.-M., Ali, E. G., Youssef, I. M., Fahmy, M. T., & Haggag, W. E. (2014). Depression and burnout among residents. *Arab Journal of Psychiatry, 25*(1), 40–51.
Moody, K., Kramer, D., Santizo, R. O., Magro, L., Wyshogrod, D., Ambrosio, J., … Stein, J. (2013). Helping the helpers: Mindfulness training for burnout in pediatric oncology – a pilot program. *Journal of Pediatric Oncology Nursing, 30*(5), 275–284.
Moreau, E., & Mageau, G. A. (2012). The importance of perceived autonomy support for the psychological health and work satisfaction of health professionals: Not only supervisors count, colleagues too! *Motivation and Emotion, 36*(3), 268–286.
Muha, T. M., & Manion, J. (2010). Using positive psychology to engage your staff during difficult times. *Nurse Leader, 8*(1), 50–54.
Mukherjee, S., Beresford, B., Glaser, A., & Sloper, P. (2009). Burnout, psychiatric morbidity, and work-related sources of stress in paediatric oncology staff: A review of the literature. *Psycho-Oncology, 18*(10), 1019–1028.
Ouweneel, E., Le Blanc, P. M., & Schaufeli, W. B. (2013). Do-it-yourself: An online positive psychology intervention to promote positive emotions, self-efficacy, and engagement at work. *The Career Development International, 18*(2), 173–195.
Oyane, N. M., Pallesen, S., Moen, B. E., Akerstedt, T., & Bjorvatn, B. (2013). Associations between night work and anxiety, depression, insomnia, sleepiness and fatigue in a sample of Norwegian nurses. *PLoS ONE, 8*(8), e70228.
Pearson, A., Pallas, L. O., Thomson, D., Doucette, E., Tucker, D., Wiechula, R., … Jordan, Z. (2006). Systematic review of evidence on the impact of nursing workload and staffing on establishing healthy work environments. *International Journal of Evidence-Based Healthcare, 4*(4), 337–384.
Pereira, S. M., Fonseca, A. M., & Carvalho, A. S. (2011). Burnout in palliative care: A systematic review. *Nursing Ethics, 18*(3), 317–326.
Pereira-Lima, K., & Loureiro, S. R. (2015). Burnout, anxiety, depression, and social skills in medical residents. *Psychology Health & Medicine, 20*(3), 353–362.

Prins, J. T., Hoekstra-Weebers, J. E. H. M., Gazendam-Donofrio, S. M., Dillingh, G. S., Bakker, A. B., Huisman, M. ... van der Heijden, F. M. (2010). Burnout and engagement among resident doctors in the Netherlands: A national study. *Medical Education, 44*(3), 236–247.

Prins, J. T., van der Heijden, F. M., Hoekstra-Weebers, J. E., Bakker, A. B., van de Wiel, H. B., Jacobs, B., & Gazendam-Donofrio, S. M. (2009). Burnout, engagement and resident physicians' self-reported errors. *Psychology Health & Medicine, 14*(6), 654–666.

Richards, K. C., Campenni, C. E., & Muse-Burke, J. L. (2010). Self-care and well-being in mental health professionals: The mediating effects of self-awareness and mindfulness. *Journal of Mental Health Counseling, 32*(3), 247–264.

Roberts, D. L., Cannon, K. J., Wellik, K. E., Wu, Q., & Budavari, A. I. (2013). Burnout in inpatient-based versus outpatient-based physicians: A systematic review and meta-analysis. *Journal of Hospital Medicine, 8*(11), 653–664.

Rogers, C. R. (1961). *On becoming a person.* Boston, MA: Houghton Muffin.

Rossi, A., Cetrano, G., Pertile, R., Rabbi, L., Donisi, V., Grigoletti, L., ... Amaddeo, F. (2012). Burnout, compassion fatigue, and compassion satisfaction among staff in community-based mental health services. *Psychiatry Research, 200*(2–3), 933–938.

Ruel, S. P. (2010). *Factors influencing nurse faculty's job satisfaction and intent to stay.* PhD dissertation, University of Southern Mississippi, USA. *Dissertation Abstracts International: Section B: The Sciences and Engineering, 70*(7-B), 4091.

Ruotsalainen, J. H., Verbeek, J. H., Mariné, A., & Serra, C. (2015). Preventing occupational stress in healthcare workers. *Cochrane Database of Systematic Reviews, 4,* Art. No.: CD002892.

Ryan, R. M., & Deci, E. L. (2000). Self-determination theory and the facilitation of intrinsic motivation, social development, and well-being. *American Psychologist, 55*(1), 68–78.

Ryan, R. M., & Deci, E. L. (2001). On happiness and human potentials: A review of research on hedonic and eudaimonic well-being. *Annual Review of Psychology, 52,* 141–166.

Ryan, R. M., Huta, V., & Deci, E. L. (2008). Living well: A self-determination theory perspective on eudaimonia. *Journal of Happiness Studies, 9*(1), 139–170.

Ryff, C. D. (1989). Happiness is everything, or is it? Explorations on the meaning of psychological well-being. *Journal of Personality and Social Psychology, 57*(6), 1069–1081.

Ryff, C. D. (1995). Psychological well-being in adult life. *Current Directions in Psychological Science, 4*(4), 99–104.

Sahraian, A., Fazelzadeh, A., Mehdizadeh, A. R., & Toobaee, S. H. (2008). Burnout in hospital nurses: A comparison of internal, surgery, psychiatry and burns wards. *International Nursing Review, 55*(1), 62–67.

Schaufeli, W. B., Salanova, M., González-Romá, V., & Bakker, A. B. (2002). The measurement of engagement and burnout: A two sample confirmatory factor analytic approach. *Journal of Happiness Studies, 3*(1), 71–92.

Scheepers, R. A., Boerebach, B. C. M., Arah, O. A., Heineman, M. J., & Lombarts, K. M. J. M. H. (2015). A systematic review of the impact of physicians' occupational well-being on the quality of patient care. *International Journal of Behavioral Medicine, 22*(6), 683–698.

Schernhammer, E. S., & Colditz, G. A. (2004). Suicide rates among physicians: A quantitative and gender assessment (meta-analysis). *The American Journal of Psychiatry, 161*(12), 2295–2302.

Scheurer, D., McKean, S., Miller, J., & Wetterneck, T. (2009). U.S. physician satisfaction: A systematic review. *Journal of Hospital Medicine, 4*(9), 560–568.

Seligman, M. E. P., & Csikszentmihalyi, M. (2000). Positive psychology: An introduction. *American Psychologist, 55*(1), 5–14.

Shapiro, S. L., & Carlson, L. E. (2009). Mindfulness and self-care for clinicians. *The art and science of mindfulness: Integrating mindfulness into psychology and the helping professions.* (pp. 107–117). Washington, DC: American Psychological Association.

Sherman, A. C., Edwards, D., Simonton, S., & Mehta, P. (2006). Caregiver stress and burnout in an oncology unit. *Palliative & Supportive Care, 4*(01), 65–80.

Siegrist, J., & Peter, R. (1994). Job stressors and coping characteristics in work-related disease: Issues of validity. *Work & Stress, 8*(2), 130–140.

Simpson, M. R. (2009). Engagement at work: A review of the literature. *International Journal of Nursing Studies, 46*(7), 1012–1024.

Slemp, G. R., & Vella-Brodrick, D. A. (2014). Optimising employee mental health: The relationship between intrinsic need satisfaction, job crafting, and employee well-being. *Journal of Happiness Studies*, *15*(4), 957–977.

Smith-Miller, C. A., Shaw-Kokot, J., Curro, B., & Jones, C. B. (2014). An integrative review: Fatigue among nurses in acute care settings. *Journal of Nursing Administration*, *44*(9), 487–494.

Spector, P. E. (1997). *Job satisfaction: Application, assessment, causes, and consequences.* London, UK: Sage.

Sprang, G., Clark, J. J., & Whitt-Woosley, A. (2007). Compassion fatigue, compassion satisfaction, and burnout: Factors impacting a professional's quality of life. *Journal of Loss and Trauma*, *12*(3), 259–280.

Taku, K. (2014). Relationships among perceived psychological growth, resilience and burnout in physicians. *Personality and Individual Differences*, *59*, 120–123.

Thomas, M., Kohli, V., & Choi, J. (2014). Correlates of job burnout among human services workers: Implications for workforce retention. *Journal of Sociology and Social Welfare*, *41*(4), 69–90.

Thomas, N. K. (2004). Resident burnout. *JAMA: Journal of the American Medical Association*, *292*(23), 2880–2889.

Tims, M., Bakker, A. B., & Derks, D. (2013). The impact of job crafting on job demands, job resources, and well-being. *Journal of Occupational Health Psychology*, *18*(2), 230–240.

Toh, S. G., Ang, E., & Devi, M. K. (2012). Systematic review on the relationship between the nursing shortage and job satisfaction, stress and burnout levels among nurses in oncology/haematology settings. *International Journal of Evidence-Based Healthcare*, *10*(2), 126–141.

Trépanier, S.-G., Fernet, C., & Austin, S. (2015). A longitudinal investigation of workplace bullying, basic need satisfaction, and employee functioning. *Journal of Occupational Health Psychology*, *20*(1), 105–116.

Trufelli, D. C., Bensi, C. G., Garcia, J. B., Narahara, J. L., Abrão, M. N., Diniz, R. W. … Del Giglio, A. (2008). Burnout in cancer professionals: A systematic review and meta-analysis. *European Journal of Cancer Care*, *17*(6), 524–531.

Tunc, T., & Kutanis, R. O. (2009). Role conflict, role ambiguity, and burnout in nurses and physicians at a university hospital in Turkey. *Nursing & Health Sciences*, *11*(4), 410–416.

Utriainen, K., & Kyngäs, H. (2009). Hospital nurses' job satisfaction: A literature review. *Journal of Nursing Management*, *17*(8), 1002–1010.

van Beek, I., Hu, Q., Schaufeli, W. B., Taris, T. W., & Schreurs, B. H. J. (2012). For fun, love, or money: What drives workaholic, engaged, and burned-out employees at work? *Applied Psychology: An International Review*, *61*(1), 30–55.

van Dierendonck, D., Schaufeli, W. B., & Buunk, B. P. (2001). Burnout and inequity among human service professionals: A longitudinal study. *Journal of Occupational Health Psychology*, *6*(1), 43–52.

Van Ham, I., Verhoeven, A. A., Groenier, K. H., Groothoff, J. W., & De Haan, J. (2006). Job satisfaction among general practitioners: A systematic literature review. *European Journal of General Practice*, *12*(4), 174–180.

Wallace, J. E., & Lemaire, J. (2009). Physician well being and quality of patient care: An exploratory study of the missing link. *Psychology, Health & Medicine*, *14*(5), 545–552.

Wang, X., Kunaviktikul, W., & Wichaikhum, O. a. (2013). Work empowerment and burnout among registered nurses in two tertiary general hospitals. *Journal of Clinical Nursing*, *22*(19–20), 2896–2903.

Wentzel, D., & Brysiewicz, P. (2014). The consequence of caring too much: Compassion fatigue and the trauma nurse. *Journal of Emergency Nursing*, *40*(1), 95–97.

West, C. P., Dyrbye, L. N., Rabatin, J. T., Call, T. G., Davidson, J. H., Multari, A., … Shanafelt, T. D. (2014). Intervention to promote physician well-being, job satisfaction, and professionalism: A randomized clinical trial. *JAMA Internal Medicine*, *174*(4), 527–533.

West, C. P., Shanafelt, T. D., & Kolars, J. C. (2011). Quality of life, burnout, educational debt, and medical knowledge among internal medicine residents. *JAMA: Journal of the American Medical Association*, *306*(9), 952–960.

Wikipedia. (2015). Health professional. Retrieved March 3, 2015, from Wikimedia Foundation: http://en.wikipedia.org/wiki/Health_professional

Williams, E. S., & Skinner, A. C. (2003). Outcomes of physician job satisfaction: A narrative review, implications, and directions for future research. *Health Care Management Review*, *28*(2), 119–139.

World Health Organization. (2006). The World Health Report 2006: Working together for health. Retrieved from http://www.who.int/whr/2006/whr06_en.pdf?ua=1

Wrzesniewski, A., LoBuglio, N., Dutton, J. E., & Berg, J. M. (2013). Job crafting and cultivating positive meaning and identity in work. In A. B. Bakker (Ed.), *Advances in positive organizational psychology* (Vol. *1*, pp. 281–302). Bingley, UK: Emerald.

Zwack, J., & Schweitzer, J. (2013). If every fifth physician is affected by burnout, what about the other four? Resilience strategies of experienced physicians. *Academic Medicine*, *88*(3), 382–389.

24

The Well-Being of Teachers and Professors

Brittany Branand and Jeanne Nakamura

Introduction

Educators perform an important role in cultures across the world, as the generative nature of their work provides them a unique opportunity. As Henry Adams observed, "A teacher affects eternity, he can never tell where his influence stops" (Adams, 1999, Ch. 20, para. 5). Thus, the examination of factors that contribute to the well-being of teachers and faculty, and therefore, their thriving, is a worthwhile and beneficial endeavor.

To provide context for our well-being analysis, we will describe generativity as it relates to educators and then briefly look at a serious challenge to persistence and well-being – burnout. We will then review the literature on teacher and faculty well-being at work and examine how their well-being is impacted from both hedonic and eudaimonic perspectives. The hedonic viewpoint emphasizes maximizing pleasure (Diener & Lucas, 1999; Huta & Ryan, 2010; Seligman, 2002) and focuses on subjective experiences of well-being (e.g., positive affect, life satisfaction, and low negative affect; Diener & Lucas, 1999, Fowers, Mollica, & Procacci, 2010; Ryan, Huta, & Deci, 2008). In contrast, the eudaimonic perspective emphasizes a life of meaning (Knoop, 2011; Knoop & Delle Fave, 2013; Seligman, 2002) and engagement (Delle Fave, Massimini, & Bassi, 2011; Vitterso, 2013a, 2013b) and focuses on psychological aspects of well-being, for example, autonomy, environmental mastery, personal growth, purpose in life, positive relations with others, and self-acceptance (Ryff, 1989). In addition, we will examine character strengths and personality traits that positively relate to well-being. We will also review what attempts at intervention have been advanced, highlighting mentoring, and suggest future directions that might lead to improved work environments and increased teacher well-being.

The Wiley Blackwell Handbook of the Psychology of Positivity and Strengths-Based Approaches at Work, First Edition. Edited by Lindsay G. Oades, Michael F. Steger, Antonella Delle Fave, and Jonathan Passmore.

Generativity

Generative adults are leaders, teachers, mentors, and what George Vaillant has called the "keepers of the meaning" (Vaillant & Milofsky, 1980). Erikson (1950), who introduced the multifaceted psychosocial construct of generativity, stated that it is "primarily the concern in establishing and guiding the next generation" (p. 276). Generativity, as described, certainly instructs, if not drives, teaching. Teachers are uniquely dedicated to helping the next generation. In particular, they embody cultural generativity (Kotre, 1984); they are essential to the preservation and dissemination of the knowledge, beliefs, ethics, and standards that define a culture.

Although their role is a profoundly important and generative one, a recent international survey of teachers and leaders conducted by the Organisation for Economic Co-operation and Development (OECD) in 34 countries, found that teachers love their job, but feel undervalued, unsupported, and unrecognized (OECD, 2014). Acknowledging this disparity, at least the rhetoric, if not the actions, of political leaders from across the world's cultures calls to venerate the role of teacher. England's Education Secretary, Michael Gove, in a speech outlining his goals for the Department of Education, said "teachers hold in their hands the success of our country and the well-being of its citizens" (2013), although these public statements have not always been supported by similar positive actions in teacher policy. Xi Jinping, President of China, in a speech honoring Teachers Day, urged the government to make teaching the most respected job in China and stated "The importance of teachers lies in shaping souls, forging lives and crafting humans" ("Xi calls," 2014). President of the United States, Barack Obama, commenting on studies that showed what most influenced student success, posited "The single most important factor in determining student achievement is not the color of their skin or where they come from. It's not who their parents are or how much money they have. It's who their teacher is" (Education Week, 2009). Given what should be the elevated role of teachers across the globe, the safeguarding of their well-being is both a political and a practical priority.

The education literature has documented the generative gifts of teachers, showing that the success and well-being of students is influenced by the success and well-being of their teachers. For example, teacher enthusiasm was found to promote student intrinsic motivation to learn (Cordova & Lepper, 1996; Patrick, Hisley, & Kempler, 2000; Stenlund, 1995). In another example, music students of teachers in the Netherlands who were experiencing flow (Csikszentmihalyi, 1997), measured as absorption, work enjoyment, and intrinsic motivation, experienced higher frequency of flow themselves (Bakker, 2005; Bakker & Schaufeli, 2000). Positive teachers (those who exhibit optimistic explanatory style, grit, and life satisfaction) were shown to be more effective and their students showed greater academic gains (Duckworth, Quinn, & Seligman, 2009). Additionally, teachers' positive emotions were shown to influence student motivations and behaviors (Sutton & Wheatley, 2003). In a final example, teachers' social and emotional competence was demonstrated to promote positive developmental outcomes in students (Jennings & Greenberg, 2009). In short, engaged, happy teachers foster engaged, happy students.

The Challenge of Burnout

To best understand teacher and faculty well-being in the workplace, it is instructive to first briefly look at what the literature shows as a universally salient challenge to states of teacher well-being – burnout. By first considering the scope and nature of this pervasive condition, we will have the context to better contrast its positive antithesis – teacher well-being.

The term "burnout" was first used by Herbert Freudenberger, a U.S. psychologist, to describe the complete physical depletion experienced by workers (1974). Research on burnout heightened in the 1970s when it expanded from a phenomenon observed in the blue-collar workforce to the helping professions such as nursing, law enforcement, and teaching (Bardo, 1979). Rather than emanating from understimulation and physical exhaustion, as seen in the blue-collar workers, teacher burnout was associated with emotional overload, overstimulation, and mental exhaustion (Edelwich & Brodsky, 1980; Hamann & Daugherty, 1984). Maslach and Leiter (1999) examined teacher burnout specifically and described burnout factors and influences for the profession. Maslach and Jackson (1981) developed a tripartite model, the Maslach Burnout Inventory–Human Services Survey (MBI–HSS) that has been used widely in teacher burnout research since its inception (Maslach, Jackson, & Leiter, 1996; Schaufeli, Maslach, & Marek, 1993; van Dick & Wagner, 2001).

An international survey study conducted by the OECD (OECD, 2013) identified many of the factors that influence burnout and its related attrition problem across diverse cultures. In a study entitled "Teachers Matter," a survey of teachers in 25 countries found burnout to be a universal problem and showed that workload stress was a serious and increasing indicator (McKenzie, Santiago, Sliwka, & Hiroyuki, 2005). The study found that teacher roles across cultures have expanded; not only are they charged with the individual development and learning of their students, but they must manage the learning process in the classroom, the development of the larger school into a "learning community," and they are expected to establish and maintain connections with the local community and the wider world. The study also suggests that, with no corresponding increase in support services, teachers are experiencing decreasing job satisfaction and increasing burnout.

The problem of teacher burnout has been widely investigated in the education scholarly literature from many perspectives. Studies have shown that burnout is prevalent in beginning teachers and in experienced teachers (e.g., Burke & Greenglass, 1995; Friedman, 2000; Goddard, O'Brien, & Goddard, 2006). It is a universal challenge found in diverse cultures (e.g., Jackson, Rothmann, & van de Vijver, 2006; Jiang, 2005; Li, Li, & Sun, 2013; Liu & Onwuegbuzie, 2012). It has been found to affect both genders (Purvanova & Muros, 2010). Researchers have studied it at primary and secondary levels (e.g., Ben-Ari, Krole, & Har-Even, 2003; McCarthy, Lambert, O'Donnell, & Melendres, 2009) and the post-secondary level (e.g., Bakker, Demerouti, de Boer, & Schaufeli, 2003; Bartlett, 1994; Gonzalez & Bernard, 2006; Hamann & Daugherty, 1984; Watts & Robertson, 2011). It has been viewed as an individual stress problem (Schwartz, Pickering, & Landsbergis, 1996) and as a systemic organizational one with situational factors that impact work environments (Maslach, 2003; Maslach & Leiter, 1999).

The conceptualization of the construct of burnout is metaphorical – the smothering of a fire or the expiration of a candle; something that was vital and alive with light and heat is now dark and cold. Appreciating both the breadth and depth of the problem from this negative view, we will now consider theoretical and empirical research from the positive psychology perspective. To extend the metaphor, we will examine how to keep the fires of passion and creativity burning so that teachers and faculty, and those whose lives they impact, can shine. That is, rather than study only burnout, its causes, and implications, a more fruitful and effective path also studies how to enhance well-being. This strengths-based approach includes examining factors that promote well-being and efforts that encourage positive emotions and develop positive strengths.

Theoretical Aspects of Hedonic and Eudaimonic Well-Being

In examining teacher well-being we will look at hedonic well-being, commonly referred to as subjective well-being, which acknowledges that people react and respond differently to similar experiences and that the judgment of their life is filtered through distinctive expectations and values (Diener & Lucas, 1999). Therefore, the subjective aspect of well-being is a multidimensional construct encompassing a cognitive component that assesses our life satisfaction and an affective component that relates to our positive or negative reactions (positive and negative affect) (Diener & Lucas, 1999). The formula advanced is that subjective well-being is a result of experiencing a high degree of personal satisfaction, a high-level of positive affect, and a low level of negative affect (Deci & Ryan, 2008; Diener, 2000).

Distinct from hedonic well-being, we will also examine teacher well-being comprised of eudaimonic factors that include meaning, authenticity, personal growth, competence, relatedness, and engagement (Ryan & Deci, 2001; Ryff, 1989). These psychological well-being aspects combine the Aristotelian concept of eudaimonia with elements of lifespan developmental theory (Erikson, 1959), self-actualization (Maslow, 1968), and full-functioning (Rogers, 1961). Eudaimonic well-being focuses on and explains teachers' positive psychological functioning, an essential attribute of a successful teacher. Both aspects of well-being, hedonic and eudaimonic, contribute to the overall state of positive teacher well-being and, therefore, their success and that of those they teach.

Many theoretical frameworks inform the study of well-being in teachers; however, from a positive psychology perspective four warrant highlighting in the context of this chapter: the social cognitive career theory (SCCT; Lent, Brown, & Hackett, 1994), the job demands-resources model (JD-R; Bakker & Demerouti, 2007), the self-determination theory (SDT; Deci & Ryan, 2000), and the theory of flow (Csikszentmihalyi, 1975/2000). We will discuss the tenets of these theories and review studies that confirm and enhance their findings, so that we can best identify the factors that protect and increase well-being in teachers.

Lent and Brown's (2006) integrated social cognitive model of work satisfaction combines many of the oft-studied components of job satisfaction, such as trait and work-related fit, into a unified framework that is conceptually aligned with the SCCT (Lent, Brown, & Hackett, 1994). SCCT proposes that career choice is influenced by the beliefs the person develops through four major sources: (1) personal performance accomplishments, (2) vicarious learning, (3) social persuasion, and (4) physiological states. The ongoing process through which one develops expertise for a particular endeavor and experiences success reinforces one's self-efficacy or belief that one will continue to be successful in similar future pursuits. As a result, one is more likely to develop goals that involve continuing participation in that pursuit. In their 2006 model, Lent and Brown featured five classes of predictor variables that are relatively modifiable (self-efficacy, goal participation, personality/affective traits, work conditions, and support resources) along with the outcome variable of job satisfaction.

To test the Lent and Brown (2006) model, Duffy and Lent (2009) surveyed a sample of 336 full-time school teachers in North Carolina via the Internet. They hoped to identify modifiable precursors to their work satisfaction. Their findings confirmed that teachers with more confidence in performing their work-related tasks and fulfilling their work-related goals may be more satisfied at work. They also found, consistent with other studies (Connolly & Viswesvaran, 2000; Thoresen, Kaplan, Barsky, Warren, & de Chermont, 2003), that teachers with higher levels of trait-positive affect are more likely to have positive attitudes toward their job. Also significant was the link between perceived organizational support and work satisfaction. These three predictors accounted for 75% of the variance in work satisfaction. The authors suggest that working with teachers to strengthen their self-efficacy and design achievable work-related goals and then rewarding their progress could help teachers gain positive work experiences and increased hedonic well-being.

Using a sample of 235 Italian school teachers, researchers found additional support for the Lent and Brown (2006) social cognitive model predicting job satisfaction in teachers (Lent et al., 2011). Their survey results identified that, just as in the North Carolina study above, the two strongest predictors were perceived organizational support and trait-positive affect.

In a further test of the Lent and Brown model, Badri, Mohaidat, Ferrandino, and El Mourad (2013) surveyed 5,022 teachers in Abu Dhabi in the United Arab Emirates via the Internet. Results revealed that the model was a strong fit for the data and accounted for 82% of the variance in work satisfaction, and thus the model received support as applied to explaining teacher job satisfaction. However, this study differed from the Duffy and Lent (2009) study in that it did not find a direct path between self-efficacy and job satisfaction. The authors suggest that this is because in Abu Dhabi there was no performance-based pay system, only job tenure determined a teacher's salary; however, recent school reforms have modified this system. In suggesting implications and future directions, this study suggests prioritizing teacher development programs to strengthen skills, but also the necessity of accompanying them with appropriate organizational support.

The JD-R model posits that every job has two classes of characteristics: job demands and job resources. Job demands are the physical, psychological, social, or organizational aspects of the job that require physical or psychological effort (costs). Job resources are the physical, psychological, social, or organizational aspects of the job that are needed to achieve work goals, reduce job demands and the related costs, and stimulate personal growth and development (Bakker & Demerouti, 2014).

The basic premise of the JD-R model is that these two categories of work characteristics induce two relatively independent psychological processes that impact teachers' well-being: an energetic or health impairment process, in which high job demands exhaust mental, physical, and emotional resources leading to ill health and burnout; and a motivational process, in which job resources foster growth, learning, and development and influence teachers to achieve their work goals, which in turn leads to work engagement (absorption, vigor, and dedication). Thus job resources can buffer the impact of high job demands, as they provide support for the realization of the highly demanding work activities involved in the teaching profession (Bakker & Demerouti, 2014).

The JD-R model has been supported in a number of studies. For example, in an effort to examine the energetic process of the JD-R model, researchers surveyed 697 Italian teachers looking to identify the determinants of teachers' well-being (Guglielmi, Panari, & Simbula, 2012). The study looked at mental fatigue as a mediator between three job demands of teachers (workload, inequity, and work/family conflict) and three consequences of stress (psychological, physical symptoms, and work satisfaction). The results confirmed that mental fatigue has a mediating role.

In another test of the JD-R, Simbula (2010) examined whether the daily fluctuations of co-worker support and the daily fluctuations of work/family conflict would predict day levels of job satisfaction and mental health through work engagement and exhaustion. A total of 61 Italian teachers completed a general questionnaire and daily surveys over five consecutive work days. With regard to the motivational process, social support benefited individual well-being and job satisfaction. The results also confirmed that social support acts as an important job resource because, despite fluctuations daily, it was shown to relate to work engagement, job satisfaction, and mental health. Teachers who reported receiving adequate support from colleagues were more likely to be engaged, and in turn they reported more job satisfaction and better mental health. With regard to the health impairment (energetic) process, the results confirmed that teachers who were unable to manage their family and teacher roles were more likely to be exhausted, which negatively affected their job satisfaction.

SDT (Deci & Ryan, 2000) is particularly salient from the perspective of positive psychology. SDT suggests that people inherently possess a need to grow personally and gain fulfillment; people are actively directed toward gaining mastery over challenges and taking in new experiences. According to the theory, this dynamic is essential for developing a cohesive sense of self and eudaimonic well-being. While many people are motivated to act by external rewards such as money and acclaim (extrinsic motivation), SDT focuses on internal sources of motivation such as independence and a need to gain knowledge (intrinsic motivation). SDT suggests that teachers, like other workers, have basic human needs that must be met to achieve this growth. The three essential needs are: competence – the need to gain mastery and understanding of one's environment and develop the needed skills; connection or relatedness – a universal need to belong and have an attachment to other people and to experience caring for others; and autonomy – the sense that one is in control of one's own behavior and goals. Deci and Ryan (2000) argued that in the work environment, job resources support the worker's pursuit of need fulfillment through their work activity and, as such, are essential. Although growth is a basic human drive, they hold that it does not happen automatically; rather, social support is the key. Through relationships and interactions with others, we can either build or stunt well-being and personal growth. Applying the theory to the teaching domain argues strongly for supplying resources that not only balance the job's demands, but stimulate growth so that teachers can thrive.

In a study testing the application of SDT, researchers in Israel (Eyal & Roth, 2011) found that leadership styles of school principals (heads) greatly impacted teachers' motivation and well-being. The researchers concluded that if school principals are delegated power and trained to be autonomy supportive towards their teachers, then the teachers demonstrate increased autonomous motivation, satisfaction, and well-being, perceiving their engagement in various tasks as interesting and meaningful. As a further benefit, Roth, Assor, Kanat-Maymon, and Kaplan (2007) found that autonomous motivation was negatively related to burnout and that teachers' autonomous motivation toward teaching predicted students' autonomous motivation toward learning.

A further SDT study hypothesized that, at the momentary level, self-concordance buffers the negative impact of work demands on happiness (Tadić, Bakker, & Oerlemans, 2013). Using diaries, 132 teachers participated for three consecutive work days. Results partially explained why teachers can remain happy and satisfied in their work even though they simultaneously report high levels of stress. When there is self-concordance motivation, which comes from one's authentic choices, personal values, and interests, teachers remain happy even during stressful tasks. Positive motivation and the sense that one is in control of one's own behavior and goals, as SDT posits, increases well-being and averts burnout.

Finally, the theory of flow (Csikszentmihalyi, 1975/2000) describes an experiential state of deep absorption in the present moment that is intrinsically rewarding, promotes growth, and can give value and meaning to one's experiences, thus increasing eudaimonic well-being. Flow theory suggests that people experience an extreme form of well-being when engaged in highly challenging tasks, but their resources and skills must be equal to the challenge of that task. The conditions for flow, or optimal human experience, include: perceived challenges, or opportunities for action, that stretch (neither overmatching nor underutilizing) existing skills; a sense that one is engaging challenges at a level appropriate to one's capacities; and clear proximal goals and immediate feedback about the progress being made. Under these conditions one enters a subjective state with the following characteristics: intense and focused concentration on what one is doing in the present moment, merging actions and awareness, loss of reflective self-consciousness, a sense that one can control one's actions, distortion of temporal experience, and experiencing the activity as intrinsically rewarding. Because the flow state is intrinsically rewarding, individuals seek to replicate and enhance flow experiences. As individuals seek to master new challenges, they develop greater levels of skills. Once mastered, they seek progressively more complex challenges, thus fostering growth (e.g., Jones, 2013), in line with the eudaimonic perspective on well-being.

Considerable research has been conducted applying the theory of flow to educators. Descriptively, teaching in the classroom and individual work such as lesson preparation (two core aspects of the teaching role) were identified as the main contexts for experiencing flow at work by a sample of 184 teachers in Italy (Bassi & Delle Fave, 2012). In terms of occupational differences in flow, in two studies conducted in Spain university lecturers reported experiencing flow at work as much as managers did, and both university lecturers and secondary school teachers reported experiencing flow more than production workers (Llorens, Salanova, & Rodríguez, 2013; Salanova Martinez, Cifre, & Schaufeli, 2005, cited in Llorens et al., 2013). In contrast, flow was associated with work (vs. other activities, notably leisure) by fewer teachers than physicians in a study in Italy (Delle Fave & Massimini, 2003).

It has been suggested that an essential goal of teaching is to cultivate students' love of learning and this is fostered by teachers' own experience of joy in learning (Csikszentmihalyi, 1997; Nakamura & Csikszentmihalyi, 2005). Both teachers and faculty appear to find flow in learning. Delle Fave and Massimini (2003) found that teachers most often mentioned reading as a source of flow. Neumann (2006) distilled descriptions of flow from interviews with 40 U.S. professors about their scholarly work. Teachers' frequency of flow has been shown to correlate with the proportion of their students who are cognitively engaged (Basom & Frase, 2004; cf. Bakker, 2005).

Researchers have identified factors that make it more likely teachers will experience flow. In several studies, teachers perceived relatively high skill and challenge in their work, and perceiving high challenge and high skill was associated with experiencing flow (Bakker, 2005; Bassi & Delle Fave, 2012; Beard & Hoy, 2010; Rodríguez-Sánchez, Salanova, Cifre, & Schaufeli, 2011). Beyond proximal conditions, in U.S. studies teachers' frequency of flow experience was associated with their perception of the effectiveness of their school and fellow teachers and with the frequency of classroom visits by the school head (Basom & Frase, 2004). In the JD-R research cited earlier (Bakker, 2005), job resources of music teachers in the Netherlands, including autonomy, social support, performance feedback, and supervisory coaching, were associated with flow. Consistent with prediction, the impact of job resources on teachers' experience of flow was mediated by the perceived balance of challenge and skill. The study of teachers in Spain (Salanova, Bakker, & Llorens, 2006) also found an association between organizational resources and flow. The resources included goal-directedness, social support, and an orientation toward innovation.

Finally, the longitudinal study conducted in Spain provided evidence of an "upward spiral" in which available personal and organizational resources were associated with flow at work, and flow at work was associated with subsequent levels of resources (Rodríguez-Sánchez et al., 2011; Salanova et al., 2006).

External or Organizational Resources

Consistent and central across the theoretical frameworks regarding teacher well-being is the necessity of having resources to meet the significant challenges associated with teaching. We will look at various resources cited in the literature as contributors to teacher well-being. Resources can be external and organizational, such as having a supportive climate in which teachers perceive they have autonomy and development opportunities. They can also include procedural and distributive justice, where teachers feel that the decision-making process is fair and transparent and that rewards are given based on individual merit and responsibility. Important additional resources include internal or personal ones such as optimism and resilience.

Turning first to external resources, insight into the relationship between several organizational resources and teacher well-being was demonstrated in a large online survey study of Croatian university teachers (Slišković, Seršić, & Burić, 2011). Specifically, the researchers examined the relationship between distinct sources of occupational stress, work locus of control (control over and possibility of decision-making about events in the workplace), and well-being. They considered the importance of a supportive environment and feeling control over one's work environment. Difficulty teaching students (e.g., due to lack of motivation or interest) and poor relationships with colleagues, supervisors, and/or mentors (e.g., excessive power of supervisor) were found to have direct negative effects on job satisfaction. However, these relationships were further explained by teachers' perception of work locus of control. Interpersonal pressures related to relationships with students and colleagues were found to impact job satisfaction indirectly, via work locus of control. In other words, the association between poor interpersonal relationships at work and job satisfaction can be partially explained by the perception of lack of control and decision-making in the workplace.

In another study, Turkish elementary school teachers' perceptions about quality of school life and supportive environment along with burnout levels were examined as predictors of subjective well-being (Cenkseven-Onder & Sari, 2009). The Quality of School Life Scale (QSLS) assessed teachers' perceptions of their administrator, status, other teachers, student–student relationships, curriculum, and affect toward school. The Teacher Burnout Scales provided data on perceived administrative support, career satisfaction, attitudes toward students, and ability to cope with job-related stress. In general, results revealed that teachers' subjective well-being was predicted by their perceptions of status, the administrator, the curriculum, other teachers, affects toward the school, and their ability to cope with job-related stress. These findings suggest several different routes for improving teacher well-being. The significance of a teacher's perceptions of interpersonal relationships with other teachers suggests creating a work environment conducive to positive relationships that bring about development and growth.

Job enrichment occurs when employees are able to gain more self-sufficiency, responsibility, achievement, and control over the tasks they perform (Riches, 1993). Rashid and Rashid (2011) investigated the role of job enrichment factors in faculty job satisfaction in a sample of Pakistani academic faculty members. Specifically, they looked at the factors of responsibility, achievement, and career development (i.e., opportunities for promotion and professional development). While career development was not found to be a significant predictor (possibly due to an overall lack of it), faculty members' perceived levels of responsibility and achievement were positively and significantly related to their job satisfaction.

Du, Lai, and Lo (2010) investigated the relationship between job satisfaction of Chinese university professors and the organizational characteristics of the university. Organizational climate was found to be a strong and significant predictor of job satisfaction. Specifically, greater participation in both school policymaking and curriculum development led to higher job satisfaction. Furthermore, interpersonal relationships were also found to impact faculty job satisfaction. If professors felt that staff–professor coordination was good, then they experienced greater satisfaction. In a study of school culture in China (Zhu, Devos, & Li, 2011), goal orientation, leadership, and shared vision affected teacher commitment to a large degree. This finding further credits the importance of organizational resources and the impact of school leadership and teacher participation on commitment and teacher well-being.

Internal or Personal Resources

In addition to organizational and environmental resources, teachers draw on personal resources. Personal resources are those psychological underpinnings that help a teacher to more easily adapt to change and demands (Hobfoll, 2002). For example, optimism and resilience were found to be personal characteristics that can contribute to the reduction of stress at work (van den Heuvel, Demerouti, Bakker, & Schaufeli, 2010). Resilience refers to one's ability to "bounce back" despite being continuously exposed to stressors and adversity (Tugade & Fredrickson, 2004). Optimism can be described as a generalized expectation of positive events and outcomes in one's life (Scheier, Carver, & Bridges, 2001). Resilient and optimistic individuals possess personal strengths that allow them to view their environment positively in a more active way. In the workplace, resilient and optimistic people have been found to perceive job demands as challenges rather than as threats (Scheier, Carver, & Bridges, 1994). Their positive view has even been demonstrated to register less perceived demands at work (Lazarus & Folkman, 1984).

In a study testing an integrated model of psychological health at work (Boudrias et al., 2011), researchers in France found that personal resources show important direct and indirect impact on teachers' psychological health. They measured well-being, satisfaction of needs, individual resources of optimism and resilience, social organizational resources, and job demands. School teachers with high levels of optimism and resilience tended to perceive the demands of their jobs as less taxing. These individuals perceived more social-organizational resources and also took more personal action to make sure their needs were met. To see if the results of this study generalized across cultures, the researchers then asked Canadian teachers to complete the same questionnaires (Boudrias et al., 2011). Results from structural equation modeling analyses showed that the studies' findings were invariant across the two samples from different cultures, thus verifying and extending the original study's findings.

In terms of teachers' personal resources for experiencing flow at work, a longitudinal study of 258 secondary school teachers in Spain showed a relationship between teacher self-efficacy and flow, mediated by the combination of perceived challenges and skills (Rodríguez-Sánchez et al., 2011; cf. Basom & Frase, 2004). Relatedly, academic optimism – one element of which is teacher self-efficacy – was related to flow at work in a sample of 260 U.S. elementary school teachers, while dispositional optimism was not (Beard & Hoy, 2010).

Given the constant challenges teachers face, such as high workload, lack of control, and emotional exhaustion, the role of resilience was examined in another study. Pretsch, Flunger, and Schmitt (2012) tested whether resilience would predict well-being (i.e., job satisfaction, general health perception) above and beyond neuroticism in a sample of teachers and non-teachers. The findings showed that among teachers, resilience was a better predictor of general health perception than neuroticism; however, job satisfaction was explained equally well by both resilience and neuroticism.

In a further study of personal resources, Parker and Martin (2009) examined the roles of coping and buoyancy in predicting teacher well-being. They found that "direct" coping strategies, such as mastery orientation and planning, predicted high levels of buoyancy (everyday resilience), well-being, and engagement. They also reported that "palliative" coping strategies, such as self-handicapping and failure avoidance, predicted low levels of these measures.

Beyond these oft-studied personal resources, a major initiative in positive psychology was to develop a classification of strengths and virtues that contribute to optimal human development and, therefore, may function as a personal resource for teachers. The Values in Action (VIA) Classification of Strengths and Virtues provides a vocabulary and framework for understanding positive human strengths – what people do well. The strengths are classified under six overarching virtues: wisdom/knowledge, courage, humanity, justice, temperance, and transcendence (Seligman, Park, & Peterson, 2004).

Studies have found that certain character strengths positively relate to life satisfaction (Park, Peterson & Seligman, 2004), and when individuals' signature strengths are used in new ways as interventions they can increase happiness (Seligman, Steen, Park, & Peterson, 2005). In a study of Chinese school teachers, the researcher examined the relationship between subjective well-being and the 24 VIA character strengths (Chan, 2009). The courage strengths of integrity, bravery, persistence, and zest, as well as the specific strengths of forgiveness, hope, self-regulation, and love of learning, were all associated strongly with the three components of subjective well-being. Additionally, the transcendence strengths (appreciation of beauty, gratitude, hope) seemed to add significantly to greater life satisfaction, while the wisdom/knowledge (creativity, curiosity, open-mindedness, love of learning, perspective) and justice (fairness, leadership, teamwork) strengths added significantly to the experience of more positive emotions.

In contrast to a large Internet sample of adults in the UK (Linley et al., 2007), this sample of Chinese teachers seemed to endorse the humanity (kindness, love, social intelligence) and the transcendence domains (hope, gratitude, appreciation of beauty) to a greater degree, and reported higher levels of the specific strengths of love, hope, gratitude, teamwork, and spirituality. Per Park and Peterson's (2008) explanations of the individual character strengths, these specific strengths suggest that these teachers valued close relations with others, expected the best and worked to achieve it, were aware of and thankful for good things that happen, worked well as members of a group or team, and had coherent beliefs about the higher purpose and meaning of life – all seemingly key characteristics for teachers to cultivate and embrace.

In a further study, Chan (2013a) examined the joint contribution of two specific character strengths – gratitude and forgiveness – to teachers' subjective well-being. The two are conceptually linked as prosocial, relational, and empathy-based character strengths that are closely associated with both psychological and physical health (Breen, Kashdan, Lenser, & Fincham, 2010). Furthermore, the combination of the two character strengths has particular relevance and potential in Chinese society due to Confucian teachings that emphasize both. In the Chan study, a sample of Chinese school teachers completed five self-report questionnaires including the gratitude questionnaire. Above and beyond the contributions of the orientations to happiness (known to be associated with subjective well-being [Vella-Brodrick, Park & Peterson, 2009]), both gratitude and forgiveness were found to be strong and significant predictors of teachers' life satisfaction and positive affect. Furthermore, forgiveness contributed significantly to the prediction of negative affect, far above all other predictors. While forgiveness could help reduce the harmful consequences of teachers' interpersonal conflicts through the reduction of negative emotions, gratitude could assist teachers in savoring the benefits from their relations with others and enhancing the positive emotions felt.

In addition to focusing on character strengths that encourage well-being, studies have also examined individual personality characteristics that are associated with well-being and also function as personal resources. In a study of Norwegian high school teachers, the extent to which teacher and school socio-demographic characteristics (e.g., age, tenure, school location, school size), organizational climate (e.g., work demands, goal congruence), and personality traits (neuroticism and extraversion) were related to a teacher's subjective well-being (PANAS) was examined. Multilevel analyses, with teachers grouped within rural, suburban and city school locations, indicated that it was personality that was most strongly associated with employee well-being. Specifically, extraversion was associated with positive affect, while neuroticism was associated with negative affect. These findings suggest teachers have some control over their well-being: the less easily upset and emotionally reactive, and more sociable and outgoing, they can be, the greater their well-being – unsurprising given the interpersonal nature of their work (Burns & Machin, 2013).

Corroborating these findings, Albuquerque, de Lima, Matos, and Figueiredo (2012) found that for a sample of Portuguese primary and high school teachers, the personality facets of extraversion, neuroticism, and conscientiousness differentially predicted the three components of teachers' subjective well-being. Results revealed that neuroticism facets were the strongest predictors of negative affect, but were also strongly associated with positive affect and life satisfaction. Extraversion and conscientiousness facets were the most related to positive affect, but still significantly related to negative affect, and life satisfaction to a lesser degree. Given these results, all aspects of teacher's subjective well-being may benefit from lessening neuroticism and increasing extraversion and conscientiousness.

The Mindset of Engagement

The underlying attitude with which teachers approach their work influences their performance, their sense of well-being, and the meaning they attach to their pursuits. As posited in the theories and documented in the empirical research, the intense challenges faced by teachers must be balanced with productive and consistently available resources. One of the major impacts of availability of resources is its influence on the mindset of the teachers. The ideal attitude is one of engagement, defined as a positive, fulfilling, work-related mind-set that is characterized by vigor, dedication, and absorption (Bakker, Hakanen, Demerouti, & Xanthopoulou, 2007). Vigor in this context relates to high energy levels and mental focus while working, and the willingness to invest effort in one's work even when facing difficulty. Dedication refers to feeling a sense of significance, pride, challenge, and enthusiasm for one's work. The third aspect, absorption, is characterized by the feeling of full concentration on one's work and being happily engrossed, during which time flies by and one has difficulty stopping work. This dimension mirrors the positive psychology construct of flow.

Looking at work engagement, in a study of 805 Finnish teachers researchers were able to discern that supervisory support, opportunity for innovation, appreciation by colleagues, and a supportive school environment are all considered impactful resources for teachers, because each was shown to buffer the negative impact of pupil misbehavior on teacher engagement (Bakker et al., 2007). Further, they discovered that these job resources are particularly relevant to engagement in times of high stress. They found that the school environment and innovativeness may be crucial for work engagement, because they keep teachers' work interesting and challenging and provide growth opportunities. Their study further confirmed the JD-R model in that it suggested that teachers facing demanding work situations can be helped to be more engaged by providing these resources.

In another study of engagement, the intra-individual relationship between job resources, work engagement, and job performance of Dutch teachers was examined (Bakker & Bal, 2010). Findings showed that weekly job resources can provide motivation and enhance teachers' week-levels of engagement. Week-levels of autonomy and development opportunities were positively related to this and next week's engagement levels. This finding also further supports both the JD-R and the SDT models in showing that a work environment that provides appropriate and supportive resources creates confidence in teachers that their goals can be accomplished and also fulfills their need to belong (Bakker & Demerouti, 2007). This satisfaction of needs increases work engagement in teachers and the study found that it does so on a weekly basis.

Finally, insight into the importance of engagement in teachers is found in a Finnish study that sought to discern what kinds of situations teachers experienced that empowered them and engaged rather than burdened them (Soini, Pyhalto, & Pietarinen, 2010), and what strategies they adopted when challenged that they reported were empowering and engaging. The results showed that the operative situations were interaction with their pupils, their colleagues, and their pupils' parents. While these situations can also burden teachers, it was suggested that flexible and reflective strategies in dealing with challenges on these fronts generated feelings of empowerment and engagement. When the school environment and the interaction between teachers is supportive and collaborative, teachers have the resources they need and their interactions are reported as empowered and engaged.

Interventions

Thus, as the literature vividly demonstrates, empowered and engaged teachers, ones who persist and positively impact the lives of the many students they teach, are teachers whose jobs challenge them enough to keep their creative interests burning and who also possess the needed support and other resources to meet those challenges. Recognizing the importance of this balance, and the assets that allow it to dynamically function, there have been many attempts at planning and implementing interventions. Interventions can take the form of primary, secondary, and tertiary levels (Cartwright & Cooper, 2005). Primary interventions focus on eliminating sources of work stress or modifying the workplace environment, while secondary interventions focus on developing the personal resources of individuals to arm them with tools to prevent stress overload or improve their coping mechanisms. Tertiary interventions deal with the rehabilitation of individuals who have already suffered stress-related health problems. From a positive psychology vantage point, secondary interventions hold particular promise.

For example, in an intervention study designed to investigate the impact of a gratitude program on the life satisfaction and burnout of Hong Kong Chinese school teachers, the "count-your-blessings" exercise was shown to be an effective strategy (Chan, 2013a). The count-your-blessings approach (Emmons & McCullough, 2003) required teachers to record a weekly log of three good things or events that happened to them during the week and then reflect on them with three Naikan-meditation like questions (e.g., "What did I receive and what did the receiving tell about me?") for an 8-week time period. A pre-test and a post-test questionnaire were completed that included the Satisfaction with Life Scale as a measure of well-being (Diener, Emmons, Larsen, & Griffin, 1985) and the three components of the Maslach Burnout Inventory (Maslach et al., 1996). Significant increases in life satisfaction and sense of personal satisfaction were observed, as well as significant decreases in emotional exhaustion and depersonalization. Furthermore, at pre-test, teachers were asked to complete the three orientations to happiness scales (Peterson, Park, & Seligman, 2005) – the life of pleasure, meaning, and engagement scales – to assess their views on happiness. A significant interaction was found between the meaningful-life orientation and the intervention, such that those teachers who placed more value on the meaningful life as contributing to happiness had greater changes in life satisfaction and emotional exhaustion throughout the 8-week intervention. These findings suggest that interventions targeting both weekly gratitude and meaning in life could be effective in combating teacher burnout.

As an extension of the previous study, Chan (2013b) conducted a follow-up study that included two 8-week positive intervention approaches with the goal of promoting subjective well-being – the coping approach (count-your-misfortunes condition) and the gratitude approach (count-your blessings condition). Hong Kong Chinese school teachers were randomly assigned to the two conditions. Teachers in the gratitude approach condition would focus on journaling the good things or events that happened to them in that past week, while teachers in the coping approach condition would focus on bad things or events. The two groups again used three Naikan-meditation-like questions to reflect on their experiences. However, in the gratitude approach condition, teachers concentrated on the benefits they received and on cultivating appreciation and gratitude, whereas in the coping approach condition, teachers concentrated on finding benefits and the lessons they learned from the bad or adverse events. While both the gratitude and coping approaches resulted in increased life satisfaction, only the gratitude approach led to statistically significant changes in life satisfaction and in the experience of negative emotions. This study suggests that counting misfortunes, as well as counting blessings, could be successful in enhancing life satisfaction, although the meaning-making, gratitude approach appears more effective than the benefit-finding, coping approach.

Also in Hong Kong, 50 primary and secondary teachers participated in a study assessing the effectiveness of a stress management training program that focused on teaching recovery strategies (Siu, Cooper, & Phillips, 2014). This entailed learning to participate in meaningful activities outside of work. This exercise encourages periods of psychological detachment from work and participating in mastering experiences that do not involve teaching. The study used a quasi-experimental method with a control group, using a pre- and post-test design. Teachers in the experimental group scored significantly higher in recovery experiences (mastery) compared to the control group. They also scored higher on positive emotions, lower on emotional exhaustion, and reported fewer physical and/or psychological symptoms. The implications of this study include the findings that recovery experiences can be trained by teaching strategies. Learning nonwork new skills leading to a feeling of mastery is a personal resource that can be developed. This study corroborates the recent study on recovery in the United States (Hahn, Binnewies, Sonnentag, & Mojza, 2011).

A study analyzing the relationship between outcomes of teacher well-being and the implementation of school-wide positive behavioral interventions and supports (SWPBIS) was conducted at elementary schools in Oregon (Ross, Romer, & Horner, 2012). This intervention is designed to improve school climate and social behavior through the implementation of various support resources. The intervention worked on, among many other resources, the development of team skills, collaboration, positive relationships, and the use of effective practices. When 184 teachers completed a 54-item survey that covered aspects of the school-wide interventions, results indicated strong relationships between SWPBIS implementation and teacher perceptions of efficacy and well-being. An interesting further finding was that the well-being of teachers in schools of lower economic status may benefit the most from this type of intervention.

Mindfulness interventions build on the personal resource of present-moment awareness and have been successfully utilized to reduce work-related stress. A mixed-method study in Germany examined the outcomes of a mindfulness-based intervention for teachers (Taylor et al., 2015). In it, 59 public school teachers participated in pre- and post-training, and follow-up interviews. The training included increasing their efficacy for regulating emotion on the job, improving their coping skills, improving their efficacy for forgiving colleagues and students, and increasing their capacity to feel compassion. Results showed that efficacy beliefs and the tendency to forgive improved for teachers, and partially mediated reductions in stress from baseline to a 4-month follow-up. Teachers also reported utilizing more adaptive strategies for coping.

A recent study in the United States reports results from a randomized controlled pilot trial of a modified Mindfulness-Based Stress Reduction course (mMBSR) adapted specifically for teachers (Flook, Goldberg, Pinger, Bonus, & Davidson, 2013). Results suggest that the course may be a promising intervention, with participants showing significant reductions in psychological symptoms and burnout, improvements in observer-rated classroom organization and performance on a computer task of affective attentional bias, and increases in self-compassion.

In a quantitative study in Wales investigating the effect of teaching a mindfulness-based stress relief course to primary school teachers, researchers measured its effect on anxiety, depression, and stress, as well as movement toward a stated goal and changes in awareness (Gold et al., 2010). The results showed statistically significant improvement for most participants and also an increase in mindfulness skills inventory. This study adds further corroboration that mindfulness interventions for teachers are a productive and beneficial tool that can positively impact teacher well-being.

Teacher Mentoring

Finally in our review of intervention strategies, we now turn to an examination of mentoring, one of the more widely utilized, easily adapted, and flexible intervention programs for teachers. Because of its broad appeal and potential for mentors to function as a source of referrals to other resources needed by teachers and faculty, an in-depth review of this important intervention is warranted. As previous sections showed, teaching holds promise of great satisfaction, but its considerable challenges, especially during the early career, can be hard to navigate. Attention has been devoted to identifying possible supports for early-career educators that may smooth the transition. One intervention fostered in many countries as a component of teacher induction, and to a lesser extent faculty development, is the formal mentoring program. This section addresses mentoring in and beyond the field of education and indicates what is known about its impact on teacher and faculty well-being. Supporting the relevance of mentoring to worker well-being, Allen, Eby, Poteet, Lentz, and Lima (2004) conducted a meta-analysis of organizational studies examining both objective and subjective benefits of being mentored and concluded that "the most consistent benefits of mentoring may be the impact on affective reactions to the workplace and positive psychological feelings regarding one's career" (p. 133).

Mentoring occurs in many contexts and definitional consensus is lacking within as well as across contexts. Eby, Rhodes, and Allen (2007) suggested that five defining features apply to mentoring at work: there is (1) a dyadic relationship, (2) characterized by learning and

(3) defined by the "types of support [centrally, psychosocial and instrumental] provided by the mentor to the protégé"; the relationship is (4) "reciprocal, yet asymmetrical … the primary goal is protégé growth and development" and it (5) changes over time (p. 10).

One key distinction is between informal, spontaneously occurring mentor–protégé relationships, and the formal, organizationally initiated ones intended to institutionalize and broaden access to the benefits of mentoring. A second distinction is between the goals of providing support to the individual (mentee well-being may be a closely associated outcome) and strengthening the profession or organization by reducing attrition (mentee well-being may be a mediator).

Because mentoring occurs in different contexts, takes different forms, and may serve different goals in different fields, caution is called for in drawing on knowledge about mentoring outside education. However, as others have noted (e.g., Ghosh, 2013; Zellers, Howard, & Barcic, 2008), the field of education should not ignore organizational studies, in which knowledge about mentoring began early (e.g., Kram, 1985) and is more fully developed (see Passmore, Peterson, & Freire, 2013 for a wide-ranging review on mentoring). Major differences from the organizational context are the greater emphasis on formal mentoring and the goal of reducing early-career attrition, in the mentoring of teachers.

Concerning the benefits of mentoring in work organizations and focusing specifically on protégé well-being, systematic reviews suggest that mentoring at work has modest but consistent associations with positive outcomes (Allen et al., 2004; Dougherty & Dreher, 2007; Kammeyer-Mueller & Judge, 2008). Allen et al. (2004) reported that having a mentor is associated with protégé career satisfaction and career commitment. Further, protégé job and career satisfaction are significantly associated with the *amount* of mentoring that is received. Kammeyer-Mueller and Judge's (2008) meta-analysis showed that small but significant positive relationships between mentoring and both job and career satisfaction persist even when multiple covariates are taken into account. There is some evidence that mentoring fosters positive job attitudes in part by reducing the impact of work role ambiguity and conflict (Lankau, Carlson, & Nielson, 2006).

Relevant to the teacher attrition problem, Allen et al. (2004) also examined research on intention to stay with an organization, finding a significant positive association with mentoring. Longitudinal studies of other occupations have linked mentoring to both intentions to continue and (negatively) actual turnover (Higgins & Thomas, 2001; Payne & Huffman, 2005). Payne and Huffman's longitudinal study of a large sample of army officers highlighted the significance of worker well-being in this context, finding that affective commitment to the workplace partially mediated the impact of mentoring on turnover.

Organizational researchers traditionally have focused on naturally occurring, informal mentoring relationships. In general, based on longitudinal as well as correlational research, they have concluded that naturally occurring relationships are more beneficial than those established as part of formal mentoring programs (e.g., Tong & Kram, 2013; Underhill, 2006). However, some reasons for the differences seem remediable, including the lower frequency of contact, lack of participant input into the pairings made, and obligatory nature of participation that can characterize formal programs. Increasingly, research and evaluation aim to identify characteristics of effective programs. For example, in a randomized controlled trial, Egan and Song (2008) found that with respect to job satisfaction and other work outcomes, the participants in a facilitated formal program benefited more than those in an unfacilitated program (both benefited more than those in the control group).

Turning to early-career benefits of being mentored that focus specifically on the field of education, modest associations with well-being are also found for teachers and faculty.

In a study in Israel (Alhija & Fresko, 2010), for example, the formal mentoring received during the teachers' first year in the classroom correlated with their satisfaction with socialization. Similarly, in a survey of female faculty in the United States (August & Waltman, 2004), mentoring (formal or informal) was a marginally significant predictor of satisfaction among untenured faculty, while it was not a significant predictor for tenured faculty.

Correlational research has also linked mentoring to novice educators' sense of self-efficacy at work. In a U.S. survey of junior medical faculty, Feldman, Arean, Marshall, Lovett, and O'Sullivan (2010) found that having a mentor (formal or informal) was associated with self-efficacy. Among student teachers (Moulding, Stewart, & Dunmeyer, 2014), extent of perceived support from the formal workplace mentor correlated with self-efficacy.

In a survey of faculty in the Netherlands (van Emmerik, 2004a), having a mentor (formal or informal) showed small but significant relations with intrinsic job satisfaction, career satisfaction, and (negatively) burnout, over and above other factors. In addition, having a mentor buffered the impact of role conflict on work satisfaction and there was some evidence that it also moderated the impact on burnout.

With respect to teachers, formal mentoring programs have been incorporated into the induction process in many countries since the 1980s (Hobson, Ashby, Malderez, & Tomlinson, 2009; Howe, 2006). Based on an analysis of exemplary teacher induction programs in eight countries, Howe (2006) concluded that the most effective programs include the use of expert mentors. Features associated with effective programs include setting clear program goals and evaluating program effectiveness, establishing methods for selecting, training, and supporting mentors, matching mentors with teacher-mentees, emphasizing support (rather than assessment) of the mentee, and arranging regular meetings of the dyads (Hobson et al., 2009; Howe, 2006). Given the strong interest in formal programs that provide mentoring, it is not surprising that there is also growing interest in formal mentor training. It has been suggested that mentor training programs should present a conceptual model of mentoring and mentoring functions (e.g., definition, philosophy, aims, roles and responsibilities, organizational considerations), provide experience using effective mentoring practices, and formalize support for new mentors (Garvey & Westlander, 2013). Similar features appear to characterize effective faculty mentoring programs (Lumpkin, 2011).

As noted, a major goal of formal teacher mentoring programs in the United States and other countries has been improved retention (Hobson et al., 2009). Regarding retention concerns, Ingersoll and Strong (2012) reviewed U.S. research and found that among the strongest predictors of continuation beyond the first year was having a mentor who was teaching the same subject. Ingersoll and Strong (2011) also examined studies of programs in three U.S. states and reported that mentoring affected new teachers' job satisfaction as well as their commitment to continuing in the teaching profession.

Finally, because organizational research tends to show that formal mentoring is less effective than organically formed relationships (see, e.g., Baugh & Fagenson-Eland, 2007), comparison of how teachers perceive formal and informal mentors is instructive. Desimone et al. (2014) found that student teachers reported interacting more often with their informal mentors, getting more emotional support from them, and viewing these relationships as somewhat more positive. However, they also viewed the relationships with their formal mentors as very positive. In addition, formal mentors provided more lesson observation/feedback, one of the mentoring functions most valued by new teachers (Hobson et al., 2009); thus, in some respects, the two relationships may be complementary.

Given barriers to forming and sustaining traditional mentor/protégé dyadic relationships, the most frequently mentioned being lack of time on both sides (Ehrich, Hansford, & Tennent, 2004), other possible kinds of developmental relationships have been discussed. For new faculty, distributing the role across multiple mentors may be an effective substitute for a single sustained mentoring relationship (de Janasz & Sullivan, 2004; van Emmerik, 2004b). This alternative also may accommodate rising institutional mobility in academia. Illustrating the other end of the spectrum is the position that to be beneficial, teacher-mentoring must be embedded within an "integrated professional culture" (Kardos & Johnson, 2007). Research indicates that the various supports for new teachers do tend to co-occur empirically (Ingersoll & Strong, 2012) and a collegial school context benefits both mentors and mentees (Hobson et al., 2009).

Although serving as a formal mentor has potential dangers for teachers, notably work overload and attendant stress, educators frequently report benefiting from the role. Hobson et al. (2009) reviewed the literature on the rewards that teachers report deriving from being a mentor. In terms of well-being, self-reported benefits included pride and satisfaction in contributing to mentees' development, enhanced confidence, and renewed professional commitment.

This is supported by a larger body of organizational research. In addition to possible objective outcomes of being a mentor (gains in expertise, productivity, career success), Ghosh and Reio's (2013) meta-analysis indicates that being a mentor (vs. not) – and more specifically providing psychosocial support and role modeling to one's mentees – is associated with job satisfaction and organizational commitment. Chun, Sosik, and Yun (2012) found longitudinal effects on mentors' organizational commitment in a sample of Korean white-collar workers. Such research is needed to clarify to what extent worker well-being is enhanced by being a mentor, and to what extent positive feelings about one's job and workplace make one more inclined to mentor others. Less ambiguous is the contribution of being a mentor to mentors' feelings of personal satisfaction, meaning and purpose, and generativity or sense of contribution to future generations (Allen, Poteet, & Burroughs, 1997; Nakamura, Shernoff, & Hooker, 2009).

Mentoring is not a panacea. Its potential for harm as well as benefit has been documented (Tong & Kram, 2013), and measured benefits for mentee and mentor well-being are typically moderate. With respect to formal mentoring programs, more research is needed to identify effective practices and moderators of their effect on teacher/faculty well-being, and to compare the costs and benefits of mentoring programs to other forms of support. Nevertheless, mentoring has shown great promise as an intervention in diverse cultural contexts.

Future Research

While the education literature contains considerable research on how teachers burn out, there is relatively little available on how to engage teachers to prevent burnout. Further, within the current educator well-being literature, there are studies documenting support for enhancing well-being and engaging teachers, but at the faculty level, more research is needed. Addressing that gap is particularly important, given the benefits of designing programs that provide resources to foster fully engaged, top-performing educators at the higher education level.

Further research is needed to define those resources that best support educators as they tackle the inherent challenges in their demanding jobs. This should include examining organizational structures, policies, and environmental resources that support well-being, and also further examining the roles personal resources play. Here positive psychology offers many relevant constructs as yet relatively unexplored in educational contexts, such as organizational virtuousness and job crafting. Academic institutions would be well served by initiating and documenting varied experiential interventions. Additionally, research on teacher and faculty well-being needs to involve investigations into various forms of secondary interventions that will help teachers to buffer the stress, meet the challenges, and thrive in worthwhile and meaningful careers. Moreover, longitudinal studies are needed to measure how the benefits of interventions and training are sustained or depleted over time. In the mentoring arena, more research is needed to identify the different means by which informal mentoring and formal mentoring foster teacher well-being; formal programs then might be designed that glean the benefits of informal mentoring.

In sum, it would be instructive to see research directed toward further identification and enhancement of those practices, policies, personal qualities, leadership styles, and other factors that not only allow, but encourage, the teaching profession to thrive.

Conclusion

In concluding our chapter on well-being, we note again that teachers and faculty are important because of the work they do, because "they transform individual lives and improve the quality of life of the entire society" (Johnsrud, 2008, p. 489). Across cultures, their pivotal role and contributions are documented, along with the heavy demands they face and the lack of respect they perceive. We have demonstrated that to avoid "burnout," to fully thrive in their positions, teachers and faculty must deeply and fruitfully engage. We examined relevant theories and models and explored existing empirical research that tests both hedonic and eudaimonic well-being precursors. Theory and research we have reviewed suggest that the important and dynamic states of teacher and faculty well-being are a reflection of the adequacy of resources available to meet the significant challenges of the profession. Those resources have been shown to be both external or organizational and internal or personal, and a number of interventions designed to protect and promote those resources were reviewed.

There are some specific indications for action that emanate from this review. For example, based on the findings in several studies, suggestions for university management include: involving faculty members in decision-making processes, especially aspects that impact them directly; awarding faculty with acknowledgment and incentives; and ensuring adequate funds are set aside to support career development programs. Other efforts should be expended to ensure teachers have developed personal resources, such as optimism and resilience, that can help buoy them against the known stress of their position. To support well-being, mentoring programs could be instituted to help alleviate the pervasive stress found in the first few years of a teacher's career.

Finally, in an article celebrating deeply engaged faculty members, author Eugene Rice (1986) highlights 50 professors who were nominated by their institution presidents and faculty leaders. It is a diverse group, recipients of major awards, and all sharing in the joys of teaching and a lifetime of learning. Not surprisingly, these engaged and highly motivated educators see their job as one of motivation, to help others to learn and live full lives. They are deeply convinced that their teaching has significance in contexts far beyond their classrooms and further that their professional lives have meaning. It is this powerful feeling of engagement that we must strive to promote and enhance in our teachers so that those in the position of teaching can also inspire.

References

Adams, H. (1999). *The education of Henry Adams* [Online ed]. Retrieved from http://www.bartleby.com/159/20.html

Albuquerque, I., de Lima, M. P., Matos, M., & Figueiredo, C. (2012). Personality and subjective well-being: What hides behind global analyses? *Social Indicators Research, 105*(3), 447–460.

Alhija, F. N., & Fresko, B. (2010). Socialization of new teachers: Does induction matter? *Teaching and Teacher Education, 26*, 1592–1597.

Allen, T. D., Eby, L. T., Poteet, M. L., Lentz, E., & Lima, L. (2004). Career benefits associated with mentoring for protégés: A meta-analytic review. *Journal of Applied Psychology, 89*, 127–136.

Allen, T. D., Poteet, M. L., & Burroughs, S. M. (1997). The mentor's perspective: A qualitative inquiry and future research agenda. *Journal of Vocational Behavior, 51*, 70–89.

August, L., & Waltman, J. (2004). Culture, climate, and contribution: Career satisfaction among female faculty. *Research in Higher Education, 45*, 177–192.

Badri, M. A., Mohaidat, J., Ferrandino, V., & El Mourad, T. (2013). The social cognitive model of job satisfaction among teachers: Testing and validation. *International Journal of Educational Research, 57*, 12–24.

Bakker, A. B. (2005). Flow among music teachers and their students: The crossover of peak experiences. *Journal of Vocational Behavior, 66*, 26–44.

Bakker, A. B., & Bal, P. M. (2010). Weekly work engagement and performance: A study among starting teachers. *Journal of Occupational and Organizational Psychology, 83*(1), 189–206.

Bakker, A. B., & Demerouti, E. (2007). The job demands-resources model: State of the art. *Journal of Managerial Psychology, 22*(3), 309–328.

Bakker, A. B., & Demerouti, E. (2014). Job demands-resources theory. In P. Y. Chen & C. L. Cooper (Eds.), *Work and wellbeing* (Vol. *3*, pp. 37–64). Oxford, UK: Wiley-Blackwell.

Bakker, A. B., Demerouti, E., de Boer, E., & Schaufeli, W. B. (2003). Job demands and job resources as predictors of absence duration and frequency. *Journal of Vocational Behavior, 62*(2), 341–356.

Bakker, A. B., Hakanen, J. J., Demerouti, E., & Xanthopoulou, D. (2007). Job resources boost work engagement, particularly when job demands are high. *Journal of Educational Psychology, 99*(2), 274–284.

Bakker, A. B., & Schaufeli, W. B. (2000). Burnout contagion processes among teachers. *Journal of Applied Social Psychology, 30*(11), 2289–2308.

Bardo, P. (1979). The pain of teacher burnout: A case history. *Phi Delta Kappan, 61*(4), 252–254.

Bartlett, S. J. (1994). The psychology of faculty demoralization in the liberal arts: Burnout, acedia, and the disintegration of idealism. *New Ideas in Psychology, 12*(3), 277–289.

Basom, M. R., & Frase, L. (2004). Creating optimal work environments: Exploring teacher flow experiences. *Mentoring & Tutoring: Partnership in Learning, 12*, 241–258.

Bassi, M., & Delle Fave, A. (2012). Optimal experience among teachers: New insights into the work paradox. *The Journal of Psychology: Interdisciplinary and Applied, 146*, 533–557.

Baugh, S. G., & Fagenson-Eland, E. A. (2007). Formal mentoring programs: A "poor cousin" to informal relationships? In B. R. Ragins & K. E. Kram (Eds.), *The handbook of mentoring at work* (pp. 249–272). Thousand Oaks, CA: Sage.

Beard, K. S., & Hoy, W. K. (2010). The nature, meaning, and measure of teacher flow in elementary schools: A test of rival hypotheses. *Educational Administration Quarterly, 46*(3), 426–458.

Ben-Ari, R., Krole, R., & Har-Even, D. (2003). Differential effects of simple frontal versus complex teaching strategy on teachers' stress, burnout, and satisfaction. *International Journal of Stress Management, 10*(2), 173–195.

Boudrias, J., Desrumaux, P., Gaudreau, P., Nelson, K., Brunet, L., & Savoie, A. (2011). Modeling the experience of psychological health at work: The role of personal resources, social-organizational resources, and job demands. *International Journal of Stress Management, 18*(4), 372–395.

Breen, W. E., Kashdan, T. B., Lenser, M. L., & Fincham, F. D. (2010). Gratitude and forgiveness: Convergence and divergence on self-report and informant ratings. *Personality and Individual Differences, 49*(8), 932–937.

Burke, R. J., & Greenglass, E. R. (1995). A longitudinal study of psychological burnout in teachers. *Human Relations, 48*(2), 187–202.

Burns, R. A., & Machin, M. A. (2013). Employee and workplace well-being: A multi-level analysis of teacher personality and organizational climate in Norwegian teachers from rural, urban and city schools. *Scandinavian Journal of Educational Research, 57*(3), 309–324.

Cartwright, S., & Cooper, C. (2005). Individually targeted interventions. In J. Barling, E. Kelloway, & M. Frone (Eds.), *Handbook of work stress* (pp. 607–623). Thousand Oaks, CA: Sage.

Cenkseven-Onder, F., & Sari, M. (2009). The quality of school life and burnout as predictors of subjective well-being among teachers. *Educational Sciences: Theory and Practice, 9*(3), 1223–1235.

Chan, D. W. (2009). The hierarchy of strengths: Their relationships with subjective wellbeing among Chinese teachers in Hong Kong. *Teaching and Teacher Education, 25*(6), 867–875.

Chan, D. W. (2013a). Counting blessings versus misfortunes: Positive interventions and subjective well-being of Chinese school teachers in Hong Kong. *Educational Psychology, 33*(4), 504–519.

Chan, D. W. (2013b). Subjective well-being of Hong Kong Chinese teachers: The contribution of gratitude, forgiveness, and the orientations to happiness. *Teaching and Teacher Education, 32*, 22–30.

Chun, J. U., Sosik, J. J., & Yun, N. Y. (2012). A longitudinal study of mentor and protégé outcomes in formal mentoring relationships. *Journal of Organizational Behavior, 33*, 1071–1094.

Connolly, J. J., & Viswesvaran, C. (2000). The role of affectivity in job satisfaction: A meta-analysis. *Personality and Individual Differences, 29*(2), 265–281.

Cordova, D. I., & Lepper, M. (1996). Intrinsic motivation and the process of learning: Beneficial effects of contextualization, personalization, and choice. *Journal of Educational Psychology, 88*(4), 715–730.

Csikszentmihalyi, M. (1975/2000). *Beyond boredom and anxiety.* San Francisco, CA: Jossey-Bass.

Csikszentmihalyi, M. (1997). Intrinsic motivation and effective teaching: A flow analysis. In J. L. Bess (Ed.), *Teaching well and liking it: Motivating faculty to teach effectively* (pp. 72–89). Baltimore, MD: Johns Hopkins University Press.

Deci, E. L., & Ryan, R. M. (2000). The "what" and "why" of goal pursuits: Human needs and the self-determination of behavior. *Psychological Inquiry, 11*(4), 227–268.

Deci, E. L., & Ryan, R. M. (2008). Hedonia, eudaimonia, and well-being: An introduction. *Journal of Happiness Studies, 9*(1), 1–11.

de Janasz, S. C., & Sullivan, S. E. (2004). Multiple mentoring in academe: Developing the professorial network. *Journal of Vocational Behavior, 64*, 263–283.

Delle Fave, A., & Massimini, F. (2003). Optimal experience in work and leisure among teachers and physicians: Individual and bio-cultural implications. *Leisure Studies, 22*, 323–342.

Delle Fave, A., Massimini, F., & Bassi, M. (2011). *Psychological selection and optimal experience across cultures: Social empowerment through personal growth.* New York, NY: Springer.

Desimone, L. M., Hochberg, E. D., Porter, A. C., Polikoff, M. S., Schwartz, R., & Johnson, L. J. (2014). Formal and informal mentoring: Complementary, compensatory, or consistent? *Journal of Teacher Education, 65*, 88–110.

Diener, E. (2000). Subjective well-being: The science of happiness and a proposal for a national index. *American Psychologist, 55*(1), 34–43.

Diener, E., Emmons, R. A., Larsen, R. J., & Griffin, S. (1985). The Satisfaction with Life Scale. *Journal of Personality Assessment, 49*(1), 71–75.

Diener, E., & Lucas, R. E. (1999). Personality and subjective well-being. In D. Kahneman, E. Diener, & N. Schwarz (Eds.), *Well-being: The foundations of hedonic psychology* (pp. 213–229). New York, NY: Russell Sage Foundation.

Dougherty, T. W., & Dreher, G. F. (2007). Mentoring and career outcomes. In B. R. Ragins & K. E. Kram (Eds.), *The handbook of mentoring at work* (pp. 51–93). Thousand Oaks, CA: Sage.

Du, P., Lai, M., & Lo, L. K. (2010). Analysis of job satisfaction of university professors from nine Chinese universities. *Frontiers of Education in China, 5*(3), 430–449.

Duckworth, A. L., Quinn, P. D., & Seligman, M. P. (2009). Positive predictors of teacher effectiveness. *The Journal of Positive Psychology, 4*(6), 540–547.

Duffy, R. D., & Lent, R. W. (2009). Test of a social cognitive model of work satisfaction in teachers. *Journal of Vocational Behavior, 75*(2), 212–223.

Eby, L. T., Rhodes, J. E., & Allen, T. D. (2007). Definition and evolution of mentoring. In T. D. Allen & L. T. Eby (Eds.), *The Blackwell handbook of mentoring* (pp. 7–20). New York, NY: Wiley.

Edelwich, J., with Brodsky, A. (1980). *Burn-out: Stages of disillusionment in the helping professions.* New York, NY: Human Science Press.

Education Week. (2009). *The Obama Education Plan: An Education Week guide.* San Francisco, CA: Jossey-Bass.

Egan, T. M., & Song, Z. (2008). Are facilitated mentoring programs beneficial? A randomized experimental field study. *Journal of Vocational Behavior, 72,* 351–362.

Ehrich, L. C., Hansford, B. C., & Tennent, L. (2004). Formal mentoring programs in education and other professions: A review of the literature. *Educational Administration Quarterly, 40,* 518–540.

Emmons, R. A., & McCullough, M. E. (2003). Counting blessings versus burdens: An experimental investigation of gratitude and subjective well-being in daily life. *Journal of Personality and Social Psychology, 84*(2), 377–389.

Erikson, E. H. (1950). *Childhood and society,* New York, NY: Norton.

Erikson, E. H. (1959). *Identity and the life cycle: Selected papers.* Oxford, UK: International Universities Press.

Eyal, O., & Roth, G. (2011). Principals' leadership and teachers' motivation: Self-determination theory analysis. *Journal of Educational Administration, 49*(3), 256–275.

Feldman, M. D., Arean, P. A., Marshall, S. J., Lovett, M., & O'Sullivan, P. (2010). Does mentoring matter? Results from a survey of faculty mentees at a large health sciences university. *Medical Education Online, 15,* 1–8.

Flook, L., Goldberg, S. B., Pinger, L., Bonus, K., & Davidson, R. J. (2013). Mindfulness for teachers: A pilot study to assess effects on stress, burnout, and teaching efficacy. *Mind, Brain, and Education, 7*(3), 182–195.

Fowers, B. J., Mollica, C. O., & Procacci, E. N. (2010). Constitutive and instrumental goal orientations and their relations with eudaimonic and hedonic well-being. *The Journal of Positive Psychology, 5*(2), 139–153.

Freudenberger, H. (1974). Staff burnout. *Journal of Social Issues, 30,* 150–166.

Friedman, I. A. (2000). Burnout in teachers: Shattered dreams of impeccable professional performance. *Journal of Clinical Psychology, 56*(5), 595–606.

Garvey, R., & Westlander, G. (2013). Training mentors: Behaviors which bring positive outcomes in mentoring. In J. Passmore, D. B. Peterson, & T. Freire (Eds.), *The Wiley-Blackwell handbook of the psychology of coaching and mentoring* (pp. 243–265). Oxford, UK: Wiley.

Ghosh, R. (2013). Mentors providing challenge and support: Integrating concepts from teacher mentoring in education and organizational mentoring in business. *Human Resource Development Review, 12,* 144–176.

Ghosh, R., & Reio, T. G. (2013). Career benefits associated with mentoring for mentors: A meta-analysis. *Journal of Vocational Behavior, 83,* 106–116.

Goddard, R., O'Brien, P., & Goddard, M. (2006). Work environment predictors of beginning teacher burnout. *British Educational Research Journal, 32*(6), 857–874.

Gold, E., Smith, A., Hopper, I., Herne, D., Tansey, G., & Hulland, C. (2010). Mindfulness-Based Stress Reduction (MBSR) for primary school teachers. *Journal of Child and Family Studies, 19*(2), 184–189.

Gonzalez, S., & Bernard, H. (2006). Academic workload typologies and burnout among faculty in Seventh-Day Adventist colleges and universities in North America. *Journal of Research on Christian Education, 15*(1), 13–37.

Gove, M. (2013). *The importance of teachers.* Retrieved from https://www.gov.uk/government/speeches/michael-gove-speaks-about-the-importance-of-teaching

Guglielmi, D., Panari, C., & Simbula, S. (2012). The determinants of teachers' well-being: The mediating role of mental fatigue. *European Journal of Mental Health, 7*(2), 204–220.

Hahn, V. C., Binnewies, C., Sonnentag, S., & Mojza, E. J. (2011). Learning how to recover from job stress: Effects of a recovery training program on recovery, recovery-related self-efficacy, and well-being. *Journal of Occupational Health Psychology, 16,* 202–216.

Hamann, D, L., & Daugherty, E. (1984). Teacher burnout: The cost of caring. *UPDATE, 2*(3), 7–10.

Higgins, M. C., & Thomas, D. A. (2001). Constellations and careers: Toward understanding the effects of multiple developmental relationships. *Journal of Organizational Behavior, 22,* 223–247.

Hobfoll, S. E. (2002). Social and psychological resources and adaptation. *Review of General Psychology*, *6*(4), 307–324.
Hobson, A. J., Ashby, P., Malderez, A., & Tomlinson, P. D. (2009). Mentoring beginning teachers: What we know and what we don't. *Teaching and Teacher Education*, *25*, 207–216.
Howe, R. E. (2006). Exemplary teacher induction: An international review. *Educational Philosophy and Theory*, *38*, 287–297.
Huta, V., & Ryan, R. M. (2010). Pursuing pleasure or virtue: The differential and overlapping well-being benefits of hedonic and eudaimonic motives. *Journal of Happiness Studies*, *11* (6), 735–762.
Ingersoll, R., & Strong, M. (2011). The impact of induction and mentoring programs for beginning teachers: A critical review of the research. *Review of Educational Research*, *81*, 201–233.
Ingersoll, R., & Strong, M. (2012). What the research tells us about the impact of induction and mentoring programs for beginning teachers. *Yearbook of the National Society for the Study of Education*, *111*, 466–490.
Jackson, L. B., Rothmann, S., & van de Vijver, F. R. (2006). A model of work-related well-being for educators in South Africa. *Stress and Health: Journal of the International Society for the Investigation of Stress*, *22*(4), 263–274.
Jennings, P. A. & Greenberg, M. T. (2009). The prosocial classroom: Teacher social and emotional competence in relations to student and classroom outcomes. *Review of Educational Research*, *79*(1), 491–525.
Jiang, Y. (2005). The influencing and effective model of early childhood: Teachers' job satisfaction in China. *US-China Education Review*, *2*(11), 65–74 [online submission].
Johnsrud, L. K. (2008). Faculty work: Making our research matter – more. *The Review of Higher Education*, *31*(4), 489–504.
Jones, J. K. (2013). Re-discovering the arts: The impact of engagement in a natural environment upon pre-service teacher perceptions of creativity. *Thinking Skills and Creativity*, *8*, 102–108.
Kammeyer-Mueller, J. D., & Judge, T. A. (2008). A quantitative review of mentoring research: Test of a model. *Journal of Vocational Behavior*, *72*, 269–283.
Kardos, S., & Johnson, S. M. (2007). On their own and presumed expert: New teachers' experience with their colleagues. *The Teachers College Record*, *109*, 2083–2106.
Knoop, H. H. (2011). Education in 2025: How positive psychology can revitalize education. In S. I. Donaldson, M. Csikszentmihalyi, & J. Nakamura (Eds.), *Applied positive psychology: Improving everyday life, health, schools, work, and society* (pp. 97–115). New York, NY: Routledge.
Knoop, H. H. & Delle Fave, A. (2013). *Well-being and cultures: Perspectives from positive psychology* New York, NY: Springer.
Kotre, J. N. (1984). *Outliving the self: How we live on in future generations.* New York, NY: Norton.
Kram, K. E. 1985. *Mentoring at work.* Glenview, IL: Scott, Foresman.
Lankau, M. J., Carlson, D. S., & Nielson, T. R. (2006). The mediating influence of role stressors in the relationship between mentoring and job attitudes. *Journal of Vocational Behavior*, *68*, 308–322.
Lazarus, R. S., & Folkman, S. (1984). *Stress appraisal and coping.* New York, NY: Springer.
Lent, R. W., & Brown, S. D. (2006). Integrating person and situation perspectives on work satisfaction: A social-cognitive view. *Journal of Vocational Behavior*, *69*(2), 236–247.
Lent, R. W., Brown, S. D., & Hackett, G. (1994). Toward a unifying social cognitive theory of career and academic interest, choice, and performance. *Journal of Vocational Behavior*, *45*(1), 79–122.
Lent, R. W., Nota, L., Soresi, S., Ginevra, M. C., Duffy, R. D., & Brown, S. D. (2011). Predicting the job and life satisfaction of Italian teachers: Test of a social cognitive model. *Journal of Vocational Behavior*, *79*(1), 91–97.
Li, Y., Li, J., & Sun, Y. (2013). Young faculty job perceptions in the midst of Chinese higher education reform: The case of Zhejiang University. *Asia Pacific Journal of Education*, *33*(3), 273–294.
Linley, P. A., Maltby, J., Wood, A. M., Joseph, S., Harrington, S., Peterson, C., & … Seligman, M. P. (2007). Character strengths in the United Kingdom: The VIA Inventory of Strengths. *Personality and Individual Differences*, *43*(2), 341–351.
Liu, S., & Onwuegbuzie, A. J. (2012). Chinese teachers' work stress and their turnover intention. *International Journal of Educational Research*, *53*, 160–170.

Llorens, S., Salanova, M., & Rodríguez, A. M. (2013). How is flow experienced and by whom? Testing flow among occupations. *Stress and Health, 29*, 125–137.
Lumpkin, A. (2011). A model for mentoring university faculty. *The Educational Forum, 75*, 357–368.
Maslach, C. (2003). Job burnout: New directions in research and intervention. *Current Directions in Psychological Science, 12*(5), 189–192.
Maslach, C., & Jackson, S. E. (1981). *Maslach Burnout Inventory: "Human Services Survey"* (research ed.). Palo Alto, CA: Consulting Psychologists Press.
Maslach, C., Jackson, S. E., & Leiter, M. P. (1996). *Maslach Burnout Inventory Manual* (3rd ed.). Palo Alto, CA: Consulting Psychologists Press.
Maslach, C., & Leiter, M. P. (1999). Teacher burnout: A research agenda. In R. Vandenberghe & A. M. Huberman (Eds.), *Understanding and preventing teacher burnout* (pp. 296–303). Cambridge, UK: Cambridge University Press.
Maslow, A. H. (1968). *Toward a psychology of being* (2nd ed.). Oxford, UK: Van Nostrand.
McCarthy, C. J., Lambert, R. G., O'Donnell, M., & Melendres, L. T. (2009). The relation of elementary teachers' experience, stress, and coping resources to burnout symptoms. *Elementary School Journal, 109*(3), 282–300.
McKenzie, P., Santiago, P., Sliwka, & Hiroyuki, H. (2005). *Teachers matter: Attracting, developing and retaining effective teachers.* Paris, France: OECD.
Moulding, L. R., Stewart, P. W., & Dunmeyer, M. L. (2014). Pre-service teachers' sense of efficacy: Relationship to academic ability, student teaching placement characteristics, and mentor support. *Teaching and Teacher Education, 41*, 60–66.
Nakamura, J., & Csikszentmihalyi, M. (2005). Engagement in a profession: The case of undergraduate teaching. *Daedalus, 134*, 60–67.
Nakamura, J., & Shernoff, D., with Hooker, C. (2009). *Good mentoring.* San Francisco, CA: Jossey-Bass.
Neumann, A. (2006). Professing passion: Emotion in the scholarship of professors at research universities. *American Educational Research Journal, 43*, 381–424.
OECD (2013). *OECD Teaching and Learning International Survey (TALIS).* Retrieved from http://www.oecd.org/edu/school/talis-2013-results.htm
OECD (2014). *OECD Teaching and Learning International Survey (TALIS).* Retrieved from http://www.oecd.org/newsroom/teachers-love-their-job-but-feel-undervalued-unsupported-and-unrecognised.htm
Park, N., & Peterson, C. (2008). The cultivation of character strengths. In M. Ferrari & G. Potworowski (Eds.), *Teaching for wisdom: Cross-cultural perspectives on fostering wisdom* (pp. 59–77). New York, NY: Springer.
Park, N., Peterson, C., & Seligman, M. P. (2004). Strengths of character and well-being. *Journal of Social and Clinical Psychology, 23*(5), 603–619.
Parker, P. D., & Martin, A. J. (2009). Coping and buoyancy in the workplace: Understanding their effects on teachers' work-related well-being and engagement. *Teaching and Teacher Education: An International Journal of Research and Studies, 25*(1), 68–75.
Passmore, J., Peterson, D., & Freire, T. (Eds.) (2013). *The Wiley-Blackwell handbook of the psychology of coaching and mentoring.* Oxford, UK: Wiley-Blackwell.
Patrick, B. C., Hisley, J., & Kempler, T. (2000). "What's everybody so excited about?": The effects of teacher enthusiasm on student intrinsic motivation and vitality. *Journal of Experimental Education, 68*(3), 217–236.
Payne, S. C., & Huffman, A. H. (2005). A longitudinal examination of the influence of mentoring on organizational commitment and turnover. *Academy of Management Journal, 48*, 158–168.
Peterson, C., Park, N., & Seligman, M. P. (2005). Orientations to happiness and life satisfaction: The full life versus the empty life. *Journal of Happiness Studies, 6*(1), 25–41.
Pretsch, J., Flunger, B., & Schmitt, M. (2012). Resilience predicts well-being in teachers, but not in non-teaching employees. *Social Psychology of Education, 15*(3), 321–336.
Purvanova, R. K., & Muros, J. P. (2010). Gender differences in burnout: A meta-analysis. *Journal of Vocational Behavior, 77*(2), 168–185.
Rashid, U., & Rashid, S. (2011). The effect of job enrichment on job satisfaction: A case study of faculty members. *Interdisciplinary Journal of Contemporary Research in Business, 3*(4), 106–117.

Rice, E. (1986). Those who gladly serve. *Change*, *18*(4), 12–20.
Riches, V. C. (1993). *Standards of work performance: A functional assessment and training manual for training people with disabilities for employment.* Baltimore, MD: Paul H. Brookes.
Rodríguez-Sánchez, A., Salanova, M., Cifre, E., & Schaufeli, W. B. (2011). When good is good: A virtuous circle of self-efficacy and flow at work among teachers. *Revista de Psicología Social*, *26*, 427–441.
Rogers, C. (1961). *On becoming a person.* Oxford, UK: Houghton Mifflin.
Ross, S. W., Romer, N., & Horner, R. H. (2012). Teacher well-being and the implementation of school-wide positive behavior interventions and supports. *Journal of Positive Behavior Interventions*, *14*(2), 118–128.
Roth, G., Assor, A., Kanat-Maymon, Y., & Kaplan, H. (2007). Autonomous motivation for teaching: How self-determined teaching may lead to self-determined learning. *Journal of Educational Psychology*, *99*(4), 761–774.
Ryan, R. M., & Deci, E. L. (2001). On happiness and human potentials: A review of research on hedonic and eudaimonic well-being. *Annual Review of Psychology*, *52*, 141–166.
Ryan, R. M., Huta, V., & Deci, E. L. (2008). Living well: A self-determination theory perspective on eudaimonia. *Journal of Happiness Studies*, *9*(1), 139–170.
Ryff, C. D. (1989). Happiness is everything, or is it? Explorations on the meaning of psychological well-being. *Journal of Personality and Social Psychology*, *57*(6), 1069–1081.
Salanova, M., Bakker, A. B., & Llorens, S. (2006). Flow at work: Evidence for an upward spiral of personal and organizational resources. *Journal of Happiness Studies*, *7*, 1–22.
Schaufeli, W. B., Maslach, C., & Marek, T. (1993). *Professional burnout: Recent developments in theory and research.* Philadelphia, PA: Taylor & Francis.
Scheier, M. F., Carver, C. S., & Bridges, M. W. (1994). Distinguishing optimism from neuroticism (and trait anxiety, self-mastery, and self-esteem): A reevaluation of the Life Orientation Test. *Journal of Personality and Social Psychology*, *67*(6), 1063–1078.
Scheier, M. F., Carver, C. S., & Bridges, M. W. (2001). Optimism, pessimism, and psychological well-being. In E. C. Chang (Ed.), *Optimism and pessimism: Implications for theory, research, and practice* (pp. 189–216). Washington, DC: American Psychological Association.
Schwartz, J. E., Pickering, T. G., & Landsbergis, P. A. (1996). Work-related stress and blood pressure: Current theoretical models and considerations from a behavioral medicine perspective. *Journal of Occupational Health Psychology*, *1*(3), 287–310.
Seligman, M. P. (2002). *Authentic happiness: Using the new positive psychology to realize your potential for lasting fulfillment.* New York, NY: Free Press.
Seligman, M. P., Park, N., & Peterson, C. (2004). The Values in Action (VIA) classification of character strengths. *Ricerche Di Psicologia*, *27*(1), 63–78.
Seligman, M. P., Steen, T. A., Park, N., & Peterson, C. (2005). Positive psychology progress: Empirical validation of interventions. *Tidsskrift For Norsk Psykologforening*, *42*(10), 874–884.
Simbula, S. (2010). Daily fluctuations in teachers' well-being: A diary study using the job demands-resources model. *Anxiety, Stress & Coping: An International Journal*, *23*(5), 563–584.
Siu, O. L., Cooper, C. L., & Phillips, D. R. (2014). Intervention studies on enhancing work well-being, reducing burnout, and improving recovery experiences among Hong Kong health care workers and teachers. *International Journal of Stress Management*, *21*(1), 69–84.
Slišković, A., Seršić, D. M., & Burić, I. (2011). Work locus of control as a mediator of the relationship between sources and consequences of occupational stress among university teachers. *Review of Psychology*, *18*(2), 109–118.
Soini, T., Pyhalto, K., & Pietarinen, J. (2010). Pedagogical well-being: Reflecting learning and well-being in teachers' work. *Teachers and Teaching: Theory and Practice*, *16*(6), 735–751.
Stenlund, K. V. (1995). Teacher perceptions across cultures: The impact of students on teacher enthusiasm and discouragement in a cross-cultural context. *Alberta Journal of Educational Research*, *41*(2), 145–161.
Sutton, R. E., & Wheatley, K. F. (2003). Teachers' emotions and teaching: A review of the literature and directions for future research. *Educational Psychology Review*, *15*(4), 327–358.
Tadić, M., Bakker, A. B., & Oerlemans, W. M. (2013). Work happiness among teachers: A day reconstruction study on the role of self-concordance. *Journal of School Psychology*, *51*(6), 735–750.

Taylor, C., Harrison, J., Haimovitz, K., Oberle, E., Thomson, K., Schonert-Reichl, K., & Roeser, R. W. (2015). Examining ways that a mindfulness-based intervention reduces stress in public school teachers: A mixed-methods study. *Mindfulness*, *7*(1), 115–129.

Thoresen, C. J., Kaplan, S. A., Barsky, A. P., Warren, C. R., & de Chermont, K. (2003). The affective underpinnings of job perceptions and attitudes: A meta-analytic review and integration. *Psychological Bulletin*, *129*(6), 914–945.

Tong, C., & Kram, K.E. (2013). The efficacy of mentoring: The benefits for mentees, mentors, and organizations. In J. Passmore, D. B. Peterson, & T. Freire (Eds.), *The Wiley-Blackwell handbook of the psychology of coaching and mentoring* (pp. 217–242). Oxford, UK: Wiley-Blackwell.

Tugade, M. M., & Fredrickson, B. L. (2004). Resilient individuals use positive emotions to bounce back from negative emotional experiences. *Journal of Personality and Social Psychology*, *86*(2), 320–333.

Underhill, C. M. (2006). The effectiveness of mentoring programs in corporate settings: A meta-analytical review of the literature. *Journal of Vocational Behavior*, *68*, 292–307.

Vailliant, G. E., & Milofsky, E. (1980). Natural history of male psychological health: IX. Empirical evidence for Erikson's model of the life cycle. *The American Journal of Psychiatry*, *137*, 1348–1359.

van den Heuvel, M., Demerouti, E., Bakker, A. B., & Schaufeli, W. B. (2010). Personal resources and work engagement in the face of change. In J. Houdmont & S. Leka (Eds.), *Contemporary occupational health psychology: Global perspectives on research and practice* (Vol. *1*, pp. 124–150). Oxford, UK: Wiley-Blackwell.

van Dick, R., & Wagner, U. (2001). Stress and strain in teaching: A structural equation approach. *British Journal of Educational Psychology*, *71*(2), 243–259.

van Emmerik, H. (2004a). For better and for worse: Adverse working conditions and the beneficial effects of mentoring. *Career Development International*, *9*, 358–373.

van Emmerik, H. (2004b). The more you can get the better: Mentoring constellations and intrinsic career success. *Career Development International*, *9*, 578–594.

Vella-Brodrick, D. A., Park, N., & Peterson, C. (2009). Three ways to be happy: Pleasure, engagement, and meaning – Findings from Australian and US samples. *Social Indicators Research*, *90*(2), 165–179.

Vitterso, J. (2013a). Feelings, meanings, and optimal functioning: Some distinctions between hedonic and eudaimonic well-being. In A. S. Waterman (Ed.), *The best within us: Positive psychology perspectives on eudaimonia* (pp. 39–55). Washington, DC: American Psychological Association.

Vitterso, J. (2013b). Functional well-being: Happiness as feelings, evaluations, and functioning. In S. A. David, I. Bonwell, & A. Conley Ayers (Eds.), *The Oxford handbook of happiness* (pp. 227–244). New York, NY: Oxford University Press.

Watts, J., & Robertson, N. (2011). Burnout in university teaching staff: A systematic literature review. *Educational Research*, *53*(1), 33–50.

Xi calls for greater respect for teachers. (2014). Retrieved from http://www.chinadaily.com.cn/china/2014-09/10/content_18570761.htm

Zellers, D. F., Howard, V. M., & Barcic, M. A. (2008). Faculty mentoring programs: Reenvisioning rather than reinventing the wheel. *Review of Educational Research*, *78*, 552–588.

Zhu, C., Devos, G., & Li, Y. (2011). Teacher perceptions of school culture and their organizational commitment and well-being in a Chinese school. *Asia Pacific Education Review*, *12*(2), 319–328.

25

The Well-Being of Information Technology Professionals

Kamlesh Singh and Mohita Junnarkar

Introduction

Globally about a billion people work in information technology (IT), however the sector still faces a shortfall of employees (Young, Marriott, & Huntley, 2008). India has established itself as the premier and de facto location for offshoring activities (National Association of Software and Service Companies and McKinsey & Company, 2005) and its booming IT industries have contributed to the rapid growth of the country's economy since 1990. In 2006, India captured two thirds of the market share in IT development, maintenance, and support. The remaining market was shared by other countries such as Canada, Ireland, China, Vietnam, the Philippines, and Brazil (Tholons Inc., 2006). Global changes and new managerial challenges have motivated organizational researchers to focus on employees' health (physical and mental) and well-being for further investigation.

Employees in many parts of the sector, particularly in the developing economies, face long working hours (up to 14 hours a day; Santhi & Sundar, 2012), which leads to physical health issues such as sleeping disorders, voice loss, ear problems, digestive disorders, sight problems (Kamp, 1992), and psychological distress (Guna Seelan & Ismail, 2008). Employees strive hard to achieve success and organizational objectives, and this affects their physical health, and social and psychological well-being. The dynamic nature of the industry affects employees' well-being through job insecurity and increase in stress levels (Fatimah, Noraisha, Nair, & Khairuddin, 2012).

The empirical evidence indicates that IT employees face mental health and well-being concerns, which are presented in five sections in this chapter. The first section discusses the theoretical construct of well-being and different allied models such as quality of life, job/career satisfaction, and job/career commitment. Secondly, the chapter establishes the linkages between well-being and different job-related factors such as self-efficacy, motivation to work, quality of work life, and work–home balance. The third section deliberates the factors that affect, correlate, and predict the well-being outcomes of IT employees,

The Wiley Blackwell Handbook of the Psychology of Positivity and Strengths-Based Approaches at Work,
First Edition. Edited by Lindsay G. Oades, Michael F. Steger, Antonella Delle Fave, and Jonathan Passmore.

and the fourth section discusses different initiatives that have positively enhanced well-being among IT employees. The penultimate section of the chapter considers the future research agenda for this area, followed by a short conclusion.

The Meaning of Well-Being and Its Factors

In recent years, understanding and exploring the well-being (psychological, social, and emotional) of different sections of society has become a central focus of positive psychology research with the aim of enhancing people's lives (Diener, Suh, Lucas, & Smith, 1999; Kahneman, Diener, & Schwarz, 1999; Linley, Maltby, Wood, Osborne, & Hurling, 2009). The term well-being represents a broader biopsychosocial construct that includes physical, mental, and social well-being, and it is more than the mere avoidance of becoming physically sick (Tehrani, Humpage, Willmott, & Haslam, 2011). Well-being has been defined in several ways such as "ability to fulfil goals" (Foresight Mental Capital and Well-being Project, 2008), "happiness" (Pollard & Lee, 2003), and "life satisfaction" (Diener & Suh, 1998; Seligman, 2002).

Research on well-being is based on two theoretical approaches. The hedonic tradition is focused on feelings of happiness, and the eudaimonic tradition emphasizes optimal functioning in individual and social life. The conceptualization of well-being characterizing the hedonic tradition is also known as subjective well-being, comprising the predominance of positive emotions compared to negative ones (hedonic balance) and cognitive judgment about one's life satisfaction (Diener, et al., 1999; Linley et al., 2009). The eudaimonic tradition encompasses several constructs. The most prominent one is known as psychological well-being. It was initially conceptualized by Ryff (1989) based on the work of humanistic and lifespan psychologists such as Carl Jung, Abraham Maslow, Gordon Allport, Carl Rogers, and Erik Erikson (Lamers, Westerhof, Bohlmeijer, Klooster, & Keyes, 2011). It includes six dimensions: self-acceptance, personal growth, purpose in life, positive relations with others, autonomy, and environmental mastery. Psychological well-being reflects the challenges that individuals encounter as they strive to achieve an optimal level of functioning. Keyes (2002) stated that, when both these traditions of well-being converge, mental health can be globally defined as the presence of emotional, psychological, and social well-being. This definition is in accordance with the definition of the World Health Organization (WHO, 2004). According to WHO, mental health is "a state of well-being in which the individual realizes his or her own abilities, can cope with the normal stresses of life, can work productively and fruitfully and is able to make a contribution to his or her community" (WHO, 2004, p. 12). The definition consists of three core components, namely: well-being, effective functioning in individual life, and effective functioning in community life.

Positive psychology has promoted a shift of focus from negative aspects or what is wrong with people, to positive aspects or what is right with people. Keyes (2005, 2007) proposed a mental health model by analogy with the mental illness model, consisting of a syndrome of symptoms. He also used the term diagnosis to identify mental health categories such as flourishing, moderate mental health, and languishing (Keyes, 2005). In a similar vein, Seligman (2002) indicated three elements of well-being: pleasure, engagement, and meaning. The recent development of this theory decomposes the construct of well-being into five elements which are essential for people to experience lasting happiness, namely: positive emotion, engagement, relationships, meaning, and accomplishment (PERMA; Seligman, 2011).

The application of these positive psychology theories in the work domain led to the development of positive organizational behavior (POB) research, aimed at enhancing the knowledge and investigating the intervention potentials of psychological resources such as hope (Snyder, 2002), resilience (Masten, 2001), optimism (Seligman, 1998), and self-efficacy (Bandura, 1997). Studies in POB research have led to the identification of a higher-order factor comprising the four components mentioned above, and labeled Psychological Capital (PsyCap; Luthans & Youssef, 2007; Larson, Norman, Hughes, & Avey, 2013).

Luthans, Youssef, and Avolio (2007, p. 10) defined PsyCap as:

> an individual's positive psychological state of development … characterized by (1) having confidence (self-efficacy) to take on and put in the necessary effort to succeed at challenging tasks; (2) making a positive attribution (optimism) about succeeding now and in the future; (3) persevering toward goals and, when necessary, redirecting paths to goals (hope); and (4) when beset by problems and adversity, sustaining and bouncing back and even beyond (resilience) to attain success.

A meta-analytic study highlighted that PsyCap was positively correlated with desirable employee attitudes (job satisfaction, organizational commitment, and psychological well-being), desirable employee behaviors (citizenship), and multiple measures of performance (evaluated by the person, the supervisors, and through objective indicators). In contrast, it was negatively correlated with undesirable employee attitudes (cynicism, turnover intentions, job stress, and anxiety) and undesirable employee behaviors (deviance; Avey, Reichard, Luthans, & Mhatre, 2011).

The quality of life model encompasses satisfaction with life and health, social relationships, psychological well-being, physical health, and environmental health (WHO, 1996; Skevington, 2001). This model has been extended to the working class. Quality of work life (QoWL) is the level of happiness or satisfaction with one's career. It also encompasses a relationship between employees and the total working environment that promotes the growth of employees along with organizational growth (Pugalendhi, Umaselvi, & Senthil, 2011; Vijaimadhavan & Raju, 2013a, b). Guna Seelan and Ismail (2008) stated that QoWL is a multidimensional construct that is closely associated with job satisfaction, job involvement, motivation, productivity, health, safety and well-being, job security, competence development, and balance between work and nonwork life. The absence of QoWL results in job dissatisfaction. The QoWL construct considers that people are trustworthy, responsible, and capable of making a valuable contribution to their organization, and that they treat other people too with respect (Vijaimadhavan & Raju, 2013b).

Well-Being and IT Employees

The UK's Chartered Institute for Personnel and Development (CIPD, 2006) stated that well-being at work means creating an environment in the workplace to promote a state of contentment for employees to flourish and achieve their full potential for the benefit of themselves and their organization (Tehrani et al., 2011). According to Easton and Van Laar (2013), well-being is conceptualized as influencing and being influenced by work. Well-being is also conceptualized as a person's overall subjective feeling of good or bad. The spectrum covers a range from positive feelings – such as pleased, satisfied, happy, energetic – to negative feelings – such as sad, depressed, stressed, and anxious (Bogdanova, Enfors, & Namovska, 2008; Vijaimadhavan & Raju, 2013b).

Physically and mentally healthy employees are more likely to engage in work and contribute more at work. Employee engagement is observed to influence employee turnover and absence. Well-being at work entails managing the physical and cultural environment and employees' needs to achieve the optimum level of physical, mental,

Table 25.1 Five domains and elements of well-being.

Domain	*Elements*
Physical	Physical health, mental health, working environment, physical safety, and accommodation
Values	Ethical standards, diversity, psychological contract, and spiritual expression
Personal development	Autonomy, career development, lifelong learning, and creativity
Emotional	Positive relationships, resilience, emotional intelligence, and social responsibility
Work/organization	Change management, work demands, autonomy, and job security

Source: Based on Tehrani et al. (2011).

social, intellectual, and spiritual potential. Therefore, organizations need to actively assist employees to enhance their physical and mental health. The promotion of well-being as a subjective experience involves practical measures such as the introduction of healthy food, gym facilities at the workplace, and organizing workshops for new employees so that organizational values and beliefs and the individual's values and beliefs match. Employee well-being needs to be embedded in the day-to-day business of the organization, (Tehrani et al., 2011). The Canadian Centre for Management Development (2002) stated that employee well-being involves maintaining a healthy body by making healthy lifestyle choices with respect to diet, exercise and leisure, and developing an attitude that will enable employees to enhance self-confidence and self-respect, to become emotionally resilient, to develop a sense of purpose, fulfillment, and meaning, to possess an active mind that is alert, open to new ideas and experiences, curious and creative, and to possess a network of supportive and nurturing relationships.

Tehrani et al. (2011) mentioned that well-being at work consists of five domains: physical, values, personal development, emotional, and work/organization, each with its own elements as illustrated in Table 25.1.

Diedericks and Rothmann (2014) investigated flourishing among information technology professionals. They found that flourishing influenced job satisfaction, organizational commitment, and organizational citizenship behavior directly as well as indirectly. In addition, job satisfaction strongly affected organizational commitment (positively) and turnover intention (negatively), and had a moderate negative effect on counterproductive work behavior. What was also interesting was that flourishing affected turnover intention indirectly and negatively via organizational commitment. These results indicate that flourishing individuals engage in citizenship behavior – that is, they do things for the organization and other individuals outside of the parameters of their jobs – whereas languishing employees engage in less citizenship behavior.

Well-Being and Job-Related Factors

A high QoWL helps to reduce absenteeism, accidents, and attrition and, on the other hand, it improves production, organizational effectiveness, and employee morale (Vijaimadhavan & Raju, 2013b). Mayo (1960) was the first researcher who used the term 'quality of work' in the literature. Subsequently, many researchers have conceptualized and proposed models for QoWL. Hackman and Oldham (1974) suggested that psychological growth is composed of task identity, task significance, autonomy, and feedback, and it is important for any worthwhile attempt to increase QoWL. On the other hand, Taylor, Cooper, and Mumford (1979) suggested that extrinsic factors, such as wages, hours and working conditions, and intrinsic factors associated with the nature of work, such as employee participation in management, fairness, social support, self-development and social relevance, formed the different facets of QoWL. Warr, Cook, and Wall (1979) demonstrated correlations between factors such as work involvement and job satisfaction, intrinsic job motivation and job satisfaction, and perceived intrinsic job characteristics and job satisfaction. As the literature and research in this field has grown, a list of possible sub-factors such as equal employment opportunities, administrative system, work-role ambiguity, turnover intentions, relevance of training, supervision, job enrichment, equitable pay, flexible work schedules, and integrated socio-technical systems have also emerged (Cunningham & Eberle, 1990; Katzell, 1983; Mirvis & Lawler, 1984).

Different models such as the transfer model or spillover effect (Kavanagh & Halpern, 1977), the compensation model (Schmitt & Mellon, 1980), the segmentation model (George & Brief, 1990), and the accommodation model (Lambert, 1990) were studied by Martel and Dupuis (2006) and synthesized in a new conceptualization of QoWL. As the research has unfolded in this area, there have been conceptual refinements that have led to the development of the WRQoL (work-related quality of life) scale. The WRQoL scale seeks to measure the quality of life of employees (Edwards, Webster, Van Laar, & Easton, 2008) through different dimensions such as job and career satisfaction (JCS), general well-being (GWB), stress at work (SAW), control at work (CAW), home–work interface (HWI), and working conditions (WC). In a research study conducted at the University of Huddersfield, UK, by administering the QoWL questionnaire it was demonstrated that healthy well-being and low stress levels among staff improve working practices and encourage changes in Human Resources (HR) to improve management (Wolff, 2009).

Motivation too can be hypothesized to affect the quality of work life. Herzberg, Mausner, and Snyderman (1959) proposed a two-factor theory of motivation. The theory proposes that at work employees have two types of needs: hygiene needs (satisfied by certain conditions called hygiene factors, such as supervision, interpersonal relations, physical working conditions, salary, company policies and administrative practices, benefits, and job security) and motivator needs (achievement, recognition, the work task assigned, responsibility, and advancement). Hygiene factors result in a neutral state of satisfaction, and they do not cause satisfaction or dissatisfaction among employees. In contrast, positive motivator factors contribute to positive gains in job satisfaction.

Thus, the well-being of employees is highly dependent upon their motivation in the work place and their QoWL. However, several factors such as self-efficacy, work–home balance, social environment, physical health, and psychological environment also affect well-being. These are discussed in detail in the next section.

Factors Affecting the Well-Being of IT Professionals

Over a period of years, different studies have identified different constructs of QoWL. For instance, Rose, Beh, Uli, and Idris (2006a) stated that career satisfaction, career achievement, and career balance are significant predictors of the career-related dimensions that affect QoWL. In contrast, in a study of Italian health workers Argentero, Miglioretti, and Angilletta (2007) identified professional relationships, work organization, taking care of patients, professional ability, and professional growth as indicators of QoWL, putting significant emphasis on professional relationships. Reddy and Reddy (2010) suggested health and well-being, job security, job satisfaction, competence development, and balance between work and nonwork life as emerging dimensions of QoWL. Several research studies have employed Walton's eight major conceptual categories: adequate and fair compensation, safe and healthy working conditions, immediate opportunity to use and develop human capacities, opportunity for continued growth and security, social integration in the work organization, constitutionalism in the work organization, work and total life space, and social relevance of work life relating to QoWL (Bolhari, Rezaeean, Bolhari, Bairamzadeh, & Soltan, 2011; Sofi, Razzaghi & Hajelo, 2012; Tabassum, 2012). Swapna and Gomathi (2013) proposed six dimensions for QoWL: job and career satisfaction, working conditions, general well-being, home–work interface/work–life balance, career prospects and compensation, and training development.

Vijaimadhavan and Raju (2013b) undertook an extensive study to identify the factors which influence the quality of the work life of IT professionals. The results of the study indicated that job satisfaction (employee relationships, work nature, job autonomy, and job security), working conditions (work environment, social environment, and psychological environment), general well-being (physical health, depressive symptoms, and work stress), work–life balance (work to family interference and family to work interference), career prospects and compensation (motivation, career satisfaction, interpersonal communication, and efforts by employer), and training and development (training specified to job purpose and self-efficacy) were the components of QoWL. The different dimensions of QoWL are discussed in further detail below.

Employee relationship is correlated with job purpose, job autonomy, work nature, job security, self-efficacy, social environment, motivation, career satisfaction, and efforts by the employer (Erwee, 1990; Vijaimadhavan & Raju, 2013b). Zhang and Huang (2013) stated that close interpersonal relations with managers make subordinates more productive and more willing to accept and give feedback. Interpersonal relationships facilitate developing and maintaining smooth group work, whereas the lack of interpersonal harmony hinders teamwork that requires contribution from all members to achieve organizational objectives.

Work nature is positively correlated with job autonomy, job security, social environment, training specified to job purpose, motivation, career satisfaction, self-efficacy, efforts by the employer, interpersonal communication, physical health, work environment, family to work interference and work to family interference (Vijaimadhavan & Raju, 2013b). Similarly, Erwee (1990) found that the nature of the work had a significant influence on job autonomy. Warr (2010) too reported a positive relationship between job autonomy, job security, specific job purpose competencies, self-efficacy, and work nature.

Job autonomy shows a high and positive correlation with job security, motivation, social environment, career satisfaction, training specified to job purpose, interpersonal communication, self-efficacy, and efforts by the employer, whereas positive moderate correlations were observed with physical health, work environment, and family to work environment. In contrast, a negative correlation was observed between job autonomy and depressive symptoms and work stress (Vijaimadhavan & Raju, 2013b). Holz-Clause, Koundinya, Nancy, and Borich (2012) found that job autonomy and control significantly contribute to sustaining and improving employee contribution to the organization, and job autonomy is also essential for creating a supportive work environment.

Job security is positively correlated with social environment, motivation, career satisfaction, interpersonal communication, training specified to job purpose, efforts by the employer, self-efficacy, physical health, and work environment, and it is negatively correlated with work stress and depressive symptoms (Vijaimadhavan & Raju, 2013b). Job security, especially in the case of women employees, depends on the social environment that includes exposure to and action against harassment, and the issue of giving up leisure time or other activities for work. Sinha (2012) states that even though employers are unable to promise job security, they can aid in maintaining and enhancing the skills that are essential for the job market. It can be noted that job security has a greater impact on the job autonomy of IT professionals. Job security comprises job tenure and the fear of losing one's job. Erwee (1990) too reported a relationship between job security and job autonomy among women employees.

Work environment was correlated positively and moderately with family–work interference, depressive symptoms, physical health, work–family interference, work stress, job purpose-focused training, social environment, self-efficacy, efforts by the employer, motivation, career satisfaction, and interpersonal communication. However, a negative correlation was noted between work environment and psychological environment (Vijaimadhavan & Raju, 2013b). Bogdanova et al. (2008) demonstrated that job performance influenced the work environment. Kiriago and Bwisa (2013), in a study on work environment and its effect on quality of life, demonstrated that poor safety, physical health, work pressure or stress, and provision of inadequate working tools are the environmental aspects that bring about experiences of poor QoWL.

Social environment is positively correlated with job purpose-focused training, motivation, career satisfaction, self-efficacy, efforts by the employer, interpersonal communication, physical health, family–work interference, and work–family interference, and negatively correlated with the social environment and psychological environment (Vijaimadhavan & Raju, 2013b). Such correlations indicate that the work-based identity of the collective labor force has an indirect and significant impact on organizational performance. Ahmad (2011) stated that higher satisfaction and performance of the subordinate depend upon the superior–subordinate relationship, supporting the positive correlation between social environment and training specified to job purpose.

Psychological environment is the set of work environment characteristics that affect how the worker feels, thinks, and behaves (Briner, 2000). Psychological environment was found to be significantly correlated with work–family interference, family–work interference, work stress, depressive symptoms, physical health, job purpose-focused training, motivation, and self-efficacy (Vijaimadhavan & Raju, 2013b). Healthy occupations and workplaces contribute to individual's physical, psychological, and social well-being through benefits such as higher levels of satisfaction, and lowers level of absenteeism and health issues. At the same time, they allow the organization to reduce its turnover and improve employees' job performance (Graham, 2005).

Physical health is one of the most important factors that enhance well-being. Sickness absence rates across sectors are remarkable. In 2013, in the sectors of finance, banking, and insurance, it was estimated that over a 3-month period, sickness absence accounted for 6.1, 7.4, and 7.4 days per employee respectively. Hence, even the proverb "Health is wealth" proves that physical health is important for employees' contribution to an organization. Employees' physical health has an impact on company turnover and customer relations. Physical health is moderately yet significantly correlated with family–work interference, training specified to job purpose, work–family interference, motivation, depressive symptoms, efforts by the employer, self-efficacy, interpersonal communication, work stress, and career satisfaction (Vijaimadhavan & Raju, 2013b). However, contradictory findings were reported in other studies (Beutell, 2010), showing a negative correlation between physical health and family–work interference.

Depressive symptoms are positively correlated with work stress, work–family interference, and family–work interference, but negatively correlated with career satisfaction, interpersonal communication, and efforts by the employer (Vijaimadhavan & Raju, 2013b). Stress is related to a wide variety of health-related problems including anxiety, headaches, depression, influenza, coronary disease, and substance abuse (De Bruin, 2006). In a survey, IT employees reported that they experienced minor health problems (such as sleep problems) that affected their work performance, stress, inability to achieve a work–family balance, inability to overcome difficulties, and depression (Vijaimadhavan & Raju, 2013b).

Work stress is defined as "a situation wherein job-related factors interact with the worker to change (i.e. disrupt or enhance) his or her psychological and/or physiological condition such that the person (i.e. mind–body) is forced to deviate from normal functioning" (Newman & Beehr, 1979, pp. 1–2). Ivancevich and Matteson (1980) defined job stress as "an adaptive response, mediated by individual differences and/or psychological processes, that is a consequence of any external (environmental) action, situation, or event that places excessive psychological and/or physical demands upon a person" (pp. 24–25). Finally, the European Commission (1999) defined work-related stress as "the emotional, cognitive, behavioural and physiological reaction to aversive and noxious aspects of work, work environments and work organizations. It is characterised by high levels of arousal and distress and often by feelings of not coping" (quoted in Levi, 2002, pp. 5). The definition of work-/job-related stress illuminates that stress, as an emotional, cognitive and behavioral response to an event, is highly influenced by a person's adaptive strategies (Sugumar, Kumaran, Raj, & Xavier, 2013). The multiple roles played by an individual in family, work, and community often create conflicting demands and expectations. It can be hypothesized that work stress would follow the law of optimal arousal (Yerkes & Dodson, 1908). This law states that performance increases with physiological or mental arousal up to an optimal point; when the levels of arousal further increase beyond this point, performance decreases. This relationship is represented through an inverted-U-shaped curve. The law finds its application in the context of work stress. A certain level of stress would bring out work efficiency in an employee, but at the same time if the employee's stress crosses his or her optimal threshold level, then work efficiency is likely to decline. Pai, Yeh, and Huang (2012) stated that 40% of IT employees were worried about job security and experienced higher stress levels at work, engaging in long working hours. Moreover, work stress adversely affects the professional commitment of employees. The stress levels were also seen to be higher in females as compared to males. Stress is inversely correlated to work–family interference and family–work interference (Vijaimadhavan & Raju, 2013b). A study conducted among African employees highlighted that respondents aged 26–30 faced stress related to work, behavior, and health, and reported the highest level of stress compared to other age groups, whereas respondents aged 31–35 faced high levels of psychological stress (Sugumar et al., 2013). Gender differences were observed as well; while males reported higher levels of overall stress, females had high levels of psychological stress. In another study, it was observed that inactive participation in the stage of process change caused stress and strain on IT employees and reduced their satisfaction levels (Korunka & Vitouch, 1999). Qualitative data in the form of in-depth interviews confirmed the exposure of IT professionals to a huge amount of work stress that arises from heavy workload, inadequate staffing, role ambiguity which affects their family life, time pressure, role conflict, and a high attrition rate. The employees' coping strategies included involving themselves in some form of recreation that is personally enjoyable or rewarding (Dhar & Dhar, 2010).

Work–family interference positively correlates with family–work interference, training specified to job purpose, motivation, self-efficacy, interpersonal communication, and efforts by the employer (Vijaimadhavan & Raju, 2013b). Work–family and family–work interference is strongly associated with job demands. Another aspect related to this factor is work–life balance, that refers to setting priorities between "work" (career and ambition) on the one hand and "life" (pleasure, leisure, family, and spiritual development) on the other (Santhi & Sundar, 2012). This balance affects employees' attitudes toward their organization and, when achieved to an optimum level, it can enhance their performance at work and at home. As specifically concerns women working in the IT sector, their work–life balance is affected by several factors, such as support system, child care facilities, benefits, relocation, working hours, recreation, and job environment (Santhi & Sundar, 2012).

Family–work interference is correlated positively with specific job purpose-focused training, self-efficacy, motivation, and interpersonal communication (Vijaimadhavan & Raju, 2013b). Especially among female employees, high levels of home pressure, negative feelings, and a lack of autonomy at home were found to affect their work domain (Van Aarde & Mostert, 2008). The energy drained at the workplace does not get replenished at home, giving rise to a vicious cycle of allostatic load.

Motivation is positively correlated with career satisfaction, job purpose-focused training, employer efforts, interpersonal communication, and self-efficacy (Vijaimadhavan & Raju, 2013b), and it strongly contributes to achieving career satisfaction (Adnan & Mubarak, 2010).

Career satisfaction consists of the individual's comparison between his or her career and life expectations and those offered by the work context (Rose, Beh, Uli, & Idris, 2006b). It is significantly and positively correlated with interpersonal communication, training specified to job purpose, efforts by the employer, self-efficacy (Vijaimadhavan & Raju, 2013b), and professional commitment (Pai et al., 2012). Supervisors who have a clear vision and facilitate the acceptance of group goals foster employees' career satisfaction, at the same time enhancing the quality of the relationship between supervisor and employee (Adnan & Mubarak, 2010). Incentives and positive rewards enhance employees' career growth and compensation, as well as supervisors' satisfaction. However, in the case of poor performance, the same factors that enhance career satisfaction may reduce it (Vijaimadhavan & Raju, 2013b). Career satisfaction is considered an indicator of career commitment and turnover among information centers' personnel (Gupta, Guimaraes, & Raghunathan, 1992).

Career commitment is the degree to which someone identifies with and values his or her profession or vocation (Blau & Lunz, 1998). It comprises three components: affective, normative, and continuance commitment (Cho & Huang, 2012). IT professionals need to develop sophisticated expertise that requires them to be constantly devoted to the related activities for a long period of time. Individuals who possess a high career commitment tend to show less intention of leaving their jobs, and they spend more time in developing skills that are reflected in better performance (Wright & Bonett, 2002). However, in the IT sector it is not very easy for employees to commit to their career. Work exhaustion and stress, unexpected ever-changing user demands, unrealistic deadlines, and struggling to keep up with ever-advancing technology are common experiences among IT professionals; these sources of pressure and uncertainty make job commitment difficult (Major, Morganson, & Bolen, 2013; Shih, Jiang, Klein, & Wang, 2013). Shropshire and Kadlec (2012) reported that IT employees who suffer from stress or burnout, or are concerned about the security of their jobs, are more likely to consider a career change. Career commitment is also positively related to job satisfaction (Duffy, Dik, & Steger, 2011; Reid, Riemenschneider, Allen, & Armstrong, 2008) and job involvement (Reid et al., 2008). Fu and Chen (2015) confirmed previous results showing that IT professionals' career commitment is determined by career satisfaction. Loh, Sankar, and Yeong (1995) demonstrated that the relationship between technical orientation and job satisfaction was mediated by professionals' job perception (occupation fairness, occupational advancement prospects, organizational progressiveness posture, and organizational cohesiveness). Among Pakistani IT professionals, it was observed that employees' professional compensation, training and development, and supervisor support were significantly correlated with organizational and career commitment (Naqvi & Bashir, 2015).

Interpersonal communication refers to the quality of interaction and relationships, as well as the employer's efforts toward employees. Conflicts in interpersonal communication may cause lose–lose situations and barriers to global success (Zhang & Huang, 2013). A positive correlation was identified between interpersonal communication and interpersonal relationships, and interpersonal communication and efforts by the employer, specific job purpose-focused training, and self-efficacy (Vijaimadhavan & Raju, 2013b).

Efforts by the employer were found to correlate positively with training specified to job purpose and self-efficacy (Vijaimadhavan & Raju, 2013b). Additional efforts by employers in terms of on-the-job training were shown to influence employees' wage growth and job performance. These results suggest that training efforts undertaken by employers have a positive impact on the job.

Self-efficacy refers to an individual's belief that he or she is capable of performing a task. Self-efficacy is the foundation and motive power in producing and increasing the autonomy of working motivation, and it plays an important role in enhancing human performance (Paraskeva, Mysirlaki, & Choustoulakis, 2009). Although high self-efficacy may lead to high motivation in positive and negative ways, low self-efficacy always leads to low motivation. Higher levels of self-efficacy lead to higher levels of confidence to succeed in a task. Self-efficacious employees are more likely to take efforts to complete a task and will engage in the task for a longer time (Hees, Koeter, de Vries, Ooteman, & Schene, 2010). Individuals who lack self-efficacy in difficult situations are more likely to lessen their effort or give up altogether, while those with high self-efficacy will try harder to master the challenge. Furthermore, it was observed that specific job purpose training was found to be positively correlated with self-efficacy that represents one's own perceived ability to complete tasks and reach goals (Vijaimadhavan & Raju, 2013b). Employees' self-efficacy and level of education play a key role in how employees discharge their duties and responsibilities, and they also affect employees' QoWL (Mensah & Lebbaeus, 2013).

Well-Being Initiatives

Well-being initiatives targeted at employees aim to lower negative well-being facets such as stress, depression, and anxiety, and enhance positive well-being dimensions such as quality of life, social relationships, social well-being, psychological well-being, emotional well-being, physical health, environmental health, self-efficacy, interpersonal communication, and so on. Following Kerr and Boyd (2012), Vijaimadhavan and Raju (2013a) suggested that well-being initiatives could be classified into four categories: HR policy, training programs, corporate social responsibility, and health promotion.

HR policy consists of initiatives aimed at promoting workers' well-being through health and safety improvement measures, career development and talent management, career breaks, flexible working, special leave and child care vouchers, and welfare support services. These initiatives include providing equal opportunities for people with disabilities, preventing bullying and harassment, managing attendance and performance, and conducting staff attitude surveys and stress surveys (Vijaimadhavan & Raju, 2013a).

Training programs include first aid, time management, stress awareness management, assertiveness, people management, leadership development, managing attendance, coaching and mentoring, change management, conflict management, and team building (Vijaimadhavan & Raju, 2013a).

Health promotion includes events and seminars providing information on health promotion, as well as interventions to improve the safety and hygiene of workplaces, and to build exercise or gym spaces (Vijaimadhavan & Raju, 2013a). Sharma and Majumdar (2010) conducted a study showing that to decrease the ailments caused by occupational postures, employees should avoid sitting for long hours, take frequent breaks for walking and stretching, and involve themselves in physical activity.

Corporate social responsibility includes community outreach, blood donation, charitable fundraising, recycling, family days, and sporting events (Vijaimadhavan & Raju, 2013a).

The intervention strategies primarily aim to reduce employees' stress and increase their productivity. The productivity of employees is dependent on their psychosocial well-being. Stress, as reviewed earlier, has adverse effects on employees' physical health, work performance, social life, and relationships with co-workers and family members. Stressors and their consequences need to be understood at both the individual and organizational levels. Since workplace stress incidence is highly common among employees, organizations should undertake initiatives to prevent stress, as well as to train employees through stress reduction techniques. An extensive review article (Deshpande, 2012) highlighted the potential of yoga, meditation, and soothing humor as an antidote to workplace stress. The major outcome of the review was that work-related stressors (interpersonal, role-related, task-control related, and derived from organizational-physical environment), nonwork stressors (time-based, strain-based, role-based, etc.), and individual differences (health, knowledge skills, coping skills, resilience, and work holism) caused stress which was exhibited in the form of physiological problems (heart disease, ulcers, high blood pressure, headaches, sleep disturbance, and increased illness), psychological problems (job dissatisfaction, low commitment, exhaustion, depression, moodiness, and burnout), and behavioral problems (low job performance, more accidents, faulty decisions, higher absenteeism, workplace aggression, and turnover). The practice of coping strategies like yoga, meditation, and soothing behavior at individual and organizational levels benefited the organization by having stress-free employees who could perform better and work harder, were happier than before, and gave long-term commitment to the organization as compared to their counterparts who did not adopt these techniques. Findings showed that yoga, meditation, and soothing behavior promoted feelings of euphoria, tranquility and relaxation, delay in the aging process, increased energy levels, reduced fatigue, decreased anxiety and depression, and improved learning ability and memory among the employees.

Mental health programs aim to reduce stress in the workplace, improve working conditions, and build resilience. Work-based health promotion intervention programs have reduced depression and anxiety among employees. Some of the mental health intervention programs in organizations focus on increasing physical activity, reducing work stress through problem-solving techniques and changes to the work environment, motivational interviewing, improving knowledge in respect of mental health, counseling, and meditation. These interventions bring about positive effects on mental well-being, and contribute to reducing depression and anxiety among employees (City of London Corporation, 2014).

The different well-being initiatives devised by researchers for companies highlight that flexibility, individuality, shared benefits, accountability, values at the workplace (honesty, trust, openness, and justice), positive and open two-way communication, and work with fun and excitement enhance employees' well-being. Well-being does not require big actions or steps to be undertaken by organizations, but small steps based on the holistic approach of catering to the mental, emotional, social, and physical health of employees. When organizational well-being initiatives are translated into expected behavior and actions from the top management of the organization, they are valued and rewarded more by all employees.

Future Research

The current research on the well-being of IT employees focuses on work-related quality of life, stress, organizational climate, job satisfaction, career satisfaction, self-efficacy, work–home balance, social environment, physical health, and psychological environment. As discussed earlier, various models of well-being exist but the work-related quality of life model is extensively researched. However, there is a scarcity of research using recently developed models such as the Mental Health Continuum (MHC) and PERMA in measuring employees' well-being. Future studies need to explore these models of well-being in the IT sector, and to identify correlates and predictors of employees' well-being at the individual, work, and organization levels. Some of the key research gaps in this area are listed below.

1 Identification of factors that have significant impact on employees' well-being, in particular as concerns family environment and organizational climate. These studies would enable the development of relevant coping strategies to enhance both employees' well-being and work performance.
2 Investigation of employees' well-being through the application of new models. The MHC (Keyes, 2005) could be used to understand how flourishing, moderately mentally healthy, and languishing IT professionals perceive career satisfaction, job satisfaction, stress, and working conditions. Related studies could lead to the identification of the different correlates and predictors of emotional, social, and psychological well-being among IT employees. This line of research could also contribute to designing effective intervention models. Through the PERMA model, Seligman (2011) proposed that positive emotion, engagement, relationships, meaning, and accomplishment are essential for people to experience lasting happiness. There is, however, little evidence as regards the contribution of work–home balance, working conditions, job and income satisfaction toward lasting happiness. Future studies could address the importance and effect of these factors on the PERMA components.
3 Development and validation of well-being scales among IT employees. Validation of scales is important to establish the applicability of construct validity in specific populations. However, the papers reviewed in this chapter did not provide information about scale validation. Future studies should address this gap, reporting the psychometric properties of scales administered to IT employees. Moreover, mixed methodology based on the collection of quantitative and qualitative data is currently promoted in psychological research. Such an approach reduces methodological flaws and increases the understanding of the constructs and populations under examination. Empirical studies in the IT domain have so far adopted a quantitative approach. Inclusion of qualitative data would allow for detecting further factors contributing to distress or promoting well-being among employees.
4 Identification of relevant coping strategies and development of interventions that enhance well-being. Even though mindfulness intervention strategies and yoga have been observed to enhance well-being by lowering stress levels, yet more coping strategies need to be implemented to enhance satisfaction and happiness among employees.

Conclusion

Guna Seelan and Ismail (2008) stated that an unstrained work environment ensures good health and psychological conditions that enable employees to perform job-related and non-job-related functions without inhibitions, thus leading to a less stressful work environment. A healthy lifestyle can help to combat stress, depression, and anxiety through a proper balanced diet, physical activity, and attunement with one's biological clock. Vijaimadhavan and Raju (2013b) suggested the relevance of good sleep to employees' health, productivity, and safety. Altogether, from the above review it can be concluded that a variety of factors, ranging from work environment to organizational climate and work–family balance, play an important role in promoting well-being and/or reducing stress in an employee. However, future research with more scientific rigor and exploration of new well-being models would allow us to better delve into this complex issue, and design intervention strategies that may enhance the mental health and well-being of IT employees.

References

Adnan, R., & Mubarak, H. H. (2010). Role of transformational and transactional leadership on job satisfaction and career satisfaction. *Business and Economic Horizons*, *1*(1), 29–38.

Ahmad, K. Z. (2011). Warmth in groups and satisfaction with supervision. *International Journal of Business and Management* *6*(5), 129–134.

Argentero, P., Miglioretti, M., & Angilletta, C. (2007). Quality of work life in a cohort of Italian health workers. *Giornale Italiano di Medicina del Lavoro ed Ergonomia*, *29*(1 Suppl. A), A50–A54.

Avey, J. B., Reichard, R. J., Luthans, F., & Mhatre, K. H. (2011). Meta-analysis of the impact of positive psychological capital on employee attitudes, behaviours and performance. *Human Resource Development Quarterly*, *22*(2), 127–152.

Bandura, A. (1997). *Self-efficacy: The exercise of control.* New York, NY: Freeman.

Beutell, N. J. (2010). Health, supervisory support, and workplace culture in relation to work–family conflict and synergy, 1. *Psychological Reports*, *107*(1), 3–14.

Blau, G. J., & Lunz, M. (1998). Testing the incremental effect of professional commitment on intent to leave one's profession beyond the effects of external, personal, and work-related variables. *Journal of Vocational Behavior*, *52*(2), 260–269.

Bogdanova, A., Enfors, H., & Naumovska, S. (2008). *Work environment stressors: The link between employees' well-being and job performance?* Bachelor thesis, Jönköping International Business School, Jönköping University, Sweden.

Bolhari, A., Rezaeean, A., Bolhari, J., Bairamzadeh, S., & Soltan, A. A. (2011). The relationship between QWL and demographic characteristics of information technology staffs. In *International Conference on Computer Communication and Management: Proceedings of CSIT* (Vol. 5). Singapore: IACSIT Press.

Briner, R. B. (2000). Relationships between work environments, psychological environments and psychological well-being. *Occupational Medicine*, *50*(5), 299–303.

Canadian Centre for Management Development (2002). *A fine balance: A manager's guide to workplace well-being* [online]. Retrieved March 13, 2007, from http://www.csps-efpc.gc.ca/research/publications/pdfs/workplace_e.pdf?bcsi_scan_8CB51C24B19595DD =0&bcsi_scan_filename=workplace_e.pdf

Chartered Institute for Personnel and Development (CIPD) (2006). *Absence management: Annual survey report.* London, UK: Author.

Cho, V., & Huang, X. (2012). Professional commitment, organizational commitment, and the intention to leave for professional advancement: An empirical study on IT professionals. *Information Technology & People*, *25*(1), 31–54.

City of London Corporation in association with Cavill Associates and University of Salford, Manchester (2014). *Best practice in promoting employee health and well-being in the City of London.* London, UK: Author. Retrieved April 1, 2015 from www.cityoflondon.gov.uk/economicresearch

Cunningham, J. B., & Eberle, T. (1990). A guide to job enrichment and redesign. *Personnel*, *67*(2), 56-61.

De Bruin, G. P. (2006). The dimensionality of the general work stress scale: A hierarchical exploratory factor analysis. *SA Journal of Industrial Psychology*, *32*(4), 68.

Deshpande, R. C. (2012). A healthy way to handle work place stress through yoga, meditation and soothing humour. *International Journal of Environmental Sciences*, *2*(4), 2143–2154.

Dhar, R. L., & Dhar, M. (2010). Job stress, coping process and intentions to leave: A study of information technology professionals working in India. *The Social Science Journal*, *47*, 560–577.

Diedericks, E., & Rothmann, S. (2014). Flourishing of information technology professionals: Effects on individual and organizational outcomes. *South African Journal of Business Management*, *45*(1), 27–41.

Diener, E., & Suh, E. M. (1998). Subjective well-being and age: An international analysis. In K. W. Schaie & M. P. Lawton (Eds.), *Annual review of gerontology and geriatrics: Vol. 17. Focus on emotion and adult development* (pp. 304–324). New York, NY: Springer.

Diener, E., Suh, E. M., Lucas, R. E., & Smith, H. E. (1999). Subjective well-being: Three decades of progress. *Psychological Bulletin*, *125*, 276–302.

Duffy, R. D., Dik, B. J., & Steger, M. F. (2011). Calling and work-related outcomes: Career commitment as a mediator, *Journal of Vocational Behavior*, *78*(2), 210–218.

Easton, S., & Van Laar, D. (2013). QoWL (Quality of Working Life): What, how and why? *Psychology Research*, *3*(10), 596–605.

Edwards, J. A., Webster, S., Van Laar, D. L., & Easton, S. (2008). Psychometric analysis of the health and safety executive management standards work-related stress indicator tool. *Work & Stress*, *22*(2), 96–107.

Erwee, R. (1990). Career anchor profiles of a sample of business and professional women. *SA Journal of Industrial Psychology*, *16*(1), 5–12.

Fatimah, O., Noraishah, D., Nasir, R., & Khairuddin, R. (2012). Employment security as moderator on the effect of job security on worker's job satisfaction and well being. *Asian Social Science*, *8*(9), 50–56.

Foresight Mental Capital and Wellbeing Project. (2008). *Final project report.* London, UK: The Government Office for Science.

Fu, J. R., & Chen, J. H. F. (2015). Career commitment of information technology professionals: The investment model perspective. *Information and Management*, *52*, 537–610. http://dx.doi.org 10.1016/j.im.2015.03.005

George, J. M., & Brief, A. P. (1990). The economic instrumentality of work: An examination of the moderating effects of financial requirements and sex on the pay–life satisfaction relationship. *Journal of Vocational Behavior*, *37*(3), 357–368.

Graham, C. (2005). The economics of happiness. *World Economics*, *6*(3), 41–55.

Guna Seelan R., & Ismail, M. (2008). Constructs of quality of work life: A perspective of information and technology professionals. *European Journal of Social Sciences*, *7*(1), 58–70.

Gupta, Y. P., Guimaraes, T., & Raghunathan, T. S. (1992). Attitudes and intentions of information center personnel, *Information & Management*, *22*(3), 151–160.

Hackman, J. R., & Oldham, G. R. (1974). *The job diagnostic survey.* New Haven, CT: Yale University Press.

Hees, H. L., Koeter, M. W. J., De Vries, G., Ooteman, W., & Schene, A. H. (2010). Effectiveness of adjuvant occupational therapy in employees with depression: Design of a randomized controlled trial. *BMC Public Health*, *10*, 558–574.

Herzberg, F., Mausner, B., & Snyderman, B. (1959). *The motivation to work.* New York, NY: Wiley.

Holz-Clause, M. S., Koundinya, V. S. C., Nancy, K., & Borich, T. O. (2012). Employee job autonomy and control in a restructured extension organization. *International Journal of Agricultural Management & Development*, *2*(4), 277.

Ivancevich, J. M., & Matteson, M. T. (1980, Fall). Optimizing human resources: A case for preventive health and stress management. *Organizational Dynamics*, 5–25.

Kahneman, D., Diener, E., & Schwarz, N. (Eds.). (1999). *Well-being: Foundations of hedonic psychology.* New York, NY: Russell Sage Foundation.

Kamp, J. K. S. (1992). *American worker under pressure technical report.* St. Paul, MN: St. Paul Fire and Marine Insurance Company.

Katzell, R. A. (1983). Improving quality of work life. *American Psychologist*, *38*, 126.

Kavanagh, M. J., & Halpern, M. (1977). The impact of job level and sex differences on the relationship between life and job satisfaction. *Academy of Management Journal*, *20*(1), 66–73.

Kerr, R., & Boyd, S. (2012). *Managing employee stress* (North Ireland ed.). Retrieved May 17, 2015 from http://www.managingwellbeing.com/sites/default/files/manage%20employee%20 stress%20(NI).pdf

Keyes, C. L. M. (2002). The mental health continuum: From languishing to flourishing in life. *Journal of Health and Social Behavior*, *43*(2), 207–222.

Keyes, C. L. M. (2005). Mental illness and/or mental health? Investigating axioms of the complete state model of health. *Journal of Consulting and Clinical Psychology*, *73*, 539–548.

Keyes, C. L. M. (2007). Promoting and protecting mental health as flourishing: A complementary strategy for improving national mental health. *American Psychologist*, *62*, 95–108.

Kiriago, A. N., & Bwisa, H. M. (2013). Working environment factors that affect quality of work life among attendants in petrol stations in Kitale Town in Kenya. *International Journal of Academic Research in Business & Social Sciences*, *3*(5), 289–296.

Korunka, C., & Vitouch, O. (1999). Effects of the implementation of information technology on employees' strain and job satisfaction: A context-dependent approach. *Work & Stress*, *34*(4), 341–363.

Lambert, S. J. (1990). Processes linking work and family: A critical review and research agenda. *Human Relations*, *43*(3), 239–257.

Lamers, S., Westerhof, G. J., Bohlmeijer, E. T., ten Klooster, P. M., & Keyes, C. L. (2011). Evaluating the psychometric properties of the mental health continuum – short form (MHC–SF). *Journal of Clinical Psychology*, *67*(1), 99–110.

Larson, M. D., Norman, S. M., Hughes, L. W., & Avey, J. B. (2013). Psychological capital; A new lens for understanding employee fit and attitudes. *International Journal of Leadership Studies*, *8*(1), 28–43.

Levi, L. (2002). The European Commission's guidance on work-related stress: From words to action. *TUTB Newsletter*, *19*(20), 12–17.

Linley, P. A., Maltby, J.,Wood, A. M., Osborne, G., & Hurling, R. (2009). Measuring happiness: The higher order factor structure of subjective and psychological well-being measures. *Personality and Individual Differences*, *47*, 878–884.

Loh, L., Sankar, C. S., & Yeong, W. Y. (1995). Job orientation, perceptions, and satisfaction: A study of information technology professionals in Singapore. *Information & Management*, *29*, 239–250.

Luthans, F., & Youssef, C. M. (2007). Emerging positive organizational behavior. *Journal of Management*, *33*(3), 321–349.

Luthans, F., Youssef, C. M., & Avolio, B. J. (2007). *Psychological capital: Developing the human competitive edge*. Oxford, UK: Oxford University Press.

Major, D. A., Morganson, V. J., & Bolen, H. M. (2013). Predictors of occupational and organizational commitment in information technology: Exploring gender differences and similarities, *Journal of Business and Psychology*, *28*(3), 301–314.

Martel, J. P., & Dupuis, G. (2006). Quality of work-life: Theoretical and methodological problems, and presentation of a new model and measuring instrument. *Social Indicators Research*, *77*, 333–368.

Masten, A. S. (2001). Ordinary magic: Resilience processes in development. *American Psychologist*, *56*, 227–239.

Mayo, E. (1960). *The human problems of an industrial civilisation*. New York, NY: Viking Press.

Mensah, A. O., & Lebbaeus, A. (2013). The influence of employees' self-efficacy on their quality of work life: The case of Cape Coast, Ghana. *International Journal of Business and Social Science*, *4*(2), 195–204.

Mirvis, P. H., & Lawler, E. E. (1984). Accounting for the quality of work life. *Journal of Occupational Behaviour*, *5*, 197–212.

Naqvi, S. M. M. R., & Bashir, S. (2015). IT-expert retention through organizational commitment: A study of public sector information technology professionals in Pakistan. *Applied Computing and Informatics*, *11*, 60–75. doi:10.1016/j.aci.2011.11.001

National Association of Software and Service Companies and McKinsey & Company. (2005). *NASSCOM-McKinsey report 2005: Extending India's leadership of the global IT and BPO industries*. Retrieved April 29, 2015 from www.McKinsey.com/Locations/India/Mckinseyonindia/

Newman, J. E., & Beehr, T. A. (1979). Personal and organizational strategies for handling job stress: A review of research and opinion. *Personnel Psychology*, *3*(1), 1–43.
Pai, F. Y., Yeh, T. M., & Huang, K. I. (2012). Professional commitment of information technology employees under depression environments. *International Journal of Electronic Business Management*, *10*(1), 17.
Paraskeva, F., Mysirlaki, S., & Choustoulakis, E. (2009). Designing collaborative learning environments using educational scenarios based on SR. *International Journal of Advanced Corporate Learning*, *2*(1), 42–49. doi:10.3991%2Fijac.v2i1.606
Pollard, E., & Lee, P. (2003). Child well-being: A systematic review of the literature. *Social Indicators Research*, *61*(1), 9–78.
Pugalendhi, S. B., Umaselvi, M., & Senthil, N. (2011). Quality of work life: Perception of college teachers. *Indian Journal of Commerce & Management Studies*, *2*(1), 47–65.
Reddy, M. L., & Reddy, P. M. (2010). Quality of work life of employees: emerging dimensions. *Asian Journal of Management Research*, 827–839.
Reid, M. F., Riemenschneider, C. K., Allen, M. W., & Armstrong, D. J. (2008). Information technology employees in state government. *The American Review of Public Administration*, *38*(1), 41–61.
Rose, R. C., Beh, L., Uli, J., & Idris, K. (2006a). An analysis of quality of work life (QWL) and career-related variables. *American Journal of Applied Sciences*, *3*(12), 2151–2159.
Rose, R. C., Beh, L., Uli, J., & Idris, K. (2006b). Quality of work life: Implications of career dimensions. *Journal of Social Sciences*, *2*(2), 61–67.
Ryff, C. D. (1989). Happiness is everything, or is it? Explorations on the meaning of psychological wellbeing. *Journal of Personality and Social Psychology*, *57*(6), 1069–1081.
Santhi, T. S., & Sundar, K. (2012). A study on the work life balance of women employees in information technology industry. *International Journal of Business Economics and Management Research*, *2*(1), 82–96.
Schmitt, N., & Mellon, P. M. (1980). Life and job satisfaction: Is the job central? *Journal of Vocational Behavior*, *16*(1), 51–57.
Seligman, M. E. P. (1998). *Learned optimism*. New York, NY: Pocket Books.
Seligman, M. E. P. (2002). *Authentic happiness: Using the new positive psychology to realize your potential for lasting fulfilment*. London, UK: Nicholas Brealey.
Seligman, M. E. P. (2011). *Flourish: A visionary new understanding of happiness and well-being*. New York, NY: The Free Press.
Sharma, M., & Majumdar, P. K. (2010). Occupational lifestyle diseases: An emerging issue. *Indian Journal of Occupational Environmental Medicine*, *13*(3), 109. doi:10.4103/0019-5278.58912
Shih, S. P., Jiang, J. J., Klein, G., & Wang, E. (2013). Job burnout of the information technology worker: Work exhaustion, depersonalization, and personal accomplishment. *Information & Management*, *5*(7), 582–589.
Shropshire, J., & Kadlec, C. (2012). Leaving the IT field: The impact of stress, job insecurity, and burnout on IT professionals. *International Journal of Information*, *2*(1), 6–16.
Sinha, C. (2012). Factors affecting quality of work life: Empirical evidence from Indian organizations. *Australian Journal of Business and Management Research*, *1*(11), 31–40.
Skevington, S. M. (2001). Added validation of the WHOQOL-100: Pain management improves quality of life for chronic pain patients. *Clinical Journal of Pain*, *17*(3), 264–275.
Snyder, C. R. (2002). Hope theory: Rainbows in the mind. *Psychological Inquiry*, *13*(4), 249–276.
Sofi, Y., Razzaghi, S., & Hajelo, J. (2012). A survey of relationship between work life quality and staffs participation in Payame Noor University, Iran. *Journal of Basic Applied Science Research*, *2*(9), 9314–9320.
Sugumar, D., Kumaran, C. K. M., Raj, J., & Xavier, J. (2013). Addressing health related challenges faced by the business process outsourcing (BPO) employees by stress. *African Journal of Business Management*, *7*(12), 906–914.
Swapna, M., & Gomathi, S. (2013). A study on the interplay between the constructs of quality of work life: With special reference to IT professionals in Bangalore City. *Asian Social Science*, *9*(9), 107–122.

Tabassum, A. (2012). Interrelations between quality of work life dimensions and faculty member job satisfaction in private universities of Bangladesh. *European Journal of Business and Management, 4*(2), 78–89.

Taylor, J. C., Cooper, C. L., & Mumford, E. (1979). *The quality of working life in Western and Eastern Europe*. Heerlen, the Netherlands: Algemeen Burgerlijk Pensioenfonds.

Tehrani, N., Humpage, S., Willmott, B., & Haslam, I. (2011). *What's happening with well-being at work?* London, UK: Chartered Institute of Personnel and Development.

Tholons Inc. (2006). Emergence of centers of excellence. Tholons Knowledgebase Article #040601. Retrieved May 13, 2008 from www.tholons.com/pdfs/tholons_ar_centersofexcellence_0406.pdf

Van Aarde, A., & Mostert, K. (2008). Work–home interaction of working females: What is the role of job and home characteristics? *SA Journal of Industrial Psychology, 34*(3) 1–10.

Vijaimadhavan, P., & Raju, V. (2013a). An empirical study on relationship among quality of work life and its factors. *IOSR Journal of Business and Management, 12*(3), 20–28.

Vijaimadhavan, P., & Raju, V. (2013b). Significance of general well-being of IT professionals in India. *International Journal of Business and Management Invention, 81*, 28–33.

Warr, P. (2010). Jobs and job-holders: Two sources of happiness and unhappiness. In A. Conley, S. David, & I. Boniwell (Eds.), *Oxford handbook of happiness* (pp. 733–750). Oxford, UK: Oxford University Press.

Warr, P., Cook, J., & Wall, T. (1979). Scales for the measurement of some work attitudes and aspects of psychological well-being. *Journal of Occupational Psychology, 52*, 129–148.

WHO (1996, December). *WHOQoL-BREF: Introduction, Administration, Scoring and Generic Version of the Assessment Field Trial Version*. Geneva, Switzerland: World Health Organization.

WHO (2004). *Promoting mental health: Concepts, emerging evidence, practice* (Summary Report). Geneva, Switzerland: World Health Organization.

Wolff, C. (2009). Measuring wellbeing brings rewards at the University of Huddersfield. *Intelligent Research Solutions Employment Review*, 916.

Wright, T. A., & Bonett, D. G. (2002). The moderating effects of employee tenure on the relation between organizational commitment and job performance: A meta-analysis, *Journal of Applied Psychology, 87*(6), 1183–1190.

Yerkes, R. M., & Dodson, J. D. (1908). The relation of strength of stimulus to rapidity of habit-formation. *Journal of Comparative Neurology and Psychology, 18*, 459–482.

Young, A., Marriott, I., & Huntley, H. (2008). *Offshoring IT services can cut costs: Options for a potential economic downturn*. Report Number G00155776. Stamford, CT: Gartner Inc.

Zhang, X., & Huang, L. (2013). Cross-culture influences on interpersonal relationship in communication management a case study: Foreign supervisors PK Chinese employees in foreign-invested enterprises. *International Journal of Business and Management, 8*(12), 117–125.

26

Well-Being in the Arts and Crafts Sector

Antonella Delle Fave and Gaja Zager Kocjan

Introduction

The investigation of positive work experiences and environments is attracting the interest of both researchers and practitioners in the sector of work psychology. Over the last two decades, a vast literature has been produced on these topics. Studies have investigated individual characteristics, task features, and aspects of the work environment that may be related to employee well-being. Despite the variety of human work activities, substantially differing in structure, organization, and outcomes at the individual and social levels, psychologists have mostly devoted their attention to office and factory jobs, typical of modern urban contexts. In contrast, arts and crafts have been largely neglected. In the present chapter, we will attempt to partially fill this gap by summarizing the sparse studies investigating well-being among people who work as artists or skilled craftsmen, both in Western societies and in other countries and cultures.

The review of the literature highlights an intriguing paradox: the dearth of psychological studies investigating the job experience of professional artists and especially craftsmen is counterbalanced by a relatively rich literature on the positive outcomes of arts and crafts as non-professional leisure activities or therapeutic practices. A synthetic overview of these findings was deemed as relevant to the purposes of this book, due to their potential usefulness in designing well-being focused interventions in the organizational domain. The chapter is therefore articulated in two main sections. In the first one, attention will be devoted to the studies addressing the work experience and well-being of professional artists and craftsmen. The second section will instead focus on the studies referring to arts and crafts as non-professional activities, practiced within rehabilitation programs or during free time.

The Wiley Blackwell Handbook of the Psychology of Positivity and Strengths-Based Approaches at Work, First Edition. Edited by Lindsay G. Oades, Michael F. Steger, Antonella Delle Fave, and Jonathan Passmore.

Arts and Crafts Professions beyond Leisure and Therapy

A review of the literature revealed that approximately 80% of the studies on arts and crafts deal with these activities as leisure opportunities or therapeutic and rehabilitation tools. Only rarely are they investigated as professions or vocations. While little is known about the demands that people in arts and crafts are challenged by in their work environment, and the resources that help them face these demands, considerable attention has been given to the work conditions and experience of office and factory workers. This approach entails the risk of using the related findings as the standard criterion to understand the work experience of people occupied in a much broader range of job domains and conditions all around the world. Billions of people on this planet work in conditions and environments that differ greatly from those investigated within the mainstream psychological literature. Although technology and computers have replaced manpower in many job tasks, traditional craft activities such as sewing, weaving, carpentry, construction, shoemaking, and jewelry production remain a basic means of sustenance for a large number of families and communities (Sengupta, 2011). Even in modern urban societies many people work in handicrafts (for example hairdressers, bakers, fashion stylists and tailors, florists) or in creative art activities (dancers, writers, painters, and musicians). These people play an invaluable role in the co-creation of both traditional rural as well as modern urban lifestyle, yet they often remain invisible for much of the contemporary research. Most of the papers referring to professional craftsmen are written by economists, sociologists and anthropologists, thus addressing socio-economic issues, rather than the psychological resources and experience of these workers.

This lack of attention to the quality of work experience of professional artists and craftsmen is partially grounded in the stereotypical view of these workers as lucky people, who perform creative tasks and enjoy freedom and independence (Markusen, 2013; Sennett, 2008). Within the modern understanding of work, this stereotype can be partially justified by the fact that employees working in factories and tertiary sector companies face constraints in personal initiative and self-expression, a problem frequently highlighted by mainstream research in work psychology. This evidence supports the view of work as means for satisfying basic "deficiency" human needs, such as the need for safety or social recognition (Maslow, 1968). Work is considered as compulsory activity, instrumental in reaching other life goals. Self-actualization is usually pursued through other activities that people practice in their free time.

Creativity and technique: The two sides of arts and crafts

Arts and crafts indeed represent two work sectors that may provide positive experiences similar to those associated with leisure activities (Delle Fave, Massimini, & Bassi, 2011). Compared to modern factory or office work, these professions impose fewer restrictions in goal setting and task performance, and provide opportunities for creativity and self-expression. The creative side of arts and crafts is, however, inextricably intertwined with perseverance, strict discipline, and hard practice, necessary prerequisites for acquiring professional competences and mastering technicalities (Holmes, 2015).

At the psychological level, this twofold structure of arts and crafts can be well explained adopting Gollwitzer's (2012) mindset theory of action phases in the process of goal pursuit. The theory proposes a distinction between deliberative and implementation mindsets, that operate through different cognitive processes. The deliberative mindset is related to goal setting, and it implies choosing among a variety of potential outcomes, while the implementation mindset refers to performing practical tasks in order to achieve the goals previously set. The deliberating process, characterized by higher receptiveness and open-mindedness, can be related to the creative phase, when the workers get "inspiration" and build a mental image of their products. The subsequent implementation phase instead requires commitment to goal pursuit, focus on goal-oriented actions, and sustained effort.

Practicing technicalities represents the necessary pathway toward obtaining both high-level products and optimal states of consciousness such as flow, described as "the holistic sensation that people feel when they act with total involvement" (Csikszentmihalyi, 1975, p. 36). However, repeated practice is not always enjoyable, as it can be associated with fatigue, boredom, or even exhaustion. Hard practice in pursuit of accuracy and perfection can even result in physical injuries (Guptill, 2012) or high levels of anxiety (Kenny, Driscoll, & Ackermann, 2014).

The spatial and social environments in which artists and craftsmen work also contribute to their experience. Studies conducted by economists showed that professional artists often work under severe objective conditions, such as low income and lack of regular employment (Alper & Wassall, 2006). In addition, structural aspects of the profession, such as the prolonged eyestrain of tailors and goldsmiths, the standing position of hairdressers, and the sitting posture of shoemakers, may directly affect health (Areeudomwong, Puntumetakul, Kaber, Wanpen, Leelayuwat, & Chatchawan, 2012).

This evidence suggests that art and craft professions need to be investigated within a complex framework, overcoming simplistic and unilateral views focusing either on the creative and enjoyable features of these activities, or on their problematic aspects and demands. Indeed, professional artists and craftsmen are faced with difficult objective conditions, and their work is often anything but enjoyable. At the same time, art and craft activities may represent opportunities for engagement, promote problem solving, self-expression, and skill development, and contribute to the sense of achievement and development of personal identity (e.g., Csikszentmihalyi & Csikszentmihalyi, 1988; Griffiths, 2008; MacDonald, Byrne, & Carlton, 2006). Based on these positive features, these activities can be considered as exemplary conditions of strength promotion and resource development, from which to derive practical insights for designing interventions to promote well-being in other work contexts.

Professional Artists: Opportunities for Well-Being in a Challenging Environment

The focus on deficits rather than well-being has characterized for decades the study of human behavior and experience. Also in the field of creativity and arts, researchers have predominantly investigated ill-being indicators, such as stress, depression, and performance anxiety. More recently, however, several studies have highlighted that, though faced with difficult objective conditions such as low incomes and job insecurity, professional artists report higher job satisfaction as compared to non-artists, based on higher perceived autonomy (Bille, Bryld Fjællegaard, Frey, & Steiner, 2013), self-employment, task variety, and exposure to novelty and learning opportunities (Steiner & Schneider, 2013).

The scientific interest in the work experience of professional artists is also highly sectorial. Research is predominantly focused on dancers and musicians, whereas other artistic occupations such as writing, painting, and acting have received considerably less attention. The existing studies rely on a broad range of well-being indicators, assessed through techniques widely varying as concerns empirical validity. In addition, the theoretical conceptualizations and operationalizations of well-being differ across studies, and often a single study refers to more than one theory or construct. Therefore, the available research findings are often difficult to evaluate and rather hard to compare. In the following pages, we will attempt to group studies according to the prominent constructs investigated. We will start with flow, which is undoubtedly the positive work experience and well-being indicator most frequently examined among professional artists.

Flow among professional artists and art students

Flow is a positive experience characterized by intense concentration and deep involvement in an activity, merging of action and awareness, distorted perception of time, clear goals, constant feedback on one's own performance, intrinsic motivation, and a feeling of oneness with the task at hand (Csikszentmihalyi, 1975; Nakamura & Csikszentmihalyi, 2009). The crucial antecedent of flow experience is the match between the level of challenges perceived in the ongoing activity and the level of skills mobilized to face these challenges (Bassi & Delle Fave, 2012; Fong, Zaleski, & Leach, 2015; Inkinen, Lonka, Hakkarainen, Muukkonen, Litmanen, & Salmela-Aro, 2014; Kawabata & Mallett, 2011; Massimini, Csikszentmihalyi, & Carli, 1987).

An interpretative phenomenological analysis (IPA) performed on semi-structured interviews exploring flow among professional dancers from various genres (Hefferon & Ollis, 2006) highlighted three main higher-order themes: the autotelic nature of the experience, challenges–skills balance, and absorption. In addition, facilitators of flow onset in dance were investigated, leading to the identification of six main categories: confidence, music and choreography features, pre-performance routine, costumes and make-up, stage setting, and relationships with others. In another IPA-based study, professional ballet dancers reported merging of action and awareness (absorption), autotelic perception of the experience, and loss of self-consciousness as the prominent flow dimensions of dance (Panebianco-Warrens, 2014). Some of the participants also referred to deep awareness of music as a component of flow. For the vast majority of these dancers music promoted flow onset. However, dislike of the music and recorded music could inhibit flow experience.

Flow was also adopted as the basic theoretical framework of studies on the bodily experience of artists. Simoens and Tervaniemi (2013) focused on the close relationship often developed by musicians and singers with their work instruments, considering it as advantageous for professionals' well-being. The incorporation of the instrument into the musician's body was conceptually related to the experience of flow, and it was interpreted as a prerequisite to promote the shift in attention focus from technicalities to music itself. According to the degree of identification with their instruments/voices, participants in the study were categorized into four groups: united group (no difference between the person and the instrument/voice), person group (person rather than instrument/voice facing the audience), hiding group (personal identity hidden behind the instrument), and obstacle group (instrument as an obstacle between the musician and the audience). The results highlighted the psychological benefits derived from a relationship of unity between the person and the instrument/voice. Compared to the other groups, the "united group" reported higher performance confidence, lower performance anxiety and social phobia, lower perception of pressure, and feelings of primarily performing for the audience (rather than for themselves, for the other musicians of the ensemble, or others). Moreover, "united" participants reported a highly structured academic training that was assumed to facilitate the onset of flow, further leading to the fused relationship between the musicians and their instruments/voices.

Some studies have discussed the detrimental role of flow for musicians. A qualitative study conducted among artists suffering from playing-related injuries highlighted that entering the state of flow could entail a dissociation from body and time, leading to a lower perception of pain and excessively prolonged and uninterrupted practice (Guptill, 2012). Musicians in this study described the strategies adopted to interrupt or avoid flow in order to protect their own health.

Flow-like experiences were also detected among poets. Rathunde (2010) investigated the role of flow in the process of lifelong learning, analyzing interviews with professionals participating in a study on creativity in later life (Csikszentmihalyi, 1996). Among them, the Pulitzer prizewinning poet Mark Strand associated flow with writing poetry, describing several dimensions of optimal experience.

Other studies examined flow in students pursuing a professional career as musicians. Due to the long-term commitment and daily involvement in practice that this training entails, we decided to include these studies in the present section. Data collected among teenagers and young adults attending music academy courses by means of the Flow Questionnaire and Life Theme Questionnaire (Massimini & Delle Fave, 1995) highlighted that musical activities were associated with pervasive flow experiences by 73% of the participants, who described them as opportunities for intense concentration, deep involvement and self-expression, as well as sources of challenges. In a longitudinal study with music students, a positive relationship was detected between challenge–skill balance and flow experience, and a negative one between flow and performance anxiety during preparation for a juried recital that included musical compositions varying in complexity and technical demands (Fullagar, Knight, & Sovern, 2013). Studies conducted with a real-time sampling procedure, Experience Sampling Method (ESM; Hektner, Schmidt, & Csikszentmihalyi, 2007), highlighted a significantly positive relationship between students' flow experience and the creativity ratings of their musical compositions (Byrne, MacDonald, & Carlton 2003; MacDonald et al., 2006). The role of emotions in the flow experience of piano students was also investigated (Marin & Bhattacharya, 2013). Findings showed that trait emotional intelligence positively predicted dispositional flow, but flow did not represent a significant predictor of high performance. Moreover, high arousal emotions (both pleasant and unpleasant; Russell, 1980) expressed or induced by music, specific musical styles (romantic style, followed by classical and contemporary styles), and specific composers (Chopin, followed by Beethoven, Debussy, and Bach) were related to a higher occurrence of flow.

Finally, based on the job demands-resources model (JD-R; Demerouti, Bakker, Nachreiner, & Schaufeli, 2001), the joint investigation of the experience reported by music teachers and their students highlighted that job resources promote teachers' perceived balance between challenges and skills, thus facilitating flow (Bakker, 2005). The results suggested a conceptual convergence between the two theoretical perspectives, in terms of a higher probability of achieving flow in situations characterized by a perceived equilibrium between job demands and individual/contextual resources in the work setting. In addition, these results suggested a mechanism of flow transfer from music teachers to their students, a phenomenon described as emotional contagion (Hatfield, Cacioppo, & Rapson, 1994).

Self-determination among professional artists and students

Self-determination theory (Deci & Ryan, 1985) represents the conceptual framework underlying various studies conducted among dancers and dance students. The primary aim of these studies was to identify the individual and environmental factors allowing for the satisfaction of the three basic needs for autonomy, competence, and relatedness postulated by the theory (Deci & Ryan, 2000). The role of autonomy support and basic needs satisfaction was investigated among professional dancers in a one-month diary study (Quested, Duda, Ntoumanis, & Maxwell, 2013). Three genres were compared: ballet and Chinese dance (both regarded as controlled and structured dance forms), and contemporary dance (considered a more self-expressive and free genre). The lowest levels of autonomy support and basic needs satisfaction were detected in Chinese dance as compared to ballet and contemporary dance, suggesting that genre and environmental opportunities for basic needs satisfaction are intimately related. Moreover, the degree of autonomy support and basic needs satisfaction was related to dancers' affective experiences across genres.

This relationship was partially confirmed at the within-person level in the learning context. Different learning situations (classes, rehearsals, and performances) were characterized by the salience of different basic needs in predicting affective states. In addition, task-involving climate played a beneficial role in dancers' satisfaction of basic needs through the promotion of self-improvement, learning, and individual effort. Basic needs satisfaction in its turn contributed to well-being in terms of high positive and low negative affect. A significant relationship was also detected between perceived autonomy support and satisfaction of autonomy and relatedness needs (Quested & Duda, 2010). Other studies investigating the relationship between dance motivational climate and anxiety supported these results (Draugelis, Martin, & Garn, 2014; Nordin-Bates, Quested, Walker, & Redding, 2012). The full mediational role of basic needs satisfaction in the relationship between perceived autonomy support and burnout was further detected among dance students (Quested & Duda, 2011). Finally, a negative relationship was highlighted between basic needs satisfaction, and cortisol levels and anxiety, representing physiological and psychological parameters respectively (Quested, Bosch, Burns, Cumming, Ntoumanis, & Duda, 2011). More specifically, challenge appraisal mediated the association between basic needs satisfaction and cortisol levels, while threat appraisal mediated the relationship between basic needs satisfaction and anxiety intensity.

Studies assessing well-being indicators among professional musicians and dancers have also highlighted the importance of autonomy and autonomy-supportive environments for the quality of work experience. Semi-structured interviews administered to jazz and classical students and professionals allowed exploration of the differences in the work-related demands these artists are faced with (Dobson, 2010). The perceived degree of self-expression during the performance emerged as a relevant theme. Jazz musicians reported sufficient levels of autonomy, higher spontaneity and creativity, and a sense of exploration, while classical musicians – particularly those playing in orchestras – perceived lack of direct autonomy, high restrictions related to the demands for complete accuracy, and external control related to constant evaluations. Classical music students experienced practicing as emotionally demanding, and reported negative feelings toward it. In order to cope with these challenges, classical professionals reported adopting strategies such as emotional distancing and limited self-investment in order to maintain control over technicalities. These findings were consistent with those obtained among professional orchestra musicians, who reported high levels of trait anxiety, performance anxiety, and depression, more evident among younger women (Kenny et al., 2014). The primary causes for performance anxiety were pressure from self, excessive physical arousal before or during performance, and inadequate preparation. Intensive practice, deep breathing, and positive self-talk were used as strategies to cope with these work challenges.

A different perspective emerged from one of the few studies comparing musicians with other professionals, including clerks, factory workers, and employees of the human relations sector (Kivimaki & Jokinen, 1994). No differences were detected between musicians and the other occupational groups in the perceived levels of autonomy, conflicts, and stressors at work. However, perceived skill variety was significantly higher among musicians, who also reported higher job satisfaction, in spite of more frequent musculoskeletal symptoms. The authors argued that high skill variety represents a relevant opportunity for self-realization, thus contributing to job satisfaction. Among musicians, at the individual level perceived autonomy and lack of conflicts were also related to higher job satisfaction.

Job satisfaction, well-being, and work environment

As previously noted, in spite of disadvantageous work conditions, artists report higher job satisfaction as compared to non-artists. Some researchers specifically investigated the relationship between work environment and job satisfaction among these professionals. A study conducted through an online survey and focus groups addressed the positive and negative attitudes reported by Irish dancers toward their occupation (Cahalan & O'Sullivan, 2013). Although faced with job insecurity and short career, physical and psychological ill-being, and logistical problems related to their touring lifestyle, dancers reported high levels of job satisfaction. The main positive aspects of their work were exposure to various cultures, enduring friendships, the transformation of dance as a hobby into a career with financial benefits, personal development, and physical fitness.

The relationship between job satisfaction and health was specifically explored among orchestra musicians (Liljeholm Johansson & Theorell, 2003). Three health indicators were considered: the sum of total illness symptoms, musculoskeletal symptoms, and well-being (operationalized as a combination of low levels of fatigue, worry, frustration, and concentration difficulties, as well as high momentary satisfaction). Global positive evaluations of the work content (conductor, rehearsals, and repertoire) predicted higher levels of health. Demographic variables (gender, type of instrument, and role in the orchestra) and perceived features of the psychosocial environment (including social support and employer's engagement with the orchestra work environment) were also predictors of health levels. Specifically, women reported higher illness symptom scores than men. Musicians playing wind instruments reported lower musculoskeletal symptoms than string-players. Finally, musicians working in elite orchestras reported lower well-being than members of less prestigious orchestras, possibly due to higher job demands and lower autonomy.

This last finding is consistent with the results obtained in a study comparing professional and amateur singers (Grape, Sandgren, Hansson, Ericson, & Theorell, 2003). Cardiovascular and hormonal-biochemical measures collected before and after a singing lesson showed that participants in both groups were more energetic and relaxed after the lessons. However, amateur singers reported higher well-being and lower arousal than professionals. The answers to short semi-structured interviews clarified these findings by showing that professionals were more achievement oriented, whereas for amateurs singing lesson represented an opportunity for self-expression and self-actualization.

Overall, high job satisfaction was reported by most artists. These findings indicate the great potential of artistic professions to foster well-being and a high quality of work experience. The variety of quantitative and qualitative methodologies used across the studies makes any definitive conclusion impossible. Nevertheless, these studies represent important starting points paving the way to more systematic explorations of well-being among art professionals.

Professional Craftsmen: Invisible though Significant Workers

Moving from research on the work experience of professional artists to research on craft professions, the number of studies drops considerably. However, the activities, services, and products provided by professional craftsmen substantially contribute to individuals' and communities' quality of life worldwide. People all around the world at one time or another visit hairdressers and manicurists, order custom-made cakes for special celebrations, need a tailor to shorten or enlarge clothes, buy flower arrangements or hand-made jewelry, engage a carpenter to build a bookshelf to fit an uneven wall. Nevertheless, psychological research is seldom concerned with the job experience of these professionals. Their life and work conditions are more frequently investigated from the socio-economical and anthropological perspectives, and predominantly within non-Western societies. Most studies adopt a phenomenological approach, analyzing narratives of craftsmen's work experiences, thus making comparisons with other studies and research lines very difficult. Yet, the few studies addressing the work experience of craft professionals represent a unique and thus valuable source of information, and can serve as a basis for further explorations of this topic.

Craft, well-being, and personal identity: A gender issue

Some of the studies conducted among professional artisans focus on the relationship between engagement in craft activities and well-being outcomes from a gender perspective, prominently focusing on the relevance of work for the promotion of women's identity and emancipation. In an ethnographic fieldwork involving Trinidadian women who made their living from clothes production, sewing emerged as a source of personal satisfaction and identity (Prentice, 2012). Learning how to sew was beneficial at two different levels. It provided participants with economic power, thus enhancing their self-reliance, adaptability, and resourcefulness; it was also an opportunity for enjoyment, excitement, and development of personal talents. In the long term, the acquisition and practice of sewing skills positively contributed to shaping participants' identities.

The meaning of sewing (performed as leisure, employment, contribution to the household economy, or a means to fulfill cultural expectations) was also explored among first-generation non-English-speaking immigrant women in South Australia (Boerema, Russell, & Aguilar, 2010). Qualitative analyses of individual and group interviews revealed that sewing represented an opportunity to express creativity, a source of pleasure and satisfaction, as well as a useful means to contribute to family subsistence. In addition, sewing played an important role in shaping participants' identities, in that it provided them with a feeling of cultural continuity during the transition phase of the acculturation process, thus supporting their adaptation to the new environment.

The process of worker identity formation was explored through participant observations and interviews with people (primarily women) performing crafts at home, thus lacking contextual markers related to job and workplace (Dickie, 2003). Findings showed that the definition of a clear schedule, as well as logistic and marketing rules, substantially contributed to building participants' work identity. In particular, participants mentioned the importance of designating specific rooms or areas of the house for the work-related activities and materials; of acquiring the right equipment and supplies; of establishing a clear work timetable, as well as a legal business identity. This work identity was adequately recognized and supported by members of their households and communities.

One of the few studies investigating the meaning of work and work values among men involved retired workers of a paper mill in Massachusetts, who had been employed in the same company for at least 25 years (LeBlanc, 2009). Papermakers had developed awareness of their job as both a craft activity and a channel for creative expression. Participants also emphasized the importance of family support for the promotion of their work–life balance.

Other studies have examined the opposite phenomenon, namely the loss or downplay of craftmanship identity. A study conducted at a carpet-weaving factory in the UK (Sayce, Ackers, & Greene, 2007) highlighted that organizational changes and the introduction of automated technology forced male weavers to rebuild their work identity anew, since their craft identities were tightly related to their sense of masculinity and higher social status. The issue of identity fragmentation in relation to gender was also addressed in an ethnographic study conducted among Indian women working in jewelry production (Soni-Sinha, 2011). The study shed light on the gendered division of labor according to which men are viewed as breadwinners and women as housewives, though they often work at home. These women, whose activity was considered a low-skill and low-value leisure task, were able to assert their worker status by deconstructing their traditional gender role and achieving a more complex and multifaceted identity.

Another field research work conducted through individual narratives and group discussions within the framework of human geography explored the struggle of Indian self-employed craftswomen in challenging local gendered ideologies and economic strategies (Acharya, 2003, 2004). Finally, an interview-based study highlighted the negative impact of cultural, gender, and racial stereotypes on the work identity of Caribbean women, enrolled in micro-business empowerment programs as street vendors (Karides, 2005). The frequent failures of these programs were related to their unrealistic expectations. More specifically, promoters of these initiatives overlooked women's struggle in balancing household and business without any formal support.

Work organization and craftsmen's well-being

Policymakers and citizens of affluent societies are becoming increasingly sensitive to the issue of fair trade organization (FTO) and its potential in promoting equity and welfare in developing countries. Two studies have explored the impact of FTO on the well-being of workers. Among Peruvian producers, participation in FTO was positively related with professional self-esteem, happiness, and self-reported standard of living (Becchetti, Castriota, & Solferino, 2011). Objective benefits were also detected, such as the increase of weekly food consumption, and the decrease of the amount of income consumed for food expenditure. The second study involved Indian artisans who had acquired entrepreneurial skills while working for a parent FTO and subsequently applied them to develop a new business organization (Strawn & Littrell, 2006).

The impact of work restructuring on artisans' psychosocial well-being was also investigated in the context of social system transitions. A study involving craft-based entrepreneurs from Kyrgyzstan explored their work experience within the post-Soviet market environment (Botoeva & Spector, 2013). Narrative analysis highlighted participants' satisfaction with their ability to reallocate local knowledge and skills and to adjust to the demands of a competitive market environment. Their contribution to both family subsistence and client happiness was quoted as an important source of meaning. Similar findings were obtained from Guadalajara's artisans (Rivas-Jimenez, 2008), who were able to preserve their craft production and adjust it to the changes brought by economic liberalism by virtue of community cohesion and family support. Finally, a study conducted among pottery workshop owners in China showed that the sharing practices introduced by collectivization were preserved in spite of the privatization of handicraft, promoting knowledge transmission among community members (Gowlland, 2012).

This brief overview highlighted the dearth of studies on professional craftsmen in the scientific literature, especially in the domain of psychology. These workers seem to be unattractive for researchers, even though their social contribution is essential. Therefore, the investigation of craftsmen's work experience represents an open and challenging research avenue for psychologists, which could enrich the existing body of knowledge on human work activities.

Well-Being Promotion through the Non-Professional Practice of Arts and Crafts

A thorough review of the literature addressing the experience associated with the practice of arts and crafts sheds light on an intriguing paradox: while these activities are substantially overlooked as professions, they are much more frequently investigated as therapeutic or leisure practices. In addition, the range of activities taken into consideration becomes remarkably broader, compared to those investigated as professions. As regards arts, besides music and dancing psychologists have paid attention to poetry, song-writing, and theater acting. In most cases, however, studies referred to both arts and crafts, addressed together as creative activities.

The beneficial effects of these practices were investigated through a variety of measurement instruments and techniques. Well-being was explored in terms of experience associated to art performance and craft-making, meaning attributed to them, and their contribution to physical and mental health. Analogously to research conducted among professionals, most studies do not rely on specific theories and constructs. The only important exception is flow experience, frequently examined among non-professionals as well.

The majority of studies addressing the benefits of arts and crafts for well-being promotion can be contextualized within two domains: therapeutic or rehabilitation intervention, and free time or extra-curricular education. The beneficial role of arts and crafts as leisure activities was investigated in a variety of cultural contexts and life stages.

The therapeutic role of arts and crafts

The potential of arts and crafts as therapeutic and rehabilitation tools has been largely investigated in the scientific literature. However, in most of these studies well-being is operationalized as the absence or reduction of negative symptoms, rather than the presence of mental health indicators (Brillantes-Evangelista, 2013; Mohammadian et al., 2011; Tegner, Fox, Philipp, & Thorne, 2009). Only during the last two decades has the assessment of positive indicators of well-being become part of quantitative and qualitative studies conducted in these domains.

In acute psychiatric setting, the Warwick-Edinburgh Mental Well-being Scale (WEMWBS, Tennant et al., 2007) has been used to detect a significant improvement of patients' self-reported well-being after a 10-week creative art intervention (Crone et al., 2013). In the context of a psychiatric rehabilitation program conducted in a residential setting, a real-time study using ESM highlighted that participants perceived high challenges and flow experiences during the daily practice of artistic and expressive tasks (painting, drawing, dancing, photography), while the other daily activities were associated with less positive experiential profiles (Bassi, Ferrario, Ba, Delle Fave, & Viganò, 2012). The findings suggested that some core features of rehabilitation activities, such as clear rules, high structure, and complexity, promote participants' perception of high challenges, widely acknowledged as a major prerequisite for flow onset.

Researchers have also evaluated the outcomes of art workshops and programs organized in outpatient settings. Users associated creative arts workshops with the perception of purpose and hope, self-worth, social agency, and strengthened personal identity (Stickley, Hui, Morgan, & Bertram, 2007). A qualitative investigation of a community-based art program suggested its potential in facilitating participants' recovery process through the promotion of self-expression and self-knowledge, empowerment (control over one's own life and influence on others), self-validation (sense of identity, self-confidence, and changes in lifestyle), and spiritual fulfillment (meaning, purpose, hope, and acceptance). Supportive relationships and contexts were also involved in this process (Lloyd, Wong, & Petchkovsky, 2007). Another qualitative study suggested that participation in art programs may facilitate recovery from mental illness through identity reconstruction and the development of adaptive coping mechanisms, sense of achievement, meaning and purpose (Spandler, Secker, Kent, Hackings, & Shenton, 2007).

In a mixed-methods study, a 6-month randomized control trial with treatment and control groups was conducted among adults with chronic mental disorders, to evaluate the outcomes of an art therapy program. Participants' narratives highlighted that treatment promoted self-esteem and a sense of commitment and achievement. However, the program's effectiveness was not supported by the quantitative measures, possibly because of the small size and high heterogeneity of the sample (Odell-Miller, Hughes, & Westacott, 2006).

Finally, some studies have examined the relationship between art-based intervention and physiological indicators of well-being. A training program in visual art production offered to healthy retirees was found to enhance functional connectivity in the brain's default mode network (DMN), which was further associated with higher resilience scores (Bolwerk, Mack-Andrick, Lang, Dörfler, & Maihöfner, 2014). In an experimental study, the evaluation of salivary IgA levels before and after a singing session highlighted an enhanced immune system activity immediately after singing in different populations, including amateurs, music students, and professionals (Beck, Cesario, Yousefi, & Enamoto, 2000; Beck, Gottfried, Hall, Cisler, & Bozeman 2006; Kreutz, Bongard, Rohrmann, Hodapp, & Grebe, 2004; Kuhn, 2002).

Similar findings were obtained from studies investigating the therapeutic role of craft-making among users of mental health services. Woodwork workshops were associated with high intrinsic motivation, derived from meaning-making, time structuring, and positive environmental features (Mee & Sumsion, 2001). A case study showed that creating a tapestry representation of a photograph connected to personal grief helped the client face and accept the grief-related loss (Reynolds, 1999). A narrative inquiry investigating the meaning of craft-based interventions from the therapist's perspective (Harris, 2008) suggested that craft-making promotes the pursuit of meaningful goals, self-efficacy, hope, and sense of achievement through the creation of tangible products. The interpretation of findings was based on the assumption that craft-making fulfills the innate human need for creativity.

Through studies grounded in the phenomenological approach, Frances Reynolds examined the role of arts and crafts practice in promoting well-being among people experiencing a chronic illness. Textile work was associated with participants' development of a positive identity as artists and successful adaptation to disease through a sense of personal growth, achievement, and social connection. It also represented a means for structuring time, a distraction from worries, and contribution to others (Reynolds, 2002, 2003). Women with depression associated needlecraft practice with a condition of relaxation, deep concentration, and absorption that can be easily related to flow experience (Reynolds, 2000). Among the benefits of needlecraft, participants also mentioned self-esteem, sense of mastery and competence, as well as social recognition, connectedness and support. Women with cancer associated the practice of visual arts and crafts (such as textile work, painting, pottery, or collage) with a flow-like state of deep immersion that contributed to stress alleviation and provided sense of control, mastery, and achievement (Reynolds & Prior, 2006). Finally, women diagnosed with chronic fatigue syndrome described art and craft practice (painting, pottery, card-making, embroidery, and tapestry) as an opportunity to experience life satisfaction, enhanced self-image and self-confidence, sense of hope, and social connection (Reynolds, Vivat, & Prior, 2008).

The therapeutic meaning of creative activities was specifically investigated through a qualitative approach among patients with cancer attending occupational therapy sessions within a palliative care setting. Participants perceived creative engagement as a useful coping strategy, promoting concentration on positive targets and awareness of personal abilities and competences. Creative activities helped them attain an adaptive adjustment to illness and its contextualization within a broader perspective (La Cour, Josephsson, Tishelman, & Nygård, 2007). The positive role of creative activities was also explored from both the therapist's and the client's perspective during an occupational treatment practice (Griffiths, 2008). Among the benefits and health-related gains, participants mentioned the facilitation of flow, skill development, sense of achievement, self-confidence, purpose, control over negative thoughts, and contribution to personal identity and social relationships. Occupational therapists emphasized the importance of offering occupations that were deemed meaningful by clients. Clients underscored the opportunity to develop social connections, experience creative engagement, and transform an interest into an occupation.

Personal and social well-being in arts and crafts as leisure activities

A variety of studies have highlighted that the practice of arts and crafts during free time promotes well-being in its different facets: hedonic dimensions, eudaimonic ones, as well as social well-being. These three facets represent the components of flourishing, according to Keyes' model of mental health (Keyes, 2007). In particular, social well-being includes the perception of social support, cultural belongingness and acceptance, community coherence, and personal contribution to the society (Keyes, 1998).

The analysis of written narratives highlighted that the process of craft-making is pleasant, satisfactory, and conducive to flow; it offers opportunities for self-expression and personal growth; its outcome is represented by concrete products that provide manufacturers with a sense of achievement. Craft-making is also an opportunity for structuring time, and for acquiring physical and cognitive skills, self-esteem, self-confidence, internal locus of control, and a sense of meaning. Finally, engagement in craft is related to cultural and social awareness (Pöllänen, 2013, 2015).

Women regularly engaging in artistic activities such as painting, pottery, and photography associated both the process of art-making and the final product to positive emotions, enhanced self-image, and social connections (Titus & Sinacore, 2013). Middle-aged women perceived psychological and spiritual benefits in jewelry-making, associating this activity with social recognition, hedonic and eudaimonic dimensions of well-being, and a sense of connection with God and other people. They also underscored the meditative function of the practice (Adams-Price & Steinman, 2007). Mothers of young children described craft-making as an opportunity for self-expression as well as a relief from parenting and work responsibilities. The process of craft-making provided them with challenges, joy, and time for themselves. Offering their products as gifts allowed them to connect with others and to transmit the related values to younger generations (Grace, Gandolfo, & Candy, 2009; Mason, 2005).

Other studies focused on the personal and social values embedded in arts and crafts practice. A mixed-method study revealed that textile creation and use were perceived by women as sources of meaning and motivation. Participants described their products as symbols of their own personal identity, imbued with both tangible and intangible values (Johnson & Wilson, 2005). Iranian women immigrants to Australia, who had preserved the habit of reproducing the cypress tree pattern typical of their culture in everyday cooking and embroidery, described this pattern as a symbol of life continuity, and a memory of home to be transmitted to younger generations (Warin & Dennis, 2005). In the same vein, young Kazakh women associated the acquisition of domestic textile production skills with the construction of their personal identity and status in family and society (Portisch, 2009).

Fewer studies were focused on single indicators of well-being, usually assessed through scaled questionnaires. Choir singers reported both positive affect and personal growth and vitality after a single choir rehearsal (Busch & Gick, 2012). The joint perception of engagement and loss of self-awareness – indicative of flow experience – was reported by amateur musicians, professional musicians, and non-musicians in free descriptions and quantitative assessments of intense experiences related to music (Gabrielsson & Lindström Wik, 2003). Students' descriptions of strong experiences of music performance were investigated from the perspective of the orientation to happiness model, distinguishing between pleasant, engaged, and meaningful life (Seligman, 2002). The eudaimonic route to happiness, comprising personal and social meanings, as well as flow, was predominant in participants' descriptions. The hedonic route was also mentioned, but it was given lower relevance (Lamont, 2012). In a study conducted through ESM with adolescents enrolled in a music education program, a positive relationship was found between levels of achievement in music performance and the frequency of flow occurrence (O'Neill, 1999). Among students enrolled in extra-curricular art programs, choral singing was associated with flow (Freer, 2009) and acting with intrinsic motivation, high concentration, and clear goals (Martin & Cutler, 2002).

Future Directions

Taken together, these findings represent a plea for researchers in the domain of work psychology to expand their attention focus toward the inclusion of arts and crafts, professions so far largely neglected in spite of their great potential to promote well-being in the work context. Researchers in other social sciences, such as anthropology and sociology, show higher sensitivity and commitment to understanding the work experience of professional artists and craftsmen. Yet, related studies remain overall few in number.

The fact that office and factory workers are given much more attention by work psychologists compared to other occupations can be related, among other reasons, to the debated issue of business-driven research aimed at empowering large-scale productivity. Research grants are often funded by companies interested in understanding work conditions, experience, and employee satisfaction in their own context. Moreover, in several countries large companies are bound to legal provisions that include recurrent monitoring of employees' health indicators, such as work-related stress and, more recently, also well-being. Most professional artists and craftsmen are instead engaged in smaller-scale production workshops, they are often self-employed, and they are rarely organized in trade unions, thus running the risk of remaining invisible to government, social, and health services.

The review of the limited research literature addressing the work experience and well-being in professional arts and crafts allowed for the identification of methodological and conceptual shortcomings. As concerns methodology, the variety of measurement instruments and techniques employed, together with the dearth of rigorous quantitative studies, makes the comparison and integration of results extremely difficult. This problem is further intensified at the conceptual level by the broad range of mental health models and constructs adopted as theoretical frameworks of the studies. In addition, while a certain number of studies are grounded in well-established approaches, such as flow theory and self-determination theory, many others – especially those based on narratives and interviews – are theoretically vague. Some themes emerging from participants' descriptions can be easily subsumed under existing theories and models. For example, participants' frequent mention of self-expression and self-actualization can be referred to the concepts of personal expressiveness and development of potentials characterizing the eudaimonist identity theory (Waterman, 1990) and Maslow's theory of human motivation (1968). Themes including perceived personal abilities and success can be connected to the concept of self-efficacy (Bandura, 1997). However, authors rarely refer to these theoretical conceptualizations in their interpretation of findings.

This lack of a unified theoretical approach can be partially justified by the fact that mental health and well-being are still relatively undetermined constructs, lacking a definitive and universally accepted definition. In addition, psychological conceptualizations of mental health and well-being are often intermingled with the perspectives of other disciplines. For example, economists are more interested in the study of objective indicators of well-being, such as workers' material and social circumstances, whereas anthropologists pay specific attention to the impact of sociocultural features on individual happiness.

Overall, these findings suggest the need for further research conducted with rigorous methodology, and aimed at reaching a shared definition and operationalization of well-being and mental health encompassing different theoretical perspectives, and applicable to the different domains and contexts of human experience.

Conclusions

Despite methodological and structural limitations, the studies summarized in this chapter show that arts and crafts have pervasive beneficial effects on people's mental health, promoting high engagement, sense of growth and achievement, and personal development. These positive outcomes are related to the high complexity of these activities, which require energy investment and skill cultivation, and to the personal and social meanings and goals that individuals can autonomously attach to their practice.

These benefits are often missing in the context and structure of office and factory jobs, the occupations prominently investigated by industrial/organizational psychologists. These jobs often fail to provide workers with personal and social meanings, high challenges, and self-determined goals. Several work tasks become repetitive actions with low relevance and complexity, thus preventing workers from achieving high-quality work experiences. Therefore, findings derived from studies conducted on artists and craftsmen may provide useful suggestions for designing interventions aimed at increasing job satisfaction and work-related well-being among other professional categories, more exposed to the risk of disengagement, repetitiveness, and lack of meaningful challenges.

The research findings presented in this chapter also encourage the adoption of a broader view of work, beyond the narrow focus on office employees living in modern urban contexts. Many people worldwide devote their time and energy to ignored yet essential occupations, and through their work they shape our society and daily life.

Finally, at the wider social level these findings underscore the need for paying attention to workers who function in low-power positions, thus having no influence on research and policy programs, though they perform their job with competence and dedication.

References

Acharya, J. (2003). Women's well-being and gendered practices of labour and workspace in traditional craft productions in Orissa, India. *Gender Technology and Development, 7*, 333–357.

Acharya, J. (2004). *Gendered spaces: Craftswomen's stories of self-employment in Orissa, India.* Doctoral dissertation, Norwegian University of Science and Technology, Trondheim. Retrieved April 8, 2015, from http://www.diva-portal.org/smash/get/diva2:124213/FULLTEXT01.pdf

Adams-Price, C. E., & Steinman, B. A. (2007). Crafts and generative expression: A qualitative study of the meaning of creativity in women who make jewelry in midlife. *International Journal of Aging and Human Development, 65*, 315–333.

Alper, N. O., & Wassall, G. H. (2006). Artists' careers and their labor markets. In V. A. Ginsburgh & D. Throsby (Eds.), *Handbook of the economics of arts and culture* (Vol. *1*, pp. 813–864). Amsterdam, the Netherlands: North-Holland.

Areeudomwong, P., Puntumetakul, R., Kaber, D. B., Wanpen, S., Leelayuwat, N., & Chatchawan, U. (2012). Effects of handicraft sitting postures on lower trunk muscle fatigue. *Ergonomics, 55*, 693–703.

Bakker, A. (2005). Flow among music teachers and their students. The cross-over of peak experiences. *Journal of Vocational Behavior, 66*, 26–44.

Bandura, A. (1997). *Self efficacy: The exercise of control.* New York, NY: Freeman.

Bassi, M., & Delle Fave, A. (2012). Optimal experience and self-determination at school: Joining perspectives. *Motivation and Emotion, 36*, 425–438.

Bassi, M., Ferrario, N., Ba, G., Delle Fave, A., & Viganò, C. (2012). Quality of experience during psychosocial rehabilitation: A real time investigation with experience sampling method. *Psychiatric Rehabilitation Journal, 6*, 447–453.

Becchetti, L., Castriota, S., & Solferino, N. (2011). Development projects and life satisfaction: An impact study on fair trade handicraft producers. *Journal of Happiness Studies, 12*, 115–138.

Beck, R. J., Cesario, T. C., Yousefi, A., & Enamoto, H. (2000). Choral singing, performance perception, and immune system changes in salivary immunoglobulin A and cortisol. *Music Perception, 18*, 87–106.

Beck, R. J., Gottfried, T. L., Hall, D. J., Cisler, C. A., & Bozeman, K. W. (2006). Supporting the health of college solo singers: The relationship of positive emotions and stress to changes in salivary IgA and cortisol during singing. *Journal of Learning through the Arts: A Research Journal on Arts Integration in Schools and Communities, 2*(1). Retrieved April 14, 2015, from https://escholarship.org/uc/item/003791w4

Bille, T., Bryld Fjællegaard, C., Frey, B. S., & Steiner, L. (2013). Happiness in the arts: International evidence on artists' job satisfaction. *Economics Letters, 121*, 15–18.

Boerema, C., Russell, M., & Aguilar, A. (2010). Sewing in the lives of immigrant women. *Journal of Occupational Science, 17*, 78–84.

Bolwerk, A., Mack-Andrick, J., Lang, F. R., Dörfler, A., & Maihöfner, C. (2014). How art changes your brain: Differential effects of visual art production and cognitive art evaluation on functional brain connectivity. *PLoS ONE, 9*, e101035.

Botoeva, A., & Spector, R. A. (2013). Sewing to satisfaction: Craft-based entrepreneurs in contemporary Kyrgyzstan. *Central Asian Survey, 32*, 487–500.

Brillantes-Evangelista, G. (2013). An evaluation of visual arts and poetry as therapeutic interventions with abused adolescents. *The Arts in Psychotherapy, 40*, 71–84.

Busch, S., & Gick, M. (2012). A quantitative study of choral singing and psychological well-being. *Canadian Journal of Music Therapy, 18*, 45–61.

Byrne, C., MacDonald, R. A. R., & Carlton, L. (2003). Assessing creativity in musical compositions: The importance of flow. *British Journal of Music Education, 20*, 277–290.

Cahalan, R., & O'Sullivan, K. (2013). Job satisfaction of professional Irish dancers: Implications for performer health and well-being. *Journal of Dance Medicine and Science, 17*, 139–149.

Crone, D. M., O'Connell, E. E., Tyson, P. J., Clark-Stone, F., Opher, S., & James, D. V. (2013). "Art Lift" intervention to improve mental well-being: An observational study from UK general practice. *International Journal of Mental Health Nursing, 22*, 279–286.

Csikszentmihalyi, M. (1975). *Beyond boredom and anxiety*. San Francisco, CA: Jossey-Bass.

Csikszentmihalyi, M. (1996). *Creativity: Flow and the psychology of discovery and invention*. New York, NY: HarperCollins.

Csikszentmihalyi, M., & Csikszentmihalyi, I. (Eds.) (1988). *Optimal experience: Psychological studies of flow in consciousness*. Cambridge, UK: Cambridge University Press.

Deci, E. L., & Ryan, R. M. (1985). *Intrinsic motivation and self-determination in human behavior*. New York, NY: Plenum Press.

Deci, E. L. & Ryan, R. M. (2000). The "what" and "why" of goal pursuits: Human needs and the self-determination of behavior. *Psychological Inquiry*, *11*, 227–268.

Delle Fave, A., Massimini, F., & Bassi, M. (2011). *Psychological selection and optimal experience across cultures: Social empowerment through personal growth*. Dordrecht, the Netherlands: Springer.

Demerouti, E., Bakker, A. B., Nachreiner, F., & Schaufeli, W. B. (2001). The job demands-resources model of burnout. *Journal of Applied Psychology*, *86*, 499–512.

Dickie, V. A. (2003). Establishing worker identity: A study of people in craftwork. *American Journal of Occupational Therapy*, *57*, 250–261.

Dobson, M. C. (2010). Performing your self? Autonomy and self-expression in the work of jazz musicians and classical string players. *Music Performance Research*, *3*, 42–60.

Draugelis, S., Martin, J., & Garn, A. (2014). Psychosocial predictors of well-being in collegiate dancers. *The Sport Psychologist*, *28*, 1–9.

Fong C. J., Zaleski D. J., & Leach J. K. (2015). The challenge–skill balance and antecedents of flow: A meta-analytic investigation. *The Journal of Positive Psychology*, *10*(5), 425–446.

Freer, P. K. (2009). Boys' descriptions of their experiences in choral music. *Research Studies in Music Education*, *31*, 142–160.

Fullagar, C. J., Knight, P. A., & Sovern, H. S. (2013). Challenge/skill balance, flow, and performance anxiety. *Applied Psychology*, *62*, 236–259.

Gabrielsson, A., & Lindström Wik, S. (2003). Strong experiences related to music: A descriptive system. *Musicae Scientiae*, *7*, 157–217.

Gollwitzer, P. M. (2012). Mindset theory of action phases. In P. Van Lange, A.W. Kruglanski, & E.T. Higgins (Eds.), *Handbook of theories of social psychology* (Vol. *1*, pp. 526–545). London, UK: Sage.

Gowlland, G. (2012). Learning craft skills in China: Apprenticeship and social capital in an artisan community of practice. *Anthropology & Education Quarterly*, *43*, 358–371.

Grace, M., Gandolfo, E., & Candy, C. (2009). Crafting quality of life: Creativity and wellbeing. *Journal of the Association for Research on Mothering*, *11*, 239–250.

Grape, C., Sandgren, M., Hansson, L. O., Ericson, M., & Theorell, T. (2003). Does singing promote well-being? An empirical study of professional and amateur singers during a singing lesson. *Integrative Physiological & Behavioral Science*, *38*, 65–74.

Griffiths, S. (2008). The experience of creative activity as a treatment medium. *Journal of Mental Health*, *17*, 49–63.

Guptill, C. (2012). Injured professional musicians and the complex relationship between occupation and health. *Journal of Occupational Science*, *19*, 258–270.

Harris, E. (2008). The meanings of craft to an occupational therapist. *Australian Occupational Therapy Journal*, *55*, 133–142.

Hatfield, E., Cacioppo, J., & Rapson, R. L. (1994). *Emotional contagion*. Cambridge, UK: Cambridge University Press.

Hefferon, K. M., & Ollis, S. (2006). "Just clicks": An interpretive phenomenological analysis of professional dancers' experience of flow. *Research in Dance Education*, *7*, 141–159.

Hektner, J. M., Schmidt, J. A., & Csikszentmihalyi, M. (2007). *Experience sampling method: Measuring the quality of everyday life*. Thousand Oaks, CA: Sage.

Holmes, H. (2015). Transient craft: Reclaiming the contemporary craft worker. *Work, Employment and Society*, *29*, 479–495.

Inkinen, M., Lonka, K., Hakkarainen, K., Muukkonen, H., Litmanen, T., & Salmela-Aro, K. (2014). The interface between core affects and the challenge–skill relationship. *Journal of Happiness Studies*, *15*, 891–913.

Johnson, J. S., & Wilson, L. E. (2005). "It says you really care": Motivational factors of contemporary female handcrafters. *Clothing and Textiles Research Journal, 23*, 115–130.
Karides, M. (2005). Whose solution is it? Development ideology and the work of micro-entrepreneurs in Caribbean context. *International Journal of Sociology and Social Policy, 25*, 30–62.
Kawabata, M., & Mallett, C. J. (2011). Flow experience in physical activity: Examination of the internal structure of flow from a process-related perspective. *Motivation and Emotion, 35*, 393–402.
Kenny, D., Driscoll, T., & Ackermann, B. (2014). Psychological well-being in professional orchestral musicians in Australia: A descriptive population study. *Psychology of Music, 42*, 210–232.
Keyes, C. L. M. (1998). Social well-being. *Social Psychology Quarterly, 61*, 121–140.
Keyes, C. L. M. (2007). Promoting and protecting mental health as flourishing: A complementary strategy for improving national mental health. *American Psychologist, 62*, 95–108.
Kivimaki, M., & Jokinen, M. (1994). Job perceptions and well-being among symphony orchestra musicians: A comparison with other occupational groups. *Medical Problems of Performing Artists, 9*, 73–76.
Kreutz, G., Bongard, S., Rohrmann, S., Hodapp, V., & Grebe, D. (2004). Effects of choir singing or listening on secretory immunoglobulin A, cortisol, and emotional state. *Journal of Behavioral Medicine, 27*, 623–635.
Kuhn, D. (2002). The effects of active and passive participation in musical activity on the immune system as measured by salivary immunoglobulin A (SigA). *Journal of Music Therapy, 39*, 30–39.
La Cour, K., Josephsson, S., Tishelman, C., & Nygård, L. (2007). Experiences of engagement in creative activity at a palliative care facility. *Palliative and Supportive Care, 5*, 241–250.
Lamont, A. (2012). Emotion, engagement and meaning in strong experiences of music performance. *Psychology of Music, 40*, 574–594.
LeBlanc, C. J. (2009). Men-of-the-mill, work, craft and meaning: A qualitative case study of paper mill workers in Fitchburg, Massachusetts. *Dissertation Abstracts International Section B: The Sciences and Engineering, 69*, 7176.
Liljeholm Johansson, Y., & Theorell, T. (2003). Satisfaction with work task quality correlates with employee health: A study of 12 professional orchestras. *Medical problems of performing artists, 18*, 141–149.
Lloyd, C., Wong, S. R., & Petchkovsky, L. (2007). Art and recovery in mental health: A qualitative investigation. *British Journal of Occupational Therapy, 70*, 207–214.
MacDonald, R. A. R., Byrne, C., & Carlton, L. (2006). Creativity and flow in musical composition: An empirical investigation. *Psychology of Music, 34*, 292–306.
Marin, M. M., & Bhattacharya, J. (2013). Getting into the musical zone: Trait emotional intelligence and amount of practice predict flow in pianists. *Frontiers in Psychology/Cognitive Science, 4*, 1–14.
Markusen, A. (2013). Artists work everywhere. *Work and Occupations, 40*, 481–495.
Martin, J., & Cutler, K. (2002). An exploratory study of flow and motivation in theater actors. *Journal of Applied Sport Psychology, 14*, 344–352.
Maslow, A. H. (1968). *Toward a psychology of being*. New York, NY: Van Nostrand.
Mason, R. (2005). The meaning and value of home-based craft. *International Journal of Art & Design Education, 24*, 261–268.
Massimini, F., Csikszentmihalyi, M., & Carli, M. (1987). Optimal Experience: A tool for psychiatric rehabilitation. *Journal of Nervous and Mental Disease, 175*, 545–549.
Massimini, F., & Delle Fave, A. (1995). Qualità dell'esperienza e coltivazione di attività musicali [Quality of experience and cultivation of musical activities]. *Comunicazioni Scientifiche di Psicologia Generale, 14*, 157–180.
Mee, J., & Sumsion, T. (2001). Mental health clients confirm the motivating power of occupation. *British Journal of Occupational Therapy, 64*, 121–128.
Mohammadian, Y., Shahidi, S., Mahaki, B., Mohammadi, A. Z., Baghban, A. A., & Zayeri, F. (2011). Evaluating the use of poetry to reduce signs of depression, anxiety and stress in Iranian female students. *The Arts in Psychotherapy, 38*, 59–63.
Nakamura, J., & Csikszentmihalyi, M. (2009). Flow theory and research. In S. Lopez & C. R. Snyder (Eds.), *The Oxford handbook of positive psychology* (pp. 195–206). Oxford, UK: Oxford University Press.

Nordin-Bates, S. M., Quested, E., Walker, I. J., & Redding, E. (2012). Climate change in the dance studio: Findings from the UK centres for advanced training. *Sport, Exercise and Performance Psychology, 1*, 3–16.

Odell-Miller, H., Hughes, P., & Westacott, M. (2006). An investigation into the effectiveness of the arts therapies for adults with continuing mental health problems. *Psychotherapy Research, 16*, 122–139.

O'Neill, S. (1999). Flow theory and the development of musical performance skills. *Bulletin of the Council for Research in Music Education, 141*, 129–134.

Panebianco-Warrens, C. (2014). Exploring the dimensions of flow and the role of music in professional ballet dancers. *Muziki: Journal of Music Research in Africa, 11*, 58–78.

Pöllänen, S. (2013). The meaning of craft: Craft makers' descriptions of craft as an occupation. *Scandinavian Journal of Occupational Therapy, 20*, 217–227

Pöllänen, S. (2015). Elements of crafts that enhance well-being: Textile craft makers' descriptions of their leisure activity. *Journal of Leisure Research, 47*, 58–78.

Portisch, A. (2009). Techniques as a window onto learning: Kazakh women's domestic textile production in western Mongolia. *Journal of material culture, 14*, 471–493.

Prentice, R. (2012). "No one ever showed me nothing": Skill and self-making among Trinidadian garment workers. *Anthropology & Education Quarterly, 43*, 400–414.

Quested, E., Bosch, J., Burns, V., Cumming, J., Ntoumanis, N., & Duda, J. L. (2011). Basic psychological need satisfaction, stress-related appraisals, and dancers' cortisol and anxiety responses. *Journal of Sport and Exercise Psychology, 33*, 828–846.

Quested, E., & Duda, J. L. (2010). Exploring the social-environmental determinants of well and ill-being in dancers: A test of Basic Needs Theory. *Journal of Sport and Exercise Psychology, 32*, 39–60.

Quested, E., & Duda, J. L. (2011). Antecedents of burnout among elite dancers: A longitudinal test of basic needs theory. *Psychology of Sport and Exercise, 12*, 159–167.

Quested, E., Duda, J. L., Ntoumanis, N., & Maxwell, J. P. (2013). Daily fluctuations in the affective states of dancers: A cross-situational test of basic needs theory. *Psychology of Sport and Exercise, 14*, 586–595.

Rathunde, K. (2010). Experiential wisdom and optimal experience: Interviews with three distinguished lifelong learners. *Journal of Adult Development, 17*, 81–93.

Reynolds, F. (1999). Cognitive behavioral counseling of unresolved grief through the therapeutic adjunct of tapestry making. *The Arts in Psychotherapy, 26*, 165–171.

Reynolds, F. (2000). Managing depression through needlecraft creative activities: A qualitative study. *The Arts in Psychotherapy, 27*, 107–114.

Reynolds, F. (2002). Symbolic aspects of coping with chronic illness through textile arts. *The Arts in Psychotherapy, 29*, 99–106.

Reynolds, F. (2003). Reclaiming a positive identity in chronic illness through artistic occupation. *OTJR: Occupation, Participation and Health, 23*, 118–127.

Reynolds, F., & Prior, S. (2006). Creative adventures and flow in art-making: A qualitative study of women living with cancer. *British Journal of Occupational Therapy, 69*, 255–262.

Reynolds, F., Vivat, B., & Prior, S. (2008). Women's experiences of increasing subjective well-being in CFS/ME through leisure-based arts and crafts activities: A qualitative study. *Disability & Rehabilitation, 30*, 1279–1288.

Rivas-Jimenez, C. P. (2008). *Defense of craft: Guadalajara's artisans in the era of economic liberalism, 1842–1907.* PhD dissertation, Florida State University, Tallahassee, USA. Retrieved from http://search.proquest.com/docview/250805223

Russell, J. A. (1980). A circumplex model of affect. *Journal of Personality and Social Psychology, 39*, 1161–1178.

Sayce, S., Ackers, P., & Greene, A. M. (2007). Work restructuring and changing craft identity: The tale of the disaffected weavers. *Work, Employment & Society, 21*, 85–101.

Seligman, M. E. P. (2002). *Authentic happiness: Using the new positive psychology to realize your potential for lasting fulfilment.* New York, NY: Free Press/Simon & Schuster.

Sengupta, J. (2011, July). Indian handicrafts and handloom workers: Life and working conditions in villages – a brief survey. *Observer Research Foundation, Working Paper Series.* Retrieved from http://www.orfonline.org/wp-content/uploads/2016/02/life_1427101564486.pdf

Sennett, R. (2008). *The craftsman*. London, UK: Penguin.

Simoens, V., & Tervaniemi, M. (2013). Musician–instrument relationship as a candidate index for professional well-being in musicians. *Psychology of Aesthetics, Creativity, and the Arts*, *7*, 171–180.

Soni-Sinha, U. (2011). Invisible women: A study of jewellery production in West Bengal, India. *Journal of Gender Studies*, *20*, 105–123.

Spandler, H., Secker, J., Kent, L., Hackings, S., & Shenton, J. (2007). Catching life: The contribution of arts initiatives to recovery approaches in mental health. *Journal of Psychiatric and Mental Health Nursing*, *14*, 791–799.

Steiner, L., & Schneider, L. (2013). The happy artist: An empirical application of the work preference model. *Journal of Cultural Economics*, *37*, 225–246.

Stickley, T., Hui, A., Morgan, J., & Bertram, G. (2007). Experiences and constructions of art: A narrative-discourse analysis. *Journal of Psychiatric and Mental Health Nursing*, *14*, 783–790.

Strawn, S., & Littrell, M. (2006). Beyond capabilities: A case study of three artisan enterprises in India. *Clothing and Textiles Research Journal*, *24*, 207–213.

Tegner, I., Fox, J., Philipp, R., & Thorne, P. (2009). Evaluating the use of poetry to improve well-being and emotional resilience in cancer patients. *Journal of Poetry Therapy*, *22*, 121–131.

Tennant, R., Hiller, L., Fishwick, R., Platt, S., Joseph, S., Weich, S., … Stewart-Brown, S. (2007). The Warwick-Edinburgh Mental Well-being Scale (WEMWBS): Development and UK validation. *Health & Quality of Life Outcomes*, *5*(63).

Titus, J., & Sinacore, A. L. (2013). Art making and well-being in healthy young adult women. *The Arts in Psychotherapy*, *40*, 29–36.

Warin, M., & Dennis, S. (2005). Threads of memory: Reproducing the cypress tree through sensual consumption. *Journal of Intercultural Studies*, *26*, 159–170.

Waterman, A. S. (1990). Personal expressiveness: Philosophical and psychological foundations. *Journal of Mind and Behavior*, *11*, 47–74.

27

The Well-Being of Workers in the Agricultural Sector

Lawrence Soosai-Nathan and Antonella Delle Fave

Introduction

Farmers are indispensable, as they cater to a basic human need – food. It is claimed that the agricultural sector will remain significant as long as humans eat. In 2014, people living in rural areas accounted for 47% of the world population and about 38% of the planet consisted of agricultural land (World Bank, 2015). Almost one billion people are officially employed in the agricultural sector, but the real amount is difficult to estimate, due to the large number of part-time and full-time workers (especially women and children) who provide an unpaid though substantial contribution in many parts of the developing world (Food and Agriculture Organization, 2015).

Notwithstanding both their indispensable role and their populous nature, farmers are a largely neglected category in industrial/organizational research. Only during the last two decades have the new and compelling challenges posed by the climate changes and worsening conditions of the planet's ecosystem drawn the attention of scientists from different disciplines toward the health of the natural environment and of the people living and working in rural areas.

The problems of nutrition and planet resources were identified as the central theme of the 2015 Universal Exposition, which took place in Milan, Italy under the motto "Feeding the Planet, Energy for Life." The Milan Charter, the official manifesto of the event, emphasizes the need for raising awareness of rural workers' conditions, and for balancing tradition with innovation in agriculture: "farmers, livestock keepers and fishers all play a crucial role in nutrition; they have equal rights and duties in their work, whether they are small-scale enterprises or large-scale businesses"; "knowledge and practical experience of both traditional and advanced production methods is critical to the efficiency of agricultural systems, from family farms to industrial farms" (Milan Charter, 2015).

The Wiley Blackwell Handbook of the Psychology of Positivity and Strengths-Based Approaches at Work, First Edition. Edited by Lindsay G. Oades, Michael F. Steger, Antonella Delle Fave, and Jonathan Passmore.

Responding to this gross neglect of the most populous working class of our planet, this chapter provides a review of the available literature, underscoring the importance of urgent and varied explorations of farmers' well-being that go beyond the traditional economic and sociologic measures. It offers some hints on the resources and potentials of the people working in the agricultural sector from the eudaimonic and hedonic perspectives of well-being. More specifically, though limited in number, studies conducted among farmers highlight the important role of positive relationships, mastery and self-efficacy, connection with nature, and resilience in facing the unpredictability of natural changes that directly affect work outcomes. It also points to some challenges and problems that could greatly benefit from interventions focused on well-being promotion.

The Paradoxes of Farming

Farmers represent a paradoxical workforce on three levels. First, agriculture is ancient yet modern. As early as 8000 BCE, humans shifted to dependence on cultivated crops and domesticated animals for their subsistence. Evidences show that by 3500 BCE, the agricultural sector in the Middle East could support sufficient numbers of non-cultivating specialists to give rise to the first civilizations (Balter, 2013). After replacing the hunter-gatherer economy, agriculture was the major human occupation across millennia. It preserved this role even after the industrial revolution, by virtue of the increasing demand for food production due to overall population growth. In many African and Asian countries, agriculture remains the most prominent work opportunity even in the 21st century (World Bank, 2015).

Second, the agricultural workforce is populous yet neglected. Although the number of people employed in agriculture varies widely on a per-country basis (ranging from less than 2% in the US and Canada to over 80% in many African and Asian nations), the agricultural sector remains the largest global employer, engaging one third of the available work force (International Labour Organization, 2011). In addition, agriculture remains the main source of income and employment for the 70% of the world's poor who live in rural areas (World Bank, 2015). Nevertheless, in many countries farm workers represent one of the most neglected categories of citizens as evidenced by inadequate housing, poor health and education facilities, low income, and relative social isolation.

Third, the agricultural sector is peaceful yet endangered. Farming often elicits an image of a peaceful and healthy way of life surrounded by nature and its beauty. In contrast to this idealized and partial image, farmers are considered as the most endangered working class today due to their exposure to physical injuries, malnutrition, acute and chronic diseases, adverse events due to both natural causes and human modifications of the ecosystem, and aggressive competition including the pervasive use of genetically modified organisms (GMO).

Taking into account these three paradoxes, it is not surprising that farming ranks among the 10 most stressful occupations in the world (Kolstrup et al., 2013), leading to negative consequences at the psychological level. Several studies have explored this issue across countries, though most of them were focused on the assessment of mental disorders and ill-being, rather than mental health and well-being (Crain et al., 2012; Dongre & Deshmukh, 2012; Feng, Ji, & Xu, 2015; Judd, et al., 2006; Thomas et al., 2003). Special attention was given to the increasing incidence of farmers' suicides across nations. This worrying phenomenon is related to the progressive worsening of farmers' financial conditions caused by the aggressive market dominance of multinational companies and large-scale food producers, as well as natural challenges such as drought or epidemics affecting farm animals (Fraser et al., 2005; Miller & Burns, 2008; Mishra, 2007; Peck, 2005). Despite the populous nature of this working class, the potential impact of farmers' suicides on families and larger communities has not been substantially investigated yet (Kennedy, Maple, McKay, & Brumby, 2014).

An additional risk factor for farmers' (and consumers') health and well-being is represented by the widespread use of potentially toxic substances in agriculture. Scientists, commercial companies, technicians, and policymakers often do not provide farmers with complete and correct information on the risks and benefits of procedures and instruments (such as mechanical tools, agrochemicals, and food supplements for animals) that affect both the amount and quality of products, as well as the health and well-being of workers, animals, and consumers. This aspect is often overlooked, though its consequences can be harmful for humans, animals, and whole ecosystems. For example, a study conducted among Thai rice farmers based on the health belief model (Raksanam, Taneepanichskul, Robson, & Siriwong, 2014) showed that participants held several erroneous beliefs regarding perceived safety of agrochemicals and pesticides, maintenance of spraying equipment, and use of appropriate clothing while performing related operations.

The Multidimensional Structure of Farmers' Well-Being

Given the manifold challenges that farmers face in their daily life, the importance of developing studies, policies, and interventions aimed at exploring and promoting their well-being is increasingly perceived by international institutions. Unfortunately, these initiatives prominently focus on economic factors and stop with economic well-being, disregarding the multidimensional nature of the concept (Nimpagaritse & Culver, 2010). It is often ignored that farmers' psychological resources may promote the capacity to thrive at work and make good financial decisions, regardless or in spite of environmental and social conditions. In an extensive review of literature very little was found on the enabling factors within the agricultural sector (Goffin & ACC Policy Team, 2014). The potential of this work domain in contributing to individual and community well-being seems still unexplored.

Nevertheless, thanks to the efforts of a few, there is a growing emphasis on a broader outlook of well-being within farming communities. In particular, studies on the mental health of farmers are pitching for a multidimensional approach as farmers are subjected to complex, intertwined, and multiple stressors. Researchers suggest that a wider area of exploration – such as the content and organization of work, workers' competence, their needs, cultural beliefs and practices, and personal issues – is needed to understand farmers' physical and mental health, work performance, and satisfaction (Kolstrup et al., 2013).

One of the pioneer studies on this topic (Wozniak, Draughn, & Knaub, 1993) involved U.S. husband and wife farm residents, who were asked to rate their level of satisfaction in eight life domains. Perceived control of one's own life and family emerged as the domains characterized by the highest levels of satisfaction, while the lowest ratings were reported for financial aspects.

A more recent study was conducted among South African farmers (Thekiso, Botha, Wissing, & Kruger, 2013). Participants reported remarkably low levels of satisfaction with life, positive affect, vitality (measured through the Subjective Vitality Scale [SVS]; Ryan & Frederick, 1997), and fulfillment of the three basic psychological needs of competence, autonomy, and relatedness (La Guardia, Ryan, Couchman, & Deci, 2000). At the same time, they described some positive resources, such as interpersonal relationships, support derived from religious beliefs and practice, as well as flow-like experiences of deep absorption and enjoyment related to the practice of crafts and sports. Nevertheless, these participants seemed to be constrained in a vicious cycle of poverty and dependence that seriously affected their physical and mental health.

The importance of objective outcomes for promoting farmers' well-being was further confirmed, though in a very different setting, among Australian dryland farmers and irrigators (Peel, Berry, & Schirmer, 2015). Data were selected from the Regional Well-being Survey 2013, and were collected through the Personal Wellbeing Index (PWI, International Wellbeing Group, 2013). Findings highlighted a significant relationship between higher farm profitability, greater well-being levels, and lower distress. A three-wave longitudinal study conducted among Dutch farmers partially contradicted this evidence (Gorgievski-Duijvesteijn, Bakker, Schaufeli, & van der Heijden, 2005), showing that well-being levels were more stable than perceived financial conditions at the intra-individual level, and that an increase in financial problems led to an only temporary increase of distress levels, without affecting self-reported illness.

The relationship between well-being and physical health was also explored. A study conducted in New Zealand among livestock farmers highlighted that satisfaction with work was positively related to higher incidence of loss of control events while driving quad bikes (Clay, Treharne, Hay-Smith, & Milosavljevic, 2014). This rather surprising finding could be related to the assessment strategy. Workplace satisfaction was measured through a 15-item scale, extrapolated from the Whole Body Vibration Health Surveillance Questionnaire (WBVHSQ; Pope et al., 2002). The analysis of item loadings led to the identification of three factors: job satisfaction, colleague support, and job demands. Only job demands was significantly associated with loss of control events, and especially among self-employed farmers. As substantiated by several models (such as the job demands-resource model; Demerouti, Bakker, Nachreiner, & Schaufeli, 2001), work demands may represent gratifying opportunities for engagement and flow experiences, but also sources of distress. The self-employed participants in this study faced more stressful demands compared with employees, in relation to higher financial pressures, responsibilities toward employed personnel, and complex decision-making management. Due to these demands, and in line with the literature (Personick & Windau, 1995), they were more at risk of driving accidents. This finding further highlights the importance of assessing different facets of well-being at work, including aspects – such as perceived challenges and demands – that may have a twofold valence when referred to a specific occupation or work role.

The role of socio-economic conditions

The impact of socio-economic conditions on the well-being of agricultural workers was more clearly highlighted by comparative studies investigating well-being indicators among rural and urban groups within the same country. Several studies showed that that farmers have higher rates of mental illness (Fraser et al., 2005; Hounsome, Edwards, Hounsome, & Edwards-Jones, 2012). Even farmers scoring positively on mental health or well-being measures appear more likely than non-farmers to feel hopeless about the future, have suicidal ideation, or commit suicide – a contradiction not yet fully understood but apparent in several countries (Thomas et al., 2003).

In South Africa, four cross-sectional studies conducted between 1998 and 2010 on urban and rural populations identified recurrent constellations of well-being patterns in each group (Wissing, Temane, & Khumalo, 2013). Across studies, the hedonic dimensions of satisfaction with life (measured through the Satisfaction with Life Scale [SWLS]; Diener, Emmons, Larsen, & Griffin, 1985) and hedonic balance (measured through the Affectometer 2; Kammann & Flett, 1983) were steadily and significantly lower among rural participants. Similar findings were detected for social well-being, measured through the Mental Health Continuum (MHC-SF; Keyes, 2005), contradicting the stereotype of higher levels of social support, cohesion, and solidarity in rural communities compared with cities. As concerns eudaimonic dimensions, the pattern was more complex. Spiritual well-being, measured with the JAREL Spiritual Well-Being Scale (SWS), which is prominently focused on the feeling of interconnectedness (Hungelmann, Kenkel-Rossi, Klassen, & Stollenwerk, 1996), was steadily higher among rural participants. Sense of coherence (SOC; Antonovsky, 1993) did not significantly differ between groups in one of the studies, and the same was true of general self-efficacy and psychological well-being, the latter (assessed through MHC-SF) attaining significantly higher values in the rural group in the 2010 study. In contrast, in the same study rural participants reported significantly lower levels of global mental health (assessed through The Warwick-Edinburgh Mental Well-Being Scale [WEMWBS]; Tennant et al., 2007), while urban participants (especially women) reported higher levels of distress and depression across studies. These findings suggest that rather than urbanization per se, its positive implications in terms of better infrastructures and opportunities in the domains of jobs, health, and leisure may explain the higher levels of well-being (including its social components) reported by urban participants. The findings also provide suggestions for intervention, highlighting that improving the objective working and life conditions of farmers could promote their hedonic well-being and general mental health, capitalizing on eudaimonic resources already available, such as self-efficacy, feelings of interconnectedness, and sense of coherence.

Another cross-sectional study was conducted with the PWI in a group of Australian farmers facing a period of drought, compared with participants selected from the general population (O'Brien, Berry, & Hogan, 2012). Findings showed that in both groups the levels of satisfaction perceived in eight different life domains loaded onto two separate supra-domains: satisfaction with connectedness, and satisfaction with efficacy; moreover, analyses highlighted that efficacy mediated the link between connectedness and global satisfaction. The authors suggested that strengthening individuals' connectedness to the community may foster higher efficacy and thus drive satisfaction with life as a whole. These findings are especially relevant for interventions addressed to farmers, who live in relative isolation and have limited access to social services and health facilities.

The role of relationships and interconnectedness

The studies reported in the previous sections have identified relationships as one of the major sources of well-being for farmers. This finding is consistent with the bulk of literature focused on positive relations, which imply strong feelings of empathy and affection for all human beings and the capacity for greater love, deeper friendship, and warm relationships to others (Ryff, 1989). From birth until old age, relationships play a crucial role in meeting basic needs that range from personal care to affiliation. The importance of relationships for well-being was emphasized in various theories and models in well-being research (Deci, La Guardia, Moller, Scheiner, & Ryan, 2006; Delle Fave, Wissing, Brdar, Vella-Brodrick & Freire, 2013; Forgeard, Jayawickreme, Kern & Seligman, 2011; Ryff & Singer, 2008).

The agricultural sector offers opportunities for relationships at a unique and complex level, as the individual roles between work, home, and family are more intertwined and integrated than in industrial and service occupations. Unlike any other workforce, varied human spheres merge and interact within the agricultural sector. An individual farmer is located in the centre of the micro sphere of farming and family, closely embedded in the meso-level sphere of community, ecology/place (the natural and physical elements of the environment), and industry. In turn these are embedded in the macro sphere of government, economy, and society (Greenhill, King, Lane, & MacDougall, 2009). These peculiar features are highlighted by the increasing number of urban people who choose farming as a job out of personal interest. They have been discussed through the concept of "ambiguity work," using Swedish horse-farmers as an exemplary case (Andersson Cederholm, 2015). The analysis of narratives collected among self-employed women who provide service work with and through horses highlighted that these workers are engaged in a continuous balancing act between family roles, personal interests, and the commercial aspects of their job. In so doing, they are able to overcome the work/life juxtaposition in favor of a positive spillover and blurring of boundaries between the different life spheres and components of personal identity.

Although some studies identify the "dark side" of social capital as the reciprocal burden that strong social bonds bring to those with poor resources or resilience (Berry, 2008; Schulman & Anderson, 1999), relationships are mostly found to enhance mental health and well-being among farmers (Berry & Welsh, 2010). Qualitative studies based on interviews showed that positive relations and community connectedness represented a unique resource for farm workers, significantly contributing to their well-being along with health, standard of living, and self-efficacy (Berry, Hogan, Ng, & Parkinson, 2011; Greenhill et al., 2009).

Social support was found to be an important variable in the relationship between agricultural stress and job satisfaction. Farmers reported that they handled stress effectively through the search for support from others working in the agricultural sector, such as veterinary surgeons (Peck, 2005). In contrast, farmers experiencing a highly demanding work environment coupled with low control and low social support reported stress and strain, mental health problems, and depression (Kolstrup et al., 2013). Perceived community bonds and social cohesion represent both a strategy for sustaining well-being and a resource under adverse circumstances, when they need a boost (King, Lane, MacDougall, & Greenhill, 2009). Kilpatrick, Willis, Johnsa, and Peek (2012) found that health interventions addressed to rural workers were most successful if access to them was facilitated by local community groups and industry associations. Suicide rates were lower among Indian farmers who perceived higher social support (Mishra, 2007). Australian drought-stricken farmers perceived social capital and social cohesion as the prominent adaptive resources and resilient boosters helping their families to handle the adverse climatic conditions (Caldwell & Boyd, 2009; Rolfe, 2006).

The relational dimension of farmers' life further stretches to the ecosystem, as the agricultural sector has to evolve in harmony with nature and its dynamics. Some studies have highlighted that farmers develop a unique, close, and strong sense of connection to the land as a part of their identity, so that caring for their land is part of caring for themselves (Albrecht et al., 2007; Berry et al., 2011). Their sense of worth is dependent on their success as stewards of land and agricultural producers (Burton & Wilson, 2006; Schirmer, Berry, & O'Brien, 2013). Australian farmers experiencing severe drought expressed readiness to cope with social and economic challenges in order to maintain their generational bond to the property, based on the belief that the well-being of themselves and their families should only be addressed after addressing the well-being of the farm (DPRESP, 2008).

The opportunity for connections extends still further, as the mutuality of religion and agriculture has been repeatedly described (Zeder, 2008). In fact, from antiquity sowing seed, tending fields, and harvesting crops are often done seeking divine guidance and help. In Asian traditions, nature itself is considered as God. In a qualitative study conducted among Australian farmers, participants reported that family relationships, gardening, and the environment in which they lived all contributed to their sense of connection with life beyond themselves (Greenhill et al., 2009).

The role of mastery and self-efficacy

The concept of environmental mastery was first introduced by Phillips (1961), who described it as an instinct that progresses through five stages: isolation, dependency, autonomy, cooperation, and independence. However, the concept received significant attention through its inclusion in Ryff's (1989) construct of psychological well-being. According to Ryff's formulation, environmental mastery is defined as the "capacity to manage effectively one's life and surrounding world" (Ryff & Keyes, 1995, p. 720). It is an ability to manipulate, control, and effectively use resources and opportunities, creating environments suitable to one's psychic conditions. It is a state of mind, rather than a just a behavior, that serves as an antidote to feelings of helplessness. Environmental mastery has gained increased attention in the health and social science research as it is considered an important psychological resource.

The uncertainty and unpredictability of agricultural processes and outcomes may lead to the claim that farmers enjoy less environmental mastery in comparison to other working sectors. Suicides, for example, are often related to financial difficulties and subsequent loss of control and a sense of helplessness. This apprehension calls for a clarification of the concept that can better delineate the type of mastery characterizing the agricultural sector.

Western philosophical traditions propose a hierarchical model of environmental mastery where humans, and especially men, are the masters of the universe, called forth to direct and shape the entire natural realm. Within such a perspective, mastery is primarily perceived as a capacity to manipulate, modify, and use the environment according to the needs and wants of humans because the world is made to serve them. Consequently, self-efficacy (Bandura, 1997) represents the perceived ability to control and master environmental challenges. In contrast, Eastern philosophical traditions underscore a circular model of mastery, wherein man is not the master on the top of the universe, but is part of it. Such a worldview is synthesized in the concept of *Ṛta* found in Rg Veda. *Ṛta* in Sanskrit means "that which is properly joined" – order, rule, truth, and the principle of natural order that regulates and coordinates the activities of the universe and of its components (Mahony, 1998). It refers to the ultimate cosmic order that knits together everything, from galaxies to atomic subparticles, influencing their nature and course. This worldview of interconnectedness is currently supported by studies in systems biology, epigenetics, and biocultural evolution (Jablonka & Lamb, 2014; Richerson & Boyd, 2005). Within such a perspective, environmental mastery is not control, but adaption and collaboration, and studies in cross-cultural psychology have repeatedly highlighted its prominence among non-Western participants (Bond, 2013; Markus & Kitayama, 1991).

The hierarchical model can be credited for its technological advancement in predicting, manipulating, and modifying the environment, making life comfortable and easy. However, it has adverse effects as well, as highlighted by the growing concerns for the future of the planet expressed by international agencies, scientists, and politicians. According to the circular model of mastery, instead, humans are endowed with a mindset to cope with and adapt to the environment, rather than a superior capacity over nature. Within this model, self-efficacy is not the capacity for control and manipulation of the environment, but for collaboration and coordination.

Given its dependency on nature, the agricultural sector is a "work-with" nature process, prominently based on a circular or collaborative environmental mastery. Farming requires, for example, a constant decision-making process with large financial and material implications. Farmers have to make decisions within a world that is not entirely certain or knowable, and is almost always complex. Farmers make their decisions on bounded rationality (Greenhill et al., 2009), a cognitive strategy that underscores a circular mastery, as decisions must be made considering various interconnected variables.

Industrialization and modernization of farming have introduced a hierarchical mastery model, in the attempt to transform farming from being a lifestyle to a business. However, a business-oriented farm is expected to make utilitarian decisions, while a lifestyle-oriented farm will make decisions based on identity and family concerns (Davis-Brown & Salamon, 1987). Most of the crucial problems that farmers are facing today represent side effects of the hierarchical control–mastery approach. A collaborative model of mastery is useful not only to deal effectively with the current environmental concerns, but also to enhance the well-being of farmers. Within such a paradigm, mastery does not merely consist of a person's capacity for autonomy or control over life, but also of the capacity to gracefully adapt to life as it unfolds (Schirmer et al., 2013).

Moreover, the "workmanship of risk" (Schwalbe, 2010) that characterizes the agricultural sector due to nature's unpredictability presents opportunities for developing openness, creativity, satisfaction, and personal growth. Australian farmers participating in a qualitative study showed a healthy skepticism and preparedness for the worst, reporting openness to change and readiness to work on continued improvement (Greenhill et al., 2009). These features are components of resilience, defined as the process wherein individuals display positive adaptation despite experiences of significant adversity. Various studies find that the resilience process of farmers across countries is significantly higher than average, and that farmers, in general, nurture a realistic optimism (Caldwell & Boyd, 2009; Sobels, 2007).

The role of the natural environment

Within the assessment of population well-being conducted at regular intervals by the UK Office of National Statistics, farmers emerged as the happiest working category, compared with any other profession (Hope, 2012). Could this make sense, notwithstanding the varied hardships that farmers currently face in several countries and world regions? As repeatedly highlighted in this chapter, these workers live outside the urban environment in which most industrial/organizational research studies are conducted. Findings must therefore be contextualized within the socio-economic and cultural milieu in which these people live and work, taking into account the facilities and social services available to them, their social status, as well as the features of the natural and built environment surrounding them.

In fact farmers, unlike any other profession, have the unique privilege of closely associating with nature. Nature relatedness is found to have psychological benefits, predicting happiness regardless of other psychological factors. Practicing activities connected with nature is described by farmers as an inherently satisfying task, and part of their own personal identity (King et al., 2009; Schirmer et al., 2013).

The role of nature in enhancing physical and psychological well-being has been repeatedly ascertained, and a whole new field of eco-psychology is emerging to delineate the link between well-being and the nature. Being in natural places fosters recovery from mental fatigue, improves outlook and life satisfaction, helps one to cope with and recover from stress, improves ability to recover from illness and injury, restores concentration, and improves productivity (Burls, 2007). Multiple studies have shown that natural areas such as community gardens grant a variety of mental health benefits, and that connection to nature is correlated with most measures of well-being and physical health (Butler & Friel, 2006; Chevalier, Sinatra, Oschman, Sokal, & Sokal, 2012; Zelenski & Nisbet, 2014). Exposure to green space reduces stress and increases a sense of wellness and belonging (Bremer, Jenkins, & Kanter, 2003). Crime decreases in communities as the amount of green space increases, and vegetation alleviates mental fatigue, one of the precursors to violent behavior (Kuo & Sullivan, 2001). Simply viewing plants was shown to reduce fear, anger, blood pressure, and muscle tension (Ulrich, 1979, 1986).

The restorative effects of natural environments on cognitive functioning were specifically studied in two experiments based on attention restoration theory (ART; Berman, Jonides, & Kaplan, 2008). According to ART, nature offers stimuli that modestly grab attention in a bottom-up fashion, fostering replenishment of top-down directed-attention abilities. Urban stimuli instead capture attention dramatically, and ceaselessly require its quick and selective direction.

Empowerment Programs and Farmers' Well Being

International agencies, local institutions, and the general public are becoming increasingly aware of the ecosystem's critical conditions, and of the challenges faced by the endangered population of farmers. As discussed in the previous pages, a major problem hindering farmers' well-being is related to the poor socio-economic conditions they experience in most countries. This awareness has given rise to a number of governmental and non-governmental initiatives, prominently aimed at developing sustainable and ecologically respectful food production, as well as a participatory approach to farming, fostering the empowerment, social recognition, financial emancipation, and ultimately well-being of the people working in the agricultural sector. Other initiatives, prominently launched in Western countries, capitalize on the well-being potential of farming activities to offer farmers a way to diversify their source of income through agritourism and occupational therapy opportunities.

Promoting farmers' well-being through participation

Participatory farming programs, often supported by international agencies, are spreading across countries, and their potential for promoting rural populations' empowerment has been highlighted by several studies. A study conducted among 29 stakeholders practicing organic family farming in Brazil investigated the workers' quality of life through the World Health Organization Quality of Life scale (WHOQoL Group, 1998) and a semi-structured interview (Queiroz Pessoa & Alchieri, 2014). While participants' monthly income was remarkably lower compared with other occupations, housing facilities and the participatory and collaborative organization of work represented environmental assets. Participants reported an overall positive quality of life in the psychological domain of WHOQoL. This finding was confirmed through the interviews, in which 82% of the participants reported having a positive view of their life and social relationships. When asked to describe the prominent feeling associated with reflections about life as a whole, 41% of the interviewees reported hope, 31% pleasure/satisfaction, 12% wishes and joy of living, and only 13% referred to financial worries.

Another study was conducted among Cambodian farmers enrolled in an organic farming program (Beban, 2012), with the aim of understanding their view of the "good life," and the extent to which their expectations were congruent with the local development initiatives. Participants described happiness as a set of different capabilities, ranging from objective resources (good health, access to land, adequate income) to psychological assets, such as internal locus of control, autonomy in decision-making, and self-sufficiency.

In developing countries, farming programs are often specifically addressed to women, identified by a variety of studies as the most vulnerable members of poor farming communities (Armendariz & Morduch, 2005; World Bank, 2001). Innumerable micro-credit projects in Asian, African, and Latin American countries involve women, based on the consideration that, compared to men, they are characterized by lower mobility, higher risk averseness, and spending patterns more oriented to family needs and children's health and education (Farnworth, 2009; Lott, 2009; Mahmud, Parvez, Hilton, Kabir, & Wahid, 2014; Nussbaum, 2001; Rahman & Milgram, 1999). Women's relational skills and their contribution to the development of social capital within rural communities of the developing world were explored through interviews involving 385 heads of household in Zimbabwe (Mupetesi, Francis, Gomo, & Mudau, 2012). Findings highlighted women's higher competences in building trustful relations with family members, friends, neighbors, and formal institutions compared to men. In light of this evidence, several participatory projects purposefully involved women farmers. An ethnographic study (Galie, 2014) discussed the positive outcomes of a plant breeding program launched in Syria with the aim of enhancing women's recognition as farmers, and facilitating their access to agricultural knowledge and decision-making.

Another participatory approach is represented by Community Supported Agriculture (CSA). CSA is an alternative agricultural system that emphasizes organic and environmentally friendly farming and a direct connection between consumers and farmers (Brown & Miller, 2008). The approach is gaining momentum in several countries, as consumers are increasingly turning toward local food systems that are built around an ethos of food security, self-reliance, and community (Hunt, Geiger-Oneto, & Varca, 2012). CSA aims at making consumers aware of and more directly engaged with the process of food production. Two different models of CSA have been implemented, the distribution share and the working share (Shi, Cheng, Lei, Wen, & Merrifield, 2011). In the former, customer members regularly receive a box of produce according to the farm's cultivation plan. They thus develop a sort of value-laden partnership with the farmers through their commitment to purchase a share of the food products (Charles, 2011). In the latter, a household rents a plot of land at the farm, receives technical guidance, material equipment, seeds, and organic fertilizers from the farm, and becomes directly responsible for cultivation and production. Interviews involving consumer members of farms adopting the distribution share showed that participants derive a sense of ethical value and civic responsibility through their support of farmers and local communities (Hayden & Buck, 2012). Another study explored the values perceived in CSA by members of units based on the working share model (Chen, 2013). The author identified five distinct dimensions: functional value, emotional value, social value, epistemic value, and educational value for children. In particular, the emotional value, rated as the most important of the five dimensions, included components such as happiness, freedom, life enrichment, stress relief, and sense of accomplishment.

Agritourism and voluntourism: Fostering the well-being of hosts and guests

Opportunities for incrementing income and enhancing the socio-economic conditions of farmers are provided by the spreading phenomenon of agritourism or farm tourism, matched with the increasing awareness of the need for an ecologically sustainable food economy. This is especially true in post-industrial societies, where the agricultural labor force is steadily decreasing, its costs are growing, large-scale farming enterprises are becoming predominant and family farms cannot compete with them at the production and business levels (Di Domenico & Miller, 2012). Hosting tourists and volunteers represents for small-scale farmers a profitable solution, allowing them to preserve their jobs and even improve the quality of their products by adopting organic cultivation strategies (Haugen & Vik, 2008). A related phenomenon is the so-called volunteer tourism, or "voluntourism," in which tourists are expected to more actively participate in the farm work for a certain amount of time (ranging between 20 and 30 hours per week), receiving free food and lodging. In order to promote but also regulate the diffusion of this kind of initiative a specific organization was founded, the "World Wide Opportunities on Organic Farms" (WWOOF), that presently operates in over 60 countries with the aim of matching host farms with tourist volunteers (WWOOF-USA, 2013). An increasing number of studies are currently devoted to the investigation of this practice, from the perspective of both farm tourists and farmers.

Tourists report a variety of benefits from spending free time in an agricultural context, ranging from enjoying a closer contact with nature to physical exercise, agricultural skill acquisition, and increased ecological awareness. As concerns farmers, hosting tourists provides them with benefits at the economic level, but also at the psychological and social levels, with local variations related to climate, production patterns, cultural specificities, and socio-economic conditions (Forbord, Schermer & Grießmair, 2012; Sharpley & Vass, 2006).

Most of the related literature is based on qualitative findings, collected through narratives and semi-structured interviews. A study conducted in the USA (Tew & Barbieri, 2012) highlighted that through agritourism farmers were able to achieve a variety of goals related to economic, social, and personal dimensions of well-being, such as capturing new farm customers, educating the public about agriculture, and enhancing the quality of life of their family. Another U.S. study involving farmers who host volunteers for more or less prolonged periods (Terry, 2014) highlighted benefits at the financial, relational, and emotional levels. Participants enjoyed the collaboration of young and enthusiastic people, the chance to teach them farming skills, and the sense of responsibility derived from this role. A UK-based study involving farm families was focused on the impact of farm tourism on family organization and lifestyle through the conceptual lens of experiential authenticity. The findings highlighted participants' perception of a creative and positive convergence between the changes required to adapt the traditional farm activities to the tourism goals and organization, on the one hand, and the changes in personal and family identity, on the other hand (Di Domenico & Miller, 2012).

The therapeutic role of farming: sharing benefits and well-being

The potential of farming activities as rehabilitation and therapeutic tools has been repeatedly confirmed by the positive outcomes of collaboration projects between health and social services and farmers developed in European countries. Farming activities are included in treatment programs aimed at the most vulnerable members of the society, such as people diagnosed with mental disorders, people recovering from substance abuse and addiction, and people released from prison. In these contexts, farming activities may help to achieve the twofold outcome of promoting clients' well-being and farmers' empowerment, knowledge expansion, social recognition, and socio-economic conditions (Hassink, Grin, & Hulsink, 2015).

The therapeutic effects of farming activities were investigated among users of UK mental health services, who were administered scaled questionnaires and interviews before and after a "care farm program" (Leck, Upton, & Evans, 2015). The WEMWBS (Tennant et al., 2007) was used to quantitatively measure changes in well-being; the interviews helped to identify which features of the farm experience primarily contributed to these changes. Significant positive relationships were detected between length of participation in the program and well-being enhancement. Reported benefits included empowerment, personal growth, and positive social interactions. The real-life context and the possibility of customizing activities based on the individual's health conditions and potentials are major strengths of these programs, together with the opportunity to promote collaboration between productive sectors of society – farmers and health services – which otherwise seldom interact (Iancu, Zweekhorst, Veltman, van Balkom, & Bunders, 2015).

Future Research

As repeatedly highlighted throughout this chapter, the well-being and quality of life of farmers are largely neglected topics in psychology. Awareness of the importance to address this issue is nevertheless increasing among psychologists, based on the acknowledgment of the variety of psychosocial facets that influence the quality of life of rural workers as risk factors or resources, and that cannot be adequately investigated from other disciplinary perspectives (Landini, Leeuwis, Long, & Murtagh, 2014).

Interventions to promote the well-being of farmers should be designed, taking into account their living conditions and exposure to specific local risk factors, related to both the features of the natural environment and the availability of social and health services (Hossain, Eley, Coutts, & Gorman, 2008; Robinson et al., 2009). Intervention programs should be focused on the enhancement of collaborative mastery and self-efficacy (Roy, 2014), and the promotion of adaptive strategies to successfully cope with the economic challenges and structural social changes that undermine the traditional work organization of the agriculture sector worldwide.

The need for more exhaustive studies, taking into account the various dimensions of farmers' well-being together with ill-being indicators, is further corroborated by meta-analyses showing the lack of conclusive data regarding the incidence of mental health problems among farmers compared with non-farmers (Fraser et al., 2005). Despite the relatively stable and well-defined features of farming activities and related risk factors, specific attention must be devoted to the variety of local conditions, cultural attitudes, and unexplored social and personal resources that may counterbalance the impact of these risks, or increase farmers' resilience and personal development, as their broad variations across countries and societies do not allow for easy generalizations.

In order to adequately investigate the facets and components of farmers' well-being, researchers should carefully take into consideration the cultural milieu in which data are collected, and interpret findings from a culture-fair perspective. More than other occupations, agriculture is strongly rooted in local traditions, habits, and relationship with land. In developing societies, characterized by a higher degree of social stratification than post-industrial ones, farmers' status is often disadvantaged, thus requiring a broader, interdisciplinary approach that goes beyond the specific boundaries of psychological investigation.

As concerns methodology, in the majority of world regions farmers do not enjoy high levels of education. The use of standardized scales may thus be problematic in these contexts, and qualitative approaches based on open-ended questions should be privileged. Language issues should be taken into account, and local researchers should be actively involved, based on both their knowledge of the language and their awareness of the sociocultural context in which the study is conducted.

Some specific constructs explored in positive psychology could represent good starting points to conduct studies among farmers. As suggested by the few findings summarized in this chapter, the perceived quality of interpersonal relationships in the work context (often including family members), the level of mastery and self-efficacy perceived in work-related decision-making, facets of individual resilience (such as adaptive coping strategies, optimism, perceived meaning in life, goal setting and pursuit), as well as the affective balance in daily life could represent important targets of investigation, in order to obtain a global representation of farmers' well-being encompassing eudaimonic and hedonic dimensions. A particular component to be explored is the relationship with the natural environment that specifically distinguishes farming activities from other occupations which primarily take place within built environments.

A more general understanding of farmers' well-being may be obtained through cross-cultural studies, comparing findings collected in different ecosystems and cultural contexts with the aim of identifying commonalities and differences. This approach could provide a representation of farmers' assets and resources both exhaustive and respectful of cultural differences, specificities, and intervention needs.

An important area requiring investigation is farm animal welfare (FAW), which is inextricably connected with farmers' attitudes to, relationships with, and behavior toward the animals they work and live with. A recent literature review (Hansson & Lagerkvist, 2014) suggests that this domain is potentially relevant for researchers and practitioners adopting a positive psychology approach, as it includes aspects such as interspecific relations and animal well-being that are largely unexplored.

Conclusions

Overall, the studies reviewed in this chapter highlight that the challenges and resources perceived by workers of the agricultural sector are inextricably intertwined with the socio-cultural environment in which these people live, thus leading to potentially broad variations in the perception of well-being. Nevertheless, the vast majority of farmers live in developing countries, and represent one of the poorest working categories. Empowerment, social recognition, and active participation of farmers in agricultural development and sustainability are thus basic prerequisites to foster the well-being of these workers in the long term.

To this purpose, farmers should be carefully listened to as experts in their own work. Their first-person and tradition-based knowledge should be taken into consideration in order to develop truly participative programs and promote their self-efficacy, autonomy, and mastery perceptions (Horseman et al., 2014; Reyes-García et al., 2014). This issue is far from being addressed, since barriers to knowledge exchange and collaboration between technicians/agronomists and farmers are still strong, with the former being considered as the expert holders of scientific knowledge, and the latter as low-educated followers of unscientific traditions (Cockburn, 2015). This widespread attitude substantially prevents farmers from attaining psychological and social well-being, in terms of personal growth, social recognition, and an active role in decision-making. Farmers' agency must be strengthened through their direct involvement in devising the rules and strategies to implement sustainable agriculture, food production, as well as workers and consumers' well-being (Farnworth, 2009).

The resourcefulness of nature, particularly that of the land, is unique and tremendous. Nature never runs out of stock. It is a pity if humanity misses such a rich reservoir. Insulated by the apparent abundance of food that has come from new technologies for growing and storing, mankind's fundamental dependence on agriculture is often overlooked. Human communities, no matter how sophisticated, cannot ignore the importance of agriculture, which is inseparably connected to daily human survival. To be far from dependable sources of food means to risk malnutrition and starvation. Efforts to preserve and sustain the well-being of agricultural workers will not only enhance social justice, but also offer a model of work culture to other sectors that are marked with dissatisfaction.

References

Albrecht, G., Sartore, G. M., Connor, L., Higginbotham, N., Freeman, S., Kelly, B., … Pollard, G. (2007). Solastalgia: The distress caused by environmental change. *Australasian Psychiatry, 15*, 95–98.

Andersson Cederholm, E. (2015). Lifestyle enterprising: The "ambiguity work" of Swedish horse-farmers. *Community, Work & Family, 18*, 317–333.

Antonovsky, A. (1993). The structure and the properties of the sense of coherence scale (SOC). *Social Science & Medicine, 366*, 725–733.

Armendariz, B., & Morduch, J. (2005). *The economics of microfinance*. Cambridge, MA: MIT Press.

Balter, M. (2013, July 4). Farming was so nice, it was invented at least twice. *Science News*.

Bandura, A. (1997). *Self-efficacy: The exercise of control*. New York, NY: Freeman.

Beban, A. (2012). The politics of wellbeing in international development: Research with organic farmers in Cambodia. In H. Selin & G. Davey (Eds.), *Happiness across cultures: Views of happiness and quality of life in non-Western cultures* (pp. 149–165). Dordrecht, the Netherlands: Springer.

Berman, M. G., Jonides, J., & Kaplan, S. (2008). The cognitive benefits of interacting with nature. *Psychological Science, 19*, 1207–1212.

Berry, H. L. (2008). Social capital elite, excluded participators, busy working parents and aging, participating less: Types of community participators and their mental health. *Social Psychiatry and Psychiatric Epidemiology, 43*, 527–537.

Berry, H. L., Hogan, A., Ng, S. P., & Parkinson, A. (2011). Farmer health and adaptive capacity in the face of climate change and variability. Part 1: Health as a contributor to adaptive capacity and as an outcome from pressures coping with climate related adversities. *International Journal of Environmental Research and Public Health, 8*, 4039–4054.

Berry, H. L., & Welsh, J. A. (2010). Social capital and health in Australia: An overview from the household income and labour dynamics in Australia Survey. *Social Science and Medicine, 70*, 588–596.

Bond, M. H. (2013). The pan-culturality of well-being: But how does culture fit into the equation? *Asian Journal of Social Psychology, 16*, 158–162.

Bremer, A., Jenkins, K., & Kanter, D. (2003). *Community gardens in Milwaukee: Procedures for their long-term stability and their import to the city*. Milwaukee, WI: University of Wisconsin, Department of Urban Planning.

Brown, C., & Miller, S. (2008). The impacts of local markets: A review of research on farmers markets and community supported agriculture (CSA). *American Journal of Agricultural Economics, 90*, 1296–1302.

Burls, A. (2007). People and green spaces: Promoting public health and mental well-being through ecotherapy. *Journal of Public Mental Health, 6*, 24–39.

Burton, R. J. F., & Wilson, G. A. (2006). Injecting social psychology theory into conceptualisations of agricultural agency: Towards a post-productivist farmer self-identity? *Journal of Rural Studies, 22*, 95–155.

Butler, C. D., & Friel, S. (2006). Time to regenerate: Ecosystems and health promotion. *PLoS Med, 3*, e394. doi:10.1371/journal.pmed.0030394

Caldwell, K., & Boyd, C. P. (2009). Coping and resilience in farming families affected by drought. *Rural and Remote Health*. Retrieved from http://www.rrh.org.au

Charles, L. (2011). Animating community supported agriculture in North East England: Striving for a "caring practice." *Journal of Rural Studies, 27*, 362–371.

Chen, W. (2013). Perceived value of a community supported agriculture (CSA) working share: The construct and its dimensions. *Appetite, 62*, 37–49.

Chevalier, G., Sinatra, S. T., Oschman, J. L., Sokal, K., & Sokal, P. (2012). Earthing: Health implications of reconnecting the human body to the earth's surface electrons. *Journal of Environmental and Public Health*, Article ID 291541. doi:10.1155/2012/291541

Clay, L., Treharne, G. J., Hay-Smith, E. J. C., & Milosavljevic, S. (2014). Is workplace satisfaction associated with self-reported quad bike loss of control events among farm workers in New Zealand? *Applied Ergonomics, 45*, 496–502.

Cockburn, J. (2015). Local knowledge/lacking knowledge: Contradictions in participatory agroecology development in Bolivia. *Anthropologica, 57*, 169–183.

Crain, R., Grzywacz, J. G., Schwantes, M., Isom, S., Quandt, S. A., & Arcury, T. A. (2012). Correlates of mental health among Latino farmworkers in North Carolina. *The Journal of Rural Health, 28*, 277–285.

Davis-Brown, K., & Salamon, S. (1987). Farm families in crisis: An application of stress theory to farm family research. *Family Relations, 36*, 368–373.

Deci, E. L., La Guardia, J. G., Moller, A. C., Scheiner, M. J., & Ryan, R. M. (2006). On the benefits of giving as well as receiving autonomy support: Mutuality in close friendships. *Personality and Social Psychology Bulletin, 32*, 313–327.

Delle Fave, A., Wissing, M. P., Brdar, I., Vella-Brodrick, D., & Freire, T. (2013). Perceived meaning and goals in adulthood: Their roots and relation with happiness. In A. Waterman (Ed.), *The best within us: Positive psychology perspectives on eudaimonia* (pp. 227–248). Washington, DC: American Psychological Association.

Demerouti, E., Bakker, A. B., Nachreiner, F., & Schaufeli, W. B. (2001). The job demands-resources model of burnout. *Journal of Applied Psychology, 86*, 499–512.

Di Domenico, M. L., & Miller, G. (2012). Farming and tourism enterprise: Experiential authenticity in the diversification of independent small-scale family farming. *Tourism Management, 33*, 285–294.

Diener, E., Emmons, R., Larsen, R., & Griffin, S. (1985). The Satisfaction with Life Scale. *Journal of Personality Assessment, 47*, 1105–1117.

Dongre, A. R., & Deshmukh, P. R. (2012). Farmers' suicides in the Vidarbha region of Maharashtra, India: A qualitative exploration of their causes. *Journal of Injury & Violence Research, 4*, 2–6.

DPRESP (Drought Policy Review Expert Social Panel) (2008). *It's about people: Changing perspectives on dryness.* Report to the Minister for Agriculture, Fisheries and Forestry. Canberra, Australia: Department of Agriculture, Fisheries, and Forestry. Retrieved from http://www.agriculture.gov.au/ag-farm-food/drought/drought-policy/history/national_review_of_drought_policy/dryness-report

Milan Charter (2015). Retrieved October 10, 2015 from http://carta.milano.it/en/

Farnworth, C. R. (2009). Well-being is a process of becoming: Respondent-led research with organic farmers in Madagascar. *Social Indicators Research, 90*, 89–106.

Feng, D., Ji, L., & Xu, L. (2015). Effect of subjective economic status on psychological distress among farmers and non-farmers of rural China. *The Australian Journal of Rural Health, 23*, 215–220.

Food and Agriculture Organization of the United Nations (2015). *FAO statistical pocketbook 2015: World food and agriculture.* Rome: Author.

Forbord, M., Schermer, M., & Grießmair, K. (2012). Stability and variety: Products, organization and institutionalization in farm tourism. *Tourism Management, 33*, 895–909.

Forgeard, M. J. C., Jayawickreme, E., Kern, M. L., & Seligman, M. E. P. (2011). Doing the right thing: Measuring well-being for public policy. *International Journal of Well-being, 1*, 79–106.

Fraser, C. E., Smith, K. B., Judd, F., Humphreys, J. S., Fragar, L. J., & Henderson, A. (2005). Farming and mental health problems and mental illness. *International Journal of Social Psychiatry, 51*, 340–349.

Galie, A. (2014). Feminist research approaches to empowerment in Syria. In S. Brisolara, D. Seigart, & S. SenGupta (Eds.), *Feminist evaluation and research: Theory and practice* (pp. 284–310). New York, NY: Guilford Press.

Goffin A., & ACC Policy Team (2014). *Farmers' mental health: A review of the literature.* Report prepared for the Farmers' Mental Wellbeing Stakeholder Group by the Accident Compensation Corporation. Retrieved from http://www.acc.co.nz/preventing-injuries/at-work/index.htm

Gorgievski-Duijvesteijn, M. J., Bakker, A. B., Schaufeli, W. B., & van der Heijden, P. G. M. (2005). Finances and well-being: A dynamic equilibrium model of resources. *Journal of Occupational Health Psychology, 10*, 210–224.

Greenhill, J., King, D. Lane, A., & MacDougall, C. (2009). Understanding resilience in South Australian farm families. *Rural Society, 19*, 318–325.

Hansson, H., & Lagerkvist, C. J. (2014). Defining and measuring farmers' attitudes to farm animal welfare. *Animal Welfare, 23*, 47–56.

Hassink, J., Grin, J., & Hulsink, W. (2015). New practices of farm-based community-oriented social care services in the Netherlands. *Journal of Social Service Research, 41*, 49–63.

Haugen, M., & Vik, J. (2008). Farmers as entrepreneurs: The case of farm-based tourism. *International Journal of Entrepreneurship and Small Business, 6*, 321–336.

Hayden, J., & Buck, D. (2012). Doing community supported agriculture: Tactile space, affect and effects of membership. *Geoforum, 43*, 332–341.

Hope, C. (2012, July 22). Farmers, forestry workers and fishermen happier than the rest of us, ONS study to find. *The Telegraph*.

Horseman, S. V., Roe, E. J., Huxley, J. N., Bell, N. J., Mason, C. S, & Whay, H. R. (2014). The use of in-depth interviews to understand the process of treating lame dairy cows from the farmers' perspective. *Animal Welfare, 23*, 157–165.

Hossain, D., Eley, R., Coutts, J., & Gorman, D. (2008). Mental health of farmers in Southern Queensland: Issues and support. *The Australian Journal of Rural Health, 16*, 343–348.

Hounsome, B., Edwards, R. T., Hounsome, N., & Edwards-Jones, G. (2012). Psychological morbidity of farmers and non-farming population: Results from a UK survey. *Community Mental Health Journal, 48*, 503–510.

Hungelmann, J., Kenkel-Rossi, E., Klassen, L., & Stollenwerk, R. (1996). Focus on spiritual well-being: Harmonious interconnectedness of mind-body-spirit – use of the JAREL Spiritual Well-Being Scale. *Geriatric Nursing, 17*, 262–266.

Hunt, D. M., Geiger-Oneto, S., & Varca, P. E. (2012). Satisfaction in the context of customer co-production: A behavioral involvement perspective. *Journal of Consumer Behaviour, 11*, 347–356

Iancu, S. C., Zweekhorst, M. B., Veltman, D. J., van Balkom, A. J. L. M., & Bunders, J. F. G. (2015). Outsourcing mental health care services? The practice and potential of community-based farms in psychiatric rehabilitation. *Community Mental Health Journal, 51*, 175–184.

International Labour Organization (2011). *ILO initiative to address rural labour statistics in the context of national development for decent work*. Retrieved September 23, 2015 from http://www.ilo.org/stat/Areasofwork/Compilation/WCMS_153119/lang--en/index.htm

International Wellbeing Group (2013). *Personal wellbeing index* (5th ed.). Melbourne, Australia: Australian Centre on Quality of Life, Deakin University.

Jablonka, E., & Lamb, M. J. (2014). *Evolution in four dimensions: Genetic, epigenetic, behavioural and symbolic variations in the history of life* (2nd ed.). Cambridge, MA: MIT Press.

Judd, F., Jackson, H., Fraser, C., Murray, G., Robins, G., & Komiti, A. (2006). Understanding suicide in Australian farmers. *Social Psychiatry and Psychiatric Epidemiology, 41*, 1–10.

Kammann, N. R., & Flett, R. (1983). Affectometet 2: A scale to measure current level of general happiness. *Australian Journal of Psychology, 35*, 259–265.

Kennedy, A., Maple, M. J., McKay, K., & Brumby, S. (2014). Suicide and accidental death in Australia's rural farming communities: A review of the literature. *Rural and Remote Health, 14*, 2517.

Keyes, C. L. M. (2005). Mental illness and/or mental health? Investigating axioms of the complete state model of health. *Journal of Consulting and Clinical Psychology, 73*, 539–548.

Kilpatrick, S. Willis, K., Johnsa, S., & Peek, K. (2012). Supporting farmer and fisher health and wellbeing in "difficult times": Communities of place and industry associations. *Rural Society, 22*, 31–44.

King, D., Lane, A., MacDougall, C., & Greenhill, J. (2009). *The resilience and mental health and wellbeing of farm families experiencing climate variation in South Australia*. Adelaide, Australia: National Institute of Labour Studies, Flinders University.

Kolstrup, C., Lallioniemi, M., Lundqvist, P., Kymalainene, H., Stallones, L., & Brumby, S. (2013). International perspectives on psychosocial working conditions, mental health, and stress of dairy farm operators. *Journal of Agromedicine, 18*, 244–255.

Kuo, F., & Sullivan, W. (2001). Aggression and violence in the inner city: Impacts of environment via mental fatigue. *Environment & Behavior, 33*, 543–571.

La Guardia, J., Ryan, R. M., Couchman, M. R., & Deci, E. L. (2000). Within-person variation in security of attachment: A self-determination theory perspective on attachment, need fulfillment, and well-being. *Journal of Personality and Social Psychology, 79*, 367–384.

Landini, F., Leeuwis, C., Long, N., & Murtagh, S. (2014). Towards a psychology of rural development: Processes and interventions. *Journal of Community and Applied Social Psychology, 24*, 534–546.

Leck, C., Upton, D., & Evans, N. (2015). Growing well-beings: The positive experience of care farms. *British Journal of Health Psychology, 20*, 745–762.

Lott, C. E. (2009). Why women matter: The story of microcredit. *Journal of Law and Commerce, 27*, 219–230.

Mahmud, K. T., Parvez, A., Hilton, D., Kabir G. M. S., & Wahid I. S. (2014). The role of training in reducing poverty: The case of agricultural workers receiving microcredit in Bangladesh. *International Journal of Training and Development, 18*, 282–290.

Mahony, W. K. (1998). *The artful universe: An introduction to the vedic religious imagination.* Albany, NY: State University of New York Press.

Markus, R., & Kitayama, S. (1991). Culture and the self: Implications for cognition, emotion, and motivation. *Psychological Review, 98*, 224–253.

Miller, K., & Burns, C. (2008). Suicides on farms in South Australia, 1997–2001. *Australian Journal of Rural Health, 16*, 327–331.

Mishra, S. (2007). *Risks, farmers' suicides and agrarian crisis in India: Is there a way out?* Mumbai, India: Indira Gandhi Institute of Development Research.

Mupetesi, T., Francis, J., Gomo, R., & Mudau, J. (2012). Gendered patterns of social capital among farmers in Guruve District of Zimbabwe. *Gender & Behaviour, 10*, 4832–4848.

Nimpagaritse, F., & Culver, D. (2010, May). *A broader perspective of measuring well-being of rural farm and non-farm households.* Paper presented at the Third Wye Global Conference, Washington, DC. Retrieved October 1, 2015 from http://www.fao.org/fileadmin/templates/ess/pages/rural/wye_city_group/2010/May/WYE_2010

Nussbaum, M. C. (2001). *Woman and human development: The capabilities approach.* Cambridge, UK: Cambridge University Press.

O'Brien L. V., Berry, H. L., & Hogan, A. (2012). The structure of psychological life satisfaction: Insights from farmers and a general community sample in Australia. *BMC Public Health, 12*, 976.

Peck, D. (2005). Foot and mouth outbreak: Lessons for mental health services. *Advances in Psychiatric Treatment, 11*, 270–276.

Peel, D., Berry, H. L., & Schirmer, J. (2015). Perceived profitability and well-being in Australian dryland farmers and irrigators. *The Australian Journal of Rural Health, 23*, 207–214.

Personick, M. E., & Windau, J. A. (1995). Self-employed individuals fatally injured at work. *Monthly Labor Review, 118*, 24.

Phillips, R. H. (1961). Environmental mastery and personality development. *Archives of General Psychiatry, 5*, 146–150.

Pope, M., Magnusson, M., Lundström, R., Hulshof, C., Verbeek, J., & Bovenzi, M. (2002). Guidelines for whole-body vibration health surveillance. *Journal of Sound and Vibration, 253*, 131–167.

Queiroz Pessoa, Y. S. R., & Alchieri, J. C. (2014). Qualidade de vida em agricultores organicos familiares no interior Paraibano [Quality of life in organic family farmers in rural Paraiba]. *Psicologia: Ciencia e Profissao, 34*, 330–343.

Rahman, A., & Milgram, B. L. (1999). *Women and microcredit in rural Bangladesh: An anthropological study of Grameen Bank lending.* Boulder, CO: Westview Press.

Raksanam, B., Taneepanichskul, S., Robson, M. G., & Siriwong, W. (2014). Health risk behaviors associated with agrochemical exposure among rice farmers in a rural community, Thailand: A community-based ethnography. *Asia-Pacific Journal of Public Health, 26*, 588–595.

Reyes-García, V., Aceituno-Mata, L., Calvet-Mir, L., Garnatje, T., Gómez-Baggethun, E., Lastra, J. J., & Parada, M. (2014). Resilience of traditional knowledge systems: The case of agricultural knowledge in home gardens of the Iberian Peninsula. *Global Environmental Change, 24*, 223–231.

Richerson P. J., & Boyd R. (2005). *Not by genes alone: How culture transformed human evolution.* Chicago, IL: University of Chicago Press.

Robinson, T., Kurtz, H., Kelly, B., Fuller, J., Fragar, L., Roy, S., ... Hedger, B. (2009). Clinical leadership in rural psychiatry: Farmers' mental health and well-being. *Australian Journal of Rural Health, 17*, 284–285.

Rolfe, R. E. (2006). *Social cohesion and community resilience: A multi-disciplinary review of literature for rural health research.* Halifax, Canada: Department of International Development Studies, Faculty of Graduate Studies and Research, Saint Mary's University. (Full text available from author on request via https://www.researchgate.net/researcher/2025694742_Rebecca_Eve_Rolfe)

Roy, D. D. (2014). Agro-psychological counseling: Concept and process. *Journal of the Indian Academy of Applied Psychology, 40,* 20–26.

Ryan, R. M., & Frederick, C. M. (1997). On energy, personality, and health: Subjective vitality as a dynamic reflection of well-being. *Journal of Personality, 65,* 529–565.

Ryff, C. D. (1989). Happiness is everything, or is it? Explorations on the meaning of psychological well-being. *Journal of Personality and Social Psychology, 57,* 1069–1081.

Ryff, C. D., & Keyes, C. L. M. (1995). The structure of psychological well-being revisited. *Journal of Personality and Social Psychology, 69,* 719–727.

Ryff, C. D., & Singer, B. H. (2008). Know thyself and become what you are: A eudaimonic approach to psychological well-being. *Journal of Happiness Studies, 9,* 13–39.

Schirmer, J., Berry, H. L., & O'Brien, L. V. (2013). Healthier land, healthier farmers: Considering the potential of natural resource management as a place-focused farmer health intervention. *Health & Place, 24,* 97–109.

Schulman, M. D., & Anderson, C., (1999). The Dark Side of the force: A case study of restructuring and social capital. *Rural Sociology, 64,* 351–372.

Schwalbe, M. (2010). In search of craft. *Social Psychology Quarterly, 73,* 107–111.

Sharpley, R., & Vass, A. (2006). Tourism, farming and diversification: An attitudinal study. *Tourism Management, 27,* 1040–1052.

Shi, Y., Cheng, C. W., Lei, P., Wen, T. J., & Merrifield, C. (2011). Safe food, green food, good food: Chinese community supported agriculture and the rising middle class. *International Journal of Agricultural Sustainability, 9,* 551–558.

Sobels, J. D. (2007). *Social impacts of drought: Lower Murray: A scoping study for the Lower Murray Drought Impact Community Reference Group.* Australia: Primary Industries and Resources South Australia (PIRSA). Retrieved from: http://www.mdba.gov.au/kid/files/726-Social-Impact-Lower-Murray-Lakes-Region.pdf

Tennant, R., Hiller, L., Fishwick, R., Platt, S., Joseph, S., Weich, S., ... Stewart-Brown, S. (2007). The Warwick-Edinburgh mental well-being scale (WEMWBS): Development and UK validation. *Health and Quality of Life Outcomes, 51,* 63–75.

Terry, W. (2014). Solving labor problems and building capacity in sustainable agriculture through volunteer tourism. *Annals of Tourism Research, 49,* 94–107.

Tew, C., & Barbieri, C. (2012). The perceived benefits of agritourism: The provider's perspective. *Tourism Management, 33,* 215–224.

Thekiso, S. M., Botha, K. F. H., Wissing, M. P., & Kruger, A. (2013). Psychological well-being, physical health, and the quality of life of a group of farm workers in South Africa: The FLAGH study. In M. P. Wissing (Ed.), *Well-being research in South Africa* (pp. 293–313). Dordrecht, the Netherlands: Springer.

Thomas, H. V., Lewis, G., Thomas, D. R., Salmon, R. L., Chalmers, R. M., Coleman, T. J., ... Softley, P. (2003). Mental health of British farmers. *Occupational and Environmental Medicine, 60,* 181–186.

Ulrich, R. S. (1979). Visual landscapes and psychological well-being. *Landscape Research, 4,* 17–23.

Ulrich, R. S. (1986). Human responses to vegetation and landscapes. *Landscape and Urban Planning, 13,* 29–44.

WHOQoL Group (1998). The World Health Organization quality of life assessment (WHOQoL): Development and general psychometric properties. *Social Science & Medicine, 46,* 1569–1585.

Wissing, M. P., Temane, Q. M., & Khumalo, I. P. (2013). Psychosocial health: Disparities between urban and rural communities. In M. P. Wissing (Ed.), *Well-being research in South Africa* (pp. 415–438). Dordrecht, the Netherlands: Springer.

World Bank (2001). *Engendering development through gender equality in rights, resources and voice.* World Bank Policy Research Report. Washington, DC: Author. Retrieved from http://documents.worldbank.org/curated/en/2001/01/891686/engendering-development-through-gender-equality-rights-resources-voice

World Bank (2015). *Data: Agriculture and rural development.* Retrieved October 2, 2015 from http://data.worldbank.org/topic/agriculture-and-rural-development

Wozniak, P. J., Draughn, P. S., & Knaub, P. K. (1993). Domains of subjective well-being in farm men and women. *Journal of Family and Economic Issues, 14*, 97–114.

WWOOF-USA (2013). *Factsheet: Worldwide opportunities on organic farms, USA*. San Francisco, CA: WWOOF.

Zeder, M. A. (2008). Domestication and early agriculture in the Mediterranean Basin: Origins, diffusion, and impact. *Proceedings of the National Academy of Sciences, 105*, 11597–11604

Zelenski, J. M., & Nisbet, E. K. (2014). Happiness and feeling connected: The distinct role of nature relatedness. *Environment and Behavior, 46*, 3–23.

Index

Page numbers in **bold** indicate figures and/or tables

The Wiley Blackwell Handbook of the Psychology of Positivity and Strengths-Based Approaches at Work, First Edition. Edited by Lindsay G. Oades, Michael F. Steger, Antonella Delle Fave, and Jonathan Passmore.